edition 14

Managing Human Resources

George Bohlander
Professor of Management, Arizona State University

Scott Snell
Professor and Director of Executive Education, Cornell University

THOMSON

Australia · Brazil · Canada · Mexico · Singapore · Spain · United Kingdom · United States

Managing Human Resources, Fourteenth Edition
George Bohlander, Scott Snell

VP/Editorial Director:
Jack W. Calhoun
VP/Editor-in-Chief:
Dave Shaut
Senior Acquisitions Editor:
Joe Sabatino
Senior Developmental Editor:
Susanna C. Smart
Senior Marketing Manager:
Kimberly Kanakes
Production Project Manager:
Heather Mann
Sr. Marketing Communications Manager:
Jim Overly

Manager of Technology, Editorial:
Vicky True
Technology Project Editor:
Kristen Meere
Web Coordinator:
Karen Schaffer
Manufacturing Coordinator:
Diane Lohman
Production House:
Lachina Publishing Services, Inc.
Printer:
RR Donnelley
Willard, OH

Art Director:
Tippy McIntosh
Internal Designer:
Grannan Graphic Design, LTD
Cover Designer:
Tippy McIntosh
Cover Image:
Diana Ong/Superstock
Photography Manager:
Deanna Ettinger
Photo Researcher:
Susan Van Etten

Printed in the United States of America
1 2 3 4 5 08 07 06 05

Student Edition:
ISBN 0-324-31463-9
Instructor's Edition:
ISBN 0-324-42238-5

Library of Congress Control Number:
2005931605

For more information about our products, contact us at:
Thomson Learning Academic Resource Center
1-800-423-0563

Thomson Higher Education
5191 Natorp Boulevard
Mason, OH 45040
USA

brief contents

HUMAN RESOURCES MANAGEMENT IN PERSPECTIVE

MEETING HUMAN RESOURCES REQUIREMENTS

DEVELOPING EFFECTIVENESS IN HUMAN RESOURCES

IMPLEMENTING COMPENSATION AND SECURITY

ENHANCING EMPLOYEE-MANAGEMENT RELATIONS

EXPANDING HUMAN RESOURCES MANAGEMENT HORIZONS

contents

HUMAN RESOURCES MANAGEMENT IN PERSPECTIVE

chapter 1

The Challenge of Human Resources Management, 3

DEVELOPING EFFECTIVENESS IN HUMAN RESOURCES

IMPLEMENTING COMPENSATION AND SECURITY

chapter 9

ENHANCING EMPLOYEE-MANAGEMENT RELATIONS

chapter 13

chapter 14

EXPANDING HUMAN RESOURCES MANAGEMENT HORIZONS

preface

The 14th edition of *Managing Human Resources* will place your students at the forefront in understanding how organizations can gain sustainable competitive advantage through people. The role of HR managers is no longer limited to service functions such as recruiting and selecting employees. Today, HR managers assume an active role in the strategic planning and decision making at their organizations. Meeting challenges head-on and using human resources effectively are critical to the success of any work organization. In this edition of the book, we've made improvements that make these points even more strongly.

In the first chapter, we begin by explaining the key challenges to HRM in developing the flexible and skilled workforce needed to compete effectively. Side by side with the competitive challenges, HRM must also address important employee concerns such as managing a diverse workforce, recognizing employee rights, and adjusting to new work attitudes. The chapter also discusses the important partnership with line managers and the competencies required of HR management. Then the textbook continues with the introduction, explanation, and discussion of the individual practices and policies that make up HRM. We recognize the manager's changing role, and emphasize current issues and real-world problems and the policies and practices of HRM used to meet them.

Although we focus on the HR role of managers, we do not exclude the impact and importance of the HR department's strategic role in developing, coordinating, and enforcing policies and procedures relating to HR functions. Whether the reader becomes a manager, a supervisor, or an HR specialist, or is employed in other areas of the organization, *Managing Human Resources* provides a functional and practical understanding of HR programs to enable readers to see how HR affects all employees, the organization, the community, and the larger society.

Issues of strategy and talent have become such central concerns of HR today that we have reorganized and reemphasized the topics in this edition of the book. The second chapter of the book specifically addresses the issues of HR strategy and planning. Chapter 5 focuses on expanding and managing the talent pool in organizations. The detailed coverage of these topics solidifies *Managing Human Resources* as perhaps the premier text for thought leadership.

Organizations in today's competitive world are discovering that it is *how* the individual HR topics are combined that makes all the difference. Managers typically don't focus on HR issues such as staffing, training, and compensation in isolation from one another. Each of these HR practices is combined into an overall system to enhance employee involvement and productivity. *Managing Human Resources* ends with a final chapter that focuses on development of high-performance work systems (HPWS). We outline the various components of the systems including work-flow design, HR practices, management processes, and supporting technologies. We also discuss the strategic processes used to implement high-performance work systems and the outcomes that benefit both the employee and the organization as a whole.

What's Dynamic in the 14th Edition

Many new features and much new information are provided in this revision. We introduce overall text improvements that more accurately reflect HRM in today's business world and help the reader understand HRM issues more effectively.

- HRM Experience: We build upon a popular addition to the previous edition of *Managing Human Resources* by including many new experiential exercises to explore significant issues in HRM. These skill-building exercises will help students gain practical experience when dealing with employee/management concerns such as pay-for-performance; effective teaming; employee benefits; reducing employee stress; employee rights; balancing competitive challenges and employee concerns; customizing HR for different types of human capital; designing selection criteria and methods; and assessing the strategic fit of HPWS. Students can work through these new exercises on either an individual or a team basis.
- Human Resources Information Systems (HRIS): Throughout the text, we have specifically highlighted the use of HRIS to facilitate the managing of employees and the efficient performance of HR functions. For example, the impact of information technology on HR and the role of HRIS in such areas as compensation, recruitment and selection, training, job analysis, and safety are discussed.
- Diversity: Because we believe that diversity issues are an integral part of every HRM activity, updated and expanded coverage is included throughout the text.
- HRM Strategy: The increasingly important role HRM plays in strategic planning is covered specifically in Chapter 2. However, elsewhere we also discuss the role of human capital and Six Sigma; HR benchmarking; balanced scorecard, strategy mapping, and performance diagnosis; global HR strategy; as well as strategic alignment and the implementation of high-performance work systems.
- Contemporary employment issues such as global sourcing, offshoring, alternative work arrangements, temporary workers, contractors, and the like are covered throughout the book.
- Global and international HR concerns are covered in more detail in this edition. This includes issues such as the World Trade Organization, China, and the impact of globalization on HR; multinationals, joint ventures, and the like; and global rights issues such as data protection, property rights, and intellectual property. Although these issues have perhaps been peripheral to HRM in the past, they are increasingly seen as "front and center" in many organizations.
- A complete update of all laws, administrative rulings and guidelines, and court decisions governing HRM includes such recent developments as legislation regarding sexual orientation; the U.S. Supreme Court decision on affirmative action and the promotion of diversity; FLSA changes governing exemptions from overtime payments; stock option reporting requirements; new medical privacy legislation; camera-equipped phones; and other employee rights issues.
- The latest versions of the posters of all major federal regulations governing HRM are included.
- We have readdressed the important role of compensation in HRM by heightening our discussion of pay-for-performance, healthcare cost savings, strategic pension planning, and effective employee awards. For example, in Chapter 11 we have added an important new section on consumer-driven health plans such as medical saving accounts and flexible spending accounts.

- Expanded discussions cover major issues, including:

aggressive union organizing	offshoring and outsourcing
balanced scorecard	pension plans and underfunding
competency assessment for training	performance diagnosis
cumulative trauma disorders	person-organization fit
EEO reporting requirements	promotion of workplace fitness and health
employee leasing	role of human capital
executive compensation reform	strategic planning
globalization	violence and terrorism in the workplace
incentive rewards and employee recognition	

- Many new Highlights in HRM boxes present the reader with up-to-date, real-world examples from a variety of large and small organizations.
- Internet: The ever-growing role of the Internet in HR activities is evident throughout the text. A few examples include online recruiting in Chapter 5; online staffing in Chapter 6; web-based training and e-learning in Chapter 7; and online 360-degree performance appraisal in Chapter 8.
- Each chapter has at least one new end-of-chapter case study highlighting chapter content. These cases have been selected to provide students with both current and practical HR problems and issues.
- Six new extended cases are included at the end of the book. These cases have been carefully selected to reflect current issues in managing human resources, and explore the important topics of virtual HR, diversity, workforce mobility, employment downsizing, wrongful discharge, ethics, performance appraisal, and the arbitration of employee complaints.
- New Ancillaries: There are new online ancillaries for instructors and students. A completely revised test bank plays a strategic role in the Integrated Learning System. A new set of PowerPoint presentation slides and acetates makes teaching and preparation easier and more convenient.

Features of the Book

Use of the Integrated Learning System (which is described on the front inside cover) continues for the new edition. This integrated structure creates a comprehensive teaching and testing system. Designed to facilitate understanding and retention of the material presented, each chapter contains the following pedagogical features:

- **Learning objectives** listed at the beginning of each chapter provide the basis for the Integrated Learning System. Icons that identify the learning objectives appear throughout the text and end-of-chapter material, and all print ancillaries.
- **Highlights in HRM.** This popular boxed feature provides real-world examples of how organizations perform HR functions. The Highlights are introduced in the text discussion and include topics such as small businesses and international issues.
- **Using the Internet.** All chapters include new government, research, and business Internet references and addresses.
- **Key terms** appear in boldface and are defined in margin notes next to the text discussion. The key terms are also listed at the end of the chapter and appear in the glossary at the end of the text.

- **Figures.** An abundance of graphic materials and flowcharts provides a visual, dynamic presentation of concepts and HR activities. All figures are systematically referenced in the text discussion.
- **Summary.** A paragraph or two for each learning objective provides a brief and focused review of the chapter.
- **Discussion questions** following the chapter summary offer an opportunity to focus on each of the learning objectives in the chapter and stimulate critical thinking. Many of these questions allow for group analysis and class discussion.
- **HRM Experience.** An experiential activity (described earlier) is included in each chapter.
- **Two or more case studies** per chapter present current HRM issues in real-life settings that allow for student consideration and critical analysis.
- **Extended cases.** Eleven extended cases are provided at the end of the main text. These cases use material covered in more than one text chapter and provide capstone opportunities.

Ancillary Teaching and Learning Materials

For Students

Study Guide* to Accompany *Managing Human Resources (ISBN: 0-324-31469-8). Thomas Lloyd of Westmoreland County Community College has again revised the *Study Guide.* His many years of teaching experience allow him to bring a special insight to this popular student supplement. It includes review questions that can be used to check understanding and prepare for examinations on each chapter in this textbook. Using the Integrated Learning System, *Study Guide* questions are arranged by chapter learning objective so the student can quickly refer back to the textbook if further review is needed. A sample chapter of the *Study Guide* as well as online purchase are available at http://bohlander.swlearning.com.

New for this edition are three exceptional online tools: **Xtra!, HRM in the News** on the product support site, and **InfoTrac® College Edition:**

xtra!

Xtra! Web Site

This robust site provides a wealth of online learning tools including *BizFlix* and Workplace Videos; HRM in the News; interactive chapter-by-chapter quizzes; digitized *Author Insight* videos to further clarify difficult concepts from the text; *HR Measurement Lab Exercises, powered by InfoHRM,* that ask students to analyze various workforce metrics to reinforce theories presented in the text; and much more! For more information, visit http://bohlanderxtra.swlearning.com.

HRM in the News

Provides summaries of the latest human resource management–related news stories, indexed by topic for your convenience. Each HRM News summary contains a headline, subject category, key words, three-to-five-paragraph summary of a news article, article source line, and questions to spur further thought.

InfoTrac® College Edition

An InfoTrac® College Edition four-month subscription card is automatically packaged free with new copies of this text. With InfoTrac® College Edition, sources such as *Forbes, Fortune,* and *The New York Times* are just a click away! InfoTrac® College Edition provides students with anytime, anywhere access to 20 years' worth of full-text articles (*more than 10 million!*) from nearly *4,000* scholarly and popular sources! In addition to receiving the latest business news as reported in the popular business press, students also have access to many other journals, among them those that are particularly valuable to the human resources discipline—including *Human Resource Planning, Human Resource Department Management Report, HR Focus, Employee Benefits, HR Magazine,* and more. For more information on InfoTrac® College Edition, visit http://infotrac-college.thomsonlearning.com.

***Managing Human Resources, 14e* Support Web Site**
http://bohlander.swlearning.com

This comprehensive, resource-rich web site provides ongoing learning and teaching resources and support for both instructors and students. You'll find it filled with practice quizzes, links to online HR management resources, and much more!

For Instructors

The following instructor support materials are available to adopters from your Thomson South-Western Representative, from the Academic Resource Center at 800-423-0563, or through http://www.swlearning.com. All printed ancillary materials were prepared by or under the direction of the text authors to guarantee full integration with the text. Multimedia supplements were prepared by experts in those fields.

- ***Instructor's Resource Guide*** (ISBN: 0-324-31464-7). For each chapter in the textbook, the *Instructor's Resource Guide* contains a chapter synopsis and learning objectives; a very detailed lecture outline; answers to the end-of-chapter discussion questions and case studies; solutions to the extended cases in the textbook; and suggested answers for the chapter video exercises.
- **Test Bank** (ISBN: 0-324-31465-5). The new test bank was prepared by Satish P. Deshpande of Western Michigan University. Each test bank chapter provides over 100 questions and includes a matrix table that classifies each question according to type and learning objective. There are true/false, multiple-choice, and essay items for each chapter, arranged by learning objective. Page references from the text are included. Each objective question is coded to indicate whether it covers knowledge of key terms, understanding of concepts and principles, or application of principles.
- **Computerized Test Bank** (ISBN: 0-324-31467-1). *ExamView*™ testing software contains all the questions from the printed test bank and allows the instructor to edit, add, delete, or randomly mix questions for customized tests.
- **PowerPoint™ Presentation Slides** (ISBN: 0-324-42243-1). Created specifically for the new edition by Charlie T. Cook of the University of West Alabama, these presentation slides will add color and interest to lectures. The transparencies are also included within the presentation slide package.
- **Instructor's Resource CD** (ISBN: 0-324-31466-3). The *Instructor's Resource Guide,* test bank, *ExamView,* and PowerPoint slides are provided on a single CD-ROM.

  Real to Reel Video Package. The video package consists of two separate sets of videos:

  - **BizFlix Videos.** BizFlix are short film clips taken from popular Hollywood movies that provide real-world examples of the human resource management concepts students are learning. End-of-chapter BizFlix exercises in the text stimulate students to see how the filmed scenarios apply to chapter topics.

- **Workplace Videos.** This video collection features both small and large companies with innovative HR practices, many of which have been recognized for their excellence in HR practices.
- Real to Reel DVD package: 0-324-42248-2
- Real to Reel VHS package: 0-324-42249-0

- ***JoinIn*™ on TurningPoint®.** Transform any lecture into a truly interactive student experience with *JoinIn.* Combined with your choice of several leading keypad systems, *JoinIn* turns your ordinary PowerPoint® application into powerful audience response software. With just a click on a handheld device, your students can respond to multiple-choice questions, short polls, interactive exercises, and peer review questions. You can take attendance, check student comprehension of difficult concepts, collect student demographics to better assess student needs, and even administer quizzes without collecting papers or grading. In addition, we provide interactive text-specific slide sets that you can modify and merge with any existing PowerPoint lecture slides for a seamless classroom presentation. This interactive tool is available to qualified college and university adopters. For more information, contact your Thomson representative or visit http://turningpoint.thomsonlearningconnections.com.
- **Transparency Acetates** (ISBN: 0-324-31468-X). A set of transparencies is also available with this edition.
- **WebTutor™.** WebTutor is used by an entire class under the direction of the instructor and is particularly convenient for distance learning courses. It provides web-based learning resources to students as well as powerful communication and other course management tools including course calendar, chat, and e-mail for instructors. WebTutor is available on WebCT (0-324-42245-8) and Blackboard (0-324-42244-X). See http://webtutor.thomsonlearning.com for more information.
- **TextChoice Cases and Exercises.** TextChoice is the home of Thomson Learning's digital content. This Management Cases and Exercises database allows you to easily evaluate and select cases, experiential exercises, and activities and to even include your own material to create a tailor-fit course companion. See http://www.textchoice.com for more information.
- **E-Coursepacks.** E-Coursepacks is a completely online collection of articles and resources tailored specifically to selected South-Western management textbooks. E-Coursepacks goes beyond the book by providing access to three to five full-length articles for each chapter of the text, chosen from hundreds of scholarly, practitioner, and popular periodicals by a team of management content specialists. These articles relate and reinforce key topics and examples from the text. In addition, e-Coursepacks allows instructors to access the most current articles and biographical and background information on key companies or important individuals in HRM through links to predefined searches on the databases.

Acknowledgments

Because preparation of manuscript for a project as large as *Managing Human Resources* is a continuing process, we would like to acknowledge the work of those colleagues who provided thoughtful feedback for this and the previous editions of the text. We were fortunate to have the results of an extensive survey whose participants offered suggestions based on their actual use of this and other texts in their courses, as well as the careful evaluations of our colleagues. Our appreciation and thanks go to:

Michael Bedell, California State University, Bakersfield
Sharon Davis, Central Texas College
Angela L. Farrar, University of Nevada, Las Vegas
Lou Firenze, Northwood University
Judith Gordon, Boston College
Mike Griffith, Cascade College
Daniel Grundmann, Indiana University
Sally Hackman, Central Methodist College
Rich Havranek, SUNY Institute of Technology
Kim Hester, Arkansas State University
Stephen Hiatt, Catawba College
Alyce Hochhalter, St. Mary Woods College
David J. Hudson, Spalding University
Avan Jassawalla, SUNY at Geneseo
Pravin Kamdar, Cardinal Stritch University
Jordan J. Kaplan, Long Island University
Steve Karau, Southern Illinois University at Carbondale
Joseph Kavanaugh, Sam Houston State University
John Kelley, Villanova University
Dennis Lee Kovach, Community College of Allegheny County
Kenneth Kovach, University of Maryland
Chalmer E. Labig, Jr., Oklahoma State University
Scott W. Lester, University of Wisconsin, Eau Claire
J. Jonathan Lewis, Texas Southern University
Barbara Luck, Jackson Community College
Michael Matukonis, SUNY Oneonta
Doug McCabe, Georgetown University
Marjorie L. McInerney, Marshall University
Veronica Meyers, San Diego State University
Julia Morrison, Bloomfield College
David Nye, Kennedy-Western University
Paul Olsen, Saint Michael's College
Donald Otto, Lindenwood University
Dane Partridge, University of Southern Indiana
Bryan J. Pesta, Cleveland State University
Alex Pomnichowski, Ferris State University
Victor Prosper, University of the Incarnate Word
Michael Raphael, Central Connecticut State University
Charles Rarick, Barry University
June Roux, Salem Community College
Kelli Schutte, Calvin College
Tom Sedwick, Indiana University of Pennsylvania
Jim Sethi, University of Montana-Western

William L. Smith, Emporia State University
Emeric Solymossy, Western Illinois University
Howard Stanger, Canisius College
Scott L. Stevens, Detroit College of Business
Nanette Swarthout, Fontbonne College
Karen Ann Tarnoff, East Tennessee State University
Thomas Taveggia, University of Arizona
Alan Tillquist, West Virginia State College
Sue Toombs, Weatherford College
Richard Trotter, University of Baltimore
William Turnley, Kansas State University
Catherine L. Tyler, Oakland University
Barbara Warschawski, Schenectady County Community College
Steve Werner, University of Houston
L. A. Witt, University of New Orleans
Evelyn Zent, University of Washington, Tacoma

In the manuscript for this edition, we have drawn not only on the current literature but also on the current practices of organizations that furnished information and illustrations relating to their HR programs. We are indebted to the leaders in the field who have developed the available heritage of information and practices of HRM and who have influenced us through their writings and personal associations. We have also been aided by students in our classes, by former students, by the participants in the management development programs with whom we have been associated, by HR managers, and by our colleagues. In particular, we would like to express our appreciation to Dorothy Galvez and Amy Ray for their helpful insights and support for this edition of the text. We appreciate the efforts of everyone at Thomson South-Western who helped to develop and produce this text and its supplements. They include Joe Sabatino, Senior Acquisitions Editor; Susan Smart, Senior Developmental Editor; Kimberly Kanakes, Senior Marketing Manager; Heather Mann, Production Project Manager; Tippy McIntosh, Art Director; and Kristen Meere, our Technology Project Manager.

Our greatest indebtedness is to our wives—Ronnie Bohlander and Marybeth Snell—who have contributed in so many ways to this book over the years. They are always sources of invaluable guidance and assistance. Furthermore, by their continued enthusiasm and support, they have made the process a more pleasant and rewarding experience. We are most grateful to them for their many contributions to this publication, to our lives, and to our families.

George W. Bohlander
Arizona State University

Scott A. Snell
Cornell University

about the authors

George Bohlander

George Bohlander is Professor of Management at Arizona State University. He received his M.B.A. from the University of Southern California and his Ph.D. from the University of California at Los Angeles. His areas of expertise include employment law, training and development, work teams, public policy, and labor relations. He has received the Outstanding Undergraduate Teaching Excellence Award presented by the College of Business at ASU and also received the prestigious ASU Parents Association Professorship for his contributions to students and teaching.

Dr. Bohlander is an active researcher and author. He has published over 50 articles and monographs in professional and practitioner journals such as *National Productivity Review, HR Magazine, Labor Law Journal, The Journal of Collective Bargaining in the Public Sector,* and others. Dr. Bohlander continues to be a consultant to public and private organizations including the U.S. Postal Service, American Productivity & Quality Center, BFGoodrich, McDonnell Douglas, Rural/Metro Corporation, and Del Webb. He is also an active labor arbitrator.

Scott Snell

Scott A. Snell is Professor of Human Resource Studies and Director of Executive Education in the School of Industrial and Labor Relations at Cornell University. He received a B.A. in Psychology from Miami University as well as M.B.A. and Ph.D. degrees in Business Administration from Michigan State University. Prior to joining the faculty at Cornell, Dr. Snell was on the faculty of business at Penn State University. During his career, he has taught courses in human resource management and strategic management to undergraduates, graduates, and executives.

Professor Snell has worked with companies such as AT&T, GE, IBM, Merck, and Shell to address the alignment of human resource systems with strategic initiatives such as globalization, technological change, and knowledge management. His research and teaching interests focus on the development and deployment of intellectual capital as a foundation of an organization's core competencies. He has published a number of articles in professional journals and is the author of two textbooks. In addition, Dr. Snell has served on the editorial boards of *Journal of Managerial Issues, Digest of Management Research, Human Resource Management Review, Human Resource Planning,* and *Academy of Management Journal.*

edition 14

Managing Human Resources

chapter 1

The Challenge of Human Resources Management

After studying this chapter, you should be able to

Identify how firms gain sustainable competitive advantage through people.

Explain how globalization is influencing human resources management.

Describe the impact of information technology on managing people.

Identify the importance of change management.

State HR's role in developing intellectual capital.

Differentiate how TQM and reengineering influence HR systems.

Discuss the impact of cost pressures on HR policies.

Discuss the primary demographic and employee concerns pertaining to HRM.

Provide examples of the roles and competencies of today's HR managers.

There's an old joke that goes . . .

The organization of the future will be so technologically advanced that it will be run by just one person and a dog. The person will be there to feed the dog, and the dog will be there to make sure that the person doesn't touch anything.

In the past, observers feared that machines might one day eliminate the need for people at work. In reality, just the opposite has been occurring. People are more important in today's organizations than ever before. As Ed Gubman, author of *The Talent Solution,* points out, "In many fast-growing economies, it may be easier to access money and technology than good people." Competitive advantage belongs to companies that know how to attract, select, deploy, and develop talent.[1]

human resources management (HRM) The process of managing human talent to achieve an organization's objectives

We use a lot of words to describe the importance of people to organizations. The term *human resources* implies that people have capabilities that drive organizational performance (along with other resources such as money, materials, and information). Other terms such as *human capital* and *intellectual assets* all have in common the idea that people make the difference in how an organization performs. Successful organizations are particularly adept at bringing together different kinds of people to achieve a common purpose. This is the essence of **human resources management (HRM).**

Why Study Human Resources Management?

As you embark on this course, you may be wondering how the topic of human resources management relates to your interests and career aspirations. The answer to the question "Why study HRM?" is pretty much the same regardless of whether you plan on working in an HR department or not. Staffing the organization, designing jobs and teams, developing skillful employees, identifying approaches for improving their performance, and rewarding employee successes—all typically labeled HRM issues—are as relevant to line managers as they are to managers in the HR department.

To work with people effectively, we have to understand human behavior, and we have to be knowledgeable about the various systems and practices available to help us build a skilled and motivated workforce. At the same time, we have to be aware of economic, technological, social, and legal issues that either facilitate or constrain our efforts to achieve organizational goals.[2] Because employee skills, knowledge, and abilities are among the most distinctive and renewable resources on which a company can draw, their strategic management is more important than ever. As Thomas J. Watson, the founder of IBM, said, "You can get capital and erect buildings, but it takes people to build a business."[3]

While "competing through people" may be a theme for human resources management, the idea remains only a framework for action. On a day-to-day basis, managers focus on specific challenges and issues that pertain to human resources. Figure 1.1 provides an overall framework for human resources management. From this figure, we can see that HRM has to help blend many aspects of management; at this point we will simply classify them as either "competitive challenges" or "employee concerns." By balancing sometimes competing demands, HRM plays an important role in getting the most from employees and providing a work environment that meets

Figure 1.1 Overall Framework for Human Resources Management

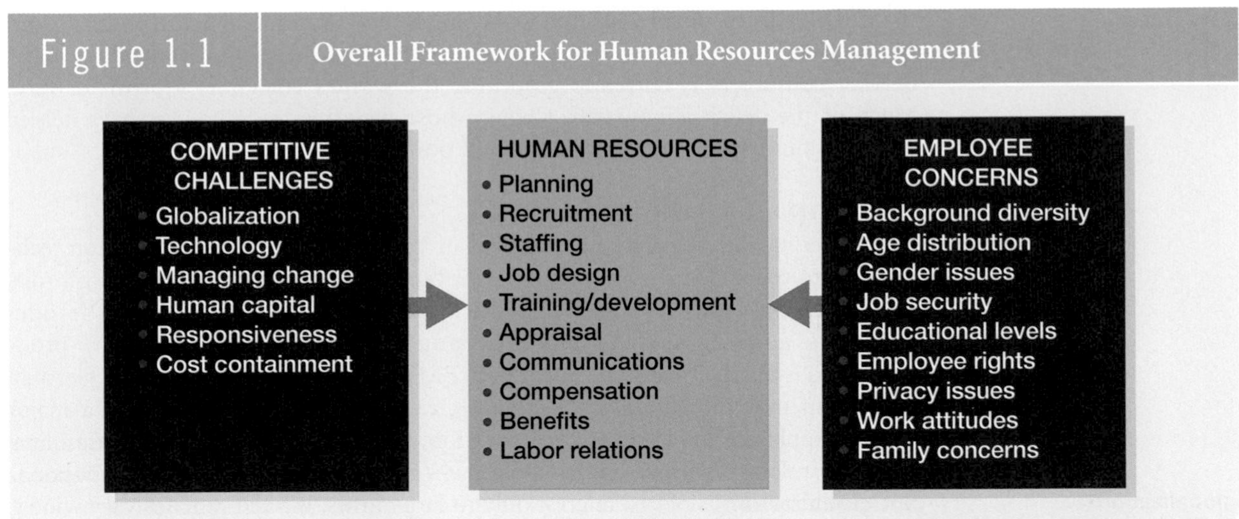

their short-term and long-term needs. We will use this framework as a basis for our discussion throughout the rest of this chapter.

Competitive Challenges and Human Resources Management

Professional organizations such as the Society for Human Resource Management (SHRM) and the Human Resource Planning Society (HRPS) conduct ongoing studies of the most pressing competitive issues facing firms. By seeking the input of chief executives and HR managers, these organizations keep a finger on the pulse of major trends. For the past decade or so, there has been a constant theme around the following issues:

USING THE INTERNET

The Society for Human Resource Management's web site provides membership information, resources, and links to others in the HR field. Go to the Student Resources at:

http://bohlander.swlearning.com

- Going global
- Embracing new technology
- Managing change
- Managing talent, or human capital
- Responding to the market
- Containing costs

These trends extend beyond "people issues" per se, but they all focus on the need to develop a skilled and flexible workforce in order to compete in the twenty-first century.

Challenge 1: Going Global

In order to grow and prosper, many companies are seeking business opportunities in global markets. Competition—and cooperation—with foreign companies has become an important focal point for business. Indeed, exporting accounts for a large portion of the U.S. economy, and totaled more than $1,146.1 billion in 2004. On the flip side, the United States has imported more than it has exported every year since the early 1970s. Between 2003 and 2004 alone, the U.S. trade deficit increased from nearly $500 billion to more than $600 billion. By all accounts, the insatiable demand of U.S. consumers is currently propelling the world's economic growth forward. Much of the deficit is now with China, whose new free-trade policies have helped turn the country into an economic growth powerhouse.[4]

The Impact of Globalization

By partnering with firms in other regions of the world and using information technologies to coordinate distant parts of their businesses, companies such as Motorola, General Electric, and Toyota have shown that their vision for the future is to offer customers "anything, anytime, anywhere" around the world. Even well-known products are losing their national identities: BMW has traditionally been a German brand, but now the automaker is building cars in South Carolina; Hafer, a major Chinese appliance and electronics corporation, has opened a plant in North Carolina; and Chevrolets—as American as apple pie—are now being assembled in Mexico.[5] But **globalization** is not of interest only to large firms. While estimates vary widely, approximately 70–85 percent of the U.S. economy today is affected by international competition. Even small companies partner with organizations in other countries; for example, SpringHill Greenhouses in Lodi, Ohio, partners with florists through associations such as FTD and Teleflora to work with growers in Holland (tulips and lilies) and Colombia (roses) to serve customers around the world. Even though they produce only 30 percent of the total value of American manufactured exports, nearly 97 percent of all U.S. exporters are small and medium-sized companies, and their numbers are growing rapidly, up from 65,000 in 1987 to almost 250,000 today, according to the National Small Business Association.

globalization
The trend toward opening up foreign markets to international trade and investment

USING THE INTERNET

To learn more about NAFTA, go to the Student Resources at:
http://bohlander.swlearning.com

Numerous free-trade agreements forged between nations in the last half-century have helped quicken the pace of globalization. The first major trade agreement of the twentieth century was made in 1948, following World War II. Called the General Agreement on Tariffs and Trade (GATT), it established rules and guidelines for global commerce between nations and groups of nations. Since GATT began, world trade has increased more than sixfold. GATT paved the way for the formation of the European Union in 1986; the North American Free Trade Agreement (NAFTA), encompassing the United States, Canada, and Mexico in 1994; and the Asia-Pacific Economic Cooperation (APEC) in 1989, which loosened trade restrictions among Pacific Rim countries. The World Trade Organization (WTO), headquartered in Lausanne, Switzerland, now has more than 148 member countries, accounting for more than 97 percent of world trade.[6]

Globalization and Corporate Social Responsibility. Even though globalization has led to a great improvement in people's living standards in the last half-century, free-trade agreements still stir fierce debate. When NAFTA talks were first underway, U.S. and Canadian citizens worried that the agreement would lead to a loss of jobs to Mexico, where labor costs are cheaper. Other people worry that free trade is creating a "have/have not" world economy, in which the people in developing economies and the world's environment are being exploited by companies in richer, more developed countries. This has sparked anti-free-trade protests in many nations.

Concerns such as these, coupled with numerous scandals plaguing U.S. corporations in recent years, have led to a new focus on **corporate social responsibility,** or good citizenship. Companies are discovering that being socially responsible helps the

corporate social responsibility
The responsibility of the firm to act in the best interests of the people and communities affected by its activities

Highlights in HRM 1

A Guide to HR Internet Sites

HR professionals can access the following web sites for current information related to human resources.

Codes of Conduct

Asia-Pacific Economic Cooperation Forum Business Code of Conduct (http://www.cauxroundtable.org/APECForumBusinessCodeofConduct.html)
Caux Round Table Principles for Business (http://www.cauxroundtable.org)
European Corporate Code of Conduct (European Union Parliament, http://www.europa.eu.int)
Fair Labor Association Workshop Code of Conduct (http://www.fairlabor.org)
Global Sullivan Principles (http://www.thegsp.org)
ILO Tripartite Declaration of Principles Concerning Multinational Enterprises and Social Policy (http://www.ilo.org)
OECD Guidelines for Multinational Enterprises—2002 (http://www.corporate-accountability.org)
OECD, Principles of Corporate Governance—2004 (http://www.oecd.org)
Rules of Conduct on Extortion and Bribery in International Business Transactions (International Chamber of Commerce, http://www.iccwbo.org)
United Nations Universal Declaration of Human Rights (http://www.un.org)

General

- AFL-CIO (http://www.aflcio.org/home.htm)—Union news, issue papers, press releases, links to labor sites.
- American Management Association (http://www.amanet.org/index.htm)—AMA membership, programs, training, and so on.
- FedWorld (http://www.fedworld.gov)—A gateway to many government web sites.
- HR Professional's Gateway to the Internet (http://www.prosgateway.com/www/index2.html)—Links to HR-related web pages.
- Occupational Safety and Health Resources (http://osh.net)—OSHA-related sites, government pages, resources, and so on.
- Society for Human Resource Management (http://www.shrm.org)—Current events, information, connections, and articles.
- Telecommuting, Telework, and Alternative Officing (http://www.gilgordon.com)—Telecommuting and flexible hours.
- Training & Development Resource Center (http://www.tcm.com/trdev/)—Job mart, training links, and T&D electronic mailing list links.
- U.S. Department of Labor (http://www.dol.gov)—Job bank, labor statistics, press releases, grants, and contract information.

bottom line. Moreover, workers applying for jobs are saying corporate responsibility is now more important to their job selection. One of HR's leadership roles is to spearhead the development and implementation of corporate citizenship throughout the organization.[7] Highlights in HRM 1 lists a number of Internet sites of organizations with different conduct codes firms internationally are striving to adhere to. Also listed are a number of general web sites useful to HR professionals.

Effect of Globalization on HRM

For all of the opportunities afforded by international business, when managers talk about "going global," they have to balance a complicated set of issues related to different geographies, cultures, employment laws, and business practices. Human resources issues underlie each of these concerns and include such things as gauging the knowledge and skill base of foreign workforces and figuring out how best to hire and train them, sometimes with materials that must be translated into a number of different languages. Relocating managers and other workers to direct the efforts of a foreign workforce is a challenge as well. HR personnel are frequently responsible for implementing training programs and development opportunities to enhance managers' understanding of foreign cultures and practices. In many cases, HR managers must adjust the compensation plans of employees working abroad to ensure that they receive fair and equitable pay in parts of the world where living costs differ. Perhaps the most difficult task is retaining these employees in the face of the culture shock they and their families are likely to experience.

So while managing across borders provides new and broader opportunities for organizations, it also represents a quantum leap in the complexity of human resources management. In fact, the international arena for HRM is so involved that we have devoted an entire chapter (Chapter 15) to discussing its competitive, cultural, and practical implications.

Challenge 2: Embracing New Technology

Advancements in information technology have enabled organizations to take advantage of the information explosion. With computer networks, unlimited amounts of data can be stored, retrieved, and used in a wide variety of ways, from simple record keeping to controlling complex equipment. The effect is so dramatic that at a broader level, organizations are changing the way they do business. Use of the Internet to transact business has become so pervasive for both large and small companies that e-commerce is rapidly becoming the organizational challenge of the new millennium. Even following the "dot-com bust," in which many promising new Internet companies failed rapidly, the Web is transforming the way traditional brick-and-mortar companies do business. Organizations are connected via computer-mediated relationships, and they are giving rise to a new generation of "virtual" workers who work from home, in hotels, in their cars, or wherever their work takes them. The implications for HRM are at times mind boggling.

From Touch Labor to Knowledge Workers

knowledge workers
Workers whose responsibilities extend beyond the physical execution of work to include planning, decision making, and problem solving

The introduction of advanced technology tends to reduce the number of jobs that require little skill and to increase the number of jobs that require considerable skill. In general, this transformation has been referred to as a shift from "touch labor" to **"knowledge workers,"** in which employee responsibilities expand to include a richer array of activities such as planning, decision making, and problem solving.[8] In many cases, current employees are being retrained to assume new roles and responsibilities. Even when employees are displaced, they also require retraining.

USING THE INTERNET

For more information about Manpower, go to the Student Resources at:

http://bohlander.swlearning.com

Technology, transportation, communications, and utilities industries tend to spend the most on training. Knowledge-based training has become so important that Manpower Inc., the largest employment agency in the United States, offers free information technology training through its Manpower Global Learning Center (http://www.manpowernet.com), an online university for its 2.5 million employees worldwide. The Manpower site features more than 5,000 hours of online instruction in technology applications, along with professional-development and business skills, and telecommunications courses. In fact, Manpower is so focused on developing technical skills in potential employees that it has set up the system so that some training and career-planning information is available to those who simply send the company a resume. A trend toward "just-in-time" learning delivered via the Internet to employees' desktops has developed, as well. Cisco, for example, has online digital videos its employees can download from its Intranet when and where they need them to do their jobs.[9]

Influence of Technology in HRM

human resources information system (HRIS) A computerized system that provides current and accurate data for purposes of control and decision making

Information technology has, of course, changed the face of HRM in the United States and abroad. Perhaps the most central use of technology in HRM is an organization's **human resources information system (HRIS).** Organizations determined to improve productivity and lower costs are finding HR a good place to start. Because HR affects the entire workforce—everyone who works for the company must be hired, trained, and paid, usually through HR—the impact of HRIS can be dramatic. It can be a potent weapon for lowering administrative costs, increasing productivity, speeding up response times, and improving decision making and customer service.

Source: © 1998 by Nick Downes; from *Harvard Business Review.*

Highlights in HRM 2

Most Common HR Information Systems Applications

Payroll	76.7%
Benefits administration	57.1
Benefits enrollment	41.4
Recruiting—applicant tracking	39.1
Personnel administration	39.1
Training and development	31.6
Employee self-service	24.8
Manager self-service	18.0
Other	3.8

Source: "How HR Managers Use Technology Applications to Control HR Department Costs," *Human Resource Department Management Report,* no. 4–5 (May 2004).

The most obvious impact has been operational—that is, automating routine activities, alleviating administrative burdens, reducing costs, and improving productivity internal to the HR function itself. As shown in Highlights in HRM 2, the most frequent uses include automating payroll processing, maintaining employee records, and administering benefits programs. One of the big trends in recent years has been toward HRIS "self-service"—setting up systems, usually on an Intranet, to allow managers to access employee records themselves for administrative purposes, and to allow employees to access and change their own benefits and other personal information. Merck's HR system was redesigned to enable line managers and employees to enter, retrieve, and edit data in order to make better decisions faster. This has helped alleviate many of the paper burdens Merck's HR group previously faced and offered greater convenience to both managers and their employees.

Today, however, software applications are available to automate far more HR activities than just payroll, records, and benefits information. All sorts of routine HR activities, from front to back, have seen some sort of automation. Companies are now using software to recruit, screen, and pretest applicants online before hiring them as well as to train and promote employees once they've been hired. For example, Merck's staffing management system supports the hiring process by tracking applicants' information, scanning resumes, and making the information immediately accessible to line managers so they can search systematically for the people whose skills they want. Managers can search online for internal and external talent by running searches of candidates who have been categorized by skill set. An outside vendor that specializes in web-based recruiting administers the system and acts as a conduit between Merck and broader databases such as Monster.com and Hotjobs.com.[10]

Corning, Inc., uses HR software, among other things, to set the developmental goals of its employees once they've been hired and gauge how well they are meeting them. Employees can look online to see their own goals and mark their progress as well as see everyone else's goals in the command chain, from the CEO down to their immediate supervisors. This "cascading" of goals has helped Corning's employees align their personal goals with the organization's overall objectives in order to reach higher levels. "Like any large company, we tended to get 'silo-ed' and fragmented the more we grew," said one vice president at a company using a system similar to Corning's. "We needed a better way to pull our global team together and get people focused on what the priorities are for our business." Brown and Williamson Tobacco uses a program called Career Tracker not only to trace the performance of employees but also to allow them to create a personalized learning curriculum from materials online. Similarly, Merck worked with a software vendor to develop a system that provides coaching tips and learning tools and resources for employees and managers based on their goals.[11]

Highlights in HRM 3 shows just a partial list of software companies and the products they provide for managing people. According to a survey by Cedar Group, a technology consulting firm, prepackaged, or "canned," HR web-based solutions are as commonly used as custom-designed systems. Generally, companies also have the choice of hosting the applications on their own servers or having a vendor do it for them. Most companies have outside vendors such as Oracle-PeopleSoft (sometimes called *ASPs,* which stands for *application service providers*) support the applications, instead of the IT groups within their own organizations.

So what sort of system should HR professionals choose from among the many options available to them? Expert say the first step in choosing an HRIS is for HR personnel to evaluate the biggest "headaches" they experience, or most time-consuming tasks, and then choose the applications that can have the strongest impact on the firm's financial measures—that is, the ones that get the "biggest bang for the buck." These applications are more likely to get "buy-in" from the firm's top managers. HR managers should then calculate the costs based on average salaries, or HR hours, that could be saved by using an HRIS, along with the hours of increased productivity that would occur as a result.

Other factors that need to be evaluated include the following:

- *Fit of the application to the firm's employee base.* If many of the firm's employees work on a factory floor, is the system appropriate, or does HR need to install kiosks in employee areas? How will the information be secured? Will employees need to be assigned passwords? Can they access the information from offsite, say, from their homes?
- *Ability to upgrade or customize the software.* What sorts of costs will be involved to upgrade the software in the coming years?
- *Compatibility with current systems.* Does the HRIS link into existing, or planned, information systems easily and inexpensively?
- *User friendliness.* Does the software provide additional features such as links to learning resources or help for managers who might need it?
- *Availability of technical support.* Should the HRIS system be supported internally or should the vendor host it? What are the vendor's technical support capabilities?
- *Time required to implement and train staff members to use the HRIS, including HR and payroll personnel, managers, and employees.* Who is responsible for training employees and how will it be done?
- *Initial costs and annual maintenance costs.* Is a "suite" of applications needed or just a few key applications? Experts advise HR managers to price each application separately and then ask vendors for a "bundled" price.[12]

Human Resources Information System Companies

ADP
http://www.adp.com
Roseland, NJ
(973) 974-5000
Provides solutions and services for payroll, tax, and HR benefits administration, including 401k/retirement services.

Best Software Inc.
http://www.bestsoftware.com
Irvine, CA
(800) 854-3415
Provider of software for accounting, budgeting and planning, fixed assets, customer relationship, analytics, human resources, and payroll.

Ceridian
http://www.ceridian.com
Minneapolis, MN
(952) 853-8100
Integrated human resources, payroll, tax, time, benefits management, and employee effectiveness services.

Employease
http://www.employease.com
Norcross, GA
(770) 325-7700
Hosted, web-based human resources software and services benefits administration, reporting, and applicant tracking applications.

Human Concepts
http://www.orgplus.com/company/index.htm
Sausalito, CA
(888) 821-1261
Solutions for managing organizational change and supporting critical business decisions. Software integrates with HR databases to automatically create and publish organizational charts.

Kronos
http://www.kronos.com
Chelmsford, MA
(978) 250-9800
Provider of systems that collect attendance data and automatically post it to payroll. Labor management analysis software and payroll processing applications.

NuView Systems, Inc.
http://www.nuviewinc.com
Wilmington, MA
(978) 988-7884
Applications for human resources and benefits administration, recruitment, applicant tracking and resume scanning, training administration, succession planning, employee and manager self-service, and corporate performance metrics.

Oracle-PeopleSoft
http://www.oracle.com/peoplesoft/index.html
Redwood City, CA
(650) 506-7000
Software for data center management, business intelligence, corporate governance, information security, supply chain management, and relationship management.

People Trak, by Technical Difference
http://www.people-trak.com
Bonsall, CA
(760) 941-5800
Offers tools for personnel management, time and attendance, COBRA administration, workplace safety management, recruitment applicant tracking, and training administration.

SAS Institute
http://www.sas.com
Cary, NC
(919) 677-8000
Human capital software that can gather and analyze information on headcount, retention, churn, compensation, staffing, recruiting, budgeting, employment history, and affirmative action and EEO issues.

Spectrum Human Resource Systems Corporation
http://www.spectrumhr.com
Denver, CO
(303) 592-3200
Offers a variety of web-based and desktop-based software products for human resource management that allow for employee self-service. Spectrum also provides in-house support services for its software, including planning, training, and a hotline.

Ultimate Software Group
http://www.ultimatesoftware.com
Weston, FL
(954) 331-7000
Provider of web-based software that manages employee communications, benefits, payroll, and staffing functions.

When an effective HRIS is implemented, perhaps the biggest advantage gained is that HR personnel can concentrate more effectively on the firm's strategic direction instead of on routine tasks. This can include forecasting personnel needs (especially for firms planning to expand, contract, or merge), planning for career and employee promotions, and evaluating the impact of the firm's policies—both those related to HR functions and other functions—to help improve the firm's earnings and strategic direction. "We wanted our HR teams to focus on people issues instead of data problems," explains Sandra Hoffman, CIO of MAPICS, an HR applications provider.

The initial drive to adopt human resources information systems was related to cutting HR costs. But HR managers have since discovered that the systems have allowed them to share information with line managers, who, by having access to it, have been able to come up with better production practices and cost control solutions. As a result, HR managers are now asking their application providers to develop additional software to meet certain goals, such as lowering a company's total spending on employee health care and improving customer service.[13]

Challenge 3: Managing Change

Technology and globalization are only two of the forces driving change in organizations and HRM. Today, being able to manage change has become paramount to the firm's success. As one pundit put it, "No change means chance." Successful companies, says Harvard Business School professor Rosabeth Moss Kanter, develop a culture that just keeps moving all the time.[14] Given the pace of today's commerce, organizations can rarely stand still for long. In highly competitive environments, where competition is global and innovation is continuous, change has become a core competency of organizations.

Types of Changes

reactive change
Change that occurs after external forces have already affected performance

proactive change
Change initiated to take advantage of targeted opportunities

Programs focused on total quality, continuous improvement, downsizing, reengineering, outsourcing, and the like are all examples of the means organizations are using to modify the way they operate in order to be more successful. Some of these changes are **reactive change,** resulting when external forces have already affected an organization's performance. Other changes are **proactive change,** initiated by managers to take advantage of targeted opportunities, particularly in fast-changing industries in which followers are not successful. Bob Nardelli, for example, recognized the need for change when he took over as CEO of Home Depot. Even though the company was the leader in the home improvement industry, Nardelli recognized the unrealized potential of the company and its capacity for growth. In the first year of his term, Nardelli and Dennis Donovan, executive vice president of HR, utilized their experience at GE (working under Jack Welch) to initiate organization-wide transformation of the company. The main thrust of the change-management program was to involve employees in instituting continuous innovation and excellent customer service. These types of change initiatives are not designed to fix problems that have arisen in the organization so much as they are designed to help renew everyone's focus on key success factors.[15]

Managing Change through HR

In a survey by the American Management Association (AMA), 84 percent of executives polled said that they have at least one change initiative going on in their organizations.

© STOCKBYTE GOLD/GETTY IMAGES

Formal change management programs help to keep employees focused on the success of the business.

Yet surprisingly, in contrast to the Home Depot experience, only about two-thirds said that their companies have any sort of formal change-management program to support these initiatives![16] This is unfortunate because successful change rarely occurs naturally or easily. Most of the major reasons why change efforts can fail come down to HR issues. Some of the top reasons are as follows:[17]

1. Not establishing a sense of urgency
2. Not creating a powerful coalition to guide the effort
3. Lacking leaders who have a vision
4. Lacking leaders who communicate the vision
5. Not removing obstacles to the new vision
6. Not systematically planning for and creating short-term "wins"
7. Declaring victory too soon
8. Not anchoring changes in the corporate culture

Most employees—regardless of occupation—understand that the way things were done five or ten years ago is very different from how they are done today (or will be done five or ten years from now). Responsibilities change, job assignments change, and work processes change. And this change is continuous—a part of the job—rather than temporary. Nevertheless, people often resist change because it requires them to modify or abandon ways of working that have been successful or at least familiar to them. As Dr. Marilyn Buckner, the immediate past president of the Human Resource Planning Society in New York City, put it: "Non-technical, unattended human factors are, in fact, most often the problem in failed change projects." To manage change, executives and managers, including those in HR, have to envision the future, communicate this vision to employees, set clear expectations for performance, and develop the capability to execute by reorganizing people and reallocating assets. Organizations that have been successful in engineering change typically build into their change-management planning these key elements:

- They link the change to the business strategy.
- They create quantifiable benefits.
- They engage key employees, customers, and their suppliers, early.
- They integrate required behavior changes.
- They lead clearly, unequivocally, and consistently.
- They invest to implement and sustain change.
- They communicate continuously and personally.
- They sell commitment to the change, not communication about the change.[18]

human capital
The knowledge, skills, and capabilities of individuals that have economic value to an organization

Challenge 4: Managing Talent, or Human Capital

The idea that organizations "compete through people" highlights the fact that success increasingly depends on an organization's ability to manage talent, or **human capital.**

The term *human capital* describes the economic value of employees' knowledge, skills, and capabilities. Although the value of these assets may not show up directly on a company's balance sheet, it nevertheless has tremendous impact on an organization's performance. The following quotations from notable CEOs illustrate this point:[19]

- "If you look at our semiconductors and melt them down for silicon, that's a tiny fraction of the costs. The rest is intellect and mistakes." (Gordon Moore, Intel)
- "An organization's ability to learn, and translate that learning into action rapidly, is the ultimate competitive business advantage." (Jack Welch, General Electric)
- "Successful companies of the 21st century will be those who do the best jobs of capturing, storing and leveraging what their employees know." (Lew Platt, Hewlett-Packard)

Human Capital and HRM

Human capital is intangible and elusive and cannot be managed the way organizations manage jobs, products, and technologies. One of the reasons for this is that the employees, *not* the organization, own their own human capital. If valued employees leave a company, they take their human capital with them, and any investment the company has made in training and developing those people is lost.

To build human capital in organizations, managers must continue to develop superior knowledge, skills, and experience within their workforce. Staffing programs focus on identifying, recruiting, and hiring the best and the brightest talent available. Training programs complement these staffing practices to provide skill enhancement, particularly in areas that cannot be transferred to another company if an employee leaves.[20] In addition, employees need opportunities for development on the job. The most highly valued intelligence tends to be associated with competencies and capabilities that are learned from experience and are not easily taught.[21] Consequently, managers have to do a good job of providing developmental assignments to employees and ensuring their job duties and requirements are flexible enough to allow for growth and learning.

Beyond the need to invest in employee development, organizations have to find ways of using the knowledge that currently exists. Too often, employees have skills that go unused. As Robert Buckman (who served as CEO of Buckman Laboratories for twenty-two years, a period of unprecedented growth for the company) noted, "If the greatest database in the company is housed in the individual minds of the associates of the organization, then that is where the power of the organization resides. These individual knowledge bases are continually changing and adapting to the real world in front of them. We have to connect these individual knowledge bases together so that they do whatever they do best in the shortest possible time."[22] Efforts to empower employees and encourage thier participation and involvement more fully utilize the human capital available. (Employee empowerment is discussed fully in later chapters.)

In companies such as Texas Instruments and Toys "R" Us, managers are evaluated on their progress toward meeting developmental goals. These goals focus on skill development and gaining new competencies and capabilities. In a growing number of instances, pay is attached to this knowledge and skill acquisition. Skill-based pay, for example, rewards employees for each new class of jobs they are capable of performing. We will discuss skill-based pay (or pay-for-knowledge) more in Chapter 9.

Developmental assignments, particularly those involving teamwork, can also be a valuable way of facilitating knowledge exchange and mutual learning. Effective communication (whether face to face or through information technology) is instrumental in sharing knowledge and making it widely available throughout the organization. As Dave Ulrich, professor of business at the University of Michigan, noted: "Learning capability is *g* times *g*—a business's ability to *generate* new ideas multiplied by its adeptness at *generalizing* them throughout the company."[23]

HR programs and assignments are often the conduit through which knowledge is transferred among employees. A recent survey by the Human Resource Planning Society revealed that 65 percent of responding companies believed that their HR group plays a key role in developing human capital. Boeing Satellite Systems, for example, has created a "lessons learned" site on its Intranet where all areas of the company can store the knowledge they have learned. As information and intellectual capital are posted to the company's electronic newsgroups, they can be analyzed and consolidated by editorial teams. Employees can access and use this new codified knowledge directly from the Internet. Executives at Boeing estimate that this form of intellectual capital has reduced the cost of developing a satellite by as much as $25 million.[24]

HR managers and line managers each play an important role in creating an organization that understands the value of knowledge, documents the skills and capabilities available to the organization, and identifies ways of utilizing that knowledge to benefit the firm. We will address these issues throughout the text, but particularly in Chapters 5 and 7 on career development and training.

Challenge 5: Responding to the Market

Meeting customer expectations is essential for any organization. In addition to focusing on internal management issues, managers must also meet customer requirements of quality, innovation, variety, and responsiveness. These standards often separate the winners from the losers in today's competitive world. How well does a company understand its customers' needs? How fast can it develop and get a new product to market? How effectively has it responded to special concerns? "Better, faster, cheaper"—these standards require organizations to constantly align their processes with customer needs. Management innovations such as total quality management (TQM) and process reengineering are but two of the comprehensive approaches to responding to customers. Each has direct implications for HR.

Total Quality Management, Six Sigma, and HRM

total quality management (TQM)
A set of principles and practices whose core ideas include understanding customer needs, doing things right the first time, and striving for continuous improvement

Total quality management (TQM) is a set of principles and practices whose core ideas include understanding customer needs, doing things right the first time, and striving for continuous improvement. Total quality management techniques were developed in the mid-1940s by Dr. W. Edward Deming after studying Japanese companies rebuilding following WWII. The TQM revolution in the United States began in the mid-1980s, led by companies such as Motorola, Xerox, and Ford. But since that time, criteria spelled out in the Malcolm Baldrige National Quality Award have provided the impetus for both large and small companies to rethink their approach to HRM. Currently, the Baldrige Award is given annually in each of five categories: manufacturing, service, small business, education, and healthcare.[25]

Unfortunately, early TQM programs were no panacea for responding to customer needs and improving productivity. In many cases, managers viewed quality as a quick fix and became disillusioned when results did not come easily. When TQM initiatives do work, it is usually because managers have made major changes in their philosophies and HR programs. More recently, companies such as Motorola, GE, Dow Chemical, and Home Depot have adopted a more systematic approach to quality, called **Six Sigma,** which includes major changes in management philosophy and HR programs. Six Sigma is a statistical method of translating a customer's needs into separate tasks and defining the best way to perform each task in concert with the others. By examining the optimal process, Six Sigma can have a powerful effect on the quality of products, the performance of customer service, and the professional development of employees. What makes Six Sigma different from other quality efforts is that it catches mistakes before they happen. In a true Six Sigma environment, variation from standard is reduced to only 3.4 defects per million.[26]

Six Sigma
A process used to translate customer needs into a set of optimal tasks that are performed in concert with one another

The importance of HR to Six Sigma begins with the formation of teams, and extends to training, performance management, communication, culture, and even rewards. As individuals progress through Six Sigma training, they can move up from "green belt" to eventually achieve "black belt" status. Many of Dow's key HR slots require black-belt certification, for example. If this all sounds a bit hokey, take note of the successful companies that have made cultural—and performance—transformation as a result: Motorola credits Six Sigma with $16 billion in savings over the past twelve years; Ford reports that it saved more than $4 billion in one year alone; Motorola is so committed to Six Sigma that it now conducts Six Sigma training for employees of other firms who attend its Motorola University.[27] The most important quality-improvement techniques stress employee motivation, change in corporate culture, and employee education. Organizations known for product and service quality strongly believe that employees are the key to that quality.

One of the reasons that HR programs are so essential to programs such as Six Sigma is that they help balance two opposing forces. According to Laurie Broedling, an organizational psychologist and human resources expert, "One set of forces (the need for order and control) pulls every business toward stagnation, while another set of forces (the need for growth and creativity) drives it toward disintegration." Six Sigma's focus on continuous improvement drives the system toward disequilibrium, while Six Sigma's focus on customers, management systems, and the like provide the restraining forces that keep the system together. HR practices help managers balance these two forces. Like human resources information systems, TQM has helped HR departments progress from a focus on functional activities to strategic planning. Better business thinking builds more strategic HR thinking.[28]

Reengineering and HRM

In addition to TQM and Six Sigma programs, some companies take a more radical approach to process redesign called reengineering. **Reengineering** has been described as "the fundamental rethinking and radical redesign of business processes to achieve dramatic improvements in cost, quality, service and speed."[29] Reengineering often requires that managers start over from scratch in rethinking how work should be done, how technology and people should interact, and how entire organizations should be structured. HR issues are central to these decisions. First, reengineering requires that managers create an environment for change, and, as we mentioned previously, HR issues drive change. Second, reengineering efforts depend on effective leadership and communication processes, two other areas related to HRM. Third, reengineering requires that administrative systems be reviewed and modified. Selection, job descriptions, training, career planning, performance appraisal, compensation, and

reengineering
Fundamental rethinking and radical redesign of business processes to achieve dramatic improvements in cost, quality, service, and speed

labor relations are all candidates for change to complement and support reengineering efforts. We will return to these issues, and speak more directly to the organizational development tools necessary for reengineering, in later chapters.

Challenge 6: Containing Costs

Investments in reengineering, TQM, human capital, technology, globalization, and the like are all very important for organizational competitiveness. Yet at the same time, there are increasing pressures on companies to lower costs and improve productivity to maximize efficiency. Like other functional department managers, human resources managers are now under pressure to show top managers the "bottom line" financial results their departments are achieving. Labor costs are one of the largest expenditures of any organization, particularly in service- and knowledge-intensive companies. Moreover, the healthcare costs of insuring workers and their families have skyrocketed in the past decade, posing a much bigger burden to firms. Organizations are taking many approaches to lowering labor-related costs. In addition to shifting some of the rising costs of healthcare back onto employees, firms are also downsizing, outsourcing, offshoring, and engaging in employee leasing in an attempt to enhance productivity. Each of these efforts has a big impact on HR policies and practices.

Downsizing

downsizing
Planned elimination of jobs

Downsizing is the planned elimination of jobs. For example, when L. L. Bean saw that sales had fallen, the company undertook a number of efforts to identify what it called "smart cost reductions." Bean's TQM activities helped the company target quality problems and saved an estimated $30 million. But the cuts were not enough, and ultimately Leon Gorman, president of the firm, and Bob Peixotto, vice president of HR and quality, realized the company needed to eliminate some jobs. Instead of simply laying off people, however, the company started early retirement and "sweetened" voluntary separation programs. Then the company offered employee sabbaticals for continuing education.[30]

These efforts, combined with better employee communication, helped soften the blow of layoffs at L. L. Bean. But the pain of downsizing has been widespread throughout the United States. Virtually every major corporation within the country has undergone some cycle of downsizing. During the period from 1995 to 2002, about 2 million U.S. manufacturing jobs were lost—an 11 percent drop. One-third of companies downsized following 9/11. And it's not just U.S. firms that are losing manufacturing jobs. China lost 15 percent of its industrial jobs during the 1995–2002 period as well.

Historically, layoffs tended to affect manufacturing firms and line workers in particular, but in the 1990s, the layoffs began to encompass white-collar workers in greater numbers. In fact, in the largest U.S. firms, most of the jobs lost in the last decade have been white-collar jobs. One of the hardest-hit industries has been information technology.[31]

But downsizing is no longer being regarded as a short-term fix when times are tough. It's now become a tool continually used by companies to adjust to changes in technology, globalization, and the firm's business direction. For example, in a study that surveyed 450 senior HR executives at companies that had downsized in the past three years, only 21 percent said that financial difficulties had spurred the cutbacks, compared to 78 percent in a similar study in 1994. In fact, 34 percent of the executives said that the downsizing was done to strengthen their companies' future positions; 21 percent said it was done to achieve fundamental staff realignment; 17 percent said it was due to a merger or acquisition.

Whatever the reason, while some firms improve efficiency (and lower costs) with layoffs, many others do not obtain such benefits. These kinds of trade-offs have led some firms to establish a policy of "no layoffs." For example, in an industry that has seen layoffs in the tens of thousands, Southwest Airlines hasn't laid off a single employee. In fact, the company hasn't had layoffs in thirty years. Nucor Steel is another company with a no-layoff policy. These practices are admittedly an exception, but some firms are taking such an approach because of downsizing's toll on retention and recruitment. A study by Watson Wyatt of 750 companies showed that companies with excellent recruiting and retention policies provide a nearly 8% higher return to shareholders compared to those that don't. Those with a strong commitment to job security earned an additional 1.4% for shareholders.

Advocates of a no-layoff policy often note that layoffs may backfire after taking into account such hidden costs as the following:

- Severance and rehiring costs
- Accrued vacation and sick-day payouts
- Pension and benefit payoffs
- Potential lawsuits from aggrieved workers
- Loss of institutional memory and trust in management
- Lack of staffers when the economy rebounds
- Survivors who are risk averse, paranoid, and political

In contrast, companies that avoid downsizing say they get some important benefits from such policies:

- A fiercely loyal, more productive workforce
- Higher customer satisfaction
- Readiness to snap back with the economy
- A recruiting edge
- Workers who aren't afraid to innovate, knowing their jobs are safe[32]

More than one executive has concluded that you don't get dedicated and productive employees if at the first sign of trouble you show them that you think they are expendable.

To approach downsizing more intelligently, companies such as Continental Airlines, Dial Corporation, and L. L. Bean have made special efforts to reassign and retrain employees for new positions when their jobs are eliminated. This is consistent with a philosophy of employees as assets, as intellectual capital.

Outsourcing, Offshoring, and Employee Leasing

outsourcing
Contracting outside the organization to have work done that formerly was done by internal employees

Over the past twenty-five years, the employment relationship between companies and employees has shifted from relationship-based to transaction-based. Fewer people are working for one employer over the course of their lifetimes, and the Internet has created a workforce that is constantly scanning for new opportunities. More people are choosing to work on a freelance or contract basis, or to work part-time, especially women. Outsourcing is evidence of this trend.[33] **Outsourcing** simply means hiring

© AMIT BHARGAVE/BLOOMBERG NEWS/LANDOV

Dell Computer has thousands of employees located at call centers in India and elsewhere around the world. In fact, the Austin, Texas, computer maker has more employees working outside the United States than within it.

someone outside the company to perform tasks that could be done internally. Companies often hire the services of accounting firms, for example, to take care of financial services. They may hire advertising firms to handle promotions, software firms to develop data-processing systems, or law firms to handle legal issues. Maintenance, security, catering, and payroll are being outsourced in order to increase the organization's flexibility and lower its overhead costs. Interest in outsourcing has been spurred by executives who want to focus their organization's activities on what they do best versus peripheral activities. Increasingly, outsourcing is changing the way HR departments operate as well. Indeed, outsourcing has been one of the most prominent HR trends of the last 10 years, and will continue to be until the last dollar of excess costs has been wrung out. HR outsourcing is already is a $25 billion market, according to the research firm Gartner, Inc. In 2005, more than 85 percent of U.S. employers expected to outsource at least one HR function.[34]

Offshoring
The business practice of sending jobs to other countries

Offshoring, also referred to as "global sourcing," is the controversial practice of moving jobs overseas. Nonetheless, almost half of 500 senior finance and HR leaders surveyed said their firms are either offshoring or are considering offshoring in the next three years, according to a study by Hewitt Associates.[35] Figure 1.2 shows the huge number of jobs estimated to be offshored in the coming years, along with the fields most likely to be affected. Cost reduction is the overwhelming motivator for doing so—companies estimate that they can save 40–60 percent on labor costs by offshoring work to countries such as India, where highly educated workers can perform the same jobs as U.S. workers at half the price. Other markets include the Philippines, Russia, China, Mexico, Brazil, and Hungary. But hidden costs can chew up most, if not all, of the profits gained from offshoring, including those associated with finding foreign vendors, productivity lost during the transition, domestic layoff costs, language difficulties, foreign regulatory challenges, and political and economic instability that can threaten operations.

In Chapter 2, you will learn about the other ways firms can get a competitive edge besides just cutting labor costs. But offshoring is going to continue to be a fact

Figure 1.2 Estimated Number and Types of U.S. Jobs Moving Offshore by 2015

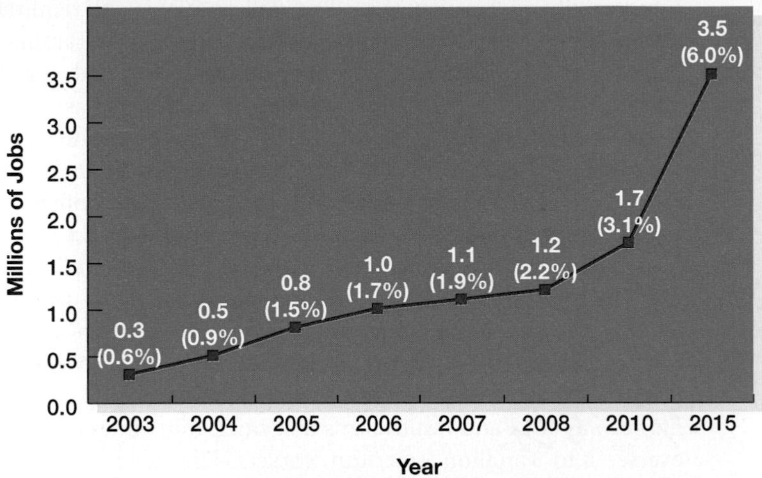

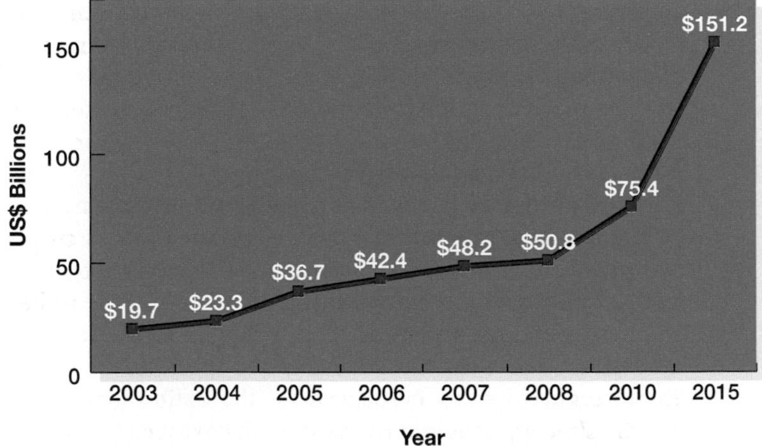

NUMBER OF U.S. JOBS MOVING OFFSHORE BY JOB CATEGORY, 2003–2015

	2003	2004	2005	2006	2007	2008	2010	2015
Management	3,500	15,000	34,000	42,000	48,000	64,000	106,000	259,000
Business	30,000	55,000	91,000	105,000	120,000	136,000	176,000	356,000
Computer	102,000	143,000	181,000	203,000	228,000	247,000	322,000	542,000
Architecture	14,000	27,000	46,000	54,000	61,000	70,000	93,000	191,000
Life sciences	300	2,000	4,000	5,500	6,500	9,000	16,000	39,000
Legal	6,000	12,000	20,000	23,000	26,000	29,000	39,000	79,000
Art, design	2,500	4,500	8,000	9,000	10,000	11,000	15,000	30,000
Sales	11,000	22,000	38,000	47,000	55,000	67,000	97,000	218,000
Office	146,000	256,000	410,000	475,000	541,000	616,000	815,000	1,600,000
Total	**315,000**	**540,000**	**830,000**	**960,000**	**1,100,000**	**1,200,000**	**1,700,000**	**3,400,000**

Source: *Near-Term Growth of Offshoring Accelerating,* Forester Research, Inc., May 2004.

of life as the global economy shifts and the lure of low labor costs continues to entice U.S. corporations. Too often, however, the decision to offshore is made by top managers and finance, without HR's initial input: "Companies can minimize hidden costs and maximize their returns by enabling HR to have a seat at the table early so they can carefully address issues such as skill and language requirements, labor costs by market, alternative talent pools, workforce training, retraining and change management," says Mark Arian, a corporate restructuring and change practice leader for Hewitt. To minimize problems, line and HR managers have to work together with the firm's other functional groups to define and communicate transition plans, minimize the number of unknowns, and help employees identify their employment options.[36]

employee leasing
The process of dismissing employees who are then hired by a leasing company (which handles all HR-related activities) and contracting with that company to lease back the employees

As an alternative to downsizing, outsourcing, and offshoring, many companies, especially small ones, have decided to sign **employee leasing** agreements with professional employer organizations (PEOs). A PEO—typically a larger company—takes over the management of a smaller company's HR tasks and becomes a co-employer to its employees. The PEO performs all the HR duties of an employer—hiring, payroll, and performance appraisal. Because PEOs can co-employ a large number of people working at many different companies, they can provide employees with benefits such as 401k and health plans that small companies can't afford. Today 700 PEOs oversee 2 to 3 million American workers. The value of employee leasing lies in the fact that an organization can essentially maintain its working relationships with its employees but shift some employment costs to the PEO, in return for a fee. Full-service PEOs sell an even broader range of services, including high-end benefits such as adoption assistance, usually found only at the largest corporations. More details on employee leasing will be discussed in Chapter 5.[37]

Productivity Enhancements

Pure cost-cutting efforts such as downsizing, outsourcing, and leasing may prove to be disappointing interventions if managers use them as simple solutions to complex performance problems. Overemphasis on labor costs perhaps misses the broader issue of productivity enhancement.

Employee productivity is the result of a combination of employees' abilities, motivation, and work environment, and the technology they have to work with. Since productivity can be defined as "the output gained from a fixed amount of inputs," organizations can increase productivity either by reducing the inputs (the cost approach) or by increasing the amount that employees produce, by adding more human and/or physical capital to the process. Nonetheless, it is quite possible for managers to cut costs only to find that productivity falls even more rapidly. Conversely, managers may find that increasing investment in employees (raising labor costs) may lead to even greater returns in enhanced productivity.

In absolute terms, the United States remains the world's most productive nation. Figure 1.3 shows how markedly U.S. productivity per person (in dollars) has increased since the 1930s. That said, the growth in output per worker is now climbing faster in less-developed countries such as China that have lacked expertise and technology in the past but are making strides to close the gap. Even in the wake of the last U.S. recession, however, new investments in technology kept the productivity of U.S. workers climbing upward. The problem is that this rapid investment in faster computers and more-efficient machine tools is beginning to level off. This will limit how much assistance technology can offer U.S. employee in terms of their productivity in the years to come. And employees are already working more hours than they

Figure 1.3 U.S. Productivity/Output per Worker

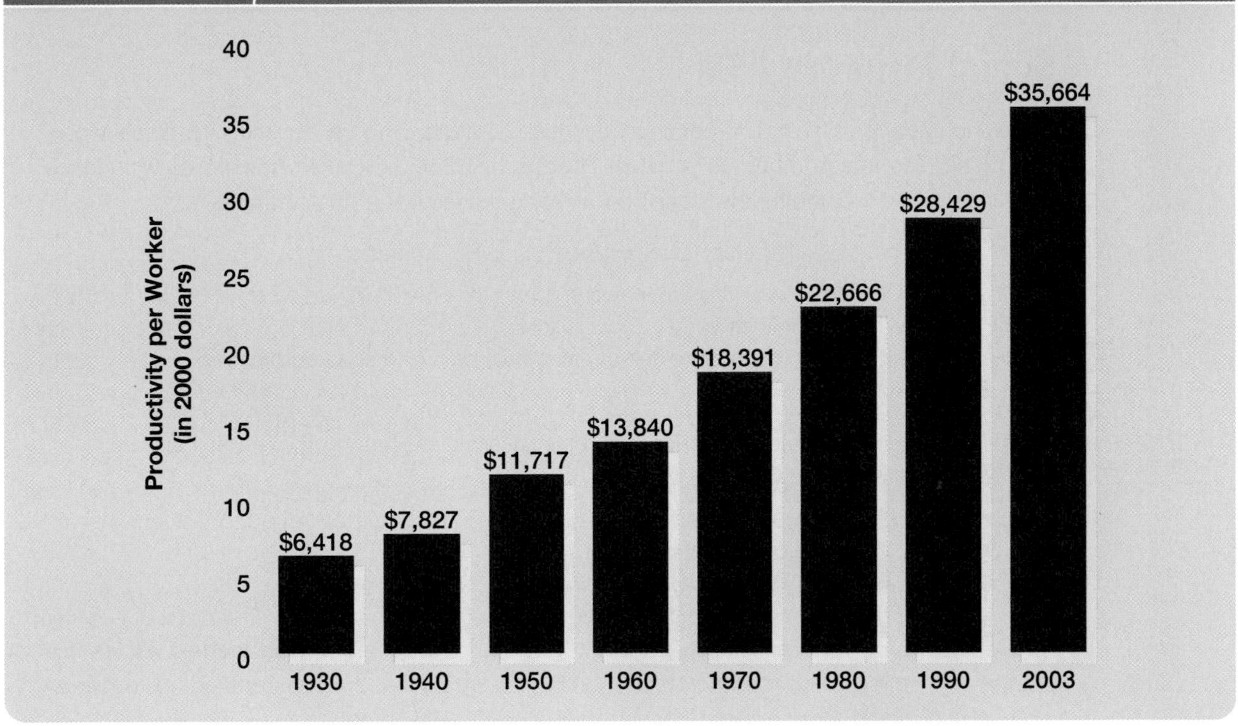

Productivity per Worker (in 2000 dollars)

Year	Productivity per Worker
1930	$6,418
1940	$7,827
1950	$11,717
1960	$13,840
1970	$18,391
1980	$22,666
1990	$28,429
2003	$35,664

Source: Derived from U.S. Department of Commerce data

have at any time since 1973. This means that that any additional productivity will have to come from the enhanced ability of employees, their motivation, and their work environment—which makes the job of the HR manager in the coming years all the more crucial.[38] Figure 1.4 shows some of the topics that we cover in this textbook that help managers increase productivity in their organizations.

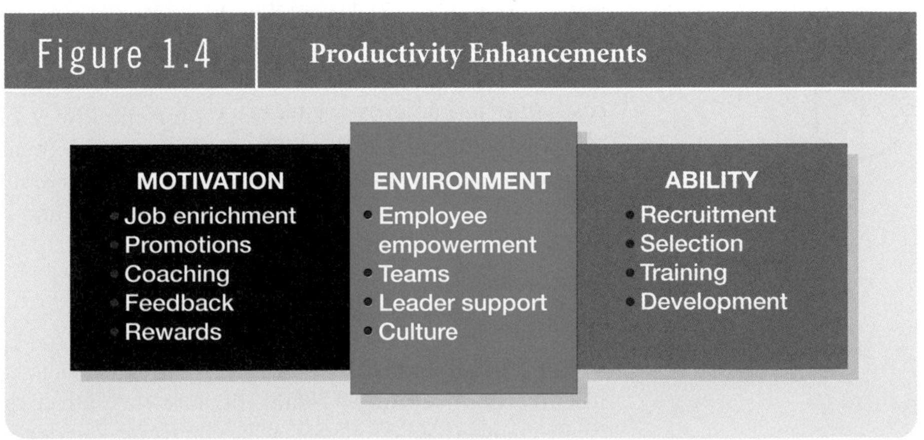

Figure 1.4 Productivity Enhancements

Highlights in HRM 4

Social Issues in HRM

Changing Demographics: The coming decades will bring a more diverse and aging workforce. This has major implications for all aspects of HRM as it alters traditional experience and expectations regarding the labor pool. Among the issues in this area are:

- Shrinking pool of skilled entry-level workers
- Diversity strategies
- Continual skills development
- Outsourcing, offshoring, and the use of temporary and part-time employees
- Globalization
- Social Security and retirement issues

Employer/Employee Rights: This area reflects the shift toward organizations and individuals attempting to define rights, obligations, and responsibilities. Among the issues here are:

- Relationship employment versus transactional-based employment
- Ethics
- Whistle-blowing
- Comparable worth
- Concern for privacy
- Legal compliance
- Mandated benefits

Attitudes toward Work and Family: Because of the increase of working women as well as employee mobility and a growing concern about family issues, there is demand for recognizing and supporting family-related concerns. Among the issues are:

- Daycare and elder care
- Job sharing
- Job rotation
- Parental leave
- Flextime
- Alternative work schedules
- Telecommuting

Demographic and Employee Concerns

In addition to the competitive challenges facing organizations, managers in general—and HR managers in particular—need to be concerned about changes in the makeup and the expectations of their employees. As we noted at the beginning of this chapter, HRM involves being an advocate for employees, being aware of their concerns, and making sure that the exchange between the organization and its employees is *mutually* beneficial. Highlights in HRM 4 shows a summary of social concerns in HRM. We will discuss some of these issues here and address all of them in greater detail throughout the book.

Demographic Changes

Among the most significant challenges to managers are the demographic changes occurring in the United States. Because they affect the workforce of an employer, these changes—in employee background, age, gender, and education—are important topics for discussion.

Because the U.S. population is becoming more diverse, companies that don't hire minorities reflecting the change are likely to find themselves at a competitive disadvantage.

The Diversity Challenge

As shown in Figure 1.5, minorities in the United States are increasing relative to the total population. It comes as no surprise, then, that American workers are becoming more diverse as well. The U.S. Census Bureau estimates that in 2012, minorities will make up an even larger share of the U.S. labor force than they do today, and the white non-Hispanic labor force will continue to comprise a smaller share. For example, between 2002 and 2012, the Hispanic labor force is expected to grow by more than 30 percent versus just 10 percent for the white, non-Hispanic labor force. Much of the growth of the minority workforce is due to the arrival of immigrants who often are of working age but have different educational and occupational backgrounds from those of the U.S. population.[39] In cities such as New York, Houston, Chicago, Los Angeles, Atlanta, and Detroit, minorities currently represent more than half the population.

To accommodate the shift in demographics, many organizations have increased their efforts to recruit and train a more diverse workforce. In this regard, a group of 600 firms such as Chevron, AT&T, and Monsanto has developed an organization called Inroads, which for the past twenty-five years has identified promising minority students during their senior year in high school and offered them summer internships. Darden Restaurants, best known for its Olive Garden and Red Lobster chains, has a long history of recruiting minority employees. Denny's and 7-Eleven have stepped up their efforts to attract minority owners of their franchises.[40]

USING THE INTERNET

For more information about 7-Eleven's success attracting minority franchisees, go to the Student Resources at:

http://bohlander.swlearning.com

Age Distribution of Employees

Past fluctuations in American birthrates are producing abrupt changes in the makeup of the labor force. The U.S. Census Bureau projects that between 2002 and 2012, the annual growth rate of the 55-and-older group will be 4.1 percent—four times the annual growth rate for the overall labor force.[41] Imbalance in the age distribution of the labor force has significant implications for employers. Companies such as Pacific Gas and Electric and Dow Chemical are finding that large portions of their workforces are nearing

Figure 1.5 Growth of the U.S. Minority Population

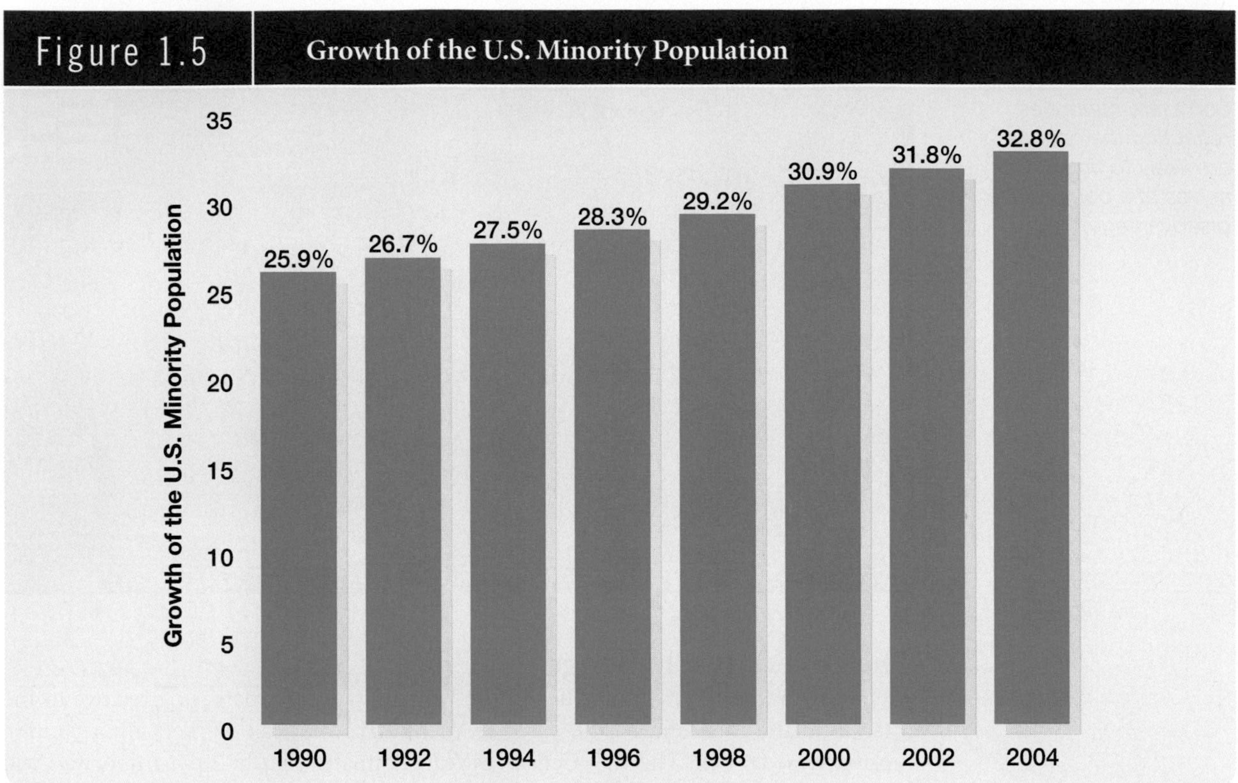

Source: U.S. Census Bureau

retirement. Beyond the sheer number of employees they will have to replace, managers are concerned that the expertise of these employees is likely to be drained too rapidly from the company. As a stopgap measure, employers are making positive efforts to attract older workers, especially those who have taken early retirement. And workers are taking them up on the on the offer. AARP has reported that 68 percent of workers between ages 50 and 70 plan to work in retirement or never retire. Good health and longer life expectancies play the biggest role in extended work lives. But some retirees have returned to the workforce because of economic needs.

Home Depot is one company participating in a pilot program with AARP in an effort to attract older workers. As part of the program, AARP's web site matches AARP members with corporations looking to hire them. Bob Nardelli, Home Depot's CEO, said he intends to hire older employees in direct proportion to their increase as a share of the population. Borders, the national bookseller, is attempting to do likewise. "Whenever our demographics match up with a community, sales are better," says Borders senior vice president Dan Smith.

Recruiting older workers may sound counterintuitive because they incur higher healthcare costs. But older workers also have fewer dependents and offer other cost savings. "Our over-50 employee turnover is 10 times less than those under 30," says Smith. "So when you think about the savings you have in training costs, transitions costs, and recruitment costs, you save a lot more on that for the over-50 workers than you do for others."[42]

The other problem that accompanies age imbalances in the workforce might be referred to as the "echo boom" effect. Similar to the trends with baby boomers, those who constitute the new population bulge are experiencing greater competition for advancement from others of approximately the same age. This situation challenges the ingenuity of managers to develop career patterns for employees to smooth out gaps in the numbers and kinds of workers.[43]

Gender Distribution of the Workforce

Sixty percent of women participate in the labor force, and as a group they represent 47 percent of the total U.S. labor force. Approximately 80 percent of mothers with school-age children are employed in some capacity. As shown in Figure 1.6, projections by the Bureau of Labor Statistics suggest that women will continue to join the U.S. labor force and are expected to account for just under 48 percent by 2012.[44] Educational attainment of women is also increasing relative to men. Employers who want to attract the talent that women have to offer are taking measures to ensure that women are treated equally in the workplace in terms of advancement opportunities

Figure 1.6 Labor Force and Gender Distributions

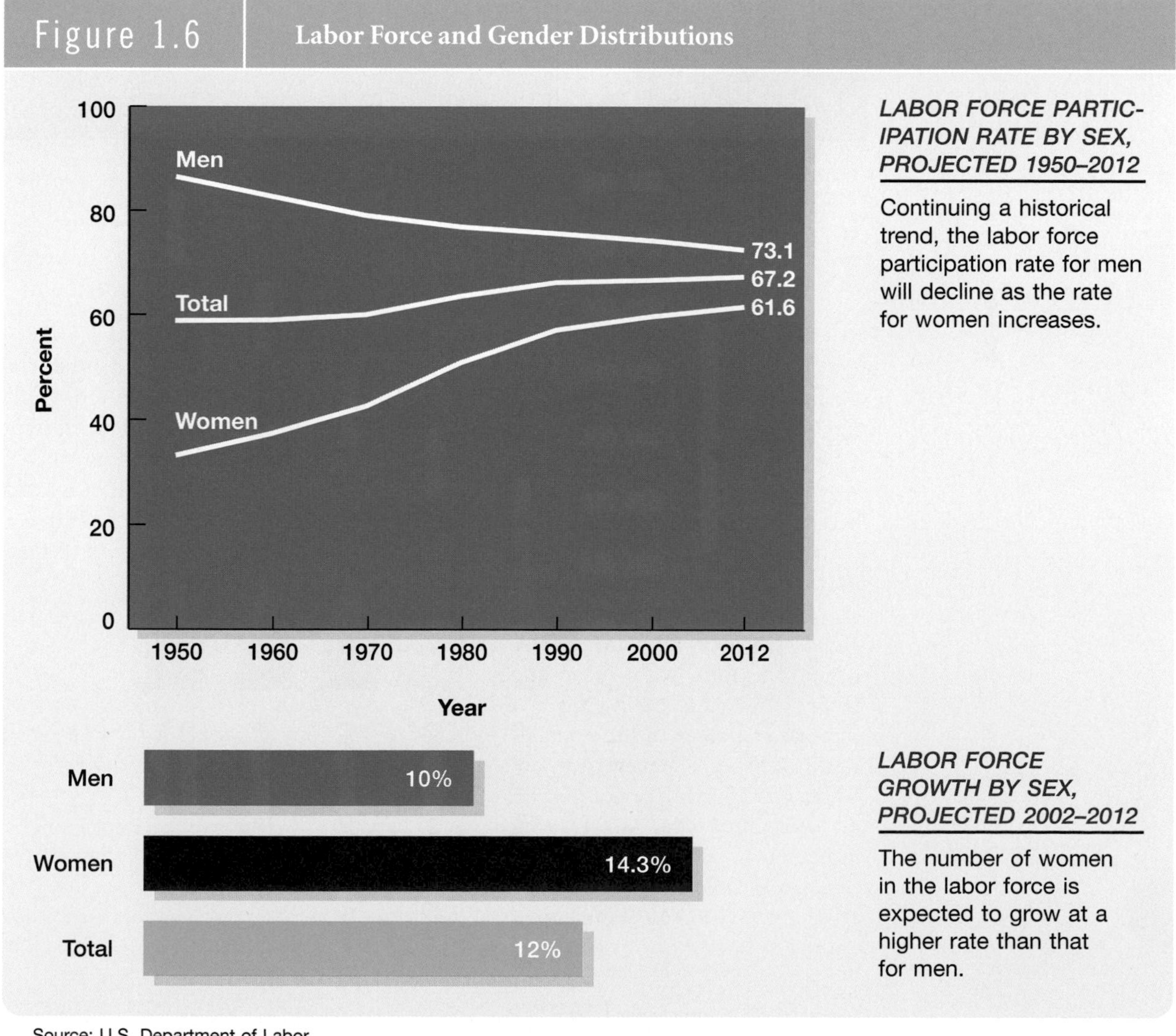

Source: U.S. Department of Labor.

> **USING THE INTERNET**
>
> The U.S. Department of Labor and U.S. Department of Education web sites are helpful for providing more information about employment and education. Go to the Student Resources at:
>
> http://bohlander.swlearning.com

and compensation. They also need to accommodate working parents through parental leaves, part-time employment, flexible work schedules, job sharing, telecommuting, and child and elder care assistance.

Rising Levels of Education

Over the years, the educational attainment of the U.S. labor force has risen dramatically. Not coincidentally, some of the fastest-growing sectors of employment over the past few decades have been in areas requiring higher levels of education.[45] Figure 1.7 shows the average payoff in annual earnings from education. It is important to note, however, that while the complexity of jobs is increasing significantly, the skills gap is huge and widening. One study by the U.S. Department of Education found that less than half of all high school seniors can handle mathematics problems involving fractions, decimals, percents, elementary geometry, and simple algebra. Between 45 and 50 percent of adults in the United States have only limited reading and writing abilities needed to handle the minimal demands of daily living or job performance. As a result, busi-

Figure 1.7 Education Pays

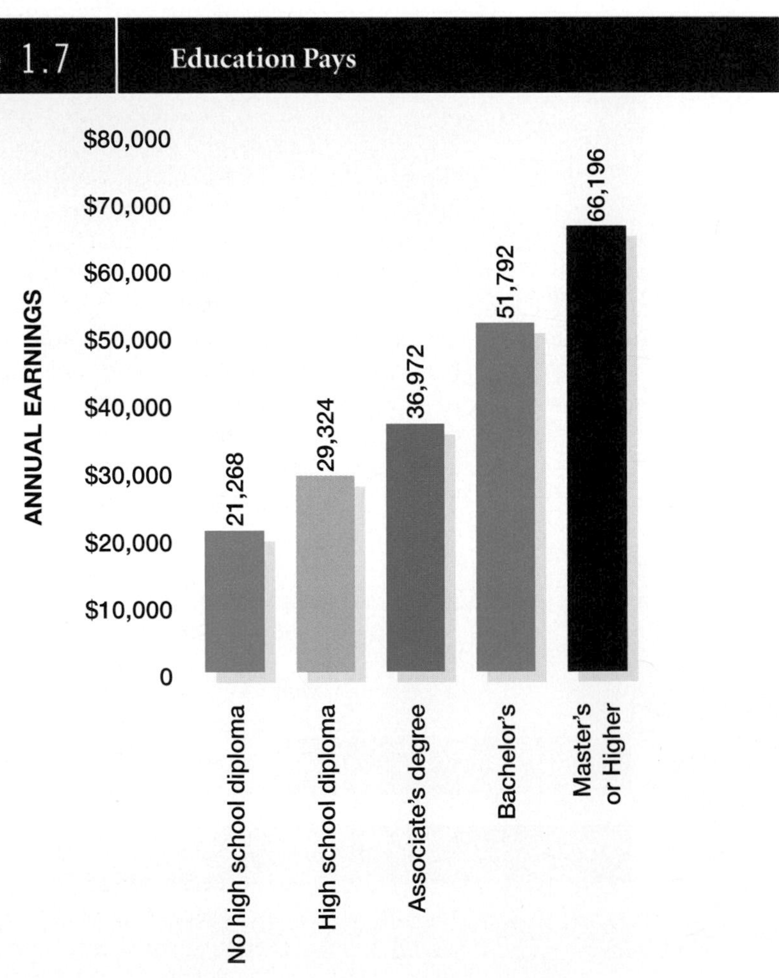

Source: U.S. Department of Labor

nesses now spend billions of dollars on basic skills training for their employees. In a speech to the Commonwealth Club of California, David Kearns, the renowned former CEO of Xerox Corporation and ardent education advocate, said, "The American workforce is in grave jeopardy. We are running out of qualified people. If current demographic and economic trends continue, American business will have to hire a million new workers a year who can't read, write, or count."[46]

And it's not just workers with four-year degrees that are in great demand. Companies are having trouble finding trained and certified workers such as pipe fitters, motorcycle mechanics, and air traffic controllers. As the baby boomer generation retires, the problem will likely worsen. HR departments will have to offer higher compensation packages to attract qualified candidates, and recruiting and selection systems will have to function much more competitively in order to identify talent. Given the recession the United States experienced earlier in the decade, this might sound strange. But demographic shifts can, and will, have a huge impact on HR and society.

HR managers are interested in these trends because the economy and job market are critical to HR's operations. For example, given that minorities and women have increased their share of the labor force, HR managers frequently analyze how each group is represented in both fast-growing and slow-growing occupations. Women, for example, are fairly well represented in fast-growing occupations such as health services but are also represented in some slow-growth occupations such as secretarial, computer processing, and financial records processing. For blacks and Hispanics, the data are less encouraging. Blacks and Hispanics have been heavily concentrated in several of the slow-growth and declining groups. Given these data, a number of efforts have been undertaken to encourage minority recruitment, selection, and training.

managing diversity
Being aware of characteristics common to employees, while also managing employees as individuals

But these are only the initial efforts to provide an overall environment that values and utilizes a diverse workforce. **Managing diversity** means being acutely aware of characteristics *common* to employees, while also managing these employees as *individuals.* It means not just tolerating or accommodating all sorts of differences but supporting, nurturing, and utilizing these differences to the organization's advantage.[47] Figure 1.8 summarizes a model for developing a diversity strategy in organizations. While there are important social reasons for including a broader spectrum of workers, there are some essential business reasons as well. Highlights in HRM 5 shows the primary business reasons for diversity management.

Cultural Changes

The attitudes, beliefs, values, and customs of people in a society are an integral part of their culture. Naturally, their culture affects their behavior on the job and the environment within the organization, influencing their reactions to work assignments, leadership styles, and reward systems. Like the external and internal environments of which it is a part, culture is undergoing continual change. HR policies and procedures therefore must be adjusted to cope with this change.

Employee Rights

Over the past few decades, federal legislation has radically changed the rules for management of employees by granting them many specific rights. Among these are laws granting the right to equal employment opportunity (Chapter 3), union representation if desired (Chapter 14), a safe and healthful work environment (Chapter 12), pension plans regulated by the government (Chapter 11), equal pay for men and

Figure 1.8 Model of Diversity Management Strategy

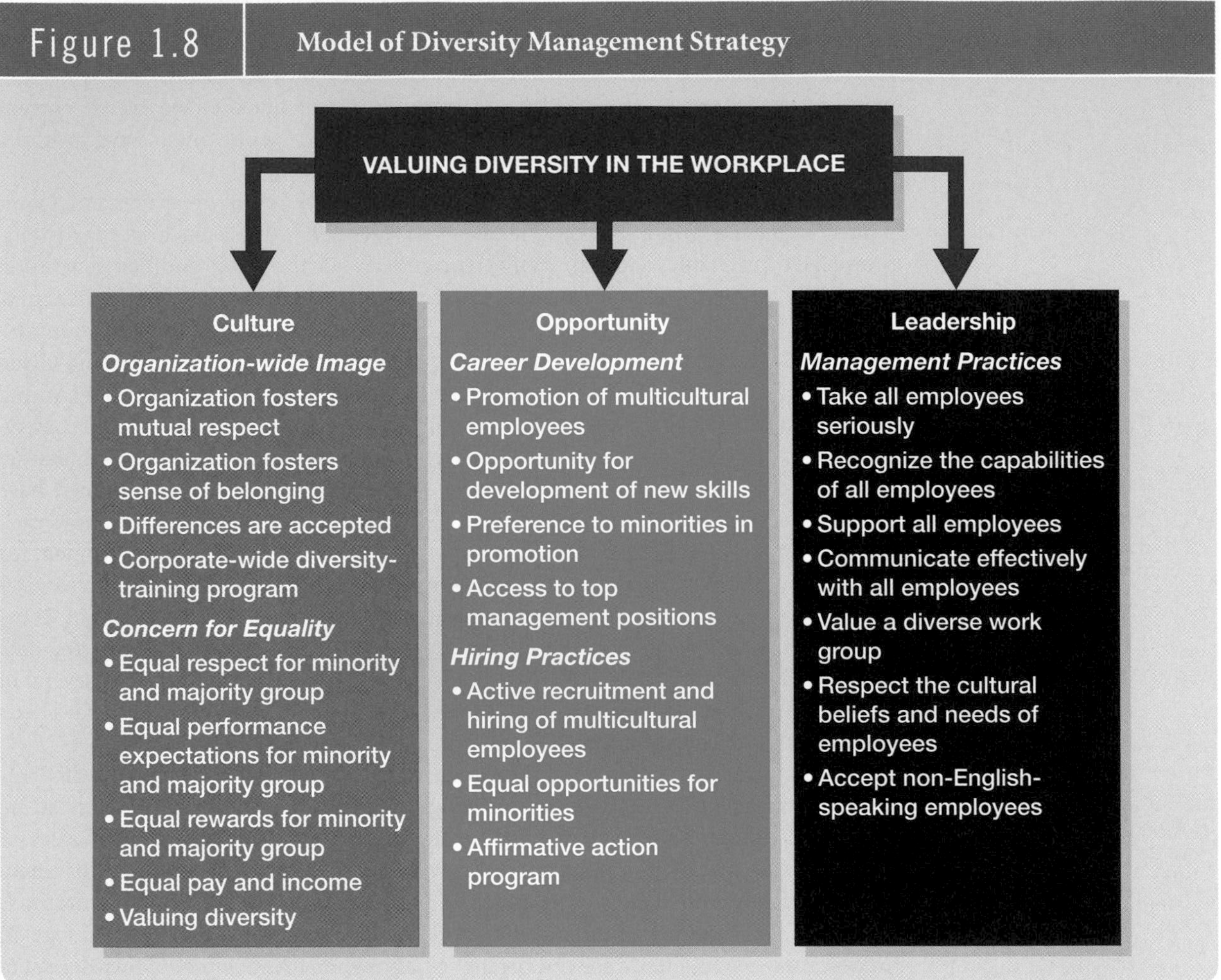

Source: Reprinted by permission of Elsevier from "Managing for Effective Workforce Diversity" by Kathleen Iverson from *The Cornell Hotel and Restaurant Administration Quarterly* 41, no. 2 (April 2000): 31–38.

women performing essentially the same job (Chapter 9), and privacy in the workplace. An expanded discussion of the specific areas in which rights and responsibilities are of concern to employers and employees, including the often-cited employment-at-will doctrine, will be presented in Chapter 13.

Concern for Privacy

HR managers and their staffs, as well as line managers in positions of responsibility, generally recognize the importance of discretion in handling all types of information about employees. Since the passage of the federal Privacy Act of 1974, increased attention to privacy has been evident, heightened by the increase in identity theft in recent years. While the act applies almost exclusively to records maintained by federal agencies, it has drawn attention to the importance of privacy and has led to the passage of additional privacy legislation, including the Health Insurance Portability and Accountability Act of 1996 (HIPAA) and the associated privacy rule issued by the U.S. Department of Health and Human Services, which protects the use and disclosure of personal medical information. (Although the Electronic Communications

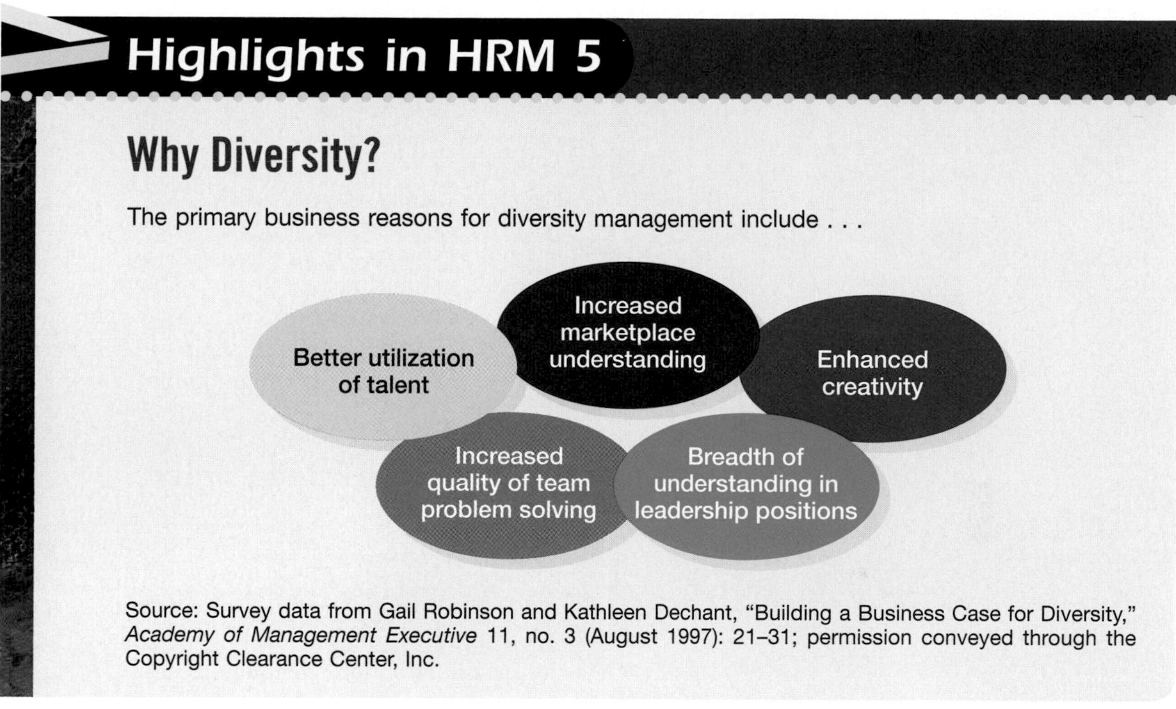

Privacy Act of 1986 legislated the protection of electronic communications such as e-mail, the rules are different when it comes to the privacy that employees can expect with regard to their electronic communications at work.) Globalization has added another twist to privacy compliance. For example, EU countries prohibit the transfer of personal data to countries with inadequate data protection laws, such as China.

According to the Society for Human Resources Management, of more than 400 human resources professionals, 54 percent said they now have written privacy policies safeguarding employee data. IBM was one of the first companies to show concern for how personal information about employees was handled. It began restricting the release of information as early as 1965, and in 1971 it developed a comprehensive privacy policy. Other things companies are doing to protect their employees include limiting the use of Social Security numbers on time sheets, log-in sheets, and other employment forms. Some companies lock up employee files, conduct background checks on employees who have access to others' files, educate employees in fraud prevention, and contract with outside firms specializing in identity theft.[48] In Chapter 13, we will discuss the content of such programs, along with the privacy employees can expect while on the job, and present some recommended privacy guidelines.

Changing Attitudes toward Work

Employees today are less likely to define their personal success only in terms of financial gains. This trend has been evolving for some time, but observers have noted that it has peaked since the terrorist attacks of September 11, 2001. Personal fulfillment and self-expression—as well as a balance between work and family—are key factors in a complex array of job attitudes. Many people view life satisfaction as more likely to result from balancing the challenges and rewards of work with those in their personal lives. Though most people still enjoy work, and want to excel at it, they tend to

© PHOTODISC GREEN/GETTY IMAGES

Parents today face real challenges in balancing work and home life.

be focused on finding interesting work and may pursue multiple careers rather than being satisfied with just "having a job." In fact, in a survey of more than 3,000 workers, 86 percent said work fulfillment and work-life balance were their top priorities. Only 35 percent said being successful at work and moving up the ladder were their top priorities. People also appear to be seeking ways of living that are less complicated but more meaningful. These new lifestyles cannot help having an impact on the way employees must be motivated and managed. Consequently, HRM has become more complex than it was when employees were concerned primarily with economic survival.

Balancing Work and Family

Work and the family are connected in many subtle and not-so-subtle social, economic, and psychological ways. Because of the new forms that the family has taken—such as the two-wage-earner and the single-parent family—work organizations find it necessary to provide employees with more family-friendly options. "Family friendly" is a broad term that may include unconventional hours, daycare, part-time work, job sharing, pregnancy leave, parental leave, executive transfers, spousal involvement in career planning, assistance with family problems, and telecommuting.

Flextime options for employees are on the rise, according to the Society for Human Resource Management. More than half of all companies—American Express, Levi Strauss, PepsiCo, and Schering-Plough among them—now offer such programs. In general, these companies calculate that accommodating individual needs and circumstances is a powerful way to attract and retain top-caliber people. Aetna Life and Casualty, for example, cut turnover by 50 percent after it began offering six-month parental leaves, coupled with an option for part-time work when employees return to the job. Bank of America encourages all its employees to visit their children's schools or volunteer at any school—on company time. Still, there are acknowledged costs. In professional firms such as law, career paths and promotions are programmed in a lockstep manner. Time away from work can slow down—and in some cases derail—an individual's career advancement.[49]

Furthermore, family-friendly companies have to balance the benefits they provide to families versus their single employees. A majority of employees have no children under 18. A Conference Board survey of companies with family-friendly programs found that companies acknowledge that childless employees harbor resentment against employees with children who are able to take advantage of these programs.[50]

The Partnership of Line Managers and HR Departments

We have taken a good deal of time up front in this book to outline today's competitive and social challenges to reinforce the idea that managing people is not something that occurs in a back room called the HR department. Managing people is every manager's business, and successful organizations combine the experience of line managers with the expertise of HR specialists to develop and utilize the talents of employees to their greatest potential. Addressing HR issues is rarely the exclusive responsibility of HR departments acting alone. Instead, HR managers work side by side with line managers to address people-related issues of the organization. And while this relationship has not always achieved its ideal, the situation is rapidly improving. HR managers are assuming a greater role in top-management planning and decision making, a trend that reflects the growing awareness among executives that HRM can make important contributions to the success of an organization.

Responsibilities of the Human Resources Manager

Although line managers and HR managers need to work together, their responsibilities are different, as are their competencies and expertise. The major activities for which an HR manager is typically responsible are as follows:

1. *Advice and counsel.* The HR manager often serves as an in-house consultant to supervisors, managers, and executives. Given their knowledge of internal employment issues (policies, labor agreements, past practices, ethics and corporate governance, and the needs of employees) as well as their awareness of external trends (economic and employment data, new legal and regulatory issues, and the like), HR managers can be an invaluable resource for making decisions. For example, larger companies have begun appointing "chief ethics officers" to help their employees wade through gray areas when it comes to right and wrong. The firm's top HR manager is in a good position for this job. In smaller companies, however, this task frequently falls on the shoulders of individual HR managers. These managers need to counsel both employees and executives in this area and areas in which Congress has passed new *corporate governance* laws to prevent, among other things, top executives from abusing their power. (Corporate governance relates to the way rights and responsibilities are shared within corporations, especially between managers and shareholders.) HR managers are also being relied on more heavily to advise compensation committees, which are more closely scrutinizing executives' pay than they have in years past.
2. *Service.* HR managers also perform a host of service activities such as recruiting, selecting, testing, planning and conducting training programs, and hearing employee concerns and complaints. Technical expertise in these areas is essential for HR managers and forms the basis of HR program design and implementation. Moreover, managers must be convinced that the HR staff is there to help them increase their productivity rather than to impose obstacles to their goals. This requires not only the ability on the part of the HR executive to consider problems from the viewpoint of line managers and supervisors but also skill in communicating with the managers and supervisors.
3. *Policy formulation and implementation.* HR managers generally propose and draft new policies or policy revisions to cover recurring problems or to prevent anticipated problems. Ordinarily, these are proposed to the senior executives of the organization, who actually issue the policies. HR managers may monitor performance of line departments and other staff departments to ensure conformity with established HR policies, procedures, and practices. Perhaps more important, they are a resource to whom managers can turn for policy interpretation.

4. *Employee advocacy.* One of the enduring roles of HR managers is to serve as an employee advocate—listening to employees' concerns and representing their needs to managers. Effective employee relations provides a support structure when disruptive changes interfere with normal daily activities.

In the process of managing human resources, increasing attention is being given to the personal needs of the participants. Thus throughout this book we will not only emphasize the importance of the contributions that HRM makes to the organization but also give serious consideration to its effects on the individual and on society.

Increasingly, employees and the public at large are demanding that employers demonstrate greater social responsibility in managing their human resources. Complaints that job stress is devitalizing the lives and injuring the health of employees are not uncommon. Charges of discrimination against women, minorities, the physically and mentally disabled, and the elderly with respect to hiring, training, advancement, and compensation are being leveled against some employers. Issues such as comparable pay for comparable work, the high cost of health benefits, daycare for the children of employees, elder care for their parents, and alternative work schedules are concerns that many employers must address as the workforce grows more diverse. All employers are finding that privacy and confidentiality of information about employees are serious matters and deserve the greatest protection that can be provided.

Where employees are organized into unions (covered in Chapter 14), employers can encounter costly collective bargaining proposals, threats of strike, and charges of unfair labor practices. Court litigation, demands for corrective action by governmental agencies, sizable damage awards in response to employee lawsuits, and attempts to erode the employment-at-will doctrine valued by employers are still other hazards that contemporary employers must try to avoid. (We will discuss these issues in detail in Chapter 13.)

Top management generally recognizes the contributions that the HR program can make to the organization and thus expects HR managers to assume a broader role in the overall organizational strategy. Thus HR managers must remember the bottom line if they are to fulfill their role.

Competencies of the Human Resources Manager

As top executives expect HR managers to assume a broader role in overall organizational strategy, many of these managers will need to acquire a complementary set of competencies. These competencies are summarized here and shown graphically in Figure 1.9.

1. *Business mastery.* HR professionals need to know the business of their organization thoroughly. This requires an understanding of its economic and financial capabilities so that they can "join the team" of business managers in order to develop the firm's strategic direction. It also requires that HR professionals develop skills at external relations focused on their customers.
2. *HR mastery.* HR professionals are the organization's behavioral science experts. In areas such as staffing, development, appraisal, rewards, team building, and communication, HR professionals should develop competencies that keep them abreast of changes.
3. *Change mastery.* HR professionals have to be able to manage change processes so that HR activities are effectively merged with the business needs of the organi-

Figure 1.9 Human Resource Competency Model

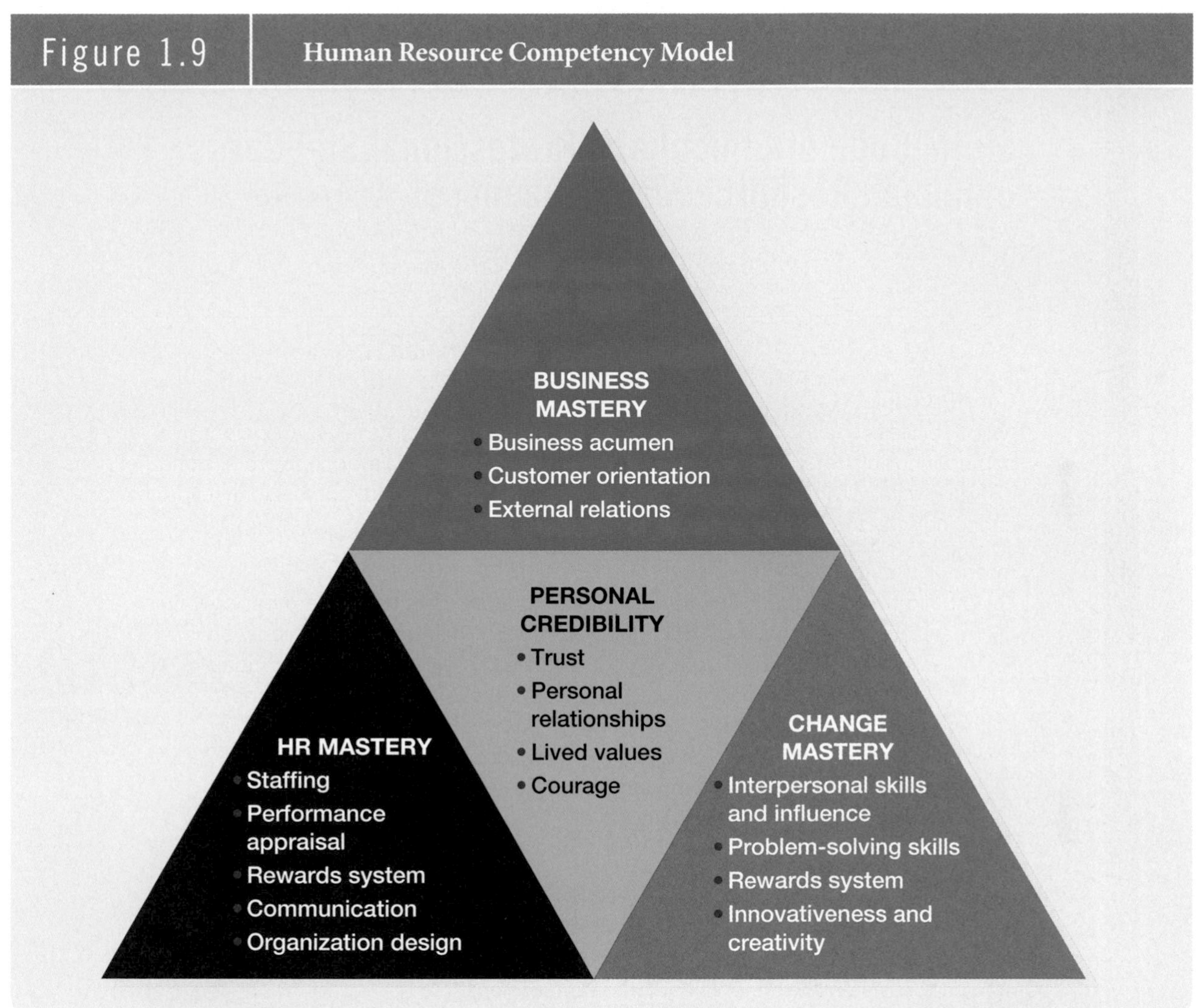

Source: Arthur Yeung, Wayne Brockbank, and Dave Ulrich, "Lower Cost, Higher Value: Human Resource Function in Transformation." Reprinted with permission from *Human Resource Planning,* Vol. 17, No. 3 (1994). Copyright 1994 by The Human Resource Planning Society, 317 Madison Avenue, Suite 1509, New York, NY 10017, Phone: (212) 490-6387, Fax: (212) 682-6851.

zation. This involves interpersonal and problem-solving skills, as well as innovativeness and creativity.

4. *Personal credibility.* HR professionals must establish personal credibility in the eyes of their internal and external customers. Credibility and trust are earned by developing personal relationships with customers, by demonstrating the values of the firm, by standing up for one's own beliefs, and by being fair-minded in dealing with others. Highlights in HRM 6 outlines the code of ethics HR professionals should follow, according to the Society for Human Resource Management.

The ability to integrate business, HR, and change competencies is essential. By helping their organizations build a sustained competitive advantage and by learning to manage many activities well, HR professionals are becoming full business partners. Forward-looking CEOs such as Bob Nardelli at Home Depot; Herb Kelleher, the

SHRM Code of Ethical and Professional Standards in Human Resource Management

Society for Human Resource Management
CODE PROVISIONS

PROFESSIONAL RESPONSIBILITY

Core Principle

As HR professionals, we are responsible for adding value to the organizations we serve and contributing to the ethical success of those organizations. We accept professional responsibility for our individual decisions and actions. We are also advocates for the profession by engaging in activities that enhance its credibility and value.

Intent

- To build respect, credibility and strategic importance for the HR profession within our organizations, the business community, and the communities in which we work.
- To assist the organizations we serve in achieving their objectives and goals.
- To inform and educate current and future practitioners, the organizations we serve, and the general public about principles and practices that help the profession.
- To positively influence workplace and recruitment practices.
- To encourage professional decision-making and responsibility.
- To encourage social responsibility.

Guidelines

1. Adhere to the highest standards of ethical and professional behavior.
2. Measure the effectiveness of HR in contributing to or achieving organizational goals.
3. Comply with the law.
4. Work consistent with the values of the profession.
5. Strive to achieve the highest levels of service, performance and social responsibility.
6. Advocate for the appropriate use and appreciation of human beings as employees.
7. Advocate openly and within the established forums for debate in order to influence decision-making and results.

PROFESSIONAL DEVELOPMENT

Core Principle

As professionals we must strive to meet the highest standards of competence and commit to strengthen our competencies on a continuous basis.

Intent

- To expand our knowledge of human resource management to further our understanding of how our organizations function.
- To advance our understanding of how organizations work ("the business of the business").

Guidelines

1. Pursue formal academic opportunities.
2. Commit to continuous learning, skills development and application of new knowledge related to both human resource management and the organizations we serve.
3. Contribute to the body of knowledge, the evolution of the profession and the growth of individuals through teaching, research and dissemination of knowledge.
4. Pursue certification such as CCP, CEBS, PHR, SPHR, etc. where available, or comparable measures of competencies and knowledge.

ETHICAL LEADERSHIP

Core Principle

HR professionals are expected to exhibit individual leadership as a role model for maintaining the highest standards of ethical conduct.

Intent

- To set the standard and be an example for others.
- To earn individual respect and increase our credibility with those we serve.

Guidelines

1. Be ethical; act ethically in every professional interaction.
2. Question pending individual and group actions when necessary to ensure that decisions are ethical and are implemented in an ethical manner.
3. Seek expert guidance if ever in doubt about the ethical propriety of a situation.
4. Through teaching and mentoring, champion the development of others as ethical leaders in the profession and in organizations.

FAIRNESS AND JUSTICE

Core Principle

As human resource professionals, we are ethically responsible for promoting and fostering fairness and justice for all employees and their organizations.

Intent

To create and sustain an environment that encourages all individuals and the organization to reach their fullest potential in a positive and productive manner.

Guidelines

1. Respect the uniqueness and intrinsic worth of every individual.
2. Treat people with dignity, respect and compassion to foster a trusting work environment free of harassment, intimidation and unlawful discrimination.
3. Ensure that everyone has the opportunity to develop their skills and new competencies.
4. Assure an environment of inclusiveness and a commitment to diversity in the organizations we serve.
5. Develop, administer and advocate policies and procedures that foster fair, consistent and equitable treatment for all.
6. Regardless of personal interests, support decisions made by our organizations that are both ethical and legal.
7. Act in a responsible manner and practice sound management in the country(ies) in which the organizations we serve operate.

(continued on next page)

(continued from previous page)

CONFLICTS OF INTEREST

Core Principle

As HR professionals, we must maintain a high level of trust with our stakeholders. We must protect the interests of our stakeholders as well as our professional integrity and should not engage in activities that create actual, apparent or potential conflicts of interest.

Intent

To avoid activities that are in conflict or may appear to be in conflict with any of the provisions of this Code of Ethical and Professional Standards in Human Resource Management or with one's responsibilities and duties as a member of the human resource profession and/or as an employee of any organization.

Guidelines

1. Adhere to and advocate the use of published policies on conflicts of interest within your organization.
2. Refrain from using your position for personal, material or financial gain or the appearance of such.
3. Refrain from giving or seeking preferential treatment in the human resources processes.
4. Prioritize your obligations to identify conflicts of interest or the appearance thereof; when conflicts arise, disclose them to relevant stakeholders.

USE OF INFORMATION

Core Principle

HR professionals consider and protect the rights of individuals, especially in the acquisition and dissemination of information while ensuring truthful communications and facilitating informed decision-making.

Intent

To build trust among all organization constituents by maximizing the open exchange of information, while eliminating anxieties about inappropriate and/or inaccurate acquisition and sharing of information

Guidelines

1. Acquire and disseminate information through ethical and responsible means.
2. Ensure only appropriate information is used in decisions affecting the employment relationship.
3. Investigate the accuracy and source of information before allowing it to be used in employment related decisions.
4. Maintain current and accurate HR information.
5. Safeguard restricted or confidential information.
6. Take appropriate steps to ensure the accuracy and completeness of all communicated information about HR policies and practices.
7. Take appropriate steps to ensure the accuracy and completeness of all communicated information used in HR-related training.

founder of Southwest Airlines; and Daniel Carp at Eastman Kodak make certain that their top HR executives report directly to them and help them address key issues.

At lower levels in the organization, a rapidly growing number of companies such as Ford, Intel, and Corning assign HR representatives to business teams to make certain that HR issues are addressed on the job and that HR representatives, in turn, are knowledgeable about business issues rather than simply focusing on the administrative function.

Role of the Line Manager

As much as we might say about the role of the HR department, in the final analysis managing people depends on effective supervisors and line managers. As one executive at Merck put it, "Human resources are far too important to be left to the personnel department." Although HR managers have the responsibility for coordinating programs and policies pertaining to people-related issues, managers and employees themselves are ultimately responsible for performing these functions.

We understand that most readers of this book will be line managers and supervisors, rather than HR specialists. The text is, therefore, oriented to *helping people manage people more effectively,* whether they become first-line supervisors or chief executive officers. Students now preparing for careers in organizations will find that the study of HRM provides a background that will be valuable in managerial and supervisory positions. Discussions concerning the role of the HR department can provide a better understanding of the functions performed by this department. A familiarity with the role of HR should help facilitate closer cooperation with the department's staff and fuller utilization of the assistance and services available from this resource.

SUMMARY

objective 1 People have always been central to organizations, but their strategic importance is growing in today's knowledge-based industries. An organization's success increasingly depends on the knowledge, skills, and abilities of its employees.

objective 2 Globalization influences approximately 70–85 percent of the U.S. economy and affects the free flow of trade among countries. This influences the number and kinds of jobs that are available and requires that organizations balance a complicated set of issues related to managing people in different geographies, cultures, legal environments, and business conditions. HR functions such as staffing, training, compensation, and the like have to be adjusted to take into account the differences in global management.

objective 3 Advanced technology has tended to reduce the number of jobs that require little skill and to increase the number of jobs that require considerable skill, a shift we refer to as moving from touch labor to knowledge work. This displaces some employees and requires that others be retrained. In addition, information technology has influenced HRM through human resources information systems (HRIS) that streamline HR processes, make information more readily available to managers and employees, and enable HR departments to focus on the firm's strategies.

objective 4 Both proactive and reactive change initiatives require HR managers to work with line managers and executives to create a vision for the future, establish an architecture that enables change, and communicate with employees about the processes of change.

objective 5 In order to "compete through people," organizations have to do a good job of managing human capital: the knowledge, skills, and capabilities that have value to organizations. Managers must develop strategies for identifying, recruiting, and hiring the best talent available; for developing these employees in ways that are firm-specific; for helping them to generate new ideas and generalize them through the company; for encouraging information sharing; and for rewarding collaboration and teamwork.

objective 6 In order to respond to customer needs better, faster, and more cheaply, organizations have instituted total quality management (TQM) and reengineering programs. Each of these programs requires that HR be involved in changing work processes, training, job design, compensation, and the like. HR issues also arise when communicating with employees about the new work systems, just as with any change initiative. Better business thinking builds more strategic HR thinking.

objective 7 In order to contain costs, organizations have been downsizing, outsourcing, offshoring, and leasing employees, and enhancing productivity. HR's role is to maintain the relationship between a company and its employees while implementing the changes.

objective 8 The workforce is becoming increasingly diverse, and organizations are doing more to address employee concerns and to maximize the benefit of different kinds of employees. Demographic changes, social and cultural differences, and changing attitudes toward work can provide a rich source of variety for organizations. But to benefit from diversity, managers need to recognize the potential concerns of employees and make certain that the exchange between the organization and employees is mutually beneficial.

objective 9 In working with line managers to address the organization's challenges, HR managers play a number of important roles; they are called on for advice and ethics counsel, for various service activities, for policy formulation and implementation, and for employee advocacy. To perform these roles effectively, HR managers must contribute business competencies, state-of-the-art HR competencies, and change-management competencies. Ultimately, managing people is rarely the exclusive responsibility of the HR function. Every manager's job is managing people, and successful companies combine the expertise of HR specialists with the experience of line managers to develop and utilize the talents of employees to their greatest potential.

KEY TERMS

corporate social responsibility
downsizing
employee leasing
globalization
human capital
human resources information system (HRIS)
human resources management (HRM)
knowledge workers
managing diversity
offshoring
outsourcing
proactive change
reactive change
reengineering
Six Sigma
total quality management (TQM)

HRM Experience

Balancing Competitive Challenges and Employee Concerns

Today, human resources management is not just the responsibility of the personnel department. If people are a competitive resource, then line managers play an increasingly important role in managing the workforce. But this is not an either/or situation. Rather than seeing line managers take over responsibility from HR managers, we see both groups working together to handle workforce issues. But how do they work together?

Assignment

1. Working in teams of four to six individuals, identify what role the HR department would play and what role line managers would play in the following activities. Where would overlaps occur, and would there be any likely problems?
   a. Recruiting and selection
   b. Training and development
   c. Compensation
   d. Performance evaluation
   e. Labor relations
2. How would potential problems be resolved?
3. Write the groups' findings on flip charts and post for all to see. One member from each team should explain his or her findings to all class members.
4. Point out the similarities and differences across the teams. Save these points and revisit them—possibly revising them—as you study subsequent chapters in this textbook.

DISCUSSION QUESTIONS

1. Are people always an organization's most valuable asset? Why or why not?

2. Suppose your boss asked you to summarize the major people-related concerns in opening an office in Tokyo. What issues would be on your list?

3. Will technology eliminate the need for human resources managers?

4. What are the pros and cons of change? Does it help or hurt organizational performance? Do you like change? Why or why not?

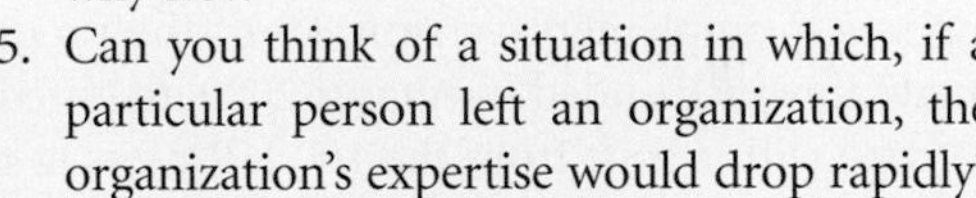

5. Can you think of a situation in which, if a particular person left an organization, the organization's expertise would drop rapidly?

6. Someone once said that TQM "is like paving cow paths." What do you suppose this means in relation to reengineering?

7. Do pressures on cost containment work against effective management of people? Why or why not?

8. What are the pros and cons of having a more diverse workforce? Is the United States in a better position to compete globally because of its diverse population?

9. In your opinion, what is the most important role of HR managers?

BIZFLIX EXERCISES

Babe: Herding Sheep, Babe's Way

This chapter's introduction to human resources management emphasized its role in helping managers bring together different types of people to reach a common purpose. An earlier chapter section, "Demographic and Employee Concerns," highlighted those differences. Watch this scene from *Babe* while recalling those discussions.

Babe is a charming Australian film featuring eccentric, quiet Farmer Hoggett (James Cromwell), who trains a pig he won at the fair to herd his sheep. His eccentricity turns to determination when he enters the pig in the Australian National Sheepdog Championships. The Academy Award–winning visual effects include a seamless mixture of animatronic doubles, computer images, and live animals.

This scene comes from the "a pig that thinks it's a dog" segment that appears about 40 minutes into the film. Farmer Hoggett's sheepdogs, Rex (voiced by Hugo Weaving) and Fly (voiced by Miriam Margolyes), along with Babe (voiced by Christine Cavanaugh) the pig, accompany him to his sheep herd. Hoggett needs to gather the sheep into a pen so he can shear their wool. Before leaving for the pasture, Farmer Hoggett saw Babe carefully divide some chickens into two groups based on their color. Hoggett suspects that perhaps Babe has some herding skills.

What to Watch for and Ask Yourself

- Are Babe's methods of herding sheep different from those used by the sheepdogs? If yes, what are the differences?
- Does Babe discover that he cannot successfully herd sheep as a sheepdog herds them? What does he do?
- Does Farmer Hoggett accept Babe for what he is—a pig not a sheepdog?

case study 1

Self-Service System Works Out Well for WellPoint

When Tom Van Berkem, senior vice president, HR, arrived at WellPoint (Thousand Oaks, Calif., $20.4 billion in 2003 revenue) seven years ago, he was faced with the challenge of cost-effectively managing human resources for a company of about 6,000 employees that planned to quadruple in size.

"We faced the strategic challenge to build an [HR] infrastructure for a Fortune 500 company to become Fortune 100," says Van Berkem. "Our existing system wasn't up to that challenge."

Van Berkem's vision for meeting that challenge was to centralize HR services, along with instituting sweeping self-service functionality and 24/7 call center capability—an ambitious set of requirements for that time. Having vetted all the vendor players in the marketplace, Van Berkem relates, WellPoint chose PeopleSoft (Pleasanton, Calif.) because, "We were looking for a vendor we thought shared our vision and most closely matched what we wanted."

Lacking internal resources, WellPoint relied on "a major accounting firm" for PeopleSoft version 7 in January 1998, according to Chuck Moore, staff vice president, HR information systems and administration. It went live on the client/server system in October 1998, with about 100 HR staff users.

In 2000, when WellPoint was ready to make the leap to Web-based self-service, it turned to PeopleSoft Global Services to implement version 8.0 of the vendor's solution. The five-month implementation, which ended in August 2000, required a significant investment in hardware to cope with a shift from the 100 HR users to the entire employee population of over 14,000. But it was at that time that WellPoint also achieved a large payback from the system. A month after going live, the carrier was able to use the PeopleSoft solution to bring its open enrollment process in-house, saving $25-per-head—or roughly $400,000.

That kind of gain was possible because of the strategic role envisioned for the system, according to Moore. "At the beginning, we made the decision that the PeopleSoft database was going to be the source of all [employee] information," he says. "Over time, we have more and more systems dependent on PeopleSoft to become the source of accurate information." The solution is tied into tertiary budgeting and expense report systems, and it plays an important role in employee communications. For example, by tying into PeopleSoft, "a vendor can contact scores of our employees on a moment's notice with voicemail messages," Moore explains.

WellPoint turned to PeopleSoft Global Services again in the summer of 2003 to manage an upgrade to PeopleSoft version 8.3, which enabled all HR manager transactions to be immediately uploaded to the solution's database. The carrier is currently in the process of launching a PeopleSoft portal, which delivers more personalized information than the standard self-service interface. WellPoint is also about to move to a PeopleSoft-driven paperless paycheck system that will save the company $1.17 per employee per check. With about 20,000 employees currently, savings for open-enrollment add up to $500,000 annually, and paperless paychecks amount to a savings of $608,400 per year.

Full-Service Strategic Solution

Added to these benefits is a savings of about 40 to 50 human resources employees, plus related facilities expenses not needed within a self-service HR paradigm. With productivity benefits owing to the efficiency of the self-service process, the solution more than pays back an investment of about $8.5 million plus undisclosed annual maintenance fees, says Van Berkem. "We have transformed a traditional payroll [and] personnel record solution into a full-service strategic solution at a cost not substantially higher than a traditional solution," he asserts.

QUESTIONS

1. What problems do you think WellPoint might have encountered by moving so many employees to a web-based HR system?
2. What do you think WellPoint's HR department should try to achieve in moving forward?
3. How can PeopleSoft make certain that WellPoint is happy with its service?

Source: Anthony O'Donnell, "WellPoint Grows with PeopleSoft: Self-Service Functionality and Centralized HR Services Help the Health Insurer Navigate the Challenges of Its Aggressive Growth Strategy Cost-Effectively," *Insurance & Technology* 29, no. 5 (May 2004): 17.

case study 2

Florida Company Fastens Its Sights on Global Growth

When Robert Kilbey began selling medical supplies out of his twenty-four-foot Airstream trailer in the early 1960s, he came upon a brilliant idea: make the braces and wraps with a new sort of closure—Velcro fasteners—instead of the common laces and hooks-and-eyes. The new hook-and-loop fastener, invented in the early 1940s and now used on everything from automobiles to footwear, caught on with the medical world. Kilbey moved Professional Products, Inc., from his base in Miami to DeFuniak Springs, Florida, where it quietly has become one of Walton

County's largest and most stable employers. Forty-two years later his son, Bryan Kilbey, is expanding the company and taking it international. "We will build a new 100,000-square-foot building this year," the company's CEO said. "And we are going to open a new sales office for the European market."

"From order to shipping, we can fill an order in 4½ hours," Kilbey said. "These are often specific requests from doctors who like a piece of equipment to work a certain way. So we don't have a lot of inventory." Instead, as general manager Dean Stanton says, the company is vertical in its operations, designing and making most of its own components.

"We make our own elastic," Kilbey said. "We have the thread, the rubber, and we make our own." He said new technology and equipment will be used to streamline production. Some work will be outsourced to other countries, possibly Mexico and Honduras. That decision hasn't been made. But no jobs will disappear.

"We have never laid off anyone," Kilbey said. "We have worked short weeks, although we haven't done that in 15 years. But we have kept our people." Neither does he go into panic-hiring mode and add employees at crunch time.

"These are highly skilled jobs," Stanton said. "We can't just go out and hire anyone." Stanton said, "We will cross-train people to do other jobs" when some work moves to possibly Mexico, Honduras, and other countries.

QUESTIONS

1. How would you describe Professional Products' growth strategy?
2. Why would Professional Products commit to no layoffs in its expansion? Is this a positive move, or could it be detrimental to the company?
3. In addition to training employees for other jobs, what other HR strategies might the firm employ to maintain its relationship with its domestic employees?

Source: Excerpted from Fraser, Morris, "DeFuniak Springs Company Fastens Its Sight on Growth," *Northwest Florida (Fort Walton Beach) Daily News* (via Knight-Ridder/Tribune Business News), March 7, 2005.

case study 3

Deloitte & Touche: Managing Diversity for a Competitive Advantage

In 1992, Deloitte & Touche, LLP, was celebrating the tenth year in which approximately 50 percent of its new hires were women. Because it takes nearly a decade to become a partner, the accounting firm based in Wilton, Connecticut, was now sitting back waiting for all the women in the pipeline to start making bids for partnership. But something unexpected happened. Instead of seeing an increase in the number of women applying for partnership, Deloitte & Touche saw a *decline*. Talented women were leaving the firm and this represented a huge drain of capable people. In a knowledge-intensive business such as theirs, this problem went beyond social consciousness. They could not afford to lose valued partners.

The company formed the Task Force on the Retention and Advancement of Women to pinpoint the reason women were leaving. The task force conducted a massive information-gathering initiative, interviewing women at all levels of the company, even contacting women who had left the firm. It uncovered three main areas of complaint: (1) a work environment that limited opportunity for advancement, (2) exclusion from mentoring and networking, and (3) work and family issues.

The networking and mentoring concerns seemed to be the most troublesome. In a male-dominated business, men often network, sometimes to the exclusion of women. To tackle this problem, Deloitte & Touche retooled the work environment. It made changes such as a renewed commitment to flexible work arrangements, reduced workload, and flextime. The firm also developed plans for company-sponsored networking and formal career planning for women. In addition, the firm's 5,000 partners and managers attended two-day workshops called "Men and Women as Colleagues" at a price to the company of approximately $3 million.

The results were terrific. Retention of women at all levels rose, and for the first time in the history of the firm, turnover rates for senior managers (just before making partner) were lower for women than for men. In addition to winning an Optima Award, it was cited as one of the top places for women to work in a New York City survey by McKinsey & Company. Deloitte not only had one of the highest proportions of women employees among those surveyed—more than 75 percent—but received especially high marks for its leadership in work/life quality and effectiveness. The firm was singled out as the only company to have a full suite of skills training and succession planning programs specifically for women. Deloitte also ranked number six on *Training* magazine's 2005 "Training Top 100" list.

QUESTIONS

1. How did the problems at Deloitte & Touche occur in the first place?
2. Did their changes fix the underlying problems? Explain.
3. What other advice would you give their managers?

Source: Excerpted from "Deloitte Earns #6 Ranking on 'Training Top 100' List,"*PR Newswire* (March 2, 2005); "Deloitte Recognized by City of New York as One of the Five Best Employers in New York City for Women," *PR Newswire* (October 27, 2003); "Firm's Diversity Efforts Even the Playing Field," *Personnel Journal* (January 1996): 56.

NOTES AND REFERENCES

1. Edward L. Gubman, *The Talent Solution: Aligning Strategy and People to Achieve Extraordinary Results* (New York: McGraw-Hill Professional Publishing, 1998).
2. "Retiring Workforce, Widening Skills Gap, Exodus of 'Critical Talent' Threaten Companies: Deloitte Survey," *Canadian Corporate News* (February 15, 2005); "The Importance of HR," *HRFocus* 73, no. 3 (March 1996): 14.
3. T. J. Watson, Jr., *A Business and Its Beliefs: The Ideas That Helped Build IBM* (New York: McGraw-Hill, 1963).
4. William L. Helkie, "U.S. International Transactions in 2001," *Federal Reserve Bulletin* 88, no. 5 (May 2002): 235–47; John S. McClenahen and Traci Purdum, "U.S. Trade Deficit to Deepen," *Industry Week* 251, no. 4 (May 2002): 56; "Goods and Services Deficit Increases in 2004," *U.S. International Trade in Goods and Services Highlight,* U.S. Census Bureau (February 10, 2005).
5. Fay Hansen, "U.S. Firms Extend Global Reach," *Workforce Management* 83, no. 13 (December 1, 2004): 138; Susan Meisinger, "Going Global: A Smart Move for HR Professionals," *HRMagazine* 49, no. 3 (March 2004): 6.
6. "FTAA Progress Report," *The New American* 18, no. 12 (June 17, 2002): 7. For more information, see the web page for the World Trade Organization at http://www.wto.org/english/thewto_e/whatis_e/10ben_e/10b07_e.htm; Christian Doeringer, "Going Global? Let HR Pave the Way," *China Staff* 10, no. 8 (July–August 2004): 36–42.
7. Nancy R. Lockwood, "Corporate Social Resonsibility: HR's Leadership Role," *HRMagazine* 49, no. 2 (December 2004): S1–11.
8. Peter F. Drucker, "Knowledge-Worker Productivity: The Biggest Challenge," *California Management Review* 41, no. 2 (Winter 1999): 79–94; A. D. Amar, *Managing Knowledge Workers* (Westport, CT: Quorum, 2002); Cynthia C. Froggat, *Work Naked: Eight Essential Principles for Peak Performance in the Virtual Workplace* (New York: John Wiley and Sons, 2002); Mary Ann Roe, "Cultivating the Gold-Collar Worker," *Harvard Business Review* 79, no. 5 (May 2001): 32–33. See also D. P. Lepak and S. A. Snell, "The Human Resource Architecture: Toward a Theory of Human Capital Development and Allocation," *Academy of Management Review* 24, no. 1 (1999): 31–48; "China Engineers

Next Great Leap with Wave of 'Knowledge Workers,'" *Milwaukee Journal Sentinel* (via Knight-Ridder/Tribune News Service), December 31, 2003; "Edward Yourdon's New Book Helps 'Knowledge Workers' Put Emotion Aside to Look at the Facts of the New Economic Reality," *PR Newswire* (October 4, 2004).

9. "Industry Report 1998: Information-Technology Training," *Training* 35, no. 10 (October 1998): 63–68; Barb Cole-Gomolski, "Recruiters Lure Temps with Free IT Training," *Computerworld* 33, no. 31 (August 2, 1999): 10; Ben Worthen, "Measuring the ROI of Training," *CIO* 14, no. 9 (February 15, 2001): 128–36.
10. Scott A. Snell, Donna Stueber, and David P. Lepak, "Virtual HR Departments: Getting Out of the Middle," in R. L. Heneman and D. B. Greenberger (eds.), *Human Resource Management in Virtual Organizations* (Columbus, OH: Information Age Publishing, forthcoming); Samuel Greengard, "How to Fulfill Technology's Promise," *Workforce* (February 1999): *HR Software Insights* supplement, 10–18.
11. Drew Robb, "Building a Better Workforce: Performance Management Software Can Help You Identify and Develop High-Performing Workers," *HRMagazine* 49, no. 10 (October 2004): 86–92.
12. Robb, "Building a Better Workforce," 86–92; "How to Implement an Effective Process for a New HR Management System," *HRFocus* (January 2005): 3–4.
13. Bruce Shutan, "HRMS Flexibility Unlocks Secret to Success," *Employee Benefits* (August 1, 2004).
14. John P. Kotter, "Ten Observations," *Executive Excellence* 16, no. 8 (1999): 15–16.
15. Chad Terhune, "Home Depot's Home Improvement—Retail Giant Aims to Spur Sales with Less-Cluttered Stores, Increased Customer Service," *The Wall Street Journal,* March 8, 2001, B1.
16. Jennifer J. Laabs, "Change," *Personnel Journal* (July 1996): 54–63.
17. John P. Kotter, "Leading Change: Why Transformation Efforts Fail," *Harvard Business Review* (March–April 1995): 59–67; Kotter, "Ten Observations," 15–16; Edward E. Lawler III, Alec Levenson, and John W. Boudreau, "HR Metrics and Analytics: Use and Impact," *Human Resource Planning* 27, no. 4 (December 2004): 27–36.
18. Lee G. Bolman and Terry E. Deal, "Four Steps to Keeping Change Efforts Heading in the Right Direction," *Journal of Quality and Participation* 22, no. 3 (May/June 1999): 6–11; "Coaching Employees through the Six Stages of Change," *HRFocus* 79, no. 5 (May 2002): 9; Stefan Stern, "Forever Changing," *Management Today* (February 7, 2005): 40; Dennis Smillie, "Managing Change, Maximizing Technology," *Multi-Housing News* 40, no. 1 (January 2005): 4.
19. For information on a company that does measure its intellectual capital, see the Skandia AFS web site and look at the company's Business Navigator at http://www.skandia.com/en/index; Donald C. Busi, "Assignment Reviews (ARs): Moving toward Measuring Your Most Valuable Asset," *Supervision* 66, no. 1 (January 2005): 3–7.
20. David Lepak and Scott Snell, "Knowledge Management and the HR Architecture," in S. Jackson, M. Hitt, and A. DeNisi (eds.), *Managing Knowledge for Sustained Competitive Advantage: Designing Strategies for Effective Human Resource Management* (SIOP Scientific Frontiers Series, forthcoming); David Lepak and Scott Snell, "Examining the Human Resource Architecture: The Relationship among Human Capital, Employment, and Human Resource Configurations," *Journal of Management,* forthcoming; Steve Bates, "Study Links HR Practices with the Bottom Line," *HRMagazine* 46, no. 12 (December 2001): 14; Ann Pomeroy, "Cooking Up Innovation: When It Comes to Helping Employees Create New Products and Services, HR's Efforts Are a Key Ingredient," *HRMagazine* 49, no. 11 (November 2004): 46–54.
21. Gary S. Becker, *Human Capital* (New York: Columbia University Press, 1964); Charles A. O'Reilly III and Jeffrey Pfeffer, "Cisco Systems: Acquiring and Retaining Talent in Hypercompetitive Markets," *Human Resource Planning* 23, no. 3 (2000): 38–52.
22. For more on Buckman Labs and their approach to managing human capital, visit their web site at http://www.buckman.com. The company is also well known for its knowledge management initiatives, called Knowledge Nurture, as well as its knowledge management system, called K'Netix; see http://www.knowledge-nurture.com.
23. Dave Ulrich, Steve Kerr, and Ron Ashkenas, *The GE Work-Out: How to Implement GE's Revolutionary Method for Busting Bureaucracy & Attacking Organizational Problems* (New York: McGraw-Hill Professional Publishing, 2002).
24. Joseph E. McCann, *Managing Intellectual Capital: Setting the Agenda for Human Resource Professionals* (New York: Human Resource Planning Society, 1999); Benoit Guay, "Knowledge Management Is a Team Sport," *Computing Canada* 27, no. 3 (July 13, 2001): 23; Pimm Fox, "Making Support Pay," *Computerworld* 36, no. 11 (March 11, 2002): 28.
25. C. W. Russ Russo, "Ten Steps to a Baldrige Award Application," *Quality Progress* 34, no. 8 (August 2001): 49–56; "Nonprofits Aim to Apply for Baldrige Award," *Quality* 43, no. 11 (November 2004): 11–13.
26. The term *Six Sigma* is a registered trademark of Motorola. It is based on the Greek letter sigma, used as a symbol of variation in a process (the standard deviation). For more information see Peter S. Pande, Robert P. Neuman, and Roland R. Cavanagh, *The Six Sigma Way: How GE, Motorola, and Other Top Companies Are Honing Their Performance* (New York: McGraw-Hill, 2000).
27. Joseph A. Defeo, "Six Sigma: Road Map for Survival," *HRFocus* 76, no. 7 (July 1999): 11–12; Michele V. Gee and Paul C. Nystrom, "Strategic Fit between Skills Training and Levels of Quality Management: An Empirical Study of American Manufacturing Plants," *Human Resource Planning* 22, no. 2 (1999): 12–23; Linda Heruing," Six Sigma in Sight," *HRMagazine* 49, no. 3 (March 2004): 76–81.
28. Ed Gubman, "HR Strategy and Planning: From Birth to Business Results," *Human Resource Planning* 27, no. 1 (March 2004): 13–21.
29. M. Hammer and J. Champy, *Reengineering the Corporation* (New York: HarperCollins, 1994). See also Michael Hammer, *Beyond Reengineering: How the Process-Centered Organization Is Changing Our Work and Our Lives* (New York: Harper Business, 1996); William M. James, "Best HR Practices for Today's Innovation Management," *Research-Technology Management* 45, no. 1 (January–Februrary 2002): 57–61.

30. "Up to Speed: L. L. Bean Moves Employees as Workloads Shift," *Chief Executive* (July–August 1996): 15; Darrell Rigby, "Look before You Lay Off," *Harvard Business Review* 80, no. 4 (April 2002): 20–21.
31. "WorldatWork Finds One-Third of Companies Downsized after 9/11," *Report on Salary Surveys* (December 2002): 2.
32. Stephanie Armour, "Some Companies Choose No-Layoff Policy," *USA Today,* December 17, 2001, B-1; Gene Koretz, "Hire Math: Fire 3, Add 5," *Business Week Online* (March 13, 2000); Michelle Conlin, "Where Layoffs Are a Last Resort," *Business Week Online* (October 8, 2001); Lynn Miller, "Downsizing Trend Brings New Change to HR Directors," *HRMagazine* 45, no. 1 (January 2001); Norman E. Amundson, William A. Borgen, Sharalyn Jordan, and Anne C. Erlebach, "Survivors of Downsizing: Helpful and Hindering Experiences," *Career Development Quarterly* 52, no. 3 (March 2004): 256–72.
33. Gubman, "HR Strategy and Planning," 13–21.
34. Gubman, "HR Strategy and Planning," 13–21; Thomas W. Gainey, Brian S. Klaas, and Darla Moore, "Outsourcing the Training Function: Results from the Field," *Human Resource Planning* 25, no. 1 (2002): 16–23; Helen G. Drinan, "Outsourcing: Opportunity or Threat?" *HRMagazine* 47, no. 2 (February 2002): 8–9; George Tischelle and Elisabeth Goodridge, "Prudential Financial Expects Savings by Outsourcing HR," *InformationWeek* (January 28, 2002): 873, 881; Denise Pelham, "Is It Time to Outsource HR?" *Training* 39, no. 4 (April 2002): 50–52; Tom Anderson, "HR Outsourcing Expected to Surge this Year," *Employee Benefit News* (February 1, 2005).
35. Karyn Siobhan Robinson, "HR Needs Large Role in Offshoring," *HRMagazine* 590, no. 45 (May 2004): 30–32.
36. Gainey, Klaas, and Moore, "Outsourcing the Training Function," 16–23; Drinan, "Outsourcing: Opportunity or Threat?" 8–9; Tischelle and Goodridge, "Prudential Financial Expects Savings by Outsourcing HR," 873, 881; Pelham, "Is It Time to Outsource HR?" 50–52; Pam Babcock, "America's Newest Export: White-Collar Jobs," *HRMagazine* 49, no. 4 (April 2004): 50–54.
37. Elliot Spagat, "Procter & Gamble to Outsource about 80% of Back-Office Work," *The Wall Street Journal Online* (June 14, 2002); "Outsourcing HR," *Industry Week* 249, no. 10 (May 15, 2000): 71; Carolyn Hirschman, "For PEOs, Business Is Booming," *HRMagazine* 45, no. 2 (February 2000): 42–47; Brian Klaas, "Trust and the Role of Professional Employer Organizations: Managing HR in Small and Medium Enterprises," *Journal of Managerial Issues* 14, no. 1 (Spring 2002): 31–49; Chris Pentilla, "Got It Covered: If You Can't Afford to Offer Employee Benefits on Your Own, Why Not Joint Forces with a PEO?" *Entrepreneur* 32, no. 2 (February 2004): 66–68.
38. Patrick Barta and Andrew Caffrey, "Productivity Leap Shows Potential of U.S. Economy—Rise at 8.6 Percent Pace, Positive for Profits, Doesn't Bode Very Well for Employment," *The Wall Street Journal,* May 8, 2002, A1; Jon E. Hilsenrath, "The Economy: Big U.S. Service Sectors Boosted Late 1990s Surge in Productivity," *The Wall Street Journal,* April 22, 2002, A2; Karen Lowry Miller, "Economy: Out of Steam—A Dip in U.S. Productivity Provokes Anxious Questions," *Newsweek International* (February 21, 2005): 34.
39. Mitra Tooss, "Labor Force Projections to 2012: The Graying of the U.S. Workforce," *The U.S. Department of Labor's Bureau of Labor Statistics* 127 (February 2004).
40. Charlotte Thomas, "Challenges to Diversity: Recruiting and Retaining Minorities," *Pharmaceutical Executive* (July 2001): 10–14. For more information about Inroads, visit their web site at http://www.inroads.org; Gail Johnson, "Time to Broaden Diversity," *Training* 41, no. 9 (September 2004): 16; Irwin Speizer, "Diversity on the Menu: Rachelle Hood, Denny's Chief Diversity Officer, Has Boosted the Company's Image. But That Hasn't Sold More Breakfasts," *Workforce Management* 83, no. 12 (November 1, 2004): 41.
41. The U.S. Department of Labor's Bureau of Labor Statistics keeps up-to-date projections and percentages in these categories. Interested readers can access this information at http://www.bls.gov.
42. "Work Force Reflects How Much Gray Matters," *The Kansas City Star* (via Knight-Ridder/Tribune Business News), March 6, 2005; Kevin G. Hall, "Age-Old Dilemma," *Fort Worth Star-Telegram* (via Knight-Ridder/Tribune News Service), March 7, 2005, C3–C4.
43. Peter Francese, "My, You've Grown: The Teen Economy Is Like Totally Awesome," *The Wall Street Journal,* June 28, 2000, S3.
44. The U.S. Department of Labor's Bureau of Labor Statistics keeps up-to-date projections and percentages in these categories. Interested readers can access this information at http://www.bls.gov; Robert Schwab, "Dancing on the Glass Ceiling," *Colorado Biz* 31, no. 5 (May 2004): 18–23.
45. The U.S. Department of Labor's Bureau of Labor Statistics keeps up-to-date projections and percentages on educational requirements for different kinds of jobs. Interested readers can access this information at http://www.bls.gov; Louis Uchitelle, "College Degree Still Pays, but It's Leveling Off," *The New York Times,* January 13 2005, C1.
46. The U.S. Department of Education has either commissioned or conducted several studies on literacy rates in the United States (http://www.ed.gov). In addition, the National Institute for Literacy (NIFL) is a federal organization that shares information about literacy and supports the development of high-quality literacy services (http://www.nifl.gov). See also "Corporate America Can't Write," *Work & Family Newsbrief* (January 2005): 4.
47. Kathleen Iverson, "Managing for Effective Workforce Diversity," *Cornell Hotel and Restaurant Administration Quarterly* 41, no. 2 (April 2000): 31–38; Gail Johnson, "Time to Broaden Diversity Training," *Training* 41, no. 9 (September 2004): 16.
48. "Avoiding Identity Theft," *Aftermarket Business* 114, no. 12 (December 2004): 10.
49. Todd Raphael, "The Drive to Downshifting," *Workforce* 80, no. 10 (October 2001): 23; Jim Olsztynski, "Flexible Work Schedules May Make More Sense: One in Six Americans Qualifies as a Caregiver Who May Benefit from Flextime," *National Driller* 26, no. 2 (February 2005): 16–19.
50. Leah Carlson, "Flextime Elevated to National Issue," *Employee Benefit News* (September 15, 2004).

chapter 2

Strategy and Human Resources Planning

After studying this chapter, you should be able to

Identify the advantages of integrating human resources planning and strategic planning.

Understand how an organization's competitive environment influences strategic planning.

Recognize the importance of internal resource analysis.

Describe the basic tools for human resources forecasting.

Explain the linkages between competitive strategies and HR.

Understand the requirements of strategy implementation.

Recognize the methods for assessing and measuring the effectiveness of strategy.

One of the clichés about company annual reports is that they often claim that "people are our most important asset." Although we might believe this to be true, the fact is that historically managers often have not acted as though they themselves really believed it. In the past, executives often tried to remove human resources from the strategy equation, by substituting capital for labor where possible, or by creating hierarchical structures that separated those who think from those who actually do the work. But much is changing today.

In a recent survey by *USA Today* and Deloitte & Touche, nearly 80 percent of corporate executives said the importance of HRM in their firms has grown substantially over the past ten years, and two-thirds said that HR expenditures are now viewed as a strategic investment rather than simply a cost to be minimized.[1]

Strategic Planning and Human Resources

As we explained in Chapter 1, "competing through people" is the theme for this book. But the idea remains only a premise for action until we put it into practice. To deliver on this promise, we need to understand some of the systems and processes in organizations that link human resources management and strategic management. A few definitions may be helpful up front.

First of all, **strategic planning** involves a set of procedures for making decisions about the organization's long-term goals and strategies. In this chapter, we discuss strategic plans as having a strong external orientation that covers major portions of the organization. They especially focus on how the organization will position itself relative to competitors in order to achieve long-term survival, value, and growth. **Human resources planning (HRP),** by comparison, is the process of anticipating and making provision for the movement of people into, within, and out of an organization. Overall, its purpose is to help managers deploy human resources as effectively as possible, where and when they are needed, in order to accomplish the organization's goals. **Strategic human resources management (SHRM),** then, combines strategic planning and HR planning. It can be thought of as the pattern of human resources deployments and activities that enable an organization to achieve its strategic goals.

strategic planning
Procedures for making decisions about the organization's long-term goals and strategies

human resources planning (HRP)
The process of anticipating and providing for the movement of people into, within, and out of an organization

strategic human resources management (SHRM)
The pattern of human resources deployments and activities that enable an organization to achieve its strategic goals

Although planning has always been an essential process of management, increased emphasis on HR issues becomes especially critical when organizations consider global strategies, mergers, relocation of plants, innovation, downsizing, outsourcing, offshoring, or the closing of operating facilities. Dramatic shifts in the composition of the labor force require that managers become more involved in planning, since such changes affect the full range of HR practices (such as employee recruitment, selection, training, compensation, and motivation).

Strategic Planning and HR Planning: Linking the Processes

As organizations plan for their future, HR managers must be concerned with meshing HRP and strategic planning for the organization as a whole.[2] Through strategic planning, organizations set major objectives and develop comprehensive plans to achieve those objectives. Human resources planning relates to strategic planning in several ways, but at a fundamental level we can focus on two issues: strategy formulation and strategy implementation. Human resources planning provides a set of inputs into the strategic *formulation* process in terms of what is possible; that is, whether the types and numbers of people are available to pursue a given strategy. For example, when Barnes & Noble executives contemplated the move into web-based commerce to compete with Amazon.com, one of the issues they had to address was whether they had the talent needed to succeed in that arena.

In addition to strategy formulation, HRP is important in terms of strategy *implementation* as well. Once the strategy is devised, executives must make primary resource allocation decisions, including those pertaining to structure, processes, and human resources.[3] Companies such as GE, IBM, and CIGNA have taken strides to combine these two aspects of strategic management.[4]

All the available evidence suggests that the integration of HRP and strategic planning tends to be most effective when there is a reciprocal relationship between the two processes. In this relationship, the top management team recognizes that strategic-planning decisions affect—and are affected by—HR concerns. Figure 2.1 illustrates the basic outline of how companies have begun aligning HRP and strategic planning in this way. While this figure begins to address this issue of strategic alignment, we will raise the issue at several points throughout the chapter.

As we look at trends in the best of companies, there is virtually no distinction between strategic planning and HRP; the planning cycles are the same and HR issues

Figure 2.1 Linking Strategic Planning and Human Resources

	BUSINESS/CORPORATE	HUMAN RESOURCES
Mission, Vision and Values	• Identify purpose and scope • Clarify long-term direction • Establish enduring beliefs and principles	• Capture underlying philosophy • Establish foundation of culture • Guide ethical codes of conduct
SWOT Analysis: External Analysis	• Opportunities and threats (OT) • Environmental scanning (legal, etc.) • Industry/competitor analysis	• Demographic trends • External supply of labor • Competitor benchmarking
SWOT Analysis: Internal Analysis	• Strengths and weaknesses (SW) • Core competencies • Resources: People, process, systems	• Culture, competencies, composition • Forecast demand for employees • Forecast supply of employees
Strategy Formulation	• Corporate strategy • Business strategy • Functional strategy: Alignment	• Productivity and efficiency • Quality, service, speed, innovation • External fit/alignment and internal fit
Strategy Implementation	• Design structure, systems, etc. • Allocate resources • Leadership, communication, and change	• Reconcile supply and demand • Downsizing, layoffs, etc. • HR practice: Staffing, training, rewards, etc.
Evaluation	• Assessment and benchmarking • Ensuring alignment • Agility and flexibility	• Human capital metrics • Balanced Scorecard

are seen as inherent in the management of the business. As James Walker, noted HRP expert, put it, "Today, virtually *all* business issues have people implications; *all* human resource issues have business implications."[5] HR managers are important facilitators of the planning process and are viewed as credible and important contributors to creating the organization's future. This positive linkage occurs when the HR manager becomes a member of the organization's management steering committee or strategic-planning group. Once this interactive and dynamic structure exists, HR managers are recognized as contributing strategic planners alongside other top managers.[6]

This is an important element for the rest of our discussion in this chapter. Traditionally, authors—and too many HR managers—have treated HR planning and strategic planning as separate activities. Instead, we provide a step-by-step process to show how the two aspects of planning can be integrated.

Step One: Mission, Vision, and Values

mission
The basic purpose of the organization as well as its scope of operations

The first step in strategic planning is establishing a mission, vision, and values for the organization. The **mission** is the basic purpose of the organization, as well as its scope of operations. It is a statement of the organization's reason for existing. The mission often is written in terms of general clients it services. Depending on the scope of the organization, the mission may be broad or narrow. For example, the mission of Merck and Company is as follows:

> The mission of Merck is to provide society with superior products and services by developing innovations and solutions that improve the quality of life and satisfy customer needs, and to provide employees with meaningful work and advancement opportunities, and investors with a superior rate of return.[7]

strategic vision
A statement about where the company is going and what it can become in the future; clarifies the long-term direction of the company and its strategic intent

The **strategic vision** of the organization moves beyond the mission statement to provide a perspective on where the company is headed and what the organization can become in the future. Although the terms *mission* and *vision* often are used interchangeably, the vision statement ideally clarifies the long-term direction of the company and its strategic intent.

core values
The strong and enduring beliefs and principles that the company uses as a foundation for its decisions

Organizational **core values** are the strong enduring beliefs and principles that the company uses as a foundation for its decisions. Starbucks, for example, lists the following core values:

- Provide a great work environment and treat each other with respect and dignity.
- Embrace diversity as an essential component in the way we do business.
- Apply the highest standards of excellence to the purchasing, roasting, and fresh delivery of our coffee.
- Develop enthusiastically satisfied customers all of the time.
- Contribute positively to our communities and our environment.
- Recognize that profitability is essential to our future success.

These are the underlying parameters for how the company will act toward customers, employees, and the public in general. In many cases, the values capture the underlying philosophy of the company culture and give direction to its employees. The values also place limits on what behavior is seen as ethical and acceptable. Highlights in HRM 1 shows the results of IBM's recent effort to reexamine and reinforce its values.

Highlights in HRM 1

Our Values at Work on Being an IBMer

Business Value and a Company's Values

We've been spending a great deal of time thinking, debating and determining the fundamentals of this company. It has been important to do so. When IBMers have been crystal clear and united about our strategies and purpose, it's amazing what we've been able to create and accomplish. When we've been uncertain, conflicted or hesitant, we've squandered opportunities and even made blunders that would have sunk smaller companies.

It may not surprise you, then, that last year we examined IBM's core values for the first time since the company's founding. In this time of great change, we needed to affirm IBM's reason for being, what sets the company apart and what should drive our actions as individual IBMers.

Importantly, we needed to find a way to engage everyone in the company and get them to speak up on these important issues. Given the realities of a smart, global, independent-minded, 21st-century workforce like ours, I don't believe something as vital and personal as values could be dictated from the top.

So, for 72 hours last summer, we invited all 319,000 IBMers around the world to engage in an open "values jam" on our global intranet. IBMers by the tens of thousands weighed in. They were thoughtful and passionate about the company they want to be a part of. They were also brutally honest. Some of what they wrote was painful to read, because they pointed out all the bureaucratic and dysfunctional things that get in the way of serving clients, working as a team or implementing new ideas. But we were resolute in keeping the dialog free-flowing and candid. And I don't think what resulted—broad, enthusiastic, grass-roots consensus—could have been obtained in any other way.

In the end, IBMers determined that our actions will be driven by these values:

- Dedication to every client's success
- Innovation that matters, for our company and for the world
- Trust and personal responsibility in all relationships

I must tell you, this process has been very meaningful to me. We are getting back in touch with what IBM has always been about—and always will be about—in a very concrete way. And I feel that I've been handed something every CEO craves: a mandate, for exactly the right kinds of transformation, from an entire workforce.

Where will this lead? It is a work in progress, and many of the implications remain to be discovered. What I can tell you is that we are rolling up our sleeves to bring IBM's values to life in our policies, procedures and daily operations.

I've already touched on a number of things relating to clients and innovation, but our values of trust and personal responsibility are being managed just as seriously—from changes in how we measure and reward performance, to how we equip and support IBMers' community volunteerism.

Our values underpin our relationships with investors, as well. In late February, the board of directors approved sweeping changes in executive compensation. They include innovative programs that ensure investors first receive meaningful returns—a 10 percent increase in the

(continued on next page)

(continued from previous page)

stock price—before IBM's top 300 executives can realize a penny of profit from their stock option grants. Putting that into perspective, IBM's market value would have to increase by $17 billion before executives saw any benefit from this year's option awards. In addition, these executives will be able to acquire market-priced stock options only if they first invest their own money in IBM stock. We believe these programs are unprecedented, certainly in our industry and perhaps in business.

Clearly, leading by values is very different from some kinds of leadership demonstrated in the past by business. It is empowering, and I think that's much healthier. Rather than burden our people with excessive controls, we are trusting them to make decisions and to act based on values—values they themselves shaped.

To me, it's also just common sense. In today's world, where everyone is so interconnected and interdependent, it is simply essential that we work for each other's success. If we're going to solve the biggest, thorniest and most widespread problems in business and society, we have to innovate in ways that truly matter. And we have to do all this by taking personal responsibility for all of our relationships—with clients, colleagues, partners, investors and the public at large. This is IBM's mission as an enterprise, and a goal toward which we hope to work with many others, in our industry and beyond.

Samuel J. Palmisano
Chairman, President and Chief Executive Officer

Source: http://www.ibm.com/ibm/values/us/.

Step Two: Environmental Analysis

environmental scanning Systematic monitoring of the major external forces influencing the organization

The mission, vision, and values drive the second component of the strategic management process: analysis of external opportunities and threats. Changes in the external environment have a direct impact on the way organizations are run and people are managed. Some of these changes represent opportunities, and some of them represent real threats to the organization. Because of this, successful strategic management depends on an accurate and thorough evaluation of the environment. **Environmental scanning** is the systematic monitoring of the major external forces influencing the organization.[8] Managers attend to a variety of external issues; however, the following six are monitored most frequently:

1. Economic factors, including general, regional, and global conditions
2. Industry and competitive trends, including new processes, services, and innovations
3. Technological changes, including information technology, innovations, and automation
4. Government and legislative issues, including laws and administrative rulings
5. Social concerns, including child care, elder care, the environment, and educational priorities
6. Demographic and labor market trends, including age, composition, and literacy

By scanning the environment for changes that will likely affect an organization, managers can anticipate their impact and make adjustments early.

Competitive Environment

While many factors in the general environment may influence strategic decisions, analysis of the firm's competitive environment is central to strategic planning. The competitive environment includes the specific organizations with which the firm interacts. As shown in Figure 2.2, the competitive environment includes customers, rival firms, new entrants, substitutes, and suppliers. In strategic planning, firms analyze the competitive environment in order to adapt to or influence the nature of competition. A general rule of thumb about this analysis is: The more power each of these forces has, the less profitable (and therefore attractive) the industry will be. Let's look at each of the five forces.

Customers

One of the most important assessments a firm can make is identifying the needs of its customers. At a fundamental level, strategy focuses on creating customer value—and different customers often want different things. For example, in the hotel industry, business travelers may want convenient locations with meeting facilities. Vacationers may want resort locations with swimming pools, golf courses, and luxury spas. Other travelers may just want an inexpensive room next to the highway. The point is that increasingly, "one size does not fit all," and organizations need to know how they are going to provide value to customers. That is the foundation for strategy, and it influences the kind of skills and behavior that will be needed from employees. For example, actions and attitudes that lead to excellent customer service can include the following:

- Speed of delivering normal orders
- Willingness to meet extraordinary needs
- Merchandise delivered in good condition
- Readiness to take back defective goods and resupply new goods quickly
- Availability of installation and repair services and parts

Figure 2.2 Five Forces Framework

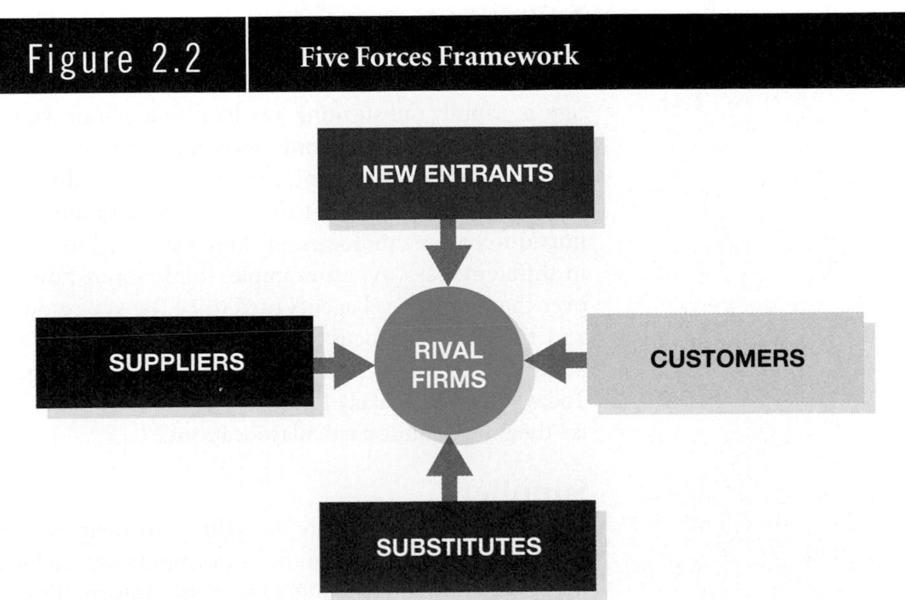

Rival Firms

In addition to customer analysis, perhaps the most obvious element of industry analysis is examining the nature of competition. The first question to consider is: Who is the competition? Often the answer is clear to everyone, but sometimes it is not. For example, for many years, Toys "R" Us viewed its main competitors to be other toy stores such as FAO Schwarz or KB Toys. However, other retailers such as Target and Wal-Mart soon moved into this space very successfully. This had a direct effect on human resources planning for Toys "R" Us. While in the past, Toys "R" Us had been successful with a volume-based approach (that is, "stack it high, and let it fly"), bigger retailers soon gained an advantage—who can beat Wal-Mart's volume and cost advantage? As a consequence, Toys "R" Us had to modify its strategy to compete more on customer service and the expertise of its employees. But did Toys "R" Us have the number and kind of employees required to compete in this way? Were its staffing, training, performance management, and compensation practices aligned with this strategy?

New Entrants

As suggested previously, new companies can sometimes enter an industry to compete with established firms. And sometimes they can't. To protect their position, companies often try to establish entry barriers to keep new firms out of the industry. However, when new firms do enter an industry it is often because they have a different—and perhaps better—way to provide value to customers. For example, when JetBlue entered the airline business, it distinguished itself by providing excellent service and low prices in regions where customers did not have many options. The HR implications of this are clear. When we look at the challenges faced by traditional airlines because of the threat of low-cost carriers such as JetBlue, Alaska Air, and Southwest Airlines, we can clearly see that new entrants can change the "rules of the game" in an industry. The impact on labor costs, productivity, skills required, and work design are important considerations in both strategic planning and human resources planning.

Substitutes

At times, the biggest opportunity or threat in an industry is not with direct competition, but from substitution. In the telephone industry, for example, cellular technology is rapidly substituting for land-line phone systems. Similarly, some firms are using new technology to offer telephone service over the Internet (VOIP). These substitutes offer the same service or function as traditional firms, but through a different method. That implies that firms may need to adjust their skill base in order to support different technologies. Or they may need to think about how they will compete in different ways. As an example, think about how the travel business has changed over the years. Travel agents used to be the key resource for flights, hotels, rental cars, and the like. The focus was almost exclusively on transactions. However, with the advent of online reservation systems, travel agents have had to adapt their approach. Today, they are as likely to compete based on the service they provide and the expertise they have about particular locations.

Suppliers

Organizations rarely create everything on their own, but instead have suppliers that provide them with key inputs. These inputs can include raw materials for production, money (from banks and stockholders), information, and people. This last factor—

people, or labor as it is historically called—has direct implications for strategic planning and human resources planning. Because of its central role in both strategic planning and HRP, we explore it next in much more detail.

External Supply of Labor

Many factors influence the labor supply, including demographic changes in the population, national and regional economics, education level of the workforce, demand for specific employee skills, population mobility, and governmental policies. National and regional unemployment rates are often considered a general barometer of labor supply. Consider these U.S. Census Bureau facts about American workers:

- By 2012, employment will rise to more than 163 million workers. And while the labor force is expected to grow at a rate of 12 percent, the growth rate for college graduate–level jobs is expected to grow by more than double that.
- By 2012, the average ages of the workforce will be 41, up from 34.7 in 1979. Yet while the group of workers ages 45 to 54 will have increased by 52 percent, the group between ages 35 and 44 will have shrunk by more than 10 percent.
- The fastest-growing segments of the workforce in terms of race will be Asian Americans and Hispanics (an increase primarily effected through immigration).
- By 2012, nearly one in five American workers will be age 55 or older.
- On average nationwide, high school graduates can expect to earn about $27,280 annually. Those with a bachelor degrees can expect to earn, on average, nearly double that amount.
- Women will make up approximately 48 percent of the workforce in 2012. Today, three of every five college graduates are women.
- Nearly 25 percent of the workforce is composed of part-timers, and the number has been steadily rising. But only one in five of these workers has access to medical coverage.
- Over the next ten years another 1 million-plus computer, Internet, and software technology job openings will be created. However, the fastest-growing sector will be in service industries.
- Between 45 and 50 percent of adults in the United States have only limited reading and writing abilities needed to handle the minimal demands of daily living or job performance.

These labor force trends illustrate the importance of monitoring demographic changes as a part of environmental scanning. Fortunately, labor market analysis is aided by various published documents. Unemployment rates, labor force projection figures, and population characteristics are reported by the U.S. Department of Labor.[9] The *Monthly Labor Review* and *Occupational Outlook Handbook,* both published by the Bureau of Labor Statistics (BLS) of the U.S. Department of Labor, contain information on jobholder characteristics and predicted changes in the workforce. In addition, local chambers of commerce and individual state development and planning agencies also may assist both large organizations and new business ventures with labor market analysis.

These sources of information are invaluable. In a rapidly changing environment, it is extremely risky to be caught off guard. Such changes are important for many reasons, some related to operational issues and some to strategic issues. HRP has to focus on both. At an operational level, the change in labor supply directly influences hiring plans that must take into account the demographic composition of the population in the area where the organization is located. Similarly, with a "maturing" workforce, HRP must consider the implications for recruitment and replacement policies.

From a strategic standpoint, changes in the labor supply can limit the strategies available to firms. High-growth companies in particular may find it difficult to find the talent they need to expand their businesses. While unemployment rates vary by sector, the shortage of talent in high-skill jobs continues to create real challenges for firms.

Step Three: Internal Analysis

As organizations conduct external analyses of environmental opportunities and threats, they also analyze their internal strengths and weaknesses. Internal analysis provides strategic decision makers with an inventory of organizational skills and resources as well as their performance levels.

To be sure, many resources combine to give organizations a competitive advantage. But in contrast to the past, the advantages due to physical assets are being supplanted by intangible assets, including people. As James Brian Quinn noted, "With rare exceptions, the economic and producing power of firms lies more in its intellectual and service capabilities than in its hard assets—land, plant, and equipment."[10]

The Three Cs: Culture, Competencies, and Composition

In the context of human resource planning, internal analysis focuses especially on "the three Cs": culture, competencies, and composition.

Culture: Auditing Values, Beliefs, and Attitudes

Think about our initial discussion (in Step One) of mission, vision, and values. Because managers increasingly understand that employee-oriented cultures are critical to success, they often conduct **cultural audits** to examine the attitudes and beliefs of the workforce as well as the activities they engage in. At one level, this analysis focuses on whether critical values are embraced and demonstrated by employees throughout the organization. Employee surveys, for example, can measure how employees feel on a number of critical issues, and can be very useful for upward assessment and feedback of (and for) management.

cultural audits
Audits of the culture and quality of work life in an organization

However, these audits can go much deeper. Sears, for example, found that positive employee attitudes on ten essential factors—including workload and treatment by bosses—are directly linked to customer satisfaction and revenue increases.[11]

Cultural audits essentially involve discussions among top-level managers of how the organization's culture reveals itself to employees and how it can be influenced or improved. The cultural audit may include such questions as the following:

- How do employees spend their time?
- How do they interact with each other?
- Are employees empowered?

- What is the predominant leadership style of managers?
- How do employees advance within the organization?

By conducting in-depth interviews and making observations over a period of time, managers are able to learn about the culture of their organization and the attitudes of its employees. With the increased diversity of the U.S. workplace, cultural audits can be used to determine whether there are different groups, or subcultures, within the organization that have distinctly different views about the nature of work, the quality of managers, and so on. Before any HR planning can take place, managers have to gain a clear idea of how employees view their organization.

Competencies: People as a Strategic Resource

core competencies
Integrated knowledge sets within an organization that distinguish it from its competitors and deliver value to customers

A growing number of experts now argue that the key to a firm's success is based on establishing a set of **core competencies**—integrated skills and knowledge sets within an organization that distinguish it from its competitors and deliver value to customers. McDonald's, for example, has developed core competencies in management efficiency and training. Federal Express has core competencies in package routing, delivery, and employee relations. Royal Dutch Shell has core competencies in oil exploration and production.[12] Core competencies tend to be limited in number, but they provide a long-term basis for technology innovation, product development, and service delivery.

In many cases, people are a key resource that underlies a firm's core competencies. Particularly in knowledge-based industries such as software and information services, success increasingly depends on "people-embodied know-how." This includes the knowledge, skills, and abilities of employees. Organizations can achieve a sustained competitive advantage through people if they are able to meet the following criteria:[13]

1. *The resources must be valuable.* People are a source of competitive advantage when they improve the efficiency or effectiveness of the company. Value is increased when employees find ways to decrease costs, provide something unique to customers, or some combination of the two. Empowerment programs, total-quality initiatives, and continuous improvement efforts at companies such as Nordstrom and UPS are intentionally designed to increase the value that employees represent on the bottom line.
2. *The resources must be rare.* People are a source of competitive advantage when their knowledge, skills, and abilities are not equally available to competitors. Companies such as Microsoft, McKinsey, and Four Seasons Hotels invest a great deal to hire and train the best and the brightest employees in order to gain an advantage over their competitors.
3. *The resources must be difficult to imitate.* People are a source of competitive advantage when employee capabilities and contributions cannot be copied by others. Disney, Southwest Airlines, and Starbucks are each known for creating unique cultures that get the most from employees (through teamwork) and are difficult to imitate.
4. *The resources must be organized.* People are a source of competitive advantage when their talents can be combined and deployed to work on new assignments at a moment's notice. Companies such as IBM and GE have invested in information technology to help allocate and track employee assignments to temporary projects. Teamwork and cooperation are two other pervasive methods for ensuring an organized workforce.

These four criteria highlight the importance of people and show the closeness of HRM to strategic management.

Composition: The Human Capital Architecture

A related element of internal analysis for organizations that compete on competencies is determining the composition of the workforce. That is, managers need to determine whether people are available, internally or externally, to execute an organization's strategy. In some respects, this has traditionally been the focal point of human resources planning. Managers have to make tough decisions about whom to employ internally, whom to contract externally, and how to manage different types of employees with different skills who contribute in different ways to the organization.

Figure 2.3 shows that different skill groups in any given organization can be classified according to the degree to which they create strategic value and are unique to the organization. As a general rule, managers often consider contracting externally (or outsourcing) skill areas that are not central to the firm's core competence. HRP

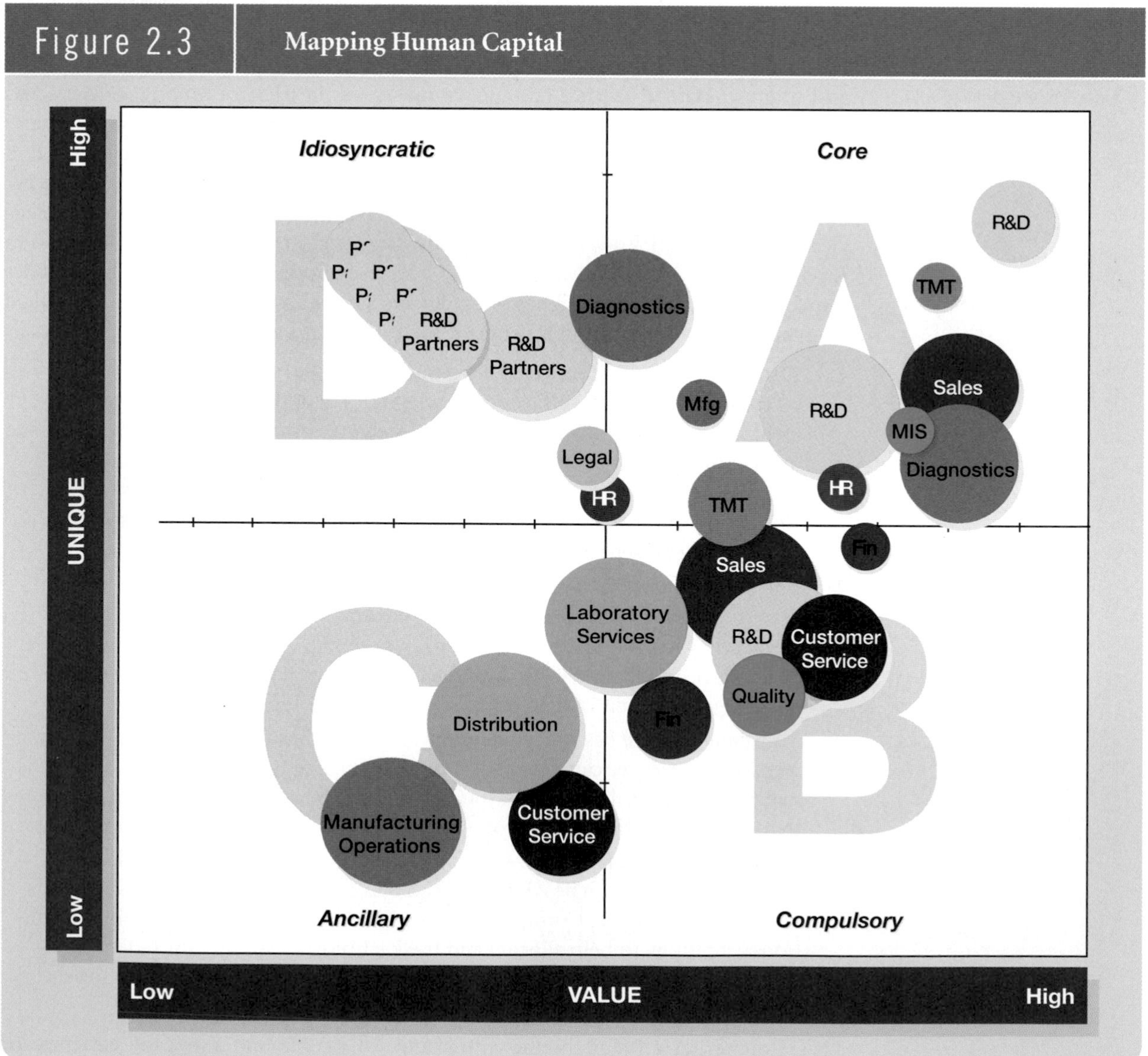

Figure 2.3 Mapping Human Capital

plays an important role in helping managers weigh the costs and benefits of using one approach to employment versus another.

Evidence from research suggests that employment relationships and HR practices for different employees vary according to which segment they occupy in this matrix. Here are some general trends:

Core Knowledge Workers. This group of employees tends to have firm-specific skills that are directly linked to the company's strategy (such as R&D scientists in a pharmaceuticals company or computer scientists in a software development company). These employees typically are engaged in knowledge work that involves considerable autonomy and discretion. Companies tend to make long-term commitments to these employees, investing in their continuous training and development and perhaps giving them an equity stake in the organization.

Traditional Job-Based Workers. This group of employees has skills that are quite valuable to a company, but not particularly unique (such as salespeople in a department store or truck drivers for a courier service). These employees tend to be employed to perform a predefined job. As it is quite possible that they could leave to go to another firm, managers frequently make less investment in training and development and tend to focus more on paying for short-term performance achievements.

USING THE INTERNET

For more information about contract employees, go to the Student Resources at:

http://bohlander.swlearning.com

Contract Labor. This group of employees typically has skills that are of less strategic value and generally available to all firms (such as clerical workers, maintenance workers, and staff workers in accounting and human resources). Individuals in these jobs are increasingly hired from external agencies on a contract basis, and the scope of their duties tends to be limited. Employment relationships tend to be transactional, focused on rules and procedures, with less investment in development.

Alliance Partners. This group of individuals has skills that are unique, but frequently not directly related to a company's core strategy (such as attorneys, consultants, and research lab scientists). Although companies perhaps cannot justify their internal employment, given their tangential link to strategy, these individuals have skills that are specialized and not readily available to all firms. As a consequence, companies tend to establish longer-term alliances and partnerships with them and nurture an ongoing relationship focused on mutual learning. Considerable investment is made in the exchange of information and knowledge.[14]

Forecasting: A Critical Element of Planning

While internal analysis of the three Cs (culture, competencies, and composition) may reveal a great deal about where the organization is today, things change. And in an important sense strategic planning is about managing that change. Managers must continually forecast both the needs and the capabilities of the firm for the future in order to do an effective job at strategic planning. As shown in Figure 2.4, managers focus on (at least) three key elements: (a) forecasting the demand for labor, (b) forecasting the supply of labor, and (c) balancing supply and demand considerations. Careful attention to each factor helps top managers meet their human resources requirements.

Figure 2.4 Model of HR Forecasting

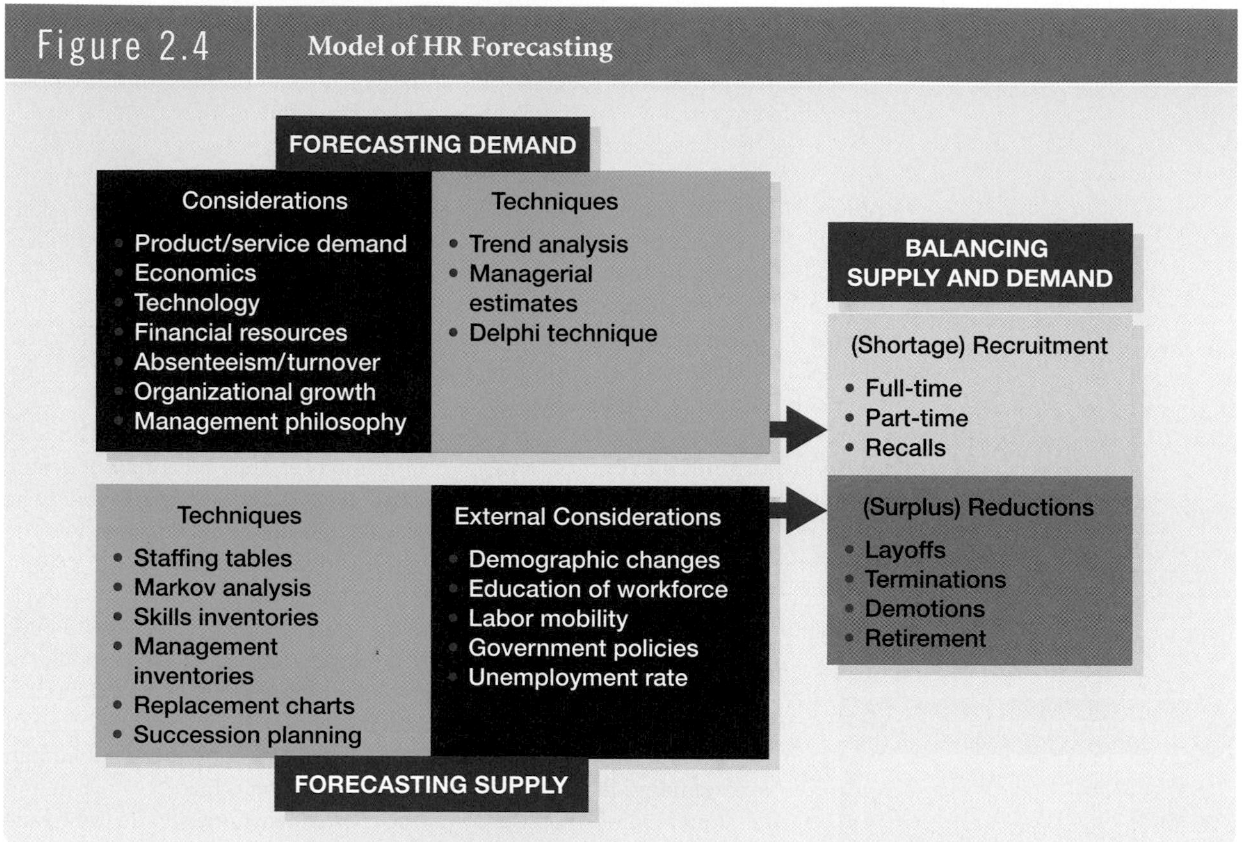

Consider for a moment the high costs of not forecasting—or forecasting poorly. If job vacancies are left unfilled, the resulting loss in efficiency can be very costly, particularly when lead time is required to train replacements. As ridiculous as it may sound, we have seen situations in which employees are laid off in one department while applicants are hired for similar jobs in another department. This kind of mistake can be frustrating, to say the least, and can be confounded when overhiring results in having to lay off employees who were just recently hired. Poor forecasting also makes it difficult for employees to effectively assess their own careers and development. As a result, some of the more competent and ambitious workers may seek other employment where they feel they will have better career opportunities.[15]

On the plus side, accurate forecasting provides the kind of information managers need to make sound decisions. It can help them ensure that they have the right number and right kind of people in the right places at the right times, doing things that provide value to both the organization and the employees.

Forecasting Demand for Employees

If a key component of forecasting is predicting the number and type of people needed to meet organizational objectives, the question remains: "How can this be done?" A variety of factors, including competitive strategy, technology, structure, and productivity, can influence the demand for labor. For example, as noted in Chapter 1, use of advanced technology is generally accompanied by less demand for low-skilled workers and more demand for knowledge workers. External factors such as business cycles—economic and seasonal trends—can also play a role. For example, retailers such as The Gap, Bath & Body Works, and Marks & Spencer rely heavily on temporary employees between November and January, during the holiday season.

There are two approaches to HR forecasting: quantitative and qualitative. When concentrating on human resources needs, forecasting is primarily quantitative in nature and, in large organizations, is accomplished by highly trained specialists. Quantitative approaches to forecasting can employ sophisticated analytical models, although forecasting may be as informal as having one person who knows the organization anticipate future HR requirements. Organizational demands will ultimately determine which technique is used. Regardless of the method, however, forecasting should not be neglected, even in relatively small organizations.

trend analysis
A quantitative approach to forecasting labor demand based on an organizational index such as sales

Quantitative Approaches. Quantitative approaches to forecasting involve the use of statistical or mathematical techniques; they are the approaches used by theoreticians and professional planners. One example is **trend analysis,** which forecasts employment requirements on the basis of some organizational index and is one of the most commonly used approaches for projecting HR demand. Trend analysis is typically done in the following several stages:

First, select an appropriate business factor. This should be the best available predictor of human resources needs. Frequently, sales or value added (selling price minus costs of materials and supplies) is used as a predictor in trend analysis. Second, plot a historical trend of the business factor in relation to the number of employees. The ratio of employees to the business factor will provide a labor productivity ratio (for example, sales per employee). Third, compute the productivity ratio for at least the past five years. Fourth, calculate human resources demand by multiplying the business factor by the productivity ratio. Finally, project human resources demand out to the target year. This procedure is illustrated in Figure 2.5 for a hypothetical building contractor.

Figure 2.5 Example of Trend Analysis of HR Demand

YEAR	BUSINESS FACTOR (SALES IN THOUSANDS)	÷ LABOR PRODUCTIVITY (SALES/EMPLOYEE)	= HUMAN RESOURCES DEMAND (NUMBER OF EMPLOYEES)
2000	$2,351	14.33	164
2001	$2,613	11.12	235
2002	$2,935	8.34	352
2003	$3,306	10.02	330
2004	$3,613	11.12	325
2005	$3,748	11.12	337
2006	$3,880	12.52	310
2007*	$4,095	12.52	327
2008*	$4,283	12.52	342
2009*	$4,446	12.52	355

*Projected figures

Other, more-sophisticated statistical planning methods include modeling or multiple predictive techniques. Whereas trend analysis relies on a single factor (such as sales) to predict employment needs, the more-advanced methods combine several factors, such as interest rates, gross national product, disposable income, and sales, to predict employment levels. While the costs of developing these forecasting methods used to be quite high, advances in technology and computer software have made rather sophisticated forecasting tools affordable to even small businesses.

Qualitative Approaches. Admittedly, forecasting is frequently more an art than a science, providing inexact approximations rather than absolute results. The ever-changing environment in which an organization operates contributes to this situation. For example, estimating changes in product or service demand is a basic forecasting concern, as is anticipating changes in national or regional economics. A community hospital anticipating internal changes in technology, organization, or administration must consider these environmental factors in its forecasts of staffing needs. Also, the forecasted staffing needs must be in line with the organization's financial resources.

In contrast to quantitative approaches, qualitative approaches to forecasting are less statistical, attempting to reconcile the interests, abilities, and aspirations of individual employees with the current and future staffing needs of an organization. In both large and small organizations, HR planners may rely on experts who help prepare forecasts to anticipate staffing requirements. **Management forecasts** are the opinions (judgments) of supervisors, department managers, experts, or others knowledgeable about the organization's future employment needs. For example, at the Ripe Tomato, a growing family dining chain, each restaurant manager is responsible for employment forecasts.

management forecasts
The opinions (judgments) of supervisors, department managers, experts, or others knowledgeable about the organization's future employment needs

Another qualitative forecasting method, the Delphi technique, attempts to decrease the subjectivity of forecasts by soliciting and summarizing the judgments of a preselected group of individuals. The final forecast thus represents a composite group judgment. The Delphi technique requires a great deal of coordination and cooperation in order to ensure satisfactory forecasts. This method works best in organizations in which dynamic technological changes affect staffing levels.

Ideally, forecasting should include the use of both quantitative and qualitative approaches. In combination, the two approaches complement each other, providing a more complete forecast by bringing together the contributions of both theoreticians and practitioners.

Forecasting Supply of Employees

Just as an organization must forecast its future requirements for employees, it must also determine whether sufficient numbers and types of employees are available to staff anticipated openings. As with demand forecasts, the process involves both tracking current levels and making future projections.

staffing tables
Graphic representations of all organizational jobs, along with the numbers of employees currently occupying those jobs and future (monthly or yearly) employment requirements

Markov analysis
A method for tracking the pattern of employee movements through various jobs

Staffing Tables and Markov Analysis. An internal supply analysis may begin with the preparation of staffing tables. **Staffing tables** are graphic representations of all organizational jobs, along with the numbers of employees currently occupying those jobs (and perhaps also future employment requirements derived from demand forecasts). Another technique, called **Markov analysis,** shows the percentage (and actual number) of employees who remain in each job from one year to the next, as well as the proportions of those who are promoted, demoted, or transferred, or exit the

In addition to qualitative, or statistical, approaches, HR managers also rely on the opinions of managers in their organizations to help forecast the demand for future employees.

organization. As shown in Figure 2.6, Markov analysis can be used to track the pattern of employee movements through various jobs and to develop a transition matrix for forecasting labor supply.

Forecasting the supply of human resources requires that managers have a good understanding of employee turnover and absenteeism. We have included formulas for

Figure 2.6 **Hypothetical Markov Analysis for a Retail Company**

2005 → 2006	Store Managers	Asst. Store Managers	Section Managers	Dept. Managers	Sales Associates	Exit
Store Managers (*n* = 12)	90% 11					10% 1
Assistant Store Managers (*n* = 36)	11% 4	83% 30				6% 2
Section Managers (*n* = 96)		11% 11	66% 63	8% 8		15% 14
Department Managers (*n* = 288)			10% 29	72% 207	2% 6	16% 46
Sales Associates (*n* = 1440)				6% 86	74% 1066	20% 288
Forecasted Supply	15	41	92	301	1072	351

Transition percentage / Actual number of employees

computing turnover and absenteeism rates in an appendix to this chapter. The calculations are easily made and used by managers of both large and small organizations.

skill inventories
Files of personnel education, experience, interests, skills, and so on that allow managers to quickly match job openings with employee backgrounds

Skill Inventories and Management Inventories. While staffing tables, Markov analysis, turnover rates, and the like tend to focus on the number of employees in particular jobs, other techniques are more oriented toward the types of employees and their skills, knowledge, and experiences. **Skill inventories** can also be prepared that list each employee's education, past work experience, vocational interests, specific abilities and skills, compensation history, and job tenure. Of course, confidentiality is a vital concern in setting up any such inventory. Nevertheless, well-prepared and up-to-date skill inventories allow an organization to quickly match forthcoming job openings with employee backgrounds. When data are gathered on managers,

Figure 2.7 An Executive Replacement Chart

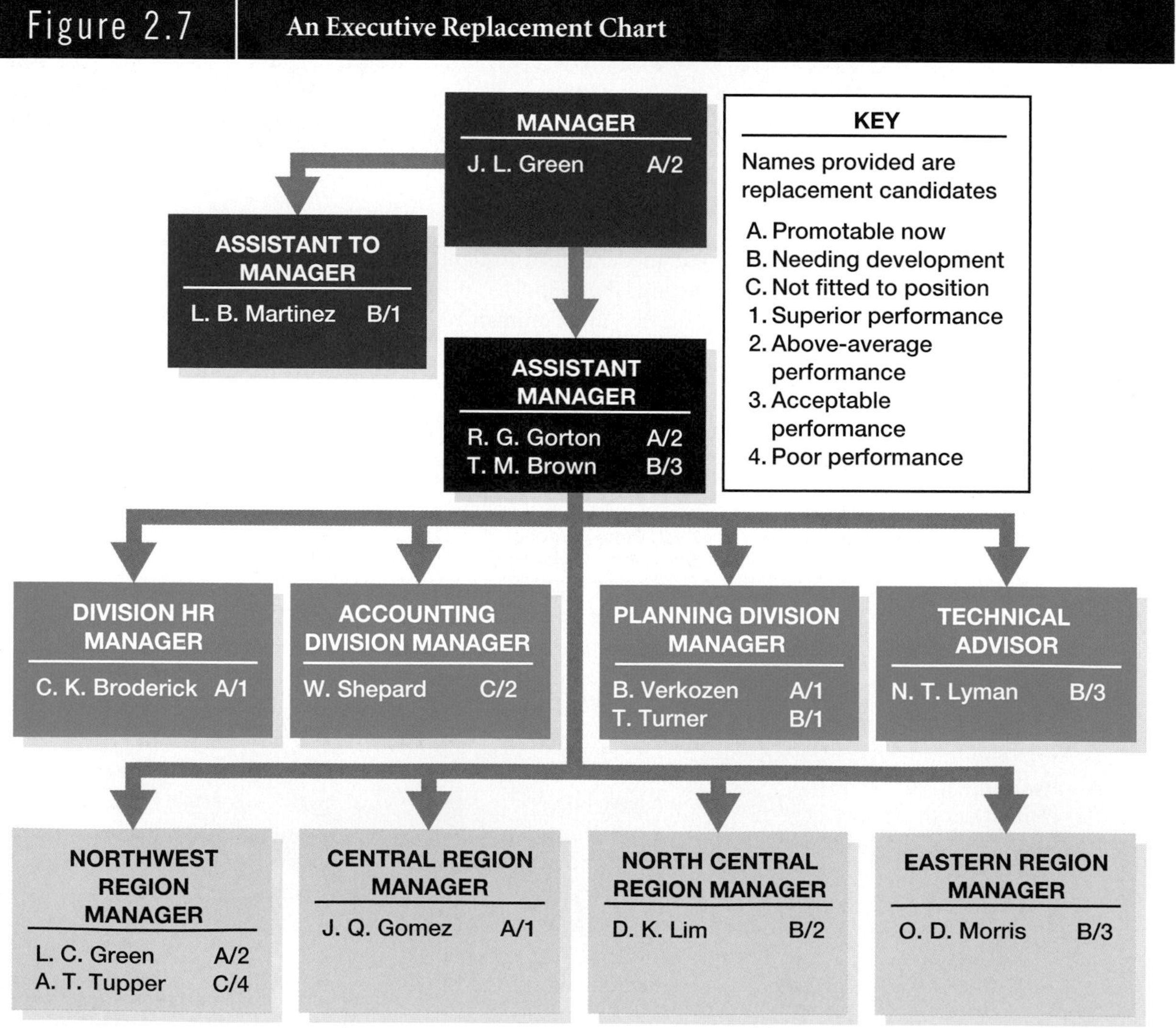

these inventories are called *management inventories.* And all of this analysis is made simpler these days through the use of HR information systems and enterprise systems provided by companies such as Oracle-PeopleSoft and SAP.

replacement charts
Listings of current jobholders and people who are potential replacements if an opening occurs

succession planning
The process of identifying, developing, and tracking key individuals for executive positions

Replacement Charts and Succession Planning. Both skill and management inventories—broadly referred to as talent inventories—can be used to develop employee **replacement charts,** which list current jobholders and identify possible replacements should openings occur. Figure 2.7 shows an example of how an organization might develop a replacement chart for the managers in one of its divisions. Note that this chart provides information on the current job performance and promotability of possible replacements. As such, it can be used side by side with other pieces of information for **succession planning**—the process of identifying, developing, and tracking key individuals so that they may eventually assume top-level positions.

In today's fast-moving environment, succession planning may be more important—and more difficult to conduct—than ever before. Executives frequently lament that their firms are chronically short of talent. Yet in a recent survey of 150 executives with the nation's 1,000 largest companies, while all agreed on the value of identifying successors, only 72 percent said they are currently preparing someone to take their place. According to William Byham, CEO of Development Dimensions International (DDI), the typical company expects 33 percent turnover in the executive ranks in the next five years and, among these companies, roughly one-third are worried that they will not be able to find suitable replacements. And the cost of replacing these managers is extremely high, says Byham. "The average one-year estimated replacement cost is $750,000. That includes finding the new [person], training and development costs and opportunity costs of getting the new hire up to speed." Highlights in HRM 2 shows a checklist for evaluating the "success" of succession planning.[16]

Step Four: Formulating Strategy

The forecasting techniques discussed previously provide critical information for strategic planning. Recall that we noted at the beginning of the chapter that HR analysis is an input to strategy formulation. However, a word of caution is needed here. Because HR forecasting techniques take us deep into the specifics of labor supply and demand, we need to be careful not to lose sight of the larger strategic picture. One of the biggest concerns among executives is that (at times) HR managers cannot "see the forest for the trees" because they become mired in the administrative details of their planning models. SWOT analysis, discussed shortly, helps managers combine various sources of information into a broader framework for analysis.

SWOT analysis
A comparison of strengths, weaknesses, opportunities, and threats for strategy formulation purposes

After managers have analyzed the internal strengths and weaknesses of the firm, as well as external opportunities and threats, they have the information they need to formulate corporate, business, and HR strategies for the organization. A comparison of *strengths, weaknesses, opportunities,* and *threats* normally is referred to as a **SWOT analysis.** SWOT analysis helps executives summarize the major facts and forecasts derived from external and internal analyses. Strategy formulation builds on SWOT analysis to use the strengths of the organization to capitalize on opportunities, counteract threats, and alleviate internal weaknesses. In short, strategy formulation moves from simple analysis to devising a coherent course of action.

Highlights in HRM 2

Succession-Planning Checklist

RATE THE SUCCESS OF YOUR SUCCESSION PLANNING

For each characteristic of a best-practice succession-planning and management program appearing in the left column below, enter a number to the right to indicate how well you believe your organization manages that characteristic. Ask other decision makers in your organization to complete this form individually. Then compile the scores and compare notes.

Characteristics of a Best-Practice Succession-Planning and Management Program		How Would You Rate Your Organization's Succession Planning and Management Program on the Characteristic?				
Your organization has successfully...		Very Poor (1)	Poor (2)	Neither Poor Nor Good (3)	Good (4)	Very Good (5)
1	Clarified the purpose and desired results of the succession-planning and management program.					
2	Determined what performance is required now for all job categories in the organization by establishing competency models.					
3	Established a means to measure individual performance that is aligned with the competencies currently demonstrated by successful performers.					
4	Determined what performance is needed in the future by establishing future competency models for all job categories.					
5	Created an ongoing means by which to assess individual potential against future competency models.					
6	Established a means by which to narrow gaps through the use of individual development plans (IDPs).					
7	Created a means to follow up and hold people accountable.					
8	Created a means by which to document competence and find organizational talent quickly when needed.					
9	Created and sustained rewards for developing people.					
10	Established a means by which to evaluate the results of the succession planning and management program.					

Total (add up the scores for items 1–10 and place in the box on the right)

SCORES

Score	Interpretation
50–40	Congratulations. The succession-planning and management program in your organization conforms with best practices.
29–20	Okay. While your organization could make improvements, you appear to have some of the major pieces in place for a succession-planning and management program.
39–30	Pretty good. Your organization is on the way toward establishing a first-rate succession-planning and management program.
19–10	Not good at all. Your organization is probably filling positions on an as-needed basis.
9–0	Give yourself a failing grade. You need to take steps immediately to improve the succession-planning and management practices of your organization.

Source: From William J. Rothwell, "Putting Success into Your Succession Planning," *The Journal of Business Strategy* 23, no. 3 (May/June 2002): 32–37. Republished with permission—Thomson Media, One State Street, 26th Floor, New York, NY 10004.

Corporate Strategy

In any industry, firms decide where and how they will compete. Corporate strategy focuses on domain selection; that is, where they will compete. Some firms choose a concentration strategy that focuses on only a limited portion of the industry. For example, Visteon Corporation specializes in electronics, climate, and power train technologies for the automotive industry. In contrast, Henry Ford at one time had fully integrated his company from the ore mines needed to make steel all the way to the showrooms where his cars were sold.

Growth and Diversification

As companies grow, their strategic choices tend to focus on geographic, volume, and product expansion. HR planning is a vital input to these decisions. Growth hinges on three related elements: (a) increased productivity, (b) a greater number of employees, and (c) developing or acquiring new skills. Concerns about staffing, training, motivation, performance, and the like can either enable growth or limit its potential. As companies diversify into new businesses, managers inevitably are faced with a "make or buy" decision. That is, should they develop the capabilities in-house or contract externally? For example, when IBM entered the personal computer market in the early 1980s, it contracted with (startup companies) Intel and Microsoft to make the hardware and operating systems for its PC. The decision did not rest solely on human resources issues, but they were an important part of the equation.

Some companies diversify far beyond their core businesses. GE, for example, has diversified from its original base in electrical and home appliance products to such wide-ranging industries as health, finance, insurance, truck and air transportation, and even media, with its ownership of NBC. In order to manage such a diverse portfolio, GE has invested heavily in the development of general management skills and leadership ability. CEO Jeffrey Immelt has stated that GE's future depends on pursuing businesses that leverage human capital (in contrast to its traditional focus on manufacturing). This new strategy is strongly linked to human resources. In fact, the strategy is viable only because the company has done such an enviable job developing talent over the years.

Mergers and Acquisitions

In addition to strategies of growth and diversification, corporate America has seen a host of mergers and acquisitions in recent years. These include such firms as Hewlett-Packard and Compaq, Daimler-Benz and Chrysler, Walt Disney and ABC, Kmart and Sears, and Procter & Gamble and Gillette. And while there are some important competitive reasons for mergers such as these, it is unfortunate to note that many of them have not gone well. Not surprisingly, perhaps, the failure rate among firms is very high. Some estimates suggest that only about 15 percent; of all mergers achieve their objectives (measured by return on investment, shareholder value, and the like). Often the failure is due to cultural inconsistencies, as well as conflicts among the managers of each firm. Clearly, these concerns point directly to the importance of effective HR planning prior to—and during—the merger process. Highlights in HRM 3 shows key HR activities associated with different phases of a merger or acquisition.

© ASSOCIATED PRESS/AP

Like many mergers and acquisitions, the acquisition of Compaq by Hewlett-Packard didn't turn out to be quite as successful as many people hoped it would be—especially the employees who found themselves laid off as a result.

Strategic Alliances and Joint Ventures

Sometimes firms do not acquire or merge with another firm, but instead pursue cooperative strategies such as a strategic alliance or joint venture. Especially when firms enter into international joint ventures, the issues of culture (both company culture and national culture) become paramount. On the front end, HR plays a vital role in assessing the compatibility of cultures and potential problems. As the alliance is formed, HR helps select key executives and develop teamwork across the respective workforces. In addition, HR is typically involved in the design of performance assessment and mutual incentives for the alliance. And, of course, one of the controversial issues related to such alliances is the inevitable issue of outsourcing or offshoring work to other locations.

Business Strategy

While we think about corporate strategy as domain selection, business strategy is viewed in terms of domain navigation. It is more focused on how the company will compete against rival firms in order to create value for customers. We can think of **value creation** in a cost/benefit scenario (that is, value = benefits − costs). Companies can increase customer value either by decreasing costs to customers or by increasing their benefits (or some combination of the two). And their business strategies reflect these choices.

value creation
What the firm adds to a product or service by virtue of making it; the amount of benefits provided by the product or service once the costs of making it are subtracted

Low-Cost Strategy: Compete on Productivity and Efficiency

A low-cost strategy means keeping your costs low enough so that you can offer an attractive price to customers (relative to competitors). Organizations such as Dell, Wal-Mart, and Southwest Airlines have been very successful at using a low-cost strategy. Critical success factors for this strategy focus on efficiency, productivity, and minimizing waste. These types of companies often are large and try to take advantage of economies of scale in production and distribution. In many cases, the large

Key HR Activities Associated with Merger or Acquisition Phases

HR Issues	Key HR Activities
Stage 1—Precombination	
• Identifying reasons for the M&A • Forming M&A team/leader • Searching for potential partners • Selecting a partner • Planning for managing the process • Planning to learn from the process	• Participate in preselection assessment of target firm • Assist in conducting thorough due diligence assessment • Participate in planning for combination • Assist in developing HR practices that support rapid learning and knowledge transfer
Stage 2—Combination	
• Selecting the integration manager(s) • Designing/implementing transition teams • Creating the new structure/strategies/leadership • Retaining key employees • Managing the change process • Communicating to and involving stakeholders • Developing new policies and practices	• Assist in recruiting and selecting integration manager(s) • Assist with transition team design and staffing • Develop retention strategies and communicate to top talent • Assist in deciding who goes • Facilitate establishment of a new culture • Provide assistance to ensure implementation of HR policies and practices
Stage 3—Solidification and Assessment	
• Solidifying leadership and staffing • Assessing the new strategies and structures • Assessing the new culture • Assessing the concerns of stakeholders • Revising as needed • Learning from the process	• Participate in establishing criteria and procedures for assessing staff effectiveness • Monitor the new culture and recommend approaches to strengthen it • Participate in stakeholder satisfaction • Assist in developing and implementing plans for continuous adjustment and learning

Source: Susan E. Jackson and Randall S. Schuler, *Managing Human Resources through Strategic Partnerships,* 9th ed. (Mason, OH: Thomson/South-Western, 2006), 50.

size allows them to sell their products and services at a lower price, which leads to higher market share, volume, and (hopefully) profits. However, even a low-cost leader must offer a product or service that customers find valuable. As Gordon Bethune, CEO of Continental Airlines, put it, "You can make a pizza so cheap that no one will buy it."[17] Ultimately organizations need to use a cost strategy to increase value to customers, rather than take it away.

A low-cost strategy has several links to HR planning. The first has to do with productivity. A common misconception about low-cost strategies is that they inevitably require cutting labor costs. On the contrary, there are several good examples of companies that pay their employees "top dollar," but gain back cost advantages because of excellent productivity. That is, they get a terrific "bang for the buck." Either they produce more from the workforce they have, or they can produce the same amount with a smaller workforce. Starbucks is an often-recognized example of a company that pays its employees among the highest wages in its industry, yet still has the lowest overall costs among all competitors. This is because highly motivated employees can often work more efficiently, ensure better quality, eliminate waste, and provide better service.

The second way that low-cost strategies are linked to HR pertains to outsourcing. In some cases, companies seeking low cost may consider contracting with an external partner that can perform particular activities or services as well (or better) at a lower cost. This decision directly links strategic planning to human resources planning. Decisions such as these often result in layoffs, transfers, and the like. As noted before, organizations need to have a clear understanding of their core processes and skills in order to make these decisions. Too often, firms approach outsourcing decisions based on costs alone, but this can lead to detrimental effects in the long run if core skills and capabilities are eroded.

Differentiation Strategy: Compete on Value Added

While decreasing costs is one important way to enhance customer value, another involves providing something unique and distinctive to customers. A differentiation strategy is often based on high product quality, innovative features, speed to market, or superior service. Ritz-Carlton's commitment to quality and luxury, FedEx's focus on speed and flexible delivery, Neiman Marcus's commitment to fashion and customer service, and Sony's emphasis on innovation and product development are all easily identifiable examples of differentiation strategies.

Each of these strategies is rooted in the management of human resources. Companies that focus on service, for example, need to identify and support ways to empower employees to serve customers better. In contrast to the company that emphasizes low cost and efficiencies, you may find that differentiating companies will bend the rules a bit more, allow more flexibility to let you "have it your way," and customize products and services around the customer's particular needs. In place of rigid rules, service-oriented companies often try to embed their values in the cultural values of the company. David Pace, executive vice president of partner resources at Starbucks, noted that the key feature he looks for in new employees is "discernment," the ability to make good decisions on their own.

Functional Strategy: Ensuring Alignment

In addition to formulating corporate and business-level strategies, managers also need to "translate" strategic priorities into functional areas of the organization (such as marketing, manufacturing, human resources, and the like). This involves all aspects of the business, but in particular there needs to be a clear alignment between HR and the requirements of an organization's strategy. In this regard, HR policies and practices need to achieve two types of fit: external and internal.[18]

External Fit/Alignment

External fit (or *external alignment*) focuses on the connection between the business objectives and the major initiatives in HR. For example, as noted earlier, if a company's strategy focuses on achieving low cost, HR policies and practices need to reinforce this idea by reinforcing efficient and reliable behavior, enhanced productivity, and the like. On the other hand, if the organization competes through innovation and new product development, then HR policies and practices would be more aligned with the notion of enabling creating creativity and flexibility. Highlights in HRM 4 shows the external fit between major business objectives and HR imperatives at Continental Airlines.

Internal Fit/Alignment

In addition to external alignment or fit, managers need to ensure that HR practices are all aligned with one another internally to establish a configuration that is mutually reinforcing. Job design, staffing, training, performance appraisal, and compensation—the entire range of HR practices—need to focus on the same workforce objectives (such as efficiency, creativity, and loyalty). Unfortunately, often one HR practice, such as training, might be focused on teamwork and sharing, while another HR practice, such as appraisal and compensation programs, reinforces the ideas of individual achievement. Charles Schwab and Company, for example, faced this very situation. The company has a reputation in the financial services industry for developing a culture of teamwork that has been important to its strategy. However, when it changed its compensation strategy to provide more rewards to high-performing brokers, it ran into a potential problem of sending mixed signals to employees: Which is more important, teamwork or individual high flyers?[19]

While we raise the issue of alignment and fit here as an element of strategy formulation, it clearly links directly to strategy implementation as well. At the end of this chapter, we raise the issue again in the context of evaluating and assessing the success of strategic planning.

Step Five: Strategy Implementation

As the old saying goes, "Well begun is half done." But only half. Like any plan, formulating the appropriate strategy is not enough. Managers must also ensure that the new plans are implemented effectively. Recently organizations have been paying more attention to implementation and execution. As Larry Bossidy, the former CEO of Honeywell, noted, "My job these days is to restore the discipline of execution to a company that had lost it. Many people regard execution as detail work that's beneath the dignity of a business leader. That's wrong. To the contrary, it's the leader's most important job."[20]

Figure 2.8 shows the now classic 7-S framework and reveals that human resources management is instrumental to almost every aspect of strategy implementation, whether it pertains to structure, systems, style, skills, staff, or shared values. While *strategy* lays out the route that the organization will take in the future, organizational *structure* is the framework in which activities of the organization members are coordinated.

Highlights in HRM 4

Achieving Strategic Fit at Continental Airlines

Continental Airlines ***The "Go Forward" Plan***

WORKING TOGETHER	MAKE RELIABILITY A REALITY	FLY TO WIN	FUND THE FUTURE
• Focus on safer work environment • Make payroll and benefit programs easy to use • Establish front-line supervisors as leaders and credible source of information • Open, honest, direct communication of information with all employees • Compensation that is fair to the employees and fair to the company • All employees treat each other with dignity and respect	• Perform in top 3 (out of 10) airlines on key customer/DOT metrics –On-time arrivals/departures –Baggage –Complaints • Continue to improve our image –Clean airplanes –Refurbish planes –Upgrade Pres. Clubs –Upgrade advertising/sponsorships –Improve Trans-Atlantic product –Complete new image upgrade • Enhance product with low-cost improvements	• Allocate flying to maximize profit –Grow hubs in IAH, EWR, CLE –Grow Europe and Air Mic • Improve customer mix –Backpacks and flipflops to coats and ties –Align travel agents and sales force • Develop an alliance network across the Atlantic • Aggressively eliminate non-value-added costs	• Eliminate excess lease/interest expense • Develop and implement five-year fleet plan • Acquire sufficient real estate in our hubs to support growth • Build cash balances to achieve long-term stability • Eliminate GECC covenants
Company where employees enjoy coming to work and are valued for contributions	Have an industry-leading product that we are proud to sell	Industry average RASM with bottom quartile CASM	Reduce interest expense, own our markets, and lay foundation for growth

Source: Company document.

Figure 2.8 The 7-S Model

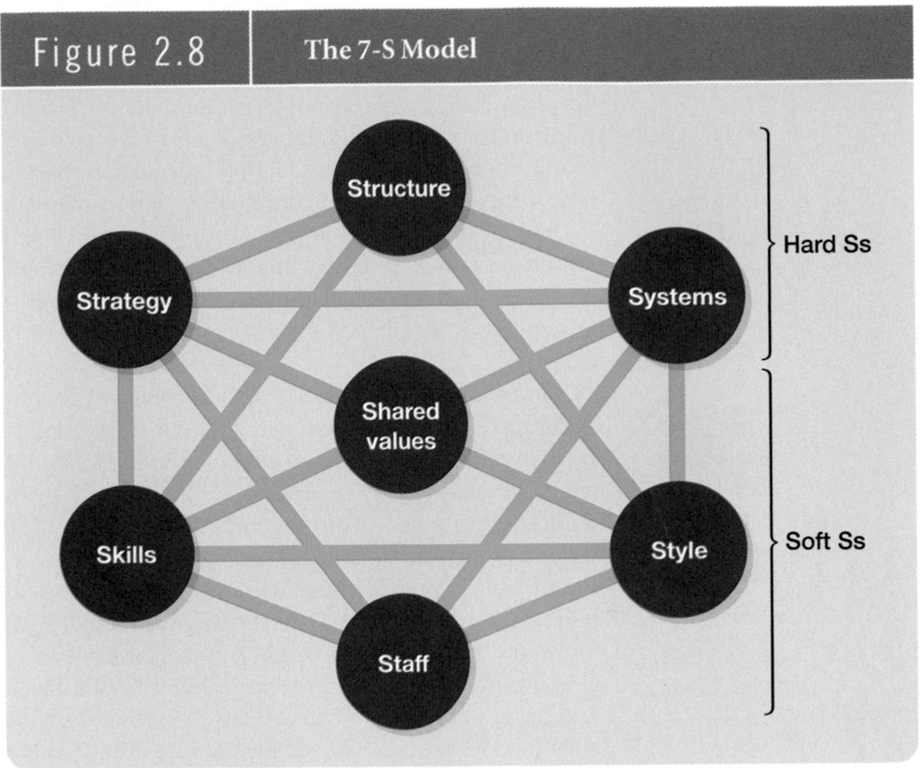

Source: McKinsey & Company

If the strategy requires redeployment or reorganization of employees, HR will be intimately involved. Closely related to structure are *systems* and processes. These include formal and informal procedures that govern everyday activity. As organizations consider reengineering and process redesign to implement strategies, HR helps ensure that the best workflow models are in place and—importantly—that employees are involved in sharing their advice.

Shared values were discussed earlier in the chapter as a guiding parameter for strategic planning. They arise again as an important issue in implementation as well. Strategic change often requires employees and managers to modify, or abandon, their old ways of doing things. HR managers play a central role as guardians of the corporate culture, the principles on which the company is founded, the fundamental ideas around which the business is built. This is tightly connected to the issue of *style,* which refers not only to the leadership approach of top managers, but also the way in which employees present themselves to the outside world (to suppliers, customers, and so on.).

Skills and *staff* relate directly to the concerns of human resources management and point to the critical role that HR plays in strategy implementation. At a fundamental level, HR's role in strategy implementation focuses on reconciling (1) human resources demanded and (2) human resources available.

Taking Action: Reconciling Supply and Demand

Through HRP, organizations strive for a proper balance between demand considerations and supply considerations. Demand considerations are based on forecasted trends in business activity. Supply considerations involve determining where and how candidates with the required qualifications can be found to fill vacancies. Because of the difficulty in locating applicants for the increasing number of jobs that require advanced training, this aspect of planning has been receiving a great deal more attention. Greater planning effort is also needed in recruiting members of protected classes for managerial jobs and technical jobs that require advanced levels of education.

In an effort to meet the demand for human resources, organizations have several staffing possibilities, including hiring full-time employees, having current employees work overtime, recalling laid-off workers, and using temporary employees. However, when forecasts show a surplus of employees, organizations may restrict hiring; reduce work hours; institute work sharing; or consider layoffs, demotions, and/or terminations. Additionally, over time organizations may try to reduce their workforce by relying on attrition (a gradual reduction of employees through resignations, retirements, and deaths). Over the past two decades, early retirements have become a more and more common means for organizations to reduce excess labor supply. Organizations as diverse as state colleges, healthcare facilities, and travel companies encourage employees to accept early retirement by offering "sweetened" retirement benefits. The various types of benefits are discussed in Chapter 11.

Organizational Downsizing, Outsourcing, and Offshoring

As discussed in Chapter 1, organizations have undertaken the extremely painful task of downsizing and restructuring over the past decade to reduce "head count." Because of either economic or competitive pressures, organizations have found themselves with too many employees or with employees who have the wrong kinds of skills. In an effort to reconcile labor supply and demand considerations, companies such as Motorola, Corning, and Hewlett-Packard have eliminated thousands of jobs.[21] These job cuts are not simply restricted to hourly workers. Technical, professional, and managerial positions have been (and are still being) eliminated at an unprecedented rate. In many cases, the move is part of a longer-term process of restructuring to take advantage of new technology, corporate partnerships, and cost minimization.

Making Layoff Decisions

Decisions about employee layoffs are usually based on seniority and/or performance. In some organizations, especially those with labor agreements, seniority may be the primary consideration. In other organizations, such factors as ability and fitness may take precedence over seniority in determining layoffs.

In the case of unionized organizations, the criteria for determining an employee's eligibility for layoff are typically set forth in the union agreement. As a rule, seniority on the job receives significant weight in determining which employees are laid off first. Similar provisions in the union agreement provide for the right of employees to be recalled for jobs that they are still qualified to perform. Organizational policy, as well as provisions in the labor agreement, should therefore establish and define clearly the employment rights of each individual and the basis on which layoff selections will be made and reemployment effected. The rights of employees during layoffs, the conditions concerning their eligibility for recall, and their obligations in accepting recall should also be clarified. It is common for labor agreements to preserve the reemployment rights of employees laid off for periods of up to two years, providing that they do not refuse to return to work if recalled sooner.

It has become customary, however, for employers to give some degree of recognition to seniority even among employees who are not unionized. Unions generally advocate recognition of seniority because they feel that their members should be entitled to certain rights proportionate to the years they have invested in their jobs. Nevertheless, whenever seniority provides a basis for determining or even influencing HR decisions, the discretion of management is reduced accordingly. One of the major disadvantages of overemphasizing seniority is that the less-competent employees receive the same rewards and security as the more-competent ones. Also, the practice of using seniority as the basis for deciding which workers to lay off may well have a disparate impact on women and minority workers, who often have less seniority than other groups.[22]

In cases where economic conditions have brought about layoffs, employees who were let go while in good standing may be recalled to their jobs when the economic outlook brightens and job openings occur. However, in many cases these new jobs require a different set of skills than the jobs they replace. Identifying individuals for these jobs can be accomplished by searching among previous employees or among current employees who can be transferred, but frequently it requires searching externally in the broader labor market.

Step Six: Evaluation and Assessment

At one level, it might seem that assessing effectiveness is the final step in the planning process. That is true. But it is also the first step. Planning is cyclical, of course, and while we've somewhat conveniently placed evaluation at the end, it actually provides the inputs to the next cycle in the planning process. Issues of measurement, benchmarking, alignment, fit, and flexibility are central to the evaluation process.

Evaluation and Assessment Issues

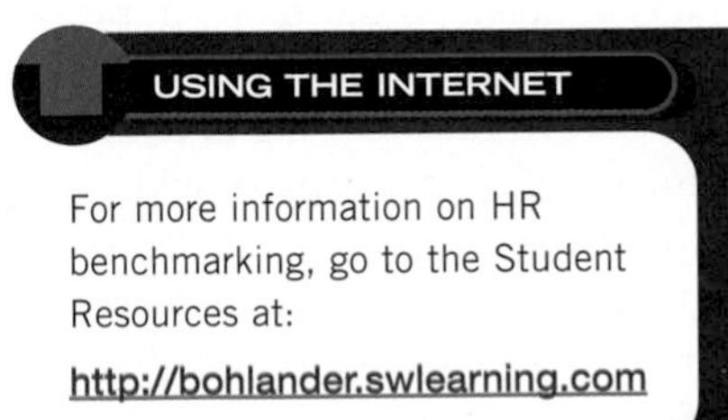

In order to evaluate their performance, firms need to establish a set of parameters that focus on the "desired outcomes" of strategic planning, as well as the metrics they will use to monitor how well the firm delivers against those outcomes. Because strategic management is ultimately aimed at creating a competitive advantage, many firms evaluate their performance against other firms. **Benchmarking** is the process of identifying "best practices" in a given area—say, productivity, logistics, brand management, training, and so on—and then comparing your practices and performance to those of other companies. To accomplish this, a benchmarking team

benchmarking
The process of comparing the organization's processes and practices with those of other companies

would collect information on its own company's operations and those of the other firm in order to determine gaps. The gaps help determine the causes of performance differences, and ultimately the team would map out a set of best practices that lead to world-class performance.

Interestingly, the target company for benchmarking does not need to be a competitor. For example, when Xerox wanted to learn about excellent customer service, it benchmarked L. L. Bean. By working with noncompeting companies, Xerox was able to get access to information a competitor would not divulge.

In the context of HR strategy, metrics fall into two basic categories: human capital metrics and HR metrics. Human capital metrics assess aspects of the workforce, while HR metrics assess the performance of the HR function itself. The Saratoga Institute publishes the annual *Human Capital Benchmarking Report,* which includes benchmarking information from almost 900 companies (see Highlights in HRM 5). Clients can use the information from studies of such areas as pay structure, return on investment per employee, turnover rates, and cost-per-hire and time-to-fill for key employees. This kind of detailed information clarifies potential bases of competitive advantage and reveals a path for developing future HR strategies.[23]

Measuring Strategic Alignment

Earlier in the chapter, we discussed the importance of strategic alignment and fit as an element of strategy formulation and implementation. As an element of evaluation, some very useful techniques help managers assess the extent to which they have achieved these objectives.

Strategy Mapping and the Balanced Scorecard

Balanced Scorecard (BSC)
A measurement framework that helps managers translate strategic goals into operational objectives

One of the most enthusiastically adopted tools for mapping a firm's strategy in order to ensure strategic alignment is the **Balanced Scorecard (BSC).** Developed by Harvard professors Robert Kaplan and David Norton, the BSC is a framework that helps managers translate strategic goals into operational objectives. The model has four related cells: (1) financial, (2) customer, (3) processes, and (4) learning. The logic of the BSC is firmly rooted in human resources management. People management and learning help organizations improve their internal processes and provide excellent customer service. Internal processes—product development, service, and the like—are critical for creating customer satisfaction and loyalty, and they are also important for ensuring productivity to contain costs for better financial performance. Customer value creation, in turn, drives up revenues, which enhances profitability.

Figure 2.9 shows how this might work at Starbucks. In each cell, Starbucks would identify the key metrics that help translate strategic goals to operational imperatives. For example, under customer metrics, Starbucks might look at percentage of repeat customers, number of new customers, growth rate, and the like. Under people metrics, managers might measure the numbers of suggestions provided by employees, participation in Starbucks' stock sharing program, employee turnover, training hours spent, and the like. Each of these cells links vertically. People management issues such as rewards, training, and suggestions can be linked to efficient processes (brewing the perfect cup, delivering top-notch customer service, and so forth). These processes then lead to better customer loyalty and growth. Growth and customer loyalty in turn lead to higher profitability and market value.

Highlights in HRM 5

The Top Ten Measures of Human Capital

The top ten areas to measure, as recommended by Jac Fitz-enz, chair of the Saratoga Institute (now part of Spherion's Human Capital Consulting Group), in an issue of *Workforce* magazine (http://www.workforce.com), won't all apply to your company, but some will:

1. **Your most important issues.** These are the targets of all lower-level measures. Focus on them and ensure that your metrics lead in a direct line to them.
2. **Human capital value added.** How do your workers optimize themselves for the good of the company and for themselves? This is the primary measure of an individual's contribution to profitability.
3. **Human capital ROI.** This is the ratio of dollars spent on pay and benefits to an adjusted profit figure.
4. **Separation cost.** How many people are leaving? From which departments? What does it cost the company? The average cost of separation for an employee is at least six months' equivalent of revenue per employee.
5. **Voluntary separation rate.** Lost personnel equal potential lost opportunity, lost revenue, and the cost of workers having to fill the gaps under greater stress. Cutting the separation rate saves the cost of hiring and keeps customer service quality high.
6. **Total labor-cost/revenue percentage.** This is total benefits and compensation cost as a percentage of organizational revenue and shows how much of what you are taking in through revenue goes to support the company's total labor cost, including temporary, seasonal, and contract or contingent workers. This metric can help you track changes in your workforce. Best approach: Compare it to your revenue factor and compensation, benefits, and contingent off-payroll costs. If the metric is rising, determine whether compensation or benefits costs are up or revenue is down. This will help you decide what actions to take.
7. **Total compensation/revenue percentage.** This is the percentage of the company's revenues allocated to the direct costs of employees. It excludes costs for off-payroll employees who receive a 1099 form (as does the metric in item 6). Before creating strategies to address concerns, compare this metric to your revenue factor, compensation costs, and benefits costs to analyze what is happening with workers.
8. **Training investment factor.** Basic skills are crucial: Workers who cannot read, write, do simple calculations, or talk intelligently with customers need to have these skill deficiencies addressed.
9. **Time to start.** Recruitment will continue to be a challenge. The amount of the time it takes from approval of a job requisition until the person is on the job is a strategic indicator of revenue production.
10. **Revenue factor.** This is the basic measure understood by managers.

Source: "The Top 10 Measures of Human Capital Management," *HRFocus* 78, no. 5 (May 2001): 8.

Figure 2.9 Balanced Scorecard

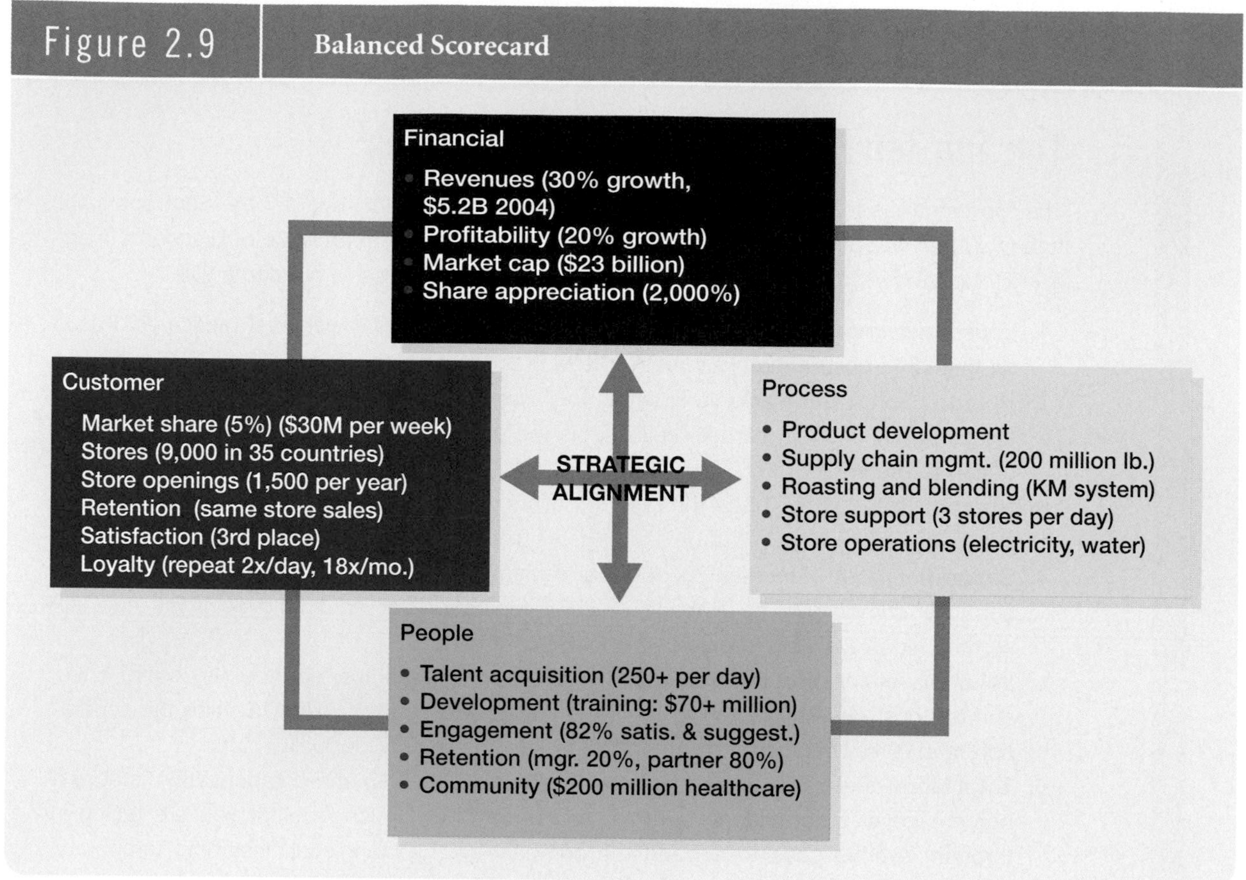

Measuring Internal Fit

Recall that internal fit means that HR practices are all aligned with one another to establish a configuration that is mutually reinforcing. Figure 2.10 shows an example of how organizations can assess the internal fit of their HR practices. There are essentially three steps. First, managers need to identify the key workforce objectives they hope to achieve. Often this information can come from the people/learning cell of the Balanced Scorecard, and might include loyalty, customer service, productivity, and creativity. Second, managers would identify each of the HR practices used to elicit or reinforce those workforce objectives (job design, staffing, training, appraisal, compensation, and so on). Third, managers would evaluate each HR practice on a scale of −5 (not supportive) to 5 (supportive). By tallying up the ratings across managers, organizations can get a very clear idea of which HR practices are working together to achieve the workforce objectives, and which are not.

An important caveat to this analysis is that internal fit is a necessary, but insufficient, cause of strategic alignment. A company could have nearly perfect alignment among its HR practices, and they still might not be aligned with the competitive strategy. For that reason, it is important for managers to assess both internal fit and external alignment.

Figure 2.10 Assessing Internal Fit

WORKFORCE OBJECTIVES

ORGANIZATION	SALES PRODUCTIVITY	CUSTOMER SERVICE	MERCHANDISE INFORMATION	STOCK MAINTENANCE	TOTAL
Structure/Workflow					
• Cross-functional teams	3	2	0	−1	4
• Rotation (Depts.)	3	3	−1	−1	4
Staffing					
• Test battery	2	2	1	1	6
• Select for experience	5	3	2	2	12
Training					
• Retail selling skills	4	5	1	1	11
Rewards					
• Results appraisal	5	−4	−2	−5	−6
• Individual incentives	5	−5	−3	−5	−8
Leadership					
• Corporate	3	3	1	0	7
• Store manager	4	2	2	2	10
Technologies					
• Merchandise IS	5	2	5	1	13
• Daily postings	4	−3	4	−1	4
	43/55	10/55	10/55	26/55	57/220
		SYSTEM COHERENCE			***26%***

FUNCTIONAL COHESION

5 = Strongly supports the priority
0 = Neutral
−5 = Strongly counterproductive

Ensuring Strategic Flexibility for the Future

organizational capability The capacity of the organization to act and change in pursuit of sustainable competitive advantage

Apart from the need to establish and measure fit between HR and strategy, HR is also focused on ensuring flexibility and agility when the environment changes. Ultimately, successful HRP helps increase **organizational capability**—the capacity of the organization to continuously act and change in pursuit of sustainable competitive advantage.[24]

Flexibility can be achieved in two primary ways: coordination flexibility and resource flexibility. *Coordination flexibility* occurs through rapid reallocation of resources to new or changing needs. Through HRP, managers can anticipate upcoming events, keep abreast of changes in legal regulations, forecast economic trends, recognize competitor moves, and the like. With advance notice, managers can move people into and out of jobs, retrain them for new skill requirements, and modify the kinds of incentives they use. Use of a contingency workforce composed of part-timers, temporary employees, and external partners also helps achieve coordination flexibility.[25] *Resource flexibility*, on the other hand, results from having people who can do many different things in different ways. Cross-training, job rotations, team-based work modes, and the like are all focused on establishing a flexible workforce.

We will draw on these ideas throughout the text. But at this point we want to close the chapter by emphasizing that strategic planning is a process designed to ensure superior performance today, as well as establishing the capability and agility to respond tomorrow. As the great hockey player Wayne Gretsky used to say, "I don't skate to where the puck is. I skate to where the puck is going to be."

SUMMARY

objective 1 Strategic human resources management (SHRM) integrates strategic planning and HR planning. It can be thought of as the pattern of human resources deployments and activities that enable an organization to achieve its strategic goals. HR planning and strategies becomes especially critical when organizations consider global strategies, mergers, relocation of plants, innovation, and downsizing, or when dramatic shifts in the composition of the labor force are occurring.

objective 2 Analyzing the firm's competitive environment is central to strategic planning. The competitive environment includes the specific organizations with which the firm interacts. Firms analyze the competitive environment in order to adapt to or influence the nature of competition.

objective 3 Conducting an internal analysis to gauge the firm's strengths and weaknesses involves looking a firm's "three Cs"—its culture, competencies, and composition. An internal analysis enables strategic decision makers to inventory the organization's skills and resources as well as their performance levels.

An organization's success increasingly depends on the knowledge, skills, and abilities of employees, particularly as they help establish a set of core competencies that distinguish an organization from its competitors. When employees' talents are valuable, rare, difficult to imitate, and organized, an organization can achieve a sustained competitive advantage through people.

objective 4 HRP is a systematic process that involves forecasting demand for labor, performing supply analysis, and balancing supply and demand considerations. Forecasting demand requires using either quantitative or qualitative methods to identify the number and type of people needed to meet organizational objectives. Supply analysis involves determining whether sufficient employees are available within the organization to meet demand and also whether potential employees are available on the job market. Reconciling supply and demand requires a host of activities, including internal and external recruitment.

objective 5 As organizations plan for their future, top management and strategic planners must recognize that strategic-planning decisions affect—and are affected by—HR functions. On one hand, HRP plays a reactive role in ensuring that the right number and type of employees are available to implement a chosen business plan. On the other hand, HRP can proactively identify and initiate programs needed to develop organizational capabilities on which future strategies can be built. HRP and strategic planning tend to be most effective when there is a reciprocal relationship between the two processes.

Formulating an HR strategy is only half of the HR battle: The strategy must also be implemented. Employment forecasts must be reconciled against the internal and the external supplies of labor the firm faces. This can include hiring, downsizing, outsourcing, and offshoring. If there is a labor shortage, the firm might have to reformulate its long- and short-term strategic plans.

Firms need to establish a set of parameters that focus on the "desired outcomes" of strategic planning, as well as the metrics they will use to monitor how well the firm delivers against those outcomes. Issues of measurement, benchmarking, alignment, fit, and flexibility are central to the evaluation process. Firms use benchmarking, strategy mapping, and the Balanced Scorecard (BSC) as tools to gauge their outcomes.

KEY TERMS

Balanced Scorecard (BSC)
benchmarking
core competencies
core values
cultural audits
environmental scanning
human resources planning (HRP)
management forecasts
Markov analysis
mission
organizational capability
replacement charts
skill inventories
staffing tables
strategic human resources management (SHRM)
strategic planning
strategic vision
succession planning
SWOT analysis
trend analysis
value creation

DISCUSSION QUESTIONS

1. Identify the three key elements of the human resources planning model and discuss the relationships among them.

2. What competitive environmental forces influence the firm's strategy?

3. What criteria must be met if firms are to achieve a competitive advantage through their employees?

4. Which approach do you think should be relied on more heavily for strategy formulation—the quantitative or qualitative approach?

5. Explain the difference between a firm's corporate strategy and business strategy. Why do firms need to look at both aspects?

6. What steps does the firm need to take to reconcile labor supply and labor demand?

7. Why is organizational capability important to firm and how can HR managers enhance it?

HRM Experience

Customizing HR for Different Types of Human Capital

Part of strategic planning in HR is mapping an organization's human capital. When we look at the strategic value of a person's skills as well as their uniqueness, we soon discover that organizations comprise different kinds of workers who have very different kinds of skills. Some are core knowledge workers; some are more traditional job-based employees; some are contract workers; and some are external partners. In this context, it is unlikely that we would manage all of these employees the same way (as much as we might want to for fairness). There are differences in HR practices for different groups. That's not bad, but it makes the job of HR managers more difficult.

Assignment

The following are descriptions of three different employees. How would you characterize each worker? What role does each play when it comes to the organization's strategy?

Andrea Bascomb is a highly talented computer programmer for MiniFluff, Inc. She is among the elite set of engineers in the computer industry that is doing leading-edge work on advanced computer modeling. In truth, CEO Bill Ding believes that the future of the company rests on the innovative work that Andrea and her team are doing. He worries that someone might lure Andrea away to work for them. So he wants to give her all the room she needs to grow and stay committed to MiniFluff.

Calvin Duff is a salesperson on the retail side of MiniFluff. He has daily contact with customers and is responsible for making sales and communicating with service personnel. Make no mistake: To many customers, Calvin and his co-workers are the "face" of MiniFluff. Always on the lookout for a better situation, Calvin has thought about working for PeachTree Computing, MiniFluff's main competitor. In truth, other salespeople have found that they can leave MiniFluff and get "up to speed" easily at other firms. Their skills are very transferable and the transition is not difficult. Bill Ding and other managers at MiniFluff recognize this fact, so they try to keep salespeople loyal and productive, recognizing that many of them do eventually leave.

Evelyn Frank is a part-time secretary for MicroFluff. She handles routine typing and filing work for the company, particularly in peak periods in the summer and around the holidays. She usually works for a few weeks at a time and then takes time off. The executives at MicroFluff have considered either outsourcing the job to an agency or automating it through a new computer system. But for now things are steady.

BIZFLIX EXERCISES

U-571: Setting Strategy

Watch the scene from *U-571.* It shows several aspects of strategic planning described earlier in this chapter.

This action-packed World War II thriller shows a U.S. submarine crew's efforts to retrieve an Enigma encryption device from a disabled German submarine. After the crew gets the device, a German vessel torpedoes and sinks the U.S. submarine. The survivors must now use the disabled German submarine to escape from the enemy with their prize. The film's almost nonstop action and extraordinary special effects look and sound best with a home theater system.

The scene comes from the "160 meters" segment toward the film's end. Lt. Andrew Tyler (Matthew McConaughey) is now the submarine's commander following the drowning death of Lt. Commander Mike Dahlgren (Bill Paxton), the original commander. Lt. Tyler says, "Chief." Chief Petty Officer Henry Klough (Harvey Keitel) approaches the map table. The film continues to its dramatic end with the execution of the strategy Tyler describes.

What to Watch for and Ask Yourself

- Does Lt. Tyler analyze the submarine's external environment? Does he engage in environmental scanning as described earlier in this chapter?
- What is Lt. Tyler's assessment of the submarine's strengths and weaknesses?
- Does Lt. Tyler consider threats and opportunities in forming his strategic plan? Has he done a SWOT analysis as described earlier in this chapter?

case study 1

Benchmarking Benefits at Mazda

Mazda Motors UK (United Kingdom) is only too aware of the importance of staying up to date with competitor developments and so its HR department conducts a benchmarking analysis every two years. This involves comparing its pay and benefits packages against twenty-two blue-chip companies, including other automotive firms, and against a more general service industry database. The fact that Mazda Motors UK gives every employee a car was found to be a major differentiating factor from some competitors, which provide a car only for employees at certain levels. Its benefits package, which is the same for all of its ninety employees, was also found to be much flatter than usual.

Jemma Galbraith-Marten, HR officer at Mazda Motors UK, says: "You must benchmark regularly because current information may not be valid in a few years' time. We've found the exercise very useful in terms of recognizing our general position in the marketplace and it has fuelled a lot of internal debate about how we recognize and reward our employees. It has helped us to set grades within the company and to pitch effectively for recruitment. It has also stimulated conversations about whether to provide a flex scheme because, in view of our benefits package, some individuals may find that more flexibility better addresses work-life balance issues."

QUESTIONS

1. What do you think of Mazda Motors UK's efforts to benchmark its benefits package on an annual basis?
2. As a prospective employee, would you have more interest in working for a company that conducts such benchmarking?
3. What are the benefits and costs associated with giving employees a free car to drive? In what way does it give Mazda a competitive edge in terms of recruiting and retaining employees?
4. Should Mazda offer different benefits for employees who, say, use public transportation or would prefer other benefits such as flextime? How do you think such an alternate package could be crafted?

Source: Edmund Tirbutt, "Brimming with Confidence: Benchmarking Your Perks against Your Rivals' Can Provide HR with Added Reassurance," *Employee Benefits* (November 2004): 49–52.

case study 2

Matching Talent with Tasks: Dole Implements Succession Planning

With 61,000 workers in more than ninety countries, Dole Food Company has talent all over the world. Only a few hundred of those employees are in top management at the 151-year-old company headquartered in Westlake Village, California. Trouble is, Dole doesn't have comprehensive knowledge of who these managers are or what they can do. If a key job opens up in North America, the business unit leader wouldn't know if the perfect candidate worked in another Dole unit in South America. Dole has no way to match its top managerial talent with its executive needs.

But that is changing. The highly decentralized company is launching a succession-planning process, supported by web-based software, through which Dole executives hope to rectify their inability to promote the best and the brightest across the corporation. The process itself requires a change of culture and could become an agent for further culture change. "The idea of succession planning is contrary to being highly decentralized," says Sue Hagen, vice president of HR for North American operations, who led the effort.

Hagen talked informally to all corporate executives and the leaders and staffs of each business unit to generate consensus for succession planning for corporate positions—corporate officers, business unit presidents, and their direct reports. The initial group would be about 100, she says. Next year, another few hundred will be included.

The reaction was mostly positive, Hagen says. Hagen's next step was to hold a series of in-depth interviews with the executives to determine which succession-planning processes were needed and how often they should be conducted. The goal was to reflect as much of their thinking as possible. "One division wanted to review succession plans on their people six times a year. Another didn't want to do it at all," she says. Hagen compromised: Succession planning will be conducted twice a year. She also identified four competencies on which everyone would be evaluated: accountability, business acumen, multifunctionality (cross-training), and vision/originality.

Many HRMS software suites have an optional succession-planning module, but neither Dole nor its business units have an HRMS. Since most employees are farm or factory workers, there is not much need for the detailed information an HRMS provides, says Hagen. "It would be overkill." In a way, the succession-planning software Dole adopted will become a mini-HRMS for top personnel, she adds.

Hagen also wanted an application service provider (ASP) model. Outsourcing, including payroll, is common at Dole. Hagen didn't want to own and support technology, and she didn't want the small corporate information technology staff to have to work on it.

The users of the system—top managers—access the program from the Web with a password. They fill out a resume, including career interests, and note any mobility restrictions. They assess themselves on the four competencies. When they are done, the system automatically notifies their manager, who does an assessment and indicates whether he or she thinks the individual could be promoted. The manager also assesses overall potential and the risk of losing the user. This assessment then goes automatically to the division head, then the divisional HR director, and then Hagen. Hagen will use the information to create a career development plan for each individual, including seminars she'll organize. She'll also direct business unit leaders to potential candidates in other units when they have appropriate openings. "The beauty is, for the first time we'll have a database that ties together these talent metrics and can serve as a clearinghouse for people available for opportunities," Hagen says.

Dole's corporate management hopes all business units will eventually adopt similar succession-planning processes and software, Hagen says. "I view this as a pilot, a very visible pilot," she says. "To get the buy-in of individual business units, we'll show them that this was adopted by their senior management and that it works."

QUESTIONS

1. Why do you think companies like Dole need succession planning?
2. Do you see any disadvantage of "automating" succession planning?

Source: Excerpted from Bill Roberts, "Matching Talent with Tasks: Dole Implements Succession Planning to Get Ready for Changes at the Top," *HRMagazine* 47, no. 11 (November 2002): 91–95.

NOTES AND REFERENCES

1. "The Importance of HR," *HRFocus* 73, no. 3 (March 1996): 14; "Retiring Workforce, Widening Skills Gap, Exodus of 'Critical Talent' Threaten Companies: Deloitte Survey," *Canadian Corporate News* (February 15, 2005).
2. Scott A. Snell, Mark Shadur, and Patrick M. Wright, "Human Resources Strategy: The Era of Our Ways," in M. A. Hitt, R. E. Freeman, and J. S. Harrison (eds.), *Handbook of Strategic Management* (Oxford, UK: Blackwell, 2002), 627–49; Patrick M. Wright, Benjamin Dunford, and Scott A. Snell, "Human Resources and the Resource-Based View of the Firm," *Journal of Management* 27, no. 6 (2002): 701–21.
3. "The Importance of HR," 14. For data from a similar survey conducted in Canada, see David Brown, "HR's Role in Business Strategy: Still a Lot of Work to Be Done," *Canadian HR Reporter* 14, no. 19 (November 5, 2001): 1–20; "How Should the HR Dept. of 2004 Be Structured?" *Human Resource Department Management Report*, no. 3 (November 2003): 1.
4. T. J. Watson, Jr., *A Business and Its Beliefs: The Ideas That Helped Build IBM* (New York: McGraw-Hill, 1963).
5. James W. Walker, "Integrating the Human Resource Function with the Business," *Human Resource Planning* 14, no. 2 (1996): 59–77; James W. Walker, "Perspectives," *Human Resource Planning* 25, no. 1 (2002): 12–14.
6. Patrick Wright, Gary McMahan, Scott Snell, and Barry Gerhart, "Comparing Line and HR Executives' Perceptions of HR Effectiveness: Services, Roles, and Contributions," *Human Resource Management* 40, no. 2 (2001): 111–23; Ryan Langlois, "Fairmont Hotels: Business Strategy Starts with People," *Canadian HR Reporter* 14, no. 19 (November 5, 2001): 19–25.
7. http://www.merck.com/about/mission.html.
8. Eileen Abels, "Hot Topics: Environmental Scanning," *Bulletin of the American Society for Information Science* 28, no. 3 (February/March 2002): 16–17; William M. James, "Best HR Practices for Today's Innovation Management," *Research-Technology Management* 45, no. 1 (January/February 2002): 57–60; Jay J. Jamrog and Miles H. Overholt, "Building a Strategic HR Function: Continuing the Evolution," *Human Resource Planning* 27, no. 1 (March 2004): 51.
9. For example, see U.S. Department of Labor, Bureau of Labor Statistics, *Geographic Profiles of Employment and Unemployment.* The data and information are accessible via the Office of Employment Projections home page at http://www.bls.gov/emp/.
10. J. B. Quinn, "The Intelligent Enterprise: A New Paradigm," *Academy of Management Executive* 6, no. 4 (2002): 48–63.
11. Jennifer Laabs, "The HR Side of Sears' Comeback," *Workforce* 78, no. 3 (March 1999): 24–29; Anthony Early, Jr., "A Passion for Personal Success," *Vital Speeches of the Day* 65, no. 6 (January 1, 1999): 184–87.
12. For more information on methods to identify a firm's core competencies, see Khalid Hafeez, YanBing Zhang, and Naila Malak, "Core Competence for Sustainable Competitive Advantage: A Structured Methodology for Identifying Core Competence," *IEEE Transactions on Engineering Management* 49, no. 1 (February 2002): 28–35. See also Geert Duysters and John Hagedoorn, "Core Competences and Company Performance in the World-Wide Computer Industry," *Journal of High Technology Management Research* 11, no. 1 (Spring 2000): 75–91; Quinn, "The Intelligent Enterprise," 48–63; Jane Wollman

Rusoff, "Outsourced Solutions: Brokerage Firms Looking to Focus on Their Core Competencies Find the Most Value in a Resource-Rich Clearing Partner," *Research* 27, no. 11 (November 2004): 37–40.

13. Snell, Shadur, and Wright, "Human Resources Strategy," 627–49; Wright, Dunford, and Snell, "Human Resources and the Resource-Based View of the Firm," 701–21.
14. D. P. Lepak and S. A. Snell, "The Human Resource Architecture: Toward a Theory of Human Capital Development and Allocation," *Academy of Management Review* 24, no. 1 (1999): 31–48; David Lepak and Scott Snell, "Examining the Human Resource Architecture: The Relationship among Human Capital, Employment, and Human Resource Configurations," *Journal of Management* 24, no. 1 (January 1999): 31; Mike Berry, "HR must push for Change to Drive Human Capital Strategy," *Personnel Today* (April 6, 2004): 4.
15. Stephenie Overman, "Gearing Up for Tomorrow's Workforce," *HRFocus* 76, no. 2 (February 1999): 1, 15; Kathryn Tyler, "Evaluate Your Next Move," *HRMagazine* 46, no. 11 (November 2001): 66–71; Bill Leonard, "Turnover at the Top," *HRMagazine* 46, no. 5 (May 2001): 46–52.
16. Robert Grossman, "Heirs Unapparent," *HRMagazine* 44, no. 2 (February 1999): 36–44; "Succession Planning Is the Top Issue for Executives," *HRFocus* 79, no. 6 (June 2002): 9; Sarah Fister Gale, "Bringing Good Leaders to Light," *Training* 38, no. 6 (June 2001): 38–42; William J. Rothwell, "Putting Success into Your Succession Planning," *Journal of Business Strategy* 23, no. 3 (May/June 2002): 32–37; Mary Maxwell, "Putting Success into Succession Planning," *Nursing Economics* 22, no. 5 (September–October 2004): 285–87.
17. John Huey, "Outlaw Flyboy CEOs," *Fortune* 142, no. 11 (November 13, 2000): 237–50.
18. Brian Becker, Mark Huselid, and Dave Ulrich, *The HR Scorecard: Linking People, Strategy, and Performance* (Cambridge, MA: Harvard Business School Press, 2001). See also Shari Caudron, "How HR Drives Profits," *Workforce* 80, no. 12 (December 2001): 26–31.
19. "A Singular Sensation for Schwab Brokers," *Business Week Online* (January 24, 2002).
20. Larry Bossidy, Ram Charan, and Charles Burck, *Execution: The Art of Getting Things Done* (New York: Crown Business, 2002).
21. Jesse Drucker, "Motorola to Cut 7,000 More Jobs and Take $3.5 Billion in Charges," *The Wall Street Journal,* June 28, 2002, B6; Dennis K. Berman, "Corning Sets a $1 Billion Charge to Cut 4,000 More Employees," *The Wall Street Journal,* October 4, 2001, B2; Jaikumar Vijayan, "HP/Compaq Brace Workers for Integration, Layoffs," *Computerworld* 36, no. 14 (April 1, 2002): 6; "Planning to Outsource," *HRFocus* 81, no. 5 (May 2004): 1.
22. Lisa Bransten, "U.S. Examining Sun Microsystems over Complaint," *The Wall Street Journal,* June 25, 2002, B6; Matthew Miklave and A. Jonathan Trafimow, "Expecting Problems from This Dismissal," *Workforce* 80, no. 12 (December 2001): 81–83.
23. Ray Brillinger, "Best Practices: Human Resources Benchmarking," *Canadian HR Reporter* 14, no. 12 (June 18, 2001): 12; Chris Mahoney, "Benchmarking Your Way to Smarter Decisions," *Workforce* 79, no. 10 (October 2000): 100–103.
24. P. M. Wright and S. A. Snell, "Toward a Unifying Framework for Exploring Fit and Flexibility in Strategic Human Resource Management," *Academy of Management Review* 22, no. 4 (1998): 756–72; Snell, Shadur, and Wright, "Human Resources Strategy," 627–49; Wright, Dunford, and Snell, "Human Resources and the Resource-Based View of the Firm," 701–21.
25. R. Sanchez, "Strategic Flexibility in Product Competition," *Strategic Management Journal* 16 (1995): 135–59; Wright and Snell, "Toward a Unifying Framework."

appendix

Calculating Turnover and Absenteeism

Throughout this chapter we have emphasized that HRP depends on having an accurate picture of both the supply of and the demand for employees. Two factors, employee turnover and absenteeism, have a direct impact on HR planning strategy and recruitment processes. In this appendix, we provide a detailed discussion of turnover and absenteeism, methods for measuring them, and suggestions for managing their impact.

Employee Turnover Rates

Employee turnover refers simply to the movement of employees out of an organization. It is often cited as one of the factors behind the failure of U.S. employee productivity rates to keep pace with those of foreign competitors. It is also one of the chief determinants of labor supply. Even if everything else about an organization stays the same, as employees turn over, its supply of labor goes down. This involves both direct and indirect costs to the organization.

Computing the Turnover Rate

The U.S. Department of Labor suggests the following formula for computing turnover rates:

$$\frac{\text{Number of separations during the month}}{\text{Total number of employees at midmonth}} \times 100$$

Thus, if there were 25 separations during a month and the total number of employees at midmonth was 500, the turnover rate would be:

$$\frac{25}{500} \times 100 = 5 \text{ percent}$$

Turnover rates are computed on a regular basis to compare specific units such as departments, divisions, and work groups. In many cases, comparisons are made with data provided by other organizations. The *Bureau of National Affairs Quarterly Report on Job Absence and Turnover* is a very good source of comparative turnover data.[1]

Another method of computing the turnover rate is one that reflects only the avoidable separations (S). This rate is computed by subtracting unavoidable separations (US)—for example, due to pregnancy, return to school, death, or marriage—from all separations. The formula for this method is as follows:

$$\frac{S - US}{M} \times 100 = T \text{ (turnover rate)}$$

where M represents the total number of employees at midmonth. For example, if there were 25 separations during a month, 5 of which were US, and the total number of employees at midmonth (M) was 500, the turnover rate would be:

$$\frac{25 - 5}{500} \times 100 = 4 \text{ percent}$$

In looking at the impact of turnover on HR planning and recruitment, it is vitally important to recognize that quantitative rates of turnover are not the only factor to be considered. The *quality* of employees who leave an organization is equally important. If poor employees leave, what experts refer to as "functional turnover," this can prove to be beneficial to the organization. The costs of keeping unproductive workers may be far more than the costs to recruit and train a new, more effective performer.

Determining the Costs of Turnover

Replacing an employee is time-consuming and expensive. Costs can generally be broken down into three categories: separation costs for the departing employee, replacement costs, and training costs for the new employee. These costs are conservatively estimated at two to three times the monthly salary of the departing employee, and they do not include indirect costs such as low productivity prior to quitting and lower morale and overtime for other employees because of the vacated job. Consequently, reducing turnover could result in significant savings to an organization. Highlights in HRM 6 details one organization's costs associated with the turnover of a single computer programmer. Note that the major expense is the cost involved in training a replacement.

Employee Absenteeism Rates

How frequently employees are absent from their work—the absenteeism rate—is also directly related to HR planning and recruitment. When employees miss work, the organization incurs direct costs of lost wages and decreased productivity. It is not uncommon for organizations to hire extra workers just to make up for the number of absences totaled across all employees. In addition to these direct costs, indirect costs may underlie excessive absenteeism. A certain amount of absenteeism is, of course, unavoidable. There will always be some who must be absent from work because of sickness, accidents, serious family problems, or other legitimate reasons. However, chronic absenteeism may signal deeper problems in the work environment.

Highlights in HRM 6

Costs Associated with the Turnover of One Computer Programmer

Turnover costs = Separation costs + Replacement costs + Training costs

Separation costs

1. Exit interview = cost for salary and benefits of both interviewer and departing employee during the exit interview = $30 + $30 = $60
2. Administrative and record-keeping action = $30

   Separation costs = $60 + $30 = $90

Replacement costs

1. Advertising for job opening = $2,500
2. Preemployment administrative functions and record-keeping action = $100
3. Selection interview = $250
4. Employment tests = $40
5. Meetings to discuss candidates (salary and benefits of managers while participating in meetings) = $250

   Replacement costs = $2,500 + $100 + $250 + $40 + $250 = $3,140

Training costs

1. Booklets, manuals, and reports = $50
2. Education = $240/day for new employee's salary and benefits × 10 days of workshops, seminars, or courses = $2,400
3. One-to-one coaching = ($240/day per new employee + $240/day per staff coach or job expert) × 20 days of one-to-one coaching = $9,600
4. Salary and benefits of new employee until he or she gets "up to par" = $240/day for salary and benefits × 20 days = $4,800

   Training costs = $50 + $2,400 + $9,600 + $4,800 = $16,850

Total turnover costs = $90 + $3,140 + $16,850 = $20,080

Source: Adapted from the book *Turning Your Human Resources Department into a Profit Center™* by Michael Mercer, Ph.D. (Castlegate Publishers, Inc., Barrington, Illinois). Copyright 2002 Michael Mercer. Reproduced with permission from Michael Mercer, Ph.D., www.DrMercer.com.

Computing Absenteeism Rates

Managers should determine the extent of the absenteeism problem, if any, by maintaining individual and departmental attendance records and by computing absenteeism rates. Although there is no universally accepted definition of "absence" or a standard formula for computing absenteeism rates, the method most frequently used is that recommended by the U.S. Department of Labor:

$$\frac{\text{Number of worker-days lost through job absence during period}}{\text{Average number of employees} \times \text{number of workdays}} \times 100$$

If 300 worker-days are lost through job absence during a month having 25 scheduled working days at an organization that employs 500 workers, the absenteeism rate for that month is:

$$\frac{300}{500 \times 25} \times 100 = 2.4 \text{ percent}$$

The Department of Labor defines job absence as the failure of employees to report to work when their schedules require it, whether or not such failure to report is excused. Scheduled vacations, holidays, and prearranged leaves of absence are not counted as job absence.

Comparing Absenteeism Data

The Bureau of Labor Statistics of the U.S. Department of Labor receives data on job absences from the Current Population Survey of Households conducted by the Bureau of the Census, and analyses of these data are published periodically. These analyses permit the identification of problem areas—industries, occupations, or groups of workers with the highest incidence of absence or with rapidly increasing rates of absence. Comparison with other organizations may be made by referring to Bureau of Labor Statistics data reported in the *Monthly Labor Review* or by consulting such reporting services as the Bureau of National Affairs and Commerce Clearing House.[2]

Costs of Absenteeism

Traditional accounting and information systems often do not generate data that reflect the costs of absenteeism. Consequently, their usefulness in HR planning is often limited. To accentuate the impact of absenteeism on organizational performance, managers should translate the data into dollar costs. A system for computing absenteeism costs for an individual organization is available. Organizations with computerized absence-reporting systems should find this additional information easy and inexpensive to generate. The cost of each person-hour lost to absenteeism is based on the hourly weighted-average salary, costs of employee benefits, supervisory costs, and incidental costs.

For example, XYZ Company, with 1,200 employees, has 78,000 person-hours lost to absenteeism; the total absence cost is $560,886. When this figure is divided by 1,200 employees, the cost per employee is $467.41. (In this example, we are assuming the absent workers are paid. If absent workers are not paid, their salary figures are omitted from the computation.)

Absenteeism and HR Planning

While an employer may find that the overall absenteeism rate and costs are within an acceptable range, it is still advisable to study the statistics to determine whether there are patterns in the data. Rarely does absenteeism spread itself evenly across an organization. It is very likely that employees in one area (or occupational group) may have nearly perfect attendance records, while others in a different area may be absent frequently. By monitoring these differential attendance records, managers can assess where problems might exist and, more important, begin planning ways to resolve or improve the underlying causes. For example, incentives could be provided for perfect attendance. Alternatively, progressive discipline procedures might be used with employees having a record of recurring absenteeism.

By establishing a comprehensive absenteeism policy, Allen-Bradley cut absenteeism 83.5 percent in a twenty-five-month period. This reduced the strain on labor costs and increased productivity. Part of the company's attendance policy reads:

> It is important to the successful operation of the Motion Control Division that employees be at work each scheduled workday. Each employee is performing an important set of tasks or activities. Excessive and/or avoidable absenteeism places unfair burdens on co-workers and increases the company's cost of doing business by disruption of work schedules, [creating] inefficiency and waste, delays, costly overtime, job pressures and customer complaints.[3]

NOTES AND REFERENCES

1. This quarterly report is part of the *BNA Bulletin to Management.* For an excellent review of the relationship between performance and voluntary turnover, see Charles R. Williams and Linda Parrack Livingstone, "Another Look at the Relationship between Performance and Voluntary Turnover," *Academy of Management Journal* 37, no. 2 (April 1994): 269–98.
2. The looseleaf publications of these organizations are sources of invaluable information for managers and HR professionals. These publications may be found in most libraries containing business reference books.
3. *Allen-Bradley Employee Handbook.*

chapter 3

Equal Employment Opportunity and Human Resources Management

After studying this chapter, you should be able to

Explain the reasons behind passage of EEO legislation.

Prepare an outline describing the major laws affecting equal employment opportunity. Describe bona fide occupational qualification and religious preference as EEO issues.

Discuss sexual harassment and immigration reform and control as EEO concerns.

Explain the use of the *Uniform Guidelines on Employee Selection Procedures.*

Provide examples illustrating the concept of adverse impact and apply the four-fifths rule.

Discuss significant court cases affecting equal employment opportunity.

Illustrate the various enforcement procedures affecting equal employment opportunity.

Describe affirmative action and the basic steps in developing an affirmative action program.

equal employment opportunity
The treatment of individuals in all aspects of employment—hiring, promotion, training, etc.—in a fair and nonbiased manner

Within the field of HRM perhaps no topics continue to receive more attention than equal employment opportunity (EEO) and affirmative action (AA). **Equal employment opportunity,** or the employment of individuals in a fair and nonbiased manner, has consumed the attention of the media, the courts, practitioners, and legislators. Not surprisingly, a more diverse and multicultural workforce has mandated that managers know and comply with a myriad of legal requirements affecting all aspects of the employment relationship. These mandates create legal responsibilities for an organization and each of its managers to comply with various laws and administrative guidelines. Importantly, practitioners agree that when all functions of HRM comply with the law, the organization becomes a fairer and more effective place to work.

However, when managers ignore the legal aspects of HRM, they risk incurring costly and time-consuming litigation, negative public attitudes, and damage to their individual careers.[1] Two highly publicized cases illustrate these points. In 2004, Wal-Mart Stores, Inc., the nation's largest employer, was hit with a gender-discrimination lawsuit. The charge, originally filed by six women, was granted class-action status and will cover as many as 1.6 million current and former Wal-Mart employees—the largest civil rights case in U.S. history. The suit claims that the retail giant used a pay system that paid female workers 5–15 percent less than their male counterparts for comparable jobs and favored men for promotions despite women having higher performance ratings and seniority.[2] In a black eye for Boeing Co., the Seattle airplane manufacturer was charged, in a 2004 lawsuit filed on behalf of 28,000 women, with systematic pay discrimination and a hostile sexual work environment. Depositions from multiple employees describe groping, fondling, and offensive language on the part of male colleagues.[3] These prominent examples overshadow the hundreds of discrimination lawsuits filed by employees of smaller organizations. For example, a federal jury in Florida awarded $1.55 million in damages to five former waitresses and hostesses of the Rio Bravo Cantina in Clearwater, Florida. The women claimed they were sexually harassed on the job over a four-year period. Each of the five women was awarded $10,000 in compensation for emotional pain and suffering. Punitive damages of $500,000 each were awarded to three of the five women. Delner Franklin-Thomas, EEOC regional attorney in Miami, noted, "This is the largest jury verdict for the EEOC in Florida in a sexual harassment case."[4]

Equal employment opportunity is not only a legal topic, it is also an emotional issue. It concerns all individuals, regardless of their sex, race, religion, age, national origin, color, physical condition, or position in an organization. Supervisors should be aware of their personal biases and how these attitudes can influence their dealings with subordinates. It should be emphasized that covert, as well as blatantly intentional, discrimination in employment is illegal.

To comply with the mandates of EEO legislation, employers have been compelled to develop employment policies that incorporate different laws, executive orders (EOs), administrative regulations, and court decisions (case law) designed to end job discrimination. The role of these legal requirements in shaping employment policies will be emphasized in this chapter. We will also discuss the process of affirmative action, which attempts to correct past practices of discrimination by actively recruiting minority-group members, and the importance of supporting diversity as a proactive business goal.

Historical Perspective of EEO Legislation

Equal employment opportunity as a national priority has emerged slowly in the United States. Not until the mid-1950s and early 1960s did nondiscriminatory employment become a strong social concern. Three factors seem to have influenced the growth of EEO legislation: (1) changing attitudes toward employment discrimination; (2) published reports highlighting the economic problems of women, minorities, and older workers; and (3) a growing body of disparate laws and government regulations covering discrimination.

Changing National Values

The United States was founded on the principles of individual merit, hard work, and equality. The Constitution grants to all citizens the right to life, liberty, and the pursuit of happiness. A central aim of political action has been to establish justice for all people of the nation.

In spite of these constitutional guarantees, employment discrimination has a long history in the United States. Organizations that claim to offer fair treatment to employees have openly or covertly engaged in discriminatory practices. Well-known organizations such as Dow Chemical, Westinghouse Electric Corporation, Mitsubishi Motor Manufacturing of America, the U.S. Army, the City of Los Angeles, Lockheed Martin, Amtrak, Home Depot, and American Airlines have violated equal employment laws.

Civil rights marches have long been used to protest discrimination.

Public attitudes changed dramatically with the beginning of the civil rights movement. During the late 1950s and early 1960s, minorities—especially blacks—publicized their low economic and occupational position through marches, sit-ins, rallies, and clashes with public authorities.[5] The low employment status of women also gained recognition during this period. Supported by concerned individuals and church and civic leaders, the civil rights movement and the women's movement received wide attention through television and print media. These movements had a pronounced influence on changing the attitudes of society at large, of the business community, of civic leaders, and of government officials, resulting in improvements in the civil rights of all individuals. No longer was blatant discrimination to be accepted.

Economic Disparity

The change in government and societal attitudes toward discrimination was further prompted by increasing public awareness of the economic imbalance between nonwhites and whites. Even today, civil rights activists cite government statistics to emphasize this disparity. For example, the March 2004 unemployment rate for black males over age 20 was 9.2 percent, compared with 4.7 percent for white males of the same age.[6] When employed, nonwhites tend to hold unskilled or semiskilled jobs characterized by unstable employment, low status, and low pay. In the fourth quarter of 2003, the median weekly earnings of white males were $702; of black males, $524; and, of Hispanic males, $451.[7] Remarking on the disparity in wages between whites and minorities, Steve Hipple, a Bureau of Labor Statistics economist, notes, "There's still a huge gap and it hasn't improved over the last 20 years."[8]

Early Legal Developments

Since as early as the nineteenth century, the public has been aware of discriminatory employment practices in the United States. In 1866 Congress passed the Civil Rights Act, which extended to all people the right to enjoy full and equal benefits of all laws, regardless of race. Beginning in the 1930s and 1940s, more-specific federal policies covering nondiscrimination began to emerge. In 1933 Congress enacted the Unemployment Relief Act, which prohibited employment discrimination on account of race, color, or creed. In 1941 President Franklin D. Roosevelt issued Executive Order 8802, which was to ensure that every American citizen, "regardless of race, creed, color, or national origin," would be guaranteed equal employment opportunities in World War II defense contracts. Over the next twenty years a variety of other legislative efforts were promoted to resolve inequities in employment practices.

Unfortunately, these early efforts did little to correct employment discrimination. First, at both the state and federal levels, nondiscrimination laws often failed to give any enforcement power to the agency charged with upholding the law. Second, the laws that were passed frequently neglected to list specific discriminatory practices or methods for their correction. Third, employers covered by the acts were required only to comply voluntarily with the equal employment opportunity legislation. Without a compulsory requirement, employers often violated legislation with impunity. Despite these faults, however, early executive orders and laws laid the groundwork for passage of the Civil Rights Act of 1964.

Government Regulation of Equal Employment Opportunity

Significant laws have been passed barring employment discrimination. These laws influence all of the HRM functions, including recruitment, selection, performance appraisal, training opportunities, promotion, and compensation. Because today's managers and supervisors are involved in employment activities, knowledge and application of these statutes are critical. It should be understood that managers and supervisors perform their jobs as agents of the employer.[9] Under the business concept of agency, managers and supervisors authorized to deal with employees on the employers' behalf subject themselves, and their employers, to responsibility for illegal acts taken against employees. Both the manager and the organization can be sued by an employee alleging discrimination.[10] Organizations cannot afford to have managers make HRM decisions without considering the possible legal implications of their actions for the organization and themselves. Highlights in HRM 1 will test your current understanding of EEO laws.

Major Federal Laws

protected classes
Individuals of a minority race, women, older people, and those with disabilities who are covered by federal laws on equal employment opportunity

Major federal equal employment opportunity laws have attempted to correct social problems of interest to particular groups of workers, called **protected classes.**[11] Defined broadly, these include individuals of a minority race, women, older people, and those with physical or mental disabilities. Separate federal laws cover each of these classes. Figure 3.1 lists the major federal laws and their provisions governing equal employment opportunity.

Equal Pay Act of 1963

The Equal Pay Act outlaws discrimination in pay, employee benefits, and pensions based on the worker's gender. Employers are prohibited from paying employees of one gender at a rate lower than that paid to members of the other gender for doing equal work. Jobs are considered "equal" when they require substantially the same skill, effort, and responsibility under similar working conditions and in the same establishment. For example, male and female plastic molders working for Medical Plastics Laboratory, a company of 125 employees manufacturing medical education products, must not be paid differently because of their gender. However, other employers in this specialized industry may pay their plastic molders wage rates that differ on the basis of different job content or economic conditions from those of Medical Plastics.

Employers do not violate the Equal Pay Act when differences in wages paid to men and women for equal work are based on seniority systems, merit considerations, or quantity or quality of production. However, these exceptions must not be based on the employee's gender or serve to discriminate against one particular gender. Employers may not lower the wages of one gender to comply with the law; rather, they must raise the wages of the gender being underpaid.[12]

USING THE INTERNET

Review the details explaining the responsibilities of the EEOC and complete texts of all the EEO laws. Go to the Student Resources at:

http://bohlander.swlearning.com

The Equal Pay Act was passed as an amendment to the Fair Labor Standards Act (FLSA) and is administered by the Equal Employment Opportunity Commission (EEOC). It covers employers engaged in interstate commerce and most government employees.

Highlights in HRM 1

Test Your Knowledge of Equal Employment Opportunity Law

The following questions have been used as "icebreakers" by employers and consultants when training supervisors and managers in EEO legislation. What is your knowledge of EEO laws? Answers are found at the end of this chapter.

1. Two male employees tell a sexually dirty joke. The joke is overheard by a female employee who complains to her supervisor that this is sexual harassment. Is her complaint legitimate?
   ___Yes ___No
2. To be covered by Title VII of the Civil Rights Act, an employer must be engaged in interstate commerce and employ twenty-five or more employees.
   ___True ___False
3. People addicted to illegal drugs are classified as disabled under the Americans with Disabilities Act of 1990.
   ___Yes ___No
4. The Equal Pay Act of 1963 allows employers to pay different wages to men and women who are performing substantially similar work. What are the three defenses for paying a different wage?
   1. ______________________________
   2. ______________________________
   3. ______________________________
5. A person applies with you for a job as a janitor. During the interview the person mentions that since birth he has sometimes experienced short periods of memory loss. Must you consider this individual a disabled person under the Americans with Disabilities Act of 1990?
   ___Yes ___No
6. On Friday afternoon you tell Nancy Penley, a computer analyst, that she must work overtime the next day. She refuses, saying that Saturday is her regular religious holiday and she can't work. Do you have the legal right to order her to work on Saturday?
   ___Yes ___No
7. You have just told an applicant that she will not receive the job she applied for. She claims that you denied her employment because of her age (she's 52). You claim she is not protected under the age discrimination law. Is your reasoning correct?
   ___Yes ___No
8. As an employer, you can select those applicants who are the most qualified in terms of education and experience.
   ___Yes ___No
9. As a manager, you have the legal right to mandate dates for pregnancy leaves.
   ___True ___False
10. State fair employment practice laws cover smaller employers not covered by federal legislation.
    ___True ___False

Figure 3.1 Major Laws Affecting Equal Employment Opportunity

LAW	PROVISIONS
Equal Pay Act of 1963	Requires all employers covered by the Fair Labor Standards Act and others to provide equal pay for equal work, regardless of sex.
Title VII of Civil Rights Act of 1964 (amended in 1972, 1991, and 1994)	Prohibits discrimination in employment on the basis of race, color, religion, sex, or national origin; created the Equal Employment Opportunity Commission (EEOC) to enforce the provisions of Title VII.
Age Discrimination in Employment Act of 1967 (amended in 1986 and 1990)	Prohibits private and public employers from discriminating against people age 40 or older in any area of employment because of age; exceptions are permitted when age is a bona fide occupational qualification.
Equal Employment Opportunity Act of 1972	Amended Title VII of Civil Rights Act of 1964; strengthens EEOC's enforcement powers and extends coverage of Title VII to government employees, employees in higher education, and other employers and employees.
Pregnancy Discrimination Act of 1978	Broadens the definition of sex discrimination to include pregnancy, childbirth, or related medical conditions; prohibits employers from discriminating agaist pregnant women in employment benefits if they are capable of performing their job duties.
Americans with disabilities Act of 1990	Prohibits discrimination in employment against people with physical or mental disabilities or the chronically ill; enjoins employers to make reasonable accommodation to the employment needs of the disabled; covers employers with fifteen or more employees.
Civil Rights Act of 1991	Provides for compensatory and punitive damages and jury trials in cases involving intentional discrimination; requires employers to demonstrate that job practices are job-related and consistent with business necessity; extends coverage to U.S. citizens working for American companies overseas.
Uniformed Services Employment and Reemployment Rights Act of 1994	Protects the employment rights of individuals who enter the military for short periods of service.

Civil Rights Act of 1964

Title VII of the Civil Rights Act of 1964 is the broadest and most significant of the antidiscrimination statutes. The act bars discrimination in all HR activities, including hiring, training, promotion, pay, employee benefits, and other conditions of employment. Discrimination is prohibited on the basis of race, color, religion, sex (also referred to as gender), or national origin. Importantly, in response to the growing number of immigrant workers and workplace cultural and ethnic awareness, the EEOC has issued new guidelines on national origin discrimination.[13] A "national origin group" is defined as a group of people sharing a common language, culture,

Source: Cartoon by Ted Goff. Reprinted with permission.

ancestry, and/or similar social characteristics. This definition includes people born in the United States who are not racial or ethnic minorities.[14] Also prohibited under the act is discrimination based on pregnancy.[15] The law protects hourly employees, supervisors, professional employees, managers, and executives from discriminatory practices. Section 703(a) of Title VII of the Civil Rights Act specifically provides that

> It shall be unlawful employment practice for an employer:
> 1. To fail or refuse to hire or to discharge any individual, or otherwise to discriminate against any individual with respect to his [or her] compensation, terms, conditions, or privileges of employment because of such individual's race, color, religion, sex, or national origin. . . .

While the purpose and the coverage of Title VII are extensive, the law does permit various exemptions. For example, as with the Equal Pay Act, managers are permitted to apply employment conditions differently if those differences are based on such objective factors as merit, seniority, or incentive payments. For example, the law would permit the promotion of a male office worker over a female office worker if the promotion was based on the superior skills and abilities of the male. Nowhere does the law require employers to hire, promote, or retain workers who are not qualified to perform their job duties. And managers may still reward employees differently, provided these differences are not predicated on the employees' race, color, sex, religion, or national origin.

The Civil Rights Act of 1964, as amended by the Equal Employment Opportunity Act of 1972 and the Civil Rights Act of 1991, covers a broad range of organizations. The law includes under its jurisdiction the following:

1. All private employers in interstate commerce who employ fifteen or more employees for twenty or more weeks per year
2. State and local governments
3. Private and public employment agencies, including the U.S. Employment Service
4. Joint labor-management committees that govern apprenticeship or training programs
5. Labor unions having fifteen or more members or employees
6. Public and private educational institutions
7. Foreign subsidiaries of U.S. organizations employing U.S. citizens

Certain employers are excluded from coverage of the Civil Rights Act. Broadly defined, these are (1) U.S. government–owned corporations, (2) bona fide, tax-exempt private clubs, (3) religious organizations employing people of a specific religion, and (4) organizations hiring Native Americans on or near a reservation.

The Civil Rights Act of 1964 established the Equal Employment Opportunity Commission to administer the law and promote equal employment opportunity. The commission's structure and operations will be reviewed later in this chapter.

Bona Fide Occupational Qualification. Under Title VII of the Civil Rights Act, employers are permitted limited exemptions from antidiscrimination regulations if employment preferences are based on a bona fide occupational qualification. A **bona fide occupational qualification (BFOQ)** permits discrimination when employer hiring preferences are a reasonable necessity for the normal operation of the business. However, a BFOQ is a suitable defense against a discrimination charge only when age, religion, sex, or national origin is an actual qualification for performing the job. For example, an older person could legitimately be excluded from consideration for employment as a model for teenage designer jeans. It is reasonable to expect the San Francisco 49ers of the National Football League to hire male locker-room attendants or for Macy's department store to employ females as models for women's fashions. Likewise, religion is a BFOQ in organizations that require employees to share a particular religious doctrine.

bona fide occupational qualification (BFOQ)
Suitable defense against a discrimination charge only when age, religion, sex, or national origin is an actual qualification for performing the job

The EEOC does not favor BFOQs, and both the EEOC and the courts have construed the concept narrowly. The exception does not apply to discrimination based on race or color. When an organization claims a BFOQ, it must be able to prove that hiring on the basis of sex, religion, age, or national origin is a business necessity. **Business necessity** has been interpreted by the courts as a practice that is necessary to the safe and efficient operation of the organization. A commercial driver's license required for over-the-road truck drivers would ensure proper handling of the vehicle and safety to the driver and other motorists. Students often ask, "Why do Asian restaurants hire only Asian American food servers?" While restaurants generally cannot prefer one nationality over another (because the job of serving food can be performed equally well by all nationalities), to ensure the "authenticity" of the dining experience, an Asian restaurant may legitimately use the business-necessity defense to support the preference for hiring Asian American servers.

business necessity
A work-related practice that is necessary to the safe and efficient operation of an organization

Religious Preference. Freedom to exercise religious choice is guaranteed under the U.S. Constitution. Title VII of the Civil Rights Act also prohibits discrimination based on religion in employment decisions, though it permits employer exemptions.

The act defines religion to "include all aspects of religious observance and practice, as well as belief."

Title VII does not require employers to grant complete religious freedom in employment situations. Employers need only make a reasonable accommodation for a current employee's or job applicant's religious observance or practice without incurring undue hardship in the conduct of the business. Managers or supervisors may have to accommodate an employee's religion in the specific areas of (1) holidays and observances (scheduling), (2) personal appearance (wearing beards, veils, or turbans), and (3) religious conduct on the job (missionary work among other employees).

USING THE INTERNET

To view the EEOC's Facts about Religious Discrimination, go to the Student Resources at:

http://bohlander.swlearning.com

What constitutes "reasonable accommodation" has been difficult to define.[16] In 1977, in the leading case of *TWA v Hardison,* the Supreme Court attempted to settle this dispute by ruling that employers had only to bear a minimum cost to show accommodation.[17] The Court said that to require otherwise would be discrimination against other employees for whom the expense of permitting time off for religious observance was not incurred. The *Hardison* case is important because it supported union management seniority systems in which the employer had made a reasonable attempt to adjust employee work schedules without undue hardship. While *Hardison* permits reasonable accommodation and undue hardship as a defense against religious discrimination charges, the EEOC investigates complaints on a case-by-case basis; employers are still responsible for supporting their decisions to deny an employee's religious requests.

Age Discrimination in Employment Act of 1967

With the aging of the baby boomers—76 million people—the chances of age discrimination by employers increase dramatically. Recent figures from the EEOC show that age discrimination complaints compose about 23.5 percent of all discrimination charges. Managers or supervisors may discriminate against older employees by

- Excluding older workers from important work activities
- Making negative changes in the performance evaluations of older employees
- Denying older employees job-related education, career development, or promotional opportunities
- Selecting younger job applicants over older, better-qualified candidates
- Pressuring older employees into taking early retirement
- Reducing the job duties and responsibilities of older employees
- Terminating older employees through downsizing[18]

Additionally, since older workers are less likely to agree to relocate or adapt to new job demands, they are prone to employer discrimination.

To make employment decisions based on age illegal, the Age Discrimination in Employment Act (ADEA), as amended, was passed in 1967. The act prohibits specific employers from discriminating against people age 40 or older in any area of employment, including selection, because of age. Employers affected are those with twenty or more employees; unions with twenty-five or more members; employment agencies; and federal, state, and local governments.

Exceptions to the law are permitted when age is a bona fide occupational qualification. A BFOQ may exist when an employer can show that advanced age may

USING THE INTERNET

AARP offers a number of resources to employers who want to maximize their use of older workers. Go to the Student Resources at:

http://bohlander.swlearning.com

affect public safety or organizational efficiency. For example, such conditions might exist for bus or truck drivers or for locomotive engineers. The greater the safety factor, measured by the likelihood of harm thorough accidents, the more stringent may be the job qualification designed to ensure safety. A BFOQ does not exist when an employer argues that younger employees foster a youthful or more energetic organizational image. Employers must also be careful to avoid making offhand remarks (such as "the old man" or our "aging graying sales force") or expressing negative opinions (such as "People over 50 years old have more accidents") about older individuals. These remarks and attitudes can be used as proof of discrimination in age-bias suits.[19]

Equal Employment Opportunity Act of 1972

In 1972 the Civil Rights Act of 1964 was amended by the Equal Employment Opportunity Act. Two important changes were made. First, the coverage of the act was broadened to include state and local governments and public and private educational institutions. Colleges and universities such as Central Texas College in Killeen; San Diego State University; and Bloomfield College in Bloomfield, New Jersey, are now covered by this statute. Second, the law strengthened the enforcement powers of the EEOC by allowing the agency itself to sue employers in court to enforce the provisions of the act. Regional litigation centers now exist to provide faster and more effective court action.

Pregnancy Discrimination Act of 1978

Before the passage of the Pregnancy Discrimination Act, pregnant women could be forced to resign or take a leave of absence because of their condition. In addition, employers did not have to provide disability or medical coverage for pregnancy. The Pregnancy Discrimination Act amended the Civil Rights Act of 1964 by stating that pregnancy is a disability and that pregnant employees in covered organizations must be treated on an equal basis with employees having other medical conditions. Under the law, it is illegal for employers to deny sick leave for morning sickness or related pregnancy illness if sick leave is permitted for other medical conditions such as flu or surgical operations. Specifically, the Pregnancy Discrimination Act affects employee benefit programs including (1) hospitalization and major medical insurance, (2) temporary disability and salary continuation plans, and (3) sick leave policies.

Furthermore, the law prohibits discrimination in the hiring, promotion, or termination of women because of pregnancy. Women must be evaluated on their ability to perform the job, and employers may not set arbitrary dates for mandatory pregnancy leaves. Leave dates are to be based on the individual pregnant employee's ability to work.

Americans with Disabilities Act of 1990

Discrimination against the disabled was first prohibited in federally funded activities by the Vocational Rehabilitation Act of 1973 (to be discussed later). However, the disabled were not among the protected classes covered by the Civil Rights Act of 1964. To remedy this shortcoming, Congress in 1990 passed the Americans with Disabilities Act (ADA), prohibiting employers from discriminating against individuals with physical and mental handicaps and the chronically ill.[20] The law defines a disability as "(a) a physical or mental impairment that substantially limits one or more of the major life activities; (b) a record of such impairment; or (c) being regarded as having such an impairment." Note that the law also protects people "regarded" as having a disability—for example, individuals with disfiguring burns.

Managers and supervisors remark that the ADA is difficult to administer because of the ambiguous definition of a disability, particularly mental impairment. The issue is, what is a disability? It sounds like a simple question, yet it is not. Not every mental or physical impairment is considered a disability under the law. For example, significant personality disorders are covered under the EEOC's "Enforcement Guidance on the Americans with Disabilities Act and Psychiatric Disabilities."[21] Covered personality disorders include schizophrenia, bipolar disorders, major affective disorders, personality disorders, and anxiety disorders. These impairments are characterized by aberrant behavior, self-defeating behavior, manipulation of others, and troublesome manners of behavior. However, mental impairments described as "adjustment disorders" or attributed to stress have generally not been subject to ADA coverage.[22] Therefore, employees who claim to be "stressed" over marital problems, financial hardships, demands of the work environment, job duties, or harsh, unreasonable treatment from a supervisor would not be classified as disabled under the ADA.

Does the ADA protect individuals who use medication or corrective devices to control the effects of their physical or mental impairments—for example, individuals wearing eyeglasses or those taking medication to ameliorate illnesses such as asthma, diabetes, or epilepsy? In a significant Supreme Court case, *Toyota v Williams* (2002),[23] the Court ruled that if physical or mental impairments are correctable, then they are not a disability. Specifically, the Court held that (1) to be substantially limited in performing work tasks, an individual must have an impairment that prevents or severely restricts the individual from doing activities that are of central importance to most people's daily lives and (2) it is insufficient for individuals attempting to prove disability status to merely submit evidence of a medical diagnosis of an impairment. Therefore, coverage of the act is restricted to only those whose impairments are not mitigated by corrective measures. To decide whether a person's conditions substantially limit a major life activity, managers must consider how the person functions with medication or assistive devices, not in the individual's uncorrected state.

The act does not cover

1. Homosexuality or bisexuality
2. Gender-identity disorders not resulting from physical impairment or other sexual-behavior disorders
3. Compulsive gambling, kleptomania, or pyromania
4. Psychoactive substance-use disorders resulting from current illegal use of drugs
5. Current illegal use of drugs
6. Infectious or communicable diseases of public health significance (applied to food-handling jobs only and excluding AIDS)

reasonable accommodation
An attempt by employers to adjust, without undue hardship, the working conditions or schedules of employees with disabilities or religious preferences

In the cases it does cover, the act requires employers to make a reasonable accommodation for disabled people who are otherwise qualified to work, unless doing so would cause undue hardship to the employer. "Undue hardship" refers to unusual work modifications or excessive expenses that might be incurred by an employer in providing an accommodation. **Reasonable accommodation** "includes making facilities accessible and usable to disabled persons, restructuring jobs, permitting part-time or modified work schedules, reassigning to a vacant position, changing equipment, and/or expense."[24] "Reasonable" is to be determined according to (1) the nature and cost of the accommodation and (2) the financial resources, size, and profitability of the facility and parent organization. Furthermore, employers cannot use selection procedures that screen out or tend to screen out disabled people, unless the selection procedure "is shown to be job-related for the position in question and is consistent with business necessity" and acceptable job performance cannot be achieved through reasonable accommodation. ("Essential functions," a pivotal issue for ensuring reasonable accommodation, will be discussed in Chapter 4.)

USING THE INTERNET

Retailer Sears has long had a commitment to hiring people with disabilities. Go to the Student Resources at:

http://bohlander.swlearning.com

The act prohibits covered employers from discriminating against a qualified individual regarding application for employment, hiring, advancement, discharge, compensation, training, or other employment conditions. The law incorporates the procedures and remedies found in Title VII of the Civil Rights Act, allowing job applicants or employees initial employment, reinstatement, back pay, and other injunctive relief against employers who violate the statute. The act covers employers with fifteen or more employees. The EEOC enforces the law in the same manner that Title VII of the Civil Rights Act is enforced.

Employers subject to the ADA, and those who value the varied abilities of the disabled, approach the law in a proactive manner. Because of the success experienced in the employment of disabled people, the slogan "Hire the disabled—it's good business" is a standard policy for organizations such as Little Tykes Co. of Hudson, Ohio; Fry's Food Stores of Phoenix, Arizona; and Magnum Assembly Inc. of Austin, Texas.[25] Jennifer Sheehy of the federal Office of Special Education and Rehabilitative Services advocates hiring disabled students as a way to enhance diversity recruitment and offset labor shortages.[26] Hiring the disabled emphasizes what these individuals *can* do rather than what they *cannot* do. It is not suggested that disabled people can be placed in any job without giving careful consideration to their disabilities, nor that employers can always make the workplace "user-friendly," but rather that it is good business to hire qualified disabled people who can work safely and productively. Fortunately, there exist today manual and electronic devices to aid hearing-impaired, visually impaired, and mobility-impaired employees. In many cases, the simple restructuring of jobs permits disabled persons to qualify for employment. Figure 3.2 identifies specific ways to make the workplace more accessible to the disabled.

Civil Rights Act of 1991

After extensive U.S. House and Senate debate, the Civil Rights Act of 1991 was signed into law. The act amends Title VII of the Civil Rights Act of 1964. One of the major elements of the law is the awarding of damages in cases of intentional discrimination or unlawful harassment. For the first time under federal law, damages are provided to victims of intentional discrimination or unlawful harassment on the basis of sex, religion, national origin, and disability. An employee who claims intentional discrimination can seek compensatory or punitive damages. Compensatory damages include payment for future money losses, emotional pain, suffering, mental anguish, and other nonmonetary losses. Punitive damages are awarded if it can be shown that the employer engaged in discrimination with malice or reckless indifference to the law. Most significantly, the act allows juries rather than federal judges to decide discrimination claims. Compensatory or punitive damages cannot be awarded in cases when

Figure 3.2 ADA Suggestions for an Accessible Workplace

- Install easy-to-reach switches.
- Provide sloping sidewalks and entrances.
- Install wheelchair ramps.
- Reposition shelves for the easy reach of materials.
- Rearrange tables, chairs, vending machines, dispensers, and other furniture and fixtures.
- Widen doors and hallways.
- Add raised markings on control buttons.
- Provide designated accessible parking spaces.
- Install hand controls or manipulation devices.
- Provide flashing alarm lights.
- Remove turnstiles and revolving doors or provide alternative accessible paths.
- Install holding bars in toilet areas.
- Redesign toilet partitions to increase access space.
- Add paper cup dispensers at water fountains.
- Replace high-pile, low-density carpeting.
- Reposition telephones, water fountains, and other needed equipment.
- Add raised toilet seats.
- Provide a full-length bathroom mirror.

an employment practice not intended to be discriminatory is shown to have an unlawful adverse impact on members of a protected class. The total damages any one person can receive cannot be more than

$50,000 for employers having between 15 and 100 employees
$100,000 for employers having between 101 and 200 employees
$200,000 for employers having between 201 and 500 employees
$300,000 for employers having more than 500 employees

In each case the aggrieved individual must have been employed with the organization for twenty or more calendar weeks.

Under its other provisions, the law

- Prohibits employers from adjusting employment test scores or using different cutoff test scores on the basis of race, color, religion, sex, or national origin
- Prohibits litigation involving charges of reverse discrimination when employers are under a consent order (court order) to implement an affirmative action program
- Requires that employers defending against a charge of discrimination demonstrate that employment practices are *job-related* and consistent with *business necessity.*

The Civil Rights Act of 1991 states that employees who are sent abroad to work for American-based companies are protected by U.S. antidiscrimination legislation governing age and disability and Title VII of the Civil Rights Act of 1964. Thus employees can sue their American employers for claims of discriminatory treatment while employed in a foreign country. This could occur, for example, in Middle Eastern countries where women are prohibited from holding certain jobs or when a foreign country's mandatory retirement law conflicts with the Age Discrimination in Employment Act.

Passed jointly with the Civil Rights Act of 1991 was the Glass Ceiling Act of 1991. The "glass ceiling" represents an invisible barrier that prohibits protected-class members from reaching top organizational positions. The act created the Glass Ceiling Commission to study and report on the status of and obstacles faced by minorities as they strive for top-level management jobs. Additional discussion of the glass ceiling can be found in Chapter 5.

Uniformed Services Employment and Reemployment Rights Act of 1994

Under this act, individuals who enter the military for a short period of service can return to their private-sector jobs without risk of loss of seniority or benefits.[27] For example, military reservists called up to active duty during the Iraq conflict would qualify for reemployment rights under this law. The act protects against discrimination on the basis of military obligation in the areas of hiring, job retention, and advancement. Other provisions under the act require employers to make reasonable efforts to retrain or upgrade skills to qualify employees for reemployment, expand health care and employee pension plan coverage, and extend the length of time an individual may be absent for military duty from four to five years. For their part, service members must provide their employers advance notice of their military obligations in order to be protected by the reemployment rights statute. The Labor Department's Veterans Employment and Training Service is responsible for enforcing the law.

Other Federal Laws and Executive Orders

Because the major laws affecting equal employment opportunity do not cover agencies of the federal government and because state laws do not apply to federal employees, it has at times been necessary for the president to issue executive orders to protect federal employees. Executive orders are also used to provide equal employment opportunity to individuals employed by government contractors. Since many large employers—such as General Dynamics, AT&T, Honeywell, and Motorola—and numerous small companies have contracts with the federal government, managers are expected to know and comply with the provisions of executive orders and other laws. The federal laws and executive orders that apply to government agencies and government contractors are summarized in Figure 3.3.

Vocational Rehabilitation Act of 1973

People with disabilities experience discrimination both because of negative attitudes regarding their ability to perform work and because of physical barriers imposed by organizational facilities. The Vocational Rehabilitation Act was passed in 1973 to correct these problems by requiring private employers with federal contracts over $2,500 to take affirmative action to hire individuals with a mental or physical disability. Recipients of federal financial assistance, such as public and private colleges and universities, are also covered. Employers must make a reasonable accommodation to hire disabled individuals but are not required to employ unqualified people. In applying the safeguards of this law, the term **disabled individual** means "any person who (1) has a physical or mental impairment which substantially limits one or more of such person's major life activities, (2) has a record of such an impairment, or (3) is regarded as having such an impairment." This definition closely parallels the definition of disabled individual provided in the Americans with Disabilities Act, just discussed.

disabled individual
Any person who (1) has a physical or mental impairment that substantially limits one or more of the person's major life activities, (2) has a record of such impairment, or (3) is regarded as having such an impairment

Figure 3.3 EEO Rules Applicable to Federal Contractors and Agencies

LAW	PROVISIONS
Vocational Rehabilitation Act of 1973 (amended in 1974)	Prohibits federal contractors from discriminating against disabled individuals in any program or activity receiving federal financial assistance; requires federal contractors to develop affirmative action plans to hire and promote disabled people.
Executive Order 11246 (1965), as amended by Order 11375 (1966)	Prohibits employment discrimination based on race, color, religion, sex, or national origin by government contractors with contracts exceeding $10,000; requires contractors employing fifty or more workers to develop affirmative action plans when government contracts exceed $50,000 a year.
Executive Order 11478 (1969)	Obligates the federal government to ensure that all personnel actions affecting applicants for employment be free from discrimination based on race, color, religion, sex, or national origin.

In a significant 1987 decision, the Supreme Court ruled in *Nassau County, Florida v Arline* that employees afflicted with contagious diseases, such as tuberculosis, are disabled individuals and subject to the act's coverage.[28] In cases when people with contagious diseases are "otherwise qualified" to do their jobs, the law requires employers to make a reasonable accommodation to allow the disabled to perform their jobs.[29] Individuals with AIDS are also disabled within the meaning of the Rehabilitation Act. Therefore, discrimination on the basis of AIDS violates the law, and employers must accommodate the employment needs of people with AIDS. Public interest in AIDS has presented management with a challenge to address work-related concerns about AIDS. Many organizations have developed specific policies to deal with the issue of AIDS in the workplace.

The Rehabilitation Act does not require employers to hire or retain a disabled person if he or she has a contagious disease that poses a direct threat to the health or safety of others and the individual cannot be accommodated. Also, employment is not required when some aspect of the employee's disability prevents that person from carrying out essential parts of the job; nor is it required if the disabled person is not otherwise qualified.

Executive Order 11246

Federal agencies and government contractors with contracts of $10,000 or more must comply with the antidiscrimination provisions of Executive Order 11246. The order prohibits discrimination based on race, color, religion, sex, or national origin in all employment activities. Furthermore, it requires that government contractors or subcontractors having fifty or more employees with contracts in excess of $50,000 develop affirmative action plans; such plans will be discussed later in the chapter.

Executive Order 11246 created the Office of Federal Contract Compliance Programs (OFCCP) to ensure equal employment opportunity in the federal procurement area. The agency issues nondiscriminatory guidelines and regulations similar to those issued by the EEOC. Noncompliance with OFCCP policies can result in the cancellation or suspension of contracts. The OFCCP is further charged with requiring that contractors provide job opportunities to the disabled, disabled veterans, and veterans of the Vietnam War.

Fair Employment Practice Laws

fair employment practices (FEPs)
State and local laws governing equal employment opportunity that are often more comprehensive than federal laws

Federal laws and executive orders provide the major regulations governing equal employment opportunity. But, in addition, almost all states and many local governments have passed laws barring employment discrimination. Referred to as **fair employment practices (FEPs),** these statutes are often more comprehensive than the federal laws. While state and local laws are too numerous to review here, managers should be aware of them and how they affect HRM in their organizations.

State and local FEPs also promote the employment of individuals in a fair and unbiased way. They are patterned after federal legislation, although they frequently extend jurisdiction to employers exempt from federal coverage and therefore pertain mainly to smaller employers. While Title VII of the Civil Rights Act exempts employers with fewer than fifteen employees, many states extend antidiscrimination laws to employers with one or more workers. Thus managers and entrepreneurs operating a small business must pay close attention to these laws. Local or state legislation may bar discrimination based on physical appearance, marital status, arrest records, color blindness, or political affiliation. Maryland recently joined states such as California, Vermont, Hawaii, Nevada, New Mexico, and Wisconsin in protecting employees from discrimination based on sexual orientation.

More than 100 fair employment practices agencies (FEPAs) administer and enforce equal employment opportunity statutes. The Ohio Civil Rights Commission, the Massachusetts Commission against Discrimination, the Colorado Civil Rights Division, and the Pittsburgh Commission on Human Relations are examples. State agencies play an important role in the investigation and resolution of employment discrimination charges. FEPAs and the Equal Employment Opportunity Commission often work together to resolve discrimination complaints.[30]

Other Equal Employment Opportunity Issues

Federal laws, executive orders, court cases, and state and local statutes provide the broad legal framework for equal employment opportunity. Within these major laws, specific issues are of particular interest to supervisors and managers. The situations discussed here occur in the day-to-day supervision of employees.

Sexual Harassment

Sexual situations in the work environment are not new to organizational life. Sexual feelings are a part of group dynamics, and people who work together may come to develop these kinds of feelings for one another. Unfortunately, however, often these encounters are unpleasant and unwelcome, as witnessed by the many reported instances of sexual harassment.[31] Nationwide, 13,136 sexual harassment complaints were filed in 2004 with the EEOC and state fair employment practice agencies by

© DAVE L. RYAN/INDEX STOCK IMAGERY

Sexual harassment encounters are unpleasant, causing personal and organizational hardships.

employees of both small and large employers.[32] About 15 percent of these charges were filed by males. Problems often arise from lack of knowledge of the specific on-the-job behaviors that constitute sexual harassment under the law. Through a questionnaire it is possible to test employee understanding of what is and what is not sexual harassment. Highlights in HRM 2 is a sampling of questions that could be used during a sexual harassment audit. Such an instrument, which is essentially a test, is a valuable tool for determining what employees know and do not know about sexual harassment.

The EEOC guidelines on sexual harassment are specific, stating that "unwelcome advances, requests for sexual favors, and other verbal or physical conduct of a sexual nature" constitute **sexual harassment** when submission to the conduct is tied to continuing employment or advancement. The EEOC recognizes two forms of sexual harassment as being illegal under Title VII. The first, *quid pro quo harassment,* occurs when "submission to or rejection of sexual conduct is used as a basis for employment decisions."[33] This type of harassment involves a tangible or economic consequence, such as a demotion or loss of pay. If a supervisor promotes a female employee only after she agrees to an after-work date, the conduct is clearly illegal.

The second type of harassment, *hostile environment,* can occur when unwelcome sexual conduct "has the purpose or effect of unreasonably interfering with job performance or creating an intimidating, hostile, or offensive working environment."[34] Thus dirty jokes, vulgar slang, nude pictures, swearing, and personal ridicule and insult constitute sexual harassment when an employee finds them offensive.

sexual harassment
Unwelcome advances, requests for sexual favors, and other verbal or physical conduct of a sexual nature in the working environment

For example, the Paradise Valley Unified School District of Phoenix, Arizona, defines sexual harassment as including, but not limited to, suggestive or obscene letters, notes, or invitations; derogatory comments, slurs, jokes, and epithets; assault; blocking movements; leering gestures; and displays of sexually suggestive objects, pictures, or cartoons where such conduct may create a hostile environment for the employee.[35] Interestingly, with the intrusion of pornographic spam at work, Eugene Volokh, professor of law at UCLA, cautions employers to operate as if porn spam does create a hostile work environment.[36]

The EEOC considers an employer guilty of sexual harassment when the employer knew or should have known about the unlawful conduct and failed to remedy it or to take corrective action. Employers are also guilty of sexual harassment when they allow nonemployees (customers or salespeople) to sexually harass employees.[37]

It is noteworthy that both the Supreme Court and the EEOC hold employers strictly accountable to prevent sexual harassment of both female and male employees. In 1998, the Supreme Court held in *Oncale v Sundowner Offshore Services* that same-sex sexual harassment (male-to-male, female-to-female) is covered under Title VII.[38] In the opinion of Justice Antonin Scalia, "What matters is the conduct at issue, not the sex of the people involved and not the presence or absence of sexual desire, whether heterosexual or homosexual."[39] When charges of sexual harassment have

Highlights in HRM 2

Questions Used in Auditing Sexual Harassment

ACTIVITY	IS THIS SEXUAL HARASSMENT?			ARE YOU AWARE OF THIS BEHAVIOR IN THE ORGANIZATION?	
• Employees post cartoons on bulletin boards containing sexually related material.	Yes	No	Uncertain	Yes	No
• A male employee says to a female employee that she has beautiful eyes and hair.	Yes	No	Uncertain	Yes	No
• A male manager habitually calls all female employees "sweetie" or "darling."	Yes	No	Uncertain	Yes	No
• A manager fails to promote a female (male) employee for not granting sexual favors.	Yes	No	Uncertain	Yes	No
• Male employees use vulgar language and tell sexual jokes that are overheard by, but not directed at, female employees.	Yes	No	Uncertain	Yes	No
• A male employee leans and peers over the back of a female employee when she wears a low-cut dress.	Yes	No	Uncertain	Yes	No
• A supervisor gives a female (male) subordinate a nice gift on her (his) birthday.	Yes	No	Uncertain	Yes	No
• Two male employees share a sexually explicit magazine while observed by a female employee.	Yes	No	Uncertain	Yes	No
• Female office workers are "rated" by male employees as they pass the men's desks.	Yes	No	Uncertain	Yes	No
• Revealing female clothing is given as a gift at an office birthday party.	Yes	No	Uncertain	Yes	No
• A sales representative from a supplier makes "suggestive" sexual remarks to a receptionist.	Yes	No	Uncertain	Yes	No

Basic Components of an Effective Sexual Harassment Policy

1. Develop a comprehensive organization-wide policy on sexual harassment and present it to all current and new employees. Stress that sexual harassment will not be tolerated under any circumstances. Emphasis is best achieved when the policy is publicized and supported by top management.
2. Hold training sessions with supervisors to explain Title VII requirements, their role in providing an environment free of sexual harassment, and proper investigative procedures when charges occur.
3. Establish a formal complaint procedure in which employees can discuss problems without fear of retaliation. The complaint procedure should spell out how charges will be investigated and resolved.
4. Act immediately when employees complain of sexual harassment. Communicate widely that investigations will be conducted objectively and with appreciation for the sensitivity of the issue.
5. When an investigation supports employee charges, discipline the offender at once. For extremely serious offenses, discipline should include penalties up to and including discharge. Discipline should be applied consistently across similar cases and among managers and hourly employees alike.
6. Follow up on all cases to ensure a satisfactory resolution of the problem.

been proved, the EEOC has imposed remedies including back pay; reinstatement; and payment of lost benefits, interest charges, and attorney's fees. Sexual harassment involving physical conduct can invite criminal charges, and damages may be assessed against both the employer and the individual offender.

Sexual harassment investigations are one of the most sensitive responsibilities faced by managers. When to investigate, who should handle the investigation, how to interview the complainant and the accused, and the availability of witnesses are a few of the critical elements affecting harassment cases. One HR professional described the investigating manager as playing the multiple roles of prosecutor, defender, judge, and jury.[40] Additionally, to determine whether the misconduct is hostile or offensive, the manager must look at all the circumstances surrounding the charge of harassment. Important factors include the frequency of the misconduct; the severity of the misconduct; whether it is physically threatening or humiliating, as opposed to merely offensive; and whether it unreasonably interferes with the employee's work performance.[41]

Despite legislation against it, however, sexual harassment is still common in the workplace. Managers and supervisors must take special precautions to try to prevent it.[42] Highlights in HRM 3 presents the Court's suggestions and the EEOC guidelines for an effective policy to minimize sexual harassment in the work environment.

Sexual Orientation

A culture of "changing lifestyles," a growing diversified workforce, and continual employee demands for equal workplace rights has sparked an emotional debate over employment guarantees for homosexuals. The debate intensifies as growing numbers of gays and lesbians openly announce their sexual orientation and legislatures, courts, and company leaders discuss the merits of "gay rights." Presently, what laws protect employees from discrimination based on their sexual orientation?

While Title VII of the Civil Rights Act of 1964 lists "sex" as a protected class, court cases have consistently held that sexual orientation is not a valid defense against discrimination. Currently, no federal law bars discrimination based on one's sexual orientation. For homosexual employees protection from discrimination largely comes from fair employment practice laws passed at the state or local level. Furthermore, state and local same-sex statutes vary regarding the protection afforded homosexuals and who is covered under the laws. For example, in some states, public—but not private—sector employees are protected from discrimination based on their sexual orientation.[43] Therefore, it becomes important for managers and supervisors to know and follow the legal rights of homosexuals in their geographic area.

Regardless of their legal obligations toward homosexuals, companies—in support of their diversity initiatives—increasingly are fostering "gay-friendly" work places.[44] Organizations such as S. C. Johnson and Sons, Eastman Kodak, Lucent Technologies, Microsoft, and Southern California Edison hold training sessions aimed at overcoming the stereotypes affecting gay and lesbian workers. Defense contractors Raytheon and Lockheed Martin sponsor homosexual support groups, and Wal-Mart has adopted a nondiscrimination policy toward homosexuals.[45] Of the nation's top 500 companies, 70 percent now offer health benefits to same-sex couples (see Chapter 10). A safe prediction is that employment rights for gays and lesbians will intensify, becoming a dynamic area for future legislation.

Immigration Reform and Control

Good employment is the magnet that attracts many people to the United States. Unfortunately, illegal immigration has adversely affected welfare services and educational and Social Security benefits. To preserve our tradition of legal immigration while closing the door to illegal entry, in 1986 Congress passed the Immigration Reform and Control Act. The act was passed to control unauthorized immigration by making it unlawful for a person or organization to hire, recruit, or refer for a fee people not legally eligible for employment in the United States.[46]

Employers must comply with the law by verifying and maintaining records on the legal rights of applicants to work in the United States. The *Handbook for Employers*, published by the U.S. Department of Justice, lists five actions that employers must take to comply with the law:

1. Have employees fill out their part of Form I-9.
2. Check documents establishing an employee's identity and eligibility to work.
3. Complete the employer's section of Form I-9.
4. Retain Form I-9 for at least three years.
5. Present Form I-9 for inspection to an Immigration and Naturalization Service officer or to a Department of Labor officer upon request.[47]

Section 102 of the law also prohibits discrimination. Employers with four or more employees may not discriminate against any individual (other than an unauthorized alien) in hiring, discharge, recruiting, or referring for a fee because of that individual's national origin or, in the case of a citizen or intending citizen, because of citizenship status. Employers found to have violated the act will be ordered to cease the discriminatory practice. They may also be directed to hire, with or without back pay, individuals harmed by the discrimination and pay a fine of up to $1,000 for each person discriminated against. Charges of discrimination based on national origin or citizenship are filed with the Office of Special Counsel in the Department of Justice.

Uniform Guidelines on Employee Selection Procedures

Uniform Guidelines on Employee Selection Procedures
A procedural document published in the *Federal Register* to help employers comply with federal regulations against discriminatory actions

Employers are often uncertain about the appropriateness of specific selection procedures, especially those related to testing and selection. To remedy this concern, in 1978 the Equal Employment Opportunity Commission, along with three other government agencies, adopted the current **Uniform Guidelines on Employee Selection Procedures.**[48] Since it was first published in 1970, the *Uniform Guidelines* has become a very important procedural document for managers because it applies to employee selection procedures in the areas of hiring, retention, promotion, transfer, demotion, dismissal, and referral. It is designed to help employers, labor organizations, employment agencies, and licensing and certification boards comply with the requirements of federal laws prohibiting discrimination in employment.[49]

Essentially the *Uniform Guidelines* recommends that an employer be able to demonstrate that selection procedures are valid in predicting or measuring performance in a particular job. It defines "discrimination" as follows:

> The use of any selection procedure which has an adverse impact on the hiring, promotion, or other employment or membership opportunities of members of any race, sex, or ethnic group will be considered to be discriminatory and inconsistent with these guidelines, unless the procedure has been validated in accordance with these guidelines (or, certain other provisions are satisfied).[50]

Validity

adverse impact
A concept that refers to the rejection of a significantly higher percentage of a protected class for employment, placement, or promotion when compared with the successful, nonprotected class

When using a test or other selection instrument to choose individuals for employment, employers must be able to prove that the selection instrument bears a direct relationship to job success. This proof is established through validation studies that show the job relatedness or lack thereof for the selection instrument under study. The *Uniform Guidelines,* along with several of the court cases we discuss later, provides strict standards for employers to follow as they validate selection procedures. The different methods of testing validity are reviewed in detail in Chapter 6.

Adverse Impact and Disparate Treatment

For an applicant or employee to pursue a discrimination case successfully, the individual must establish that the employer's selection procedures resulted in an adverse impact on a protected class. **Adverse impact** refers to the rejection for employment, placement, or promotion of a significantly higher percentage of a protected class when compared with a nonprotected class.[51] Additionally, when pursuing an adverse impact claim, an individual is alleging that the employer's selection practice has *unintentionally* discriminated against a protected group.

While the *Uniform Guidelines* does not require an employer to conduct validity studies of selection procedures where no adverse impact exists, it does encourage employers to use selection procedures that are valid. Organizations that validate their selection procedures on a regular basis and use interviews, tests, and other procedures in such a manner as to avoid adverse impact will generally be in compliance with the principles of equal employment legislation. Affirmative action programs also reflect employer intent. The motivation for using valid selection procedures, however, should be the desire to achieve effective management of human resources rather than the fear of legal pressure.

There are two basic ways to show that adverse impact exists:

Adverse Rejection Rate, or Four-Fifths Rule. According to the *Uniform Guidelines,* a selection program has an adverse impact when the selection rate for any racial, ethnic, or sex class is less than four-fifths (or 80 percent) of the rate of the class with the highest selection rate. The Equal Employment Opportunity Commission has adopted the **four-fifths rule** as a rule of thumb to determine adverse impact in enforcement proceedings. The four-fifths rule is not a legal definition of discrimination; rather, it is a method by which the EEOC or any other enforcement agency monitors serious discrepancies in hiring, promotion, or other employment decisions. The appendix at the end of this chapter explains how adverse impact is determined and gives a realistic example of how the four-fifths rule is computed.

four-fifths rule
A rule of thumb followed by the EEOC in determining adverse impact for use in enforcement proceedings

An alternative to the four-fifths rule, and one increasingly used in discrimination lawsuits, is to apply *standard deviation analysis* to the observed applicant flow data. In 1977, the Supreme Court, in *Hazelwood School District v United States,* set forth a standard deviation analysis that has been followed by numerous lower courts.[52] This statistical procedure determines whether the difference between the expected selection rates for protected groups and the actual selection rates could be attributed to chance. If chance is eliminated for the lower selection rates of the protected class, it is assumed that the employer's selection technique has an adverse impact on the employment opportunities of that group.

Restricted Policy. Any evidence that an employer has a selection procedure that excludes members of a protected class, whether intentional or not, constitutes adverse impact. For example, hiring individuals who must meet a minimum height or appearance standard (at the expense of protected-class members) is evidence of a restricted policy. In one case known to the authors, an organization when downsizing discharged employees primarily age 40 or older. These employees filed a class-action suit claiming adverse impact under the Age Discrimination in Employment Act.

In EEO cases it is important to distinguish between adverse impact and disparate treatment discrimination. Adverse impact cases deal with unintentional discrimination; **disparate treatment** cases involve instances of purposeful discrimination. For example, disparate treatment would arise when an employer hires men, but no women, with school-age children. Allowing men to apply for craft jobs, such as carpentry or electrical work, but denying this opportunity to women would also show disparate treatment. To win a disparate treatment case, the plaintiff must prove that the employer's actions intended to discriminate, a situation often difficult to substantiate.

disparate treatment
A situation in which protected-class members receive unequal treatment or are evaluated by different standards

McDonnell Douglas Test. Individuals who believe they have been unjustly rejected for employment may demonstrate disparate treatment through the McDonnell Douglas test. This test, named for the Supreme Court case *McDonnell Douglas Corp. v Green* (1973), provides four guidelines for individuals to follow in establishing a case:[53]

1. The person is a member of a protected class.
2. The person applied for a job for which he or she was qualified.
3. The person was rejected, despite being qualified.
4. After rejection, the employer continued to seek other applicants with similar qualifications.

Provided these four guidelines are met, then a prima facie (before further examination) case of discrimination is shown. The burden now shifts to the employer to prove that the action taken against the individual was not discriminatory. For example, in a selection case in which female applicants were denied employment, the supervisor may claim that the male hired was the only applicant qualified to perform the job.

Workforce Utilization Analysis

While employers must be aware of the impact of their selection procedures on protected-class members, they must also be concerned with the composition of their internal workforce when compared with their external labor market. The EEOC refers to this comparison as **workforce utilization analysis.** This concept simply compares an employer's workforce by race and sex for specific job categories against the surrounding labor market. The employer's relevant labor market is that area from which employees are drawn who have the skills needed to successfully perform the job. For example, if the Vision Track Golf Corporation is hiring computer technicians from a labor market composed of 10 percent black workers, 8 percent Hispanic workers, and 2 percent Native American workers, all of whom possess the qualifications for the job, the employer's internal workforce should reflect this racial composition. When this occurs, the employer's workforce is said to be *at parity* with the relevant labor market. If the employer's racial workforce composition is below external figures, then the protected class is said to be *underutilized* and the employer should take affirmative steps to correct the imbalance.

workforce utilization analysis
A process of classifying protected-class members by number and by the type of job they hold within the organization

Significant Court Cases

The *Uniform Guidelines* has been given added importance through two leading Supreme Court cases. Each case is noteworthy because it elaborates on the concepts of adverse impact, validity testing, and job-relatedness. Managers of both large and small organizations must constantly be alert to new court decisions and be prepared to implement those rulings. The Bureau of National Affairs, Commerce Clearing House, and Prentice Hall provide legal information on a subscription basis to interested managers. Local and regional seminars offered by professional organizations such as the American Management Association also provide information.

The benchmark case in employment selection procedures is *Griggs v Duke Power Company* (1971). Willie Griggs had applied for the position of coal handler with the Duke Power Company. His request for the position was denied because he was not a high school graduate, a requirement for the position. Griggs claimed the job standard was discriminatory because it did not relate to job success and because the standard had an adverse impact on a protected class.

In the *Griggs* decision, the Supreme Court established two important principles affecting equal employment opportunity.[54] First, the Court ruled that employer discrimination need not be overt or intentional to be present. Rather, employment practices can be illegal even when applied equally to all employees. For example, under this ruling, a new venture pharmaceuticals company requiring all salespeople to be six feet tall would impose an adverse impact on Asians and women, limiting their employment opportunities.

Second, under *Griggs,* employment practices must be job-related. When discrimination charges arise, employers have the burden of proving that employment requirements are job-related or constitute a business necessity. When employers use education, physical, or intelligence standards as a basis for hiring or promotion, these requirements must be absolutely necessary for job success. Under Title VII, good intent, or absence of intent to discriminate, is not a sufficient defense.

In 1975 the Supreme Court decided *Albemarle Paper Company v Moody.*[55] The Albemarle Paper Company required job applicants to pass a variety of employment tests, some of which were believed to be poor predictors of job success. The *Albemarle* case is important because in it the Supreme Court strengthened the principles established in *Griggs.* Specifically, more-stringent requirements were placed on employers to demonstrate the job-relatedness of tests. When tests are used for hiring or promotion decisions (tests are defined to include performance appraisals), they must be valid predictors of job success.

Enforcing Equal Employment Opportunity Legislation

Along with prohibiting employment discrimination, Title VII of the Civil Rights Act created the Equal Employment Opportunity Commission. As the federal government's leading civil rights agency, the EEOC is responsible for ensuring that covered employers comply with the intent of this act. The commission accomplishes this goal primarily by (1) issuing various employment guidelines and monitoring the employment practices of organizations and (2) protecting employee rights through the investigation and prosecution of discrimination charges.[56] Figure 3.4 illustrates the caseload of the EEOC for recent years.

It is important to remember that the EEOC's guidelines are not federal law but administrative rules and regulations published in the *Federal Register.* However, the different guidelines have been given weight by the courts as they interpret the law and therefore should not be taken lightly. In addition to enforcing Title VII, the EEOC has the authority to enforce the Age Discrimination in Employment Act and the Equal Pay Act. Executive Order 12067, which requires the coordination of all federal equal employment opportunity regulations, practices, and policies, is also administered by the EEOC.

The Equal Employment Opportunity Commission

The EEOC consists of five commissioners and a general counsel, all appointed by the president of the United States and confirmed by the Senate. The president appoints

Figure 3.4 U.S. Equal Employment Opportunity Commission Case Figures, Fiscal Years 1997–2003

BASIS	FY 1998	FY 1999	FY 2000	FY 2001	FY 2002	FY 2003	FY 2004
Race	28,820	28,819	28,945	28,912	29,910	28,526	27,696
Sex	24,454	23,907	24,194	25,140	25,536	24,362	24,249
Disability	17,806	17,007	15,864	16,470	15,964	15,377	15,346
Age	15,191	14,141	16,008	17,405	19,921	19,124	17,837
Retaliation	19,114	19,694	21,613	22,257	22,768	22,690	22,740
National origin	6,778	7,108	7,792	8,025	9,046	8,450	8,361
Religion	1,786	1,811	1,939	2,217	2,572	2,532	2,466
Equal pay	1,071	1,044	1,270	1,251	1,256	1,167	1,011
Total*	**79,591**	**77,444**	**79,896**	**80,840**	**84,442**	**81,293**	**79,432**

*The number for total charges reflects the number of individual charge filings. Because individuals often file charges under multiple bases, the number of total charges for any given fiscal year will be less than the total of the eight bases listed.

Source: Data compiled by the Office of Research, Information and Planning from EEOC's Charge Data System's national database.

commissioners for staggered five-year terms, and no more than three members of the commission can be of the same political party. One commissioner is appointed to be the EEOC chairperson, who is responsible for the overall administration of the agency. The commission's work consists of formulating EEO policy and approving all litigation involved in maintaining equal employment opportunity.

Appointed for a four-year term, the general counsel is responsible for investigating discrimination charges, conducting agency litigation, and providing legal opinions, in addition to reviewing EEOC regulations, guidelines, and contracts.

The day-to-day operation of the commission is performed through administrative headquarters, districts, and area offices. *District offices* handle discrimination charges and all compliance and litigation enforcement functions. *Area offices* are less than full-service organizations and generally serve as charge-processing and initial investigation units. Much of the EEOC's work is delegated to the district offices and other designated representatives. District directors have authority to receive or consent to the withdrawal of Title VII charges, issue subpoenas, send notices of the filing of charges, dismiss charges, enter into and sign conciliation agreements (voluntary employer settlements), and send out notices of the employee's right to sue. Employees who wish to file discrimination charges and employers responding to complaints work with district or area office personnel.

Record-Keeping and Posting Requirements

Organizations subject to Title VII are required by law to maintain specific employment records and reports. In addition, employers are required to post selected equal employment opportunity notices and to summarize the composition of their workforce in order to determine the distribution of protected individuals. These records are for establishing minority-group statistical reports. Equal employment opportunity legislation covering federal contractors and subcontractors has special reporting requirements for these employers. Those failing to comply with record-keeping and

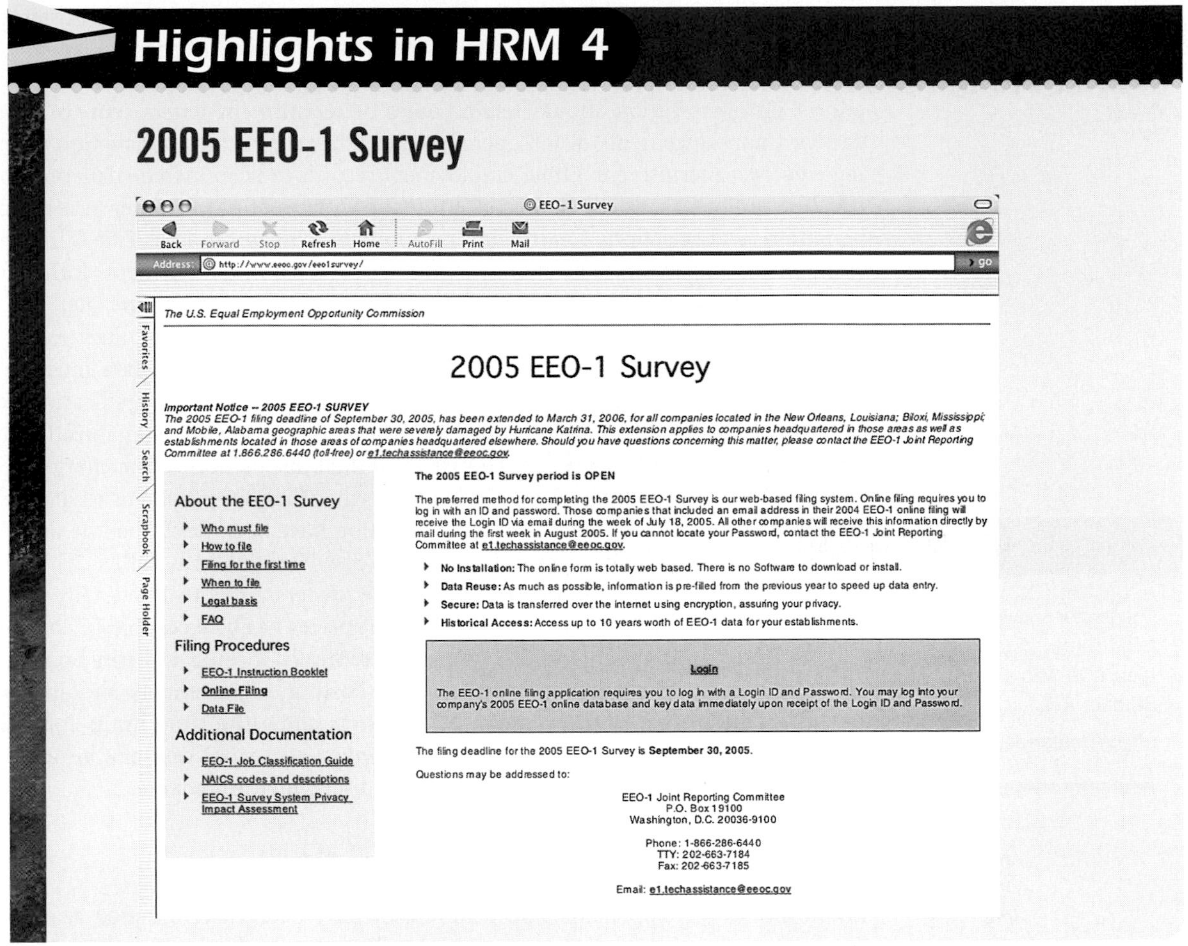

Highlights in HRM 4

2005 EEO-1 Survey

posting requirements or willfully falsifying records can incur penalties, including fines and imprisonment.

It is important to note that record-keeping requirements are both detailed and comprehensive. For example, managers must generate and retain for specific time periods different employment data under each of the following laws: Title VII, the Age Discrimination in Employment Act, and the Equal Pay Act. When federal contractors are required to have written affirmative action programs, these must be retained along with supporting documents (such as names of job applicants, rejection ratios, and seniority lists).

EEO-1 report
An employer information report that must be filed annually by employers of 100 or more employees (except state and local government employers) and government contractors and subcontractors to determine an employer's workforce composition

Employers of 100 or more employees (except state and local government employees) and government contractors and subcontractors subject to Executive Order 11286 must file annually an **EEO-1 report** (Employer Information Report) that requires the reporting of minority employees. This comprehensive report is the EEOC's basic document for determining an employer's workforce composition, investigating charges of discrimination, and providing information about the employment status of minorities and women.[57] Employers can now submit the EEO-1 report through the agency's Web-based filing system. Highlights in HRM 4 discusses the new Web-based reporting system. In preparing the EEO-1 report, the organization may collect records concerning racial or ethnic identity either by visual survey or through postemployment questionnaires, if not prohibited by state fair employment practice law.

To show evidence of its equal employment opportunity and affirmative action efforts, an organization should retain copies of recruitment letters sent to minority agencies, announcements of job openings, and other significant information concerning employee recruitment. Other employment records to keep include data on promotions, demotions, transfers, layoffs or terminations, rates of pay or other terms of compensation, and selections for training or apprenticeship programs. Title VII requires retention of all personnel or employment records, including application forms, for at least six months or until resolution of any HR action, whichever occurs later.

During the employment process, employers are permitted to collect racial data on job applicants for compiling statistical reports; however, these data must be collected on a separate information sheet, not on the formal job application form. When a charge of discrimination has been filed, the respondent organization must retain all HR records relevant to the case until final disposition of the charge.

USING THE INTERNET

The poster shown in Highlights in HRM 5 may be downloaded from the EEOC web site. Go to the Student Resources at:

http://bohlander.swlearning.com

Posters explaining to individuals what their employment rights are and how to file complaints of discrimination have been developed by the EEOC and other administrative agencies. (See Highlights in HRM 5.) The law requires that employers display these posters and other federally required posters related to HRM in prominent places easily accessible to employees. HR employment offices, cafeterias, centrally located bulletin boards, and time clocks are popular locations. Posting requirements should not be taken lightly. For example, EEO posters show the time limits for filing a charge of discrimination. Failure to post these notices may be used as a basis for excusing the late filing of a discrimination charge.

Processing Discrimination Charges

charge form
A discrimination complaint filed with the EEOC by employees or job applicants

Employees or job applicants who believe they have been discriminated against may file a discrimination complaint, or **charge form,** with the EEOC. Filing a charge form initiates an administrative procedure that can be lengthy, time-consuming, and costly for the employer.[58] Both parties, the plaintiff (employee) and the defendant (organization), must be prepared to support their beliefs or actions. If litigation follows, employers will normally take an aggressive approach to defend their position.[59]

Figure 3.5 summarizes the process of filing a discrimination charge with the EEOC. Under the law, charges must be filed within 180 days (300 days in deferral states)[60] of the alleged unlawful practice. The processing of a charge includes notifying the employer that a charge of employment discrimination has been filed. Employers will receive a copy of the charge within ten days of filing.

In states that have FEP laws with appropriate enforcement machinery, the discrimination charge is deferred to the state agency for resolution before action is taken by the EEOC. The EEOC will accept the recommendation of the state agency because deferral states must comply with federal standards. If the state agency fails to resolve the complaint or if the sixty-day deferral period lapses, the case is given back to the EEOC for final investigation.

EEOC investigations are conducted by fully trained equal opportunity specialists (EOSs) who have extensive experience in investigative procedures, theories of discrimination, and relief and remedy techniques. The EOS will gather facts from both sides through telephone calls, letters and questionnaires, field visits, or jointly arranged meetings. While it is generally advisable for them to cooperate in EEOC

Highlights in HRM 5

EEOC Poster

Equal Employment Opportunity is THE LAW

Employers Holding Federal Contracts or Subcontracts

Applicants to and employees of companies with a Federal government contract or subcontract are protected under the following Federal authorities:

RACE, COLOR, RELIGION, SEX, NATIONAL ORIGIN

Executive Order 11246, as amended, prohibits job discrimination on the basis of race, color, religion, sex or national origin, and requires affirmative action to ensure equality of opportunity in all aspects of employment.

INDIVIDUALS WITH HANDICAPS

Section 503 of the Rehabilitation Act of 1973, as amended, prohibits job discrimination because of handicap and requires affirmative action to employ and advance in employment qualified individuals with handicaps who, with reasonable accommodation, can perform the essential functions of a job.

VIETNAM ERA AND SPECIAL DISABLED VETERANS

38 U.S.C. 4212 of the Vietnam Era Veterans Readjustment Assistance Act of 1974 prohibits job discrimination and requires affirmative action to employ and advance in employment qualified Vietnam era veterans and qualified special disabled veterans.

Any person who believes a contractor has violated its nondiscrimination or affirmative action obligations under the authorities above should contact immediately:

The Office of Federal Contract Compliance Programs (OFCCP), Employment Standards Administration, U.S. Department of Labor, 200 Constitution Avenue, N.W., Washington, D.C. 20210 or call (202) 523-9368, or an OFCCP regional or district office, listed in most telephone directories under U.S. Government, Department of Labor.

Private Employment, State and Local Governments, Educational Institutions

Applicants to and employees of most private employers, state and local governments, educational institutions, employment agencies and labor organizations are protected under the following Federal laws:

RACE, COLOR, RELIGION, SEX, NATIONAL ORIGIN

Title VII of the Civil Rights Act of 1964, as amended, prohibits discrimination in hiring, promotion, discharge, pay, fringe benefits, job training, classification, referral, and other aspects of employment, on the basis of race, color, religion, sex or national origin.

DISABILITY

The Americans with Disabilities Act of 1990, as amended, protects qualified applicants and employees with disabilities from discrimination in hiring, promotion, discharge, pay, job training, fringe benefits, classification, referral, and other aspects of employment on the basis of disability. The law also requires that covered entities provide qualified applicants and employees with disabilities with reasonable accommodations that do not impose undue hardship.

AGE

The Age Discrimination in Employment Act of 1967, as amended, protects applicants and employees 40 years of age or older from discrimination on the basis of age in hiring, promotion, discharge, compensation, terms, conditions or privileges of employment.

SEX (WAGES)

In addition to sex discrimination prohibited by Title VII of the Civil Rights Act (see above), the Equal Pay Act of 1963, as amended, prohibits sex discrimination in payment of wages to women and men performing substantially equal work in the same establishment.

Retaliation against a person who files a charge of discrimination, participates in an investigation, or opposes an unlawful employment practice is prohibited by all of these Federal laws.

If you believe that you have been discriminated against under any of the above laws, you immediately should contact:

The U.S. Equal Employment Opportunity Commission (EEOC), 1801 L Street, N.W., Washington, D.C. 20507 or an EEOC field office by calling toll free (800) 669-4000. For individuals with hearing impairments, EEOC's toll free TDD number is (800) 800-3302.

Programs or Activities Receiving Federal Financial Assistance

RACE, COLOR, NATIONAL ORIGIN, SEX

In addition to the protection of Title VII of the Civil Rights Act of 1964, Title VI of the Civil Rights Act prohibits discrimination on the basis of race, color or national origin in programs or activities receiving Federal financial assistance. Employment discrimination is covered by Title VI if the primary objective of the financial assistance is provision of employment, or where employment discrimination causes or may cause discrimination in providing services under such programs. Title IX of the Education Amendments of 1972 prohibits employment discrimination on the basis of sex in educational programs or activities which receive Federal assistance.

INDIVIDUALS WITH HANDICAPS

Section 504 of the Rehabilitation Act of 1973, as amended, prohibits employment discrimination on the basis of handicap in any program or activity which receives Federal financial assistance. Discrimination is prohibited in all aspects of employment against handicapped persons who, with reasonable accommodation, can perform the essential functions of a job.

If you believe you have been discriminated against in a program of any institution which receives Federal assistance, you should contact immediately the Federal agency providing such assistance.

★U.S. GOVERNMENT PRINTING OFFICE 1993-0-339-476

EEOC–P/E–1

Figure 3.5 Filing a Charge of Employment Discrimination

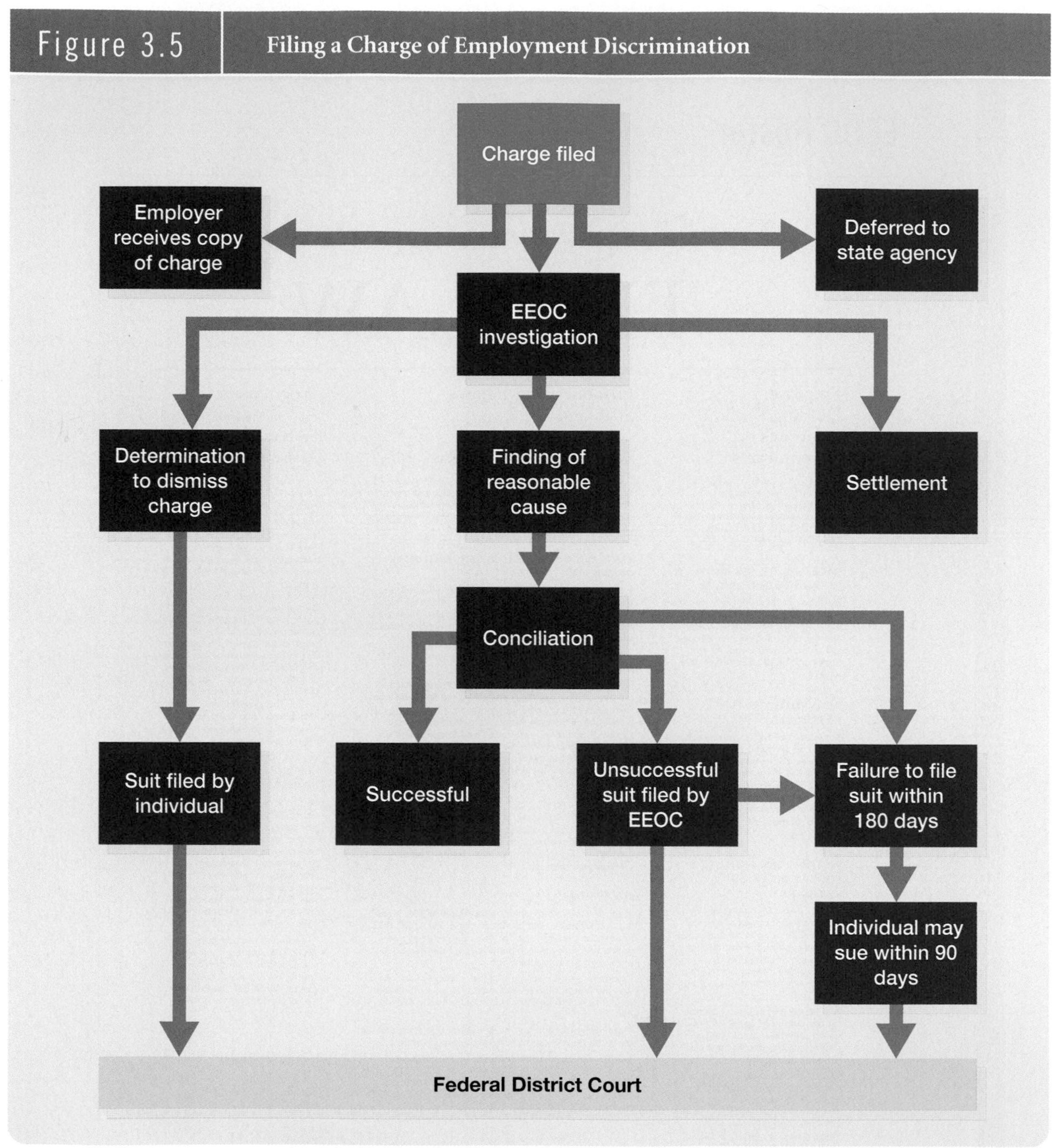

investigations, employers may legally resist the commission's efforts by refusing to submit documents or give relevant testimony. However, the EEOC may obtain this information through a court subpoena. Employers who then refuse to supply the information will face contempt-of-court charges.

Once the investigation is under way or completed, several decision points occur. First, the employer may offer a settlement to resolve the case without further investigation. If the offer is accepted, the case is closed. Second, the EEOC may find no violation of law and dismiss the charge. In this case, the charging party is sent a *right-to-sue notice,* which permits the individual to start private litigation, if he or she so desires, in federal court within ninety days. Third, if the EEOC finds "reasonable cause" of discrimination, the commission will attempt to conciliate (settle) the matter between the charging party and the employer. The conciliation process is a voluntary procedure and will not always lead to a settlement.

Employers should keep in mind that when the EEOC negotiates a settlement, it will attempt to obtain full remedial, corrective, and preventive relief. Back pay, reinstatement, transfers, promotions, seniority rights, bonuses, and other "make whole" perquisites of employment are considered appropriate remedies. These settlements can frequently be costly.

If the employer and the EEOC cannot reach a negotiated settlement, the commission has the power to prosecute the organization in court. However, this decision is made on a case-by-case basis and may depend on the importance of the issue. Failure of the EEOC to take court action or to resolve the charge in 180 days from filing permits employees to pursue litigation within 90 days after receiving a right-to-sue letter issued by the commission.[61]

Retaliation

Importantly, managers and supervisors must not retaliate against individuals who invoke their legal rights to file charges or to support other employees during EEOC proceedings.[62] Title VII of the Civil Rights Act states that an employer may not

> discriminate against any of his employees because the employee has opposed any unlawful employment practice, or because the employee has made a charge, testified, assisted, or participated in any manner in an investigation, proceedings, or hearing under this Act.

In one case, a pilot working for Ryan International Airlines was awarded $400,000 in damages when she was fired in violation of Title VII of the Civil Rights Act of 1964 for complaining about sex discrimination and harassment to her employer.[63] Retaliation can include any punitive action taken against employees who elect to exercise their legal rights before any EEO agency. These actions include discharge, demotion, salary reduction, reduced work responsibilities, and transfer to a less desirable job.[64]

Preventing Discrimination Charges

Both large and small employers understand that the foundation to preventing any form of discrimination is a comprehensive EEO policy. The Supreme Court's emphasis on the prevention and correction of discrimination means that employers that do not have an EEO policy are legally vulnerable. Antidiscrimination policy statements must be inclusive; they must cover all applicable laws and EEOC guidelines and contain practical illustrations of specific inappropriate behavior. For the policy to have value it must be widely disseminated to managers, supervisors, and all nonmanagerial employees. A complete policy will include specific sanctions for those found guilty of discriminatory behavior.

Since managers and supervisors are key to preventing and correcting discrimination, they, in particular, must be trained to understand employee rights and managerial obligations.[65] A comprehensive training program will include (1) the prohibitions covered in the various EEO statutes, (2) guidance on how to respond to complaints of discrimination, (3) procedures for investigating complaints (see Chapter 13), and (4) suggestions for remedying inappropriate behavior. Perhaps the ultimate key to preventing employment discrimination is for managers and supervisors to create an organizational climate in which the principles of dignity, respect, and the acceptance of a diverse workforce are expected.

Diversity Management: Affirmative Action

affirmative action
A policy that goes beyond equal employment opportunity by requiring organizations to comply with the law and correct past discriminatory practices by increasing the numbers of minorities and women in specific positions

Equal employment opportunity legislation requires managers to provide the same opportunities to all job applicants and employees regardless of race, color, religion, sex, national origin, or age. While EEO law is largely a policy of nondiscrimination, **affirmative action** requires employers to analyze their workforce and develop a plan of action to correct areas of past discrimination. Affirmative action is achieved by having organizations follow specific guidelines and goals to ensure that they have a balanced and representative workforce. To achieve these goals, employers must make a concerted effort to recruit, select, train, and promote members of protected classes. Employers must locate not only minority candidates who are qualified, but also those who, with a reasonable amount of training or physical accommodation, can be made to qualify for job openings.

Establishing Affirmative Action Programs

Employers establish affirmative action programs for several reasons. As noted in Figure 3.3, affirmative action programs are required by the OFCCP for employers with federal contracts greater than $50,000. The OFCCP provides regulations and suggestions for establishing affirmative action plans. Specifically, employers must (1) provide an organizational profile that graphically illustrates their workforce demographics, (2) establish goals and timetables for employment of underutilized protected classes, (3) develop actions and plans to reduce underutilization, including initiating proactive recruitment and selection methods, and (4) monitor progress of the entire affirmative action program.

reverse discrimination
The act of giving preference to members of protected classes to the extent that unprotected individuals believe they are suffering discrimination

Affirmative action programs may also be required by court order when an employer has been found guilty of past discrimination. Court-ordered programs will require the setting of hiring and promotion quotas along with stated timetables for compliance. Finally, many employers voluntarily develop their own affirmative action programs to ensure that protected-class members receive fair treatment in all aspects of employment. General Electric, the City of Portland, and Hilton Hotels use these programs as a useful way of monitoring the progress of employees while demonstrating good-faith employment effort. The EEOC recommends that organizations developing affirmative action programs follow specific steps, as shown in Highlights in HRM 6.

In pursuing affirmative action, employers may be accused of **reverse discrimination,** or giving preference to members of protected classes to the extent that unprotected individuals believe they are suffering discrimination. When these charges occur, organizations are caught between attempt-

USING THE INTERNET

For information on the Office of Federal Contract Compliance Programs (OFCCP), go to the Student Resources at:

http://bohlander.swlearning.com

Highlights in HRM 6

Basic Steps in Developing an Effective Affirmative Action Program

1. Issue a written equal employment opportunity policy and affirmative action commitment.
2. Appoint a top official with responsibility and authority to direct and implement the program.
3. Publicize the policy and affirmative action commitment.
4. Survey present minority and female employment by department and job classification.
5. Develop goals and timetables to improve utilization of minorities and women in each area where underutilization has been identified.
6. Develop and implement specific programs to achieve goals.
7. Establish an internal audit and reporting system to monitor and evaluate progress in each aspect of the program.
8. Develop supportive in-house and community programs.

Source: *Affirmative Action and Equal Employment: A Guidebook for Employers,* vol. 1 (Washington, DC: Equal Employment Opportunity Commission, 1974), 16–17.

ing to correct past discriminatory practices and handling present complaints from unprotected members alleging that HR policies are unfair. It is exactly this "catch-22" that has made affirmative action one of the most controversial issues of the past fifty years. Two highly publicized cases illustrate the controversy.

In *University of California Regents v Bakke* (1978), the Supreme Court settled one of the most famous reverse discrimination cases.[66] Allen Bakke, a white male, charged that the University of California at Davis was guilty of reverse discrimination by admitting minority-group members he believed were less qualified than he. The central issue before the Court was equal treatment under the law as guaranteed in the equal protection clause of the Fourteenth Amendment. The Court ruled that applicants must be evaluated on an individual basis, and race can be one factor used in the evaluation process as long as other competitive factors are considered. The Court stated that affirmative action programs were not illegal per se as long as rigid quota systems were not specified for different protected classes.

One year later the Supreme Court decided *United Steelworkers of America v Weber.*[67] In 1974 Kaiser Aluminum and its union, the United Steelworkers, had joined in a voluntary affirmative action program designed to increase the number of black workers in craft jobs at Kaiser's Louisiana plant. Brian Weber, a white production employee who was passed over for craft training in favor of a less-senior black worker, filed a suit charging violation of Title VII. The Supreme Court ruled against Weber, holding that under Title VII voluntary affirmative action programs are permissible where they attempt to eliminate racial imbalances in "traditionally segregated job categories." In *Weber,* the Supreme Court did not endorse all voluntary affirmative action programs, but it did give an important push to programs voluntarily implemented and designed to correct past racial imbalances.

Managing Diversity: Affirmative Action

Affirmative action is a highly emotional and controversial subject because affirmative action programs affect all employees regardless of gender, race, or ethnicity. At the core of the debate is the concern that affirmative action leads to preferential treatment and quotas for selected individuals and thus results in reverse discrimination against others. Additionally, affirmative action as a national priority has been challenged for the following reasons:

- Affirmative action has not consistently resulted in improvement of the employment status of protected groups.
- Individuals hired under affirmative action programs sometimes feel prejudged and assumed capable only of inferior performance, and, in fact, these individuals *are* sometimes viewed by others as "tokens."
- Affirmative action programs of either voluntary or forced compliance have failed to effectively assimilate protected classes into an organization's workforce.
- Preferences shown toward one protected class may create conflicts between other minority groups.

Judicial support for affirmative action as a worthy national goal has changed remarkably over the years.[68] For example, early support for affirmative action was demonstrated through the *Bakke* and *Weber* decisions. However, during the mid-1990s, federal courts increasingly restricted the use of race and ethnicity in awarding scholarships, determining college admissions, making layoff decisions, selecting employees, promoting employees, and awarding government contracts. Several important court cases illustrate this point.

In *Adarand Constructors v Peña* (1995), the court ruled that federal programs that use race or ethnicity as a basis for decision making must be strictly scrutinized to ensure that they promote "compelling" governmental interests.[69] In the majority opinion the Court declared that "strict scrutiny of all governmental racial classifications is essential" to distinguish between legitimate programs that redress past discrimination and programs that "are in fact motivated by illegitimate notions of racial inferiority or simple racial politics."

In a 1996 decision affecting admission standards at the University of Texas law school, the Court ruled in *Hopwood v State of Texas* that diversity could not constitute a competing state interest justifying racial preference in selection decisions.[70] The Court noted that the school could not discriminate "because there was no compelling justification under the Fourteenth Amendment or Supreme Court precedent for such conduct even if it was designed to correct perceived racial imbalance in the student body."

Then, in a landmark and highly significant 2003 affirmative action ruling, the Supreme Court held in *Grutter v Bollinger* that colleges and universities *can* consider an applicant's race as a factor in admission decisions.[71] The decision upheld an admission policy at the University of Michigan Law School in which officials considered an applicant's race along with other factors when making admission decisions.[72] Writing for the Court, Justice Sandra Day O'Connor noted that colleges and universities have compelling educational reasons for seeking a diverse student body in light of a growing diverse society and a global business environment. Justice O'Connor stated, "Effective participation by members of all racial and ethnic groups in the civil life of our nation is essential if the dream of one nation, indivisible, is to be realized."

The Supreme Court decision was supported by legal briefs filed by more than thirty companies such as GM, Microsoft, KPMG International, and Bank One.[73]

The future of affirmative action may rest not in voluntary programs or judicial decisions but in managerial attitudes that value diversity in the workforce. Managers who embrace a diverse workforce acknowledge individual employee differences and the contributions made by people of varied abilities. Organizations that approach diversity from a practical, business-oriented perspective (rather than a court-ordered affirmative action mandate) will employ and promote protected-class members as a means for developing competitive advantage. Viewed in this manner, greater workforce diversity will significantly enhance organizational performance through knowledge of diverse marketplaces and creative problem solving. For example, Michael Goldstein, chairman of the Toys "R" Us Children's Fund, supports both affirmative action and diversity because "our customers are not one group; they comprise all of America. It's important to be able to serve them." Eastman Kodak maintains that it is committed to diversity because the composition of its customer base and of the workforce is changing. For both of these organizations, commitment to the advantages of diversity automatically achieves the goals of affirmative action.[74]

SUMMARY

objective 1 Employment discrimination against blacks, Hispanics, women, and other groups has long been practiced by U.S. employers. Prejudice against minority groups is a major cause in their lack of employment gains. Government reports show that the wages and job opportunities of minorities typically lag behind those for whites.

objective 2 Effective management requires knowing the legal aspects of the employment relationship. Pertinent legislation includes the Equal Pay Act, Title VII of the Civil Rights Act of 1964, Age Discrimination in Employment Act, Equal Employment Opportunity Act of 1972, Pregnancy Discrimination Act, Americans with Disabilities Act, Civil Rights Act of 1991, and various executive orders. Employers are permitted to discriminate against selected protected classes when hiring preferences are a reasonable necessity, constituting a bona fide occupational qualification for normal business operation. The religious preferences of employees must be accommodated as required by law.

Sexual harassment is an area of particular importance to managers and supervisors. Extensive efforts should be made to ensure that both male and female employees are free from all forms of sexually harassing conduct. The Immigration Reform and Control Act was passed to control unauthorized immigration into the United States. The law requires managers to maintain various employment records, and they must not discriminate against job applicants or present employees because of national origin or citizenship status.

The *Uniform Guidelines on Employee Selection Procedures* is designed to help employers comply with federal prohibitions against employment practices that discriminate on the basis of race, color, religion, gender, or national origin. The *Uniform Guidelines* provides employers a framework for making legally enforceable employment decisions. Employers must be able to show that selection procedures are valid in predicting job performance.

objective 5 Adverse impact plays an important role in proving employment discrimination. Adverse impact means that an employer's employment practices result in the rejection of a significantly higher percentage of members of minority and other protected groups for some employment activity. When charges of discrimination are filed, plaintiffs bear the initial responsibility to show proof of employer discrimination. Once this requirement has been met, managers must defend their actions by showing the action taken was not discriminatory to any protected class.

objective 6 The United States court system continually interprets employment law, and managers must formulate organizational policy in response to court decisions. Violations of the law will invite discrimination charges from protected groups or self-initiated investigation from government agencies. *Griggs v Duke Power* and *Albemarle Paper Company v Moody* provided added importance to the *Uniform Guidelines*. *Oncale v Sundowner Offshore Services* and *TWA v Hardison* are instructive in the areas of sexual harassment and religious preference. Important cases in affirmative action include *University of California Regents v Bakke, United Steelworkers of America v Weber, Adarand Constructors v Peña, Hopwood v State of Texas*, and *Grutter v Bollinger*.

objective 7 To ensure that organizations comply with antidiscrimination legislation, the EEOC was established to monitor employers' actions. Employers subject to federal laws must maintain required records and report requested employment statistics where mandated. The EEOC maintains a complaint procedure for individuals who believe they have been discriminated against. Figure 3.5 illustrates the steps in filing a charge of employment discrimination.

objective 8 Affirmative action goes beyond providing equal employment opportunity to employees. Affirmative action requires employers to become proactive and correct areas of past discrimination. This is accomplished by employing protected classes for jobs in which they are underrepresented. The employer's goal is to have a balanced internal workforce representative of the employer's relevant labor market.

KEY TERMS

adverse impact
affirmative action
bona fide occupational qualification (BFOQ)
business necessity
charge form
disabled individual
disparate treatment
EEO-1 report
equal employment opportunity
fair employment practices (FEPs)
four-fifths rule
protected classes
reasonable accommodation
reverse discrimination
sexual harassment
Uniform Guidelines on Employee Selection Procedures
workforce utilization analysis

DISCUSSION QUESTIONS

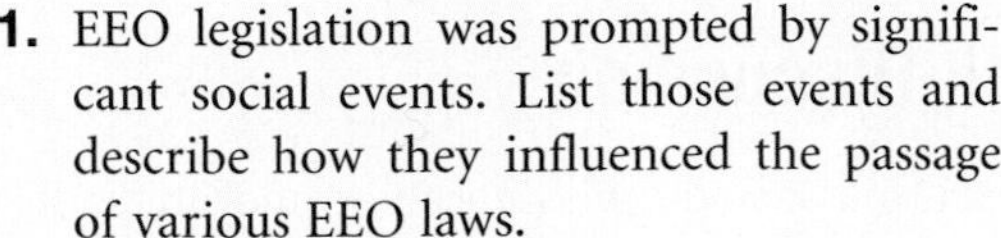

1. EEO legislation was prompted by significant social events. List those events and describe how they influenced the passage of various EEO laws.

2. Cite and describe the major federal laws and court decisions that affect the employment process of both large and small organizations.

3. After receiving several complaints of sexual harassment, the HR department of a city library decided to establish a sexual harassment policy. What should be included in the policy? How should it be implemented?

4. What is the *Uniform Guidelines on Employee Selection Procedures?* To whom do the guidelines apply? What do they cover?

5. Explain the difference between adverse impact and disparate treatment. Provide examples illustrating how adverse impact and disparate treatment discrimination can exist.

6. Throughout the chapter, specific court cases have been highlighted to signify their impact on shaping federal antidiscrimination policy. Identify these cases and explain their significance in defining employee or employer rights and duties.

7. As a marketing manager you have recently turned down Nancy Conrad for a position as sales supervisor. Nancy believes the denial was due to her gender and she has filed a sex discrimination charge with the EEOC. Explain the steps the EEOC will use to process the charge; include Nancy's options during the process.

8. Affirmative action is both a legal and emotional issue affecting employees and employers. Develop as many arguments as you can both supporting and opposing affirmative action as an employer policy. If you were asked to implement such a program, what steps would you follow?

BIZFLIX EXERCISES

Legally Blonde: Sexual Harassment

Review the earlier section "Sexual Harassment" before watching this scene from *Legally Blonde.* Several aspects of that discussion appear in the scene.

Elle Woods' (Reese Witherspoon) boyfriend, Warner Huntington III (Matthew Davis), wants to go to Harvard Law School instead of keeping their relationship alive. Elle pursues him vigorously by applying to and getting accepted to Harvard Law School. This is a charming comedy, dedicated to blonde women everywhere in the world. It is filled with stereotyping, giving many delightful twists to its surprise conclusion.

This scene comes from the "Poor Judgment" segment near the end of the film. It follows the successful use of Elle's hunch about key witness Enrique Salvatore (Greg Serano) in Brooke Windam's (Ali Larter) trial. The film continues after she leaves Professor Callahan's (Victor Garber) office. Elle sees Emmett (Luke Wilson) in the building lobby and tells him she is quitting the internship.

What to Watch for and Ask Yourself

- Does Professor Callahan sexually harass Elle? If yes, what is the evidence in these scenes?
- If these scenes show sexual harassment, what type of harassment is it? Quid pro quo harassment or hostile environment harassment?
- Did Elle behave appropriately or inappropriately in Professor Callahan's office?

HRM Experience

Sexual Harassment: A Frank Discussion

Over the past decade the problem of sexual harassment has captured the attention of all managers and employees. While it is widely known that sexual harassment is both unethical and illegal, the incidents of sexual harassment continue to plague business. Unfortunately, when these cases arise, they cause morale problems among employees, embarrassment to the organization, and costly legal damages. Consequently, all managers and supervisors play a central role in preventing sexual harassment complaints. It is important that managers understand the definition of sexual harassment, who is covered by sexual harassment guidelines, and how to prevent its occurrence. This skill-building exercise will provide you knowledge in each of these areas.

Assignment

1. Working in teams of female and male members, develop a list of behaviors that could be classified as quid pro quo harassment or hostile environment. Explore the possibility that some sexual harassing behaviors might be viewed differently by female and male employees. Give examples.
2. Many sexual harassment incidents go unreported. Fully discuss why this can occur and what might be done to reduce this problem.
3. The cornerstone to addressing sexual harassment is achieving organizational awareness through training. Develop a sexual harassment training program for a company of 250 employees that covers, at a minimum, the following: (1) who should attend the training sessions, (2) the content outline for the training program (the list of materials your team wants to teach), (3) specific examples to illustrate the training materials, and (4) how to investigate sexual harassment complaints.
4. This chapter will assist you with this assignment. You can obtain additional materials from EEOC offices and from various HR magazines.
5. Be prepared to present your training outline to other class members.

case study 1

You Be the Judge: Was the Discharge Legal?

Work-related charges often seen as justified by employers can lead to EEO court cases. Take, for example, the following case on disability discrimination.

Robert Johnson began working for CompTech in Glendale, Colorado, in 1999. His position, at the time of his discharge, was senior electrical technician. In 2003, Johnson was diagnosed with attention deficit disorder (ADD), a medical condition that caused him severe work stress and anxiety.

After a work reorganization plan implemented by CompTech in 2004, Johnson was placed under a new manager, after which he experienced increased levels of workplace stress and tension. According to Johnson, his new manager's supervisory style was "harsh, autocratic, and very demanding." Johnson requested a transfer to accommodate his disability. The request was supported by a letter from his personal physician noting that Johnson should be assigned to "a more relaxing work setting." The transfer and accommodation were not granted.

On June 14, 2004, Johnson was required to attend a meeting to discuss important design changes to the company's core products. Johnson missed the meeting due to "personal reasons," which he refused to discuss with his manager. On June 15, 2004, after his manager discussed the missed meeting with members of human resources, Johnson was terminated for insubordination. On June 26, 2004, Johnson filed a court case claiming both disability discrimination and retaliatory discharge.

QUESTIONS

1. In your opinion, does Johnson have a viable claim of disability discrimination? Explain. Does he have a claim of retaliatory discharge? Explain.
2. Does the fact that Johnson refused to discuss his personal reasons for missing the meeting affect this case?
3. Do you believe Johnson was insubordinate in this case? Explain.
4. How do you believe the court decided this case? What might be the basis for the court's decision?

Source: This case is adapted from a 2003 circuit court decision. All names are fictitious.

case study 2

Misplaced Affections: Discharge for Sexual Harassment

Peter Lewiston was terminated on July 15, 2004, by the governing board of the Pine Circle Unified School District (PCUSD) for violation of the district's sexual harassment policy. Prior to Lewiston's termination he was a senior maintenance employee with an above-average work record who had worked for the PCUSD for eleven years. He had been a widower since 1998 and was described by his co-workers as a friendly, outgoing, but lonely individual. Beverly Gilbury was a fifth-grade teacher working in the district's Advanced Learning Program. She was 28 years old and married, and had worked for PCUSD for six years. At the time of the incidents, Lewiston and Gilbury both worked at the Simpson Elementary School, where their relationship was described as "cooperative." The following sequence of events was reported separately by Lewiston and Gilbury during the district's investigation of this sexual harassment case.

Gilbury reported that her relationship with Lewiston began to change during the last month of the 2003-2004 school year. She believed that Lewiston was paying her more attention and that his behavior was "out of the ordinary" and "sometimes weird." He began spending more time in her classroom talking with the children and with her. At the time she didn't say anything to Lewiston because "I didn't want to hurt his feelings since he is a nice, lonely, older man." However, on May 25, when

Lewiston told Gilbury that he was "very fond" of her and that she had "very beautiful eyes," she replied, "Remember, Peter, we're just friends." For the remainder of the school year there was little contact between them; however, when they did see each other, Lewiston seemed "overly friendly" to her.

June 7, 2004. On the first day of summer school, Gilbury returned to school to find a dozen roses and a card from Lewiston. The card read, "Please forgive me for thinking you could like me. I played the big fool. Yours always, P.L." Later in the day Lewiston asked Gilbury to lunch. She replied, "It's been a long time since anyone sent me roses, but I can't go to lunch. We need to remain just friends." Gilbury told another teacher that she was uncomfortable about receiving the roses and card and that Lewiston wouldn't leave her alone. She expressed concern that Lewiston might get "more romantic" with her.

June 8, 2004. Gilbury arrived at school to find another card from Lewiston. Inside was a handwritten note that read, "I hope you can someday return my affections for you. I need you so much." Later in the day Lewiston again asked her to lunch and she declined saying, "I'm a happily married woman." At the close of the school day, when Gilbury went to her car, Lewiston suddenly appeared. He asked to explain himself but Gilbury became agitated and shouted, "I have to leave right now." Lewiston reached inside the car, supposedly to pat her shoulder, but touched her head instead. She believed he meant to stroke her hair. He stated that he was only trying to calm her down. She drove away, very upset.

June 9, 2004. Gilbury received another card and a lengthy letter from Lewiston, stating that he was wrong in trying to develop a relationship with her and he hoped they could still remain friends. He wished her all happiness with her family and job.

June 11, 2004. Gilbury obtained from the Western Justice Court an injunction prohibiting sexual harassment by Lewiston. Shortly thereafter Lewiston appealed the injunction. A notice was mailed to Gilbury giving the dates of the appeal hearing. The notice stated in part, "If you fail to appear, the injunction may be vacated and the petition dismissed." Gilbury failed to appear at the hearing and the injunction was set aside. Additionally, on June 11 she had filed with the district's EEOC officer a sexual harassment complaint against Lewiston. After the investigation the district concluded that Lewiston's actions created an "extremely sexually hostile" environment for Gilbury. The investigative report recommended dismissal based upon the grievous conduct of Lewiston and the initial injunction granted by the Justice Court.

QUESTIONS

1. Evaluate the conduct of Peter Lewiston against the EEOC's definition of sexual harassment.
2. Should the intent or motive behind Lewiston's conduct be considered when deciding sexual harassment activities? Explain.
3. If you were the district's EEOC officer, what would you conclude? What disciplinary action, if any, would you take?

Source: This case is adapted from an actual experience. The background information is factual. All names are fictitious.

NOTES AND REFERENCES

1. Alison Stein Wellner, "Costco Piercing Case Puts a New Face on the Issue of Wearing Garb at Work," *Workforce Management* 84, no. 6 (June 2005): 76–78. See also Paul Salvatore and Andrew M. Gutterman, "The Risk of Intentional Torts," *HRMagazine* 48, no. 8 (August 2003): 109–14.
2. Lisa Takeuchi and Cullen Wilson, "Wal-Mart's Gender Gap," *Time*, July 5, 2004, 44. See also Melissa Nelson, "Wal-Mart Sex-Bias Case May Reshape Retail World," *The Arizona Republic*, June 28, 2004, D-1; Douglas P. Shuit, "Wal-Mart Women Win a Round," *Workforce* 83, no. 7 (July 2004): 21; and Wendy Zeller, "A Wal-Mart Settlement: What It Might Look Like," *Business Week*, July 15, 2004, 48.
3. Stanley Holmes, "A New Black Eye for Boeing?" *Business Week*, April 26, 2004, 90–92; Stanley Holmes and Mike France, "Cover-up at Boeing?" *Business Week*, June 28, 2004, 84–90.
4. "Jury Awards $1.55 Million to Waitresses in Florida Case," *Fair Employment Practices*, Bureau of National Affairs, Inc., 38, no. 976 (July 3, 2004): 84.
5. Roger O. Crockett, "Putting Words to the Dream," *Business Week*, July 12, 2004, 16. See also William C. Symonds, "A Bittersweet Birthday," *Business Week*, May 17, 2004, 60.
6. "Current Labor Statistics," *Monthly Labor Review* 127, no. 5 (May 2004): Table 6.
7. Bureau of Labor Statistics, "Median Usual Weekly Earnings of Full-Time Wage and Salary Workers by Selected Characteristics, Quarterly Average Not Adjusted," *Labor Force Statistics from Current Population Survey*, Fourth Quarter 2004, http://www.bls.gov/cps/.
8. Robert J. Grossman, "Race in the Workplace," *HRMagazine* 45, no. 3 (March 2002): 43.
9. "'Supervisor' May Be Broadly Defined in Employer Liability," *HRFocus* 80, no. 6 (June 2003): 2.
10. Jathan Janove, "The Faragher/Ellerth Decision Tree," *HRMagazine* 48, no. 9 (September 2003): 149–155.
11. For a practical overview of EEO law, see David J. Walsh, *Employment Law for Human Resource Practice* (Mason, OH: South-Western, 2004).
12. Aaron Bernstein, "Women's Pay: Why the Gap Remains a Chasm," *Business Week*, June 14, 2004, 58. See also "Reasons for Gender Pay Gap Still Unclear," *HRFocus* 81, no. 2 (February 2004): 12.
13. Patrick Mirza, "A Bias That's Skin Deep," *HRMagazine* 48, no. 12 (December 2003): 63–67.
14. "EEOC Guidance on National Origin Bias," *HRFocus* 80, no. 1 (January 2003): 2. Information on national origin guidelines is available on the EEOC's web site at http://www.eeoc.gov.
15. For an overview of EEO law, see David P. Twomey, *Employment Discrimination Law: A Manager's Guide*, 6th ed. (Mason, OH: South-Western, 2005).
16. Patricia Digh, "Religion in the Workplace: Making a Good-Faith Effort to Accommodate," *HRMagazine* 43, no. 13 (December 1998): 85–91.
17. *TWA v Hardison*, 432 U.S. 63 (1977).
18. Elizabeth Becker and Debo Sarkar, "Look Before You RIF: Managing the Risk of ADA Collective Action," *Labor Law Journal* 54, no. 2 (Summer 2003): 101–107. See also Peter H. Wingate, George C. Thornton III, Kelly S. McIntyre, and Jennifer H. Frame, "Organizational Downsizing and Age Discrimination Litigation: The Influence of Personal Practices and Statistical Evidence on Litigation Outcomes," *Law and Human Behavior* 27, no. 1 (February 2003): 87–105.
19. "Age-Based Comments Proof of Discrimination," *Workforce Management* 83, no. 2 (February 2002): 16.
20. *The Americans with Disabilities Act: A Primer for Small Business* contains examples, tips, and do's and don'ts. Published by the EEOC, the handbook explains who is protected, how to avoid mistakes during interviews, when employers may ask questions about a medical condition, how to address safety issues, reasonable accommodation obligations, and tax incentives for businesses that hire and retain individuals with disabilities. It's available on the Web or in printed format. Call 202-663-4900 or go to http://www.eeoc.gov.
21. According to the ADA, an employer is not required to retain an employee who presents a "direct threat," implying a significant risk of substantial harm to the health and safety of the individual or others that cannot be eliminated or reduced by reasonable accommodation. Also, some court cases have held that an employee with a psychiatric disability is not a qualified individual because he or she cannot perform the essential functions of the job.
22. Gina Gupta Srivastava, "'Stress' Does Not Equal 'Duress'," *HRMagazine* 49, no. 4 (April 2004): 127.
23. *Toyota Motors v Williams*, 122 S.Ct. 681 (2002).
24. "How To Cope with the ADA's 'Reasonableness' Requirement," *HRFocus* 79, no. 8 (August 2002): 3–4.
25. "Advantages and Opportunities in Hiring Disabled Workers," *HRFocus* 80, no. 6 (June 2003): 11–13.
26. Jim Barthold, "Waiting in the Wings," *HRMagazine* 49, no. 4 (April 2004): 89–95. The Department of Labor's Office of Disability Employment Policy has a database of college students and recent graduates with disabilities who are seeking jobs (http://www.wrpjobs.com or (202) 693-7880).

27. "Know the Rights of Reservists Who Are Called to Duty," *HRFocus* 80, no. 5 (May 2003): 10–13. Find additional information on the law at the USERRA Advisor at the Department of Labor web site (http://www.dol.gov/elaws).
28. *Nassau County, Florida v Arline*, 480 U.S. 273, 43 FEP 81 (1987).
29. As currently defined, an "otherwise qualified" employee is one who can perform the "essential functions" of the job under consideration.
30. To learn more about fair employment practice agencies, go to http://www.eeoc.gov. Under the title "Employers & EEOC," click on "Small Businesses," then click on "State and Local Agencies."
31. Luci Scott, "Dial Settles Case for $10 Mil," *Arizona Republic*, April 30, 2003, D1.
32. EEOC charge statistics can be found at http://www.eeoc.gov. EEOC figures do not include the thousands of sexual harassment incidents not reported to governmental agencies or complaints reported to employers and settled internally through in-house complaint procedures.
33. *Guidelines on Discrimination Because of Sex*, 29 C.F.R. Sec. 1604.11(a) (1955).
34. *Guidelines on Discrimination*, Sec. 1605.11(a). See also Jathan W. Janove, "Sexual Harassment and the Three Big Surprises," *HRMagazine* 46, no. 11 (November 2001): 123–26.
35. Paradise Valley Unified School District N. 69, Phoenix, Arizona.
36. "Obscene Spam Has Potential to Create Hostile Environment," *Bureau of National Affairs*, May 22, 2004, 64–65.
37. Gillian Flynn, "Third-Party Sexual Harassment: Commonplace and Laden with Liability," *Workforce* 79, no. 11 (November 2000): 88–92.
38. *Oncale v Sundowner Offshore Services, Inc.*, 72 PED ¶45, 175; WL 88039 (U.S. 1998).
39. Jon D. Bible, "Same-Sex Sexual Harassment: When Does a Harasser Act 'Because of Sex'?" *Labor Law Journal* 53, no. 1 (Spring 2002): 3–10.
40. Jonathan A. Segal, "HR as Judge, Jury, Prosecutor and Defender," *HRMagazine* 46, no. 10 (October 2001): 141–52.
41. Amy Oppenheimer, "Investigating Workplace Harassment and Discrimination," *Employee Relations Law Journal* 29, no. 4 (Spring 2004): 56–68.
42. Arthur Gross-Schaefer, Renée Florsheim, and Judi Pannetier, "The Swinging Pendulum: Moving from Sexual Harassment to Respectful Workplace Relationships," *Employee Relations Law Journal* 29, no. 2 (Fall 2003): 50–67. See also Laura A. Reese and Karen E. Lindenberg, "The Importance of Training on Sexual Harassment Policy Outcomes," *Review of Public Personnel Administration* 23, no. 3 (September 2003): 175–91.
43. Richard Lacayo, "For Better or Worse?" *Time*, March 8, 2004, 27–33.
44. "Sexual Orientation: The Latest Diversity Challenge," *HRFocus* 79, no. 6 (June 2002): 3–4.
45. Cliff Edwards, "Coming Out in Corporate America," *Business Week*, December 15, 2003, 64–72.
46. Chuck Bartels, "Wal-Mart Stores Raided Nationwide," *The* [Hemet, California] *Press-Enterprise*, Friday, October 24, 2003, C-10.
47. U.S. Department of Justice, Immigration and Naturalization Service, *Handbook for Employers: Instructions for Completing Form I-9* (Washington, DC: U.S. Government Printing Office, 1987).
48. Equal Employment Opportunity Commission, Civil Service Commission, Department of Labor, and Department of Justice, Adoption by Four Agencies of *Uniform Guidelines on Employee Selection Procedures* (1978), as reproduced in the *Federal Register* 43, no. 166 (August 25, 1978): 38290–315. Discussion relating to the adoption of the *Uniform Guidelines* by four agencies comprises several pages. The guidelines themselves are published on pages 38295–309. Further clarification and expansion on the guidelines may be found in the *Federal Register* 44, no. 43 (March 2, 1979): 11996–12009.
49. David Twomey, *Labor and Employment Law*, 12th ed. (Mason, OH: South-Western, 2004).
50. *Uniform Guidelines*, Sec. 3A.
51. *Uniform Guidelines*, Sec. 40. Adverse impact need not be considered for groups that constitute less than 2 percent of the relevant labor force.
52. *Hazelwood School District v United States*, 433 U.S. 299, 15 FEP 1 (1977).
53. *McDonnell Douglas Corp. v Green*, 411 U.S. 792, 80 (1973).
54. *Griggs v Duke Power Company*, 401 U.S. 424 (1971).
55. *Albemarle Paper Company v Moody*, 422 U.S. 405 (1975).
56. The primary web site for the EEOC is http://www.eeoc.gov. This web site contains a wealth of information about the EEOC including the agency's history and administration, how discrimination charges are filed and processed, training and outreach programs, litigation statistics, and various pamphlets and posters offered free of charge to interested parties.
57. "EEOC Proposes Changes to Employer Reporting Form," *Fair Employment Practices* 39, no. 975: 78.
58. Robert J. Grossman, "How Will You Be Treated by the EEOC?" *HRMagazine* 48, no. 12 (December 2003): 69–73.
59. Timothy S. Bland, "Anatomy of an Employment Lawsuit," *HRMagazine* 46, no. 3 (March 2001): 145–54.
60. A *deferral state* is one in which the state EEOC office complies with minimum operating guidelines established by the federal agency. In a deferral state, discrimination charges filed with the federal EEOC office will be deferred to the state agency for investigation and determination. If the state agency is unwilling or unable to resolve the complaint in a specified time period,

the complaint is referred back to the federal EEOC office for final disposition.

61. Carol T. Kulik, Elissa L. Perry, and Molly B. Pepper, "Here Comes the Judge: The Influence of Judge Personal Characteristics on Federal Sexual Harassment Case Outcomes," *Law and Human Behavior* 27, no. 1 (February 2003): 69–85.
62. Wilfred J. Benoit, Jr., and James W. Negle, "Retaliation Claims," *Employee Relations Law Journal* 29, no. 3 (Winter 2003): 13–72.
63. "Seventh Circuit Affirms $400,000 Verdict for Female Pilot Fired after Complaint Letter," *Fair Employment Practices* 38, no. 953 (September 2003): 115.
64. Alan L. Rupe, "The Life Cycle of the 'Twofer,'" *Workplace Management* 83, no. 6 (June 2004): 16–17.
65. Sue K. Willman, "The New Law of Training," *HRMagazine* 49, no. 5 (May 2004): 115–118.
66. *University of California Regents v Bakke*, 438 U.S. 265 (1978).
67. *United Steelworkers of America v Weber*, 443 U.S. 193 (1979).
68. Kenneth A. Kovach, David A. Kravitz, and Allen A. Hughes, "Affirmative Action: How Can We Be So Lost When We Don't Even Know Where We Are Going?" *Labor Law Journal* 55, no. 1 (Spring 2004): 53–60.
69. *Adarand Constructors v Peña*, 515 U.S. 200, 67 FEP 1828 (1995).
70. *Hopwood v State of Texas*, 78 F. 3d 932 (5th Cir. 1996).
71. *Grutter v Bollinger*, 123 S.Ct. 2325 (2003).
72. "Court Preserves Affirmative Action," *The Wall Street Journal Online*, June 24, 2003, http://www.wsj.com. See also Jan Crawford Greenburg, "High Court Backs Affirmative Action," *The Arizona Republic*, June 24, 2003, A-1.
73. Lisa E. Chang, "*Grutter v Bollinger*, et al.: Affirmative Action's Lessons for the Private Employer," *Employer Relations Law Journal* 30, no. 1 (Summer 2004): 3–11.
74. Jennifer Schramm, "Acting Affirmatively," *HRMagazine* 48, no. 9 (September 2003): 192.

appendix

Determining Adverse Impact:
The Four-Fifths Rule

Employers can determine adverse impact by using the method outlined in the interpretive manual for the *Uniform Guidelines on Employee Selection Procedures.*

A. Calculate the rate of selection for each group (divide the number of people selected from a group by the number of total applicants from that group).

B. Observe which group has the highest selection.

C. Calculate the impact ratios by comparing the selection rate for each group with that of the highest group (divide the selection rate for a group by the selection rate for the highest group).

D. Observe whether the selection rate for any group is substantially less (usually less than four-fifths, or 80 percent) than the selection rate for the highest group. If it is, adverse impact is indicated in most circumstances.

Example

	JOB APPLICANTS	**NUMBER HIRED**	**SELECTION RATE PERCENT HIRED**
Step A	Whites 100	52	52/100 = 52%
	Blacks 50	14	14/50 = 28%
Step B	The group with the highest selection rate is whites, 52 percent.		
Step C	Divide the black selection rate (28 percent) by the white selection rate (52 percent). The black rate is 53.8 percent of the white rate.		
Step D	Since 53.8 percent is less than four-fifths, or 80 percent, adverse impact is indicated.		

Source: Adoption of Questions and Answers to Clarify and Provide a Common Interpretation of the *Uniform Guidelines on Employee Selection Procedures, Federal Register* 44, no. 43 (March 2, 1979): 11998.

ANSWERS TO HIGHLIGHTS IN HRM 1

1. Yes
2. False
3. No
4. Merit, seniority, incentive pay plans
5. Yes
6. Yes, if no reasonable accommodation can be made
7. No
8. Yes, except if under a court order
9. False
10. True

chapter 4

Job Analysis, Employee Involvement, and Flexible Work Schedules

After studying this chapter, you should be able to

Discuss the relationship between job requirements and the performance of HRM functions.

Indicate the methods by which job analysis typically is completed.

Identify and explain the various sections of job descriptions.

Provide examples illustrating the various factors that must be taken into account in designing a job.

Discuss the various job characteristics that motivate employees.

Describe the different group techniques used to maximize employee contributions.

Differentiate and explain the different adjustments in work schedules.

Organizations are "reengineering" themselves in an attempt to become more effective. Companies such as Samsung, United Technologies, and Sports Authority are breaking into smaller units and getting flatter. There is emphasis on smaller scale, less hierarchy, fewer layers, and more decentralized work units. As organizational reshaping takes place, managers want employees to operate more independently and flexibly to meet customer demands. To do this, they require that decisions be made by the people who are closest to the information and who are directly involved in the product or service delivered. The objective is to develop jobs and basic work units that are adaptable enough to thrive in a world of high-velocity change.

In this chapter, we will discuss how jobs can be designed so as to best contribute to the objectives of the organization and at the same time satisfy the needs of the employees who are to perform them. Clearly, the duties and responsibilities present in jobs greatly influence employee productivity, job satisfaction, and employment retention.[1] Therefore, the value of job analysis, which defines clearly and precisely the requirements of each job, will be stressed. We will emphasize that these job requirements provide the foundation for making objective and legally defensible decisions in managing human resources. The chapter concludes by reviewing several innovative job design and employee contribution techniques that increase job satisfaction while improving organizational performance. Teamwork and the characteristics of successful teams are highlighted. Stacy Sullivan, director of HR at Google, notes that "the work environment and the sense of team spirit have become a critical job element."[2]

Relationship of Job Requirements and HRM Functions

job
A group of related activities and duties

position
The different duties and responsibilities performed by only one employee

job family
A group of individual jobs with similar characteristics

job specification
A statement of the needed knowledge, skills, and abilities of the person who is to perform the job

A **job** consists of a group of related activities and duties. Ideally, the duties of a job should consist of natural units of work that are similar and related. They should be clear and distinct from those of other jobs to minimize misunderstanding and conflict among employees and to enable employees to recognize what is expected of them. For some jobs, several employees may be required, each of whom will occupy a separate position. A **position** consists of different duties and responsibilities performed by only one employee. In a city library, for example, four employees (four positions) may be involved in reference work, but all of them have only one job (reference librarian). Where different jobs have similar duties and responsibilities, they may be grouped into a **job family** for purposes of recruitment, training, compensation, or advancement opportunities.

Recruitment

Before they can find capable employees for an organization, recruiters need to know the job specifications for the positions they are to fill.[3] A **job specification** is a statement of the knowledge, skills, and abilities required of the person performing the job. In the HR department for the City of Mesa, Arizona, the job specification for senior HR analyst includes the following:

1. Graduation from a four-year college with major course work (minimum fifteen hours) in human resources management
2. Three to five years' experience in employee classification and compensation or selection or recruitment
3. Two years' experience in developing/improving job-related compensation and testing instruments and procedures[4]

Because job specifications establish the qualifications required of applicants for a job opening, they serve an essential role in the recruiting function. These qualifications typically are contained in the notices of job openings. Whether posted on organizational bulletin boards or HRIS Internet sites or included in help-wanted advertisements or employment agency listings, job specifications provide a basis for attracting qualified applicants and discourage unqualified ones.

Selection

job description
A statement of the tasks, duties, and responsibilities of a job to be performed

In addition to job specifications, managers and supervisors use job descriptions to select employees and orient them to jobs. A **job description** is a statement of the tasks, duties, and responsibilities of a job. (See "Job Descriptions" later in this chapter.)

In the past, job specifications used as a basis for selection sometimes bore little relation to the duties to be performed under the job description. Examples of such nonjob-related specifications abounded. Applicants for the job of laborer were required to have a high school diploma. Firefighters were required to be at least six feet tall. And applicants for skilled craft positions—plumbers, electricians, machinists—were required to be male. These kinds of job specifications discriminated against members of certain protected classes, many of whom were excluded from these jobs.

Since the landmark *Griggs v Duke Power* case and the Civil Rights Act of 1991 (see Chapter 3), employers must be able to show that the job specifications used in selecting employees for a particular job relate specifically to the duties of that job. An organization must be careful to ensure that managers with job openings do not hire employees on the basis of "individualized" job requirements that satisfy personal whims but bear little relation to successful job performance. In one case known to the authors, a company desired to hire only tall salespeople—male or female—on the assumption that tall individuals presented a more authoritative stature.

Training and Development

Any discrepancies between the knowledge, skills, and abilities (often referred to as KSAs) demonstrated by a jobholder and the requirements contained in the description and specification for that job provide clues to training needs. Also, career development as a part of the training function is concerned with preparing employees for advancement to jobs where their capacities can be utilized to the fullest extent possible. The formal qualification requirements set forth in high-level jobs indicate how much more training and development are needed for employees to advance to those jobs.

Performance Appraisal

The requirements contained in the description of a job provide the criteria for evaluating the performance of the holder of that job. The results of performance appraisal may reveal, however, that certain requirements established for a job are not completely valid. As we have already stressed, these criteria must be specific and job-related. If the criteria used to evaluate employee performance are vague and not job-related, employers may find themselves being charged with unfair discrimination.

Compensation Management

In determining the rate to be paid for performing a job, the relative worth of the job is one of the most important factors. This worth is based on what the job demands of an employee in terms of skill, effort, and responsibility, as well as the conditions and hazards under which the work is performed. The systems of job evaluation by which this worth may be measured are discussed in Chapter 9.

Job Analysis

job analysis
The process of obtaining information about jobs by determining the duties, tasks, or activities of jobs

Job analysis is sometimes called the cornerstone of HRM because the information it collects serves so many HRM functions. **Job analysis** is the process of obtaining information about jobs by determining the duties, tasks, or activities of those jobs.[5] The procedure involves systematically investigating jobs by following a number of predetermined steps specified in advance of the study.[6] When completed, job analysis results in a written report summarizing the information obtained from the analysis of twenty or thirty individual job tasks or activities.[7] HR managers use these data to develop job descriptions and job specifications. These documents, in turn, are used to perform and enhance the different HR functions such as the development of performance appraisal criteria or the content of training classes. The ultimate purpose of job analysis is to improve organizational performance and productivity. Figure 4.1 illustrates how job analysis is performed, including the functions for which it is used.

As contrasted with job design, which reflects subjective opinions about the ideal requirements of a job, job analysis is concerned with objective and verifiable information about the actual requirements of a job. The job descriptions and job specifications developed through job analysis should be as accurate as possible if they are to be of value to those who make HRM decisions. These decisions may involve any of the HR functions—from recruitment to termination of employees.

Job Analysis and Essential Job Functions

It should be emphasized that a major goal of modern job analysis is to help the organization establish the *job-relatedness* of its selection and performance requirements. Job analysis helps both large and small employers meet their legal duty under EEO law. Section 14.C.2 of the *Uniform Guidelines* states: "There shall be a job analysis which includes an analysis of the important work behaviors required for successful performance. . . . Any job analysis should focus on work behavior(s) and the tasks associated with them." (The *Uniform Guidelines* are discussed more fully in Chapter 3.)

The passage of the Americans with Disabilities Act (ADA) also had a marked impact on the process of job analysis. Specifically, when preparing job descriptions and job specifications managers and supervisors must adhere to the legal mandates

Figure 4.1 The Process of Job Analysis

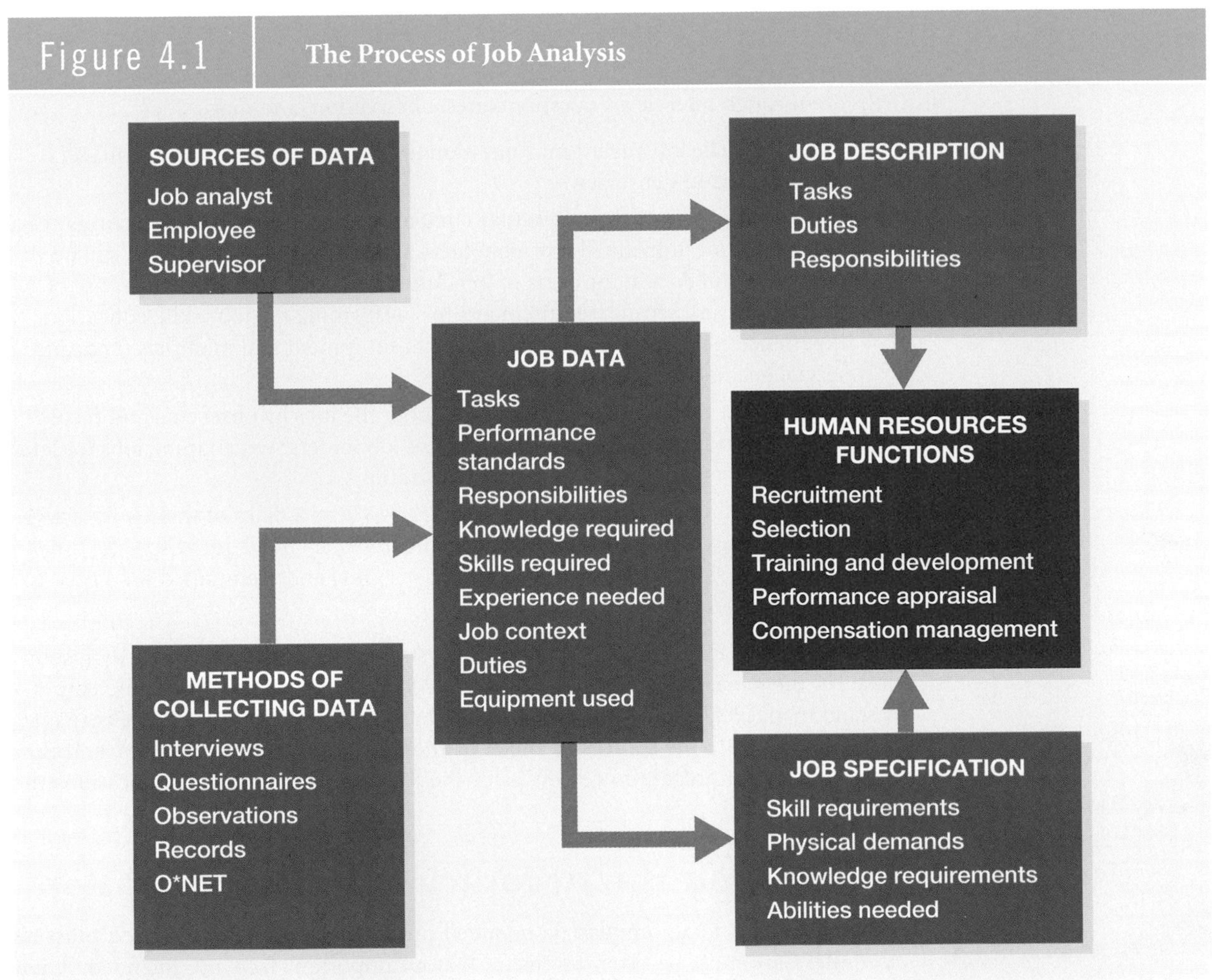

of the ADA. The act requires that job duties and responsibilities be *essential functions* for job success. The purpose of essential functions is to help match and accommodate human capabilities to job requirements. For example, if the job requires the jobholder to read extremely fine print, to climb ladders, or to memorize stock codes, these physical and mental requirements should be stated within the job description. Section 1630.2(n) of the act gives three guidelines for rendering a job function essential: (1) the reason that the position exists is to perform the function, (2) a limited number of employees are available among whom the performance of the function may be distributed, and (3) the function may be highly specialized, requiring needed expertise or abilities to complete the job.[8] Managers who write job descriptions and job specifications in terms of essential functions reduce the risk of discriminating on the basis of a disability. Remember also that once essential functions for a job are defined, the organization is legally required to make a reasonable accommodation to the disability of the individual.

Gathering Job Information

Job data may be obtained in several ways. The more common methods of analyzing jobs are through interviews, questionnaires, observation, and diaries.

- *Interviews.* The job analyst may question individual employees and managers about the job under review.
- *Questionnaires.* The job analyst may circulate carefully prepared questionnaires to be filled out individually by jobholders and managers. These forms will be used to obtain data in the areas of job duties and tasks performed, purpose of the job, physical setting, requirements for performing the job (skill, education, experience, physical and mental demands), equipment and materials used, and special health and safety concerns.
- *Observation.* The job analyst may learn about the jobs by observing and recording on a standardized form the activities of jobholders. Videotaping jobs for later study is an approach used by some organizations.
- *Diaries.* Jobholders themselves may be asked to keep a diary of their work activities during an entire work cycle. Diaries are normally filled out at specific times of the work shift (such as every half hour or hour) and maintained for a two- to four-week period.

Although HR specialists, called job analysts, are the personnel primarily responsible for the job analysis program, they usually enlist the cooperation of the employees and managers in the departments where jobs are being analyzed. These managers and employees are the sources of much of the information about the jobs, and they may be asked to prepare rough drafts of the job descriptions and specifications the job analysts need.

Controlling the Accuracy of Job Information

If job analysis is to accomplish its intended purpose, the job data collected must be accurate. Care must be taken to ensure that all important facts are included. A job analyst should be alert for employees who tend to exaggerate the difficulty of their jobs in order to inflate their egos and their paychecks. When interviewing employees or reviewing their questionnaires, the job analyst must look for any responses that do not agree with other facts or impressions the analyst has received. Furthermore, when job information is collected from employees, a representative group of individuals should be surveyed. For example, the results of one study indicated that the information obtained from job analysis was related to race. In another study, the experience level of job incumbents influenced job analysis outcomes.

A job analyst who doubts the accuracy of information provided by employees should obtain additional information from them, from their managers, or from other individuals who are familiar with or perform the same job. It is common practice to have the descriptions for each job reviewed by the jobholders and their managers. The job description summaries contained in O*NET, compiled by the U.S. Department of Labor, can also serve as a basis for the job analyst's review.

O*NET and Job Analysis

For many years the U.S. Department of Labor published the *Dictionary of Occupational Titles,* commonly referred to as the *DOT.* This book contained standardized

USING THE INTERNET

To explore the Department of Labor's new O*NET database, including how to convert from the *DOT* to O*NET, go to the Student Resources at:

http://bohlander.swlearning.com

and comprehensive descriptions of about 20,000 jobs. The purpose of the *DOT* was to group occupations into a systematic occupational classification structure based on interrelationships of job tasks and requirements. The *DOT* helped bring about a great degree of uniformity in the job titles and descriptions used by employers nationwide.

The Department of Labor has replaced the *DOT* with the O*NET online database.[9] The O*NET database includes all occupations from the *DOT* plus an update of more than 3,500 additional occupations. The database job descriptors include skill abilities, knowledge, tasks, work activities, and experience level requirements. Importantly, in order to remain current with occupational change, the O*NET program collects and publishes data continuously, a feature not available with the old *DOT*. The O*NET database is useful for a variety of HR activities including career counseling and training as well as job analysis.

Approaches to Job Analysis

The systematic and quantitative definition of job content that job analysis provides is the foundation of many HRM practices. Specifically, the job analysis serves to justify job descriptions and other HRM selection procedures. Several different job analysis approaches are used to gather data, each with specific advantages and disadvantages.[10] Five of the more popular methods are functional job analysis, the position analysis questionnaire system, the critical incident method, task inventory analysis, and computerized job analysis.

Functional Job Analysis

functional job analysis (FJA)
A quantitative approach to job analysis that utilizes a compiled inventory of the various functions or work activities that can make up any job and that assumes that each job involves three broad worker functions: (1) data, (2) people, and (3) things

Developed by the U.S. Training and Employment Service, the **functional job analysis (FJA)** approach utilizes an inventory of the various types of functions or work activities that can constitute any job. FJA thus assumes that each job involves performing certain functions. Specifically, three broad worker functions form the bases of this system: (1) data, (2) people, and (3) things. These three categories are subdivided to form a hierarchy of worker-function scales, as shown in Figure 4.2. The job analyst, when studying the job under review, indicates the functional level for each of the three categories (for example, "copying" under DATA) and then reflects the relative involvement of the worker in the function by assigning a percentage figure to each function (such as 50 percent to "copying"). This is done for each of the three areas, and the three functional levels must equal 100 percent. The result is a quantitatively evaluated job. FJA can easily be used to describe the content of jobs and to assist in writing job descriptions and specifications.

The Position Analysis Questionnaire System

position analysis questionnaire (PAQ)
A questionnaire covering 194 different tasks that, by means of a five-point scale, seeks to determine the degree to which different tasks are involved in performing a particular job

The **position analysis questionnaire (PAQ)** is a quantifiable data collection method covering 194 different worker-oriented tasks. Using a five-point scale, the PAQ seeks to determine the degree, if any, to which the different tasks, or job elements, are involved in performing a particular job.

A sample page from the PAQ covering eleven elements of the Information Input Division is shown in Figure 4.3. The person conducting an analysis with this questionnaire would rate each of the elements using the five-point scale shown in the upper-right-hand corner of the sample page. The results obtained with the PAQ are

Figure 4.2 **Difficulty Levels of Worker Functions**

DATA (4TH DIGIT)	PEOPLE (5TH DIGIT)	THINGS (6TH DIGIT)
0 Synthesizing	0 Mentoring	0 Setting up
1 Coordinating	1 Negotiating	1 Precision working
2 Analyzing	2 Instructing	2 Operating-controlling*
3 Compiling	3 Supervising	3 Driving-operating*
4 Computing	4 Diverting	4 Manipulating
5 Copying	5 Persuading	5 Tending
6 Comparing	6 Speaking-signaling*	6 Feeding-offbearing*
	7 Serving	7 Handling
	8 Taking instructions–helping*	

*Hyphenated factors are single factors.

Source: U.S. Department of Labor, Employment and Training Administration, *Revised Handbook for Analyzing Jobs* (Washington, DC: U.S. Government Printing Office, 1991), 5.

quantitative and can be subjected to statistical analysis. The PAQ also permits dimensions of behavior to be compared across a number of jobs and permits jobs to be grouped on the basis of common characteristics.

The Critical Incident Method

critical incident method
A job analysis method by which important job tasks are identified for job success

The objective of the **critical incident method** is to identify critical job tasks. Critical job tasks are those important duties and job responsibilities performed by the jobholder that lead to job success. Information about critical job tasks can be collected through interviews with employees or managers or through self-report statements written by employees.

Suppose, for example, that the job analyst is studying the job of reference librarian. The interviewer will ask the employee to describe the job on the basis of what is done, how the job is performed, and what tools and equipment are used. The reference librarian may describe the job as follows:

> I assist patrons by answering their questions related to finding books, periodicals, or other library materials. I also give them directions to help them find materials within the building. To perform my job I may have to look up materials myself or refer patrons to someone who can directly assist them. Some individuals may need training in how to use reference materials or special library facilities. I also give library tours to new patrons. I use computers and a variety of reference books to carry out my job.

After the job data are collected, the analyst then writes separate task statements that represent important job activities. For the reference librarian one task statement

Figure 4.3 A Sample Page from the PAQ

INFORMATION INPUT

1 INFORMATION INPUT

1.1 Sources of Job Information

	Extent of Use (U)
NA	Does not apply
1	Nominal/very infrequent
2	Occasional
3	Moderate
4	Considerable
5	Very substantial

Rate each of the following items in terms of the extent to which it is used by the worker as a source of information in performing his job.

1.1.1 Visual Sources of Job Information

01 U Written materials (books, reports, office notes, articles, job instructions, signs, etc.)

02 U Quantitative materials (materials which deal with quantities or amounts, such as graphs, accounts, specifications, tables of numbers, etc.)

03 U Pictorial materials (pictures or picturelike materials used as *sources* of information, for example, drawings, blueprints, diagrams, maps, tracings, photographic films, x-ray films, TV pictures, etc.)

04 U Patterns/related devices (templates, stencils, patterns, etc., used as *sources* of information when *observed* during use; do *not* include here materials described in item 3 above)

05 U Visual displays (dials, gauges, signal lights, radarscopes, speedometers, clocks, etc.)

06 U Measuring devices (rulers, calipers, tire pressure gauges, scales, thickness gauges, pipettes, thermometers, protractors, etc., used to obtain visual information about physical measurements; do *not* include here devices described in item 5 above)

07 U Mechanical devices (tools, equipment, machinery, and other mechanical devices which are *sources* of information when *observed* during use or operation)

08 U Materials in process (parts, materials, objects, etc., which are *sources* of information when being modified, worked on, or otherwise processed, such as bread dough being mixed, workpiece being turned in a lathe, fabric being cut, shoe being resoled, etc.)

09 U Materials *not* in process (parts, materials, objects, etc., not in the process of being changed or modified, which are *sources* of information when being inspected, handled, packaged, distributed, or selected, etc., such as items or materials in inventory, storage, or distribution channels, items being inspected, etc.)

10 U Features of nature (landscapes, fields, geological samples, vegetation, cloud formations, and other features of nature which are observed or inspected to provide information)

11 U Man-made features of environment (structures, buildings, dams, highways, bridges, docks, railroads, and other "man-made" or altered aspects of the indoor or outdoor environment which are *observed or inspected* to provide job information; do *not* consider equipment, machines, etc., that an individual uses in his work, as covered by item 7)

Source: *Position Analysis Questionnaire,* copyright 1969, 1989 by Purdue Research Foundation, West Lafayette, IN 47907. Reprinted with permission.

might be, "Listens to patrons and answers their questions related to locating library materials." Typically the job analyst writes five to ten important task statements for each job under study. The final product is written task statements that are clear, complete, and easily understood by those unfamiliar with the job. The critical incident method is an important job analysis method because it teaches the analyst to focus on employee behaviors critical to job success.

Task Inventory Analysis

task inventory analysis An organization-specific list of tasks and their descriptions used as a basis to identify components of jobs

The **task inventory analysis** method can be considered a job-oriented type of job analysis. The technique was pioneered by the U.S. Air Force to analyze jobs held by Air Force specialists. Unlike the PAQ, which uses a standardized form to analyze jobs in different organizations, a task inventory questionnaire can be tailor-made to a specific organization.

The technique is developed by identifying—with the help of employees and managers—a list of tasks and their descriptions that are components of different jobs. The goal is to produce a comprehensive list of task statements that are applicable to all jobs. Task statements then are listed on a task inventory survey form to be completed by the person analyzing the job under review. A task statement might be, "Inventories current supplies to maintain stock levels." The job analysis would also note the importance and frequency of use of the task to the successful completion of the job.

HRIS and Job Analysis

Human resource information systems have greatly facilitated the job analysis process. Available today are various software programs designed specifically to analyze jobs and to write job descriptions and job specifications based on those analyses. These programs normally contain generalized task statements that can apply to many different jobs. Managers and employees select those statements that best describe the job under review, indicating the importance of the task to the total job where appropriate. Advanced computer applications of job analysis combine job analysis with job evaluation (see Chapter 9) and the pricing of organizational jobs. Computerized job analysis systems can be expensive to initiate, but where the organization has many jobs to analyze the cost per job may be low. HR publications such as *HRMagazine* and *Workforce* contain advertisements from numerous software companies offering HRIS job analysis packages.

Job Outlook
Computer Programmers
Prospects should be best for college graduates with knowledge of a variety of programming languages and tools; those with less formal education or its equivalent in work experience should face strong competition for programming jobs. Earnings ranged between $45,960 and $78,140 a year.

Source: *Occupational Outlook Handbook,* 2004–05 Edition. http://www.bls.gov/oco

Job Analysis in a Changing Environment

The traditional approach to job analysis assumes a static job environment where jobs remain relatively stable apart from incumbents who might hold these jobs. Here, jobs can be meaningfully defined in terms of tasks, duties, processes, and behaviors necessary for job success. This assumption, unfortunately, discounts technological advances that are often so accelerated that jobs, as they are defined today, may be obsolete tomorrow. The following statement by two HR professionals highlights this concern: "Typically, job analysis looks at how a job is currently done. But the ever-changing business market makes it difficult to keep a job analysis up-to-date. Also, companies are asking employees to do more, so there is a question of whether 'jobs' as we know them are obsolete. This means we must do an analysis of work as quickly as possible, leading to more emphasis on technology-related options, such as web-based job analysis."[11]

Furthermore, downsizing, the demands of small organizations, and the need to respond to global change can alter the nature of jobs and the requirements of individuals needed to successfully perform them. For organizations using "virtual jobs" and "virtual teams" there is a shift away from narrow job specifications and descriptions to a world where work is "dejobbed" and emphasis is placed on the distribution of work. In a dynamic environment where job demands rapidly change, obsolete job analysis information can hinder an organization's ability to adapt to change.

When organizations operate in a fast-moving environment, several novel approaches to job analysis may accommodate needed change. First, managers might adopt a future-oriented approach to job analysis. This "strategic" analysis of jobs requires that managers have a clear view of how jobs should be restructured in terms of duties and tasks in order to meet future organizational requirements. Second, organizations might adopt a competency-based approach to job analysis, in which emphasis is placed on characteristics of successful performers rather than on standard job duties, tasks, and so on. These competencies would match the organization's culture and strategy and might include such things as interpersonal communication skills, decision-making ability, conflict resolution skills, adaptability, and self-motivation.[12] This technique of job analysis serves to enhance a culture of TQM and continuous improvement, because organizational improvement is the constant aim. Either of these two approaches is not without concerns, including the ability of managers to accurately predict future job needs, the necessity of job analysis to comply with EEOC guidelines, and the possibility of role ambiguity created by generically written job descriptions.

Job Descriptions

As previously noted, a job description is a written description of a job and the types of duties it includes. Since there is no standard format for job descriptions, they tend to vary in appearance and content from one organization to another. However, most job descriptions will contain at least three parts: the job title, a job identification section, and a job duties section. If the job specifications are not prepared as a separate document, they are usually stated in the concluding section of the job description. Highlights in HRM 1 shows a job description for an HR employment assistant. This sample job description includes both job duties and job specifications and should satisfy most of the job information needs of managers who must recruit, interview, and orient a new employee.

Job descriptions are of value to both the employees and the employer. From the employees' standpoint, job descriptions can be used to help them learn their job duties and to remind them of the results they are expected to achieve.[13] From the employer's standpoint, written job descriptions can serve as a basis for minimizing the misunderstandings that occur between managers and their subordinates concerning job requirements. They also establish management's right to take corrective action when the duties covered by the job description are not performed as required.

Job Title

Selection of a job title is important for several reasons. First, the job title is of psychological importance, providing status to the employee. For instance, "sanitation engineer" is a more appealing title than "garbage collector." Second, if possible, the

Highlights in HRM 1

Job Description for an Employment Assistant

Job Identification

JOB TITLE: Employment Assistant

Division:	Southern Area
Department:	Human Resources Management
Job Analyst:	Virginia Sasaki
Date Analyzed:	12/3/05
Wage Category:	Exempt
Report to:	HR Manager
Job Code:	11-17
Date Verified:	12/17/05

Brief Listing of Major Job Duties

JOB STATEMENT

Performs professional human resources work in the areas of employee *recruitment and selection, testing, orientation, transfers, and maintenance of employee human resources files.* May handle special assignments and projects in *EEO/Affirmative Action, employee grievances, training,* or *classification and compensation.* Works under general supervision. Incumbent exercises initiative and independent judgment in the performance of assigned tasks.

Essential Functions and Responsibilities

ESSENTIAL FUNCTIONS

1. Prepares recruitment literature and job advertisements for applicant placement.
2. Schedules and conducts personal interviews to determine applicant suitability for employment. Includes reviewing mailed applications and resumes for qualified personnel.
3. Supervises administration of testing program. Responsible for developing or improving testing instruments and procedures.
4. Presents orientation program to all new employees. Reviews and develops all materials and procedures for orientation program.
5. Coordinates division job posting and transfer program. Establishes job posting procedures. Responsible for reviewing transfer applications, arranging transfer interviews, and determining effective transfer dates.
6. Maintains a daily working relationship with division managers on human resources matters, including recruitment concerns, retention or release of probationary employees, and discipline or discharge of permanent employees.
7. Distributes new or revised human resources policies and procedures to all employees and managers through bulletins, meetings, memorandums, and/or personal contact.
8. Performs related duties as assigned by the human resources manager.

Job Specifications and Requirements

JOB SPECIFICATIONS

1. Four-year college or university degree with major course work in human resources management, business administration, or industrial psychology; OR a combination of experience, education, and training equivalent to a four-year college degree in human resources management.
2. Considerable knowledge of principles of employee selection and assignment of personnel.
3. Ability to express ideas clearly in both written and oral communications.
4. Ability to independently plan and organize one's own activities.
5. Knowledge of human resources computer applications desirable.

title should provide some indication of what the duties of the job entail. Titles such as *meat inspector, electronics assembler, salesperson,* and *engineer* obviously hint at the nature of the duties of these jobs. The job title also should indicate the relative level occupied by its holder in the organizational hierarchy. For example, the title *junior engineer* implies that this job occupies a lower level than that of *senior engineer.* Other titles that indicate the relative level in the organizational hierarchy are *welder's helper* and *laboratory assistant.*

Job Identification Section

The job identification section of a job description usually follows the job title. It includes such items as the departmental location of the job, the person to whom the jobholder reports, and the date the job description was last revised. Sometimes it also contains a payroll or code number, the number of employees performing the job, the number of employees in the department where the job is located, and the O*NET code number. "Statement of the Job" usually appears at the bottom of this section and distinguishes the job from other jobs—something the job title may fail to do.

Job Duties, or Essential Functions, Section

Statements covering job duties are typically arranged in order of importance. These statements should indicate the weight, or value, of each duty. Usually, but not always, the weight of a duty can be gauged by the percentage of time devoted to it. The statements should stress the responsibilities all the duties entail and the results they are to accomplish. It is also general practice to indicate the tools and equipment used by the employee in performing the job. Remember, the job duties section must comply with law by listing only the essential functions of the job to be performed (see "Job Analysis and Essential Job Functions" earlier in this chapter).[14]

Job Specifications Section

As stated earlier, the personal qualifications an individual must possess in order to perform the duties and responsibilities contained in a job description are compiled in the job specification. Typically the job specification covers two areas: (1) the skill required to perform the job and (2) the physical demands the job places on the employee performing it.

Skills relevant to a job include education or experience, specialized training, personal traits or abilities, and manual dexterities. The physical demands of a job refer to how much walking, standing, reaching, lifting, or talking must be done on the job. The condition of the physical work environment and the hazards employees may encounter are also among the physical demands of a job.

Job specifications should also include interpersonal skills or specific behavioral attributes necessary for job success. For example, behavioral competencies might include the ability to make decisions on imperfect information, decisiveness, the ability to handle multiple tasks, and conflict-resolution skills. Behavioral attributes can be assessed by asking applicants situational interview questions (see Chapter 6). For example, a manager could ask an applicant about a time he or she had to make a critical decision quickly.

Problems with Job Descriptions

Managers consider job descriptions a valuable tool for performing HRM functions. Nevertheless, several problems are frequently associated with these documents, including the following:

1. If they are poorly written, using vague rather than specific terms, they provide little guidance to the jobholder.
2. They are sometimes not updated as job duties or specifications change.
3. They may violate the law by containing specifications not related to job success.
4. They can limit the scope of activities of the jobholder, reducing organizational flexibility.

Writing Clear and Specific Job Descriptions

When writing a job description, it is essential to use statements that are terse, direct, and simply worded.[15] Unnecessary words or phrases should be eliminated. Typically, the sentences that describe job duties begin with a present-tense verb, with the implied subject of the sentence being the employee performing the job. The term "occasionally" is used to describe duties that are performed once in a while. The term "may" is used in connection with duties performed only by some workers on the job.

Even when set forth in writing, job descriptions and specifications can still be vague. To the consternation of many employers, however, today's legal environment has created what might be called an "age of specifics." Federal guidelines and court decisions now require that the specific performance requirements of a job be based on *valid* job-related criteria.[16] Personnel decisions that involve either job applicants or employees and are based on criteria that are vague or not job-related are increasingly successfully challenged. Managers of small businesses, in which employees may perform many different job tasks, must be particularly concerned about writing specific job descriptions.

Managers may find that writing job descriptions is a tedious process that distracts from other supervisory responsibilities. Fortunately, software packages are available to simplify this time-consuming yet necessary task. One program provides an initial library of more than 2,500 prewritten job descriptions. Since the program works much like a word processor, text can be easily deleted, inserted, or modified to user demands.

Job Design

job design
An outgrowth of job analysis that improves jobs through technological and human considerations in order to enhance organization efficiency and employee job satisfaction

It is not uncommon for managers and supervisors to confuse the processes of job analysis and job design. Job analysis is the study of jobs as currently performed by employees. It identifies job duties and the requirements needed to perform the work successfully. **Job design,** which is an outgrowth of job analysis, is concerned with structuring jobs in order to improve organization efficiency and employee job satisfaction. Job design is concerned with changing, modifying, and enriching jobs in order to capture the talents of employees while improving organization performance.[17] For example, companies such as Harley-Davidson, Lucent Technologies, and PageNet, which are engaged in continuous improvement, or process reengineering, may revamp their jobs in order to eliminate unnecessary job tasks or find better ways of performing work. Job design should facilitate the achievement of organizational objectives.[18] At the same time, the design should recognize the capabilities and needs of those who are to perform the job.

As Figure 4.4 illustrates, job design is a combination of four basic considerations: (1) the organizational objectives the job was created to fulfill; (2) industrial engineering considerations, including ways to make the job technologically efficient; (3) ergonomic concerns, including workers' physical and mental capabilities; and (4) behavioral concerns that influence an employee's job satisfaction.

Figure 4.4 Basis for Job Design

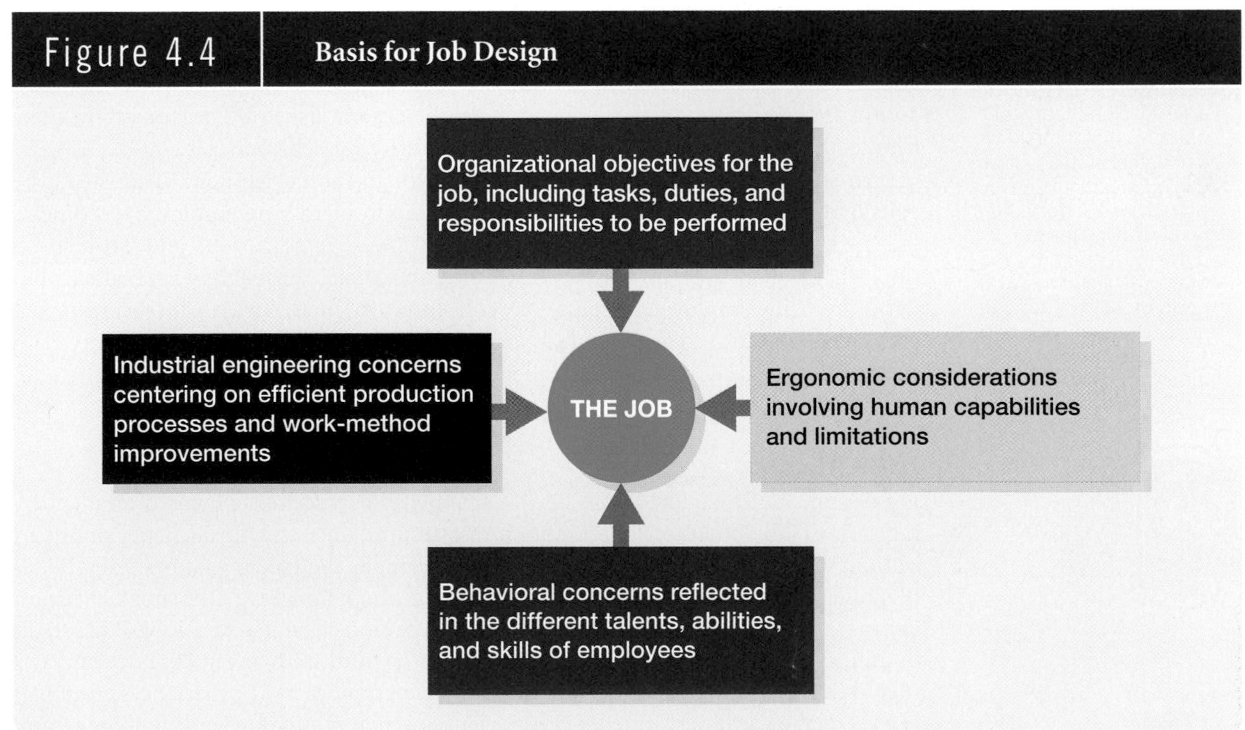

Behavioral Concerns

Two job design methods seek to incorporate the behavioral needs of employees as they perform their individual jobs. Both methods strive to satisfy the intrinsic needs of employees. The job enrichment model and the job characteristics model have long been popular with researchers and practitioners as ways to increase the job satisfaction of employees.

Job Enrichment

job enrichment
Enhancing a job by adding more meaningful tasks and duties to make the work more rewarding or satisfying

Any effort that makes work more rewarding or satisfying by adding more meaningful tasks to an employee's job is called **job enrichment.** Originally popularized by Frederick Herzberg, job enrichment is touted as fulfilling the high motivational needs of employees, such as self-fulfillment and self-esteem, while achieving long-term job satisfaction and performance goals.[19] Job enrichment, or the *vertical expansion* of jobs, may be accomplished by increasing the autonomy and responsibility of employees. Herzberg discusses five factors for enriching jobs and thereby motivating employees: achievement, recognition, growth, responsibility, and performance of the whole job versus only parts of the job. For example, managers can use these five factors to enrich the jobs of employees by

- Increasing the level of difficulty and responsibility of the job
- Allowing employees to retain more authority and control over work outcomes
- Providing unit or individual job performance reports directly to employees
- Adding new tasks to the job that require training and growth
- Assigning individuals specific tasks, thus enabling them to become experts

job characteristics model
A job design theory that purports that three psychological states (experiencing meaningfulness of the work performed, responsibility for work outcomes, and knowledge of the results of the work performed) of a jobholder result in improved work performance, internal motivation, and lower absenteeism and turnover

These factors allow employees to assume a greater role in the decision-making process and become more involved in planning, organizing, directing, and controlling their own work. Vertical job enrichment can also be accomplished by organizing workers into teams and giving these teams greater authority for self-management.

In spite of the benefits to be achieved through job enrichment, it must not be considered a panacea for overcoming production problems and employee discontent. Job enrichment programs are more likely to succeed in some jobs and work situations than in others. They are *not* the solution to such problems as dissatisfaction with pay, with employee benefits, or with employment security. Moreover, not all employees object to the mechanical pacing of an assembly line, nor do all employees seek additional responsibility or challenge. Some prefer routine jobs because they can let their minds wander while performing their work.

Job Characteristics

Job design studies explored a new field when behavioral scientists focused on identifying various job dimensions that would improve simultaneously the efficiency of organizations and the job satisfaction of employees. Perhaps the theory that best exemplifies this research is the one advanced by Richard Hackman and Greg Oldham.[20] Their **job characteristics model** proposes that three psychological states of a jobholder result in improved work performance, internal motivation, and lower absenteeism and turnover. A motivated, satisfied, and productive employee (1) experiences *meaningfulness* of the work performed, (2) experiences *responsibility* for work outcomes, and

(3) has *knowledge of the results* of the work performed. Hackman and Oldham believe that five core job dimensions produce the three psychological states. The five job characteristics are as follows:

1. *Skill variety:* The degree to which a job entails a variety of different activities, which demand the use of a number of different skills and talents by the jobholder
2. *Task identity:* The degree to which the job requires completion of a whole and identifiable piece of work, that is, doing a job from beginning to end with a visible outcome
3. *Task significance:* The degree to which the job has a substantial impact on the lives or work of other people, whether in the immediate organization or in the external environment
4. *Autonomy:* The degree to which the job provides substantial freedom, independence, and discretion to the individual in scheduling the work and in determining the procedures to be used in carrying it out
5. *Feedback:* The degree to which carrying out the work activities required by the job results in the individual being given direct and clear information about the effectiveness of his or her performance

The job characteristics model appears to work best when certain conditions are met. One of these conditions is that employees must have the psychological desire for the autonomy, variety, responsibility, and challenge of enriched jobs. When this personal characteristic is absent, employees may resist the job redesign effort. In addition, job redesign efforts almost always fail when employees lack the physical or mental skills, abilities, or education needed to perform the job. Forcing enriched jobs on individuals lacking these traits can result in frustrated employees.

Employee Empowerment

Job enrichment and job characteristics are specific programs by which managers or supervisors can formally change the jobs of employees. A less structured method is to allow employees to initiate their own job changes through the concept of empowerment. **Employee empowerment** is a technique of involving employees in their work through the process of inclusion. Empowerment encourages employees to become innovators and managers of their own work, and it involves them in their jobs in ways that give them more control and autonomous decision-making capabilities (see Highlights in HRM 2). As described by one manager, employee empowerment involves "pushing down decision-making responsibility to those close to internal and external customers."

employee empowerment
Granting employees power to initiate change, thereby encouraging them to take charge of what they do

While defining empowerment can become the first step to achieving it, in order for empowerment to grow and thrive, organizations must encourage these conditions:

- *Participation.* Employees must be encouraged to take control of their work tasks. Employees, in turn, must care about improving their work process and interpersonal work relationships.
- *Innovation.* The environment must be receptive to people with innovative ideas and encourage people to explore new paths and to take reasonable risks at reasonable costs. An empowered environment is created when curiosity is as highly regarded as is technical expertise.

Highlights in HRM 2

Empowered Employees Achieve Results

In today's highly competitive and dynamic business environment, employers as diverse as Home Depot, Wal-Mart, Cigna HealthCare, Costco, AutoZone, Disney, and Applebee's have turned to their employees to improve organizational performance. Empowered employees have made improvements in product or service quality, have reduced costs, and have modified or, in some cases, designed products.

- At Kraft Foods, employees at the company's Sussex, Wisconsin, food plant participated in work-redesign changes and team building that increased productivity, reduced overhead, and cut assembly time.
- Avon Products empowered its minority managers to improve sales and service in inner-city markets. Grounded in the belief that minority managers better understand the culture of inner-city residents, Avon turned an unprofitable market into a highly productive sales area.
- Dorothy Galvez, administrative assistant to Robert E. Mittelstaedt, Jr., dean of the W.P. Carey School of Business at Arizona State University, has empowered her position by planning college activities and events, preparing special college reports, learning new educational and business technology, and serving as the dean's representative at college and business events.
- At Ford's factory in Wayne, Michigan, one group of employees made a suggestion saving $115,000 a year on the purchase of gloves used to protect workers who handle sheet metal and glass. The group figured out how to have the gloves washed so they could be used more than once.
- Home Depot's Special Project Support Teams (SPST) work to improve the organization's business and information services. Employees with a wide range of backgrounds and skills collaborate to address a wide range of strategic and tactical business needs.
- American Airlines' "Rainbow Team" of gay employees brought in $192 million in annual revenue by targeting the gay community.

- *Access to information.* Employees must have access to a wide range of information. Involved individuals decide what kind of information they need for performing their jobs.
- *Accountability.* Empowerment does not involve being able to do whatever you want. Empowered employees should be held accountable for their behavior toward others, producing agreed-on results, achieving credibility, and operating with a positive approach.

Additionally, employee empowerment succeeds when the culture of the organization is open and receptive to change. An organization's culture is largely created through the philosophies of senior managers and their leadership traits and behaviors. Effective leadership in an empowered organization is highlighted by managers who are honest, caring, and receptive to new ideas and who exhibit dignity and respect for employees as partners in organizational success.

Industrial Engineering Considerations

industrial engineering
A field of study concerned with analyzing work methods and establishing time standards

The study of work is an important contribution of the scientific management movement. **Industrial engineering,** which evolved with this movement, is concerned with analyzing work methods and establishing time standards. Specifically, it involves the study of work cycles to determine which, if any, elements can be modified, combined, rearranged, or eliminated to reduce the time needed to complete the cycle. Next, time standards are established by recording the time required to complete each element in the work cycle, using a stopwatch or work-sampling technique. By combining the times for each element, observers can determine the total time required. This time is subsequently adjusted to allow for the skill and effort demonstrated by the observed worker and for interruptions that may occur in performing the work. The adjusted time becomes the time standard for that particular work cycle.

Industrial engineering constitutes a disciplined and objective approach to job design. Unfortunately, the concern of industrial engineering for improving efficiency and simplifying work methods may cause the behavioral considerations in job design to be neglected. What may be improvements in job design and efficiency from an engineering standpoint can sometimes prove psychologically unsound. For example, the assembly line with its simplified and repetitive tasks embodies sound principles of industrial engineering, but these tasks are often not psychologically rewarding for those who must perform them. Thus, to be effective, job design must also provide for the satisfaction of behavioral needs.

ergonomics
An interdisciplinary approach to designing equipment and systems that can be easily and efficiently used by human beings

Ergonomic Considerations

Ergonomics attempts to accommodate the human capabilities and limitations of those who are to perform a job. It is concerned with adapting the entire job system—the work, the work environment, the machine and equipment, and the processes—to

Alan Hedge, a professor of ergonomics at Cornell University, sits in a special chair with a floating arms keyboard designed to be ergonomically correct. In the background are other ergonomic chairs that Hedge and students tested.

match human characteristics. In short, it seeks to fit the job to the person rather than the person to the job.[21] Ergonomics attempts to minimize the harmful effects of carelessness, negligence, and other human fallibilities that otherwise may cause product defects, damage to equipment, or even the injury or death of employees.

Equipment design must consider the physical ability of operators to use the equipment and to react through vision, hearing, and touch to the information the equipment conveys. Designing equipment controls to be compatible with both the physical characteristics and the reaction capabilities of the people who must operate them and the environment in which they work is increasingly important. Ergonomics also considers the requirements of a diverse workforce, accommodating, for example, women who may lack the strength to operate equipment requiring intense physical force or Asian Americans who may lack the stature to reach equipment controls. Managers must adapt the workplace to the labor force or risk sacrificing quality and productivity.

Ergonomics improves productivity and morale and yields positive return on investment (ROI). Peter Budnick, president of ErgoWeb, Inc., notes, "At our company we look at ergonomics as much more than a musculoskeletal issue. Injuries are one of the natural outcomes of poor workplace design. But so is lost productivity, loss of efficiency, errors and increased waste. We really look at ergonomics as a broad approach to improving human performance."[22] Ergonomics has proven cost-effective at organizations such as Compaq Computer, 3M, Pratt and Whitney, and the U.S. Postal Service. Unfortunately, more than 1.8 million workplace injuries occur yearly resulting from motions such as lifting, bending, and typing. Therefore, ergonomics has recently focused on elimination, or at least reduction, of many repetitive-motion injuries, particularly those related to the back and wrist. For example, with the increased use of computers, ergonomics has particular application at employee workstations. Figure 4.5 provides a checklist of potential repetitive-motion problem areas for employees using computers.

Designing Work for Group/Team Contributions

Although a variety of group techniques have been developed to involve employees more fully in their organizations, all of these techniques have two characteristics in common—enhancing collaboration and increasing synergy. In increasing the degree of collaboration in the work environment, these techniques can improve work processes and organizational decision making. In increasing group synergy, the techniques underline the adage that the contributions of two or more employees are greater than the sum of their individual efforts. Furthermore, research has shown that working in a group setting strengthens employee commitment to the organization's goals, increases employee acceptance of decisions, and encourages a cooperative approach to workplace tasks.[23] Two collaborative techniques are discussed here: employee involvement groups and employee teams.

Employee Involvement Groups

employee involvement groups (EIs)
Groups of employees who meet to resolve problems or offer suggestions for organizational improvement

Groups of five to ten employees doing similar or related work who meet regularly to identify, analyze, and suggest solutions to shared problems are often referred to as **employee involvement groups (EIs).** Also widely known as *quality circles (QCs),* EIs are used principally as a means of involving employees in the larger goals of the organization through their suggestions for improving product or service quality and

Figure 4.5 **Computer Workstation Ergonomics Checklist**

Use the following list to identify potential problem areas that should receive further investigation. Any "no" response may point to a problem.

1. Does the workstation ensure proper worker posture, such as
   - Thighs in the horizontal position?
   - Lower legs in the vertical position?
   - Feet flat on the floor or on a footrest?
   - Wrists straight and relaxed?
2. Does the chair
   - Adjust easily?
   - Have a padded seat with a rounded front?
   - Have an adjustable backrest?
   - Provide lumbar support?
   - Have casters?
3. Are the height and tilt of the work surface on which the keyboard is located adjustable?
4. Is the keyboard detachable?
5. Do keying actions require minimal force?
6. Is there an adjustable document holder?
7. Are armrests provided where needed?
8. Are glare and reflections minimized?
9. Does the monitor have brightness and contrast controls?
10. Is there sufficient space for knees and feet?
11. Can the workstation be used for either right- or left-handed activity?

Source: The National Institute for Occupational Safety and Health (NIOSH), *Elements of Ergonomics Programs: A Primer Based on Workplace Evaluations of Musculoskeletal Disorders* (Washington, DC: U.S. Government Printing Office, March 1997).

cutting costs.[24] Generally, EIs recommend their solutions to management, which decides whether to implement them.

The employee involvement group process, illustrated in Figure 4.6, begins with EI members brainstorming job-related problems or concerns and gathering data about these issues. The process continues through the generation of solutions and recommendations that are then communicated to management. If the solutions are implemented, results are measured, and the EI and its members are usually recognized for the contributions they have made. EIs typically meet four or more hours per month, and the meetings are chaired by a group leader chosen from the group. The leader does not hold an authority position but instead serves as a discussion facilitator.

Although EIs have become an important employee contribution system, they are not without their problems and their critics. First, in order to achieve the results desired, those participating in EIs must receive comprehensive training in problem identification, problem analysis, and various decision-making tools such as statistical analysis and cause-and-effect diagrams. Comprehensive training for EIs is often cited

Figure 4.6 The Dynamics of Employee Involvement Groups

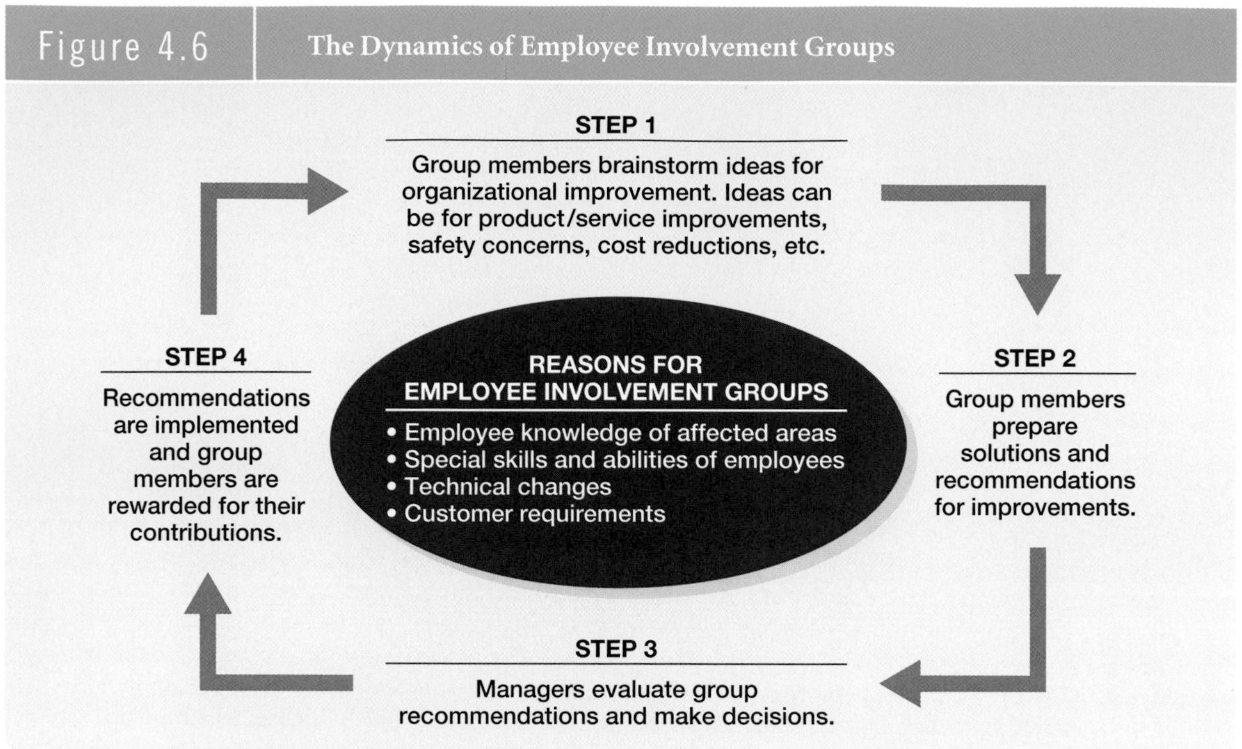

Source: Adapted from materials prepared by The Family and Relationship Center, 7946 Ivanhoe Avenue, La Jolla, CA 92037.

as the most important factor leading to their success. Second, managers should recognize the group when a recommendation is made, regardless of whether the recommendation is adopted. This approach encourages the group to continue coming up with ideas even when they are not all implemented by management. Third, some organizations have found that EIs run out of ideas, and management must feed them ideas to keep the process going. Finally, and most important, managers and supervisors must exhibit a participative/democratic leadership style in which employees are encouraged to work collaboratively with management to improve organizational performance.

Employee Teams

employee teams
An employee contributions technique whereby work functions are structured for groups rather than for individuals and team members are given discretion in matters traditionally considered management prerogatives, such as process improvements, product or service development, and individual work assignments

During the past decade perhaps one of the more radical changes to how work is done is the introduction of organizational teams. Jim Barksdale, president and CEO of Netscape Communications, states, "These days it seems as if every time a task needs to be accomplished within an organization, a team is formed to do it." This statement simply emphasizes the increasing importance of teams to organizational success in an ever-dynamic business climate. At such diverse organizations as Federal Express, Hewlett-Packard, the City of Phoenix, Calvin Klein, and Lockheed Martin Aeronautics in Fort Worth, Texas, the benefits of employee teams have included more integration of individual skills, better performance in terms of quality and quantity, solutions to unique and complex problems, reduced delivery time, reduced turnover and absenteeism, and accomplishments among team members.[25]

Team members brainstorm, support, and challenge each other, and interact as they work together for a common goal.

Employee teams are a logical outgrowth of employee involvement and the philosophy of empowerment. Although many definitions of teams exist, we define a work team as a group of individuals working together toward a common purpose, in which members have complementary skills, members' work is mutually dependent, and the group has discretion over tasks performed. Furthermore, teams seek to make members of the work group share responsibility and accountability for their group's performance. Inherent in the concept of employee teams is that employees, not managers, are in the best position to contribute to workplace performance. With work teams, managers accept the notion that the group is the logical work unit to apply resources to resolve organizational problems and concerns.[26]

Teamwork also embraces the concept of *synergy.* Synergy occurs when the interaction and outcome of team members is greater than the sum of their individual efforts.[27] Unfortunately, synergy may not automatically happen, but rather, it must be nurtured within the team environment.[28] Figure 4.7 lists the factors contributing to a synergistic team setting.

Teams can operate in a variety of structures, each with different strategic purposes or functional activities. Figure 4.8 describes common team forms. One form, self-directed teams, is often championed as being the highest form of team structure. Self-directed teams, also called *autonomous work groups, self-managed teams,* or *high-performance teams,* are groups of employees who are accountable for a "whole" work process or segment that delivers a product or service to an internal or external

Figure 4.7 Synergistic Team Characteristics

Team synergy is heightened when team members engage in these positive behaviors.

- *Support.* The team exhibits an atmosphere of inclusion. All team members speak up and feel free to offer constructive comments.
- *Listening and Clarification.* Active listening is practiced. Members honestly listen to others and seek clarification on discussion points. Team members summarize discussions held.
- *Disagreement.* Disagreement is seen as natural and is expected. Member comments are nonjudgmental and focus on factual issues rather than personality conflicts.
- *Consensus.* Team members reach agreements through consensus decision making. Consensus decisions require finding a proposal that is acceptable to all team members, even if not the first choice of individual members. Common ground among ideas is sought.
- *Acceptance.* Team members are valued as individuals, recognizing that each person brings a valuable mix of skills and abilities to team operations.
- *Quality.* Each team member is committed to excellent performance. There is emphasis on continuous improvement and attention to detail.

Figure 4.8 Forms of Employee Teams

Cross-Functional Teams. A group staffed with a mix of specialists (e.g., marketing, production, engineering) and formed to accomplish a specific objective. Cross-functional teams are based on assigned rather than voluntary membership.

Project Teams. A group formed specifically to design a new product or service. Members are assigned by management on the basis of their ability to contribute to success. The group normally disbands after task completion.

Self-Directed Teams. Groups of highly trained individuals performing a set of interdependent job tasks within a natural work unit. Team members use consensus decision making to perform work duties, solve problems, or deal with internal or external customers.

Task Force Teams. A task force is formed by management to immediately resolve a major problem. The group is responsible for developing a long-term plan for problem resolution that may include a charge for implementing the solution proposed.

Process-Improvement Teams. A group made up of experienced people from different departments or functions and charged with improving quality, decreasing waste, or enhancing productivity in processes that affect all departments or functions involved. Team members are normally appointed by management.

USING THE INTERNET

To obtain a wide variety of information on teams, including free pamphlets and articles, view the Center for the Study of Work Teams. Go to the Student Resources at:

http://bohlander.swlearning.com

customer. Team members acquire multiple skills enabling them to perform a variety of job tasks. To varying degrees, team members work together to improve their operations, handle day-to-day concerns, and plan and control their work. Typical team functions include setting work schedules, dealing directly with external customers, training team members, setting performance targets, budgeting, and purchasing equipment or services.

Self-directed teams are designed to give the team "ownership" of a product or service. In a manufacturing environment, a team might be responsible for a whole product or a clearly defined segment of the production process. Similarly, in a service environment, a team is usually responsible for entire groupings of products and services, often serving clients in a designated geographic area. Providing employees this type of ownership usually requires broader job categories and the sharing of work assignments.

virtual team
A team with widely dispersed members linked together through computer and telecommunications technology

To compete in today's national and international markets, managers have formed virtual teams.[29] **Virtual teams** use advanced computer and telecommunications technology to link team members who are geographically dispersed—often worldwide.[30] Management may form a cross-functional team (see Figure 4.8) to develop a new pharmaceutical drug and have the team operate in a virtual environment to achieve its goal. Virtual teams provide new opportunities for training, product development, and product market analysis. Importantly, virtual teams provide access to previously unavailable expertise and enhance cross-functional interactions.[31] However, although virtual teams have many benefits, they are not without their problems. Paulette Tichenor, president of Organizational Renaissance, a team training organization, notes these concerns with virtual teams: language and cultural barriers, unclear objectives, time conflicts due to diverse geographical locations, selecting people who are self-starters and have technological skills, and behavioral problems caused by a lack of close interpersonal contact.[32]

Source: ©Randy Glasbergen. Reprinted with permission.

Regardless of the structure or purpose of the team, the following characteristics have been identified with successful teams:

- Commitment to shared goals and objectives
- Motivated and energetic team members
- Open and honest communication
- Shared leadership
- Clear role assignments
- Climate of cooperation, collaboration, trust, and accountability
- Recognition of conflict and its positive resolution

Unfortunately, not all teams succeed or operate to their full potential. Therefore, in adopting the work-team concept, organizations must address several issues that could present obstacles to effective team function, including overly high expectations, group compensation, training, career movement, and power.[33] For example, new team members must be retrained to work outside their primary functional areas, and compensation systems must be constructed to reward individuals for team accomplishments. Since team membership demands more general skills and since it moves an employee out of the historical career path, new career paths to general management must be created from the team experience. Finally, as the team members become capable of carrying out functions, such as strategic planning, that were previously restricted to higher levels of management, managers must be prepared to utilize their newfound expertise.

Another difficulty with work teams is that they alter the traditional manager-employee relationship.[34] Managers often find it hard to adapt to the role of leader rather than supervisor and sometimes feel threatened by the growing power of the team and the reduced power of management. Furthermore, some employees may also have difficulty adapting to a role that includes traditional supervisory responsibilities. Therefore, from our experience in working with teams, extensive attention must be given to training team members as they move through the four stages of team development—forming, storming, norming, and performing.[35] *Complete* training would cover the importance of skills in (1) team leadership, (2) mission/goal setting, (3) conduct of meetings, (4) team decision making, (5) conflict resolution, (6) effective communication, and (7) diversity awareness.[36]

Flexible Work Schedules

Flexible work schedules are not a true part of job design because job tasks and responsibilities are not changed. Nevertheless, we discuss adjustments in work schedules here because they alter the normal workweek of five eight-hour days in which all employees begin and end their workday at the same time. Employers may depart from the traditional workday or workweek in their attempt to improve organizational productivity and morale by giving employees increased control over the hours they work.

Speaking on the importance of flexible work schedules, Lois Brakon, codirector of the Families and Work Institute, notes, "Flexible schedules are going to be the way good, competitive businesses work."[37] Flexible work schedules may be assigned by the organization or requested by individual employees (see Highlights in HRM 3). The more common flexible work schedules are the compressed workweek, flextime, job sharing, and telecommuting.

The Compressed Workweek

Under the compressed workweek, the number of days in the workweek is shortened by lengthening the number of hours worked per day. This schedule is best illustrated by the four-day, forty-hour week, generally referred to as 4/10 or 4/40. Employees working a four-day workweek might work ten hours a day, Monday through Thursday. Although the 4/10 schedule is probably the best known, other compressed arrangements include reducing weekly hours to thirty-eight or thirty-six hours or scheduling eighty hours over nine days (9/80), taking one day off every other week.

Several examples illustrate this popular work arrangement.[38] At AVT Document Exchange Software Group in Tucson, Arizona, all general workers work four ten-hour days, with workers choosing the day they would like off. The organization's information technology employees, working swing and midnight shifts, work four nine-hour days. Working one less hour is comparable to offering a pay differential. In comparison, employees at Nahan Printing Inc., in St. Cloud, Minnesota, work three twelve-hour shifts, while employees at Marcel Dekker in New York City are employed on a Monday-through-Thursday office schedule with employees working a total of thirty-eight hours. At Marcel Dekker, employees are given the option of starting their workday between 7:30 A.M. and 9:30 A.M.

Managers cite the following reasons for implementing compressed workweek schedules:

- Recruitment and retention of employees[39]
- Coordinating employee work schedules with production schedules

Highlights in HRM 3

How to Request a Flexible Work Schedule

You may be thinking, "My manager would never agree to a flexible work schedule." But that's not necessarily so. When valued employees make reasonable scheduling requests, managers often try to accommodate employee proposals. Here are some proven strategies for securing different types of flexible work hour arrangements.

- *Investigate.* Look into similar arrangements others have made within your company or industry. Research company policy. Be realistic by providing a schedule that will fit the demands of your organization.
- *Be Professional.* Treat your request as a business proposal. Be positive and assume a "can-do" attitude. Be serious and present the proposal as a benefit to both you and your company. Present your idea as a "win-win" arrangement.
- *Write It Out.* Submit your request for a flexible work hour arrangement in a well-organized, detailed written proposal.
- *Promote Yourself.* Explain your value to your organization. Have others speak to your abilities—especially those in authority. Ask to be evaluated based on your quantity and quality of work rather than on the hours you actually spend on the job.
- *Anticipate Questions.* Be prepared for potential problems and have specific answers on how to deal with these issues. For example, how will you communicate or coordinate with other employees?
- *Propose a Review.* Propose review dates to evaluate your new flexible schedule. Continually assess how you work with others and your manager.

Source: Adapted from Julie Shields, "Showing How to Flex It," *Incentive* 178, no. 3 (March 2004): 47.

- Accommodating the leisure-time activities of employees while facilitating employee personal appointments—medical, dental, financial[40]
- Improvements in employee job satisfaction and morale

The major disadvantage of the compressed workweek involves federal laws regarding overtime.[41] The Fair Labor Standards Act has stringent rules requiring the payment of overtime to nonsupervisory employees who work more than forty hours a week. (See Chapter 9.) Another disadvantage of the compressed workweek is that it increases the amount of stress on managers and employees, and long workdays can be exhausting.

flextime
Flexible working hours that permit employees the option of choosing daily starting and quitting times, provided that they work a set number of hours per day or week

Flextime

Flextime, or flexible working hours, permits employees the option of choosing daily starting and quitting times, provided that they work a certain number of hours per day or week.[42] With flextime, employees are given considerable latitude in scheduling their work. However, there is a "core period" during the morning and afternoon when *all* employees are required to be on the job. Flexible working hours are most common in service-type organizations—financial institutions, government agencies, and other organizations with large clerical operations. The regional office of Sentry Insurance Company in Scottsdale, Arizona, has found that flextime provides many advantages for employees working in claims, underwriting, and HR areas. At Sentry Insurance, employees work a core period from 9 A.M. to 3 P.M. Flexible time periods are 6 A.M. to 9 A.M. and 3 P.M. to 7 P.M.

Flextime provides both employees and employers with several advantages. By allowing employees greater flexibility in work scheduling, employers can reduce some of the traditional causes of tardiness and absenteeism. Employees can adjust their work to accommodate their particular lifestyles and, in doing so, gain greater job satisfaction. Employees can also schedule their working hours for the time of day when they are most productive. In addition, variations in arrival and departure times can help reduce traffic congestion at the peak commuting hours. In some cases, employees require less time to commute, and the pressures of meeting a rigid schedule are reduced.

From the employer's standpoint, flextime can be most helpful in recruiting and retaining personnel. It has proved invaluable to organizations wishing to improve service to customers or clients by extending operating hours. Qwest, a telecommunications company, uses flextime to keep its business offices open for customers who cannot get there during the day. Research demonstrates that flextime can have a positive impact on the performance measures of reliability, quality, and quantity of employee work.

There are, of course, several disadvantages to flextime. First, it is not suited to some jobs. It is not feasible, for example, where specific workstations must be staffed at all times. Second, it can create problems for managers in communicating with and instructing employees. Flextime schedules may also force these managers to extend their workweek if they are to exercise control over their subordinates.

Job Sharing

The arrangement whereby two part-time employees perform a job that otherwise would be held by one full-time employee is called *job sharing.* Job sharers usually work three days a week, "creating an overlap day for extended face-to-face conferencing." Their pay is three-fifths of a regular salary; however, job sharers usually take on additional responsibilities beyond what the original job would require. Companies that use job sharing are primarily in the legal, advertising, and financial-services businesses. Among more notable national programs, Sprint began an extensive job sharing program for its attorneys, and Kaiser Permanente, one of the nation's largest health maintenance organizations, developed a job sharing program for physicians in its Northern California region. American Express, Lotus Development Company, and Carter Hawley Hale Stores also use job sharing extensively. Employers note that without job sharing two good employees might otherwise be lost.

Job sharing is suited to the needs of families in which one or both spouses desire to work only part-time.[43] It is suited also to the needs of older workers who want to phase into retirement by shortening their workweek. For the employer, the work of part-time employees can be scheduled to conform to peaks in the daily workload. Job sharing can also limit layoffs in hard economic times. A final benefit is that employees engaged in job sharing have time off during the week to accommodate personal needs, so they are less likely to be absent.

© BOB DAEMMERICH/PHOTOEDIT

Telecommuting allows employees to balance both work and family responsibilities.

Job sharing does have several problems, however. Employers may not want to employ two people to do the work of one because the time required to orient and train a second employee constitutes an added burden. They may also want to avoid prorating employee benefits between two part-time employees. This problem may be reduced, however, by permitting the employees to contribute the difference between the health insurance (or life insurance) premiums for a full-time employee and the pro rata amount the employer would otherwise contribute for a part-time employee. The key to making job sharing work is good communications between partners, who can use a number of ways to stay in contact—phone calls, written updates, e-mail, and voice mail.[44]

Telecommuting

One of the more dynamic changes and potentially the most far-reaching is telecommuting. **Telecommuting** is the use of personal computers, networks, and other communications technology such as fax machines to do work in the home that is traditionally done in the workplace.

telecommuting
Use of personal computers, networks, and other communications technology such as fax machines to do work in the home that is traditionally done in the workplace

A variant of telecommunicating is the *virtual office,* where employees are in the field helping customers or are stationed at other remote locations working as if they were in the home office.[45]

Both managers and HR professionals note the following advantages of telecommuting:[46]

- Increased flexibility for employees
- Ability to attract workers who might not otherwise be available
- Lessened burden on working parents
- Less time and money wasted on physical commuting
- Increased productivity
- Reduced absenteeism

Perhaps the strongest economic reason in favor of telecommuting is its power to retain valued employees. Retention is a top priority for employers largely because the costs of replacing employees are far higher than those involved in installing a telecommunicating arrangement. Figure 4.9 presents suggestions for establishing a successful telecommuting program.

While telecommuting offers significant benefits to employers, it also presents potential drawbacks. These include the loss of creativity as employees are not interacting with one another on a regular basis, the difficulty of developing appropriate performance standards and evaluation systems for telecommuters, and the need to formulate an appropriate technology strategy for allocating the necessary equipment.[47] Additionally, managers may believe that telecommuting negatively affects employee-supervisor relationships through loss of knowledge or information, trust,

Figure 4.9 Keys for Successful Telecommuting

- *Identify jobs best suited to distance work.* Those involving sales, customer service, and auditing are logical choices.
- *Select responsible employees.* Employees who are self-starters, motivated, and trustworthy and who can work independently are ideal candidates. Establish employee feedback procedures and performance review methods for employee evaluation.
- *Establish formalized telecommuting procedures.* Telecommuting guidelines could cover hours of availability, office reporting periods, performance expectations, and weekly progress reports or e-mail updates.
- *Begin a formal training program.* Training for both telecommuters and managers should include the technical aspects of equipment usage and relationship factors such as how and when to contact the office or availability and location of support facilities.
- *Keep telecommuters informed.* Physical separation can make telecommuters feel isolated and invisible. Department and staff updates, inclusion of telecommuters on project teams, required attendance at meetings, and "chat room" discussions all keep telecommuters "in the loop."
- *Recognize when telecommuting isn't working.* State in telecommunicating policies that the arrangement may be terminated when it no longer serves company needs or if the employee's performance declines.

Source: Adapted from Barbara Hemphill, "Telecommuting Productivity," *Occupational Health and Safety* 73, no. 3 (March 2004): 16.

and a sense of connectedness.[48] Employers wishing to have their employees telecommute must also comply with wage and hour laws, workers' compensation regulations, equipment purchase or rental agreements with employees, and federal EEO posting requirements (see Chapter 3). Employees who are denied the opportunity to work from home may feel discriminated against and elect to pursue legal action or simply become disgruntled employees.

SUMMARY

objective 1 Job requirements reflect the different duties, tasks, and responsibilities contained in jobs. Job requirements, in turn, influence HR functions performed by managers, including recruitment, selection, training and development, performance appraisal, compensation, and various labor relations activities.

objective 2 Job analysis data may be gathered using several collection methods—interviews, questionnaires, observations, and diaries. Other more quantitative approaches include use of the functional job analysis, the position analysis questionnaire system, the critical incident method, task inventory analysis, and computerized job analysis. It is the prevailing opinion of the courts that HRM decisions on employment, performance appraisal, and promotions must be based on specific criteria that are job-related. These criteria can be determined objectively only by analyzing the requirements of each job.

objective 3 The format of job descriptions varies widely, often reflecting the needs of the organization and the expertise of the writer. As a minimum, job descriptions should contain a job title, a job identification section, and an essential functions section. A job specification section also may be included. Job descriptions should be written in clear and specific terms with consideration given to their legal implications.

objective 4 Job design is a combination of four basic considerations: organizational objectives; industrial engineering concerns of analyzing work methods and establishing time standards; ergonomic considerations, which accommodate human capabilities and limitations to job tasks; and employee contributions.

objective 5 In the job characteristics model, five job factors contribute to increased job performance and satisfaction—skill variety, task identity, task significance, autonomy, and feedback. All factors should be built into jobs, since each factor influences different employee psychological states. When jobs are enriched through the job characteristics model, employees experience more meaningfulness in their jobs, acquire more job responsibility, and receive direct feedback from the tasks they perform.

objective 6 To improve the internal process of organizations and increase American productivity, greater efforts are being made by organizations to involve groups of employees in work operations. Employee involvement groups are composed of employees in work units charged with offering suggestions for improving product or service quality or fostering workplace effectiveness. Employee teams stress employee collaboration over individual accomplishment. Teams rely on the expertise and different abilities of members to achieve a specific goal or objective. Self-directed teams are characterized by their willingness to perform traditional managerial tasks.

objective 7 Changes in work schedules—which include the compressed workweek, flextime, job sharing, and telecommuting—permit employees to adjust their work periods to accommodate their particular lifestyles. Employees can select from among these HR techniques to accommodate diverse employee needs while fostering organizational effectiveness.

KEY TERMS

critical incident method
employee empowerment
employee involvement groups (EIs)
employee teams
ergonomics
flextime
functional job analysis (FJA)
industrial engineering
job
job analysis
job characteristics model
job description
job design
job enrichment
job family
job specification
position
position analysis questionnaire (PAQ)
task inventory analysis
telecommuting
virtual team

DISCUSSION QUESTIONS

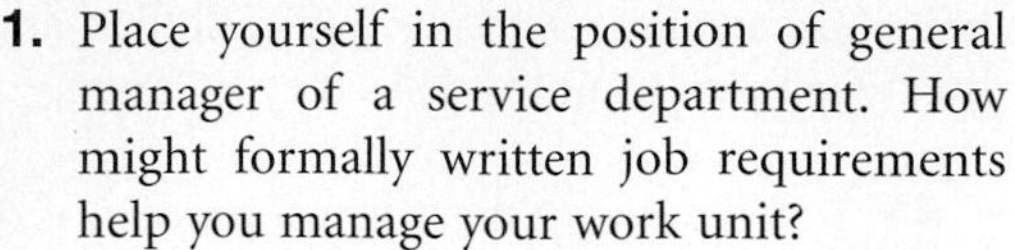

1. Place yourself in the position of general manager of a service department. How might formally written job requirements help you manage your work unit?

2. Discuss the various methods by which job analysis can be completed. Compare and contrast these methods, noting the pros or cons of each.

3. Working with a group of three or four students, collect at least five different job descriptions from organizations in your area. Compare the descriptions, highlighting similarities and differences.

4. Explain how industrial engineering and ergonomics can both clash with and complement each other in the design of jobs.

5. The job characteristics model has five components that enhance employee jobs—skill variety, task identity, task significance, autonomy, and feedback. Give an example illustrating how each component can be used to improve the organization and the job of the employee. (Suggestion: Consider your present or a recent job to answer this question.)

6. Figure 4.8 shows the different forms of employee teams. Provide an example of where each type of team can be used. How do teams create synergy?

7. As a small-business employer, explain how nontraditional work schedules might make it easier for you to recruit employees.

BIZFLIX EXERCISES

Intolerable Cruelty: Just Doing My Job

This chapter discussed several aspects of job analysis and job design. Try to apply much of that discussion to this scene from the film *Intolerable Cruelty.* Use the questions below as guides to your viewing.

Ruthless, beautiful Marilyn Rexroth (Catherine Zeta-Jones) matches the brilliance of divorce attorney Miles Massey (George Clooney). Conflict rises and falls as the two try to outwit each other in this charming romantic comedy. The film twists and turns in typical Coen brothers (co-screenwriters; Joel Cohen, director) fashion as it reaches its predictable end.

This scene comes from "The War Room" segment that occurs about 20 minutes into the film. It follows Rex Rexroth's (George Herrmann) escapade with a young woman (Kristen Dattilo). His wife, Marilyn Rexroth, hired private detective Gus Petch (Cedric the Entertainer) to videotape the event. He now needs some legal help. Miles Massey meets his new client and discusses the case. The film continues with some women sitting by The Waters swimming pool talking about their ex- and present husbands.

What to Watch for and Ask Yourself

- What knowledge, skills, and abilities (KSAs) are required for the successful performance of Miles Massey's job?
- Recall the earlier chapter section "Job Analysis." Apply some observations from that section to this scene. What duties, tasks, and activities do you infer from the scene for Massey's job?
- Job design views certain job characteristics as important for a person's motivation and satisfaction (see the earlier section "Job Design"). Which of the five core job dimensions appear(s) in Miles Massey's job?

HRM Experience

Establishing Ground Rules for Team Success

Professional trainers understand that setting ground rules for teams is a cornerstone for continued team success. Ground rules—or team norms—are agreed-on formal rules that guide group member behavior. Norms established prior to the team's task regulate the behavior of group members. Ground rules simply state how members want to be treated and how members agree to treat others. When team members follow the established norms, then norms help maintain order, promote positive behavior, and can be used to correct undesirable actions. Remember, because teams operate in different settings, different norms may be appropriate in different arrangements.

Assignment

1. Working within your team, select what you believe are the ten most important norms for team behavior.
2. From the following Behavior List, have each team member *silently* select two lists of ten items each of the behaviors they believe most critical for team success. The first list of ten items (your A list) is considered the most important for group conduct. The second list (the B list) is desired items but those not of major importance.
3. In a group discussion, have all team members select a final list of ten items from both lists. These become your team's final norms. Select no more than ten items. During your discussion, items can be modified or combined to meet your team's specific needs.
4. Prepare a written document of chosen behaviors and have all team members sign the form. You have now established a written contract for positive team conduct.

Behavior List

While working in our team, individuals should . . .

1. Do their fair share of the work.
2. Check to ensure that everyone clearly understands what is to be done.
3. Encourage planning, including short-range agendas as well as long-range goals.
4. Encourage open and candid opinions about issues.
5. Listen willingly and carefully to other people's ideas, even if those people have a different viewpoint.
6. Prepare thoroughly before meetings.
7. Make team members feel at ease in discussion.
8. Ask questions when they do not clearly understand tasks or procedures.
9. Propose specific analyses of the pros and cons of decisions faced by the team.
10. Follow through on task assignments.
11. Help other members when assistance is requested.
12. Treat all team members as equals.
13. Paraphrase or restate what someone else says in order to check meaning.
14. Openly voice opinions and share ideas.
15. Be flexible in arranging meeting schedules.

16. Compliment others for things they have said or done.
17. Be willing to meet whenever it is necessary to discuss a problem.
18. Deal with conflict directly, bringing it to the attention of the team.
19. Express enthusiasm about what the team is doing.
20. Encourage budgeting of the team's time.
21. At the end of a meeting, restate their own responsibilities to check for agreement.
22. Be serious about the team's work.
23. Arrive on time for regularly scheduled meetings.
24. Be willing to listen to other team members' ideas.
25. Get the team's approval on important matters before proceeding.

case study 1

Building a Stealth Fighter with Virtual Teams

On October 26, 2001, defense contractor Lockheed Martin Aeronautics of Fort Worth, Texas, won its largest manufacturing contract ever—a whopping $200 million. The contract, received from the U.S. Department of Defense, is to build a new family of supersonic stealth fighter planes. Success of the megaproject will hinge greatly on intricate teamwork. For example, more than eighty suppliers will be working at 187 locations worldwide to design and build components of the Joint Strike Fighter. A seventy-five-member technology group at Lockheed's aeronautics division will link the suppliers, along with the U.S. Air Force, Navy, and Marines, to Britain's Defense Ministry to track progress and make midstream design and production changes if necessary. Individuals working at more than 40,000 computer stations will collaborate to get the first plane airborne in just four years. Speaking of the teamwork involved, Mark Peden, vice president for information systems at Lockheed Aeronautics, said, "It's the true virtual connection."

Teams working both nationally and internationally will interact as if team members were working in the same room. Teams will communicate via their computers while looking at shared documents, carry on e-mail chats, and use electronic whiteboards on which geographically separated team members can draw pictures or charts, in real time, as others watch and respond. The Internet is designed to allow people from different companies with incompatible computing systems to interface on web sites that speak a common language.

QUESTIONS

1. What advantages will Lockheed Martin gain by using virtual teams? Explain.
2. Identify and discuss potential problems with using virtual teams—for example, interpersonal, technical, or geographical concerns.
3. Discuss specific training that virtual teams could receive.

Source: This case was written by George Bohlander, based on information found in Faith Keenan and Spencer E. Ante, "The New Teamwork," *Business Week* (February 18, 2002): EB 12.

case study 2

But My Job Has Changed

Job descriptions are a critical tool used for job orientation and training and, importantly, in annual employee performance evaluations. When the duties and responsibilities listed in the job description do not reflect current job content employee/management disagreements can arise, as this case illustrates.

Both employees and managers agree that Brenda Batten has been an exceptional employee. As a senior technical representative (STR) for Blackhawk Aironics, she is valued for her knowledge in airplane instrumentation. One manager described her as "simply an expert in the complex technology of satellite weather systems."

In May 2004, Blackhawk Aironics implemented a new work reorganization plan. STRs such as Brenda now work largely by telecommuting with managers and engineers at company headquarters in Denton, Texas, and with customers scattered throughout the United States. Additionally, under the new work plan, STRs were given more freedom to deal directly with customers and engineers without supervisory intervention. This freedom greatly facilitated customer service needs and demands in an aviation market everyone considers highly dynamic.

Brenda's current job description reflects the technical dimensions of her position but not the telecommuting requirements now performed. Personal competencies such as decision-making, self-motivation, problem-solving, and communication skills are not covered.

In May 2005, Brenda met with her manager, Martin Eaton, for her annual performance review. Unfortunately, unlike past meetings, which were highly satisfactory, this meeting quickly developed into a disagreement. At the center of the controversy were the factors to be used to measure Brenda's new job demands. Martin wanted to place major emphasis on the tasks and duties listed in her current job description. As he explained to Brenda, "I hardly see you anymore, and I have no objective criteria or performance data by which to measure those behaviors you now use." Brenda, in response, acknowledged that some things in the current job description were still important aspects of her job, but overall the current job description did not capture the full scope of her new duties and responsibilities. Brenda concluded that she was satisfied with Martin's evaluation of the technical aspects of her job, but she was clearly not pleased with the overall evaluation of her performance. As she told Martin, "It's simply not fair, you just don't know what I do now."

QUESTIONS

1. Given the facts of this case, is it possible for Brenda and Martin to reach a satisfactory result? Explain.
2. How could an organization go about identifying and measuring the personal competencies of employees?
3. How could the company prevent this problem from occurring in the future? Explain.

Source: Based on an actual case known to the authors. All names and locations are fictitious.

NOTES AND REFERENCES

1. Arnold B. Bakker, Evangelia Demeroob, and Willem Verbeke, "Using the Job Demands Resources Model to Predict Burnout and Performance," *Human Resources Management* 43, no. 1 (Spring 2004): 83.
2. Pam Withers, "Retention Strategies That Respond to Worker Values," *Workforce* 80, no. 7 (July 2001): 37–41.
3. Thiagarajan Srinivasan and Brian H. Kleiner, "How to Hire Employees Effectively," *Management Research News* 25, no. 5 (2002): 65–75.
4. Adapted from job description for "Senior HR Analyst," City of Mesa, Arizona.
5. Donald M. Truxillo, Matthew E. Paronto, Michelle Collins, and Jefferson L. Sulzer, "Effects of Subject Matter Expert Viewpoint on Job Analysis Results," *Public Personnel Management* 33, no. 1 (Spring 2004): 33–44.
6. George T. Milkovich and Jerry M. Newman, *Compensation*, 8th ed. (Boston: McGraw-Hill Irwin, 2005).
7. Richard Henderson, *Compensation Management in a Knowledged-Based World*, 9th ed. (Englewood Cliffs, NJ: Prentice Hall, 2003).
8. Information on the technical aspects of the Americans with Disabilities Act can be obtained from the Equal Employment Opportunity Commission. See, for example, *The ADA: Questions and Answers, ADA Technical Assistance and Resource Manual,* and *The ADA: Your Responsibility as an Employer*. Publications can be ordered from the EEOC web site at http://www.eeoc.gov.
9. The O*NET database Internet site is at http://www.doleta.gov/programs/onet/.
10. A detailed description of different job analysis techniques is beyond the scope of this text. For those interested in more comprehensive information or job analysis tools, see Michael T. Bannick and Edward Levine, *Job Analysis: Methods, Research, and Applications for Human Resource Management in the New Millennium* (Thousand Oaks, CA: Sage, 2002).
11. Helen Palmer and Will Valet, "Job Analysis: Targeting Needed Skills," *Employment Relations Today* 28, no. 3 (Autumn 2001): 85–92.
12. Erich P. Prien, Kristin O. Prien, and Louis G. Gamble, "Perspectives on Nonconventional Job Analysis Methodologies," *Journal of Business and Psychology* 18, no. 3 (Spring 2004): 337.
13. Chris Burand, "Good Job Descriptions Can Boost Productivity," *American Agent and Broker* 74, no. 10 (October 2002): 8.
14. Chi Ming Chow and Brian H. Kleiner, "How to Differentiate Essential Job Duties from Marginal Job Duties," *Managerial Law* 44, no. 1/2 (2002): 121–26.
15. Jamie Swedberg, "Put It in Writing," *Credit Union Management* 26, no. 12 (December 2003): 50–53.
16. Chapter 3 discusses the *Uniform Guidelines on Employee Selection Procedures* and the necessity for performance standards to be based on valid job-related criteria.
17. Sharon K. Parker, Toby D. Wall, and John L. Cordery, "Future Work Design Research and Practice: Toward an Elaborated Model of Work," *Journal of Occupational and Organizational Psychology* 74 (November 2001): 413–40.
18. A. S. Evangelista and Lisa A. Burke, "Work Redesign and Performance Management in Times of Downsizing," *Business Horizons* 46, no. 2 (March/April 2003): 71.
19. For Herzberg's important article on job enrichment, see Frederick Herzberg, "One More Time: How Do You Motivate Employees?" *Harvard Business Review* 46, no. 2 (January–February 1968): 53–62.
20. For the original article on the job characteristics model, see J. Richard Hackman and Greg R. Oldham, "Motivation through the Design of Work: Test of a Theory," *Organizational Behavior and Human Performance* 16, no. 2 (August 1976): 250–79.
21. Scott Smith, "Ergonomics and Manufacturing Excellence," *Occupational Hazards* 64, no. 9 (September 2002): 47–48.
22. Bernie Knill, "Practical Ergonomics for Plant People," *Material Handling Management* 57, no. 2 (September 2002): 53.
23. Andrew J. DuBrin, *Fundamentals of Organizational Behavior*, 3rd ed. (Cincinnati, OH: South-Western, 2005): Chapter 10.
24. Ann Pomeroy, "Great Places, Inspired Employees," *HRMagazine* 49, no. 7 (July 2004): 46.
25. Debbie D. Dufrene and Carol M. Lehman, *Building High Performance Teams*, 2nd ed. (Cincinnati, OH: South-Western, 2005).
26. Debra J. Housel, *Team Dynamics* (Mason, OH: South-Western, 2002).
27. Alden M. Hayashi, "Building Better Teams," *Sloan Management Review* 45, no. 2 (Winter 2004): 5.
28. Jon R. Katzenbach and Douglas Smith, "The Discipline of Teams," *Harvard Business Review* 83, no. 7 (July–August 2005): 162. See also Leigh Thompson, "Improving the Creativity of Organizational Work Groups," *The Academy of Management Executive* 17, no. 1 (February 2003): 96.
29. Michael Hansen, "Virtual Teams That Work: Creating Conditions for Virtual Team Effectiveness," *Personal Psychology* 57, no. 1 (Spring 2004): 243.
30. Ruth Wageman, "Multinational Work Teams: A New Perspective," *Administrative Science Quarterly* 48, no. 2 (June 2003): 332.
31. Stacie A. Furst, Martha Reeves, Benson Rosen, and Richard S. Blackburn, "Managing the Life Cycle of Virtual Teams," *Academy of Management Executive* 18, no. 2 (May 2004): 6.
32. Interview with Paulette Tichenor, Arizona State University, Tempe, Arizona, January 18, 2004. See also Bradley L. Kirkman, Benson Rosen, Paul E. Tesluk, and Cristina B. Gibson, "The Impact of Team Empowerment on Virtual Team Performance: The Moderating Role of Face-to-Face Interaction," *Academy of Management Journal* 47, no. 2 (April 2004): 175.
33. David Clutterbuck, "Teams and Learning: The Agenda Has Changed," *Training Strategies for Tomorrow* 17, no. 2 (2003): 10.

34. Glenn Parker, "Leading a Team of Strangers," *Training and Development* 57, no. 2 (February 2003): 21.
35. For a discussion of the stages of team development, see Don Hellriegel and John W. Slocum, Jr., *Organizational Behavior,* 10th ed. (Cincinnati, OH: South-Western, 2004): 203–206.
36. Charles E. Naguin and Renee O. Tynan, "The Team Halo Effect: Why Teams Are Not Blamed for Their Failures," *Journal of Applied Psychology* 88, no. 2 (April 2003): 332.
37. Vicki Powers, "Keeping Work and Life in Balance," *Training and Development* 58, no. 7 (July 2004): 32.
38. "The Latest Data on Gen X Women and Their Perceptions," *HRFocus* 79, no. 2 (February 2002): 9.
39. Rosalind Chait Barnett and Douglas T. Hall, "How to Use Reduced Hours to Win the War for Talent," *Organizational Dynamics* 29, no. 3 (Winter 2001): 101.
40. Michael White, Stephen Hill, Patrick McGovern, and Colin Mills, "'High Performance' Management Practices: Working Hours and Work-Life Balance," *British Journal of Industrial Relations* 41, no. 2 (June 2003): 175. See also Virginia Smith Major, Katherine J. Klein, and Mark G. Ehrhart, "Work Time, Work Interference with Family, and Psychological Distress," *Journal of Applied Psychology* 87, no. 3 (June 2002): 427.
41. Overtime provisions of the Fair Labor Standards Act can be found at the Department of Labor web site at http://www.dol.gov.
42. Sara Fisher Gale, "Formalized Flextime: The Perk That Brings Productivity," *Workforce* 80, no. 2 (February 2001): 39–42.
43. Sherry E. Sullivan, David F. Martin, William A. Carden, and Lisa A. Mainiero, "The Road Less Traveled: How to Manage the Recycling Career Stage," *Journal of Leadership and Organizational Studies* 10, no. 2 (Fall 2003): 34.
44. Kenneth L. Schultz, John O. McClain, and L. Joseph Thomas, "Overcoming the Dark Side of Worker Flexibility," *Journal of Operations Management* 21, no. 1 (January 2003): 81.
45. Anne-Mette Jhalager, "Virtual Working: Traditional and Emerging Institutional Framework for the Contingent Workforce," *International Journal of Manpower* 24, no. 2 (2003): 422–39.
46. "Time to Take Another Look at Telecommuting," *HRFocus* 79, no. 5 (May 2002): 6.
47. Gus Manchehri and Theresa Pinkerton, "Managing Telecommuters: Opportunities and Challenges," *American Business Review* 21, no. 1 (January 2003): 9.
48. Jathan W. Janove, "Managing by Remote Control," *HRMagazine* 49, no. 3 (April 2004): 119–24.

chapter 5

Expanding the Talent Pool: Recruitment and Careers

After studying this chapter, you should be able to

Explain the advantages and disadvantages of external recruitment.

Explain the advantages and disadvantages of recruiting from within the organization.

Discuss how job opportunities can be inventoried and employee potential assessed.

Explain how a career management program integrates individual and organizational needs.

Describe the conditions that help make a career management program successful.

Explain why diverse recruitment and career development activities are important to companies.

In earlier chapters we stressed that many HR challenges center on the idea that organizations increasingly compete on the basis of their employee talents and capabilities. Even though workers seemed to be in plentiful supply following the recession of 2001, that began changing as the economy recovered. Moreover, as the baby boomers begin retiring, the demand for labor is expected to grow by between 9 and 22 percent—far outstripping supply.

Increased competition for talent means that recruiting has acquired new importance for managers. Today, many jobs require higher skill levels, and no longer can managers rely solely on unsolicited applications to fill these positions. To stay apace of their competitors and expand their operations around the world, companies are also having to look globally for workers. It is therefore essential that organizations do a good job of broadening their pools of talent—the number and kinds of people able to contribute to the success of the organization, and the variety of ways in which they recruit and retain them.

Of course, unlike physical assets, human assets (employees) can decide to leave the firm of their own accord as well as join it. And in the war for talent, rival firms are likely to lure valued employees away. Employees may find that their options and opportunities are more attractive across firms rather than within only one firm. Flatter organization structures mean that there are fewer positions for promotion, so individuals must look for advancement opportunities outside the firm. At the same time, as economic cycles lead organizations first to hire—and then to lay off—and then to hire again, employment security can be assured only when individuals take control of their own careers. The upshot is that individuals are less likely to work in the same job for extended periods and, in fact, most are unlikely to spend their entire careers with only one firm. In other words, today's labor market—for both employees and employers—has become more "free agent" oriented.[1]

In this chapter we will discuss various sources and approaches to expanding the talent pool in organizations. Specifically, we will discuss both external sources of recruitment and internal sources (such as promotion, transfers, and the like). But beyond recruiting itself, we will also discuss the approaches that organizations take toward career management over time. As organizations consider the long-term implications for managing talent, career progressions are taking on new importance. Finally, at the end of the chapter, we devote special attention to the recruitment and career development of minorities and women.

Recruiting Talent Externally

Recruitment is the process of locating potential individuals who might join an organization and encouraging them to apply for existing or anticipated job openings. During this process, efforts are made to inform the applicants fully about the qualifications required to perform the job and the career opportunities the organization can offer its employees. Whether a particular job vacancy will be filled by someone from within the organization or from outside will, of course, depend on the availability of personnel, the organization's HR policies, and the requirements of the job to be staffed. Highlights in HRM 1 outlines Marriott's principles for recruiting.

Unless managers intend to reduce the size of the workforce, any job vacancy is a cue that a replacement from outside must be found to replace a departing employee. An old adage goes something like this: "When the president or CEO of the organization retires, a chain reaction of promotions occurs. Everyone moves up a slot, and someone new is hired into a starting position in the mailroom." Of course this almost never occurs, but the story provides a framework for how some companies approach their recruiting philosophy. More realistically, when there is an opening, managers must make careful decisions about whom to bring into the position, and how best to approach the decision. The question therefore is not whether to bring people into the organization, but rather at which level they are to be brought in.

In the past few years, an astonishing number of the nation's largest companies, including McDonald's, Hewlett-Packard, Home Depot, and 3M, have brought in outsiders to be their new CEOs. Stock prices rose and fell based on a CEO's appointment. Hiring someone from the outside was seen as essential for revitalizing organizations.[2]

Outside Sources for Recruitment

The outside sources from which employers recruit will vary with the type of position to be filled. A computer programmer, for example, is not likely to be recruited from the same source as a machine operator. Trade schools can provide applicants for entry-level positions, though these recruitment sources are not as useful when highly skilled employees are needed. Some firms keep detailed statistics by job type on the sources from which their employees are hired. This helps human resources managers make better decisions about the places to begin recruiting when different job openings arise.

The condition of the labor market may also help determine which recruiting sources an organization will use. During periods of high unemployment, organizations may be able to maintain an adequate supply of qualified applicants from unsolicited resumes alone. A tight labor market, one with low unemployment, may force the employer to advertise heavily and/or seek assistance from local employment agencies. How successful an organization has been in reaching its affirmative action goals may be still another factor in determining the sources from which to recruit. Typically, an employer at any given time will find it necessary to use several recruitment sources.

Several other studies have suggested that an employee's recruitment source can affect that employee's subsequent tenure and job performance in both large and small organizations.[3] In general, applicants who find employment through referral by a current employee tend to remain with the organization longer and give higher-quality performance than employees recruited through the formal recruitment sources of advertisements and employment agencies. Informal recruiting sources may also yield higher selection rates than formal sources. Employers are cautioned, however, that relying on only one or two recruitment sources to secure job applicants could have an adverse effect on protected classes.

Advertisements

One of the most common methods of attracting applicants is through advertisements. Although web sites, newspapers, and trade journals are the media used most

Highlights in HRM 1

Marriott's Recruitment Principles

#1: Get It Right the First Time. Marriott "hires friendly" and "trains technical." It's better to hire people with "the spirit to serve" and train them to work than hire people who know business and try to teach them to enjoy serving guests. Marriott hires cooks who love to cook and housekeepers who love to clean. They have learned that this approach works both for delivering excellent service and for retaining their employees.

#2: Money Is a Big Thing, But . . . The top concern of Marriott associates is total compensation. But intangible factors taken together, such as work-life balance, leadership quality, opportunity for advancement, work environment, and training, far outweigh money in their decisions to stay or leave. Pay matters less and the other factors matter more the longer someone works for Marriott. From flexible schedules to tailored benefit packages and development opportunities, Marriott has built systems to address these nonmonetary factors.

#3: A Caring Workplace Is a Bottom-Line Issue. When employees come to work, they feel safe, secure, and welcome. Committed associates are less likely to leave. And associate work commitment is one of the key drivers of guest satisfaction. Managers are accountable for associate satisfaction ratings and for turnover rates. Every day, associates in each of Marriott's full-service hotels participate in a fifteen-minute meeting to review basic values such as respect. Managers also encourage associates to raise their personal concerns. They take the time to celebrate birthdays and anniversaries. Marriott calls this the loyalty program, because it builds loyalty among associates and repeat business from customers. The result is that everyone has a stake in making the hotel a success.

#4: Promote from Within. More than 50 percent of Marriott's current managers have been promoted from within. All associates are given the opportunity to advance as far as their abilities will carry them. Elevating veterans to positions of leadership helps Marriott pass on the soul of its business—its corporate culture—from one generation to the next. In addition, promoting from within is a powerful tool for recruitment and retention. Associates cite "opportunity for advancement" as a key factor in their decisions to stay with Marriott. (Accompanying that is a $100-million-a-year commitment to training.)

#5: Build the Employment Brand. Marriott attracts employees the same way it attracts customers. Just as consumers buy experiences, not just products, potential employees are looking for a great work experience when they shop for jobs. Communicating the promise of a great work experience is what employment branding is all about. It's basically a value proposition. According to CEO J. W. Marriott, "For more than 70 years, we've lived by a simple motto: If we take care of our associates they'll take care of our guests. That isn't just a sentiment. It's a strategy—one all businesses must adopt to remain competitive in an environment where our most valuable resource, human capital, drives economic value for our company."

Source: J. W. Marriott, "Competitive Strength," *Executive Excellence* 18, no. 4 (April 2001): 3–4; J. W. Marriott, "Our Competitive Strength: Human Capital," *Executive Speeches* 15, no. 5 (April/May 2001): 18–21.

often, radio, television, billboards, posters, and e-mail are also used. Advertising has the advantage of reaching a large audience of possible applicants. Some degree of selectivity can be achieved by using newspapers and journals directed toward a particular group of readers. Professional journals, trade journals, and publications of unions and various fraternal or nonprofit organizations fall into this category.

The preparation of recruiting advertisements not only is time-consuming, but also requires creativity in developing design and message content. Well-written advertisements highlight the major assets of the position while showing the responsiveness of the organization to the job and career needs of the applicants. Also, there appears to be a correlation between the accuracy and completeness of information provided in advertisements and the recruitment success of the organization. Among the information typically included in advertisements is that the recruiting organization is an equal opportunity employer.

Advertising can sometimes place a severe burden on an organization's employment office. Even though the specifications for the openings are described thoroughly in the advertisement, many applicants who know they do not meet the job requirements may still be attracted. They may apply with the hope that the employer will not be able to find applicants who do meet the specifications.

Unsolicited Applications and Resumes

Many employers receive unsolicited applications and resumes from individuals who may or may not be good prospects for employment. Even though the percentage of acceptable applicants from this source may not be high, it is a source that cannot be ignored. In fact, it is often believed that individuals who contact the employer on their own initiative will be better employees than those recruited through college placement services or newspaper advertisements.

Good public relations dictates that any person contacting an organization for a job be treated with courtesy and respect. If there is no possibility of employment in the organization at present or in the future, the applicant should be tactfully and frankly informed of this fact. Telling an applicant to "fill out an application, and we will keep it on file" when there is no hope for his or her employment is not fair to the applicant. Research has shown that a candidate who has been treated well by a potential employer will, on average, tell one other person. On the other hand, a candidate who has been treated poorly—perhaps receiving a tardy rejection letter or no letter all—will, on average, tell eleven other people.[4]

Internet Recruiting

According to a Society for Human Resource Management study, looking on the Internet is the most commonly used search tactic by job seekers; nine out of ten recruiters use the Internet to get the word out about new positions. Both companies and applicants find the approach cheaper, faster, and potentially more effective.

There are now more than 4,000 web sites where applicants can submit their resumes and potential employers can check for qualified applicants. Applicant tracking systems can match the job requirements with the experiences and skills of applicants. Monster.com is the leading job site, with more than 25 million resumes online. Other job sites include Jobcentral.com, created by a group of Fortune 500 companies to bypass intermediaries such as Monster.com. Specialty Internet recruiting sites such as AttorneyJobs.com, AMFMJobs.com (for radio personnel), Vets4Hire.com,

Figure 5.1 **Top Internet Recruiting Sites**

SITE	VISITORS PER MONTH
Monster.com	10,774,000
Yahoo! Hot Jobs	3,545,000
CareerBuilder	3,342,000
USAJobs	1,270.000
AOL Career	1,120,000

Source: "Hot Internet Recruiting Sites," *HRFocus* 8, no. 2 (August 2004): 8.

and 6FigureJobs.com (for executives) are seeing increasing traffic. Figure 5.1 shows the top Internet job sites and the number of visitors each typically gets per month.[5]

Employee Referrals

The recruitment efforts of an organization can be greatly aided by employee referrals, or recommendations from the firm's current employees about potential candidates. In fact, word-of-mouth recommendations are the way most job positions are filled. (Apparently there is truth to the phrase, "It's not what you know, but who you know.") Managers have found that the quality of employee-referred applicants is normally quite high, since employees are generally hesitant to recommend individuals who might not perform well.

There are several suggested ways to increase the effectiveness of employee referral programs:

- *Up the ante.* Companies pay high commissions to employment agencies and search firms, so why not do the same thing with employees when they provide a good referral? Other recruitment incentives used by organizations include complimentary dinners, discounts on merchandise, all-expenses-paid trips, and free insurance. When employers pay higher bonuses for "hot" skills, employees are more likely to focus on people they know in that area.
- *Pay for performance.* Some firms save part of the referral bonus until the new hire has stayed for six months. This encourages referring employees to help the new hires succeed.
- *Tailor the program.* Companies typically need more of certain types of skills than others, but the referral programs do not always reflect this. Part of a good referral program is educating employees about the kinds of people the organization wants to hire. This includes some communication of the skills required, but also a reaffirmation of the values and ethics sought in applicants.
- *Increase visibility.* One of the best ways to publicize a referral program is to celebrate successes. Some companies use novel approaches such as "job of the month" or "celebrity endorsements" from managers. The idea is to keep everyone thinking about bringing in good people.

- *Keep the data.* Even if a referral does not get the job, it might be a good idea to keep the resume on file just in case another vacancy arises.
- *Rethink your taboos.* Some companies are reluctant to take on certain potential hires, such as former employees, relatives, and the like. In a tight labor market, it is a good idea to broaden the search.
- *Widen the program.* Just as it may make sense to consider hiring former employees, it may make sense to ask them for referrals even if they are not candidates for the jobs themselves. A number of companies have mailing lists of "corporate friends" that can be used to seek out potential candidates.
- *Measure results.* No surprise here. After the program is implemented, managers need to take a hard look at the volume of referrals, the qualifications of candidates, and the success of new hires on the job. These results are then fed back to fine-tune the program.[6]

Some potential negative factors are associated with employee referrals. They include the possibility of inbreeding and the violation of EEO regulations. Since employees and their referrals tend to have similar backgrounds, employers who rely heavily on employee referrals to fill job openings may intentionally or unintentionally screen out, and thereby discriminate against, protected classes. Furthermore, organizations may choose not to employ relatives of current employees. The practice of hiring relatives, referred to as **nepotism,** can invite charges of favoritism, especially in appointments to desirable positions. Nepotism, however, gets mixed reviews, in part, because family members are in an ideal position to pass job knowledge and skills on to one another. Many corporate dynasties (Ford Motor Company and the Rockefeller Foundation among them) have been built on nepotism. Labor unions would not have flourished without it. In recent years, a number of law firms and universities have dropped restrictions against hiring spouses on the basis that they are prejudicial.[7]

nepotism
A preference for hiring relatives of current employees

Executive Search Firms

In contrast to public and private employment agencies, which help job seekers find the right job, executive search firms (often called "headhunters") help employers find the right person for a job. Firms such as Korn/Ferry International, Heidrick & Struggles, MercerDelta Consulting, and the Hunter Group seek out candidates with qualifications that match the requirements of the positions their client firm is seeking to fill. Executive search firms do not advertise in the media for job candidates, nor do they accept a fee from the individual being placed.

The fees charged by search firms may range from 30 to 40 percent of the annual salary for the position to be filled. For the recruitment of senior executives, this fee is paid by the client firm, whether or not the recruiting effort results in a hire. It is for this practice that search firms receive the greatest criticism.

Nevertheless, as noted earlier, hiring new chief executive officers (CEOs) from outside the organization has become commonplace. A large number of these new CEOs are placed in those positions through the services of an executive search firm. Because high-caliber executives are in short supply, a significant number of the nation's largest corporations, including BMW, Texaco, Pillsbury, and MONEY Financial Services, have used search firms to fill their top positions. However, newer data suggest that CEOs who are promoted from within their organizations actually outperform those hired from the outside. In light of the numerous CEO-related scandals that have occurred in recent times, human resources personnel are increasingly being called on to demand more from executive search firms and to assist boards of directors in the careful selection of top executives.[8]

Educational Institutions

Educational institutions typically are a source of young applicants with formal training but relatively little full-time work experience. High schools are usually a source of employees for clerical and blue-collar jobs. Community colleges, with their various types of specialized training, can provide candidates for technical jobs. These institutions can also be a source of applicants for a variety of white-collar jobs, including those in the sales and retail fields. Some management-trainee jobs are also staffed from this source.

For technical and managerial positions, colleges and universities are generally the primary source. About 30 percent of workers in the United States hold a bachelor's degree—about the same percentage as in 1980. Given these numbers and the strong demand for high-skilled employees, colleges are likely to remain a good recruiting source. However, the suitability of college graduates for open positions often depends on their major field of study. Organizations seeking applicants in the technical and professional areas, for example, frequently face a shortage of qualified candidates. Not surprisingly, graduates in these areas command higher pay. For example, in 2004, the average salary offered to information science graduates was $44,075, versus $28,388 offered to communications grads.[9] Figure 5.2 shows the number of people employed in the United States in various occupations, and what their average annual wages are. To attract high-demand graduates, in addition to higher pay, firms sometimes employ innovative recruitment techniques such as work-study programs, internships, low-interest loans, and scholarships.

USING THE INTERNET

All types of media releases, including weekly unemployment figures and special reports, are available at the Department of Labor's web site. Go to the Student Resources at:

http://bohlander.swlearning.com

Some employers fail to take full advantage of college and university resources because of a poor recruitment program.[10] Consequently, their recruitment efforts fail to attract many potentially good applicants. Another common weakness is the failure to maintain a planned and continuing effort on a long-term basis. Furthermore, some recruiters sent to college campuses are not sufficiently trained or prepared to talk to interested candidates about career opportunities or the requirements of specific openings. Attempts to visit too many campuses instead of concentrating on selected institutions and the inability to use the campus placement office effectively are other recruiting weaknesses. Mismanagement of applicant visits to the organization's headquarters and the failure to follow up on individual prospects or to obtain hiring commitments from higher management are among other mistakes that have caused employers to lose well-qualified prospects.

Professional Associations

Many professional associations and societies offer a placement service to members as one of their benefits. Listings of members seeking employment may be advertised in their journals or publicized at their national meetings. A placement center is usually established at national meetings for the mutual benefit of employers and job seekers. The Society for Human Resource Management, for example, helps employers and prospective HR employees come together. Mediabistro.com is an association that allows creative people, including editors, writers, television producers, graphic designers,

Figure 5.2 U.S. Employment and Pay by Occupation

OCCUPATION	NUMBER EMPLOYED	MEAN ANNUAL WAGE
Management	6,439,530	$83,400
Legal	945,440	$78,590
Computer and mathematical	2,830,550	$64,150
Architecture and engineering	2,354,580	$60,390
Healthcare practitioners and technical	6,258,560	$56,240
Business and financial operations	5,045,860	$56,000
Life, physical, and social science	1,102,070	$54,930
Arts, design, entertainment, sports, and media	1,583,250	$43,350
Education, training, and library	7,852,030	$41,390
Construction and extraction	6,099,360	$37,000
Installation, maintenance, and repair	5,207,650	$36,560
Community and social services	1,654,420	$35,800
Protective service	2,983,230	$34,430
Sales and related	13,522,460	$31,560
Production	10,246,130	$28,930
Office and administrative support	22,607,360	$28,540
Transportation and material moving	9,361,690	$27,630
Healthcare support	3,235,840	$22,960
Personal care and service	3,040,060	$21,570
Building and grounds cleaning and maintenance	4,274,480	$21,290
Farming, fishing, and forestry	460,820	$20,290
Food preparation and serving	10,314,820	$17,400

Source: "November 2003 National Cross-Industry Estimates of Employment and Mean Annual Wage for SOC Major Occupational Groups," U.S. Bureau of Labor Statistics.

and book publishers, to meet personally and online to showcase their work and hire one another for projects.

Labor Unions

Labor unions can be a principal source of applicants for blue-collar and some professional jobs. Some unions, such as those in the maritime, printing, and construction industries, maintain hiring halls that can provide a supply of applicants, particularly for short-term needs. Employers wishing to use this recruitment source should contact the local union under consideration for employer-eligibility requirements and applicant availability.

Public Employment Agencies

Each of the fifty states maintains an employment agency that administers its unemployment insurance program. Many of the state agencies bear such titles as Department of Employment or Department of Human Resources. They are subject to certain regulations and controls administered by the U.S. Employment Service (USES).

State agencies maintain local public employment offices in most communities of any size. Individuals who become unemployed must register at one of these offices and be available for "suitable employment" in order to receive their weekly unemployment checks. Consequently, public employment agencies are able to refer to employers with job openings those applicants with the required skills who are available for employment.

The USES has developed a nationwide computerized job bank that lists job openings, and state employment offices are connected to this job bank. The computerized job bank helps facilitate the movement of job applicants to different geographic areas. Most of the local employment offices have a local job bank book published as a daily computer printout. Many of the jobs can also be found on the Internet at cooperative web sites such as America's Job Bank (AJB), America's Career InfoNet (ACINet), and America's Service Locator. Employer openings are listed along with other pertinent information, such as number of openings, pay rates, and job specifications. Employment interviewers in an agency can access a list of all job openings in the geographic area for which applicants assigned to them might qualify. Furthermore, applicants looking for a specific job can review the lists and apply directly to organizations with openings.

USING THE INTERNET

This computerized job bank is called America's Job Bank and can be used to access all of the individual state employment agencies. Go to the Student Resources at:

http://bohlander.swlearning.com

In addition to matching unemployed applicants with job openings, public employment agencies may assist employers with employment testing, job analysis, evaluation programs, and community wage surveys.

Private Employment and Temporary Agencies

Charging a fee enables private employment agencies to tailor their services to the specific needs of their clients. Snelling Personnel Services, Manpower, Kelly Services, and Olsten Staffing Services are among the largest private employment agencies. However, it is common for agencies to specialize in serving a specific occupational area or professional field. Aquent, for example, specializes in providing businesses with the computer experts they need and in helping skilled employees find temporary and permanent positions. (For more on temporary help, see the next section.) Depending on who is receiving the most service, the fee may be paid by the employer, the job seeker, or both. It is not uncommon for private employment agencies to charge an employer a 25–30 percent fee, based on the position's annual salary, if the employer hires an applicant found by the agency.

Private employment agencies differ in the services they offer, their professionalism, and the caliber of their counselors. If counselors are paid on a commission basis, their desire to do a professional job may be offset by their desire to earn a commission. Thus they may encourage job seekers to accept jobs for which they are not suited. Because of this, job seekers would be wise to take the time to find a recruiter who is knowledgeable, experienced, and professional. When talking with potential recruiters, individuals should discuss openly their philosophies and practices with regard to recruiting strategies, including advertising, in-house recruiting, screening procedures, and costs for these efforts. They should try to find a recruiter who is flexible and who will consider their needs and wants.

In addition to placing permanent workers, many private agencies hire and place workers in temporary positions. The temporary services industry is one of the fastest-growing recruitment sources, employing 2 to 3 million people annually.[11] This form of employment grew at a roaring pace in the 1990s and is likely to remain

Figure 5.3 Occupational Breakdowns of Temporary Help Agency Placements

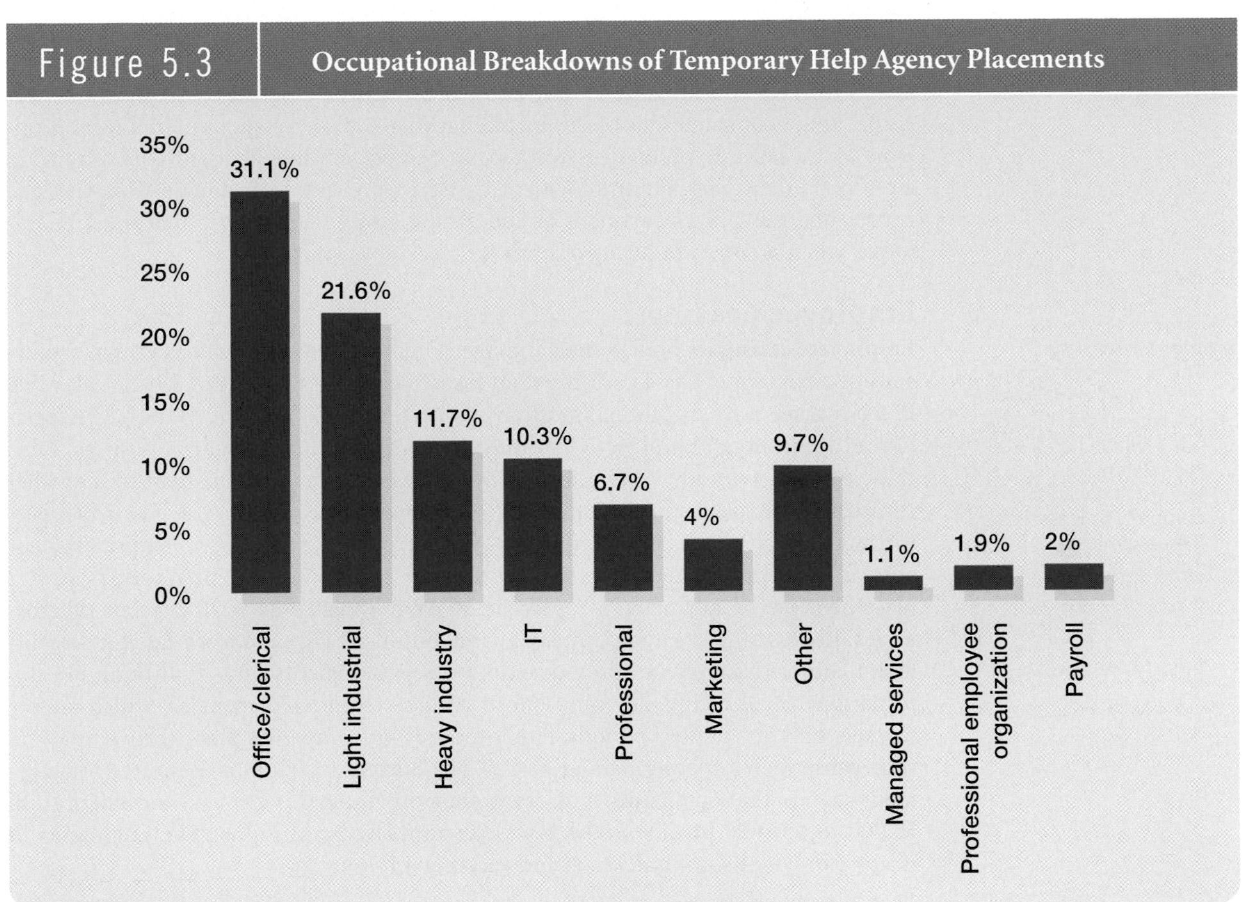

Source: Steve Jones, "You've Come a Long Way, Baby: What the Staffing Industry Offers Today," *Canadian HR Reporter* 14, no. 19 (November 5, 2001): 15. © Copyright *Canadian HR Reporter,* November 5, 2001, by permission of Carswell, Toronto, Ontario 1-800-387-5164. Web: http://www.hrreporter.com. Data supplied by Association of Canadian Search, Employment Staffing Services.

strong. Figure 5.3 shows the results of a Canadian study that lays out the breakdown of occupations most represented by temporary employment agencies.[12]

An estimated nine out of ten U.S. companies, including both large and small firms, make some use of temporary employees. "Temps" are typically used for short-term assignments or to help when managers cannot justify hiring a full-time employee, such as for vacation fill-ins, for peak work periods, or during an employee's pregnancy leave or sick leave. Increasingly, temps are being employed to fill positions once staffed by permanent employees. This practice is growing because temporaries can be laid off quickly, and with less cost, when work lessens. Some companies use a just-in-time staffing approach in which a core staff of employees is augmented by a trained and highly skilled supplementary workforce. The use of temporaries thus becomes a viable way to maintain proper staffing levels. Also, the employment costs of temporaries are often lower than those of permanent employees because temps are not provided with benefits and can be dismissed without the need to file unemployment insurance claims.

Temporary employment arrangements can be advantageous to both employees and employers. Because many temporary employees are eventually hired full-time, it allows workers and firms to try one another out before a permanent commitment is made. Some companies, however, including Microsoft, have encountered legal problems by mislabeling permanent workers as "temps" or "independent contractors" in an effort to cut back on employment costs. To prevent such abuses Congress, the courts, and the U.S. Department of Labor have established criteria that must be followed when it comes to hiring temps.

Employee Leasing

employee leasing
The process of dismissing employees who are then hired by a leasing company (which handles all HR-related activities) and contracting with that company to lease back the employees

Employee leasing by professional employer organizations (PEOs) has grown rapidly since the passage of the Tax Equity and Fiscal Responsibility Act of 1982. Today 700 PEOs oversee 2 to 3 million American workers, according to the National Association of Professional Employer Organizations (NAPEO) in Alexandria, Virginia. Basically, a PEO—typically a larger company—takes over the management of a smaller company's HR tasks and becomes a co-employer to its employees. The PEO performs all the HR duties of an employer—hiring, payroll, performance appraisal, benefits administration, and other day-to-day HR activities—and in return is paid a placement fee of normally 4–8 percent of payroll cost plus 9–20 percent of gross wages. Because PEOs can co-employ a large number of people working at many different companies, they can provide employees with benefits such as 401k and health plans that small companies can't afford. Unlike temporary agencies, which supply workers only for limited periods, employee-leasing companies place their employees with subscribers on a permanent basis.[13] The Society for Human Resource Management reports that companies with fewer than 50 employees can save anywhere from $5,000 to $50,000 in time and labor costs annually by hiring a PEO. Highlights in HRM 2 provides some guidelines for selecting a PEO.

Improving the Effectiveness of External Recruitment

With all of the uncertainties inherent in external recruiting, it is sometimes difficult to determine whether an organization's efforts to locate promising talent are effective and/or cost-efficient. However, managers can do several things to maximize the probability of success. These include calculating yield ratios on recruiting sources, calculating costs of recruitment, training organizational recruiters, and conducting realistic job previews.

Yield Ratios

yield ratio
The percentage of applicants from a recruitment source that make it to the next stage of the selection process

Yield ratios help indicate which recruitment sources are most effective at producing qualified job candidates. Quite simply, a **yield ratio** is the percentage of applicants from a particular source that make it to the next stage in the selection process. For example, if 100 resumes were obtained from an employment agency, and 17 of the applicants submitting those resumes were invited for an on-site interview, the yield ratio for that agency would be 17 percent (17/100). This yield ratio could then be recalculated for each subsequent stage in the selection process (for example, after the interview and again after the final offer), which would result in a cumulative yield ratio. By calculating and comparing yield ratios for each recruitment source, it is possible to find out which sources produce qualified applicants.

Highlights in HRM 2

Guidelines for Selecting a PEO

1. Assess your workplace to determine human resources and risk management needs.
2. Make sure the PEO is capable of meeting your goals. Sales brochures and fancy proposals are easy to print. Meet the people who will be serving you.
3. Check the firm's financial background. Ask for banking and credit references. Ask the PEO to demonstrate that payroll taxes and insurance premiums have been paid.
4. Ask for client and professional references.
5. Check to see whether the company is a member of the National Association of Professional Employer Organizations (NAPEO), the national trade association of the PEO industry. (See http://www.napeo.org for a list of members.)
6. Investigate the company's administrative and risk management service competence. What experience and depth does their internal staff have? Have any of the senior staff of the PEO been certified as Certified Professional Employer Specialists or other relevant professional designations?
7. Understand how the employee benefits are funded. Are they fully insured or partially self-funded? Who is the third-party administrator (TPA) or carrier? If required in your state, is their TPA or carrier licensed?
8. Understand how the employee benefits are tailored. Determine whether they fill the needs of your employees.
9. Review the service agreement carefully. Are the respective parties' responsibilities and liabilities clearly laid out? What guarantees are provided? What provisions permit you or the PEO to cancel the terms of the contract?
10. If your state requires a PEO to be licensed or registered, make sure the company you are considering meets all such requirements.

Source: Carolyn Hirschman, "For PEOs, Business Is Booming," *HRMagazine* 45, no. 2 (February 2000): 43. Reprinted with the permission of *HRMagazine*, published by the Society for Human Resource Management, Alexandria, VA, via Copyright Clearance Center.

Costs of Recruitment

The cost of various recruiting procedures can be computed using a fairly simple set of calculations. For example, the average source cost per hire (SC/H) can be determined by the following formula:

$$\frac{SC}{H} = \frac{AC + AF + RB + NC}{H}$$

where AC = advertising costs, total monthly expenditure (example: $28,000)

AF = agency fees, total for the month (example: $19,000)

RB = referral bonuses, total paid (example: $2,300)

NC = no-cost hires, walk-ins, nonprofit agencies, etc. (example: $0)

H = total hires (example: 119)

Substituting the example numbers into the formula gives

$$\frac{SC}{H} = \frac{\$28{,}000 + \$19{,}000 + \$2{,}300 + \$0}{119}$$

$$= \frac{\$49{,}300}{119}$$

$$= \$414 \text{ (source cost of recruits per hire)}$$

When combined with information about yield ratios, these calculations can provide invaluable information to managers about the utility of different approaches to and sources of recruitment. In that way, they can make more informed decisions about both controlling the costs of recruitment and increasing its effectiveness. For example, although advertisements and employee referrals may both yield qualified applicants, managers may find that referral bonuses are a more economical alternative.

Organizational Recruiters

The size of an organization influences who performs the recruitment function. For large employers, professional HR recruiters are hired and trained to find new employees. In smaller organizations, recruitment may be done by an HR generalist; if the organization has no HR position, recruitment may be carried out by managers and/or supervisors. At companies such as Macy's and Williams-Sonoma, members of work teams take part in the selection of new team members.

Regardless of who does the recruiting, it is imperative that these individuals have a good understanding of the knowledge, skills, abilities, experiences, and other characteristics required for the job. All too often, a new person in the HR department or a line manager may be given a recruitment assignment, even before that person has been given interview training, before he or she fully understands the job, and before he or she fully comprehends the values and goals of the organization.

It is important to remember that recruiters have an influence on an applicant's job decision. Because recruiters can often enhance the perceived attractiveness of a job and an organization, they are often a main reason why applicants select one organization over another. On this basis we can conclude that personable, enthusiastic, and competent recruiters have an impact on the success of an organization's recruitment program.

Realistic Job Previews

realistic job preview (RJP) Informing applicants about all aspects of the job, including both its desirable and undesirable facets

Another way organizations may be able to increase the effectiveness of their recruitment efforts is to provide job applicants with a **realistic job preview (RJP).** An RJP informs applicants about all aspects of the job, including both its desirable and undesirable facets. In contrast, a typical job preview presents the job in only positive terms. The RJP may also include a tour of the working area, combined with a discussion of any negative health or safety considerations. Proponents of the RJP believe that applicants who are given realistic information regarding a position are more likely to remain on the job and be successful, because there will be fewer unpleasant surprises. In fact, a number of research studies on RJP report these positive results:

- Improved employee job satisfaction
- Reduced voluntary turnover
- Enhanced communication through honesty and openness
- Realistic job expectations

To help new recruits know what to realistically expect on the job and improve their retention rates, National City Corporation implemented a series of workshops for its entry-level banking employees. Hiring managers were taught how to prepare for the arrival of new employees and make their transition to their new jobs smoother. New employees were also paired with experienced "sponsor" employees. As a result, new employee turnover at National City Corporation fell by 50 percent.[14]

Recruiting Talent Internally

While we typically think about recruiting being focused on attracting potential employees from outside the organization, most organizations try to follow a policy of filling job vacancies above the entry-level position through promotions and transfers. By filling vacancies in this way, an organization can capitalize on the investment it has made in recruiting, selecting, training, and developing its current employees, who might look for jobs elsewhere if they lack promotion opportunities. Procter & Gamble is one organization that recruits its top managers exclusively from within the company. Companies are also more likely to promote from within than they have been in the past, one survey of executives found.[15]

Advantages and Limitations of Recruiting from Within

Promotion-from-within policies at Marriott, Nordstrom's, Nucor Steel, and Wal-Mart have contributed to the companies' overall growth and success.[16] Promotion rewards employees for past performance and is intended to encourage them to continue their efforts. It also gives other employees reason to anticipate that similar efforts by them will lead to promotion, thus improving morale within the organization. This is particularly true for members of protected classes who have encountered difficulties in finding employment and have often faced even greater difficulty in advancing within an organization. Most organizations have integrated promotion policies as an essential part of their EEO/AA programs.

If an organization's promotion policy is to have maximum motivational value, employees must be made aware of that policy. The following is an example of a policy statement that an organization might prepare:

> "Promotion from within" is generally recognized as a foundation of good employment practice, and it is the policy of our organization to promote from within whenever possible when filling a vacancy. The job vacancy will be posted for five calendar days to give all qualified full- and part-time personnel an equal opportunity to apply.

While a transfer lacks the motivational value of a promotion, it sometimes can serve to protect employees from layoff or to broaden their job experiences. Furthermore, the transferred employee's familiarity with the organization and its operations can eliminate the orientation and training costs that recruitment from the outside would entail. Most important, the transferee's performance record is likely to be a more accurate predictor of the candidate's success than the data gained about outside applicants.

Side by side with the potential advantages of internal recruitment, managers need to be aware of potential limitations as well. For example, certain jobs at the middle and upper levels that require specialized training and experience cannot be easily filled from within the organization and may need to be filled from the outside. This is especially common in small organizations. Also, for certain openings it may be necessary to hire individuals from the outside who have gained from another employer the knowledge and expertise required for these jobs.

Even though HR policy encourages job openings to be filled from within the organization, potential candidates from the outside should be considered in order to prevent the inbreeding of ideas and attitudes. Applicants hired from the outside, particularly for certain technical and managerial positions, can be a source of new ideas and may bring with them the latest knowledge acquired from their previous employers. Indeed, excessive reliance on internal sources can create the risk of "employee cloning." Furthermore, it is not uncommon for firms to attempt to gain secrets from their competitors by hiring away their employees: Procter & Gamble sued a rival papermaker when it hired former employees who had a great deal of knowledge about the making of Charmin toilet paper and Bounty paper towels—both P&G products. Amazon.com was sued by Wal-Mart, which accused it of hiring away employees who had in-depth knowledge about Wal-Mart's sophisticated inventory systems.[17]

Methods for Identifying Qualified Candidates

The effective use of internal sources requires a system for locating qualified job candidates and for enabling those who consider themselves qualified to apply for the opening. Qualified job candidates within the organization can be located in a number of ways, which we discuss next.

Human Resources Information Systems

As discussed in Chapter 2, information technology has made it possible for organizations to create databases that contain the complete records and qualifications of each employee within an organization. Combined with increasingly user-friendly search engines, managers can access this information and identify potential candidates for available jobs. Organizations as diverse as Sun Microsystems, Merck, and the U.S. military have developed resume-tracking systems that allow managers to query an online database of resumes. Companies such as PeopleSoft and SAP are leaders in developing automated staffing and skills management software. Similar to the skills inventories mentioned earlier, these information systems allow an organization to rapidly screen its entire workforce to locate suitable candidates to fill an internal opening. These data can also be used to predict the career paths of employees and to anticipate when and where promotion opportunities may arise. Since the value of the data depends on its being kept up to date, the systems typically include provisions for recording changes in employee qualifications and job placements as they occur.[18]

Job Posting and Bidding

job posting and bidding Posting vacancy notices and maintaining lists of employees looking for upgraded positions

Organizations may communicate information about job openings through a process referred to as **job posting and bidding.** The jobs are frequently posted on electronic bulletin boards or on regular bulletin boards where employees congregate. Job openings can also be announced in employee publications, special handouts, direct mail, and public-address messages. Many companies have developed online job posting systems whereby employees looking for upgraded positions can post their names, resumes, and the positions they are interested in applying for. As a position becomes available, the list of employees seeking that position is retrieved, and the records of these employees reviewed to select possible candidates for interviews. The employees can be electronically notified about interview schedules and track their progress electronically through the various hiring stages.[19]

The system of job posting and bidding can provide many benefits to an organization. However, these benefits may not be realized unless employees believe the system is being administered fairly. Furthermore, job bidding is more effective when it is part of a career development program in which employees are made aware of opportunities available to them within the organization. For example, HR departments may provide new employees with information on job progression that describes the lines of job advancement, training requirements for each job, and skills and abilities needed as they move up the job progression ladder.

Identifying Talent through Performance Appraisals

Performance appraisals are discussed more fully in Chapter 8. For our purposes here, we want to note that managers measure and evaluate an employee's performance for several reasons, none more important than for making developmental and career decisions. Successful performers are often good candidates for a promotion. In contrast, poorly performing employees may need—and benefit from—a transfer to another area or even a demotion.

Identifying and developing talent in individuals is a role that all managers should take seriously. As they conduct formal appraisals, they should be concerned with their subordinates' potential for managerial or advanced technical jobs and encourage their growth in that direction. In addition to immediate managers, others in the organization should have the power to evaluate, nominate, and sponsor employees with promise.

Inventorying Management Talent

As we discussed in Chapter 2, skill inventories are an important tool for succession planning. These inventories provide an indication of the skills employees have as well as their interests and experiences. In this way, they help managers pay better attention to the developmental needs of employees, both in their present jobs and in managerial jobs to which they may be promoted. An equally important part of this process is identifying high-potential employees who may be groomed as replacements for managers who are reassigned, retire, or otherwise vacate a position. At GE, for every position at or above a director level, two or three people are usually identified who can easily step in when the current jobholder moves on.

Unfortunately, many companies do a poor job of managing their talent. In a study conducted by McKinsey and Company, three-quarters of corporate officers

Figure 5.4 Warning Signs of a Weak Talent "Bench"

1. It takes a long time to fill key positions
2. Key positions can be filled only by hiring from the outside.
3. Vacancies in key positions cannot be filled with confidence in the abilities of those chosen for them.
4. Replacements for positions often are unsuccessful in performing their new duties.
5. Promotions are made on the basis of whim, favoritism, or nepotism.

Source: Adapted from William Rothwell, *Effective Succession Planning* (New York: AMACOM, 2000).

said their companies were chronically short of talent. At the same time, half of the respondents to a similar survey acknowledged that they were not doing effective succession planning and were unprepared to replace key executives.[20] Some signs that the firm needs to work harder at grooming internal talent are shown in Figure 5.4.

Using Assessment Centers

assessment center
A process by which individuals are evaluated as they participate in a series of situations that resemble what they might be called on to handle on the job

There are other very effective ways to assess a person's career potential. Pioneered in the mid-1950s by Douglas Bray and his associates at AT&T, assessment centers are considered one of the most valuable methods for evaluating personnel. An **assessment center** is a process (not a place) by which individuals are evaluated as they participate in a series of situations that resemble what they might be called on to handle on the job. The popularity of the assessment center can be attributed to its capacity for increasing an organization's ability to select employees who will perform successfully in management positions or to assist and promote the development of skills for their current position. These centers may use in-basket exercises, leaderless group discussions, and other approaches:

- *In-basket exercises.* This method is used to simulate a problem situation. The participants are given several documents, each describing some problem or situation requiring an immediate response. They are thus forced to make decisions under the pressure of time and also to determine what priority to give each problem.
- *Leaderless group discussions.* With this activity, trainees are gathered in a conference setting to discuss an assigned topic, either with or without designated group roles. The participants are given little or no instruction in how to approach the topic, nor are they told what decision to reach. Leaderless group trainees are evaluated on their initiative, leadership skills, and ability to work effectively in a group setting.
- *Role playing.* The exercise might involve preparing for and engaging in a customer meeting or a team-leader meeting with one's subordinates. A trained assessor then assesses the participant using a structured rating scale.
- *Behavioral interviews.* The interviewer asks the participant a series of question about what he or she would do in particular work circumstances. Sometimes behavioral interviews are combined with videos showing work simulations, and participants are asked at intervals to make choices about what they would do in the situations shown.

Participation in these activities provides samples of behavior that are representative of what is required for advancement. At the end of the assessment center period, the assessors' observations are combined and integrated to develop an overall picture of the strengths and needs of the participants. A report is normally submitted to senior management, and feedback is given to the participants.

Increasing attention is being given to the validity of assessment center procedures. Before the assessment center is run, the characteristics or dimensions to be studied should be determined through job analyses. The exercises used in the center should reflect the job for which the person is being evaluated; that is, the exercises should have content validity. While the assessment center methodology lends itself readily to content validation, predictive validity has also been observed in many instances. A strong positive relationship is found between assessments and future performance on the job.[21]

While assessment centers have proved quite valuable in identifying managerial talent and in helping with the development of individuals, it should be noted that the method tends to favor those who are strong in interpersonal skills and have the ability to influence others. Some individuals find it difficult to perform at their best in a situation that for them is as threatening as taking a test. The manner in which assessment center personnel conduct the exercises and provide feedback to the participants will play a major role in determining how individuals react to the experience.

Career Management: Developing Talent over Time

While we can think of recruitment as a stand-alone activity, limited to a single job at a single point in time, often this is not the case. Inevitably decisions about talent—regardless of whether they pertain to recruiting, transferring, promoting, developing, or deploying people—need to be considered within the context of long-term priorities of the business and the employees. Increasingly, managers are not making these decisions on a "one-off" basis, but rather as part of a comprehensive approach to career management.

Integrating career development with other HR programs creates synergies in which all aspects of HR reinforce one another. Figure 5.5 illustrates how HR structures relate to some of the essential aspects of the career management process. For example, in planning careers, employees need organizational information—information that strategic planning, forecasting, succession planning, and skills inventories can provide. Similarly, as they obtain information about themselves and use it in career planning, employees need to know the career paths within the organization and how management views their performance.[22]

The Goal: Matching Individual and Organizational Needs

In the final analysis, a career development program should be viewed as a dynamic process that matches the needs of the organization with the needs of employees.

Figure 5.5 HR's Role in Career Management

The Employee's Role

Although some firms play a role in the planning of their employees' careers, ultimately, employees are responsible for initiating and managing their own career planning. Because having a successful career involves creating your own career path—not just following a path that has been established by the organization—it is up to each individual to identify his or her own knowledge, skills, abilities, interests, and values and seek out information about career options in order to set goals and develop career plans. Managers should encourage employees to take responsibility for their own careers, offering continuing assistance in the form of feedback on individual performance and making available information about the organization, the job, and career opportunities that might be of interest.

The organization is responsible for supplying information about its mission, policies, and plans and for providing support for employee self-assessment, training, and development. Significant career growth can occur when individual initiative combines with organizational opportunity. Career development programs benefit managers by giving them increased skill in managing their own careers, greater retention of valued employees, increased understanding of the organization, and enhanced reputations as people developers. As with other HR programs, the inauguration of a career development program should be based on the organization's needs as well.

Assessment of needs should take a variety of approaches (surveys, informal group discussions, interviews, and so on) and should involve personnel from different groups, such as new employees, managers, longtime employees, minority employees, and technical and professional employees. Identifying the needs and problems of these groups provides the starting point for the organization's career development efforts. As shown in Figure 5.6, organizational needs should be linked with individual career needs in a way that joins personal effectiveness and satisfaction of employees with the achievement of the organization's strategic objectives.

The Organization's Role: Establishing a Favorable Context

If career development is to succeed, it must receive the complete support of top management. Ideally, senior line managers and HR department managers should work together to design and implement a career development system. The system should reflect the goals and culture of the organization, and the HR philosophy should be woven throughout. An HR philosophy can provide employees with a clear set of expectations and directions for their own career development. For a program to be effective, managerial personnel at all levels must be trained in the fundamentals of job design, performance appraisal, career planning, and counseling.

One of the most important indicators of management support comes in the form of mentoring. This is true regardless of whether it is done formally as part of an ongoing program or informally as merely a kind gesture to a less experienced employee. Dealing with uncertainty is one of the biggest challenges any individual

Figure 5.6 Balancing Individual and Organizational Needs

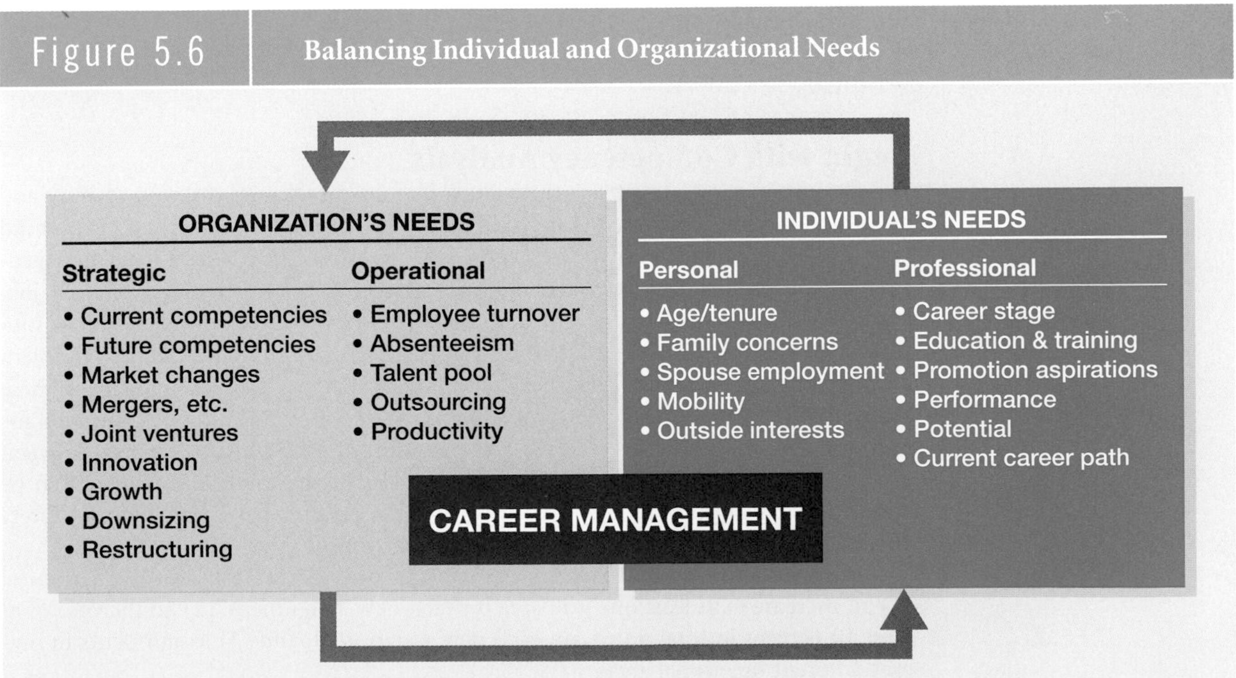

faces in his or her career. Receiving advice and counsel from someone who has gone through similar experiences can prove to be invaluable to employees. We devote an entire section to mentoring later in this chapter.

Blending Individual and Organizational Goals

Before individuals can engage in meaningful career planning, not only must they have an awareness of the organization's philosophy, but they must also have a good understanding of the organization's more immediate goals. Otherwise, they may plan for personal change and growth without knowing whether or how their own goals match those of the organization. For example, if the technology of a business is changing and new skills are needed, will the organization retrain to meet this need or hire new talent? Is there growth, stability, or decline in the number of employees needed? How will turnover affect this need? Clearly, an organizational plan that answers these kinds of questions is essential to support individual career planning.

At the same time, it would be unrealistic to expect that individuals can establish their career goals with *perfect* understanding of where they are going or—for that matter—where the organization is going. Individuals change over time, and because of that, their needs and interests change. Similarly, organizations also change their directions and adjust their strategies to cope with change. So while goal setting is critical, building in some flexibility is probably a good idea.

Identifying Career Opportunities and Requirements

While talent management integrates a number of related HR activities, those who direct the process have to keep a steady watch on the needs and requirements of the organization. This involves an analysis of the competencies required for jobs, the progression among related jobs, and the supply of ready (and potential) talent available to fill those jobs.

Begin with Competency Analysis

It is important for an organization to study its jobs carefully in order to identify and assign weights to the knowledge and skills that each one requires. This can be achieved with job analysis and evaluation systems such as those used in compensation programs. The system used at Sears measures three basic competencies for each job: know-how, problem solving, and accountability. Know-how is broken down into three types of job knowledge: technical, managerial, and human relations. Problem solving and accountability also have several dimensions. Scores for each of these three major competencies are assigned to each job, and a total value is computed for each job. For any planned job transfer, the amount of increase (or decrease) the next job represents in each of the skill areas, as well as in the total point values, can be computed. This information is then used to make certain that a transfer to a different job is a move that requires growth on the part of the employee.

Sears designs career development paths to provide the following experiences: (1) an increase in at least one skill area on each new assignment, (2) an increase of at least 10 percent in total points on each new assignment, and (3) assignments in several different functional areas.[23]

Identify Job Progressions

job progressions
The hierarchy of jobs a new employee might experience, ranging from a starting job to jobs that successively require more knowledge and/or skill

career paths
Lines of advancement in an occupational field within an organization

Once the skill demands of jobs are identified and weighted according to their importance, it is then possible to plan **job progressions.** A new employee with no experience is typically assigned to a "starting job." After a period of time in that job, the employee can be promoted to one that requires more knowledge and/or skill. While most organizations concentrate on developing job progressions for managerial, professional, and technical jobs, progressions can be developed for all categories of jobs. These job progressions then can serve as a basis for developing **career paths**—the lines of advancement within an organization—for individuals.

Figure 5.7 illustrates a typical line of advancement in the human resources area of a large multinational corporation. It is apparent that one must be prepared to move geographically in order to advance very far in the human resources department of this firm. This would also be true of other career fields within the organization.

Many organizations prepare interesting and attractive brochures to describe the career paths that are available to employees. General Motors has prepared a career development guide that groups jobs by fields of work such as engineering, manufacturing, communications, data processing, financial, HR, and scientific. These categories give employees an understanding of the career possibilities in the various fields.

Although these analyses can be quite helpful to employees—and are perhaps essential for organizations—a word of caution is appropriate here for readers. Many successful careers are not this methodical, nor do they proceed in a lockstep manner. In today's working world, career progressions often occur as much through creating and capitalizing on arising opportunities as they do through rational planning. So while it is a good idea for organizations to map out a career path, and individuals would do well to establish a strategy for advancement, many successful individuals

Figure 5.7 Typical Line of Advancement in HR Management

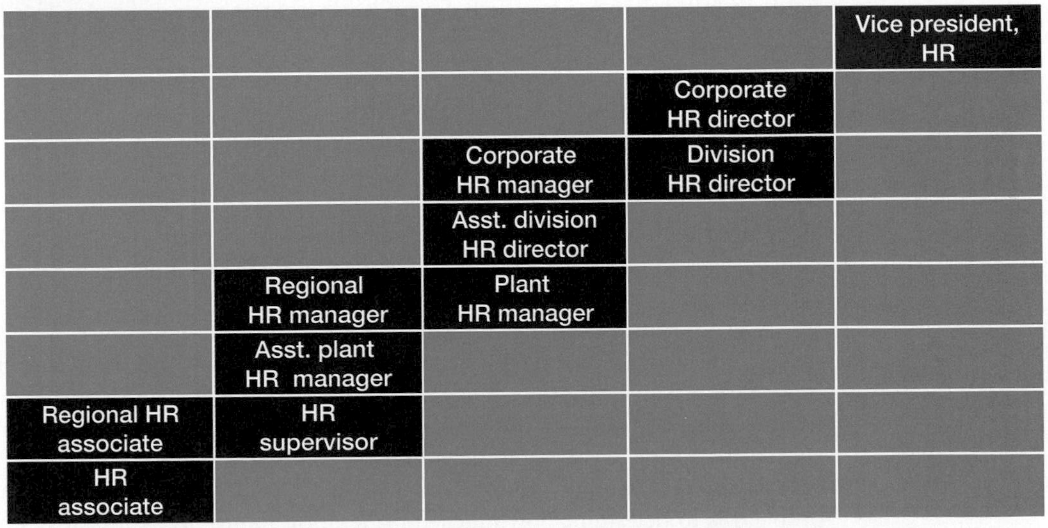

				Vice president, HR
			Corporate HR director	
		Corporate HR manager	Division HR director	
		Asst. division HR director		
	Regional HR manager	Plant HR manager		
	Asst. plant HR manager			
Regional HR associate	HR supervisor			
HR associate				

Highlights in HRM 3

Career Path of Colin Powell

1954	Joins ROTC program
1957	Enrolls in City College of New York
1963	Tour of duty in Vietnam
1968	Graduates from U.S. Army Command and General Staff College (CGSC)
1971	Graduate School at the George Washington University
1972	White House Fellow under President Richard Nixon
1974	Commander of 1st Battalion, 32nd Infantry in Korea
1977	Colonel, Commander of 2nd Brigade, 101st Infantry
1978	Works in Office of Secretary of Defense under President Jimmy Carter
1982	Brigadier General, Commander of 4th Infantry Division
1982	Deputy Commanding General of Combined Arms Combat Developments Activity
1987	National Security Advisor under President Ronald Reagan
1989	Chairman, Joint Chiefs of Staff under President George Bush
1992	Approached to be Bill Clinton's vice presidential running mate (declined)
1993	Chairman, Joint Chiefs of Staff under President Bill Clinton
1993	Retired from military service
2000	Secretary of State under President George W. Bush
2005	Resigned as Secretary of State

readily admit that their career paths are quite idiosyncratic to their circumstances. These people often note that they have been fortunate to be "in the right place at the right time." Of course, others describe them as being extremely career savvy. Highlights in HRM 3 shows one such example—the career path of former U.S. secretary of state Colin Powell.

Recognize Lots of Possibilities

Career development and planning systems were once primarily focused on promotions and hierarchical advancement. However, in today's flatter organizations and more dynamic work environment, an individual's career advancement can occur along several different paths: transfers, demotions—even exits—and promotions. HR policies have to be flexible enough to adapt as well as helpful enough to support the career change.

promotion
A change of assignment to a job at a higher level in the organization

A **promotion** is a change of assignment to a job at a higher level in the organization. The new job normally provides an increase in pay and status and demands more skill or carries more responsibility. Promotions enable an organization to utilize the skills and abilities of its personnel more effectively, and the opportunity to gain a promotion serves as an incentive for good performance. The three principal criteria for determining promotions are merit, seniority, and potential. Often the problem is to determine how much consideration to give to each factor. A common problem in organizations that promote primarily on past performance and seniority is called the Peter Principle. This refers to the situation in which individuals are promoted as long as they have done a good job in their previous job. The trouble is this continues until someone does poorly in his or her new job. Then he or she is no longer promoted. This results in people being promoted to their level of incompetence. There are other intrafirm challenges related to promotions. Sometimes extremely good employees are prevented from being promoted to other departments because their current managers are reluctant to lose them. At other firms, an employee who tries, but fails, to advance to a position in another department is earmarked for the next round of layoffs.[24]

transfer
Placement of an individual in another job for which the duties, responsibilities, status, and remuneration are approximately equal to those of the previous job

In flatter organizations, there are fewer promotional opportunities, so many individuals find career advancement through lateral moves. A **transfer** is the placement of an employee in another job for which the duties, responsibilities, status, and remuneration are approximately equal to those of the previous job (although as an incentive, organizations may offer a salary adjustment). Individuals who look forward to change or want a chance to learn more may seek out transfers. In addition, transfers frequently provide a broader foundation for individuals to prepare them for an eventual promotion. A transfer may require the employee to change work group, workplace, work shift, or organizational unit; it may even necessitate moving to another geographic area. Transfers make it possible for an organization to place its employees in jobs where there is a greater need for their services and where they can acquire new knowledge and skills.

A downward transfer, or *demotion,* moves an individual into a lower-level job that can provide developmental opportunities. Although such a move is ordinarily considered unfavorable, some individuals actually may request it in order to return to their "technical roots." It is not uncommon, for example, for organizations to appoint temporary leaders (especially in team environments) with the proviso that they will eventually step down from this position to resume their former position.

relocation services
Services provided to an employee who is transferred to a new location, which might include help in moving, selling a home, orienting to a new culture, and/or learning a new language

Transfers, promotions, and demotions require individuals to adjust to new job demands and usually to a different work environment. A transfer that involves moving to a new location within the United States or abroad places greater demands on an employee because it requires that employee to adapt not only to a new work environment but also to new living conditions. The employee with a family has the added responsibility of helping family members adjust to the new living arrangements. Even though some employers provide all types of **relocation services**—including covering moving expenses, helping to sell a home, and providing cultural orientation and language training—there is always some loss of productive time. Pretransfer training, whether related to job skills or to lifestyle, has been suggested as one of the most effective ways to reduce lost productivity.

When one considers the numerous changes that may accompany a career move within an organization, it should come as no surprise that many individuals are opting to accept career changes that involve *organizational exit.* Given limited career opportunities within firms, coupled with the need for talent in other companies, many individuals are discovering that their best career options may involve switching companies.

outplacement services
Services provided by organizations to help terminated employees find a new job

While some employees leave voluntarily, other employees are forced to leave. Even so, many organizations now provide **outplacement services** to help terminated employees find a job elsewhere. These services can be used to enhance a productive employee's career as well as to terminate an employee who is unproductive. If an organization cannot meet its career development responsibilities to its productive workers, HR policy should provide for assistance to be given them in finding more suitable career opportunities elsewhere. Jack Welch, chairman of General Electric, was one of the first executives to make a commitment to employees that while the company could no longer guarantee lifetime employment, it would try to ensure *employability.* That is, GE has committed to providing employees with the skills and support they would need to find a job in another organization.[25]

Consider Dual Career Paths for Employees

One of the most obvious places where career paths have been changing is in technical and professional areas. One of the ironies of organizations in the past has been that the most successful engineers, scientists, and professionals were often promoted right out of their area of specialization into management. Instead of doing what they were good at, they were promoted into a job they often didn't understand and often didn't enjoy. It has become apparent that there must be another way to compensate such individuals without elevating them to a management position. The solution has been to develop dual career paths, or tracks, that provide for progression in special areas such as information technology, finance, marketing, and engineering, with compensation that is comparable to that received by managers at different levels.

Many organizations have found that this is the solution to keeping employees with valuable knowledge and skills performing tasks that are as important to the organization as those performed by managers. Highlights in HRM 4 show the dual career path devised by Xenova Group, a biopharmaceuticals company, to recognize both the scientific and the managerial paths of employees.

Pursue the Boundaryless Career

A generation ago, the "organization man" served as a popular career icon. Career success was synonymous with ascending a corporate hierarchy over the course of a lifetime spent in a single firm. Today, however, individuals pursuing *boundaryless careers* may prefer to see themselves as self-directed "free agents" who develop a portfolio of employment opportunities by proactively moving from employer to employer, simultaneously developing and utilizing their marketable skills. As shown in Figure 5.8, it is possible to map the different career profiles. Employees pursuing boundaryless careers develop their human capital along dimensions of industry and occupational knowledge. That is, they may be experts in computer programming or have great insights into trends in the banking industry. In contrast, individuals pursuing more traditional careers develop their knowledge in ways specific to a given firm.

Both approaches can be beneficial, but they are not the same. Under the boundaryless career model, success depends on continually learning new skills, developing new relationships, and capitalizing on existing skills and relationships. These individuals place a premium on flexibility and the capacity to do several different types of tasks, to learn new jobs, to adjust quickly to different group settings and organizational cultures, and to move from one firm, occupation, or industry to another. Their employment security depends on their marketable skills rather than their dedication to one organization over time. A number of studies have shown that people with boundaryless careers find them very satisfying. Organizations can also benefit from boundaryless careers because it allows them to attract top talent from all over the world on a project-by-project basis.[26]

Highlights in HRM 4

Dual Career Tracks: Xenova System

Scientist
Plans and undertakes laboratory work to achieve agreed-on project goals, using inputs from colleagues, the external scientific community, literature, and suppliers.

↓

Senior Scientist
Plans and undertakes experimental programs and laboratory work to achieve agreed-on project or scientific goals, uses inputs from and provides outputs to colleagues, community, and suppliers.

Section Leader
Leads and manages a team of scientists from both science and operational management standpoint; makes significant contribution to management of groups of scientists and the general management of the department.

↓

Department Head
Leads and manages a department of scientists to provide Xenova with a well-managed and motivated scientific resource; makes a significant contribution to the general management of the company or division of the company.

Research Associate
Provides expertise and direction to programs and projects through in-depth understanding of a scientific specialism; leads or forms part of a scientific team with the main purpose of providing expertise in a scientific discipline.

↓

Principal Scientist
Provides scientific expertise and understanding of the highest level to ensure scientific leadership and direction; maintains a personal standing as a world-recognized and highly respected scientist and uses this to further the aims of the company through science.

Source: Adapted from Alan Garmonsway and Michael Wellin, "Creating the Right Natural Chemistry," *People Management* 1, no. 19 (September 21, 1995): 36–39.

Track Career Stages

Knowledge, skills, abilities, and attitudes as well as career aspirations change as one matures. While the work that individuals in different occupations perform can vary significantly, the challenges and frustrations that they face at the same stage in their careers are remarkably similar. A model describing these stages is shown in Figure 5.9. The stages are (1) preparation for work, (2) organizational entry, (3) early career,

Figure 5.8 Human Capital Profiles for Two Different Careers

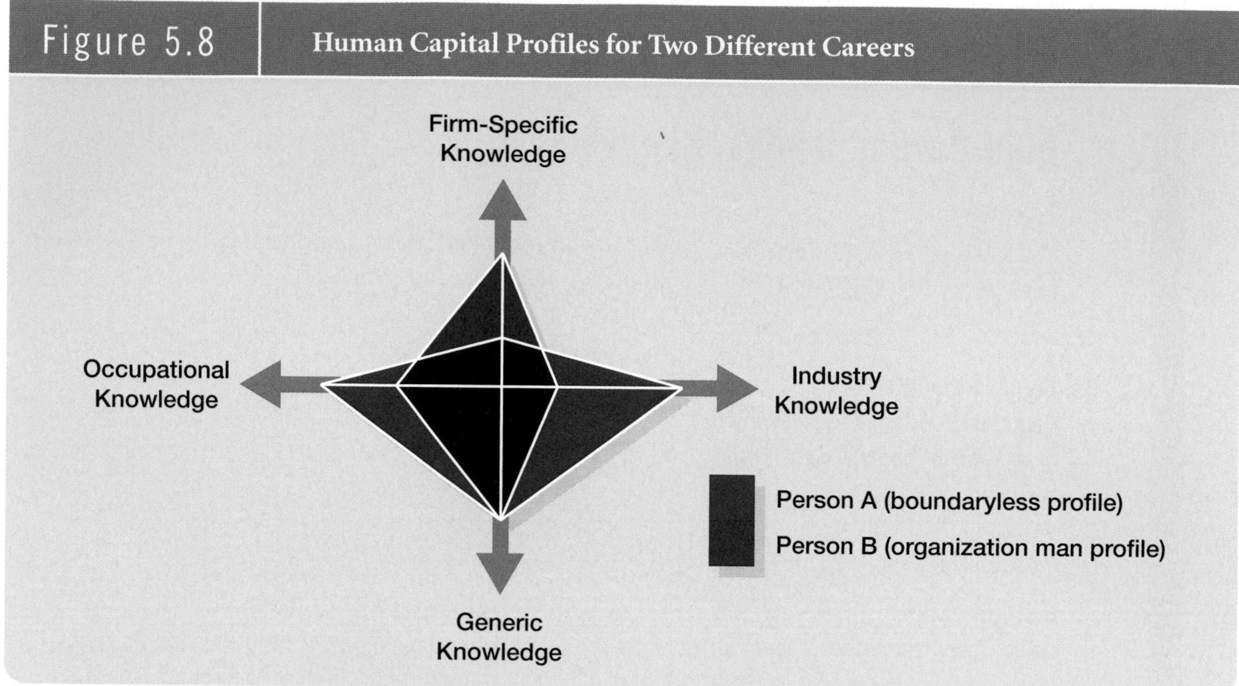

Source: Scott Snell, Cornell University.

(4) midcareer, and (5) late career. The typical age range and the major tasks of each stage are also presented in the figure.

The first stage—preparation for work—encompasses the period prior to entering an organization, often extending until age 25. It is a period in which individuals must acquire the knowledge, abilities, and skills they will need to compete in the marketplace. It is a time when careful planning, based on sound information, should be the focus. The second stage, typically from ages 18 to 25, is devoted to soliciting job offers and selecting an appropriate job. During this period one may also be involved in preparing for work. The next three stages entail fitting into a chosen occupation and organization, modifying goals, making choices, remaining productive, and finally, preparing for retirement. In the remainder of the chapter we will examine some of the activities of primary concern to the student, who is likely to be in the early stages. Retirement planning will be discussed in Chapter 11.

Avoid the Plateau Trap

career plateau
A situation in which for either organizational or personal reasons the probability of moving up the career ladder is low

Author Judith Bardwick was the first to label the "plateauing" phenomenon.[27] A **career plateau** is a situation in which for either organizational or personal reasons the probability of moving up the career ladder is low. According to Bardwick, only 1 percent of the labor force will not plateau in their working lives. There are three types of plateaus: structural, content, and life. A *structural plateau* marks the end of promotions; one will now have to leave the organization to find new opportunities and challenges. A *content plateau* occurs when a person has learned a job too well and is bored with day-to-day activities. A *life plateau* is more profound and may feel like a midlife crisis. People who experience life plateaus often have allowed work or some other major factor to become the most significant aspect of their lives, and

Figure 5.9 Stages of Career Development

Stage 5: Late Career (ages 55–retirement):
Remain productive in work, maintain self-esteem, prepare for effective retirement.

Stage 4: Midcareer (ages 40–55):
Reappraise early career and early adulthood goals, reaffirm or modify goals, make choices appropriate to middle adult years, remain productive.

Stage 3: Early Career (ages 25–40):
Learn job, learn organizational rules and norms, fit into chosen occupation and organization, increase competence, pursue goals.

Stage 2: Organizational Entry (ages 18–25):
Obtain job offer(s) from desired organization(s), select appropriate job based on complete and accurate information.

Stage 1: Preparation for Work (ages 0–25):
Develop occupational self-image, assess alternative occupations, develop initial occupational choice, pursue necessary education.

they experience a loss of identity and self-esteem when there is no longer success in that area. Figure 5.10 lists some probing questions employees can ask themselves if they find themselves in, or trying to overcome, a career plateau.

Organizations can help individuals cope with plateaus by providing opportunities for lateral growth when opportunities for advancement do not exist. Companies with international divisions can encourage employees to take assignments abroad to expand their horizons. Career enrichment programs can help people learn more about what gives them satisfaction within a company, as well as what kinds of opportunities will make them happiest if they go elsewhere.

Career Development Initiatives

Although career management involves a good deal of analysis and planning, the reality is that it needs to provide a set of tools and techniques that help employees gauge their potential for success in the organization. Informal counseling by HR staff and supervisors is used widely. As we mentioned earlier in the chapter, many organizations give

Figure 5.10 Career Plateau Questions

1. Do I accept high-visibility assignments?
2. Do I continue to advance my education, both formal and vocational?
3. Am I recognized by other leaders in my organization?
4. Am I routinely promoted?
5. Am I known as a versatile employee?
6. Do I continue to get larger-than-normal raises?
7. Do I rate at the high end of the performance ratings?
8. Do I have a plan with measurable objectives, and have I updated it recently?

Source: John Rosche, "Who's Managing Your Career?" *Contract Management* 44, no. 2 (February 2004): 20–22.

their employees information on educational assistance, EEO/AA programs and policies, salary administration, and job requirements. Career planning workbooks and workshops are also popular means of helping employees identify their potential and the strength of their interests.

In a recent study undertaken by Drake Beam Morin, the six most successful career-management practices used within organizations are as follows:

- Placing clear expectations on employees so that they know what is expected of them throughout their careers with the organization.
- Giving employees the opportunity to transfer to other office locations, both domestically and internationally.
- Providing a clear and thorough succession plan to employees.
- Encouraging performance through rewards and recognition.
- Giving employees the time and resources they need to consider short- and long-term career goals.
- Encouraging employees to continually assess their skills and career direction.

In contrast, organizations also need to be mindful of the internal barriers that inhibit employees' career advancement. Generally, these barriers can include such things as the following:

- Lack of time, budgets, and resources for employees to plan their careers and to undertake training and development.
- Rigid job specifications, lack of leadership support for career management, and a short-term focus.
- Lack of career opportunities and pathways within the organization for employees.[28]

Career-Planning Workbooks

Several organizations have prepared workbooks to guide their employees individually through systematic self-assessment of values, interests, abilities, goals, and personal development plans. General Motors' *Career Development Guide* contains a section called "What Do You Want Your Future to Be?" in which the employee makes a personal evaluation. General Electric has developed an extensive set of career development programs, including workbooks to help employees explore life issues that affect career decisions.

Some organizations prefer to use workbooks written for the general public. Popular ones include Richard N. Bolles's *What Color Is Your Parachute?*, Andrew H. Souerwine's *Career Strategies: Planning for Personal Growth,* John Holland's *Self-Directed Search,* and John W. Slocum and G. Scott King's *How to Pack Your Career Parachute.*[29] These same books are recommended to students for help in planning their careers.

Career-Planning Workshops

Workshops offer experiences similar to those provided by workbooks. However, they have the advantage of providing a chance to compare and discuss attitudes, concerns, and plans with others in similar situations. Some workshops focus on current job performance and development plans. Others deal with broader life and career plans and values.

As mentioned earlier, employees should be encouraged to assume responsibility for their own careers. A career workshop can help them do that. It can also help them learn how to make career decisions, set career goals, create career options, seek career-planning information, and at the same time build confidence and self-esteem.[30]

Career Counseling

career counseling
The process of discussing with employees their current job activities and performance, their personal and career interests and goals, their personal skills, and suitable career development objectives

Career counseling involves talking with employees about their current job activities and performance, their personal and career interests and goals, their personal skills, and suitable career development objectives. While some organizations make counseling a part of the annual performance appraisal, career counseling is usually voluntary. Career counseling may be provided by the HR staff, managers and supervisors, specialized staff counselors, or outside consultants. Several techniques for career counseling are outlined at the end of this chapter. (See the chapter appendix titled "Personal Career Development.") As employees approach retirement, they may be encouraged to participate in preretirement programs, which often include counseling along with other helping activities. Preretirement programs will be discussed in Chapter 11.

One interesting development in recent years has been the establishment of the Workforce Investment Act of 1998. With the signing of this act, Congress established a new law that consolidates a wide variety of federally sponsored career development and job training programs. Under the new arrangement, one-stop service centers have been set up in cooperation among businesses and local governments to provide job seekers with a variety of services, including career counseling, skill assessments, training, job search assistance, and referrals to related programs and services. For example, CTWorks, based in Bridgeport, Connecticut, is one of hundreds of non-profit career centers across the country where unemployed and underemployed workers can apply for unemployment and training benefits, meet with career counselors, and mail and fax resumes to prospective employers free of charge.[31]

Determining Individual Development Needs

Because the requirements of each position and the qualifications of each person are different, no two individuals will have identical developmental needs. For one individual, self-development may consist of developing the ability to write reports, give talks, and lead conferences. For another, it may require developing interpersonal skills in order to communicate and relate more effectively with a diverse workforce. Periodic performance appraisals can provide a basis for determining each employee's progress. Conferences in which these appraisals are discussed are an essential part of self-improvement efforts.

In helping individuals plan their careers, it is important for organizations to recognize that younger employees today seek meaningful training assignments that are interesting and involve challenge, responsibility, and a sense of empowerment. They also have a greater concern for the contribution that their work in the organization will make to society. Unfortunately, they are frequently given responsibilities they view as rudimentary, boring, and composed of too many "make-work" activities. Some organizations are attempting to retain young managers with high potential by offering a **fast-track program** that enables them to advance more rapidly than those with less potential. A fast-track program may provide for a relatively rapid progression—lateral transfers or promotions—through a number of managerial positions requiring exposure to different organizational functions; it may also provide opportunities to make meaningful decisions.

fast-track program
A program that encourages young managers with high potential to remain with an organization by enabling them to advance more rapidly than those with less potential

Career Self-Management Training

In response to the growing view that employees should assume greater responsibility for their own career management, many organizations are establishing programs for employees on how they can engage in *career self-management.* The training focuses on two major objectives: (1) helping employees learn to continuously gather feedback and information about their careers and (2) encouraging them to prepare for mobility.

The training is not geared to skills and behaviors associated with a specific job, but rather toward long-term personal effectiveness. Employees typically undertake self-assessments to increase awareness of their own career attitudes and values. In addition, they are encouraged to widen their viewpoint beyond the next company promotion to broader opportunities in the marketplace. For many, these external opportunities have not been seen as viable options, much less something the company would acknowledge. Participants might be encouraged to engage in career networking or to identify other means to prepare for job mobility, such as hearing reports from employees who made transitions to new job opportunities both within and outside the organization.[32]

Mentoring

When one talks with men and women about their employment experiences, it is common to hear them mention individuals at work who influenced them. They frequently refer to immediate managers who were especially helpful as career developers. But they also mention others at higher levels in the organization who provided guidance and support to them in the development of their careers. These executives and managers who coach, advise, and encourage employees of lesser rank are called **mentors.**

mentors
Executives who coach, advise, and encourage individuals of lesser rank

At times, individuals can be overly restrictive in their definitions of who constitutes a mentor, or what that mentor can do. The top ten myths about mentors are shown in Figure 5.11. In reality, informal mentoring goes on daily within every type of organization. Generally, the mentor initiates the relationship, but sometimes an

Figure 5.11 **Top Ten Myths about Mentors**

Myth 1: *Mentors exist only for career development.* Sometimes the mentor focuses on formal career development. Sometimes the mentor is teacher, counselor, and friend. Some mentors assume all these roles. This enhances both personal and professional development.

Myth 2: *You need only one mentor.* We can have multiple mentors in our lives. Different mentors provide different things and tap different facets of our lives.

Myth 3: *Mentoring is a one-way process.* Learning flows both ways. The mentor often learns from the protégé, so the growth is reciprocal.

Myth 4: *A mentor has to be older than the protégé.* Age does not matter. Experience and wisdom matter. Don't deprive yourself of learning opportunities from others who have rich experiences.

Myth 5: *A mentor has to be the same gender and race as the protégé.* The purpose of mentoring is to learn. Don't deprive yourself. Seek mentors who are different from you.

Myth 6: *Mentor relationships just happen.* Being in the right place at the right time can help, but the key to selecting a good mentor is what (not whom) you need. Don't be afraid to actively seek a mentor.

Myth 7: *Highly profiled people make the best mentors.* Prestige and success can be good, but good advice, leadership styles, work ethics, and the like vary by individuals. Good mentors are people who challenge you according to your needs, readiness, and aspirations.

Myth 8: *Once a mentor, always a mentor.* Over time, the mentor should pull back and let the protégé go his or her own way. Although the two may maintain contact, the relationship changes over time.

Myth 9: *Mentoring is a complicated process.* The most complicated part is getting out of a bad mentor relationship. If the relationship is not productive, find a tactful way to disengage.

Myth 10: *Mentor-protégé expectations are the same for everyone.* Individuals seek mentors for the same reasons: resources, visibility, enhanced skills, and counsel. But each individual brings different expectations. The key is understanding where the protégé is *now*, not where he or she *should be.*

employee will approach a potential mentor for advice. Most mentoring relationships develop over time on an informal basis. They frequently end that that way, too. However, proactive organizations emphasize formal mentoring plans that assign a mentor to employees considered for upward movement in the organization. GE, for example, selects the top 20 percent of its performers and allows these people to choose their own mentors from a list of top executives. Under a good mentor, learning focuses on goals, opportunities, expectations, standards, and assistance in fulfilling one's potential.[33]

Figure 5.12 shows a list of the most effective features of mentors as well as partners. In order to form an effective mentoring relationship, an employee seeking a mentor should follow a few general guidelines:

1. *Research the person's background.* Do your homework. The more you know about your potential mentor, the easier it will be to approach him or her and establish a relationship that will work for both of you.
2. *Make contact with the person.* Have a mutual friend or acquaintance introduce you, or get involved with your potential mentor in business settings. That will help the mentor see your skills in action.

Figure 5.12 **Mentoring Functions**

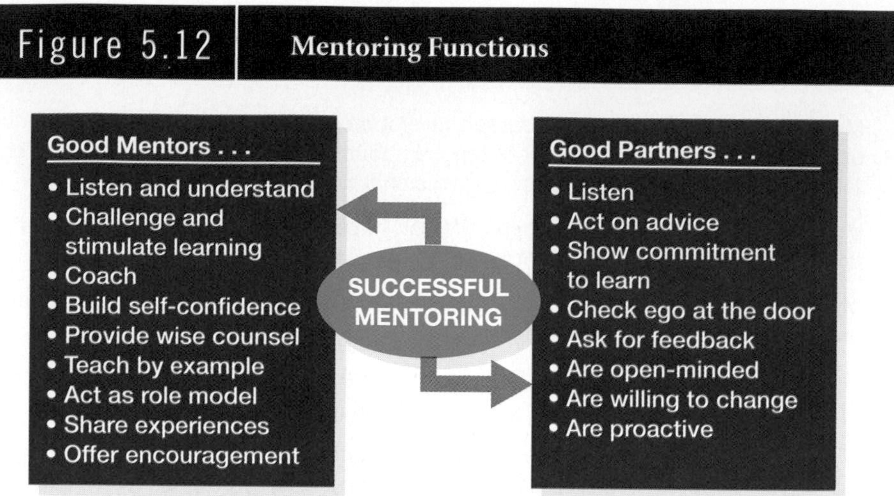

Source: Matt Starcevich, Ph.D. and Fred Friend, "Effective Mentoring Relationships from the Mentee's Perspective," *Workforce,* supplement (July 1999): 2–3. Used with permission of the Center for Coaching and Mentoring, Inc., http://coachingandmentoring.com.

3. *Request help on a particular matter.* Let the mentor know that you admire him or her, and ask for help in that arena. For example, you might say, "You're good at dealing with customers. Would it be OK if I came to you for advice on my customers?" Keep your request simple and specific.
4. *Consider what you can offer in exchange.* Mentoring is a two-way street. If you can do something for your potential mentor, then by all means, tell him or her.
5. *Arrange a meeting.* Once your specific request has been accepted, you're ready to meet with your potential mentor. Never go into this meeting cold. Set goals, identify your desired outcomes, and prepare a list of questions. Listen attentively. Then ask your prepared questions and request specific suggestions.
6. *Follow up.* After the meeting, try some of your potential mentor's suggestions and share the results. Express appreciation by identifying something in particular that was significant to you.
7. *Ask to meet on an ongoing basis.* After your potential mentor has had a chance not only to meet and interact with you, but also to see the value of what he or she can provide, you're in a good position to request an ongoing relationship. Suggest that you meet with him or her regularly, or ask permission to get help on an ad hoc basis.[34]

Organizations with formal mentoring programs include Shell International, Sun Microsystems, Johnson & Johnson, the federal Government Accounting Office, and the Bank of Montreal. Alternatively, given the importance of the issue, a number of mentoring organizations have begun to spring up. One such organization, Menttium Corporation, helps create and monitor mentoring partnerships so that the right people are matched with one another. When done well, the mentoring process is beneficial for both the pupil and the mentor. One survey found, for example, that 77 percent of companies with successful mentoring programs reported that they effectively increased employee retention.[35]

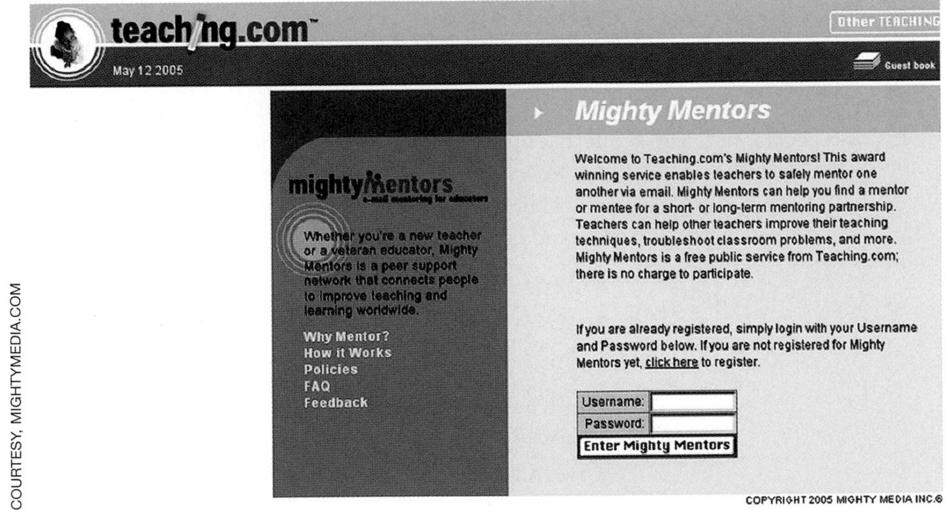

*Mighty Mentors, launched by Mighty Media, facilitates online mentoring for teachers.**

COURTESY, MIGHTYMEDIA.COM

A new form of mentoring, sponsored by the MS Foundation for Women, provides an opportunity for boys and girls ages 8 to 12 to spend a day with their parents or their parents' friends on the job. "Take Our Daughters and Sons to Work Day" is designed to give children career role models. People and companies across the country participate in the event every April 28. Other groups, such as the Girl Scouts in the Washington, D.C., area, have longer-term mentoring plans in which young women ages 12 to 18 spend up to a month during one year in the offices of women scientists, accountants, and other professionals. It is hoped that through such programs, young women will think more broadly in their career planning.

Not surprisingly, mentoring is also being done over the Internet. *E-mentoring* brings experienced business professionals together with individuals needing counseling. A few examples include the following:

- *Women in Technology International (WITI)* is an association that has assembled thousands of women in technology fields in the United States and internationally to act as online mentors to visitors to its web site.
- *Mighty Mentors* is a program by Mighty Media (Minneapolis, Minnesota) that provides interactive educational technology. The mentor service lets teachers mentor one another via e-mail after they connect online.
- *NursingNet* is an online nursing forum that has mentoring programs for those in healthcare. The site hooks up experienced nurses with those who need guidance.[36]

Even though participants in e-mentoring typically never meet in person, many form long-lasting e-mail connections that tend to be very beneficial. Still, most participants see these connections as supplements to—rather than substitutes for—in-company mentors.

*Mighty Mentors is part of the Teaching.com family of online educational services provided by Mighty Media, Inc., an interactive and creative communications firm in Minneapolis, MN (www.mightymedia.com). Mighty Media provides non-commercial Web services for K-12 students, educators, and families (www.teaching.com), and these services are used by hundreds of thousands of teachers, parents, and youth from over 100 different countries annually. Mighty Media also co-sponsors a series of online education events every year with national non-profit organizations and concerned corporations to promote youth leadership, volunteerism, and innovation in teaching and learning.

Networking

career networking The process of establishing mutually beneficial relationships with other business people, including potential clients and customers

As the number of contacts grows, mentoring broadens into a process of **career networking.** As a complement to mentoring, in which relationships are more selective, networking relationships tend to be more varied and temporary. The networks can be internal to a particular organization or connected across many different organizations.

According to the Monster.com Career Center (http://content.monster.com/career/networking/), there are many ways to identify networking contacts. Some of the best places to consider are the following:

- Your college alumni association or career office networking lists
- Your own extended family
- Your friends' parents and other family members
- Your professors, advisors, coaches, tutors, and clergy
- Your former bosses and your friends' and family members' bosses
- Members of clubs, religious groups, and other organizations to which you belong
- All of the organizations near where you live or go to school

Through networking, individuals often find out about new jobs, professional trends, and other opportunities. In a survey of executives by the human resources firm Drake Beam Morin, 61 percent said that they had found new positions in the previous year through networking. Another study of 15 high-ranking executive women found that although many of them lacked formal mentors, they had successfully engaged in a kind of "360-degree" networking: The women made it a point to form and maintain relationships with people above, below, and at the same level as themselves, which helped advance their careers.[37]

Developing a Diverse Talent Pool

In meeting their legal obligation to provide equal employment opportunity, employers often develop a formal EEO/AA program. An essential part of any EEO/AA policy must be an affirmative effort to recruit members of protected classes. The steps the EEOC recommends for organizations to follow in developing such a program were discussed in Chapter 3. But the reasons to develop a diverse talent pool aren't merely legal ones. Today, ethnic groups represent approximately 30 percent of the total U.S. population. In the next ten years, however, the number is expected to grow to 50 percent. By 2060, the U.S. Census bureau estimates that ethnic minorities will account for an astounding 90 percent of the population. These groups have a huge amount of buying power, and that power is growing. Some researchers predict that companies failing to diversify their talent pools will have a hard time identifying with their target customers and competing. As they face tougher competition in the United States and abroad, businesses will need all the leadership, productivity, innovation, and creativity the talent pool has to offer.

Recruitment and Development of Women

Women constitute the largest number among the protected classes. Sixty percent of women participate in the labor force, and as a group, they represent 47 percent of the total U.S. labor force. The participation rate of working mothers is significantly higher: Approximately 80 percent of mothers with school-age children (ages 6 to 17) are employed in some capacity, and three out of five are the heads of households. In many of the latter cases, these women have the employment disadvantage of having completed, on average, fewer years of school than married women not in the workforce, and they are concentrated in lower-skilled, lower-paying jobs.[38]

A major employment obstacle for women, both skilled and unskilled, is the stereotyped thinking that persists within our society. Still another barrier has been that women in the past had fewer years of experience in the workforce and were not as likely as men to have professional training and preparation for entrance or advancement into management positions. This situation is changing, however. Today, three out of five college graduates are women, and there have been significant increases in the enrollment of women in programs leading to degrees in management and other professional fields. Figure 5.13 shows women as a percentage of people in the U.S. earning professional degrees at select intervals during the course of the last three decades. In addition, more women are enrolling in management seminars and certification programs that will further prepare them for higher managerial positions.

As a consequence of these changes, an increasing number of women enter the labor force in managerial positions. The largest percentage of employed women (38 percent) work in management, professional, and related occupations, while 35 percent work in sales and office occupations. Today women account for between 45 and 50 percent of all managers. About 13 percent of board of directors' seats in Fortune 500 firms are held by women—up from around 8 percent in 1995.[39]

Eliminating Women's Barriers to Advancement

Despite some of the changes taking place, women in management traditionally have been at a disadvantage because they have not been part of the so-called "good old

Figure 5.13 Women as a Percentage of People Earning Selected Professional Degrees, 1970–1971, 1987–1988, and 2000–2001

FIELD OF STUDY	1970–1971	1987–1998	2000–2001
Engineering	0.8	15.3	19.9
Dentistry	1.2	26.1	38.6
Optometry	2.4	34.3	54.5
Law	7.3	40.4	47.3
Veterinary Medicine	7.8	50.0	69.8
Medicine	9.2	33.0	45.3
Accounting	10.1	52.6	60.5
Economics	11.2	32.8	34.1
Architecture	12.0	38.7	35.8
Pharmacy	25.2	59.7	66.1

Source: Commission of Professionals in Science and Technology, *Professional Women and Minorities* (Washington, DC: CPST, 1987); U.S. Department of Education, *Digest of Education Statistics,* 1990 and 2002 (Washington, DC: U.S. Government Printing Office).

GETTY IMAGES

Artificial barriers or "glass ceilings" are being shattered by successful women executives and entrepreneurs.

boys'" network, an informal network of interpersonal relationships that has traditionally provided a means for senior (male) members of the organization to pass along news of advancement opportunities and other career tips to junior (male) members. Women have typically been outside the network, lacking role models to serve as mentors.

To combat their difficulty in advancing to management positions, women in several organizations have developed their own women's networks. At Burlington Northern Santa Fe Railway, a women's network serves as a system for encouraging and fostering women's career development and for sharing information, experiences, and insights. Women in lower levels of the company are mentored by women at higher levels. Corporate officers are invited to regularly scheduled network meetings to discuss such matters as planning, development, and company performance. Network members view these sessions as an opportunity to let corporate officers know of women who are interested in and capable of furthering their careers. Other corporations in which women's networks have been established include Metropolitan Life Insurance, Ralston Purina, Atlantic Richfield Company, and CBS.[40]

As we mentioned previously, several online e-mentoring networks are available. One that is expressly devoted to working women is Advancing Women (http://www.advancingwomen.com). In addition, an organization devoted to helping employers break down barriers to upward mobility for women is Catalyst, a New York City–based not-for-profit organization. Catalyst (http://www.catalystwomen.org) not only courts corporate officers but also offers career advice, job placement, continuing education, and related professional development for women of all ages. At its New York headquarters, Catalyst houses an extensive library and audiovisual center that is regarded as the country's leading resource for information on women and work.

There is substantial evidence that stereotyped attitudes toward women are changing. As women pursue career goals assertively and attitudes continue to change, the climate for women in management will be even more favorable. Research has shown that newer male managers tend to be more receptive to the advancement of women managers. That said, and despite the fact that more women hold managerial positions than they have in years past, the proportion of women in top echelons of management—board chair, CEO, president, executive VP—still remains extremely low, around 3 percent. Although these data suggest that there has been some progress, there is much left to do to break the "glass ceiling"—the invisible barrier of attitudes, prejudices, and "good old boys'" networks that blocks the progress of women who seek important positions in an organization.

Glass-Ceiling Audits

The U.S. Department of Labor defines the glass ceiling as "those artificial barriers based on attitudinal or organizational bias that prevent qualified individuals from advancing upward in their organizations into management level positions."[41] "Glass-ceiling reviews," also known as "corporate reviews," are conducted by the Department of Labor to identify practices that appear to hinder the upward mobility of qualified women (and minorities). The Department of Labor looks for such things as equal access to the following:

- Upper-level management and executive training
- Rotational assignments
- International assignments
- Opportunities for promotion
- Opportunities for executive development programs at universities
- Desirable compensation packages
- Opportunities to participate on high-profile project teams
- Upper-level special assignments

Organizations are increasingly conducting their own glass-ceiling audits prior to government review to avoid fines and externally imposed corrective action. These audits can document any ceilings and the reasons they exist. Self-audits are one step to tapping the potentials of a diversified workforce. Women are also breaking through the glass ceiling by starting their own businesses. As one entrepreneur put it, "It's not hard to break through the glass ceiling when you own it."

Preparing Women for Management

As noted earlier, opportunities for women to move into management positions are definitely improving. In addition to breaking down the barriers to advancement, the development of women managers demands a better understanding of women's needs and the requirements of the management world.

Many employers now offer special training to women who are on a management career path. They may use their own staff or outside firms to conduct this training. Opportunities are also available for women to participate in seminars and workshops that provide instruction and experiences in a wide variety of management topics.

In addition to formal training opportunities, women today are provided with a wealth of information and guidance in books and magazines. Business sections in bookstores are stocked with numerous books written especially for women who want a better idea of the career opportunities available to them. Many books are devoted to the pursuit of careers in specific fields.[42]

Popular magazines that contain many articles about women and jobs include *Working Woman, New Woman, Savvy, The Executive Female,* and *Enterprising Women.*

These magazines are also recommended reading for men who want a better understanding of the problems that women face in the world of work.

USING THE INTERNET

Many organizations today realize the importance of families to both male and female managers. See how quality-of-life and family-resource programs are included in career planning at DuPont. Go to the Student Resources at:

http://bohlander.swlearning.com

Accommodating Families

One of the major problems women have faced is that of having both a managerial career and a family. Women managers whose children are at an age requiring close parental attention often experience conflict between their responsibility to the children and their duty to the employer. If the conflict becomes too painful, they may decide to forgo their careers, at least temporarily, and leave their jobs.

In recent years many employers, including AFLAC, SunTrust Banks, Quaker Oats Company, Abbott Labs, Bristol-Myers Squibb, IBM, and the accounting firm KPMG, have inaugurated programs that are mutually advantageous to the career-oriented woman and the employer. These programs, which include alternative career paths, extended leave, flextime, job sharing, and telecommuting, provide new ways to balance career and family. AFLAC, for example, offers families hot take-home meals at their onsite cafeterias to ease the burden of employees' having to prepare dinner after leaving the office for the day. The company also subsidizes babysitting for parents on Saturday nights so they can spend some free time together.[43] These efforts are paying off. Both IBM and KPMG, for example, report that their programs have helped them retain and increase their numbers of women workers.

Nonetheless, maintaining a balance between work and family still appears difficult for employees. After reaching a high in 1998, the number of working women with children under age 1 has dropped off slightly. And it's now not just mothers who are feeling the tug-of-war between work and family. The number of stay-at-home dads has increased dramatically as well.[44]

Recruitment and Development of Minorities

Since the passage of the Civil Rights Act of 1964, many members of minority groups have been able to realize a substantial improvement in their social and economic well-being. According to the EEOC, the employment of women and African Americans as officials and managers has increased by 33 percent in the past decade. The employment of Hispanic and Asian American managers has increased by more than 50 percent. Increasing numbers of blacks and Hispanics are now in the upper income tax brackets by virtue of their entrance into professional, engineering, and managerial positions. However, the proportion of minorities in these areas is still substantially below their proportions in the total population. Moreover, unemployment among minorities, particularly youth, continues to be critically high. The rates climb even higher during economic downturns when employment opportunities become harder to find. For many minorities employment opportunities still remain exceedingly limited because of educational and societal disadvantages. Also, mainstream, traditional recruitment methods may prove ineffective in reaching them. Community action agencies, civil rights organizations, and church groups within communities can provide a means for recruiters to reach inner-city residents. Special media advertising targeted to this group also may prove effective. Highlights in HRM 5 shows how to design a tailored approach to diversity planning.

Diversity Recruitment That Works

Workforce diversity will help your organization reach new markets and develop greater intellectual capital. But to leverage diversity, you must first have it—at all levels.

Making It Real

To tap into and retain a diverse pool of top talent, HR professionals must:

- Understand demographic changes in the workforce.
- Ensure that majority groups aren't marginalized in the process.
- Educate staff that *diversity* is not synonymous with *minority*, and at the same time try to increase access and opportunities for people of color and other minorities.
- Build long-term relationships with minority organizations, not look for quick fixes.
- Learn how to effectively interview diverse groups.
- Make sure that they're not just "grafting" minorities onto the organization without making appropriate internal culture changes that will enable them to thrive.
- Become the employer of choice for a diverse workforce.
- Ensure retention by developing a diversity-friendly culture.
- Foster a culturally sensitive work environment.
- Network for strategic alliances to enable long-term diversity recruitment.
- Measure the effectiveness of their recruitment efforts.

Putting Theory into Action

To maximize the effectiveness of diversity at all levels of an organization, the diversity has to first exist. Here are some methods an organization may want to try:

- Establish networks with minority colleges.
- Offer corporate internships and scholarships.
- Sponsor job fairs in minority communities. Develop partnerships with minority student professional organizations.
- Develop partnerships with minority organizations, such as the National Black MBA Association.
- Tap all known web sites where resumes of diverse individuals can be found, such as http://www.HireDiversity.com.

Steps to Take Now

Consider implementing the following initiatives:

- Identify and begin building connections with national minority organizations, not only for access to college-age minority students, but for access to the organization's members who might be viable candidates for mid- and senior-level positions.
- Target recruitment advertising to minority publications such as *The Advocate* and *Hispanic Times*.
- Use your internal employee resource groups. Ask minority employees to provide insight on effective places and ways to recruit diverse candidates. Obviously, this strategy depends on how your existing minority employees view the organization's commitment to diversity.
- Develop training for hiring leaders to ensure that diverse applicants aren't discounted in the interviewing process because they are different.
- Understand the "cultural norms" of diverse candidates.
- Partner with your marketing group to ensure that all marketing—not just recruitment advertising—features a diverse mix of individuals.

Source: Condensed from Patricia Digh, "Getting People in the Pool: Diversity Recruitment That Works," *HRMagazine* 44, no. 10 (October 1999): 94–98. Reprinted with the permission of *HRMagazine*, published by the Society for Human Resource Management, Alexandria, VA, via Copyright Clearance Center.

Providing Minority Internships

Unless minorities can be retained within an organization, diversity programs are likely to prove ineffective. If minority employees are to be retained, they, like any employee, must be made to feel welcome in their jobs and to feel that their efforts contribute to the success of the organization. To build ongoing relationships with prospective employees, many companies have increased their sponsorship of internship programs. An internship program offers students an opportunity to learn on the job and gain hands-on experience. For example, in the media industry ABC, NBC, CBS, and Fox made substantial contributions to the Emma L. Bowen Foundation, which provides internships, college scholarships, and postgraduate employment for minorities. The program mentors students from their junior year in high school through college graduation. Similarly, *Newsday* works with other news publications to offer an internship program for minority news reporters and copyeditors, who are underrepresented in the print journalism field. Prospective reporters are trained at *The Los Angeles Times*, and aspiring copyeditors are trained at *Newsday*. In another effort, Lockheed Martin teamed up with Operation Enterprise, the American Management Association's summer program for high school and college students, to offer ten-week paid internships to students of America's historically black colleges and universities.[45]

Since 1973, Inroads, Inc., an internship organization, has arranged for minority college students to get tutoring, counseling, and summer internships with large corporations. Inroads sponsors approximately 5,500 salaried interns at more than 600 companies annually. The program considers only students who graduate in the top 10 percent of their high school class. In college, the students must maintain a 3.0 grade-point average out of a possible 4.0. Participants report that Inroads has raised their aspirations and has taught them how to adjust to the corporate world, and 83 percent of them end up taking permanent jobs with companies with whom they've interned. Benefits for the corporation include early access to talented minorities, opportunities to hire college graduates who understand the company's business and its culture, and a greater number of minorities pursuing careers in the traditionally underrepresented fields of engineering and business.[46]

Advancing Minorities to Management

The area of employment that has been the slowest to respond to affirmative action appeals is the advancement of minorities to middle- and top-management positions. For example, while blacks and Hispanics constitute approximately 30 percent of the employed U.S. civilian population, they hold only a very small percentage of executive, administrative, and managerial positions. That will likely change as the demographics of the United States changes and the percentage of people with minority backgrounds increases. Abbott Laboratories, Sara Lee, and BankBoston are among a growing number of companies that are committed to increasing their ranks of minority managers. These companies believe that increasing the number of the minorities they hire and promote today is critical to their future success.[47]

Training opportunities for minority managers are also offered by such organizations as the American Management Association. Specifically addressing the advancement difficulties of blacks, the AMA conducts a course titled "Self-Development Strategies for Black Managers" in several cities throughout the country. Major topics include the realities of corporate life, race-related stresses, effective interpersonal relationships, situational leadership, handling racial discrimination, and personal self-assessment. In recent years black women have been rising more rapidly than black men in corporate America. Over the past decade, this group has grown dramatically. The reasons black women are overtaking black men are many and complex. However, in spite of their progress, both black women and black men need continued support in their development and advancement.[48]

While minority managers do play a part in creating a better climate for groups that are discriminated against in advancement opportunities, top managers and the HR department have the primary responsibility for creating conditions within their organizations that are favorable for recognizing and rewarding performance on the basis of objective, nondiscriminatory criteria.

Other Important Talent Concerns

Recruitment of the Disabled

The disabled have more $200 billion in discretionary spending power. Employers who identify job opportunities within their organizations for the disabled and recruit them will undoubtedly benefit. Currently, however, only about 30 percent of disabled Americans between ages 21 and 64 are working. The participation rate of those who are severely disabled is lower (about 25 percent). The greatest numbers have impairments that are hearing-, vision-, or back-related.

Of those who do not work, the majority would like to. These individuals have often been rejected for employment because of the mistaken belief that there were no jobs within an organization that they might be able to perform effectively. Fears that the disabled might have more accidents or that they might aggravate existing disabilities have also deterred their employment. The lack of special facilities for physically impaired people, particularly those who use wheelchairs, has been a further employment restriction. However, physical obstructions are being eliminated as employers are making federally legislated improvements to accommodate disabled workers.

Efforts to eliminate discrimination in hiring, promotion, and compensation of people with disabilities are increasing as organizations comply with the Americans with Disabilities Act of 1990 (see Chapter 3). Thanks to federal regulations, many organizations are beginning to recognize that physical disabilities may constitute limitations only with respect to certain job requirements. An employee in a wheelchair who might not be able to perform duties that involve certain physical activities may be quite capable of working at a bench or a desk. Highlights in HRM 6 lists tips from employers that have been successful in hiring and retaining talented employees with disabilities.

The most frequently cited advantages of employing disabled people include their dependability, superior attendance, loyalty, and low turnover. IBM hired its first disabled employee in 1914. This is not surprising, as the company makes software and other products that help eliminate workplace barriers for the disabled. IBM's

Highlights in HRM 6

Tips for Hiring and Retaining Employees with Disabilities

- *Get the facts and don't make assumptions.* Myths or assumptions are also major barriers to employment. For example, some employers think their workers' compensation insurance will increase if they hire someone with a disability. Not true. Insurance rates are based on the hazards of the operation and the organization's accident experience, not on whether workers have disabilities. Another frequent assumption is that people with disabilities do not have training or education. In fact, many people have college degrees and/or extensive experience making them qualified.
- *Make sure your company is accessible.* This means more than wide doors and ramps. It also means making sure job postings and promotion opportunities are accessible to people with disabilities. Forms and applications should be within reach and interview locations fully accessible. Most important, do not assume accessibility will create a financial hardship. Visit the U.S. Office of Disability Employment Policy (http://www.dol.gov/odep) and JobAccess (http://www.jobaccess.org) for success stories achieved inexpensively.
- *Write job descriptions for all positions.* Written job descriptions identify essential job functions and help applicants identify which jobs he or she would be qualified for and enjoy.
- *Set standards and expectations.* Many people believe that individuals with disabilities receive special treatment and unfair advantages. Be fair and responsible, but do not lower standards or expectations simply because someone has a disability. The purpose of accommodations is to enhance an individual's ability to accomplish work tasks, not to lower expectations.
- *Make a company-wide commitment.* The best employment success stories are always found in companies in which the president, CEO, or owner is publicly committed to hiring people with disabilities.
- *Get connected with people who can help.* Several organizations throughout Washington State can help business owners and human resources personnel recruit, interview, hire, train, and retain skilled employees with disabilities. Contact the Washington State Developmental Disabilities Council (http://www.ddc.wa.gov) at (800) 634-4473 or Rehabilitation Enterprises of Washington at (360) 943-7654.

Source: Ed Holen and Penny Jo Haney, "Consider Employing People with Disabilities," *Wenatchee Business Journal* 17, no. 10 (October 2003): A19.

viewpoint is that no employee should be overlooked because of a disability, because he or she might be the person to develop the next generation of hardware or software from which the company will profit. Indeed, several of the company's deaf researchers are doing world-class work with new technologies, including voice recognition technology.

IBM also participates in mentoring and internships for the disabled. The Workforce Recruitment Program for College Students with Disabilities (WRP) is one internship organization. WRP puts together profiles of more than 1,500 college students and recent graduates from 200 colleges seeking summer internships or permanent employment nationwide with federal agencies. These profiles are then made available free of charge to business owners. The candidates are skilled in a wide variety of fields, and each has a disability. This effort to help employers find workers and help the disabled find jobs is cosponsored by the U.S. Department of Labor and the Office of Disability Employment Policy. The American Association for the Advancement of Science has a program called Entry Point, which has placed more than 400 science and engineering students with disabilities in internships in the public and private sectors. More than 90 percent of these students have gone on to graduate schools or jobs in science and technology.[49]

Many organizations are finding that hiring disabled workers is a good investment.

Less Publicized Disadvantages

In addition to the widely recognized forms of disability, employees have other physical characteristics that can limit their hiring and advancement opportunities. One such disadvantage is unattractiveness, against which employers can be biased even if unconsciously. "Unattractive" individuals are those whose facial features are considered unpleasant but who do not possess physical disfiguration that would put them in the physically disabled category. Another less publicized disadvantage is obesity. Although the EEOC has said that obesity is not a disability per se, in some cases, courts have held obesity to be a legitimate physical disability. A number of cities and states, including San Francisco and Washington, D.C., have outlawed discrimination based on body weight or height. Countless employees, including Pam Am flight attendants who had hoped to work for Delta when it acquired Pan Am in 1991, have sued their employers over weight-related issues. The Pan Am flight attendants sued Delta, claiming the company's weight standards were discriminatory, and won.

Employment attorneys say that to some extent, the looks-related criteria depend on what you're selling. A Las Vegas club hiring showgirls, for example, is more likely to be in a better position to argue that thinness and good looks are necessary for the job than Delta Air Lines would be. When facing such a situation, attorneys say employers should ask themselves the following question: "Do you think that *not* hiring the person will do so much good for your company that you are willing to take the risk of being sued?"[50]

Finally, there is the illiteracy handicap. Between 45 and 50 percent of adults in the United States have only limited reading and writing abilities needed to handle the minimal demands of daily living or job performance. Employers are encountering increasing numbers of employees, including college graduates, whose deficient reading and writing skills limit their performance on the job. A survey of Fortune 1000 CEOs found that 90 percent recognized the problems of illiteracy—yet just 38 percent acknowledged that it was a problem for their workers.[51]

The U.S. Department of Labor estimates that illiteracy costs U.S. businesses $60 billion a year in lost productivity. To address literacy problems, organizations such as Smith and Wesson, Hewlett-Packard, Motorola, and the City of Phoenix instituted basic-skill assessment programs to teach reading, math, and communication skills to employees who show some level of deficiency. America's Literacy Directory (ALD), sponsored by the National Institute for Literacy, connects employers, learners, volunteers, social service providers, and others with literacy programs in all 50 states and U.S. territories. Employees and employers need only go to ALD's online directory and type in their locations to find the literacy help centers nearest them.

Employing the Older Workforce

The U.S. Bureau of Labor Statistics anticipates that more than 25 percent of the working population will have reached retirement age by 2010. This is estimated to create a worker shortfall of about 10 million people. Even today, however, there is a definite trend by organizations to hire older people. The move has come both as a result of changing workforce demographics and as a change in the attitudes of employers and employees. Organizations realize that older workers have proven employment experience, have job "savvy," and are reliable employees. They are also an excellent recruitment source to staff part-time and full-time positions that are otherwise hard to fill. In addition, more older employees want to continue working, especially in light of the financial concerns facing the U.S. Social Security system.

Retirees often return to the workforce at the behest of their employers, who can't afford to lose the knowledge accumulated by longtime employees or their reliable work habits that have a positive effect on the entire work group. To prevent an exodus of talent, employers will need to implement human resources strategies to help retain and attract the talent older workers have to offer. Moreover, as the workforce ages, employers will need to make workplace adaptations to help older workers cope with the physical problems they will experience, such as poorer vision, hearing, and mobility. For some firms, especially in jobs for which it's difficult to attract and retain skilled, reliable employees, older workers can be the permanent solution to an intractable problem. Many older workers gravitate to non-full-time forms of work, especially independent contracting or consulting, on-call work (such as substitute nursing or teaching), and temporary work in administrative or IT roles.[52]

Employing Dual-Career Couples

As discussed throughout this book, the employment of both members of a couple has become a way of life in North America. Economic necessity and social forces have encouraged this trend to the point that over 80 percent of all marriages are now **dual-career partnerships** in which both members follow their own careers and actively support each other's career development.

dual-career partnerships
Couples in which both members follow their own careers and actively support each other's career development

As with most lifestyles, the dual-career arrangement has its positive and negative sides. A significant number of organizations are concerned with the problems facing dual-career couples and offer assistance to them. Flexible working schedules are the most frequent organizational accommodation to these couples. Other arrangements include leave policies under which either parent may stay home with a newborn, policies that allow work to be performed at home, daycare on organization premises, and job sharing.

The difficulties that dual-career couples face include the need for quality child care, the time demands, and the emotional stress. However, the main problem these

"How do you do, sir? My name is John L. Flagman, and I run a successful executive search firm."

Source: From *The Wall Street Journal*—Permission, Cartoon Features Syndicate.

couples face is the threat of relocation. Many large organizations now offer some kind of job-finding assistance for spouses of employees who are relocated, including payment of fees charged by employment agencies, job counseling firms, and executive search firms. Organizations are also developing networking relationships with other employers to find jobs for the spouses of their relocating employees. These networks can provide a way to "share the wealth and talent" in a community while simultaneously assisting in the recruitment efforts of the participating organizations.[53]

Relocating dual-career couples to foreign facilities is a major issue that international employers face. Fewer employees are willing to relocate without assistance for their spouses. Many employers have developed effective approaches for integrating the various allowances typically paid for overseas assignments when husband and wife work for the same employer. Far more complex are the problems that arise when couples work for two different employers. The problems associated with overseas assignments of dual-career couples will be examined in greater detail in Chapter 15.

SUMMARY

objective 1 In order to expand the talent pool of organizations—the number and kind of people available for employment—organizations must focus on multiple approaches to recruitment and career management. Outside sources for recruitment are especially useful for filling jobs with special qualifications and to acquire individuals with new skills, ideas, and perspectives. Which outside sources and methods are used in recruiting will depend on the recruitment goals of the organization, the conditions of the labor market, and the specifications of the jobs to be filled.

objective 2 Employers usually find it advantageous to use internal promotion and transfer to fill as many openings as possible above the entry level. By recruiting from within, an organization can capitalize on previous investments made in recruiting, selecting, training, and developing its current employees. Further, internal promotions can reward employees for past performance and send a signal to other employees that their future efforts will pay off. However, potential candidates from the outside should occasionally be considered in order to prevent the inbreeding of ideas and attitudes.

The legal requirements governing EEO make it mandatory that employers exert a positive effort to recruit and promote members of protected classes so that their representation at all levels within the organization will approximate their proportionate numbers in the labor market. These efforts include recruiting not only those members who are qualified but also those who can be made qualified with reasonable training and assistance.

Job opportunities may be identified by studying jobs and determining the knowledge and skills each one requires. Once that is accomplished, it is possible to plan job progressions. These progressions can then serve as a basis for developing career paths. Once career paths are developed and employees are identified on the career ladders, it is possible to inventory the jobs and determine where individuals with the required skills and knowledge are needed or will be needed.

Identifying and developing talent is a responsibility of all managers. In addition to immediate superiors, there should be others in the organization who can nominate and sponsor employees with promise. Many organizations use assessment centers to identify managerial talent and recommend developmental experiences in order that each individual may reach her or his full potential. Mentoring has been found to be valuable for providing guidance and support to potential managers.

Beyond recruiting per se, organizations also need to consider the progression of employees through a series of jobs. In this way, they can manage not only the immediate contribution of individuals to the organization, but the long-term contribution throughout their careers. A career development program is a dynamic process that should integrate individual employee needs with those of the organization. It is the responsibility of the employee to identify his or her own KSAs as well as interests and values and to seek out information about career options. The organization should provide information about its mission, policies, and plans and what it will provide in the way of training and development for the employee.

In order to be successful, a career management program must receive the support of top management. The program should reflect the goals and the culture of the organization, and managerial personnel at all levels must be trained in the fundamentals of job design, performance appraisal, career planning, and counseling. Employees should be aware of the organization's philosophy and its goals; otherwise they will not know how their goals match those of the organization. HRM policies, especially those concerning rotation, transfers, and promotions, should be consistent with the goals. The objectives and opportunities of the career development program should be announced widely throughout the organization.

The first step in facilitating the career development of women is to eliminate barriers to advancement. Forming women's networks, providing special training for women, accepting women as valued members of the organization, providing mentors for women, and accommodating families have been found to be effective ways to facilitate a woman's career development.

While a diversified workforce is composed of many different groups, an important segment is minority groups. In addition to creating conditions that are favorable for recognizing and rewarding performance, many organizations have special programs such as internships that provide hands-on experience as well as special training opportunities. Other groups that require the attention of management are the disabled, older workers, and dual-career couples, who often need flexible working schedules.

KEY TERMS

assessment center
career counseling
career networking
career paths
career plateau
dual-career partnerships
employee leasing
fast-track program
job posting and bidding
job progressions
mentors
nepotism
outplacement services
promotion
realistic job preview (RJP)
relocation services
transfer
yield ratio

DISCUSSION QUESTIONS

1. In what ways do executive search firms differ from the traditional employment agencies?

2. Explain how realistic job previews (RJPs) operate. Why do they appear to be an effective recruitment technique?

3. More than 50 percent of all MBAs leave their first employer within five years. While the change may mean career growth for the individuals, it represents a loss to the employers. What are some of the probable reasons an MBA would leave his or her first employer?

4. What are the advantages and disadvantages of filling openings from internal sources?

5. How might retired executives in any organization assist in the career management of current employees?

6. Give some reasons for the trend toward increased emphasis on career management programs.

7. What contributions can a career management program make to an organization that is forced to downsize its operations?

8. What are some of the barriers to advancement opportunities for women in many organizations?

9. How are the career challenges of minorities both similar to and different from those of women?

BIZFLIX EXERCISES

In Good Company: Carter Manages His Career

This chapter described many ways a company can recruit employees. The scenes from the film *In Good Company* show other ways a company can find new employees. Use the questions below as guides while viewing these scenes.

A corporate takeover brings star advertising executive Dan Foreman (Dennis Quaid) a new boss who is half his age. Carter Duryea (Topher Grace)—Dan's new boss—wants to prove his worth as the new marketing chief at *Sports America,* Waterman Publishing's flagship magazine. Carter applies his unique approaches while dating Dan's daughter, Alex (Scarlett Johansson).

These scenes come from the "breaking news" segment that appears in about the first five minutes of the film. They follow Carter's presentation of his concepts for marketing cell phones to children under age five. Mark Steckle (Clark Greg) tells his staff that Teddy K. (Malcolm McDowell) asked him to take over marketing at the magazine division of Waterman Publishing, Teddy K.'s recent acquisition. Carter Duryea discusses Mark's move to Waterman Publishing and the prospect of Carter following him to head advertising sales for *Sports America.* The film continues with Dan Foreman soon learning that Carter is his new boss.

What to Watch for and Ask Yourself

- Do these scenes show external or internal recruitment?
- Recall an earlier discussion in this chapter of the employee's role in career planning. What does Carter do to help his career?
- Review the earlier section "Career Development Initiatives." Which of those initiatives appear in these scenes? What is Mark Steckle's role in Carter's career development?

HRM Experience

Career Management

We often think that successful people plan their careers out in advance and then work toward their goals in a very logical, sequential manner. Although some successes are designed and implemented this way, others are created through insight, preparedness, and taking advantages of opportunities as they arise.

Assignment

1. Form teams of four to six members. Identify three different people to interview about their careers. One person should be in the early stages of his or her career; one should be in midcareer; and one should be in the final stages of his or her career.
2. Ask each person to identify his or her career goals and how they have changed or are expected to change over time.
3. Ask each person to describe the sequence of events that led to where he or she is. How well does that story align with the traditional model of careers?
4. Ask each person what (if anything) he or she would do differently. Ask what advice he or she has for you about how to approach your career.

case study 1

UPS Delivers the Goods

When Jordan Colletta joined UPS in 1975, fresh out of school and newly married, he wasn't thinking about building a career. He just wanted some security. A former tracing clerk, Colletta managed to go a long way—to vice president of the shipper's e-commerce sales team. His advancement in the company was steady, the result of careful planning through UPS's career development programs. By putting resources into such programs and helping reps set goals and develop skills, businesses can allow employees to grow within their organization and reduce turnover rates in the process, as UPS has found: its turnover rate among full-time workers is just 4 percent.

Developing salespeople starts with a clear mission. At UPS, employees meet annually with managers to identify their strengths and decide what skills they need for a new job within the company. "We lay the foundation for future development and map out immediate, midterm, and future goals," Colletta says. "When I was a tracing clerk, I told my supervisor that my goal was to become a district sales manager. I then became a driver, then a salesperson, and in 1986 I reached my goal."

UPS spends $300 million annually on classroom and online training for its employees. Career development entails implementing training programs and Internet career centers that can help companies grow their staffs. Employees take courses in order to acquire the pedigree that will make them candidates for management positions. But learning isn't just in the classroom. Mentoring programs in which managers coach lower-level employees are also valuable. "Mentors are especially important," Colletta says. "They help you understand the opportunities that are out there. They helped me see what I couldn't because I couldn't look that far ahead yet."

Progress must be routinely monitored. Employee reviews and 360-degree reports are good ways to track improvement. So is a manager's involvement. "Have an open door policy to keep the communication lines open," he says.

Finally, when it comes to encouraging participation in these programs, companies should highlight successes. Colletta announces promotions during weekly calls with UPS directors and immediately sends messages to his employees throughout the country. "It can't be about talk," Colletta says. "You can't say 'We have opportunities to develop you' and then look around and not see anyone getting ahead. You have to celebrate it."

Source: Adapted from Eduardo Javier Canto, "Rising through the Ranks," *Sales and Marketing Management* 153, no. 7 (July 2001): 66. Copyright © 2001. Reprinted by permission of Reprint Management Services; Lea N. Soupata, "Prepare for the Future," *Executive Excellence* 21, no. 11 (November 2004): 15–16.

QUESTIONS

1. What do you think are the main strengths of UPS's career development program?
2. What are the key outcomes that UPS wants to achieve?
3. What suggestions do you have for improving the program?

case study 2

Preparing a Career Development Plan

Sue Ann Scott was a receptionist at the headquarters of a large corporation. A high school graduate, she had no particular skills other than an ability to organize her job duties and a pleasant personality. Unfortunately, she did not have any particular plan for career development; nevertheless, she wanted very much to improve her economic position. Recognizing her educational limitations, she began taking accounting courses on a random basis in an evening adult education program.

Scott also took advantage of the corporation's job bidding system by applying for openings that were posted, even though in many instances she did not meet the specifications listed for them. After being rejected several times, she became discouraged. Her depressed spirits were observed by Elizabeth Burroughs, one of the department managers in the corporation. Burroughs invited Scott to come to her office for a talk about the problems she was having. Scott took full advantage of this opportunity to express her frustrations and disappointments. As she unburdened herself, it became apparent both to her and to Burroughs that during interviews she repeatedly apologized for having "only a high school education," an attitude that had probably made it difficult for the interviewers to select her over other candidates who were more positive about their backgrounds and skills. Burroughs suggested that Scott might try taking a more positive approach during her interviews. For example, she could stress her self-improvement efforts at night school and the fact that she was a dependable and cooperative person who was willing to work hard to succeed in the job for which she was applying.

Following Burroughs's advice, Scott applied for a position as invoice clerk, a job for which she felt she was qualified. She made a very forceful and positive presentation during her interview, stressing the favorable qualities she possessed. As a result of this approach, she got the job. While the pay for an invoice clerk was not much more than that for a receptionist, the position did offer an avenue for possible advancement into the accounting field, in which the accounting courses she was taking would be of value.

QUESTIONS

1. What are some of the possible reasons Scott did not seek or receive advice from her immediate supervisor?
2. After reviewing the chapter, suggest all possible ways that Scott can prepare herself for career advancement.

NOTES AND REFERENCES

1. Sherry Sullivan, "The Changing Nature of Careers: A Review and Research Agenda," *Journal of Management* 25, no. 3 (1999): 457–84; Steve Prentice, "A Game Plan for Career Survival," *Canadian HR Reporter* 15, no. 11 (June 3, 2002): 27–28; Mark Tatge, "Prescription for Growth," *Forbes* 171, no. 4 (February 17, 2003): 64–67.
2. Jill Jusko, "CEO Turnover Slows in 2003," *Industry Week* 253, no. 7 (July 2004): 20; Yan Zhang and Nandini Rajagopalan, "When the Known Devil Is Better Than an Unknown God: An Empirical Study of the Antecedents and Consequences of Relay CEO Successions," *Academy of Management Journal* 47, no. 4 (August 2004): 483–500; Nicholas Varchaver, "Glamour! Fame! Org Chart!" *Fortune* 150, no. 10 (November 15, 2004): 136–143.
3. Douglas P. Shuit, "Monster Board Games," *Workforce Management* 82, no. 2 (November 2003): 37–42.
4. Rob Yeung, "Finders Keepers," *Accountancy Magazine* 134, no. 1335 (November 2004): 42–44.
5. Ibid.
6. Keith Swenson, "Maximizing Employee Referrals," *HRFocus* 76, no. 1 (January 1999): 9–10.
7. "In Praise of Nepotism?" *Business Ethics Quarterly* 15, no. 1 (January 2005): 153–161; Richard Reeve and Gavin Sheridan, "Nepotism: Is It Back?" *New Statesman* 135 (September 29, 2003): 22–25.
8. Roger Kenny, "The Boardroom Role of Human Resources," *Corporate Board* 25, no. 150 (January–February 2005): 12–17.
9. Magali Rheault, "The Kiplinger Monitor," *Kiplinger's Personal Finance* 58, no. 7 (July 2004): 26.
10. Louis Uchitelle, "College Degree Still Pays, but It's Leveling Off," *The New York Times*, January 13, 2005, C1.
11. John Owens, "With Hard Work, Temp Employees Can Land Full-Time Jobs," *Knight Ridder/Tribune News Service* (June 10, 2003): K7953.
12. Judith E. Bendich, "When Is a Temp Not a Temp?" *Employee Rights Quarterly* 3, no. 2 (Fall 2002): 13–20.
13. Chris Pentilla, "Got It Covered: If You Can't Afford to Offer Employee Benefits on Your Own, Why Not Join Forces with a PEO?" *Entrepreneur* 32, no. 2 (February 2004): 66–68.
14. "Workforce Optima Awards 2003," *Workforce* 82, no. 3 (March 2003): 45–48.
15. Max Messmer, "Recognizing Potential Stars by Promoting from Within," *Strategic Finance* 86, no. 5 (October 2004): 9–11.
16. J. W. Marriott, "Our Competitive Strength: Human Capital," *Executive Speeches* 15, no. 5 (April–May 2001): 18–21.
17. Debbie Mack, "P&G Fights to Protect Its Bounty," *Corporate Legal Times* 13, no. 135 (February 2003): 64.
18. "How to Implement an Effective Process for a New HR Management System," *HRFocus* 82, no. 1 (January 2005): 3–4.
19. "The Pros and Cons of Online Recruiting," *HR Focus* 81 (April 2004 Supplement): S2.
20. Robert Rodriguez, "Filling the HR Pipeline," *HRMagazine* 49, no 9 (September 2004): 78–84; James W. Walker, "Perspectives," *Human Resource Planning* 25, no. 1 (2002): 12–14.
21. Paul W. B. Atkins and Robert E. Wood, "Self versus Others' Ratings as Predictors of Assessment Center Ratings: Validation Evidence for 360-Degree Feedback Programs," *Personnel Psychology* 55, no. 4 (Winter 2002): 871–905.
22. Ellen Ernst Kossek, Karen Roberts, Sandra Fisher, and Beverly Demarr, "Career Self-Management: A Quasi-Experimental Assessment of the Effects of a Training Intervention," *Personnel Psychology* 51, no. 4 (Winter 1998): 935–62; Shelly Green, "Attracting Top Talent Despite Business Challenges," *Journal of Career Planning and Employment* 62, no. 4 (Summer 2002): 24–28; Cynthia Jones, "Step by Step: Creating a Strategic Management System for Career Services Delivery," *Journal of Career Planning and Employment* 62, no. 3 (Spring 2002): 21–27.

23. Peg O'Herron and Peggy Simonsen, "Career Development Gets a Charge at Sears Credit," *Personnel Journal* 74, no. 5 (May 1995): 103–106. See also Jules Abend, "Behind the Scenes at: Sears," *Bobbin* 39, no. 11 (June 1998): 22–26; Shari Caudron, "The De-Jobbing of America," *Industry Week* 243, no. 16 (September 5, 1994): 30–36; Edward E. Lawler III, "From Job-Based to Competency-Based Organizations," *Journal of Organizational Behavior* 15, no. 1 (January 1994): 3–15; Douglas T. Hall, "Accelerate Executive Development—At Your Peril!" *Career Development International* 4, no. 4 (1999): 237–39.
24. "How a Talent Management Plan Can Anchor Your Company's Future," *HR Focus* 81, no. 10 (October 2004): 7–10.
25. Elizabeth Craig, John Kimberly, and Hamid Bouchikhhi, "Can Loyalty Be Leased?" *Harvard Business Review* 80, no. 9 (September 2002): 24–34; Edward Potter, "Improving Skills and Employability in the 21st Century," *Industrual and Labor Relations Review* 55, no. 4 (July 2002): 739–45.
26. Suzanne C. de Janasz, Shery E. Sullivan, and Vicki Whiting, "Mentor Networks and Career Success: Lessons for Turbulent Times," *Academy of Management Executive* 17, no. 4 (November 2003): 78–92.
27. Judith Bardwick, *The Plateauing Trap* (New York: AMACOM, 1986). See also Judith Bardwick, *Danger in the Comfort Zone: From Boardroom to Mailroom—How to Break the Entitlement Habit That's Killing American Business* (New York: AMACOM Book Division, 1995); Max Messmer, "Moving beyond a Career Plateau," *National Public Accountant* 45, no. 7 (September 2000): 20–21; John Rosche, "Who's Managing Your Career?" *Contract Management* 44, no. 2 (February 2004): 20–22.
28. Larry Cambron, "Career Development Pays," *Far Eastern Economic Review* 164, no. 42 (October 25, 2001): 83.
29. For up-to-date career information and guidance as well as an opportunity for self-analysis, see Richard Bolles, *What Color Is Your Parachute 2005: A Practical Manual for Job-Hunters & Career-Changers* (Berkeley, CA: Ten Speed Press, 2004).
30. Susan Wells, "Smoothing the Way," *HRMagazine* 46, no. 6 (June 2001): 52–58; Heath Row, "Market Yourself," *Fast Company* 58 (May 2002): 24.
31. Bonnie Rothman Morris, "New Skills, and Paying for Them," *The New York Times*, October 29, 2002, G6.
32. Thomas A. Stewart, "What's in It for Me?" *Harvard Business Review* 83, no. 1 (January 2005): 8.
33. de Janasz, Sullivan, and Whiting, "Mentor Networks and Career Success," 78–92.
34. Jeff Barbian, "The Road Best Traveled," *Training* 39, no. 5 (May 2002): 38–42; Kathleen Barton, "Will You Mentor Me?" *Training and Development* 56, no. 5 (May 2002): 90–92.
35. Elaine Biech, "Executive Commentary," *Academy of Management Executive* 17, no. 4 (November 2003): 92–94.
36. Anne Field, "No Time to Mentor? Do It Online," *Business Week*, no. 3822 (March 3, 2003): 26, Rhea Borija; "E-Mentors Offer Online Support, Information for Novice Instructors," *Education Week* 21, no. 29 (April 3, 2002): 12. For more information, see the web sites for these organizations: Mighty Mentors (http://K6educators.about.com/b/a/090852.htm), Nursing Net (http://www.nursingnet.org), and Women in Technology International (http://www.witi.org).
37. de Janasz, Sullivan, and Whiting, "Mentor Networks and Career Success," 78–92.
38. Julianne Maveaux, "Whose Revolution?" *Working Woman* 26, no. 8 (September 2001): 56–58; Ann Crittendon, "Motherload," *Working Woman* 26, no. 8 (September 2001): 66–68.
39. "Growth in Managerial Positions May Help Close the Gender Pay Gap," *Human Resources Department Management Report* 3, no. 5 (May 2003): 8; Laura D'Andrea Tyson, "New Clues to the Pay and Leadership Gap," *Business Week*, no. 3855 (October 27, 2003): 6–7.
40. Anne M. Walsh and Susan C. Borkowski, "Cross-Gender Mentoring and Career Development in the Health Care Industry," *Health Care Management Review* 24, no. 3 (Summer 1999): 7–17.
41. Robert Schwab, "Dancing on the Glass Ceiling," *Colorado Biz* 31, no. 5 (May 2004): 18–23. A host of reports on glass ceiling issues can be found on the U.S. Department of Labor's web site at http://www.dol.gov.
42. The interested reader should find the following books very informative: Johanna Hunsaker and Phillip Hunsaker, *Strategies and Skills for Managerial Women* (Cincinnati, OH: South-Western, 1991); Marian Ruderman and Patricia Ohlott, *Standing at the Crossroads: Next Steps for High-Achieving Women* (New York: John Wiley and Sons, 2002).
43. Alison Stein Wellner, "Welcoming Back Mom," *HRM Magazine* 49, no. 6 (June 2004): 76–83.
44. "Mothers' Labor Force Participation," *Monthly Labor Review* 137, no. 5 (May 2004): 2.
45. "Recruiting Minorities," *Black Enterprise* 35, no. 6 (January 2005): 53; Debbie Smith, "Building a New Diversity Road Map," *Multichannel News* 25, no. 38 (September 20, 2004): 82.
46. "IFD, INROADS Partner for Summer Enrichment Program Internships," *AHA News* 40, no. 18 (September 6, 2004): 8.
47. Miles White, "Paying More Than Lip Service to Diversity," *Chief Executive* 242, no. 16 (October 2002): 20–22.
48. Yeung, "Finders Keepers," 42–44; Janny Scott, "Nearly Half of Black Men Found Jobless," *The New York Times*, February 28, 2004, B1.
49. Joe Mullich, "Hiring without Limits," *Workforce Management* 83, no. 6 (June 1, 2004): 53–60; Julie Hotchkiss, "Growing Part-Time Employment among Workers with Disabilities," *Economic Review* 89, no. 3 (July 2004): 25–42; "Entry Point Interns Top 400 in Seventh Year," *Science* 301, no. 5637 (August 29, 2003): 1195.
50. Michael Barrier, "Should Looks Count?" *HRM Magazine* 49, no. 9 (September 2004): 64–69; "Be Cautions about Weighing Weight in Your Employment Decisions," *Staff Leader* 17, no. 9 (May 2004): 1–4.
51. Dannah Baynton, "America's $60 Billion Problem," *Training* 38, no. 5 (May 2001): 50–55.
52. Christopher Reynolds, "Boomers, Act II," *American Demographics* 27, no. 8 (October 2004): 10–12; Theresa Minton-Eversole, "Senate Forum Explores Ways to Keep Aging Workforce Working," *HR Magazine* 48, no. 10 (October 2003): 30.
53. Darin E. Hartley, "Tools for Talent," *Training and Development* 58, no. 4 (April 2004): 20–23.

appendix

Personal Career Development

We have observed that there are numerous ways for an employer to contribute to an individual employee's career development and at the same time meet the organization's HR needs. The organization can certainly be a positive force in the development process, but the primary responsibility for personal career growth still rests with the individual. One's career may begin before and often continue after a period of employment with an organization. To help you, as students and prospective employees, achieve your career objectives, this appendix is included to provide some background for your personal development and decisions.

Developing Personal Skills and Competencies

In planning a career, one should attend to more than simply acquiring specific job knowledge and skills. Job know-how is clearly essential, but one must develop other skills to be successful as an employee. To succeed as a manager, one must achieve a still higher level of proficiency in such major areas as communication, time management, self-motivation, interpersonal relationships, and the broad area of leadership.

Source: Copyright 1983 Pat Brady. Reprinted by permission.

Highlights in HRM 7

Career Competencies at Caterpillar

During the Caterpillar business unit's career development training process in Joliet, Illinois, the company compiled the following competencies as necessary for success within the reorganized, changing organization:

- *Interpersonal skills:* Possesses team-building and leadership skills; can effectively lead groups and facilitate group interaction
- *Problem-solving skills:* Can analyze and use problem-solving approaches
- *Communication skills:* Can verbalize articulately, make presentations, and write cogently
- *Leadership skills:* Is recognized by peers as a natural leader; accomplishes results without formal authority
- *Organization and planning skills:* Can manage time; sets and achieves goals
- *Technical skills:* Possesses education specific to assignments and job content; understands and uses appropriate level of technical skills
- *Responsibility:* Takes initiative; accepts accountability for own work and additional tasks for the good of the group
- *Assertiveness:* Able and comfortable with communicating openly and directly; demonstrates self-confidence and awareness of others' perceptions
- *Flexibility:* Can adapt to organizational changes and changing market needs; willingly considers new ideas and implements new ways of doing things
- *Judgment:* Can determine level of risk and appropriate action; accepts accountability for significant decisions

Source: Peggy Simonsen and Cathy Wells, "African Americans Take Control of Their Careers," *Personnel Journal* 73, no. 4 (April 1994): 99–108. See also David Dubois, "The Seven Stages of One's Career," *Training and Development* 54, no. 12 (December 2000): 45–50.

Hundreds of self-help books have been written on these topics, and myriad opportunities to participate in workshops are available, often sponsored by one's employer.[1] One should not overlook sources of valuable information such as articles in general-interest magazines and professional journals. For example, the pointers on the basic skills of successful career management listed in Highlights in HRM 7 are taken from a competency assessment conducted at Caterpillar.

Choosing a Career

Many years ago, when Peter Drucker was asked about career choice, he said, "The probability that the first job choice you make is the right one for you is roughly one in a million. If you decide your first choice is the right one, chances are that you are just plain lazy."[2] The implications of this statement are just as true today. One must often do a lot of searching and changing to find a career path that is psychologically and financially satisfying. According to the U.S. Bureau of Labor Statistics (BLS), education, health services, and professional and business services represent the industry divisions with the strongest projected employment from now until 2012. These industries are projected to grow twice as fast as the overall economy. Information technology, leisure and hospitality, and transportation and warehousing are also projected to grow faster than average. Highlights in HRM 8 shows a list of some of the hottest (and not-so-hot) career tracks according to CareerBuilder.com and John A. Challenger, chief executive officer of the global outplacement firm Challenger, Gray & Christmas, Inc.[3]

Use of Available Resources

A variety of resources are available to aid in the process of choosing a satisfying career. Counselors at colleges and universities, as well as those in private practice, are equipped to assist individuals in evaluating their aptitudes, abilities, interests, and values as they relate to career selection. There is broad interest among business schools in a formal instructional program in career planning and development, and other units in the institutions, such as placement offices and continuing education centers, offer some type of career planning assistance.

Accuracy of Self-Evaluation

Successful career development depends in part on an individual's ability to conduct an accurate self-evaluation. In making a self-evaluation, one needs to consider factors that are personally significant. The most important internal factors are one's academic aptitude and achievement, occupational aptitudes and skills, social skills, communication skills, leadership abilities, and interests and values. The latter should include consideration of salary level, status, opportunities for advancement, and growth on the job. External factors that should be assessed include family values and expectations, economic conditions, employment trends, job market information, and perceived effect of physical or psychological disabilities on success.

Significance of Interest Inventories

Psychologists who specialize in career counseling typically administer a battery of tests. The *Strong Vocational Interest Blank* (SVIB), developed by E. K. Strong, Jr., was among the first of the interest tests.[4] Somewhat later, G. Frederic Kuder developed inventories to measure degree of interest in mechanical, clerical, scientific, and persuasive activities, among others. Both the Strong and the Kuder interest inventories have been used widely in vocational counseling.

Strong found substantial differences in interests that vary from occupation to occupation and that a person's interest pattern, especially after age 21, tends to become quite stable. By taking his test, now known as the *Strong Interest Inventory*, one can learn the degree to which his or her interests correspond with those of successful people in a wide range of occupations. Personality type can also be obtained by using a special scoring key on an individual's Strong Interest Inventory answer sheet. This key, developed by John Holland, provides scores on six personality types: (1) realistic, (2) investigative, (3) artistic, (4) social, (5) enterprising, and (6) conven-

Highlights in HRM 8

Hot and Not-So-Hot Career Tracks

What's Hot:

Healthcare—nurses, radiology technicians, finance administrators
Construction—carpenters, electricians, contractors
Manufacturing—machine tool specialists, welders, machinists
Tech services—tech support, network administrators, security specialists
Education—teachers, child care workers, administrators

What's Not:

Automotive—manufacturing and sales
Travel—airlines, travel agents
Telemarketing
Apparel
Computer, telecommunications—manufacturing, sales

tional. These categories characterize not only a type of personality, but also the type of working environment that a person would find most satisfying. In the actual application of Holland's theory, combinations of the six types are examined. For example, a person may be classified as realistic-investigative-enterprising (RIE). Jobs in the RIE category include mechanical engineer, lineperson, and air-traffic controller. To facilitate searching for occupations that match one's category, such as RIE, Holland has devised a series of tables that correlate the Holland categories with jobs in the *Dictionary of Occupational Titles (DOT)*, described in Chapter 4.[5]

Another inventory that measures both interests and skills is the *Campbell Interest and Skill Survey (CISS)*.[6] The CISS can be used not only to assist employees in exploring career paths and options but to help organizations develop their employees or to reassign them because of major organizational changes. In completing the inventory, individuals report their levels of interest and skill using a six-point response scale on 200 interest items and 120 skill items. CISS item responses are translated into seven orientations—influencing, organizing, helping, creating, analyzing, producing, and adventuring—and further categorized into twenty-nine basic scales such as leadership and supervision, to identify occupations that reflect today's workplace.

Highlights in HRM 9 shows a sample profile for one individual. Note that at the top of the profile the range of scores is from 30 to 70, with 50 in the midrange. Corresponding verbal descriptions of scores range from very low to very high. Also note that on the profile two types of scores are profiled: interest (a solid diamond ♦) and skill (an open diamond ◇). The interest score ♦ shows how much the individual likes the specified activities; the skill score ◇ shows how confident the individual feels about performing these activities.

Highlights in HRM 9

Campbell Interest and Skill Survey: Individual Profile

SAMPLE ORIENTATIONS AND BASIC SCALES DATE SCORED 6/9/2005

ORIENTATIONS AND BASIC SCALES	INTEREST ◆	SKILL ◇	INTEREST/SKILL PATTERN
Influencing	**39**	**47**	
Leadership	42	49	
Law/Politics	42	46	
Public Speaking	36	40	Avoid
Sales	44	36	Avoid
Advertising/Marketing	52	42	
Organizing	**47**	**58**	Explore
Supervision	52	56	Explore
Financial Services	51	52	
Office Practices	58	65	Pursue
Helping	**59**	**63**	Pursue
Adult Development	48	56	Explore
Counseling	58	59	Pursue
Child Development	44	59	Explore
Religious Activities	42	49	
Medical Practice	68	61	Pursue
Creating	**59**	**58**	Pursue
Art/Design	66	64	Pursue
Performing Arts	54	52	
Writing	36	34	Avoid
International Activities	57	48	Develop
Fashion	69	70	Pursue
Culinary Arts	66	70	Pursue
Analyzing	**32**	**36**	Avoid
Mathematics	34	36	Avoid
Science	38	38	Avoid
Producing	**57**	**62**	Pursue
Mechanical Crafts	45	51	
Woodworking	63	58	Pursue
Farming/Forestry	54	60	Explore
Plants/Gardens	66	74	Pursue
Animal Care	62	71	Pursue
Adventuring	**47**	**57**	Explore
Athletics/Physical Fitness	56	56	Pursue
Military/Law Enforcement	52	54	
Risks/Adventure	59	58	Pursue

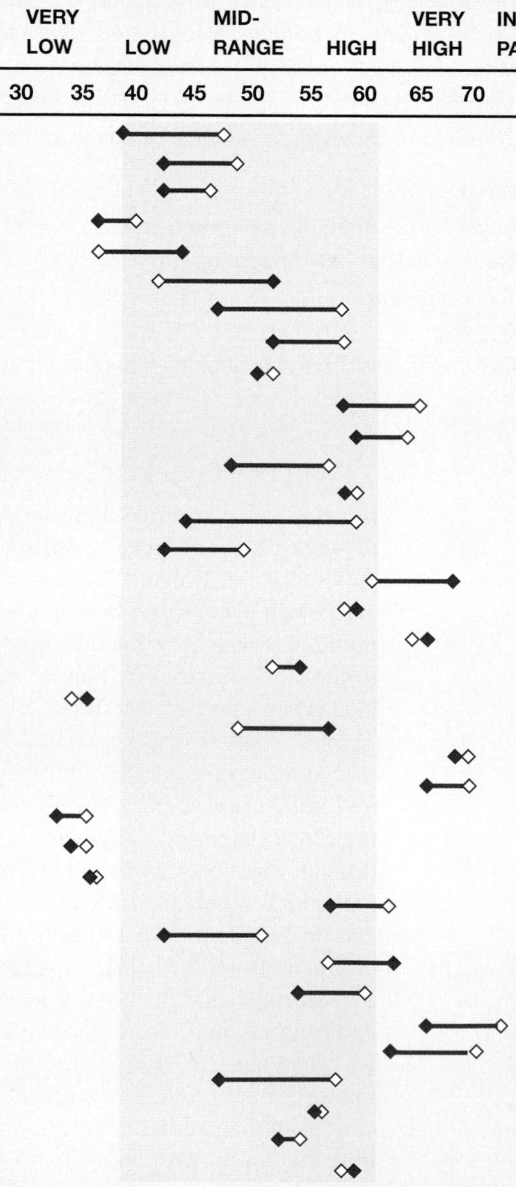

There are four noteworthy patterns of combinations of the interest and skill scores as shown in Figure 5.A1: Pursue, Develop, Explore, and Avoid. For the individual whose scores are profiled in Highlights in HRM 9, one would interpret the scores on the seven orientation scales (as shown in the left-hand column of the profile) as follows:

Influencing	Pursue
Organizing	Indeterminate
Helping	Pursue
Creating	Avoid
Analyzing	Avoid
Producing	Indeterminate
Adventuring	Develop

On the basis of such profiles, individuals can see how their interests and skills compare with those of a sample of people happily employed in a wide range of occupations. Completed answer sheets can be mailed to a scoring center, or software is available and may be obtained for in-house scoring.

Evaluating Long-Term Employment Opportunities

In making a career choice, one should attempt to determine the probable long-term opportunities in the occupational fields one is considering. While even the experts can err in their predictions, one should give at least some attention to the opinions that are available. A source of information that has proved valuable over the years is the *Occupational Outlook Handbook*, published by the U.S. Department of Labor and available at most libraries. Many libraries also have publications that provide details about jobs and career fields. In recent years, a considerable amount of computer software has been developed to facilitate access to information about career fields and to enable individuals to match their abilities, aptitudes, interests, and experiences with the requirements of occupational areas.

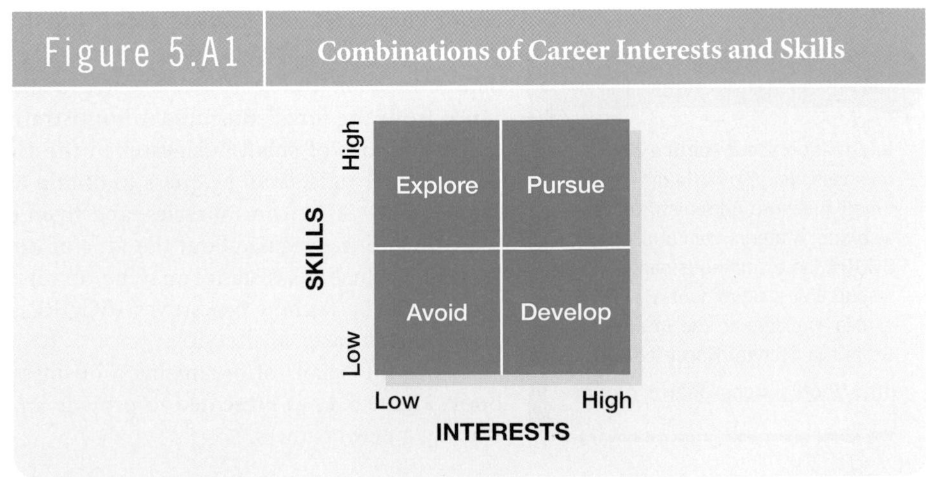

Choosing an Employer

Once an individual has made a career choice, even if only tentatively, the next major step is deciding where to work. The choice of employer may be based primarily on location, on immediate availability of a position, on starting salary, or on other basic considerations. However, the college graduate who has prepared for a professional or managerial career is likely to have more sophisticated concerns. Douglas Hall proposes that people frequently choose an organization on the basis of its climate and how it appears to fit their needs. According to Hall, people with high needs for achievement may choose aggressive, achievement-oriented organizations. Power-oriented people may choose influential, prestigious, power-oriented organizations. Affiliative people may choose warm, friendly, supportive organizations. We know that people whose needs fit with the climate of an organization are rewarded more and are more satisfied than those who fit in less well, so it is natural to reason that fit would also be a factor in one's choice of an organization. As noted at the outset of this chapter, it is increasingly unlikely that individuals will remain with only one organization for their entire career. The old model of "the organization man" who starts and stays with the same company is being replaced by a more flexible career model that Hall calls a "protean" career (based on the Greek god Proteus, who could change shape at will).[7]

Becoming an Entrepreneur

entrepreneur
One who starts, organizes, manages, and assumes responsibility for a business or other enterprise

At the opening of the century, no discussion of careers would be complete if entrepreneurship opportunities were not mentioned. Being an **entrepreneur**—one who starts, organizes, manages, and assumes responsibility for a business or other enterprise—offers a personal challenge that many individuals prefer over being an employee. Small businesses are typically run by entrepreneurs who accept the personal financial risks that go with owning a business but who also benefit directly from the success of the business.[8]

Small businesses are actually big employers. They employ half of all private-sector employees and account for a little less than half of the total U.S. private payrolls. They also generate 60–80 percent of new jobs annually.[9] The individual who considers starting a small business can obtain assistance from the Small Business Administration (SBA), which advises and assists millions of small businesses in the United States. It is essential for one considering a small business to obtain as much information as possible from the SBA, from libraries, and from organizations and individuals who are knowledgeable about the type of business one is considering. For instance, valuable assistance may be obtained from members of the Service Corps of Retired Executives (SCORE), who offer advisory services under the auspices of the SBA.

USING THE INTERNET

Information about starting a business can also be found at the Small Business Administration's web site. Material concerning SCORE (as a small-business resource or a retirement activity) is also available on the Internet. Go to the Student Resources at:

http://bohlander.swlearning.com

Since the details of organizing a business are beyond the scope of this book, Figure 5.A2 is presented to provide an overview of the basic steps in starting a new business.[10]

Figure 5.A2 Twelve Steps for Starting a New Business

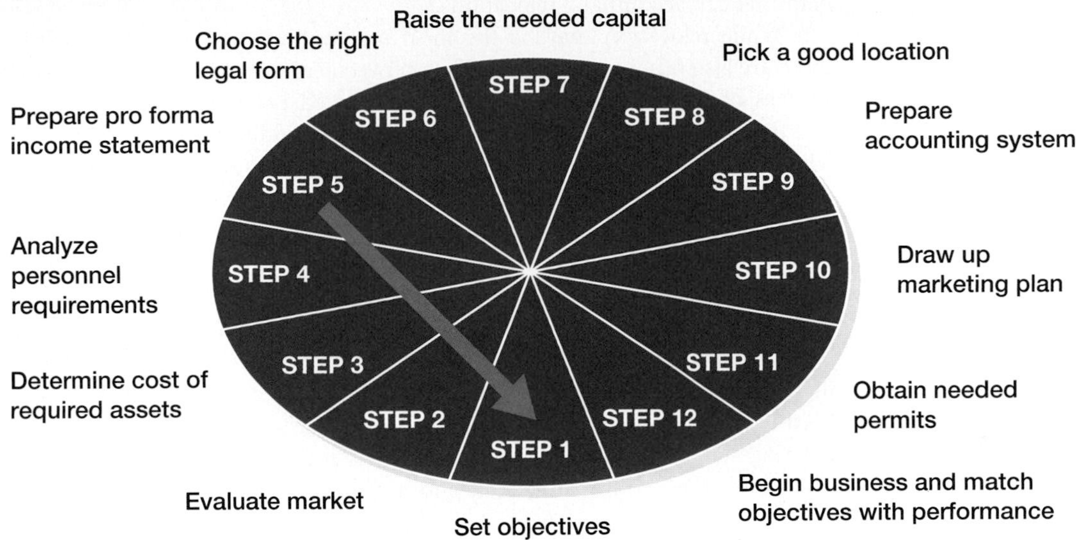

Source: From *Business in a Changing World,* 3rd edition, by W. Cunningham, R. Aldag, and S. Block: 139 © 1993. Reprinted with permission of South-Western, a division of Thomson Learning: http://www.thomsonrights.com.

Keeping a Career in Perspective

For most people, work is a primary factor in the overall quality of their lives. It provides a setting for satisfying practically the whole range of human needs and is thus of considerable value to the individual. Nevertheless, it is advisable to keep one's career in perspective so that other important areas of life are not neglected.

Developing Off-the-Job Interests

Satisfaction with one's life is a product of many forces. Some of the more important ingredients are physical health, emotional well-being, financial security, harmonious interpersonal relationships, freedom from too much stress, and achievement of one's goals. While a career can provide some of the satisfaction that one needs, most people find it necessary to turn to interests and activities outside their career. Off-the-job activities not only provide a respite from daily work responsibilities but also offer satisfaction in areas unrelated to work.

Balancing Marital and/or Family Life

The career development plans of an individual as well as of an organization must take into account the needs of spouses and children. As we have said, the one event that often poses the greatest threat to family needs is relocation. Conflict between a desire to advance in one's career and a desire to stay in one place and put down family roots often borders on the disastrous. Many employers now provide assistance in this area, including relocation counseling, in an effort to reduce the severity of the pain that can accompany relocations.

While relocation may be the most serious threat to employees with families, there are also other sources of conflict between career and family. Some work-related sources of conflict are number of hours worked per week, frequency of overtime, and the presence and irregularity of shift work. In addition, ambiguity and/or conflict within the employee's work role, low level of leader support, and disappointments due to unfulfilled expectations affect one's life away from the job. Some family-related sources of conflict include the need to spend an unusually large amount of time with the family and its concerns, spouse employment patterns, and dissimilarity in a couple's career orientations. Those who are "married" to their jobs to the extent that they fail to provide the attention and caring essential to marriage and family relationships can be said to lack an appreciation for the balance needed for a satisfying life. One should always be aware that "to be a success in the business world takes hard work, long hours, persistent effort, and constant attention. To be a success in marriage takes hard work, long hours, persistent effort, and constant attention. . . . The problem is giving each its due and not shortchanging the other."[11]

Planning for Retirement

While retirement appears to be a long way off for the individual who is still in the early stages of a career, it is never too early to plan for it. In order to enjoy retirement one should prepare for it by giving careful attention to health, finances, family, and interpersonal relationships throughout one's adult life. While most large organizations have preretirement programs, many participants in those programs are unfortunately already too close to actual retirement. Thus it is each individual's responsibility to plan early in order to have time to set the stage for a healthy and satisfying retirement as free as possible from worries—especially those that could have been avoided or minimized earlier in life. While employer-sponsored preretirement programs are usually considered very helpful by the participants, as we will see in Chapter 11, they are not a substitute for continual personal concern for oneself.

KEY TERM

entrepreneur

NOTES AND REFERENCES

1. A selection of self-help publications on a variety of topics may be found in any bookstore. College and university bookstores typically have a wide selection in their trade or general books department. Two particularly useful books might be Edward Crip and Richard Mansfield, *The Value-Added Employee: 31 Competencies to Make Yourself Irresistible to Any Company* (London: Butterworth-Heinemann, 2001); Daniel Goleman, *Emotional Intelligence* (New York: Bantam Books, 1995).
2. Mary Harrington Hall, "A Conversation with Peter Drucker," *Psychology Today* (March 1968): 22.
3. Kate Lorenz, "Where the Jobs Are—2005," CareerBuilder.com; Eilene Zimmerman, "Know the Job Market of 2012," *Workforce* 81, no. 10 (October 2002): 18.
4. E. K. Strong, Jr., of Stanford University, was active in the measurement of interests from the early 1920s until his death in 1963. Since then his work has been carried on by the staff of the Measurement Research Center, University of Minnesota. The Strong Interest Inventory is distributed by Consulting Psychologists Press, Inc., P.O. Box 60070, Palo Alto, CA 94306, to qualified people under an exclusive license from the publisher, Stanford University Press.
5. Gary D. Gottfredson and John L. Holland, *Dictionary of Holland Occupational Codes* (Lutz, FL: Psychological Assessment Resources, December 1996).
6. The *Campbell Interest and Skill Survey* (copyright 1992) is published and distributed by NCS Assessments, P.O. Box 1416, Minneapolis, MN 55440. For recent research in this area, see David Lubinski, Camilla P. Benbow, and Jennifer Ryan, "Stability of Vocational Interests among the Intellectually Gifted from Adolescence to Adulthood: A 15-Year Longitudinal Study," *Journal of Applied Psychology* 80, no. 1 (February 1995): 196–200.
7. Douglas T. Hall and Jonathan E. Moss, "The New Protean Career Contract: Helping Organizations and Employees Adapt," *Organizational Dynamics* 26, no. 3 (Winter 1998): 22–37. See also Douglas T. Hall, *The Career Is Dead, Long Live the Career: A Relational Approach to Careers* (San Francisco: Jossey-Bass, 1996); Douglas T. Hall, "Protean Careers of the 21st Century," *Academy of Management Executive* 10, no. 4 (1996): 8–16; Douglas T. Hall and Associates, *Career Development in Organizations* (San Francisco: Jossey-Bass, 1986); Yue-Wah Chay and Samuel Aryee, "The Moderating Influence of Career Growth Opportunities on Careerist Orientation and Work Attitudes: Evidence of the Protean Career Era in Singapore," *Journal of Organizational Behavior* 20, no. 5 (September 1999): 613–23.
8. Abraham Sagie and Dov Abraham, "Achievement Motive and Entrepreneurial Orientation: A Structural Analysis," *Journal of Organizational Behavior* 20, no. 3 (May 1999): 375–87; Eleni T. Stavrous, "Succession in Family Businesses: Exploring the Effects of Demographic Factors on Offspring Intentions to Join and Take Over the Business," *Journal of Small Business Management* 37, no. 3 (July 1999): 43–61; Julie Rose, "The New Risk Takers," *Fortune Small Business* 12, no. 2 (March 2002): 28–34.
9. U.S. Bureau of the Census; Advocacy-funded research by Joel Popkin and Company (Research Summary #211); U.S. Department of Labor, Bureau of Labor Statistics, Current Population Survey; U.S. Department of Commerce, International Trade Administration.
10. For information on starting a business, the interested reader might look into Bob Adams, *Adams Streetwise Small Business Startup* (Holbrook, MA: Adams Media Corporation, 1996); Linda Pinson and Jerry Jinnett, *Anatomy of a Business Plan: Starting Smart, Building a Business and Securing Your Company's Future* (Chicago: Upstart, 1996); Kenneth Cook, *AMA Complete Guide to Strategic Planning for Small Business* (Lincolnwood, IL: NTC Business Books, 1995); Priscilla Y. Huff, *101 Best Small Businesses for Women* (Rocklin, CA: Prima, 1996); Constance Jones, *The 220 Best Franchises to Buy: The Sourcebook for Evaluating the Best Franchise Opportunities* (New York: Bantam Doubleday Dell, 1993).
11. Christopher Caggiano, "Married . . . with Companies," *Inc.* 17, no. 6 (May 1995): 68–76; Sue Shellenbarger, "Sustaining a Marriage When Job Demands Seem to Be Endless," *The Wall Street Journal*, December 8, 1999, B1.

ME ZIKOMO/SUPERSTOCK

chapter 6

Employee Selection

After studying this chapter, you should be able to

Explain the objectives of the personnel selection process.

Identify the various sources of information used for personnel selection.

Compare the value of different types of employment tests.

Illustrate the different approaches to conducting an employment interview.

Describe the various decision strategies for selection.

There is perhaps no more important topic in HRM than employee selection. If it is true that organizations succeed or fail on the basis of talents of employees, then managers directly influence that success by the people they hire. Regardless of whether the company is large or small, hiring the best and the brightest employees lays a strong foundation for excellence. Alternatively, it is common to hear managers who don't recognize this point lament the inordinate amount of time they spend trying to fix bad selection decisions. In addition, equal employment opportunity legislation, court decisions, and the Uniform Guidelines (discussed in Chapter 3) have also provided an impetus for making sure that the selection process is done well. The bottom line is, good selection decisions make a difference. So do bad ones.

Matching People and Jobs

selection
The process of choosing individuals who have relevant qualifications to fill existing or projected job openings

In conjunction with the recruiting process, which is designed to increase the number of applicants whose qualifications meet job requirements and the needs of the organization, **selection** is the process of reducing that number and choosing from among those individuals who have the relevant qualifications.

Figure 6.1 shows in broad terms that the overall goal of selection is to maximize "hits" and avoid "misses." Hits are accurate predictions and misses are inaccurate ones. The cost of one type of miss would be the direct and indirect expense of hiring an employee who turns out to be unsuccessful. The cost of the other type of miss is an opportunity cost—someone who could have been successful didn't get a chance.

While the overall selection program is often the formal responsibility of the HR department, line managers typically make the final decision about hiring people in their unit. It is important therefore that managers understand the objectives, policies, and practices used for selection. In that way, they can be highly involved in the process from the very beginning. Those responsible for making selection decisions should have adequate information upon which to base their decisions. Information about the jobs to be filled, knowledge of the ratio of job openings to the number of applicants, and as much relevant information as possible about the applicants themselves are essential for making sound decisions.

Person-Job Fit: Beginning with Job Analysis

In Chapter 4 we discussed the process of analyzing jobs to develop job descriptions and specifications. Job specifications, in particular, help identify the *individual competencies* employees need for success—the knowledge, skills, abilities, and other factors (KSAOs) that lead to superior performance. By identifying competencies through job analysis, managers can then use selection methods such as interviews, references, psychological tests, and the like to measure applicant KSAOs against the competencies required for the job. This is often referred to as *person-job fit.* Research has demonstrated that complete and unambiguous specification of required competencies (via job analysis) reduces the influence of racial and gender stereotypes and helps the interviewer differentiate between qualified and unqualified applicants.

Figure 6.1 The Goal of Selection: Maximize "Hits"

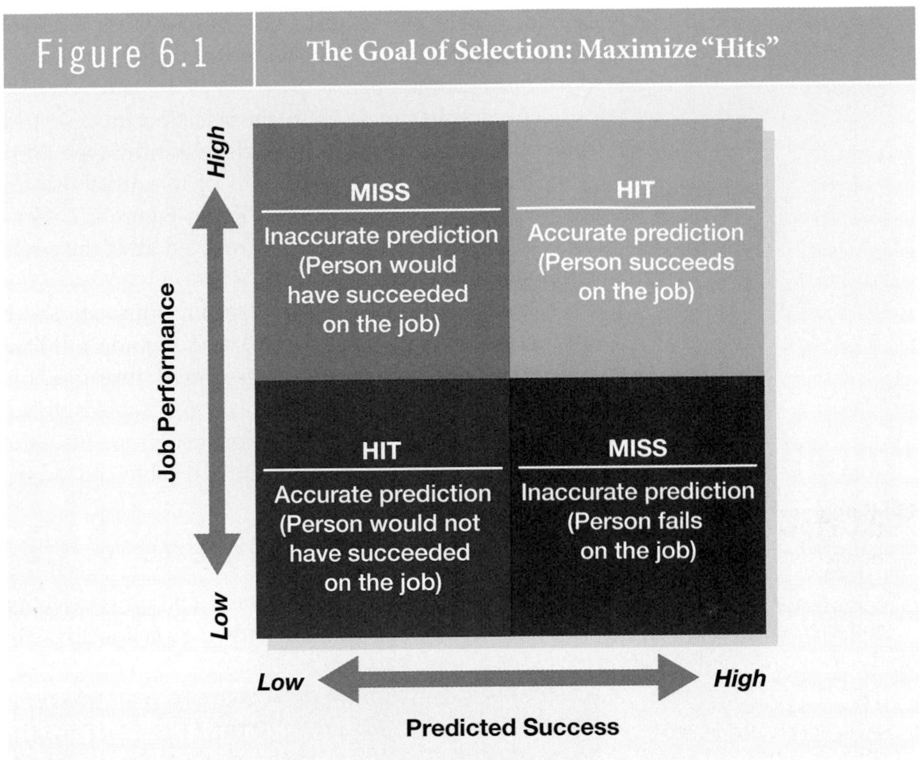

Research also shows that applicants whose KSAOs are well matched to the jobs they are hired for perform better and are more satisfied.[1]

Person-Organization Fit

In addition to the requirements of the job, many organizations also place a priority on finding individuals that meet broader organizational requirements. Companies such as Texas Instruments, Merck, Southwest Airlines, and Starbucks place a high priority on selecting individuals who match the values and culture of the organization. Although there are at times potential concerns that this may create an overly uniform workforce (and raises diversity concerns), the need for teamwork and flexibility has created a keen interest in this type of person-organization fit. In many instances, managers will pass up potential employees if they don't embrace the values of the organization—even if they have excellent technical skills for the job.[2]

Ordinarily, managers are well acquainted with the requirements pertaining to skill, physical demands, and other factors for jobs in their organizations. Interviewers and other members of the HR department who participate in selection should maintain a close liaison with the various departments so that they can become thoroughly familiar with the jobs and competencies needed to perform them.

The Selection Process

In most organizations, selection is an ongoing process. Turnover inevitably occurs, leaving vacancies to be filled by applicants from inside or outside the organization or by individuals whose qualifications have been assessed previously. It is common to have a waiting list of applicants who can be called when permanent or temporary positions become open.

The number of steps in the selection process and their sequence will vary, not only with the organization but also with the type and level of jobs to be filled. Each step should be evaluated in terms of its contribution. The steps that typically make up the selection process are shown in Figure 6.2. Not all applicants will go through all of these steps. Some may be rejected after the preliminary interview, others after taking tests, and so on.

As shown in Figure 6.2, organizations use several different means to obtain information about applicants. These include application blanks, interviews, tests, medical examinations, and background investigations. Regardless of the method used, it is essential that it conform to accepted ethical standards, including privacy and confidentiality, as well as legal requirements. Above all, it is essential that the information obtained be sufficiently reliable and valid.

reliability
The degree to which interviews, tests, and other selection procedures yield comparable data over time and alternative measures

Obtaining Reliable and Valid Information

The degree to which interviews, tests, and other selection procedures yield comparable data over a period of time is known as **reliability.** For example, unless interviewers

Figure 6.2 Steps in the Selection Process

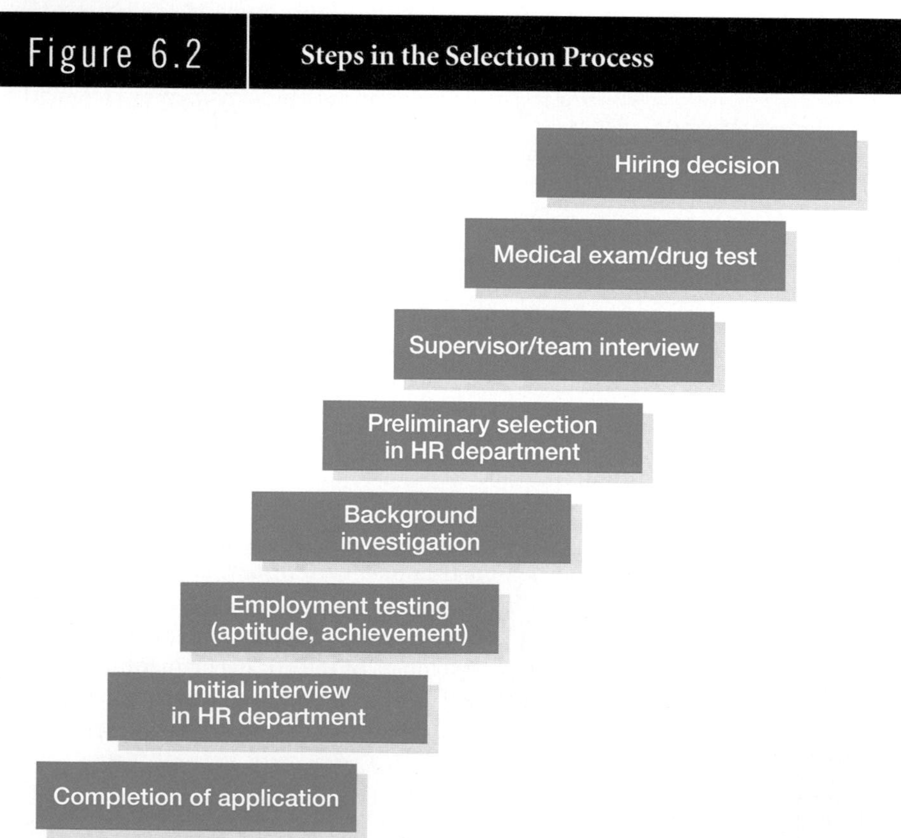

Note: Steps may vary. An applicant may be rejected after any step in the process.

judge the capabilities of a group of applicants to be the same today as they did yesterday, their judgments are unreliable (that is, unstable). Likewise, a test that gives widely different scores when it is administered to the same individual a few days apart is unreliable.

Reliability also refers to the extent to which two or more methods (interviews and tests, for example) yield similar results or are consistent. Interrater reliability—agreement between two or more raters—is one measure of a method's consistency. Unless the data on which selection decisions are based are reliable, in terms of both stability and consistency, they cannot be used as predictors.

validity
The degree to which a test or selection procedure measures a person's attributes

In addition to having reliable information pertaining to a person's suitability for a job, the information must be as valid as possible. **Validity** refers to what a test or other selection procedure measures and how well it measures it. In the context of personnel selection, validity is essentially an indicator of the extent to which data from a procedure (interview or test, for example) are predictive of job performance. Like a new medicine, a selection procedure must be validated before it is used. There are two reasons for validating a procedure. First, validity is directly related to increases in employee productivity, as we will demonstrate later. Second, EEO regulations emphasize the importance of validity in selection procedures.[3] Although we commonly refer to "validating" a test or interview procedure, validity in the technical sense refers to the inferences made from the use of a procedure, not to the procedure itself.

The *Uniform Guidelines* (see Chapter 3) recognizes and accepts different approaches to validation: criterion-related validity, content validity, and construct validity.

Criterion-Related Validity

criterion-related validity
The extent to which a selection tool predicts, or significantly correlates with, important elements of work behavior

concurrent validity
The extent to which test scores (or other predictor information) match criterion data obtained at about the same time from current employees

predictive validity
The extent to which applicants' test scores match criterion data obtained from those applicants/employees after they have been on the job for some indefinite period

cross-validation
Verifying the results obtained from a validation study by administering a test or test battery to a different sample (drawn from the same population)

The extent to which a selection tool predicts, or significantly correlates with, important elements of work behavior is known as **criterion-related validity.** Performance on a test, for example, is compared with actual production records, supervisory ratings, training outcomes, and other measures of success that are appropriate to each type of job. In a sales job, for example, it is common to use sales figures as a basis for comparison. In production jobs, quantity and quality of output may provide the best criteria of job success.

There are two types of criterion-related validity: concurrent and predictive. **Concurrent validity** involves obtaining criterion data from *current employees* at about the same time that test scores (or other predictor information) are obtained. For example, a supervisor is asked to rate a group of clerical employees on the quantity and quality of their performance. These employees are then given a clerical aptitude test, and the test scores are compared with the supervisory ratings to determine the degree of relationship between them. **Predictive validity,** on the other hand, involves testing *applicants* and obtaining criterion data *after* those applicants have been hired and have been on the job for some indefinite period. For example, applicants are given a clerical aptitude test, which is then filed away for later study. After the individuals have been on the job for several months, supervisors, who should not know the employees' test scores, are asked to rate them on the quality and quantity of their performance. Test scores are then compared with the supervisors' ratings.

Regardless of the method used, cross-validation is essential. **Cross-validation** is a process in which a test or battery of tests is administered to a different sample (drawn from the same population) for the purpose of verifying the results obtained from the original validation study.

Correlational methods are generally used to determine the relationship between predictor information such as test scores and criterion data. The correlation scatterplots in Figure 6.3 illustrate the difference between a selection test of zero validity (A) and one of high validity (B). Each dot represents a person. Note that in scatterplot A there is no relationship between test scores and success on the job; in other words, the validity is zero. In scatterplot B, those who score low on the test tend to have low success on the job, whereas those who score high on the test tend to have high success on the job, indicating high validity. In actual practice we would apply a statistical formula to the data to obtain a coefficient of correlation referred to as a *validity coefficient.* Correlation coefficients range from 0.00, denoting a complete absence of relationship, to +1.00 and to −1.00, indicating a perfect positive and perfect negative relationship, respectively.

A thorough survey of the literature shows that the averages of the maximum validity coefficients are 0.45 where tests are validated against *training* criteria and 0.35 where tests are validated against job *proficiency* criteria. These figures represent the predictive power of single tests.[4] A higher validity may be obtained by combining two or more tests or other predictors (interview or biographical data, for instance), using the appropriate statistical formulas. The higher the overall validity, the greater the chances of hiring individuals who will be the better performers. The criterion-related method is generally preferred to other validation approaches because it is based on empirical data.

validity generalization The extent to which validity coefficients can be generalized across situations

For several decades, personnel psychologists believed that validity coefficients had meaning only for the specific situation (job and organization). More recently, as a result of several research studies—many involving clerical jobs—it appears that validity coefficients can often be generalized across situations, hence the term **validity generalization.** When there are adequate data to support the existence of validity generalization, the development of selection procedures can become less costly and

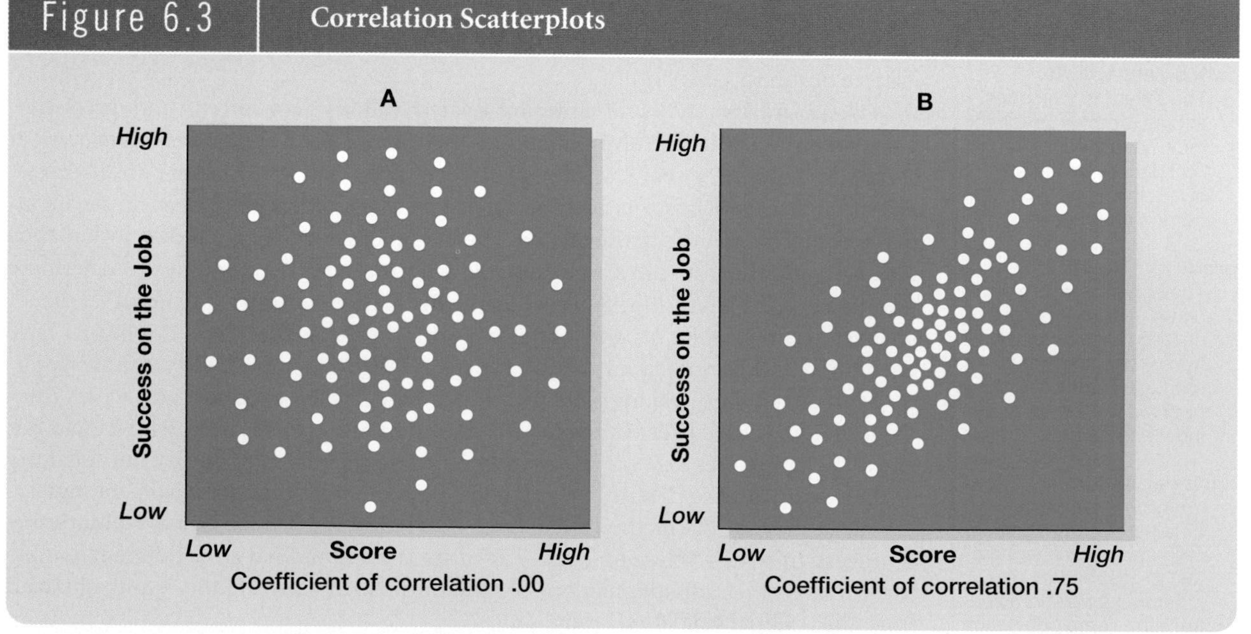

time-consuming. The process involves analyzing jobs and situations and, on the basis of these analyses, consulting tables of generalized validities from previous studies using various predictors in similar circumstances. It is advisable for organizations to employ the services of an industrial-organizational psychologist experienced in test validation to develop the selection procedures.[5]

Content Validity

content validity
The extent to which a selection instrument, such as a test, adequately samples the knowledge and skills needed to perform a particular job

When it is not feasible to use the criterion-related approach, often because of limited samples of individuals, the content method is used. **Content validity** is assumed to exist when a selection instrument, such as a test, adequately samples the knowledge and skills needed to perform a particular job.

The closer the content of the selection instrument is to actual work samples or behaviors, the greater its content validity. For example, a civil service examination for accountants has high content validity when it requires the solution of accounting problems representative of those found on the job. Asking an accountant to lift a sixty-pound box, however, is a selection procedure that has content validity only if the job description indicates that accountants must be able to meet this requirement.

Content validity is the most direct and least complicated type of validity to assess. It is generally used to evaluate job knowledge and skill tests, to be described later. Unlike the criterion-related method, content validity is not expressed in correlational terms. Instead, an index is computed (from evaluations of an expert panel) that indicates the relationship between the content of the test items and performance on the job.[6] While content validity does have its limitations, it has made a positive contribution to job analysis procedures and to the role of expert judgment in sampling and scoring procedures.

Construct Validity

construct validity
The extent to which a selection tool measures a theoretical construct or trait

The extent to which a selection tool measures a theoretical construct, or trait, is known as **construct validity.** Typical constructs are intelligence, mechanical comprehension, and anxiety. They are in effect broad, general categories of human functions that are based on the measurement of many discrete behaviors. For example, the Bennett Mechanical Comprehension Test consists of a wide variety of tasks that measure the construct of mechanical comprehension.

Measuring construct validity requires showing that the psychological trait is related to satisfactory job performance and that the test accurately measures the psychological trait. There is a lack of literature covering this concept as it relates to employment practices, probably because it is difficult and expensive to validate a construct and to show how it is job-related.[7]

Sources of Information about Job Candidates

Many sources of information are used to provide as reliable and valid a picture as possible of an applicant's potential for success on the job. Figure 6.4 shows the results of a recent survey that asked HR executives to evaluate the effectiveness of various selection techniques. In this section, we will study the potential contributions of application forms; biographical information blanks; background investigations;

Figure 6.4 The Effectiveness of Selection Methods

In a survey of 201 HR executives, participants were asked which selection methods produce the best employees. The mean rating for nine methods on a 5-point scale (1 = not good, 3 = average, 5 = extremely good):

Work samples	3.68
References/recommendations	3.49
Unstructured interviews	3.49
Structured interviews	3.42
Assessment centers	3.42
Specific aptitude tests	3.08
Personality tests	2.93
General cognitive ability tests	2.89
Biographical information blanks	2.84

Source: David E. Terpstra, "The Search for Effective Methods," *HRFocus* (May 1996).

polygraph, or lie detector, tests; honesty and integrity tests; graphology; and medical examinations. Because interviewing plays such a major role in selection and because testing presents unique challenges, there will be expanded discussions of these sources of information later in the chapter. Assessment centers, which are often used in managerial selection, were discussed in Chapter 5.

Application Forms

Most organizations require application forms to be completed because they provide a fairly quick and systematic means of obtaining a variety of information about the applicant. As with interviews, the EEOC and the courts have found that many questions asked on application forms disproportionately discriminate against females and minorities and often are not job-related. Application forms should therefore be developed with great care and revised as often as necessary. Because of differences in state laws on fair employment practices (FEPs) (see Chapter 3), organizations operating in more than one state will find it difficult to develop one form that can be used nationally.

Application forms serve several purposes. They provide information for deciding whether an applicant meets the minimum requirements for experience, education, and so on. They provide a basis for questions the interviewer will ask about the applicant's background. They also offer sources for reference checks. For certain jobs, a short application form is appropriate. For example, McDonald's uses a form that is quite brief but asks for information that is highly relevant to job performance. It also provides information regarding the employer's conformity with various laws and regulations. For scientific, professional, and managerial jobs, a more extended form is likely to be used.

Even when applicants come armed with elaborate resumes, it is important that they complete an application form early in the process. Individuals frequently exaggerate or overstate their qualifications on a resume. They also omit unflattering information. The consequences of falsifying information on applications and resumes are frequently high. For example, George O'Leary had to resign as head football coach at Notre Dame after admitting to falsely claiming he had played football at New Hampshire and had a master's degree from New York University. Similarly, Sandra Baldwin resigned as U.S. Olympic Committee chair after it came to light that she had listed a Ph.D. she hadn't earned.[8]

USING THE INTERNET

You can practice reading and analyzing resumes online. Go to the Student Resources at:

http://bohlander.swlearning.com

Other cases highlight the importance of integrity in job applications. Some staffing experts estimate that at least 30 percent of applicants "stretch" the truth on their resumes. Others estimate that the percentage is much higher. One technique for anticipating problems of misrepresentation is to ask applicants to transcribe specific resume material onto a standardized application form. The applicant is then asked to sign a statement that the information contained on the form is true and that he or she accepts the employer's right to terminate the candidate's employment if any of the information is subsequently found to be false.[9]

Many managers remain unclear about the questions they can ask on an application blank. While most know they should steer clear of issues such as age, race, marital status, and sexual orientation, other issues are less clear. The following are some suggestions for putting together an application form:

- *Application date.* The applicant should date the application. This helps managers know when the form was completed and gives them an idea of the time limit (for example, one year) that the form should be on file.
- *Educational background.* The applicant should provide grade school, high school, college, and postcollege attendance—but not the dates attended, since that can be connected with age.
- *Experience.* Virtually any questions that focus on work experience related to the job are permissible.
- *Arrests and criminal convictions.* Questions about arrests alone are not permissible. But questions about convictions are fine. However, the Rehabilitation of Offenders Act of 1974 allows that, for some crimes (generally, minor convictions), the applicant has no duty to disclose the conviction to a prospective employer after a certain time period has passed. Certain professions, such as teaching and nursing, are exceptions to this rule.
- *Country of citizenship.* Such questions are not permitted. It is allowable to ask whether the person is legally prevented from working in the United States.
- *References.* It is both permissible and advisable that the names, addresses, and phone numbers of references be provided. (We will cover this in more detail later.)
- *Disabilities.* This is a potentially tricky area. The Americans with Disabilities Act prohibits discriminating against a person with a disability who, with or without reasonable accommodation, can perform essential job functions. But employers are not allowed to ask applicants questions designed to elicit information about the existence, nature, or severity of a disability. Inquiries about the ability of the person to perform job functions, however, are acceptable. And under most recent guidelines issued by the EEOC, employers can ask whether an applicant needs reasonable accommodation—*if* the disability is obvious or *if* the applicant has voluntarily disclosed the disability.

Many of these issues will be addressed again, particularly in the section on employment interviews.

Some organizations use what is referred to as a *weighted application blank (WAB)*. The WAB involves the use of a common standardized employment application that is designed to distinguish between successful and unsuccessful employees. If managers can identify application items (such as where someone went to school) that have predicted employee success in the past, they may use that information to screen other applicants. Some evidence suggests that use of the WAB has been especially helpful for reducing turnover costs in the hospitality industry.

Online Applications

Perhaps the biggest change in the hiring process in recent years has been the proliferation of the online applications process. In 1998, fewer than a third of Fortune 500 companies had adapted their web sites to accept job applications. Today, about 95 percent of them have done so, reports RecruitSoft/iLogos, an Internet recruiting firm. Early web sites merely collected resumes and offered rudimentary search capabilities. Today's systems enable employers to mine resumes, spot qualified applicants, and conduct screening tests online.

Companies that don't want to host their own career web sites frequently contract with job board companies such as Monster.com, CareerBuilder, Hotjobs.com, or more specialized companies such as Medzilla.com, a medical personnel job board. Others contract with third-party application service providers (ASPs) such as Oracle-PeopleSoft, and SAP to handle the posting, application, and tracking process. Some companies use a combination of the two. H&R Block uses Hire.com but also collects

Employers can post a job for 60 days; purchase job inventories for later posting within a year; search resumes to find specific job qualifications; and view, save, and organize resumes online.

resumes through its own corporate web site. Using keywords, the tax preparation company also searches the Web for resumes posted at various sites and then invites individuals to apply for certain positions.

One of the key advantages of accepting applications online is that companies can recruit candidates and fill their job openings much faster. Discount broker Charles Schwab claims that using the Internet, it can now fill a job opening in just one week. Posting job openings online is also significantly cheaper than advertising them in newspapers. Woolworths, for example, reduced its cost per hire by 70 percent by advertising online.

Companies report that the downside of posting jobs and accepting online applications is that it can lead to a large volume of them being submitted—many of which fail to meet minimum qualifications. The upside, however, is that generating a larger number of applicants tends to promote greater employee diversity. Home Depot, for example, successfully implemented an online application system called the Job Preference Program to get a broader pool of applicants than it previously had been getting. It ultimately enabled the company to hire more women.[10]

Biographical Information Blanks

One of the oldest methods for predicting job success uses biographical information about job applicants. As early as 1917, the Life Insurance Agency Management Association constructed and validated a biographical information blank (BIB) for life insurance salespeople. BIBs cover such issues as family life, hobbies, club memberships, sales experience, and investments. Like application blanks, BIBs reveal information about a person's history that may have shaped his or her behavior. Sample questions from a BIB might include the following:

- At what age did you leave home?
- How large was the town/city in which you lived as a child?
- Did you ever build a model airplane that flew?
- Were sports a big part of your childhood?
- Do you play any musical instruments?

Both the BIB and the application form can be scored like tests. And because biographical questions rarely have obviously right or wrong answers, BIBs are difficult to fake. The development of a scoring system requires that the items that are valid predictors of job success (positively or negatively correlated) be identified and that weights be established for different responses to these items. By totaling the scores for each item, it is possible to obtain a composite score on the BIB as a whole for each applicant. Studies have shown that an objective scoring of BIB and application forms is one of the most potentially valid methods of predicting job success. This method has been useful in predicting all types of behavior, including employee theft, turnover, and performance in jobs such as sales, nursing, and management.[11]

Background Investigations

When the interviewer is satisfied that the applicant is potentially qualified, information about previous employment as well as other information provided by the applicant is investigated. Following 9/11 and a rash of corporate scandals at companies such as Enron, Tyco, and WorldCom, background investigations have become standard procedure for many companies to prevent a variety of problems ranging from embezzlement and theft of merchandise to workplace violence. Moreover, state courts have ruled that companies can be held liable for negligent hiring if they fail to do adequate background checks. Federal law requires comprehensive background checks for all child care providers, for example. It also prohibits convicted felons from engaging in financial and security-oriented transactions.

Among the checks are Social Security verification, past employment and education verification, and a criminal records check. A number of other checks can be conducted if they pertain to the job being hired for. They include a motor vehicle record check (for jobs involving driving), a credit check (for money-handling jobs), and a military records check. Figure 6.5 shows the various screening tools used by Fortune 1000 companies, according to a recent survey by Pinkerton Consulting and Investigations.

Like the application process, many checks that were once done manually are now being done online using existing computer databases. However, this frequently requires checking many different databases on a county-by-county basis. Information on international applicants is even harder to come by. Additionally, delving into areas of an applicant's background irrelevant to the job requirements he or she is applying for can leave the firms explosed to violation-of-privacy claims.

To comply with different state laws regarding privacy and treat all applicants fairly and consistently, most large companies now outsource at least part of the background screening process. According to the Pinkerton survey, 39 percent outsource background screening entirely, 17 percent conduct the screening in-house, and 41 percent use a combination of the two. A third-party background screen can cost between \$4 and \$80, depending on the types of checks requested, the number of references contacted, and the number of counties searched for criminal activity. They can generally be e-mailed to the company within a few hours or a few days. In addition, a number of job boards such as Yahoo! and Hotjobs.com now have online

Figure 6.5 **Use of Pre-Employment Selection Tools by Fortune 1000 Companies***

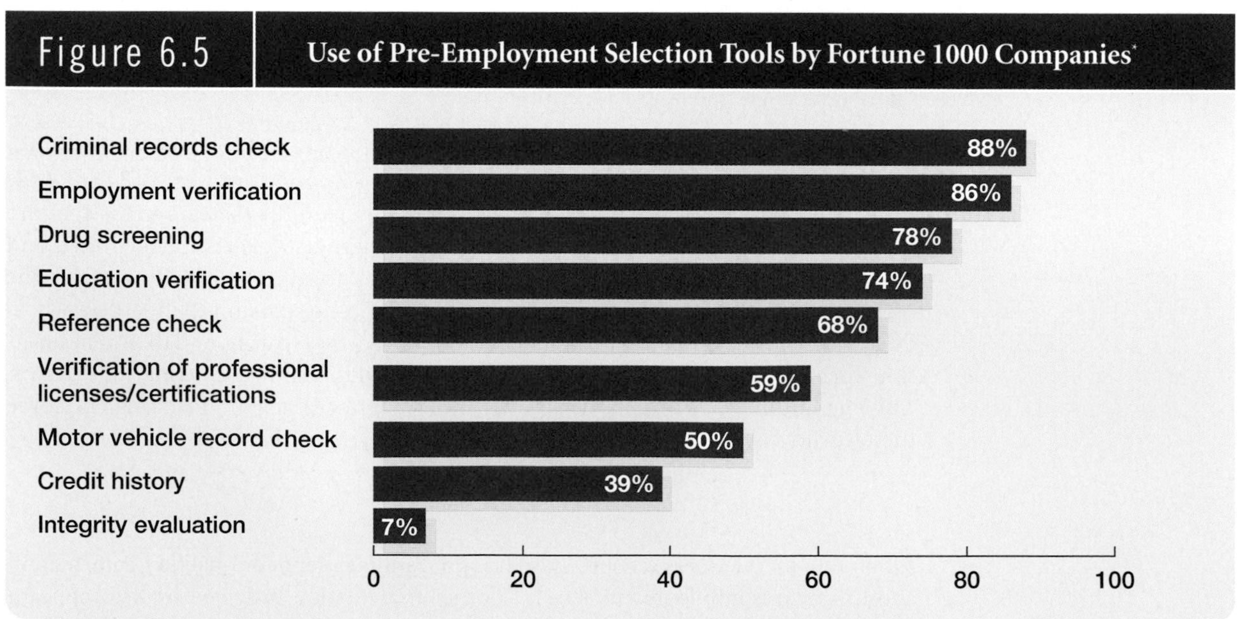

*Tools that 212 security representatives at Fortune 1000 companies said their companies use consistently.

Source: *Top Security Threats and Management Issues Facing Corporate America,* Pinkerton Consulting and Investigations, Inc.

screening tools allowing an applicant to conduct his or her own self-background check and post it online prior to any sort of interview. The idea is to to demonstrate upfront to prospective employers that the applicant has a clean criminal record, a good job history, and would make a good employee.[12]

Checking References

Organizations ranging from Canon to the Boston Philharmonic use both mail and the telephone to check references. But while references are commonly used to screen and select employees, they have not proved successful for predicting employee performance. Written letters of reference are notoriously inflated, and this limits their validity. Generally, telephone checks are preferable because they save time and provide for greater candor. But faxes and e-mail are also used. InfoTech, a computer-systems managing company in Fairfax, Virginia, first calls references to establish contact, then faxes or e-mails them a two-page questionnaire, asking them to numerically rank the applicant's various job-related attributes. There's room at the end of the questionnaire for comments and recommendations. The most reliable information usually comes from supervisors, who are in the best position to report on an applicant's work habits and performance. Written verification of information relating to job titles, duties, and pay levels from the former employer's HR office is also very helpful. Highlights in HRM 1 includes a list of helpful questions to ask about applicants when checking their references.[13]

Based on the Privacy Act of 1974, individuals have a legal right to examine letters of reference about them (unless they waive the right to do so). Although the Privacy Act applies only to the records maintained by federal government agencies, other forms of privacy legislation in most states have influenced employers to "clean up" personnel files and open them up to review and challenge by the employees concerned.[14]

As a legal protection for all concerned, it is important to ask the applicant to fill out forms permitting information to be solicited from former employers and other reference sources. Even with these safeguards, many organizations are reluctant to put into writing an evaluation of a former employee, and some employers even hesitate to answer questions and/or verify information about former employees over the phone. A survey by the SHRM found that although 75 percent of companies do provide references, many reported that the information consists only of employment dates and position. One reason is that firms have been sued by former employees who discovered that they had been given poor recommendations. But even firms that have failed to give an employee a recommendation have found themselves sued.

Under these circumstances, it may be nearly impossible for potential employers to learn enough about the candidate to avoid hiring mistakes. There are really two problems here. First, new employers may be liable for negligent hiring if they fail to screen out applicants with histories of instability who become dangerous in the workplace. Second, numerous court cases have held former employers liable when they knew an individual was dangerous but failed to disclose this fact to the new employer. Recognizing this predicament, thirty-seven states so far have enacted statutes offering protection from liability for employers who give references in good faith.[15]

Using Credit Reports

Credit checks are more widely available and cheaper in the United States today than in other countries because the United States has a national credit reporting system. But the Fair and Accurate Credit Transactions Act of 2003 (which was designed, among other things, to make identity theft more difficult), along with the Consumer

Highlights in HRM 1

Sample Reference-Checking Questions

Just the Facts

What were the candidate's dates of employment?

What was the candidate's title?

What were the candidate's general responsibilities?

What is your relationship to the candidate (peer, subordinate, superior)?

How long have you known the candidate?

On the Job

How would you describe the overall quality of the candidate's work? Can you give me some examples?

(For superiors) What areas of performance did you have to work on?

What would you say are the candidate's strengths?

What would you say are the candidate's weaknesses?

How would you compare the candidate's work to the work of others who performed the same job?

What kind of environment did the candidate work in?

How much of a contribution do you think the candidate made to your company or department?

How would you describe the candidate's ability to communicate?

How does the candidate handle pressure/deadlines?

How well does the candidate get along with co-workers?

How well does the candidate get along with managers?

How well does the candidate supervise others? Can you give me your impressions of his or her management style? Describe the candidate's success in motivating subordinates.

How does the candidate handle conflict situations?

Based on the candidate's performance with your company, do you think he or she would be good in the type of position we're considering him or her for?

What motivates the candidate? How ambitious is he or she?

The Bottom Line

Why did the candidate leave your company?

Would you rehire this person?

Would you recommend this candidate for this type of position?

What type of work is the candidate ideally suited for?

Were there any serious problems with the candidate that we need to be aware of before making a hiring decision?

Do you have any additional information to share with us about this candidate?

Source: Carolyn Hirschman, "The Whole Truth," *HRMagazine* 45, no. 6 (June 2000): 86–72.

Reporting Employment Clarification Act of 1998, and the Consumer Credit Reporting Reform Act of 1996 now restrict the sharing of some credit information. In terms of hiring, a "credit report" extends beyond the financial arena to include almost any compilation of information on an individual that is prepared by a third-party agency. To rely on a report such as this in making employment decisions, organizations must follow four important steps.

First, organizations must advise and receive written consent from applicants if such a report will be requested. If an employer plans to use a more comprehensive type of third-party report, such as an investigative consumer report, the applicant must be advised in writing. An investigative consumer report includes information based on personal interviews with the applicant's friends, neighbors, and associates rather than just from an existing database. The applicant must be told that additional disclosure concerning the complete nature and scope of the investigation will be provided to the applicant on written request.

Second, the organization must provide a written certification to the consumer reporting agency (the agency providing the information) about the purpose of the report and must assure them that it will not be used for any other purpose. In the case of investigative reports, the employer also has to certify that it will give an applicant the information if he or she asks for it.

Third, before taking any adverse action due to information in the report, organizations must provide applicants a copy of the consumer report as well as a summary of their rights.

Fourth, if the organization decides not to hire the applicant based on the report, it must provide an adverse-action notice to that person. Although the notice can be provided verbally, in writing, or electronically, it must contain the name, address, and phone number of the agency that provided the report. The employer must also provide a statement that the reporting agency didn't make the hiring decision, that the applicant has a right to obtain an additional free copy of the report, and that the applicant has a right to dispute the accuracy of information with the reporting agency.[16]

Polygraph Tests

The polygraph, or lie detector, is a device that measures the changes in breathing, blood pressure, and pulse of a person who is being questioned. It consists of a rubber tube around the chest, a cuff around the arm, and sensors attached to the fingers that record the physiological changes in the examinee as the examiner asks questions that call for an answer of yes or no. Questions typically cover such items as whether a person uses drugs, has stolen from an employer, or has committed a serious undetected crime.

The growing swell of objections to the use of polygraphs in employment situations culminated in the passage of the federal Employee Polygraph Protection Act of 1988. The act generally prohibits the use of a lie detector for prehire screening and random testing and applies to all private employers except pharmaceutical companies and companies that supply security guards for health and safety operations as well as government agencies.[17] It defines the term *lie detector* to include the polygraph, deceptograph, voice stress analyzer, psychological stress evaluator, and any similar mechanical or electrical device used to render a diagnostic opinion about the honesty or dishonesty of an individual.

Other provisions of the act set qualification standards for polygraph examiners, conditions for examinations, and disclosure of information when the use of the polygraph is authorized. Because of the law, employers have had to resort to such alternatives as written tests of honesty and background checks of applicants. Among the organizations most affected are Wall Street firms, banks, and retail companies, which used to rely heavily on polygraphs. Polygraphs are used by only a small percentage of firms in the general population, although their use is prevalent among law enforcement agencies.[18]

Honesty and Integrity Tests

Job Outlook
Law Enforcement Civil service regulations govern the appointment of police in most states. Candidates must be U.S. citizens, at least 20 years old, meet rigorous physical and personal qualifications, and have at least a high school diploma. Federal and state agencies usually require a college degree.

Source: *Occupational Outlook Handbook,* 2004-05 Edition. http://www.bls.gov/oco

In response to the Employee Polygraph Protection Act, many employers have dramatically increased their use of pencil-and-paper honesty and integrity tests. These tests have commonly been used in settings such as retail stores where employees have access to cash or merchandise. Common areas of inquiry include beliefs about frequency and extent of theft in our society, punishment for theft, and perceived ease of theft. For example, Payless ShoeSource, based in Topeka, Kansas, has used a paper-and-pencil honesty test to reduce employee theft. When the company began its program, losses totaled nearly $21 million per year among its 4,700 stores. Within only one year of implementing its screening program, inventory shrinkage fell by 20 percent to less than 1 percent of sales. Nordstrom, the Seattle-based department store, also uses an integrity test, called the Reid Report Assessment, which takes only about fifteen minutes to complete. Nordstrom contends that, using the Reid Report Assessment, the company has about a 90 percent chance of screening out undesirable candidates. The popularity of the Reid test grew substantially in the 1990s. Its developer, Reid Systems, saw the number of its clients, ranging from retailers to airlines, fully double prior to its 2001 merger with one of its competitors (London House).[19]

Potential items that might be used on an integrity test are shown in Figure 6.6. A comprehensive analysis of honesty tests reveals that they are valid for predicting job performance as well as a wide range of disruptive behaviors such as theft, disciplinary problems, and absenteeism.[20] Nevertheless, honesty tests have come under fire, too. According to Lewis Maltby, president of the National Work Rights Institute, a nonprofit organization, "There are questions that will ask you for your reaction to hypothetical dishonest situations, and if you are a particularly kindhearted person who isn't sufficiently punitive, you fail. Mother Teresa would never have passed some of these honesty tests." Given this possibility, HRM specialists should use the results from honesty tests very cautiously and most certainly in conjunction with other sources of information.[21]

Graphology

USING THE INTERNET

To see how handwriting analysis is used for employment purposes, go to the Student Resources at:

http://bohlander.swlearning.com

Graphology, a term that refers to a variety of systems of handwriting analysis, is used by some employers to make employment decisions. Graphologists obtain a sample of handwriting and then examine such characteristics as the size and slant of letters, amount of pressure applied, and placement of the writing on the page. From their observations, graphologists draw inferences about such things as the writer's personality traits, intelligence, energy level, organizational abilities, creativity, integrity, emotional maturity, self-image, people skills, and entrepreneurial tendencies. Graphology is used

Figure 6.6 Integrity Test Question Examples

TO TEST TENDENCY TO	DESCRIPTION
Protect	Contains items that require individuals to indicate whether they would protect friends or co-workers who had engaged in counterproductive behaviors. *Example:* I would turn in a fellow worker I saw stealing money.
Be lenient	Contains items in which test takers indicate whether they would be lenient with respect to the wrongdoings of others. *Example:* An employee should be fired if the employer finds out the employee lied on the application bank.
Admit thought	Includes items that require test takers to indicate the degree to which they would engage in counterproductive thoughts or behaviors. *Example:* I've thought about taking money from an employer without actually doing it.
Admit behavior	Contains items in which individuals admit to directly participating in actual counterproductive behaviors. *Example:* Over the last three years, what's the total amount of money you've taken without permission from your employer?
Consider common	Includes items that require the individual to indicate whether there are excuses or justifications for stealing or performing other questionable behaviors. *Example:* Most people I've worked with have stolen something at one time or another.
Excuse	Contains items in which individuals indicate whether there are excluses or justifications for stealing or performing other questionable behaviors. *Example:* Someone who steals because his family is in need should not be treated the same as a common thief.
Lie	Contains items that measure the extent to which the test taker is responding in a socially desirable manner. *Example:* Never in my whole life have I wished for anything I was not entitled to.

Note: The number of items in each category was 2, 8, 13, 9, 17, 8, and 7 respectively.

Source: Stephen Dwight and George Alliger, "Reactions to Overt Integrity Test Items," *Educational and Psychological Measurement* 57, no. 6 (December 1977): 937–48, copyright © 1997 by Sage Publications, Inc. Reprinted with the permission of Sage Publications, Inc.

extensively in France, Germany, Switzerland, Israel, and the United Kingdom in making employment decisions.[22] Now handwriting analysis is quietly spreading through corporate America. Companies such as Ford and General Electric have used it for selection, as has the U.S. Central Intelligence Agency (CIA).

Organizations using handwriting analysis say they prefer it to typical personality tests because it requires only that job candidates take a few minutes to jot down a short essay. By contrast, a battery of personality tests and interviews with psychologists can take several hours and can cost thousands of dollars. In addition, the available

Because medical examinations are costly, they are usually reserved for final candidates.

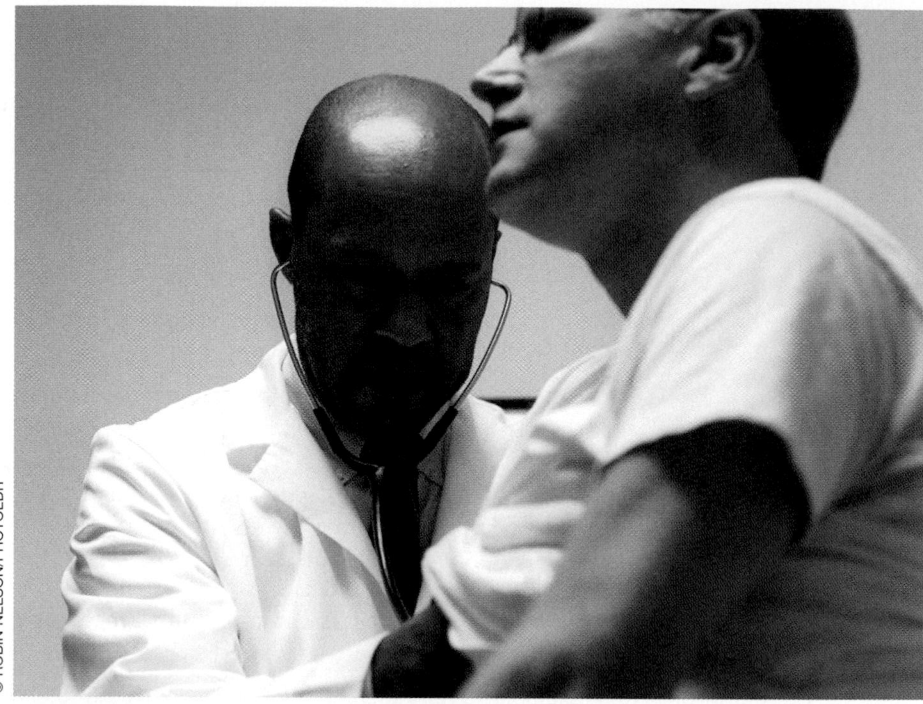

© ROBIN NELSON/PHOTOEDIT

evidence shows graphology to be a reliable predictor of personality when compared with other psychological tests. However, its predictive validity for job performance and occupational success remains questionable. In the academic community, where formal and rigorous validity studies are customary, use of graphology for employment decisions has been viewed with considerable skepticism.[23]

Medical Examinations

The medical examination is one of the later steps in the selection process because it can be costly. A medical examination is generally given to ensure that the health of an applicant is adequate to meet the job requirements. It also provides a baseline against which subsequent medical examinations can be compared and interpreted. The latter objective is particularly important in determinations of work-caused disabilities under workers' compensation law.

In the past, requirements for such physical characteristics as strength, agility, height, and weight were often determined by an employer's unvalidated notion of what should be required. Many such requirements that tend to discriminate against women have been questioned and modified so as to represent typical job demands.[24]

In some cases, medical testing can be considered an invasion of privacy and may be in violation of the law. For example, the Americans with Disabilities Act severely limits the types of medical inquiries and examinations that employers may use. Wal-Mart, for example, paid $6 million to settle one lawsuit involving an ADA claim. According to the EEOC, Wal-Mart's hiring questionnaire violated an ADA provision restricting the kinds of medical information companies can request from prospective employees. The law explicitly states that all exams must be directly related to the requirements of the job and that a medical exam cannot be given until an offer of employment has been extended. Further, the ADA prohibits companies from screening out a prospective employee because he or she has an elevated risk of on-the-job injury or a medical condition that could be aggravated because of job demands. However, the ADA does not prevent testing of applicants or employees for illegal drug use, a topic discussed next.[25]

Drug Testing

Since passage of the Drug-Free Workplace Act of 1988, applicants and employees of federal contractors, Department of Defense contractors, and those under Department of Transportation regulations are subject to testing for illegal drug use. (See Chapter 12 for an extended discussion of this topic, including a sample policy statement for a drug-free workplace.) Urine sampling is the normal method used for drug testing, but testing hair, saliva, and sweat are becoming more commonplace. Hair testing, for example, can show drug use going back months. Saliva, or oral fluid, testing works well at accident scenes involving drug use by current employees when urine testing is inconvenient. Sweat testing is efficient for workers returning to duty after testing positive because it captures drug use within a specific window of weeks or days.

Well over half of all U.S. companies conduct pre-employment drug tests. According to a survey of companies conducted by the American Management Association, drug testing (of both applicants and employees) increased in the 1990s, but then fell in the early 2000s. A number of studies have failed to show that that drug testing makes the workplace safer or leads to improvements in the performance of workers. Moreover, relatively few applicants test positive for drugs (less than 5 percent). Alcohol use, in fact, appears to create more problems than illegal drugs in the workplace. Testing also involves a cost, ranging from more than $50 for a urine test to more than $100 for a hair test.[26]

Consequently, some companies no longer conduct drug tests. Hewlett-Packard is one of them. Cisco and Sun Microsystems have never conducted drug tests. Dell Computer, on the other hand, tests every one of its 40,000-plus employees. The weight of the evidence suggests that testing is most appropriate for staff members in safety-critical positions.

Employment Tests

As the United States mobilized for World War I in the summer of 1917, some of the most talented psychologists in the country worked together to develop what later became known as the Army Alpha and Beta Tests of intelligence. (The Alpha exam was written for the general population and the Beta was designed for internationals and those with poor reading skills.) The tests were used to help identify potential officer candidates as well as select and place other potential recruits. Since that time, employment tests have played an important part in the HR programs of both public and private organizations.

Before the passage of the Civil Rights Act of 1964, more than 90 percent of companies surveyed by the Bureau of National Affairs reported using tests. By the 1980s, however, far less than half were using tests. In the 1990s there was a dramatic resurgence of

Organizations use a variety of tests to determine an applicant's abilities, knowledge, and skills.

employment testing. Although a survey of the American Management Association showed that the percentage of companies doing employment testing fell during 2001, according to the Association of Test Publishers, overall employment testing ticked upward 10–15 percent annually during 2002–2004. PepsiCo, Sara Lee, and Hewlett-Packard have all used such tests.[27]

One of the drawbacks of pre-employment testing is that it creates the potential for legal challenges. Many companies have been taken to court by candidates claiming that the tests they took were discriminatory. There is also some evidence that the more tests that are required, the higher the likelihood of a lawsuit. The relative frequency of discrimination suits also appears to vary by industry and job type. Police, firefighting, and teaching areas—which generally require applicants to pass more tests—appear to be more prone to discrimination litigation.[28]

Nonetheless, tests have played a more important part in government HR programs in which hiring on the basis of merit is required by law. Government agencies experienced the same types of problems with their testing programs as did organizations in the private sector. However, their staffs were forced to improve their testing programs rather than to abandon them.

Many organizations use professional test consultants such as Wonderlic Inc. in Libertyville, Illinois, to improve their testing programs and to meet EEO requirements. While it is often advisable to use consultants, especially if an organization is considering the use of personality tests, managers should have a basic understanding of the technical aspects of testing and the contributions that tests can make to the HR program. They should also do a thorough job analysis to determine the crucial job requirements and related skills that actually need to be tested for and eliminate any unnecessary or duplicate tests.

Nature of Employment Tests

An employment test is an objective and standardized measure of a sample of behavior that is used to gauge a person's knowledge, skills, abilities, and other characteristics (KSAOs) in relation to other individuals.[29] The proper sampling of behavior—whether verbal, manipulative, or some other type—is the responsibility of the test author. It is also the responsibility of the test author to develop tests that meet accepted standards of reliability.[30] Data concerning reliability are ordinarily presented in the manual for the test. While high reliability is essential, it offers no assurance that the test provides the basis for making valid judgments—that is, that the test actually measures the knowledge, skills, and abilities necessary to do a job successfully. It is the responsibility of the HR staff to conduct validation studies before a test is adopted for regular use. Again, this involves doing a thorough job analysis. One way to measure a test's validity is to test current employees and create a benchmark score to which applicants' scores can be compared. Other considerations are cost, time, ease of administration and scoring, and the apparent relevance of the test to the individuals being tested—commonly referred to as "face validity." While face validity is desirable, it is no substitute for technical validity, described earlier in this chapter. Adopting a test just because it appears relevant is bad practice; many a "good-looking" test has poor validity.

Classification of Employment Tests

aptitude tests
Measures of a person's capacity to learn or acquire skills

achievement tests
Measures of what a person knows or can do right now

Employment tests may be classified in different ways. Generally, they are viewed as measuring either aptitude or achievement. **Aptitude tests** measure a person's capacity to learn or acquire skills. **Achievement tests** measure what a person knows or can do right now.

Cognitive Ability Tests

Cognitive ability tests measure mental capabilities such as general intelligence, verbal fluency, numerical ability, and reasoning ability. A host of paper-and-pencil tests measure cognitive abilities, including the General Aptitude Test Battery (GATB), the Scholastic Aptitude Test (SAT), the Graduate Management Aptitude Test (GMAT), and the Bennett Mechanical Comprehension Test. Figure 6.7 shows some items that could be used to measure different cognitive abilities.

Figure 6.7 Is That Your Final Answer?

Verbal

1. What is the meaning of the word "surreptitious"?
   a. covert c. lively
   b. winding d. sweet

2. How is the noun clause used in the following sentence? "I hope that I can learn this game."
   a. Subject c. direct object
   b. predicate nominative d. object of the preposition

Quantitative

3. Divide 50 by 0.5 and add 5. What is the result?
   a. 25 c. 95
   b. 30 d. 105

4. What is the value of 144^2?
   a. 12 c. 95
   b. 72 d. 20736

Reasoning

5. ___________ is to *boat* as *snow* is to_________.
   a. Sail, ski c. Water, ski
   b. Water, winter d. Engine, water

6. Two women played 5 games of chess. Each woman won the same number of games, yet there were no ties. How can this be?
   a. There was a forfeit. c. They played different people.
   b. One player cheated. d. One game is still in progress.

Mechanical

7. If gear A and gear C are both turning counterclockwise, what is happening to gear B?
   a. It is turning counterclockwise. c. It remains stationary.
   b. It is turning clockwise. d. The whole system will jam.

A B C

Answers: 1. a, 2. c, 3. d, 4. d, 5. c, 6. c, 7. b

Although cognitive ability tests can be developed to measure very specialized areas such as reading comprehension and spatial relations, many experts believe that the validity of cognitive ability tests simply reflects their connection to general intelligence. However, measures of general intelligence (such as IQ) have been shown to be good predictors of performance across a wide variety of jobs.[31]

Personality and Interest Inventories

Whereas cognitive ability tests measure a person's mental capacity, personality tests measure disposition and temperament. During 1990s, for example, testing by the U.S. Army found that cognitive ability tests were the best predictors of how well soldiers were able to acquire job knowledge and, ultimately, of their technical proficiencies. But personality tests were the better predictors of their motivation, such as their leadership efforts and propensity to adhere to rules. Years of research show that five dimensions can summarize personality traits. The "Big Five" factors are the following:

1. *Extroversion*—the degree to which someone is talkative, sociable, active, aggressive, and excitable
2. *Agreeableness*—the degree to which someone is trusting, amiable, generous, tolerant, honest, cooperative, and flexible
3. *Conscientiousness*—the degree to which someone is dependable and organized and perseveres in tasks
4. *Neuroticism*—the degree to which someone is secure, calm, independent, and autonomous
5. *Openness to experience*—the degree to which someone is intellectual, philosophical, insightful, creative, artistic, and curious[32]

Figure 6.8 illustrates facets and sample items from the well-known California Psychological Inventory (CPI). Other personality tests include the Myers-Briggs Type Indicator (MBTI) and the 180-question Caliper test, whose users range from FedEx to the Chicago Cubs. The predictive validity of personality and interest inventories historically has been quite low. However, when used in combination with cognitive ability tests, measures of personality traits (such as conscientiousness) can lead to a better prediction of job performance.[33]

It is important to note that personality tests can be problematic if they inadvertently discriminate against individuals who would otherwise perform effectively. Demonstrating job-relatedness and validity of some personality characteristics is not always easy. The use of personality tests may also be seen as an invasion of privacy.[34] Several states severely restrict their usage because of this.

Beyond the initial hiring decision, personality and interest inventories may be most useful for helping with occupational selection and career planning. Interest tests such as the Kuder Inventory measure an applicant's preferences for certain activities over others (such as sailing versus poker).

USING THE INTERNET

Find additional information about the administration and interpretation of the Kuder Inventory. Go to the Student Resources at:

http://bohlander.swlearning.com

Physical Ability Tests

In addition to learning about a job candidate's mental capabilities, employers frequently need to assess a person's physical abilities. These types of tests are reportedly being used more widely today for selection than ever before. Particularly for demanding and potentially dangerous jobs such as those held by firefighters and police officers, physical abilities such as strength

Figure 6.8 CPI Personality Facets and Sample Items

Agreeableness
- Consideration—I like to do little things for people to make them feel good.
- Empathy—I take other people's circumstances and feelings into consideration before making a decision.
- Interdependence—I tend to put group goals first and individual goals second.
- Openness—I do not have to share a person's values to work well with that person.
- Thought agility—I think it is vital to consider other perspectives before coming to conclusions.
- Trust—I believe people are usually honest with me.

Conscientiousness
- Attention to detail—I like to complete every detail of tasks according to the work plans.
- Dutifulness—I conduct my business according to a strict set of ethical principles.
- Responsibility—I can be relied on to do what is expected of me.
- Work focus—I prioritize my work effectively so the most important things get done first.

Extroversion
- Adaptability—For me, change is exciting.
- Competitiveness—I like to win, even if the activity isn't very important.
- Desire for achievement—I prefer to set challenging goals, rather than aim for goals I am more likely to reach.
- Desire for advancement—I would like to attain the highest position in an organization some day.
- Energy level—When most people are exhausted from work, I still have energy to keep going.
- Influence—People come to me for inspiration and direction.
- Initiative—I am always looking for opportunities to start new projects.
- Risk-taking—I am willing to take big risks when there is potential for big returns.
- Sociability—I find it easy to start up a conversation with strangers.
- Taking charge—I actively take control of situations at work if no one is in charge.

Neuroticism
- Emotional control—Even when I am very upset, it is easy for me to control my emotions.
- Negative affectivity—I am easily displeased with things at work.
- Optimism—My enthusiasm for living life to its fullest is apparent to those with whom I work.
- Self-confidence—I am confident about my skills and abilities.
- Stress tolerance—I worry about things that I know I should not worry about.

Openness to Experience
- Independence—I tend to work on projects alone, even if others volunteer to help me.
- Innovativeness/creativity—I work best in an environment that allows me to be creative and expressive.
- Social astuteness—I know what is expected of me in different social situations.
- Thought focus—I quickly make links between causes and effects.
- Vision—I can often foresee the outcome of a situation before it unfolds.

Source: Mark J. Schmit, Jenifer A. Kihm, and Chet Robie, "Development of a Global Measure of Personality," *Personnel Psychology* 53, no.1 (Spring 2000): 153–93. Reprinted by permission.

and endurance tend to be good predictors not only of performance, but of accidents and injuries.[35]

Despite their potential value, physical ability tests tend to work to the disadvantage of women and disabled job applicants, a tendency that has led to several recent lawsuits. Evidence suggests that the average man is stronger, faster, and more powerful than the average woman, but women tend to have better balance, manual dexterity, flexibility, and coordination than men. On the basis of these differences, it is clear that (as with other methods for screening potential employees) the use of physical ability tests should be carefully validated on the basis of the essential functions of the job.[36]

Job Knowledge Tests

Government agencies and licensing boards usually develop job knowledge tests, a type of achievement test designed to measure a person's level of understanding about a particular job. The uniform CPA Examination used to license certified public accountants is one such test. Most civil service examinations, for example, are used to determine whether an applicant possesses the information and understanding that will permit placement on the job without further training.[37] Job knowledge tests also play a major role in the enlisted personnel programs of the U.S. Army, Navy, Air Force, and Marines. Anyone who wants to become a pilot in the armed services and fly multimillion-dollar jets, for example, must undergo extensive job knowledge testing.

Work Sample Tests

Work sample tests, or job sample tests, require the applicant to perform tasks that are actually a part of the work required on the job. Like job knowledge tests, work sample tests are constructed from a carefully developed outline that experts agree includes the major job functions; the tests are thus considered content-valid. Organizations that are interested in moving toward *competency-based selection*—that is, hiring based on observation of behaviors previously shown to distinguish successful employees—increasingly use work samples to see potential employees "in action."[38]

Work samples have been devised for many diverse jobs: a map-reading test for traffic control officers, a lathe test for machine operators, a complex coordination test for pilots, an in-basket test for managers, a group discussion test for supervisors, and a judgment and decision-making test for administrators, to name a few. The City of Miami Beach has used work sample tests for jobs as diverse as plumbers, planners, and assistant chief accountants. The U.S. Air Force has used work samples for enlisted personnel in eight different specialty areas. In an increasing number of cases, work sample tests are aided by computer simulations, particularly when testing a candidate might prove dangerous. The reports are that this type of test is cost-effective, reliable, valid, fair, and acceptable to applicants.[39]

The Employment Interview

Traditionally, the employment interview has a central role in the selection process—so much so that it is rare to find an instance in which an employee is hired without some sort of interview. Depending on the type of job, applicants may be interviewed by one person, members of a work team, or other individuals in the organization. While

Source: Cartoon by Ted Goff. Reprinted with permission.

researchers have raised some doubts about its validity, the interview remains a mainstay of selection because (1) it is especially practical when there are only a small number of applicants; (2) it serves other purposes, such as public relations; and (3) interviewers maintain great faith and confidence in their judgments. Nevertheless, the interview can be plagued by problems of subjectivity and personal bias. In those instances, the judgments of different interviewers may vary dramatically and the quality of the hire can be called into serious question.

In this section, we review the characteristics, advantages, and disadvantages of various types of employment interviews. We highlight the fact that the structure of the interview and the training of interviewers strongly influence the success of the hiring process.[40]

Interviewing Methods

Interview methods differ in several ways, most significantly in terms of the amount of structure, or control, exercised by the interviewer. In highly structured interviews, the interviewer determines the course that the interview will follow as each question is asked. In the less structured interview, the applicant plays a larger role in determining the course the discussion will take. An examination of the different types of interviews from the least structured to the most structured reveals these differences.

The Nondirective Interview

nondirective interview An interview in which the applicant is allowed the maximum amount of freedom in determining the course of the discussion, while the interviewer carefully refrains from influencing the applicant's remarks

In the **nondirective interview,** the interviewer carefully refrains from influencing the applicant's remarks. The applicant is allowed the maximum amount of freedom in determining the course of the discussion. The interviewer asks broad, open-ended questions—such as "Tell me more about your experiences on your last job"—and permits the applicant to talk freely with a minimum of interruption. Generally, the nondirective interviewer listens carefully and does not argue, interrupt, or change the subject abruptly. The interviewer also uses follow-up questions to allow the applicant to elaborate, makes only brief responses, and allows pauses in the conversation; the pausing technique is the most difficult for the beginning interviewer to master.

The greater freedom afforded to the applicant in the nondirective interview is particularly valuable in bringing to the interviewer's attention any information, attitudes, or feelings that may often be concealed by more structured questioning. However, because the applicant determines the course of the interview and no set procedure is followed, little information that comes from these interviews enables interviewers to cross-check agreement with other interviewers. Thus the reliability and validity of the nondirective interview may be expected to be minimal. This method is most likely to be used in interviewing candidates for high-level positions and in counseling, which we will discuss in Chapter 13.

The Structured Interview

structured interview An interview in which a set of standardized questions having an established set of answers is used

More attention is being given to the structured interview as a result of EEO requirements and a concern for maximizing validity of selection decisions.[41] Because a **structured interview** has a set of standardized questions (based on job analysis) and an established set of answers against which applicant responses can be rated, it provides a more consistent basis for evaluating job candidates. For example, staff members of Weyerhaeuser Company's HR department have developed a structured interviewing process with the following characteristics:

1. The interview process is based exclusively on job duties and requirements critical to job performance.
2. It uses four types of questions: situational questions, job knowledge questions, job sample/simulation questions, and worker requirements questions.
3. There are sample (benchmark) answers, determined in advance, to each question. Interviewee responses are rated on a five-point scale relative to those answers.
4. The process involves an interview committee so that interviewee responses are evaluated by several raters.
5. It consistently follows the same procedures in all instances to ensure that each applicant has exactly the same chance as every other applicant.
6. The interviewer takes notes and documents the interview for future reference and in case of a legal challenge.

A structured interview is more likely to provide the type of information needed for making sound decisions. According to a report by the U.S. Merit Systems Protection Board, a quasi-judicial agency that serves as the guardian of federal merit systems, structured interviews are twice as likely as nondirective interviews to predict on-the-job performance. Structured interviews are also less likely than nondirective interviews to be attacked in court.[42]

Most employment interviewers will tend toward either a nondirected or a structured format. However, within the general category of structured interviews, there are more specific differences that relate to the format of questions. These include the situational interview and behavioral description interview, discussed next.

The Situational Interview

situational interview An interview in which an applicant is given a hypothetical incident and asked how he or she would respond to it

One variation of the structured interview is called the **situational interview.** With this approach, an applicant is given a *hypothetical* incident and asked how he or she would respond to it. The applicant's response is then evaluated relative to pre-established benchmark standards. Interestingly, many organizations are using the situational interview to select new college graduates. Highlights in HRM 2 shows a sample question from a situational interview used to select systems analysts at a chemical plant. Highlights in HRM 3 on page 271 lists some of the biggest blunders made by job applicants.

The Behavioral Description Interview

behavioral description interview (BDI) An interview in which an applicant is asked questions about what he or she actually did in a given situation

In contrast to a situational interview, which focuses on hypothetical situations, a **behavioral description interview (BDI)** focuses on *actual* work incidents in the interviewee's past. The BDI format asks the job applicant what he or she actually did in a given situation. For example, to assess a potential manager's ability to handle a problem employee, an interviewer might ask, "Tell me about the last time you disci-

Highlights in HRM 2

Sample Situational Interview Question

QUESTION:

It is the night before your scheduled vacation. You are all packed and ready to go. Just before you get into bed, you receive a phone call from the plant. A problem has arisen that only you can handle. You are asked to come in to take care of things. What would you do in this situation?

RECORD ANSWER:

____

____

____

SCORING GUIDE:

Good: "I would go in to work and make certain that everything is OK. Then I would go on vacation."

Good: "There are no problems that *only* I can handle. I would make certain that someone qualified was there to handle things."

Fair: "I would try to find someone else to deal with the problem."

Fair: "I would go on vacation."

plined an employee." Such an approach to interviewing, based on a critical-incidents job analysis, assumes that past performance is the best predictor of future performance. It also may be somewhat less susceptible to applicant faking. In addition, recent research indicates that the behavioral description interview is more effective than the situational interview for hiring higher-level positions such as general managers and executives.[43]

The Panel Interview

panel interview
An interview in which a board of interviewers questions and observes a single candidate

Another type of interview involves a panel of interviewers who question and observe a single candidate. In a typical **panel interview** the candidate meets with three to five interviewers who take turns asking questions. After the interview the interviewers pool their observations and their rating scores if the interview is structured to reach a consensus about the suitability of the candidate. HRM specialists using this method at Philip Morris USA and Virginia Power report that panel interviews provide several significant advantages over traditional one-to-one interviews, including higher reliability because of multiple inputs, greater acceptance of the decision, and shorter decision time. Studies also suggest that if the panels are composed of a diverse group of interviewers, hiring discrimination is minimized.[44]

The Computer Interview

With advances in information technology, more and more organizations are using computers and the Internet to help with the interviewing process. Nike (see the

In this panel interview, one of the participants is connecting by videoconference.

end-of-chapter case), Cigna Insurance, and Pinkerton Security have all developed expert systems to gather preliminary information as well as compare candidates.

Typically, a computer interview requires candidates to answer a series (75 to 125) of multiple-choice questions tailored to the job. These answers are compared either with an ideal profile or with profiles developed on the basis of other candidates' responses. The computer interview can also be used as a screening device to help filter out unqualified applicants applying online who don't merit a personal interview. Depending on the vendor and the software used, a computer interview conducted in conjunction with online tests can measure everything from contradictory responses and latent responses (time delays related to answering a question) to the applicant's typing speed and ability to use different kinds of software. CareerBuilder.com, for example, offers a service called IntelligentHire that screens out the ten most qualified and interested applicants posting for a job on CareerBuilder's site. IntelligentHire then generates a report for the employer that includes the applicants' resumes, answers to questions, background check results, and their overall rankings against one another.[45]

A few years ago, Pic 'n Pay Shoe Stores created a computerized interview that could be conducted over the phone using an 800 number. The interview focused on honesty, work attitude, drug use, candor, dependability, and self-motivation. After implementing the system, the company cut turnover by 50 percent and reduced employee theft by almost 40 percent. In addition to the benefits of objectivity, some research evidence suggests that applicants may be less likely to engage in "impression management" in computerized interviews than in face-to-face interviews. So far, organizations have used the computer mainly as a complement to, rather than as a replacement for, conventional interviews.[46]

Video Interviews

Companies such as AT&T, Dell Computer, Shell Oil, and Nike are using videoconference technologies to evaluate job candidates. While some use their own in-house systems, others use outside service partners. Kinko's, for example, rents videoconferencing

Hiring Managers Reveal Top Five Biggest Mistakes Candidates Make During Job Interviews in CareerBuilder.com Survey

Chicago, January 21, 2004. What is the biggest mistake you ever made during a job interview? Show up late? Insult the interviewer? How about eat a snack? In its survey of more than 400 hiring managers completed in December 2003, CareerBuilder.com asked respondents to share the most memorable blunders that caused them to pass on a particular candidate.

"Job interviews are intimidating and even the most-practiced job seeker can sometimes forget proper interview etiquette," said Kirk Scott, Senior Career Advisor for CareerBuilder.com. "To help job seekers gain insights into the minds of potential employers, CareerBuilder.com asked hiring managers nationwide to identify interview pitfalls that should be avoided. Most interview blunders fell under five key categories: communication, performance, attitude, appearance and honesty."

#1—Communication

Hiring managers report concerns with some candidates' abilities to communicate effectively, citing poor language skills and a tendency to reveal too much or too little information.

Examples:

- "The candidate said he had days he could not give 100 percent."
- "She kept telling me about her personal problems."
- "He spoke to me as if he was in prison—very bad grammar and manners."

Scott's Tip: Choose your words wisely and listen closely. Hiring managers look for candidates who pay attention, think quickly on their feet, and effectively communicate why their skills and accomplishments are the best fit for the job.

#2—Performance

The candidate's professionalism throughout the interview process plays an important role in the hiring decision. Hiring managers say candidates who are unprepared, distracted, or a little too comfortable are not considered for recruitment.

Examples:

- "The candidate kept looking around the room and knew nothing about the job being offered."
- "The woman answered her cell phone during the interview."
- "One guy ate a sandwich."

Scott's Tip: Maintain eye contact and do your homework. Research the company, its industry, and competitors prior to your arrival. Make sure to eat a solid meal beforehand to keep up your energy, and leave your cell phone or pager at home.

(continued on next page)

#3—Attitude

Candidates who display bored or arrogant attitudes during the interview are also a turn-off for these hiring managers.

Examples:

- "He asked me to speed up the interview because he had a lunch date."
- "He told me the only reason he was here was because his mother wanted him to get a job. He was 37."
- "The candidate used profanity when describing something negative about a previous boss."

Scott's Tip: Keep positive. Avoid saying anything negative about a previous employer. Show enthusiasm when speaking and being spoken to, and let the employer know that you are really interested in the opportunity.

#4—Appearance

For hiring managers, proper dress is always required—a lesson they feel some job seekers have not yet grasped.

Examples:

- "One candidate did not wear shoes to the interview."
- "A woman came in with open toe shoes and a slit on her dress up to her backside."
- "He showed up in jeans and a T-shirt with dirty fingernails and looked like he just woke up. He also smelled of alcohol."

Scott's Tip: Leave the Levis at home. Even if the company dress is casual, you don't want to seem casual about the job opportunity. Wear a business suit or other appropriate attire. Groom properly and change out of last night's clubbing clothes.

#5—Honesty

Hiring managers state that candidates who lie or give the impression that they are dishonest in any way are dismissed.

Examples:

- "One guy mentioned his arrest during the interview after stating on his application that he had never been arrested."
- "One guy asked if we drug-tested and if we gave advance notice (we are a drug treatment facility)."

Scott's Tip: Honesty is always the best policy, and think before you speak. Even the most innocent question, if not worded properly, can give the wrong impression.

Source: CareerBuilder.com.

rooms at a quarter of its 900 stores for about $150 per hour. National Career Centers has partnered with Radisson and Hilton to offer videoconferencing to customers in hotels.

Video interviews have several potential advantages related to flexibility, speed, and cost. Employers can make preliminary assessments about candidates' technical abilities, energy level, appearance, and the like before incurring the costs of a face-to-face meeting. The goal, of course, is to enable faster, higher-quality decisions at lower cost.

A number of companies, including Employment Video Stream (EVS) and Hire Intelligence, a Web-based recruiting firm in Houston, allow recruiters to videotape job applicants and post video interviews to a web site. Corporations log on to the sites and check out candidates free of charge or for a small fee, depending on the vendor. By recording and playing back the interviews to several companies' executives, firms can eliminate complications involved in setting up many more interviews.[47]

Guidelines for Employment Interviewers

Apart from the characteristics of the interviews themselves, there are several important tips for interviewers. Organizations should be cautious in selecting employment interviewers. Qualities that are desirable include humility, the ability to think objectively, maturity, and poise. Given the importance of diversity in the workforce, experience in associating with people from a variety of backgrounds is also desirable. Qualities to avoid in interviewers include overtalkativeness, extreme opinions, and biases.

A Review of the Best

There have been several reviews of research studies on the employment interview.[48] Each of these reviews discusses and evaluates numerous studies concerned with such questions as "What traits can be assessed in the interview?" and "How do interviewers reach their decisions?" Highlights in HRM 4 on page 275 presents some of the major findings of these studies. It shows that information is available that can be used to increase the validity of interviews.

Figure 6.9 summarizes the variables and processes involved in the employment interview. The figure shows that a number of applicant characteristics may influence the perception of the interviewer and thus the hiring decision. In addition, many interviewer and situational factors may also influence the perceptual and judgmental processes. For example, the race and sex of an applicant may shape the expectations, biases, and behaviors of an interviewer, which in turn may affect the interview outcome. Even a limited understanding of the variables shown in Figure 6.9 can help increase the interviewing effectiveness of managers and supervisors.

Interviewer Training

Training has been shown to dramatically improve the competence of interviewers. If not done on a continuing basis, training should at least be done periodically for managers, supervisors, and HR representatives who conduct interviews. Interviewer training programs should include practice interviews conducted under guidance. Practice interviews may be recorded on videotape and evaluated later in a group training session. Some variation in technique is only natural. However, the following list presents ten ground rules for employment interviews that are commonly accepted and supported by research findings. Their apparent simplicity should not lead one to underestimate their importance.

1. *Establish an interview plan.* Examine the purposes of the interview and determine the areas and specific questions to be covered. Review job requirements, application-form data, test scores, and other available information before seeing the applicant.
2. *Establish and maintain rapport.* This is accomplished by greeting the applicant pleasantly, by explaining the purpose of the interview, by displaying sincere interest in the applicant, and by listening carefully.

Figure 6.9 Variables in the Employment Interview

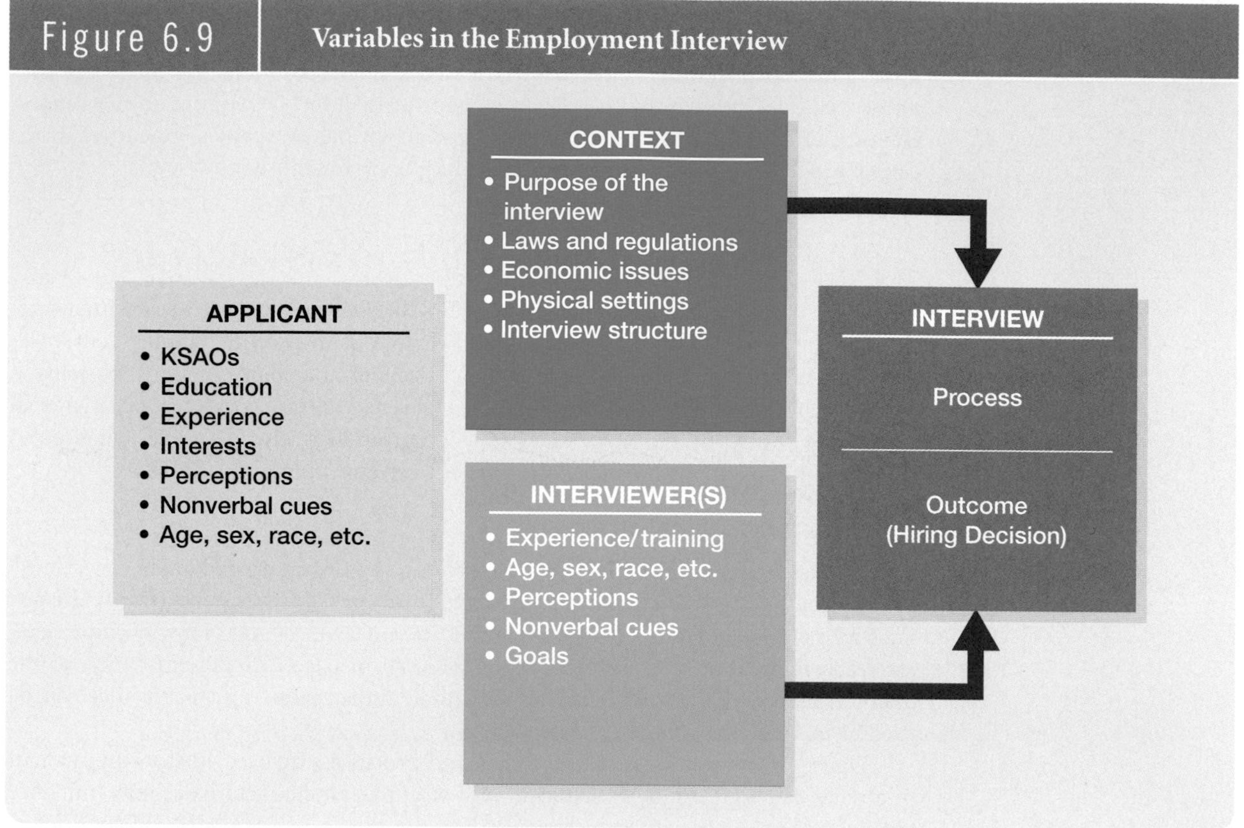

3. *Be an active listener.* Strive to understand, comprehend, and gain insight into what is only suggested or implied. A good listener's mind is alert, and face and posture usually reflect this fact.
4. *Pay attention to nonverbal cues.* An applicant's facial expressions, gestures, body position, and movements often provide clues to that person's attitudes and feelings. Interviewers should be aware of what they themselves are communicating nonverbally.
5. *Provide information as freely and honestly as possible.* Answer fully and frankly the applicant's questions. Present a realistic picture of the job.
6. *Use questions effectively.* To elicit a truthful answer, questions should be phrased as objectively as possible, giving no indication of what response is desired.
7. *Separate facts from inferences.* During the interview, record factual information. Later, record your inferences or interpretations of the facts. Compare your inferences with those of other interviewers.
8. *Recognize biases and stereotypes.* One typical bias is for interviewers to consider strangers who have interests, experiences, and backgrounds similar to their own to be more acceptable. Stereotyping involves forming generalized opinions of how people of a given gender, race, or ethnic background appear, think, feel, and act. The influence of sex-role stereotyping is central to sex discrimination in employment. Avoid the influence of "beautyism." Discrimination against unattractive

Some Major Findings from Research Studies on the Interview

1. Structured interviews are more reliable than unstructured interviews.
2. Interviewers are influenced more by unfavorable than by favorable information.
3. Interrater reliability is increased when there is a greater amount of information about the job to be filled.
4. A bias is established early in the interview, and this tends to be followed by either a favorable or an unfavorable decision.
5. Intelligence is the trait most validly estimated by an interview, but the interview information adds nothing to test data.
6. Interviewers can explain why they feel an applicant is likely to be an unsatisfactory employee but not why the applicant may be satisfactory.
7. Factual written data seem to be more important than physical appearance in determining judgments. This increases with interviewing experience.
8. An interviewee is given a more extreme evaluation (positive/negative) when preceded by an interviewee of opposing value (position/negative).
9. Interpersonal skills and motivation are probably best evaluated by the interview.
10. Allowing the applicant time to talk makes rapid first impressions less likely and provides a larger behavior sample.
11. Nonverbal as well as verbal interactions influence decisions.
12. Experienced interviewers rank applicants in the same order, although they differ in the proportion that they will accept. Experienced interviewers tend to be more selective than less experienced ones.

people is a persistent and pervasive form of employment discrimination. Also avoid "halo error," or judging an individual favorably or unfavorably overall on the basis of only one strong point (or weak point) on which you place high value.

9. *Control the course of the interview.* Establish an interview plan and stick to it. Provide the applicant with ample opportunity to talk, but maintain control of the situation in order to reach the interview objectives.
10. *Standardize the questions asked.* To increase reliability and avoid discrimination, ask the same questions of all applicants for a particular job. Keep careful notes; record facts, impressions, and any relevant information, including what was told to the applicant.

Diversity Management: Are Your Questions Legal?

The entire subject of what is legal or illegal in an employment interview gets pretty complicated. There are differing and sometimes contradictory interpretations by the courts, the EEOC, and the OFCCP about what you can ask in an interview. Under federal laws no questions are expressly prohibited. However, the EEOC looks with disfavor on direct or indirect questions related to race, color, age, religion, sex, or national origin. Some questions that interviewers once felt free to ask are now potentially hazardous. Federal courts have severely limited the area of questioning. An interviewer, for example, can ask about physical disabilities if the job involves manual labor, but not otherwise. Several states have fair employment practice laws that are more restrictive than federal legislation. In general, if a question is job-related, is asked of everyone, and does not discriminate against a certain class of applicants, it is likely to be acceptable to government authorities.

Particular care has to be given to questions asked of female applicants about their family responsibilities. It is inappropriate, for example, to ask, "Who will take care of your children while you are at work?" or "Do you plan to have children?" or "What is your husband's occupation?" or "Are you engaged?" It is, in fact, inappropriate to ask applicants of either gender questions about matters that have no relevance to job performance.

Employers have found it advisable to provide interviewers with instructions on how to avoid potentially discriminatory questions in their interviews. The examples of appropriate and inappropriate questions shown in Highlights in HRM 5 may serve as guidelines for application forms as well as pre-employment interviews. Complete guidelines may be developed from current information available from district and regional EEOC offices and from state FEP offices. Once the individual is hired, the information needed but not asked in the interview may be obtained if there is a valid need for it and if it does not lead to discrimination.

Reaching a Selection Decision

While all of the steps in the selection process are important, the most critical step is the decision to accept or reject applicants. Because of the cost of placing new employees on the payroll, the short probationary period in many organizations, and EEO/AA considerations, the final decision must be as sound as possible. Thus it requires systematic consideration of all the relevant information about applicants. It is common to use summary forms and checklists to ensure that all of the pertinent information has been included in the evaluation of applicants.

Summarizing Information about Applicants

Fundamentally, an employer is interested in what an applicant can do and will do. An evaluation of candidates on the basis of assembled information should focus on these two factors, as shown in Figure 6.10. The "can-do" factors include knowledge and skills, as well as the aptitude (the potential) for acquiring new knowledge and skills. The "will-do" factors include motivation, interests, and other personality characteristics. Both factors are essential to successful performance on the job. The employee who has the ability (can do) but is not motivated to use it (will not do) is little better than the employee who lacks the necessary ability.

It is much easier to measure what individuals can do than what they will do. The can-do factors are readily evident from test scores and verified information. What

Highlights in HRM 5

Appropriate and Inappropriate Interview Questions

	APPROPRIATE QUESTIONS	INAPPROPRIATE QUESTIONS
National origin	What is your name? Have you ever worked under a different name? Do you speak any foreign languages that may be pertinent to this job?	What's the origin of your name? What is your ancestry?
Age	Are you over 18? If hired, can you prove your age?	How old are you? What is your date of birth?
Gender	(Say nothing unless it involves a bona fide occupational qualification.)	Are you a man or a woman?
Race	(Say nothing.)	What is your race?
Disabilities	Do you have any disabilities that may inhibit your job performance? Are you willing to take a physical exam if the job requires it?	Do you have any physical defects? When was your last physical? What color are your eyes, hair, etc?
Height and weight	(Not appropriate unless it is a bona fide occupational qualification.)	How tall are you? How much do you weigh?
Residence	What is your address? How long have you lived there?	What are the names/relationships of those with whom you live?
Religion	(You may inform a person of the required work schedule.)	Do you have any religious affiliation?
Military record	Did you have any military education/experience pertinent to this job?	What type of discharge did you receive?
Education and experience	Where did you go to school? What is your prior work experience? Why did you leave? What is your salary history?	Is that a church-affiliated school? When did you graduate? What are your hobbies?
Criminal record	Have you ever been convicted of a crime?	Have you every been arrested?
Citizenship	Do you have a legal right to work in the United States?	Are you a U.S. citizen?
Marital/family status	What is the name, address, and telephone number of a person we may contact in case of an emergency?	Are you married, divorced, single? Do you prefer Miss, Mrs., or Ms.? Do you have any children? How old are they?

Figure 6.10 "Can-Do" and "Will-Do" Factors in Selection Decisions

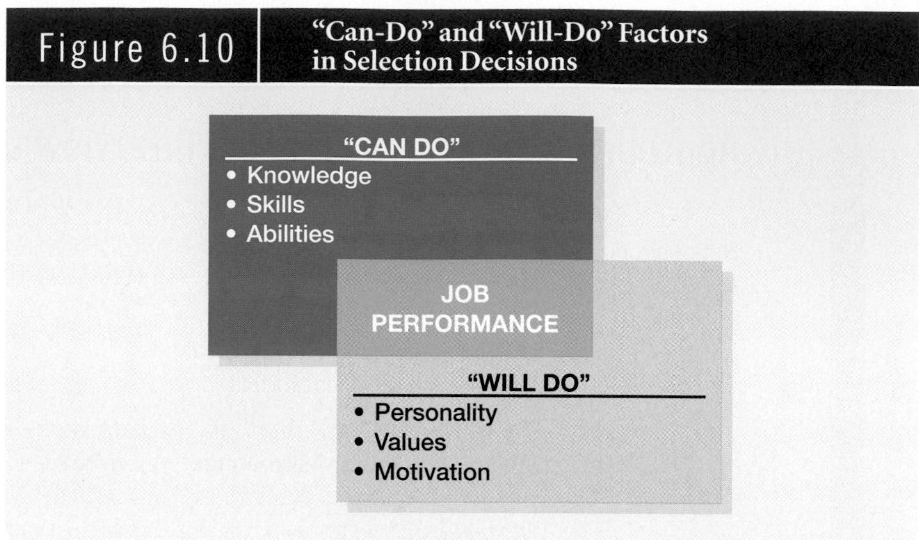

the individual will do can only be inferred. Responses to interview and application-form questions may be used as a basis for obtaining information for making inferences about what an individual will do.

Decision Strategy

The strategy used for making personnel decisions for one category of jobs may differ from that used for another category. The strategy for selecting managerial and executive personnel, for example, will differ from that used in selecting clerical and technical personnel. While many factors are to be considered in hiring decisions, the following are some of the questions that managers must consider:

1. Should the individuals be hired according to their highest potential or according to the needs of the organization?
2. At what grade or wage level should the individual be started?
3. Should initial selection be concerned primarily with an ideal match of the employee to the job, or should potential for advancement in the organization be considered?
4. To what extent should those who are not qualified but are qualifiable be considered?
5. Should overqualified individuals be considered?
6. What effect will a decision have on meeting affirmative action plans and diversity considerations?

In addition to these types of factors, managers must also consider which approach they will use in making hiring decisions. There are two basic approaches to selection: clinical (personal judgment) and statistical.

Clinical Approach

In the clinical approach to decision making, those making the selection decision review all the data on applicants. Then, on the basis of their understanding of the job and the individuals who have been successful in that job, they make a decision. Different individuals often arrive at different decisions about an applicant when they use this approach because each evaluator assigns different weights to the applicant's strengths and weaknesses. Furthermore, personal biases and stereotypes are frequently covered up by what appear to be rational bases for acceptance or rejection.

Statistical Approach

In contrast to the clinical approach, the statistical approach to decision making is more objective. It involves identifying the most valid predictors and weighting them through statistical methods such as multiple regression.[49] Quantified data such as scores or ratings from interviews, tests, and other procedures are then combined according to their weighted value. Individuals with the highest combined scores are selected. A comparison of the clinical approach with the statistical approach in a wide variety of situations has shown that the statistical approach is superior. Although this superiority has been recognized for many decades, the clinical approach continues to be the one most commonly used.

compensatory model
A selection decision model in which a high score in one area can make up for a low score in another area

multiple cutoff model
A selection decision model that requires an applicant to achieve some minimum level of proficiency on all selection dimensions

multiple hurdle model
A sequential strategy in which only the applicants with the highest scores at an initial test stage go on to subsequent stages

With a strictly statistical approach, a candidate's high score on one predictor (such as a cognitive ability test) will make up for a low score on another predictor (such as the interview). For this reason, this model is a **compensatory model.** However, it is frequently important that applicants achieve some minimum level of proficiency on all selection dimensions. When this is the case, a **multiple cutoff model** can be used in which only those candidates who score above the minimum cutoff on all dimensions are considered. The selection decision is made from that subset of candidates.[50]

A variation of the multiple cutoff is referred to as the **multiple hurdle model.** This decision strategy is sequential in that after candidates go through an initial evaluation stage, the ones who score well are provisionally accepted and are assessed further at each successive stage. The process may continue through several stages (hurdles) before a final decision is made regarding the candidates. This approach is especially useful when either the testing or training procedures are lengthy and expensive.

Each of the statistical approaches requires that a decision be made about where the cutoff lies—that point in the distribution of scores above which a person should be considered and below which the person should be rejected. The score that the applicant must achieve is the cutoff score. Depending on the labor supply and diversity and antidiscrimination considerations, it may be necessary to lower or raise the cutoff score.

The effects of raising and lowering the cutoff score are illustrated in Figure 6.11. Each dot in the center of the figure represents the relationship between the test score (or a weighted combination of test scores) and the criterion of success for one individual. In this instance, the test has a fairly high validity, as represented by the elliptical pattern of dots. Note that the high-scoring individuals are concentrated in the satisfactory category on job success, whereas the low-scoring individuals are concentrated in the unsatisfactory category.

If the cutoff score is set at A, only the individuals represented by areas 1 and 2 will be accepted. Nearly all of them will be successful. If more employees are needed (that is, there is an increase in the selection ratio), the cutoff score may be lowered to point B. In this case, a larger number of potential failures will be accepted, as shown in quadrants 2 and 4. Even if the cutoff is lowered to C, the total number of satisfactory individuals selected (represented by the dots in areas 1, 3, and 5) exceeds the total number selected who are unsatisfactory (areas 2, 4, and 6). Thus the test serves

Figure 6.11 Test Score Scatterplot with Hypothetical Cutoffs

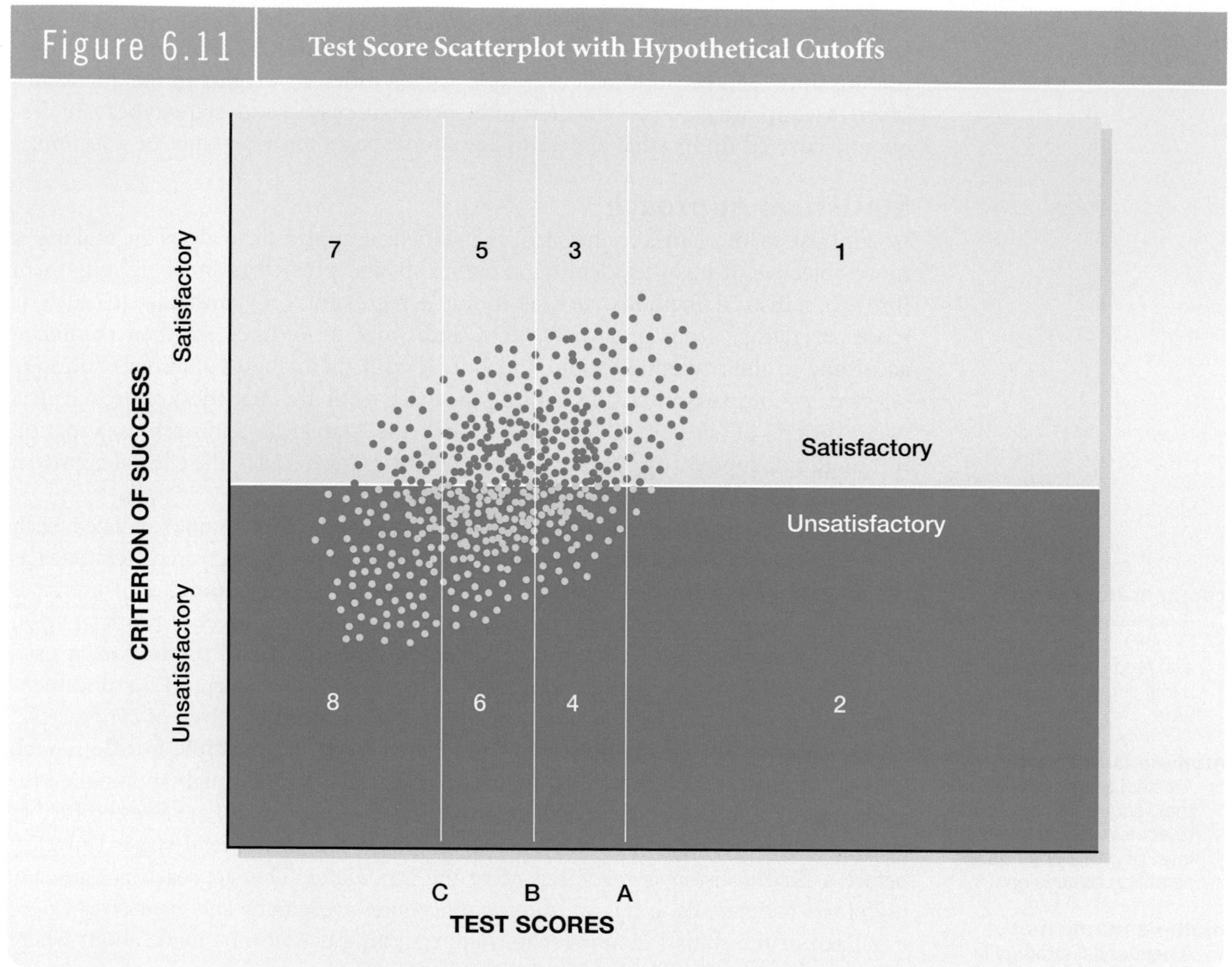

to maximize the selection of probable successes and to minimize the selection of probable failures. This is all we can hope for in predicting job success: the probability of selecting a greater proportion of individuals who will be successful rather than unsuccessful.

While the most valid predictors should be used with any selection strategy, a related factor contributes to selecting the best-qualified people: selectivity, or having an adequate number of applicants or candidates from which to make a selection. Selectivity is typically expressed in terms of a **selection ratio,** which is the ratio of the number of applicants to be selected to the total number of applicants. A ratio of 0.10, for example, means that 10 percent of the applicants will be selected. A ratio of 0.90 means that 90 percent will be selected. If the selection ratio is low, only the most promising applicants will normally be hired. When the ratio is high, very little selectivity will be possible, because even applicants having mediocre ability will have to be hired if the vacancies are to be filled.

selection ratio
The number of applicants compared with the number of people to be hired

It should be noted that how much of a contribution any predictor will make to the improvement of a given selection process is a function not only of the validity of the predictor and the selection ratio, but also of the proportion of people who are judged successful using current selection procedures.

Final Decision

After a preliminary selection has been made in the employment department, the applicants who appear most promising are then referred to departments with vacancies. There they are interviewed by the managers or supervisors, who usually make the final decision and communicate it to the employment department. Because of the weight that is usually given to their choices, managers and supervisors should be trained so that their role in the selection process does not negate the more rigorous efforts of the HR department staff.

In large organizations, notifying applicants of the decision and making job offers is often the responsibility of the HR department. This department should confirm the details of the job, working arrangements, wages, and so on, and specify a deadline by which the applicant must reach a decision. If, at this point, findings from the medical examination are not yet available, an offer is often made contingent on the applicant's passing the examination.

In government agencies, the selection of individuals to fill vacancies is made from lists or registers of eligible candidates. Ordinarily, three or more names of individuals at the top of the register are submitted to the requisitioning official. This arrangement provides some latitude for those making a selection and, at the same time, preserves the merit system.

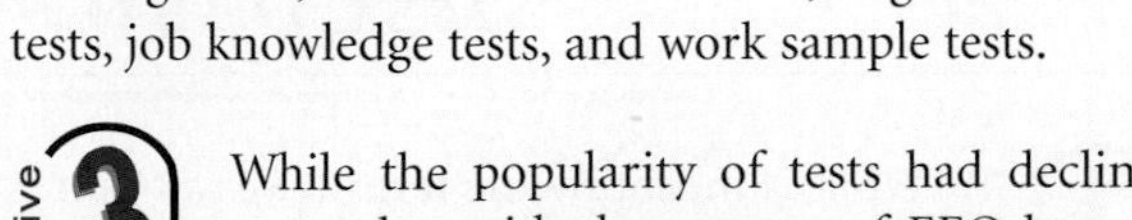

SUMMARY

objective 1

The selection process should provide as much reliable and valid information as possible about applicants so that their qualifications can be carefully matched with job specifications. The information that is obtained should be clearly job-related or predictive of success on the job and free from potential discrimination. Reliability refers to the consistency of test scores over time and across measures. Validity refers to the accuracy of measurement. Validity can be assessed in terms of whether the measurement is based on a job specification (content validity), whether test scores correlate with performance criteria (predictive validity), and whether the test accurately measures what it purports to measure (construct validity).

Interviews are customarily used in conjunction with application forms, biographical information blanks, references, background investigations, medical examinations, cognitive ability tests, job knowledge tests, and work sample tests.

objective 3

While the popularity of tests had declined somewhat with the passage of EEO laws, in recent years there has been a dramatic resurgence of testing. The value of tests should not be overlooked because they are more objective than the interview and can provide a broader sampling of behavior. Cognitive ability tests are especially valuable for assessing verbal, quantitative, and reasoning abilities. Personality and interest tests are perhaps best for placement. Physical ability tests are most useful for predicting job performance, accidents, and injuries, particularly for physically demanding work. Job knowledge and work sample tests are achievement tests that are useful for determining whether a candidate can perform the duties of the job without further training.

The interview is an important source of information about job applicants. It can be unstructured, wherein the interviewer is free to pursue whatever approach and sequence of topics might seem appropriate. Alternatively, an interview can be structured, wherein each applicant receives the same set of questions, which have pre-established answers. Some interviews are situational and can focus on hypothetical situations or actual behavioral descriptions of previous work experiences. Interviews can be conducted by a single individual, by a panel, or via a computer or video interface. Regardless of the technique chosen, those who conduct interviews should receive special training to acquaint them with interviewing methods and EEO considerations. The training should also make them more aware of the major findings from research studies on the interview and how they can apply these findings.

In the process of making decisions, all "can-do" and "will-do" factors should be assembled and weighted systematically so that the final decision can be based on a composite of the most reliable and valid information. While the clinical approach to decision making is used more than the statistical approach, the former lacks the accuracy of the latter. Compensatory models allow a candidate's high score on one predictor to make up for a low score on another. However, multiple cutoff and multiple hurdle approaches require minimal competency on each selection criterion. Whichever of these approaches is used, the goal is to select a greater proportion of individuals who will be successful on the job.

KEY TERMS

achievement tests
aptitude tests
behavioral description interview (BDI)
compensatory model
concurrent validity
construct validity
content validity
criterion-related validity
cross-validation
multiple cutoff model
multiple hurdle model
nondirective interview
panel interview
predictive validity
reliability
selection
selection ratio
situational interview
structured interview
validity
validity generalization

DISCUSSION QUESTIONS

1. What is meant by the term *criterion* as it is used in personnel selection? Give some examples of criteria used for jobs with which you are familiar.

2. What are some of the problems that arise in checking references furnished by job applicants? Are there any solutions to these problems?

3. What characteristics do job knowledge and job sample tests have that often make them more acceptable to the examinees than other types of tests?

4. Personality tests, like other tests used in employee selection, have been under attack for several decades. What are some of the reasons why applicants find personality tests objectionable? On what basis could their use for selection purposes be justified?

5. Compare briefly the major types of employment interviews described in this chapter. Which type would you prefer to conduct? Why?

6. In what ways does the clinical approach to selection differ from the statistical approach? How do you account for the fact that one approach is superior to the other?

Designing Selection Criteria and Methods

Making hiring decisions is one of the most important—and difficult—decisions a manager makes. Without good information, managers have almost no chance of making the right choice. They might as well be using a ouija board. The process begins with a sound understanding of the job: the tasks, duties, and responsibilities required and the knowledge, skills, and abilities needed to do it. Job analysis is very helpful in making certain that all the information is needed to ensure a person-job fit, but it may not be enough. Other information about company values, philosophy, and the like may be required to ensure person-organization fit.

Assignment

1. Working in teams of four to six individuals, choose a job with which you are familiar and identify the most important knowledge, skills, abilities, and other characteristics needed for someone to perform well.
2. Next, identify which methods you would use to tap these qualities. Would you use applications, interviews, psychological tests, work samples, or what? Explain why you would use these methods and justify the cost and time required.
3. After you have identified your selection criteria and methods, do a "reality check" in a real organization. Interview a manager who employs someone in that job. For example, if the job you selected is salesperson, go to a local business to learn how they select individuals for sales jobs. Compare what you thought would be a good selection approach with what you learned in the company you visited.
4. Identify the reasons for any discrepancies between your approach and theirs. Are the reasons justified and sound?

BIZFLIX EXERCISES

Bowfinger: The Lookalike

Some major learning objectives of this chapter include understanding the goals of an organization's selection process, using different types of information in employee selection, and using different employment interview approaches. Watch this humorous scene from *Bowfinger* with those learning objectives in mind.

This film, which brought Steve Martin and Eddie Murphy together for the first time, offers a funny look at Hollywood filmmaking. Bobby Bowfinger (Martin), perhaps the least successful director in films, wants to produce a low-budget film with top star Kit Ramsey (Murphy). Bowfinger's problem: Recruit a crew and cast with almost no budget and trick Kit into appearing in his film.

Bowfinger interviews several candidates for the Kit Ramsey lookalike role. He rejects everyone until Jifferson—Jiff—Ramsey (Murphy) auditions. This scene is an edited version of "The Lookalike" sequence early in the film. It includes Jiff's audition and interview, and a brief look at his first workday.

What to Watch for and Ask Yourself

- Which steps in the employee selection process shown earlier in Figure 6.2 appear in this scene? Which steps did Bobby Bowfinger skip?
- Does Bobby Bowfinger have valid selection criteria for filling the role of the Kit Ramsey lookalike? Do you predict Jiff Ramsey's success as a Kit Ramsey substitute?
- Which type of employment interview did Bowfinger use? See the earlier section "The Employment Interview" for a discussion of different employment interview approaches.

case study 1

Nike: Hiring Gets Off on the Right Foot

Technology is changing how companies recruit and select employees. Nike, the world's largest shoe manufacturer, is one example of a company using computer-assisted interviewing. The company has used an Aspen Tree product to hire some of its 24,000-plus employees, including employees for Niketowns, retail stores that showcase Nike products. At a single store opened in Las Vegas, for example, 6,000 people responded to ads for workers needed to fill 250 positions. Nike used IVR (interactive voice response) technology to make the first cut. Applicants responded to eight questions over the telephone; 3,500 applicants were screened out because they weren't available when needed or didn't have retail experience. The rest had a computer-assisted interview at the store, followed by a personal interview.

"We think it's important to give a personal interview to anyone who comes to the store," said Nike's manager of human resources for the retail division. "Applicants are customers as well as potential hires."

The computer interview identified candidates who had been in customer service environments, had a passion for sports, and would make good Nike customer service representatives. Interviews were done in batches. The computer interview (which includes a video showing three scenarios for helping a customer and asks the applicant to choose the best one) was given every forty-five minutes to a group of applicants. As applicants completed the interview, a printer in the next room printed their responses. Areas that needed to be probed further were flagged, as were areas that indicated particular strengths.

While the applicant completed an application form online, the interviewer used the printout to prepare for the applicant's human interview. Some applicants would be given only a short interview; other, more likely candidates would be interviewed at greater length. The computer not only helped interviewers screen for people who lost their temper in work situations or who demonstrated other undesirable behaviors, but it also helped the interviewers determine what to ask to reconcile inconsistencies in the computer interview or to probe applicant strengths in desired areas. Because Nike uses behavioral-based interviewing, applicants must document their areas of strength with examples from their work. Some applicants were offered jobs on the spot. Others were called back for second interviews.

Using computer-assisted interviewing has helped Nike staff up fast as well as reduce turnover in the retail division. The company saved $2.4 million during a three-year period by reducing turnover from 87 to 51 percent, although other processes for coaching and leading within the stores have also played a part.

Other areas of the company are finding ways to use recruitment technology, too. When an international division found itself besieged with as many as 400 resumes a week, it hired a solutions provider to automate the process of responding to applicants and tracking them. (Nike has a policy of responding to each potential employee with an individual letter.) Susannah Sanchez Perez applied for a job with Nike in May 2004, and remembers being impressed by how quickly the company responded to her. "I received an e-mail straightaway telling me that it would respond to me within three weeks," she said. "In fact, it only took four days for Nike to call me and invite me in for an interview. It took a long time to fill out the online form and that could be streamlined, but I was impressed by how professional the company seemed."

Source: Linda Thornburg, "Computer-Assisted Interviewing Shortens Hiring Cycle," *HRMagazine* 43, no. 2 (February 1998): 73–79. Adapted with the permission of *HRMagazine,* published by the Society for Human Resource Management, Alexandria, VA, via Copyright Clearance Center. See also Alex Blyth, "Winning Recruitment Race," *Personnel Today,* May 2004, 26.

QUESTIONS

1. What do you think are the prime advantages and disadvantages of Nike's computer-based interviewing system?
2. Are there any EEO concerns regarding this system?
3. If interviews serve a public relations role, what should Nike be concerned about?
4. How would you suggest that Nike might modify and improve its system?

case study 2

Clean Up the "Resu-mess"

Layne Buckley and Eric Muller both need to hire engineers, and those engineers need to understand electricity. But the recruiters are looking for two very different types of candidates.

Buckley, staffing manager for communications headset manufacturer Plantronics Inc. in Santa Cruz, California, wants engineers who can design the electronics for audio equipment. Muller, on the other hand, is recruiting a team leader for the energy firm Southern Company, and that calls for an engineer to run nuclear, coal, natural gas, and hydroelectric power plants. Both recruiters have one problem in common: Each has too many applicants to weed through.

"Our recruiters were overwhelmed and couldn't pinpoint who they should hire for a particular vacancy," says Muller. "They were victims of their own successful sourcing efforts."

Buckley had a similar experience. "Since we are near Silicon Valley, some [information technology] jobs have had 400 applicants," he says. "I have only a limited number of staff, and they can't be reading that many applications."

Southern has 26,000 employees operating 79 generating stations and overseeing 28,000 miles of transmission lines, as well as handling sales, clerical, financial, and other administrative tasks. About one-third of them work in the greater Atlanta area, where the company is headquartered, but the rest are scattered throughout Georgia, Alabama, Mississippi, and Florida. To maintain the required staffing levels, the company must hire more than 2,000 new permanent full-time employees each year, Muller says. But to do this, the recruiters have to sort through more than

100,000 applicants. "Our recruiters were swimming under what they called the 'resumess,'" says Muller.

Southern was doing online recruiting, but the process wasn't automated. Each recruiter would post open positions on the company's web site with instructions for candidates to send an e-mail to a generic address with the job requisition code in the subject line. The system wasn't very workable. "If that code was not in the subject line, the e-mail would go into a black hole," Muller explains.

But even when the e-mails wound up with the right recruiter, there were major problems. To begin with, some candidates would apply to every open job on the web site, some of which they were legitimately qualified for and some of which they were not. Then the resumes wouldn't necessarily list the key information the recruiter needed, such as whether the applicant had worked on a particular piece of equipment. This meant that the recruiters would have to follow up with the candidates to chase down the missing information.

In the late 1990s, the company started looking for a better way of managing applications. It sent out a request for proposals and asked the strongest companies to make an in-depth presentation. In addition to HR staff, technical staff reviewed each vendor for data security. The company decided to go with an application service provider (ASP) model so the internal information technology (IT) group wouldn't have to support the application. This decision eliminated some other vendors from the running.

Southern selected Hire.com, a privately owned recruitment ASP headquartered in Austin, Texas. Its HireEnterprise suite contains three modules: electronic recruiting, applicant tracking, and staffing analytics.

Hire.com hosts the software in its data centers, and users access it through a browser. Customers have the option of purchasing just one of the modules rather than the entire package. For example, Southern uses just the recruitment software, while Plantronics uses both the recruitment and applicant tracking modules.

Since Southern didn't have to install and configure the software at its end, it took only thirty-five days to get the initial functions up and running. (Additional functions and more in-depth integration were added later.) After that, Hire.com sent in a team to train the recruiters on the software. The two-day process consisted of half a day of briefing, half a day of training, and then a full day of practice on the system.

"The great thing is that it is designed like a public Internet web site so it didn't really take any training, just a matter of getting used to it," says Muller. "If you can use [Amazon.com], you can use this software."

When applicants apply for a job on either Plantronics's or Southern's web site and clicks on the jobs link, it takes them to the Hire.com server, though there is nothing to indicate to an applicant that he or she is accessing a different site. There they can set up an account based on their education, job preferences, location, and so on and search for open positions. Applicants can also sign up to receive e-mail alerts when jobs that meet their criteria become available in the future. Southern reports that 60 percent of its job candidates come through this push feature.

The biggest advantage, however, is not in finding applicants, but in narrowing down which ones the company should pursue. Recruiters, after all, don't have time to read through hundreds of applications for a position. To simplify this, both Plantronics and Southern use the software's testing functions to prescreen candidates.

Answers to these screening questions can take several different forms, including yes/no, true/false, multiple choice, numerical, or text. Answers can be assigned different weights, and certain answers can also automatically include or exclude the applicant. Based on the responses, the software screens out any applicants who are not qualified and ranks those who do meet the criteria.

Here are some sample questions that can be included:

- How many years' experience in the industry do you have?
- In which subject do you have a master's degree?
- Are you used to functioning independently with minimum supervision?
- In how many research studies were you involved?
- What are your former employers in this sector?

Plantronics uses, on average, seventeen questions for each open position, but these vary from job to job. There is a core set of questions, most relating to software, with project management or people management questions added for any managerial position. Plantronics also asks questions that are applicable to a particular job, such as queries about the applicant's experience operating a specific piece of equipment or knowledge of a particular field.

When Southern started using the recruitment module, it screened out only around 40 percent of the applicants. By refining the questions, the company has increased that to 65 percent. Plantronics sometimes screens out as many as 95 percent. "By using the prescreening questions, the recruiter can spend time phone screening or following up on the best 10 applicants rather than having to sort through 100," says Muller.

Source: Adapted from Drew Robb, "Screening for Speedier Selection," *HRMagazine* 49, no. 9 (September 2004): 143–147.

QUESTIONS

1. What impact do you think Hire.com's screening tools have had on the HR departments of Southern and Plantronics?
2. What competitive advantages do you see in using online screening tools to screen applicants?
3. Do you see any drawbacks associated with the Hire.com system, and, if so, how might they be addressed?

NOTES AND REFERENCES

1. Patrick D. Converse, Fredrick L. Oswald, Michael A. Gillespie, Kevin A. Field, and Elizabeth B. Bizot, "Matching Individual to Occupations Using Abilities and the O*NET," *Personnel Psychology* 57, no. 2 (Summer 2004): 451–488; George Callaghan and Paul Thompson, "'We Recruit Attitude': The Selection and Shaping of Routine Call Centre Labour," *Journal of Management Studies* 39, no. 2 (March 2002): 233–54; Terry Beehr, Lana Ivanitskaya, Curtiss Hansen, Dmitry Erofeev, and David Gudanoski, "Evaluation of 360-Degree Feedback Ratings: Relationships with Each Other and with Performance and Selection Predictors," *Journal of Organizational Behavior* 22, no. 7 (November 2001): 775–88.
2. Helena D. Cooper-Thomas, Annelies Van Vianen, and Neil Anderson, "Changes in Person-Organization Fit: The Impact of Socialization Tactics on Perceived and Actual P-O Fit," *European Journal of Work & Organizational Psychology* 13, no. 1 (March 2004): 52–79; Dan Cable and Charles Parsons, "Socialization Tactics and Person-Organization Fit," *Personnel Psychology* 54, no. 1 (Spring 2001): 1–23; Amy Kristof-Brown, "Perceived Applicant Fit: Distinguishing between Recruiters' Perceptions of Person-Job and Person-Organization Fit," *Personnel Psychology* 53, no. 3 (Autumn 2000): 643–71.
3. Mary-Kathryn Zachary, "Discrimination without Intent," *Supervision* 64, no. 5 (May 2003): 23–29; Neal Schmitt, William

Rogers, David Chan, Lori Sheppard, and Danielle Jennings, "Adverse Impact and Predictive Efficiency of Various Predictor Combinations," *Journal of Applied Psychology* 82, no. 5 (October 1997): 719–30; Charlene Marmer Solomon, "Testing at Odds with Diversity Efforts?" *Personnel Journal* 75, no. 4 (April 1996): 131–40; Scott E. Maxwell and Richard D. Arvey, "The Search for Predictors with High Validity and Low Adverse Impact: Compatible or Incompatible Goals?" *Journal of Applied Psychology* 78, no. 3 (June 1993): 433–37.

4. Namok Choi, "A Psychometric Examination of the Personal Attributes Questionnaire," *Journal of Social Psychology* 144, no. 3 (June 2004): 348–52; Frank J. Landy, "Test Validity Yearbook," *Journal of Business Psychology* 7, no. 2 (1992): 111–257. See also Edwin E. Ghiselli, "The Validity of Aptitude Tests in Personnel Selection," *Personnel Psychology* 26, no. 4 (Winter 1973): 461–77; J. E. Hunter and R. H. Hunter, "Validity and Utility of Alternative Predictors of Job Performance," *Psychological Bulletin* 96 (1984): 72–98; Ivan Robertson and Mike Smith, "Personnel Selection," *Journal of Occupational and Organizational Psychology* 74, no. 4 (November 2001): 441–72.

5. Jesus F. Salgado and Neil Anderson, "Validity Generalization of GMA Tests across Countries in the European Community," *European Journal of Work & Organizational Psychology* 12, no. 1 (March 2003): 1–17; Calvin C. Hoffman and S. Morton McPhail, "Exploring Options for Supporting Test Use in Situations Precluding Local Validation," *Personnel Psychology* 51, no. 4 (Winter 1998): 987–1003; Leaetta Hough and Frederick Oswald, "Personnel Selection: Looking toward the Future—Remembering the Past," *Annual Review of Psychology* 51 (2000): 631–64.

6. Kobi Dayan, Ronen Kasten, and Shaul Fox, "Entry-Level Police Candidate Assessment Center: An Efficient Tool or a Hammer to Kill a Fly?" *Personnel Psychology* 55, no. 4 (Winter 2002): 827–50; S. Messick, "Foundations of Validity: Meaning and Consequences in Psychological Assessment," *European Journal of Psychological Assessment* 10 (1994): 1–9; Michael Lindell and Christina Brandt, "Assessing Interrater Agreement on the Job Relevance of a Test: A Comparison of the CVI, T, $r^{WG(J)}$, and $r^{*WG(J)}$ Indexes," *Journal of Applied Psychology* 84, no. 4 (August 1999): 640–47.

7. D. Brent Smith and Lill Ellingson, "Substance versus Style: A New Look at Social Desirability in Motivating Contexts," *Journal of Applied Psychology* 87, no. 2 (April 2002): 211–19; Ken Craik et al., "Explorations of Construct Validity in a Combined Managerial and Personality Assessment Programme," *Journal of Occupational and Organizational Psychology* 75, no. 2 (June 2002): 171–93.

8. "A New Assistant at Georgia Tech Made False Claims," *The New York Times,* January 29, 2002, D7; Stephanie Armour, "Security Checks Worry Workers; Padded Resumes Could Be Exposed," *USA Today,* June 19, 2002, B1.

9. Pamela Babock, "Spotting Lies," *HRMagazine* 48, no. 10 (October 2003): 46–51; Tammy Prater and Sara Bliss Kiser, "Lies, Lies, and More Lies," *A.A.M. Advance Management Journal* 67, no. 2 (Spring 2002): 9–14.

10. "The Pros and Cons of Online Recruiting," *HRFocus* 81 (April 2004): S1; Rob Drew, "Career Portals Boost Online Recruiting," *HRMagazine* 49, no. 4 (April 2004): 111–114; Samuel Greengard, "Smarter Screening Takes Technology and HR Savvy," *Workforce* 81, no. 6 (June 2002): 56–62; Scott R. Kaak, Hubert S. Field, William F. Giles, and Dwight R. Norris, "The Weighted Application Blank," *Cornell Hotel and Restaurant Administration Quarterly* 39, no. 2 (April 1998): 18–24; Brad Bingham, Sherrie Ilg, and Neil Davidson, "Great Candidates Fast: On-Line Job Application and Electronic Processing: Washington State's New Internet Application System," *Public Personnel Management* 31, no. 1 (Spring 2002): 53–64; Sarah Fister Gale, "Internet Recruiting: Better, Cheaper, Faster," *Workforce* 80, no. 12 (December 2001): 74–77; Tim Armes, "Internet Recruiting," *Canadian Manager* 24, no. 1 (Spring 1999): 21–22; "Top Firms Recruit on Web," *USA Today,* September 22, 2000, A1; Cora Daniels, "To Hire a Lumber Expert, Click Here," *Fortune* 141, no. 7 (April 3, 2000): 267–70.

11. Margaret A. McManus and Mary L. Kelly, "Personality Measures and Biodata: Evidence Regarding Their Incremental Predictive Value in the Life Insurance Industry," *Personnel Psychology* 52, no. 1 (Spring 1999): 137–48; Andrew J. Vinchur, Jeffrey S. Schippmann, Fred S. Switzer III, and Philip L. Roth, "A Meta-Analytic Review of Predictors of Job Performance for Salespeople," *Journal of Applied Psychology* 83, no. 4 (August 1998): 586–97; Gary R. Kettlitz, Imad Zbib, and Jaideep Motwani, "Validity of Background Data as a Predictor of Employee Tenure among Nursing Aides in Long-Term Care Facilities," *Health Care Supervisor* 16, no. 3 (March 1998): 26–31; Yen Chung, "The Validity of Biographical Inventories for the Selection of Salespeople," *International Journal of Management* 18, no. 3 (September 2001): 322–29; Teri Elkins and James Phillips, "Job Context, Selection Decision Outcome, and the Perceived Fairness of Selection Tests: Biodata as an Illustrative Case," *Journal of Applied Psychology* 85, no. 3 (June 2000): 479–84; Herschel Chait, Shawn Carreher, and M. Ronald Buckley, "Measuring Service Orientation with Biodata," *Journal of Managerial Issues* 12, no. 1 (Spring 2000): 109–20.

12. Doug Eisenschenk and Elaine Davis, "Background Checks in Hiring and Compensation: The Next Generation," *Benefits & Compensation Digest* 41, no 10 (October 2004): 1–4; "What's New," *HR Magazine* 49, no. 4 (April 2004): 153–156; "Why You Should Update Your Background Checks," *HR Focus* (February 2004): 12–13; Deborah L. O'Mara, "Help Yourself to Background Checks," *Security* 34, no. 3 (March 1997): 91–92; Merry Mayer, "Background Checks in Focus," *HRMagazine* 47, no. 1 (January 2002): 59–62. In addition, organizations use other resources, such as the following: *The Guide to Background Investigations: A Comprehensive Source Directory for Employee Screening and Background Investigations,* 8th ed. (TISI, 2000); *The Computerized Guide to Background Investigations,* Hi Tek Information Services, 4500 S. 129th East Avenue, Suite 200, Tulsa, OK 74134. For an article summarizing this system, see "Using Computers for Hiring," *The Futurist* 31, no. 1 (January/February 1997): 41.

13. Kathleen Samey, "A Not-So-Perfect Fit," *Adweek* 44, no. 47 (December 1, 2003): 34; Ann Fisher, "How Can We Be Sure

We're Not Hiring a Bunch of Shady Liars?" *Fortune* 147, no. 10 (May 26, 2003); Diane Lacy, Saundra Jackson, and Anne St. Martin, "References, Cafeteria Changes, Smokers," *HRMagazine* 48, no. 4 (April 2003): 37–38; Carolyn Hirschman, "The Whole Truth," *HRMagazine* 45, no. 6 (June 2000): 86–92; Samuel Greengard, "Are You Well Armed to Screen Applicants?" *Personnel Journal* (December 1995): 84–95; "The Final Rung: References," *Across the Board* (March 1996): 40; Judith Howlings, "Staff Recruitment: Your Rights and Obligations," *People Management* (May 30, 1996): 47; "Read between the Lines," *Management Today* (February 1996): 14; Diane Domeyer, "Reference Checks Offer Valuable Insight," *Women in Business* 51, no. 4 (July/August 1999): 32.

14. "Legal Issues Raised by Giving Bad References," *Fair Employment Practice Guidelines,* no. 594 (November 2004): 1–3; Robert L. Brady, "Employee Loses Defamation Suit over Bad Reference," *HRFocus* 73, no. 7 (July 1996): 20; Glenn Withiam, "Complexities of Employee References," *Cornell Hotel and Restaurant Administration Quarterly* 37, no. 3 (June 1996): 10; Mimi Moon, "Justices Consider FERPA in Student's Privacy Claim," *News Media and the Law* 26, no. 2 (Spring 2002): 37–38; Mary Connerley, Fred Mael, and Ray Morath, "Don't Ask—Please Tell: Selection Privacy from Two Perspectives," *Journal of Occupational and Organizational Psychology* 72, no. 4 (December 1999): 405–22. For a continuously updated listing of employment policy changes, see *Bulletin to Management* (Washington, DC: Bureau of National Affairs).

15. Diane Cadrian, "HR Professionals Stymied by Vanishing Job References," *HRMagazine* 49, no. 11 (November 2004): 31–32; Jane Easter Bahls, "Available upon Request?" *HRMagazine* 44, no. 1 (January 1999): H2–H6; Ellen Duffy McKay, "Reference Checks: A Legal Minefield," *HRFocus* 74, no. 12 (December 1997): S11–S12.

16. Barry J. Nadell, "The Cut of His Jib Doesn't Jibe," *Security Management* 48, no. 9 (September 2004): 108–114; William Atkinson, "Who Goes There?" *LP/Gas* 64, no. 9 (September 2004): 16–24; Amelia Deligiannis, "Fair Credit Reporting Act Pre-Emption Debate Heats Up," *Corporate Legal Times* 13, no. 139 (June 2003): 22–24; Gillian Flynn, "Are You Legal under the Fair Credit Reporting Act?" *Workforce* 77, no. 3 (March 1998): 79, 81; Scott F. Cooper, "The Fair Credit Reporting Act—Time for Employers to Change Their Use of Credit Information," *Employee Relations Law Journal* 24, no. 1 (1998): 57–71; Joyce Ostrosky, Linda Leinicke, W. Max Rexroad, and Jim Baker, "The Fair Credit Reporting Act: Time to Mind the Details," *Internal Auditor* 58, no. 6 (December 2001): 50–55.

17. "Pretext for Discrimination: How to Avoid Looking Like a Liar," *Fair Employment Practices Guidelines,* no. 592 (September 1, 2004): 1–3; Gillian Flynn, Diane D. Hatch, and James E. Hall, "Know the Background of Background Checks," *Workforce* 81, no. 9 (September 2002): 96–98; Bob Rosner, "How Do You Feel about the Use of Lie Detectors at Work?" *Workforce* 78, no. 6 (June 1999): 24–25; David Terpstra, R. Bryan Kethley, Richard Foley, and Wanthanee Limpaphayom, "The Nature of Litigation Surrounding Five Screening Devices," *Public Personnel Management* 29, no. 1 (Spring 2000): 43–54. With some exceptions for jobs in law enforcement, government agencies, and drug-dispensing firms, the following states have banned compulsory or involuntary polygraphing in employment situations: Alaska, California, Connecticut, Delaware, Georgia, Hawaii, Idaho, Iowa, Kansas, Maine, Maryland, Massachusetts, Michigan, Minnesota, Montana, Nebraska, Nevada, New Jersey, New York, Oregon, Pennsylvania, Rhode Island, Tennessee, Texas, Utah, Vermont, Virginia, Washington, West Virginia, and Wisconsin. The District of Columbia also prohibits such testing. Several states have some restrictions. See *BNA Policy and Practice Series—Personnel Management,* 1988, 201–51.

18. Paul Zielbauer, "Small Changes Could Improve Police Hiring, Panel Says," *The New York Times,* January 7, 1999, 8; Lynn McFarland and Ann Marie Ryan, "Variance in Faking across Noncognitive Measures," *Journal of Applied Psychology* 85, no. 5 (October 2000): 812–21; David Arnold and John Jones, "Who the Devil's Applying Now?" *Security Management* 46, no. 3 (March 2002): 85–88; "Polygraph Testing Considered Personnel Tool," *Crime Control Digest* 33, no. 14 (April 9, 1999): 4.

19. Constance L. Hays, "Tests Are Becoming Common in Hiring," *The New York Times,* November 28, 1997, D1. See also Gregory M. Lousig-Nont, "Avoid Common Hiring Mistakes with Honesty Tests," *Nation's Restaurant News* 31, no. 11 (March 17, 1997): 30; "If the Shoe Fits," *Security Management* 40, no. 2 (February 1996): 11; Michelle Cottle, "Job Testing: Multiple Choices," *The New York Times,* September 5, 1999, 3: 10.

20. Thomas J. Ryan, "Nerves of Steal," *SGB* 37, no. 6 (June 2004): 8–10; D. S. Ones, C. Viswesvaran, and F. L. Schmidt, "Comprehensive Meta-Analysis of Integrity Test Validities: Findings and Implications for Personnel Selection and Theories of Job Performance," *Journal of Applied Psychology* 78 (August 1993): 679–703. See also Deniz S. Ones and Chockalingam Viswesvaran, "Gender, Age and Race Differences on Overt Integrity Tests: Results across Four Large-Scale Job Applicant Data Sets," *Journal of Applied Psychology* 83, no. 1 (February 1998): 35–42; McFarland and Ryan, "Variance in Faking across Noncognitive Measures."

21. "Honesty Tests Flawed," *People Management* 3, no. 2 (January 23, 1997): 15; Hays, "Tests Are Becoming Common in Hiring"; Stephen A. Dwight and George M. Alliger, "Reactions to Overt Integrity Test Items," *Educational and Psychological Measurement* 57, no. 6 (December 1997): 937–48.

22. Klass Hogenesch, "A New Science for Finding the Right Employee?" *NZ Business* 18, no. 2 (March 2004): 10; Bill Leonard, "Reading Employees," *HRMagazine* 44, no. 4 (April 1999): 67–73; Steven Thomas and Steve Vaught, "The Write Stuff: What the Evidence Says about Using Handwriting Analysis in Hiring," *S.A.M. Advanced Management Journal* 66, no. 4 (Autumn 2001): 31–35.

23. Dirk D. Steiner and Stephen W. Gilliland, "Fairness Reactions to Personnel Selection Techniques in France and the United States," *Journal of Applied Psychology* 81, no. 2 (April 1996): 134–41.

24. Michael Adams, Ben Van Houten, Robert Klara, and Elizabeth Bernstein, "Access Denied?" *Restaurant Business* 98, no. 2 (January 15, 1999): 36–48; "Medical Screening: Are Employers Going Too Far?" *Employee Benefit Plan Review* 53, no. 11 (May 1999): 42–43.

25. "Accommodating Hearing-Impaired," *Fair Employment Practices Guidelines,* no. 587 (April 1, 2004): 1–3; Terpstra, Kethley, Foley, and Limpaphayom, "The Nature of Litigation Surrounding Five Screening Devices"; Teresa Burke Wright, "ADA Restricts Medical Inquiries," *Credit Union Magazine* 68, no. 3 (March 2002): 89.

26. "New Developments Question the Use of Drug Tests in the Workplace," *Safety Director's Report* 4, no. 9 (September 2004): 3–6; Sandy Smith, "What Every Employer Should Know about Drug Testing in the Workplace," *Occupational Hazards* 66, no. 8 (August 2004): 45–48; David May, "Testing by Necessity," *Occupational Health & Safety* 68, no. 4 (April 1999): 48–51; Ken Kunsman, "Cafeteria Plan Testing," *Occupational Health & Safety* 68, no. 4 (April 1999): 44–47; Bill Leonard, "Pot Smokers See Job Offers Go Up in Smoke," *HRMagazine* 44, no. 4 (April 1999): 30–32.

27. Rod Kurtz, "Testing, Testing . . . ," *Inc.* 26, no. 6 (June 2004): 35–38; Gillian Flynn, "A Legal Examination of Testing," *Workforce* 81, no. 6 (June 2002): 92–94; Gillian Flynn, "Pre-Employment Testing Can Be Unlawful," *Workforce* 78, no. 7 (July 1999): 82–83; Gilbert Nicholsen, "Screen and Glean: Good Screening and Background Checks Help Make the Right Match for Every Open Position," *Workforce* 79, no. 10 (October 2000): 70–72.

28. Ely A. Leightling and Pamela M. Ploor, "When Applicants Apply through the Internet." *Employee Relations Law Journal* 30, no. 2 (Autumn 2004): 3–13; "EEOC Clarifies the Definition of Who Is an 'Applicant' in the Context of Internet Recruiting and Hiring," *Fair Employment Practices Guidelines,* no. 587 (April 1, 2004): 3–13; Kathryn Tyler, "Put Applicants' Skills to the Test," *HRMagazine* 45, no. 1 (January 2000): 74–80. For a counterargument, see Kevin R. Murphy and Ann Harris Shiarella, "Implications of the Multidimensional Nature of Job Performance for the Validity of Selection Tests: Multivariate Frameworks for Studying Test Validity," *Personnel Psychology* 50, no. 4 (Winter 1997): 823–54.

29. For books with comprehensive coverage of testing, including employment testing, see Anne Anastasi and Susana Urbina, *Psychological Testing,* 7th ed. (New York: Macmillan, 1997); Gary Groth-Marnat, *Handbook of Psychological Assessment* (New York: John Wiley and Sons, 1996); Lee J. Cronbach, *Essentials of Psychological Testing,* 5th ed. (New York: HarperCollins, 1990).

30. Standards that testing programs should meet are described in *Standards for Educational and Psychological Tests* (Washington, DC: American Psychological Association, 1986). HR managers who want to examine paper-and-pencil tests should obtain specimen sets that include a test manual, a copy of the test, an answer sheet, and a scoring key. The test manual provides the essential information about the construction of the test; its recommended use; and instructions for administering, scoring, and interpreting the test. Test users should not rely entirely on the material furnished by the test author and publisher. A major source of consumer information about commercially available tests—the *Mental Measurements Yearbook (MMY)*—is available in most libraries. Published periodically, the *MMY* contains descriptive information plus critical reviews by experts in the various types of tests. The reviews are useful in evaluating a particular test for tryout in employment situations. Other sources of information about tests include *Test Critiques,* a set of volumes containing professional reviews of tests, and *Tests: A Comprehensive Reference for Assessments in Psychology, Education, and Business.* The latter describes more than 3,100 tests published in the English language. Another source, *Principles for the Validation and Use of Personnel Selection Procedures,* published by the Society for Industrial and Organizational Psychology, is a valuable guide for employers who use tests. Other publications present detailed information on how to avoid discrimination and achieve fairness in testing.

31. Harold W. Goldstein, Kenneth P. Yusko, Eric P. Braverman, D. Brent Smith, and Beth Chung, "The Role of Cognitive Ability in the Subgroup Differences and Incremental Validity of Assessment Center Exercises," *Personnel Psychology* 51, no. 2 (Summer 1998): 357–74; Sara Rynes, Amy Colbert, and Kenneth Brown, "HR Professionals' Beliefs about Effective Human Resource Practices: Correspondence between Research and Practice," *Human Resource Management* 41, no. 2 (Summer 2002): 149–74; Mary Roznowski, David Dickter, Linda Sawin, Valerie Shute, and Sehee Hong, "The Validity of Measures of Cognitive Processes and Generalizability for Learning and Performance on Highly Complex Computerized Tutors: Is the g Factor of Intelligence Even More General?" *Journal of Applied Psychology* 85, no. 6 (December 2000): 940–55.

32. Kris Frieswick, "Casting to Type," *CFO* 20, no. 9 (July 2004): 71– 73; Timothy Judge and Joyce Bono, "Five-Factor Model of Personality and Transformational Leadership," *Journal of Applied Psychology* 85, no. 5 (October 2000): 751–65; J. Michael Crant and Thomas S. Bateman, "Charismatic Leadership Viewed from Above: The Impact of Proactive Personality," *Journal of Organizational Behavior* 21, no. 1 (February 2000): 63–75.

33. Arielle Emmett, "Snake Oil or Science? The Raging Debate on Personality Testing," *Workforce Management* 83, no. 10 (October 2004): 90–93; Gregory Hurtz and John Donovan, "Personality and Job Performance: The Big Five Revisited," *Journal of Applied Psychology* 85, no. 6 (December 2000): 869–79.

34. George B. Yancey, "The Predictive Power of Hiring Tools," *Credit Union Executive Journal* 40, no. 4 (July–August 2000): 12–18; In the case of *Soroka v Dayton Hudson Corporation* (1993), plaintiffs sued on the grounds that the selection test violated California's Fair Employment laws and that certain items, especially MMPI items, constituted an unlawful invasion of privacy. Although the case was settled out of court, the California state appellate court, in a preliminary injunction, found that certain questions violated the plaintiffs' rights to privacy and that Target Stores had not shown these questions to be job-related. See Dwight and Alliger, "Reactions to Overt Integrity Test Items"; Daniel P. O'Meara, "Personality Tests Raise Questions of Legality and Effectiveness," *HRMagazine* 39, no. 1 (January 1994): 97–100; Jeffrey A. Mello, "Personality Tests and Privacy Rights," *HRFocus* 73, no. 3 (March 1996): 22–23.

35. Walter C. Borman, Mary Ann Hanson, and Jerry W. Hedge, "Personnel Selection," *Annual Review of Psychology* 48 (1997): 299–337; Charles Sproule and Stephen Berkley, "The Selection of Entry-Level Corrections Officers: Pennsylvania Research," *Public Personnel Management* 30, no. 3 (Fall 2001): 377–418.

36. M. S. Sothmann, D. L. Gebhardt, T. A. Baker, G. M. Kastello, and V. A. Sheppard, "Performance Requirements of Physically Strenuous Occupations: Validating Minimum Standards for Muscular Strength," *Ergonomics* 47, no. 8 (June 22, 2004): 864–76; T. L. Stanley, "The Wisdom of Employment Testing," *Supervision* 65, no. 2 (February 2004): 11–14.
37. It may be interesting to note that the origins of the civil service system go back to 2200 B.C., when the Chinese emperor examined officials every three years to determine their fitness for continuing in office. In 1115 B.C. candidates for government posts were examined for their proficiency in music, archery, horsemanship, writing, arithmetic, and the rites and ceremonies of public and private life.
38. Rachel Suff, "Testing the Water: Using Work Sampling for Selection," *IRS Employment Review,* no. 802 (June 18, 2004): 44–49; Leonard D. Goodstein and Alan D. Davidson, "Hiring the Right Stuff: Using Competency-Based Selection," *Compensation & Benefits Management* 14, no. 3 (Summer 1998): 1–10.
39. Linda Marsh, "By Their Actions Shall Ye Know Them," *Works Management* 50, no. 11 (November 1997): 52–53; Florence Berger and Ajay Ghei, "Employment Tests: A Facet of Hospitality Hiring," *Cornell Hotel and Restaurant Administration Quarterly* 36, no. 6 (December 1995): 28–31; Malcolm James Ree, Thomas R. Carretta, and Mark S. Teachout, "Role of Ability and Prior Job Knowledge in Complex Training Performance," *Journal of Applied Psychology* 80, no. 6 (December 1995): 721–30.
40. James Bassett, "Stop, Thief!" *Gifts & Decorative Accessories* 104, no. 1 (January 2003): 130–34; Cynthia Kay Stevens, "Antecedents of Interview Interactions, Interviewers' Ratings, and Applicants' Reactions," *Personnel Psychology* 51, no. 1 (Spring 1998): 55–85; Laura Gollub Williamson, James E. Campion, Stanley B. Malos, and Mark V. Roehling, "Employment Interview on Trial: Linking Interview Structure with Litigation Outcomes," *Journal of Applied Psychology* 82, no. 6 (December 1997): 900–12; Richard A. Posthuma, Frederick Morgeson, and Michael Campion, "Beyond Employment Interview Validity: A Comprehensive Narrative Review of Recent Research and Trends over Time," *Personnel Psychology* 55, no. 1 (Spring 2002): 1–8.
41. David E. Terpstra and Bryan R. Kethley, "Organizations' Relative Degree of Exposure to Selection Discrimination Litigation," *Public Personnel Management* 31, no. 3 (February 2002): 277–94; Schmidt and Rader, "Exploring the Boundary Conditions for Interview Validity"; Williamson, Campion, Malos, and Roehling, "Employment Interview on Trial."
42. "MSPB Calls for Use of Structured Interviews to Assess Candidates for Federal Jobs," *PA Times* 26, no. 5 (May 2003): 13; Robert J. Lavigna and Steven W. Hays, "Recruitment and Selection of Public Workers: An International Compendium of Modern Management Trends and Practices," *Public Personnel Management* 33, no. 3 (Fall 2004): 237–54; For an excellent review of research on the structured interview, see Michael A. Campion, David K. Palmer, and James E. Campion, "A Review of Structure in the Selection Interview," *Personnel Psychology* 50, no. 3 (Autumn 1997): 655–702. See also Karen van der Zee, Arnold Bakker, and Paulien Bakker, "Why Are Structured Interviews So Rarely Used in Personnel Selection?" *Journal of Applied Psychology* 87, no. 1 (February 2002): 176–84.
43. Jesus F. Salgado and Silvia Moscoso, "Compreshensive Meta-Analysis of the Construct Validity of the Employment Interview," *European Journal of Work and Organizational Psychology* 11, no. 3 (September 2002): 299–325; Allen Huffcutt, Jeff Weekley, Willi Wiesner, Timothy Degroot, and Casey Jones, "Comparison of Situational and Behavior Description Interview Questions for Higher-Level Positions," *Personnel Psychology* 54, no. 3 (Autumn 2001): 619–44.
44. Peter Herriot, "Assessment by Groups: Can Value Be Added?" *European Journal of Work & Organizational Psychology* 12, no. 2 (June 2003): 131–46; Salgado and Moscoso, "Comprehensive Meta-Analysis"; Amelia J. Prewett-Livingston, John G. Veres III, Hubert S. Field, and Philip M. Lewis, "Effects of Race on Interview Ratings in a Situational Panel Interview," *Journal of Applied Psychology* 81, no. 2 (April 1996): 178–86. See also Damodar Y. Golhar and Satish P. Deshpande, "HRM Practices of Large and Small Canadian Manufacturing Firms," *Journal of Small Business Management* 35, no. 3 (July 1997): 30–38; Philip L. Roth and James E. Campion, "An Analysis of the Predictive Power of the Panel Interview and Pre-Employment Tests," *Journal of Occupational and Organizational Psychology* 65 (March 1992): 51–60.
45. Michele V. Rafter, "Candidates for Jobs in High Places Sit for Tests That Size Up Their Mettle," *Workforce Management* 83, no. 5 (May 2004): 70–73; Patricia Buhler, "Computer Interview: Managing in the New Millennium," *Supervision* 63, no. 10 (October 2002): 20–23; For more information about Interactive Information Services, see their web site at http://www.iiserve.com/about.html.
46. Victoria Reitz, "Interview without Leaving Home," *Machine Design* 76, no. 7 (April 1, 2004): 66; Linda Thornburg, "Computer-Assisted Interviewing Shortens Hiring Cycle," *HRMagazine* 43, no. 2 (February 1998): 73–79; Dan Hanover, "Hiring Gets Cheaper and Faster," *Sales and Marketing Management* 152, no. 3 (March 2000): 87; Jessica Clark Newman et al., "The Differential Effects of Face-to-Face and Computer Interview Modes," *American Journal of Public Health* 92, no. 2 (February 2002): 294; David Mitchell, "ijob.com Recruiting Online," *Strategic Finance* 80, no. 11 (May 1999): 48–51.
47. Hanover, "Hiring Gets Cheaper and Faster."
48. Posthuma, Morgeson, Campion, "Beyond Employment Interview Validity"; Schmidt and Rader, "Exploring the Boundary Conditions for Interview Validity."
49. Multiple regression is a statistical method for evaluating the magnitude of effects of more than one independent variable (e.g., selection predictors) on a dependent variable (e.g., job performance) using principles of correlation and regression.
50. David E. Bowen and Cheri Ostroff, "Understanding HRM—Firm Performance Linkages: The Role of the Strengths of the HRM System," *Academy of Management Review* 29, no. 2 (April 2004): 203–22; Ann Marie Ryan, Joshua Sacco, Lynn McFarland, and David Kriska, "Applicant Self-Selection: Correlates of Withdrawal from a Multiple Hurdle Process," *Journal of Applied Psychology* 85, no. 2 (April 2000): 163–79.

chapter 7

Training and Development

After studying this chapter, you should be able to

Discuss the systems approach to training and development.

Describe the components of training-needs assessment.

Identify the principles of learning and describe how they facilitate training.

Identify the types of training methods used for managers and nonmanagers.

Discuss the advantages and disadvantages of various evaluation criteria.

Describe the special training programs that are currently popular.

Training has become increasingly vital to the success of modern organizations. Recall that in Chapter 2 we noted that organizations often compete on competencies—the core sets of knowledge and expertise that give them an edge over their competitors. Training plays a central role in nurturing and strengthening these competencies, and in this way has become part of the backbone of strategy implementation. In addition, rapidly changing technologies require that employees continuously hone their knowledge, skills, and abilities (KSAs) to cope with new processes and systems. Jobs that require little skill are rapidly being replaced by jobs that require technical, interpersonal, and problem-solving skills. Other trends toward empowerment, total-quality management, teamwork, and international business make it necessary for managers, as well as employees, to develop the skills that will enable them to handle new and more demanding assignments.

The Scope of Training

Many new employees come equipped with most of the KSAs needed to start work. Others may require extensive training before they are ready to make much of a contribution to the organization. Almost any employee, however, needs some type of ongoing training to maintain effective performance or to adjust to new ways of work.

The term *training* is often used casually to describe almost any effort initiated by an organization to foster learning among its members. However, many experts distinguish between *training*, which tends to be more narrowly focused and oriented toward short-term performance concerns, and *development*, which tends to be oriented more toward broadening an individual's skills for future responsibilities. The two terms tend to be combined into a single phrase—*training and development*—to recognize the combination of activities organizations use to increase the skill base of employees.

The primary reason that organizations train new employees is to bring their KSAs up to the level required for satisfactory performance. As these employees continue on the job, additional training provides opportunities for them to acquire new knowledge and skills. As a result of this training, employees may be even more effective on the job and may be able to perform other jobs in other areas or at higher levels.

Investments in Training

Research shows that an organization's revenues and overall profitability are positively correlated to the amount of training it gives its employees. According to *Training* magazine's ongoing industry report, U.S. businesses spend more than $50 billion annually to provide each of their employees with twenty-six hours, on average, of formal training. By contrast, the 100 best U.S. companies to work for, as cited by *Fortune* magazine in 2004, provide employees with nearly double that amount of training—forty-five hours, on average. While a good deal of money is spent on executive development and management training, Figure 7.1 shows that by far the greatest proportion of training is spent on rank-and-file employees and supervisors. Technology, trans-

Figure 7.1 Training Dollars Spent by Employee Type

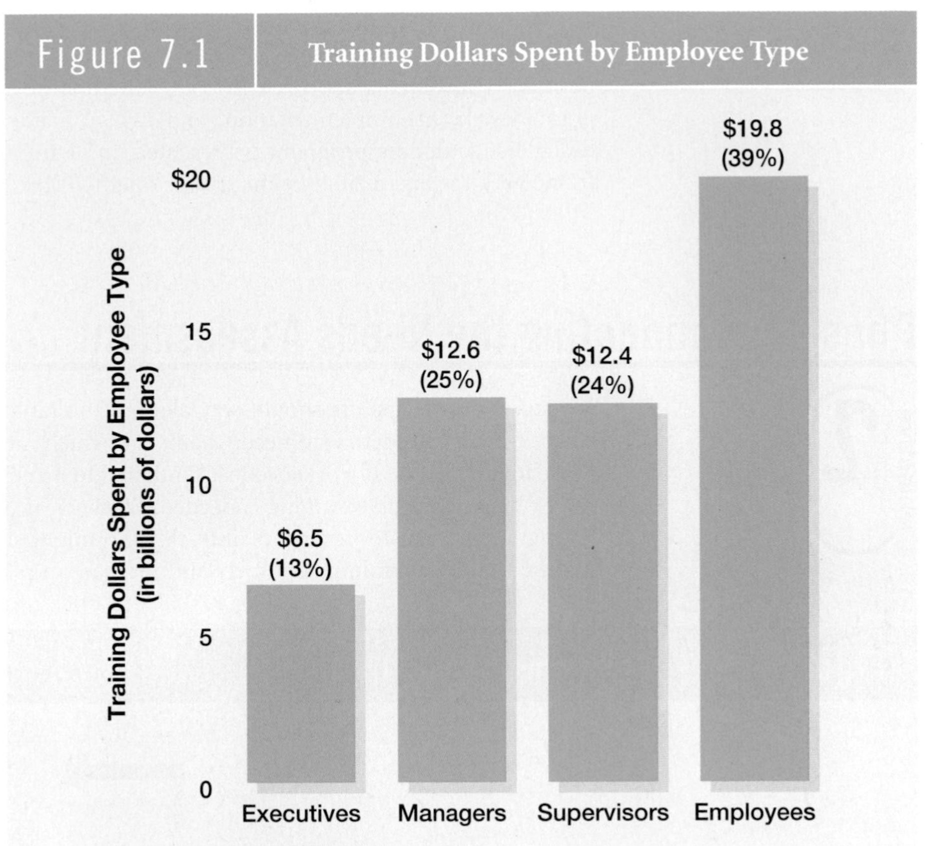

Source: Holly Dolezalek, "2004 Industry Report," *Training* (October 2004): 28.

portation, communications, and utilities industries tend to spend the most on training. In addition to the more than $50 billion spent by U.S. businesses each year on formal training, nearly *four times* that amount is spent on informal instruction. The types of training given employees range from simple, on-the-job instruction to sophisticated skills training conducted on multimillion-dollar simulators. Other types of training include customer service, sales and management training, personal growth, and communication skills training.[1]

A Systems Approach to Training

From the broadest perspective, the goal of training is to contribute to the organization's overall goals. Training programs should be developed with this in mind. Managers should keep a close eye on organizational goals and strategies and orient training accordingly. Unfortunately, many organizations never make the connection between their strategic objectives and their training programs. Instead, fads, fashions, or "whatever the competition is doing" can sometimes be the main drivers of an organization's training agenda. As a result, much of an organization's investment can be wasted—training programs are often misdirected, poorly designed, and inadequately evaluated—and these problems directly affect organizational performance.

To ensure that investments in training and development have maximum impact on individual and organizational performance, a systems approach to training should be used. The systems approach involves four phases: (1) needs assessment, (2) program design, (3) implementation, and (4) evaluation. A model that is useful to designers of training programs is presented in Figure 7.2. We will use this model as a framework for organizing the material throughout this chapter.

Phase 1: Conducting the Needs Assessment

Managers and HR staffs should stay alert to the kinds of training that are needed, where they are needed, who needs them, and which methods will best deliver needed KSAs to employees. If workers consistently fail to achieve productivity objectives, this might be a signal that training is needed. Likewise, if organizations receive an excessive number of customer complaints, this too might suggest inadequate training. To make certain that training is timely and focused on priority issues, managers should

Figure 7.2 Systems Model of Training

PHASE 1:
Needs Assessment
• Organization analysis
• Task analysis
• Person analysis

PHASE 2:
Design
• Instructional objectives
• Trainee readiness
• Learning principles

PHASE 3:
Implementation
• On-the-job methods
• Off-the-job methods
• Management development

PHASE 4:
Evaluation
• Reactions
• Learning
• Behavior (transfer)
• Results

Note:
U.S. organizations spend more than $50 billion annually on training. Much of that investment is wasted because it is not done in a systematic way.

approach needs assessment systematically by utilizing the three different types of analysis shown in Figure 7.3: organization analysis, task analysis, and person analysis. Each of these is discussed next.

To ensure that their firms' training dollars are spent wisely, about half of managers surveyed by the Institute of Management and Administration (IOMA) say their companies engage in needs assessment before initiating a training program. But much of the money spent on training still goes wasted. A separate study by the American Society for Training and Development (ASTD) found that, unfortunately, because of the costs, expertise, and time required, organizations conduct needs assessment less than 50 percent of the time. Ironically, as the speed of change increases, and time and resources are at a premium, the need for good needs assessment actually increases. In these cases, the process need not be so daunting and laborious. Highlights in HRM 1 provides some tips for rapidly assessing training needs.[2]

Organization Analysis

organization analysis Examination of the environment, strategies, and resources of the organization to determine where training emphasis should be placed

The first step in needs assessment is identifying the broad forces that can influence training needs. **Organization analysis** is an examination of the environment, strategies, and resources of the organization to determine where training emphasis should be placed.

Economic and public policy issues influence training needs. For example, since the September 11 attacks, the training of airport security personnel has increased substantially. It has also increased for flight crews of airlines, employees in the transportation industry, workers in nuclear power plants, and even security staff at theme parks.

According to Chris Rogers, senior consultant for loss control in the Entertainment Practices Group of Aon Corporation (a risk management firm), there is an emphasis today on training theme park security in a tactic called "aggressive hospitality," which calls for staff to greet people and look them in the eye and offer to assist, rather than waiting to be approached by visitors. "This is one of the best and simplest security measures," he says. When staff members engage visitors, they become more aware of them. This heightened level of attention also discourages troublemakers from coming to the facility, because they generally go where they can remain anonymous.[3]

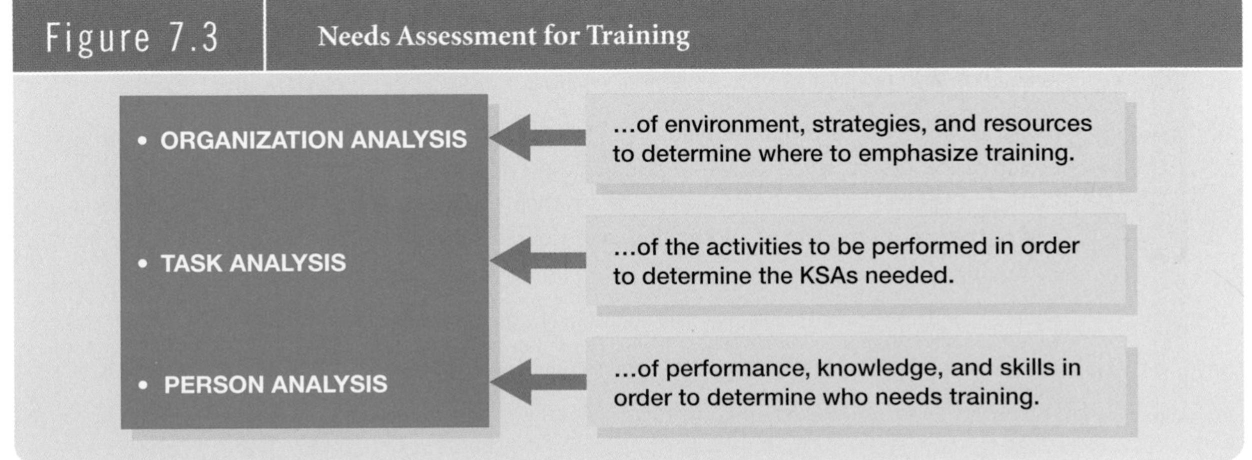

Highlights in HRM 1

Notes on Rapid Needs Assessment

NOTE 1: Look at the problem scope. Common sense suggests that small, local matters may require less information gathering than big problems with a major impact on the organization. Ask managers a series of questions about the nature of the problem and its impact on the organization and gear your analysis accordingly.

NOTE 2: Do organizational scanning. Stay connected with what is going on in the organization in order to anticipate upcoming training needs. If a new technology is about to be launched, the need for training should take no one by surprise. In short, needs assessment isn't an event with a start-and-stop switch. It is the process of being engaged in your business.

NOTE 3: Play "give and take." Get the information you need, but don't drag your feet with excessive analysis before reporting back to managers. Show them that you are sensitive to their need for action by giving them updates on the information you have collected. If necessary, explain that better value may be gained by further analysis.

NOTE 4: Check "lost and found." Often, information gathered for a different purpose may bear on your training issue. Performance data (such as errors, sales, and customer complaints) and staffing data (such as proficiency testing, turnover, and absenteeism) can be very helpful as a starting point.

NOTE 5: Use plain talk. Instead of using clinical terms such as *analysis* or *assessment*, use straight talk with managers that tells them what you are doing: (1) Identify the problem, (2) identify alternative ways to get there, (3) implement a solution based on cost/benefit concerns, and (4) determine the effectiveness and efficiency of the solution.

NOTE 6: Use the Web. Information technology allows you to communicate with others, perhaps by setting up an electronic mailing list to post questions, synthesize responses, share resources, get feedback, gather information on trends, and the like.

NOTE 7: Use rapid prototyping. Often the most effective and efficient training is that which is "just-in-time, just enough, and just for me." Create a rapid prototype of a training program, evaluating and revising as you implement and learn more about the problems.

NOTE 8: Seek out exemplars. Find those in the organization that currently demonstrate the performance the organization wants. Bring others together with them to talk about the performance issues, and let the exemplars share their experiences and insights. This avoids the risk of packaging the wrong information, and people learn just what they need to know from each other.

Source: Condensed from Ron Zemke, "How to Do a Needs Assessment When You Think You Don't Have Time," *Training* 35, no. 3 (March 1998): 38–44. Reprinted with permission from the March 1998 issue of *Training Magazine*.

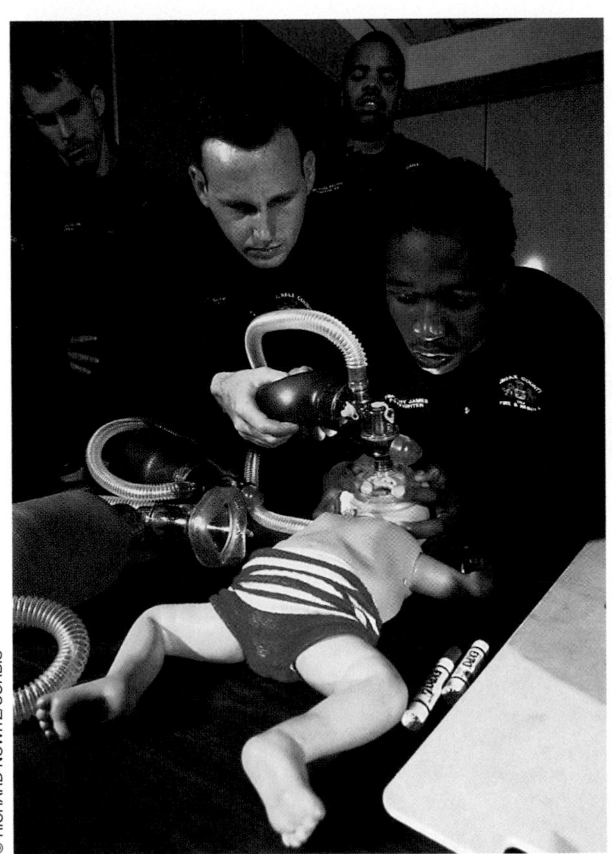
© RICHARD NOWITZ/CORBIS

A company must carefully analyze the job duties of its employees to determine their training needs.

Other training issues tend to revolve around the strategic initiatives of an organization. Mergers and acquisitions, for example, frequently require that employees take on new roles and responsibilities and adjust to new cultures and ways of conducting business. Nowhere is this more prevalent than in grooming new leaders within organizations. Other issues such as technological change, globalization, reengineering, and total quality management all influence the way work is done and the types of skills needed to do it. Still other concerns may be more tactical, but no less important in their impact on training. Organizational restructuring, downsizing, empowerment, and teamwork, for example, have immediate training requirements. Finally, trends in the workforce itself have an impact on training needs. As older workers near retirement, younger workers need to focus on gaining the skills and knowledge needed to take their place. Organizations as diverse as Intel and Boeing are facing situations in which they need to prepare the next generations of employees as the current groups approach retirement.

Side by side with forces that influence training needs, organization analysis involves close examination of the resources—technological, financial, and human—that are available to meet training objectives. Organizations typically collect data to use in the analysis, data such as information on direct and indirect labor costs, quality of goods or services, absenteeism, turnover, and number of accidents. The availability of potential replacements and the time required to train them are other important factors in organization analysis.

In recent years, as organizations continue to keep a tight rein on costs, training budgets are often constrained—even while organizations recognize the need for more and better training. To cope with resource constraints while contributing to strategic imperatives, managers have to be more focused and efficient with their training budgets. Companies such as Motorola, Ford, and Merck have found that by using information technology wisely, they cut their training budget by as much as 30 to 50 percent while keeping service levels high. In order to "do more with less," managers have to plan carefully where they will spend their training dollars, and this means doing rigorous organization analysis. Other companies have outsourced their training programs to external partners in order to cut costs. However, evidence suggests that while many companies find they can provide equal or better service to employees in this way, surprisingly few actually reduce their training costs as a result.[4]

task analysis
The process of determining what the content of a training program should be on the basis of a study of the tasks and duties involved in the job

Task Analysis

The second step in training-needs assessment is task analysis. **Task analysis** involves reviewing the job description and specifications to identify the activities performed in a particular job and the KSAs needed to perform them. Task analysis often becomes more detailed than job analysis, but the overall purpose is to determine the exact content of the training program.

The first step in task analysis is to list all the tasks or duties included in the job. The second step is to list the steps performed by the employee to complete each task. Once the job is understood thoroughly, the type of performance required (such as speech, recall, discrimination, and manipulation), along with the skills and knowledge necessary for performance, can be defined. For example, in the task of taking a chest x-ray, a radiologist correctly positions the patient (manipulation), gives special instructions (speech), and checks the proper distance of the x-ray tube from the patient (discrimination). The types of performance skills and knowledge that trainees need can be determined by observing and questioning skilled jobholders and/or by reviewing job descriptions. This information helps trainers select program content and choose the most effective training method.

competency assessment
Analysis of the sets of skills and knowledge needed for decision-oriented and knowledge-intensive jobs

However, like job analysis, task analysis appears to be shifting from an emphasis on a fixed sequence of tasks to the more flexible sets of competencies required for superior performance. Companies such as Case Financial and the Principal Financial Group have found that as jobs change toward teamwork, flexibility requires that employees adjust their behavior as needed. **Competency assessment** focuses on the sets of skills and knowledge employees need to be successful, particularly for decision-oriented and knowledge-intensive jobs. But competency assessment goes beyond simply describing the traits an employee must have to successfully perform the work. It also captures elements of how those traits should be used within an organization's context and culture. That might include an employee's motivation levels, personality traits, interpersonal skills, and so on. General Electric, for example, uses a formal competency assessment program based on forty-five different employee behaviors. While training programs based on work-oriented task analysis can become dated as work undergoes dynamic change, training programs based on competency assessment are more flexible and perhaps have more durability. The practice has been adopted extensively in the healthcare industry. Highlights in HRM 2 shows an example of a competency assessment used for designing training programs for public health professionals. The American Public Human Services Association has adopted the model as an infrastructure for training universal skills.[5]

Person Analysis

person analysis
Determination of the specific individuals who need training

Along with organization and task analyses, it is necessary to perform a person analysis. **Person analysis** involves determining which employees require training and, equally important, which do not. In this regard, person analysis is important for several reasons. First, thorough analysis helps organizations avoid the mistake of sending all employees into training when some do not need it. In addition, person analysis helps managers determine what prospective trainees are able to do when they enter training so that the programs can be designed to emphasize the areas in which they are deficient.

Companies such as Teradyne and Hewlett-Packard have used performance appraisal information as an input for person analysis. However, while performance appraisal may reveal who is not meeting expectations, it typically does not reveal why. If performance deficiencies are due to ability problems, training may likely be a good intervention. However, if performance deficiencies are due to poor motivation or factors outside an employee's control, training may not be the answer. Ultimately

Competency Assessment for Training Public Health Workers

- Analytic discipline
  - Determining appropriate use of data and statistical methods
  - Making relevant inferences from data
- Communication discipline
  - Communicating effectively both in writing and orally
  - Presenting accurately and effectively demographic, statistical, programmatic, and scientific information for professional and lay audiences
- Policy and program-planning discipline
  - Developing mechanisms to monitor and evaluate programs (effectiveness, quality)
- Culture discipline
  - Developing and adapting approaches that take into account cultural differences
- Basic science discipline
  - Understanding research methods in all basic public health sciences
  - Applying the basic public health sciences, including behavioral and social sciences, biostatistics, epidemiology, environmental public health, and prevention of chronic and infectious diseases and injuries
- Finance and management discipline
  - Monitoring program performance
- Orientation to public health
  - Public health process
  - Core functions and essential services
  - Ethics and values of public health
  - Legal basis of public health

Source: Margaret Potter, Christine Pistella, Carl Fertman, and Virginia Dato, "Needs Assessment and a Model Agenda for Training the Public Health Workforce," *American Journal of Public Health* 90, no. 8 (August 2000): 1294–96. Reprinted by permission of American Public Health Association.

managers have to sit down with employees to talk about areas for improvement so that they can jointly determine the developmental approaches that will have maximum benefit.[6]

Phase 2: Designing the Training Program

Once the training needs have been determined, the next step is to design the type of learning environment necessary to enhance learning. The success of training programs depends on more than the organization's ability to identify training needs.

Success hinges on taking the information gained from needs analysis and utilizing it to design first-rate training programs. Experts believe that training design should focus on at least four related issues: (1) instructional objectives, (2) trainee readiness and motivation, (3) principles of learning, and (4) characteristics of instructors.

Instructional Objectives

instructional objectives Desired outcomes of a training program

As a result of conducting organization, task, and person analyses, managers will have a more complete picture of the training needs. On the basis of this information, they can more formally state the desired outcomes of training through written instructional objectives. Generally, **instructional objectives** describe the skills or knowledge to be acquired and/or the attitudes to be changed. One type of instructional objective, the performance-centered objective, is widely used because it lends itself to an unbiased evaluation of results. For example, the stated objective for one training program might be that "Employees trained in team methods will be able to perform these different jobs within six months." Performance-centered objectives typically include precise terms, such as "to calculate," "to repair," "to adjust," "to construct," "to assemble," and "to classify."

Robert Mager, an internationally known training expert, emphasizes the importance of instructional objectives by noting that "before you prepare for instruction, before you select instructional procedures or subject matter or material, it is important to be able to state clearly just what you intend the results of that instruction to be. A clear statement of instructional objectives will provide a sound basis for choosing methods and materials and for selecting the means for assessing whether the instruction will be successful."[7]

Trainee Readiness and Motivation

Two preconditions for learning affect the success of those who are to receive training: readiness and motivation. *Trainee readiness* refers to both maturity and experience factors in the trainee's background. Prospective trainees should be screened to determine that they have the background knowledge and the skills necessary to absorb what will be presented to them. Recognizing individual differences in readiness is as important in organizational training as it is in any other teaching situation. It is often desirable to group individuals according to their capacity to learn, as determined by test scores, and to provide an alternative type of instruction for those who need it.

The receptiveness and readiness of participants in training programs can be increased by having them complete questionnaires about why they are attending training and what they hope to accomplish. Participants may also be asked to give copies of their completed questionnaires to their managers.

The other precondition for learning is *trainee motivation.* Individuals who are conscientious, goal-oriented, self-disciplined, and persevering are more likely to perceive a link between effort they put into training and higher performance on the job. For optimum learning to take place, trainees must recognize the need for new knowledge or skills, and they must maintain a desire to learn as training progresses. By focusing on the trainees themselves rather than on the trainer or training topic, managers can create a training environment that is conducive to learning. Six strategies can be essential:

1. Use positive reinforcement.
2. Eliminate threats and punishment.
3. Be flexible.
4. Have participants set personal goals.
5. Design interesting instruction.
6. Break down physical and psychological obstacles to learning.

While most employees are motivated by certain common needs, they differ from one another in the relative importance of these needs at any given time. For example, new college graduates often have a high desire for advancement, and they have established specific goals for career progression. Training objectives should be clearly related to trainees' individual needs to succeed in training programs.[8]

Principles of Learning

As we move from needs assessment and instructional objectives to employee readiness and motivation, we shift from a focus on the organization to a focus on employees. Ultimately, training has to build a bridge between employees and the organization. One important step in this transition is giving full consideration to the psychological principles of learning—that is, the characteristics of training programs that help employees grasp new material, make sense of it in their own lives, and transfer it back to the job.

Because the success or failure of a training program is frequently related to certain principles of learning, managers as well as employees should understand that different training methods or techniques vary in the extent to which they utilize these principles. All things considered, training programs are likely to be more effective if they incorporate the principles of learning shown in Figure 7.4.

Goal Setting

The value of goal setting for focusing and motivating behavior extends into training. When trainers take the time to explain the goals and objectives to trainees—or when trainees are encouraged to set goals on their own—the level of interest, understanding, and effort directed toward training is likely to increase. In some cases, goal setting can simply take the form of a "road map" of the course/program, its objectives, and its learning points.[9]

Meaningfulness of Presentation

One principle of learning is that the material to be learned should be presented in as meaningful a manner as possible. Quite simply, trainees are better able to learn new information (from training) if they can connect it with things that are already familiar to them. Trainers frequently use colorful examples to which trainees can relate. The examples make the material meaningful. In addition, material should be arranged so that each experience builds on preceding ones. In this way, trainees are able to integrate the experiences into a usable pattern of knowledge and skills.

Modeling

The old saying "A picture is worth a thousand words" applies to training. Just as examples increase the meaningfulness of factual material or new knowledge in a training environment, modeling increases the salience of behavioral training. Work by

Figure 7.4 Principles of Learning

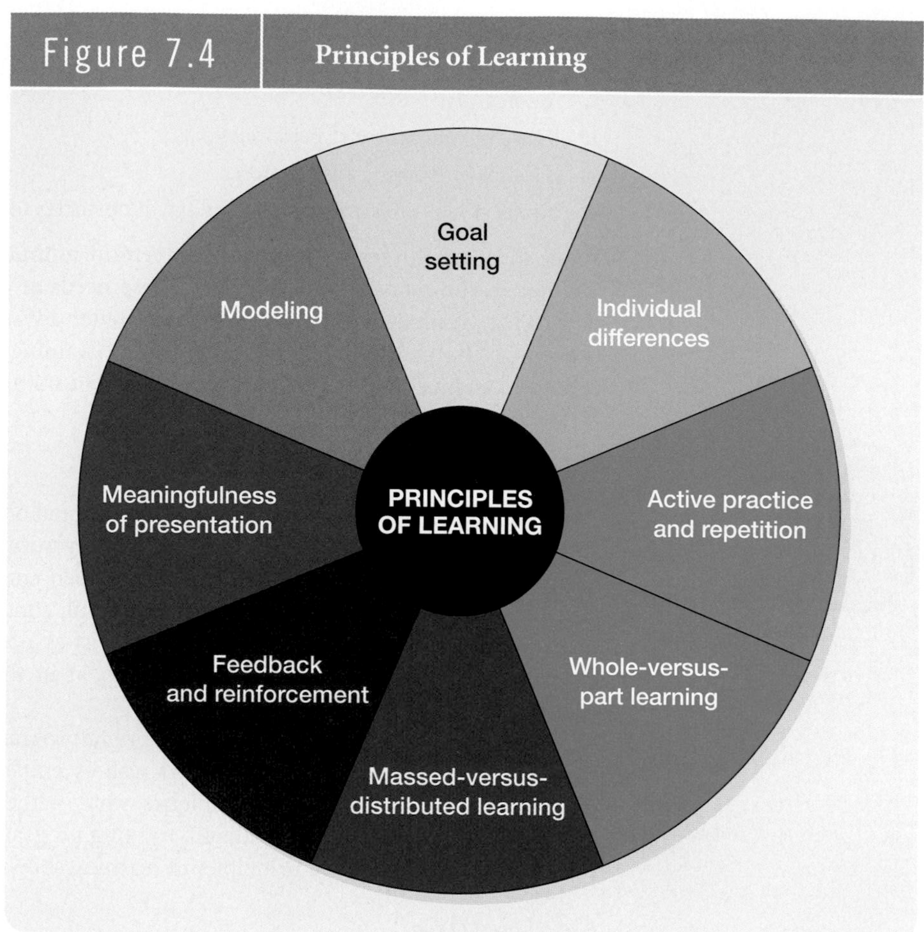

Albert Bandura and others on social learning theory underscores the point that we learn vicariously. Quite simply, we learn by watching. For example, if you were learning to ride a horse, it would be much easier to watch someone do it—and then try it yourself—than to read a book or listen to a lecture and hope you can do it right.[10]

Modeling can take many forms. For example, real-life demonstrations or videotapes are often helpful; even pictures and drawings can get the visual message across. The point is that modeling demonstrates the desired behavior or method to be learned. In some cases, modeling the wrong behavior can even be helpful if it shows trainees what not to do and then clarifies the appropriate behavior.

Individual Differences

People learn at different rates and in different ways. For example, some individuals can remember new information after hearing it only once (echoic memory) or seeing it only once (iconic memory). Others may have to work longer or find other techniques for retrieving the information, but this may have nothing to do with their intelligence. Some students do horribly in large lecture settings but then excel in small discussion classes. Others may have the opposite ability. To the extent possible, training programs should try to account for and accommodate these individual differences in order to facilitate each person's style and rate of learning.[11]

Active Practice and Repetition

Those things we do daily become a part of our repertoire of skills. Trainees should be given frequent opportunity to practice their job tasks in the way that they will ultimately be expected to perform them. The individual who is being taught how to operate a machine should have an opportunity to practice on it. The manager who is being taught how to train should be given supervised practice in training.

In some cases, the value of practice is that it causes behaviors to become second nature. For example, when you first learned to drive a car, you focused a great deal on the mechanics: "Where are my hands, where are my feet, how fast am I going?" As you practiced driving, you began to think less about the mechanics and more about the road, the weather, and the traffic. Other forms of learning are no different—by practicing, a trainee can forget about distinct behaviors and concentrate on the subtleties of how they are used.

Whole-versus-Part Learning

Most jobs and tasks can be broken down into parts that lend themselves to further analysis. Determining the most effective manner for completing each part then provides a basis for giving specific instruction. Learning to sell a product, for example, is made up of several skills that are part of the total process. Although the process sounds daunting, it can essentially be broken down into a few discrete steps: finding customer opportunities; eliciting a prospective customer's needs by learning the proper questions to ask him or her; presenting the firm's product in a way that meets those needs; and finally, learning how and when to ask the customer to buy the product (closing the deal). In evaluating whole-versus-part learning, it is necessary to consider the nature of the task to be learned. If the task can be broken down successfully, it probably should be broken down to facilitate learning; otherwise, it should probably be taught as a unit.

Massed-versus-Distributed Learning

Another factor that determines the effectiveness of training is the amount of time devoted to practice in one session. Should trainees be given training in five two-hour periods or in ten one-hour periods? It has been found in most cases that spacing out the training will result in faster learning and longer retention. This is the principle of *distributed learning*. Since the efficiency of the distribution will vary with the type and complexity of the task, managers should refer to the rapidly growing body of research in this area when they require guidance in designing a specific training situation.

Feedback and Reinforcement

Can any learning occur without feedback? Some feedback comes from self-monitoring while other feedback comes from trainers, fellow trainees, and the like. As an employee's training progresses, feedback serves two related purposes: (1) knowledge of results and (2) motivation.

The informational aspects of feedback help individuals focus on what they are doing right and what they are doing wrong. In this way, feedback serves a "shaping" role in helping individuals approach the objectives of training. Think about when you first learned how to throw a baseball, ride a bicycle, or swim. Someone, perhaps a parent, told you what you were doing right and what things to correct. As you did, you perhaps got better.

In addition to its informational aspects, feedback also serves an important motivational role. At times, progress in training, measured in terms of either mistakes or successes, may be plotted on a chart commonly referred to as a "learning curve." Figure 7.5 presents an example of a learning curve common in the acquisition of many job skills. In many learning situations there are times when progress does not occur. Such periods show up on the curve as a fairly straight horizontal line called a *plateau.* A plateau may be the result of reduced motivation or of ineffective methods of task performance. It is a natural phenomenon of learning, and there is usually a spontaneous recovery, as Figure 7.5 shows.

Verbal encouragement or more extrinsic rewards may help reinforce desired behavior over time. At times, reinforcement is simply the feeling of accomplishment that follows successful performance. (In some cases it may be impossible to distinguish between feedback and rewards.) Reinforcement is generally most effective when it occurs immediately after a task has been performed.

behavior modification
A technique that operates on the principle that behavior that is rewarded, or positively reinforced, will be exhibited more frequently in the future, whereas behavior that is penalized or unrewarded will decrease in frequency

In recent years some work organizations have used **behavior modification,** a technique that operates on the principle that behavior that is rewarded—positively reinforced—will be exhibited more frequently in the future, whereas behavior that is penalized or unrewarded will decrease in frequency. For example, in safety training it is possible to identify "safe" behavioral profiles—that is, actions that ensure fewer accidents—as well as unsafe profiles. As a follow-up to training, or as part of the training itself, managers can use relatively simple rewards to encourage and maintain desired behavior. Companies such as Monsanto, GE, and Bowater (the largest newsprint maker in America) have found that nothing more than words of encouragement and feedback are needed to strengthen the behaviors required and desired from training. Other more formal rewards such as awards and ceremonies may prove useful as well. However, the idea with behavior modification is that behavior can be motivated and gradually shaped toward the desired profile using reinforcement.[12]

Figure 7.5 A Typical Learning Curve

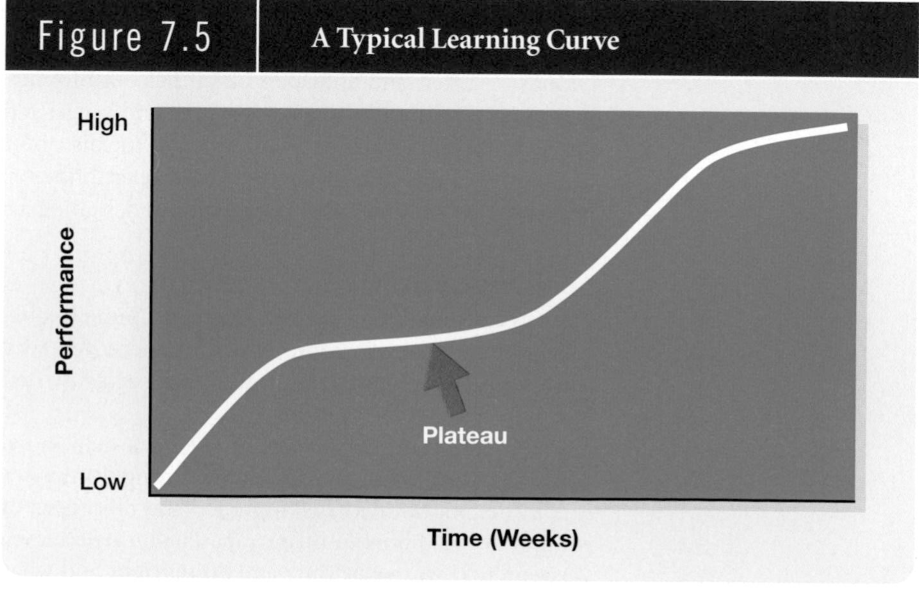

Characteristics of Instructors

The success of any training effort will depend in large part on the teaching skills and personal characteristics of those responsible for conducting the training. What separates good trainers from mediocre ones? Often a good trainer is one who shows a little more effort or demonstrates more instructional preparation. However, training is also influenced by the trainer's personal manner and characteristics. Here is a short list of desirable traits:

1. *Knowledge of subject.* Employees expect trainers to know their job or subject thoroughly. Furthermore, they are expected to demonstrate that knowledge (what some experts call "active intelligence").
2. *Adaptability.* Some individuals learn faster or slower than others, and instruction should be matched to the trainee's learning ability.
3. *Sincerity.* Trainees appreciate sincerity in trainers. Along with this, trainers need to be patient with trainees and demonstrate tact in addressing their concerns.
4. *Sense of humor.* Learning can be fun; very often a point can be made with a story or anecdote.
5. *Interest.* Good trainers have a keen interest in the subject they are teaching; this interest is readily conveyed to trainees.
6. *Clear instructions.* Naturally, training is accomplished more quickly and retained longer when trainers give clear instructions.
7. *Individual assistance.* When training more than one employee, successful trainers always provide individual assistance.
8. *Enthusiasm.* A dynamic presentation and a vibrant personality show trainees that the trainer enjoys training; employees tend to respond positively to an enthusiastic climate.[13]

For training programs to be most successful, organizations should reward managers who prove to be excellent trainers. Too often managers are not recognized for their contributions to this important aspect of HRM. Likewise, training specialists in the HR function should be recognized for their role in the training program.

Phase 3: Implementing the Training Program

Despite the importance of needs assessment, instructional objectives, principles of learning, and the like, choices regarding instructional methods are where "the rubber meets the road" in implementing a training program. A major consideration in choosing among various training methods is determining which ones are appropriate for the KSAs to be learned. For example, if the material is mostly factual, methods such as lecture, classroom, or programmed instruction may be fine. However, if the training involves a large behavioral component, other methods such as on-the-job training, simulation, or computer-based training (CBT) might work better.[14]

In order to organize our discussion of various training methods, we will break them down into two primary groups: those used for nonmanagerial employees and those used for managers.

Training Methods for Nonmanagerial Employees

A wide variety of methods are available for training employees at all levels. Some methods have a long history of usage. Newer methods have emerged over the years out of a greater understanding of human behavior, particularly in the areas of learning, motivation, and interpersonal relationships. More recently, technological advances, especially in computer hardware and software, have resulted in training devices that in many instances are more effective and economical than the traditional training methods.

On-the-Job Training

on-the-job training (OJT) A method by which employees are given hands-on experience with instructions from their supervisor or other trainer

By far, the most common method used for training nonmanagerial employees is **on-the-job training (OJT).** In fact, one estimate suggests that organizations spend three to six times as much on OJT as on classroom training. OJT has the advantage of providing hands-on experience under normal working conditions and an opportunity for the trainer—a manager or senior employee—to build good relationships with new employees. As time becomes a critical resource—and "just-in-time training" is needed most—OJT is viewed by some to be potentially the most effective means of facilitating learning in the workplace.[15]

Although it is used by all types of organizations, OJT is often one of the most poorly implemented training methods. Three common drawbacks are (1) the lack of a well-structured training environment, (2) poor training skills of managers, and (3) the absence of well-defined job performance criteria. To overcome these problems, training experts suggest the following:

1. Develop realistic goals and/or measures for each OJT area.
2. Plan a specific training schedule for each trainee, including set periods for evaluation and feedback.
3. Help managers establish a nonthreatening atmosphere conducive to learning.
4. Conduct periodic evaluations, after training is completed, to prevent regression.[16]

Highlights in HRM 3 shows the basic steps of an OJT program. The method is used frequently in organizations to ensure that new employees have adequate guidance before taking on work responsibilities on their own. For example, KLM Royal Dutch Airlines uses on-the-job training to train its cabin attendants. The airline started a program that places cabin attendant trainees in the classroom for a certain period and then gives them additional training during an evaluation flight. On these flights, experienced cabin attendants provide the trainees with on-the-job training, based on a list of identified job tasks. Some tasks, such as serving meals and snacks, are demonstrated during the actual delivery of services to passengers. Other tasks are presented to trainees away from passengers between meal service.[17]

Apprenticeship Training

apprenticeship training A system of training in which a worker entering the skilled trades is given thorough instruction and experience, both on and off the job, in the practical and theoretical aspects of the work

An extension of OJT is **apprenticeship training.** With this method, individuals entering industry, particularly in the skilled trades such as machinist, laboratory technician, and electrician, are given thorough instruction and experience, both on and off the job, in the practical and theoretical aspects of the work. For example, Bonneville Power Administration and General Physics Corporation developed an apprenticeship program for substation operators to give employees both a strong

Highlights in HRM 3

The PROPER Way to Do On-the-Job Training

P	**Prepare.** Decide what employees need to be taught. Identify the best sequence or steps of the training. Decide how best to demonstrate these steps. Have materials, resources, and equipment ready.
R	**Reassure.** Put each employee at ease. Learn about his or her prior experience, and adjust accordingly. Try to get the employee interested, relaxed, and motivated to learn.
O	**Orient.** Show the employee the correct way to do the job. Explain why it is done this way. Discuss how it relates to other jobs. Let him or her ask lots of questions.
P	**Perform.** When employees are ready, let them try the job themselves. Give them an opportunity to practice the job and guide them through rough spots. Provide help and assistance at first, then less as they continue.
E	**Evaluate.** Check the employees' performance, and question them on how, why, when, and where they should do something. Correct errors; repeat instructions.
R	**Reinforce and Review.** Provide praise and encouragement, and give feedback about how the employee is doing. Continue the conversation and express confidence in his or her doing the job.

Source: Scott Snell, Cornell University.

technical foundation in the fundamentals of electricity and a hands-on ability to operate equipment within the power substation. Ultimately the program was also designed to help future electrical operators respond to emergencies. In Europe, organizations such as BAE Systems and Ford Motor Company use apprenticeship programs extensively for their engineers. Highlights in HRM 4 gives an overview of the usage and benefits of apprenticeship training in the state of Washington.[18]

Interestingly, a Detroit-based organization called Focus: HOPE provides young, low-income, unemployed adults apprenticeship opportunities to learn advanced manufacturing skills for today's high-tech jobs. Among other opportunities, Focus: HOPE has established the Center for Advanced Technology, which offers a six-year curriculum that integrates structured work experience and study in applied engineering with computer-integrated manufacturing in collaboration with companies such as Cisco, Microsoft, and the Computer Technology Industry Association.[19]

While apprenticeship programs originated in Europe as part of its guild system, they have been adapted for use in the United States. Typically, the programs involve cooperation between organizations and their labor unions, between industry and government, or between organizations and local school systems. In the United States today, nearly 31,000 organizations have registered their programs with the U.S. Department of Labor's Bureau of Apprenticeship and Training (BAT), including

Job Outlook

Electronics Installer Complex electronic equipment—such as in generating plants, defense systems, and air traffic control—are installed, maintained, and repaired by electrical/electronics installers and repairers. Knowledge of electrical equipment and electronics is necessary for employment, and many applicants learn through one- to two-year programs at vocational schools or community colleges. Salaries range from $18,000 to $85,000 per year, depending on the specialty.

Source: *Occupational Outlook Handbook,* 2004–05 Edition, http://www.bls.gov/oco.

Highlights in HRM 4

About Apprenticeship in Washington State

Apprenticeship is an age-old way of learning something new that has proven successful over the centuries. Apprenticeship can lead us into the future with a highly skilled, diverse workforce. Apprenticeship offers several unique benefits:

- You "earn while you learn"—making a living wage with healthcare, retirement, and other benefits while learning skills in a trade.
- Wages increase progressively as your skill level increases by learning the trade both in the classroom and working under the guidance of a journey-level worker on the job site.
- After completion of an apprenticeship program, your journey-level status provides an additional benefit of nationwide mobility at journey-wage scale.

Apprenticeship is not just a job, but a career choice and commitment. Once you have decided on a trade, apply to the Washington State–approved apprenticeship program in your area offering training in that trade. There may not be immediate openings in that program, and you may need to put your name on a waiting list. Apprenticeship programs usually bring in new apprentices only when there are enough jobs to keep all apprentices working. Some trades accept applications only at certain times of the year. Others require that you find a job in the trade before you are accepted into the program.

Apprenticeship is a rewarding but demanding choice that requires determination, commitment, attitude, and physical conditioning to succeed. Because construction work is seasonal, if you choose a career in this field, you will need to stretch your budget in preparation for layoffs. You need to stay in excellent physical shape, and remain drug and alcohol free, even when you are not working.

For those who meet the challenges of apprenticeship, the rewards are substantial. A journey-level worker is guaranteed excellent wages and benefits anywhere in the United States. He or she is a highly trained, skilled worker whose qualifications are recognized and respected throughout the industry. Apprenticeship is one of the best ways to acquire work experience and training to establish yourself in a career.

Training—Classroom and On-the-Job

Classroom training requires six to forty-eight hours each week, depending on the trade. These classes may run evenings, during the day, or on weekends.

On-the-job training involves working with and learning from experienced journey-level workers. During this training period, you will receive wages for your work. The starting wage for beginning apprentices is usually about 50 percent of the journey-level rate; it increases regularly as you satisfactorily progress through the program. Near the end of the training, an apprentice is performing as a skilled worker and is earning close to the journey-level wage.

Programs

- Asbestos Workers
- Associated General Contractors
- Avista Line Construction
- Boilermakers
- Bricklayers/Tilesetters
- Carpenters
- Cement Masons
- Electrical Workers
- Homebuilders/Residential Carpenters
- Ironworkers
- Laborers
- Painters
- Plumbers/Steamfitters
- Roofers
- Sheet Metal Workers
- Tree Trimmers

Source: Adapted from Spokane Community College web site, http://www.scc.spokane.edu/tech/apprent/default.htm.

employers, and the number of apprentices, including minorities, women, youth, and dislocated workers, totals more than 480,000. (Approximately two-thirds of these are in construction and manufacturing industries.) Generally, an apprentice is paid 50 percent of a skilled journey worker's wage to start with, but the wage increases at regular intervals as the apprentice's job skills increase. When the apprentice successfully completes the apprenticeship, he or she becomes a certified journey-level worker earning full pay. According to BAT, many journey workers earn as much as college graduates and some earn more.[20]

cooperative training A training program that combines practical on-the-job experience with formal educational classes

Cooperative Training, Internships, and Governmental Training

Similar to apprenticeships, **cooperative training** programs combine practical on-the-job experience with formal classes. However, the term *cooperative training* is typically

© PETER HVIZDAK/THE IMAGE WORKS

Apprenticeships are a good way to train employees, especially in skilled-trade industries.

used in connection with high school and college programs that incorporate part- or full-time experiences. In recent years there has been an increased effort to expand opportunities that combine on-the-job skill training with regular classroom training so that students can pursue either technical work or a college degree program. Many organizations, including Fannie Mae, Burger King, Champion International, Cray Research, and First UNUM Life Insurance, have invested millions of dollars in educational cooperative training programs in conjunction with public schools.

internship programs
Programs jointly sponsored by colleges, universities, and other organizations that offer students the opportunity to gain real-life experience while allowing them to find out how they will perform in work organizations

Internship programs, jointly sponsored by colleges, universities, and a variety of organizations, offer students the chance to get real-world experience while finding out how they will perform in work organizations. Organizations benefit by getting student-employees with new ideas, energy, and eagerness to accomplish their assignments. Arizona State University, Cornell University, and many other universities and community colleges allow students to earn college credits on the basis of successful job performance and fulfillment of established program requirements. Highlights in HRM 5 shows how to make the most from internship opportunities.[21]

The federal government and various state governments have begun working together with private employers to sponsor a multitude of training programs for new and current employees through approximately 1,900 career centers nationwide. Funded by the Workforce Investment Act of 1998 (discussed in Chapter 5), these One Stop career centers (sometimes called "Job Service" or "Workforce Development" centers) have enabled thousands of organizations to help local citizens get jobs and job training assistance. The One Stop centers were modeled on Minnesota's successful program to help workers find jobs, help employers find qualified workers, and provide job training and other employment services all under one roof (hence the name *One Stop*). 3M, Northwest Airlines, Honeywell, and General Mills are just a few of the companies involved in the One Stop program.[22]

Classroom Instruction

When most people think about training, they think about classrooms. There is good reason for this. Beyond its pervasiveness in education, classroom training enables the maximum number of trainees to be handled by the minimum number of instructors. This method lends itself particularly well to what is called "blended" learning in which lectures and demonstrations are combined with films, DVDs, videotapes, or computer instruction. When it is not possible to obtain videotapes, audiotapes can be very valuable. For example, to instruct flight-crew trainees, airlines might play actual cockpit tapes recorded on airplanes involved in accidents. After listening to the tape, the trainees discuss the behavior of the crew during the crisis. By listening to the recorded statements of others and observing their failure to operate as a team, pilot trainees will develop an understanding of the need for balancing their sense of self-reliance with an ability to listen to subordinates. Despite the rise of many other types of learning—electronic and otherwise—classroom instruction is still the number one training method, as Figure 7.6 shows.[23]

Programmed Instruction

One method of instruction that is particularly good for allowing individuals to work at their own pace is programmed instruction. Programmed instruction—increasingly referred to as *self-directed learning*—involves the use of books, manuals, or computers to break down subject matter content into highly organized, logical sequences that demand continuous response on the part of the trainee. After being presented with a small segment of information, the trainee is required to answer a

Highlights in HRM 5

Making the Most of Internships

Today, many colleges and universities encourage students to apply for internships as part of the curriculum. Done well, internships provide advantages to students, universities, and potential employers.

Benefits for Students

Those who intern with organizations before graduation have higher starting salaries, more job offers, a shorter time in which they obtain their first position, faster movement into jobs with more prestige, greater challenges and financial rewards, and faster promotion. They are better prepared for the world of work.

Benefits for Universities

Internships help colleges get in touch with the marketplace. As students succeed in the workplace, student recruitment improves. Strong internship programs increase the retention of students and their placement after graduation.

Benefits for Potential Employers

Interns can provide your organization with competent assistance without a large financial outlay. Internships also let organizations evaluate a prospective employee nearly risk-free. At the end of the internship, there are no obligations to continue the relationship, but if it's a good match the organization has a leg up on hiring the person—it eliminates recruitment expenses and greatly reduces the cost per hire.

How to Increase the Value of Interns

To increase the internal value of your internship programs, take the following steps:

1. Assign the intern to projects that are accomplishable and provide training as required.
2. Involve the intern in the project-planning process.
3. Appoint a mentor or supervisor to guide the intern.
4. Invite project suggestions from other staff members.
5. Ask interns to keep a journal of their work activities.
6. Rotate interns throughout the organization.
7. Explain the rationale behind work assignments.
8. Hold interns accountable for projects and deadlines.
9. Treat interns as part of the organizational staff and invite them to staff meetings.
10. Establish a process for considering interns for permanent hire.

Source: Condensed from John Byrd and Rob Poole, "Highly Motivated Employees at No Cost? It's Not an Impossible Dream," *Nonprofit World* 19, no. 6 (November/December 2001): 312–32. Reprinted by permission of *Nonprofit World*, http://www.snpo.org, telephone: 734-451-3582.

question, either by writing it in a response screen or by pushing a button. If the response is correct, the trainee is told so and is presented with the next step (screen) in the material. If the response is incorrect, further explanatory information is given and the trainee is told to try again.

Figure 7.6 Delivery Method of Training

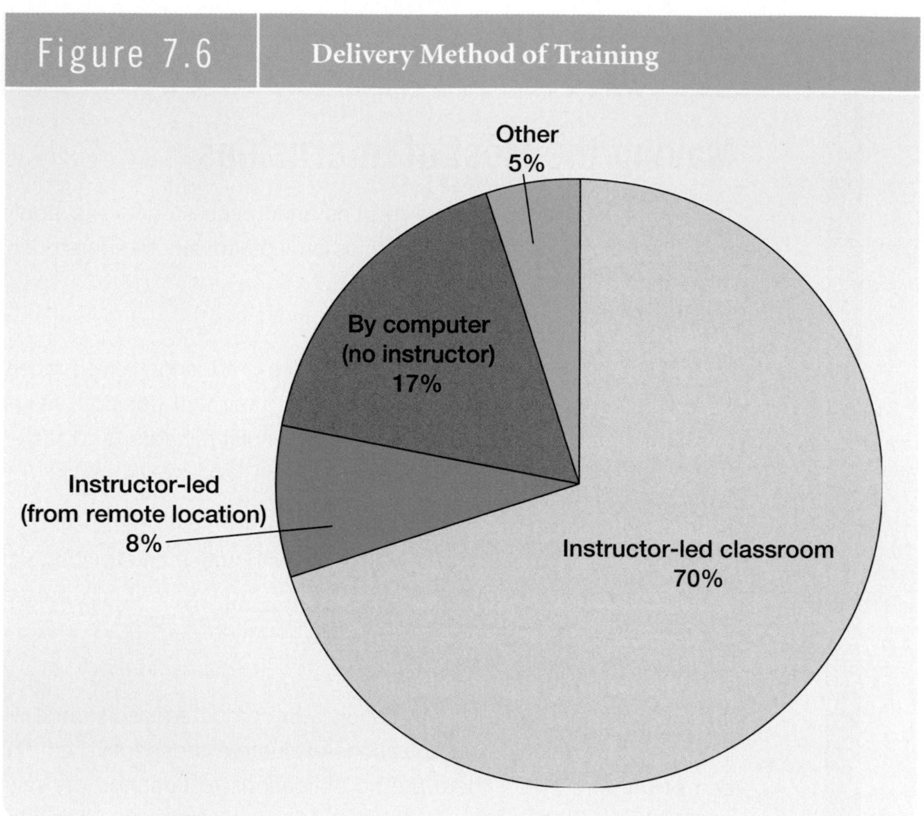

Source: Holly Dolezalek, "2004 Industry Report," *Training* (October 2004): 32.

A major advantage of programmed instruction is that it incorporates a number of the established learning principles discussed earlier in the chapter. With programmed instruction, training is individualized, trainees are actively involved in the instructional process, and feedback and reinforcement are immediate. While programmed instruction may not increase the amount an individual learns, it typically increases the speed at which he or she learns.

Audiovisual Methods

To teach skills and procedures for many production jobs, certain audiovisual devices can be used. At the simplest level, videotapes are often used to illustrate the steps in a procedure such as assembling electronic equipment or working with a problem employee. Using camcorders permits trainers and trainees to view an on-the-spot recording and to get immediate feedback about progress toward learning objectives. Golf and tennis coaches frequently tape their students to let them see their mistakes.

Other technologies, such as CDs and DVDs, allow trainees to access any segment of the instructional program, which is especially useful for individualized instruction when employees have different levels of knowledge and ability. Such technology is currently used to teach doctors to diagnose illness, to help dairy farmers increase their productivity, and to teach CPR trainees to revive victims of heart attacks. More recent applications tackle the difficult managerial skills of leadership, supervision, and interpersonal relations.

Interestingly, the South Dakota Army National Guard has used "teletraining" to teach its multiple-launch rocket system conversion process. In the past, soldiers would wait several months to complete a typical correspondence course. Teletraining enabled soldiers to breeze through CD-ROMs during weekend drills and interact with an instructor during the telephone sessions to get immediate feedback on their progress. Soldiers can complete the modules at their own pace and review the modules as necessary. Audio and video clips on the CD-ROMs enhance the instruction by capturing the soldier's attention and provide a visual demonstration of the task to be performed. The teletraining sessions allow the soldier to ask a qualified, experienced instructor questions on the material covered on the CD-ROMs from a list the soldiers have written in advance.[24]

Extending these kinds of video technologies with a teleconferencing infrastructure allows an instructional program to be transmitted to many locations simultaneously and permits immediate interaction among trainees. These methods are becoming quite powerful as tools for bringing continuing- and distance-education to life. The School of Industrial and Labor Relations at Cornell University, for example, has successfully used teleconferencing and technologies to connect executives at companies such as IBM, General Motors, Motorola, and Boeing and students in real time from around the globe in order to discuss issues, share ideas and best-practices models, and engage in web chats and bulletin board and videoconference exchanges.[25]

E-Learning

e-learning
Learning that takes place via electronic media

The simpler, audiovisual, programmed, and computer-oriented training methods just discussed are evolving into what trainers today refer to as e-learning. **E-learning** covers a wide variety of applications such as web and computer-based training (CBT) and virtual classrooms. It includes delivery of content via the Internet, intranets and extranets, audiotape, videotape, satellite and broadcast interactive TV, DVD, and CD-ROM. E-learning makes it possible to provide drill and practice, problem solving, simulation, gaming forms of instruction, and certain very sophisticated forms of individualized tutorial instruction in a way that's more engaging for learners than traditional classroom instruction. It is also cheaper for employers to administer because, in many instances, it can be delivered directly via employees' PCs. Companies are engaging in more e-learning than ever before and are reporting that they are saving anywhere from 30 to 70 percent on their training costs by doing so.[26]

USING THE INTERNET

Motorola is a high-tech firm, and much of its training uses multimedia technologies. Read how Motorola University extends training worldwide by using the Internet and CD-ROM technologies; go to the Student Resources at:

http://bohlander.swlearning.com

E-learning transforms the learning process in several ways. First, as we have said, it allows the firm to bring the training to employees rather than vice versa, which is generally more efficient and cost-effective. The nuclear power plant industry is a case in point: Nuclear power plant training is frequent and time-consuming. For workers just to remove their protective gear and commute to a separate training venue can take anywhere from an hour to more. One nuclear power company that switched to e-learning reported that it saved nearly $1 million and 10,000 employee hours in just a year by doing so.

E-learning also allows employees to search through a virtual sea of information in order to customize their own learning in their own time and space. More companies are demanding access to individual training components for employees to use when and where they need them. This helps alleviate the boredom trainees experience during full-blown training courses, and employees are more likely to retain the information when they can immediately put it to use. When one of TimeWarner Cable's service representatives is unsure about how to a process a work order, he or she can click on an e-learning simulation and get a step-by-step tutorial. Similarly, Cisco has 3,000 training VoDs (videos on demand) that employees can download off the company's intranet as needed. As new training VoDs are published by managers at Cisco, older, less requested VoDs are automatically removed and archived.[27]

Although e-learning systems can be very sophisticated, they need not be overly expensive. Many e-learning training programs use existing applications employees are familiar with such as PowerPoint, Word, and Adobe Acrobat and convert them into Flash programs so they can be easily viewed online with any web browser. Web-based training can also be revised rapidly, thereby providing continuously updated training material. This not only makes it easier and cheaper to revise training curricula, but also saves travel and classroom costs. When combined with other communications technology such as e-mail, teleconferencing, videoconferencing, and groupware, web-based training can be even more effective. A summary of these advantages includes the following:

- Learning is self-paced.
- The training comes to the employee.
- The training is interactive.
- Employees do not have to wait for a scheduled training session.
- The training can focus on specific needs as revealed by built-in tests.
- Trainees can be referred to online help or written material.
- It is easier to change a web site than to retype, photocopy, and distribute new classroom-training materials.
- Record keeping is facilitated.
- The training can be cost-effective if used for both large and small numbers of employees.

One catch to e-learning is that it requires some planning so that both employees in-house connecting through a fast corporate Internet connection and employees offsite with wireless modems or slow dialup connections are able to access the training material. To cope with this limitation, companies frequently supply their offsite personnel with CDs and DVDs containing the training material employees onsite are able to download. Or, like AT&T, they offer low-bandwidth employees alternate training presentations with still photos versus streamed video for downloading. Highlights in HRM 6 shows the different types of media firms use to train their employees and the frequency with which they use the media.

Simulation Method

Sometimes it is either impractical or unwise to train employees on the actual equipment used on the job. An obvious example is training employees to operate aircraft, spacecraft, and other highly technical and expensive equipment. The simulation method emphasizes realism in equipment and its operation at minimum cost and maximum safety.

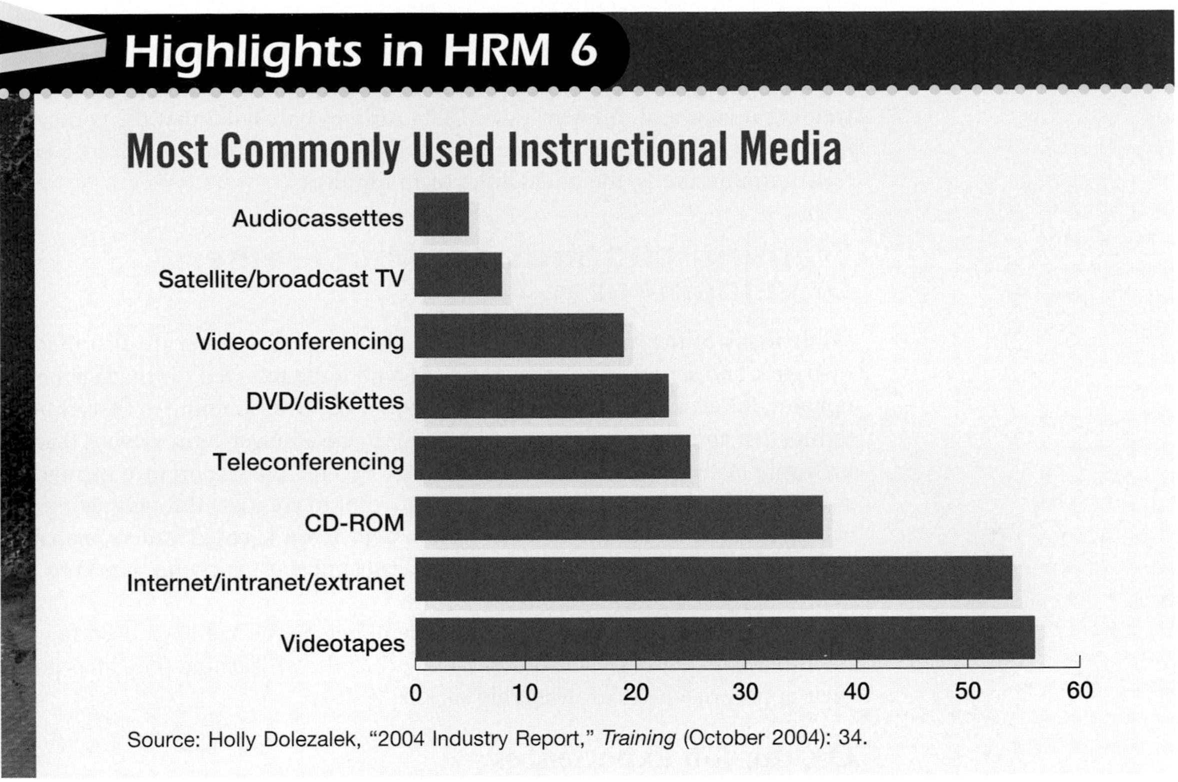

Source: Holly Dolezalek, "2004 Industry Report," *Training* (October 2004): 34.

Southwest Airlines boasts perhaps the most technologically advanced flight simulator in the airline industry: a $10.8 million full-motion Boeing 737-700 unit housed in an 110,000-square-foot flight operations training center adjacent to Southwest's headquarters at Dallas's Love Field. The facility can house up to six 737 simulators and can train up to 300 (of Southwest's 4,100) pilots at one time. The center has a staff of 110 employees. In addition to the simulators and their associated briefing and computer programming rooms, the training center houses eight classrooms, each fully equipped with closed-circuit TV, computers, conventional audiovisual equipment, and telephone and Internet hookups. On an average day, the flight operations training center will have 80 to 120 pilots in its classrooms and on its simulators. Facing a serious worker shortage, the Federal Aviation Administration developed a sophisticated simulator to dramatically speed up the training of air traffic controllers, a process that used to take as long as five years. Variables such as wind speed, precipitation, and the number of airplanes to be guided can be adjusted on the simulator to test the ability of trainees. Trainees who do poorly in certain situations are then targeted for additional training in those areas. The U.S. military has invested heavily in simulators to train soldiers for combat. The computerized devices, among other things, can simulate the interior of tanks, fighting vehicles, and other equipment, which can then be linked together to train an entire platoon, company, or battalion.[28]

As with e-learning and computer-based training, the distinction between simulation and computer-based training has blurred. For example, a simulation developed by Wicat in partnership with Airbus and Singapore Airlines runs on a PC and replicates a cockpit with control displays and throttle/flap controls. Even though the

PC-based simulation is relatively inexpensive, it is powerful. Pilots are taken through a self-paced program that simulates "taxi, takeoff, climb, cruise, descent, approach, landing, and go-around." These types of technologies are making it easier to offer training in new and different ways. Delta Airlines has stated that the company's goal is to deliver simulation training to employees at their homes. Given advances in telecommunications, the possibilities seem limitless.[29]

Training Methods for Management Development

While many of the methods used to train first-level employees are also used to train managers and supervisors, other methods tend to be reserved for management development. Recall that development differs somewhat from training in that its purpose is to broaden an individual's experience and provide a longer-term view of that individual's role in the organization. Over the past decade, the importance of management development has grown as organizations attempt to compete through people. Organizational change and strategic revitalization depend on talented leaders, managers, and supervisors. Management development is instrumental for giving managers the skills and perspectives they need to be successful.[30]

As with training for nonmanagerial employees, the methods used for management development differ in terms of the principles of learning they incorporate and their appropriateness for delivering various KSAs.

On-the-Job Experiences

Some skills and knowledge can be acquired just by listening and observing or by reading. But others must be acquired through actual practice and experience. By presenting managers with the opportunities to perform under pressure and to learn from their mistakes, on-the-job development experiences are some of the most powerful and commonly used techniques.

However, just as on-the-job training for first-level employees can be problematic if not well planned, on-the-job management development should be well organized, supervised, and challenging to the participants. Methods of providing on-the-job experiences include the following:

1. *Coaching* involves a continuing flow of instructions, comments, and suggestions from the manager to the subordinate. (*Mentoring*, discussed in Chapter 5, is a similar approach to personal and informal management development.)
2. *Understudy assignments* groom an individual to take over a manager's job by gaining experience in handling important functions of the job.
3. *Job rotation* provides, through a variety of work experiences, the broadened knowledge and understanding required to manage more effectively.
4. *Lateral transfer* involves horizontal movement through different departments, along with upward movement in the organization.
5. *Special projects* and *junior boards* provide an opportunity for individuals to become involved in the study of current organizational problems and in planning and decision-making activities.
6. *Action learning* gives managers release time to work full-time on projects with others in the organization. In some cases, action learning is combined with classroom instruction, discussions, and conferences.

7. *Staff meetings* enable participants to become more familiar with problems and events occurring outside their immediate area by exposing them to the ideas and thinking of other managers.
8. *Planned career progressions* (discussed in Chapter 5) utilize all these different methods to provide employees with the training and development necessary to progress through a series of jobs requiring higher and higher levels of knowledge and/or skills.[31]

Although these methods are used most often to develop managers for higher-level positions, they also provide valuable experiences for those who are being groomed for other types of positions in the organization. And while on-the-job experiences constitute the core of management training and development, other off-the-job methods of development can be used to supplement these experiences.

Seminars and Conferences

Seminars and conferences, like classroom instruction, are useful for bringing groups of people together for training and development. In management development, seminars and conferences can be used to communicate ideas, policies, or procedures, but they are also good for raising points of debate or discussing issues (usually with the help of a qualified leader) that have no set answers or resolutions. In this regard, seminars and conferences are often used when attitude change is a goal.

Outside seminars and conferences are often conducted jointly with universities and consulting firms. One such program that focuses on management development is the Leadership Grid. The seminars focus on two dimensions of effective leadership: *concern for people* and *concern for production.* These two dimensions are represented in the grid shown in Figure 7.7. The developers of the grid, Robert Blake and Jane Srygley Mouton, use a combination of seminars, discussions, and personal reflection to help managers achieve what they refer to as the "9, 9" leadership style ("Team Management" in Figure 7.7). By participating in seminars, managers and supervisors learn to identify necessary personal and organizational changes and to become more effective in their interpersonal relationships and their work groups.

Other seminars, on topics ranging from communications to strategic planning, are offered by organizations such as the American Management Association, the Conference Board, and the Center for Creative Leadership.

Case Studies

A particularly useful method used in classroom learning situations is the case study. The FBI, for example, uses its Integrated Case Scenario method to bring together new agents in a logical way. Using documented examples, participants learn how to analyze (take apart) and synthesize (put together) facts, to become conscious of the many variables on which management decisions are based, and, in general, to improve their decision-making skills. Experienced educators and trainers generally point out that the case study is most appropriate when:

1. Analytic, problem-solving, and critical-thinking skills are most important.
2. The KSAs are complex and participants need time to master them.
3. Active participation is desired.
4. The process of learning (questioning, interpreting, and so on) is as important as the content.
5. Team problem solving and interaction are possible.[32]

Figure 7.7 The Leadership Grid

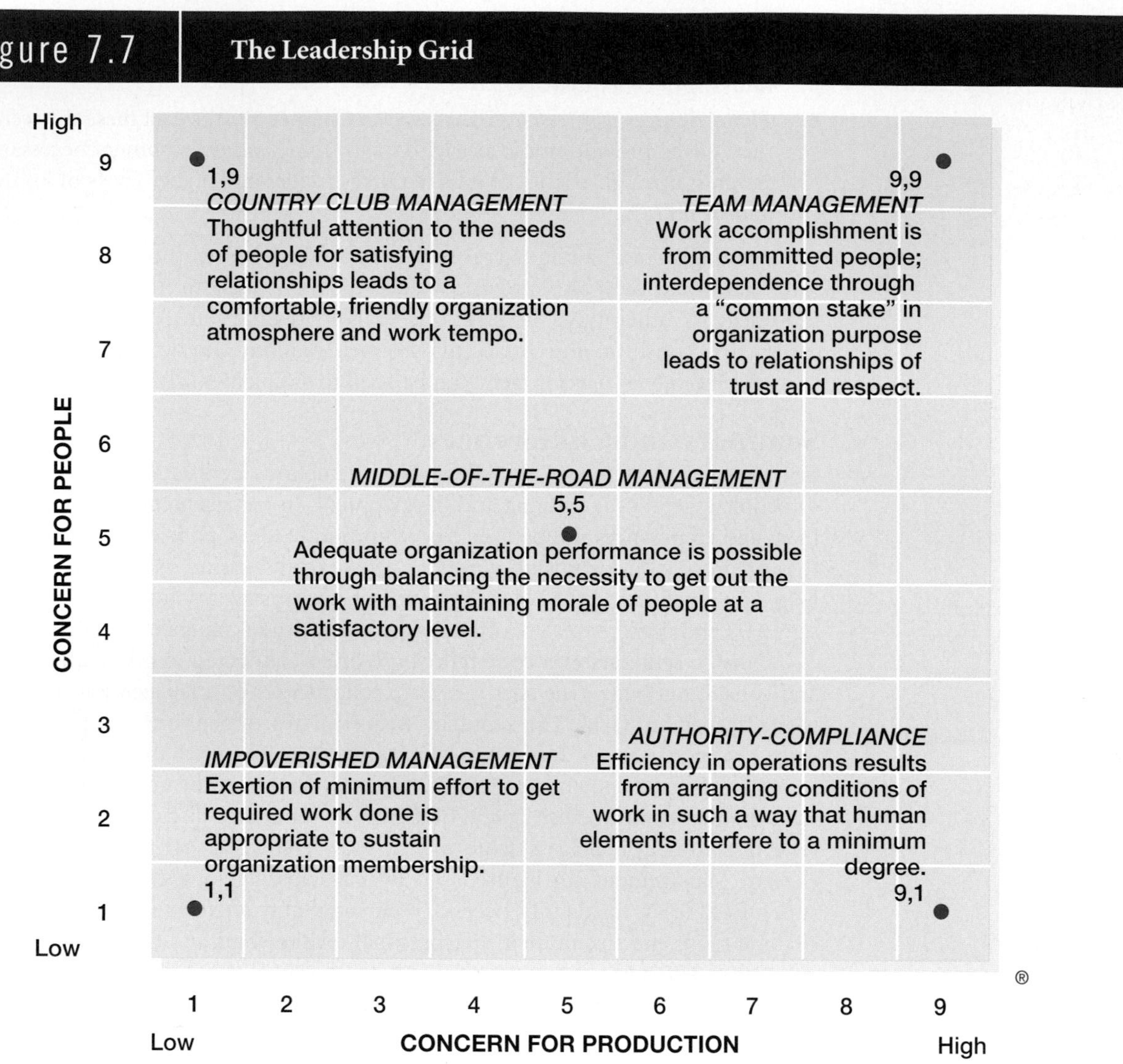

Source: Robert R. Blake and Anne Adams McCanse, *Leadership Dilemmas—Grid Solutions* (Houston: Gulf Publishing, 1991), 29. (First published as *The Managerial Grid Figure* by Robert R. Blake and Jane S. Mouton.) Courtesy of Grid International, Austin, TX. All rights reserved.

Even when case studies may be appropriate, they are often mismanaged. As with any other development technique, implementation is crucial for effectiveness. Figure 7.8 provides a set of guidelines for conducting case studies.

Management Games

Training experiences have been brought to life and made more interesting through the development of management games, in which players are faced with the task of making a series of decisions affecting a hypothetical organization. The effects that every decision has on each area within the organization can be simulated with a computer programmed for the game. A major advantage of this technique is the high degree of participation it requires.

Figure 7.8 Case Studies

WHEN USING CASE STUDIES . . .

- Be clear about learning objectives, and list possible ways to achieve the objectives.
- Decide which objectives would be best served by the case method.
- Identify available cases that might work, or consider writing your own.
- Set up the activity—including the case material, the room, and the schedule.
- Follow the principles of effective group dynamics.
- Provide a chance for all learners to take part and try to keep the groups small.
- Stop for process checks and be ready to intervene if group dynamics get out of hand.
- Allow for different learning styles.
- Clarify the trainer's role.
- Bridge the gap between theory and practice.

Source: Adapted from Albert A. Einsiedel, Jr., "Case Studies: Indispensable Tools for Trainers," *Training and Development* (August 1995): 50–53.

Games are now widely used as a management development method. Many of them have been designed for general use but more recently have been adapted for specific industries. It might be amusing to learn that the Marine Corps's basic warfare group has used the computer game Doom to help trainees learn how to develop strategies. Similarly, Bell Canada has its managers play TeleSim, a computer simulation for the telecommunications industry developed by Thinking Tools and Coopers & Lybrand to teach executives how to act in an increasingly open, competitive market.[33]

As the development of industry-specific games has increased, there are now simulations for a wide variety of organizations. For example, Lufthansa Airlines and Delta Air Lines have each developed management games designed to teach participants business issues related to today's stiff competition and low or no profits in their industry. Managers working in teams compete with one another running fictitious airline companies and have to balance issues of routing, schedules, costs, profits, and the like. Delta's game was so popular that after the company's managers were trained, the game was rolled out to front-line employees.[34]

The game method does not always require a computer, however. Motorola developed a game called "EEO: It's Your Job" to teach the basic principles of equal employment opportunity. Originally devised to fill Motorola's own affirmative action needs, it is now commercially available for use in training programs. The game kit accommodates up to twenty-four players, divided into teams of four, at a single session. The players get caught up in the competitive spirit of a game and at the same time absorb and remember government regulations. They also become aware of how their own daily decisions affect their employer's compliance with these regulations. Red Robin, a gourmet burger chain based in Colorado, holds an *Iron Chef*–like cook-off at its training conferences held annually. Contestants from various regions show off their gourmet burger presentation skills and win trips and cash prizes.[35]

Role Playing

Role playing consists of assuming the attitudes and behavior—that is, playing the role—of others, often a supervisor and a subordinate who are involved in a particular problem. By acting out another's position, participants in the role playing can improve their ability to understand and cope with others. Role playing should also help them learn how to counsel others by helping them see situations from a different point of view. Role playing is used widely in training healthcare professionals to be empathic and sensitive to the concerns of patients. It is also used widely in training managers to handle employee issues relating to absenteeism, performance appraisal, and conflict situations.

At times, participants may be hesitant to try role playing. Successful role play takes planning. Instructors should do the following:

1. Ensure that members of the group are comfortable with each other.
2. Select and prepare the role-players by introducing a specific situation.
3. To help participants prepare, ask them to describe potential characters.
4. Realize that volunteers make better role-players.
5. Prepare the observers by giving them specific tasks (such as evaluation or feedback).
6. Guide the role-play enactment through its bumps (because it is not scripted).
7. Keep it short.
8. Discuss the enactment and prepare bulleted points of what was learned.[36]

Role play is a versatile teaching model, applicable to a variety of training experiences. Planned and implemented correctly, role play can bring realism and insight into dilemmas and experiences that otherwise might not be shared. Computer programs that simulate role playing have also been developed. Virtual Leader, a product by SimuLearn, is one such program: Management trainees interact with animated "employees"—some of whom are more cooperative than others. The trainees are then given feedback as to how well they applied their managerial skills to each situation.

Behavior Modeling

behavior modeling
An approach that demonstrates desired behavior and gives trainees the chance to practice and role-play those behaviors and receive feedback

One technique that combines several different training methods, and therefore multiple principles of learning, is the behavior modeling technique. **Behavior modeling** involves four basic components:

1. *Learning points.* At the beginning of instruction, the essential goals and objectives of the program are enumerated. In some cases, the learning points are a sequence of behaviors that are to be taught. For example, the learning points might describe the recommended steps for giving employees feedback.
2. *Modeling.* Participants view films, DVDs, or videotapes in which a model manager is portrayed dealing with an employee in an effort to improve his or her performance. The model shows specifically how to deal with the situation and demonstrates the learning points.
3. *Practice and role play.* Trainees participate in extensive rehearsal of the behaviors demonstrated by the models. The greatest percentage of training time is spent in these skill-practice sessions.

4. *Feedback and reinforcement.* As the trainee's behavior increasingly resembles that of the model, the trainer and other trainees provide social reinforcers such as praise, approval, encouragement, and attention. Videotaping behavior rehearsals provides feedback and reinforcement. Emphasis throughout the training period is placed on transferring the training to the job.

Does behavior modeling work? Several controlled studies have demonstrated success in helping managers interact with employees, handle discipline, introduce change, and increase productivity. Military training is a classic example of how behavior modeling can work. Drill sergeants model the behavior expected of new recruits, who, in turn, by emulating them, develop discipline and confidence.[37]

Phase 4: Evaluating the Training Program

Training, like any other HRM function, should be evaluated to determine its effectiveness. A variety of methods are available to assess the extent to which training programs improve learning, affect behavior on the job, and impact the bottom-line performance of an organization. Unfortunately, few organizations adequately evaluate their training programs. In many ways, this goes beyond poor management; it is poor business practice. Given the substantial monetary stake that organizations have in training, it would seem prudent that managers would want to maximize the return on that investment.

Figure 7.9 shows that four basic criteria are available to evaluate training: (1) reactions, (2) learning, (3) behavior, and (4) results. Some of these criteria are easier to measure than others, but each is important in that it provides different information about the success of the programs. The combination of these criteria can give a total picture of the training program in order to help managers decide where problem areas lie, what to change about the program, and whether to continue with a program.[38]

Figure 7.9 Criteria for Evaluating Training

Criterion 1: Reactions

One of the simplest and most common approaches to training evaluation is assessing participant reactions. Happy trainees will be more likely to want to focus on training principles and to utilize the information on the job. Conversely, dissatisfaction with job training contributes to low employee job satisfaction. Trainees can do more than tell you whether they liked a training program, though. They can give insights into the content and techniques they found most useful. They can critique the instructors or make suggestions about participant interactions, feedback, and the like. Potential questions might include the following:

- What were your learning goals for this program?
- Did you achieve them?
- Did you like this program?
- Would you recommend it to others who have similar learning goals?
- What suggestions do you have for improving the program?
- Should the organization continue to offer it?

While evaluation methods based on reactions are improving, too many conclusions about training effectiveness are still based on broad satisfaction measures that lack specific feedback. Furthermore, it should be noted that positive reactions are no guarantee that the training has been successful. It may be easy to collect glowing comments from trainees, but gratifying as this information is to management, it may not be useful to the organization unless it somehow translates into improved behavior and job performance that is measurable. In the final analysis, reaction measures should not stop with assessing the training's entertainment value.[39]

Criterion 2: Learning

Beyond what participants *think* about the training, it might be a good idea to see whether they actually learned anything. Testing knowledge and skills before beginning a training program gives a baseline standard on trainees that can be measured again after training to determine improvement. However, in addition to testing trainees before and after training, parallel standards can be measured for individuals in a control group to compare with those in training to ensure that improvements are due to training and not some other factor (such as changes in jobs or compensation). The control group should be made up of employees who have not received the training but who match the trainees in such areas as experience, past training, and job level. Federal Express took this approach by studying twenty van drivers who attended a weeklong new-hire training program. The company then compared the performance of these drivers with a control group of twenty drivers who had received only on-the-job training. FedEx found that the drivers who had been formally trained made fewer package processing errors, saving the company about $500 per trained driver.[40]

Criterion 3: Behavior

You might be surprised to learn that much of what is learned in a training program never gets used back on the job. It's not that the training was necessarily ineffective.

In fact, on measures of employee reactions and learning, the program might score quite high. But for several reasons, trainees may not demonstrate behavior change back on the job. **Transfer of training** refers to the effective application of principles learned to what is required on the job. To maximize transfer, managers and trainers can take several approaches:

transfer of training
Effective application of principles learned to what is required on the job

1. *Feature identical elements.* Transfer of training to the job can be facilitated by having conditions in the training program come as close as possible to those on the job.
2. *Focus on general principles.* When jobs change or the work environment cannot be matched exactly, trainers often stress the general principles behind the training rather than focusing on rote behavior. This approach helps trainees learn how to apply the main learning points to varying conditions on the job.
3. *Establish a climate for transfer.* In some cases, trained behavior is not implemented because old approaches and routines are still reinforced by other managers, peers, and employees. To prevent this kind of problem, the manager should ensure that the work environment supports, reinforces, and rewards the trainee for applying the new skills or knowledge.
4. *Give employees transfer strategies.* Particularly in settings that are not conducive to transfer, managers should also provide trainees with strategies and tactics for dealing with their transfer environment. One approach, called *relapse prevention (RP)*, teaches individuals how to anticipate and cope with the inevitable setbacks they will encounter back on the job—that is, a relapse into former behaviors. By identifying high-risk situations that jeopardize transfer and developing coping strategies, relapse prevention can help employees gain better control over maintaining learned behaviors.[41]

There are several methods for assessing transfer of learned skills back to the job. At Xerox, for example, managers use multiple methods, including observations of trainees once they return to their regular positions, interviews with the trainees' managers, and examination of trainees' post-training performance appraisals. They combine these indices to ascertain whether training and development have influenced job behaviors.

Criterion 4: Results, or Return on Investment (ROI)

Training managers are under pressure to show that their programs produce "bottom-line" results.[42] Most organizations today measure their training in terms of its return on investment (ROI), which is also sometimes referred to as the *utility* the firm gets for its training dollars. A company's ROI refers to the benefits derived from training relative to the costs incurred. HR managers are responsible for calculating and presenting these benefits to the company's top managers. The benefits can include higher revenues generated, increased productivity, improved quality, lower costs, more satisfied customers, higher job satisfaction, and lower employee turnover.

The following are the types of questions HR managers should try to answer as they calculate a training program's benefits:

- How much did quality improve because of the training program?
- How much has it contributed to profits?

- What reduction in turnover and wasted materials did the company get after training?
- How much has productivity increased and by how much have costs been reduced?

To answer these questions, HR managers use various types of data such as sales data, human resources and financial data, and employee-survey and control-group data gathered from various sources within the organization. Of course, the costs of the training program need to be measured, too. The costs of training include the various expenses incurred as a result of training, including the direct costs of the programs (materials, travel, meeting site, meals, equipment, trainer salary or fee, and so on) as well as the indirect costs of the programs (participants' salaries, lost productivity while attending the training, and so on). The ROI formula can then be calculated fairly simply:

$$\text{ROI} = \text{Results/Training Costs}$$

If the ROI ratio is >1, the benefits of the training exceed the cost of the program; if the ROI ratio is <1, the costs of the training exceed the benefits. ROI can also be measured in terms of how long it takes before the benefits of the training pay off. This payback analysis is done by adding the costs and dividing the benefits realized in a single month. The result will indicate the overall time required for the training to pay for itself. Highlights in HRM 7 shows some simple examples of ROI calculations.[43]

Benchmarking

benchmarking
The process of measuring one's own services and practices against the recognized leaders in order to identify areas for improvement

Closely related to calculating the firm's training ROI is the process of **benchmarking** developmental services and practices against those of recognized leaders in industry. While no single model for exact benchmarking exists, the simplest models are based on the late W. Edwards Deming's classic four-step process. The four-step process advocates that managers:

1. *Plan.* Conduct a self-audit to define internal processes and measurements; decide on areas to be benchmarked and choose the comparison organization.
2. *Do.* Collect data through surveys, interviews, site visits, and/or historical records.
3. *Check.* Analyze data to discover performance gaps and communicate findings and suggested improvements to management.
4. *Act.* Establish goals, implement specific changes, monitor progress, and redefine benchmarks as a continuous improvement process.

To use benchmarking successfully, managers must clearly define the measures of competency and performance and must objectively assess the current situation and identify areas for improvement. To this end, experts in this area are attempting to work out ways of measuring what training departments do. Three broad areas that most HR training and developmental practitioners consider essential to measure are as follows:

1. *Training activity:* How much training is occurring?
2. *Training results:* Do training and development achieve their goals?
3. *Training efficiency:* Are resources utilized in the pursuit of this mission?

Calculating Training ROI: Examples

If the ROI ratio is >1, the benefits of the training exceed the cost of the program, and if the ratio is <1, the costs of the training program outweigh the benefits

Example 1: A program to train new machine operators costs $15,000 to develop and implement. After completing the training program, the average number of parts produced each year increased by 3,000, and the profit on each new part is $10, producing a net result of $30,000.

ROI = $30,000/$15,000 = 2

Example 2: A safety program costs the company $25,000 to develop and implement. One year later, there had been a small decrease in accidents, saving the company a total of $10,000.

ROI = $10,000/$25,000 = 0.4

In Example 1, the program resulted in a ROI of 2, indicating that the benefits of the program outweigh its cost. However, in Example 2, the ROI was only 0.4, indicating that the costs of the program outweigh the benefits.

Source: Richard J. Wagner and Robert J. Weigand, "Can the Value of Training Be Measured? A Simplified Approach to Evaluating Training," *The Health Care Manager* 23, no.1 (January–March 2004): 71–78.

The ASTD and its Institute for Workplace Learning have established a project that allows organizations to measure and benchmark training and development activities against each other. This benchmarking forum, which shares findings from more than 800 companies, compares data on training costs, staffing, administration, design, development, and delivery of training programs. Not only do initiatives such as these help organizations evaluate their training programs, but the process serves as a feedback loop to reinitiate needs assessment and design of future training.[44] Highlights in HRM 8 shows several aspects of training that can be benchmarked against organizations considered superior in the training function, and how those aspects are calculated.

Special Topics in Training and Development

While we have focused almost exclusively on the processes underlying a systems model of training—needs assessment, principles of learning, implementation methods, evaluation—it may be useful to discuss some of the more popular topics that are covered in these training programs. As we noted in the beginning of this chapter, there is a wide

Highlights in HRM 8

Benchmarking HR Training

MEASUREMENT	HOW TO CALCULATE
Percent of payroll spent on training	Total training expenditures ÷ total payroll
Training dollars spent per employee	Total training expenditures ÷ total employees served
Average training hours per employee	Total number of training hours (hours × participants) ÷ total employees served
Percent of employees trained per year	Total number of employees receiving training ÷ total employee population
HRD staff per 1,000 employees	Number of human resource development staff ÷ total employee population × 1,000
Cost savings as a ratio of training expenses	Total savings in scrap or waste ÷ dollars invested in training
Profits per employee per year	Total yearly gross profits ÷ total number of employees
Training costs per student hour	Total costs of training ÷ total number of hours of training

variety of training programs. In addition to training that addresses KSAs reflecting the demands of a particular job, many employers develop training programs to meet the needs of a broader base of employees. In this final section, we summarize some of these programs, including orientation training, basic skills training, team training, and diversity training. Global training will be covered in Chapter 15.

Orientation Training

orientation
The formal process of familiarizing new employees with the organization, their jobs, and their work units

To get new employees off to a good start, organizations generally offer a formal orientation program. **Orientation** is the formal process of familiarizing new employees with the organization, their jobs, and their work units. Most executives, 82 percent in one survey conducted by Robert Half International, believe that formal orientation programs are effective in helping to retain and motivate employees. These and other reported benefits include the following:

1. Lower turnover
2. Increased productivity
3. Improved employee morale
4. Lower recruiting and training costs
5. Facilitation of learning
6. Reduction of the new employee's anxiety[45]

Southwest Airlines buys into the idea that employee orientation is important. The company approaches the new hire orientation program as a welcoming party. Explained Dena Wilson, a learning facilitator with the company, "We celebrate the individual becoming a part of our family at Southwest and what that signifies. . . . It's not easy to become a Southwest employee." In fact, Southwest can get as many as 200,000 applications in some years and hire fewer than a thousand people.[46]

The more time and effort spent in helping new employees feel welcome, the more likely they are to identify with the organization and become valuable members of it. Unlike training, which emphasizes the *what* and the *how*, orientation often stresses the *why*. It is designed to influence employee attitudes about the work they will be doing and their role in the organization. It defines the philosophy behind the organization's rules and provides a framework for job-related tasks. And as plans, policies, and procedures change in organizations, even current employees need to be kept up to date and continually reoriented to changing conditions.

For a well-integrated orientation program, cooperation between line and staff is essential. The HR department ordinarily is responsible for coordinating orientation activities and for providing new employees with information about conditions of employment, pay, benefits, and other areas not directly under a supervisor's direction. However, the supervisor has the most important role in the orientation program. New employees are interested primarily in what the supervisor says and does and what their new co-workers are like. Before the arrival of a new employee, the supervisor should inform the work group that a new worker is joining the unit. It is also common practice for supervisors or other managerial personnel to recruit co-workers to serve as volunteer "sponsors," or mentors, for incoming employees. In addition to providing practical help to newcomers, experienced colleagues represent an important source of information about the norms and nuances of the work group, the culture of the organization, and what it expects from its employees. These relationships are vital to the socialization of new employees and contribute significantly to their long-term success within the organization.

Given the immediate and lasting impact of orientation programs, careful planning—with emphasis on program goals, topics to be covered, and methods of organizing and presenting them—is essential. In many cases, organizations devise checklists for use by those responsible for conducting the orientation so that no item of importance to employees is overlooked. The checklist would include such things as (1) an introduction to other employees, (2) an outline of training, (3) expectations for attendance, conduct, and appearance, (4) the conditions of employment, such as hours and pay periods, (5) an explanation of job duties, standards, and appraisal criteria, (6) safety regulations, (7) a list of the chain of command, and (8) an explanation of the organization's purpose and strategic goals. Highlights in HRM 9 shows the types of materials new hires can be given and the various steps that can ease their transition into the workplace.[47]

Some organizations combine orientation programs with computer-based training. Lazarus Department Stores (now Macy's) cut its orientation-training time in half this way, orienting 2,500 new employees in just six weeks. New hires at SumTotal Systems, an e-learning company based in Bellevue, Washington, go online for virtual tours of the company's various departments, with introductions to company leaders sprinkled throughout. Of course, these types of programs *supplement*—but do not replace—the value of face-to-face orientation.[48]

Checklist for Orienting New Employees

Items in Orientation Packet

- Welcome letter with company background
- Map of facility, including parking information
- IDs, keys, and parking decals
- Current organization chart
- Telephone numbers, e-mail addresses, and locations of key personnel
- Copy of employee's specific job goals and descriptions
- List of unique terms in the industry, company, and job
- Training class schedules
- Safety and emergency procedures
- Copy of policy handbook, including office hours and telephone and e-mail rules
- List of employee benefits, including insurance plans
- Holiday schedule

Follow-Up Activities

- Ensure that employee has completed required paperwork, including benefit enrollment forms
- Revisit performance standards
- Schedule first performance appraisal meeting

Basic Skills Training

Remedial training for adults has grown to be a full-blown educational industry on which businesses now spend about $3.1 billion annually. Between 45 and 50 percent of adults in the United States have only limited reading and writing abilities needed to handle the minimal demands of daily living or job performance. Furthermore, the U.S. Department of Education reports that illiteracy will grow in the workforce because each year 1 million teenagers leave school without elementary skills and another 1.3 million non-English-speaking people arrive in the United States. As the baby boom generation retires, the situation will only be exacerbated. Businesses report that they are already having a harder time finding workers with the basic skills they seek. Many businesses say it's their top problem.[49]

These figures have important implications for society at large and for organizations that must work around these skill deficiencies. Never has this been more true. Basic skills have become essential occupational qualifications, having profound implications for product quality, customer service, internal efficiency, and workplace and environmental safety. A list of typical basic skills includes the following:

- Reading
- Writing
- Computing

Job-specific and general skills are both essential for career success.

© GETTY IMAGES

- Speaking
- Listening
- Problem solving
- Managing oneself
- Knowing how to learn
- Working as part of a team
- Leading others

Ford, Polaroid, United Technologies, and AT&T are among the many companies who now offer remedial courses to their employees. Although there are different possible approaches to ensuring that employees have basic skills, the establishment of in-house basic skills programs has come increasingly into favor.[50] Recognizing that the skills gap is increasing, colleges and companies have begun teaming up to bridge the gap. For example, Pierce College, a two-year college in California (which had previously concentrated on preparing students for four-year colleges), now provides remedial instruction to employees at the offices of more than thirty companies in the San Fernando Valley area, where the college is located.[51] To implement a successful program in basic and remedial skills, managers should do the following:

1. Explain to employees why and how the training will help them in their jobs.
2. Relate the training to the employees' goals.
3. Respect and consider participant experiences, and use these as a resource.
4. Use a task-centered or problem-centered approach so that participants "learn by doing."
5. Give feedback on progress toward meeting learning objectives.

The key to developing a successful basic-skills program is *flexibility*, reinforcing the principle of individual differences while acknowledging the reality of work and family constraints.

Team Training and Cross-Training

As we discussed earlier in the book, organizations rely on teams to attain strategic and operational goals. Whether the team is an aircrew, a research team, or a manufacturing or service unit, the contributions of the individual members of the team are not only a function of the KSAs of each individual but of the interaction of the team members. Teamwork behaviors that differentiate effective teams are shown in Figure 7.10. They include both process dynamics and behavioral dynamics. The fact that these behaviors are observable and measurable provides a basis for training team members to function more effectively in the pursuit of their goals.[52]

Coca-Cola's Fountain Manufacturing Operation (which makes the syrup for Coke and Diet Coke) developed team training for its manufacturing employees. The program focused on three skill categories: (1) technical, (2) interpersonal, and (3) team action. The technical component, called Four-Deep Training, meant that each individual should learn four different jobs to allow for team flexibility. The interpersonal skills component, called Adventures in Attitudes, focused on listening, conflict resolution, influence, and negotiation. Team-action training focused on team leadership, management of meetings, team roles, group dynamics, and problem solving—all skills needed to function effectively as a team. The training not only increased quality and customer satisfaction, but has also helped decrease costs and set up a model for preparing employees for the future.[53]

Figure 7.10 Team Training Skills

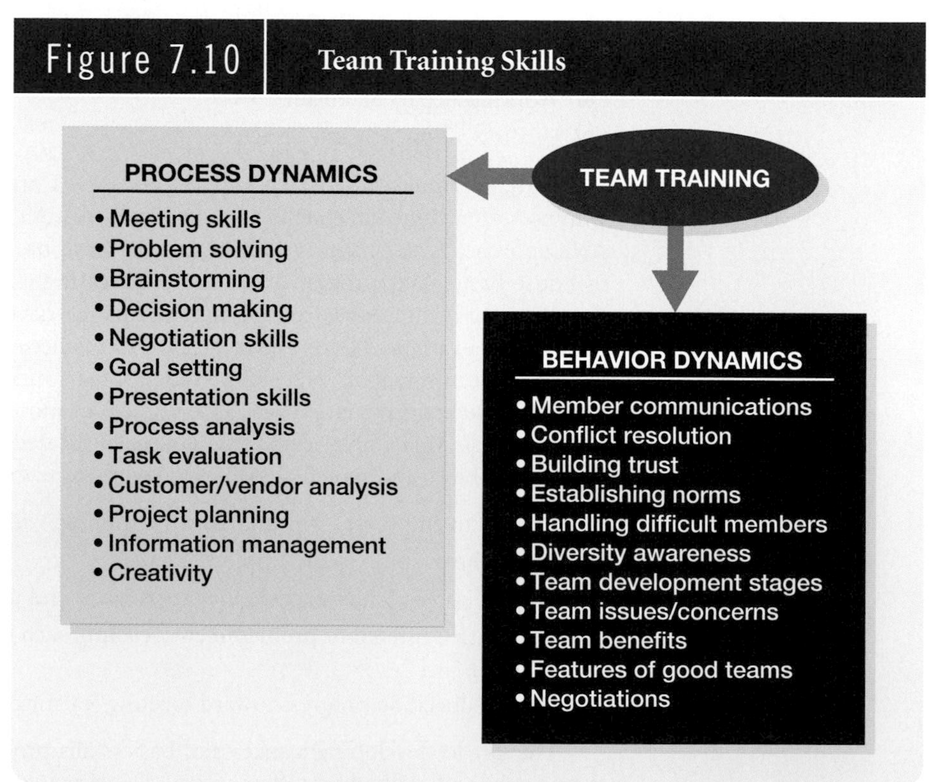

Source: George Bohlander and Kathy McCarthy, "How to Get the Most from Team Training," *National Productivity Review* (Autumn 1996): 25–35.

In the last few years other organizations have developed exercises to generate enthusiasm and enhance team participation. Managers who want to design team training for their organization should keep the following points in mind:

1. Team building is a difficult and comprehensive process. Since many new teams are under pressure to produce, there is little time for training. You cannot cover everything in a twenty-four-hour blitz. Team training works best when it is provided over time and parallels team development.
2. Team development is not always a linear sequence of "forming, storming, norming, and performing." Training initiatives can help a team work through each of these stages, but managers must be aware that lapses can occur.
3. Additional training is required to assimilate new members. Large membership changes may result in teams reverting to a previous developmental stage.
4. Behavioral and process skills need to be acquired through participative exercises. Team members cannot internalize subjects such as conflict resolution through passive listening. Hands-on experiences are much better.[54]

cross-training
The process of training employees to do multiple jobs within an organization

Closely related to team training is **cross-training.** Cross-trained employees learn how to do different jobs within an organization as well as their own. Part of the motivation for cross-training is that it gives firms flexible capacity. Workers can be dynamically shifted when and where they are needed, unlike specialized workers and equipment, which cannot. Moreover, by keeping workers interested and motivated, cross-training can cut turnover, increase productivity, pare down labor costs, and lay the foundation for careers rather than dead-end jobs. For example, at The Gourmet Pizza restaurants in Boston, employees begin cross-training their first day on the job. Staffers run through every function in the back and front of the restaurant and then plot their own course of cross-training. If they're interested in the bar, they have the opportunity to work there in various positions; those who want to become managers or franchise owners learn the entire operation, a process that takes eight to twelve months.[55]

In a sense, cross-training represents a shift from Henry Ford's assembly line production to flexible production. Some companies are using cross-training to keep their workers and plants in the United States versus offshoring them. Pace, a Maryland company that sells soldering equipment, watched all of its competitors move offshore. To keep up with the productivity of its low-cost rivals abroad, Pace grouped workers into teams and trained each team to build an entire product as well as different products. "Some of the people could only do certain things and if they had no work, they would just sit and wait," said one Pace manager. "Now they have ownership of it all." Employees have an incentive to learn because their hourly wages get bumped up as they master more skills. Now Pace builds products to meet actual customer demand, rather than storing inventory, which is more costly, and it has been able to shorten its production times and move its operations into one building versus two. Other companies that have been able to successfully utilize cross-training include IBM, John Deere, and GE Financial Assurance. In addition to making them more productive, research shows that cross-training gives employees the "big picture," making them more creative and better problem solvers.[56]

Diversity Training

Two out of three U.S. companies have broadened their diversity programs because of increasing globalization, according to a survey of 1,780 human resources and training executives by the Boston-based consulting firm Novations/J. Howard & Associates. Of those that have not done so, most expect to update diversity efforts in the near future. Sixty-three percent of training and human resources executives surveyed report a need to broaden the scope of their company's diversity programs, and 22 percent plan to do so in the near future. This emphasis is sparked by an awareness of the varied demographics of the workforce, the challenges of affirmative action, the dynamics of stereotyping, the changing values of the workforce, and the potential competitive payoffs from bringing different people together for a common purpose. There are basically two types of diversity training: (1) awareness building, which helps employees appreciate the benefits of diversity, and (2) skill building, which provides the KSAs necessary for working with people who are different. For example, a skill-building diversity program might teach managers how to conduct performance appraisals with people from different cultures or teach male supervisors how to coach female employees toward better career opportunities. All of the diverse dimensions—race, gender, age, disabilities, lifestyles, culture, education, ideas, and backgrounds—should be considered in the design of a diversity training program.[57]

After its highly public—and costly—$54 million discrimination lawsuit, Denny's Restaurants and its parent company, Advantica, took a first step toward changing the culture of the company through intensive diversity training. Everyone—from the board of directors to every cook, hostess, and server—was required to participate in varying levels of training. Servers and cooks, for example, were required to watch a video on diversity, while the board of directors received a full day of training. Restaurant managers received the most extensive training: two nonconsecutive days of training lasting seven to nine hours each day. The training covered diversity awareness and diversity skills. A 1996 company survey found that only a third of African Americans gave Denny's good marks on measures such as respectful service. Today, satisfaction totals from African Americans range from the mid-70s to more than 80 percent. Following a couple of highly publicized incidents of intolerance, the San Francisco 49ers football team underwent diversity training: In 2002, 49ers running back Garrison Hearst said in a newspaper interview that he would never accept a gay teammate. Lindsey McLean, a retired gay trainer with the team, admitted publicly that he was gay and that he had endured taunts and humiliation from players at times during his twenty-four years with the 49ers. "We're trying to create an environment where we can talk about these things and eliminate the problems and violence that can take place and help them understand that they can create an environment that people can work in, even if they are different," said one 49ers manager.[58]

USING THE INTERNET

The focus of GE's commitment to leadership development is the John F. Welch Leadership Center at Crotonville, the world's first major corporate business school. To find information about the development programs offered at the center, go to the Student Resources at:

http://bohlander.swlearning.com

Highlights in HRM 10 shows some characteristics of effective diversity training programs. Increasingly, diversity training is being combined with other training programs, an occurrence that some believe represents the "mainstreaming" of diversity with other strategic issues facing organizations. Honeywell, for example, subsumes diversity training within a week-long advanced management program and as part of its sales training programs. General Electric trains mentors and protégés in a program that isn't explicitly a diversity initiative but nevertheless clearly helps women and ethnic minorities.

Organizations that have been successful with diversity training realize that it is a long-term process that requires the highest level of skill. Ineffective training in this

Highlights in HRM 10

Characteristics of Effective Diversity Training Programs

- Steering committee represents all levels of the organization and a mix of races, ages, and gender.
- Workshops include the following:
  - Top executives demonstrate their commitment by early participation.
  - Each participant is given a workbook with support materials.
  - Participants are made aware of key topics and company policies.
  - Participants are asked to describe specific steps they would take to support diversity.
  - Participants create a list of diversity ground rules or behavioral norms.
  - Managers discuss and revise rules for their areas.
  - Participants link diversity training to other HR initiatives such as recruitment and selection, career management, and compensation.
- Managers are accountable for achieving goals of diversity training.

area can be damaging and can create more problems than it solves. Unfortunately, many consulting firms have added diversity training to their list of programs without adequate personnel to handle the assignment. To avoid the pitfalls of substandard diversity training, managers will want to do the following:

1. *Forge a strategic link.* Begin by establishing the reasons for diversity training. Clarify the links between diversity and business goals in order to provide a context for training. Affirmative action and valuing diversity are not the same thing. Ultimately diversity enhances differences and unites those differences toward a common goal.
2. *Check out consultant qualifications.* Recognize that there are no certification criteria for consultants, so ensure that they are qualified. Background and experience checks are essential.
3. *Don't settle for "off the shelf" programs.* Each company has somewhat different goals, and the training should reflect this.
4. *Choose training methods carefully.* Most diversity training is really education (awareness building). Managers may hope they are developing skills, but this requires more in-depth training. Employees may benefit from either awareness or skill building, but they are not the same.
5. *Document individual and organizational benefits.* Diversity training, when done well, can enhance communications, improve responsiveness to social issues, reduce lawsuits, create a climate of fairness, improve productivity on complex tasks, and increase revenues and profits. These criteria extend beyond affirmative action goals and support the competitive capability of the organization.

SUMMARY

objective 1

Today we find that organizational operations cover a broad range of subjects and involve personnel at all levels, from orientation through management development. In addition to providing the training needed for effective job performance, employers offer training in such areas as personal growth and wellness. In order to have effective training programs, the systems approach is recommended. This approach consists of four phases: (1) needs assessment, (2) program design, (3) implementation, and (4) evaluation.

objective 2

Needs assessment begins with organization analysis. Managers must establish a context for training by deciding where training is needed, how it connects with strategic goals, and how organizational resources can best be used. Task analysis is used to identify the knowledge, skills, and abilities that are needed. Person analysis is used to identify which people need training.

objective 3

In designing a training program, managers must consider the two fundamental preconditions for learning: readiness and motivation. In addition, principles of learning should be considered in order to create an environment that is conducive to learning. These principles include goal setting, meaningfulness of presentation, modeling, individual differences, active practice and repetition, whole-versus-part learning, massed-versus-distributed learning, and feedback and reinforcement.

objective 4

In the training of nonmanagerial personnel a wide variety of methods are available. On-the-job training is one of the most commonly used methods because it provides the advantage of hands-on experience and an opportunity to build a relationship between supervisor and employee. Apprenticeship training and internships are especially effective because they provide both on- and off-the-job experiences. Other off-the-job methods include the conference or discussion method, classroom training, programmed instruction, computer-based training, simulation, closed-circuit TV, teletraining, and interactive e-learning. All of these methods can make a contribution to the training effort with relatively little cost per trainee.

The training and development of managers is a multibillion-dollar business. As with nonmanagerial personnel, a wide variety of training methods are used for developing managers. On-the-job experiences include coaching, understudy assignment, job rotation, lateral transfer, project and committee assignments, and staff meetings. Off-the-job experiences include analysis of case studies, management games, role playing, and behavior modeling.

objective 5

Evaluation of a training program should focus on several criteria: participant reactions, learning, behavior change on the job, and bottom-line results such as return on investment. Transfer of training is measured via examination of the degree to which trained skills are demonstrated back on the job. Benchmarking and utility analysis help evaluate the impact of training and provide the information for further needs assessment.

objective 6

Special issues in training involve programs that are important to a broad range of employees. Orientation training, for example, begins and continues throughout an employee's service with an organization. By participating in a formal orientation program, employees acquire the knowledge, skills, and attitudes that increase the probabilities of their success with the organization. To make an orientation effective there should be close cooperation between the HR department and other departments in all phases of the program, from initial planning through follow-up and evaluation. Basic skills training, team training, and diversity training are also critically important in today's organizations.

HRM Experience

Training and Learning Principles

It is surprising how many training programs don't explicitly incorporate principles of learning into their design (such as goal setting, modeling, individual differences, and feedback). It is not that difficult to build learning principles into the training process, even for very simple instructional programs. To prove this point, do the following assignment for building a paper airplane.

Assignment

1. Form teams of four to six members. Identify someone on the team who knows how to make a paper airplane. That person will be the *trainer.*
2. Identify someone who will be the *observer/recorder.* That person will not participate in the training, but will write down how many (and how effectively) principles of learning are used in the instruction:
   a. Goal setting
   b. Modeling
   c. Meaningfulness
   d. Individual differences
   e. Whole-versus-part learning
   f. Distributed learning
   g. Active practice
   h. Feedback
3. Give the trainer ten to fifteen minutes to train the group in making a paper airplane. The observer will keep notes of effective and ineffective training techniques (demonstrated learning principles).
4. Have someone from each team—not the trainer—volunteer to come before the class for a friendly competition. The instructor will give each team member two minutes to make a paper airplane. And then just for fun, they can compete by seeing which one flies the farthest. As always, no wagering, please.
5. To finish the exercise, the observer/recorders will lead a discussion of the learning principles that were demonstrated. Discuss also, if they were done in this setting, why they might not be done in other training settings.

KEY TERMS

apprenticeship training
behavior modeling
behavior modification
benchmarking
competency assessment
cooperative training
cross-training
e-learning
instructional objectives
internship programs
on-the-job training (OJT)
organization analysis
orientation
person analysis
task analysis
transfer of training

DISCUSSION QUESTIONS

1. What economic, social, and political forces have made employee training even more important today than it was in the past?

2. What analyses should be made to determine the training needs of an organization? After the needs are determined, what is the next step?

3. Which principles of learning do you see demonstrated in your own class? In what ways might you bring other principles into the class?

4. Indicate what training methods you would use for each of the following jobs. Give reasons for your choices.
   - **a.** File clerk
   - **b.** Computer operator
   - **c.** Automobile service station attendant
   - **d.** Pizza maker
   - **e.** Nurse's aide

5. Compare computer-based instruction with the lecture method in regard to the way the two methods involve the different psychological principles of learning.

6. Suppose that you are the manager of an accounts receivable unit in a large company. You are switching to a new system of billing and record keeping and need to train your three supervisors and twenty-eight employees in the new procedures. What training method(s) would you use? Why?

7. Participants in a training course are often asked to evaluate the course by means of a questionnaire. What are the pros and cons of this approach? Are there better ways of evaluating a course?

8. A new employee is likely to be anxious the first few days on the job.
   - **a.** What are some possible causes of this anxiety?
   - **b.** How may the anxiety be reduced?

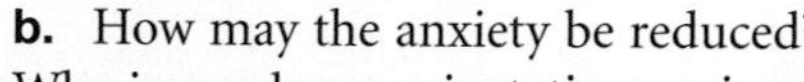

9. Why is employee orientation an important process? What are some benefits of a properly conducted orientation program?

BIZFLIX EXERCISES

Backdraft: Probie's Training Experiences

Watch the scenes from the film *Backdraft* to see examples of the training and development discussions in this chapter. Use the discussion questions below as guides to your viewing of the scenes.

Two brothers follow their late father, a legendary Chicago firefighter, and join the City of Chicago Fire Department. Stephen "Bull" McCaffrey (Kurt Russell) joins first and rises to the rank of lieutenant. Younger brother Brian (William Baldwin) joins later. After graduation from the fire academy, Brian becomes a member of Bull's Engine Company 17. Sibling rivalry tarnishes their work relationships, but they continue to fight Chicago fires successfully. Add a plot element about a mysterious arsonist, and you have the basis for an extraordinary film. The intense, unprecedented special effects give the viewer an unparalleled experience of what it is like to fight a fire. Chicago firefighters applauded the realism of the fire scenes.

These scenes are an edited composite built from two parts of the film. Part I: "On-the-Job Training: Probie's First Day" appears early in *Backdraft* as part of "The First Day" sequence. This part shows Engine Company 17 preparing to fight a garment factory fire. Part II: "Back at Station 17: Probie Continues Training" comes from "The Probie's Life" segment that appears about 30 minutes later in the film. The term *probie* is jargon for a probationary firefighter—someone just starting with the department.

What to Watch for and Ask Yourself

- Which training methods described earlier in this chapter appear in these scenes? Link the training methods discussed to specific moments and examples in the scenes.
- Did Brian McCaffrey receive any classroom instruction?
- Review the earlier section "Phase 4: Evaluating the Training Program." Assess the training Brian received using the criteria discussed in that section.

case study 1

Learning to Walk in the Customer's Shoes

Problem: Like most high-tech companies, semiconductor giant Texas Instruments rode the technology boom in a state of bliss. As customers waited in line for its products, TI became more product- and technology-centric, and admittedly less concerned about its customers. Then came the bust. TI was suddenly forced to compete for new business, yet elements of its management simply wouldn't adjust to the market's new demands. How could TI jolt its people into a renewed awareness of the customer?

Solution: Texas Instruments called on BTS USA, a global supplier of computer-based simulations for learning. The provider developed a customer loyalty course for TI's top 300 executives aimed at raising awareness about customer-centric thinking. The course was so successful that it was expanded to an additional 2,000 TI managers and earned BTS a coveted Supplier Excellence Award from a grateful TI.

They call it a "Customer Loyalty Boot Camp." The title is appropriate because much like the army's indoctrination for recruits, it represents the Tough Love approach to employee learning. And for Texas Instruments, it seemed that nothing less would do.

Picture the scene: a classroom of 25 TI executives, all chastened by a stern lecture from the company's senior vice president of worldwide sales and marketing, Jeffrey S. McCreary. "This company is broken," McCreary railed. But the audience wasn't getting the message. The year was 2001, the bottom was dropping out of the semiconductor industry, and TI's fortunes were plummeting along with it. It was no time for the company to be dismissive of its valued customers—or perceived as such.

Also in the classroom were consultants and trainers from BTS USA. BTS had been invited to help develop and deliver a course for TI executives on customer loyalty. The two-and-a-half-day course had been painstakingly created by BTS following extensive interviews with TI executives, key account managers, and customers to gain an accurate picture of the problems facing the company. The customized course was designed and created with active participation from TI's training department.

The twenty-five assembled managers were divided into five teams, each assigned to simulate executives of a fictitious company called Streaming Wireless Video (STREAVO). The concern "manufactured" a handheld product that included chips supplied by another fictitious company called Terrific Instruments (TI). It was now time for the TI managers to walk a mile in their customer's shoes.

Each team was responsible for a different department within STREAVO, including engineering, finance, supplier management, manufacturing, and marketing. Using laptop computers and a simulation to analyze data, such as engineering specifications, financial statements, and customer and market reports, they pondered the purchasing decision for three hours before hitting a button named "commit."

"Little did they know that upon return from their coffee break, the teams would walk into a valley of darkness," recalls Daniel Parisi, senior vice president of BTS USA and general manager of its San Francisco office. Parisi was in charge of the seminar, and was about to make their lives miserable by delivering information about Terrific Instruments' execution missteps, including failure to meet time, cost, and performance commitments.

The simulated learning concept he was using got its start in 1985, when Swedish entrepreneur Henrik Ekelund launched BTS to help companies meet strategic business goals. Ekelund found simulation to be a useful tool to communicate complex business strategies to executives, and apparently clients agree. BTS has since expanded to the United States, the United Kingdom, Finland, South Africa, Australia, and Spain.

At the heart of the learning exercise are custom-designed computer-based simulations that replicate the actual business processes of the client company. Each management team is assisted in the decision-making process with a laptop on which they can perform budgeting and "what-if" analysis and scenarios. Over the course of a three-month development process, the simulation was co-created by BTS and the client and inserted into a platform of Excel and Visual Basic software. "It simulates the technical and business interrelationships that exist between TI and its client," says Parisi. "In this case, the semiconductor's performance and functionality are realistically linked into the handheld's design specifications," he says. "Also, the impacts of the supplier execution missteps are extremely realistic," adds Parisi.

The concept often uses a kind of shock therapy to jolt executives into reality. At Texas Instruments, for example, many executives were not sensitive to the impact TI's execution missteps could have on the customer. There also were gaps in their knowledge regarding their customers' drivers of profitability and competitive advantage. In many cases, they lacked a long-term view of TI's customer relationships.

When the TI executives returned from their break, Parisi was there to greet them, a scowl on his face and a baseball cap that read Terrific Industries on his head. "There are problems with your order," he told the assembled "STREAVO" management teams. Not only would there be a five-week delay in delivery, but alas, the chip would not meet specifications, he told the horrified group.

What's more, Parisi was brutally unsympathetic to the customer's predicament. "Count your blessings," he sneered. "After all, we're Terrific. We're Number One." Then came the clincher: an ultimatum from STREAVO's retail customer, "Circus City," which was affected by Terrific's delays. "We don't care about your problems," grumbled Circus. "You will either help us or we will cut you off."

The effect of the simulation exercise was written on the faces of the Texas Instruments executives, who felt betrayed and frustrated at the arrogance on display. Some also felt that the excuses sounded distressingly familiar, as indeed they should have. To complete the session, Parisi played a five-minute video of comments from actual TI customers. "TI's own customers said almost exactly what the TI managers in the STREAVO simulation were saying," said Parisi. Indeed, hearing customers echo their own experience in the simulation "was like hitting them in the stomach," he said.

The boot camp was so successful that it has since been rolled out to more than 2,000 TI managers and engineers, says Parisi, who claims the results speak for themselves. "In 2001, TI had some dissatisfied customers. But at the end of 2003, it was receiving supplier excellence awards from the very same customers," says Parisi. "Within 24 months, TI turned the entire company in a much more customer-centric direction."

Source: Adapted from Paul Harris, "BTS Helps Companies Walk in Customers' Shoes," *Learning Circuits* (June 2004), http://www.learningcircuits.org/2004/jun2004/harris.htm.

QUESTIONS

1. Do you think that TI took the right approach to achieving better customer satisfaction by training its executives first? Would TI have achieved quicker results by training its front-line employees prior to its executives?

2. If you were an HR manager at TI, to what sources would you have looked to find information with which to calculate the program's ROI?

case study 2

Kodak Gets the Picture in Executive Education

Eastman Kodak is changing dramatically to compete in a world of new technologies, emerging markets, and global customers. As a result, Kodak's efforts in executive education have pushed the limits to create innovative "learning events" for senior management. According to June Delano, Kodak's director of Executive Education and Development, these learning events are designed to be as dynamic and future-oriented as the company's business environment.

In the past, the highly successful Kodak was a citadel of stability. It enjoyed market dominance, worldwide brand recognition, extraordinary customer loyalty, and enviable profits. Understandably, few employees (or managers) wanted to do anything to upset the status quo as most of them looked forward to a lifetime of employment and security.

Then things changed. The company restructured in order to go head-to-head with competitors in a much tougher digital marketplace and, in the process, there has been a one-third reduction in executive positions. These events have driven complacency far from the environs of Rochester, New York, Kodak's headquarters city. *Agility* has replaced *stability* as the watchword of the future.

As a consequence of Kodak's transformation—not to mention the personnel changes—the majority of senior managers have been in their positions for less than three years. Executive education is viewed as a critical tool for improving the managerial ranks. But Delano believed that the development programs needed to be as active, innovative, and future-oriented as the company. Off-the-shelf materials were out, as were case studies, lectures, and other passive learning approaches. A new approach meant inventing from scratch, letting go of control, and taking monumental risks. Skills in anticipating the business, pushing the culture, and networking were demanded. Delano wanted executive education to optimize opportunities to think collectively and to experiment and explore implications as a team. These objectives led to the creation of three new programs for the senior management team:

- *The Kodak Prosperity Game.* This program was developed in partnership with the Prosperity Institute and was conducted in June 1996 using staff drawn from industry and academia. Focusing on the imaging industry, the program innovatively teamed fifty Kodak executives with twenty-five peer executives from other companies. These "reality-based" teams worked on meaningful, implementable strategies, alliances, and deals.
- *The Digital Executive.* This program consisted of a "scavenger hunt" exploring Kodak's digital present and future. Using digital products and the Internet, small teams researched digital competitors and interacted with a consumer focus group via videoconferencing. One innovative feature of this program was the upward mentoring of the participants by technology "whiz kids."

- *The Future of the Company.* This was a two-part program, developed in partnership with the Global Business Network and focused on learning about possible futures for the industry and the company. Part I was a two-day "conversation" about Kodak and its environment in the coming years. Industry scenarios for growth were developed in small team discussions involving Kodak executives and customers, alliance partners, and futurists. The resulting scenarios launched Part II, in which additional outsiders and provocative thinkers mixed ideas with the participants. The outcomes were a set of new ideas and potential strategies for the Kodak businesses.

So far, the program seems to be working for the company that invented consumer photography more than a century ago. After Kodak's executives committed to an all-out digital strategy, the company's revenues climbed. In 2004, Kodak surpassed Sony, the market leader, in the number of digital cameras shipped in the United States.

Sources: William G. Stopper, "Agility in Action: Picturing the Lessons Learned from Kodak and 23 Other Companies." Adapted with permission from *Human Resource Planning*, Vol. 21, No. 1 (1998). Copyright 1998 by The Human Resource Planning Society, 317 Madison Avenue, Suite 1509, New York, NY 10017, Phone: (212) 490-6387, Fax: (212) 682-6851; "Kodak Overtakes Sony in U.S. Digital Camera Shipments," *Kyodo News International (Tokyo, Japan)* (via *Knight-Ridder/Tribune Business News*) (February 3, 2005).

QUESTIONS

1. What can you tell about how Kodak did needs assessment for executive education? What recommendations would you give June Delano for improving this analysis?
2. From what you read, what principles of learning do you believe are embedded in the three new programs?
3. How would you go about evaluating the effectiveness of these educational experiences? Do you believe that company profitability should be used as a criterion?

NOTES AND REFERENCES

1. "Spending on Training Remains Steady in 2004 According to ASTD," *Lifelong Learning Market Report* 10, no. 1 (January 7, 2005): 3–4; "What to Do Now That Training Is Becoming a Major HR Force," *HR Focus* (February 2005): 5–6.
2. David Dubois and William Rothwell, "Competency-Based or a Traditional Approach to Training?" *Training and Development* 58, no. 4 (April 2004): 46–59; Bob Rosner, "Training Is the Answer . . . But What Was the Question?" *Workforce* 78, no. 5 (May 1999): 42–52. See also Irwin L. Goldstein and J. Kevin Ford, *Training in Organizations: Needs Assessment, Development and Evaluation*, 4th ed. (Belmont, CA: Wadsworth, 2002). For the classic citation on needs assessment, see William McGehee and Paul W. Thayer, *Training in Business and Industry* (New York: John Wiley and Sons, 1961).
3. Laurie Bassi and Daniel McMurrer, "How's Your Return on People?" *Harvard Business Review* 8, no. 3 (March 2004): 18; Tracy Mauro, "Helping Organizations Build Community," *Training and Development* 56, no. 2 (February 2002): 25–29; Liam Lahey, "RFIDs Touted as Standard for Airport Security," *Computing Canada* 28, no. 13 (June 21, 2002): 21; Caroline Wilson, "Ensuring a Smooth Ride," *Security Management* 46, no. 8 (August 2002): 92.
4. "E-Learning and Teleconferencing Join Needs Assessment to Control Training Costs," *Managing Training & Development*, no. 3 (December 2003): 1; Thomas Gainey, Brian Klaas, and Darla Moore, "Outsourcing the Training Function: Results from the Field," *Human Resource Planning* 25, no. 1 (2002): 16; Sarah Fister Gale, "Creative Training: Doing More with Less," *Workforce* 80, no. 10 (October 2001): 82–88.
5. Patty Davis, Jennifer Naughton, and William Rothwell, "New Roles and New Competencies for the Profession: Are You Ready for the Next Generation," *Training and Development* 58, no. 4 (April 2004): 26–38; David Dubois and William Rothwell, "Competency-Based or a Traditional Approach to Training?" *Training and Development* 58, no. 4 (April 2004): 46-59; Cather-

ine Robbins, Elizabeth Bradely, Maryanne Spicer, and Gary Mecklenburge, "Developing Leadership in Healthcare Administration: A Competency Assessment Tool/Practitioner Application," *Journal of Healthcare Management* 46, no. 3 (May/June 2001): 188–202; Margaret Potter, Christine Pistella, Carl Fertman, and Virginia Dato, "Needs Assessment and a Model Agenda for Training the Public Health Workforce," *American Journal of Public Health* 90, no. 8 (August 2000): 1294–96.

6. Thomas Hoffman, "Motivation: These IT Leaders Keep Staffers Upbeat during Lean Times by Targeting What Drives Them: Technology and Training," *Computerworld* 38, no. 1 (January 5, 2004): 39; Elwood Holton, Reid Bates, and Sharon Naquin, "Large-Scale Performance-Driven Training Needs Assessment: A Case Study," *Public Personnel Management* 29, no. 2 (Summer 2000): 249–67.

7. Gail Johnson, "The Development Framework: Booz Allen Hamilton's Holistic Method of Employee Development Gives Its Employee a Roadmap to Success—Both Professionally and Personally," *Training* 40, no. 2 (February 2003): 32–34; Robert Mager, "Contract Training Tips," *Security Management* 45, no. 6 (June 2001): 30; Robert Mager, *What Every Manager Should Know about Training: An Insider's Guide to Getting Your Money's Worth from Training* (Atlanta, GA: Center for Effective Performance, 1999).

8. Debbie Schachter, "How to Set Performance Goals: Employee Reviews Are More Than Annual Critiques," *Information Outlook* 8, no. 9 (September 2004): 26–30; "Burger Olympics," *Training* 41, no. 7 (July 2004): 20; Jason A. Colquitt and Marcia J. Simmering, "Conscientiousness, Goal Orientation, and Motivation to Learn during the Learning Process: A Longitudinal Study," *Journal of Applied Psychology* 83, no. 4 (August 1998): 654–65; Sherry Ryan, "A Model of the Motivation for IT Retraining," *Information Resources Management Journal* 12, no. 4 (October–December 1999): 24–32; Kimberly A. Smith-Jentsch, Florian G. Jentsch, Stephanie C. Payne, and Eduardo Salas, "Can Pretraining Experiences Explain Individual Differences in Learning?" *Journal of Applied Psychology* 81, no. 1 (February 1996): 110–16.

9. J. Kevin Ford, Eleanor M. Smith, Daniel A. Weissbein, Stanley M. Gully, and Eduardo Salas, "Relationships of Goal Orientation, Metacognitive Activity, and Practice Strategies with Learning Outcomes and Transfer," *Journal of Applied Psychology* 83, no. 2 (April 1998): 218–33; Annette Towler and Robert Dipboye, "Effects of Trainer Expressiveness, Organization, and Trainee Goal Orientation on Training Outcomes," *Journal of Applied Psychology* 86, no. 4 (August 2001): 664–73; Steve Kozlowski, Stanley Gully, Kenneth Brown, and Eduardo Salas, "Effects of Training Goals and Goal Orientation Traits on Multidimensional Training Outcomes and Performance Adaptability," *Organizational Behavior and Human Decision Processes* 85, no. 1 (May 2001): 1–31.

10. The classics by Albert Bandura here include *Social Foundations of Thought and Action: A Social Cognitive Theory* (Englewood Cliffs, NJ: Prentice Hall, 1986) and *A Social Learning Theory* (Englewood Cliffs, NJ: Prentice Hall, 1977). See also Melesa Altizer Bolt, Larry Killough, and Hian Chye Koh, "Testing the Interaction Effects of Task Complexity in Computer Training Using the Social Cognitive Model," *Decision Sciences* 32, no. 1 (Winter 2001): 1–20; Susan Pedersen and Min Liu, "The Transfer of Problem-Solving Skills from a Problem-Based Learning Environment: The Effect of Modeling an Expert's Cognitive Processes," *Journal of Research on Technology in Education* 35, no. 2 (Winter 2002): 303–21.

11. M. K. Kacmar, P. W. Wright, and G. C. McMahan, "The Effect of Individual Differences on Technological Training," *Journal of Managerial Issues* 9, no. 1 (Spring 1997): 104–20; Stanley Gully, Stephanie Payn, K. Lee Kiechel Koles, and John-Andrew Whiteman, "The Impact of Error Training and Individual Differences on Training Outcomes: An Attribute-Treatment Interaction Perspective," *Journal of Applied Psychology* 87, no. 1 (February 2002): 143–55; Steven John Simon, "The Relationship of Learning Style and Training Method to End-User Computer Satisfaction and Computer Use: A Structural Equation Model," *Information Technology, Learning, and Performance Journal* 18, no. 1 (Spring 2000): 41–59.

12. "Can Technology Actually Boost Behavior Change?" *Managing Training & Development* no. 3 (November 2003): 3; Don Hartshorn, "Reinforcing the Unsafe Worker," *Occupational Hazards* 62, no. 10 (October 2000): 125–28; Fred Luthan and Alexander Stajkovic, "Reinforce for Performance: The Need to Go beyond Pay and Even Rewards," *Academy of Management Executive* 13, no. 2 (May 1999): 49–57.

13. Greg Hopkins, "How to Design an Instructor Evaluation," *Training and Development* 53, no. 3 (March 1999): 51–52; Beth Thomas, "How to Hire Instructors Who Love Training," *Training and Development* 53, no. 3 (March 1999): 14–15; John L. Bennett, "Trainers as Leaders of Learning," *Training and Development* 55, no. 3 (March 2001): 42–45; Ruth Palombo Weiss, "Deconstructing Trainers' Self-Image," *Training and Development* 55, no. 12 (December 2001): 34–39.

14. Eduardo Salas and Janis Cannon-Bowers, "The Science of Training: A Decade of Progress," *Annual Review of Psychology* 52 (2001): 471–99.

15. Diane Walter, *Training on the Job* (Alexandria, VA: American Society for Training and Development, 2001); Toni Hodges, *Linking Learning and Performance: A Practical Guide to Measuring Learning and On-the-Job Application* (Burlington, MA: Butterworth-Heinemann, 2001); Gary Sisson, *Hands-On Training: A Simple and Effective Method for On-the-Job Training* (San Francisco: Barrett-Koehler, 2001).

16. Teresa M. McAleavy, "U.S. Schools Fail to Provide Job Training," *Knight-Ridder/Tribune Business News* (June 9, 2004); "Eight Steps to Better On-the-Job Training," *HRFocus* 80, no. 7 (July 2003): 11; Alison Booth, Yu-Fu Chen, and Gylfi Zoega, "Hiring and Firing: A Tale of Two Thresholds," *Journal of Labor Economics* 20, no. 2 (April 2002): 217–48.

17. Ronald L. Jacobs and Michael J. Jones, "Teaching Tools: When to Use On-the-Job Training," *Security Management* 41, no. 9 (September 1997): 35–39.

18. Information found on the Apprenticeship page, Spokane Community College web site, February 9, 2005, http://www.scc.spokane.edu/tech/apprent/.

19. "Agilisys Automotive Helps to Build Tomorrow's Leaders Through Focus: HOPE Sponsorship at Important Auto Industry Event," *PR Newswire* (August 4, 2003).
20. For more information about the Bureau of Apprenticeship and Training, see the bureau's web site at http://bat.doleta.gov. See also Glenn Burkins, "A Special News Report about Life on the Job—and Trends Taking Shape There," *The Wall Street Journal*, November 2, 1999, A1.
21. John Byrd and Rob Poole, "Highly Motivated Employees at No Cost? It's Not an Impossible Dream," *Nonprofit World* 19, no. 6 (November/December 2001): 312–32.
22. "Workforce Investment Act: One-Stop Centers Implemented Strategies to Strengthen Services and Partnerships, but More Research and Information Sharing Is Needed," *General Accounting Office Reports & Testimony* 2003, no. 7 (July 2003).
23. Phil Britt, "E-Learning on the Rise in the Classroom: Companies Move Content Online: Cisco Systems' Employees and Partners Routinely Watch Videos on the Internet," *EContent* 27, no. 11 (November 2004): 36–41; Heather Johnson, "The Whole Picture: When It Comes to Finding Out How Employees Feel about Training, Many Companies Fail to Get a Clear Picture," *Training* 47, no. 7 (July 2004): 30–35.
24. Robert Markovetz, Jr., "Distance Learning: MLRS 3x6 Conversion for the Army National Guard," *Field Artillery* 5 (September/October 1999): 42–43.
25. For more information about Cornell University's Global Education program, visit the program's web site at http://www.ilr.cornell.edu/dl/globaled/.
26. "What to Do Now That Training Is Becoming a Major HR Force," *HRFocus* (February 2005): 5–6; Britt, "E-Learning on the Rise in the Classroom," 36–41; Tammy Galvin, "The Delivery," *Training* 38, no. 10 (October 2001): 66–72; Kenneth G. Brown, "Using Computers to Deliver Training: Which Employees Learn and Why?" *Personnel Psychology* 54, no. 2 (Summer 2001): 271–96; Bill Roberts, "E-Learning New Twist on CBT," *HRMagazine* 46, no. 4 (April 2001): 99–106.
27. Scott A. Snell, Donna Stueber, and David P. Lepak, "Virtual HR Departments: Getting Out of the Middle," in R. L. Heneman and D. B. Greenberger (eds.), *Human Resource Management in Virtual Organizations* (Greenwich, CT: Information Age Publishing, 2002).
28. "Soup to Nuts: Simulator Manufacturing Is a Lucrative but Risky Business, Which Is Why Market Leader CAE Has Tapped into the More Stable World of Flight Training," *Air Transport World* 40, no. 5 (May 2003): 69–71; "SimsSir: Modeling and Simulation Are Leading the Assault on New Learning Technologies That Are Winning Favor with the U.S. Military," *Training and Development* 57, no. 10 (October 2003): 46–52.
29. For other applications of simulation in training used at Boeing and Eastman Kodak, see George Tischelle, "E-Learning Gets a Dose of Reality," *InformationWeek* 895 (July 1, 2002): 57. For applications of simulation training used in the U.S. Navy, see John Flink, "This Is Really Neat Stuff," *United States Naval Institute Proceedings* 128, no. 7 (July 2002): 68–69. For applications of simulation training used in medical schools, see David Noonan, "Is the Cadaver Dead?" *Newsweek* 139, no. 25 (June 24, 2002): 62. For applications of simulation training used in the police force, see Jim Weiss and Mickey Davis, "Deadly Force Decision-Making," *Law and Order* 50, no. 6 (June 2002): 58–62.
30. Martin Delahoussaye, Kristine Ellis, and Matt Bolch, "Measuring Corporate Smarts," *Training* 39, no. 8 (August 2002): 20–35; Daniel Crepin, "From Design to Action: Developing a Corporate Strategy," *Quality Progress* 35, no. 2 (February 2002): 49–56; Brad Miller, "Making Managers More Effective Agents of Change," *Quality Progress* 34, no. 5 (May 2001): 53–57.
31. Joseph Alutto, "Just-in-Time Management Education in the 21st Century," *HRMagazine* 44, no. 11 (1999): 56–57; Gordon Dehler, M. Ann Welsh, and Marianne W. Lewis, "Critical Pedagogy in the 'New Paradigm,'" *Management Learning* 493, no. 4 (December 2001): 493–511.
32. Chris Whitcomb, "Scenario-Based Training to the F.B.I.," *Training and Development* 53, no. 6 (June 1999): 42–46; Anne Hoag, Dale Brickley, and Joanne Cawley, "Media Management Education and the Case Method," *Journalism and Mass Communication Educator* 55, no. 4 (Winter 2001): 49–59.
33. Jenny C. McCune, "The Game of Business," *Management Review* 87, no. 2 (February 1998): 56–58; Phaedra Brotherton, "Let the Games Begin," *American Gas* 81, no. 3 (April 1999): 19–20; A. J. Faria, "The Changing Nature of Business Simulation/Gaming Research: A Brief History," *Simulation and Gaming* 32, no. 1 (March 2001): 97–110.
34. Matt Bolch, "Games Employees Play: Delta Air Lines Uses a Blended e-Learning Program to Teach Employees the Economic Realities of the Airline Industry," *Training* 40, no. 4 (April 2003): 44–48; Leonard Hill, "Games People Play," *Air Transport World* 37, no. 3 (March 2000): 97–98.
35. Dan Heilman, "Putting Games to Work: Game-Based Training Is Shaping Up to Be One of This Generation's Primary Teaching Tools, in Business and Elsewhere," *Computer User* 22, no. 2 (February 2004): 14–16.
36. Christopher Hosford, "Serious Fun: Computer Training Finds a Niche," *Meeting News* 28, no. 7 (December 2004): 16; Rick Sullivan, "Lessons in Smallness," *Training and Development* 56, no. 3 (March 2002): 21–23; James W. Walker, "Perspectives," *Human Resource Planning* 23, no. 3 (2000): 5–7.
37. T. L. Stanley, "Be a Good Role Model for Your Employees," *Supervision* 65, no. 5 (January 2004): 5–8; Gary May and William Kahnweiler, "The Effect of a Mastery Practice Design on Learning and Transfer in Behavior Modeling Training," *Personnel Psychology* 53, no. 2 (Summer 2000): 353–73.
38. Wendy Larlee, "Training Programs: Key to Collections: Companies in the Collections Business Face Significant Challenges: Putting Solid Training Program in Place Can Help," *Collections & Credit Risk* 9, no. 2 (December 2004): 42–44; Heather Johnson, "The Whole Picture: When It Comes to Finding Out How Employees Feel about Training, Many Companies Fail to Get a Clear Picture," *Training* 47, no. 7 (July 2004): 30–35; Martin Delahoussaye, "Show Me the Results," *Training* 39, no. 3 (March 2002): 28–29; Reinout van Brakel, "Why ROI Isn't Enough," *Training and Development* 56, no. 6 (June 2002): 72–74.

39. "Dissatisfaction with Job Training Contributes to Low Job Satisfaction," *Managing Training & Development* (November 2003): 8; James Pershing and Jana Pershing, "Ineffective Reaction Evaluation," *Human Resource Development Quarterly* 12, no. 1 (Spring 2001): 73–90.
40. Andreas Putra, "Evaluating Training Programs: An Exploratory Study of Transfer of Learning onto the Job at Hotel A and Hotel B, Sydney, Australia," *Journal of Hospitality and Tourism Management* 11, no. 1 (April 2004): 77–78; Thomas Hoffman, "Simulations Revitalize e-Learning," *Computerworld* 37, no. 31 (August 4, 2003): 26–28; Donna Abernathy, "Thinking outside the Evaluation Box," *Training and Development* 53, no. 2 (February 1999): 18–23.
41. Jathan Janove, "Use It or Lose It," *HRMagazine* 47, no. 4 (April 2002): 99–104; Max Montesino, "Strategic Alignment of Training, Transfer-Enhancing Behaviors, and Training Usage: A Posttraining Study," *Human Resource Development Quarterly* 13, no. 1 (Spring 2002): 89–108; Siriporn Yamnill and Gary McLean, "Theories Supporting Transfer of Training," *Human Resource Development Quarterly* 12, no. 2 (Summer 2001): 195–208.
42. Delahoussaye, "Show Me the Results," 28–29; van Brakel, "Why ROI Isn't Enough," 72–74.
43. Richard J. Wagner and Robert J. Weigand, "Can the Value of Training Be Measured? A Simplified Approach to Evaluating Training," *The Health Care Manager* 23, no. 1 (January–March 2004): 71–79; van Brakel, "Why ROI Isn't Enough," 72–74; Sarah Fister Gale, "Measuring the ROI of E-Learning," *Workforce* 81, no. 8 (August 2002): 74–77; Earl Honeycutt, Kiran Karande, Ashraf Attia, and Steven Maurer, "A Utility-Based Framework for Evaluating the Financial Impact of Sales Force Training Programs," *Journal of Personal Selling and Sales Management* 21, no. 3 (Summer 2001): 229–38.
44. "Three Quick and Easy Ways to Gauge Your Training Outcomes," *IOMA's Report on Managing Training & Development* (January 2005): 4–5; "Use This Eight-Step Process to Predict the ROI of Your Training Programs," *IOMA's Human Resource Department Management Report* (December 2004): 4–5; Ellen Drost, Colette Frayne, Keven Lowe, and J. Michael Geringer, "Benchmarking Training and Development Practices: A Multi-Country Comparative Analysis," *Human Resource Management* 41, no. 1 (Spring 2002): 67–86; Daniel McMurrer, Mark Van Buren, and William Woodwell, "Making the Commitment," *Training and Development* 54, no. 1 (January 2000): 41–48.
45. Lisa Bertagnoli, "Basic Training: Orientation Is Proving to Be an Important First Step in Establishing Employee Bonds That Last," *WWD* (September 30, 2004): 40S; Jonathan Thom, "Creating Effective Orientation Programs," *San Diego Business Journal* 25, no. 33 (August 16, 2004): A6; Howard Klein and Natasha Weaver, "The Effectiveness of an Organizational-Level Orientation Training Program in the Socialization of New Hires," *Personnel Psychology* 53, no. 1 (Spring 2000): 47–66.
46. Kathryn Tyler, "Take New Employee Orientation off the Back Burner," *HRMagazine* 43, no. 6 (May 1998): 49–57; Noel Tichy, "No Ordinary Boot Camp," *Harvard Business Review* 79, no. 4 (April 2001): 63–70.
47. Mike Frost, "Creative New Employee Orientation Programs," *HRMagazine* 47, no. 8 (August 2002): 120–21; Marilyn Moats Kennedy, "Setting the Right Tone, Right Away," *Across the Board* 36, no. 4 (April 1999): 51–52.
48. Tim Ouellette, "Multimedia Jolts Duracell Training Program," *Computerworld* 29, no. 40 (October 2, 1995): 64; Norm Tollinsky, "Technology Puts Employees in Orientation Program's Driver Seat," *Canadian HR Reporter* 14, no. 7 (April 9, 2001): 19; Alan Horowitz, "Up to Speed—Fast," *Computerworld* 33, no. 7 (February 15, 1999): 48.
49. "How to Prepare for Training's Critical Role in the Labor Force of the Future," *IOMA's Report on Managing Training & Development* (September 2004): 2–3; Steve Hook, "Basic Skills Training on Target," *Times Educational Supplement* 4444 (August 31, 2001): 39.
50. "Corporate America Can't Write," *Work & Family Newsbrief* (January 2005): 4; Matt Bolch, "School at Work," *Training* 39, no. 2 (February 2002); Slav Kanyba, "Community Colleges React to Job-Training Request," *San Fernando Valley Business Journal* 9, no. 2 (June 7, 2004): 1–2.
51. Michael A. Verespej, "The Education Difference," *Industry Week* 245, no. 9 (May 6, 1996): 11–14; Richard D. Zalman, "The Basics of In-House Skills Training," *HRMagazine* 34, no. 2 (February 1990): 74–78; Ron Zemke, "Workplace Illiteracy—Shall We Overcome?" *Training* 26, no. 6 (June 1989): 33–39.
52. "What Makes Teams Work?" *HRFocus* 79, no. 4 (April 2002): S1–S3; John Annett, David Cunningham, and Peter Mathias-Jones, "A Method for Measuring Team Skills," *Ergonomics* 43, no. 8 (August 2000): 1076–94; Alan Auerbach, "Making Decisions under Stress: Implications for Individual and Team Training," *Personnel Psychology* 52, no. 4 (Winter 1999): 1050–53.
53. "Behavior-Based Sales Team Training Produces a 56% Increase in Revenues," *Managing Training & Development* (April 2004): 1; Sandra N. Phillips, "Team Training Puts Fizz in Coke Plant's Future," *Personnel Journal* 75, no. 1 (January 1996): 87–92.
54. Gail Johnson, "Time to Broaden Diversity," *Training* 41, no. 9 (September 2004): 16; George W. Bohlander and Kathy McCarthy, "How to Get the Most from Team Training," *National Productivity Review* (Autumn 1996): 25–35.
55. Lisa Bertagnoli, "The Ten-Minute Manager's Guide to . . . Cross-Training Staff," *Restaurants & Institutions* 114, no. 18 (August 15, 2004): 26–28; Wallace J. Hopp and Mark P. Van Oyen, "Agile Workforce Evaluation: A Framework for Cross-Training and Coordination," *IIE Transactions* 36, no. 10 (October 2004): 919–41.
56. Lorraine Mirabella, "Productivity Gains in Maryland Mean Less Hiring But More Job Cross-Training," *The Baltimore Sun (via Knight-Ridder/Tribune Business News)* (April 17, 2004).
57. Gary Stern, "Small Slights Bring Big Problems," *Workforce* 81, no. 8 (August 2002): 17; Bill Leonard, "Ways to Tell If a Diversity Program Is Measuring Up," *HRMagazine* 47, no. 7 (July 2002): 21.
58. "49ers Decide to Add Diversity to Training Camp," *The New York Times*, July 8, 2004, D3; Irwin Speizer, "Diversity on the Menu: Rachelle Hood, Denny's Chief Diversity Officer, Has Boosted the Company's Image. But That Hasn't Sold More Breakfasts," *Workforce Management* 83, no. 12 (November 1, 2004): 41.

chapter 8

Appraising and Improving Performance

After studying this chapter, you should be able to

Explain the purposes of performance appraisals and the reasons they can sometimes fail.

Explain the various methods used for performance evaluation.

Identify the characteristics of an effective appraisal program.

Outline the characteristics of an effective performance appraisal interview.

Describe the different sources of appraisal information.

In the preceding chapters, we have discussed some of the most effective methods available to managers for acquiring and developing top-notch employees. But talented employees are not enough—successful organizations are particularly adept at engaging their workforce to achieve goals that benefit the organization as well as the individuals.

In this chapter we turn to performance appraisal programs, which are among the most helpful tools an organization can use to maintain and enhance productivity and facilitate progress toward strategic goals. While we will focus mainly on formal performance appraisal procedures, the processes of managing and evaluating performance can be informal as well. All managers monitor the way employees work and assess how this matches organizational needs. They form impressions about the relative value of employees to the organization and seek to maximize the contribution of every individual. Yet while these ongoing informal processes are vitally important, most organizations also have a formal performance appraisal once or twice a year. In fact, in a survey of employees conducted by Mercer Human Resources Consulting, only a third of the 2,600 respondents had received a formal performance appraisal in the past year, and only 26 percent receive regular coaching from their manager on improving performance. Of those who said they'd had a formal performance appraisal in the past twelve months, 62 percent expressed a strong sense of commitment to their organization, compared to 49 percent of employees who hadn't.[1]

The success or failure of a performance appraisal program depends on the philosophy underlying it, its connection with business goals, and the attitudes and skills of those responsible for its administration. Many different methods can be used to gather information about employee performance. However, gathering information is only one step in the appraisal process. The information must be evaluated in the context of organizational needs and communicated to employees so that it will result in high levels of performance.

Performance Appraisal Programs

performance appraisal
A process, typically performed annually by a supervisor for a subordinate, designed to help employees understand their roles, objectives, expectations, and performance success

performance management
The process of creating a work environment in which people can perform to the best of their abilities

The **performance appraisal** can be defined as a process, typically delivered annually by a supervisor to a subordinate, designed to help employees understand their roles, objectives, expectations and performance success. **Performance management** is the process of creating a work environment in which people can perform to the best of their abilities. It is a whole work system that begins when a job is defined. Formal programs for performance appraisal and merit ratings are by no means new to organizations. The federal government began evaluating employees in 1842, when Congress passed a law mandating yearly performance reviews for department clerks. From this early beginning, performance appraisal programs have spread to large and small organizations in both the public and private sectors. Advocates see these HR programs as among the most logical means to appraise, develop, and effectively utilize the knowledge and abilities of employees. However, a growing number of observers point out that performance appraisals frequently fall short of their potential. In an ongoing survey of employee attitudes by the HR consulting firm Watson Wyatt, only 30 percent of employees said they thought their company's performance management process actually improved employee performance; only one in five thought it helped poorly performing employees do better.[2]

The push toward teamwork, continuous improvement, learning, and the like has caused numerous organizations to rethink their approach to appraisal. Some argue that performance appraisal discourages teamwork because it frequently focuses on individual achievement and produces a self-focus rather than a team focus. Others contend that appraisals are useful only at the extremes—highly effective or highly ineffective employees—and are not as useful for the majority of employees in the middle. Others point out that appraisals may focus on short-term achievements rather than long-term improvement and learning. They are sometimes too subjective or inconsistent or autocratic in that they create a distance between manager and employee rather than creating a team environment. Companies such as Xerox, Motorola, and Procter & Gamble have modified their performance appraisals to better acknowledge the importance of teamwork, continuous improvement, quality, and the like. Each of these issues is discussed at greater length throughout the chapter.[3]

Purposes of Performance Appraisal

It might seem at first glance that performance appraisals are used for a rather narrow purpose—to evaluate who is doing a good job (or not). But in reality performance appraisals are one of the most versatile tools available to managers. They can serve many purposes that benefit both the organization and the employee whose performance is being appraised.

Figure 8.1 shows the most common uses of performance appraisals. In general, these can be classified as either *administrative* or *developmental.*

Administrative Purposes

From the standpoint of administration, appraisal programs provide input that can be used for the entire range of HRM activities. For example, research has shown that

Figure 8.1 Purposes for Performance Appraisal

DEVELOPMENTAL	ADMINISTRATIVE
Provide performance feedback	Document personnel decisions
Identify individual strengths/weaknesses	Determine promotion candidates
Recognize individual performance	Determine transfers and assignments
Assist in goal identification	Identify poor performance
Evaluate goal achievement	Decide retention or termination
Identify individual training needs	Decide on layoffs
Determine organizational training needs	Validate selection criteria
Reinforce authority structure	Meet legal requirements
Allow employees to discuss concerns	Evaluate training programs/progress
Improve communication	Personnel planning
Provide a forum for leaders to help	Make reward/compensation decisions

performance appraisals are used most widely as a basis for compensation decisions.[4] The practice of "pay-for-performance" is found in all types of organizations. Performance appraisal is also directly related to a number of other major HR functions, such as promotion, transfer, and layoff decisions. Performance appraisal data may also be used in HR planning, in determining the relative worth of jobs under a job evaluation program, and as criteria for validating selection tests. Performance appraisals also provide a "paper trail" for documenting HRM actions that may result in legal action. Because of government EEO/AA directives, employers must maintain accurate, objective records of employee performance in order to defend themselves against possible charges of discrimination in connection with such HRM actions as promotion, salary determination, and termination. Finally, it is important to recognize that the success of the entire HR program depends on knowing how the performance of employees compares with the goals established for them. This knowledge is best derived from a carefully planned and administered HR appraisal program. Appraisal systems have the capability to influence employee behavior, thereby leading directly to improved organizational performance.[5]

Developmental Purposes

From the standpoint of individual development, appraisal provides the feedback essential for discussing strengths and weaknesses as well as improving performance. Regardless of the employee's level of performance, the appraisal process provides an opportunity to identify issues for discussion, eliminate any potential problems, and set new goals for achieving high performance. Newer approaches to performance appraisal emphasize training as well as development and growth plans for employees. A developmental approach to appraisal recognizes that the purpose of a manager is to improve job behavior, not simply to evaluate past performance. Having a sound basis for improving performance is one of the major benefits of an appraisal program.

Companies such as Best Buy and EDS have redesigned their performance appraisal systems to focus more on employee development and learning. EDS, for example, integrated its performance appraisal system to work in concert with learning and career management objectives. The new system, called the Career Resource System, includes a detailed job description, a performance review, and a career planner to track long-term goals, as well as access to the company's automated career library. The system is ultimately linked to the company's succession policies. By creating this overall system, EDS hopes to shift the role of manager from that of "judge" to one of "coach."[6]

Reasons Appraisal Programs Sometimes Fail

In actual practice, and for a number of reasons, formal performance appraisal programs sometimes yield disappointing results. Figure 8.2 shows that the primary culprits include lack of top-management information and support, unclear performance standards, rater bias, too many forms to complete, and use of the program for conflicting purposes. For example, if an appraisal program is used to provide a written appraisal for salary action and at the same time to motivate employees to improve their work, the administrative and developmental purposes may be in conflict. As a result, the appraisal interview may become a discussion about salary in which the manager seeks to justify the action taken. In such cases, the discussion might have little influence on the employee's future job performance.

Figure 8.2 Let Me Count the Ways . . .

There are many reasons why performance appraisal systems might not be effective. Some of the most common problems include the following:

- Inadequate preparation on the part of the manager.
- Employee is not given clear objectives at the beginning of performance period.
- Manager may not be able to observe performance or have all the information.
- Performance standards may not be clear.
- Inconsistency in ratings among supervisors or other raters.
- Rating personality rather than performance.
- The halo effect, contrast effect, or some other perceptual bias.
- Inappropriate time span (either too short or too long).
- Overemphasis on uncharacteristic performance.
- Inflated ratings because managers do not want to deal with "bad news."
- Subjective or vague language in written appraisals.
- Organizational politics or personal relationships cloud judgments.
- No thorough discussion of causes of performance problems.
- Manager may not be trained at evaluation or giving feedback.
- No follow-up and coaching after the evaluation.

Sources: Patricia Evres, "Problems to Avoid during Performance Evaluations," *Air Conditioning, Heating & Refrigeration News* 216, no. 16 (August 19, 2002): 24–26; Clinton Longnecker and Dennis Gioia, "The Politics of Executive Appraisals," *Journal of Compensation and Benefits* 10, no. 2 (1994): 5–11; "Seven Deadly Sins of Performance Appraisals," *Supervisory Management* 39, no. 1 (1994): 7–8.

As with all HR functions, if the support of top management is lacking, the appraisal program will not be successful. Even the best-conceived program will not work in an environment where appraisers are not encouraged by their superiors to take the program seriously. To underscore the importance of this responsibility, top management should announce that effectiveness in appraising subordinates is a standard by which the appraisers themselves will be evaluated.

Other reasons performance appraisal programs can fail to yield the desired results include the following:

1. There is little face-to-face discussion between the manager and the employee being appraised.
2. The relationship between the employee's job description and the criteria on the appraisal form isn't clear.
3. Managers feel that little or no benefit will be derived from the time and energy spent in the process, or they are concerned only with bad performances.
4. Managers dislike the face-to-face confrontation of appraisal interviews.
5. Managers are not sufficiently adept at rating employees or providing them with appraisal feedback.

6. The judgmental role of appraisal conflicts with the helping role of developing employees.
7. The appraisal is just a once-a-year event, and there is little follow-up afterward.

In many organizations, performance appraisals are conducted only once a year—but that is changing. More organizations are beginning to conduct them on a semiannual basis, and even quarterly. An important principle of performance appraisal is that continual feedback and employee coaching must be a positive daily activity. The annual or semiannual performance review should simply be a logical extension of the day-to-day supervision process.

One of the main concerns of employees is the fairness of the performance appraisal system, as the process is central to so many HRM decisions. Employees who believe the system is unfair may consider the appraisal interview a waste of time and leave the interview with feelings of anxiety or frustration. Also, they may view compliance with the appraisal system as perfunctory and thus play only a passive role during the interview process. By addressing these employee concerns during the planning stage of the appraisal process, the organization will help the appraisal program succeed in reaching its goals.[7]

Finally, organizational politics can introduce a bias even in fairly administered employee appraisals.[8] For example, managers may inflate evaluations because they desire higher salaries for their employees or because higher subordinate ratings make them look good as managers. Alternatively, managers may want to get rid of troublesome employees, passing them off to another department by inflating their ratings.

Developing an Effective Appraisal Program

The HR department ordinarily has the primary responsibility for overseeing and coordinating the appraisal program. Managers from the operating departments must also be actively involved, particularly in helping to establish the objectives for the program. Furthermore, employees are more likely to accept and be satisfied with the performance appraisal program when they have the chance to participate in its development. Their concerns about fairness and accuracy in determining raises, promotions, and the like tend to be alleviated somewhat when they have been involved at the planning stage and have helped develop the performance standards themselves.

What Are the Performance Standards?

Before any appraisal is conducted, the standards by which performance is to be evaluated should be clearly defined and communicated to the employee. As discussed in Chapter 4, these standards should be based on job-related requirements derived from job analysis and reflected in an employee's job description and job specifications. When performance standards are properly established, they help translate organizational goals and objectives into job requirements that convey acceptable and unacceptable levels of performance to employees.

As shown in Figure 8.3, there are four basic considerations in establishing performance standards: strategic relevance, criterion deficiency, criterion contamination, and reliability.

Figure 8.3 Establishing Performance Standards

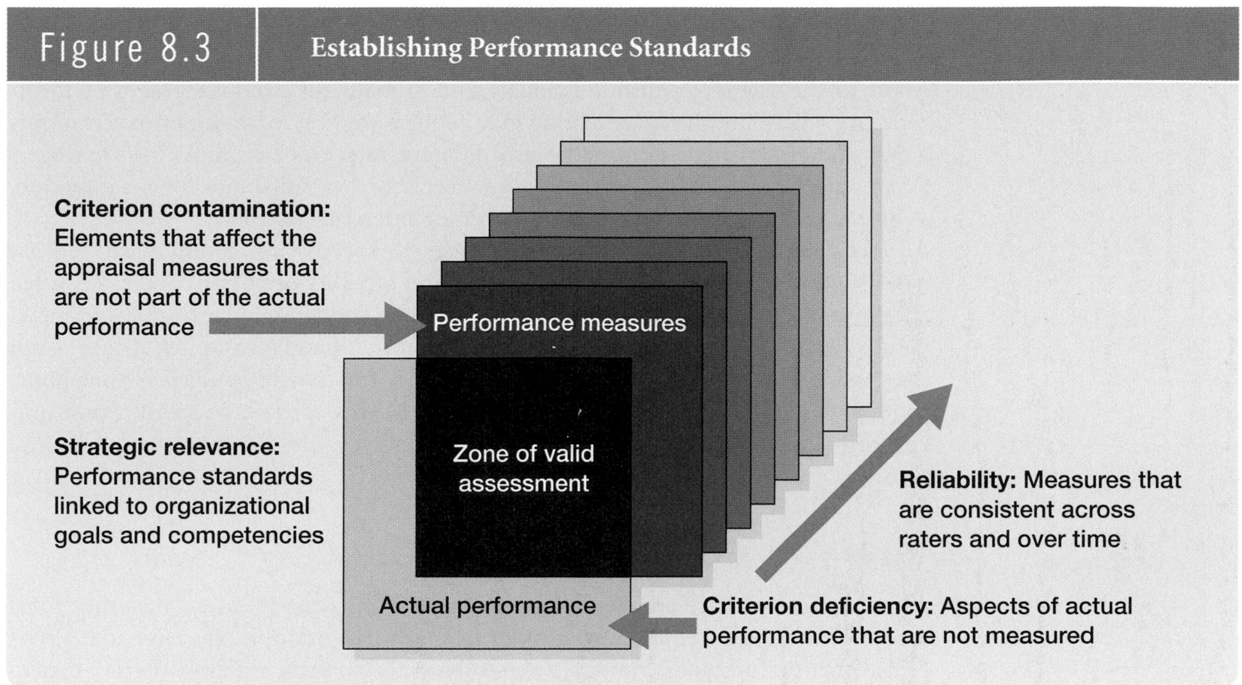

Strategic Relevance

Strategic relevance refers to the extent to which standards relate to the strategic objectives of the organization. For example, if an organization has established a standard that "95 percent of all customer complaints are to be resolved in one day," then it is relevant for the customer service representatives to use such a standard for their evaluations. Companies such as 3M and Buckman Laboratories have strategic objectives that 25–30 percent of their sales are to be generated from products developed within the past five years. These objectives are translated into performance standards for their employees. General Motors and Whirlpool include other objectives such as cost, quality, and speed. They develop metrics to identify and compare their performance around the world on these measures.[9]

Criterion Deficiency

A second consideration in establishing performance standards is the extent to which the standards capture the entire range of an employee's responsibilities. When performance standards focus on a single criterion (such as sales revenues) to the exclusion of other important but less quantifiable performance dimensions (such as customer service), then the appraisal system is said to suffer from criterion deficiency.[10]

Criterion Contamination

Just as performance criteria can be deficient, they can also be contaminated. There are factors outside an employee's control that can influence his or her performance. A comparison of performance of production workers, for example, should not be contaminated by the fact that some have newer machines than others do. A comparison of the performance of traveling salespeople should not be contaminated by the fact that territories differ in sales potential.[11]

Reliability

As discussed in Chapter 6, reliability refers to the stability or consistency of a standard, or the extent to which individuals tend to maintain a certain level of performance over time. In ratings, reliability may be measured by correlating two sets of ratings made by a single rater or by two different raters. For example, two managers may rate the same individual and estimate his or her suitability for a promotion. Their ratings could be compared to determine interrater reliability.

Performance standards permit managers to specify and communicate precise information to employees regarding quality and quantity of output. Therefore, when performance standards are written, they should be defined in quantifiable and measurable terms. For example, "ability and willingness to handle customer orders" is not as good a performance standard as "all customer orders will be filled in four hours with a 98 percent accuracy rate." When standards are expressed in specific, measurable terms, comparing the employee's performance against the standard results in a more justifiable appraisal.

Are You Complying with the Law?

Because performance appraisals are used as one basis for HRM actions, they must meet certain legal requirements. In *Brito v Zia*, for example, the Supreme Court ruled that performance appraisals were subject to the same validity criteria as selection procedures.[12] As the courts have made clear, a central issue is to have carefully defined and measurable performance standards. In one landmark case involving test validation, *Albemarle Paper Company v Moody* (discussed in Chapter 3), the U.S. Supreme Court found that employees had been ranked against a vague standard, open to each supervisor's own interpretation. The Court stated that "there is no way of knowing precisely what criteria of job performance the supervisors were considering, whether each supervisor was considering the same criteria, or whether, indeed,

Specific, measurable job standards help remove vagueness and subjectivity from performance appraisals.

any of the supervisors actually applied a focused and stable body of criteria of any kind."[13] This decision has prompted organizations to try to eliminate vagueness in descriptions of traits such as attitude, cooperation, dependability, initiative, and leadership. For example, the trait "dependability" can be made much less vague if it is spelled out in terms of employee tardiness and/or unexcused absences. In general, reducing room for subjective judgments will improve the entire appraisal process.

Furthermore, other court decisions show that employers might face legal challenges to their appraisal systems when appraisals indicate acceptable or above-average performance but employees are later passed over for promotion, disciplined for poor performance, discharged, or laid off from the organization. In these cases, the performance appraisals can undermine the legitimacy of the subsequent personnel decision. Intel, for example, was recently taken to court by a group of former employees on grounds that the performance appraisal system (used for layoff decisions) was unreliable and invalid. Other companies such as Goodyear and Ford have also faced legal battles because their performance appraisals were viewed as discriminatory against older workers.[14] In light of court cases such as these, performance appraisals should meet the following legal guidelines:

- Performance ratings must be job-related, with performance standards developed through job analysis.
- Employees must be given a written copy of their job standards in advance of appraisals.
- Managers who conduct the appraisal must be able to observe the behavior they are rating. This implies having a measurable standard with which to compare employee behavior.
- Supervisors should be trained to use the appraisal form correctly. They should be instructed in how to apply appraisal standards when making judgments.
- Appraisals should be discussed openly with employees and counseling or corrective guidance offered to help poor performers improve their performance.
- An appeals procedure should be established to enable employees to express disagreement with the appraisal.[15]

To comply with the legal requirements of performance appraisals, employers must ensure that managers and supervisors document appraisals and reasons for subsequent HRM actions. This information may prove decisive should an employee take legal action. An employer's credibility is strengthened when it can support performance appraisal ratings by documenting instances of poor performance.

Who Should Appraise Performance?

Just as there are multiple standards by which to evaluate performance, there are also multiple candidates for appraising performance. Given the complexity of today's jobs, it is often unrealistic to presume that one person can fully observe and evaluate an employee's performance. At IBM, employees with high potential are regularly reviewed by a broad cross-section of the company's leaders, not just their immediate bosses. As shown in Figure 8.4, raters may include supervisors, peers, team members, self, subordinates, customers, vendors, and suppliers. And each may be more or less useful for the administrative and developmental purposes we discussed earlier. Companies such as Cigna, Black & Decker, and Disney have used a multiple-rater

Figure 8.4 Alternative Sources of Appraisal

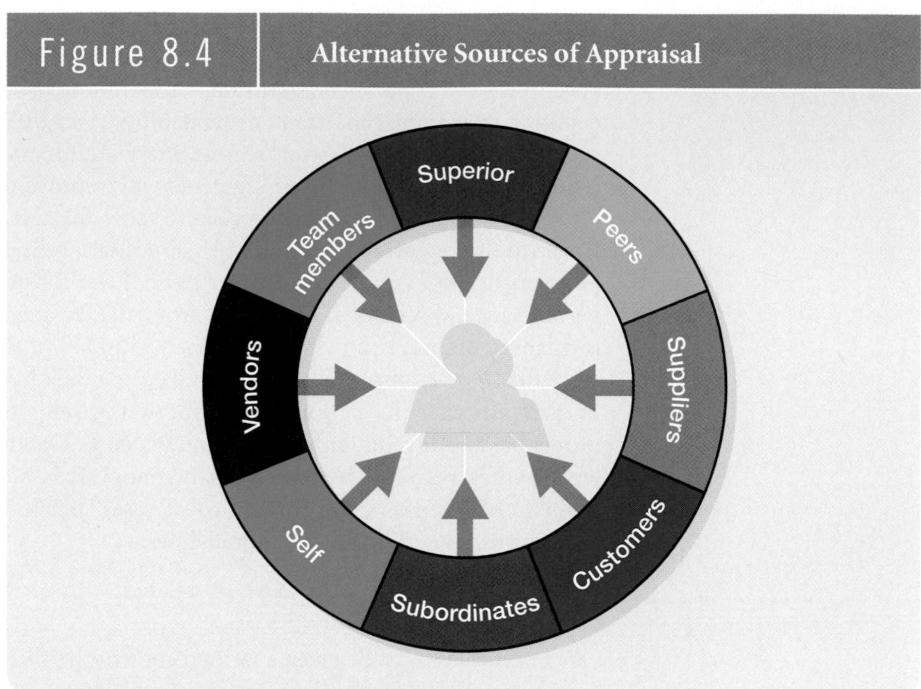

approach—or 360-degree appraisal—to evaluate employee performance.[16] We will talk more about 360-degree appraisal at the end of this section.

Manager/Supervisor Appraisal

manager and/or supervisor appraisal A performance appraisal done by an employee's manager and often reviewed by a manager one level higher

Manager and/or supervisor appraisal has been the traditional approach to evaluating an employee's performance. In most instances supervisors are in the best position to perform this function, although it may not always be possible for them to do so. Managers often complain that they do not have the time to fully observe the performance of employees. These managers must then rely on performance records to evaluate an employee's performance. If reliable and valid measures are not available, the appraisal may be less than accurate. (Recall our earlier discussion of criterion deficiency and contamination.)

When a supervisor appraises employees independently, provision is often made for a review of the appraisals by the supervisor's superior. Having appraisals reviewed by a supervisor's superior reduces the chance of superficial or biased evaluations. Reviews by superiors generally are more objective and provide a broader perspective of employee performance than do appraisals by immediate supervisors.

Self-Appraisal

self-appraisal A performance appraisal done by the employee being evaluated, generally on an appraisal form completed by the employee prior to the performance interview

Sometimes employees are asked to evaluate themselves on a self-appraisal form. The **self-appraisal** is beneficial when managers seek to increase an employee's involvement in the review process. A self-appraisal system requires an employee to complete the appraisal form prior to the performance interview. At a minimum, this gets the employee thinking about his or her strengths and weaknesses and may lead to discussions about barriers to effective performance. During the performance interview,

Source: From *The Wall Street Journal*—permission, Cartoon Features Syndicate.

the manager and the employee discuss job performance and agree on a final appraisal. This approach also works well when the manager and the employee jointly establish future performance goals or employee development plans. Critics of self-appraisal argue that self-raters are more lenient than managers in their assessments and tend to present themselves in a highly favorable light. There is also evidence that self-appraisals can lead employees to believe that they will have more influence over the appraisal's outcome. If that expectation isn't met, the employee can become frustrated. For this reason, self-appraisals may be best for developmental purposes rather than for administrative decisions. Used in conjunction with other methods, self-appraisals can be a valuable source of appraisal information. They at least serve as a catalyst for discussion during the appraisal.[17]

Subordinate Appraisal

subordinate appraisal
A performance appraisal of a superior by an employee, which is more appropriate for developmental than for administrative purposes

Subordinate appraisal has been used by both large organizations (such as Xerox and Honeywell) and small organizations (such as Hyde Manufacturing and Alliance Funding) to give managers feedback on how their subordinates view them.[18] Subordinates are in a good position to evaluate their managers because they are in frequent contact with their superiors and occupy a unique position from which to observe many performance-related behaviors. Subordinate appraisals have also been shown to improve the performance of managers. The performance dimensions judged most appropriate for subordinate appraisals include leadership, oral communication, delegation of authority, coordination of team efforts, and interest in subordinates. However, dimensions related to managers' specific job tasks, such as planning and organizing, budgeting, creativity, and analytical ability, are not usually seen as appropriate for subordinate appraisal. Because subordinate appraisals give employees power over their bosses, managers may be hesitant to endorse such a system, particularly when it might be used as a basis for compensation decisions. However, when the information is used for developmental purposes, managers tend to be more open to the idea. And available evidence suggests that when managers heed the advice of their subordinates, their own performance can improve substantially. Nevertheless, to avoid potential problems, subordinate appraisals should be submitted anonymously and combined across several individual raters.[19]

Peer Appraisal

peer appraisal
A performance appraisal done by one's fellow employees, generally on forms that are compiled into a single profile for use in the performance interview conducted by the employee's manager

Individuals of equal rank who work together are increasingly asked to evaluate each other. A **peer appraisal** provides information that differs to some degree from ratings by a superior, since peers often see different dimensions of performance. Peers can readily identify leadership and interpersonal skills along with other strengths and weaknesses of their co-workers. A superior asked to rate a patrol officer on a dimension such as "dealing with the public" may not have had much opportunity to

USING THE INTERNET

A lengthy but insightful description of the implementation of a peer appraisal system in conjunction with self-directed work teams at the Racine liquid manufacturing facility of S. C. Johnson & Son, Inc., appears at their web site. Go to the Student Resources at:

bohlander.swlearning.com

observe it. Fellow officers, on the other hand, have the opportunity to observe this behavior regularly.

One advantage of peer appraisals is the belief that they furnish more accurate and valid information than appraisals by superiors. The supervisor often sees employees putting their best foot forward, while those who work with their fellow employees on a regular basis may see a more realistic picture. With peer appraisals, co-workers complete an evaluation on the employee. The forms are then usually compiled into a single profile, which is given to the supervisor for use in the final appraisal. For employees who have trouble confronting their co-workers about problems, the reviews provide a forum in which to address issues and resolve conflicts. They also provide an opportunity to hand out praise.[20]

Despite the evidence that peer appraisals are possibly the most accurate method of judging employee behavior, there are reasons why they have not been used more frequently.[21] The reasons commonly cited include the following:

1. Peer ratings are simply a popularity contest.
2. Managers are reluctant to give up control over the appraisal process.
3. Those receiving low ratings might retaliate against their peers.
4. Peers rely on stereotypes in ratings.

When peers are in competition with one another, such as with sales associates, peer appraisals may not be advisable for administrative decisions such as salary or bonuses. Employers using peer appraisals must also be sure to safeguard confidentiality in handling the review forms. Any breach of confidentiality can create interpersonal rivalries or hurt feelings and bring about hostility among fellow employees.

team appraisal
A performance appraisal, based on TQM concepts, that recognizes team accomplishment rather than individual performance

Team Appraisal

An extension of the peer appraisal is the **team appraisal.** While peers are on equal standing with one another, they may not work closely together. In a team setting, it

Some managers give their teams autonomy but hold them accountable for results.

kinko's®
Express Yourself.™

You are a valued Kinko's customer. What you have to say is important to us.
Please take a moment to let us know how we are doing by filling out this card, calling Kinko's Customer Service at 1-800-2-KINKOS or visiting our web site at www.kinkos.com.

Overall, how satisfied were you with your experience at Kinko's today? (Circle one)

1 2 3 4 5 6 7 8 9
Extremely Dissatisfied — Extremely Satisfied

What do we do well? ______

What should we change? ______

What can we do to serve you better? ______

Additional comments? ______

Date of visit: ______ Time of day: ______
Name: ______
Address: ______
City/State/Zip: ______
Area Code: ______ Telephone: ______
Occupation: ______

Thanks for visiting
Kinko's Glenview IL Glenview North Plaza
#02-08-047-3614

Kinko's invites customers to rate the company on its service.

may be nearly impossible to separate out an individual's contribution. Advocates of team appraisal argue that, in such cases, individual appraisal can be dysfunctional because it detracts from the critical issues of the team. To address this issue, organizations ranging from Boeing and Texas Instruments to Jostens and Ralston Foods have begun developing team appraisals to evaluate the performance of the team as a whole.[22]

A company's interest in team appraisals is frequently driven by its commitment to TQM principles and practices. At its root, TQM is a control system that involves setting standards (based on customer requirements), measuring performance against those standards, and identifying opportunities for continuous improvement. In this regard TQM and performance appraisal are perfectly complementary. However, a basic tenet of TQM is that performance is best understood at the level of the system as a whole, whereas performance appraisal traditionally has focused on individual performance. Team appraisals represent one way to break down barriers between individuals and encourage their collective effort.[23] Frequently, the system is complemented by the use of team incentives or group variable pay. (See Chapters 10 and 16.)

Customer Appraisal

Also driven by TQM concerns, an increasing number of organizations use internal and external **customer appraisal** as a source of performance appraisal information. External customers' evaluations, of course, have been used for some time to appraise restaurant personnel. However, companies such as Federal Express, Best Buy, and Isuzu are among the companies that have utilized external customers as well. Managers establish customer service measures (CSMs) and set goals for employees (linked to company goals). Other companies survey their vendors and suppliers as part of the appraisal process. By including the firm's business partners in the performance reviews, managers hope to produce more objective evaluations, more effective employees, more satisfied customers, and better business performance.[24]

customer appraisal
A performance appraisal that, like team appraisal, is based on TQM concepts and seeks evaluation from both external and internal customers

In contrast to external customers, internal customers include anyone inside the organization who depends on an employee's work output. For example, managers who rely on the HR department for selection and training services would be candidates for conducting internal customer evaluations of that department. For both developmental and administrative purposes, internal customers can provide extremely useful feedback about the value added by an employee or team of employees.

Putting It All Together: 360-Degree Appraisal

As mentioned previously, many companies are combining various sources of performance appraisal information to create multirater—or 360-degree—appraisal and feedback systems. Jobs are multifaceted, and different people see different things. As

USING THE INTERNET

Software used to help prepare 360-degree appraisal systems is available from a number of companies. For example, Quality coach/360 software developed by Leadership Software Corp. combines total quality management (TQM), the coaching style of management, and 360-degree performance assessment. Go to the Student Resources at:

bohlander.swlearning.com

the name implies, 360-degree feedback is intended to provide employees with as accurate a view of their performance as possible by getting input from all angles: supervisors, peers, subordinates, customers, and the like. Although in the beginning, 360-degree systems were purely developmental and were restricted mainly to management and career development, they have migrated to performance appraisal and other administrative applications. An estimated 25 percent of U.S. employers and more than 90 percent of Fortune 1000 companies have implemented some form of 360-degree feedback system for career development, performance appraisal, or both. Because the system combines more information than a typical performance appraisal, it can become administratively complex. For that reason, organizations have recently begun using employee management software (EPM) to compile and aggregate the information. Approximately 20 percent use the Web or other software for their performance management systems; another 33 percent plan to do so in the near future.[25] For example, PerformancePlus and CompetencyPlus, developed by Exxceed, a Chicago company, allow managers and employees to develop performance plans, goals, and objectives, and then track their progress over time. Managers can see all of an employee's goals and action steps on a single screen, and self-appraisals and multiple-rater reviews can be combined into a 360-degree format. After rating an employee's performance on each goal, raters can provide summary comments in three categories: victories and accomplishments, setbacks and frustrations, and general comments. To ensure security, a user ID and password are required and all the data are captured and saved in the employee's history file. Other types of EPM software can calculate and manage financial rewards based on how well employees perform as well as identify their performance gaps and manage their education, certification, and training.[26]

Although 360-degree feedback can be useful for both developmental and administrative purposes, most companies start with an exclusive focus on development. Employees may be understandably nervous about the possibility of everyone "ganging up" on them in their evaluations. In addition, organizations sometimes implement 360-feedback without clearly defining the strategic mission of the program—either the competencies on the 360-feedback form are not relevant to the firm's business objectives or they are so broad that they can't be linked to an individual employee's performance. Therefore, 360-feedback programs should be implemented only after a close scrutiny of their purposes and conducted with proper planning and evaluation. Figure 8.5 shows a list of pros and cons of 360-degree appraisal.

When Intel established a 360-degree system, the company observed the following safeguards to ensure its maximum quality and acceptance:

- *Assure anonymity.* Make certain that no employee ever knows how any evaluation-team member responded. (The supervisor's rating is an exception to this rule.)
- *Make respondents accountable.* Supervisors should discuss each evaluation-team member's input, letting each member know whether he or she used the rating scales appropriately, whether his or her responses were reliable, and how other participants rated the employee.
- *Prevent "gaming" of the system.* Some individuals may try to help or hurt an employee by giving either too high or too low an evaluation. Team members may try to collude with one another by agreeing to give each other uniformly high ratings. Supervisors should check for obviously invalid responses.

Figure 8.5 Pros and Cons of 360-Degree Appraisal

PROS

- The system is more comprehensive in that responses are gathered from multiple perspectives.
- Quality of information is better. (Quality of respondents is more important than quantity.)
- It complements TQM initiatives by emphasizing internal/external customers and teams.
- It may lessen bias/prejudice since feedback comes from more people, not one individual.
- Feedback from peers and others may increase employee self-development.

CONS

- The system is complex in combining all the responses.
- Feedback can be intimidating and cause resentment if employee feels the respondents have "ganged up."
- There may be conflicting opinions, though they may all be accurate from the respective standpoints.
- The system requires training to work effectively.
- Employees may collude or "game" the system by giving invalid evaluations to one another.
- Appraisers may not be accountable if their evaluations are anonymous.

Sources: Compiled from David A. Waldman, Leanne E. Atwater, and David Antonioni, "Has 360-Degree Feedback Gone Amok?" *Academy of Management Executive* 12, no. 2 (May 1998): 86–94; Bruce Pfau, Ira Kay, Kenneth Nowak, and Jai Ghorpade, "Does 360-Degree Feedback Negatively Affect Company Performance?" *HRMagazine* 47, no. 6 (June 2002): 54–59; Maury Peiperl, "Getting 360-Degree Feedback Right," *Harvard Business Review* 79, no. 1 (January 2001): 142–47; Joyce E. Bono and Amy E. Colbert, "Understanding Responses to Multi-Source Feedback: The Role of Core Self-Evaluations," *Personnel Psychology* 58, no. 1 (Spring 2005): 171–205.

- *Use statistical procedures.* Use weighted averages or other quantitative approaches to combining evaluations. Supervisors should be careful about using subjective combinations of data, which could undermine the system.
- *Identify and quantify biases.* Check for prejudices or preferences related to age, gender, ethnicity, or other group factors.[27]

Based on the experiences of companies such as Intel, Disney, and Monsanto, it appears that 360-degree feedback can provide a valuable approach to performance appraisal. Its success, as with any appraisal technique, depends on how managers use the information and how fairly employees are treated.

Training Appraisers

A weakness of many performance appraisal programs is that managers and supervisors are not adequately trained for the appraisal task and provide little meaningful feedback to subordinates. Because they lack precise standards for appraising subordinates' performance and have not developed the necessary observational and feedback skills, their appraisals often become nondirective and meaningless. Therefore, training appraisers can vastly improve the performance appraisal process. Says one HR manager: "What's not important is the (appraisal) form or the (measuring) scale. What's important is that managers can objectively observe people's performance and objectively give feedback on that performance." Notwithstanding, in a survey of fifty-five HR managers from medium and large companies, more than half said their companies did either little or no evaluation of how well their managers do appraisals.[28]

Establishing an Appraisal Plan

Training programs are most effective when they follow a systematic process that begins with an explanation of the objectives of the performance appraisal system. It is important for the rater to know the purpose for which the appraisal is to be used. For example, using the appraisal for compensation decisions rather than development purposes may affect how the rater evaluates the employee, and it may change the rater's opinion of how the appraisal form should be completed. The mechanics of the rating system should also be explained, including how frequently the appraisals are to be conducted, who will conduct them, and what the standards of performance are. In addition, appraisal training should alert raters to the weaknesses and problems of appraisal systems so they can be avoided.

Eliminating Rater Error

Appraisal training should focus on eliminating the subjective errors made by managers in the rating process. Gary Latham and Kenneth Wexley stress the importance of performance appraisal training by noting that

> [R]egardless of whether evaluations are obtained from multiple appraisers or from only the employee's immediate superior, all appraisers should be trained to reduce errors of judgment that occur when one person evaluates another. This training is necessary because to the degree to which a performance appraisal is biased, distorted, or inaccurate, the probability of increasing the productivity of the employee is greatly decreased. Moreover, wrong decisions could be made regarding whom to promote, retain, or replace, which in turn will penalize the organization's bottom line. In addition, when a performance appraisal is affected by rating errors, the employee may be justified in filing a discrimination charge.[29]

With any rating method, certain types of errors can arise that should be considered. The "halo error" discussed in Chapter 6 is also common with respect to rating scales, especially those that do not include carefully developed descriptions of the employee behaviors being rated. Provision for comments on the rating form tends to reduce halo error. The "horn error" is the opposite of the halo effect. It occurs when a manager focuses on one negative aspect about an employee and generalizes it into an overall poor appraisal rating. A personality conflict between a manager and his or her employees increases the probability of the horn effect, which can lead to a high level of frustration on the employee's part if it's not corrected.[30]

Some types of rating errors are *distributional errors* in that they involve a group of ratings given across various employees. For example, raters who are reluctant to assign either extremely high or extremely low ratings commit the **error of central tendency.** In this case, all employees are rated about average. To such raters it is a good idea to explain that, among large numbers of employees, one should expect to find significant differences in behavior, productivity, and other characteristics.

error of central tendency
A performance-rating error in which all employees are rated about average

In contrast to central tendency errors, it is also common for some raters to give unusually high or low ratings. For example, a manager may erroneously assert, "All my employees are excellent" or "None of my people are good enough." These beliefs give rise to what is called **leniency or strictness error.**[31] One way to reduce this error is to clearly define the characteristics or dimensions of performance and to provide meaningful descriptions of behavior, known as "anchors," on the scale. Another approach is to require ratings to conform to a *forced ranking*, a type of system initially developed by GE, purportedly with good results. Managers appraising employees under a *forced-distribution* system are required to place a certain percentage of employees into various performance categories. For example, it may be required that 10 percent of ratings be poor (or excellent). This is similar to the requirement in some schools that instructors grade on a curve. A variation of this is *peer ranking*, a system whereby employees in a work group are ranked against one another from best to worst. Although forced distribution and peer ranking may solve leniency and strictness errors, they can create other rating errors—particularly if most employees are performing above standard. Moreover, if the system has a disparate impact on a legally protected group, such as minority or older employers, it can result, and has resulted, in discrimination suits. Even so, more organizations are using forced-ranking systems. However, other companies, including Ford and Goodyear, abandoned their forced-ranking systems after lawsuits, lower morale, decreased teamwork, and destructive employee competition ensued following their use. Because of the legal issues related to forced ranking, companies that use these methods obviously need to carefully train their appraisers.[32]

leniency or strictness error
A performance-rating error in which the appraiser tends to give employees either unusually high or unusually low ratings

Some rating errors are *temporal* in that the performance review is biased either favorably or unfavorably, depending on the way performance information is selected, evaluated, and organized by the rater over time. For example, when the appraisal is based largely on the employee's recent behavior, good or bad, the rater has committed the **recency error.** Managers who give higher ratings because they believe an employee is "showing improvement" may unwittingly be committing recency error. Without work-record documentation for the entire appraisal period, the rater is forced to recall recent employee behavior to establish the rating. Having the rater routinely document employee accomplishments and failures throughout the whole appraisal period can minimize the recency error. One way for managers to do this is by keeping a diary or a log. Rater training also will help reduce this error.

recency error
A performance-rating error in which the appraisal is based largely on the employee's most recent behavior rather than on behavior throughout the appraisal period

Contrast error occurs when an employee's evaluation is biased either upward or downward because of another employee's performance, evaluated just previously. For example, an average employee may appear especially productive when compared with a poor performer. However, that same employee may appear unproductive when compared with a star performer. Contrast errors are most likely when raters are required to rank employees in order from the best to the poorest. Employees are evaluated against one another, usually on the basis of some organizational standard or guideline. For example, they may be compared on the basis of their ability to meet production standards or their "overall" ability to perform their job. As with other types of rating error, contrast error can be reduced through training that focuses on using objective standards and behavioral anchors to appraise performance.[33]

contrast error
A performance-rating error in which an employee's evaluation is biased either upward or downward because of comparison with another employee just previously evaluated

Similar-to-me error occurs when appraisers inflate the evaluations of people with whom they have something in common. For example, if both the manager and the employee are from small towns, the manager may unwittingly have a more favorable impression of the employee. The effects of a similar-to-me error can be powerful, and when the similarity is based on race, religion, gender, or some other protected category, it may result in discrimination.

similar-to-me error
A performance-rating error in which an appraiser inflates the evaluation of an employee because of a mutual personal connection

Furthermore, raters should be aware of any stereotypes they may hold toward particular groups—such as male/female or white/black—because the observation and interpretation of performance can be clouded by these stereotypes. For example, one study found that men who experience conflicts between family and work received lower overall performance ratings and lower reward recommendations than men who did not experience such conflicts. Women, on the other hand, were judged no differently, whether they experienced family-work conflicts or not. A host of organizations such as Sears and Weyerhaeuser have developed formal training programs to reduce the subjective errors commonly made during the rating process. This training can pay off, particularly when participants have the opportunity to (1) observe other managers making errors, (2) actively participate in discovering their own errors, and (3) practice job-related tasks to reduce the errors they tend to make.[34]

Feedback Training

Finally, a training program for raters should provide some general points to consider for planning and conducting the feedback interview. The interview not only provides employees with knowledge of results of their evaluation, but also allows the manager and employee to discuss current problems and set future goals.

Training in specific skills should cover at least three basic areas: (1) communicating effectively, (2) diagnosing the root causes of performance problems, and (3) setting goals and objectives.[35] A checklist can be used to assist supervisors in preparing for the appraisal interview. As shown in Highlights in HRM 1, the checklist reflects the growing tendency of organizations such as AT&T, Weyerhaeuser, and Honeywell to have employees assess their own performance prior to the appraisal interview. The performance appraisal interview will be discussed in detail later in the chapter.

Performance Appraisal Methods

Since the early years of their use by the federal government, methods of evaluating personnel have evolved considerably. Old systems have been replaced by new methods that reflect technical improvements and legal requirements and are more consistent with the purposes of appraisal. In the discussion that follows, we will examine in some detail the methods that have found widespread use, and we will briefly touch on other methods that are used less frequently. Performance appraisal methods can be broadly classified as measuring traits, behaviors, or results. Trait approaches continue to be more popular despite their inherent subjectivity. Behavioral approaches provide more action-oriented information to employees and therefore may be best for development. The results-oriented approach is gaining popularity because it focuses on the measurable contributions that employees make to the organization.

Trait Methods

Trait approaches to performance appraisal are designed to measure the extent to which an employee possesses certain characteristics—such as dependability, creativity, initiative, and leadership—that are viewed as important for the job and the organiza-

Highlights in HRM 1

Supervisor's Checklist for the Performance Appraisal

Scheduling

1. Schedule the review and notify the employee ten days to two weeks in advance.
2. Ask the employee to prepare for the session by reviewing his or her performance, job objectives, and development goals.
3. Clearly state that this will be the formal annual performance appraisal.

Preparing for the Review

1. Review the performance documentation collected throughout the year. Concentrate on work patterns that have developed.
2. Be prepared to give specific examples of above- or below-average performance.
3. When performance falls short of expectations, determine what changes need to be made. If performance meets or exceeds expectations, discuss this and plan how to reinforce it.
4. After the appraisal is written, set it aside for a few days and then review it again.
5. Follow whatever steps are required by your organization's performance appraisal system.

Conducting the Review

1. Select a location that is comfortable and free of distractions. The location should encourage a frank and candid conversation.
2. Discuss each topic in the appraisal one at a time, considering both strengths and shortcomings.
3. Be specific and descriptive, not general and judgmental. Report occurrences rather than evaluating them.
4. Discuss your differences and resolve them. Solicit agreement with the evaluation.
5. Jointly discuss and design plans for taking corrective action for growth and development.
6. Maintain a professional and supportive approach to the appraisal discussion.

tion in general. The fact that trait methods are the most popular is due in large part to the ease with which they are developed. However, if not designed carefully on the basis of job analysis, trait appraisals can be notoriously biased and subjective.

Graphic Rating Scales

graphic rating-scale method A trait approach to performance appraisal whereby each employee is rated according to a scale of characteristics

In the **graphic rating-scale method** each trait or characteristic to be rated is represented by a scale on which a rater indicates the degree to which an employee possesses that trait or characteristic. An example of this type of scale is shown in Highlights in HRM 2. There are many variations of the graphic rating scale. The differences are to be found in (1) the characteristics or dimensions on which individuals are rated, (2) the degree to which the performance dimension is defined for the rater, and (3) how clearly the points on the scale are defined. In Highlights in HRM 2 the dimensions are defined briefly, and some attempt is made to define the points on the scale. Subjectivity bias is reduced somewhat when the dimensions on the scale and

Highlights in HRM 2

Graphic Rating Scale with Provision for Comments

Appraise employee's performance in PRESENT ASSIGNMENT. Check (✔) most appropriate square. Appraisers are *urged to freely use* the "Remarks" sections for significant comments descriptive of the individual.

1. KNOWLEDGE OF WORK: Understanding of all phases of his/her work and related matters	Needs instruction or guidance		Has required knowledge of own and related work		Has exceptional knowledge of own and related work
	☐	☐	☐	✔	☐
	Remarks: *Is particularly good on gas engines.*				
2. INITIATIVE: Ability to originate or develop ideas and to get things started	Lacks imagination		Meets necessary requirements		Unusually resourceful
	☐	✔	☐	☐	☐
	Remarks: *Has good ideas when asked for an opinion, but otherwise will not offer them. Somewhat lacking in self-confidence.*				
3. APPLICATION: Attention and application to his/her work	Wastes time Needs close supervision		Steady and willing worker		Exceptionally industrious
	☐	☐	✔	☐	☐
	Remarks: *Accepts new jobs when assigned.*				
4. QUALITY OF WORK: Thoroughness, neatness, and accuracy of work	Needs improvement		Regularly meets recognized standards		Consistently maintains highest quality
	☐	☐	☐	☐	✔
	Remarks: *The work he turns out is always of the highest possible quality.*				
5. VOLUME OF WORK: Quantity of acceptable work	Should be increased		Regularly meets recognized standards		Unusually high output
	☐	☐	✔	☐	☐
	Remarks: *Would be higher if he did not spend so much time checking and rechecking his work.*				

the scale points are defined as precisely as possible. This can be achieved by training raters and by including descriptive appraisal guidelines in a performance appraisal reference packet.[36]

Also, the rating form should provide sufficient space for comments on the behavior associated with each scale. These comments improve the accuracy of the

Highlights in HRM 3

Example of a Mixed-Standard Scale

DIRECTIONS: Please indicate whether the individual's performance is above (+), equal to (0), or lower than (−) each of the following standards.

1. ______ Employee uses good judgment when addressing problems and provides workable alternatives; however, at times does not take actions to prevent problems. *(medium PROBLEM SOLVING)*
2. ______ Employee lacks supervisory skills; frequently handles employees poorly and is at times argumentative. (*low LEADERSHIP*)
3. ______ Employee is extremely cooperative; can be expected to take the lead in developing cooperation among employees; completes job tasks with a positive attitude. (*High COOPERATION*)
4. ______ Employee has effective supervision skills; encourages productivity, quality, and employee development. (*medium LEADERSHIP*)
5. ______ Employee normally displays an argumentative or defensive attitude toward fellow employees and job assignments. (*low COOPERATION*)
6. ______ Employee is generally agreeable but becomes argumentative at times when given job assignments; cooperates with other employees as expected. (*medium COOPERATION*)
7. ______ Employee is not good at solving problems; uses poor judgment and does not anticipate potential difficulties. (*low PROBLEM SOLVING*)
8. ______ Employee anticipates potential problems and provides creative, proactive alternative solutions; has good attention to follow-up. (*high PROBLEM SOLVING*)
9. ______ Employee displays skilled direction; effectively coordinates unit activities; is generally a dynamic leader and motivates employees to high performance. (*high LEADERSHIP*)

appraisal because they require the rater to think in terms of observable employee behaviors while providing specific examples to discuss with the employee during the appraisal interview.

Mixed-Standard Scales

mixed-standard scale method
A trait approach to performance appraisal similar to other scale methods but based on comparison with (better than, equal to, or worse than) a standard

The **mixed-standard scale method** is a modification of the basic rating-scale method. Rather than evaluating traits according to a single scale, the rater is given three specific descriptions of each trait. These descriptions reflect three levels of performance: superior, average, and inferior. After the three descriptions for each trait are written, they are randomly sequenced to form the mixed-standard scale. As shown in Highlights in HRM 3, supervisors evaluate employees by indicating whether their performance is better than, equal to, or worse than the standard for each behavior.

Forced-Choice Method

forced-choice method A trait approach to performance appraisal that requires the rater to choose from statements designed to distinguish between successful and unsuccessful performance

The **forced-choice method** requires the rater to choose from statements, often in pairs, that appear equally favorable or equally unfavorable. The statements, however, are designed to distinguish between successful and unsuccessful performance. The rater selects one statement from the pair without knowing which statement correctly describes successful job behavior. For example, forced-choice pairs might include the following:

1. ______ a) Works hard ______ b) Works quickly

2. ______ a) Shows initiative ______ b) Is responsive to customers

3. ______ a) Produces poor quality ______ b) Lacks good work habits

The forced-choice method is not without limitations, the primary one being the cost of establishing and maintaining its validity. The fact that it has been a source of frustration to many raters has sometimes caused the method to be eliminated from appraisal programs. In addition, it cannot be used as effectively as some of the other methods to help achieve the commonly held objective of using appraisals as a tool for developing employees by such means as the appraisal interview.

Essay Method

essay method A trait approach to performance appraisal that requires the rater to compose a statement describing employee behavior

Unlike rating scales, which provide a structured form of appraisal, the **essay method** requires the appraiser to compose a statement that best describes the employee being appraised. The appraiser is usually instructed to describe the employee's strengths and weaknesses and to make recommendations for his or her development. Often the essay method is combined with other rating methods. Essays may provide additional descriptive information on performance that is not obtained with a structured rating scale, for example.

The essay method provides an excellent opportunity to point out the unique characteristics of the employee being appraised. This aspect of the method is heightened when a supervisor is instructed to describe specific points about the employee's promotability, special talents, skills, strengths, and weaknesses. A major limitation of the essay method is that composing an essay that attempts to cover all of an employee's essential characteristics is a very time-consuming task (though when combined with other methods, this method does not require a lengthy statement). Another disadvantage of the essay method is that the quality of the performance appraisal may be influenced by the supervisor's writing skills and composition style. Good writers may simply be able to produce more-favorable appraisals. A final drawback of this appraisal method is that it tends to be subjective and may not focus on relevant aspects of job performance.

Behavioral Methods

As mentioned previously, one of the potential drawbacks of a trait-oriented performance appraisal is that traits tend to be vague and subjective. We discussed earlier that one way to improve a rating scale is to have descriptions of behavior along a scale, or continuum. These descriptions permit the rater to readily identify the point where a particular employee falls on the scale. Behavioral methods have been developed to specifically describe which actions should (or should not) be exhibited on the job. They are frequently more useful for providing employees with developmental feedback.

Critical Incident Method

The critical incident method, described in Chapter 4 in connection with job analysis, is also used as a method of appraisal. Recall that a **critical incident** occurs when employee behavior results in unusual success or unusual failure in some part of the job. A favorable critical incident is illustrated by the janitor who observed that a file cabinet containing classified documents had been left unlocked at the close of business. The janitor called the security officer, who took the necessary action to correct the problem. An unfavorable incident is illustrated by the mail clerk who failed to deliver an Express Mail package immediately, instead putting it in with regular mail to be routed two hours later. The manager keeps a log or diary for each employee throughout the appraisal period and notes specific critical incidents related to how well they perform. When completing the appraisal form, the manager refers to the critical incident log and uses this information to substantiate an employee's rating of outstanding, satisfactory, or unsatisfactory in specific performance areas and overall. This method can also help a manager counsel employees when they are having performance problems while the problem is still minor. It also increases the objectivity of the appraisal by requiring the rater to use job performance criteria to justify the ratings.[37]

critical incident
An unusual event that denotes superior or inferior employee performance in some part of the job

Behavioral Checklist Method

One of the oldest appraisal techniques is the behavioral checklist method. It consists of having the rater check the statements on a list that the rater believes are characteristic of the employee's performance or behavior. A checklist developed for computer salespeople might include a number of statements like the following:

______ Is able to explain equipment clearly

______ Keeps abreast of new developments in technology

______ Tends to be a steady worker

______ Reacts quickly to customer needs

______ Processes orders correctly

Behaviorally Anchored Rating Scale (BARS)

A **behaviorally anchored rating scale (BARS)** consists of a series of five to ten vertical scales—one for each important dimension of performance identified through job analysis. These dimensions are anchored by behaviors identified through a critical-incident job analysis. The critical incidents are placed along the scale and are assigned point values according to the opinions of experts. A BARS for the job of firefighter is shown in Highlights in HRM 4. Note that this particular scale is for the dimension described as "Firefighting Strategy: Knowledge of Fire Characteristics."

behaviorally anchored rating scale (BARS)
A behavioral approach to performance appraisal that consists of a series of vertical scales, one for each important dimension of job performance

A BARS is typically developed by a committee that includes both subordinates and managers. The committee's task is to identify all the relevant characteristics or dimensions of the job. Behavioral anchors in the form of statements are then established for each of the job dimensions. Several participants are asked to review the anchor statements and indicate which job dimension each anchor illustrates. The only anchors retained are those that at least 70 percent of the group agree belong with a particular dimension. Finally, anchors are attached to their job dimensions and placed on the appropriate scales according to values that the group assigns to them.

USING THE INTERNET

Review example of BARS used for the state of Michigan. Go to the Student Resources at:

bohlander.swlearning.com

Highlights in HRM 4

Example of a BARS for Municipal Fire Companies

FIREFIGHTING STRATEGY: Knowledge of Fire Characteristics. This area of performance concerns the ability of a firefighter to use his or her knowledge of fire characteristics to develop the best strategy for fighting a fire. It involves the following activities: Observe fire and smoke conditions and locate source of fire. Size up fire and identify appropriate extinguishing techniques and ventilation procedures. Consult preplan reports. Apply knowledge of heat and fluid mechanics to anticipate fire behavior. Identify and screen or saturate potential exposures using direct or fog streams or water curtains. Identify and remove or protect flammable or hazardous materials.

HIGH	7	—Finds the fire when no one else can
	6	—Correctly assesses best point of entry for fighting fire
		—Uses type of smoke as indicator of type of fire
	5	
		—Understands basic hydraulics
AVERAGE	4	
	3	—Cannot tell the type of fire by observing the color of flame
		—Cannot identify location of the fire
	2	
		—Will not change firefighting strategy in spite of flashbacks and other signs that accelerants are present
LOW	1	

Source: Adapted from Landy, Jacobs, and Associates. Reprinted with permission.

At present there is no strong evidence that a BARS reduces all of the rating errors mentioned previously. However, some studies have shown that scales of this type can yield more-accurate ratings. One major advantage of a BARS is that personnel outside the HR department participate with HR staff in its development. Employee participation can lead to greater acceptance of the performance appraisal process and of the performance measures that it uses.

The procedures followed in developing a BARS also result in scales that have a high degree of content validity. The main disadvantage of a BARS is that it requires considerable time and effort to develop. In addition, because the scales are specific to particular jobs, a scale designed for one job may not apply to another.

behavior observation scale (BOS)
A behavioral approach to performance appraisal that measures the frequency of observed behavior

Behavior Observation Scale (BOS)

A **behavior observation scale (BOS)** is similar to a BARS in that they are both based on critical incidents. However, Highlights in HRM 5 shows that rather than

Highlights in HRM 5

Sample Items from Behavior Observation Scales

INSTRUCTIONS: Please consider the sales representative's behavior on the job in the past rating period. Read each statement carefully, then circle the number that indicates the extent to which the employee has demonstrated this *effective* or *ineffective* behavior.

For each behavior observed, use the following scale:

5 represents *almost always*	95–100% of the time
4 represents *frequently*	85–94% of the time
3 represents *sometimes*	75–84% of the time
2 represents *seldom*	65–74% of the time
1 represents *almost never*	0–64% of the time

SALES PRODUCTIVITY	ALMOST NEVER				ALMOST ALWAYS
1. Reviews individual productivity results with manager	1	2	3	4	5
2. Suggests to peers ways of building sales	1	2	3	4	5
3. Formulates specific objectives for each contact	1	2	3	4	5
4. Focuses on product rather than customer problem	1	2	3	4	5
5. Keeps account plans updated	1	2	3	4	5
6. Keeps customer waiting for service	1	2	3	4	5
7. Anticipates and prepares for customer concerns	1	2	3	4	5
8. Follows up on customer leads	1	2	3	4	5

asking the evaluator to choose the most representative behavioral anchor, a BOS is designed to measure how frequently each of the behaviors has been observed.

The value of a BOS is that this approach allows the appraiser to play the role of observer rather than of judge. In this way, he or she may more easily provide constructive feedback to the employee. Companies such as AT&T, Weyerhaeuser, and Dayton-Hudson have used the BOS, and research shows that users of the system frequently prefer it over the BARS or trait scales for (1) maintaining objectivity, (2) distinguishing good performers from poor performers, (3) providing feedback, and (4) identifying training needs.[38]

Results Methods

Rather than looking at the traits of employees or the behaviors they exhibit on the job, many organizations evaluate employee accomplishments—the results they achieve through their work. Advocates of results appraisals argue that they are more objective and empowering for employees. Looking at results such as sales figures and production output involves less subjectivity and therefore may be less open to bias. Furthermore, results appraisals often give employees responsibility for their outcomes, while giving them discretion over the methods they use to accomplish them (within limits). This is empowerment in action.

Productivity Measures

A number of results measures are available to evaluate performance. Salespeople are evaluated on the basis of their sales volume (both the number of units sold and the dollar amount in revenues). Production workers are evaluated on the basis of the number of units they produce and perhaps the scrap rate or number of defects that are detected. Executives are frequently evaluated on the basis of company profits or growth rate. Each of these measures directly links what employees accomplish and results that benefit the organization. In this way, results appraisals can directly align employee and organizational goals.

But there are some problems with results appraisals. First, recall our earlier discussion of criteria contamination. Results appraisals may be contaminated by external factors that employees cannot influence. Sales representatives who have extremely bad markets or production employees who can't get materials will not be able to perform up to their abilities. It may be unfair to hold these employees accountable for results that are contaminated by circumstances beyond their control.

Furthermore, results appraisals may inadvertently encourage employees to "look good" on a short-term basis, while ignoring the long-term ramifications. Line supervisors, for example, may let their equipment suffer to reduce maintenance costs. If the appraisal focuses on a narrow set of results criteria to the exclusion of other important process issues, the system may suffer from criterion deficiency and may unintentionally foster the attitude that "what gets measured gets done." In fact, in any job involving interaction with others, it is not enough to simply look at production or sales figures. Factors such as cooperation, adaptability, initiative, and concern for human relations may be important to job success. If these factors are important job standards, they should be added to the appraisal review. Thus, to be realistic, both the results and the methods or processes used to achieve them should be considered.[39]

Management by Objectives

management by objectives (MBO)
A philosophy of management that rates performance on the basis of employee achievement of goals set by mutual agreement of employee and manager

One method that attempts to overcome some of the limitations of results appraisals is **management by objectives (MBO).** MBO is a philosophy of management first proposed by Peter Drucker in 1954 that has employees establish objectives (such as production costs, sales per product, quality standards, and profits) through consultation with their superiors and then uses these objectives as a basis for evaluation.[40] MBO is a system involving a cycle (Figure 8.6) that begins with setting the organization's common goals and objectives and ultimately returns to that step. The system acts as a goal-setting process whereby objectives are established for the organization (Step 1), departments (Step 2), and individual managers and employees (Step 3).

As Figure 8.6 illustrates, a significant feature of the cycle is the establishment of specific goals by the employee, but those goals are based on a broad statement of employee responsibilities prepared by the supervisor. Employee-established goals are discussed with the supervisor and jointly reviewed and modified until both parties are satisfied with them (Step 4). The goal statements are accompanied by a detailed account of the actions the employee proposes to take in order to reach the goals. During periodic reviews, as objective data are made available, the progress that the employee is making toward the goals is then assessed (Step 5). Goals may be changed at this time as new or additional data are received. At the conclusion of a period of time (usually six months or one year), the employee makes a self-appraisal of what he or she has accomplished, substantiating the self-appraisal with factual data wherever possible. The "interview" is an examination of the employee's self-appraisal by

Figure 8.6 Performance Appraisal under an MBO Program

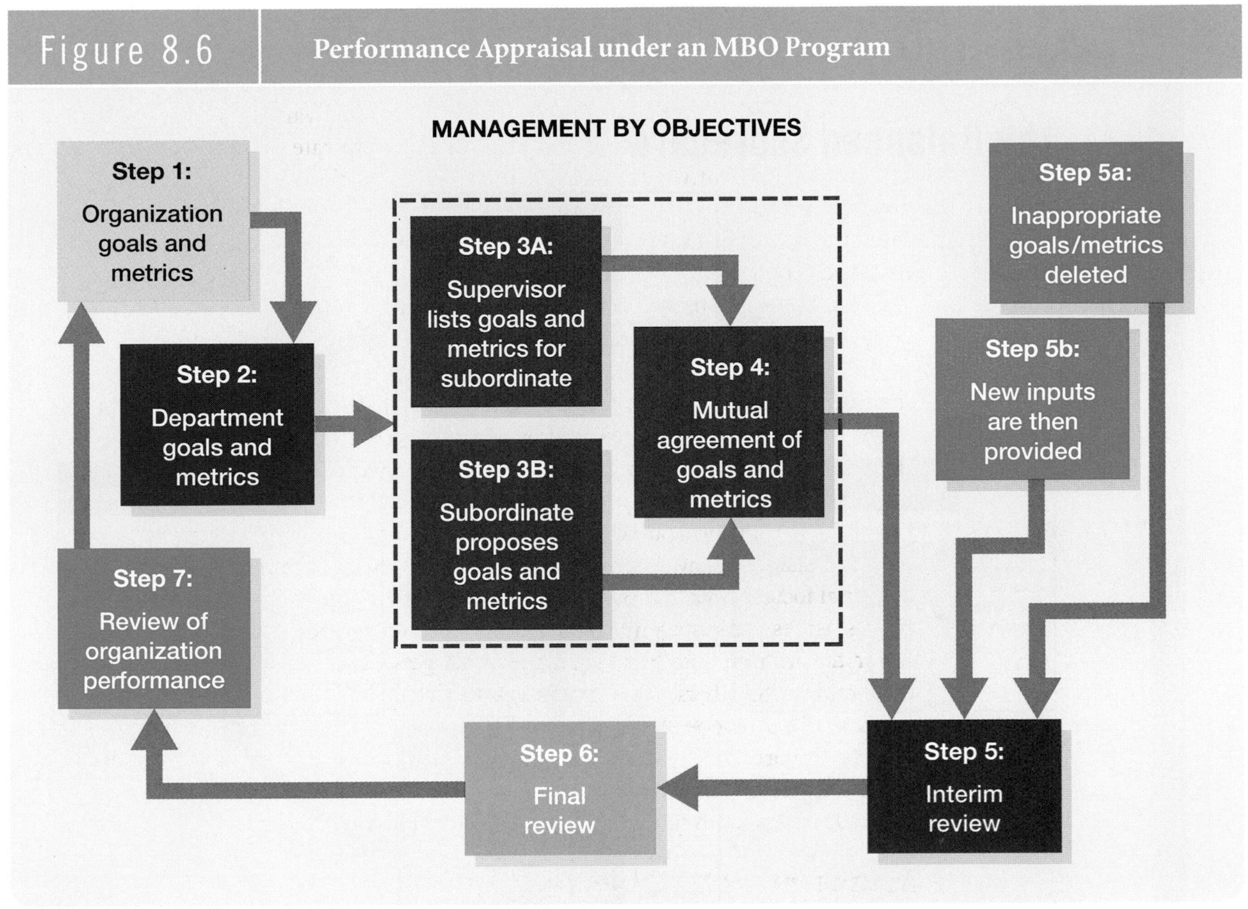

the supervisor and the employee together (Step 6). The final step (Step 7) is reviewing the connection between individual and organizational performance. To ensure success, MBO programs should be viewed as part of a total system for managing, not as merely an addition to the manager's job. Managers must be willing to empower employees to accomplish their objectives on their own, giving them discretion over the methods they use (but holding them accountable for outcomes). The following guidelines may be especially helpful:

1. Managers and employees must be willing to establish goals and objectives together. Goal setting has been shown to improve employee performance, typically ranging from 10 to 25 percent. Goal setting works because it helps employees focus on important tasks and makes them accountable for completing these tasks. It also establishes an automatic feedback system that aids learning, because employees can regularly evaluate their performance against their goals.[41]
2. Objectives should be quantifiable and measurable for the long and short term. However, goal statements should be accompanied by a description of how that goal will be accomplished.
3. Expected results must be under the employee's control. Recall our early discussion of criterion contamination.

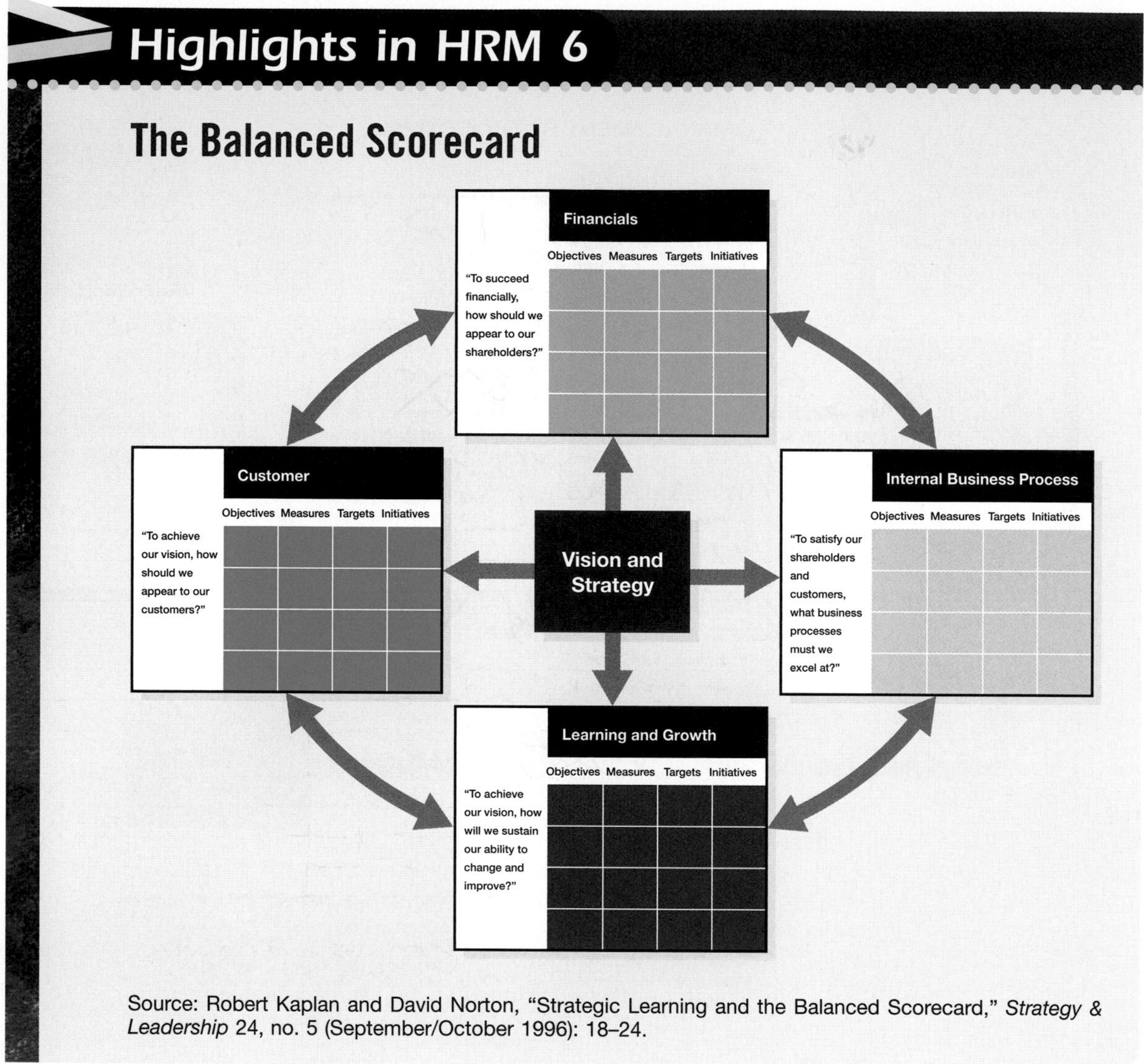

Source: Robert Kaplan and David Norton, "Strategic Learning and the Balanced Scorecard," *Strategy & Leadership* 24, no. 5 (September/October 1996): 18–24.

4. Goals and objectives must be consistent for each level (top executive, manager, and employee).
5. Managers and employees must establish specific times when goals are to be reviewed and evaluated.

The Balanced Scorecard

The Balanced Scorecard (BSC), which we first discussed in Chapter 2, can be used to appraise individual employees, teams, business units, and the corporation itself. The idea behind the Balanced Scorecard model is shown in Highlights in HRM 6. The appraisal takes into account four related categories: (1) financial, (2) customer, (3) processes, and (4) learning. These internal processes—product development, service, and the like—are critical for creating customer satisfaction and loyalty. Cus-

Highlights in HRM 7

Personal Scorecard

CORPORATE OBJECTIVES

- Double our corporate value in seven years.
- Increase our earnings by an average of 20% per year.
- Achieve an internal rate of return 2% above the cost of capital.
- Increase both production and reserves by 20% in the next decade.

☑ Corporate
❑ Business Unit
❑ Team/Individual

Corporate Targets				Scorecard Measures	Bus. Unit Targets				Team/Individual Objectives
2001	2002	2003	2004		2001	2002	2003	2004	1.
				Financial					
100	120	160	180	Earnings (millions of dollars)					
100	450	200	210	Net cash flow					
100	85	75	70	Overhead and operating costs					2.
				Operating					
100	75	73	70	Production costs/barrel					
100	97	93	90	Development costs/barrel					
100	105	108	110	Total annual production					3.
Team/Individual Measures					**Targets**				
1.									
2.									4.
3.									
4.									

Source: Robert Kaplan and David Norton, "Using the Balanced Scorecard as a Strategic Management System," *Harvard Business Review* (January–February 1996): 75–85.

tomer value creation in turn is what drives financial performance and profitability. Highlights in HRM 7 shows an example of a scorecard used for this process. As you can see, the corporation's objectives have already been spelled out on the scorecard. Then the various business unit targets are added, followed by the target objectives of the firm's teams and individual employees. The value of this is that each individual can see more clearly how his or her performance ties into the overall performance of the firm. Similar in some ways to MBO, the BSC enables managers to translate broad corporate goals into divisional, departmental, and team goals in a cascading fashion. Many firms have adopted the Balanced Scorecard approach, but it is neither a flawless nor a simple performance management system. For example, in a survey conducted by the Society for Human Resource Management, 73 percent of organizations using the approach said they had clearly articulated the strategic direction of their firm. But only 44 percent of those firms said the direction was communicated well to employees.

Some recommendations for ensuring the method's success include the following:

- *Translate the strategy into a scorecard of clear objectives.* As the BSC process begins with strategic objectives, unless these are clear the rest of the system is doomed to ambiguity and potential failure. Translating a strategy into objectives provides managers and front-line employees with goals that are more understandable and attainable. Typically, having fewer goals adds clarity and focus.
- *Attach measures to each objective.* In order for managers and employees to know if and when the objectives are achieved, clear measures must be attached to each goal. Each objective should be given at least one metric that can be measured either by a pre-existing system or manually within an organization.
- *Cascade scorecards to the front line.* It is often said that the real strategic work happens at the front line. In order for all employees to understand how their roles and job duties are aligned with higher-level goals, scorecards should be cascaded to the individual level. Cascading scorecards ensures that strategy then becomes "everyone's" job.
- *Provide performance feedback based on measures.* As with other performance management systems, unless managers provide employees with solid feedback on how they are doing, the system is likely to be ineffective. As part of this process, employees must know that they are accountable for achieving their objectives and providing an explanation when they do not hit their targets.
- *Empower employees to make performance improvements.* Individuals, on their own or working in teams, may understand ways of achieving higher performance. One of the benefits of a results-based system such as the BSC is that it gives employees the latitude to continuously improve best-practices methods.
- *Reassess strategy.* One of the key benefits of the BSC is that it is a continuous-loop process. Managers should monitor performance and use this information to reassess the strategy and make continuous adjustments. Those who have had the best success with the BSC argue that the system helps improve communication and learning rather than fixing in place a mechanical set of controls.[42]

Which Performance Appraisal Method to Use?

The choice of method should be based largely on the purpose of the appraisal. Figure 8.7 lists some of the strengths and weaknesses of trait, behavior, and results approaches to appraisal. Note that the simplest and least expensive techniques often yield the least-accurate information. However, research has not always supported a clear choice among appraisal methods. While researchers and HR managers generally believe that the more sophisticated and more time-consuming methods offer more useful information, this may not always be the case. Says Ronald Gross, an industrial psychologist and human resources consultant, "I can't judge a performance-appraisal system just by looking at the paperwork. The back of an envelope can work just fine. I've seen many systems fail miserably because they're too complex, too time-consuming, and too burdensome. I've never seen a system fail because it was too simple."[43] One way to assess whether an organization's appraisal system is effective is by doing an annual, or at least periodic, audit of the process. Highlights in HRM 8 shows a sample survey that HR managers can ask both managers and employees to complete

Figure 8.7 Summary of Various Appraisal Methods

	ADVANTAGES	DISADVANTAGES
Trait Methods	1. Are inexpensive to develop 2. Use meaningful dimensions 3. Are easy to use	1. Have high potential for rating errors 2. Are not useful for employee counseling 3. Are not useful for allocating rewards 4. Are not useful for promotion decisions
Behavioral Methods	1. Use specific performance dimensions 2. Are acceptable to employees and superiors 3. Are useful for providing feedback 4. Are fair for reward and promotion decisions	1. Can be time-consuming to develop/use 2. Can be costly to develop 3. Have some potential for rating error
Results Methods	1. Have less subjectivity bias 2. Are acceptable to employees and superiors 3. Link individual performance to organizational performance 4. Encourage mutual goal setting 5. Are good for reward and promotion decisions	1. Are time-consuming to develop/use 2. May encourage a short-term perspective 3. May use contaminated criteria 4. May use deficient criteria

on a periodic basis. This should give HR a better sense of whether the appraisal processes is improving.

Of course, having a first-rate appraisal method does no good if the manager simply "shoves it in a drawer." Even a rudimentary system, when used properly, can initiate a discussion between managers and employees that genuinely drives superior performance. These issues are discussed next under the topic of performance appraisal interviews. In addition, performance appraisals shouldn't be just for middle managers and rank-and-file employees. If the organization's goals are to cascade downward, the firm's top executives need to be involved in the appraisal process as well.

Appraisal Interviews

The appraisal interview is perhaps the most important part of the entire performance appraisal process. The appraisal interview gives a manager the opportunity to discuss a subordinate's performance record and to explore areas of possible improvement and growth. It also provides an opportunity to identify the subordinate's attitudes and feelings more thoroughly and thus to improve communication.

Unfortunately, the interviewer can become overburdened by attempting to discuss too much, such as the employee's past performance and future development goals. Dividing the appraisal interview into two sessions, one for the performance review and the other for the employee's growth plans, can alleviate time pressures. Moreover, by separating the interview into two sessions, the interviewer can give each session the proper attention it deserves. It can be difficult for a supervisor to perform the role of both evaluator and counselor in the same review period. Dividing the

Appraising the Appraisal System

Using a graphical rating scale of 1 (strongly disagree) to 5 (strongly agree), rate your performance management system in relation to the following statements:

- Our performance management system reflects our company's mission and values; it reflects our desired company culture.
- Our performance management system has the full commitment and active participation of our CEO and senior management team.
- Our business strategy is clear, including our key business drivers and the metrics used to track them (for example, financial, operational, employee engagement, customer and client).
- Our managers understand how to cascade our company goals down through the organization to ensure that they are effectively linked to individual employee goals.
- Individual goals are truly linked to our business drivers, and effective two-way communication links are clearly established.
- Our performance appraisal process distinguishes between observable behavioral dimensions and the frequency of those behaviors (for examples, appraisals based on core competencies or the mastery of certain behaviors).
- Our performance management system incorporates feedback from multiple sources (such as, 360-degree feedback and/or another form of multirater feedback).
- Our performance management system outlines clear standards of performance and rewards eligibility for high performers, solid performers, and marginal performers in the following scenarios:
    - Merit increases
    - Annual incentives
    - Long-term incentives
    - Discretionary incentives
- Our performance management system provides an ongoing comprehensive training program for:
    - Managers conducting performance appraisals
    - Individuals being appraised
- Our performance management system provides additional support services for professional and career development to managers and employees.
- We are able to accurately determine the ROI of the PMS.
- Our existing technology supports our performance management system objectives as designed (that is, in accordance with system requirements) to include:
    - The various raters and reviewers we wish to involve in the process
    - The capture of information throughout the performance cycle (including planning, forecasting, progress review, and end-of-year evaluation)
    - Sharing data across HR and other business applications (including pay, learning and development, workforce, and succession planning)
    - Providing the necessary level of data security and archiving
- Our performance management system is capable of real-time analysis of performance data to identify trends in relation to:
    - Performance differentiation
    - Pay differentiation
    - Performance gaps/developmental needs
- Our internal business partners are able to access and use the performance management system.

Source: Leslie A. Weatherly, "Performance Management: Getting It Right from the Start," *HRMagazine* 49, no. 3 (March 2004): S1–S12.

There are different approaches to performance appraisal interviews. A problem-solving approach may be the best.

© RACHEL EPSTEIN/PHOTOEDIT

sessions may also improve communication between the parties, thereby reducing stress and defensiveness.

The format for the appraisal interview will be determined in large part by the purpose of the interview, the type of appraisal system used, and the organization of the interview form. Most appraisal interviews attempt to give feedback to employees on how well they are performing their jobs and on planning for their future development. Interviews should be scheduled far enough in advance to allow the interviewee, as well as the interviewer, to prepare for the discussion. Usually ten days to two weeks is a sufficient amount of lead time.

Three Types of Appraisal Interviews

The individual who has probably studied different approaches to performance appraisal interviews most thoroughly is Norman R. F. Maier. In his classic book *The Appraisal Interview*, he analyzes the cause-and-effect relationships in three types of appraisal interviews: tell-and-sell, tell-and-listen, and problem solving.

Tell-and-Sell Interview

The skills required in the tell-and-sell interview include the ability to persuade an employee to change in a prescribed manner. This may require the development of new behaviors on the part of the employee and skillful use of motivational incentives on the part of the appraiser/supervisor.

Tell-and-Listen Interview

In the tell-and-listen interview, the skills required include the ability to communicate the strong and weak points of an employee's job performance during the first part of the interview. During the second part of the interview, the employee's feelings about the appraisal are thoroughly explored. The supervisor is still in the role of appraiser, but the method requires listening to disagreement and coping with defensive behavior without attempting to refute any statements. The tell-and-listen method assumes that the opportunity to release frustrated feelings will help reduce or remove those feelings.

Problem-Solving Interview

The skills associated with the problem-solving interview are consistent with the nondirective procedures of the tell-and-listen method. Listening, accepting, and responding to feelings are essential elements of the problem-solving interview. However, this method goes beyond an interest in the employee's feelings. It seeks to stimulate growth and development in the employee by discussing the problems, needs, innovations, satisfactions, and dissatisfactions the employee has encountered on the job since the last appraisal interview. Maier recommends this method, because the objective of appraisal is normally to stimulate growth and development in the employee.

Managers should not assume that only one type of appraisal interview is appropriate for every review session. Rather, they should be able to use one or more of the interview types, depending on the topic being discussed or on the behavior of the employee being appraised. The interview should be seen as requiring a flexible approach.

Conducting the Appraisal Interview

While there are probably no hard-and-fast rules for how to conduct an appraisal interview, some guidelines may increase the employee's acceptance of the feedback, satisfaction with the interview, and intention to improve in the future. Many of the principles of effective interviewing discussed in Chapter 6 apply to performance appraisal interviews as well. Here are some other guidelines that should also be considered.

Ask for a Self-Assessment

As noted earlier in the chapter, it is useful to have employees evaluate their own performance prior to the appraisal interview. Even if this information is not used formally, the self-appraisal starts the employee thinking about his or her accomplishments. Self-appraisal also ensures that the employee knows against what criteria he or she is being evaluated, thus eliminating any potential surprises.

Recent research evidence suggests that employees are more satisfied and view the appraisal system as providing more *procedural justice* when they have input into the process. When the employee has evaluated his or her own performance, the interview can be used to discuss areas in which the manager and the employee have reached different conclusions—not so much to resolve the "truth," but to work toward a resolution of problems.

Invite Participation

The core purpose of a performance appraisal interview is to initiate a dialogue that will help an employee improve his or her performance. To the extent that an employee is an active participant in that discussion, the more likely it is that the root causes and obstacles to performance will be uncovered, and the more likely it is that constructive ideas for improvement will be raised. In addition, research evidence suggests that participation is strongly related to an employee's satisfaction with the appraisal feedback, the extent to which the employee believes it is fair and useful, and his or her intention to improve performance. As a rule of thumb, supervisors should spend only about 30–35 percent of the time talking during the interview. The rest of the time they should be listening to employees respond to questions.

Express Appreciation

Praise is a powerful motivator, and in an appraisal interview, particularly, employees are seeking positive feedback. It is frequently beneficial to start the appraisal interview by expressing appreciation for what the employee has done well. In this way, he or she may be less defensive and more likely to talk about aspects of the job that are not going so well. However, try to avoid obvious use of the "sandwich technique" in which positive statements are followed by negative ones, which are then followed by positive statements. This approach may not work for several reasons. Praise often alerts the employee that criticism will be coming. If managers follow an appraisal form, the problem of the sandwich technique will often be avoided. Furthermore, if employees are kept informed of their behavior on a regular basis, there will be no need to use this appraisal technique.

Minimize Criticism

Employees who have a good relationship with their managers may be able to handle criticism better than those who do not. However, even the most stoic employees can absorb only so much criticism before they start to get defensive. If an employee has many areas in need of improvement, managers should focus on those few objective issues that are most problematic or most important to the job. Some tips for using criticism constructively include the following:

- *Consider whether it is really necessary.* Frustration with performance problems sometimes leads to criticism that is little more than a manager "letting off steam." Make certain that the criticism focuses on a recurrent problem or a consistent pattern of behavior.
- *Don't exaggerate.* Even managers who dislike criticizing may find that, once they get started, they tend to overdo it. Sometimes we overstate problems in order to be convincing or to demonstrate our concern. Try to keep criticism simple, factual, and to the point. Avoid using terms such as *always, completely*, and *never*.
- *Watch your timing.* Properly timed criticism can often mean the difference between success and failure. Even good criticism given late in the day, for example, can touch a raw nerve if the employee is tired.
- *Make improvement your goal.* "Laying it on the line" is not likely to be useful unless it clarifies a path to improved performance. Criticism needs to be complemented with managerial support. This point is elaborated on next.[44]

Change the Behavior, Not the Person

Managers frequently try to play psychologist, to "figure out" why an employee has acted a certain way. However, when dealing with a problem area, in particular, remember that it is not the person who is bad, but the actions exhibited on the job. Avoid suggestions about personal traits to change; instead suggest more acceptable ways of performing. For example, instead of focusing on a person's "unreliability," a manager might focus on the fact that the employee "has been late to work seven times this month." It is difficult for employees to change who they are; it is usually much easier for them to change how they act.

Focus on Solving Problems

In addressing performance issues, it is frequently tempting to get into the "blame game" in which both manager and employee enter into a potentially endless discussion of why a situation has arisen. Frequently, solving problems requires an analysis of the causes, but ultimately the appraisal interview should be directed at devising a solution to the problem.

Be Supportive

One of the better techniques for engaging an employee in the problem-solving process is for the manager to ask, "What can I do to help?" Employees frequently attribute performance problems to either real or perceived obstacles (such as bureaucratic procedures or inadequate resources). By being open and supportive, the manager conveys to the employee that he or she will try to eliminate external roadblocks and will work with the employee to achieve higher standards.

Establish Goals

Since a major purpose of the appraisal interview is to make plans for improvement, it is important to focus the interviewee's attention on the future rather than the past. In setting goals with an employee, the manager should observe the following points:

- Emphasize strengths on which the employee can build rather than weaknesses to overcome and how the employee's efforts will contribute to the organization during the coming year.
- Concentrate on opportunities for growth that exist within the framework of the employee's present position and drop unproductive tasks.
- Limit plans for growth to a few important items that can be accomplished within a reasonable period of time.
- Establish specific action plans that spell out how each goal will be achieved. These action plans may also include a list of contacts, resources, and timetables for follow-up.

Many managers are as nervous about administering appraisals as employees are about receiving them.

Follow Up Day to Day

Ideally, performance feedback should be an ongoing part of a manager's job. Feedback is most useful when it is immediate and specific to a particular situation. Unfortunately, both managers and employees are frequently happy to finish the interview and file away the appraisal form. A better approach is to have informal talks periodically, perhaps quarterly, to follow up on the issues raised in the appraisal interview. Levi Strauss, for example, offers employees informal feedback and coaching sessions on an ongoing basis. This puts managers in more of a coaching role versus that of a judge.

Improving Performance

In many instances the appraisal interview will provide the basis for noting deficiencies in employee performance and for making plans for improvement. Unless these deficiencies are brought to the employee's attention, they are likely to continue until they become quite serious. Sometimes underperformers may not understand exactly what is expected of them. However, once their responsibilities are clarified, they are in a position to take the corrective action needed to improve their performance.

Identifying Sources of Ineffective Performance

Performance is a function of several factors, but perhaps it can be boiled down to three primary concerns: ability, motivation, and environment. Each individual has a unique pattern of strengths and weaknesses that play a part. But talented employees with low motivation are not likely to succeed. In addition, other factors in the work environment—or even in the external environment, which includes personal, family, and community concerns—can affect performance either positively or negatively. Figure 8.8 may provide a better picture of how these three factors (motivation, environment, and ability) can influence performance.

It is recommended that a diagnosis of poor employee performance focus on these three interactive elements. As shown in Highlights in HRM 9, if an employee's performance is not up to standards, the cause could be a skill problem (knowledge, abilities, technical competencies), an effort problem (motivation to get the job done), and/or some problem in the external conditions of work (poor economic conditions, worker shortages due to downsizing, difficult sales territories).[45] Any one of these problem areas could cause performance to suffer.

Performance Diagnosis

Although performance appraisal systems can often tell us who is not performing well, they typically cannot reveal why. Unfortunately, research evidence suggests that managers often make wrong attributions for poor performance. They often assume that poor performance is first due to lack of ability, second to poor motivation, and then to external constraints. Ironically, research evidence also suggests that we tend to make just the opposite attributions about our own performance. We first attribute poor performance to external constraints such as bad luck or factors out of our control. If the problem is internal, then we typically attribute it to temporary factors such as motivation or energy ("I had a bad day") and only as a last resort admit that it might be due to ability.

Figure 8.8 Factors That Influence Performance

MOTIVATION	ENVIRONMENT	ABILITY
• Career ambition • Employee conflict • Frustration • Fairness/satisfaction • Goals/expectations	• Equipment/materials • Job design • Economic conditions • Unions • Rules and policies • Management support • Laws and regulations	• Technical skills • Interpersonal skills • Problem-solving skills • Analytical skills • Communication skills • Physical limitations

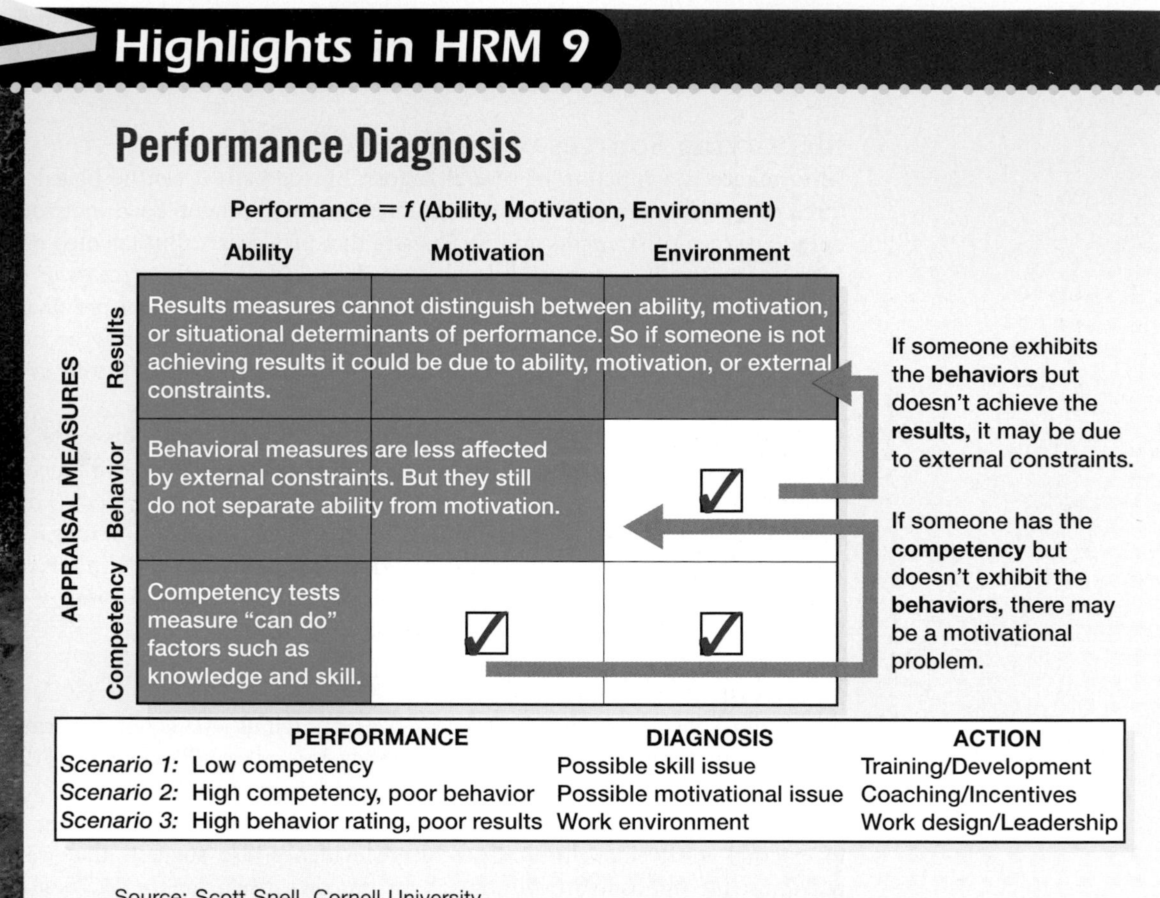

	PERFORMANCE	DIAGNOSIS	ACTION
Scenario 1:	Low competency	Possible skill issue	Training/Development
Scenario 2:	High competency, poor behavior	Possible motivational issue	Coaching/Incentives
Scenario 3:	High behavior rating, poor results	Work environment	Work design/Leadership

Source: Scott Snell, Cornell University.

So what can be done to diagnose the real reasons for poor performance? More specifically, how can managers identify the root causes and get to work on a solution that improves performance? By comparing different performance measures, managers can begin to get an idea of the underlying causes of performance problems. For example, as shown in Highlights in HRM 9, results measures cannot distinguish between ability, motivation, and situational determinants of performance. So if someone is not achieving desired results it could be due to ability, motivation, or external constraints. On the other hand, behavioral measures are less affected by external constraints. So if someone is demonstrating all the desired behaviors but is not achieving the desired results, logic suggests that it may be due to factors beyond his or her control.

Other kinds of diagnoses are possible by comparing different measures of performance. And only by correctly diagnosing the causes of performance problems can managers—and employees—hope to improve them.

Managing Ineffective Performance

Once the sources of performance problems are known, a course of action can be planned. This action may lie in providing training in areas that would increase the knowledge and/or skills needed for effective performance. A transfer to another job or department might give an employee a chance to become a more effective member of the organization. In other instances, greater attention may have to be focused on ways to motivate the individual.

If ineffective performance persists, it may be necessary to transfer the employee, take disciplinary action, or discharge the person from the organization. Not only is the ineffective behavior likely affecting the manager and the organization as a whole, it is also probably affecting the person's co-workers. Whatever action is taken to cope with ineffective performance, however, should be done with objectivity, fairness, and a recognition of the feelings of the individual involved. A new manager may also need training in this area because it is one of the most difficult of aspects of being a manager.

A final word of caution when it comes to managing performance problems: Because research consistently shows that managers often attribute poor performance to characteristics of the individuals (ability or motivation), while employees themselves typically blame external factors for their miscues, this can establish a negative cycle if not handled properly. Managers who assume that employees are not motivated or not capable may begin to treat them differently (perhaps supervising them too closely or watching for their next mistake). This can actually decrease an employee's motivation and cause him or her to withdraw. Seeing this, the manager may confirm his or her initial beliefs that the employee does not "measure up." As you can see, this "set-up-to-fail" syndrome can be self-fulfilling and self-reinforcing. It is hoped that the ideas and suggestions given in this chapter will help managers accurately identify who is performing well (and why) and give them some focus for improving employee productivity.[46]

SUMMARY

objective 1

Performance appraisal programs serve many purposes, but in general those purposes can be clustered into two categories: administrative and developmental. The administrative purposes include decisions about who will be promoted, transferred, or laid off. They can also include compensation decisions. Developmental decisions include those related to improving and enhancing an individual's capabilities. These include identifying a person's strengths and weaknesses, eliminating external performance obstacles, and establishing training needs. The combination of administrative and developmental purposes of performance appraisal reflect, in a specific way, human resources management's larger role of integrating the individual with the organization.

In many organizations, performance appraisals are seen as a necessary evil. Managers frequently avoid conducting appraisals because they dislike playing the role of judge. Further, if managers are not adequately trained, subjectivity and organizational politics can distort the reviews. This situation tends to be self-defeating in that such managers frequently do not develop good feedback skills and are often not prepared to conduct an appraisal. As a consequence, the appraisal is done begrudgingly once a year and then forgotten.

The success of an organization depends largely on the performance of its human resources. To determine the contributions of each individual, it is necessary to have a formal appraisal program with clearly stated objectives. Carefully defined performance standards that are reliable, strategically relevant, and free from either criterion deficiency or contamination are essential foundations for evaluation. Appraisal systems must also comply with the law. Appraisals should be treated with the same concerns for validity as are selection tests. For example, ratings must be job-related, employees must understand their performance standards in advance, appraisers must be able to observe job performance, appraisers must be trained, feedback must be given, and an appeals procedure must be established.

objective 3 Using multiple raters is frequently a good idea because different individuals see different facets of an employee's performance. The supervisor, for example, has legitimate authority over an employee and is in a good position to discern whether he or she is contributing to the goals of the organization. Peers and team members, on the other hand, often have an unfiltered view of an employee's work activity, particularly related to issues such as cooperation and dependability. Subordinates often provide good information about whether an employee is facilitating their work, and customers (both internal and external) can convey the extent to which an employee adds value and meets their requirements. Self-appraisal is useful, if for no other reason than it encourages employees to think about their strengths, weaknesses, and future goals. An increasing number of organizations are using multiple raters—or 360-degree appraisal—to get a more comprehensive picture of employee performance. Regardless of the source of appraisal information, appraisers should be thoroughly trained in the particular methods they will use in evaluating their subordinates. Participation in developing rating scales, such as a BARS, automatically provides such training.

objective 4 Several methods can be used for performance appraisal. These include trait approaches (such as graphic rating scales, mixed-standard scales, forced-choice forms, and essays), behavioral methods (such as critical-incident ratings, checklists, BARS, and BOS), and results methods (MBO). The choice of method depends on the purpose of the appraisal. Trait appraisals are simple to develop and complete, but they have problems in subjectivity and are not useful for feedback. Behavioral methods provide more specific information for giving feedback but can be time-consuming and costly to develop. Results appraisals are more objective and can link individual performance to the organization as a whole, but they may encourage a short-term perspective (such as annual goals) and may not include subtle yet important aspects of performance.

objective 5 The degree to which the performance appraisal program benefits the organization and its members is directly related to the quality of the appraisal interviews that are conducted. Interviewing skills are best developed through instruction and supervised practice. Although there are various approaches to the interview, research suggests that employee participation and goal setting lead to higher satisfaction and improved performance. Discussing problems, showing support, minimizing criticism, and rewarding effective performance are also beneficial practices. In the interview, deficiencies in employee performance can be discussed and plans for improvement can be made.

KEY TERMS

behavior observation scale (BOS)
behaviorally anchored rating scale (BARS)
contrast error
critical incident
customer appraisal
error of central tendency
essay method
forced-choice method
graphic rating-scale method
leniency or strictness error
management by objectives (MBO)
manager and/or supervisor appraisal
mixed-standard scale method
peer appraisal
performance appraisal
performance management
recency error
self-appraisal
similar-to-me error
subordinate appraisal
team appraisal

HRM Experience

Performance Diagnosis

Managing performance is an important—yet delicate—process for managers to undertake. They need to make tough calls at times regarding who is performing well or not. Also, they need to play the role of coach to help each employee improve his or her performance. One of the toughest aspects of performance management is assessing why someone is not performing well. Although it may be easy to spot who is not performing well, it is not always easy to diagnose the underlying causes of poor performance (such as motivation, ability, and external constraints). But without a correct diagnosis, it is nearly impossible to cure the problem.

Assignment

Following are descriptions of three different employees. Describe the potential causes of poor performance in each case. For each potential cause, identify appropriate solutions to enhance performance.

1. *Carl Spackler* is the assistant greenskeeper at Bushwood Country Club. Over the past few months, members have been complaining that gophers are destroying the course and digging holes in the greens. Although Carl has been working evenings and weekends to address the situation, the problem persists. Unfortunately, his boss is interested only in results, and because the gophers are still there, he contends that Carl is not doing his job. He has accused Carl of "slacking off" and threatened his job.
2. *Clark Griswold* works in research and development for a chemical company that makes nonnutritive food additives. His most recent assignment has been the development of a nonstick aerosol cooking spray, but the project is way behind schedule and seems to be going nowhere. CEO Frank Shirley is decidedly upset and has threatened that if things don't improve, he will suspend bonuses again this year as he did last year. Clark feels dejected, because without the bonus he won't be able to take his family on vacation.
3. *Bonnie Molloy* is the host of a local television talk show called *Morning Chicago*. Although she is a talented performer and comedienne, Bonnie has an unacceptable record of tardiness. The show's producer, David Bellows, is frustrated, because the problem has affected the quality of the show. On several occasions, Bonnie was unprepared when the show went on the air. Bellows has concluded that Bonnie is not a morning person and has thought about replacing her with a different host.

DISCUSSION QUESTIONS

1. What are the major purposes of performance appraisal? In what ways might these purposes be contradictory?

2. Describe the relationships among performance appraisal and selection, training, and development.

3. How can performance appraisals be adjusted to include the principles underlying total quality management (TQM)?

4. Describe the characteristics of the ideal appraisal system.

5. Discuss the guidelines that performance appraisals should meet in order to be legally defensible.

6. What sources could be used to evaluate the performance of people working in the following jobs?

- **a.** Sales representative
- **b.** TV repairer
- **c.** Director of nursing in a hospital
- **d.** HR manager
- **e.** Air traffic controller

7. In many organizations, evaluators submit ratings to their immediate superiors for review before discussing them with the individual employees they have rated. What advantages are there to this procedure?

8. What are the pros and cons of trait, behavior, and results appraisals?

9. Three types of appraisal interviews are described in this chapter.

- **a.** What different skills are required for each type of appraisal interview? What reactions can one expect from using these different skills?
- **b.** How can one develop the skills needed for the problem-solving type of interview?
- **c.** Which method do you feel is the least desirable? Why?

10. Discuss how you would diagnose poor performance. List several factors to consider.

BIZFLIX EXERCISES

Seabiscuit: George Rides Seabiscuit

This scene will show you several aspects of appraising and improving performance. Watch for performance standards, peer appraisal, behavior shaping, and coaching.

Combine a jockey who is blind in one eye with an undersized, ill-tempered thoroughbred and an unusual trainer. The result: the Depression-era champion racehorse Seabiscuit. This engaging film shows the training and development of Seabiscuit by trainer "Silent" Tom Smith (Chris Cooper) and jockey Red Pollard (Tobey Maguire). The enduring commitment of owner Charles Howard (Jeff Bridges) ensures the ultimate success of Seabiscuit on the racing circuit.

The *Seabiscuit* scene is a composite edited from DVD Chapter 21 toward the end of the film. In earlier scenes, Red severely injured a leg—he cannot ride Seabiscuit in the competition against War Admiral. Samuel Riddle (Eddie Jones), War Admiral's owner, has described any new rider as immaterial to the race's result. The scene begins with Red giving George Wolff (Gary Stevens), Seabiscuit's new jockey, some tips about riding him.

What to Watch for and Ask Yourself

- Does Red set clear performance standards for George? If he does, what are they?
- Red and George are both jockeys who competed against each other in earlier races. Do these scenes show peer appraisal or appraisal by people of different rank or position? Which characteristics of the performance appraisal process does this scene show?
- An earlier section, "Performance Appraisal Methods," discussed many approaches to performance appraisal. Which method or methods most closely match(es) what occurs in these scenes? Identify examples in the scenes that match the performance appraisal method or methods you picked.

case study 1

Siebel: Forcing the Issue

Siebel Systems, a U.S.-based developer of customer and employee management software, has built its forced-ranking system on the back of corporate objectives that cascade down from the top of the company. On the first day of each quarter, chairman and CEO Tom Siebel publishes his corporate objectives, generated from an off-site executive meeting. By day 3, senior managers will have reviewed the objectives and created their own targets for their specific divisions. By day 15, all 8,000 employees of the company will have created their own sets of objectives in conjunction with their managers. According to Anthony Deighton, director of Siebel Employee Relationship Management (ERM), these objectives are reviewed on a frequent basis through the quarter at both an individual and team level.

At the end of the quarter, employees write a self-assessment and discuss how effectively they hit target with their line manager. Their performance is measured against each objective, culminating in a 1-to-5 overall ranking. Managers have the ability to override the automated ranking calculation to take into account specific factors that may have influenced performance, such as an extended sickness. In addition to the formal ranking, the review also covers a range of other factors, including soft measures that are not objective-based.

Siebel employs three techniques to ensure that the ranking process is carried out as consistently as possible across the company: The HR department supplies relevant documentation, web-based training and an employee helpdesk in an effort to standardize the objectives and measurement techniques. Additionally, all objectives are reviewed by the next layer of management. Finally, the company's employee management software generates a ratings and distribution report, which highlights bands and trends. "If someone has given everybody 5, you make them justify it," says Deighton. "If the manager sees something is skewed, they can drill down, see details and reject a review."

This ranking system forms the basis of Siebel's six-monthly "cull" of the bottom 5 percent of employees. "We do the analytics, get the names, and then go and interview them to find out if this is the right 5 percent, or if there is a different set," says Deighton. "This is not math, it is people's lives. That 5 percent is a blurred boundary."

Although the process may seem ruthless, Deighton argues that it is ultimately constructive. Few people who fail to make the grade are "bad" employees—maybe one-quarter or half a percent of an organization, he believes. Most of them, however, are simply in the wrong job for their skill sets, and it may be there is no suitable alternative opening within the organization.

"There has always got to be a bottom performer. You are forcing managers to think about their people—who is more of a drain than a plus? It is certainly seen as positive by the people who remain. If you do not do it, the star performers will get frustrated and leave."

Source: Keith Rodgers, "Grade," *Personnel Today* (April 2, 2002): 21.

QUESTIONS

1. What do you think are the pros and cons of using a forced-ranking system such as Siebel's?
2. Does it make any difference that Siebel develops and sells performance management software?

3. If you were the owner-CEO of Siebel's, would it change your view on forced ranking?
4. Do you believe Deighton's claim that some of the star performers at Seibel will leave if the bottom 5 percent of employees aren't cut?

case study 2

Bank of Montreal's Balanced Scorecard

In 1990, the Bank of Montreal (BMO) had one major goal: to focus the entire workforce on success. It's a simple idea, but not so easy in execution. How would the company get entry-level tellers to think of their work not just as a means to a paycheck, but as a direct contribution to BMO shareholders? How would it remind corporate executives that their jobs were not just to boost the bottom line, but to charm entire communities?

The answer was BMO executives' balanced scorecard approach. To be competitive, executives decided, the bank had to meet the needs of four stakeholders: BMO shareholders, customers, employees, and communities. Executives translated that idea into four goals: Shareholders needed a return on equity, customers needed good service, employees needed to feel loyal and satisfied, and communities needed to feel that the bank made a difference in their neighborhoods. Return on investment would determine satisfaction for shareholders; surveys and feedback would determine satisfaction for customers, employees, and communities.

Every single department and every employee in every department had to understand how their work contributed to the success of those four goals. So each employee's and each department's performance ratings were revised to reflect their contribution toward each goal. Employees in the customer service department, for instance, were rated by their return on equity (judged by their cost-effectiveness), their customer satisfaction (judged by customer feedback), and their community involvement (judged by any outreach programs or increase in customers).

In some cases, departments were assigned a specific stakeholder. For example, HR was put in charge of the employee piece, ensuring competent, committed workers in a cost-effective way. Similarly, the company's senior vice president of HR was responsible for training and education aspects to ensure competency, and work/life and career-development programs to help with employee commitment. At the end of the year, the scores from everyone's performance ratings were translated into indexes, ratings from 1 to 10. The index for the employee stakeholder piece was determined by ratings for competency, commitment, and cost-effectiveness. The four indexes for BMO shareholders, customers, employees, and communities were then rolled up into one figure of merit to determine the bonus of BMO's CEO.

Source: Adapted from "How the Bank of Montreal Keeps Score on Success" by Gillian Flynn, copyright December 1997. Used with permission of ACC Communications/*Workforce*, Costa Mesa, CA. Web site at http://www.workforce.com.

QUESTIONS

1. What are the strengths and weaknesses of a balanced scorecard approach to performance appraisal?
2. Do you think it's fair to base the bonus paid to BMO's CEO on the four indexes comprising the firm's balanced scorecard?

3. Do you believe that a balanced scorecard approach would be more effective for the administrative or for the developmental purposes of appraisal discussed in this chapter?

NOTES AND REFERENCES

1. Susan Scherreik, "Your Performance Review: Make It Perform," *Business Week*, no. 3762 (December 17, 2001): 139; Dick Grote, "Performance Evaluations: Is It Time for a Makeover?" *HRFocus* 77, no. 11 (November 2000): 6–7; Duncan Brown, "Marking the Scorecard: Performance Appraisal Models Are Changing, Shedding Their Reputation for Being Top-Down, Demotivating Influences on a Company," *Grocer* 227, no. 7 (December 4, 2004): 72; "Employers Need to Do a Better Job of Performance Management," *Managing Training & Development* (April 2003): 8.
2. Matthew Boyle, "Performance Reviews: Perilous Curves Ahead," *Fortune* 143, no. 11 (May 28, 2001): 187–88; Susanne Scott and Walter Einstein, "Strategic Performance Appraisal in Team-Based Organizations: One Size Does Not Fit All," *Academy of Management Executive* 15, no. 2 (May 2001): 107–16; "Study Questions Performance Appraisal," *Australasian Business Intelligence* (May 1, 2003); Drew Robb, "Building a Better Workforce: Performance Management Software Can Help You Identify and Develop High-Performing Workers," *HRMagazine* 49, no. 10 (October 2004): 86–93.
3. Jonathan A. Segal, "86 Your Appraisal Process?" *HRMagazine* 45, no. 10 (October 2000): 199–206; Barry Witcher and Rosie Butterworth, "Honshin Kanri: How Xerox Manages," *Long-Range Planning* 32, no. 3 (June 1999): 323–32.
4. Janet Wiscombe, "Can Pay for Performance Really Work?" *Workforce* 80, no. 8 (August 2001): 28–34; Charlotte Garvey, "Meaningful Tokens of Appreciation: Cash Awards Aren't the Only Way to Motivate Your Workforce," *HRMagazine* 49, no. 8 (August 2004): 101–106.
5. David Allen and Rodger Griffeth, "Test of a Mediated Performance-Turnover Relationship Highlighting the Moderating Roles of Visibility and Reward Contingency," *Journal of Applied Psychology* 86, no. 5 (October 2001): 1014–21; Charles Pettijohn, Linda Pettijohn, and Michael D'Amico, "Characteristics of Performance Appraisals and Their Impact on Sales Force Satisfaction," *Human Resource Development Quarterly* 12, no. 2 (Summer 2001): 127–46; Scott and Einstein, "Strategic Performance Appraisal in Team-Based Organizations," 107–16.
6. Donna Doldwasser, "Me a Trainer?" *Training* 38, no. 4 (April 2001): 60–66; Rebecca Ganzel, "Mike Carter," *Training* 38, no. 7 (July 2001): 28–30; Carla Joinson, "Making Sure Employees Measure Up," *HRMagazine* 46, no. 3 (March 2001): 36–41; Ashish Chandra and Zachary D. Frank, "Utilization of Performance Appraisal Systems in Health Care Organizations and Improvement Strategies for Supervisors," *The Health Care Manager* 23, no. 1 (January–March 2004): 25–31; Morton D. Rosenbaum, "Gratitude Adjustment: When a Pat on the Back Isn't Enough," *Meetings & Conventions* 39, no. 7 (June 2004): 20; James W. Smither, Manuel London, and Richard R. Reilly, "Does Performance Improve Following Multisource Feedback?" *Personnel Psychology* 58, no. 1 (Spring 2005): 33–67.
7. Kathryn Bartol, Cathy Durham, and June Poon, "Influence of Performance Evaluation Rating Segmentation on Motivation and Fairness Perceptions," *Journal of Applied Psychology* 86, no. 6 (December 2001): 1106–19; Elizabeth Douthitt and John Aiello, "The Role of Participation and Control in the Effects of Computer Monitoring on Fairness Perceptions, Task Satisfaction, and Performance," *Journal of Applied Psychology* 86, no. 5 (October 2001): 867–74; Anne P. Hubbell, "Motivating Factors: Perceptions of Justice and Their Relationship with Managerial and Organizational Trust," *Communication Studies* 56, no. 1 (March 2005): 47; Rebecca M. Chory-Assad, "Room for Improvement," *Training* 40, no. 11 (December 2003): 18–20.
8. John Newman, J. Mack Robinson, Larry Tyler, David Dunbar, and Joseph Zager, "CEO Performance Appraisal: Review and Recommendations/Practitioner Application," *Journal of Healthcare Management* 46, no. 1 (January/February 2001): 21–38; Bob Losyk, "How to Conduct a Performance Appraisal," *Public Management* 84, no. 3 (April 2002): 8–12,
9. Michael Arndt, "3M: A Lab for Growth?" *Business Week*, no. 3766 (January 21, 2002): 50–51; "General Motors and Whirlpool: Two Approaches for Developing Performance Benchmarks," *HRFocus* 77, no. 6 (June 2000): 7–10; Doug Cederblom, "From Performance Appraisal to Performance Management: One Agency's Experience," *Public Personnel Management* 31, no. 2 (Summer 2002): 131–40; Sean Way and James Thacker, "The Successful Implementation of Strategic Human Resource Management Practices: A Canadian Survey," *International Journal of Management* 18, no. 1 (March 2001): 25–32; "Anonymous 360-Feedback Drives Vauxhall Strategy," *Personnel Today* (August 19, 2003): 16; Cindy Romaine, "Staying Relevant: Competencies and Employee Reviews," *Information Outlook* 8, no. 7 (April 2004): 21–25.
10. Jason D. Shaw and Nina Gupta, "Job Complexity, Performance, and Well-Being: When Does Supplies-Values Fit Matter?" *Personnel Psychology* 57, no. 4 (Winter 2004): 847–80.
11. Joel Lefkowitz, "The Role of Interpersonal Affective Regard in Supervisory Performance Ratings: A Literature Review and Proposed Causal Model," *Journal of Occupational and Organizational Psychology* 73, no. 1 (March 2000): 67–85; Scott Highhouse, "Assessing the Candidate As a Whole: A Historical and Critical Analysis of Individual Psychological Assessment for Personnel Decision Making," *Personnel Psychology* 55, no. 2 (Summer 2002): 363-397.

12. *Brito v Zia Company*, 478 F.2d 1200 (10th Cir. 1973).
13. *Albemarle Paper Company v Moody*, 422 U.S. 405 (1975).
14. Timothy Aeppel, "Goodyear Ends Ratings System ahead of Lawsuit," *The Wall Street Journal*, September 12, 2002, B8; "How to Stay 'Legal' with Performance Evaluation and Testing," *Managing Training & Development*, no. 4 (February 2004): 9.
15. Jilly Welch, "Intel Faces Fight over Termination Quotas," *People Management 3*, no. 13 (June 26, 1997): 9; David Martin, Kathryn Bartol, and Patrick Kehoe, "The Legal Ramifications of Performance Appraisal: The Growing Significance," *Public Personnel Management* 29, no. 3 (Fall 2000): 379–406; Gillian Flynn, "Getting Performance Reviews Right," *Workforce* 80, no. 5 (May 2001): 76–78. For a review of other performance appraisal court cases, see Clinton O. Longnecker and Frederick R. Post, "Effective and Legally Defensible Performance Appraisals," *Journal of Compensation and Benefits* 11, no. 6 (May/June 1996): 41–46; David C. Martin, Kathryn M. Bartol, and Patrick E. Kehoe, "The Legal Ramifications of Performance Appraisal: The Growing Significance," *Public Personnel Management* 29, no. 3 (Fall 2000): 381.
16. Joan Brett and Leanne Atwater, "360-Degree Feedback: Accuracy, Reactions, and Perceptions of Usefulness," *Journal of Applied Psychology* 86, no. 5 (October 2001): 930–42; Bruce Pfau, Ira Kay, Kenneth Nowak, and Jai Ghorpade, "Does 360-Degree Feedback Negatively Affect Company Performance?" *HRMagazine* 47, no. 6 (June 2002): 54–59; Maury Peiperl, "Getting 360-Degree Feedback Right," *Harvard Business Review* 79, no. 1 (January 2001): 142–47; Ruth Thaler-Carter, "Whither Global Leaders?" *HRMagazine* 45, no. 5 (May 2000): 82–88; Robert Gandossy and Tina Kao, "Talent Wars: Out of Mind, Out of Practice," *Human Resource Planning* 27, no. 4 (December 2004): 15–20.
17. Bob Rosner, "Squeezing More Respect out of Your Team," *Workforce* 79, no. 7 (July 2000): 80; Dick Grote, "The Secrets of Performance Appraisal: Best Practices from the Masters," *Across the Board* 37, no. 5 (May 2000): 14–20; Edward J. Inderrieden, Robert E. Allen, and Timothy J. Keaveny, "Managerial Discretion in the Use of Self-Ratings in an Appraisal System: The Antecedents and Consequences," *Journal of Managerial Issues* 16, no. 4 (Winter 2004): 460–484.
18. Jeffrey Seglin, "Reviewing Your Boss," *Fortune* 143, no. 12 (June 11, 2001): 248; Ann Harrington, "Workers of the World, Rate Your Boss!" *Fortune* 142, no. 6 (September 18, 2000): 340–42; Robert Thompson, "Management Lite: Less Control, More Innovation," *HRMagazine* 44, no. 8 (August 1999): 10.
19. Brett and Atwater, "360-Degree Feedback," 930–42; Paula Silva and Henry L. Tosi, "Determinants of the Anonymity of the CEO Evaluation Process," *Journal of Managerial Issues* 16, no. 1 (Spring 2004): 87–103.
20. Ann Pomeroy, "Great Places, Inspired Employees: The Nation's Best Employers Show That Inspiring Employee Involvement through Good HR Practices Makes Good Business Sense," *HRMagazine* 49, no. 7 (July 2004): 44–64.
21. John Drexler, Jr., Terry Beehr, and Thomas Stetz, "Peer Appraisals: Differentiation of Individual Performance on Group Tasks," *Human Resource Management* 40, no. 4 (Winter 2001): 333–45.
22. Scott and Einstein, "Strategic Performance Appraisal in Team-Based Organizations," 107–16; Debbie Kibbe and Jill Casner-Lotto, "Ralston Foods: From Greenfield to Maturity in a Team-Based Plant," *Journal of Organizational Excellence* 21, no. 3 (Summer 2002): 57–67; Simon Taggar and Mitchell Neubert, "The Impact of Poor Performers on Team Outcomes: An Empirical Examination of Attribution Theory," *Personnel Psychology* 57, no. 4 (Winter 2004): 935–69.
23. Bradley Kirkman and Benson Rosen, "Powering Up Teams," *Organizational Dynamics* 28, no. 3 (Winter 2000): 48–66; Matthew Valle and Kirk Davis, "Teams and Performance Appraisal: Using Metrics to Increase Reliability and Validity," *Team Performance Management* 5, no. 8 (1999): 238–43.
24. Michael Cohn, "Best Buy Beefs Up Customer Value at the Call Center," *Internet World* 8, no. 6 (June 2002): 42–43; Joe Kohn, "Isuzu Has IDEA for Boosting Sales," *Automotive News* 76, no. 5973 (March 4, 2002): 41; D. L. Radcliff, "A New Paradigm of Feedback," *Executive Excellence* 19, no. 4 (April 2002): 20.
25. Pfau, Kay, Nowak, and Ghorpade, "Does 360-Degree Feedback Negatively Affect Company Performance?" 54–59; Peiperl, "Getting 360-Degree Feedback Right," 142–47; Jack Kondrasuk, and Matt Graybill, "From Paper to Computer," *The Human Resource Professional* 13, no. 6 (November/December 2000): 18–19.
26. David W. Bracken, Lynn Summers, and John Fleenor, "High-Tech 360," *Training and Development* 52, no. 8 (August 1998): 42–45; Gary Meyer, "Performance Reviews Made Easy, Paperless," *HRMagazine* 45, no. 10 (October 2000): 181–84; Douglas P. Shuit, "Huddling with the Coach—Part 2," *Workforce Management* 84, no. 2 (February 1, 2005): 5; "Ceridian and Softscape Announce an Agreement to Deliver Employee Performance and Development Solutions," *Payroll Manager's Report* (May 2004): 13.
27. "Performance Appraisal," *HRMagazine* 47, no. 10 (October 2002): 146; Frank E. Kuzmits, Arthur J. Adams, Lyle Sussman, and Louis E. Raho, "360-Feedback in Health Care Management: A Field Study," *The Health Care Manager* 23, no. 321 (October–December 2004): 321–29.
28. Gary E. Roberts, "Perspectives on Enduring and Emerging Issues in Performance Appraisal," *Public Personnel Management* 27, no. 3 (Fall 1998): 301–20; William Hubbartt, "Bring Performance Appraisal Training to Life," *HRMagazine* 40, no. 5 (May 1995): 166, 168; Filip Lievens, "Assessor Training Strategies and Their Effects on Accuracy, Interrater Reliability, and Discriminant Validity," *Journal of Applied Psychology* 86, no. 2 (April 2001): 255–64; Dick Grote, "Performance Appraisals: Solving Tough Challenges," *HRMagazine* 45, no. 7 (July 2000): 145–50; Leslie A. Weatherly, "Performance Management: Getting It Right from the Start," *HRMagazine* 49, no. 3 (March 2004): S1–S12.
29. Gary P. Latham and Kenneth N. Wexley, *Increasing Productivity through Performance Appraisal*, 2nd ed. (Reading, MA: Addison-Wesley, 1994), 137.
30. Lefkowitz, "The Role of Interpersonal Affective Regard in Supervisory Performance Ratings," 67–85; Edwin Arnold and

Marcia Pulich, "Personality Conflicts and Objectivity in Appraising Performance," *The Health Care Manager* 22, no. 3 (July–September 2003): 227.

31. Deidra J. Schleicher and David V. Day, "A Cognitive Evaluation of Frame-of-Reference Rater Training: Content and Process Issues," *Organizational Behavior and Human Decision Processes* 73, no. 1 (January 1998): 76–101; Wanda Smith, K. Vernard Harrington, and Jeffery Houghton, "Predictors of Performance Appraisal Discomfort: A Preliminary Examination," *Public Personnel Management* 29, no. 1 (Spring 2000): 21–32.
32. Gail Johnson, "Forced Ranking: The Good, the Bad, and the Alternative," *Training* 41, no. 5 (May 2004): 24–31; Christine A. Amalfe and Eileen Quinn Steiner, "Forced Ranking Systems: Yesterday's Legal Target?" *New Jersey Law Journal* (March 28, 2005).
33. Lisa Keeping and Paul Levy, "Performance Appraisal Reaction: Measurement, Modeling, and Method Bias," *Journal of Applied Psychology* 85, no. 5 (October 2000): 708–23.
34. Wendy Boswell and John Boudreau, "Employee Satisfaction with Performance Appraisals and Appraisers: The Role of Perceived Appraisal Use," *Human Resource Development Quarterly* 11, no. 3 (Fall 2000): 283–99; Adam B. Butler and Amie Skattebo, "What Is Acceptable for Women May Not Be for Men: The Effect of Family Conflicts with Work on Job-Performance Ratings," *Journal of Occupational and Organizational Psychology* 77, no. 4 (December 2004): 553–64; Cheri Ostroff, Leanne E. Atwater, and Barbara J. Feinberg, "Understanding Self-Other Agreement: A Look at Rater and Ratee Characteristics, Context, and Outcomes," *Personnel Psychology* 57, no. 1 (Summer 2004): 333–37.
35. Kristina E. Chirico, M. Ronald Buckley, Anthony R. Wheeler, Jeffrey D. Facteau, H. John Bernardin, and Danielle S. Beu, "A Note on the Need for True Scores in Frame-of-Reference (FOR) Training Research," *Journal of Managerial Issues* 16, no. 3 (Fall 2004): 382–98.
36. Stephen C. Behrenbrinker, "Conducting Productive Performance Evaluations in the Assessor's Office," *Assessment Journal* 2, no. 5 (September/October 1995): 48–54; Aharon Tziner, Christine Joanis, and Kevin Murphy, "A Comparison of Three Methods of Performance Appraisal with Regard to Goal Properties, Goal Perception, and Ratee Satisfaction," *Group & Organization Management* 25, no. 2 (June 2000): 175–90.
37. Elaine Pulakos, Sharon Arad, Michelle Donovan, and Kevin Plamondon, "Adaptability in the Workplace: Development of a Taxonomy of Adaptive Performance," *Journal of Applied Psychology* 85, no. 4 (August 2000): 612–24; Leslie A. Weatherly, "Performance Management: Getting It Right from the Start," *HRMagazine* 49, no. 3 (March 2004): S1–S12; Edwin Arnold, and Marcia Pulich, "Personality Conflicts and Objectivity in Appraising Performance," *The Health Care Manager* 22, no. 3 (July–September 2003): 227.
38. Latham and Wexley, *Increasing Productivity*; Tziner, Joanis, and Murphy, "A Comparison of Three Methods of Performance Appraisal," 175–90; Simon Taggar and Travor Brown, "Problem-Solving Team Behaviors: Development and Validation of BOS and a Hierarchical Factor Structure," *Small Group Research* 32, no. 6 (December 2001): 698–726.
39. Daniel Bachrach, Elliot Bendoly, and Philip Podsakoff, "Attributions of the 'Causes' of Group Performance as an Alternative Explanation of the Relationship between Organizational Citizenship Behavior and Organizational Performance," *Journal of Applied Psychology* 86, no. 6 (December 2001): 1285–93; Susan Leandri, "Measures That Matter: How to Fine-Tune Your Performance Measures," *Journal for Quality and Participation* 24, no. 1 (Spring 2001): 39–41.
40. Peter F. Drucker, *The Practice of Management* (New York: Harper & Brothers, 1954); reissued by HarperCollins in 1993); Janice S. Miller, "High Tech and High Performance: Managing Appraisal in the Information Age," *Journal of Labor Research* 24, no. 3 (Summer 2003): 409–425.
41. E. Locke and G. Latham, *A Theory of Goal Setting and Task Performance* (Englewood Cliffs, NJ: Prentice Hall, 1990). See also John J. Donovan and David J. Radosevich, "The Moderating Role of Goal Commitment on the Goal Difficulty-Performance Relationship: A Meta-Analytic Review and Critical Reanalysis," *Journal of Applied Psychology* 83, no. 2 (April 1998): 308–15; Cindy Romaine, "Staying Relevant: Competencies and Employee Reviews," *Information Outlook* 8, no. 4 (April 2004): 21–25; Gail Johnson, "Room for Improvement," *Training* 40, no. 11 (December 2003): 18–20.
42. Jack Steele, "Transforming the Balanced Scorecard into Your Strategy Execution System," *Manage* 53, no. 1 (September/October 2001): 22–23. See also Robert Kaplan and David Norton, "Strategic Learning and the Balanced Scorecard," *Strategy & Leadership* 24, no. 5 (September/October 1996): 18–24; Robert Kaplan and David Norton, "Using the Balanced Scorecard as a Strategic Management System," *Harvard Business Review* (January–February 1996): 75–85; Joe Mullich, "Get in Line: People Talk about Aligning Corporate, Departmental and Employee Goals, But Not Many Actually Do It," *Workforce Management* 82, no. 13 (December 2003): 43; "Good Appraisal Is Simple, Happens Often, Experts Say," *The Orlando Sentinel* (via *Knight-Ridder/Tribune News Service*), December 3, 2003.
43. Deloris McGee Wanguri, "A Review, an Integration, and a Critique of Cross-Disciplinary Research on Performance Appraisals, Evaluations, and Feedback," *Journal of Business Communications* 32, no. 3 (July 1995): 267–93; Tziner, Joanis, and Murphy, "A Comparison of Three Methods of Performance Appraisal," 175–90; "Good Appraisal Is Simple, Happens Often, Experts Say."
44. Kwok Leung, Steven Su, and Michael Morris, "When Is Criticism Not Constructive? The Roles of Fairness Perceptions and Dispositional Attributions in Employee Acceptance of Critical Supervisory Feedback," *Human Relations* 54, no. 9 (September 2001): 1155–87; Ted Pollock, "Make Your Criticism Pay Off," *Electric Light & Power* 81, no. 1 (January 2003): 31.
45. "Focus on Success," *Aftermarket Business* 115, no. 2 (February 2005): 1.
46. Helen Wilkie, "The Tricky Art of Criticism," *HRMagazine* 49, no. 12 (December 2004): 77–83.

chapter 9

Managing Compensation

After studying this chapter, you should be able to

Explain employer concerns in developing a strategic compensation program.

Indicate the various factors that influence the setting of wages.

Differentiate the mechanics of each of the major job evaluation systems.

Explain the purpose of a wage survey.

Define the wage curve, pay grades, and rate ranges as parts of the compensation structure.

Identify the major provisions of the federal laws affecting compensation.

Discuss the current issues of equal pay for comparable worth, pay compression, and low wage budgets.

An extensive review of the literature indicates that important work-related variables leading to job satisfaction include challenging work, interesting job assignments, equitable rewards, competent supervision, and rewarding careers.[1] It is doubtful, however, whether many employees would continue working were it not for the money they earn. Employees desire compensation systems that they perceive as being fair and commensurate with their skills and expectations. Pay, therefore, is a major consideration in HRM because it provides employees with a tangible reward for their services, as well as a source of recognition and livelihood. Employee compensation includes all forms of pay and rewards received by employees for the performance of their jobs. *Direct compensation* encompasses employee wages and salaries, incentives, bonuses, and commissions. *Indirect compensation* comprises the many benefits supplied by employers, and *nonfinancial compensation* includes employee recognition programs, rewarding jobs, organizational support, work environment, and flexible work hours to accommodate personal needs.

Both managers and scholars agree that the way compensation is allocated among employees sends a message about what management believes is important and the types of activities it encourages.[2] Furthermore, for an employer, the payroll constitutes a sizable operating cost. In manufacturing firms compensation is seldom as low as 20 percent of total expenditures, and in service enterprises it often exceeds 80 percent. A strategic compensation program, therefore, is essential so that pay can serve to motivate employee production sufficiently to keep labor costs at an acceptable level. This chapter will be concerned with the management of a compensation program, job evaluation systems, and pay structures for determining compensation payments. Included will be a discussion of federal regulations that affect wage and salary rates. Chapter 10 will review financial incentive plans for employees. Employee benefits that are part of the total compensation package are then discussed in Chapter 11.

Strategic Compensation Planning

What is strategic compensation planning? Simply stated, it is the compensation of employees in ways that enhance motivation and growth, while at the same time aligning their efforts with the objectives, philosophies, and culture of the organization. Strategic compensation planning goes beyond determining what market rates to pay employees—although market rates are one element of compensation planning—to purposefully linking compensation to the organization's mission and general business objectives.[3] Commenting on the importance of strategic compensation planning to organizational success, Gerald Ledford and Elizabeth Hawk, two compensation specialists, note, "Companies throughout the economy have begun to rethink their compensation systems in search for competitive advantage."

Additionally, strategic compensation planning serves to mesh the monetary payments made to employees with specific functions of the HR program. For example, in the recruitment of new employees, the rate of pay for jobs can increase or limit the supply of applicants. A compensation specialist speaking to one of the authors noted, "The linkage of pay levels to labor markets is a strategic policy issue because it serves to attract or retain valued employees while affecting the organization's relative payroll budget." For example, colleges such as Idaho State University; Mesa Community College in Mesa, Arizona; and the University of Georgia know that they cannot attract or retain qualified professors unless their pay strategy is linked to competitive market rates.

Many fast-food restaurants, such as Burger King, Taco Bell, and Blimpie's—traditionally low-wage employers—have needed to raise their starting wages to attract a sufficient number of job applicants to meet staffing requirements. If pay rates are high, creating a large applicant pool, then organizations may choose to raise their selection standards and hire better-qualified employees. This in turn can reduce employer training costs. When employees perform at exceptional levels, their performance appraisals may justify an increased pay rate. For these reasons and others, an organization should develop a formal HR program to manage employee compensation.

We will discuss three important aspects of strategic compensation planning: linking compensation to organizational objectives, the pay-for-performance standard, and motivating employees through compensation.

Linking Compensation to Organizational Objectives

Compensation has been revolutionized by heightened domestic competition, globalization, increased employee skill requirements, and new technology. Therefore, an outcome of today's dynamic business environment is that managers have needed to change their pay philosophies from paying for a specific position or job title to rewarding employees on the basis of their individual competencies or work contributions to organizational success. A recent study showed that 91 percent of responding organizations had a company compensation philosophy linking their pay strategy with organizational performance. As the authors of this study noted, "A written compensation philosophy indicates senior management understands and is committed to aligning their business strategy with pay, suggesting that alignment can have a positive impact on organizational effectiveness."[4]

value-addeed compensation
Evaluating the individual components of the compensation program to see whether they advance the needs of employees and the goals of the organization

Increasingly, compensation specialists speak of value-added compensation.[5] A **value-added compensation** program, also called value-chain compensation, is one in which the components of the compensation package (benefits, base pay, incentives, and so on), both separately and in combination, create value for the organization and its employees. Using a value-added viewpoint, managers ask questions such as "How does this compensation practice benefit the organization?" and "Does the benefit offset the administrative cost?" Payments that fail to advance either the employee or the organization are removed from the compensation program.

It is not uncommon for organizations to establish very specific goals for joining their organizational objectives to their compensation program.[6] Formalized compensation goals serve as guidelines for managers to ensure that wage and benefit policies achieve their intended purpose. The more common goals of a strategic compensation policy include the following:

1. To reward employees' past performance[7]
2. To remain competitive in the labor market
3. To maintain salary equity among employees

4. To mesh employees' future performance with organizational goals
5. To control the compensation budget
6. To attract new employees[8]
7. To reduce unnecessary turnover[9]

To achieve these goals, policies must be established to guide management in making decisions. Formal statements of compensation policies typically include the following:

1. The rate of pay within the organization and whether it is to be above, below, or at the prevailing market rate
2. The ability of the pay program to gain employee acceptance while motivating employees to perform to the best of their abilities
3. The pay level at which employees may be recruited and the pay differential between new and more senior employees
4. The intervals at which pay raises are to be granted and the extent to which merit and/or seniority will influence the raises
5. The pay levels needed to facilitate the achievement of a sound financial position in relation to the products or services offered

The Pay-for-Performance Standard

pay-for-performance standard
A standard by which managers tie compensation to employee effort and performance

This quote from compensation specialist Edward E. Lawler III illustrates the importance of pay-for-performance as a strategic pay practice: "A most dramatic pay trend is the increased adoption by *Fortune* 1000 corporations of pay-for-performance programs,"[10] Why is this statement significant? A **pay-for-performance standard** serves to raise productivity and lower labor costs in today's competitive economic environment. It is agreed that managers must tie at least some reward to employee effort and performance. Without this standard, motivation to perform with greater effort will be low, resulting in higher wage costs to the organization. Additionally, most employees believe that their compensation should be directly linked to their relative performance.

The term "pay for performance" refers to a wide range of compensation options, including merit-based pay, bonuses, salary commissions, job and pay banding, team/group incentives, and various gainsharing programs.[11] (Gainsharing plans are discussed in Chapter 10.) Each of these compensation systems seeks to differentiate between the pay of average performers and that of outstanding performers. In 2002, when Plum Creek Timber Company, the second largest timberland owner in the United States, merged with The Timber Company, it emphasized a pay-for-performance philosophy by forming new salary ranges based on each job's impact on the business and incentive rewards linked more directly to individual and company performance.[12] Interestingly, productivity studies show that employees will increase their output by 15 to 35 percent when an organization installs a pay-for-performance program.

Unfortunately, designing a sound pay-for-performance system is not easy. Consideration must be given to how employee performance will be measured. For example, measuring an employee's output may be relatively easy and objective on an assembly line but more difficult (and subjective) when the employee works in a service environment. Other concerns include the monies to be allocated for compensation increases, which employees to cover, the payout method, and the periods when pay-

Lumber workers are often paid on a pay-for-performance basis.

ments will be made. A critical issue concerns the size of the monetary increase and its perceived value to employees. Rose Stanley, compensation specialist with WorldatWork, reports that annual salary budgets for 2004 averaged 3.5 percent. Projected annual salary budgets for 2005 are 3.7 percent.[13] These percentages only slightly exceed yearly increases in the cost of living. Although differences exist as to how large a wage or salary increase must be before it is perceived as meaningful, a pay-for-performance program will lack its full potential when pay increases only approximate rises in the cost of living.

Motivating Employees through Compensation

Pay constitutes a quantitative measure of an employee's relative worth. For most employees, pay has a direct bearing not only on their standard of living, but also on the status and recognition they may be able to achieve both on and off the job. Because pay represents a reward received in exchange for an employee's contributions, it is essential, according to the equity theory, that the pay be equitable in terms of those contributions. It is essential also that an employee's pay be equitable in terms of what other employees are receiving for their contributions.

Pay Equity

Simply defined, equity embraces the concept of fairness. Equity theory, also referred to as *distributive fairness*, is a motivation theory that explains how people respond to situations in which they feel they have received less (or more) than they deserve.[14] Central to the theory is the role of perception in motivation and the fact that individuals make comparisons.[15] It states that individuals form a ratio of their inputs (abilities, skills, experiences) in a situation to their outcomes (salary, benefits) in that situation. They then compare the value of that ratio with the value of the input/output ratio for other individuals in a similar class of jobs either internal or external to the organization. If the value of their ratio equals the value of another's, they perceive the situation as equitable and no tension exists. However, if they perceive their input/output ratio as inequitable relative to others', this creates tension and motivates them to eliminate or reduce the inequity. The strength of their motivation is proportional to the magnitude of the perceived inequity. Figure 9.1 illustrates pay equity and feelings of being fairly paid.

pay equity
An employee's perception that compensation received is equal to the value of the work performed

For employees, **pay equity** is achieved when the compensation received is equal to the value of the work performed. Research clearly demonstrates that employees' perceptions of pay equity, or inequity, can have dramatic effects on their motivation for both work behavior and productivity. Managers must therefore develop strategic pay practices that are both internally and externally equitable. Compensation policies are *internally* equitable when employees believe that the wage rates for their jobs approximate the job's worth to the organization. Perceptions of *external* pay equity exist when the organization is paying wages that are relatively equal to what other employers are paying for similar types of work.

Figure 9.1 Relationship between Pay Equity and Motivation

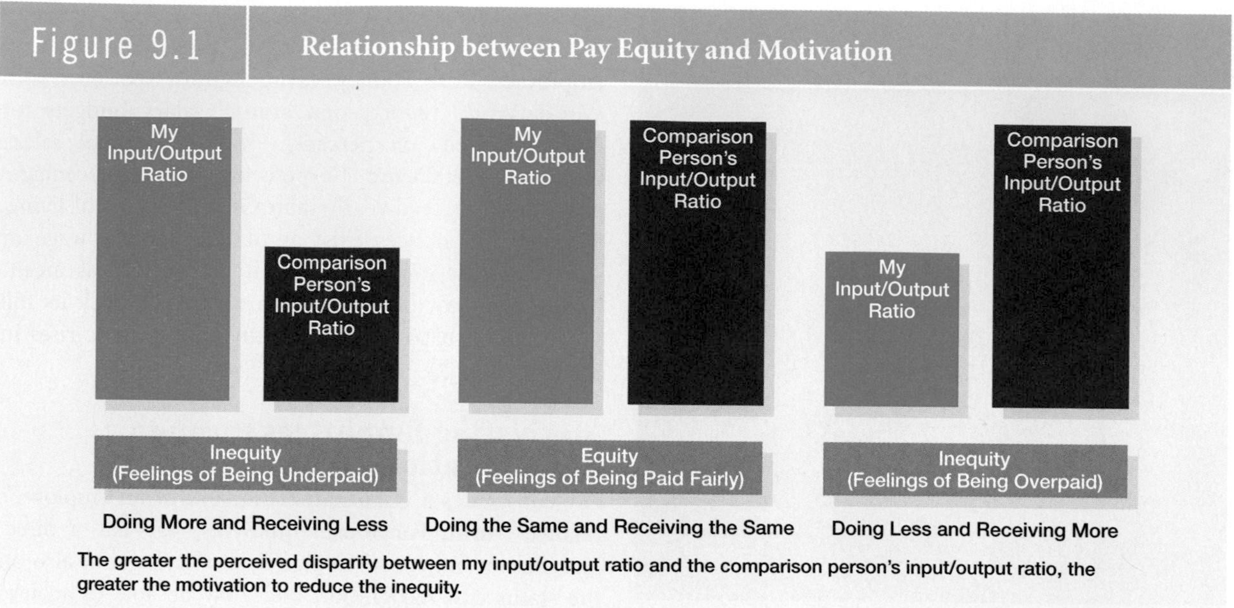

The greater the perceived disparity between my input/output ratio and the comparison person's input/output ratio, the greater the motivation to reduce the inequity.

Expectancy Theory and Pay

The expectancy theory of motivation predicts that one's level of motivation depends on the attractiveness of the rewards sought and the probability of obtaining those rewards.[16] The theory has developed from the work of psychologists who consider humans as thinking, reasoning people who have beliefs and anticipations concerning future life events. Expectancy theory therefore holds that employees should exert greater work effort if they have reason to expect that it will result in a reward that is valued.[17] To motivate this effort, the value of any monetary reward should be attractive. Employees also must believe that good performance is valued by their employer and will result in their receiving the expected reward.

Figure 9.2 shows the relationship between pay-for-performance and the expectancy theory of motivation. The model predicts, first, that high effort will lead to high performance (expectancy). For example, if an employee believes she has the skills and abilities to perform her job, and if she works hard (effort), then her performance will improve or be high. Second, high performance should result in rewards that are appreciated (valued). Elements of the compensation package are said to have *instrumentality* when an employee's high performance leads to monetary rewards that are valued. As we previously stated that pay-for-performance leads to a feeling of pay satisfaction, this feeling should reinforce one's high level of effort.

Thus, how employees view compensation can be an important factor in determining the motivational value of compensation. Furthermore, the effective communication of pay information together with an organizational environment that elicits employee trust in management can contribute to employees' having more accurate perceptions of their pay. The perceptions employees develop concerning their pay are influenced by the accuracy of their knowledge and understanding of the compensation program's strategic objectives.

Figure 9.2 Pay-for-Performance and Expectancy Theory

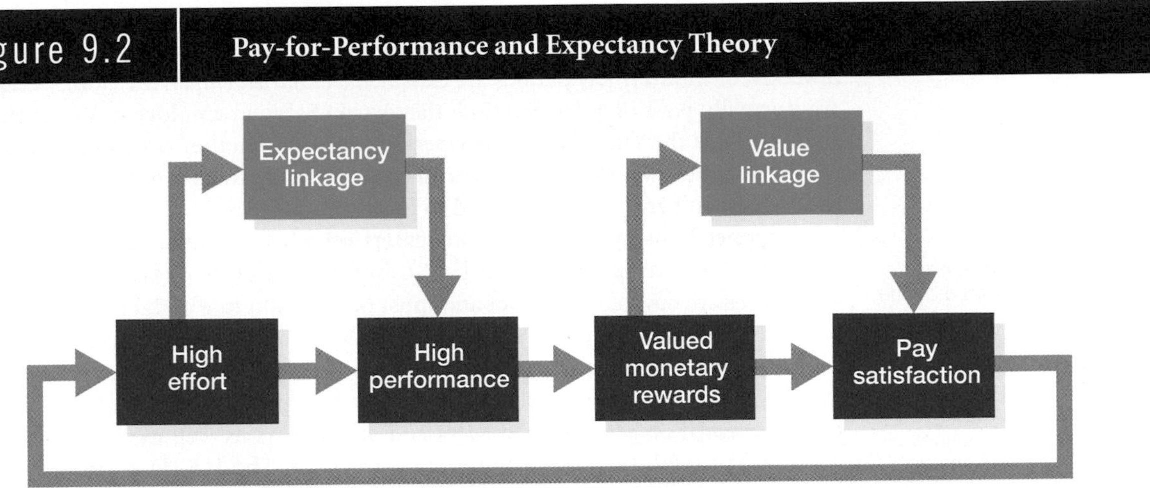

Pay Secrecy

Misperceptions by employees concerning the equity of their pay and its relationship to performance can be created by secrecy about the pay that others receive. There is reason to believe that secrecy can generate distrust in the compensation system, reduce employee motivation, and inhibit organizational effectiveness. Yet pay secrecy seems to be an accepted practice in many organizations in both the private and the public sector.

Managers may justify secrecy on the grounds that most employees prefer to have their own pay kept secret. Probably one of the reasons for pay secrecy that managers may be unwilling to admit is that it gives them greater freedom in compensation management, because pay decisions are not disclosed and there is no need to justify or defend them. Employees who are not supposed to know what others are being paid have no objective base for pursuing complaints about their own pay. Secrecy also serves to cover up inequities existing within the internal pay structure. Furthermore, secrecy surrounding compensation decisions may lead employees to believe that there is no direct relationship between pay and performance.

Pay secrecy, however, may not promote a positive strategic pay program. In one study concerning employees' knowledge of their base pay, results showed that (1) knowledge of base pay is the strongest predictor of pay satisfaction, which is highly associated with work engagement, and (2) knowledge of base pay more strongly predicts pay satisfaction than does the actual amount of pay received by employees.[18] Expectancy theory, previously discussed, would also argue for an "open" strategic pay philosophy.

The Bases for Compensation

hourly work
Work paid on an hourly basis

piecework
Work paid according to the number of units produced

Work performed in most private, public, and not-for-profit organizations has traditionally been compensated on an hourly basis. It is referred to as **hourly work,** in contrast to **piecework,** in which employees are paid according to the number of units they produce. Hourly work, however, is far more prevalent than piecework as a basis for compensating employees.

Employees compensated on an hourly basis are classified as *hourly employees*, or wage earners. Those whose compensation is computed on the basis of weekly, biweekly, or monthly pay periods are classified as *salaried employees*. Hourly employees are normally paid only for the time they work. Salaried employees, by contrast, are generally paid the same for each pay period, even though they occasionally may work more hours or fewer than the regular number of hours in a period. They also usually receive certain benefits not provided to hourly employees.

nonexempt employees
Employees covered by the overtime provisions of the Fair Labor Standards Act

exempt employees
Employees not covered by the overtime provisions of the Fair Labor Standards Act

Another basis for compensation centers on whether employees are classified as *nonexempt* or *exempt* under the Fair Labor Standards Act (FLSA).[19] **Nonexempt employees** are covered by the act and must be paid at a rate of 1½ times their *regular* pay rate for time worked in excess of forty hours in their workweek. Most hourly workers employed in interstate commerce are considered nonexempt workers under the FLSA. Employees not covered by the overtime provision of the FLSA are classified as **exempt employees.** Managers and supervisors as well as a large number of white-collar employees are in the exempt category. The U.S. Department of Labor (DOL) imposes a narrow definition of exempt status, and employers wishing to classify employees as exempt must convince the DOL that the job is exempt on the basis of the independent judgment of the jobholder and other criteria. Therefore employers should check the exact terms and conditions of exemption before classifying employees as either exempt or nonexempt. (See "Exemption from Overtime Provisions" later in this chapter.)

Determining Compensation—The Wage Mix

Employees may inquire of their managers, "How are the wages for my job determined?" In practice, a combination of *internal* and *external* factors can influence, directly or indirectly, the rates at which employees are paid. Through their interaction these factors constitute the wage mix, as shown in Figure 9.3.[20] For example, the area wage rate for administrative assistants might be $9.75 per hour. However, one employer may elect to pay its administrative assistants $11.50 per hour because of their excellent performance. The influence of government legislation on the wage mix will be discussed later in the chapter.

Internal Factors

The internal factors that influence wage rates are the employer's compensation strategy, the worth of a job, an employee's relative worth in meeting job requirements, and an employer's ability to pay.

Employer's Compensation Strategy

Highlights in HRM 1 illustrates the compensation strategies of two organizations, Tri Star Performance and Preventive Health Care. The pay strategy of Preventive Health Care is to be an industry pay leader, while Tri Star Performance seeks to be wage-competitive. Both employers strive to promote a compensation policy that is internally fair.

Tri Star Performance and Preventive Health Care, like other employers, will establish numerous compensation objectives that affect the pay employees receive. As

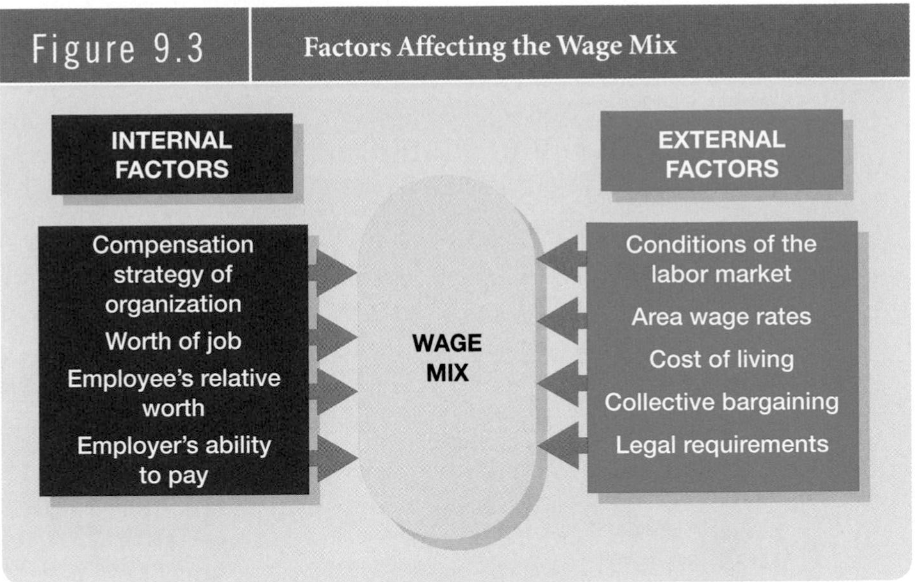

a minimum, both large and small employers should set pay policies reflecting (1) the internal wage relationship among jobs and skill levels, (2) the external competition or an employer's pay position relative to what competitors are paying, (3) a policy of rewarding employee performance, and (4) administrative decisions concerning elements of the pay system such as overtime premiums, payment periods, and short-term or long-term incentives.

Worth of a Job

Organizations without a formal compensation program generally base the worth of jobs on the subjective opinions of people familiar with the jobs. In such instances, pay rates may be influenced heavily by the labor market or, in the case of unionized employers, by collective bargaining. Organizations with formal compensation programs, however, are more likely to rely on a system of *job evaluation* to aid in rate determination. Even when rates are subject to collective bargaining, job evaluation can assist the organization in maintaining some degree of control over its wage structure.

The use of job evaluation is widespread in both the public and the private sector. The cities of Chicago and Miami use job evaluation in establishing wage structures, as do Levi Strauss and Dell Computer. The jobs covered most frequently by job evaluation are clerical, technical, and various blue-collar groups. Other jobs covered are managerial and top executive positions.

In today's competitive environment, compensation professionals believe that the worth of a job should be based on more than market prices or using only an internally driven job evaluation program. Rather, a job's value should be based on *the total value* delivered to the organization.[21] That is, some jobs may simply be more important to organizational success than others regardless of how they are internally evaluated. Valuing work not only properly enables organizations to price "important" jobs effectively, but also provides insight into how a job relates to overall organizational success. Additionally, valuing work properly serves to attract and retain the right talent to drive organizational performance.[22]

Highlights in HRM 1

Comparison of Compensation Strategies

Compensation strategies and objectives can differ widely across large and small employers as well as across employers in the private and public sectors. Here are the compensation strategies at Tri Star Performance and Preventive Health Care.

Tri Star Performance

- Promote pay-for-performance practices
- Pay market-competitive compensation
- Achieve internal and external pay equity
- Achieve simplicity in compensation programs
- Strive for employee commitment and a collaborative work environment
- Promote gender fairness in pay and benefits
- Comply with all governmental compensation regulations
- Minimize increased fixed costs

Preventive Health Care

- Be a pay leader in the healthcare industry
- Promote open and understandable pay practices
- Ensure fair employee treatment
- Offer benefits promoting individual employee needs
- Offer compensation rewarding employee creativity and achievements
- Offer compensation to foster the strategic mission of the organization
- Obtain employee input when developing compensation practices
- Emphasize performance through variable pay and stock options

Employee's Relative Worth

In both hourly and salary jobs, employee performance can be recognized and rewarded through promotion and with various incentive systems. (The incentive systems used most often will be discussed in the next chapter.) Superior performance can also be rewarded by granting merit raises on the basis of steps within a rate range established for a job class. If merit raises are to have their intended value, however, they must be determined by an effective performance appraisal system that differentiates between employees who deserve the raises and those who do not. This system, moreover, must provide a visible and credible relationship between performance and any raises received. Unfortunately, too many so-called merit systems provide for raises to be granted automatically. As a result, employees tend to be rewarded more for merely being present than for being productive on the job.

Employer's Ability to Pay

Pay levels are limited by earned profits and other financial resources available to employers. This is clearly illustrated by financially burdened companies such as United Airlines and Delta Air Lines that ask their employees for pay cuts. Furthermore, an organization's ability to pay is determined in part by the productivity of its employees. This productivity is a result not only of their performance, but also of the amount of capital the organization has invested in labor-saving equipment. Generally, increases in capital investment reduce the number of employees required to perform the work and increase an employer's ability to provide higher pay for those it employs.

Economic conditions and competition faced by employers can also significantly affect the rates they are able to pay. Competition and recessions can force prices down and reduce the income from which compensation payments are derived. In such situations, employers have little choice but to reduce wages and/or lay off employees, or, even worse, to go out of business.

External Factors

The major external factors that influence wage rates include labor market conditions, area wage rates, cost of living, collective bargaining if the employer is unionized, and legal requirements. The legal requirements of compensation will be discussed later in the chapter.

Labor Market Conditions

The labor market reflects the forces of supply and demand for qualified labor within an area. These forces help influence the wage rates required to recruit or retain competent employees. It must be recognized, however, that counterforces can reduce the full impact of supply and demand on the labor market. The economic power of unions, for example, may prevent employers from lowering wage rates even when unemployment is high among union members. Government regulations also may prevent an employer from paying at a market rate less than an established minimum.

Area Wage Rates

A formal wage structure should provide rates that are in line with those being paid by other employers for comparable jobs within the area. Data pertaining to area wage rates may be obtained from local wage surveys. For example, the Arizona Department of Economic Security conducts an annual wage survey for both large and small employers in various cities throughout the state. Wage survey data also may be obtained from a variety of sources, including the American Management Association, Administrative Management Society, U.S. Department of Labor, and Federal Reserve Banks. Smaller employers such as the Woodsmith Corporation and Golden State Container use government surveys to establish rates of pay for new and senior employees. Many organizations, such as the City of Atlanta, Northwest Airlines, and Progress Energy, conduct their own surveys. Others engage in a cooperative exchange of wage information or rely on various professional associations for these data. A high percentage of wage data surveys are inexpensive—less than $100—and are therefore available to all employers, regardless of size.

Wage surveys (discussed fully later in the chapter) serve the important function of providing external wage equity between the surveying organization and other organizations competing for labor in the surrounding labor market. Importantly, data from area wage surveys can be used to prevent the rates for jobs from drifting too far above or below those of other employers in the region. When rates rise above existing area levels, an employer's labor costs may become excessive. Conversely, if they drop too far below area levels, it may be difficult to recruit and retain competent personnel. Wage survey data must also take into account indirect wages paid in the form of benefits.

Cost of Living

Because of inflation, compensation rates have had to be adjusted upward periodically to help employees maintain their purchasing power. Employers make these changes

consumer price index (CPI)
A measure of the average change in prices over time in a fixed "market basket" of goods and services

with the help of the **consumer price index (CPI).** The CPI is a measure of the average change in prices over time in a fixed "market basket" of goods and services. The consumer price index is based on prices of food, clothing, shelter, and fuels; transportation fares; charges for medical services; and prices of other goods and services that people buy for day-to-day living. The Bureau of Labor Statistics collects price information on a monthly basis and calculates the CPI for the nation as a whole and various U.S. city averages. Separate indexes are also published by size of city and by region of the country. Employers in a number of communities monitor changes in the CPI as a basis for compensation decisions.

Changes in the CPI can have important effects on pay rates. Granting wage increases solely on the basis of the CPI helps compress pay rates within a pay structure, thereby creating inequities among those who receive the wage increase. Inequities also result from the fact that adjustments are made on a cents-per-hour basis rather than a percentage basis. For example, a cost-of-living adjustment of 50 cents represents a 7.1 percent increase for an employee earning $7 per hour, but only a 4.2 percent increase for one earning $12 per hour. Unless adjustments are made periodically in employee base rates, the desired differential between higher- and lower-paying jobs will gradually be reduced. The incentive to accept more-demanding jobs will also be reduced.

escalator clauses
Clauses in labor agreements that provide for quarterly cost-of-living adjustments in wages, basing the adjustments on changes in the consumer price index

Employees who work under a union contract may receive wage increases through **escalator clauses** found in their labor agreement. These clauses provide for quarterly cost-of-living adjustments (COLA) in wages based on changes in the CPI. The most common adjustments are 1 cent per hour for each 0.3- or 0.4-point change in the CPI. COLAs are favored by unions during particularly high periods of inflation.

Collective Bargaining

real wages
Wage increases larger than rises in the consumer price index; that is, the real earning power of wages

One of the primary functions of a labor union, as emphasized in Chapter 14, is to bargain collectively over conditions of employment, the most important of which is compensation.[23] The union's goal in each new agreement is to achieve increases in **real wages**—wage increases larger than the increase in the CPI—thereby improving the purchasing power and standard of living of its members. This goal includes gaining wage settlements that equal or exceed the pattern established by other unions within the area.

job evaluation
A systematic process of determining the relative worth of jobs in order to establish which jobs should be paid more than others within an organization

The agreements negotiated by unions tend to establish rate patterns within the labor market. As a result, wages are generally higher in areas where organized labor is strong. To recruit and retain competent personnel and avoid unionization, nonunion employers must either meet or exceed these rates. The "union scale" also becomes the prevailing rate that all employers must pay for work performed under government contract. The impact of collective bargaining therefore extends beyond the segment of the labor force that is unionized.

Job Evaluation Systems

As we discussed earlier, one important component of the wage mix is the worth of the job. Organizations formally determine the value of jobs through the process of job evaluation. **Job evaluation** is the systematic process of determining the *relative* worth of jobs in order to establish which jobs should be paid more than others within the organization. Job evaluation helps establish internal equity between various jobs. The relative worth of a job may be determined by comparing it with others within the organization or by comparing it with a scale that has been constructed for this purpose. Each method of comparison, furthermore, may be made on the basis of the jobs as a whole or on the basis of the parts that constitute the jobs.[24]

Three traditional methods of comparison provide the basis for the principal systems of job evaluation. We will begin by discussing the simpler nonquantitative approaches and conclude by reviewing the more popular quantitative system. Also discussed is a newer method of job evaluation—work evaluation. Regardless of the methodology used, it is important to remember that all job evaluation methods require varying degrees of managerial judgment. Also, those involved in evaluating jobs must consider the impact of the Americans with Disabilities Act on the process. (See Chapter 3.)

Job Ranking System

job ranking system
The simplest and oldest system of job evaluation by which jobs are arrayed on the basis of their relative worth

The simplest and oldest system of job evaluation is the **job ranking system,** which arrays jobs on the basis of their relative worth. One technique used to rank jobs consists of having the raters arrange cards listing the duties and responsibilities of each job in order of the importance of the jobs. Job ranking can be done by a single individual knowledgeable about all jobs or by a committee composed of management and employee representatives.

Another common approach to job ranking is the paired-comparison method. Raters compare each job with all other jobs by means of a paired-comparison ranking table that lists the jobs in both rows and columns, as shown in Figure 9.4. To use the table, raters compare a job from a row with the jobs from each of the columns. If the row job is ranked higher than a column job, an X is placed in the appropriate

Figure 9.4 Paired-Comparison Job Ranking Table

Row Jobs \ Column Jobs	Senior Administrative Secretary	Data-Entry Operator	Data-Processing Director	File Clerk	Systems Analyst	Programmer	Total
Senior Administrative Secretary	—	X		X		X	3
Data-Entry Operator		—		X			1
Data-Processing Director	X	X	—	X	X	X	5
File Clerk				—			0
Systems Analyst	X	X		X	—	X	4
Programmer		X		X		—	2

Directions: Place an X in the cell where the value of a row job is higher than that of a column job.

cell. After all the jobs have been compared, raters total the Xs for row jobs. The total number of Xs for a row job will establish its worth relative to other jobs. Differences in rankings should then be reconciled into a single rating for all jobs. After jobs are evaluated, wage rates can be assigned to them through use of the salary survey discussed later in the chapter.

The basic disadvantage of the job ranking system is that it does not provide a very precise measure of each job's worth. Another weakness is that the final ranking of jobs indicates the relative importance of the job, not the differences in the degree of importance that may exist between jobs. A final limitation of the job ranking method is that it can be used only with a small number of jobs, probably no more than fifteen. Its simplicity, however, makes it ideal for use by smaller employers.

Job Classification System

job classification system
A system of job evaluation in which jobs are classified and grouped according to a series of predetermined wage grades

In the **job classification system,** jobs are classified and grouped according to a series of predetermined grades. Successive grades require increasing amounts of job responsibility, skill, knowledge, ability, or other factors selected to compare jobs. For example, Grade GS-1 from the federal government grade descriptions reads as follows:

> GS-1 includes those classes of positions the duties of which are to perform, under immediate supervision, with little or no latitude for the exercise of independent judgment (A) the simplest routine work in office, business, or fiscal operations; or (B) elementary work of a subordinate technical character in a professional, scientific, or technical field.

The descriptions of each of the job classes constitute the scale against which the specifications for the various jobs are compared. Managers then evaluate jobs by comparing job descriptions with the different wage grades in order to "slot" the job into the appropriate grade. While this system has the advantage of simplicity, it is less precise than the point system because the job is evaluated as a whole. The federal civil service job classification system is probably the best-known system of this type. The job classification system is widely used by municipal and state governments.

Point System

point system
A quantitative job evaluation procedure that determines the relative value of a job by the total points assigned to it

The **point system** is a quantitative job evaluation procedure that determines a job's relative value by calculating the total points assigned to it.[25] It has been successfully used by high-visibility organizations such as Digital Equipment Company, Met Life, Johnson Wax, Prudential Financial, TransAmerica, and many other public and private organizations, both large and small. Although point systems are rather complicated to establish, once in place they are relatively simple to understand and use. The principal advantage of the point system is that it provides a more refined basis for making judgments than either the ranking or classification systems and thereby can produce results that are more valid and less easy to manipulate.

The point system permits jobs to be evaluated quantitatively on the basis of factors or elements—commonly called *compensable factors*—that constitute the job.[26] The skills, efforts, responsibilities, and working conditions that a job usually entails are the more common major compensable factors that serve to rank one job as more or less important than another. More contemporary factors might include fiscal accountability, leadership, teamwork, and project accountability. The number of compensable factors an organization uses depends on the nature of the organization and the jobs to be evaluated. Once selected, compensable factors will be assigned weights according to their relative importance to the organization. For example, if responsibility is considered extremely important to the organization, it could be assigned a weight of 40 percent. Next, each factor will be divided into a number of degrees. Degrees represent different levels of difficulty associated with each factor.

The Point Manual

The point system requires the use of a *point manual.* The point manual is, in effect, a handbook that contains a description of the compensable factors and the degrees to which these factors may exist within the jobs. A manual also will indicate—usually by means of a table—the number of points allocated to each factor and to each of the degrees into which these factors are divided. The point value assigned to a job represents the sum of the numerical degree values of each compensable factor that the job possesses.

For example, the job factors illustrated in Highlights in HRM 2 represent those covered by the American Association of Industrial Management point manual. Each of the factors listed in this manual has been divided into five degrees. The number of degrees into which the factors in a manual are to be divided, however, can be greater or smaller than this number, depending on the relative weight assigned to each factor and the ease with which the individual degrees can be defined or distinguished. A statement is provided defining each of the degrees, as well as each factor as a whole. The definitions should be concise and yet distinguish the factors and each of their degrees. Highlights in HRM 3 represents another portion of the point manual used by the American Association of Industrial Management to describe each of the degrees for the education factor. These descriptions enable those conducting a job evaluation to determine the degree to which the factors exist in each job being evaluated.

Using the Point Manual

Job evaluation under the point system is accomplished by comparing the job descriptions and job specifications, factor by factor, against the various factor-degree descriptions contained in the manual. Each factor within the job being evaluated is then assigned the number of points specified in the manual. When the points for each factor have been determined from the manual, the total point value for the job as a whole can be calculated. The relative worth of the job is then determined from the total points that have been assigned to that job.

Work Valuation

work valuation
A job evaluation system that seeks to measure a job's worth through its value to the organization

Work valuation is a relatively new job evaluation system championed to meet the demands of a dynamic business environment. The cornerstone for **work valuation** is that work should be valued relative to the business goals of the organization rather than by an internally applied point-factor job evaluation system.[27] As noted by one compensation specialist, "Valuing work properly enables organizations to not only price individual jobs effectively, but provides insight into how jobs relate to overall organizational goals and objectives and how roles ultimately contribute to organizational success."[28] Additionally, work valuation serves to direct compensation dollars to the type of work pivotal to organizational goals.

Highlights in HRM 2

Point Values for Job Factors of the American Association of Industrial Management

FACTORS	1ST DEGREE	2ND DEGREE	3RD DEGREE	4TH DEGREE	5TH DEGREE
Skill					
1. Education	14	28	42	56	70
2. Experience	22	44	66	88	110
3. Initiative and ingenuity	14	28	42	56	70
Effort					
4. Physical demand	10	20	30	40	50
5. Mental or visual demand	5	10	15	20	25
Responsibility					
6. Equipment or process	5	10	15	20	25
7. Material or product	5	10	15	20	25
8. Safety of others	5	10	15	20	25
9. Work of others	5	10	15	20	25
Job Conditions					
10. Working conditions	10	20	30	40	50
11. Hazards	5	10	15	20	25

Source: Reproduced with permission of the American Association of Industrial Management, Springfield, Mass.

With work valuations, work is measured through standards that come directly from business goals. For example, jobs might be valued relative to financial, operational, or customer service objectives. All forms of work, employee roles, and ways of organizing work (such as teams) are valued. The work evaluation process ends with a work hierarchy that is an array of work by value to the organization. The work hierarchy is eventually priced through wage surveys to determine individual pay rates.

Job Evaluation for Management Positions

Because management positions are more difficult to evaluate and involve certain demands not found in jobs at the lower levels, some organizations do not attempt to include them in their job evaluation programs for hourly employees. Rather, they employ either a standardized (purchased) program or customize a point method to fit their particular jobs. However, regardless of the approach adopted, point plans for executive and managerial employees operate similarly to those for other groups of employees.

Hay profile method
A job evaluation technique using three factors—knowledge, mental activity, and accountability—to evaluate executive and managerial positions

One of the better-known standardized job evaluation programs for evaluating executive, managerial, and professional positions is the **Hay profile method,** developed

Description of Education Factor and Degrees of the American Association of Industrial Management

1. EDUCATION

This factor measures the basic trades training, knowledge or "scholastic contact" essential as background or training preliminary to learning the job duties. This job knowledge or background may have been acquired either by formal education or by training on jobs of lesser degree or by any combination of these approaches.

1st Degree **14 points**

Requires the use of simple writing, adding, subtracting, whole numbers and the carrying out of instructions; and the use of fixed gauges and direct reading instruments and devices in which interpretation is not required.

2nd Degree **28 points**

Requires the use of commercial English, grammar and arithmetic such as addition, subtraction, multiplication and division, including decimals and fractions; simple use of formulas, charts, tables, drawings, specifications, schedules, wiring diagrams, together with the use of adjustable measuring instruments, graduates and the like requiring interpretation in their various applications; or the posting, preparation, interpretation, use and checking of reports, forms, records and comparable data.

3rd Degree **42 points**

Requires the use of shop mathematics together with the use of complicated drawings, specifications, charts, tables, various types of adjustable measuring instruments and the training generally applicable in a particular or specialized occupation. Equivalent to 1 to 3 years applied trades training.

4th Degree **56 points**

Requires the use of advanced shop mathematics, together with the use of complicated drawings, specifications, charts, tables, handbook formulas, all varieties of adjustable measuring instruments and the uses of broad training in a recognized trade or craft. Equivalent to complete, accredited, indentured apprenticeship or equivalent to high school plus a 2-year technical college education.

5th Degree **70 points**

Requires the use of higher mathematics involved in the application of engineering principles and the performance of related, practical operations, together with a comprehensive knowledge of the theories and practices of mechanical, electrical, chemical, civil or like engineering field. Equivalent to complete 4 years of technical college or university education.

Source: Reproduced with permission of the American Association of Industrial Management, Springfield, Mass.

by Edward N. Hay. The three broad factors that constitute the evaluation in the "profile" are knowledge (or know-how), mental activity (or problem solving), and accountability.[29] The Hay method uses only three factors because it is assumed that these factors represent the most important aspects of all executive and managerial positions. The profile for each position is developed by determining the percentage value to be assigned to each of the three factors. Jobs are then ranked on the basis of each factor, and point values that make up the profile are assigned to each job on the basis of the percentage-value level at which the job is ranked.

The Compensation Structure

Job evaluation systems provide for internal equity and serve as the basis for wage-rate determination. They do not in themselves determine the wage rate. The evaluated worth of each job in terms of its rank, class, points, or monetary worth must be converted into an hourly, daily, weekly, or monthly wage rate. The compensation tool used to help set wages is the wage and salary survey.

objective 4

Wage and Salary Surveys

The **wage and salary survey** is a survey of the wages paid by employers in an organization's relevant labor market—local, regional, or national, depending on the job. The labor market is frequently defined as the area from which employers obtain certain types of workers. The labor market for office personnel would be local, whereas the labor market for engineers would be national. It is the wage and salary survey that permits an organization to maintain external equity—that is, to pay its employees wages equivalent to the wages similar employees earn in other establishments.

wage and salary survey
A survey of the wages paid to employees of other employers in the surveying organization's relevant labor market

When job evaluation and wage-survey data are used jointly, they link the likelihood of both internal and external equity. Although surveys are conducted primarily to gather competitive wage data, they can also collect information on employee benefits or organizational pay practices (such as overtime rates or shift differentials).

Collecting Survey Data

While many organizations conduct their own wage and salary surveys, a variety of "preconducted" pay surveys are available to satisfy the requirements of most public and not-for-profit or private employers. The Bureau of Labor Statistics (BLS) is the major publisher of wage and salary data. The BLS publishes the National Compensation Survey (NCS), a statistically valid and comprehensive compensation program of wage, salary, and benefit information. (See Highlights in HRM 4.) As described on the BLS web site, "The National Compensation Survey is the umbrella program that combines several BLS compensation programs into a single vehicle that can produce local, regional, and national statistics on levels, trends, and characteristics of pay and benefits."[30]

USING THE INTERNET

The Bureau of Labor Statistics publishes wage and salary data and benefits information. Go to the Student Resources at:

http://bohlander.swlearning.com

Many states conduct surveys on either a municipal or county basis and make them available to employers. Besides these government surveys, trade groups such as the Dallas Personnel Association, the Administrative Management Society, the Society for Human Resource Management, the Amer-

Bureau of Labor Statistics National Compensation Survey

NCS data are used by managers and compensation specialists in large and small organizations to answer such questions as the following:

- How much must I pay accountants in Atlanta, Georgia?
- Is a 3 percent benefits increase comparable to that of other employers in the manufacturing industry?
- Is vision coverage a prevalent benefit among large employers in the Northeast?
- How have wage costs changed over the past year?

How the NCS Survey Works

The National Compensation Survey is an area-based survey. Wage and benefit data are collected from a predetermined set of 154 metropolitan and nonmetropolitan areas through the fifty states and the District of Columbia to represent the United States. Compensation information is collected from such diverse locations as Knoxville, Tennessee; Pittsburgh, Pennsylvania; Reno, Nevada; and Richland-Kennewick-Pasco, Washington. All areas are selected to produce regional estimates for nine broad geographic divisions and four broad regions.

Within each area, a scientific sample of establishments represents all area establishments. An "establishment" is a single physical location, such as a plant, a warehouse, a corporate office, or a retail outlet. State and local government offices are also included in the survey.

Once an establishment has been chosen for inclusion in the survey, a BLS economist selects occupations within that establishment to represent all occupations in the establishment. The BLS limits the selection to a small number of occupations to reduce the survey burden for employers. Data are collected for all incumbents in a selected occupation.

The selected occupations are then classified based on the Census Bureau's occupation classification system. The census classification categorizes approximately 450 individual occupations into ten major groupings such as sales, professional specialty, and technical, and machine operators, assemblers, and inspectors. For the occupations selected, wage and benefit data are collected. Items included in the collection of wages are time-based payments, piece rates, commissions, hazard pay, and other items directly related to the work being performed. A variety of benefit data are collected, including paid vacations, paid holidays, paid sick leave, shift differentials, and nonproduction bonuses.

ican Management Association, the National Society of Professional Engineers, and the Financial Executive Institute conduct special surveys tailored to their members' needs. Employers with global operations can purchase international surveys through large consulting firms. The overseas compensation survey offered by *TPF&C* reports on payment practices in twenty countries. While all of these third-party surveys provide certain benefits to their users, they also have various limitations. Two problems with all published surveys are that (1) they are not always compatible with the user's jobs and (2) the user cannot specify what specific data to collect. To overcome these problems, organizations may collect their own compensation data.

HRIS and Salary Surveys

Wage and benefits survey data can be found on numerous web sites. The previously mentioned National Compensation Survey is an example. Also readily available are commercial products such as those offered at http://www.salary.com: the Salary Wizard, Comp Analyst, and Survey Finder surveys. Survey Finder has a database of hundreds of compensation surveys offered by more than fifty independent vendors. Managers and compensation specialists can search for applicable surveys for either purchase or participation.[31]

Employer-Initiated Surveys

Employers wishing to conduct their own wage and salary survey must first select the jobs to be used in the survey and identify the organizations with whom they actually compete for employees. Since it is not feasible to survey all the jobs in an organization, normally only key jobs, also called benchmark jobs, are used. Characteristics of key jobs include the following:

1. They are important to employees and the organization.
2. They contain a large number of positions.
3. They have relatively stable job content.
4. They have the same job content across many organizations.
5. They are acceptable to employees, management, and labor as appropriate for pay comparisons.

The survey of key jobs will usually be sent to ten or fifteen organizations that represent a valid sample of other employers likely to compete for the employees of the surveying organization. A diversity of organizations should be selected—large and small, public and private, new and established, and union and nonunion—since each classification of employer is likely to pay different wage rates for surveyed jobs.

After the key jobs and the employers to be surveyed have been identified, the surveying organization must decide what information to gather on wages, benefit types, and pay policies. For example, when requesting pay data, it is important to specify whether hourly, daily, or weekly pay figures are needed.[32] In addition, those conducting surveys must state whether the wage data are needed for new hires or for senior employees. Precisely defining the compensation data needed will greatly increase the accuracy of the information received and the number of purposes for which it can be used. Once the survey data are tabulated, the compensation structure can be completed.

The Wage Curve

wage curve
A curve in a scattergram representing the relationship between relative worth of jobs and wage rates

The relationship between the relative worth of jobs and their wage rates can be represented by means of a **wage curve.** This curve may indicate the rates currently paid for jobs within an organization, the new rates resulting from job evaluation, or the rates for similar jobs currently being paid by other organizations within the labor market. A curve may be constructed graphically by preparing a scattergram consisting of a series of dots that represent the current wage rates. As shown in Figure 9.5, a freehand curve is then drawn through the cluster of dots in such a manner as to leave approximately an equal number of dots above and below the curve. The wage curve can be relatively straight or curved. This curve can then be used to determine the relationship between the value of a job and its wage rate at any given point on the line.

Figure 9.5 Freehand Wage Curve

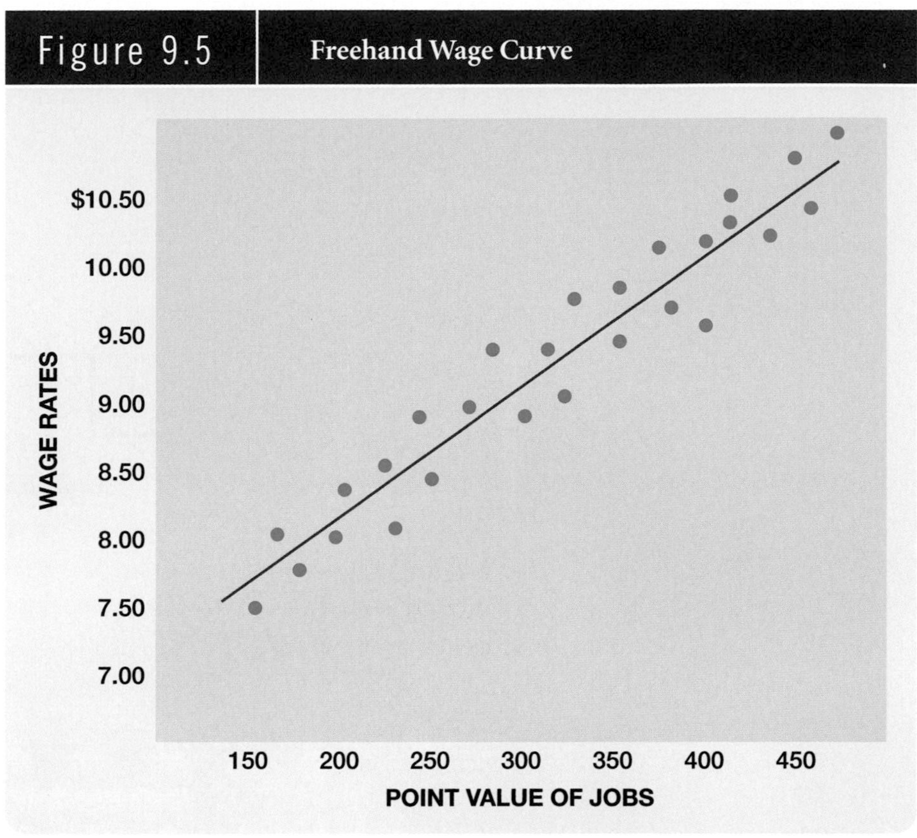

Pay Grades

pay grades
Groups of jobs within a particular class that are paid the same rate

From an administrative standpoint, it is generally preferable to group jobs into **pay grades** and to pay all jobs within a particular grade the same rate or rate range. When the classification system of job evaluation is used, jobs are grouped into grades as part of the evaluation process. When the point system is used, however, pay grades must be established at selected intervals that represent either the point or the evaluated monetary value of these jobs. The graph in Figure 9.6 illustrates a series of pay grades designated along the horizontal axis at fifty-point intervals.

The grades within a wage structure may vary in number.[33] The number is determined by such factors as the slope of the wage curve, the number and distribution of the jobs within the structure, and the organization's wage administration and promotion policies. The number utilized should be sufficient to permit difficulty levels to be distinguished, but not so great as to make the distinction between two adjoining grades insignificant.

Rate Ranges

Although a single rate may be created for each pay grade, as shown in Figure 9.6, it is more common to provide a range of rates for each pay grade. The rate ranges may be the same for each grade or proportionately greater for each successive grade, as shown in Figure 9.7. Rate ranges constructed on the latter basis provide a greater incentive for employees to accept a promotion to a job in a higher grade.

Figure 9.6 Single Rate Structure

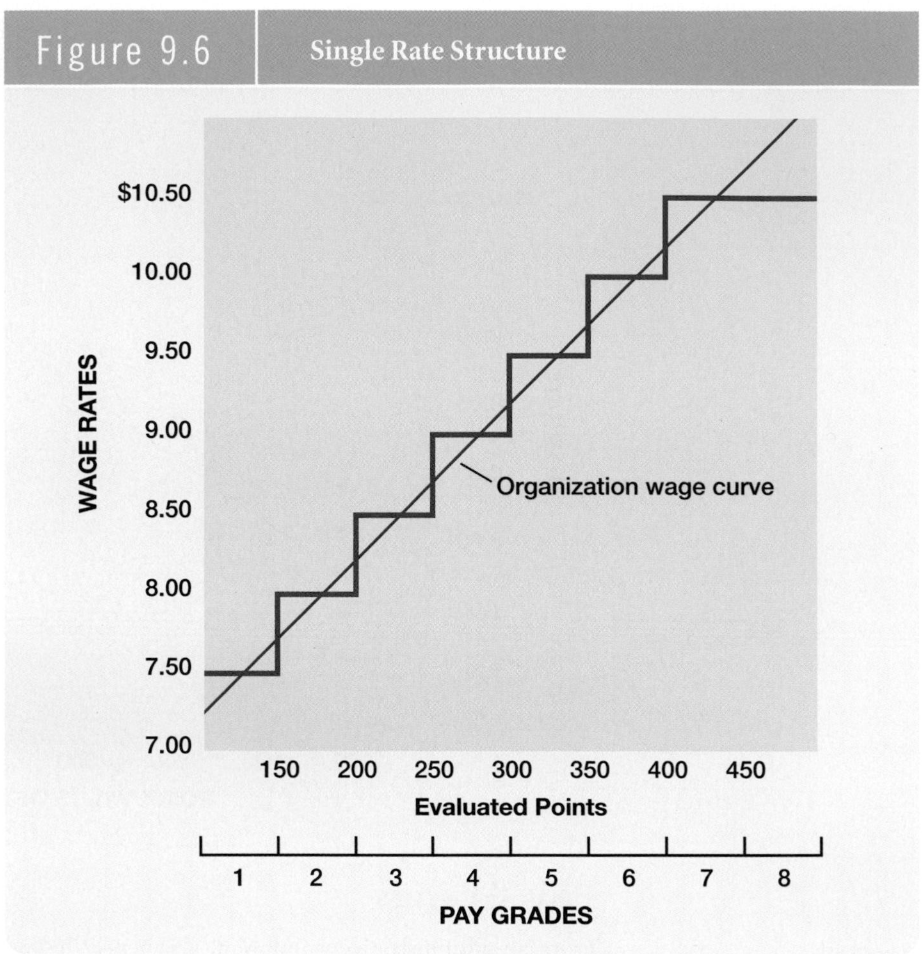

Rate ranges generally are divided into a series of steps that permit employees to receive increases up to the maximum rate for the range on the basis of merit or seniority or a combination of the two. Most salary structures provide for the ranges of adjoining pay grades to overlap. The purpose of the overlap is to permit an employee with experience to earn as much as or more than a person with less experience in the next-higher job classification.

The final step in setting up a wage structure is to determine the appropriate pay grade into which each job should be placed on the basis of its evaluated worth. Traditionally, this worth is determined on the basis of job requirements without regard to the performance of the person in that job. Under this system, the performance of those who exceed the requirements of a job may be acknowledged by merit increases within the grade range or by promotion to a job in the next-higher pay grade.

red circle rates
Payment rates above the maximum of the pay range

Organizations may pay individuals above the maximum of the pay range when employees have high seniority or promotional opportunities are scarce. Wages paid above the range maximum are called **red circle rates.** Because these rates are exceptions to the pay structure, employers often "freeze" these rates until all ranges are shifted upward through market wage adjustments.

Figure 9.7 Wage Structure with Increasing Rate Ranges

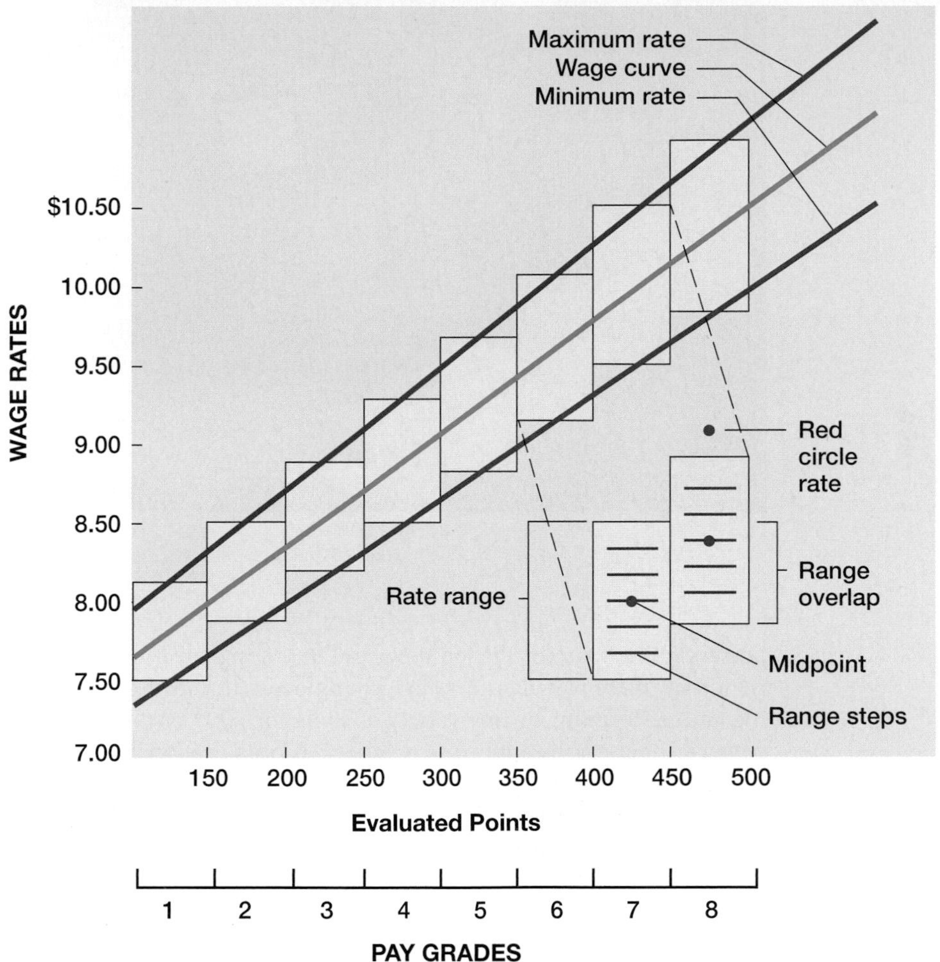

Competence-Based Pay

The predominant approach to employee compensation is still the job-based system. Unfortunately, such a system often fails to reward employees for their skills or the knowledge they possess or to encourage them to learn a new job-related skill. Additionally, job-based pay systems may not reinforce an organizational culture stressing employee involvement or provide increased employee flexibility to meet overall production or service requirements. Therefore, organizations such as Frito-Lay, Nortel Networks, Sherwin-Williams, and Honeywell have introduced competence-based pay plans.

competence-based pay Pay based on an employee's skill level, variety of skills possessed, or increased job knowledge

Competence-based pay, also referred to as skill-based pay or knowledge-based pay, compensates employees for the different skills or increased knowledge they

A competence-based pay program will encourage employees to increase their job-related knowledge and skills.

© JEFF GREENBERG/PHOTOEDIT

possess rather than for the job they hold in a designated job category.[34] Regardless of the name, these pay plans encourage employees to earn higher base wages by learning and performing a wider variety of skills (or jobs) or displaying an array of competencies that can be applied to a variety of organizational requirements. For example, in a manufacturing setting, new tasks might include various assembly activities carried out in a particular production system or a variety of maintenance functions. Within service organizations, employees might acquire new knowledge related to advanced computer systems or accounting procedures. Organizations will grant an increase in pay after each skill or knowledge has been mastered and can be demonstrated according to a predetermined standard.

Competence-based pay systems represent a fundamental change in the attitude of management regarding how work should be organized and how employees should be paid for their work efforts. The most frequently cited benefits of competence-based pay include greater productivity, increased employee learning and commitment to work, improved staffing flexibility to meet production or service demands, and the reduced effects of absenteeism and turnover, because managers can assign employees where and when needed. Competence-based pay also encourages employees to acquire training when new or updated skills are needed by an organization.

Unfortunately, competence-based plans bring some long-term difficulties.[35] Some plans limit the amount of compensation employees can earn, regardless of the new skills or competencies they acquire. Thus, after achieving the top wage, employees may be reluctant to continue their educational training. Perhaps the greatest challenge in paying individuals for their skills, knowledge, and competencies is developing appropriate measures. It is difficult to write specific knowledge and skill descriptions for jobs that employees perform and then establish accurate measures of acquired skills or knowledge.

Broadbanding

Organizations that adopt a competency-based or skill-based pay system frequently use *broadbanding* to structure their compensation payments to employees. Broadbanding simply collapses many traditional salary grades into a few wide salary bands.[36] Broadbands may have midpoints and quartiles or they may have extremely wide salary ranges or no ranges at all. Banding encourages lateral skill building while addressing the need to pay employees performing multiple jobs with different skill-level requirements. Additionally, broadbands help eliminate the obsession with grades and, instead, encourage employees to move to jobs in which they can develop in their careers and add value to the organization. Paying employees through broadbands enables organizations to consider job responsibilities, individual skills and competencies, and career mobility patterns in assigning employees to bands.

Government Regulation of Compensation

Compensation management, like the other areas of HRM, is subject to state and federal regulations. A majority of states have minimum wage laws or wage boards that fix minimum wage rates on an industry-by-industry basis. When an employee is subject to both the state and federal minimum wage laws, the employee is entitled to the higher of the two minimum wages. Most states also regulate hours of work and overtime payments.

The three principal federal laws affecting wages are the Davis-Bacon Act, the Walsh-Healy Act, and the Fair Labor Standards Act. These laws were enacted during the 1930s to prevent the payment of abnormally low wage rates and to encourage the spreading of work among a greater number of workers. The latter objective was accomplished by forcing organizations to pay a premium rate for overtime work (all hours worked in excess of a prescribed number).

Davis-Bacon Act of 1931

The Davis-Bacon Act, also referred to as the Prevailing Wage Law, was passed in 1931 and is the oldest of the three federal wage laws. It requires that the minimum wage rates paid to people employed on federal public works projects worth more than $2,000 be at least equal to the prevailing rates and that overtime be paid at 1½ times this rate. The act is criticized because the prevailing rates are often the union rates for jobs in the area and are often higher than the average (nonunion) rates.

Walsh-Healy Act of 1936

The Walsh-Healy Act, which is officially called the Public Contracts Act, was passed in 1936 and covers workers employed on government contract work for supplies, equipment, and materials worth in excess of $10,000. The act requires contractors to pay employees at least the prevailing wage rates established for the area by the Secretary of Labor, and overtime of 1½ times the regular rate for all work performed in excess of eight hours in one day or forty hours in one week, depending on which basis provides the larger premium.

The use of child labor was common by employers before passage of the FLSA.

© CORBIS

Fair Labor Standards Act of 1938 (as Amended)

The Fair Labor Standards Act (FLSA), commonly referred to as the Wage and Hour Act, was passed in 1938 and since then has been amended many times. It covers employees who are engaged in the production of goods for interstate and foreign commerce, including those whose work is closely related to or essential to such production. The act also covers agricultural workers, as well as employees of certain retail and service establishments whose sales volume exceeds a prescribed amount. The major provisions of the FLSA are concerned with minimum wage rates and overtime payments, child labor, and equal rights.[37]

Wage and Hour Provisions

The minimum wage prescribed by federal law has been raised many times, from an original figure of 25 cents per hour to $5.15 per hour on September 1, 1997. (See Highlights in HRM 5 for the federal minimum wage poster that employers are required to display.) This minimum rate applies to the actual earning rate before any overtime premiums have been added. An overtime rate of 1½ times the base rate must be paid for all hours worked in excess of forty during a given week. The base wage rate from which the overtime rate is computed must include incentive payments or bonuses that are received during the period. When employees are given time off in return for overtime work (referred to as *compensatory time off* or *comp time*), it must be granted at 1½ times the number of hours that were worked as overtime. Employees who are paid on a piece-rate base must receive a premium for overtime work. The FLSA does not, however, require severance pay, sick leave, vacation, or holidays.

Highlights in HRM 5

The Federal Minimum Wage Poster

Your Rights Under the Fair Labor Standards Act

Federal Minimum Wage

$4.75 *per hour* *beginning October 1, 1996*

$5.15 *per hour* *beginning September 1, 1997*

Employees under 20 years of age may be paid $4.25 per hour during their first 90 consecutive calendar days of employment with an employer.

Certain full-time students, student learners, apprentices, and workers with disabilities may be paid less than the minimum wage under special certificates issued by the Department of Labor.

Tip Credit – Employers of "tipped employees" must pay a cash wage of at least $2.13 per hour if they claim a tip credit against their minimum wage obligation. If an employee's tips combined with the employer's cash wage of at least $2.13 per hour do not equal the minimum hourly wage, the employer must make up the difference. Certain other conditions must also be met.

Overtime Pay

At least 1½ times your regular rate of pay for all hours worked over 40 in a workweek.

Child Labor

An employee must be at least **16** years old to work in most non-farm jobs and at least **18** to work in non-farm jobs declared hazardous by the Secretary of Labor. Youths **14** and **15** years old may work outside school hours in various non-manufacturing, non-mining, non-hazardous jobs under the following conditions:

No more than –

- **3** hours on a school day or **18** hours in a school week;
- **8** hours on a non-school day or **40** hours in a non-school week.

Also, work may not begin before **7 a.m.** or end after **7 p.m.**, except from **June 1** through **Labor Day**, when evening hours are extended to **9 p.m.** Different rules apply in agricultural employment.

Enforcement

The Department of Labor may recover back wages either administratively or through court action, for the employees that have been underpaid in violation of the law. Violations may result in civil or criminal action.

Fines of up to $10,000 per violation may be assessed against employers who violate the child labor provisions of the law and up to $1,000 per violation against employers who willfully or repeatedly violate the minimum wage or overtime pay provisions. This law prohibits discriminating against or discharging workers who file a complaint or participate in any proceedings under the Act.

Note:
- Certain occupations and establishments are exempt from the minimum wage and/or overtime pay provisions.
- Special provisions apply to workers in American Samoa.
- Where state law requires a higher minimum wage, the higher standard applies.

For Additional Information, Contact the Wage and Hour Division office nearest you — listed in your telephone directory under United States Government, Labor Department.

This poster may be viewed on the world wide web at this address: http://www.dol.gov./dol/esa/public/minwage/main.htm

The law requires employers to display this poster where employees can readily see it.

U.S. Department of Labor
Employment Standards Administration
Wage and Hour Division
Washington, D.C. 20210

WH Publication 1088
Revised October 1996

*U.S. Government Printing Office: 1996 — 414-231

Along with equal employment opportunity lawsuits, wage and hour violations are another prominent problem for managers. A major problem is violations of overtime payments. In 2003, more than 300,000 employees received back wages totaling more than $212 million as a result of DOL investigations of FLSA violations. Employees are increasingly filing charges with the DOL that accuse companies of cheating them out of overtime pay. Also, failure to include all periods of work can often lead to overtime miscalculations. Some important compensable situations include the following:

- Downtime or call-in time, during which the employee must be readily available for work
- Payment for required classes, meetings, or other periods of instruction
- Travel between job sites
- Preparation and cleanup before and after shifts
- Break periods shorter than twenty minutes

Clearly, a complete understanding of when and how to pay employees is the best protection against a DOL investigation into overtime violation. Furthermore, under the FLSA, an employer must pay an employee for whatever work the employer "suffers or permits" the employee to perform, even if the work is done away from the workplace and even if it is not specifically expected or requested. This condition could likely occur when employees work away from headquarters and are unsupervised, or when they telecommute on a frequent basis.

Some argue that the "floor" imposed by the minimum wage makes it more difficult for high school students and young adults to find jobs. Many employers who might otherwise be willing to hire these individuals are unwilling to pay them the same rate as adults because of their lack of experience. For unskilled workers, the FLSA permits employers to pay a "training wage" of $4.25 per hour for employees younger than age 20 during their first ninety days of employment, provided their employment does not displace other workers.

Child Labor Provisions

The FLSA forbids the employment of minors between ages 16 and 18 in hazardous occupations such as mining, logging, woodworking, meatpacking, and certain types of manufacturing. Minors under 16 cannot be employed in any work destined for interstate commerce except that which is performed in a nonhazardous occupation for a parent or guardian or for an employer under a temporary work permit issued by the Department of Labor.

Exemption from Overtime Provisions

The feature of the FLSA that perhaps creates the most confusion is the exemption from overtime requirements for certain groups of employees or from coverage by certain of the act's provisions. Five employee groups—executive, administrative, professional, computer, and outside salespeople—are specifically excluded from overtime provisions provided they meet defined job requirements as stated under the law. Other employees are exempt from overtime pay if their weekly or annual earnings exceed certain limits.

In August 2004, the DOL made important changes to the FLSA known as the Fair Pay Rules.[38] Fair Pay Rules were implemented to strengthen overtime protections and redefine the job requirements for exempt groups of employees. The changes affect many employees and employers and are not without controversy. Proponents note that overtime rights are now strengthened for 6.7 million American workers, including 1.3 million low-wage workers who were denied overtime under the old rules.[39] Opponents claim the new regulations will enable employers to reclassify may workers as high-level administrative or professional employees, thus exempting millions of employees from overtime protection.[40] Important changes to the act include the following:

- Overtime must be paid to employees earning less than $455 a week, or $26,660 annually.
- A new "standards test" is used to determine whether employees who earn between $26,660 and $100,000 annually are excluded from overtime requirements.
- Administrative personnel to be exempt must have primary duties that include the exercise of discretion and independent judgment *with respect to matters of significance.*

While the Fair Pay Rules are purported to "modernize" and clarify overtime regulations, they will, nevertheless, require interpretation. For example, how is "with respect to matters of significance" to be defined? Employers seeking exceptions to overtime payments should carefully monitor Fair Pay regulations. The DOL provides an online seminar that describes the new Fair Pay Rules.[41]

Equal Rights Provisions

One of the most significant amendments to the FLSA was the Equal Pay Act passed in 1963. (See Chapter 2.) The federal Age Discrimination Act of 1967, as amended, extends the equal rights provisions by forbidding wage discrimination based on age for employees age 40 and older. Neither of these acts, however, prohibits wage differentials based on factors other than age or sex. Seniority, merit, and individual incentive plans, for instance, are not affected.

In spite of the Equal Pay Act, the achievement of parity by women in the labor market has been slow in coming. As Figure 9.8 shows, in the second quarter of 2004 the usual average weekly earnings of all women workers in the United States was 80 percent of the usual average weekly earnings of men. This figure has not changed greatly since 1995. Fortunately, the average weekly earnings of young women (age 16–24) are 91 percent of those of similar-age men—up from 78 percent in 1980. However, it is still important to remember that young women, and young men as well, typically work in low-paying, entry-level jobs. For women, these are often clerical, domestic, or sales positions.[42]

Significant Compensation Issues

As with other HR activities, compensation management operates in a dynamic environment. For example, as managers strive to reward employees in a fair manner, they must consider controls over labor costs, legal issues regarding male and female wage payments, and internal pay equity concerns. Each of these concerns is highlighted in

Figure 9.8 The Equal Pay Act: The Jury's Still Out

Has the Equal Pay Act been effective in raising the wages of women relative to the wages of men? That depends on whom you ask and the importance you place on government statistics. "Fifty-nine cents on the dollar" was the rallying cry of the women's movement more than thirty years ago to illustrate the large gap between the wages of women and men. That is, for every dollar that a man made, a woman earned fifty-nine cents. Currently, government wage figures based on the usual weekly earnings of full-time wage and salary workers peg women's average pay at 80.1 percent of men's compensation. Unfortunately, the gain in women's wages relative to men's wages has not changed significantly in recent years, as the following figures show.

YEAR	AVERAGE WEEKLY WAGE (WOMEN)	AVERAGE WEEKLY WAGE (MEN)	WOMEN'S AVERAGE WAGE AS A PERCENTAGE OF MEN'S AVERAGE WAGE
1985	$277	$406	68.2%
1995	406	538	75.5
2000	493	641	76.9
2001	512	670	76.4
2002	529	679	77.9
2003	552	695	79.4
2004 (2nd quarter)	572	714	80.1

Source: Median usual weekly earnings of full-time wage and salary workers by sex, age, race, and Hispanic or Latino ethnicity, current dollars 1979–2004. Unpublished tabulations from *Current Population Survey*, Bureau of Labor Statistics, 2004. Data at www.bls.gov.

three important compensation issues: equal pay for comparable worth, wage-rate compression, and low salary budgets.

The Issue of Equal Pay for Comparable Worth

comparable worth
The concept that male and female jobs that are dissimilar, but equal in terms of value or worth to the employer, should be paid the same

One of the most important gender issues in compensation is equal pay for comparable worth. The issue stems from the fact that jobs performed predominantly by women are paid less than those performed by men. This practice results in what critics term *institutionalized sex discrimination,* causing women to receive less pay for jobs that may be different from but comparable in worth to those performed by men. The issue of **comparable worth** goes beyond providing equal pay for jobs that involve the same duties for women as for men. It is not concerned with whether a female secretary should receive the same pay as a male secretary. Rather, the argument for comparable worth is that jobs held by women are not compensated the same as those held by men, even though both job types may contribute equally to organizational success.[43]

Reasons for the gender pay gap are still entirely unclear. Discrimination against women accounts for a portion of the wage difference. Other cited reasons include women working in low-paying, sex-segregated occupations—such as cashiers and maids—and family responsibilities that require women to remain outside the workforce for extended periods.

Advocates of comparable worth argue that the difference in wage rates for predominantly male and female occupations rests in the undervaluing of traditional female occupations.[44] To remedy this situation, they propose that wages should be equal for jobs that are "somehow" equivalent in total worth or compensation to the organization. Additionally, it is argued that current job evaluation techniques simply serve to continue the differences in pay between the sexes. With these concerns the compensation gap between men and women will not disappear overnight, but the persistence of comparable-worth advocates will help shrink it.

The Issue of Wage-Rate Compression

wage-rate compression
Compression of differentials between job classes, particularly the differential between hourly workers and their managers

Earlier, when we discussed the compensation structure, it was noted that the primary purpose of the pay differentials between the wage classes is to provide an incentive for employees to prepare for and accept more-demanding jobs. Unfortunately, this incentive is being significantly reduced by **wage-rate compression**—the reduction of differences between job classes. Wage-rate compression is largely an internal pay-equity concern. The problem occurs when employees perceive that there is too narrow a difference between their compensation and that of colleagues in lower-rated jobs.

There is no single cause of wage-rate compression. For example, it can occur when unions negotiate across-the-board increases for hourly employees but managerial personnel are not granted corresponding wage differentials. Such increases can result in part from COLAs provided for in labor agreements. Other inequities have resulted from the scarcity of applicants in computers, engineering, and other professional and technical fields. Job applicants in these fields frequently have been offered starting salaries not far below those paid to employees with considerable experience and seniority. Wage-rate compression often occurs when organizations grant pay adjustments for lower-rated jobs without providing commensurate adjustments for occupations at the top of the job hierarchy.

Identifying wage-rate compression and its causes is far simpler than implementing organizational policies to alleviate its effect. Organizations wishing to minimize the problem may incorporate the following ideas into their pay policies:[45]

1. Give larger compensation increases to more-senior employees.
2. Emphasize pay-for-performance and reward meritworthy employees.
3. Limit the hiring of new applicants seeking exorbitant salaries.
4. Design the pay structure to allow a wide spread between hourly and supervisory jobs or between new hires and senior employees.
5. Provide equity adjustments for selected employees hardest hit by pay compression.

Remember, wage-rate compression can cause low employee morale, leading to issues of reduced employee performance, higher absenteeism and turnover, and even delinquent behavior such as employee theft.

The Issue of Low Salary Budgets

At a recent compensation seminar attended by one of the authors, a speaker noted, "The blank-check days for large salary increases are over." While workers may not

Figure 9.9 Salary Budgets by Type of Employee, 1994–2005

TYPE OF EMPLOYEE	1994	1995	1996	1997	1998	1999	2000	2001	2002	2003	2004	PROJECTED 2005
	ACTUAL											
Nonexempt hourly nonunion			3.8%	4.1%	4.1%	4.1%	4.3%	4.3%	3.7%	3.5%	3.5%	3.6%
Nonexempt salaried	4.0%	3.9%	4.0	4.1	4.2	4.2	4.4	4.4	3.7	3.4	3.4	3.6
Exempt salaried	4.0	4.0	4.1	4.3	4.5	4.4	4.6	4.6	3.9	3.6	3.6	3.7
Officers/ executives	4.1	4.1	4.3	4.5	4.6	4.5	4.7	4.7	4.0	3.6	3.6	3.8

Source: Reprinted from 2004–2005 Total Salary Increase Budget Survey with permission from WorldatWork, 14040 N. Northsight Blvd., Scottsdale, AZ 85260; phone (877) 951-9191; fax (480) 483-8352; http://www.worldatwork.org. © 2002 WorldatWork. Unauthorized reproduction or distribution is strictly prohibited.

have as tough a time as Dagwood in convincing employers that a raise is in order, WorldatWork reports that the sizes of salary increases have been modest compared with periods before 1990. Figure 9.9 shows salary budgets by type of employee from 1994 to 2005. These figures are not projected to increase greatly in future years. While current inflation rates have been relatively stable—allowing most employees to realize a real earnings gain—these gains are small compared with prior years.

Low salary budgets reflect a general trend toward tight compensation cost controls caused by global competition for jobs, the reduction in workforce because of technology, and the growing use of temporary and part-time employees who receive low wages and few benefits.[46] Unfortunately, low wages could portend unfavorable effects for employers and society, including increased turnover as employees change jobs for higher wages and diminished employee output as employees perceive a low pay-for-performance relationship.

SUMMARY

Establishing compensation programs requires both large and small organizations to consider specific goals—employee retention, compensation distribution, and adherence to a budget, for instance. Compensation must reward employees for past efforts (pay-for-performance) while motivating employees' future performance. Internal and external equity of the pay program affects employees' concepts of fairness. Organizations must balance each of these concerns while still remaining competitive. The ability to attract qualified employees while controlling labor costs is a major factor in allowing organizations to remain viable in the domestic or international markets.

The basis on which compensation payments are determined, and the way they are administered, can significantly affect employee productivity and the achievement of organizational goals. Internal influences include the employer's compensation policy, the worth of the job, the performance of the employee, and the employer's ability to pay. External factors influencing wage rates include labor market conditions, area wage rates, cost of living, the outcomes of collective bargaining, and legal requirements.

Organizations use one of four basic job evaluation techniques to determine the relative worth of jobs. The job ranking system arranges jobs in numerical order on the basis of the importance of the job's duties and responsibilities to the organization. The job classification system slots jobs into preestablished grades. Higher-rated grades will require more responsibilities, working conditions, and job duties. The point system of job evaluation uses a point scheme based on the compensable job factors of skill, effort, responsibility, and working conditions. The more compensable factors a job possesses, the more points are assigned to it. Jobs with higher accumulated points are considered more valuable to the organization. The work valuation system evaluates jobs based on their value relative to organizational goals—financial, customer service, and so on—and the job's contribution to organization success.

Wage surveys determine the external equity of jobs. Data obtained from surveys will facilitate establishing the organization's wage policy while ensuring that the employer does not pay more, or less, than needed for jobs in the relevant labor market.

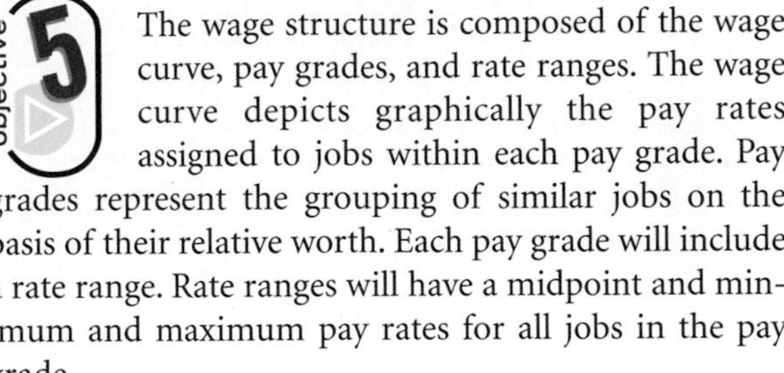

The wage structure is composed of the wage curve, pay grades, and rate ranges. The wage curve depicts graphically the pay rates assigned to jobs within each pay grade. Pay grades represent the grouping of similar jobs on the basis of their relative worth. Each pay grade will include a rate range. Rate ranges will have a midpoint and minimum and maximum pay rates for all jobs in the pay grade.

Both the Davis-Bacon Act and the Walsh-Healy Act are prevailing wage statutes. These laws require government contractors to pay wages normally based on the union scale in the employer's operating area. The Walsh-Healy Act also requires payment of 1½ times the regular pay for hours over eight per day or forty per week. The Fair Labor Standards Act contains provisions covering the federal minimum wage, hours worked, and child labor.

The concept of comparable worth seeks to overcome the fact that jobs held by women are compensated at a lower rate than those performed by men. This happens even though both types of jobs may contribute equally to organizational productivity. Wage-rate compression largely affects managerial and senior employees as the pay given to new employees or the wage increases gained through union agreements erode the pay differences between these groups. Low-wage increases are a prominent compensation strategy as employers seek to adjust to competitive challenges.

KEY TERMS

comparable worth
competence-based pay
consumer price index (CPI)
escalator clauses
exempt employees
Hay profile method
hourly work
job classification system
job evaluation
job ranking system
nonexempt employees
pay equity
pay-for-performance standard
pay grades
piecework
point system
real wages
red circle rates
value-added compensation
wage and salary survey
wage curve
wage-rate compression
work valuation

HRM Experience

Why This Salary?

A question frequently asked is, "Why is that person paid more than I am when we both perform the same job?" The answer to this question lies in understanding the components of the wage mix as discussed in this chapter. While we may disapprove of the idea that someone is paid more or less than we are for similar work, nevertheless, factors both internal and external to the organization influence the final salary paid to a job or a specific person. Often we have little control over the wage mix factors. However, at other times, we can improve our wage by gaining additional job experience or seniority, or by obtaining increases in job knowledge or skills. This project is designed to give you experience in understanding why jobs are paid different salaries.

Assignment

Shown here are the annual median salaries paid to selected occupations listed in the 2004–2005 edition of the *Occupational Outlook Handbook*. Study the salaries paid to these occupations and then answer the questions that follow as to why the differences in salaries exist. Relate these reasons to the internal and external factors of the wage mix that are discussed in the text.

Occuption	Median Annual Salary
• Flight attendant	$43,140
• Librarian	$43,090
• Construction laborer	$24,270
• Computer systems administrator	$54,810
• Police officer	$42,270
• Motor coach operator	$29,008
• Lawyer	$90,290

1. What factors may account for the wide differences among salaries for different occupations?
2. What factors may account for the differences among salaries for the identical occupation in the same organization?
3. What factors may account for the differences among salaries for the identical occupation in different organizations?

You may work individually or in teams to complete this skill-building exercise. The *Occupational Outlook Handbook* published by the U.S. Bureau of Labor Statistics can be found at http://www.bls.gov/oco.

DISCUSSION QUESTIONS

1. Tomax Corporation has 400 employees and wishes to develop a compensation policy to correspond to its dynamic business strategy. The company wishes to employ a high-quality workforce capable of responding to a competitive business environment. Suggest different compensation objectives to match Tomax's business goals.

2. Since employees may differ in terms of their job performance, would it not be more feasible to determine the wage rate for each employee on the basis of his or her relative worth to the organization? Explain.

3. What is job evaluation? Explain the differences between the major job evaluation systems, noting the advantages and disadvantages of each.

4. Describe the basic steps in conducting a wage and salary survey. What are some factors to consider?

5. One of the objections to granting wage increases on a percentage basis is that the lowest-paid employees, who are having the most trouble making ends meet, get the smallest increase, while the highest-paid employees get the largest increase. Is this objection a valid one? Explain.

6. Federal laws governing compensation raise important issues for both employers and employees. Discuss the following:
   a. The effect of paying a prevailing wage as required by the Davis-Bacon Act
   b. The effects of raising the minimum wage

7. Discuss ways that employers might seek to restrain the salary budget.

BIZFLIX EXERCISES

The Wedding Date: How Much Is Nick Mercer's Job Worth?

These scenes from *The Wedding Date* occur in two parts. Watch Part I, "Nick's Job," first. Apply the job evaluation concepts discussed in this chapter to decide the worth of Nick Mercer's (Dermot Mulroney) job.

Kat Ellis (Debra Messing) wants a date to accompany her to her sister Amy's (Amy Adams) wedding. She also wants to show her ex-fiancé that she can recover from him dumping her two years earlier. These requirements become part of her frantic search of the male escort classified advertisements. She hires Nick Mercer, who turns out to be much more dashing and charming than she expected. This lighthearted romantic comedy will entertain you from beginning to end.

There are two sets of scenes with a chalkboard between them. Part I comes from the "Trying too Hard" segment that appears in the first ten minutes of the film. Kat and Nick have arrived at Heathrow Airport, London, England. Part II comes from the "A Simple Business Transaction" segment that appears a few minutes later. They have arrived at the cocktail party honoring Amy and her fiancé, Edward Fletcher-Wooten (Jack Davenport).

The Part I chalkboard reads, "Nick's Job"; the Part II chalkboard reads, "Nick's Pay." Pause the scenes at the start of Part II to consider the first question below. Kat and Nick return to the cocktail party after Kat straightens the coats in the closet.

What to Watch for and Ask Yourself

- From your viewing of Part I, how much is Nick Mercer's job as Kat's date worth? If you have seen this film, do not try to recall how much Nick received.

- The opening of this chapter includes the following observation: "Employees desire compensation systems that they perceive as being fair and commensurate with their skills and expectations." Does Nick believe he is paid fairly in Part II of the scenes? Does he place any conditions on his job and its compensation?
- Review the earlier section "Significant Compensation Issues." Do any issues raised in that section apply to these scenes? Why or why not?

case study 1

Pay Decisions at Performance Sports

Katie Perkins's career objective while attending Rockford State College was to obtain a degree in small-business management and to start her own business after graduation. Her ultimate desire was to combine her love of sports and a strong interest in marketing to start a mail-order golf equipment business aimed specifically at beginning golfers.

In February 1998, after extensive development of a strategic business plan and a loan in the amount of $75,000 from the Small Business Administration, Performance Sports was begun. Based on a marketing plan that stressed fast delivery, error-free customer service, and large discount pricing, Performance Sports grew rapidly. At present the company employs sixteen people: eight customer service representatives earning between $9.75 and $11.25 per hour; four shipping and receiving associates paid between $7.50 and $8.50 per hour; two clerical employees each earning $7.75 per hour; an assistant manager earning $13.10 per hour, and a general manager with a wage of $14.25 per hour. Both the manager and assistant manager are former customer service representatives.

Perkins intends to create a new managerial position, purchasing agent, to handle the complex duties of purchasing golf equipment from the company's numerous equipment manufacturers. Also, the mail-order catalog will be expanded to handle a complete line of tennis equipment. Since the position of purchasing agent is new, Perkins isn't sure how much to pay this person. She wants to employ an individual with five to eight years of experience in sports equipment purchasing.

While attending an equipment manufacturers' convention in Las Vegas, Nevada, Perkins learns that a competitor, East Valley Sports, pays its customer service representatives on a pay-for-performance basis. Intrigued by this compensation philosophy, Perkins asks her assistant manager, George Balkin, to research the pros and cons of this payment strategy. This request has become a priority because only last week two customer service representatives expressed dissatisfaction with their hourly wage. Both complained that they felt underpaid relative to the large amount of sales revenue each generates for the company.

QUESTIONS

1. What factors should Perkins and Balkin consider when setting the wage for the purchasing agent position? What resources are available for them to consult when establishing this wage?
2. Suggest advantages and disadvantages of a pay-for-performance policy for Performance Sports.
3. Suggest a new payment plan for the customer service representatives.

case study 2

Mission Possible: A Competency-Based Compensation Program for Preferred and AFD Federal Credit Unions

Preferred Credit Union in Detroit, Michigan, and AFD Federal Credit Union in South Bend, Indiana, faced critical problems encountered by other credit unions nationwide—the threat of megabanks. With large financial resources, ATM networks, and online banking services, large banks threatened the very existence of smaller, locally owned and managed credit unions. The question faced by these small financial institutions was how to survive.

Based on a friendship between the CEOs of Preferred and AFD Federal, a joint venture was started. The officers of both organizations immediately realized that they needed to develop a competitive advantage, one grounded in a customer-friendly culture in which outstanding service would serve to compete with the banks. Central to achieving this strategic business goal was the design and implementation of a competency-based review and reward compensation program for credit union employees. Formerly, both financial organizations paid employees based on a traditional job title and tenure payment system. The compensation committee, composed of both managers and hourly employees, faced these concerns as they designed the competency-based reward system: (1) What competencies must employees possess to achieve strategic business objectives? (2) How should competencies be measured in order to fairly reward employees? (3) How should the new compensation program be implemented to ensure employee acceptance?

Source: Based on an actual case. All names are fictitious.

QUESTIONS

1. Develop a list of competencies needed by employees to facilitate attainment of credit union strategic goals.
2. Recommend an employee appraisal program to measure identified competencies.
3. What steps should the credit union adopt to achieve employee acceptance of the new compensation program?

NOTES AND REFERENCES

1. Don Hellriegel and John W. Slocum, Jr., *Organizational Behavior*, 10th ed. (Mason, OH: South-Western, 2004): 51.
2. Edward E. Lawler III, "Pay Practices in *Fortune* 1000 Corporations," *WorldatWork* 12, no. 4 (Fourth Quarter 2003): 45–64. See also Ann Pomeroy, "Global Compensation Strategies and HR," *HRMagazine* 50, no. 5 (May 2005): 14.
3. For a frequently referenced book on strategic compensation planning, see Edward E. Lawler III, *Strategic Pay: Aligning Organizational Strategies and Pay Systems* (San Francisco: Jossey-Bass, 1990). See also Thomas J. Bergmann and Vida Gulbinas Scarpello, *Compensation Decision Making*, 4th ed. (Mason, OH: South-Western, 2002): Chapter 2.
4. John Cumminqs and Laurie Brannen, "The New World of Compensation," *Business Finance* 11, no. 6 (January 2005): 8. See also Dow Scott, Richard S. Sperling, Thomas D. McMullen, and Marc Wallace, "Linking Compensation Policies and Programs to Organizational Effectiveness," *WorldatWork* 12, no. 4 (Fourth Quarter 2003): 35.

5. Robyn T. Costello, "Value-Added Compensation Statements: Developing Strategic Content for a Winning Communication," *Employee Benefits Journal* 27, no. 3 (September 2002): 24–29.
6. George T. Milkovich and Jerry M. Newman, *Compensation*, 8th ed. (Boston: McGraw-Hill Irwin, 2005).
7. John A. Menefee and Ryan O. Murphy, "Rewarding and Retaining the Best: Compensation Strategies for Top Performers," *Benefits Quarterly* 20, no. 3 (Third Quarter 2004): 13–15. See also Steve Bates, Patrick Mirza, and Adrienne For, "Top Pay for Best Performance," *HRMagazine* 48, no. 1 (January 2003): 30.
8. Bronwyn Fryer, "HBR Case Study: In a World of Pay," *Harvard Business Review* 81, no. 11 (November 2003): 31–38.
9. Jude T. Rich, "Sitting on a Gold Mine: Reducing Employee Turnover at All Costs," *WorldatWork* 11, no. 2 (Second Quarter 2002): 44–51. See also Claudia Zeitz Poster, "Retaining Key People in Troubled Companies," *Compensation and Benefits Review* 34, no. 1 (January–February 2002): 7–11.
10. Lawler, "Pay Practices in *Fortune* 1000 Corporations," 45.
11. Michelle Brown and John S. Heywood, *Paying for Performance: An International Comparison* (Armonk, NY: M. E. Sharpe, 2002).
12. Barbara Crowe, llene Siscovick, and Marjorie Pieper, "Designing a Work Force Architecture for Merger Success," *WorldatWork* 12, no. 3 (Third Quarter 2003): 39–46.
13. Rose Stanley, Project Manager, Benefits, WorldatWork, Scottsdale, Arizona, interview by author, September 1, 2004.
14. For one of the classic articles on equity theory, see J. Stacey Adams, "Integrity in Social Exchange," in L. Berkowitz (ed.), *Advances in Experimental Social Psychology* (New York: Academic Press, 1965): 276–99.
15. Andrew J. DuBrin, *Fundamentals of Organizational Behavior*, 3rd ed. (Mason, OH: South-Western, 2005): 114–16.
16. Victor H. Vroom, *Work and Motivation* (San Francisco: Jossey-Bass, 1994). This landmark book, originally published in 1964, integrates the work of hundreds of researchers seeking to explain choice of work, job satisfaction, and job performance.
17. Joseph Champoux, *Organizational Behavior: Essential Tenets*, 2nd ed. (Mason, OH: South-Western, 2003): Chapter 8.
18. Robert L. Heneman, Paul W. Mulvey, and Peter V. LeBlanc, "Improve Base Pay ROI by Increasing Employee Knowledge," *WorldatWork* 11, no. 4 (Fourth Quarter 2002): 23–36.
19. Detailed discussion of exempt and nonexempt rules under the Fair Labor Standards Act can be found at http://www.dol.gov.
20. Ira Feder, "Fine-Tuning the Pay Mix for Potential Cost Savings," *WorldatWork* 12, no. 2 (Second Quarter 2003): 6.
21. James R. Bowers, "Valuing Work: An Integrated Approach," *WorldatWork* 12, no. 2 (Second Quarter 2003): 28–39.
22. Robert L. Heneman, Peter V. LeBlanc, and Tim L. Reynolds, "Using Work Valuation to Identify and Protect the Talent Pool," *WorldatWork* 11, no. 2 (Third Quarter 2002): 31–41.
23. William H. Holley, Jr., Kenneth H. Jennings, and Rogert W. Wolters, *The Labor Relations Process*, 8th ed. (Mason, OH: South-Western, 2005): Chapter 6.
24. Robert L. Heneman, "Job and Work Evaluation," *Public Personnel Management* 32, no. 1 (Spring 2003): 1–25.
25. Fred Hilling, "Job Evaluation Is Here to Stay," *WorldatWork* 12, no. 3 (Third Quarter 2003): 14–21.
26. Deborah Keary, Saundra Jackson, and Vicki Neal, "Job Evaluation, Health Coverage, Discipline," *HRMagazine* 49, no. 1 (January 2004): 39–40.
27. Robert L. Heneman, Peter V. LeBlanc, and Howard Risher, "Work Valuation Addresses Shortcomings of Both Job Evaluation and Market Pricing," *Compensation and Benefits Review* 35, no. 1 (January–February 2003): 7–11.
28. James R. Bowers, "Valuing Work," *WorldatWork* 12, no. 2 (Second Quarter 2003): 28.
29. Craig Skenes and Brian H. Kleiner, "The Hay System of Compensation," *Management Research News* 26, no. 2 (2003): 109.
30. The Bureau of Labor web site is at http://www.bls.gov.
31. Nona Tobin, "Can Technology Ease the Pain of Salary Surveys?" *Public Personnel Management* 31, no. 1 (Spring 2002): 65–76.
32. Michael O'Malley, "What Is Base Salary?" *WorldatWork* 12, no. 3 (Third Quarter 2003): 22–28.
33. Gregory A. Stoskopf, "Choosing the Best Salary Structure for Your Organization," *WorldatWork* 11, no. 4 (Fourth Quarter 2004): 28–36.
34. R. Eugene Hughes, "Skill or Diploma? The Potential Influence of Skill-Based Pay Systems on Sources of Skills Acquisition and Degree Programs," *Work Study* 52, no. 4/5 (2003): 179–83.
35. Patricia K. Zingheim and Jay R. Schuster, "Reassessing the Value of Skill-Based Pay," *WorldatWork* 11, no. 3 (Third Quarter 2002): 72–77.
36. Andrew S. Rosen and David Turetsky, "Broadbanding: The Construction of a Career Management Framework," *WorldatWork* 11, no. 4 (Fourth Quarter 2002): 45–55.
37. Because the FLSA is always subject to amendment, an employer should consult the appropriate publications of one of the labor services previously mentioned or the Wage and Hour Division of the U.S. Department of Labor in order to obtain the latest information regarding its current provisions, particularly the minimum wage rate. Changes to the FLSA can also be found at the DOL web site, http://www.dol.gov.
38. "Meet the FLSA's Fair Pay Rules," *HRFocus* 81, no. 6 (June 2004): 13.
39. Yvette Armendariz, "Time Is Money: Overtime May Not Be," *The Arizona Republic*, February 8, 2004, D-1.
40. Trish Nicholson, "Kiss Your Overtime Pay Goodbye?" *AARP Bulletin* (February 2004): 6.
41. The online seminar can be viewed at the DOL web site, http://www.dol.gov/esa.
42. Aaron Bernstein, "Women's Pay: Why the Gap Remains a Chasm," *Business Week*, June 14, 2004: 58. See also "Reasons for Gender Pay Gap Still Unclear," *HRFocus* 81, no. 2 (February 2004): 12.

43. Mark R. Killingsworth, "Comparable Work and Pay Equality: Recent Developments in the United States," *Canadian Public Policy* 28 (May 2002): 171.

44. Joel P. Rudin and Kimble Byrd, "U.S. Pay Equity Legislation: Sheep in Wolves' Clothing," *Employee Responsibility and Rights Journal* 15, no. 4 (December 2003): 183.

45. Andrew L. Klein, Kimberly M. Keating, and Lisa M. Ruggiero, "The Perils of Pay Inequity: Addressing the Problems of Compression," *WorldatWork* 11, no. 4 (Fourth Quarter 2002): 56–62.

46. "How to Keep a Lid on Compensation Costs," *HRFocus* 85, no. 5 (May 2004): 3–4.

CCH
FEDERAL TAX
SERVICE

chapter 10

Pay-for-Performance: Incentive Rewards

After studying this chapter, you should be able to

Discuss the basic requirements for successful implementation of incentive programs.

Identify the types of, and reasons for implementing, individual incentive plans.

Explain why merit raises may fail to motivate employees adequately and discuss ways to increase their motivational value.

Indicate the advantage of each of the principal methods used to compensate salespeople.

Differentiate how gains may be shared with employees under the Scanlon, Rucker, and Improshare gainsharing systems.

Differentiate between profit-sharing plans and explain advantages and disadvantages of these programs.

Describe the main types of ESOP plans and discuss the advantages of ESOP to employers and employees.

In the previous chapter we emphasized that the worth of a job is a significant factor in determining the pay rate for that job. However, pay based solely on this measure may fail to motivate employees to perform to their full capacity. Unmotivated employees are likely to meet only minimum performance standards. Recognizing this fact, diverse organizations such as MasterBrand Cabinets, Sears Craftsman, Linens 'n Things, Neiman Marcus, and Liz Claiborne offer some form of incentive to workers. These organizations are attempting to get more motivational mileage out of employee compensation by tying it more closely to organizational objectives and employee performance. Jessica Smilko and Kathy Van Neck, compensation specialists, note this fact about variable pay: "Employees are embracing variable compensation as a means of aligning employee behavior with organizational goals."[1] When incentives are linked with output, workers will increasingly apply their skills and knowledge to their jobs and will be encouraged to work together as a team. Therefore, in their attempt to raise productivity, managers are focusing on the many variables that help determine the effectiveness of pay as a motivator.

In this chapter we will discuss incentive plans in terms of the objectives they hope to achieve and the various factors that may affect their success. Because many organizations have implemented broad-based incentive programs, for discussion purposes we have grouped incentive plans into three broad categories: individual incentive plans, group incentive plans, and enterprise incentive plans, as shown in Figure 10.1.[2]

Strategic Reasons for Incentive Plans

variable pay
Tying pay to some measure of individual, group, or organizational performance

A clear trend in strategic compensation management is the growth of incentive plans, also called **variable pay** programs, for employees throughout the organization. Ken Abosch, compensation specialist with Hewitt Associates LLC, notes, "There's no question that most corporations have turned away from fixed forms of compensation in favor of variable forms. There has been an abandonment of entitlement programs."[3]

Incentive rewards are based entirely upon a pay-for-performance philosophy (see Chapter 9). Incentive pay programs establish a performance "threshold" (a baseline performance level) that an employee or group of employees must reach in order to qualify for incentive payments. According to one compensation manager, "The performance threshold is the minimum level an employee must reach in order to qualify for variable pay." Additionally, incentive plans emphasize a shared focus on organizational objectives by broadening the opportunities for incentives to employees throughout the organization. Incentive plans create an operating environment that champions a philosophy of shared commitment through the belief that every individual contributes to organizational performance and success.

Incentive Plans as Links to Organizational Objectives

Contemporary arguments for incentive plans focus on linking compensation rewards, both individual and group, to organizational goals. Specific company goals or objec-

Figure 10.1 Types of Incentive Plans

INDIVIDUAL	GROUP	ENTERPRISE
Piecework	Team compensation	Profit sharing
Standard hour plan	Scanlon Plan	Stock options
Bonuses	Rucker Plan	Employee stock ownership plans (ESOPs)
Merit pay	Improshare	
Lump-sum merit pay		
Incentive awards		
Sales incentives		
Incentives for professional employees		
Executive compensation		

tives might be to lower labor costs, improve customer satisfaction, expand product markets, or maintain high levels of productivity and quality, which in turn improve the market for U.S. goods and services in a global economy. By meshing compensation and organizational objectives, managers believe that employees will assume "ownership" of their jobs, thereby improving their effort and overall job performance. Incentives are designed to encourage employees to put out more effort to complete their job tasks—effort they might not be motivated to expend under hourly and/or seniority-based compensation systems. Also, incentive pay is highly valued as a compensation strategy to attract and retain top-performing employees.[4] Figure 10.2 summarizes the major advantages of incentive pay programs as noted by researchers and HR professionals.

Figure 10.2 Advantages of Incentive Pay Programs

- Incentives focus employee efforts on specific performance targets. They provide real motivation that produces important employee and organizational gains.
- Incentive payouts are variable costs linked to the achievement of results. Base salaries are fixed costs largely unrelated to output.
- Incentive compensation is directly related to operating performance. If performance objectives (quantity and/or quality) are met, incentives are paid. If objectives are not achieved, incentives are withheld.
- Incentives foster teamwork and unit cohesiveness when payments to individuals are based on team results.
- Incentives are a way to distribute success among those responsible for producing that success.
- Incentives are a means to reward or attract top performers when salary budgets are low.

Do incentive plans work? Various studies, along with reports from individual organizations, show a measurable relationship between incentive plans and improved organizational performance. In the area of manufacturing, productivity often improves by as much as 20 percent after the adoption of incentive plans. Improvements, however, are not limited to goods-producing industries. Service organizations, not-for-profits, and government agencies also show productivity gains when incentives are linked to organizational goals. For example, after implementing a rating-based incentive program—based on customer satisfaction criteria—Shell Oil developed a consistent brand experience at thousands of independent stations. Bob Hull, program implementation director for Shell, notes, "When you have a good experience at a Shell station you'll come back."[5] Cadillac dealers who meet sales and customer satisfaction targets receive a cash bonus, merchandise awards, and a plaque to hang in the showroom.[6]

Unfortunately, studies also show that variable pay plans may not achieve their proposed objectives or lead to organizational improvements. First, incentive plans sometimes fail to satisfy employee expectations for pay gains. Second, management may have failed to give adequate attention to the design and implementation of the plan, leaving employees confused about how incentive payments are calculated. Third, employees may have little ability to affect performance standards. Furthermore, the success of an incentive plan will depend on the environment that exists within an organization. A plan is more likely to work in an organization where morale is high, employees believe they are being treated fairly, and there is harmony between employees and management.

objective 1

Requirements for a Successful Incentive Plan

For an incentive plan to succeed, employees must have some desire for the plan. This desire can be influenced in part by how successful management is in introducing the plan and convincing employees of its benefits. Encouraging employees to participate in developing and administering the plan is likely to increase their willingness to accept it.

Employees must be able to see a clear connection between the incentive payments they receive and their job performance. This connection is more visible if there are objective quality or quantity standards by which they can judge their performance. Commitment by employees to meet these standards is also essential for incentive plans to succeed. This requires mutual trust and understanding between employees and their supervisors, which can be achieved only through open, two-way channels of communication. Management should never allow incentive payments to be seen as an *entitlement.* Instead, these payments should be viewed as a reward that must be earned through effort. This perception can be strengthened if the incentive money is distributed to employees in a separate check. Compensation specialists also note the following as characteristics of a successful incentive plan:

- Financial incentives are linked to valued behavior.
- The incentive program seems fair to employees.
- Productivity/quality standards are challenging but achievable.
- Payout formulas are simple and understandable.

Highlights in HRM 1

Assessing Incentive Program Effectiveness

MasterBrand Cabinets and Waterloo Industries have spent several years broadly implementing incentive programs. With a hardworking and dedicated workforce, each company has identified broad-based incentives as a key element in achieving business goals. To ensure continued success with their incentive programs, managers at both organizations are expected to periodically review and assess their incentive programs. Here is an example of one diagnostic assessment tool.

INCENTIVE PROGRAM ASSESSMENT TOOL

GENERAL ASSESSMENT	UNSURE	LOW	SOME	HIGH
1. To what extent do incentive program measures support business and operational objectives?	☐	☐	☐	☐
2. To what extent do employees understand how to influence program measures?	☐	☐	☐	☐
3. To what extent have employee behaviors changed as a result of the program?	☐	☐	☐	☐
4. To what extent has plant leadership actively engaged employees in improving performance?	☐	☐	☐	☐
5. To what extent is there an effective infrastructure to support the program (e.g., communications, tracking)?	☐	☐	☐	☐
6. Overall, how would you rate plant management's satisfaction with the program?	☐	☐	☐	☐
7. Overall, how would you rate employee (program participant) satisfaction with the program?	☐	☐	☐	☐

Source: Christian M. Ellis and Cynthia L. Paluso, "Blazing a Trail to Broad-Based Incentives," *WorldatWork Journal* 9, no. 4 (Fourth Quarter 2000): 33–41. Used with permission, WorldatWork, Scottsdale, Arizona.

Furthermore, the best-managed incentive pay programs are clearly and continuously communicated to employees. This is true during both good and bad economic periods. According to Roisin Woolnough, compensation consultant, "Communicate what you are doing and why it is critical to success. Everyone needs to know what the goals are and what the rewards are for achieving those goals."[7] Proactive organizations find it advisable to evaluate the operation and administration of their variable pay programs. Highlights in HRM 1 provides one diagnostic tool for the periodic review and assessment of incentive programs.

Highlights in HRM 2

Setting Performance Measures—The Keys

Both large and small organizations have established performance measures to improve operational success while rewarding employees for their performance outcomes. Establishing meaningful performance measures is one of the important and difficult challenges facing management today. Before managers or supervisors develop and implement organizational measures, they should consider the following guidelines.

- *Performance measures—at all organizational levels—must be consistent with the strategic goals of the organization.* Avoid nonrelevant measures or metrics that are not closely linked to the business or what employees do in their work.
- *Define the intent of performance measures and champion the cause relentlessly.* Demonstrate that performance measures are, in fact, good business management, and hold managers and employees accountable for their success.
- *Involve employees.* A critical step in any measurement program is the development of an employee involvement strategy outlining the nature of employee participation, implementation, and ongoing management of the performance management program. Segment the workforce based on nature of work and potential for impact. Consider which metrics require customization. Acceptance of a performance measurement program is heightened when employees "buy into" the process.
- *Consider the organization's culture and workforce demographics when designing performance measures.* For example, organizations with a more traditional hierarchical structure may need more time to introduce performance metrics compared to flatter organizations, which are more fluid and less steeped in control and command characteristics.
- *Widely communicate the importance of performance measures.* Performance messages are the principles and guidelines that communicate to employees about required performance levels and why the organization needs to achieve those levels of success.

Source: Adapted from Christian M. Ellis, "Improving the Impact of Performance Management," *Workspan* 45, no. 2 (February 2002): 7–8.

Setting Performance Measures

Measurement is key to the success of incentive plans because it communicates the importance of established organizational goals. What gets measured and rewarded gets attention.[8] For example, if the organization desires to be a leader in quality, then performance indexes may focus on customer satisfaction, timeliness, or being error-free. If being a low-priced producer is the goal, then emphasis should be on cost reduction or increased productivity with lower acceptable levels of quality. While a variety of performance options are available, most focus on quality, cost control, or productivity. Highlights in HRM 2 provides five proven guidelines on how to establish and maintain an effective performance measurement program.

For some organizations, linking incentive payments to formalized performance measures has not obtained positive results for either employees or the organization.[9] Failure can often be traced to the choice of performance measures. Therefore, measures that are quantitative, simple, and structured to show a clear relationship to improved performance are best. Overly quantitative, complex measures are to be avoided. Also, when selecting a performance measure, it is necessary to evaluate the extent to which the employees involved can actually influence the measurement. Finally, employers must guard against "ratcheting up" performance goals by continually trying to exceed previous results. This eventually leads to employee frustration and employee perception that the standards are unattainable. The result will be a mistrust of management and a backlash against the entire incentive program.

Administering Incentive Plans

While incentive plans based on productivity can reduce direct labor costs, to achieve their full benefit they must be carefully thought out, implemented, and maintained. A cardinal rule is that thorough planning must be combined with a "proceed with caution" approach. Compensation managers repeatedly stress a number of points related to the effective administration of incentive plans. Three of the more important points are, by consensus, as follows:

1. Incentive systems are effective only when managers are willing to grant incentives based on differences in individual, team, or organizational performance. Allowing incentive payments to become pay guarantees defeats the motivational intent of the incentive. The primary purpose of an incentive compensation plan is not to pay off under almost all circumstances, but rather to motivate performance. Thus, if the plan is to succeed, poor performance must go unrewarded.
2. Annual salary budgets must be large enough to reward and reinforce exceptional performance. When compensation budgets are set to ensure that pay increases do not exceed certain limits (often established as a percentage of payroll or sales), these constraints may prohibit rewarding outstanding individual or group performance.
3. The overhead costs associated with plan implementation and administration must be determined. These may include the cost of establishing performance standards and the added cost of record keeping. The time consumed in communicating the plan to employees, answering questions, and resolving any complaints about it must also be included in these costs.

Individual Incentive Plans

In today's competitive world, one word, *flexibility*, describes the design of individual incentive plans.[10] For example, technology, job tasks and duties, and/or organizational goals (such as being a low-cost producer) impact the organization's choice of incentive pay programs. Incentive payments may be determined by the number of units produced, by the achievement of specific performance goals, or by productivity improvements in the organization as a whole. In addition, in highly competitive industries such as foods and retailing, low profit margins will affect the availability of monies for incentive payouts. All of these considerations suggest that tradition and philosophy, as well as economics and technology, help govern the design of individual incentive systems.

Piecework

straight piecework
An incentive plan under which employees receive a certain rate for each unit produced

differential piece rate
A compensation rate under which employees whose production exceeds the standard amount of output receive a higher rate for all of their work than the rate paid to those who do not exceed the standard amount

One of the oldest incentive plans is based on piecework. Under **straight piecework,** employees receive a certain rate for each unit produced. Their compensation is determined by the number of units they produce during a pay period. At Steelcase, an office furniture maker, employees can earn more than their base pay, often as much as 35 percent more, through piecework for each slab of metal they cut or chair they upholster. Under a **differential piece rate,** employees whose production exceeds the standard output receive a higher rate for *all* of their work than the rate paid to those who do not exceed the standard.

Employers include piecework in their compensation strategy for several reasons. The wage payment for each employee is simple to compute, and the plan permits an organization to predict its labor costs with considerable accuracy, as these costs are the same for each unit of output. The piecework system is more likely to succeed when units of output can be measured readily, when the quality of the product is less critical, when the job is fairly standardized, and when a constant flow of work can be maintained.

Computing the Piece Rate

Although time standards establish the time required to perform a given amount of work, they do not by themselves determine what the incentive rate should be. The incentive rates must be based on hourly wage rates that would otherwise be paid for the type of work being performed. Say, for example, the standard time for producing one unit of work in a job paying $11.50 per hour was set at twelve minutes. The piece rate would be $2.30 per unit, computed as follows:

$$\frac{60 \text{ (minutes per hour)}}{12 \text{ (standard time per unit)}} = 5 \text{ units per hour}$$

$$\frac{\$11.50 \text{ (hourly rate)}}{5 \text{ (units per hour)}} = \$2.30 \text{ per unit}$$

Piecework: The Drawbacks

Despite their obvious advantages—including their direct tie to a pay-for-performance philosophy—piecework systems have a number of disadvantages that offset their usefulness. One of the most significant weaknesses of piecework, as well as of other incentive plans based on individual effort, is that it may not always be an effective motivator. If employees believe that an increase in their output will provoke disapproval from fellow workers (often referred to as "rate busting"), they may avoid exerting maximum effort because their desire for peer approval outweighs their desire for more money. Also, jobs in which individual contributions are difficult to distinguish or measure, or in which the work is mechanized to the point that the employee exercises very little control over output, may be unsuited to piecework. Piecework may also be inappropriate in the following situations:

- When quality is more important than quantity
- When technology changes are frequent
- When productivity standards on which piecework must be based are difficult to develop

Importantly, piecework incentive systems can work against an organizational culture promoting workforce cooperation, creativity, or problem solving because each of these goals can infringe on an employee's time and productivity and, therefore, total incentive earned.

Standard Hour Plan

standard hour plan
An incentive plan that sets rates based on the completion of a job in a predetermined standard time

Another common incentive technique is the **standard hour plan,** which sets incentive rates on the basis of a predetermined "standard time" for completing a job. If employees finish the work in less than the expected time, their pay is still based on the standard time for the job multiplied by their hourly rate. Standard hour plans are popular in service departments in automobile dealerships. For example, if the standard time to install an engine in a truck is five hours and the mechanic completes the job in four and a half hours, the payment would be the mechanic's hourly rate times five hours. Standard hour plans are particularly suited to long-cycle operations or jobs or tasks that are nonrepetitive and require a variety of skills. However, while standard hour plans can motivate employees to produce more, employers must ensure that equipment maintenance and product quality do not suffer as employees strive to do their work faster to earn additional income.

Bonuses

bonus
An incentive payment that is supplemental to the base wage

A **bonus** is an incentive payment that is given to an employee beyond one's normal base wage. It is frequently given at the end of the year and does not become part of base pay. Bonuses have the advantage of providing employees with more pay for exerting greater effort, while at the same time the employees still have the security of a basic wage. Bonus payments are common among managerial and executive employees, but recent trends show that they are increasingly given to employees throughout the organization.

Depending on who is to receive the bonus, the incentive payment may be determined on the basis of cost reduction, quality improvement, or performance criteria established by the organization. At the executive level, for example, performance criteria might include earnings growth or enterprise-specific agreed-on objectives.

spot bonus
An unplanned bonus given for employee effort unrelated to an established performance measure

When some special employee contribution is to be rewarded, a spot bonus is used. A **spot bonus,** as the name implies, is given "on the spot," normally for some employee effort not directly tied to an established performance standard. For example, a customer service representative might receive a spot bonus for working long hours to fill a new customer's large order. Spot bonuses are championed as useful retention and motivational tools for overburdened employees, especially during lean financial times. Lauren Sejen, compensation expert with Watson Wyatt Worldwide, notes, "I think spot bonuses are one of the most underutilized forms of rewards, given how well employees respond to them. These plans make perfect sense."[11]

Merit Pay

A merit pay program (merit raise) links an increase in base pay to how successfully an employee performs his or her job. The merit increase is normally given on the basis of an employee's having achieved some objective performance standard—although a superior's subjective evaluation of subordinate performance may play a large role in the increase given. Merit raises can serve to motivate if employees perceive the raise to be related to the performance required to earn it.[12]

Theories of motivation, in addition to behavioral science research, provide justification for merit pay plans as well as other pay-for-performance programs.[13] However, research shows that a merit increase in the range of 7 to 9 percent is necessary to serve as a pay motivator. Employees may welcome lower percentage amounts, but low salary increases may not lead to significantly greater effort on the part of employees to drive business results. Consequently, with low salary budgets (see Chapter 9), organizations wishing to reward top performers will be required to distribute a large portion of the compensation budget to these individuals.[14] A meaningful merit increase will catch the attention of top performers while sending a signal to poor-performing employees. A strategic compensation policy *must differentiate* between outstanding and good or average performance. Furthermore, increases granted on the basis of merit should be distinguishable from cost-of-living or other general increases.

Problems with Merit Raises

Merit raises may not always achieve their intended purpose. Unlike a bonus, a merit raise may be perpetuated year after year even when performance declines. When this happens, employees come to expect the increase and see it as being an entitlement, unrelated to their performance. Furthermore, what are referred to as merit raises often turn out to be increases based on seniority or favoritism. A superior's biased evaluation of subordinate performance may play a large role in the increase given. Even when merit raises are determined by performance, the employee's gains may be offset by inflation and higher income taxes. Compensation specialists also recognize the following problems with merit pay plans:

1. Money available for merit increases may be inadequate to satisfactorily raise all employees' base pay.
2. Managers may have no guidance in how to define and measure performance; there may be vagueness regarding merit award criteria.
3. Employees may not believe that their compensation is tied to effort and performance; they may be unable to differentiate between merit pay and other types of pay increases.
4. The performance appraisal objectives of employees and their managers are often at odds.
5. There may be a lack of honesty and cooperation between management and employees.
6. It has been shown that "overall" merit pay plans do not motivate higher levels of employee performance.

merit guidelines
Guidelines for awarding merit raises that are tied to performance objectives

While there are no easy solutions to these problems, organizations using a true merit pay plan often base the percentage pay raise on **merit guidelines** tied to performance appraisals. For example, Highlights in HRM 3 illustrates a guideline chart

Merit Pay Guidelines Chart

A merit pay guidelines chart is a "lookup" table for awarding merit increases on the basis of (1) employee performance, (2) position in the pay range, and, in a few cases, (3) time since the last pay increase. Design of any merit guidelines chart involves several concerns. Specifically,

- What should unsatisfactory performers be paid? Because their performance is marginal or below standard, the common response is "nothing."
- What should average performers be paid? Common practice is to grant increases commensurate with cost-of-living changes (see Chapter 9). The midpoint of the merit guidelines chart should equal the local or national percentage change in the consumer price index (CPI).
- How much should superior or outstanding performers be paid? Profit levels, compensation budgets, and psychological concerns predominate here.

The following merit pay guidelines chart shows the pay range for each pay grade as divided into five levels (quintiles), with 1 at the bottom of the pay range and 5 at the top. On the left, employee performance (as determined by the annual appraisal) is arranged in five levels from high (outstanding) to low (unsatisfactory). An employee's position in his or her salary range and performance level indicates the percentage pay increase to be awarded. For example, a person at the top of the pay range (5) who gets a performance rating of "outstanding" will be awarded a 6 percent pay increase. However, an outstanding performer at the bottom of the pay range (1) will receive a 9 percent increase.

Because the purpose of the guidelines chart is to balance conflicting pay goals, it compromises, by design, the relationship between merit increases and performance appraisal ratings. The highest-rated performers will not always be the employees with the highest percentage increase. Notice that a superior performer in quintiles 1, 2, and 3 can receive a percentage increase as much as or more than that of an outstanding performer in quintile 5. As a result, employees are likely to learn that pay increases are not determined just by performance. However, as we learned in Chapter 9, if money is to serve as a motivator, top performers must receive a significant amount of the compensation budget.

MERIT PAY GUIDE CHART

	QUINTILE (POSITION IN RANGE), %				
PERFORMANCE LEVEL	**1**	**2**	**3**	**4**	**5**
Outstanding (5)	9	9	8	7	6
Superior (4)	7	7	6	5	4
Competent (3)	5	5	4	3	3
Needs improvement (2)	0	0	0	0	0
Unsatisfactory (1)	0	0	0	0	0

for awarding merit raises. The percentages may change each year, depending on various internal or external concerns such as profit levels or national economic conditions as indicated by changes in the consumer price index. Under the illustrated merit plan, to prevent all employees from being rated outstanding or above average, managers may be required to distribute the performance rating according to some preestablished formula (such as only 10 percent can be rated outstanding). Additionally, when setting merit percentage guidelines, organizations should consider individual performance along with such factors as training, experience, and current earnings.

Lump-Sum Merit Pay

lump-sum merit program program under which employees receive a year-end merit payment, which is not added to their base pay

To make merit increases more flexible and visible, organizations such as Boeing, Timex, and Westinghouse have implemented a **lump-sum merit program.** Under this type of plan, employees receive a single lump-sum increase at the time of their review, an increase that is not added to their base salary. Lump-sum merit programs offer several advantages. For employees, an advantage is that receiving a single lump-sum merit payment can provide a clear link between pay and performance. For example, a 6 percent merit increase granted to an industrial engineer earning $58,000 a year translates into a weekly increase of $66.92—a figure that looks small compared with a lump-sum payment of $3,480. For employers, lump-sum payments essentially freeze base salaries, thereby maintaining annual salary and benefit costs, as the level of benefits are normally calculated from salary levels. Organizations using a lump-sum merit program will want to adjust base salaries upward after a certain period of time. These adjustments should keep pace with the rising cost of living and increases in the general market wage.

Incentive Awards and Recognition

Awards are often used to recognize productivity gains, special contributions or achievements, and service to the organization. Merchandise awards, personalized gifts, theater tickets, vacations, gift certificates, and personalized clothing represent popular noncash incentive awards.[15] Tangible awards presented with the right message and style can make employees feel appreciated while at the same time underscoring a company's value.[16]

Research clearly shows that noncash incentive awards are most effective as motivators when the award is combined with a meaningful employee recognition program. Bob Nelson, president of Nelson Motivation, states, "Employers should take care to tie awards to performance and deliver awards in a timely, sincere and specific way."[17] Importantly, awards and employee recognition should highlight how employee performance contributes to specific organizational objectives. Greg Boswell, director of performance recognition at O. C. Tanner, notes, "Employers are now thinking of awards and employee recognition more strategically with programs closely aligned to their business goals."[18]

Sales Incentives

The enthusiasm and drive required in most types of sales work demand that sales employees be highly motivated. This fact, as well as the competitive nature of selling, explains why financial incentives for salespeople are widely used. These incentive plans must provide a source of motivation that will elicit cooperation and trust. Motivation is particularly important for employees away from the office who cannot be supervised closely and who, as a result, must exercise a high degree of self-discipline.

Unique Needs of Sales Incentive Plans

Incentive systems for salespeople are complicated by the wide differences in the types of sales jobs.[19] These range from department store clerks who ring up customer purchases to industrial salespeople from McGraw-Edison who provide consultation and other highly technical services. Salespeople's performance may be measured by the dollar volume of their sales and by their ability to establish new accounts. Other measures are the ability to promote new products or services and to provide various forms of customer service and assistance that do not produce immediate sales revenues.[20]

Performance standards for sales employees are difficult to develop, however, because their performance is often affected by external factors beyond their control. Economic and seasonal fluctuations, sales competition, changes in demand, and the nature of the sales territory can all affect an individual's sales record.[21] Sales volume alone therefore may not be an accurate indicator of the effort salespeople have expended.

In developing incentive plans for salespeople, managers are also confronted with the problem of how to reward extra sales effort and at the same time compensate for activities that do not contribute directly or immediately to sales. Furthermore, sales employees must be able to enjoy some degree of income stability.[22]

Types of Sales Incentive Plans

Compensation plans for sales employees may consist of a straight salary plan, a straight commission plan, or a combination salary and commission plan. A **straight salary plan** permits salespeople to be paid for performing various duties not reflected immediately in their sales volume. It enables them to devote more time to providing services and building up the goodwill of customers without jeopardizing their income. The principal limitation of the straight salary plan is that it may not motivate salespeople to exert sufficient effort in maximizing their sales volume.

straight salary plan
A compensation plan that permits salespeople to be paid for performing various duties that are not reflected immediately in their sales volume

On the other hand, the **straight commission plan,** based on a percentage of sales, provides maximum incentive and is easy to compute and understand. For example, total cash compensation might equal total sales volume times some percentage of total sales, say 2 percent. Under a straight commission plan salespeople may be allowed a salary draw. A *draw* is a cash advance that must be paid back as commissions are earned.

straight commission plan
A compensation plan based on a percentage of sales

However, the straight commission plan is limited by the following disadvantages:

1. Emphasis is on sales volume rather than on profits.
2. Customer service after the sale is likely to be neglected.
3. Earnings tend to fluctuate widely between good and poor periods of business, and turnover of trained sales employees tends to increase in poor periods.
4. Salespeople are tempted to grant price concessions.

The **combined salary and commission plan** is the most widely used sales incentive program. A salesperson working under a 70/30 combination plan would receive total cash compensation paid out as 70 percent base salary and 30 percent commission. The ratio of base salary to commission can be set to fit organizational objectives. The following advantages indicate why the combination salary and commission plan is so widely used:

combined salary and commission plan
A compensation plan that includes a straight salary and a commission

1. The right kind of incentive compensation, if linked to salary in the right proportion, has most of the advantages of both the straight salary and the straight commission forms of compensation.
2. A salary-plus-incentive compensation plan offers greater design flexibility and can therefore be more readily set up to help maximize company profits.
3. The plan can develop the most favorable ratio of selling expense to sales.
4. The field sales force can be motivated to achieve specific company marketing objectives in addition to sales volume.

Incentives for Professional Employees

Like other salaried workers, professional employees—engineers, scientists, and attorneys, for example—may be motivated through bonuses and merit increases. In some organizations, unfortunately, professional employees cannot advance beyond a certain point in the salary structure unless they are willing to take an administrative assignment. When they are promoted, their professional talents are no longer utilized fully. In the process, the organization may lose a good professional employee and gain a poor administrator. To avoid this situation, some organizations have extended the salary range for professional positions to equal or nearly equal that for administrative positions. The extension of this range provides a double-track wage system, as illustrated in Chapter 7, whereby professionals who do not aspire to become administrators still have an opportunity to earn comparable salaries.

Professional employees can receive compensation beyond base pay. For example, scientists and engineers employed by high-tech firms are included in performance-based incentive programs such as profit sharing or stock ownership. These plans encourage greater levels of individual performance. Cash bonuses can be awarded to those who complete projects on or before deadline dates. Payments may also be given to individuals elected to professional societies, granted patents, or meeting professional licensing standards.

The Executive Pay Package

Executive compensation plans consist of five basic components: (1) base salary, (2) short-term incentives or bonuses, (3) long-term incentives or stock plans, (4) benefits, and (5) perquisites.[24] Each of these elements may receive different emphasis in the executive's compensation package depending on various organizational goals and executive needs.

Base Executive Salaries. Executive base salaries represent between 30 and 40 percent of total annual compensation.[25] An analysis of executive salaries shows that the largest portion of executive pay is received in long-term incentive rewards and bonuses. Regardless, executives of Fortune 500 firms routinely earn an annual base salary in excess of $500,000, with executives in very large corporations earning considerably more. The levels of competitive salaries in the job market exert perhaps the greatest influence on executive base salaries. An organization's compensation committee—normally members of the board of directors—will order a salary survey to find out what executives earn in comparable enterprises. For example, by one estimate, 96 percent of companies in the Standard & Poor's 500-stock index use a technique called *competitive* *benchmarking* when setting executive pay or to remain competitive for executive talent. As noted in *Business Week*, company boards reason that a CEO who doesn't earn as much as his or her peers is likely to "take a hike."[26] Comparisons may be based on organization size, sales volume, or industry groupings. Thus, by analyzing the data from published studies, along with self-generated salary surveys, the compensation committee can determine the equity of the compensation package outside the organization.[27]

Executive Short-Term Incentives. Annual bonuses represent the main element of executive short-term incentives. A bonus payment may take the form of cash or stock and may be paid immediately (which is frequently the case), deferred for a short time, or deferred until retirement. Most organizations pay their short-term incentive bonuses in cash (in the form of a supplemental check), in keeping with their pay-for-performance strategy. By providing a reward soon after the performance, and thus linking it to the effort on which it is based, they can use cash bonuses as a significant motivator. Deferred bonuses are used to provide a source of retirement benefits or to supplement a regular pension plan.

Incentive bonuses for executives should be based on the contribution the individual makes to the organization. A variety of formulas have been developed for this purpose. Incentive bonuses may be based on a percentage of a company's total profits or a percentage of profits in excess of a specific return on stockholders' investments. In other instances the payments may be tied to an annual profit plan whereby the amount is determined by the extent to which an agreed-on profit level is exceeded. Payments may also be based on performance ratings or the achievement of specific objectives established with the agreement of executives and the board of directors.[28]

In a continuing effort to monitor the pulse of the marketplace, more organizations are tying operational yardsticks to the traditional financial gauges when computing executive pay. Called *balanced scorecards*, these yardsticks may measure things such as customer satisfaction, the ability to innovate, or product or service leadership. Notes David Cates, a compensation principal with Towers Perrin, a balanced scorecard "allows companies to focus on building future economic value, rather than be driven solely by short-term financial results." Mobil Oil uses a balanced scorecard that better indicates exactly where the company is successful and where improvement is needed.

Executive Long-Term Incentives. Stock options are the primary long-term incentive offered to executives.[29] The principal reason driving executive stock ownership is the desire of both the company and outside investors for senior managers to have a significant stake in the success of the business—to have their fortunes rise and fall with the value they create for shareholders. Stock options can also be extremely lavish for executives. Consider these examples. For 2004, Richard D. Fairbank, CEO of Capital One Financial, received long-term compensation totaling \$56.5 million; John D. Chambers, CEO of Cisco Systems, received \$52.1 million; and Louis V. Gerstner, CEO of IBM received 42.6 million.[30] Not surprisingly, the creativity in designing a stock option program seems almost limitless.[31] Figure 10.3 highlights several common forms of long-term incentives.

Short-term incentive bonuses are criticized for causing top executives to focus on quarterly profit goals to the detriment of long-term survival and growth objectives. Therefore corporations such as Sears, Combustion Engineering, Borden, and Enhart have adopted compensation strategies that tie executive pay to long-term performance measures. Each of these organizations recognizes that compensation strategies must

Figure 10.3 Types of Long-Term Incentive Plans

Stock options	Rights granted to executives to purchase shares of their organization's stock at an established price for a fixed period of time. Stock price is usually set at market value at the time the option is granted.
Stock appreciation rights (SARs)	Cash or stock award determined by increase in stock price during any time chosen by the executive in the option period; does not require executive financing.
Stock purchase	Opportunities for executives to purchase shares of their organization's stock valued at full market or a discount price, often with the organization providing financial assistance.
Phantom stock	Grant of units equal in value to the fair market value or book value of a share of stock; on a specified date the executive will be paid the appreciation in the value of the units up to that time.
Restricted stock	Grant of stock or stock units at a reduced price with the condition that the stock not be transferred or sold (by risk of forfeiture) before a specified employment date.
Performance units	Grants analogous to annual bonuses except that the measurement period exceeds one year. The value of the grant can be expressed as a flat dollar amount or converted to a number of "units" of equivalent aggregate value.
Performance shares	Grants of actual stock or phantom stock units. Value is contingent on both predetermined performance objectives over a specified period of time and the stock market.

also take into account the performance of the organization as a whole. Important to stockholders are such performance results as growth in earnings per share, return on stockholders' equity, and, ultimately, stock price appreciation. A variety of incentive plans, therefore, have been developed to tie rewards to these performance results, particularly over the long term. Additionally, stock options can serve to retain key executive personnel when exercising the options is linked to a specified vesting period, say two to four years (this type of incentive is called "golden handcuffs").

Stock options are under attack.[32] Some object to the sheer magnitude of these incentive rewards. The link between pay and performance that options are championed to provide can also be undermined when compensation committees grant additional options to executives even when company stock prices fall or performance indexes decline. Peter Clapman, chief counsel for TIAA-CREF, the world's largest pension system, notes, "It's sort of heads you win, tails let's flip again." Even worse for shareholders is the dilution problem. Every option granted to executives makes the shares of other stockholders less valuable.

Executive Benefits. The benefits package offered executives may parallel one offered to other groups of employees. Various programs for health insurance, life insurance, retirement plans, and vacations are common. However, unlike other employee groups, the benefits offered executives are likely to be broader in coverage and free of charge. Additionally, executives may be given financial assistance in the form of trusts for estate planning, payment of mortgage interest, and legal help.

perquisites
Special nonmonetary benefits given to executives; often referred to as *perks*

Executive Perquisites. **Perquisites** are nonmonetary rewards given to executives. Perquisites, or *perks*, are a means of demonstrating the executive's importance to the organization. The status that comes with perks—both inside and outside the organization—shows a pecking order and conveys authority. Corporate executives may simply consider perks a "badge of merit." Perks can also provide tax savings to executives, because some are not taxed as income.

The dark side of perks is that they are viewed as wasteful spending and overly lavish. A recent study, however, shows that perks can facilitate company productivity by saving executive time (for example, private planes and chauffeur service) or improve or maintain executive health (for example, spas, health clubs, and company cabins). Therefore, the cost of perks should be weighed against the added efficiency and managerial effectiveness they generate.[33] Highlights in HRM 4 shows the more common perks offered to executives.

Executive Compensation: Ethics and Accountability

The top executive paychecks for 2004 were, as usual, off-the-chart amazing. Consider the total annual compensation drawn in 2004 by the following executives.[34]

Terry S. Semel, Yahoo	$120,100,000
Lew Frankfort, Coach	$58,700,000
Ray R. Irani, Occidental Petroleum	$37,800,000
Paul J. Evanson, Allegheny Energy	$37,500,000
Robert L. Nardeli, Home Depot	$36,700,000

In 2003, the ratio between average CEO compensation and worker pay was 301:1, up from 282:1 in 2001 and 42:1 in 1982.[35] Figures show that in Japan the ratio is 15:1 and in Europe 20:1.[36] Management expert Peter F. Drucker has warned that the growing pay gap between CEOs and employees could threaten the very credibility of leadership. He believes that no leader should earn more than 20 times the pay of the company's lowest-paid employee.[37]

Given the large amount of these compensation packages, the question asked by many is, "Are top executives worth the salaries and bonuses they receive?" The answer may depend on whom you ask. Corporate compensation committees justify big bonuses in the following ways:

1. Large financial incentives are a way to reward superior performance.
2. Business competition is pressure-filled and demanding.
3. Good executive talent is in great demand.
4. Effective executives create shareholder value.

Others justify high compensation as a fact of business life, reflecting market compensation trends.

Nevertheless, in an era of massive downsizing, low wage increases, and increased workloads for layoff survivors, strong criticism is voiced regarding the high monetary awards given to senior executives.[38] Furthermore, with the large compensation packages awarded to senior managers and top-level executives, cries for performance accountability and openness abound. The 2004 annual Executive Pay Scoreboard published by *Business Week* argues that to justify the big bucks, CEOs and top executives should produce a surge in shareholder value. Yet in 2004 many top executives failed to beat the S&P 500 for total shareholder return over the past three years. In *Business Week*'s analysis, a large percentage of top-paid executives simply did not ace

Highlights in HRM 4

The "Sweetness" of Executive Perks

Compensation consulting firms such as Coopers and Lybrand LLP, WorldatWork, and Hewitt Associates regularly survey companies nationwide to identify the perks they provide for executives and other top managers. Below are listed popular executive perks.

- Company car
- Company plane
- Executive eating facilities
- Financial consulting
- Company-paid parking
- Personal liability insurance
- Estate planning
- First-class air travel
- Home computers
- Chauffeur service
- Children's education
- Spouse travel
- Physical exams
- Mobile phones
- Large insurance policies
- Income tax preparation
- Country club membership
- Luncheon club membership
- Personal home repairs
- Loans
- Legal counseling
- Vacation cabins

"our pay-for-performance analysis."[39] While some high-paid executives do improve performance measures, such as return on equity, earnings per share, and return to shareholders, clearly others do not.

A critical question with exorbitant executive pay is not always what is legal or externally equitable but what is right or ethical. Compensation committees sometimes fail to fulfill their obligations and corporate boards can be stacked with cronies willing to rubber-stamp high pay packages. Furthermore, the run of greed-inspired scandals beginning in 2001 with Enron has extended to such companies as Strong Capital Management, Hollinger International, and the dot-coms, raising concerns about the ethical behavior of executives at these organizations and others. While not all executive pay is exorbitant and not all executive behavior is unethical, nevertheless angry employees, government officials, and stockholders argue for change.[40]

Executive Compensation Reform

Several important changes will impact future executive compensation. First, the Internal Revenue Service (IRS) will increasingly look for tax-code violations in connection with hefty executive pay packages. The IRS intends to make executive pay a part of every corporate audit.[41] Second, in 2003, the Securities and Exchange Commission ruled that companies on the New York Stock Exchange and NASDAQ must obtain shareholder approval before granting stock options and other equity compensation to executives and employees. Third, the Financial Accounting Standards Board (FASB) now requires that stock options be recognized as an expense on income statements. Companies and compensation committees must now weigh the benefits provided by stock option programs against the potential charge to earnings.[42] Other reform measures include the following:

1. The adoption of more sophisticated formulas that peg executive compensation to organizational benchmarks other than stock price in a move to align pay more closely with performance.
2. Corporate policy changes governing how compensation committees structure executive pay packages.
3. Restraints on stock options making it harder for executives to cash out and receive windfall cash sums. A trend shows that companies are rethinking how to gain value from their options and how to deliver options to those who most deserve them.

Group Incentive Plans

The emphasis on cost reduction and total quality management has led many organizations to implement a variety of group incentive plans.[43] Group plans enable employees to share in the benefits of improved efficiency realized by major organizational units or various individual work teams. These plans encourage a cooperative—rather than individualistic—spirit among all employees and reward them for their total contribution to the organization. Such features are particularly desirable when working conditions make individual performance difficult, if not impossible, to measure.

Team Compensation

As production has become more automated, as teamwork and coordination among workers have become more important, and as the contributions of those engaged indirectly in production or service tasks have increased, team incentive plans have grown more popular. **Team incentive plans** reward team members with an incentive bonus when agreed-on performance standards are met or exceeded. Furthermore, the incentive will seek to establish a psychological climate that fosters team cooperation.

team incentive plan
A compensation plan in which all team members receive an incentive bonus payment when production or service standards are met or exceeded

One catch with setting team compensation is that not all teams are alike (see Chapter 4). For example, cross-functional teams, self-directed teams, and task force teams make it impossible to develop one consistent type of team incentive plan. And, with a variety of teams, managers find it difficult to adopt uniform measurement standards or payout formulas for team pay.[44] According to Steven Gross, Hay manager, "Each type of team requires a specific pay structure to function at its peak."

In spite of this caveat, organizations typically use the three-step approach to establishing team incentive payments. First, they set performance measures on which incentive payments are based. Improvements in efficiency, product quality, or reduction in materials or labor costs are common benchmark criteria. For example, if labor costs for a team represent 30 percent of the organization's sales dollars, and the organization pays a bonus for labor cost savings, then whenever team labor costs are less than 30 percent of sales dollars, those savings are paid as an incentive bonus to team members. Information on the size of the incentive bonus is reported to employees on a weekly or monthly basis, explaining why incentive pay was or was not earned. Second, the size of the incentive bonus must be determined. At Thrivent Financial for Lutherans, health insurance underwriters can receive team incentive bonuses of up to 10 percent of base salary; however, the exact level of incentive pay depends on overall team performance and the company's performance over one year. Team incentives at Thrivent are paid annually. Third, a payout formula is established and fully explained to employees. The team bonus may be distributed to employees equally, in proportion to their base pay, or on the basis of their relative contribution to the team. With discretionary formulas, managers, or in some cases team members themselves, agree on the payouts to individual team members. Figure 10.4 presents the commonly stated advantages and disadvantages of team incentive pay.

Gainsharing Incentive Plans

gainsharing plans Programs under which both employees and the organization share financial gains according to a predetermined formula that reflects improved productivity and profitability

Gainsharing plans are organizational programs designed to increase productivity or decrease labor costs and share monetary gains with employees. These plans are based on a mathematical formula that compares a baseline of performance with actual productivity during a given period. When productivity exceeds the baseline, an agreed-on savings is shared with employees. Inherent in gainsharing is the idea that involved employees will improve productivity through more effective use of organizational resources.

Although productivity can be measured in various ways, it is usually calculated as a ratio of outputs to inputs. Sales, pieces produced, pounds, total standard costs, direct labor dollars earned, and customer orders are common output measures. Inputs frequently measured include materials, labor, energy, inventory, purchased goods or services, and total costs. An increase in productivity is normally gained when:

- Greater output is obtained with less or equal input.
- Equal production output is obtained with less input.

Figure 10.4 The Pros and Cons of Team Incentive Plans

PROS

- Team incentives support group planning and problem solving, thereby building a team culture.
- The contributions of individual employees depend on group cooperation.
- Unlike incentive plans based solely on output, team incentives can broaden the scope of the contribution that employees are motivated to make.
- Team bonuses tend to reduce employee jealousies and complaints over "tight" or "loose" individual standards.
- Team incentives encourage cross-training and the acquiring of new interpersonal competencies.

CONS

- Individual team members may perceive that "their" efforts contribute little to team success or to the attainment of the incentive bonus.
- Intergroup social problems—pressure to limit performance (for example, team members are afraid one individual may make the others look bad) and the "free-ride" effect (one individual puts in less effort than others but shares equally in team rewards)—may arise.
- Complex payout formulas can be difficult for team members to understand.

Although gainsharing is a popular reward system for employees, experience with these techniques has pointed up a number of factors that contribute to either their success or their failure. Highlights in HRM 5 discusses common considerations when establishing a gainsharing program.[45]

There are three typical gainsharing plans. Two plans, the Scanlon and Rucker Plans, emphasize participative management and encourage cost reductions by sharing with employees any savings resulting from these reductions. The third plan, Improshare, is based on the number of finished goods that the employee work teams complete in an established period.

The Scanlon Plan

Scanlon Plan
A bonus incentive plan using employee and management committees to gain cost-reduction improvements

The philosophy behind the **Scanlon Plan** is that employees should offer ideas and suggestions to improve productivity and, in turn, be rewarded for their constructive efforts. According to Scanlon's proponents, effective employee participation, which includes the use of committees on which employees are represented, is the most significant feature of the Scanlon Plan. Improvement or gains largely come from "working smarter, not harder." Figure 10.5 illustrates the Scanlon Plan suggestion process, including the duties and responsibilities of two important groups—the *shop* and *screening* committees.

Financial incentives under the Scanlon Plan are ordinarily offered to all employees (a significant feature of the plan) on the basis of an established formula. This formula

Figure 10.5 Scanlon Plan Suggestion Process

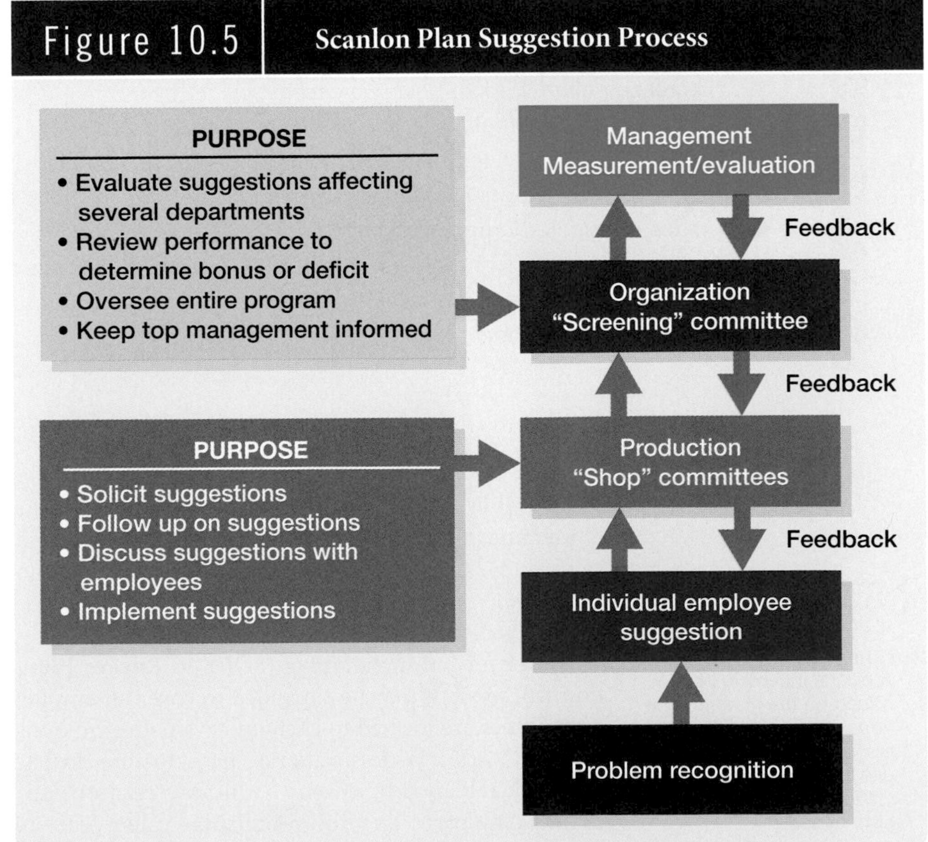

Highlights in HRM 5

Lessons Learned: Designing Effective Gainsharing Programs

Will your gainsharing program be successful? While there are no exact keys to success, gainsharing proponents cite the following as important components of a meaningful gainsharing plan.

- Enlist *total* managerial support for the gainsharing effort. While top-management support is critical, without the encouragement of middle and lower-level managers (those directly involved in program implementation), gainsharing efforts invariably fail.
- When developing new programs, include representatives from all groups affected by the gainsharing effort—labor, management, employees. Inclusion, not exclusion, serves to build trust and understanding of the program's intent and operation.
- Prevent political games in which involved parties are more interested in preserving their self-interests than in supporting the group effort. The political manipulation of the bonus calculation to hold down payouts is a certain obstacle to all gainsharing programs.
- Bonus payout formulas must be seen as fair, must be easy for employees to calculate, must offer payouts on a frequent basis, and must be large enough to encourage future employee effort. The goal is to create a pay-for-performance environment.
- Establish effective, fair, and precise measurement standards. Standards must encourage increased effort without being unreasonable.
- Be certain that employees are predisposed to a gainsharing reward system. Is there a "cultural readiness" for gainsharing? If changes are indicated, what needs to be done? Will employees need additional skills training or training in other competencies in order to make anticipated organizational improvements?
- Launch the plan during a favorable business period. Business downturns jeopardize payments. A plan is likely to fail if it does not pay out under normal conditions in its first two or three years of operation.

is based on increases in employee productivity as determined by a norm that has been established for labor costs. The Scanlon Plan (and variations of it) has become a fundamental way of managing, if not a way of life, in organizations such as American Value Company, TRW, Weyerhaeuser, and the Xaloy Corporation.[46]

The Rucker Plan

Rucker Plan
A bonus incentive plan based on the historic relationship between the total earnings of hourly employees and the production value created by the employees

The share-of-production plan (SOP), or **Rucker Plan,** normally covers just production workers but may be expanded to cover all employees. As with the Scanlon Plan, committees are formed to elicit and evaluate employee suggestions. The Rucker Plan, however, uses a far less elaborate participatory structure. The financial incentive of the Rucker Plan is based on the historic relationship between the total earnings of hourly employees and the production value that employees create. The bonus is

The Scanlon and Rucker gainsharing plans rely on employee suggestions for cost savings and productivity improvements.

© AP PHOTO/BEN MARGOT

based on any improvement in this relationship that employees are able to realize. Thus, for every 1 percent increase in production value that is achieved, workers receive a bonus of 1 percent of their total payroll costs.[47]

Lessons from the Scanlon and Rucker Plans

Perhaps the most important lesson to be learned from the Scanlon and Rucker Plans is that any management expecting to gain the cooperation of its employees in improving efficiency must permit them to become involved psychologically as well as financially in the organization. If employees are to contribute maximum effort, they must have a feeling of involvement and identification with their organization, which does not come out of the traditional manager-subordinate relationship. Consequently, it is important for organizations to realize that while employee cooperation is essential to the successful administration of the Scanlon and Rucker Plans, the plans themselves do not necessarily stimulate this cooperation. Furthermore, the attitude of management is of paramount importance to the success of either plan. For example, when managers show little confidence and trust in their employees, the plans tend to fail.

Improshare

Improshare
A gainsharing program under which bonuses are based on the overall productivity of the work team

Improshare—improved productivity through sharing—is another gainsharing program. Individual production bonuses are typically based on how much an employee produces above some standard amount, but Improshare bonuses are based on the overall productivity of the *work team*. Improshare output is measured by the number of finished products that a work team produces in a given period. Both production (direct) employees and nonproduction (indirect) employees are included in the determination of the bonus.[48]

The bonus is based on productivity gains that result from reducing the time it takes to produce a finished product. The employees and the company each receive payment for 50 percent of the improvement. Since a cooperative environment benefits all,

Improshare promotes increased interaction and support between employees and management. Companies such as Hinderliter Energy Equipment pay the bonus as a separate check to emphasize that it is extra income.

Enterprise Incentive Plans

Enterprise incentive plans differ from individual and group incentive plans in that all organizational members participate in the plan's compensation payout. Enterprise incentive plans reward employees on the basis of the success of the organization over an extended time period—normally one year, but the period can be longer. Enterprise incentive plans seek to create a "culture of ownership" by fostering a philosophy of cooperation and teamwork among all organizational members. Common enterprise incentive plans include profit sharing, stock options, and employee stock ownership plans (ESOPs).

Profit-Sharing Plans

Profit sharing is any procedure by which an employer pays, or makes available to all regular employees, special current or deferred sums based on the organization's profits. As defined here, profit sharing represents cash payments made to eligible employees at designated time periods, as distinct from profit sharing in the form of contributions to employee pension funds.

profit sharing
Any procedure by which an employer pays, or makes available to all regular employees, in addition to base pay, special current or deferred sums based on the profits of the enterprise

Profit-sharing plans are intended to give employees the opportunity to increase their earnings by contributing to the growth of their organization's profits. These contributions may be directed toward improving product quality, reducing operating costs, improving work methods, and building goodwill rather than just increasing rates of production. Profit sharing can help stimulate employees to think and feel more like partners in the enterprise and thus to concern themselves with the welfare of the organization as a whole. Its purpose therefore is to motivate a total commitment from employees rather than simply to have them contribute in specific areas.

A popular example of a highly successful profit-sharing plan is the one in use at Lincoln Electric Company, a manufacturer of arc-welding equipment and supplies. This plan was started in 1934 by J. F. Lincoln, president of the company. Each year the company distributes a large percentage of its profits to employees in accordance with their salary level and merit ratings. It is not uncommon for employees' annual bonuses to exceed 50 percent of annual wages. The success of Lincoln Electric's incentive system depends on a high level of contribution by each employee. Unquestionably there is a high degree of respect among employees and management for Lincoln's organizational goals and for the profit-sharing program.

USING THE INTERNET

Lincoln Electric's web site provides a description of its incentive management system. It also presents information concerning career opportunities with the company. Go to the Student Resources at:

http://bohlander.swlearning.com

Variations in Profit-Sharing Plans

Profit-sharing plans differ in the proportion of profits shared with employees and in the distribution and form of payment. The amount shared with employees may range from 5 to 50 percent of the net profit. In most plans, however, about 20 to 25 percent of the net profit is shared. Profit distributions may be made to all employees on an equal basis, or they may be based on regular salaries or some formula that takes into account seniority and/or merit. The payments may be disbursed in cash, deferred, or made on the basis of combining the two forms of payments.

Weaknesses of Profit-Sharing Plans

In spite of their potential advantages, profit-sharing plans are also prone to certain weaknesses. The profits shared with employees may be the result of inventory speculation, climatic factors, economic conditions, national emergencies, or other factors over which employees have no control. Conversely, losses may occur during years when employee contributions have been at a maximum. The fact that profit-sharing payments are made only once a year or deferred until retirement may reduce their motivational value. If a plan fails to pay off for several years in a row, this can have an adverse effect on productivity and employee morale.

Stock Options

What do the following companies—Apple Computer, Yahoo, Coca-Cola, Bristol-Myers Squibb, Nike, Quaker Oats, and Sara Lee—have in common? The answer: Each of these diverse organizations offers a stock option program to its employees. According to WorldatWork, a compensation association, the use of stock options is a very prevalent method of motivating and compensating hourly employees, as well as salaried and executive personnel. This appears true regardless of the industry surveyed or the organization's size.[49]

Stock option programs are sometimes implemented as part of an employee benefit plan or as part of a corporate culture linking employee effort to stock performance. However, organizations that offer stock option programs to employees do so with the belief that there is some incentive value to the systems. By allowing employees to purchase stock, the organization hopes they will increase their productivity, assume a partnership role in the organization, and thus cause the stock price to rise.[50] Furthermore, stock option programs have become a popular way to boost morale of disenfranchised employees caught in mergers, acquisitions, and downsizing.

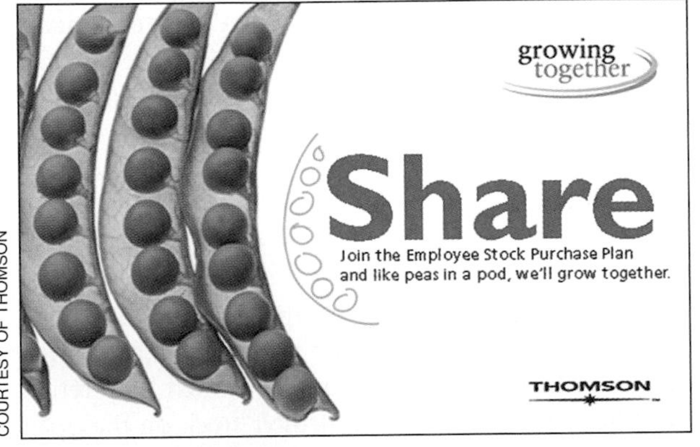

The Thomson Corporation promotes its stock option program with an attractive and comprehensive pamphlet describing eligibility requirements and program characteristics.

Stock option plans grant to employees the right to purchase a specific number of shares of the company's stock at a guaranteed price (the option price) during a designated time period. Although there are many types of options, most options are granted at the stock's fair market value. Not uncommon are plans for purchasing stock through payroll deductions.

When stock prices rise, employee stock plans can be financially rewarding to employees. In July 2004, employees in Boeing's Share Value Trust program received stock awards that paid out about $900 apiece in stock or cash to more than 200,000 current or former Boeing employees. Boeing estimated the payouts would total about $142.5 million.[51] Additionally, stock ownership plans serve as productivity incentives for booksellers at Borders, tellers at NationsBank, box packers at Pfizer, technical employees at Motorola, and espresso servers at Starbucks.

Unfortunately, in the wake of various corporate scandals, employee stock option plans have come under criticism (see "Executive Compensation: Ethics and

Accountability" earlier in this chapter). Criticism largely focuses on executive abuses and faulty accounting procedures. Fortunately, stock options continue to be a popular and effective way to pay for the performance of employees and managers.[52]

Employee Stock Ownership Plans (ESOPs)

According to Corey Rosen of the National Center for Employee Ownership, approximately 11,000 organizations have employee stock ownership plans (ESOPs) for their employees.[53] Columbia Forest Products, Southwest Airlines, Swales Aerospace, and Anderson Corporation are organizations with established ESOPs. W. L. Gore and Associates also decided that employee stock ownership was an effective and innovative way to give employees a share of the company's success.

employee stock ownership plans (ESOPs) Stock plans in which an organization contributes shares of its stock to an established trust for the purpose of stock purchases by its employees

Employee stock ownership plans take two primary forms: a stock bonus plan and a leveraged plan.[54] With either plan, the public or private employer establishes an ESOP trust that qualifies as a tax-exempt employee trust under Section 401(a) of the Internal Revenue Code. With a stock bonus plan, each year the organization gives stock to the ESOP or gives cash to the ESOP to buy outstanding stock. The ESOP holds the stock for employees, and they are routinely informed of the value of their accounts. Stock allocations can be based on employee wages or seniority. When employees leave the organization or retire, they can sell their stock back to the organization, or they can sell it on the open market if it is traded publicly. Leveraged ESOPs work in much the same way as do stock bonus plans, except that the ESOP borrows money from a bank or other financial institution to purchase stock. The organization then makes annual tax-deductible payments to the ESOP, which in turn repays the lending institution.

Advantages of ESOPs

Encouraged by favorable federal income tax provisions, employers use ESOPs to provide retirement benefits for their employees. Favorable tax incentives permit a portion of earnings to be excluded from taxation if that portion is assigned to employees in the form of shares of stock. Employers can therefore provide retirement benefits for their employees at relatively low cost, because stock contributions are in effect subsidized by the federal government. ESOPs can also increase employees' pride of ownership in the organization, providing an incentive for them to increase productivity and help the organization prosper and grow.

Problems with ESOPs

Generally, ESOPs are more likely to serve their intended purposes in publicly held companies than in privately held ones. A major problem with the privately held company is its potential inability to pay back the stock of employees when they retire. These employees do not have the alternative of disposing of their stock on the open market. Thus, when large organizations suffer financial difficulties and the value of the companies' stocks falls, so does the value of the employees' retirement plan.

Other problems with ESOPs include the following:

- The more retirement income comes from these plans, the more dependent a pensioner becomes on the price of company stock. Future retirees are vulnerable to stock market fluctuations as well as to management mistakes.

- Unlike traditional pension plans, ESOP contributions are not guaranteed by the federally established Pension Benefit Guaranty Corporation (see Chapter 11), a major drawback to employees should their employer face serious financial setbacks or closure.
- Finally, although studies show that productivity improves when ESOPs are implemented, these gains are not guaranteed. ESOPs help little unless managers are willing to involve employees in organizational decision making. Unfortunately, ESOPs are sometimes set up in ways that restrict employee decision making and expose the ESOP to risk, though providing investors with large potential gains.

SUMMARY

The success of an incentive pay plan depends on the organizational climate in which it must operate, employee confidence in it, and its suitability to employee and organizational needs. Importantly, employees must view their incentive pay as being equitable and related to their performance. Performance measures should be quantifiable, be easily understood, and bear a demonstrated relationship to organizational performance.

Piecework plans pay employees a given rate for each unit satisfactorily completed. Employers implement these plans when output is easily measured and when the production process is fairly standardized. Bonuses are incentive payments above base wages paid on either an individual or team basis. A bonus is offered to encourage employees to exert greater effort. Standard hour plans establish a standard time for job completion. An incentive is paid for finishing the job in less than the preestablished time. These plans are popular for jobs with a fixed time for completion.

Merit raises will not serve to motivate employees when they are seen as entitlements, which occurs when these raises are given yearly without regard to changes in employee performance. Merit raises are not motivational when they are given because of seniority or favoritism or when merit budgets are inadequate to sufficiently reward employee performance. To be motivational, merit raises must be such that employees see a clear relationship between pay and performance and the salary increase must be large enough to exceed inflation and higher income taxes.

Salespeople may be compensated by a straight salary, a combination of salary and commission, or a commission only. Paying employees a straight salary allows them to focus on tasks other than sales, such as service and customer goodwill. A straight commission plan causes employees to emphasize sales goals. A combination of salary and commission provides the advantages of both the straight salary and the straight commission form of payments.

The Scanlon, Rucker, and Improshare gainsharing plans pay bonuses to employees unrelated to profit levels. Each of these plans encourages employees to maximize their performance and cooperation through suggestions offered to improve organizational performance. The Scanlon Plan pays an employee a bonus based on saved labor cost measured against the organization's sales value of production. The bonus under the Rucker Plan is based on any improvement in the relationship between the total earnings of hourly employees and the value of production that employees create. The Improshare bonus is paid when employees increase production output above a given target level.

Profit-sharing plans pay to employees sums of money based on the organization's profits. Cash payments are made to eligible employees at specified times, normally yearly. The primary purpose of profit sharing is to provide employees with additional income through their participation in organizational achievement. Employee commitment to improved productivity, quality, and customer service will contribute to organizational success and, in turn, to their compensation. Profit-sharing plans may not achieve their stated gains when employee performance is unrelated to organizational success or failure. This may occur because of economic conditions, other competition, or environmental conditions. Profit-sharing plans can have a negative effect on employee morale when plans fail to consistently reward employees.

With a stock bonus ESOP, each year the organization contributes stock or cash to buy stock that is then placed in an ESOP trust. With a leveraged ESOP, the organization borrows money from a lending institution to purchase stock for the trust. With either plan, the ESOP holds the stock for employees until they either retire or leave the company, at which time the stock is sold back to the company or through a brokerage firm. Employers receive tax benefits for qualified ESOPs; they also hope to receive their employees' commitment to organizational improvement. Employees, however, may lose their retirement income should the company fail or stock prices fall. Another drawback to ESOPs is that they are not guaranteed by any federal agency.

KEY TERMS

- bonus
- combined salary and commission plan
- differential piece rate
- employee stock ownership plans (ESOPs)
- gainsharing plans
- Improshare
- lump-sum merit program
- merit guidelines
- perquisites
- profit sharing
- Rucker Plan
- Scanlon Plan
- spot bonus
- standard hour plan
- straight commission plan
- straight piecework
- straight salary plan
- team incentive plan
- variable pay

DISCUSSION QUESTIONS

1. Working individually or in groups, identify the factors for a successful incentive plan.

2. Contrast the differences between straight piecework, differential piece rate, and standard hour plans. Explain where each plan might best be used.

3. A frequently heard complaint about merit raises is that they do little to increase employee effort. What are the causes of this belief? Suggest ways in which the motivating value of merit raises may be increased.

4. What are the reasons behind the different payment methods for sales employees?

5. What are the reasons for the success of the Scanlon and Rucker Plans?

6. Because of competitive forces within your industry, you have decided to implement a profit-sharing plan for your employees. Discuss the advantages of profit sharing and identify specific characteristics that will ensure success for your plan.

7. What are some reasons for the implementation of ESOPs? Cite some of the potential problems concerning their use.

HRM Experience

Awarding Salary Increases

Because pay-for-performance is an important factor governing salary increases, managers must be able to defend the compensation recommendations they make for their employees. Merit raises granted under a pay-for-performance policy must be based on objective appraisals if they are to achieve their intended purposes of rewarding outstanding employee performance. As managers know, however, other factors that can affect salary recommendations must be dealt with. These may include the opinions of the employee's peers or extenuating circumstances such as illness or family responsibilities. The purpose of this exercise is to provide you with the experience of granting salary increases to employees based on their work performance and other information.

Assignment

Following are the work records of five employees. As their supervisor, you have just completed their annual appraisal reviews and it is now time to make recommendations for their future salary. Your department budget has $7,400 allocated for salary increases. Distribute the $7,400 among your employees based on the descriptions for each subordinate.

a. Janet Jenkins currently earns $37,000. Her performance appraisal rating was very high. She is respected by her peers and is felt to be an asset to the work group. She is divorced and has three young children to support.
b. Russell Watts earns a salary of $32,000. His annual performance appraisal was average. Several members of the work group have spoken to you about the difficulty involved in Russell's job. They feel that it is a tough and demanding job and that he is doing his best.
c. Jack Perkins earns $27,250. His performance appraisal was below average and he seems to have difficulty adjusting to his co-workers. Jack has had a difficult time this past year. His wife passed away early in the year and his father has recently been diagnosed as terminally ill.
d. Rick Jacobson earns $25,000. His performance appraisal was above average. He is respected by his peers and is generally considered to be a "good guy."
e. Paula Merrill earns $25,850. Her performance appraisal was very high. Her peers are upset because they feel that she is working only to provide a second income. Moreover, her peers see her as trying to "show them up."

Share your results with other class members. Be prepared to explain your allocation of money.

BIZFLIX EXERCISES

Scent of a Woman: Freddie Bisco's Incentives

The scene from *Scent of a Woman* shows many aspects of incentive rewards and employee performance discussed in this chapter. Watch for types of incentives and the positive and negative effects of incentives as you view the scene.

Young Charlie Simms (Chris O'Donnell) wants to earn extra money over Thanksgiving weekend for airfare to go home during his Christmas break. He becomes a guide and caretaker for ill-tempered, retired, blind Lt. Col. Frank Slade (Al Pacino). Charlie, from Gresham, Oregon, is quiet and reserved and has had little experience with the opposite sex. He attends the exclusive Baird Preparatory School on a scholarship. His wild New York City weekend with Frank Slade bonds them forever. This film is a remake of *Profumo di Donna,* a 1974 Italian film.

This scene is an edited version from the end of the "Tango Lessons" segment and the beginning of "The Ferrari" segment that appear about halfway through the film. It follows the despondent hotel room scene and the tango lesson Slade gave Donna (Gabrielle Anwar) in The Waldorf Astoria restaurant. It begins shortly after Freddie Bisco (Leonard Gaines), the Ferrari salesman, says to Charlie, "Yeah, this is a valid Oregon driver's license, . . ." Freddie does not want to let either Charlie or Slade test-drive a Ferrari. The scene ends after Slade says, "I'm a gray ghost too." The film cuts to the Ferrari rounding a New York City street corner with Charlie driving.

What to Watch for and Ask Yourself

- Assume that Freddie Bisco receives a sales incentive for each Ferrari he sells. Does Freddie appear highly motivated by this incentive reward system? What is the evidence from the scene?
- Freddie does not work for Frank Slade. Is the $2,000 that Slade gives Freddie the same as a bonus discussed earlier in this chapter? If yes, which type of bonus is it?
- Did you perceive any negative effects of Freddie Bisco's incentives that he experienced in this scene?

case study 1

Pay-for-Performance: Lenox Hits Some Problems

Merit pay programs continue to be one of the more popular pay-for-performance compensation strategies. Yet, as compensation specialists note, these programs often fail to achieve their intended objective and can "backfire" when not adminstered properly. Consider the experience of Lenox Technology when it implemented a merit pay program for its managers.

There is no debate among industry analysts that the electronics industry is fiercely competitive. Therefore, strategic compensation programs tied to organization objectives are common and prized for improving employee performance. Furthermore, as one industry executive noted, "Compensation budgets are not always large and we need to get as much 'bang for our buck' as possible."

Lenox Technology, a five-year-old company based in central Florida, had traditionally given its managers annual increases based on the consumer price index for the company's metropolian area plus general across-the-board salary increases. This payment philosophy allowed all managers to maintain their standard of living while guaranteeing them a yearly raise. However, the biggest complaint with the pay program—as voiced by company officials—concerned the lack of motivation to increase employee performance, as all managers received the same annual increases regardless of individual performance.

In June 2002, Lenox, in what was described by one manager as a "shocking" announcement, implemented a merit pay incentive plan. Across-the-board increases and cost-of-living raises were eliminated. Annual salary increases were now to be based solely on individual performance. As Joe Tittle, compensation manager for Lenox stated, "The days of entitlements are over."

While some top-performing managers welcomed the merit raise program as a way to "finally get ahead," overall the new pay plan met with general dissatisfaction. Both managers and their immediate supervisors complained about the philosophy behind the program and its administration. What was once viewed by Lenox as a strategic way to maximize the salary budget and spur managerial performance has become a headache for company officials.

QUESTIONS

1. Identify and discuss concerns managers might have with Lenox's merit pay plan. What are the advantages for starting a merit pay program?
2. Why might supervising managers resist a merit pay program?
3. Develop a program to introduce a pay-for-performance plan in an organization. Consider what should be covered, who should be involved, and so on.
4. Develop a merit pay guideline chart based on the following levels of performance evaluation: superior, above average, average, below average, and poor. Use current cost-of-living figures for your area or salary survey data available to you to guide your merit percentage increases.

case study 2

Team-Based Incentive Rewards: It's Not All Roses

Network Cable, Inc., operates throughout the central and southern portions of Florida's east coast. With approximately 43,500 subscribers, the company is a service provider for cable TV and high-speed Internet connections. Network Cable operates in an area described as a "high-growth market."

In January 2003 Tara Gilbert, vice president of human resources for Network Cable, convinced company president and CEO Jeff Lesitner that restructuring the organization workforce into teams would benefit both Network Cable and its employees. Cost savings, improved morale, and team synergy were cited as inherent benefits of teams. Based on these assessments, in June 2003 a select group of three senior managers, plus Tara Gilbert and the company's financial officer, implemented teams within the company's installation department. Here, forty service installers were formed into eight teams of five installers each. Management set performance goals for the installation teams linked to attractive incentive rewards (cash bonuses above base salaries) when performance goals are reached. Performance measures included indexes for improved installation time, customer satisfaction scores, additional sales, equipment maintenance, and repair/callback problems. Each team could earn incentive bonuses up to a maximum of $15,000 annually with cash bonuses shared equally by each team member—a possible cash reward of $3,000 for each installer. Team bonuses after the first years were as follows: two teams, $15,000; one team, $12,500; one team, $7,300; one team, $3,150.

During August 2004 Tara Gilbert sent to all installers and their supervisors a survey requesting feedback on the satisfaction with teams and, specifically, the incentive rewards program. While survey results were generally positive, not all was rosy. Problems could be grouped into the following categories:

1. Some installers believed that various team members did not "buy into" the team concept and were simply "free riders"—average employees who benefited from the efforts of superior employees.
2. There was a general feeling that several teams were routinely assigned difficult installations that prevented them from achieving high performance goals.
3. Teams did not always display the motivation and synergy expected, as "bickering" was prevalent between average performers and super performers. Average performers complained that high performers made them look bad.
4. A high percentage of survey respondents (29 percent) felt the incentive rewards program was unfair and asked for a return to fixed across-the-board salary increases.

QUESTIONS

1. Do results from the survey illustrate typical complaints about teams and specifically about team incentive rewards? Explain.
2. If appropriate, what changes would you recommend to improve the incentive reward program? Be specific.
3. Would management have benefited from employee involvement in the initial design and implementation of the program? Explain.

NOTES AND REFERENCES

1. Jessica Smilko and Kathy Van Neck, "Rewarding Excellence through Variable Pay," *Benefits Quarterly* 20, no. 3 (Third Quarter 2004): 21–25.
2. Steven E. Gross and Helen M. Friedman, "Creating an Effective Total Reward Strategy: Holistic Approach Better Supports Business Success," *Benefits Quarterly* 20, no. 3 (Third Quarter 2004): 7. See also Kathleen H. Van Neck and Jessica E. Smilko, "Variable Pay Plans: Creating a Financial Partnership with the Work Force," *WorldatWork* 11, no. 4 (Fourth Quarter 2002): 74–79.
3. Michelle Conlin and Robert Berner, "A Little Less in the Envelope This Week," *Business Week*, February 18, 2002, 64.
4. John A. Menefee and Ryan O. Murphy, "Rewarding and Retaining the Best," *Benefits Quarterly* 20, no. 3 (Third Quarter 2004): 13–21.
5. Leo Jakobson, "Shell Goes Further," *Incentive* 178, no. 5 (May 2004): 20.
6. Libby Estell, "Cadillac Standards," *Innovative* 177, no. 7 (July 2003): 22–23.
7. Roisin Woolnough, "How to Set Up an Incentive Scheme," *Personnel Today*, February 14, 2004, 22.
8. Christian M. Ellis, "Improving the Impact of Performance Management," *Workspan* 45, no. 2 (February 2002): 7–8.
9. Gregory A. Stoskopf, "Taking Performance Management to the Next Level," *Workspan* 45, no. 2 (February 2002): 26–31.
10. George T. Milkovich and Jerry M. Newman, *Compensation*, 8th ed. (Boston: McGraw-Hill Irwin, 2005).
11. Chris Taylor. "On-the-Spot Incentives," *HR Magazine* 49, no. 5 (May 2004): 80–84.
12. Don Hellriegel and John W. Slocum, Jr., *Organizational Behavior*, 10th ed. (Mason, OH: South-Western, 2004): Chapter 6.
13. Robert Vecchio, *Organizational Behavior*, 5th ed. (Mason, OH: South-Western, 2002).
14. Steve Bates, "Top Pay for Best Performance," *HRMagazine* 48, no. 1 (January 2003): 31–38.
15. Danine Alati, "Ring of Honor," *Inventive* 177, no. 11 (November 2003): 34.
16. Kenneth Hein, "Motivators of the Year," *Inventive* 177, no. 10 (October 2003): 40.
17. Charlotte Garvey, "Meaningful Tokens of Appreciation," *HRMagazine* 49, no, 8 (August 2004): 102.
18. Ibid.

19. Bill Gauthier, "The Sales Compensation Challenge: Meeting the Diverse Needs of Multiple Business Units," *Workspan* 45, no. 3 (March 2002): 34–38.
20. David H. Johnston, "Strategic Initiative in Sales Compensation," *WorldatWork* 12, no. 2 (Second Quarter 2003): 75–82.
21. Paul R. Dorf and Lisette F. Masur, "The Tough Economy Prompts Companies to Shift Their Approach to Sales Compensation," *Journal of Organizational Excellence* 23, no. 2 (Spring 2004): 35–42.
22. David Fiedler, "Should You Adjust Your Sales Compensation?" *HRMagazine* 47, no. 2 (February 2002): 79–82.
23. Ellen Neuborne, "A Compensation Plan Checkup," *Sales and Marketing Management* 155, no. 5 (May 2003): 38–41.
24. Bruce R. Ellig, "Executive Compensation 101: Considering the Many Elements," *WorldatWork* 11, no. 1 (First Quarter 2002): 11–20.
25. Total annual compensation is the sum of an executive's annual and long-term compensation. Annual compensation consists of salary, bonus, and other yearly pay. Long-term compensation consists of stock awards, the value of any stock options exercised during the year, and any other long-term compensation (such as payouts from long-term incentive plans, director's fees, and special bonuses).
26. Louis Lavelle, "The Artificial Sweetener in CEO Pay," *Business Week*, September 10, 2001, 102.
27. Blair Jones, David Leach, and Jesse Purewal, "What's Next for the Compensation Committee?" *WorldatWork* 12, no. 4 (Fourth Quarter 2003): 6–14
28. Richard Ericson, "Addressing Structural Issues in Executive Incentive Plan Design," *WorldatWork* 11, no. 1 (First Quarter 2002): 59–69.
29. Daren Fonda and Daniel Kadlec, "The Rumble over Executive Pay," *Time*, May 31, 2004, 62–64.
30. Louis Lavelle, "A Payday for Performance," *Business Week*, April 18, 2005, 78
31. Donna Stettler, "Restricted Stock: The Option to Options?" *WorldatWork* 13, no. 1 (First Quarter 2004): 19–28. See also Seymour Burchman and Blair Jones, "The Future of Stock Options," *WorldatWork* 13, no. 1 (First Quarter 2004): 29–38.
32. Louis Lavelle, "Are Options Headed for Extinction?" *Business Week*, May 2, 2005, 12. See also Louis Lavelle, Amy Borrus, Robert D. Hof, and Joseph Weber, "Options Grow Onerous," *Business Week*, December 1, 2003, 36–37; and Nanette Byrnes, Andrew Park, Joseph Weber, and David Welch, "Beyond Options," *Business Week*, July 28, 2003, 34–36.
33. "An Unfair Rap for CEO Perks?" *Business Week*, June 7, 2004, 32.
34. Lavelle, "A Pay Day for Performance," 78.
35. Fonda and Kadleg, "The Rumble over Executive Pay," 62–64.
36. Louis Aguilar, "Exec-Worker Pay Gap Widens to Gulf," *The Denver Post*, July 8, 2001, 16A.
37. Reported in *The Wall Street Journal*, April 11, 2002, B15.
38. Fonda and Kadleg, "The Rumble over Executive Pay," 64.
39. Lavelle, "A Payday For Performance," 78
40. Nanette Byrnes, "Which Is Better—Stock or Options?" *Business Week*, July 21, 2003, 25.
41. Louis Lavelle, "Everybody Should Be a Little Nervous," *Business Week*, December 22, 2003, 42.
42. Leigh Rivenback, "Responsible Executive Compensation for a New Era of Accountability," *HRMagazine* 49, no. 9 (September 2004): 178. See also Michael Savage and Terry Adamson, "Employee Stock Options: New Valuation Responsibilities and Planning Opportunities," *Benefits Quarterly* 20, no. 3 (Third Quarter 2004): 34.
43. Jerry McAdams and Elizabeth J. Hawk, "Making Group Incentive Plans Work," *WorldatWork* 9, no. 3 (Third Quarter 2002): 28–34.
44. Milkovich and Newman, *Compensation.*
45. Gregory K. Shives and K. Dow Scott, "Gainsharing and EVA: The U.S. Postal Service Experience," *WorldatWork* 12, no. 1 (First Quarter 2003): 21–30.
46. K. Dow Scott, Jane Floyd, Philip G. Gordon, and James W. Bishop, "The Impact of the Scanlon Plan on Retail Store Performance," *WorldatWork* 11, no. 3 (Third Quarter 2002): 25–31.
47. The Rucker Plan uses a somewhat more complex formula for determining employee bonuses. For a detailed example of the Rucker bonus, see Milkovich and Newman, *Compensation.*
48. The standard of Improshare's measurement system is the base productivity factor (BPF), which is the ratio of standard direct labor hours produced to total actual hours worked in a base period. The productivity of subsequent periods is then measured by enlarging standard direct labor hours earned by the BPF ratio to establish Improshare hours (IH). The IH is then compared with actual hours worked in the same period. If earned hours exceed actual hours, 50 percent of the gain is divided by actual hours worked to establish a bonus percentage for all employees in the plan.
49. Seymour Burchman and Blair Jones, "The Future of Stock Options: From Starring Role to Ensemble Player," *WorldatWork* 13, no. 1 (First Quarter 2004): 29–38.
50. "Don't Get Rid of Stock Options, Fix 'Em," *Business Week*, March 4, 2002, 120.
51. J. Lynn Lunsford, "Boeing's Workers to Get a Windfall from Stock's Rise," *The Wall Street Journal*, July 2, 2004, B2.
52. Martin J. Somelofske, Rahim Bhayani, and Sarah Levin, "Stock Options: The Reports of My Demise Are Greatly Exaggerated," *WorldatWork* 12, no. 1 (First Quarter 2003): 48–56.
53. Corey Rosen, The National Center for Employee Ownership, interview by author, September 27, 2004. The National Center for Employee Ownership (NCEO) is a private, nonprofit membership and research organization that serves as the leading source of accurate, unbiased information on employee stock ownership plans (ESOPs), broadly granted employee stock options and related programs, and ownership culture. The NCEO can be reached at http://www.nceo.org or by phone at (510) 208-1300.
54. See http://www.nceo.org for descriptions of various ESOPs.

chapter 11

Employee Benefits

After studying this chapter, you should be able to

Describe the characteristics of a sound benefits program.

Indicate management concerns about the costs of employee benefits and discuss ways to control those costs.

Identify and explain the employee benefits required by law.

Discuss suggested ways to control the costs of healthcare programs.

Describe benefits that involve payment for time not worked.

Discuss the recent trends in retirement policies and programs.

Indicate the major factors involved in the management of pension plans.

Describe the types of work/life benefits that employers may provide.

According to a recent U.S. Chamber of Commerce study on employee benefits, one of the greatest challenges in business today is attracting and retaining quality employees. While challenging work, good working conditions, and fair wages and salaries contribute to employee attraction and retention, clearly an employer's benefits program is an important "magnet" drawing employees to employers. Furthermore, the U.S. Chamber of Commerce study noted that "employees are increasingly aware of the benefits they receive and how those benefits compare to what other companies are offering."[1] Additionally, because most benefits (almost 80 percent) are provided voluntarily by employers, they become both a significant cost and an employment advantage to employers, while providing needed psychological and physical assistance to employees.[2] The importance of benefits to both sides simply cannot be overstated.

Virtually all employers provide a variety of benefits to supplement the wages or salaries paid to their employees. These benefits, some of which are required by law, must be considered a part of their total compensation. Therefore, in this chapter we examine the characteristics of employee benefits programs. We will study the types of benefits required by law, the major discretionary benefits that employers offer, the employee services they provide, and the retirement programs in use. The chapter concludes with a discussion of popular—and highly important—work/life benefit programs.

Employee Benefits Programs

Employee benefits constitute an indirect form of compensation intended to improve the quality of the work lives and the personal lives of employees. As discussed later, benefits represent approximately 42 percent of total payroll costs to employers. In return, employers generally expect employees to be supportive of the organization and to be productive. Since employees have come to expect a full benefits "package," the motivational value of these benefits depends on how the benefits program is designed and communicated. Once viewed as a gift from the employer, benefits are now considered rights to which all employees are entitled.

HRIS and Employee Benefits

With the large number of benefits offered to employees today, administering an organization's benefits program can be both costly and time-consuming. Even for small employers with thirty to forty employees, keeping track of each employee's use of a benefit, or request for a change of benefits, can be cumbersome. For example, even the rather straightforward task of monitoring employee sick-leave usage becomes complex as the size of the organization grows.

Fortunately, interactive employee benefit systems are becoming mainstream at a large majority of both large and small employers, such as Cabrini College in Radnor, Pennsylvania; Parker Services, a temporary services provider in Seattle; Wells Fargo Bank; Prudential Insurance; and the City of Cincinnati, Ohio. The technology of the

Internet permits employees to access their benefits package, allowing both greater control and ownership of the benefits offered them. Part of the advantage of an Internet benefits system is that employees can obtain information on their own timetable. Speaking specifically about HRIS and healthcare benefits, Mindy Kairey, e-business leader of the healthcare management practice for Hewitt Associates LLC, explains, "The web puts benefits information right in the hands of the people who need it. Employees want to track their claims, review their current coverage levels, and compare their options. They want to take responsibility for their health plan."[3]

Online benefits programs create a form of self-service benefits administration. One intent of online programs is to provide greater flexibility in benefits selection. An important advantage to an interactive benefits program is the significant cost savings in benefits administration. Once an online system is operational, it is easy and inexpensive to adapt to employer and employee demands. However, while the Internet can be used effectively in benefits administration, security must always be a concern when transmitting benefits information.

Perhaps no part of the HR function is more technologically advanced than the administration of employee benefits programs. A wide variety of commercially developed software packages facilitate benefits administration in such areas as pension, variable pay, workers' compensation, health benefits, and time-off programs. Descriptions of and advertisements for a variety of benefits software programs are readily found in HR journals such as *Workforce* and *HRMagazine*. Software programs represent a cost-effective way to manage employee benefits programs when employers lack the resources or expertise to manage such programs.

Requirements for a Sound Benefits Program

The soundness of a benefits programs hinges on two factors: (1) selecting benefits that target important employee needs while promoting strategic organizational objectives and (2) effective administration of benefits programs. Gone are the days of providing a particular benefit because other employers are doing it, because someone in authority believes it is a good idea, or because the benefit is "popular" at the moment. Therefore, benefit specialists recommend paying attention to certain basic considerations.

Strategic Benefits Planning

Like any other component of the HR program, an employee benefits program should be based on specific objectives. The objectives an organization establishes will depend on many factors, including the size of the firm; its location, degree of unionization, and profitability; and industry patterns. Most important, these aims must be compatible with the organization's strategic compensation plan (see Chapter 9), including its philosophy and policies.[4]

The chief objectives of most benefits programs are as follows:

- Improve employee work satisfaction
- Meet employee health and security requirements
- Attract and motivate employees
- Retain top-performing employees
- Maintain a favorable competitive position

Further, these objectives must be considered within the framework of cost containment—a major issue for today's programs.[5]

Unless an organization has a flexible benefits plan (to be discussed later), a uniform package of benefits should be developed. This involves careful consideration of the various benefits that can be offered, the relative preference shown for each benefit by management and the employees, the estimated cost of each benefit, and the total amount of money available for the entire benefits package.[6]

Allowing for Employee Involvement

Before a new benefit is introduced, the need for it should first be determined through consultation with employees.[7] Many organizations establish committees composed of managers and employees to administer, interpret, and oversee their benefits policies. Opinion surveys are also used to obtain employee input. Having employees participate in designing benefits programs helps ensure that management is moving in the direction of satisfying employee wants. For example, a medium-sized technology company used focus groups to determine employee preferences before implementing a managed-care program. Feedback from the focus groups showed that employees preferred a point-of-service plan with the option of using physicians outside the network when needed. Employees indicated that they would rather pay higher copayments as a trade-off to receiving lower premiums. The focus groups also told management that employee meetings were the best way to communicate the program.

Benefits for a Diverse Workforce

To serve their intended purpose, employee benefits programs must reflect the changes that are continually occurring within our society. Particularly significant are changes in the diversity and lifestyles of the workforce. For example, recent figures from the U.S. Census Bureau show that married-couple households have declined from nearly 80 percent in the 1950s to approximately 51 percent today. Unmarried people make up 42 percent of the workforce. These demographic shifts, and others noted throughout the text, mandate that organizations design benefit packages that match the changing U.S. population. Fortunately, more employers have begun to tailor their benefit programs to be family friendly. (Specific work/life benefits are discussed later in the chapter.) For example, more than 40 percent of the 500 largest companies have started to revise their marriage-centric policies. Merrill Lynch and Bank of America accommodate demographic shifts by offering extended family benefits.[8] At Xerox, employees receive $10,000 on joining the company, on top of a standard benefits package, to spend on whatever benefits best fit their individual or family needs. At Prudential Securities, cohabitants can receive health benefits for opposite- or same-sex partners.[9] These examples simply illustrate the need for benefits programs that take into account a highly diversified workforce in order to attract highly capable employees.

Unfortunately, benefit plans sometimes provide little advantage to employees, limiting the organization's ability to attract or retain quality employees. For example, many employers provide unneeded medical benefits to the young and single in the form of dependents' coverage. Likewise, a well-designed—and costly—defined-benefits pension program may not serve the needs of employees or the employer of a predominately younger workforce.

Providing for Flexibility

flexible benefits plans (cafeteria plans)
Benefit plans that enable individual employees to choose the benefits that are best suited to their particular needs

To accommodate the individual needs of employees, organizations may offer **flexible benefits plans,** also known as **cafeteria plans.** These plans enable individual employees to choose the benefits that are best suited to their particular needs. They also prevent certain benefits from being wasted on employees who have no need for them. Typically, employees are offered a basic or core benefits package of life and health insurance, sick leave, and vacation. Requiring a core set of benefits ensures that employees have a minimum level of coverage to protect against unforeseen financial hardships. Employees are then given a specified number of credits they may use to "buy" whatever other benefits they need.[10] Other benefit options might include prepaid legal services, financial planning, and long-term care insurance. Compensation specialists often see flexible benefits plans as ideal. Employees select the benefits of greatest value to them, while employers manage benefits costs by limiting the dollars employees have to spend. Figure 11.1 lists the most frequently cited advantages and disadvantages of flexible benefits programs.

Communicating Employee Benefits Information

Consider this research finding. A study on healthcare benefits by Towers Perrin found that many employees do not believe what their employers tell them about soaring benefits costs, and employees and employers are at loggerheads over how

Figure 11.1 Flexible Benefits Plans: Advantages and Disadvantages

ADVANTAGES

- Employees select benefits to match their individual needs.
- Benefit selections adapt to a constantly changing (diversified) workforce.
- Employees gain greater understanding of the benefits offered to them and the costs incurred.
- Employers maximize the psychological value of their benefits program by paying only for highly desired benefits.
- Employers limit benefit costs by allowing employees to "buy" benefits only up to a maximum (defined) amount.
- Employers gain competitive advantage in the recruiting and retention of employees.

DISADVANTAGES

- Poor employee benefits selection results in unwanted financial costs.
- There are certain added costs to establishing and maintaining the flexible plan.
- Employees may choose benefits of high use to them that increase employer premium costs.

effectively benefits are used. The Towers Perrin study concluded by noting that the credibility gap is largely caused by poor benefits communication and lack of employee trust.[11] Interestingly, benefit specialists remark that the true measure of a successful benefits program is the degree of trust, understanding, and appreciation it earns from the employees.[12]

The communication of employee benefits information improved significantly with passage of the Employee Retirement Income Security Act (ERISA) in 1974. The act requires that employees be informed about their pension and certain other benefits in a manner calculated to be understood by the average employee. Additionally, employees can sue their employers for misleading them about health and welfare benefits under ERISA. Problems can arise when managers discuss benefits with groups of employees or in one-on-one talks and employees receive inaccurate information. Or a manager could mislead an employee by stating that the organization's insurance policy does not cover a particular condition when, in fact, it does or that a maternity leave provision is 120 days when the plan is actually 60 days. These potential problems underscore the importance of communicating benefit information accurately and unambiguously.

Employers use an array of methods to communicate benefits to employees, such as the following:

- In-house publications (employee handbooks and organizational newsletters)
- Group meeting and training classes
- Audiocassettes/videotapes
- Bulletin boards
- Payroll inserts/pay stub messages
- Specialty brochures

Employee self-service (ESS) systems have made it possible for employees to gain information about their benefits plans, enroll in their plans of choice, change benefits coverage, alter W-4 designations, or simply inquire about the status of their various benefit accounts without ever contacting an HR representative. Coopers & Lybrand offers a Benefits Information Line that allows employers to provide employees with instant access to a wide variety of benefits and HR information by telephone. Individual account information is available upon entering a personal identification number (PIN). Other organizations use networked PCs or multimedia kiosks as the basis of their self-service system. These approaches permit employees to click on icons to access different benefits and type in new information to update their records. Once an update or change is made, the new information is permanently entered into the organization's HR information system without the need for paperwork. Highlights in HRM 1 presents suggestions for designing a professional benefits communication program.

When communicating employee benefits, the best advice is to use multiple media techniques. Different employee groups have different ways of learning and distinct preferences in how they prefer to receive information. Also, the level of complexity of the benefit will likely determine media selection.[13]

In addition to having general information, it is important for each employee to have a current statement of the status of her or his benefits. The usual means is the personalized computer-generated statement of benefits. As Highlights in HRM 2 shows, this benefits cost statement can be one of the best ways of slicing through a maze of technicalities to provide concise data to employees about the status of their personal benefits.[14]

Highlights in HRM 1

Crafting an Effective Benefits Communication Program

A well-designed benefits communication program greatly enhances employees' appreciation of their benefits while ensuring that employers receive the intended value of these offerings. An effective program provides frequent information to employees in a cost-effective and timely manner. Compensation specialists recommend the following points when administering a benefits communication program.

In building an identity:

- Design materials that are eye-catching and of high interest to employees.
- Develop a graphic logo for all material.
- Identify a theme for the benefits program.

In writing benefits materials:

- Avoid complex language when describing benefits. Clear, concise, and understandable language is a must.
- Provide numerous examples to illustrate benefit specifics.
- Explain all benefits in an open and honest manner. Do not attempt to conceal unpleasant news.
- Explain the purpose behind the benefit and the value of the benefit to employees.

In publicizing benefits information:

- Use all popular employee communication techniques.
- Maintain employee self-service (ESS) technology to disseminate benefits information and to update employee benefits selections.
- Use voice mail to send benefits information.
- Employ presentation software such as PowerPoint or Lotus Freelance to present information to groups of employees.
- Maintain a benefits hotline to answer employee questions.

Concerns of Management

Managing an employee benefits program requires close attention to the many forces that must be kept in balance if the program is to succeed. Management must consider union demands, the benefits other employers are offering, tax consequences, rising costs, and domestic partner benefits. We will briefly examine the last two concerns.

The High Cost of Providing Benefits

According to a 2003 U.S. Chamber of Commerce study, the cost of employee benefits in that year averaged 42.3 percent of payroll, as shown in Highlights in HRM 3.[15] The average distribution of these benefits was $18,000 per employee per year. Costs of benefits were higher in manufacturing than in nonmanufacturing industries. Study Highlights in HRM 3 to obtain an overview of the type of benefits to be discussed in this chapter.

Highlights in HRM 2

A Personalized Statement of Benefits Costs

Highlights of Your Telstar Global, Inc., Benefits Program

ID: 000-00-0000 Nancy Doe Statement Date: 3-15-2005

Benefits	Annual Cost You	Annual Cost Company	Total
Insurance Programs			
1. Health insurance	942.48	2,318.32	3,260.80
2. Dental insurance	254.28	301.00	555.28
3. Life insurance			
Employee—$80,000	303.80		303.80
Spouse—$10,000	457.60	37.68	495.28
Dependent—$5,000	11.04		11.04
4. Short-term disability	201.04		201.04
5. Long-term disability		207.16	207.16
6. Workers' compensation		252.84	252.84
7. Unemployment compensation		31.60	31.60
Retirement program	3,547.44	3,547.44	7,094.88
Social Security			
FICA/OASDI	2,501.20	2,501.20	5,002.40
Medicare	786.27	786.27	1,572.54
Totals	$9,005.15	$9,983.51	$18,988.66

Hourly Rate: $21.92 Annual Salary: $44,719.00

Holidays (10 Days) 80.00 Hrs. Value: $1,753.60

Because many benefits represent a fixed rather than a variable cost, management must decide whether it can afford this cost given the organization's financial position. As managers can readily attest, if an organization is forced to discontinue a benefit, the negative effects of cutting it may outweigh any positive effects that accrued from providing it.[16]

A current trend (one not universally liked by employees) is for employers to require employees to pay part of the costs of certain benefits (for example, through copayments or higher deductibles), especially medical coverage. At all times, benefit plan administrators are expected to select vendors of benefit services who have the most to offer for the cost. Furthermore, besides the actual costs of employee benefits,

U.S. Chamber of Commerce Employee Benefits Survey—2003

Type of Benefit	Percent of Payroll %: Total, All Companies	Percent of Payroll %: Total, Manufacturing	Percent of Payroll %: Total, Non-Manufacturing	Annual Dollars per Employee $: Total, All Companies	Annual Dollars per Employee $: Total, Manufacturing	Annual Dollars per Employee $: Total, Non-Manufacturing
Total Number of Companies Reporting	372	115	257	372	115	257
Total Number of Full-Time Equivalent Employees Reported	506,578	61,253	445,325	506,578	61,253	445,325
Total Benefits	42.3%	38.0%	42.9%	$18,000	$17,690	$18,043
Legally Required	8.7	9.8	8.6	3,835	4,466	3,748
Federally Required Payroll Taxes	7.2	7.5	7.2	3,169	3,445	3,131
Unemployment Compensation	0.4	0.8	0.4	175	344	151
Workers' Compensation Insurance	1.1	1.4	1.0	482	638	460
Other	0.0	0.1	0.0	10	40	6
Payments for Time Not Worked	11.6	9.7	11.9	4,970	4,371	5,053
Payments for Holidays	3.2	2.2	3.3	1,355	1,013	1,402
Paid Breaks, Etc.	0.6	1.3	0.5	240	579	193
Sick Leave Pay	2.0	0.4	2.2	775	195	855
Payments for Vacations	4.0	2.7	4.1	1,703	1,270	1,762
Paid Time Off	1.6	2.8	1.4	732	1,230	663
Family and Medical Leave Pay	0.1	0.0	0.1	43	15	47
Other	0.2	0.2	0.2	122	69	130
Medical and Medically Related Payments	15.2	14.0	15.3	6,277	6,626	6,229
STD, Sickness, or Accident Insurance	0.2	0.4	0.2	97	208	81
LTD or Wage Continuation	0.2	0.4	0.2	118	190	108
Medical Insurance Premiums	11.6	11.3	11.6	4,757	5,311	4,680
Dental Insurance Premiums	0.4	0.8	0.4	207	380	183
Vision Care	0.0	0.1	0.0	15	65	8
Retiree Medical Insurance Premiums	2.0	0.2	2.3	766	89	859
Life Insurance and Death	0.2	0.4	0.2	99	176	88
Prescription Drug Coverage	0.3	0.2	0.3	156	93	165
Other	0.0	0.0	0.0	11	2	12
Administration Costs	0.1	0.2	0.1	53	112	45
Retirement and Savings	6.2	3.5	6.6	2,634	1,694	2,763
Defined Benefit Pension Plan	4.2	1.0	4.6	1,632	448	1,795
Cash Balance or Other Hybrid Plan	0.2	0.0	0.2	69	16	76
401K and similar	1.5	2.0	1.4	712	923	683
Profit-Sharing	0.2	0.2	0.1	77	101	74
Stock Bonus/ESOP	0.1	0.2	0.0	33	129	20
Other	0.1	0.1	0.1	64	35	68
Administration Costs	0.1	0.1	0.1	46	43	47
Miscellaneous Benefit Pay	0.6	1.1	0.5	284	533	250
Severance Pay	0.2	0.7	0.2	129	365	97
Child Care	0.0	0.0	0.0	2	0	2
Employee Education Expenditures	0.2	0.3	0.2	95	124	91
Discounts	0.0	0.1	0.0	12	28	10
Other	0.1	0.0	0.1	46	15	50

Source: Reprinted with permission of the U.S. Chamber of Commerce. *The 2003 Employee Benefits Study,* prepared and published by the U.S. Chamber of Commerce. To order call 1-800-638-6582.

there are the costs of administering them. These include direct labor costs, overhead charges, office space, and equipment and technology.

Domestic Partner Benefits

According to the Society for Human Resource Management (SHRM) 2004 benefits survey, 27 percent of responding employers offer domestic partner benefits to same-sex partners and 34 percent provide them to opposite-sex partners.[17] About 40 percent of Fortune 500 companies offer domestic-partner benefits, including nearly 70 percent of the 50 top businesses.[18] With a diverse and more openly vocal work group, more employers are granting benefits to employees who establish a *domestic partnership*, including both same-sex and unmarried opposite-sex couples.[19] In some industries, domestic partner coverage is so prevalent that companies lose competitive advantage in attracting and retaining quality employees if this coverage is denied specific individuals. While the definition of a domestic partnership varies, the description used by Apple Computer is compatible with most definitions. A domestic partner, the company says, is "a person over age 18 who shares living quarters with another adult in an exclusive, committed relationship in which the partners are responsible for each other's common welfare." A standard definition of domestic partnership contains the following:

- A minimum age requirement
- A requirement that the couple live together
- A specification of financial interdependence
- A requirement that the relationship be a permanent one
- A requirement that each not be a blood relative[20]

Employers who offer domestic partnership coverage typically require employees to sign an "Affidavit of Domestic Partnership" attesting to their relationship.

Organizations that offer benefits to domestic partners are simply extending current benefits, normally full medical and dental plans, to employees. Cost increases to employers are those associated with adding new members to a current benefits plan and plan usage by employees. Costs are generally low, from less than 1 percent to about 2 percent of total benefits costs for the organization.[21] However, employer health benefits provided to unmarried partners, unlike health benefits for spouses, are taxable under federal law. This difference can be costly. Furthermore, Congress recently passed the Defense of Marriage Act, which provides that a same-sex domestic partner may not be treated as an employee's spouse for purposes of federal law.[22] One implication is that married gays are not eligible for Social Security survival benefits or other benefits governed by federal law.[23] Despite these issues, well-known organizations such as Viacom, Gannett Company (publisher of *USA Today*), Levi Strauss, Silicon Graphics, Warner Bros., Stanford University, and the City of Berkeley, California, offer benefits to domestic partners of employees.

Employee Benefits Required by Law

Legally required employee benefits constitute nearly a quarter of the benefits package that employers provide. These benefits include employer contributions to Social Security, unemployment insurance, and workers' compensation insurance. We will discuss each of these benefits.

Social Security Insurance

USING THE INTERNET

The web site of the Department of Labor provides extensive information about legally required benefits and specific requirements for compliance. Go to the Student Resources at:

http://bohlander.swlearning.com

Passed in 1935, the Social Security Act provides an insurance plan designed to protect covered individuals against loss of earnings resulting from various causes. These causes may include retirement, unemployment, disability, or, in the case of dependents, the death of the worker supporting them. Thus, as with any type of casualty insurance, Social Security does not pay off except in the case where a loss of income is actually incurred through loss of employment.

To be eligible for old-age and survivors' insurance (OASI) as well as disability and unemployment insurance under the Social Security Act, an individual must have been engaged in employment covered by the act. Most employment in private enterprise, most types of self-employment, active military service after 1956, and employment in certain nonprofit organizations and governmental agencies are subject to coverage under the act.[24] Railroad workers and civil service employees who are covered by their own systems and some occupational groups, under certain conditions, are exempted from the act.

USING THE INTERNET

At the Social Security Administration web site, you can download software that allows you to estimate your own personal SS benefit. Go to the Student Resources at:

http://bohlander.swlearning.com

The Social Security program is supported by means of a tax levied against an employee's earnings that must be matched by the employer in each pay period. The tax revenues are used to pay three major types of benefits: (1) old-age insurance benefits, (2) disability benefits, and (3) survivors' insurance benefits. Because of the continual changes that result from legislation and administrative rulings, as well as the complexities of making determinations of an individual's rights under Social Security, we will describe these benefits only in general terms.

To qualify for old-age insurance benefits, a person must have reached retirement age and be fully insured. A *fully insured person* has earned forty credits—a maximum of four credits a year for ten years, based on annual earnings, a figure adjusted annually. The amount of monthly Social Security retirement benefits is based on earnings, adjusted for inflation, over the years an individual is covered by Social Security.[25] Under Social Security insurance guidelines, an individual's *full retirement age* depends on year of birth. For example, because of longer life expectancies, full retirement age is increasing for people born after 1938. However, individuals can receive Social Security benefits as early as age 62 but the amount received each month will be less than monthly benefits received at full retirement age.

To receive old-age insurance benefits, covered individuals must also meet the *retirement earnings test.* The Senior Citizens' Freedom of Work Act of 2000 removed the earnings cap for people between ages 65 and 70; however, there is an earnings cap for those who take early retirement and collect Social Security before they reach their full retirement age.[26] This limitation on earnings does not include income from sources other than gainful employment, such as investments or pensions.

The Social Security program provides disability benefits to workers too severely disabled to engage in "substantial gainful work." To be eligible for such benefits, however, an individual's disability must have existed for at least six months and must be expected to continue for at least twelve months or be expected to result in death. After receiving disability payments for twenty-four months, a disabled person receives Medicare protection. Those eligible for disability benefits, furthermore, must have worked under Social Security long enough and recently enough before becoming disabled. Disability benefits, which include auxiliary benefits for dependents, are computed on the same basis as retirement benefits and are converted to retirement benefits when the individual reaches age 65.

Survivors' insurance benefits represent a form of life insurance paid to members of a deceased person's family who meet the eligibility requirements. Survivors' benefits can be paid only if the deceased worker had credit for a certain amount of time spent in work covered by Social Security. The exact amount of work credit needed depends on the worker's age at death. As with other benefits discussed earlier, the *amount* of benefit survivors receive is based on the worker's lifetime earnings in work covered by Social Security.

The Social Security Administration also administers the Medicare program. Retired people age 65 or older are eligible for Medicare, which includes both medical and hospital insurance. A fully insured individual pays no Medicare premiums, while those with less than forty credits pay monthly premiums of $206 for hospital insurance and $78 for medical insurance.

Unemployment Insurance

Employees who have been working in employment covered by the Social Security Act and who are laid off may be eligible for up to twenty-six weeks of unemployment insurance benefits during their unemployment. Eligible workers must submit an application for unemployment compensation with their state employment agency, register for available work, and be willing to accept any suitable employment that may be offered to them. However, the term "suitable" gives individuals considerable discretion in accepting or rejecting job offers.

The amount of compensation that workers are eligible to receive, which varies among states, is determined by their previous wage rate and previous period of employment. Funds for unemployment compensation are derived from a federal payroll tax based on the wages paid to each employee, up to an established maximum. The major portion of this tax is refunded to the individual states, which in turn operate their unemployment compensation programs in accordance with minimum standards prescribed by the federal government.

Workers' Compensation Insurance

workers' compensation insurance
Federal- or state-mandated insurance provided to workers to defray the loss of income and cost of treatment due to work-related injuries or illness

Both state and federal **workers' compensation insurance** is based on the theory that the cost of work-related accidents and illnesses should be considered one of the costs of doing business. Individual employees should not be required to bear the cost of their treatment or loss of income, nor should they be subjected to complicated, delaying, and expensive legal procedures.

Workers' compensation laws typically provide that employees will be paid a disability benefit based on a percentage of their wages. Each state also specifies the length of the period of payment and usually indicates a maximum amount that may be paid. Benefits, which vary from state to state, are generally provided for four types of disability: (1) permanent partial disability, (2) permanent total disability, (3) temporary partial disability, and (4) temporary total disability. Disabilities may result from injuries or accidents, as well as from occupational diseases such as black lung, radiation illness, and asbestosis. Before any workers' compensation claim will be allowed, though, the work-relatedness of the disability must be established. Also, the evaluation of the claimant by a physician trained in occupational medicine is an essential part of the claim process.

In addition to the disability benefits, provision is made for payment of medical and hospitalization expenses up to certain limits, and in all states, death benefits are paid to survivors of the employee. Commissions are established to resolve claims at little or no legal expense to the claimant.

A major concern to employers nationwide is the high cost of workers' compensation claims. The direct cost of claims to U.S. businesses has been around $70 billion annually. Swelling medical costs and benefits paid to workers are the major factors. In addition, there are more disorders today that are harder to assess objectively, such as back pain. Then too, claims are sometimes made for ailments that may have little to do with the workplace, such as hearing loss, stress, and cancer.

While employers in all states pay "workers' comp" insurance, the amount they pay—through payroll taxes—varies. Three factors influence the employer's insurance rate: (1) the risk of injury or illness for an occupation, (2) each state's level of benefits for injuries sustained by employees, and (3) the company's frequency and severity of employee injuries (referred to as the company's experience rating). Not surprisingly, organizations will strive to have good safety records (see Chapter 12 on creating a safe work environment) in order to pay a lower payroll tax rate. Specific steps that managers and supervisors can take to control workers' compensation costs are given in Figure 11.2.

Consolidated Omnibus Budget Reconciliation Act (COBRA)

The Consolidated Omnibus Budget Reconciliation Act of 1986 (COBRA) mandates that employers make health coverage—at the same rate the employer would pay—available to employees, their spouses, and their dependents on termination of employment, death, or divorce.[27] The coverage must be offered for between 18 and 36 months depending on qualifying guidelines. Thus, former employees and their families benefit by paying a lower premium for health coverage than is available to individual policyholders. While the former employee pays the premiums, employers have to establish procedures to collect premiums and to keep track of former employees and their dependents.

Figure 11.2 **Reducing Workers' Comp Costs: Key Areas**

1. Perform an audit to assess high-risk areas within a workplace.
2. Prevent injuries by proper ergonomic design of the job and effective assessment of job candidates.
3. Provide quality medical care to injured employees by physicians with experience and preferably with training in occupational health.
4. Reduce litigation by effective communication between the employer and the injured worker.
5. Manage the care of an injured worker from the injury until return to work. Keep a partially recovered employee at the work site.
6. Provide extensive worker training in all related health and safety areas.

Mothers of newborn children are guaranteed 12 weeks of unpaid leave under the provisions of the Family and Medical Leave Act.

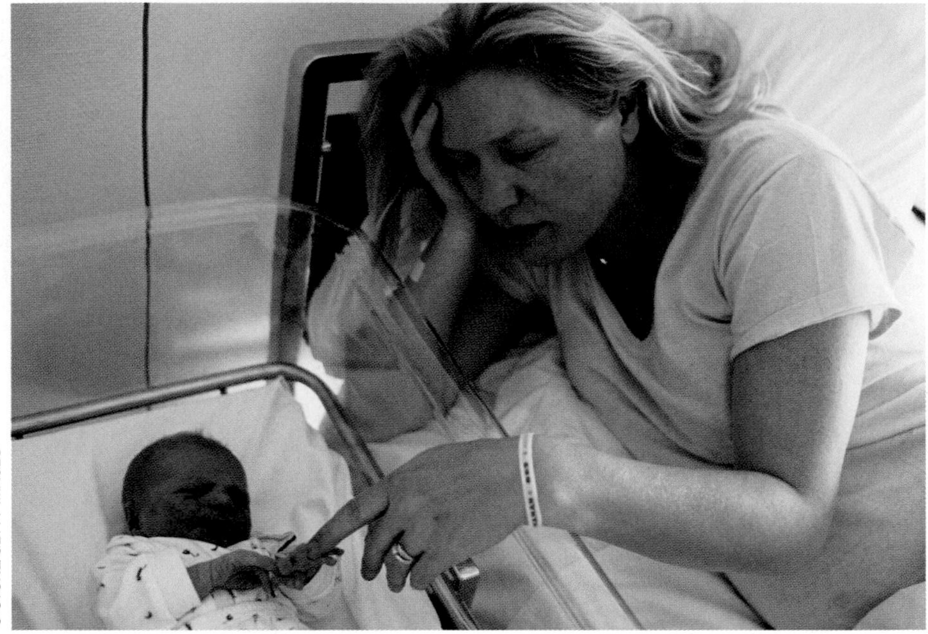

The Family and Medical Leave Act

The Family and Medical Leave Act (FMLA) was passed and became effective on August 5, 1993.[28] The FMLA applies to employers having fifty or more employees during twenty or more calendar workweeks in the current or preceding year. A covered employer must grant an eligible employee up to a total of twelve workweeks of unpaid leave in a twelve-month period for one or more of the following reasons:

- Birth of and care for a newborn child
- Adoption or foster care placement of a child
- Care for an immediate family member (spouse, child, or parent) with a serious medical condition
- Serious health condition of the employee

An employer may require that the need for medical leave be supported by a certification issued by a healthcare provider.[29] Highlights in HRM 4 shows the federally required poster for the FMLA. In studying the poster, note the other important stipulations, such as enforcement and unlawful acts, which are of direct concern to managers.

Like many laws pertaining to HRM, the FMLA is simple in principle but requires revising policies and procedures for compliance. This law affects an organization's benefits program in several of its provisions: It mandates continuation of medical coverage, it prohibits loss of accrued benefits, it provides for restoration of benefits after leave, it permits substitution of paid leave and vacation during leave, it makes communication and notice compulsory, and it prohibits waiver of benefits. On return from FMLA leave, an employee must be restored to his or her original job or to an "equivalent" job. Equivalent jobs are those identical to the original job in

Highlights in HRM 4

"Your Right": Another Federally Required Poster

Your Rights
Under The
Family and Medical Leave Act of 1993

FMLA requires covered employers to provide up to 12 weeks of unpaid, job-protected leave to "eligible" employees for certain family and medical reasons. Employees are eligible if they have worked for a covered employer for at least one year, and for 1,250 hours over the previous 12 months, and if there are at least 50 employees within 75 miles.

Reasons For Taking Leave:

Unpaid leave must be granted for *any* of the following reasons:

- to care for the employee's child after birth, or placement for adoption or foster care;
- to care for the employee's spouse, son or daughter, or parent, who has a serious health condition; or
- for a serious health condition that makes the employee unable to perform the employee's job.

At the employee's or employer's option, certain kinds of *paid* leave may be substituted for unpaid leave.

Advance Notice and Medical Certification:

The employee may be required to provide advance leave notice and medical certification. Taking of leave may be denied if requirements are not met.

- The employee ordinarily must provide 30 days advance notice when the leave is "foreseeable."
- An employer may require medical certification to support a request for leave because of a serious health condition, and may require second or third opinions (at the employer's expense) and a fitness for duty report to return to work.

Job Benefits and Protection:

- For the duration of FMLA leave, the employer must maintain the employee's health coverage under any "group health plan."
- Upon return from FMLA leave, most employees must be restored to their original or equivalent positions with equivalent pay, benefits, and other employment terms.
- The use of FMLA leave cannot result in the loss of any employment benefit that accrued prior to the start of an employee's leave.

Unlawful Acts By Employers:

FMLA makes it unlawful for any employer to:

- interfere with, restrain, or deny the exercise of any right provided under FMLA:
- discharge or discriminate against any person for opposing any practice made unlawful by FMLA or for involvement in any proceeding under or relating to FMLA.

Enforcement:

- The U.S. Department of Labor is authorized to investigate and resolve complaints of violations.
- An eligible employee may bring a civil action against an employer for violations.

FMLA does not affect any Federal or State law prohibiting discrimination, or supersede any State or local law or collective bargaining agreement which provides greater family or medical leave rights.

For Additional Information:

Contact the nearest office of the Wage and Hour Division, listed in most telephone directories under U.S. Government, Department of Labor.

U.S. Department of Labor
Employment Standards Administration
Wage and Hour Division
Washington, D.C. 20210

WH Publication 1420
June 1993

GPO : 1993 O - 355-556

Note: Other federally required posters are reproduced in Chapters 3, 9, and 12.

terms of pay, benefits, and other employment terms and conditions. It is important to remember that employers cannot penalize employees for requesting or taking FMLA leave in any employment action including hiring, promotion, transfer, training, or disciplinary action.

Since passage of the FMLA, employers, employees, and the courts have struggled with both the application and interpretation of the law. For example, what illnesses or injuries should be considered a "serious health condition"? Or, when an employee returns from leave and finds his or her job filled, what constitutes an equivalent job? Therefore, managers or supervisors faced with legal or administrative questions regarding the FMLA are advised to seek assistance from HR before proceeding with an employee's FMLA leave request.[30]

The Older Workers Benefit Protection Act

Passed by Congress in 1990, the Older Workers Benefit Protection Act (OWBPA) is a companion piece of legislation to the Age Discrimination in Employment Act (ADEA).[31] (See Chapter 3.) Specifically, the OWBPA prohibits age-based discrimination in early retirement and other benefit plans. The act imposes strict guidelines on employers who seek to have employees sign release forms waiving their right to pursue age discrimination claims under the ADEA.[32] When employers desire to obtain release waivers from employees, the OWBPA requires that a valid waiver must be voluntary and written in a manner that is understandable to the parties involved. Furthermore, employers must inform employees that they have the right to consult with an attorney before signing the waiver.

Discretionary Major Employee Benefits

Employee benefits may be categorized in different ways. In Highlights in HRM 3, we saw the categories of benefits that have been used by the U.S. Chamber of Commerce. In the following discussion, we will use a somewhat different but compatible grouping of benefits to highlight the important issues and trends in managing an employee benefits program.

Healthcare Benefits

The benefits that receive the most attention from employers today because of high costs and employee concern are healthcare benefits. In the past, health insurance plans covered only medical, surgical, and hospital expenses. Today employers include prescription drugs as well as dental, optical, and mental healthcare benefits in the package they offer their workers.

High Healthcare Costs

The concern over high healthcare costs is illustrated by the following points:

- Since 1980, the employer cost of providing medical and dental costs has increased more than 250 percent.[33]
- Health insurance costs for employees soared by 16 percent in 2004, the fifth straight year of double-digit increases.

"He's out of intensive care and back into ordinary expensive care."

Source: Used with permission of Glenn Bernhardt. From *The Saturday Evening Post* 273, no. 5 (September/October 2001).

- Double-digit increases in healthcare will likely continue through this decade.
- Healthcare spending has been steadily rising as a share of the economy, up from 5.29 percent in 1950 to more than 16 percent in 2004.[34]
- The average worker will spend $2,412 in premiums for family healthcare coverage in 2004, an increase of 49 percent since 2000.[35]

According to a U.S. Chamber of Commerce study, medical and medical-related benefits costs (employers' share) average 15.2 percent of payroll costs. This represents an annual expense of $4,757 for medical insurance premiums for each active employee. Prescription drug coverage, a growing cost factor to employers, costs $156 annually per employee (see Highlights in HRM 3).

The growth in healthcare costs is attributed to a number of factors, including federal legislation, changes in Medicare pricing, the greater need for healthcare by an aging population, the costs of technological advances in medicine, skyrocketing malpractice insurance rates, rising costs of drugs, and overuse of costly healthcare services.[36]

Cost Containment

With the significant rise in healthcare costs, it is understandable that employers seek relief from these expenses.[37] The major approaches used to contain the costs of healthcare benefits include reductions in coverage, increased deductibles or copayments, and increased coordination of benefits to make sure the same expense is not paid by more than one insurance reimbursement. Highlights in HRM 5 shows additional cost-containment strategies used by employers.[38] Furthermore, the containment of healthcare expenses can be achieved through various medical delivery systems such as health maintenance organizations, preferred provider organizations, and different consumer-driven healthcare plans.

health maintenance organizations (HMOs)
Organizations of physicians and healthcare professionals that provide a wide range of services to subscribers and dependents on a prepaid basis

preferred provider organization (PPO)
A group of physicians who establish an organization that guarantees lower healthcare costs to the employer

Health maintenance organizations (HMOs) are organizations of physicians and other healthcare professionals that provide a wide range of services to subscribers and their dependents on a prepaid basis. HMOs offer routine medical services at a specific site for a fixed fee for each employee visit. Employers pay a fixed annual fee to the HMO to cover the majority of their employees' medical costs. Because they must provide all covered services for a fixed dollar amount, HMOs generally emphasize preventive care and early intervention. As a result of the federal HMO Act of 1973, employers having twenty-five or more employees and a health insurance plan must offer a federally qualified HMO as a voluntary option.

Preferred provider organizations have also helped to contain costs. The **preferred provider organization (PPO)** is a group of physicians who establish an organization or a network of doctors that guarantees lower costs to the employer

Highlights in HRM 5

Employers Methods for Containing Healthcare Costs

- Pre-admission certification for surgical procedures.
- Financial incentives for outpatient surgery and testing.
- Mail-order prescription drug program and medical drug discount cards.
- Mandatory second opinions for surgical procedures.
- Alternative approaches to healthcare treatment such as herbal therapy or homeopathy.
- Educational programs encouraging healthcare consumers to assume more responsibility and accountability for the cost and quality of their healthcare.
- Promoting web sites or printed materials that list common conditions, treatment, drug prices, and effectiveness.
- Implementation of step therapy programs.
- Multi-tier hospital coverage networks that allow employees to choose from a variety of hospitals with small, moderate, and steep copayments at the point of service.
- Use of variable copayments (for example, $10 for physician and $25 for specialists).
- The consolidation of healthcare plans offered by employers.
- Requiring employees to pay an additional cost if a working spouse refuses coverage from his or her employer.
- Customized healthcare benefits design allowing employees to purchase riders to increase the level of benefits provided.
- Promotion of wellness and employee assistance programs.
- Automated benefits functions.
- Promoting quality, patient safety, and positive outcomes in health plans by using a variety of health plan assessment tools such as the Joint Commission on Accreditation of Healthcare Organizations.
- Implementation of a disease management program.

A survey of methods used by employers to control healthcare costs can be found in "Despite Rising Health-Care Costs, Few Companies Have Cut Benefits," *HRFocus* 81, no. 9 (September 2004): 3–5.

through lower service charges or agreed-on utilization controls (such as a reduced number of diagnostic tests per employee). Unlike HMOs, where employees may have little choice in the doctor they see, PPOs allow employees to select from a list of physicians (participating doctors) their doctor of choice. Normally, a number of physicians are available to choose from for different medical needs.

consumer-driven health plan (CDHP)
A medical insurance plan financed by employer contributions to an employee's individual healthcare spending account

Another important, and newer, medical cost containment strategy is consumer-driven health plans, also referred to as defined-contribution health plans, medical savings accounts (MSAs), health savings accounts (HSAs), flexible spending accounts (FSAs), or health reimbursement accounts (HRAs).[39] **Consumer-driven health plans (CDHPs)** are a high-deductible insurance policy tied to a limited personal healthcare spending account funded by the employer.[40] The cost-containment philosophy behind CDHPs is that with a limited amount to spend on healthcare services, employees will become more "price conscious" and more informed about where they spend their healthcare dollars. Employees can "shop" for the best cost/quality medical care available commensurate with their individual needs. According to Pete Maillet and Steve Halterman, benefits consultants, "The success of the consumer-driven health care model will ultimately be determined by its ability to modify behavior so that Americans will purchase healthcare services just as they do any other good or services."[41] Importantly, CDHPs are tax-free and can accept contributions from employers, employees, or both.[42]

A typical CDHP works like this. Each employee is assigned a personal-spending account to purchase yearly medical insurance. The account is funded by the employer. This medical budget—say $2,000 a year—can be spent on virtually any healthcare service. Unused amounts can usually be rolled over to the following year, giving employees an incentive to spend wisely and, over time, to increase the value of their medical accounts. Should an employee's annual medical expenses exceed his or her medical account, then additional employer-provided insurance is available after the employee pays certain out-of-pocket medical costs, say $500 to $2000, much like a deductible.[43]

While CDHPs are similar in structure and intent, each specific program (MSA, HSA, FSA, HRA) has its own unique design features. For example, health savings accounts, unlike flexible spending accounts, can be rolled over from year to year and are portable—employees can take them if they change jobs. HRAs are funded solely by the employer, whereas HSAs can be funded by the employee, the employer, or both. Furthermore, employees of small businesses find MSAs particularly beneficial to their healthcare needs. Under the Health Insurance Portability and Accountability Act of 1996, employees of small employers may establish a tax-free, interest-bearing MSA. Under the MSA, individuals enrolled in a plan may make tax-free contributions to an account created primarily for the purpose of paying for qualified medical expenses.

Other Health Benefits

Dental plans are designed to help pay for dental care costs and to encourage employees to receive regular dental attention. Like medical plans, dental care plans may be operated by insurance companies, dental service corporations, those administering Blue Cross/Blue Shield plans, HMOs, and groups of dental care providers. Typically, the insurance pays a portion of the charges, and the subscriber pays the remainder.

To assist employees with chronic health conditions such as diabetes, heart disease, and asthma, and to lower healthcare costs, employers may provide their employees with *disease management (DM) programs.* DM programs provide patients and their caregivers with information on monitoring and treating medical conditions, while coordinating communication between medical consumers, healthcare providers, employers, and insurers. Bank One Corporation of Chicago developed a DM program when managers experienced high absenteeism among employees with diabetes, asthma, and depression. One healthcare professional notes, "As more and more employers and employees become involved in disease management programs, it will help to change the nation's culture to one where people begin to adopt empowerment and self-management attitudes and habits related to their health—habits built from their employers' disease management programs."[44]

The Health Insurance Portability and Accountability Act

The Health Insurance Portability and Accountability Act (HIPAA) of 1996 grants employees the right to switch their medical insurance between former and present employers. Once an employee earns twelve credits with his or her former employer (one credit per month of service), he or she can transfer into the new employer's health insurance plan without a gap in coverage. Coverage is guaranteed regardless of a pre-existing health condition of the employee. An employee's medical privacy rights under HIPAA are discussed in Chapter 13.

Payment for Time Not Worked

The "payment for time not worked" category of benefits includes paid vacations, bonuses given in lieu of paid vacations, payments for holidays not worked, paid sick leave, military and jury duty, and payments for absence due to a death in the family or other personal reasons. As Highlights in HRM 3 showed, these benefits constitute another large expenditure—11.6 percent—of the employer's total payroll costs.

Vacations with Pay

It is generally agreed that vacations are essential to the well-being of an employee. Eligibility for vacations varies by industry, locale, and organization size. To qualify for longer vacations of three, four, or five weeks, one may expect to work for seven, fifteen, and twenty years, respectively.

While vacations are a relatively easy benefit to manage, employers should, nevertheless, remember that vacation scheduling must meet the employer's state wage laws and state contract law principles.

Vacations and holidays provide a break from demanding job duties and responsibilities.

Paid Holidays

Both hourly and salaried workers can usually expect to be paid for ten holidays a year. The type of business tends to influence both the number and observance of holidays. Virtually all employers in the United States, however, observe and pay their employees for New Year's Day, Memorial Day, Independence Day, Labor Day, Thanksgiving Day, and Christmas Day. Many employers give workers an additional two or three personal days off to use at their discretion.

Sick Leave

There are several ways in which employees may be compensated during periods when they are unable to work because of illness or injury. Most public employees, as well as many in private firms, receive a set number of sick-leave days each year to cover such absences. Where permitted, sick leave that employees do not use can be accumulated to cover prolonged absences. Accumulated vacation leave may sometimes be used as a source of income when sick-leave benefits have been exhausted. Group insurance that provides income protection during a long-term disability is also made available by some employers. As discussed earlier in the chapter, income lost during absences resulting from job-related injuries may be reimbursed, at least partially, through workers' compensation insurance.

Severance Pay

A one-time payment is sometimes given to employees who are being terminated. Known as *severance pay*, it may cover only a few days' wages or wages for several months. The pay received usually depends on the employee's years of service. However, severance pay can also be based on the reason for termination, the salary or grade level of the employee, the title or level in the organization, or a combination of factors. Employers that are downsizing often use severance pay as a means of lessening the negative effects of unexpected termination of employees. Other triggers for severance pay include job elimination, voluntary separation programs, or refusal of reassignment or relocation.

Supplemental Unemployment Benefits

While *not* required by law, in some industries unemployment compensation is augmented by **supplemental unemployment benefits (SUBs),** which are financed by the employer. These plans enable an employee who is laid off to draw, in addition to state unemployment compensation, weekly benefits from the employer that are paid from a fund created for this purpose. The amount of benefits is determined by length of service and wage rate. Employer liability under the plan is limited to the amount of money accumulated within the fund from employer contributions based on the total hours of work performed by employees.

supplemental unemployment benefits (SUBs)
A plan that enables an employee who is laid off to draw, in addition to state unemployment compensation, weekly benefits from the employer that are paid from a fund created for this purpose

Life Insurance

One of the oldest and most popular employee benefits is group term life insurance, which provides death benefits to beneficiaries and may also provide accidental death and dismemberment benefits. The premium costs are normally paid by the employer, with the face value of the life insurance equal to two times the employee's yearly wages. These programs frequently allow employees to purchase additional amounts of insurance for nominal charges. When employers operate a cafeteria benefits program, selection of extra life insurance may be part of the choices offered employees.

Long-Term Care Insurance

A small but growing number of employers are offering long-term care insurance as part of their benefits package.[45] Long-term care insurance is designed to pay for nursing home and other medical-related costs during old age. An advantage of employer-sponsored long-term care insurance is that enrolled employees receive coverage automatically and do not need to pass a physical examination.

Retirement Programs

A significant trend in workforce demographics is the increased age of U.S. workers. A prominent cause of this change is the "aging" of the baby boom generation—a demographic group born between 1946 and 1964. Therefore, retirement has become an important part of life for many individuals, requiring sufficient and careful preparation. In convincing job applicants, particularly older ones, that theirs is a good organization to work for, employers usually emphasize the retirement benefits that can be expected after a certain number of years of employment.

Retirement Policies

With an increasing older workforce (see Figure 11.3), a trend of recent years has been the early retirement of employees before the traditional retirement age of 65. While the United States has no law mandating a specific retirement age, there have not been an overwhelming number of older workers who remain on the job. The early retirement trend partly reflects voluntary departures. Others choose partial retirement or work part-time for a period preceding complete retirement. Recently, however, large numbers of workers have been pushed into premature retirement—the victims of organizational downsizing. Whether the trend in early retirement will continue as more baby boomers enter retirement age is open to speculation.

To avoid layoffs, particularly of more recently hired members of protected classes, and to reduce salary and benefit costs, employers often encourage early retirement. Encouragement comes in the form of increased pension benefits for several years or cash bonuses, sometimes referred to as the **silver handshake.** The cost of these retirement incentives can frequently be offset by the lower compensation paid to replacements and/or by a reduction in the workforce.

silver handshake
An early-retirement incentive in the form of increased pension benefits for several years or a cash bonus

The major factors affecting the decision to retire early are the individual's personal financial condition and health and the extent to which he or she receives satisfaction from the work. Attractive pension benefits, possibilities of future layoffs, and inability to meet the demands of their jobs are also among the reasons workers choose to retire early.

Figure 11.3 Trends Affecting Retirement

- The number of people age 65 and older tripled to about 34 million between 1940 and 1995.
- According to U.S. census projections, people age 65 and older are expected to number 86 million by 2050, an increase of 51 million since 2000.
- In 1960, 45.4 percent of male workers over age 65 were still in the labor force; in 1990, only 27.4 percent were still working. While the labor force participation rates of women between ages 55 and 64 have been rising, further increases are not expected.
- Eight baby boomers turn 50 every ten minutes.
- The U.S. net national savings rate was relatively stable at about 7 percent of GDP from 1951 to 1980. It has collapsed since 1980, most recently dropping to less than 1 percent of GDP.
- In 1900, the average life expectancy in the U.S. was 48; today, it is 80 for women and 75 for men. Virtually all of these gains can be attributed to improvements in public health and safety, such as clean water, refrigeration, seat belts, and routine vaccinations.

USING THE INTERNET

AARP is the nation's leading organization for people age 50 and older. It serves their needs through information, education, advocacy, and community service. AARP retirement information can be found at their web site. Go to the Student Resources at:

http://bohlander.swlearning.com

Preretirement Programs

While most people eagerly anticipate retirement, many are bitterly disappointed once they reach this stage of life. Employers may offer preretirement planning programs to help make employees aware of the kinds of adjustments they may need to make when they retire. These adjustments may include learning to live on a reduced, fixed income and having to cope with the problems of lost prestige, family problems, and idleness that retirement may create.

Preretirement programs typically include seminars and workshops that include lectures, videos, and printed materials. Topics covered include pension plans, health insurance coverage, Social Security and Medicare, personal financial planning, wellness and lifestyles, and adjustment to retirement. The numerous publications of AARP (formerly known as the American Association of Retired Persons), including its popular magazine, *Modern Maturity*, are valuable sources of information.

To help older workers get used to the idea of retirement, some organizations experiment with retirement rehearsal. Polaroid, for example, offers employees an opportunity to try out retirement through an unpaid three-month leave program. They also offer a program that permits employees to gradually cut their hours before retirement. Most experts agree that preretirement planning is a much-needed, cost-effective employee benefit.

Pension Plans

Originally, pensions were based on a *reward philosophy,* which viewed pensions primarily as a way to retain personnel by rewarding them for staying with the organization until they retired. Because of the vesting requirements required by law, pensions are now based on an *earnings philosophy.* This philosophy regards a pension as deferred income that employees accumulate during their working lives and that belongs to them after a specified number of years of service, whether or not they remain with the employer until retirement. Since the passage of the Social Security Act of 1935, pension plans have been used to supplement the floor of protection provided by Social Security. However, the decision whether to offer a pension plan is up to the employer.

contributory plan
A pension plan in which contributions are made jointly by employees and employers

noncontributory plan
A pension plan in which contributions are made solely by the employer

Types of Pension Plans

There are two major ways to categorize pension plans: (1) according to contributions made by the employer and (2) according to the amount of pension benefits to be paid. In a **contributory plan,** contributions to a pension plan are made jointly by employees and employers. In a **noncontributory plan,** the contributions are made solely by the employer.

When pension plans are classified by the amount of pension benefits to be paid, there are two basic types: the defined-benefit plan and the defined-contribution plan. Under a **defined-benefit plan,** the amount an employee is to receive on retirement is specifically set forth. This amount is usually based on the employee's years of service, average earnings during a specific period of time, and age at time of retirement. While a variety of formulas exist for determining pension benefits, the one used most often is based on the employee's average earnings (usually over a three- to five-year period immediately preceding retirement), multiplied by the number of

defined-benefit plan
A pension plan in which the amount an employee is to receive on retirement is specifically set forth

years of service with the organization. A deduction is then made for each year the retiree is under age 65. For example, an employee with a four-year preretirement annual salary of $55,000 and thirty years of service may receive a yearly retirement payment of $23,000. Compared to a defined-contribution plan, defined-benefit plans today are unpopular with employers because they cost more and the employer is obligated to fund the plan to the extent necessary to support future benefit payouts.

defined-contribution plan A pension plan that establishes the basis on which an employer will contribute to the pension fund

A **defined-contribution plan** establishes the basis on which an employer will contribute to the pension fund. The contributions may be made through profit sharing, thrift plans, matches of employee contributions, employer-sponsored individual retirement accounts (IRAs), and various other means. The amount of benefits employees receive on retirement is determined by the funds accumulated in their account at the time of retirement and what retirement benefits (usually an annuity) these funds will purchase. These plans do not offer the benefit-security predictability of a defined-benefit plan. However, even under defined-benefit plans, retirees may not receive the benefits promised them if the plan is not adequately funded.

401(k) Savings Plans

A significant change in pension coverage has been the tremendous growth of tax-deferred 401(k) savings plans, which are named after section 401(k) of the Internal Revenue Code. The popularity of 401(k) plans is driven primarily by (1) the ability of the employer to transfer plan funding to employees, (2) the ability to transfer responsibility for investment choices to employees, and (3) the fact that employee contributions to 401(k) plans represent tax-free investing.

The 401(k) savings plans are particularly popular with smaller employers who find these pension plans less costly than defined-benefit programs. Changes in the Fair Labor Standards Act encourage smaller employers to set up 401(k) plans by removing complicated filing rules in exchange for employer contributions of 3 percent of pay for workers who participate in the plan or 2 percent of pay for all workers whether or not they participate.

The 401(k) savings plans allow employees to save through payroll deductions and to have their contributions matched by the employer. Usually the employer matches the employee contributions at the rate of fifty cents for every worker dollar contributed. An organization's contribution can, however, run the gamut from doubling the worker's contribution to zero contribution.[46] The percentage of the employer's contribution will likely depend on the allowable saving rate of the employee (that is, higher allowable employee savings rates will decrease the percentage of the employer's contribution). A prevalent concern with 401(k) plans is the method by which employers match employee contributions, that is, with cash payments or company stock.

401(k) plans lost some luster when employees at energy giant Enron, along with employees at other scandal-plagued corporations, saw the value of their 401(k) retirement savings diminish.[47] For example, when Enron stock prices fell from a high of almost $90 to less than $1, the retirement fund deteriorated. Additionally, the stock market decline saw employees with 401(k) plans invested in company stock take heavy retirement hits. Unlike traditional defined-benefit pension plans, which guarantee payments based on years of service, the 401(k) plan guarantees nothing. Return depends entirely on how much money goes into the plan, the rate of return on investment, and, with stock-funded plans, the price of the company's stock.

USING THE INTERNET

Government guidelines that protect employers from liability for offering investment advice to employees are found in DOL Interpretative Bulletin 96-1. Go to the Student Resources at:

http://bohlander.swlearning.com

A current trend is for organizations to allow their employees considerable control over the investment of their 401(k) savings, including investing in the stock of other companies.[48] Because employees often need assistance in making informed investment decisions, Department of Labor standards provide employers with "sufficient information" standards to follow in putting participants legally in control of their investment.[49] Also, a small but growing number of 401(k) plans let employees hand the management of their 401(k) to a professional financial planner. The new service, called *managed accounts,* seeks to help employees—many of whom have little investing experience—achieve higher returns with less risk.[50] Some organizations require their benefit professionals, when they provide investing advice to employees, to be Certified Financial Planners (CFPs).

Cash-Balance Pension Plans

Along with 401(k) saving plans, a significant development in pension planning has been cash-balance saving plans.[51] Cash-balance plans work by having the employer make a yearly contribution into an employee's retirement savings account.[52] Contributions are based on a percentage of the employee's pay—typically 4 percent. Additionally, the employee's account earns annual interest, often tied to the thirty-year Treasury rate. For example, an employee earning $35,000 a year would receive a yearly contribution of $1,400 to his or her account. After a year, the account would receive an interest credit, typically 5 percent. Employees can normally roll the balance of their account into an IRA should they change jobs.

Whether an individual employee benefits from a cash-balance retirement plan depends on the employee's age and years of service with the company. Employees in their twenties or thirties with low years of service can build substantial retirement savings starting at an early age. However, employees in their forties, fifties, or sixties with lengthy years of service can lose from 20 to 50 percent of their pension by switching from a traditional pension plan to a cash-balance program.[53] Senior employees at IBM and Xerox sued over loss of retirement savings when their companies switched retirement plans.[54] To lessen the financial impact on older employees, some companies may increase the annual pay credit for older employees as compared with younger workers. Others allow older employees to remain in the traditional pension plan until retirement, or grant older employees a "boost" in their opening cash-balance account. Employers ranging from Federated Department Stores and Verizon to Colgate-Palmolive and even Harvard University now cover their employees with cash-balance plans.

Federal Regulation of Pension Plans

Private pension plans are subject to federal regulation under the Employee Retirement Income Security Act (ERISA).[55] The law governs about 7 million private pension plans. Although the act does not require employers to establish a pension plan, it provides certain standards and controls for pension plans. It requires minimum funding standards to ensure that benefits will be available when an employee retires. It also requires that the soundness of the actuarial assumptions on which the funding is based be certified by an actuary at least every three years.[56] Of special concern to the individual employee is the matter of vesting.

vesting
A guarantee of accrued benefits to participants at retirement age, regardless of their employment status at that time

Vesting is a guarantee of accrued benefits to participants at retirement age, regardless of their employment status at that time. Vested benefits that have been earned by an employee cannot be revoked by an employer. Under ERISA, all pension plans must provide that employees will have vested rights in their accrued benefits after certain minimum-years-of-service requirements have been met. However, employers can pay out a departing employee's vested benefits if the present value of the benefit is small. Also, while vesting is required by ERISA, portability—the ability to move pension funds between employers—is optional. Employees are well advised to seek out pension options that are portable if at all possible.

Three government agencies administer ERISA: the Internal Revenue Service (IRS), the Department of Labor, and the Pension Benefit Guaranty Corporation (PBGC). The IRS is concerned primarily with qualified retirement plans—those that offer employers and employees favorable income tax treatment under a special section of the tax law. The Department of Labor's main responsibility is to protect participants' rights. The PBGC ensures that if a plan is terminated, guaranteed minimum benefits are paid to participants. The PBGC is supported by premiums paid by employers.

Managers and supervisors should also remember that antidiscrimination laws (see Chapter 3) apply to the administration of benefit programs. Individuals can file a charge with the EEOC when they believe that they have been denied benefits, or received lower benefits, because of their age, disability, race, religion, sex, or national origin.

Pension Plans and Underfunding

What is one of today's biggest concerns with pension plans? The answer is inadequate funds to cover retirement obligations along with pension plan failures. For many old-line companies such as Delta Airlines, Ford, General Motors, Delphi, Cummins, and Allegheny Technologies, pension deficits are staggering. For example, in 2003, the pension deficit at Ford was $11.7 billion, at GM $8.6 billion, at Delta $5.7 billion, and at Delphi $4 billion.[57]

Equally worrisome is the number of pension plans in danger of failure. According to PBGC, as of September 2003, at least $86 billion in pension obligation was promised by companies deemed financially unstable. In 2003, 206,000 individuals became PBGC pensioners, including 95,000 from bankrupt Bethlehem Steel.[58] Unfortunately for retirees, monthly pension payments under PBGC guidelines are often significantly less than those promised under a company's original retirement plan. Furthermore, many worry that the PBGC—with a multibillion-dollar deficit of its own—will be unable to meet its financial obligations and will require a federal bailout—a bailout ultimately paid for by taxpayers.[59]

Employee Services: Creating a Work/Life Setting

ConAgra of Omaha, Nebraska, provides a home nurse for up to twelve hours to care for a sick child or elder parent. Lincoln National, a financial services company, offers a "homework-assistance help line" staffed with teachers for children of employees, and Eddie Bauer, an outdoor clothing and equipment supplier, offers its employees take-out dinners and one paid "Balance Day" off a year. These organizations, like many others, are seeking to create a work/life (also called family-friendly) organizational climate that allows employees to balance work and personal needs.

Companies are also adapting work/life programs to accommodate the entrance of Generation Y employees into the workplace. This new group of workers has its own vision for the workplace and their careers, one that work/life programs can help fulfill. A national survey conducted by Mellon Financial Human Resources and Investor Solutions found that 86 percent of surveyed employers used part-time employees, 88 percent offered work-related tuition reimbursement, 81 percent offered employee assistance programs, 71 percent offered flextime programs, 50 percent offered telecommuting and work-at-home arrangements, 44 percent offered compressed workweeks, 54 percent provided family sick days, and 47 percent offered unpaid family leave that goes beyond the requirements of the Family and Medical Leave Act. According to the study, employer reasons for offering work/life programs include raising morale (74 percent of respondents), enhancing recruitment efforts (73 percent), and remaining competitive/industry image (72 percent).[60] Figure 11.4 lists some of the more popular employer-sponsored work/life benefits.

Employee Assistance Programs

employee assistance programs (EAPs)
Services provided by employers to help workers cope with a wide variety of problems that interfere with the way they perform their jobs

To help workers cope with a wide variety of problems that interfere with the way they perform their jobs, organizations such as the New York Mets, the Los Angeles Police Department, and Levi Strauss have developed **employee assistance programs (EAPs).** An employee assistance program typically provides diagnosis, counseling, and referral for advice or treatment when necessary for problems related to alcohol or drug abuse, emotional difficulties, and financial or family difficulties.[61] (EAPs will be discussed in detail in Chapter 12.) The main intent is to help employees solve their personal problems or at least to prevent problems from turning into crises that affect their ability to work productively. To handle crises, many EAPs offer twenty-four-hour hot lines.

Counseling Services

An important part of an EAP is the counseling services it provides to employees. While most organizations expect managers to counsel subordinates, some employees

Figure 11.4 Work/Life Benefits: Balancing Work and Home Needs

- Child care/elder care referral services
- Time off for children's school activities
- Employer-paid onsite or near-site child care facilities
- Flexible work hours scheduling
- Employer-accumulated leave days for dependent care
- Customized training programs
- Subsidized temporary or emergency dependent-care costs
- Extended leave policies for child/elder care
- Sick-child programs (caregiver on call)
- Work-at-home arrangements/telecommuting
- Partial funding of child care costs
- Customized career paths

may have problems that require the services of professional counselors. Most organizations refer such individuals to outside counseling services such as family counseling services, marriage counselors, and mental health clinics. Some organizations have a clinical psychologist, counselor, or comparable specialist on staff, to whom employees may be referred.

Child and Elder Care

Consider these figures:

- Working parents take between five and twenty-nine days off work each year for sick children.
- Each day, more than 350,000 children younger than age 14 are too sick to attend school or daycare.
- The average daily cost of unscheduled absenteeism is $602 per employee, resulting in an annual business expense of more than $3 billion.[62]

elder care
Care provided to an elderly relative by an employee who remains actively at work

These figures, combined with the increased employment of women with dependent children, illustrate the unprecedented demand for child care arrangements.

Today benefits may include financial assistance, alternative work schedules, and family leave. Some employers such as Fel-Pro, Merck, Syntex, Baptist Hospital of Miami, and Ben and Jerry's, promote onsite or near-site child care centers. Employer-sponsored dependent-care spending accounts allow employees to set aside a portion of their pay before taxes to care for a dependent child.

A growing benefit offered employees with children experiencing short illnesses is mildly-ill child care. Medical supervision is the primary difference between mildly-ill facilities and traditional daycare arrangements. Mildly-ill care facilities serve children recovering from colds, flu, ear infections, strep throat, chicken pox, or other mild illnesses that temporarily prevent them from attending regular school or daycare. These facilities are either independently run, hospital based, or affiliated with child care centers.

© SUSAN VAN ETTEN/PHOTOEDIT

Caring for one's aging parents and relatives is a growing concern for both employees and their employers.

Responsibility for the care of aging parents and other relatives is another fact of life for increasing numbers of employees. According to a study of AARP and the National Alliance for Caregiving, today more than 30 million Americans are caring for an elderly parent. As noted in the study, "elder care is rapidly becoming the biggest family issue facing workers and their families."[63] The cost to U.S. employers in lost productivity and other costs may exceed $29 billion annually.[64] The term **elder care,** as used in the context of employment, occurs when an employee provides care to an elderly relative while remaining actively at work. The majority of caregivers are women.

To reduce the negative effects of caregiving on productivity, organizations may offer elder care counseling, educational fairs and seminars, printed resource material, support groups, and special flexible schedules and leaves of absence.[65] Schering-Plough, a pharmaceuticals manufacturer, uses an 800 telephone line for elder care referrals, while IBM has a national telephone network of more than 200 community-based referral agencies. Employers may also band together for better elder care. The Partnership for Elder Care—a consortium of American Express, J. P. Morgan, and Philip Morris—and other companies use the resources of the New York City Department of Aging, a public information and aging support agency.

Interest in and demand for elder care programs will increase dramatically as baby boomers move into their fifties and find themselves managing organizations and experiencing elder care problems with their own parents.[66]

Other Services

The variety of benefits and services that employers offer today is widespread. However, whether a company offers a particular service may depend on its size, ability to pay, industry pattern, or specific employee or organizational needs. Some services are fairly standard such as housing and moving expenses, various food services (such as cafeteria or vending machines), transportation pooling arrangements, and buying assistance for merchandise at a discount. Many organizations offer some type of sports program in which personnel may participate on a voluntary basis. Bowling, softball, golf, baseball, and tennis are often included in an intramural program. Four other services that employers may offer are credit unions, legal services, financial planning, and paycards.

Credit Unions

Credit unions exist in many organizations to serve the financial needs of employees. They offer a variety of deposits as well as other banking services and make loans to their members. Although the employer may provide office space and a payroll deduction service, credit unions are operated by the employees under federal and state legislation and supervision. At the end of July 2004, there were 9,542 credit unions in the United States with 85.6 million members and combined assets of $655 billion. In almost all credit unions, deposits are insured up to $100,000 per account by the National Credit Union Share Insurance Fund, a U.S. government agency.[67]

Legal Services

Legal service plans are generally of two types: access plans and comprehensive plans. Access plans provide free telephone or office consultation, document review, and discounts on legal fees for more complex matters. Comprehensive plans cover other services such as representation in divorce cases, real estate transactions, and civil and criminal trials.

Covered employees normally pay a monthly or an annual fee to be enrolled in the plan. When the need for legal assistance arises, the employee may choose an attorney from a directory of providers and incur no expenses for attorney fees. One benefits consultant remarked, "The whole idea behind prepaid legal plans is that the employer can use its purchase power and shift it to employees without incurring a lot of expense." Prepaid legal programs are typically offered as part of an employer's cafeteria benefits plan.

Financial Planning

One of the newer benefits is financial planning. As mentioned previously, financial planning has become particularly important for employees making investment decisions regarding 401(k) saving plans. Financial planning could also include (1) present position, (2) retirement planning, (3) protection planning, (4) tax planning, and (5) estate planning and related topics. Employers offer these programs through multiple forums—seminars, online tools, pamphlets, and/or face-to-face advice.[68]

Paycards

Paycards, also known as PIN-based or stored-value cards, are an electronic way to pay employees.[69] These cards are linked to an existing ATM or a point-of-service account. PIN-based cards may allow employees to purchase goods by phone, at stores, or on the Internet. Paycards are helpful to organizations moving to a 100 percent electronic payroll.[70]

SUMMARY

objective 1

Benefits are an established and integral part of the total compensation package. In order to have a sound benefits program there are certain basic considerations. It is essential that a program be based on specific objectives that are compatible with organizational philosophy and policies as well as affordable. Through committees and surveys a benefit package can be developed to meet employees' needs. Through the use of flexible benefit plans, employees are able to choose the benefits that are best suited for their individual needs. An important factor in how employees view the program is the full communication of benefits information through meetings, printed material, and annual personalized statements of benefits.

objective 2

According to a 2003 study, the costs of employee benefits in that year averaged 42.3 percent of payroll, or $18,000 per employee. Because many of the benefits represent a fixed cost, management must pay close attention in assuming more benefit expense. Increasingly, employers are requiring employees to pay part of the costs of certain benefits. Employers also shop for benefit services that are competitively priced.

objective 3

Nearly a quarter of the benefits package that employers provide is legally required. These benefits include employer contributions to Social Security, unemployment insurance, workers' compensation insurance, and state disability insurance. Social Security taxes collected from employers and employees are used to pay three major types of benefits: (1) old-age insurance benefits, (2) disability benefits, and (3) survivors' insurance benefits.

objective 4

The cost of healthcare programs has become the major concern in the area of employee benefits. Several approaches are used to contain healthcare costs, including reduction in coverage, increased coordination of benefits, increased deductible or copayments, use of health maintenance and preferred provider organizations, various consumer-driven health plans, incentives for outpatient surgery and testing, and mandatory second opinions where surgery is indicated. Employee assistance programs and wellness programs may also contribute to cutting the costs of healthcare benefits.

objective 5 Included in the category of benefits that involve payments for time not worked are vacations with pay, paid holidays, sick leave, and severance pay. The typical practice in the United States is to give ten days' vacation leave and ten holidays. In addition to vacation time, most employees, particularly in white-collar jobs, receive a set number of sick-leave days. A one-time payment of severance pay may be given to employees who are being terminated.

objective 6 Prior to 1979 employers were permitted to determine the age (usually 65) at which their employees would be required to retire. While there is now no ceiling, a growing number of workers choose to retire before age 65. Many employers provide incentives for early retirement in the form of increased pension benefits or cash bonuses. Some organizations provide preretirement programs that may include seminars, workshops, and informational materials. The National Council on Aging, AARP, and many other organizations are available to assist both employers and employees in preretirement activities.

objective 7 Whether to offer a pension plan is the employer's prerogative. However, once a plan is established it is then subject to federal regulation under ERISA to ensure that benefits will be available when an employee retires. Two traditional pension plans are available—defined-benefit and defined-contribution. The amount an employee receives on retirement is based on years of service, average earnings, and age at time of retirement. Pension benefits are typically integrated with Social Security benefits. Two of the most significant trends are the growth of 401(k) salary reduction plans and cash-balance pension plans. Pension funds may be administered through either a trusteed plan or an insurance plan. A concern today is the underfunding of pension plans and the ability of ERISA to meet its financial obligations.

objective 8 The types of service benefits that employers typically provide include employee assistance programs, counseling services, educational assistance plans, child care, and elder care. Other benefits are food services, onsite health services, prepaid legal services, financial planning, housing and moving, transportation pooling, purchase assistance, credit unions, social and recreational services, and paycards.

KEY TERMS

consumer-driven health plan
contributory plan
defined-benefit plan
defined-contribution plan
elder care
employee assistance programs (EAPs)
flexible benefits plans (cafeteria plans)
health maintenance organizations (HMOs)
noncontributory plan
preferred provider organization (PPO)
silver handshake
supplemental unemployment benefits (SUBs)
vesting
workers' compensation insurance

HRM Experience

Understanding Employer Benefit Programs

What is the best-kept secret in American today? The answer, according to a report of the U.S. Chamber of Commerce labeled "The Hidden Payroll," is employee benefits. Compensation surveys indicate that a majority of employees are unable to accurately name the benefits they receive and employees vastly underestimate the cost of benefits paid by their employers.

This exercise will help you more fully understand the benefits discussed in this chapter. Additionally, you will explore, in detail, the benefits and services offered by your employer and other employers in your area.

Assignment

Working in teams of four to six individuals, obtain information on the benefits package offered by your employer or other employers in your area. Once the information is gathered, be able to identify (1) each benefit offered, (2) what the benefit provides the employee, (3) employee eligibility (if required), and (4) how the benefit is paid for (employer, employee, or a combination of both). Compare benefit packages. Be prepared to discuss your findings with the class.

DISCUSSION QUESTIONS

1. You are a small employer wishing to establish a benefits program for your employees. What things should you consider to ensure that the program is a success for your employees?

2. Many organizations are concerned about the rising cost of employee benefits and question their value to the organization and to the employees.

- **a.** In your opinion, what benefits are of greatest value to employees? To the organization? Why?
- **b.** What can management do to increase the value to the organization of the benefits provided to employees?

3. Employers are required by law to provide specific benefits to employees. What laws mandate benefits to employees and what are the provisions of those laws?

4. Identify and contrast the various ways employers can control the costs of healthcare.

5. Do you agree with the argument that benefits for time not worked are those most readily available to reduce employer costs? Explain.

6. Prior to 1979, all employers could prescribe a mandatory retirement age—usually 65 years. What would you think are the advantages and disadvantages of a mandatory retirement age? What factors may affect an individual's decision to retire at a particular time, and what factors may affect his or her ability to adjust to retirement?

7. Describe 401(k) pension plans, listing their advantages and disadvantages. As an employee, would you want control over the investment decisions of your 401(k) plan? Explain.

8. Working in teams of three or four, assume your team was hired as a benefits consultant to a small business having fifty to sixty employees. What benefits do you believe this employer should offer, given limited resources? Justify your reasons for offering these benefits.

BIZFLIX EXERCISES

Erin Brockovich: Erin Gets Benefits, with Dental

The chapter discussed the important role of employee benefits in the employment relationship. Watch this scene from *Erin Brockovich* and assess the importance of benefits to Erin.

Erin Brockovich (Julia Roberts), a single mother of three, needs a job and convinces skeptical attorney Ed Masry (Albert Finney) to hire her. She quickly discovers a potentially large case against Pacific Gas & Electric Company (PG&E) for environmental pollution. Based on a true story, the film has many dramatic and funny moments. Roberts received the 2000 Best Actress Academy Award.

The scene comes from the "Ed comes over" segment that appears about 45 minutes into the film. It follows Erin's discussion with her neighbor George (Aaron Eckhart) about her one-year reign as Miss Wichita. This scene ends with Ed Masry saying he is drawing the line on benefits. The film continues with Ed reviewing the limited information Erin got from the Lohantan Regional Water Board office. Erin and her three children revisit the office to copy more information for the case.

What to Watch for and Ask Yourself

- The first section of this chapter, "Employee Benefits Programs," opened with this sentence: "Employee benefits constitute an indirect form of compensation intended to improve the quality of the work lives and the personal lives of employees." Does this quotation apply to Erin in this scene? If *yes,* in what way does it apply to her and her life situation?
- Erin and Ed are unclear about what benefits, except medical and dental, his firm provides. Which benefits discussed in this chapter would a typical small law firm give to its employees? See the earlier section "Discretionary Major Employee Benefits" for some ideas.
- Erin negotiates a 10 percent pay raise from Ed, suggesting that pay is important to her. Does the scene suggest that benefits are also important to Erin? Why or why not?

case study 1

Adobe's Family-Friendly Benefits: An Unexpected Backlash

Adobe Consulting Services (ACS), a provider of HR software application systems, prides itself on the variety of benefits it offers employees. In addition to healthcare, pension, and vacation benefits, the company also offers an attractive family-friendly benefits package including flexible schedules, child and elder care assistance, counseling services, adoption assistance, and extended parental leave. Unfortunately, in recent months, the company's progressive work/life policy has experienced a backlash from several employees, as the following case illustrates.

In March 2004, Teresa Wheatly was hired by Adobe as a software accounts manager. With excellent administrative and technical skills, plus four years of experience at Adaptable Software, Adobe's main competitor, Teresa became a valued addition to the company's marketing team. As a single mother with two grade-school children, Teresa received permission to take Fridays off. She was also allowed to leave work early or come in late to meet the demands of her children. Teresa is one of eleven software account managers at Adobe.

The problem for Adobe, and particularly Janis Blancero, director of marketing, began in the fall of 2004. On September 15, Dorothy McShee, citing "personal reasons"—which she refused to discuss—requested a four-day workweek for which she was willing to take a 20 percent cut in pay. When Dorothy asked for the reduced work schedule, she sarcastically quipped, "I hope I don't have to have kids to get this time off." On October 3, Juan Batista, a world-class marathon runner, requested a flexible work hours arrangement in order to accommodate his morning and afternoon training schedule. Juan is registered to run the London, England, marathon in May 2005. Just prior to Juan's request, Susan Woolf asked for, and was granted, an extended maternity leave to begin after the birth of her first child in December. If these unexpected requests were not enough, Blancero has heard comments from senior account managers about how some employees seem to get "special privileges," while the managers work long hours that often require them to meet around-the-clock customer demands. Janis has adequate reason to believe that there is hidden tension over the company's flexible work hours program. Currently, Adobe has no formal policy on flexible schedules. Furthermore, with the company's growth in business combined with the increasing workload of software account managers and the constant service demands of some customers, Blancero realizes that she simply cannot grant all the time-off requests of her employees.

Source: Adapted from Alden M. Hayashi, "Mommy-Track Backlash," Harvard Business Review 79, no. 3 (March 2001): 33–42.

QUESTIONS

1. Do managers like Janis Blancero face a more complicated decision when evaluating the personal requests of employees versus evaluating employees' individual work performance? Explain.
2. **a.** Should Adobe establish a policy for granting flexible work schedules? Explain.
   b. If you answered yes, what might that policy contain?
3. If you were Janis Blancero, how would you resolve this dilemma? Explain.

case study 2

Evaluate the Work/Life Climate in Your Company

What is the quality of the work/life environment in your company? The following survey provided by the Work and Family Connection will help provide a "case analysis" of the climate in your organization. Answers to the twenty questions will provide clear insights about your company's position in the work/life area.

Agree or Disagree with the Following Statements:

1. My manager/supervisor treats my work/life needs with sensitivity.
2. It is usually easy for me to manage the demands of both work and home life.
3. My career path at this company is limited because of the pressure of home life demands.
4. My job at this company keeps me from maintaining the quality of life I want.
5. My manager/supervisor is supportive when home life issues interfere with work.
6. My manager/supervisor focuses on results, rather than the time I am at my desk.
7. My manager/supervisor has a good understanding of flexible work hour practices.
8. If I requested a flexible work arrangement my manager/supervisor would support me.

9. My manager/supervisor is often inflexible or insensitive about my personal needs.
10. I believe my manager/supervisor treats me with respect.
11. My manager/supervisor allows me informal flexibility as long as I get the job done.
12. My manager/supervisor tends to treat us like children.
13. My manager/supervisor seldom gives me praise or recognition for the work I do.
14. My manager/supervisor seems to care about me as a person.
15. I would recommend this company to others.
16. The work I do is not all that important to this company's success.
17. If I could find another job with better pay, I would leave this organization.
18. If I could find another job where I would be treated with respect, I would take it.
19. If I could find another job where I could have more flexibility, I would take it.
20. I am totally committed to this company.

For a perfect score, you should answer **"Disagree"** to questions 3, 4, 9, 12, 13, 16, 17, 18, and 19 and **"Agree"** to all the rest (1, 2, 5, 6, 7, 8, 10, 11, 14, 15, and 20).

To score, begin by giving yourself 20 points. Then deduct one point for every "wrong" response from the total score.

If your score is 18 to 20: Congratulations! Your organization is leading the nation in flexibility and supportiveness.

If your score is 14 to 17: Your organization is probably more supportive and flexible than most, but you have room to grow.

If your score is 11 to 13: You could be open to other job offers in the race for talent among employees.

If your score is 10 or less: Your managers will need help to manage the twenty-first-century workforce.

Source: Used with permission of the Work and Family Connection, 5195 Beachside Drive, Minnetonka, Minnesota 55343; phone 1-800-487-7898 or http://www.workfamily.com.

NOTES AND REFERENCES

1. *Employee Benefits Study, 2003* (Washington, DC: U.S. Chamber of Commerce, 2003).
2. Richard I. Henderson, *Compensation Management in a Knowledge-Based World*, 9th ed. (Upper Saddle River, NJ: Prentice Hall, 2003): Chapter 17.
3. "Online Benefits Expected to Become Predominant," *Best Review* 105, no. 12 (April 2005): 106. See also Sarah Fister Gale, "Save Money: Manage Health Benefits Online," *Workforce* 80, no. 11 (November 2001): 64.
4. Steven E. Gross and Helen M. Friedman, "Creating an Effective Total Reward Strategy: Holistic Approach Better Supports Business Success," *Benefits Quarterly* 20, no. 3 (Third Quarter 2004): 7–13.
5. Lori Lucas, Minoy Kairey, and Lisa Horuczi Markos, "Integrating Benefits Decision Making," *Benefits Quarterly* 21, no. 2 (Second Quarter 2005): 2. See also Martha Frase-Blunt, "Time to Redo Your Benefits?" *HRMagazine* 47, no. 12 (December 2001): 73.
6. Laird L. Miller and Joanne E. Miller, "Designing Your Health Benefit Plan," *Employee Benefits Journal* 28, no. 1 (March 2003): 41.
7. Nina D. Cole and Douglas H. Flint, "Opportunity Knocks, Perceptions of Fairness in Employee Benefits," *Compensation and Benefits Review* 37, no. 2 (March/April 2005): 7. See also "Employee Involvement Is the Key to a Successful Work/Life Program," *HRFocus* 78, no. 2 (February 2001): 6–7.
8. Extended family benefits allow employees to add a qualified adult household member to their health plans, be it a domestic partner, an extended family member, or a grown child.
9. Michelle Conlin, "Unmarried America," *Business Week*, October 20, 2003, 106–16.

10. Pamela Babcock, "Find Out What Employees Really Want," *HRMagazine* 50, no. 4 (April 2005): 50. See also Jennifer Hutchins, "How to Make the Right Voluntary Benefit Choices," *Workforce* 81, no. 3 (March 2002): 42–48.
11. "Health Care Trust Issues," *Business Week,* August 2, 2004, 28.
12. Ann Black, "Communications Planning," *Employee Benefits Journal* 26, no. 1 (March 2001): 3–7.
13. Jeannette Swist, "Benefits Communications: Measuring Impact and Value," *Employee Benefit Plan Review* 57, no. 3 (September 2002): 24–26.
14. Computerized data also enable management to keep accurate records of the cost of each benefit. To assist employers with the administrative and communication functions, the International Foundation of Employee Benefit Plans in Brookfield, Wisconsin, maintains an extensive library of employee benefits publications. It also prepares publications on this subject. The foundation has an online database that members can use to get immediate, comprehensive responses to questions about employee benefits. For more than forty years, benefits professionals have relied on the International Foundation of Employee Benefit Plans for education and information about employee benefits. The headquarters address is P.O. Box 69, Brookfield, WI 53008-0069. Interested individuals can also learn about the organization at http://www.ifebp.org.
15. *Employee Benefits,* 11.
16. Frase-Blunt, "Time to Redo Your Benefits?," 73.
17. "Despite Rising Health-Care Costs, Few Companies Have Cut Benefits," *HRFocus* 81, no. 9 (September 2004): 3.
18. *The Arizona Republic,* May 10, 2004, D-1.
19. Todd Henneman, "Benefits for Gay Partners More Common," *Workforce Management* 84, no. 1 (July 2005): 7. See also Sue Shellenburger, "Amid Gay Marriage Debate, Companies Offer More Benefits to Same-Sex Couples," *The Wall Street Journal,* March 18, 2004, D-1.
20. "How HR Is Addressing Domestic Partner Benefits," *HRFocus* 81, no. 7 (July 2004): S-1.
21. "How HR Is Addressing Domestic Partner Benefits," S-4.
22. "What You Need to Know to Provide Domestic Partner Benefits," *HRFocus* 80, no. 8 (August 2003): 3–4.
23. "Gay Marriage Still Faces a Long Slog," *Business Week,* May 31, 2004, 16.
24. As the Social Security Act is continually subject to amendment, readers should refer to the literature provided by the nearest Social Security office for the most current details pertaining to the tax rates and benefit provisions of the act.
25. U.S. Department of Health and Human Services, *Social Security Handbook,* 14th ed. (Washington, DC: U.S. Government Printing Office, 2001): para. 212. The amount changes annually and is published in the *Federal Register.*
26. Donna G. Albrecht, "Getting Ready for Older Workers," *Workforce* 80, no. 2 (February 2001): 62. See also Charles L. Baum and William F. Ford, "The Effects of 'The Senior Citizens' Freedom to Work Act of 2000' on Delayed Retirement Incentives," *Labor Law Journal* 52, no.1 (Spring 2001): 3–8.
27. COBRA, P.L. 99-272, 100 Stat. 82 (1986).
28. FLMA, P.L. 103-3, 107 Stat. 6 (1993).
29. A "serious health condition" means an illness, injury, impairment, or physical or mental condition that involves any period of incapacity or treatment connected with patient care.
30. An expanded discussion of the FMLA can be found in David J. Walsh, *Employment Law for Human Resource Practice* (Mason, OH: South-Western, 2004): 272–82.
31. *Older Workers Benefit Protection Act* (29 U.S.C. 1990), secs. 623, 626, and 630.
32. By signing a waiver (also called a release not to sue), an employee agrees not to take any legal action against the employer. Legal action could be an age discrimination lawsuit. In return for the signed waiver, the employer gives the employee an incentive to leave voluntarily, such as a severance pay package that is larger than the company's normal offer.
33. "Health Insurance Becomes Most Costly Benefit," *Healthcare Financial Management* 10, no. 9 (September 2004): 26.
34. Christopher Farrell, "Health Is Wealth," *Business Week Online* (September 27, 2004).
35. William C. Symonds, Brian Grow, Carol Marie Cropper, and Diane Brady, "Get Used to the Pain," *Business Week,* October 20, 2003, 42–43.
36. "Despite Rising Health-Care Costs, Few Companies Have Cut Benefits," 3.
37. Leslie A. Weatherly, "The Rising Cost of Health Care: Strategic and Societal Considerations for Employers," *HRMagazine* 49, no. 9 (September 2004): A1–11.
38. Richard Ostuw, "Engaging Employees in Health Care Can Contain Costs and Improve Quality," *Benefits Quarterly* 20, no. 2 (Second Quarter 2004): 38–42.
39. Ronald E. Bachman, "Consumer-Driven Health Care: The Future Is Now," *Benefits Quarterly* 20, no. 2 (Second Quarter 2004): 15. See also Jay Green, "Assessing the Health Savings Option," *HRMagazine* 49, no. 4 (April 2004): 103–108, and Howard Gleckman, "Your New Health Plan," *Business Week,* November 8, 2004, 88–98.
40. Laura B. Benko, "Gene Shopping," *Modern Healthcare* 34, no. 36 (September 6, 2004): 28.
41. Pete Maillet and Steve Halterman, "The Consumer-Driven Approach: Defining and Measuring Success," *Benefits Quarterly* 20, no. 2 (Second Quarter 2004): 7.
42. "Periodic Checkup: Consumer-Directed Health Plans," *HRFocus* 81, no. 8 (August 2004): 1.
43. Martha Priddy Patterson, "Defined Contribution Health Plans to Consumer Driven Health Benefits: Evolution and Experience," *Benefits Quarterly* 20, no. 2 (Second Quarter 2004): 49. See also Thomas R. Beauregard, "Consumer-Driven Health Care: Tangible Employer Actions," *Benefits Quarterly* 20, no. 2 (Second Quarter 2004): 43.

44. William Atkinson, "Disease Management: A Win-Win Game Plan," *HRMagazine* 46, no. 12 (December 2001): 59–63.
45. Robert E. O'Toole, "Long-Term Care: Just What the Benefits Doctor Ordered," *Workspan* 45, no. 4 (April 2002): 58.
46. Howard Gleckman, "A Nest Egg That's a No-Brainer," *Business week*, April 25, 2005, 108.
47. Amy Borrus, "The Case of the Vanishing 401(k)s," *Business Week*, August 2, 2004, 62.
48. Anne Tergesen, "Does Your 401(k) Cost Too Much?" *Business Week*, June 7, 2004, 138.
49. Mike McNamee, "401(k)s: Workers Need Education, Not Handcuffs," *Business Week*, December 1, 2004, 108.
50. Anne Tergesen, "New Help with Your Nest Egg," *Business Week*, December 1, 2003, 108.
51. Robert J. Fulton, "Cash Balance Plus Match—A Win-Win Retirement Solution," *Workspan* 44, no. 5 (May 2001): 46–51.
52. "What You Need to Know Now about Cash-Balance Pension Plans," *HRFocus* 77, no. 7 (July 2000): 3–5.
53. With a traditional pension plan, employee benefits rise sharply during later years of employment. Remember, typical pension formulas multiply years of service by the highest final years of pay. Therefore, employees normally earn half of their pension during the last five years on the job. With a cash-balance plan, all employees receive the same steady annual credit; thus older employees lose those last big years of accruals. Companies reap financial savings because pension contributions for older employees are significantly reduced.
54. Nanette Byrnes, "Pensions That Discriminate against Older Workers," *Business Week*, August 25, 2003, 43.
55. ERISA, P.L. 93-406, 88 Stat. 829 (1974).
56. Carolyn Hirschman, "Overseeing Pension Management," *HRMagazine* 49, no. 7 (July 2004): 66.
57. Nanette Byrnes, "The Benefits Trap," *Business Week*, July 19, 2004, 64–72.
58. Ibid., 67.
59. Amy Borrus, Lorraine Woellert, Nanette Byrnes, Joseph Weber, and Brian Grow, "Pensions on a Precipice," *Business Week*, September 6, 2004, 52–53.
60. "The Return of Work/Life Plans," *HRFocus* 81, no. 4 (April 2004): 1.
61. G. Shaw Reynolds and Wayne E. K. Lehman, "Levels of Substance Abuse and Willingness to Use the Employee Assistance Program," *Journal of Behavioral Health Services and Research* 30, no. 2 (April–June 2003): 238–49.
62. Stephen LoJacono, "Mildly Ill/Back-Up Child Care: A Growing Trend in Employee Benefits," *Compensation and Benefits Review* 33, no. 5 (September/October 2001): 55.
63. Howard Gleckman, "When a Parent Needs Help," *Business Week*, July 12, 2004, 88–93.
64. Rudy M. Yandrick, "Elder Care Grows Up," *HRMagazine* 46, no. 11 (November 2001): 72–77.
65. Mirsada Pasalic, "The New Generation of Eldercare Benefits," *Bruner World* 25, no. 3 (March 2005): 52. See also Terence F. Shea, "Help with Elder Care," *HRMagazine* 48, no. 9 (September 2003): 113, and Martha Frase-Blunt, "Respecting the Elders," *HRMagazine* 48, no. 7 (July 2003): 89.
66. Dave Patel, "Just Ahead: Elder Care," *HRMagazine* 47, no. 2 (October 2002): 168.
67. Data obtained October 18, 2004, from the Credit Union National Association, P.O. Box 431, Madison, WI 53701, (608) 231-4000.
68. Steven R. Herrmann, "Financial Planning in the Workplace: The Time Is Now," *Employee Benefits Plan Review* 58, no. 4 (October 2003): 15.
69. Jeanie Caison-Tansiri, "A New Form of Paycheck," *Incentive* 178, no. 9 (September 2004): 14.
70. "Paycards Are the Wave of the Future," *HRFocus* 81, no. 8 (August 2004): 12.

chapter 12

Safety and Health

After studying this chapter, you should be able to

Summarize the general provisions of the Occupational Safety and Health Act (OSHA).

Describe what management can do to create a safe work environment.

Identify the measures that should be taken to control and eliminate health hazards.

Describe the organizational services and programs for building better health.

Explain the role of employee assistance programs in HRM.

Indicate methods for coping with stress.

Occupational safety and health accidents are both numerous and costly to employers. As one important example, workplace violence data show that more than 2 million nonfatal workplace violence incidents are reported annually in the form of assaults, robberies, thefts, hostage takings, hijackings, rapes, and sexual attacks.[1] Additionally, some 13,000 acts of domestic-related violence against women occur in the workplace annually. It is projected that employees miss 175,000 days of work per year due to domestic violence, costing employers between $3 billion and $5 billion yearly in lost productivity, greater absenteeism, and increased healthcare costs.[2] To prevent losses such as these, employers are concerned about limiting violence in the workplace along with providing working conditions—in all areas of employment—that provide for the safety and health of their employees.

While the laws safeguarding employees' physical and emotional well-being are certainly an incentive, many employers are motivated to provide desirable working conditions by virtue of their sensitivity to human needs and rights. The more cost-oriented employer recognizes the importance of avoiding accidents and illnesses wherever possible. Costs associated with sick leave, disability payments, replacement of employees who are injured or killed, and workers' compensation far exceed the costs of maintaining a safety and health program. A recent study conducted by Liberty Mutual found that employers saved $3 for each $1 invested in workplace safety.[3] Accidents and illnesses attributable to the workplace may also have pronounced effects on employee morale and on the goodwill that the organization enjoys in the community and in the business world.

Managers at all levels are expected to know and enforce safety and health standards throughout the organization. They must ensure a work environment that protects employees from physical hazards, unhealthy conditions, and unsafe acts of other personnel. Through effective safety and health programs, the physical and emotional well-being of employees may be preserved and even enhanced.

We begin this chapter by inviting readers to examine their safety and health knowledge by taking the test in Highlights in HRM 1. After discussing the legal requirements for safety and health, we shall focus in the rest of the chapter on the creation of a safe and healthy work environment and on the management of stress.

Safety and Health: It's the Law

Consider these facts:

- According to Occupational Safety and Health Administration statistics, in 2002 there were 5.5 million injuries/illnesses among private-sector firms.
- Experts estimate that back problems cost employers $50 billion yearly in workers' compensation costs and $50 billion in indirect costs (replacement workers, absenteeism, training, and so on). In 2002, more than 340,000 OSHA calls involved injuries to the back.
- In 2003, there were 609 private-sector work-related homicides.

Highlights in HRM 1

Test Your Safety Smarts

Take the following quiz to evaluate your knowledge and awareness of safety and health issues. Answers are found at the end of this chapter.

1. True or False? Employers have the right to be advised by an OSHA compliance officer of the reason for a workplace inspection.
2. True or False? Employers have the legal right to have a company representative accompany the OSHA compliance officer on an inspection.
3. True or False? OSHA requires that employers provide access to employees regarding the company's medical and exposure record.
4. What percentage of the U.S. population will be affected by back injuries?
   a. 23 b. 47 c. 60 d. 80
5. True or False? In order to correct potential health and safety problems, employers have the right to know the name of an employee who files a complaint with OSHA.
6. True or False? Employers have the legal right to request an inspection warrant before OSHA inspectors can enter a work site.
7. Which causes more accidents: unsafe acts or unsafe conditions?
8. List five areas regarding safety that should be covered during a new employee orientation.
9. True or False? Employers are required to provide employee training on OSHA standards.
10. True or False? Carpal tunnel syndrome is the fear of enclosed areas such as silos, tanks, and hallways.
11. True or False? Employers are required to allow OSHA inspectors on premises for unannounced inspections.
12. True or False? Employers have twenty-four hours to report to OSHA accidents that result in a fatality.

- In any year, approximately 75 million working days are lost because of on-the-job injuries.
- In 2003, 5,559 employees died from work accidents.

The burden on the nation's commerce as a result of lost productivity and wages, medical expenses, and disability compensation is staggering. And there is no way to calculate the human suffering involved.

It was to forestall even worse losses that Congress passed the Occupational Safety and Health Act (OSHA) in 1970.[4] The mission of OSHA is to "assure the safety and health of America's workers by setting and enforcing standards; providing training, outreach, and education; establishing partnerships; and encouraging continual improvements in workplace safety and health." In spite of the figures previously cited, the act has been very effective in reducing the number of injuries resulting in lost work time, the incident rate of specific injuries such as back problems, and the number of job-related deaths. For example, in 2004, with almost twice as many workers as in the 1960s, the 5,559 fatalities were almost one-third the number of worker deaths reported in the late 1960s.

OSHA's Coverage

OSHA covers all private-sector employees and public employees in state and local governments. Federal agencies are required to establish and maintain a safety and health program that is monitored by the Occupational Safety and Health Administration. Self-employed workers are not covered by the law. A state seeking OSHA approval of its safety and health program for the private sector must provide a similar program that covers its state and local government employees and is at least as effective as its program for private employers. Where state programs for the private sector have been approved by the federal government as meeting federal standards, the state carries out the enforcement functions that would otherwise be performed by the federal government.[5] Approximately half of the states currently have their own OSHA-approved programs.

OSHA Standards

One of the responsibilities of the Occupational Safety and Health Administration is to develop and enforce mandatory job safety and health standards. OSHA standards fall into four major categories: general industry, maritime, construction, and agriculture. These standards cover the workplace, machinery and equipment, materials, power sources, processing, protective clothing, first aid, and administrative requirements. It is the responsibility of employers to become familiar with those standards that are applicable to their establishments and to ensure that their employees use personal protective gear and equipment when required for safety. Employers can be cited and fined if they do not comply with OSHA standards. The *Federal Register* is the principal source of information on proposed, adopted, amended, and deleted OSHA standards. Large employers usually subscribe to it and/or the OSHA Subscription Service.[6]

The Occupational Safety and Health Administration can begin standards-setting procedures on its own initiative or on petition from other parties, including the Secretary of Health and Human Services (HHS) and the National Institute for Occupational Safety and Health (NIOSH). Other bodies that may also initiate standards-setting procedures are state and local governments and any nationally recognized standards-producing organization, employer, or labor representative. NIOSH, however, is the major source of standards. As an agency of the Department of Health and Human Services, it is responsible for conducting research on various safety and health problems, including the psychological factors involved.[7]

Enforcing OSHA Standards

The Occupational Safety and Health Administration is authorized to conduct workplace inspections, issue citations, and impose penalties on employers. In 2004, OSHA's staff of 1,123 inspectors conducted almost 40,000 workplace inspections. The major reason for inspections was related to high-hazard work areas (55 percent of total inspections), followed by accident-related complaints (23 percent).

Workplace Inspections

Under the act, "upon presenting appropriate credentials to the owner, operator, or agent in charge," an OSHA compliance officer is authorized to do the following:

- Enter without delay and at reasonable times any factory, plant, establishment, construction site or other areas, workplace, or environment where work is performed by an employee of an employer; and to
- Inspect and investigate during regular working hours, and at other reasonable times, and within reasonable limits and in a reasonable manner, any such place of employment and all pertinent conditions, structures, machines, apparatus, devices, equipment and materials therein, and to question privately any such employer, owner, operator, agent, or employee.[8]

OSHA has further established a system of inspection priorities:[9]

First level: Inspection of imminent danger situations

Second level: Investigation of catastrophes, fatalities, and accidents that result in hospitalization of five or more employees

Third level: Investigation of valid employee complaints of alleged violations of standards or of unsafe or unhealthful working conditions

Fourth level: Special-emphasis inspections aimed at specific high-hazard industries, occupations, or substances that are injurious to health

Typically, OSHA inspectors arrive at a work site unannounced and ask for a meeting with a representative of the employer. At the meeting the inspectors explain the purpose of the visit, describe the procedure for the inspection, and ask to review the employer's safety and health records. An employer may either agree voluntarily to the inspection or require the inspectors to obtain a search warrant.

OSHA inspectors have the authority to issue on-site citations for serious safety or health violations.

The act gives both the employer and the employees the right to accompany inspectors on their tour of the work site. After the tour the OSHA officials conduct a closing conference to inform the employer and employee representatives, if any, of the results of their inspection. They point out conditions or practices that appear to be hazardous and issue a written citation if warranted.[10]

Citations and Penalties

OSHA citations may be issued immediately following the inspection or later by mail. Citations tell the employer and employees which regulations and standards are alleged to have been violated and the amount of time allowed for their correction. The employer must post a copy of each citation at or near the place the violation occurred for three days or until the violation is abated, whichever is longer.

Under the act, OSHA may cite the following violations and propose the following penalties:

- Other-Than-Serious: A violation that has a direct relationship to job safety and health, but one unlikely to cause death or serious physical harm. OSHA may propose a penalty of up to $7,000 for each violation.
- Serious: A violation for which there is substantial probability that death or serious physical harm could result *and* the employer knew, or should have known, of the hazard. OSHA may propose a mandatory penalty of up to $7,000 for each violation.
- Willful: A violation that the employer intentionally and knowingly commits, or a violation that the employer commits with plain indifference to the law. OSHA may propose penalties of up to $70,000 for each violation.

If a willful violation results in the death of an employee, OSHA can assess penalties up to $250,000 for an individual or $500,000 for a corporation, imprisonment of up to six months, or both. The agency may adjust any penalty downward depending on the employer's good faith (such as demonstrating effort to comply with the act), history of previous violations, and size of business.[11] The law provides for appeal by employers and employees under specified circumstances. In 2003, OSHA fined employers more than $82 million for violations of the act.[12] Most penalties were for serious violations of the act (more than $52 million).

OSHA Consultation Assistance

Besides helping employers identify and correct specific hazards, OSHA can help employers develop and implement effective workplace safety and health programs that emphasize preventing worker injuries and illnesses.

Onsite Consultation

OSHA provides a free onsite consultation service. Consultants from the state government or private contractors help employers identify hazardous conditions and determine corrective measures. Employers also may receive training and education services.[13] No citations are issued in connection with a consultation, and the consultant's files cannot be used to trigger an OSHA inspection. Additionally, consultations may qualify employers for a one-year exemption from routine OSHA inspections.

Cooperative Programs

Voluntary, cooperative relationships among employers, employees, unions, and OSHA can be a useful alternative to traditional OSHA enforcement procedures, serving as an effective way to ensure worker safety and health. There are four specific cooperative programs—alliances, strategic partnerships, voluntary protection programs, and the Safety and Health Achievement Recognition Program:[14]

Alliances. Alliances enable organizations to collaborate with OSHA to prevent injuries and illnesses in the workplace. OSHA and participating organizations define, implement, and meet a set of short- and long-term goals to improve workplace safety and health.

Strategic Partnership Programs (SPPs). Strategic partnerships are long-term agreements between employers and OSHA aimed at reducing serious workplace hazards and achieving a high level of worker safety and health.

Voluntary Protection Programs (VPPs). Voluntary protection programs represent OSHA's effort to extend worker protection beyond the minimum required OSHA standards. There are three VPPs—Star, Merit, and Demonstration—each designed to recognize, motivate, or establish a cooperative relationship between employers and OSHA.

Safety and Health Achievement Recognition Program (SHARP). SHARP provides recognition to employers who demonstrate exemplary achievement in workplace safety and health.

Responsibilities and Rights under OSHA

Both employers and employees have certain responsibilities and rights under OSHA. We will discuss only those that relate directly to the management of human resources.

Employers' Responsibilities and Rights

In addition to providing a hazard-free workplace and complying with the applicable standards, employers must inform all of their employees about the safety and health requirements of OSHA. Specific employer responsibilities are listed in OSHA's publication *All About OSHA* and illustrated in Highlights in HRM 2. Employers are also required to keep certain records and to compile and post an annual summary of work-related injuries and illnesses.[15] From these records, organizations can compute their *incidence rate*, the number of injuries and illnesses per 100 full-time employees during a given year. The standard formula for computing the incidence rate is shown by the following equation, in which 200,000 equals the base for 100 full-time workers who work forty hours a week, fifty weeks a year:

$$\text{Incidence rate} = \frac{\text{Number of injuries and illnesses} \times 200{,}000}{\text{Total hours worked by all employees during period covered}}$$

It should be noted that the same formula can be used to compute incidence rates for (1) the number of workdays lost because of injuries and illnesses, (2) the number of nonfatal injuries and illnesses without lost workdays, and (3) cases involving only injuries or only illnesses.

What Are My Responsibilities under the OSH Act?

If you are an **employer** the *OSH Act* covers, you must:

- Meet your general duty responsibility to provide a workplace free from recognized hazards;
- Keep workers informed about OSHA and safety and health matters with which they are involved;
- Comply in a responsible manner with standards, rules, and regulations issued under the *OSH Act;*
- Be familiar with mandatory OSHA standards;
- Make copies of standards available to employees for review upon request;
- Evaluate workplace conditions;
- Minimize or eliminate potential hazards;
- Make sure employees have and use safe, properly maintained tools and equipment (including appropriate personal protective equipment);
- Warn employees of potential hazards;
- Establish or update operating procedures and communicate them to employees;
- Provide medical examinations when required;
- Provide training required by OSHA standards;
- Report within 8 hours any accident that results in a fatality or the hospitalization of three or more employees;
- Keep OSHA-required records of work-related injuries and illnesses, unless otherwise specified;
- Post a copy of the *OSHA 300—Log and Summary of Occupational Injuries and Illnesses* for the prior year each year during the entire month of February unless otherwise specified;
- Post, at a prominent location within the workplace, the OSHA poster (OSHA 2203) informing employees of their rights and responsibilities;
- Provide employees, former employees, and their representatives access to the OSHA 300 form at a reasonable time and in a reasonable manner;
- Provide access to employee medical records and exposure records;
- Cooperate with OSHA compliance officers;
- Not discriminate against employees who properly exercise their rights under the *OSH Act;*
- Post OSHA citations and abatement verification notices at or near the worksite involved; and
- Abate cited violations within the prescribed period.

If you are an **employee** the *OSH Act* covers, you should:

- Read the OSHA poster at the job site;
- Comply with all applicable OSHA standards;
- Follow all employer safety and health rules and regulations, and wear or use prescribed protective equipment while engaged in work;
- Report hazardous conditions to the supervisor;
- Report any job-related injury or illness to the employer, and seek treatment promptly;

- Cooperate with the OSHA compliance officer conducting an inspection; and
- Exercise your rights under the *OSH Act* in a responsible manner.

Although OSHA does not cite employees for violations of their responsibilities, each employee must follow all applicable standards, rules, regulations, and orders issued under the *OSH Act.* OSHA, however, does not expect employees to pay for guardrails, floor cleaning, equipment maintenance, respirators, training, or other safety and health measures.

Source: U.S. Department of Labor, Occupational Safety and Health Administration, *All about OSHA* (Washington, DC: U.S. Government Printing Office, 2003): 4–5.

Incidence rates are useful for comparing work groups, departments, and similar units within an organization. They also provide a basis for comparing other organizations doing similar work. The Bureau of Labor Statistics and other organizations, such as the National Safety Council, compile data that an employer can use as a basis for comparing its safety record with those of other organizations. These comparisons provide a starting point for analyzing problem areas, changing the working environment, and motivating personnel to promote safety and health.

It is the employer's responsibility to make sure employees use protective equipment when necessary. Employers must therefore engage in safety training and be prepared to discipline employees for failing to comply with safety rules. And employers must not discriminate against employees who exercise their rights under the act by filing complaints. On the other hand, employers are afforded many rights under the law, most of which pertain to receiving information, applying for variances in standards, and contesting citations.[16]

Employees' Responsibilities and Rights

Employees are required to comply with all applicable OSHA standards, to report hazardous conditions, and to follow all employer safety and health rules and regulations, including those prescribing the use of protective equipment. Workers have a right to demand safe and healthy conditions on the job without fear of punishment. They also have many rights that pertain to requesting and receiving information about safety and health conditions.[17]

Right-to-Know Laws

right-to-know laws
Laws that require employers to advise employees about the hazardous chemicals they handle

Exposure to hazardous chemicals is currently one of the most serious health concerns for both employers and employees. Therefore, most states—and federal law—require that employers provide information to employees about the hazardous chemicals they handle. Commonly known as **right-to-know laws,** these statutes address such issues as the definition of toxic and hazardous substances, the duties of employers and manufacturers to provide health-risk information to employees, trade-secret protection, and enforcement provisions. Since state right-to-know laws can be more stringent than federal law, employers are encouraged to contact their state's health and safety agency for a copy of their appropriate hazard communication standards.[18]

To understand the right-to-know laws, employers must first become familiar with OSHA-published hazardous chemical regulations known as the Hazard Communication Standard (HCS). The HCS prescribes a system for communicating data on health hazards to employees. It includes a format for **Material Safety Data Sheets (MSDSs).** MSDSs should include the chemical name of a hazardous substance; all of the risks involved in using it, including potential health risks; safe handling practices; personal protective equipment needed; first aid in the event of an accident; and information identifying the manufacturer.

Material Safety Data Sheets (MSDSs)
Documents that contain vital information about hazardous substances

OSHA's Enforcement Record

Perhaps no federal government agency has been more severely criticized than the Occupational Safety and Health Administration.[19] Complaints often concern what employers consider to be picky or unrealistic standards and the proliferation of rules under agency personnel. Another prevalent criticism is that many of OSHA's standards are dangerously outdated. According to one safety manager, "It seems OSHA administration conducts research and sets safety and health standards in an ivory tower, not knowing or caring if standards are valid for the real world." However, the complaint most registered against OSHA is uneven enforcement efforts by the agency from one political administration to the next.

Under some administrations, enforcement efforts have been seen as virtually nonexistent (or at least very lax), while under others, regulatory enforcement has seemed more proactive. Employers often view OSHA as overly zealous, while unions and safety groups continue to worry that OSHA is lax in monitoring its agreements with organizations. These groups would prefer mandatory standards instead of voluntary guidelines for problems such as injuries related to jobs involving repetitive motion—a topic to be considered later in the chapter.

Creating a Safe Work Environment

We have seen that employers are required by law to provide safe working conditions for their employees.[20] To achieve this objective, the majority of employers have a formal safety program. Typically, the HR department or the industrial relations department is responsible for the safety program. While the success of a safety program depends largely on managers and supervisors of operating departments, the HR department typically coordinates the safety communication and training programs, maintains safety records required by OSHA, and works closely with managers and supervisors in a cooperative effort to make the program a success.

Organizations with formal safety programs generally have an employee-management safety committee that includes representatives from management, each department or manufacturing/service unit, and employee representatives.[21] Committees are typically involved in investigating accidents and helping to publicize the importance of safety rules and their enforcement.

Promoting Safety Awareness

Probably the most important role of a safety awareness program is motivating managers, supervisors, and subordinates to be champions of safety considerations. In one

© KATHY FERGUSON-JOHNSON/PHOTOEDIT

Safety begins with proper instruction, as these fire-fighters demonstrate in this training exercise.

study conducted by the American Institute of Plant Engineers, "survey results showed a direct correlation between an increase in management's commitment to safety in the workplace and a decrease in accidents." If managers and supervisors fail to demonstrate awareness, their subordinates can hardly be expected to do so. Unfortunately, many managers and supervisors wear their "safety hats" far less often than their "production, quality control, and methods of improvement hats."

Most organizations have a safety awareness program that entails the use of several different media. Safety lectures, commercially produced films, specially developed videocassettes, and other media such as pamphlets are useful for teaching and motivating employees to follow safe work procedures. Highlights in HRM 3 shows a list of organizations that provide materials on safety awareness and training.

The Key Role of the Supervisor

One of a supervisor's major responsibilities is to communicate to an employee the need to work safely. Beginning with new employee orientation, safety should be emphasized continually. Proper work procedures, the use of protective clothing and devices, and potential hazards should be explained thoroughly. Furthermore, employees' understanding of all these considerations should be verified during training sessions, and employees should be encouraged to take some initiative in maintaining a concern for safety. Since training by itself does not ensure continual adherence to safe work practices, supervisors must observe employees at work and reinforce safe practices. Where unsafe acts are detected, supervisors should take immediate action to find the cause. Supervisors should also foster a team spirit of safety among the work group.

Proactive Safety Training Program

Safety training is not only good business; in certain occupational areas safety and health training is legally required. For example, employers covered by the Hazardous Liquid Pipeline and Safety Act (HLPSA) are legally required to train employees in environment safety protection. When training is mandated, employers must keep accurate records of all employee education. Violations can incur criminal penalties. For example, after a pipeline explosion killed three workers in Bellingham, Washington, Olympic Pipeline was indicted for "knowingly and willfully" violating the training and recordkeeping requirements of HLPSA.[22]

In companies that voluntarily undertake safety and health training, one study found the most frequent topics to be (1) first aid, (2) defensive driving, (3) accident prevention techniques, (4) hazardous materials, and (5) emergency procedures.[23] Most programs emphasize the use of emergency first-aid equipment and personal safety equipment.

HR professionals, and safety directors in particular, advocate employee involvement when designing and implementing safety programs.[24] Employees can offer valuable

Highlights in HRM 3

Organizations Providing Safety Awareness and Training Materials

Various public and private organizations, including those listed here, provide safety awareness and training materials. Instructional media include videos, pamphlets, posters, online instruction, and lecture materials. Materials may cover general topics such as principles of first aid or the correct use of protective clothing, or the material may be on more specific topics such as the handling of hazardous materials.

National Safety Council
Occupational Safety and Health Administration
American Society of Safety Engineers
American Industrial Hygiene Association
Canadian Society of Safety Engineering
American Conference of Governmental Industrial Hygienists
American Association of Occupational Health Nurses
American College of Occupational and Environmental Medicine
Risk and Insurance Management Society
British Occupational Hygiene Society
Drug & Alcohol Testing Industry Association
Emergency Nurses Association
International Association of Fire Chiefs
National Hearing Conservation Association
Society of Human Resource Management

ideas regarding specific safety and health topics to cover, instructional methods, and proper teaching techniques.[25] Furthermore, acceptance for safety training is heightened when employees feel a sense of ownership in the instructional program.

Information Technology and Safety Awareness and Training

Several reasons are advanced for the use of the Internet and information technology in safety and health training. First, enhanced delivery modes facilitate the development of both managers and employees.[26] Videos, PowerPoint presentations, and interactive CD-ROM training are ideal methods for standardized safety, environmental, and health instruction. Second, information technology allows organizations to customize their safety and health training needs.[27] At Stanley Works, the company's Internet is the number one tool for reducing health and safety problems. According to Kevin Nelson, employee health and safety director, "The Internet functions as the organization's SWAT team to develop and implement timely and efficient health and safety programs." Third, information technology is ideally suited for regulatory instruction. OSHA distributes information on compliance assistance through eTools, technical links, CD-ROMs, and PowerPoint presentations. OSHA's eTools are interactive, web-based training tools on various safety and health topics. These modules enable users to answer questions and receive reliable advice on how OSHA regulations apply to their work location.[28]

Enforcing Safety Rules

Specific rules and regulations concerning safety are communicated through supervisors, bulletin board notices, employee handbooks, and signs attached to equipment. Safety rules are also emphasized in regular safety meetings, at new-employee orientations, and in manuals of standard operating procedures.[29]

Penalties for violation of safety rules are usually stated in the employee handbook. In a large percentage of organizations, the penalties imposed on violators are the same as those for violations of other rules. They include an oral or written warning for the first violation, suspension for repeated violations, and, as a last resort, dismissal. However, for serious violations—such as smoking around volatile substances—even the first offense may be cause for termination.

While discipline may force employees to work safely, safety managers understand that the most effective enforcement of safety rules occurs when employees willingly obey and "champion" safety rules and procedures. This can be achieved when management actively encourages employees to participate in all aspects of the organization's safety program. For example, opportunities for employee involvement include (1) jointly setting safety standards with management, (2) participation in safety training, (3) involvement in designing and implementing special safety training programs, (4) involvement in establishing safety incentives and rewards, and (5) inclusion in accident investigations. At Federal Mogel, employees are invited to become Danger Rangers. These employees spot near-miss accidents and take corrective action. Danger Rangers who report near-miss accidents are enrolled in monthly drawings for prizes, such as gift certificates and clothing.[30]

Investigating and Recording Accidents

Every accident, even those considered minor, should be investigated by the supervisor and a member of the safety committee. Such an investigation may determine the factors contributing to the accident and reveal what corrections are needed to prevent it from happening again. Correction may require rearranging workstations, installing safety guards or controls, or, more often, giving employees additional safety training and reassessing their motivation for safety.[31]

OSHA requirements mandate that employers with eleven or more employees maintain records of work-related occupational injuries and illnesses.[32] As stated in an earlier section, OSHA also requires that a Log of Work-Related Injuries and Illnesses (OSHA Form 300) be maintained by the organization. All recordable cases are to be entered in the log. A **recordable case** is any injury or illness that results in any of the following: death, days away from work, restricted work or transfer to another job, or medical treatment beyond first aid. Other problems employers must record as work-related include loss of consciousness or diagnosis of a significant injury or illness by a healthcare professional.[33] Figure 12.1 illustrates OSHA's diagram for classifying accidents under the law. For every recordable case written in the log, an Injury and Illness Incident Report (OSHA Form 301) is to be completed. OSHA Form 301 requires answers to questions about the case. Each year OSHA Form 300-A (Summary

recordable case
Any occupational death, illness, or injury to be recorded in the log (OSHA Form 300)

Figure 12.1 Guide to Recording Cases under the Occupational Safety and Health Act

IF A CASE:

Note: A case must involve a death, or an illness, or an injury to an employee.

Results from a work accident or from an exposure in the work environment and is

Does not result from a work accident or from an exposure in the work environment

A death

An illness

An injury that involves

Medical treatment (other than first aid)

Loss of consciousness

Days away from work

Restricted work or job transfer

Diagnosis by a healthcare professional

None of these

Then case must be recorded

Then case is not to be recorded

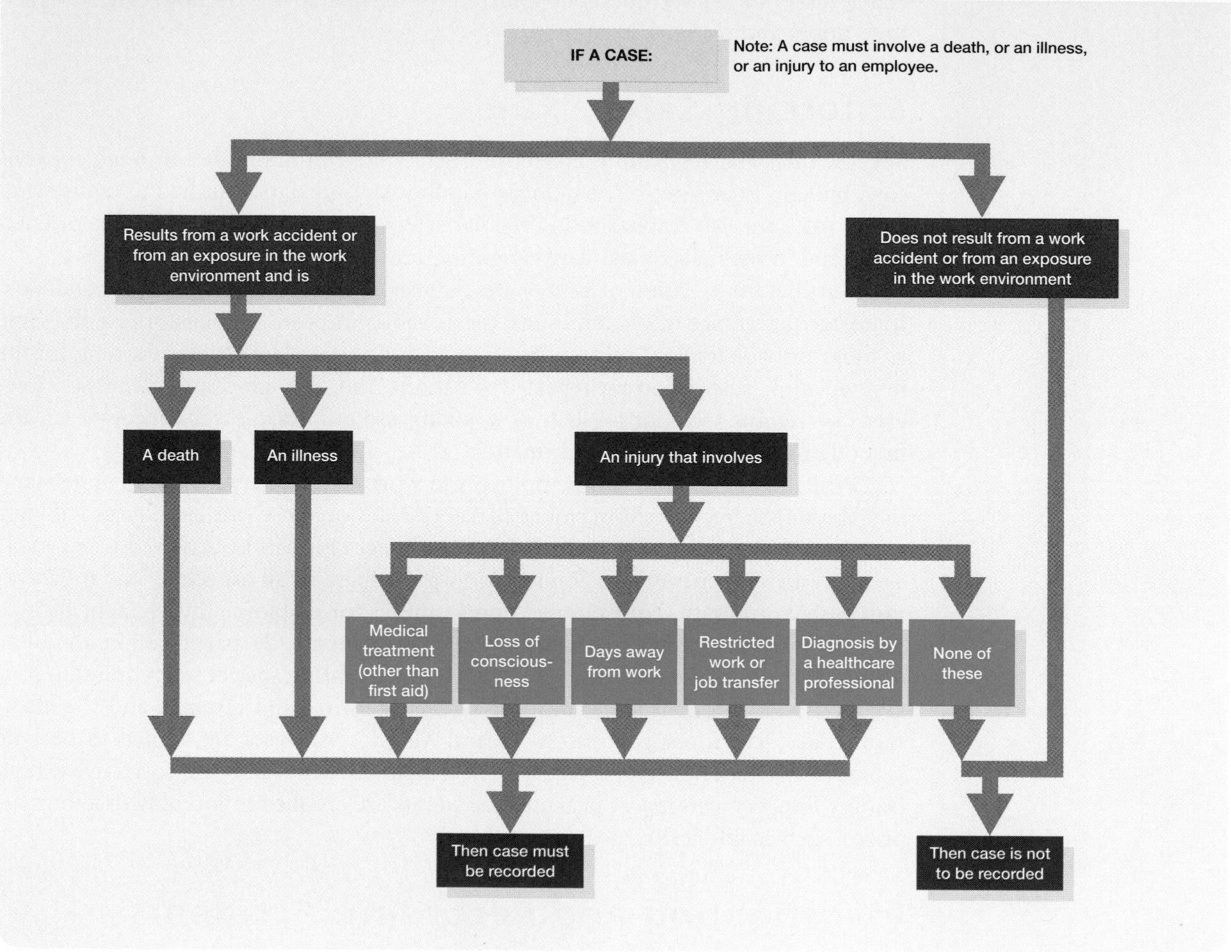

of Work-Related Injuries and Illnesses) must be completed and posted in a conspicuous place or places where notices to employees are customarily posted. Remember, when completing all OSHA forms, employers must not list the name of an injured or ill employee if the case has "privacy concerns," such as those involving sexual assault, HIV infection, and mental illness.[34]

We conclude our discussion of OSHA by showing the OSHA poster that employers are required to display at the workplace (see Highlights in HRM 4).

Creating a Healthy Work Environment

From its title alone, the Occupational Safety and Health Act was clearly designed to protect the health, as well as the safety, of employees. Because of the dramatic impact of workplace accidents, however, managers and employees alike may pay more attention to these kinds of immediate safety concerns than to job conditions that are dangerous to

Highlights in HRM 4

Job Safety and Health Protection Poster

You Have a Right to a Safe and Healthful Workplace.

IT'S THE LAW!

- You have the right to notify your employer or OSHA about workplace hazards. You may ask OSHA to keep your name confidential.
- You have the right to request an OSHA inspection if you believe that there are unsafe and unhealthful conditions in your workplace. You or your representative may participate in the inspection.
- You can file a complaint with OSHA within 30 days of discrimination by your employer for making safety and health complaints or for exercising your rights under the *OSH Act*.
- You have a right to see OSHA citations issued to your employer. Your employer must post the citations at or near the place of the alleged violation.
- Your employer must correct workplace hazards by the date indicated on the citation and must certify that these hazards have been reduced or eliminated.
- You have the right to copies of your medical records or records of your exposure to toxic and harmful substances or conditions.
- Your employer must post this notice in your workplace.

The *Occupational Safety and Health Act of 1970 (OSH Act)*, P.L. 91-596, assures safe and healthful working conditions for working men and women throughout the Nation. The Occupational Safety and Health Administration, in the U.S. Department of Labor, has the primary responsibility for administering the *OSH Act*. The rights listed here may vary depending on the particular circumstances. To file a complaint, report an emergency, or seek OSHA advice, assistance, or products, call 1-800-321-OSHA or your nearest OSHA office: • Atlanta (404) 562-2300 • Boston (617) 565-9860 • Chicago (312) 353-2220 • Dallas (214) 767-4731 • Denver (303) 844-1600 • Kansas City (816) 426-5861 • New York (212) 337-2378 • Philadelphia (215) 861-4900 • San Francisco (415) 975-4310 • Seattle (206) 553-5930. Teletypewriter (TTY) number is 1-877-889-5627. To file a complaint online or obtain more information on OSHA federal and state programs, visit OSHA's website at **www.osha.gov**. If your workplace is in a state operating under an OSHA-approved plan, your employer must post the required state equivalent of this poster.

1-800-321-OSHA

www.osha.gov

U.S. Department of Labor • Occupational Safety and Health Administration • OSHA 3165 their health. It is essential, therefore, that health hazards be identified and controlled.[35] Furthermore, pressure from the federal government and unions, as well as increased public concern, has given employers a definite incentive to provide the safest and healthiest work environment possible.

Health Hazards and Issues

At one time health hazards were associated primarily with jobs found in industrial processing operations. In recent years, however, hazards in jobs outside the plant, such as in offices, healthcare facilities, and airports, have been recognized and preventive methods adopted. Substituting materials, altering processes, enclosing or isolating a process, issuing protective equipment, and improving ventilation are some of the common preventions. This section will review several of the more important health concerns to employees and employers.

Chemical Hazards

It is estimated that more than 65,000 different chemicals are currently in use in the United States with which humans may come into contact. Many of these chemicals are harmful, lurking for years in the body with no outward symptoms until the disease they cause is well established. It is not surprising, therefore, that the OSHA Hazard Communication Standard is the most frequently cited OSHA standard for general industry as well as for the construction industry. The purpose of the law is to ensure the testing and evaluation of chemicals by producers and the distribution of the chemical hazard information to users of the chemical.

All hazardous chemical containers must be labeled with the identity of the contents and must state any appropriate hazard warnings. The labels must be in English and employees must be able to cross-reference the label to the Material Safety Data Sheet (MSDS) for the hazardous chemical. OSHA-required chemical training includes informing employees of the methods used to detect the presence or release of hazardous chemicals, the physical and health problems posed by hazardous chemicals, and the ways in which employees can protect themselves from chemical dangers.

USING THE INTERNET

Information on chemical safety can be obtained free from the Chemical Reactivity Worksheet program sponsored by NOAA. Go to the Student Resources at:

http://bohlander.swlearning.com

Chemical hazards present a significant concern when they have the potential to affect the reproductive health of either women or men. In an important case concerning women, the U.S. Supreme Court ruled in *International Union v Johnson Controls* (1991) that employers may not bar women of childbearing age from certain jobs because of potential risk to their fetuses.[36] The Court said that such policies are a form of sex bias that is prohibited by federal civil rights law. The decision has made it important for employers to inform and warn female workers about fetal health risks on the job.

Tobacco Smoke

In a recent study published in the *Journal of the American Medical Association,* research findings showed that in 2000, more than 400,000 individuals died from smoking and another 35,000 nonsmokers died from lung cancer due to breathing secondhand smoke (inhaling other people's smoke).[37] Stanton Glantz, cardiologist at the University of California at San Francisco, states that "second-hand smoke causes heart rates to rise, blood vessels to dilate less easily, and blood components to be stickier—all raising the risk of heart attack."[38]

Holsum Bakery's Workplace Smoking Policy

Purpose

The purpose of this policy is to address some of the problems and concerns voiced by smokers and non-smokers. This policy does not attempt to ban smoking, but restricts it to areas which are frequently *shared* by smokers and non-smokers. Also, this policy attempts to comply with recently enacted laws in Arizona.

Recent studies have concluded that secondary smoke can have serious health consequences. Therefore, the goal will be, to the greatest degree practicable, to obtain freedom from discomfort and irritation for those persons sensitive to tobacco smoke, while preserving a reasonable degree of freedom for those who choose to smoke.

Policy

It is the policy of Holsum Bakery to provide the space necessary for all of our associates to perform their functions in clean air spaces, as well as relax in our several break rooms in smoke-free environments, while at the same time providing separate space for those who choose to smoke.

Procedure

The designated smoking areas are the **upstairs patio** and the **back break room.** All other areas are non-smoking.

In outlying areas such as Thrift Stores and Depots, designated areas for smoking and non-smoking will be provided.

Smokers may wish to learn about our special incentive to stop smoking. Associate Services can provide the information. In order to qualify for this offer, a person must have been employed by Holsum on a full-time basis, and must be here for a minimum of six (6) months before he/she can apply.

Source: Used with permission from Holsum Bakery, Inc., 2322 West Lincoln St., Phoenix, AZ 85005.

Because of findings such as these, smokers have been banned from lighting up on airplanes, at work, in restaurants and hotels, in public buildings, and in various business establishments. More than forty states and the District of Columbia, as well as numerous cities, towns, and counties, have passed laws restricting smoking in offices and other public places.[39]

Virtually all large organizations and even smaller ones have initiated smoking policies (see Highlights in HRM 5). In developing smoking policies, it is advisable to have the involvement of both smokers and nonsmokers. Organizations emphasizing employee involvement include Merck, Comerica, Hallmark, and Southwest Airlines.

Video Display Terminals

The expanding use of computers and video display terminals (VDTs) in the workplace has generated intense debate over the possible hazards to which VDT users may be exposed. Many fears about VDT use have been shown to be unfounded, but serious health complaints remain an issue. Problems that managers have to confront in this area fall into three major groups:

1. *Visual difficulties.* VDT operators frequently complain of blurred vision, sore eyes, burning and itching eyes, and glare.
2. *Muscular aches and pains.* Pains in the back, neck, and shoulders are common complaints of VDT operators.
3. *Job stress.* Eye strain, postural problems, noise, insufficient training, excessive workloads, and monotonous work are complaints reported by three-quarters of VDT users.

To capitalize on the benefits of VDTs while safeguarding employee health, Dr. James Sheedy, a VDT and vision expert, offers these tips on how to minimize the negative effects of computer use on the eyes and body:

- Place the computer screen four to nine inches below eye level.
- Keep the monitor directly in front of you.
- Sit in an adjustable-height chair and use a copyholder that attaches to both the desk and the monitor.
- Use a screen with adjustable brightness and contrast controls.
- Use shades or blinds to reduce the computer-screen glare created by window lighting.

Cumulative Trauma Disorders

cumulative trauma disorders
Injuries involving tendons of the fingers, hands, and arms that become inflamed from repeated stresses and strains

Meat cutters, fish filleters, cooks, dental hygienists, textile workers, violinists, flight attendants, office workers at computer terminals, and others whose jobs require repetitive motion of the fingers, hands, or arms are reporting injuries in growing percentages. Known as **cumulative trauma disorders** or repetitive motion injuries, these musculoskeletal disorders (MSDs) are injuries of the muscles, nerves, tendons, ligaments, joints, and spinal discs caused by repeated stresses and strains. One of the more common conditions is *carpal tunnel syndrome*, which is characterized by tingling or numbness in the fingers occurring when a tunnel of bones and ligaments in the wrist narrows and pinches nerves that reach the fingers and the base of the thumb. Without proper treatment, employees with carpal tunnel syndrome can lose complete feeling in their hands. Another cumulative trauma disorder prevalent among tennis players is tennis elbow.

In Chapter 4, we discussed job design and ergonomics considerations as one way to accommodate the capabilities and limitations of employees. Ergonomics techniques are also successfully used to improve or correct workplace conditions that cause or aggravate cumulative trauma disorders.[40] Continuous developments in office furniture, video display terminals, tool design, computer keyboards, and adjustable workstations are all attempts to make the work setting more comfortable—and, hopefully, more productive—but also to lessen musculoskeletal disorders. Mini-breaks involving exercise and the changing of work positions have been found helpful. Importantly, these kinds of injuries often go away if they are caught early. If they are not, they may require months or years of treatment or even surgical correction. Also, when cumulative trauma disorders result from work activities, they serve to lower employee productivity, increase employer health costs, and incur workers' compensation payments.

Ergonomics and OSHA

Employee musculoskeletal injuries are classified as recordable cases and must be reported on OSHA Form 300. Additionally, OSHA will enforce removal of ergonomic hazards by issuing citations under the general duty clause of the Occupational Safety and Health Act.[41]

Currently, OSHA has issued *voluntary employer* guidelines for reducing musculoskeletal disorders in three areas—nursing homes, retail grocery stores, and poultry processing. Presently these guidelines are described as "general"; however, employers can expect OSHA to develop more industry- or task-specific guidelines for a number of industries based on current incidence rates and effective and feasible ergonomic solutions to MSD problems.[42] All future OSHA ergonomic programs are championed to be "business-friendly" and emphasize a four-pronged comprehensive approach for reducing MSD injuries and illnesses. OSHA programs will emphasize guidelines, research, outreach and assistance, and enforcement.

Beyond OSHA guidelines, proactive companies use ergonomic practices to both save costs and reduce workplace injuries. For example, at Cessna Aircraft, factory employees use specially designed hand tools to reduce hand and arm tension.[43] Rockwell Automation reduced shoulder injuries to punch-press operators by purchasing hydraulic fork trucks to lift metal dies, a process formerly done manually; Maple Landmark Woodcraft employed ergonomic education to reduce repetitive-motion injuries caused by hammering. Since 1995, Johnson & Johnson has used ergonomic techniques, saving the company $18 million. Key elements of successful ergonomic programs are shown in Figure 12.2.[44]

USING THE INTERNET

A variety of ergonomic information can be found on the Cornell University Ergonomics web site. Go to the Student Resources at:

http://bohlander.swlearning.com

Figure 12.2 Key Elements for a Successful Ergonomics Program

Companies with award-winning ergonomics programs list the following as common elements of success:

- *Provide notice and training for employees.* Implement a well-publicized ergonomics policy or present ergonomic information in safety policies or training programs. Train employees, supervisors, and managers in basic workplace ergonomics.
- *Conduct pre-injury hazard assessment.* Survey the workplace and work processes for potential hazards and adopt measures to lessen the exposure to ergonomic risk factors. Answer the question, "Are certain work areas more prone to ergonomic hazards than others?"
- *Involve employees.* Include employees in risk assessment, recognition of MSD symptoms, design of work-specific equipment or tools, and the setting of work performance rules and guidelines.
- *Plan and execute.* Integrate ergonomic responsibilities into the performance plans for all personnel. Demand accountability for program success.
- *File injury reports.* Encourage early reporting of MSD symptoms or injuries. Refer employees to the company's medical facilities or to the employee's personal physician for treatment.
- *Evaluate and assess the ergonomics program.* Periodically review the effectiveness of the ergonomics program. If the program appears to be ineffective, determine the underlying causes for failure and propose corrective changes.

AIDS

As we observed in Chapter 3, AIDS (acquired immune deficiency syndrome) is a disability covered by federal, state, and local protective statutes. Employers subject to statutes under which people with AIDS are likely to be considered disabled are required to hire or retain a person with AIDS who is qualified to perform the essential functions of his or her job. The federal Rehabilitation Act, the Americans with Disabilities Act, and statutes of several states also require employers to give reasonable accommodation to the person through such adjustments as job restructuring, modified work schedules, and less rigid physical requirements.

While there is still no evidence that AIDS can be spread through casual contact in the typical workplace, one of the major problems employers face is the concern that many people have about contracting it. Employees can express "some misgivings" or "strong resentment" about working with someone with AIDS. These reactions require employers to formulate programs to educate managers and employees about the transmission of AIDS and the legal rights and moral responsibilities of employers, employees, and people with AIDS. A wide variety of commercially produced materials (posters, pamphlets, videos, and so on) is easily obtainable. Also, the manager's job of obtaining AIDS information has been assisted by various organizations, including the Centers for Disease Control, which has a special office to assist employers and labor organizations.[45] A comprehensive and widely distributed AIDS policy contributes to reducing fears about this illness.[46]

In industries where employees may come in contact with blood or other body fluids (such as medical response teams, hospitals, and nursing homes), employers are required to follow OSHA's bloodborne pathogen standards. Covered employers must train employees in topics such as protective equipment, handling of blood and body fluids, cleaning of equipment, and waste disposal. Additionally, OSHA requires specific recordkeeping for "at-risk" employees, those with occupational exposure to bloodborne pathogens such as hepatitis B virus, and others.

Workplace Violence

In recent years, employees have been killed at these organizations: Navistar International, Ford, Edgewater Technology, Xerox, Chrysler, Fireman's Fund, Pettit and Martin (a San Francisco law firm), and the U.S. Postal Service. These examples illustrate why workplace violence has been called the "deadly virus" of crime in America. According to one study on violence perpetrators:

- 94.3 percent of violence perpetrators were men, 5.7 percent women.
- Perpetrators are normally between ages 35 and 45 and have significant job tenure.
- Normally, specific individuals are targeted for attack.
- Current employees constitute the bulk of perpetrators (43.6 percent); former employees account for 22.5 percent.[47]

Reducing Workplace Violence

A NIOSH study has identified risk factors associated with higher incidence of work-related violence. Employees who have contact with the public; exchange money; deliver passengers, goods, or services; work in healthcare, social services, or criminal settings; or work alone or in small numbers are at a greater risk of encountering workplace assaults. Employers are cautioned to afford increased protection to these individuals.

USING THE INTERNET

OSHA creates and enforces workplace safety regulations. NIOSH is concerned with research into and ways to prevent workplace hazards. You can read the NIOSH study on workplace violence via the Student Resources at:

http://bohlander.swlearning.com

OSHA has issued five recommendations for preventing workplace violence:

- Management commitment to and employee involvement in preventing acts of violence
- Analyzing the workplace to uncover areas of potential violence
- Preventing and controlling violence by designing safe workplaces and work practices
- Providing violence prevention training throughout the organization
- Evaluating violence program effectiveness[48]

In addition to following OSHA guidelines, violence-prevention specialists recommend that employers take specific actions to reduce workplace violence. First, it is recommended that organizations screen job applicants for histories showing a propensity to violence.[49] For small employers, outside investigators will perform background checks for very small fees. (Remember, employers may be found legally negligent in their hiring practices if they fail to properly investigate applicants. An employee may claim the employer was negligent in that the employer knew, or should have known, that the individual was unfit but hired and kept the person anyway.)[50]

Second, managers and supervisors can be trained to recognize violence indicators such as those given in Figure 12.3. Awareness of these threatening behaviors can

Figure 12.3 Violence Indicators: Know the Warning Signs

Most people leave a trail of indicators before they become violent. Similarly, disgruntled former employees who commit acts of violence leave warning signs of their intent before and after termination. The following behaviors should be taken seriously when assessing situations of potential violence:

- Direct or veiled threatening statements
- Recent performance declines, including concentration problems and excessive excuses
- Prominent mood or behavior changes; despondence
- Preoccupation with guns, knives, or other weapons
- Deliberate destruction of workplace equipment; sabotage
- Fascination with stories of violence
- Reckless or antisocial behavior; evidence of prior assaultive behavior
- Aggressive behavior or intimidating statements
- Written messages of violent intent; exaggerated perceptions of injustice
- Serious stress in personal life
- Obsessive desire to harm a specific group or person
- Violence against a family member
- Substance abuse

Source: Adapted from *Violence in the Workplace: Risk Factors and Prevention Strategies*, NIOSH Bulletin #59; Walter Brennan, "Sounding Off about Verbal Abuse," *Occupational Health* 55, no. 11 (November 2003): 22; and Larry J. Chavez, "Benefits That Can Prevent Workplace Violence," *Employee Benefit Plan Review* 58, no. 2 (August 2003): 6.

provide an opportunity to intervene and prevent disruptive, abusive, or violent acts.[51] Third, managers must effectively communicate a zero-tolerance policy for violence and encourage employees to report any possible or observed incidents of workplace violence.[52] Fourth, a meaningful reporting procedure with clear lines of responsibility can ensure that management is promptly notified of potential security risks in order to take immediate steps to resolve the issues. Finally, organizations such as Garden Fresh, a restaurant chain, have formalized workplace violence-prevention policies, informing employees that aggressive employee behavior will not be tolerated (see Highlights in HRM 6).

Terrorism

The September 11, 2001, attacks on the World Trade Center and the Pentagon brought home to all Americans the magnitude and horror of terrorism. Once largely confined to foreign countries, terrorism is now a major concern to U.S. employers, particularly those in high-target categories such as airlines, sporting facilities, energy plants and dams, high-tech companies, financial institutions, and public and commercial buildings. The heightened security procedures at these facilities show the importance employers place on the prevention of terrorist attacks, including those involving conventional explosives, nuclear devices, dirty bombs, chemical weapons, and bioweapons.

Many of the points recommended by NIOSH to prevent workplace violence apply equally to preventing terrorism—background checks, violence prevention policy, and so on. Additionally, counterterrorism experts recommend the following to deter terrorist attacks:

- Heightened ID checks and baggage screening
- Increased video monitoring with threat-recognition software to back up human surveillance
- Blast-resistant glass to reduce casualties
- Offsite emergency offices
- Tightened garage security with stepped-up inspections
- Staggered deliveries to reduce truck traffic[53]
- Emergency evacuation procedures, including escape routes, emergency equipment, and gathering locations[54]

Heightened security procedures are now common at high-risk environments such as this airline.

Banner Health Systems, Phoenix, Arizona, recently hired a new counterterrorism expert—Heidi. Heidi is a German shepherd trained to sniff out eighteen different bomb-making materials, including plastic explosives, ammonium nitrate, and gunpowder.[55] Interestingly, Paul Moskowitz, head of counterterrorism at Brookhaven National Laboratory, commenting on a dog's nose, stated, "That is such an exquisite instrument. A trained dog can reliably detect the slightest trace of a specific chemical even if the scent is masked by other pungent odors. We don't have anything that can touch that yet."[56]

Garden Fresh's Workplace Violence Prevention Policy

Garden Fresh is committed to conducting its operations in a safe manner. Consistent with this policy, acts or threats (either verbal or implied) of physical violence, including intimidation, harassment, and/or coercion, which involve or affect Garden Fresh or which occur on Garden Fresh property will not be tolerated.

Acts or threats of violence include, but are not limited to, the following:

- All threats or acts of violence occurring on Garden Fresh premises, regardless of the relationship between Garden Fresh and the parties involved in the incident.
- All threats or acts of violence occurring off of Garden Fresh premises involving someone who is acting in the capacity of a representative of the company.
- All threats or acts of violence occurring off of Garden Fresh premises involving an employee of GFRC if the threats or acts affect the legitimate interests of Garden Fresh.
- Any acts or threats resulting in the conviction of an employee or agent of Garden Fresh, or of an individual performing services for Garden Fresh on a contract or temporary basis, under any criminal code provision relating to violence or threats of violence which adversely affect the legitimate interests and goals of Garden Fresh.

Specific examples of conduct which may be considered threats or acts of violence include, but are not limited to, the following:

- Hitting or shoving an individual.
- Threatening an individual or his/her family, friends, associates, or property with harm.
- The intentional destruction or threat of destruction of company property.
- Harassing or threatening phone calls.
- Harassing surveillance or stalking.
- The suggestion or intimation that violence is appropriate.
- Possession or use of firearms or weapons.

Garden Fresh's prohibition against threats and acts of violence applies to all persons involved in the company's operation, including Garden Fresh personnel, contract and temporary workers, and anyone else on Garden Fresh property.

Violations of this policy by any individual on Garden Fresh's property, by any individual acting as a representative of Garden Fresh while off of Garden Fresh property, or by an individual acting off of Garden Fresh's property when his/her actions affect the company's business interests will lead to disciplinary action (up to and including termination) and/or legal action as appropriate.

Employees should learn to recognize and respond to behaviors by potential perpetrators that may indicate a risk of violence.

Employees shall place safety as the highest concern, and shall report all acts or threats of violence immediately. Every employee and every person on Garden Fresh's property is encouraged to report incidents of threats or acts of physical violence of which he/she is aware. The report should be made to the Director of Human Resources, the reporting individual's immediate supervisor, or another supervisory employee if the immediate supervisor is not available.

It is the responsibility of managers and supervisors to make safety their highest concern. When made aware of a real or perceived threat of violence, management shall conduct a thorough investigation and take specific actions to help prevent acts of violence.

Nothing in this policy alters any other reporting obligation established by Garden Fresh policies or in state, federal, or other applicable law.

Source: Used with permission from Garden Fresh, 17180 Bernardo Center Drive, San Diego, CA 92128.

Crisis Management Teams

Organizations such as AlliedSignal, Motorola, and Circle K Corporation have formal crisis management teams. These teams, composed of both hourly and managerial employees, conduct initial risk assessment surveys, develop action plans to respond to violent situations, and, importantly, perform crisis intervention during violent, or potentially violent, encounters. For example, a crisis management team would investigate a threat reported by an employee. The team's mandate would be to gather facts about the threat, decide whether the organization should intervene, and, if so, determine the most appropriate method of doing so. Occasionally, a member of the team or an individual manager will be called upon to intervene and calm an angry employee.[57] When this occurs, the steps given in Figure 12.4 will help to defuse a volatile situation.

When violent incidents, such as the death of a co-worker, happen at work, employees can experience shock, guilt, grief, apathy, resentment, cynicism, and a host of other emotions.[58] Jim Martin, an employee assistance program professional with the Detroit fire department, notes that after an incident of violence, employees

Figure 12.4 Calming an Angry Employee

If you try to defuse a tense situation, remember that anger frequently results from a person's feeling of being wronged, misunderstood, or unheard. Keep the following tips in mind to guide you.

- Strive to save the employee's dignity during an angry confrontation. Don't attack a person's rash statements or continue a muddled line of thinking.
- Hold all conversations in private. Do not allow the employee to create an embarrassing public situation for himself or herself, yourself, or other employees.
- Always remain calm. Anger or aggressiveness on your part will trigger a similar response in the employee.
- Listen to the employee with an open mind and nonjudgmental behavior. Give the employee the benefit of hearing him or her out.
- Recognize the employee's legitimate concerns or feelings. Agree that the employee has a valid point and that you will work to correct the problem.
- If the employee is very emotional or if the engagement seems out of control, schedule a delayed meeting so people can calm down.
- Keep the discussion as objective as possible. Focus on the problem at hand, not the personalities of individuals. A cornerstone of conflict resolution is to "attack the problem, not the personality."
- If the employee appears overly aggressive, withdraw immediately and seek professional help before any further discussion with the employee.
- If your efforts fail to calm the employee, report the incident to your manager, security, or human resource personnel.

Source: Adapted from professional literature on crisis management and seminars attended by the authors.

become frightened and may not want to return to work. Such incidents may require the crisis management team to perform crisis intervention through positive counseling techniques.[59]

Building Better Health

Along with improving working conditions that are hazardous to employee health, many employers provide health services and have programs that encourage employees to improve their health habits. It is recognized that better health not only benefits the individual, but also pays off for the organization in reduced absenteeism, increased efficiency, better morale, and other savings. An increased understanding of the close relationship between physical and emotional health and job performance has made broad health-building programs attractive to employers as well as to employees.

Ensuring Healthful Employees

Importantly, most large and many small employers give preemployment medical examinations to prospective employees. Generally, these examinations are required to assure employers that the health of applicants is adequate for the job. The preemployment examination should include a medical history with special reference to previous hazardous exposures. Exposure to hazards whose effects may be cumulative, such as noise, lead, and radiation, are especially relevant. For jobs involving unusual physical demands, the applicant's muscular development, flexibility, agility, range of motion, and cardiac and respiratory functions should be evaluated. The detection of back problems is of particular interest to employers. A preemployment medical examination that includes laboratory analyses can help screen applicants who abuse drugs.

Alternative Approaches to Health

In a discussion of health services as well as health benefits it should be emphasized that there are many nontraditional approaches to better health. These are typically referred to as *alternative approaches.* Many of the approaches differ from traditional medicine in that they are less invasive and they empower the patient by enlisting patient participation in healthcare decisions.

Relaxation techniques, chiropractic, acupuncture, homeopathy, herbal therapy, special diets, and many other alternative approaches are used to treat a wide variety of health problems. For example, Paula Cates, a massage therapist in Denver, Colorado, uses massage to reduce stress and tension and to improve circulation and range-of-motion activities.[60]

Promoting Workplace Fitness and Health

Appleton, a manufacturer of performance packaging products, promotes corporate fitness through its fitness facility staffed with licensed trainers and YMCA physical fitness experts. The center offers four primary areas of programming: onsite physical rehabilitation, ergonomics/injury prevention, fitness, and education.[61] Golin/Harris, a public-relations firm, offers employees a $50 monthly stipend to a gym just steps from its midtown Manhattan office.[62]

At the New York advertising agency J. Walter Thompson, the employee health management program includes both cardiovascular fitness and nutritional health. Bob Jeffrey, president of the agency's North American division, says, "Employees can work out and relax in a 'de-stress' room, get free massages and yoga or nutrition lessons, join a company sports team, and consult with a personal trainer."[63] Xerox gives its employees a publication called *Fitbook* that includes chapters on the hazards of smoking and the effects of alcohol and drug abuse, facts on nutrition and weight control, and guidelines for managing stress and learning to relax. These examples illustrate how organizations have developed programs that emphasize regular exercise, proper nutrition, rehabilitation, stress management, weight control, and avoidance of substances harmful to health. In a health and wellness survey conducted by the American Association of Occupational Health Nurses, 56 percent of respondents said that a workplace health and wellness program would be an important factor in their decision to take a job or stay in one.[64] (Small organizations may distribute wellness literature obtained from the Association for Worksite Health Promotion or the National Wellness Institute.)[65]

Overweight and Obesity. Currently, one of the more critical health and wellness issues facing employers—as well as Americans in general—is overweight and obesity.[66] The Centers for Disease Control estimate that 64 percent of Americans are overweight and 30 percent are severely overweight or obese.[67] This means that three out of every five employees have weight issues that seriously impact employer healthcare costs, employee morale, and work productivity. Overweight and obesity cost companies an estimated $5.5 billion a year in lost productivity due to absenteeism and weight-related chronic diseases such as heart attack, diabetes, high blood pressure, cancer, asthma, and other health problems. Obesity also significantly affects life expectancy. Every year, between 280,000 and 325,000 people suffer premature death related to obesity.[68]

Given the magnitude of the overweight and obesity issue, not surprisingly, employers are launching or improving programs specifically designed to help employees maintain or lose weight. All employer efforts address two lifestyle changes: (1) increasing physical exercise (walking, jogging, bicycling, and so on) and (2) adopting nutritional dietary programs that emphasize eating lots of fruits and vegetables, fish, and low-fat dairy products.[69] Stephanie Pronk, senior consultant for healthcare at Watson Wyatt Worldwide, notes that employers today are trying to create a "culture of wellness" that makes thinking about maintaining a healthy weight second nature to employees.[70] Will employer efforts be successful? Interestingly, a recent poll showed that 58 percent of Americans would like to lose weight, but only 27 percent are trying to slim down and two-thirds of those are not following a specific weight loss program.[71]

Employee Assistance Programs

A broad view of health includes the emotional as well as the physical aspects of one's life. While emotional problems, personal crises, alcoholism, and drug abuse are considered personal matters, they become organizational problems when they affect behavior at work and interfere with job performance.[72] To be able to handle such problems, organizations such as DuPont, Arizona State University, and Stewart Warner, a manufacturer of automotive parts, offer an employee assistance program (EAP). Typically, such a program refers employees in need of assistance to in-house counselors or outside professionals.[73] Supervisors are often given training and policy guidance in the type of help they can offer their subordinates. Furthermore, proactive organizations recognize that EAPs must meet the needs of a diverse population.

At United Technologies, the company's EAP reflects the culture, language, and racial makeup of its workforce.[74]

Personal Crises

The most prevalent problems among employees are personal crises involving marital, family, financial, or legal matters. Furthermore, EAPs have been directing increased attention to the problem of domestic violence. Such problems often come to a supervisor's attention. In most instances, the supervisor can usually provide the best help simply by being understanding and supportive and by helping the individual find the type of assistance he or she needs.[75] In many cases, in-house counseling or referral to an outside professional is recommended. In recent years, crisis hotlines have been set up in many communities to provide counseling by telephone for those too distraught to wait for an appointment with a counselor.

Emotional Problems

depression
A negative emotional state marked by feelings of low spirits, gloominess, sadness, and loss of pleasure in ordinary activities

While personal crises are typically fraught with emotion, most of them are resolved in a reasonable period of time and the troubled individual's equilibrium is restored. Unfortunately, when personal crises linger, stress and tension may cause or intensify a mood disorder such as depression. **Depression** is a decrease in functional activity accompanied by symptoms of low spirits, gloominess, and sadness. The National Institute of Mental Health estimates that nearly 17 million Americans, or as much as 10 percent of the adult population, experience depression each year. With available treatment, however, 70 percent of these individuals will significantly improve, usually within a matter of weeks.

Since depression lowers individual productivity, causes morale problems, increases absenteeism, and contributes to substance abuse, it is important for managers to identify signs of depression on the job and to learn to deal with depressed employees. The more likely workplace signs of depression are decreased energy, concentration and memory problems, guilt feelings, irritability, and chronic aches and pains that don't respond to treatment. When confronted with depressed employees, managers and supervisors are encouraged to be concerned with the employee's problem, be an active listener, and—should the depression persist—suggest professional help.[76] Under no circumstances should managers attempt to play amateur psychologist and try to diagnose an employee's condition. Mood disorders such as depression are complex in nature and do not lend themselves to quick diagnoses. Furthermore, in reviewing such cases, the organization should pay particular attention to workplace safety factors, because there is general agreement that emotional disturbances are primary or secondary factors in a large portion of industrial accidents and violence.

Alcoholism

Business and industry lose an estimated $20.6 billion each year because of alcoholism, according to the Conference Board. The National Council for Alcoholism reports that in this country alone there are more than 10.5 million alcoholics. Alcoholism affects workers in every occupational category—blue-collar and white-collar.

In confronting the problem, employers must recognize that alcoholism is a disease that follows a rather predictable course. Thus they can take specific actions to deal with employees showing symptoms of the disease at particular stages of its progression. Alcoholism typically begins with social drinking getting out of control. As the disease progresses, the alcoholic loses control over how much to drink and eventually cannot keep from drinking, even at inappropriate times.[77] The person uses denial to avoid facing the problems created by the abuse of alcohol and often blames others for these problems. The first step in helping the alcoholic is to awaken the person to the reality of his or her situation.

To identify alcoholism as early as possible, it is essential that supervisors monitor the performance of all personnel regularly and systematically. A supervisor should carefully document evidence of declining performance on the job and then confront the employee with unequivocal proof that the job is suffering. The employee should be assured that help will be made available without penalty. Because the evaluations are made solely in terms of lagging job performance, a supervisor can avoid any mention of alcoholism and allow such employees to seek aid as they would for any other problem.

Employers must remember that alcoholism is classified as a disability under the Americans with Disabilities Act (see Chapter 3). Alcoholism is regarded as a disease, similar to a mental impairment. Therefore, a person disabled by alcoholism is entitled to the same protection from job discrimination as any other person with a disability. However, under the ADA, employers can discipline or discharge employees when job performance is so badly affected by alcohol usage that the employee is unable to perform the job.[78]

Abuse of Illegal Drugs

Employee drug abuse is one of the major employment issues today. Once confined to a small segment of the population, drug abuse is now a national problem that has spread to every industry and occupation as well as employee level.[79] In one study it was estimated that drug abuse costs businesses between $60 billion and $140 billion annually in terms of safety risks, theft, reduced productivity, absenteeism, and accidents.[80]

Most efforts to curb workplace drug abuse are voluntary actions on the part of management.[81] However, a wide range of employers, including federal contractors and private and public transportation firms, are subject to regulations aimed at eliminating the use of illegal drugs on the job. The federal antidrug initiatives include the following:

A poster such as this is usually found in the employment office.

1. The Drug-Free Workplace Act of 1988, which requires federal contractors and recipients of federal grants to take specific steps to ensure a drug-free work environment. One of the main provisions of the act is the preparation and distribution of an antidrug policy statement, a sample of which is shown in Highlights in HRM 7.
2. Department of Defense (DOD) contract rules, which specify that employers entering into contracts with the DOD must agree to a clause certifying their intention to maintain a drug-free workplace.
3. Department of Transportation (DOT) regulations, which require that employees whose jobs include safety- or security-related duties be tested for illegal drug use under DOT rules.

To help employers benefit from being drug-free and to further its mission to help companies maintain safe, healthy, and productive workplaces, the U.S. Department of Labor created the Working Partners for an Alcohol and Drug-Free Workplace. This agency serves to raise organizational awareness about the impact of substance abuse on the workplace while providing employers with substance abuse prevention information. Additionally, the Department's Drug-Free Workplace

Highlights in HRM 7

Selected Items from Salt River Project's Substance Abuse Policy

Purpose

Salt River Project (SRP) has established substance abuse guidelines to:

- Provide a safe workplace for all employees.
- Ensure the consistent handling of employees and job applicants involved with alcohol and drugs.
- Promote a work environment entirely free from the effects of alcohol, the abuse of legal drugs, and the use, possession, or distribution of illegal drugs.
- Promote efficient operations.
- Promote high standards of employee health.
- Ensure employee performance.

Policy

1. SRP recognizes that employee off-the-job involvement with alcohol or drugs can adversely affect the workplace and SRP's ability to accomplish the goals stated above. Consequently, SRP requires that employees report for work and be on the job completely free from alcohol and unauthorized or illegal drugs in or upon their person.
2. Employees with a suspected or documented drug or alcohol problem shall be advised of and may be required to seek help through the Employee Assistance Program (EAP).
3. EAP participation does not prevent disciplinary action for violation of these guidelines and shall be considered as separate from any disciplinary action the supervisor may take prior to, during or after such participation.
4. An employee using or possessing alcohol, abusing legal or illegal drugs or selling, distributing, possessing, or using drugs on the job or on SRP property is subject to discharge. (Exception: use of alcohol at the PERA Club during the employees' after-work hours.) Illegal drugs found on the job or on SRP property will be confiscated and turned over to the appropriate law enforcement agency.
5. Any employee arrested by law enforcement officers of any state, local or federal governmental agency for off-the-job drug activity may be subject to disciplinary action, up to and including discharge. In deciding what action to take, management will consider the nature of any charge brought against the employee, the employee's present job assignment, the employee's work record, and other factors relative to the impact of the arrest on SRP's business and/or public image.
6. A supervisor who believes an employee is at work with alcohol or drugs in his/her system may require the employee to go to an SRP-designated medical professional for a medical evaluation. In the absence of an HS nurse, another supervisor, if possible, should witness and confirm any observed deficiencies in the employee's performance and behavior. With the documentation of the supervisor, a drug test can be ordered from

(continued on next page)

(continued from previous page)

the appropriate SRP-designated collection facility. Transportation will be provided for the employee for such an evaluation.

7. Supervisors may require an employee involved in an accident on the job, or on SRP premises in connection with the job, to go to an SRP-designated medical professional for a medical evaluation. A referral to EAP may be utilized by an employee's supervisor on a *mandatory* basis when an employee's performance indicates that an assessment and referral may be appropriate. The EAP counselor will determine what course of treatment will be required. Personal information and treatment plan details remain confidential. The only information available to the supervisor is that pertaining to the employee's compliance and work requirements.

9. The SRP-designated medical professional, as part of a medical evaluation, may require the employee to submit to laboratory testing procedures. If an employee refuses to go to an SRP-designated medical professional or refuses to consent to required laboratory testing, the refusal is treated as an admission that the employee is unfit to perform his/her duties.

13. An employee not fully able to operate SRP equipment due to the presence of drugs or alcohol in his/her system will not be permitted to do so. Any employee asked not to operate SRP equipment or drive a personal vehicle on SRP property or on SRP business during work time, but who insists upon doing so will be subject to disciplinary action, including discharge, and will be advised that SRP will immediately report this to the appropriate law enforcement agency.
14. Any employee using legal drugs (prescriptions or over-the-counter) which may alter his/her physical or mental ability must report this to his/her supervisor and to Health Services so that HS can determine whether it is necessary to change the employee's job assignment while he/she is using the drugs. Although the use of legal drugs is not of itself grounds for disciplinary action, improper or excessive use will not prevent disciplinary action for inadequate job performance.

New Hires

All pre-placement physical evaluations will include a lab test for substance abuse. A job applicant who tests positive, as determined in accordance with standards established at the sole discretion of SRP, will not be hired. If the job applicant refuses such testing or is unable to produce a specimen within two (2) hours, he/she will not be hired. A job applicant who has a positive test result will not be eligible for employment for one (1) year from the date of the test. A job applicant with a prior history of substance abuse will not be rejected solely on that basis. If an SRP-designated medical professional believes that the applicant has been fully rehabilitated, then the applicant will be given full consideration for employment.

Source: Adapted from Salt River Project's substance abuse policy. Used with permission from Salt River Project, Phoenix, Arizona.

Advisor provides information to employers about how to establish and maintain an alcohol- and drug-free environment.[82]

The ADA considers an individual using drugs as disabled, provided the person is enrolled in a recognized drug treatment program. The prudent employer will, therefore, make a reasonable accommodation to the specific needs of this employee. Rea-

USING THE INTERNET

The National Institute on Drug Abuse (NIDA) has information on drug awareness and prevention. Go to the Student Resources at:

http://bohlander.swlearning.com

sonable accommodation may include time off from work or a modified work schedule to obtain treatment. Illegal-drug users are, however, not covered under the ADA.

As noted earlier, employers operating under the federal requirements are required to test for drug use under certain specified conditions. However, employers that are exempt from the federal requirement may operate under state or local laws restricting or prohibiting drug tests. Issues related to drug testing under state or local laws are discussed in Chapter 13 in the context of employee rights.

While attention is usually focused on the abuse of illegal drugs, it should be noted that the abuse of legal drugs can also pose a problem for employees. Employees who abuse legal drugs—those prescribed by physicians—often do not realize they have become addicted or how their behavior has changed as a result of their addiction. Also, managers should be aware that some employees may be taking legal sedatives or stimulants as part of their medical treatment and that their behavior at work may be affected by their use of these drugs.

The Management of Stress

HR professionals are well aware of the negative effects of workplace stress on employees' health and job performance. For example, job stress places both women and men at risk for cardiovascular problems and depression and increases employee susceptibility to infectious diseases. All of these contribute to higher healthcare costs, and can

Source: Reprinted with permission of Wayne Stayskal/*Tampa Tribune*.

lower productivity, job satisfaction, and retention. Importantly, in a recent study on the magnitude of stress in the workplace, 54 percent of respondents indicated that they "often" or "always" come home from work in a state of fatigue, and nearly 50 percent come in to work tired.[83]

What Is Stress?

stress
Any adjustive demand caused by physical, mental, or emotional factors that requires coping behavior

eustress
Positive stress that accompanies achievement and exhilaration

distress
Harmful stress characterized by a loss of feelings of security and adequacy

alarm reaction
A response to stress that basically involves an elevated heart rate, increased respiration, elevated levels of adrenaline in the blood, and increased blood pressure

Stress is any demand on the individual that requires coping behavior. Stress comes from two basic sources: physical activity and mental or emotional activity. The physical reaction of the body to both types of stress is the same. Psychologists use two separate terms to distinguish between positive and negative forms of stress, even though reactions to the two forms are the same biochemically. **Eustress** is positive stress that accompanies achievement and exhilaration. Eustress is the stress of meeting challenges such as those found in a managerial, technical, or public contact job. Eustress is regarded as a beneficial force that helps us to forge ahead against obstacles. What is harmful is **distress.** Stress becomes distress when we begin to sense a loss of our feelings of security and adequacy. Helplessness, desperation, and disappointment turn stress into distress.

The stress reaction is a coordinated chemical mobilization of the entire body to meet the requirements of fight-or-flight in a situation perceived to be stressful. The sympathetic nervous system activates the secretion of hormones from the endocrine glands that places the body on a "war footing." This response, commonly referred to as the **alarm reaction,** basically involves an elevated heart rate, increased respiration, elevated levels of adrenaline in the blood, and increased blood pressure. It persists until one's estimate of the relative threat to well-being has been reevaluated. If distress persists long enough, it can result in fatigue, exhaustion, and even physical and/or emotional breakdown.[84] Some research has linked stress to heart disease. Other studies have shown a connection between chronic stress and hypertension (high blood pressure). High blood pressure, the most common cause of strokes, contributes to heart disease.

Job-Related Stress

Although the body experiences a certain degree of stress (either eustress or distress) in all situations, here we are primarily concerned with the stress related to the work setting. It is in this setting that management can use some preventive approaches.

Sources of Job-Related Stress

Causes of workplace stress are many. However, according to a study by Lluminari, a national healthcare company, four factors have a major influence on employee stress:

- *High demand:* having too much to do in too short a time.
- *High effort:* having to expend too much mental or physical energy over too long a period.
- *Low control:* having too little influence over the way a job is done on a day-to-day basis.
- *Low reward:* receiving inadequate feedback on performance and no recognition for a job well done.[85]

Other recognized job stressors include layoffs and organizational restructuring; disagreements with managers or fellow employees; prejudice because of age, gender, race, or religion; inability to voice complaints; and poor working conditions. Even minor irritations such as lack of privacy, unappealing music, and other conditions can be distressful to one person or another.

Burnout

burnout
A severe stage of distress, manifesting itself in depression, frustration, and loss of productivity

Burnout is a severe stage of distress. Career burnout generally occurs when a person begins questioning his or her own personal values. Quite simply, one no longer feels that what he or she is doing is important. Depression, frustration, and a loss of productivity are all symptoms of burnout. Burnout is due primarily to a lack of personal fulfillment in the job or a lack of positive feedback about performance.[86] In organizations that have downsized, remaining employees can experience burnout because they must perform more work with fewer co-workers. Overachievers can experience burnout when unrealistic work goals are unattainable.[87]

Coping with Stress

Many employers have developed stress management programs to teach employees how to minimize the negative effects of job-related stress. A typical program might include instruction in relaxation techniques, coping skills, listening skills, methods of dealing with difficult people, time management, and assertiveness. All of these techniques are designed to break the pattern of tension that accompanies stress situations and to help participants achieve greater control of their lives. Organizational techniques, such as clarifying the employee's work role, redesigning and enriching jobs, correcting physical factors in the environment, and effectively handling interpersonal factors, should not be overlooked in the process of teaching employees how to handle stress. Stress management counselors recommend several ways to resolve job-related stress as described in Figure 12.5.

Figure 12.5 Tips for Reducing Job-Related Stress

- Build rewarding relationships with co-workers.
- Talk openly with managers or employees about job or personal concerns.
- Prepare for the future by keeping abreast of likely changes in job demands.
- Don't greatly exceed your skills and abilities.
- Set realistic deadlines; negotiate reasonable deadlines with managers.
- Act now on problems or concerns of importance.
- Designate dedicated work periods during which time interruptions are avoided.
- When feeling stressed, find time for detachment or relaxation.
- Don't let trivial items take on importance; handle them quickly or assign them to others.
- Take short breaks from your work area as a change of pace.

Before concluding this discussion, we should observe that stress that is harmful to some employees may be healthy for others.[88] Most managers learn to handle distress effectively and find that it actually stimulates better performance. However, there will always be those who are unable to handle stress and need assistance in learning to cope with it. The increased interest of young and old alike in developing habits that will enable them to lead happier and more productive lives will undoubtedly be beneficial to them as individuals, to the organizations where they work, and to a society where people are becoming more and more interdependent.

SUMMARY

objective 1 The Occupational Safety and Health Act was designed to assure, so far as possible, safe and healthful working conditions for every working person. In general, the act extends to all employers and employees. OSHA administration involves setting standards, ensuring employer and employee compliance, and providing safety and health consultation and training where needed. Both employers and employees have certain responsibilities and rights under OSHA. Employers not only are required to provide a hazard-free work environment, but also must keep employees informed about OSHA requirements and must require their employees to use protective equipment when necessary. Under the "right to know" regulations, employers are required to keep employees informed of hazardous substances and instruct them in avoiding the dangers presented. Employees, in turn, are required to comply with OSHA standards, to report hazardous conditions, and to follow all employer safety and health regulations.

objective 2 In order to provide safe working conditions for their employees, employers typically establish a formal program that, in a large percentage of organizations, is under the direction of the HR manager. The program may have many facets, including providing safety knowledge and motivating employees to use it, making employees aware of the need for safety, and rewarding them for safe behavior. Such incentives as praise, public recognition, and awards are used to involve employees in the safety program. Maintenance of required records from accident investigations provides a basis for information that can be used to create a safer work environment.

objective 3 Job conditions that are dangerous to the health of employees are now receiving much greater attention than in the past. There is special concern for toxic chemicals that proliferate at a rapid rate and may lurk in the body for years without outward symptoms. Health hazards other than those found in industrial processing operations—such as video display terminals and cumulative trauma disorders—present special problems that must be addressed. Today tobacco smoke is rarely tolerated in the work environment. While there is no evidence that AIDS can be spread through casual contact in the workplace, employers have found that it is important to educate managers and employees about AIDS and to assist those who have it.

objective 4 Along with providing safer and healthier work environments, many employers establish programs that encourage employees to improve their health habits. Some of the larger employers have opened primary care clinics for employees and their dependents to provide better healthcare service and to reduce costs. Wellness programs that emphasize exercise, nutrition, weight control, and avoidance of harmful substances serve employees at all organizational levels.

objective 5 Virtually all of the larger organizations and many of the smaller ones have found that an employee assistance program is beneficial to all concerned. While emotional problems, personal crises, alcoholism, and drug abuse are often viewed as personal matters, it is apparent that they affect behavior at work and interfere with job performance.

An employee assistance program typically provides professional assistance by in-house counselors or outside professionals where needed.

An important dimension to health and safety is stress that comes from physical activity and mental or emotional activity. While stress is an integral part of being alive, when it turns into distress it becomes harmful. We have seen that many sources of stress are job-related. In recognizing the need for reducing stress, employers can develop stress management programs to help employees learn techniques for coping with stress. In addition, organizations need to redesign and enrich jobs, clarify the employee's work role, correct physical factors in the environment, and take any other actions that will help reduce stress on the job.

KEY TERMS

alarm reaction
burnout
cumulative trauma disorders
depression
distress
eustress
Material Safety Data Sheets (MSDSs)
recordable case
right-to-know laws
stress

DISCUSSION QUESTIONS

1. When OSHA was enacted in 1970, it was heralded as the most important new source of protection for the American worker in the second half of the twentieth century. What opinions about the effectiveness or the ineffectiveness of the act or its implementation have you heard from acquaintances who have been affected by it?

2. What steps should management take to increase motivation for safety?

3. An unhealthy work environment can lower productivity, contribute to low morale, and increase medical and workers' compensation costs. Working individually or in teams, list specific ways managers can
   a. Accommodate the desires of smokers and nonsmokers
   b. Reduce the harmful affects of VDTs
   c. Address employee fears caused by AIDS

4. To live a healthier life, medical professionals say we need to identify those things we currently do that either impair or contribute to our health. Prepare a list of those activities you do that are beneficial or harmful to your overall health. Discuss with others a way to develop a lifetime program for a healthy lifestyle.

5. In several states employers can require an employee to take a drug test only if there is a "reasonable cause" for testing. What are some behaviors that would indicate that a worker may be under the influence of drugs?

6. Identify the sources of stress in an organization.
   a. In what ways do they affect the individual employee? The organization?
   b. What can managers and supervisors do to make the workplace less stressful?

HRM Experience

Reducing Employee Stress

Job stress and its negative effect on both employees and the organization are a growing concern for managers and supervisors. As the text discusses, employee distress costs employers staggering amounts of money in lost productivity, absenteeism, turnover, increased workers' compensation claims, and healthcare costs. The cost of distress on the personal lives of employees is unmeasurable. Not surprisingly, stress management is an important aspect of any manager's job.

Stress management programs typically focus on three things to reduce workplace stress: (1) They identify factors in jobs that create stress; (2) they discuss specific techniques and managerial practices that help elevate workplace stress; and (3) they help individuals identify personal characteristics that serve to increase or decrease stress for them.

Assignment

1. Working in groups of four to six individuals, identify personal experiences that caused workplace stress. Explain exactly why these incidents were stressful. Suggest ways to reduce or eliminate these stressful conditions.
2. Stress management often begins by having individuals identify their skills and abilities and jobs that will help them succeed. Assessing our preferences and skills can help us understand why some tasks or roles are more stressful than others. Identify work-related stress by answering these questions:

   - What skills that I enjoy using am I currently using in my job?
   - What skills that I enjoy using am I currently not using?
   - What specific things about my job do I really like?
   - What are things about my job that I dislike?
   - Based on my personal skills and abilities, what would my perfect job be?

BIZFLIX EXERCISES

8 Mile: Working at North Detroit Stamping

When you view these scenes, watch for the safety of Jimmy's job and his work environment. Many aspects of safety and health discussed in this chapter appear in these scenes.

Jimmy "B-Rabbit" Smith, Jr. (Eminem) wants to succeed as a rapper and to prove that a white man can create moving sounds. His job at the North Detroit Stamping (NDS) plant fills his days while he pursues his music at night—and sometimes on the plant's grounds. The film's title refers to Detroit's northern city boundary, well known to local people. *8 Mile* is a gritty look at Detroit's hip-hop culture in 1995 and Jimmy's desire for acceptance by it.

The scene is an edited composite of two brief NDS plant sequences that appear in different places in the film. Part I appears early in the film in the sequence "The Franchise." Part II appears in the last 25 minutes of the film in the "Papa Doc Payback" sequence. Jimmy arrives late for work in the first part of the scene, after riding the city bus because his car did not start. The second part occurs after his beating by Papa Doc (Anthony Mackie) and Papa Doc's gang.

What to Watch for and Ask Yourself

- What is your perception of the safety of Jimmy's job and his work environment? What has management done about job and work environment safety at North Detroit Stamping?
- Could this job and work environment create stress for Jimmy and his co-workers? Why or why not?
- How would you react to this type of work experience?

case study 1

Safety Training at Pro's Choice: It's Not Working

While a large number of organizations have successful health and safety records, unfortunately, many companies experience unacceptable health and safety incidence rates. Furthermore, simply having a safety program does not guarantee a positive safety record, as the experience of Pro's Choice of St. Louis, Missouri, illustrates.

Pro's Choice Manufacturing produces aftermarket automobile parts for cars and trucks built during the 1950s. The company's specialty area is suspension components for Ford and Chevy vehicles. Pro's Choice Manufacturing employees work with and around a variety of machines and chemicals that have the potential to cause serious medical problems. The working environment has been described by some employees as "extremely hazardous, even life-threatening." In 2003, after an unannounced safety inspection by OSHA officials, the company received six citations for various health and safety violations and one proposed fine of $7,000 for a "serious" infraction. Additionally, OSHA noted that Pro's Choice had a higher-than-average accident rate for the manufacturing industry. The company was placed on OSHA's schedule for repeat inspections.

Between January and March 2004, Pro's Choice implemented a health and safety program specifically designed to reduce the infractions noted by OSHA. The company purchased standardized videos, posters, and safety pamphlets for viewing by employees. Supervisors were instructed to issue "safety warnings" to careless employees. (The safety warnings are jokingly referred to as "Band-Aids" by employees.) Employees with a history of safety or health injuries or illnesses were placed on a progressive discipline schedule.

During February 2005, Pro's Choice safety management team compared their injury and illness incidence rates for January 2004 and January 2005. Unfortunately, there was no meaningful improvement in the company's safety and health record. Two departments, stamping and plating, experienced incidence rates for 2005 higher than those for 2004.

Source: Adapted from a case known to the authors. All names and locations are fictitious.

QUESTIONS

1. What may have contributed to the failure of the safety training program at Pro's Choice? Explain.
2. What would you suggest doing to make the safety training program successful? Explain.
3. What role should supervisors play in any safety training program? Explain.

case study 2

Too Much Stress? You Decide

Job stress and depression are significant problems faced by employees and their managers. Unfortunately, when a case of depression arises, trying to resolve the problem may be difficult—sometimes leading to conflict—as this case illustrates.

Donald Knolls was an air traffic control supervisor for International Gateway Airport (IGA), an airport serving a major metropolitan area. In 2004, Donald began to experience depression and depression-related problems due largely to severe stress on the job. In 2005, he requested and was granted a disability leave for treatment of his illness. After eight months, his personal physician, an expert in depression treatment, and a licensed consulting psychologist agreed that he was sufficiently improved to return to his former position. IGA sent Donald to the physician it had used when Donald first requested his disability leave. After an extensive evaluation, the doctor concluded that Donald, while he had made considerable strides in overcoming his depression, should not be immediately returned to his former supervisory position because the conditions of the job had not changed and Donald was apt to find the stress too great. Instead, he recommended that Donald be returned to a nonsupervisory position on a six-month trial basis, with the case to be reviewed at the end of that time. IGA followed the advice of its doctor and did not return Donald to a supervisory position. Donald, angered by management's decision, filed a grievance through IGA's alternative dispute resolution procedure, a procedure that could end in binding arbitration.

During several meetings between Donald and management, the employer maintained that it had the right to rely on the medical opinion of "a fair and impartial" doctor who had determined that Donald should not be returned to the position that was the cause of his original stress-related emotional problems. Additionally, management pointed out to Donald that IGA's disability-leave provision states that it "may require appropriate medical documentation if it believes an employee is not fit to return to his or her former position."

Donald responded, through an attorney he hired to represent his position, that the disability-leave provisions were clear but, nevertheless, biased against an employee because they completely disregarded the opinion of his physician and psychologist. According to Donald, "Why bother to get expert medical opinions if they are dismissed?" He further noted, "I have never felt better. I'm really ready to get back to my job." Finally, Donald's lawyer contended that Donald was the victim of discrimination based on his former state of depression: "What happened to Donald would not have happened if his illness had been a more conventional physical injury."

Source: Adapted from a case known to one of the authors. All names are fictitious.

QUESTIONS

1. When conflicting medical opinions are presented, should the advice of a medical expert count more heavily than the opinion of a general physician? Explain.
2. Is the charge of discrimination presented by Donald's lawyer relevant to this case? Explain.
3. If you were presented with this case, what decision would you reach? Explain.

NOTES AND REFERENCES

1. Thomas A. Shumaker and Allison Feldstein, "Employer Liability for Workplace Violence," *P. H. Public Management* 86, no. 3 (April 2004): 3.
2. Dennis R. Falk, Melanie F. Sheppard, and Barbara A. Elliott, "Evaluation of a Domestic Violence Assessment Protocol Used by Employee Assistance Counselors," *Employee Assistance Quarterly* 17, no. 3 (2002): 1–15.
3. Adrian Gostick, "Delivering Timely Safety Recognition," *Occupational Safety and Health* 73, no. 9 (September 2004): 94.
4. P.L. 91-596, 91st Congress, S. 2193, December 29, 1970.
5. U.S. Department of Labor, Occupational Safety and Health Administration, *All about OSHA*, rev. ed. (Washington, DC: U.S. Government Printing Office, 2003): 4.
6. OSHA publishes many pamphlets pertaining to various aspects of the act, such as employee workplace rights and voluntary compliance programs. All OSHA publications can be downloaded at no cost from the agency web site at http://www.osha.gov; you may also call (800) 321-OSHA or fax a request to (202) 693-2498.
7. *All about OSHA*, 14.
8. Ibid., 21.
9. Ibid., 22.
10. Ibid., 25
11. Ibid., 27.
12. Statistics are from the OSHA web site at http://www.osha.gov.
13. A free copy of OSHA's safety and health program management guidelines can be obtained from the U.S. Department of Labor, OSHA Publications, P.O. Box 37535, Washington, DC 20013-7535.
14. *All about OSHA*, 31.
15. James L. Nash, "Court Rules OSHA Must Reveal Injury Rate," *Occupational Hazards* 66, no. 9 (September 2004): 16.
16. *All about OSHA*, 13.
17. Ibid., 5.
18. Fred S. Steingold, *The Employer's Legal Handbook*, 4th ed. (Berkeley, CA: Nolo Press, 2002): 7/27.
19. John F. Rekus, "OSHA: The Good, the Bad and the Ugly," *Occupational Hazards* 63, no. 10 (October 2001): 29–36.
20. For an overview of OSHA legislation, see David J. Walsh, *Employment Law for Human Resource Practice* (Mason, OH: South-Western, 2004): Chapter 15.
21. Mike Williamson, "Getting Results from Safety Meetings," *Occupational Safety and Health* 72, no. 2 (February 2003): 14.
22. Jane F. Barrett, "Failure to Train Employees Now a Federal Crime," *Occupational Safety and Health* 72, no. 11 (November 2003): 24.
23. Todd Nighswonger, "Is First-Aid First in Your Workplace?" *Occupational Hazards* 64, no. 4 (April 2002): 45–47.
24. Tim W. McDaniel, "Employee Participation: A Vehicle for Safety by Design," *Occupational Hazards* 6, no. 5 (May 2002): 71–76.
25. John P. Spath, "How to Get Employees Involved in the Safety Program," *Occupational Hazards* 66, no. 9 (September 2004): 63.
26. Craig Miller, "Can the Internet Improve Safety?" *Occupational Safety and Health* 73, no. 6 (June 2004): 98.
27. G. C. Shah, "Five Steps to Digital Safety," *Occupational Safety and Health* 71, no. 3 (March 2002): 22–25.
28. Roger Brooks, "OSHA's E-Tool for Lockout/Tagout," *Occupational Safety and Health* 71, no. 4 (April 2002): 22–24.
29. Larry Hansen, "How Will They Know?" *Occupational Hazards* 66, no. 10 (October 2004): 39.
30. Janet Wiscombe, "Rewards Get Results," *Workforce* 81, no. 4 (April 2002): 42–46.

31. Diana McCrohan, "Add Impact to Your Program," *Occupational Safety and Health* 73, no. 2 (February 2004): 52.
32. OSHA considers an injury or illness to be work-related if an event or exposure in the work environment either caused or contributed to the resulting condition or significantly aggravated a pre-existing injury or illness. Work-relatedness is presumed for injuries and illnesses resulting from events or exposure occurring in the work environment. OSHA defines the work environment as "the establishment and other locations where one or more employees are working or are present as a condition of their employment. The work environment includes not only physical locations, but also the equipment or materials used by the employee during the course of his or her work."
33. For complete information on the recording and reporting of illnesses and injuries, see OSHA Publication 3169, *Recording and Reporting Occupational Injuries and Illnesses*, particularly Sections 1904.5 (determination of work-relatedness) and 1904.7 (general recording criteria). See also the OSHA web site at http://www.osha.gov.
34. If employers have a "privacy concern case," they may not enter the employee's name on the OSHA 300 log. Instead, they should enter "privacy case" in the space normally used for the employee's name. This will protect the privacy of the injured or ill employee when another employee, a former employee, or an authorized employee representative is provided access to the OSHA 300 log. Privacy cases must be recorded on a separate confidential list. Employers must consider the following injuries or illnesses privacy concern cases: (i) an injury or illness to an intimate body part of the reproductive system; (ii) an injury or illness resulting from a sexual assault; (iii) mental illnesses; (iv) HIV infection, hepatitis, or tuberculosis; (v) needlestick injuries and cuts from sharp objects that are contaminated with another person's blood or other potentially infectious material; and (vi) other illnesses, if the employee independently and voluntarily requests that his or her name not be entered on the log.
35. Terese Steinback, "Workplace Strategies for Removing Obstacles to Employee Health," *Employee Benefits Journal* 25, no. 1 (March 2000): 9–10.
36. The Supreme Court decision in *International Union v Johnson Controls* may be found in 59 U.S. Law Week 4029.
37. A. H. Mokdad, J. S. Marks, D. F. Stroup, and J. L. Gerberding, "Actual Causes of Death in the United States: 2000," *Journal of the American Medical Association* 291, no. 10 (March 10, 2004): 1238.
38. "Second-Hand Smoke: A Quick Study," *Business Week* (April 19, 2004): 83. See also Paul McIntyre, "A High Price to Pay: Workers' Lives Lost to Second-Hand Smoke Far More Costly Than Possibility of Lost Profits," *National Restaurant News* 38, no. 33 (August 16, 2004): 44.
39. Kevin Tse and Dean Foust, "At Risk from Smoking: Your Job," *Business Week* (April 15, 2002): 12.
40. Greta Thornbory, "Dealing with MSDs," *Occupational Health* 56, no. 5 (May 2004): 18. See also Dave Heidorn, "Where Ergo Needs to Go," *Professional Safety* 49, no. 7 (July 2004): 14.
41. "OSHA's 'Comprehensive Plan' to Target Workplace Injuries," *HRFocus* 79, no. 5 (May 2002): 8.
42. Eva Tahmincioglu, "Ergonomics Is Back on the Radar Screen for Both Business and Regulators," *Workforce Management* 83, no. 7 (July 2004): 59.
43. Julie K. Boatman, "Kansas Born," *AOPA Pilot* 47, no. 8 (August 2004): 108.
44. James M. Stewart, "Critical Elements for Effective Ergonomics," *Occupational Safety and Health* 71, no. 1 (January 2002): 43–45.
45. CDC Business and Labor Responds to AIDS, P. O. Box 6003, Rockville, MD 20849, (800) 458–5281.
46. Catherine Arnst, "Why Business Should Make AIDS Its Business," *Business Week* (August 2, 2004): 80.
47. Larry J. Chavez, "Benefits That Can Prevent Workplace Violence," *Employee Benefit Plan Review* 58, no. 2 (August 2003): 6.
48. The NIOSH document *Violence in the Workplace: Risk Factors and Prevention Strategies*, Bulletin #59, is available from Publications Dissemination, EID, National Institute for Occupational Safety and Health, 4676 Columbia Parkway, Cincinnati, OH 45226-1998, (800) 356-4674.
49. Louis Rovner, "Are You Hiring Terrorists?" *Occupational Safety and Health* 73, no. 1 (January 2004): 18.
50. Shumaker and Feldstein, "Employer Liability for Workplace Violence," 86.
51. Gillian Flynn, "Employers Can't Look Away from Workplace Violence," *Workforce* 79, no. 7 (July 2000): 68–70; Dannie B. Fogleman, "Minimizing the Risk of Violence in the Workplace," *Employment Relations Today* 87, no. 1 (Spring 2000): 83–98.
52. Irving G. Jacob, "Defusing the Explosive Worker," *Occupational Safety and Health* 73, no. 1 (January 2004): 56.
53. Richard S. Dunham, Rick Miller, Aren Therese Palmer, and Michael Arndt, "The War on Terror: What Companies Need to Do," *Business Week* (August 16, 2004): 26. See also Lawrence D. Mankin and Ronald W. Perry, "Terrorism Challenges for Human Resource Management," *Review of Public Personnel Management* 24, no. 1 (March 2004): 3–17.
54. Stephen V. Magyar Jr., "Do You Have an Evacuation Plan That Works?" *Occupational Safety and Health* 72, no. 12 (December 2003): 44. See also Susanne M. Bruyère and William G. Stothers, "Enabling Safe Evacuations," *HRMagazine* 47, no. 1 (January 2002): 65–67.
55. Andra Eilert, "Banner's Bomb-Detection Team on Duty," *Inside Banner* (March 2003): 7.
56. David Shenk, "Watching You: The World of High-Tech Surveillance," *National Geographic* 204, no. 5 (November 2004): 6–7.
57. John C. DelBel, "Workplace Aggression," *Nursing Management* 34, no. 9 (July 2003): 30. See also Bruce T. Blythe and Terri

Butler Stivarius, "Assessing and Defusing Workplace Threats of Violence," *Occupational Safety and Health* 73, no. 2 (February 2004): 20.
58. Claire Ginther, "A Death in the Family," *HRMagazine* 46, no. 5 (May 2001): 55–58.
59. Bruce T. Blythe, "The Human Side of Crisis Management," *Occupational Hazards* 66, no. 7 (July 2004): 37.
60. Paula Cates, interview by author, Denver, Colorado, June 20, 2004.
61. Craig Halls and John Rhodes, "Employee Wellness and Beyond," *Occupational Safety and Health* 73, no. 9 (September 2004): 46. See also Julie L. Gerberding and James S. Marks, "Making America Fit and Trim—Steps Big and Small," *American Journal of Public Health* 94, no. 9 (September 2004): 1478.
62. Jonathan Pont, "Workplace Workouts," *Potentials* 36, no. 10 (October 2003): 13.
63. Carol Hymowitz, "Need to Boost Morale? Try Good Food, Fitness and Communication," *The Wall Street Journal*, May 28, 2002, B-1.
64. "Health/Wellness Plans Help Retain Workers," *HRFocus* 80, no. 6 (June 2003): 12.
65. Wellness Resources: Association for Worksite Health Promotion, 60 Revere Dr., Suite 500, Northbrook, IL 60062, (847) 637-9200; National Wellness Institute, 1045 Clark St., Suite 210, P.O. Box 827, Stevens Point, WI 54481-0828, (715) 342-2969.
66. Louise Witt, "Why We're Losing the War against Obesity," *American Demographics* 25, no. 10 (December 2003): 27.
67. Amy McKenna and Anne Maric Kuchera, "Kathy Knows She Shouldn't Eat Fatty Foods, but She Does Anyway. The Cure for America's $75 Billion Obesity Crisis: Behavioral Change," *Employee Benefit Plan Review* 59, no 2 (August 2004): 10.
68. Robert J. Grossman, "Countering a Weight Crisis," *HRMagazine* 49, no. 3 (March 2004): 42.
69. Sanjay Gupta, "Feeling the Pressure," *Time* (September 6, 2004): 102.
70. "Using Weight Management Programs to Cut Health Care Costs," *HRFocus* 81, no. 5 (May 2004): 10.
71. David Bjerklie, "America's Obesity Crisis," *Time* (June 7, 2004): 113.
72. Paul Falcone, "Dealing with Employees in Crisis," *HRMagazine* 48, no. 5 (May 2003): 117.
73. Maryann Hammers, "Banking on an In-House EAP," *Workforce* 82, no. 4 (April 2003): 18.
74. Sarah Fister Gale, "Companies Find EAPs Can Foster Diversity," *Workforce* 81, no. 2 (February 2002): 66–69.
75. Kristi D. Willbanks, "The Role of Supervisory Referral in Employee Assistance Programs," *Employee Assistance Quarterly* 15, no. 2 (1999): 13–28.
76. Zachary Meyer, "Combating Employee Depression by Integrating Behavioral, Medical, and Pharmaceutical Benefits," *Employee Benefit Plan Review* 59, no. 2 (August 2004): 13.
77. Samuel B. Bacharach, Peter A. Bamberger, and William J. Sonnenstuhl, "Driven to Drink: Managerial Control, Work-Related Work Factors, and Employee Problem Drinking," *Academy of Management Journal* 45, no. 4 (August 2002): 637.
78. Fred S. Steingold, *The Employer's Legal Handbook*, 6th ed. (Berkeley, CA: Nolo Press, 2004).
79. "What Does the Renewed Rise in Employee Drug Use Mean to HR?" *HRFocus* 79, no. 2 (February 2002): 7–8.
80. Christine L. Romero, "Elder Bush Aids Fight against Drugs at Work," *The Arizona Republic*, March 19, 2002, Section D.
81. Jay C. Thomas, "Preventing Workplace Substance Abuse: Beyond Drug Testing to Wellness," *Personnel Psychology* 57, no. 2 (Summer 2004): 553.
82. Information regarding the U.S. Department of Labor's efforts to create a drug-free workplace can be found at http://www.dol.gov.
83. "Change Your Culture and Lower Your Benefit Costs," *HRFocus* 81, no. 11 (November 2004): 6.
84. Lee Ann Jackson, "Relax, Relate, Release," *Black Enterprise* 35, no. 2 (September 2004): 61.
85. "Change Your Culture and Lower Your Benefit Costs," 6.
86. Max Messmer, "Are You Burning Out Your Best Employees?" *Strategic Finance* 85, no. 11 (May 2004): 12. See also Bob Gunn, "The Antidote to Burnout," *Strategic Finance* 86, no. 3 (September 2004): 8
87. "Stop Burnout—Before It Stops Your Employees," *HRFocus* 79, no. 2 (February 2002): 3–4.
88. Sora Song, "The Price of Pressure," *Time* (July 19, 2004): 68.

ANSWERS TO HIGHLIGHTS IN HRM 1

1. True
2. True
3. True
4. d. 80
5. False
6. True
7. Unsafe acts (85 percent of all accidents)
8. The company position on safety and health
   The identity of the safety coordinator
   Rules and regulations
   Hazard communication program elements
   Safety programs in place
   Employee and employer responsibilities
   Safety communication in the workplace
9. True
10. False
11. True
12. False (eight hours)

chapter

Employee Rights and Discipline

After studying this chapter, you should be able to

Explain the concepts of employee rights and employer responsibilities.

Explain the concepts of employment at will, wrongful discharge, implied contract, and constructive discharge.

Identify and explain the privacy rights of employees.

Explain the process of establishing disciplinary policies, including the proper implementation of organizational rules.

Discuss the meaning of discipline and how to investigate a disciplinary problem.

Differentiate between the two approaches to disciplinary action.

Identify the different types of alternative dispute resolution procedures.

Discuss the role of ethics in the management of human resources.

In this chapter we discuss employee rights, workplace privacy, and employee discipline. Managers note that these topics have a major influence on the activities of both employees and supervisors. Robert J. Deeny, an employment attorney, has stated that employee rights and workplace privacy will "continue to be the hottest employment law topics into the twenty-first century."[1] For example, while drug testing, e-mail privileges, and employee monitoring are routinely debated, employers are now using location awareness technology, global positioning systems (GPSs), and company-provided cell phones to track and locate employees.[2] Furthermore, managers are discovering that the right to discipline and discharge employees—a traditional responsibility of management—is more difficult to exercise in light of the growing attention to employee rights. Disciplining employees is a difficult and unpleasant task for most managers and supervisors; many of them report that taking disciplinary action against an employee is the most stressful duty they perform. Balancing employee rights and employee discipline may not be easy, but it is a universal requirement and a critical aspect of good management.

Because the growth of employee rights issues has led to an increase in the number of lawsuits filed by employees, we include in this chapter a discussion of alternative dispute resolution as a way to foster organizational justice. Because disciplinary actions are subject to challenge and possible reversal through governmental agencies or the courts, management should make a positive effort to prevent the need for such action. When disciplinary action becomes impossible to avoid, however, that action should be taken in accordance with carefully developed HR policies and practices. Because ethics is an important element of organizational justice, the chapter concludes with a discussion of organizational ethics in employee relations.

Employee Rights and Privacy

Various antidiscrimination laws, wage and hour statutes, and safety and health legislation have secured basic employee rights and brought numerous job improvements to the workplace. Employee rights litigation concerns such workplace issues as employees' rights to protest unfair disciplinary action, to question genetic testing, to have access to their personal files, to challenge employer searches and monitoring, and to be free from employer discipline for off-duty conduct.[3]

employee rights
Guarantees of fair treatment from employers, particularly regarding an employee's right to privacy

The current emphasis on employee rights is a natural result of the evolution of societal, business, and employee interests.[4] **Employee rights** can be defined as the guarantees of fair treatment that employees expect in protection of their employment status. These expectations become rights when they are granted to employees by the courts, legislatures, or employers. Employee rights frequently involve an employer's alleged invasion of an employee's right to privacy. For example, employees may feel they have a reasonable expectation of privacy regarding their personal phone calls made from work phones, their e-mail messages made to other employees at work, or freedom from employers' random searches of their personal belongings. However, if employers tell employees that they have no right to privacy in these areas, they probably don't. One legal commentator notes, "When employers clearly state that there is no expectation of privacy, it's hard to argue that a reasonable person could have such an expectation."[5] Furthermore, the difference between an employee's legal right to privacy and the moral or personal right to privacy is not always clear. The confusion is due to the lack of a comprehensive and consistent body of privacy protection, whether from laws or from court decisions. There are no general federal or state laws that protect the privacy of all employees in the workplace.

objective 1

Employee Rights vs. Employer Responsibilities

Balanced against employee rights is the employer's responsibility to provide a safe workplace for employees while guaranteeing safe, quality goods and services to consumers. An employee who uses drugs may exercise his or her privacy right and refuse to submit to a drug test. But should that employee produce a faulty product as a result of drug impairment, the employer can be held liable for any harm caused by that product. Employers must therefore exercise *reasonable care* in the hiring, training, and assignment of employees to jobs.[6]

It is here that employee rights and employer responsibilities can come most pointedly into conflict. The failure of employers to honor employee rights can result in costly lawsuits, damage the organization's reputation, and hurt employee morale. But failure to protect the safety and welfare of employees or consumer interests can invite litigation from both groups. Negligent-hiring lawsuits by employees have become an area of great concern for employers.

Negligent Hiring

negligence
Failure to provide reasonable care when such failure results in injury to consumers or other employees

In law, **negligence** is the failure to use a reasonable amount of care when such failure results in injury to another person. Negligent hiring is a legal doctrine that places liability on the employer for actions of its employees during the course and scope of their employment. A general responsibility exists for employers to exercise *reasonable care* in preventing employees from intentionally harming other employees during their course of work.

Unfortunately, when one employee commits a violent act on another employee or an employee willfully defames another employee through e-mail messages communicated at work, the employer may face a negligent-hiring lawsuit claiming that the employer should have used more reasonable care in the hiring of its employees.[7] While many see negligent-hiring lawsuits as a "Catch-22" for employers (that is, how can employers predict with certainty the future behavior of employees), it nonetheless forces managers to take extra care in the employment and management of the workforce. In the remainder of this section we will discuss various rights employees have come to expect from their employers.

Job Protection Rights

It is not surprising that employees should regard their jobs as an established right—a right that should not be taken away without just cause. Without the opportunity to hold a job, our personal well-being would be greatly curtailed. This line of reasoning has led to the emergence of four legal considerations regarding the security of one's job: the employment-at-will principle, the concept of the implied contract, constructive discharge, and plant closing notification.

It should be understood, however, that although employees might have cause to regard jobs as an established right, there is no legal protection affording employees a permanent or continuous job. The U.S. Constitution carries no mandate guaranteeing that jobs are among the specific property rights of employees. Regardless, employees have certain expectations regarding the employment relationship. This expectation is referred to as the **psychological contract** and includes an employee's belief about the mutual obligation between the employee and the organization.[8] For example, in exchange for their talents, energies, and technical skills, workers expect employers to provide fair compensation, meaningful work, and job training. Employees also have the right to expect sound employment practices and to be treated as individuals of dignity and substantial worth.[9] While the psychological contract is not a legal mandate, nevertheless, it strongly influences the employment relationship.

psychological contract
Expectations of a fair exchange of employment obligations between an employee and employer

Employment at Will

The employment relationship has traditionally followed the common-law doctrine of employment at will. The **employment-at-will principle** assumes that an employee has a right to sever the employment relationship for a better job opportunity or for other personal reasons. Employers, likewise, are free to terminate the employment relationship at any time—and without notice—for any reason, no reason, or even a bad reason. In essence, employees are said to work "at the will" of the employer.[10]

employment-at-will principle
The right of an employer to fire an employee without giving a reason and the right of an employee to quit when he or she chooses

The employment-at-will relationship is created when an employee agrees to work for an employer for an unspecified period of time. Because the employment is of an indefinite duration, it can, in general, be terminated at the whim of either party. This freedom includes the right of management to unilaterally determine the conditions of employment and to make personnel decisions. In 1908, the Supreme Court upheld the employment-at-will doctrine in *Adair v United States,* and this principle continues to be the basic rule governing the private-sector employment relationship.[11]

Public-sector employees have additional constitutional protection of their employment rights under the Fifth and Fourteenth Amendments to the Constitution. The Fifth Amendment applies to federal employees, while the Fourteenth applies to employees working for state, county, and local governments. Both amendments limit the methods and reasons that may be utilized to discipline or dismiss an incumbent employee in the public sector. The clauses of the Fifth Amendment that prohibit denial of life, liberty, and property without due process of law, as well as the Fourteenth Amendment, provide the principal constitutional protection afforded public-sector employees. While these guarantees apply to public-sector employees, the employment rights afforded in these amendments have, nevertheless, influenced private-sector court decisions.

Wrongful Discharge

Estimates of the American workforce subject to arbitrary discharge under the employment-at-will doctrine range from 55 million to 65 million employees. Approximately 2 million workers are discharged each year. Estimates of unfair employee dismissals range from 50,000 to 200,000 a year. In recent years, a substantial number of these employees have sued their former employers for "wrongful or unjust discharge."

The significance of wrongful discharge suits is that they challenge the employer's right under the employment-at-will concept to unilaterally discharge employees.[12]

Various state courts now recognize the following three important exceptions to the employment-at-will doctrine:

1. *Violation of public policy.* This exception occurs when an employee is terminated for refusing to commit a crime; for reporting criminal activity to government authorities; for disclosing illegal, unethical, or unsafe practices of the employer; or for exercising employment rights. (See Figure 13.1 for examples of public policy violations.)
2. *Implied contract.* This exception occurs when employees are discharged despite the employer's promise (expressed or implied) of job security or contrary to established termination procedures. An employer's oral or written statements may constitute a contractual obligation if they are communicated to employees and employees rely on them as conditions of employment.[13]
3. *Implied covenant.* This exception occurs when a lack of good faith and fair dealing by the employer has been suggested. By inflicting harm without justification, the employer violates the implied covenant. Discharged employees may seek tort damages for mental distress or defamation.

The confusion and conflict between the traditional right of employers to terminate at will and the right of employees to be protected from unjust discharge are far from resolved. Therefore, to protect themselves from wrongful discharge terminations and from large jury awards—sometimes exceeding $1 million—HR specialists recommend the suggestions given in Figure 13.2.[14]

whistle-blowing
Complaints to governmental agencies by employees about their employers' illegal or immoral acts or illegal practices

Whistle-Blowing

Employees engage in **whistle-blowing** when they report an employer's illegal actions, immoral conduct, or illegal practices to governmental agencies charged with upholding the law.[15] A number of federal and state laws protect whistle-blowers from

Figure 13.1 Discharges That Violate Public Policy

An employer may *not* terminate an employee for

- Refusing to commit perjury in court on the employer's behalf
- Cooperating with a government agency in the investigation of a charge or giving testimony
- Refusing to violate a professional code of conduct
- Reporting Occupational Safety and Health Administration (OSHA) infractions
- Refusing to support a law or a political candidate favored by the employer
- "Whistle-blowing," or reporting illegal conduct by the employer
- Informing a customer that the employer has stolen property from the customer
- Complying with summons to jury duty

Figure 13.2 Tips to Avoid Wrongful Employment Termination Lawsuits

- *Terminate an employee only if there is an articulated reason.* An employer should have clearly articulated, easily understandable reasons for discharging an employee. The reasons should be stated as objectively as possible and should reflect company rules, policies, and practices.
- *Set and follow termination rules and schedules.* Make sure every termination follows a documented set of procedures. Procedures can be from an employee handbook, a supervisory manual, or even an intra-office memorandum. Before terminating, give employees notices of unsatisfactory performance and improvement opportunities through a system of warnings and suspensions.
- *Document all performance problems.* A lack of documented problems in an employee's personnel record may be used as circumstantial evidence of pretextual discharge if the employee is "suddenly" discharged.
- *Be consistent with employees in similar situations.* Document reasons given for all disciplinary actions, even if they do not lead to termination. Terminated employees may claim that exception-to-the-rule cases are discriminatory. Detailed documentation will help employers explain why these "exceptions" did not warrant termination.

retaliation from their employer; some provide whistle-blowers with financial incentives to expose wrongdoings.[16] For example, in response to recent corporate scandals, the Sarbanes-Oxley (S-O) Act was passed in 2002 to protect whistle-blowers employed in publicly traded companies.[17] The law encourages whistle-blowing by motivating publicly held companies to promote a more open culture that is sympathetic to employees who have a "reasonable belief" that a law has been violated. Federal employees are covered by the federal Whistleblower Protection Act (WPA).[18] The Notification and Federal Employee Antidiscrimination and Retaliation Act (No Fear Act), also passed in 2002, provides whistle-blower protection under federal law at the Environmental Protection Agency (EPA),[19] and the False Claims Act (FCA) applies to employees who provide information about false or fraudulent claims made against the federal government.[20]

Not only is whistle-blowing a protected right of employees, but these cases result in embarrassment for employers, harassment for employees, and large fines for employers that are found guilty. In one whistle-blowing case, federal prosecutors fined TAP Pharmaceutical Products $875 million for fraud—conspiring with doctors to cheat the government.[21] In another case, Medical World Communications paid the government $3.7 million to settle charges of mail fraud.[22]

To prevent cases such as these, HR professionals recommend that companies implement a whistle-blowing policy that encourages employees to report illegal or immoral conduct internally rather than externally. The policy should provide for the safeguard of employee rights, a complete and unbiased investigation of the incident, a speedy report of findings, and an appeals procedure for employees who are dissatisfied with company findings.[23]

Implied Contract

Although it is estimated that 70 percent of employees in the United States work without benefit of an employment contract, under certain conditions these employees may be granted contractual employment rights. This can occur when an implied promise by the employer suggests some form of job security to the employee. These implied contractual rights can be based on either oral or written statements made during the pre-employment process or subsequent to hiring. Often these promises are contained in employee handbooks, HR manuals, or employment applications or are made during the selection interview. Once these explicit or implicit promises of job security have been made, courts have generally prohibited the employer from terminating the employee without first exhausting the conditions of the contract. For example, a leading case, *Toussaint v Blue Cross and Blue Shield of Michigan,* found an employee handbook enforceable as a unilateral contract.[24] The following are some examples of how an implied contract may become binding:

- Telling employees their jobs are secure as long as they perform satisfactorily and are loyal to the organization.
- Stating in the employee handbook that employees will not be terminated without the right of defense or access to an appeal procedure—that is, due process.
- Urging an employee to leave another organization by promising higher wages and benefits, then reneging on those promises after the person has been hired.

Fortunately, employers may lessen their vulnerability to implied-contract lawsuits by prudent managerial practices, training, and HR policies. HR experts recommend the following approaches:

1. Training supervisors and managers not to imply contract benefits in conversations with new or present employees.
2. Including in employment offers a statement that an employee may voluntarily terminate employment with proper notice and the employee may be dismissed by the employer at any time and for a justified reason. The language in this statement must be appropriate, clear, and easily understood.
3. Including employment-at-will statements in all employment documents—for example, employee handbooks, employment applications, and letters of employment.[25] (See Highlights in HRM 1.)
4. Having written proof that employees have read and understood the employment-at-will disclaimers.

Constructive Discharge

constructive discharge
An employee's voluntary termination of his or her employment because of harsh, unreasonable employment conditions placed on the individual by the employer

It is increasingly common for employees to quit or resign their employment because of acts of alleged discrimination and to subsequently claim that their employment rights were violated through a **constructive discharge.** That is, they were "forced" to resign because of intolerable working conditions purposefully placed upon them by the employer.[26] Put simply, the employer has forced on an employee working conditions so unreasonable and unfair that the employee has no choice but to quit. In a leading constructive discharge case, *Young v Southwestern Savings and Loan Association,* the court noted:

> The general rule is that if the employer deliberately makes an employee's working conditions so intolerable that the employee is forced into involuntary resignation, then the employer has encompassed a constructive discharge and is as liable for any illegal conduct involved therein as if he had formally discharged the aggrieved employee.

The courts, by formulating the constructive-discharge doctrine, attempt to prevent employers from accomplishing covertly what they are prohibited by law from

Highlights in HRM 1

Examples of Employment-at-Will Statements

Employment handbooks frequently include an opening statement that employees are employed at will; that is, there are no duration guarantees. Also no supervisors or managers, except specified individuals (that is, the HR director or company president), have the authority to promise any employment benefit—including salary, job position, and the like. All handbooks should include a disclaimer that expressly provides that all employment policies and benefits contained in the handbook are subject to change or removal at the sole and exclusive discretion of the employer.

Two examples of at-will statements are as follows:

> I acknowledge that if hired, I will be an at-will employee. I will be subject to dismissal or discipline without notice or cause, at the discretion of the employer. I understand that no representative of the company, other than the president, has authority to change the terms of an at-will employment and that any such change can occur only in a written employment contract.

> I understand that my employment is not governed by any written or oral contract and is considered an at-will arrangement. This means that I am free, as is the company, to terminate the employment relationship at any time for any reason, so long as there is no violation of applicable federal or state law. In the event of employment, I understand that my employment is not for any definite period or succession of periods and is considered an at-will arrangement. That means I am free to terminate my employment at any time for any reason, as is the company, so long as there is no violation of applicable federal or state law.

A note of caution: Because at-will employment is governed by state laws, in order for an employer to preserve its at-will status, it must follow the regulations of its jurisdiction. This includes the writing of employment-at-will statements.

achieving overtly. For example, unscrupulous employers may want to rid themselves of seemingly undesirable employees by deliberately forcing on them unfavorable working conditions so grievous that employees would rather quit than tolerate the disagreeable conditions.[27] Under this action, the employer may be attempting to limit liability should an employee seek redress through various protective employment statutes. It should be noted that the constructive-discharge doctrine does not provide employees with any new employment rights. Rather, through a constructive-discharge suit, the employee is only protecting employment safeguards previously granted through laws or court rulings.

Retaliation Discharge

Title VII of the Civil Rights Act, the Age Discrimination in Employment Act, the Americans with Disabilities Act, and other employment laws prohibit employers from retaliating against employees when they exercise their rights under these statutes (see Chapter 3). Unfortunately, more retaliation claims are succeeding in court because employers are perceived by judges and juries as imposing unfavorable working conditions on employees even when discrimination claims are meritless.[28] Employees may believe retaliation occurs when managers transfer them to lower-rated jobs, deny them salary increases or promotions, impose on them unrealistic job assignments, or become belligerent or uncommunicative with them after they file discrimination complaints or receive a favorable settlement.

To prevent retaliation charges, William Kandel, employer defense attorney, encourages employers to implement a separate anti-retaliation policy and to train managers and supervisors in acceptable and unacceptable methods to resolve employee complaints.[29] A key component to any anti-retaliation policy is to treat employees with dignity and respect.[30] Other suggestions to reduce retaliation discharges include the following:

- Take no adverse employment action against employees when they file discrimination charges. Treat employees as if nothing had happened.
- Be consistent and objective in your treatment of employees. Evaluate employees on performance, not personalities.
- Harbor no animosity toward employees when they file discrimination lawsuits. Treat every employee the way you would want to be treated—fairly.

Plant Closing Notification

The federal government, several states, and local jurisdictions have passed legislation restricting the unilateral right of employers to close or relocate their facilities. In 1989 Congress passed the Workers' Adjustment Retraining and Notification Act (WARN), which requires organizations with more than 100 employees to give employees and their communities sixty days' notice of any closure or layoff affecting fifty or more full-time employees.[31] Notice must be given to collective bargaining representatives, unrepresented employees, the appropriate state dislocated-worker agency, and the highest-elected local official. Terminated employees must be notified individually in writing.[32] The act allows several exemptions, including "unforeseeable circumstances" and "faltering businesses." For example, Michigan Industrial Holding did not violate the sixty-day notice provisions—due to unforeseeable business circumstances—when a major client cancelled a contract, causing an immediate plant closure.[33] However, failure to comply with the law can subject employers to liability for back pay, fringe benefits, prejudgment interest, and attorney's fees. WARN does not prohibit employer closings, layoffs, or loss of jobs; the law simply seeks to lessen the hardships caused by job loss.

Privacy Rights

The right of privacy can be regarded as a matter of personal freedom from unwarranted government or business intrusion into personal affairs. The right of privacy—a right well recognized in both law and legal commentary—includes the general principle of "personal autonomy." It largely involves the individual's right to be left alone.[34]

Not surprisingly, employees strongly defend their right to workplace privacy. After a U.S. Supreme Court decision ruled that the random drug-testing policy of the City of Mesa, Arizona, violated a firefighter's Fourth Amendment privacy rights,

Source: Cartoon by Ted Goff. Reprinted with permission.

Mesa fire captain Craig Peterson, who filed the suit, stated, "The way I looked at it, this policy violated my rights, and I wasn't going to submit to it. The right of privacy is one of the most basic rights we have."[35]

Employer challenges to privacy rights in the workplace have sparked a heated debate over the extent to which fundamental rights previously thought untouchable may be lessened through the employment relationship. Through company policies and court decisions, employees now realize that privacy rights on the job are more limited than those at home. According to Janis Procter-Murphy, employment attorney, "employee privacy is recognized as one of the most significant workplace issues facing companies today."[36]

Employers defend their intrusion into employee privacy by noting their legitimate interest in some of the personal affairs of employees, particularly when those affairs (such as drug use, criminal activity, and co-worker dating) may directly affect employee productivity and workplace safety and/or morale.[37] Court cases regarding workplace privacy generally attempt to balance an employee's legitimate expectation of privacy against the employer's need to supervise and control the efficient operation of the organization. In this section we address the important workplace privacy issues of substance abuse and drug testing, searches and monitoring, e-mail privacy, access to personnel files, employee conduct outside the workplace, and genetic testing.

Substance Abuse and Drug Testing

Consider these facts. Compared with nonabusing employees, substance abusers:

- are 10 times as likely to miss work than those who are clear and alert
- are 3.6 times as likely to be involved in on-the-job accidents
- are 5 times as likely to file workers' compensation claims
- are 33 percent less productive
- use 16 times as many healthcare benefits[38]

In 2003, the U.S. Department of Labor reported that three-fourths of adults who use illegal drugs are employed.[39] It is estimated that drug abuse by employees costs U.S. employers $75 billion every year in terms of safety risks, theft, reduced productivity, accidents, and benefits costs. Furthermore, in these litigious times, the failure of an employer to ensure a safe and drug-free workplace can result in astronomical liability claims when consumers are injured because of a negligent employee or a faulty product. To fight the battle of workplace drugs, 97 percent of Fortune 500 companies have drug-free workplace policies, and according to the American Medical Association, 67 percent of employers have drug-testing policies.[40]

Safety-Sensitive Jobs. Drug testing is most prevalent among employees in sensitive positions within the public sector, in organizations doing business with the federal government, and in public and private transportation companies. The definition of *sensitive position* has been formulated by the courts to include employees holding positions requiring top-secret national security clearance, those working in the interdiction of dangerous drugs, uniformed police officers and firefighters, transportation safety positions, and employees working in the nuclear power industry. These employees can be required to submit to a drug test when "reasonable suspicion" for a drug test exists and the employer's testing procedures are also reasonable. Under the Omnibus Transportation Employee Testing Act of 1991, employers are legally required to test for drugs in transportation-related occupations, including airline, railroad, trucking, and public transport facilities.

Private-Sector Employers. Managers and supervisors need to understand that legislation on drug testing in the private sector is fragmented and largely regulated by individual states. States with restrictive drug-testing laws generally prohibit testing for drugs except in very specific circumstances. Pro–drug testing states generally permit testing, provided that strict testing procedures are followed. Unless state or local laws either restrict or prohibit drug testing, private employers have a right to require employees to submit to a urinalysis or blood test when *reasonable suspicion* or *probable cause* exists.[41] Reasonable suspicion could include observable safety, conduct, or performance problems; excessive absenteeism or tardiness; or increased difficulty in working cooperatively with supervisors or co-workers. Employers who want to implement mandatory or random drug testing programs may face more stringent state court restrictions. According to one legal authority, "Employers should be especially careful in deciding whether to use random testing and will not be able to do so for non-safety-sensitive jobs in a number of states."[42]

Drug-Free Workplace Act of 1988. This federal act applies to organizations with government contracts of $25,000 or more.[43] Among other things, the act requires employers to publish and furnish to employees a policy statement prohibiting drug usage at work, to inform employees about the dangers of drugs, and to list options available for drug counseling. Additionally, employers must notify the federal contracting agency of any employees who have been convicted of a drug-related criminal offense.

Americans with Disabilities Act. Employers subject to the Americans with Disabilities Act (see Chapter 3) must comply with the law's provisions regarding drug addiction. The ADA clearly exempts from coverage any employee or job applicant who "is currently engaging in the illegal use of drugs." Illegal drug users are not considered to be "individuals with a disability." However, recovering or recovered drug addicts are included under the law's provisions. As the law states,

> Nothing in the ADA shall be construed to exclude as an individual with a disability an individual who—
>
> (1) has successfully completed a supervised drug rehabilitation program and is no longer engaging in the illegal use of drugs, or has otherwise been rehabilitated successfully and is no longer engaging in such use;
>
> (2) is participating in a supervised rehabilitation program and is no longer engaging in such use.[44]

The ADA also protects employees addicted to legal drugs obtained legally. For example, an employee who lawfully takes pain medication and subsequently becomes addicted to the medication satisfies the ADA definition of an individual with a disability.

Drug Testing. Urinalysis is by far the method of choice for employers who test for drugs, although employers also use blood sampling and hair sampling. Some of the sharpest criticism of drug testing concerns the reliability of these testing methods to identify someone currently under the influence of a drug. Three problems are noteworthy. First, employees or job applicants may attempt to beat drug-testing procedures. "Cheaters" may try to dilute urine samples, thereby helping rid the body of toxins. Another method is to add chemicals to a urine specimen, making the drugs undetectable or disrupting the testing process itself. Interestingly, nine states have laws making drug test fraud a crime.[45] Second, illegal substances remain in urine for various periods of time: cocaine for approximately 72 hours, marijuana for three weeks or longer. Therefore, an employee may test positive for a drug days or weeks after using it. Third, urine tests become problematic when testing equipment is miscalibrated or insufficiently cleaned, samples become contaminated, and chain-of-custody problems occur. (*Chain-of-custody* documentation accounts for the integrity of each urine specimen by tracking its handling and storage from point of collection to final disposition.) Any of these difficulties can cause a *false positive* test result, in which a particular drug is mistakenly identified in a specimen. Importantly, it is recommended that the results of drug tests be provided only to those who need to know—for example, supervisors or HR staff members—and not to other co-workers or disinterested managers. Boeing, 3M, United Airlines, and Motorola use an independent medical review officer (MRO) to ensure the integrity of their drug-testing programs. (MROs are required in certain states for tests mandated by the federal government.)

An alternative to drug testing is to evaluate an employee's suitability for work through *impairment testing.* Also called fitness-for-duty or performance-based testing, impairment testing measures whether an employee is alert enough for work. One impairment test requires an employee to keep a cursor on track during a video game–like simulation. Another testing technique evaluates an employee's eye movements. The employee looks into a dark viewport, then follows a light with his or her eyes. Test results, when compared against baseline data gathered earlier on the employee, mimic those of a sobriety test for probable-cause impairment. One advantage of impairment testing is that it focuses on workplace conduct rather than off-duty behavior. Furthermore, it identifies employees who are impaired because of problems that a drug test can't spot: fatigue, stress, and alcohol use.

Drug-Free Workplace Policies. Both HR professionals and legal experts highly recommend that employers implement a "zero-tolerance" drug-free workplace policy. The policy should state under what conditions employees may be subject to a drug test, the testing procedures used, and the consequences of a positive report. Figure 13.3 provides recommendations for an extensive drug-free work policy.

Employee Searches and Electronic Monitoring

- General Electric employs tiny fish-eye lenses installed behind pinholes in walls and ceilings to observe employees suspected of crimes.
- DuPont uses long-distance cameras to monitor its loading docks.

Figure 13.3 Recommendations for a Drug-Free Workplace Policy

1. Adopt a written zero-tolerance drug-free workplace policy and provide a copy to all employees. A signed copy should be placed in the employee's personnel file.
2. Post "We Are a Drug-Free Workplace" signs where employees will widely observe them.
3. Provide employees with substance-abuse prevention educational materials. Arrange substance-abuse awareness training for employees and managers.
4. Perform pre-employment drug testing on all new hires.
5. Advise employees that they are subject to drug testing when "reasonable suspicion" exists.
6. Provide for follow-up testing to ensure that an employee remains drug-free after return from a substance-abuse treatment program.
7. Provide for "post-accident" drug testing when justified by property loss or damage, serious injury, or death.
8. Use only federally or state-approved certified labs for analysis.
9. Utilize the services of a medical review officer for all positive drug test results.
10. Maintain strict confidentiality of all test results. Provide information only on a "need-to-know" basis.
11. Apply terms of a written policy strictly, fairly, and equally among employees and managers.

Source: Adapted from "Steps to a Successful Drug-Free Workplace Policy," *Occupational Hazards* 66, no. 8 (August 2004): 46.

- Mervyn's department stores issue employees clear plastic bags for carrying personal belongings. The bags are checked as they enter and leave work.
- The Cheesecake Factory, a restaurant chain, uses video monitoring of kitchens, dining rooms, and hostess stations.

While these examples may seem a violation of privacy rights, it is not uncommon for employers to monitor employee conduct through surveillance techniques. While most workplace monitoring must have some legitimate business purpose, very few federal legal controls protect workers from being watched. State laws, however, set their own regulations on how much prying employees must tolerate.

Why do companies search employees and monitor their activities? The answer is employee theft. The U.S. Chamber of Commerce estimates that employee theft (stealing merchandise, supplies, or equipment; selling information; embezzlement; "time theft"; computer crime; and so on) costs U.S. businesses $40 billion annually. According to U.S. Department of Commerce estimates, employee theft is responsible for 30 percent of all business failures.[46] In one study, results showed that "[a]n astounding 95 percent of all businesses experience employee theft."[47]

To help fight these employee crimes, the courts have allowed searches of lockers, desks, suitcases, toolboxes, and general work areas when adequate justification exists and employees have received proper notification beforehand. Employees have limited reasonable expectation of privacy in places where work rules that provide for inspections have been put into effect. They must comply with probable-cause searches by employers. And they can be appropriately disciplined, normally for insubordination, for refusing to comply with search requests. Importantly, absent emergencies or other special circumstances, random searches of employees' personal belongings or company facilities should be avoided. Random searches likely will result in employee anger and claims of privacy rights—with concomitant costs in productivity.[48]

Managers must be diligent when conducting employee searches. Improper searches can lead to employee lawsuits charging the employer with invasion of privacy, defamation of character, and negligent infliction of emotional distress. Employers are advised to develop an HR search policy based on the following guidelines:

1. The search policy should be widely publicized and should advocate a probable or compelling reason for the search.
2. The search policy should be applied in a reasonable, evenhanded manner.
3. When possible, searches should be conducted in private.
4. The employer should attempt to obtain the employee's consent prior to the search.
5. The search should be conducted in a humane and discreet manner to avoid infliction of emotional distress.
6. The penalty for refusing to consent to a search should be specified.

Some searches are more intrusive to employees than others. For example, "strip searches" are likely to inflict emotional distress and should be avoided. Likewise, any touching of employees for hidden items should be minimized and, if conducted, the search should be made by a person of the same sex.

One of the most common means of electronic monitoring by employers is telephone surveillance to ensure that customer requests are handled properly or to prevent theft.[49] Employers have the right to monitor employees, provided they do it for compelling business reasons and employees have been informed that their calls will be monitored. However, a federal law, the Electronic Communications Privacy Act (ECPA), places some major limitations on that right.[50] The ECPA restricts employers from intercepting wire, oral, or electronic communications. Under the law, if an employee receives a personal call, the employer must hang up as soon as he or she realizes the call is personal. As noted by one legal authority, "Personal calls can be monitored only to the degree needed to determine that they are indeed personal."[51]

E-Mail, Internet, and Voice Mail Privacy

The benefits of e-mail, the Internet, and voice mail are many; they provide instant delivery of messages, facilitate teamwork, increase time efficiency, offer access to global information, and promote flexible work arrangements. Unfortunately, technology also permits employees to act in unscrupulous, inappropriate, and unauthorized ways, creating ethical, productivity, and legal problems for employers. These illegitimate uses of technology cause employers to monitor the conduct of employees, creating significant privacy issues for both employees and managers.

In a survey conducted by the Society for Human Resource Management, 74 percent of respondents said they monitor the Internet usage and e-mail messages of their employees. A Privacy Foundation study found that 14 million U.S. workers are subject to continuous monitoring while online. Why do employers monitor their employees? The reasons are varied: to prevent intimidating behavior of employees, to ensure effective use of company time, to prevent employee gossip, to eliminate the surfing of pornographic web sites, to stop employees from doing personal business on company time, or to ensure employee safety including the prevention of sexual harassment or cyberstalking. For example, in a recent case, a sexual harassment suit cost Chevron $2.2 million because an employee sent coarse messages over the company e-mail system.[52] Additionally, employee monitoring is done to prevent personal information from becoming accessible to those with prying eyes or "hackers" who might use the information inappropriately.

Employers have a great latitude to monitor their own equipment. Court cases governing e-mail and the Internet generally grant to employers the right to monitor materials created, received, or sent for business-related reasons. Employees who erase their messages may wrongly assume their messages are gone when deleted. Although employees may assume that their right to privacy extends to e-mail, the Internet, or voice mail messages, it does not. Furthermore, employees can be disciplined or terminated for inappropriate e-mail messages or Internet use. HR experts and legal authorities strongly encourage employers to develop clear policies and guidelines that explain to employees how e-mail, the Internet, and voice mail are to be used, including when and under what conditions employees can be monitored[53] (see Figure 13.4). As with other employment policies, employees should sign a form indicating that they have read and understand the policy.

Figure 13.4 E-Mail, Internet, and Voice Mail: Policy Guidelines

E-mail, Internet, and voice mail policies seek to reduce an employee's reasonable expectation of privacy balanced against the employer's legitimate business reasons for monitoring employee conduct. A comprehensive e-mail, Internet, and voice mail policy would cover the following:

- Ensure compliance with federal and state legislation.
- Specify the circumstances, if any, under which the system can be used for personal business.
- Specify that confidential information not be sent on the network.
- Set forth the conditions under which monitoring will be done—by whom, how frequently, and with what notification to employees.
- Specify that e-mail and voice mail information be sent only to users who need it for business purposes.
- Expressly prohibit use of e-mail or voice mail to harass others or to send anonymous messages.
- Make clear that employees have no privacy rights in any material delivered or received through e-mail or voice mail.
- Specify that employees who violate the policy are subject to discipline, including discharge.

Monitoring employee behavior is an important deterrent to illegal conduct of employees.

© DIGITAL VISION/GETTY IMAGES

Access to Personnel Files

The information kept in an employee's personnel file can have a significant impact—positive or negative—on career development. The personnel file, typically kept by the HR department, can contain performance appraisals, salary notices, investigatory reports, credit checks, criminal records, test scores, and family data. Errors and/or omissions in personnel files, or access to the files by unauthorized people, can create employment or personal hardships.

Legislation at the federal level (see Figure 13.5) and laws in various states permit employees to inspect their own personnel files. How much access is allowed varies from state to state. For example, employers can prohibit employees from viewing information that might violate the privacy of others. Reference letters and criminal investigation reports are of this nature. A state law can limit the employee to copies of documents that he or she has signed, such as performance evaluations or job applications. The states that grant employees the privilege to see their personnel files generally provide

- The right to know of the existence of one's personnel file
- The right to inspect one's own personnel file
- The right to correct inaccurate data in the file

Typically, if a state law allows employees to examine their files, employers can insist that someone from HR, or a supervisor, be present to ensure that nothing is taken, added, or changed. Even in the absence of specific legislation, most employers give their employees access to their personnel files. Employment professionals recommend that organizations develop a policy on employee files that includes, as a minimum, the points noted in Figure 13.6.

Medical information of employees requires special handling. The Americans with Disabilities Act (discussed in Chapter 3) requires that an employee's medical history be kept in a file separate from other personal information. Also, new medical privacy

Figure 13.5 Right-to-Privacy Laws

LAW	EFFECT
Electronic Communications Privacy Act (1986)	Prohibits the interception, recording, or disclosure of wire, electronic, and aural communications through any electronic, mechanical, or other device. An interception takes place when an employer monitors a telephone call while it is occurring. Permits employer monitoring for legitimate business reasons.
Privacy Act (1974)	Applies to federal agencies and to organizations supplying goods or services to the federal government; gives individuals the right to examine references regarding employment decisions; allows employees to review their personnel records for accuracy. Employers who willfully violate the act are subject to civil suits.
Family Education Rights and Privacy Act—The Buckley Amendment (1974)	Prohibits educational institutions from supplying information about students without prior consent. Students have the right to inspect their educational records.
Fair Credit Reporting Act (1970)	Permits job applicants and employees to know of the existence and context of any credit files maintained on them. Employees have the right to know of the existence and nature of an investigative consumer report compiled by the employer.

regulations contained in the Health Insurance Portability and Accountability Act (HIPAA) mandate that covered employers safeguard health information provided to employers by insurers or healthcare providers—doctors, group medical plans, and so on. HIPAA clearly states that an individual's past, present, or future health information be used on a limited basis.[54] Therefore, as a general rule, an employee's medical information must be handled in a sensitive and confidential manner.

Figure 13.6 Personnel Files: Policy Guidelines

- Ensure compliance with applicable state laws.
- Define exactly what information is to be kept in employee files.
- Develop different categories of personnel information, depending on legal requirements and organizational needs.
- Specify where, when, how, and under what circumstances employees may review or copy their files.
- Identify company individuals allowed to view personnel files.
- Prohibit the collection of information that could be viewed as discriminatory or could form the basis for an invasion-of-privacy suit.
- Audit employment records on a regular basis to remove irrelevant, outdated, or inaccurate information.

Camera-Equipped Phones

General Motors and defense contractor Syzygy Technologies are two companies that ban employee use of camera phones, personal digital assistants, and similar digital devices. Reasons for the ban include protecting competitive proprietary information and safeguarding employee privacy. Companies routinely ban such devices from restrooms and wellness and exercise facilities because of the risk of privacy violations. John Sweeney, information specialist at SHRM, notes, "Employees using such facilities should feel safe and have no concerns that they might be photographed without their consent."[55]

Employee Conduct outside the Workplace

Consider the following case. On Monday morning the owner of ABC Corporation reads in the newspaper that a company employee has been charged with robbery and assault on a local convenience store owner. The employee has been released pending trial. A phone call to the employee's supervisor reveals that the employee has reported to work. What should the owner do?

Legal authorities generally conclude that the off-duty behavior of employees is not subject to employer disciplinary action. Case law suggests that misconduct outside the workplace may not, in some circumstances, be a lawful justification for employee discipline. Organizations that want to discipline employees for off-duty misconduct must establish a clear relationship between the misconduct and its negative effect on other employees or the organization. This might be established, for example, in cases in which off-duty criminal misconduct (such as child molestation) creates a disruptive impact on the workplace. Another example might be when the public nature of the employee's job (such as police or fire department personnel) creates an image problem for the organization. Generally, however, little of what an employee does outside the workplace bears discipline by the employer.

Workplace romances, however, create a particular dilemma for organizations. The concern is employer liability if a co-worker, supervisor-subordinate, or other power-differentiated romance goes sour, leading to charges of sexual harassment.[56] Acceptable behavior in a consensual relationship between employees can become harassing behavior if one party to the relationship no longer welcomes the conduct. Organizations may also increase the potential for workplace violence should a scorned lover seek violent revenge at the work site.

Furthermore, workplace romances can lead to employee charges of favoritism against a co-worker involved in a supervisor-subordinate romance. These "reverse harassment" claims are based on preferential treatment given an employee engaged in a romantic affair. Workplace romances can also create morale problems when other employees feel unfairly treated; such situations can lead to jealousy, resentment, and hard feelings. Supervisor romances can have profound effects on organizational operations and productivity.

Genetic Testing

Advances in genetic research now make it possible to identify the genetic basis for human diseases and illnesses.[57] Genetic findings present opportunities for individualized prevention strategies and early detection and treatment. Unfortunately, knowledge gained through genetic testing can also be used discreetly by employers to discriminate against or stigmatize individuals applying for employment or individuals currently employed. For example, genetic testing can identify an individual's risk of developing common disorders such as cancer, heart disease, or diabetes.

Because employee diseases and illnesses raise employment costs, employers may avoid hiring or retaining individuals who they believe are likely to become unduly sick, resign, or retire early, thus creating additional recruitment, training, or medical costs. Not surprisingly, when employers use genetic tests as a means to deny employment opportunities to workers, the tests raise important moral and ethical concerns, not to mention privacy issues. However, employers must remember that there is no scientific evidence to substantiate a relationship between unexpected genetic factors and an individual's ability to perform his or her job.

Few federal or state laws or court decisions govern an employer's use of genetic information. Genetic testing, however, likely violates the antidiscrimination mandates of Title VII of the Civil Rights Act and the Americans with Disabilities Act. Future legislation—either federal or state—to prohibit genetic discrimination in employment is uncertain.[58]

Disciplinary Policies and Procedures

The rights of managers to discipline and discharge employees are increasingly limited. There is thus a great need for managers at all levels to understand discipline procedures. Disciplinary action taken against an employee must be for justifiable reasons, and there must be effective policies and procedures to govern its use. Such policies and procedures assist those responsible for taking disciplinary action and help ensure that employees will receive fair and constructive treatment. Equally important, these guidelines help prevent disciplinary action from being voided or reversed through the appeal system.

Disciplinary policies and procedures should extend to a number of important areas to ensure thorough coverage. Figure 13.7 presents a disciplinary model that illustrates the areas where provisions should be established. The model also shows the logical sequence in which disciplinary steps must be carried out to ensure enforceable decisions.

A major responsibility of the HR department is to develop, and to have top management approve, its disciplinary policies and procedures. The HR department

Figure 13.7 A Disciplinary Model

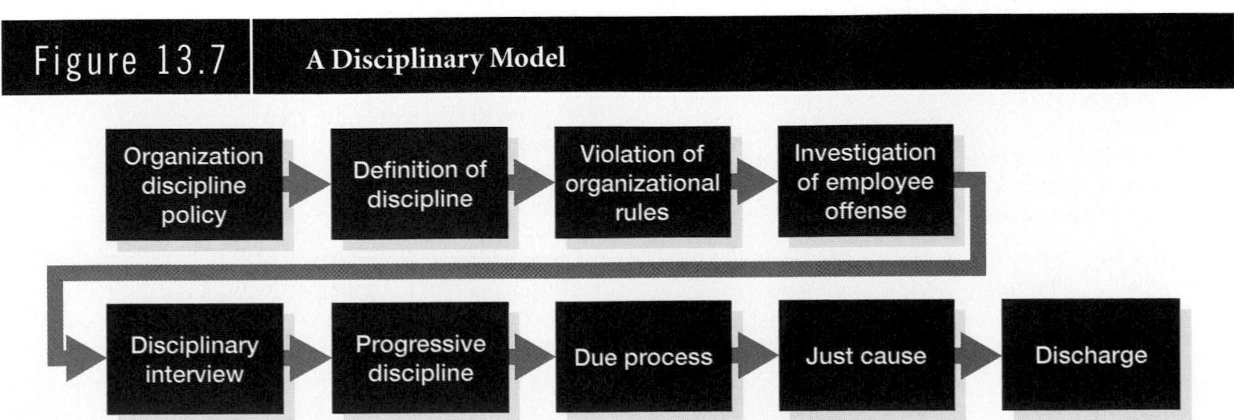

is also responsible for ensuring that disciplinary policies, as well as the disciplinary action taken against employees, are consistent with the labor agreement (if one exists) and conform to current laws. However, the primary responsibility for preventing or correcting disciplinary problems rests with an employee's immediate supervisor. This person is best able to observe evidence of unsatisfactory behavior or performance and to discuss the matter with the employee. Should discipline become necessary, the employee's immediate supervisor is the logical person to apply the company's disciplinary procedure and monitor employee improvement.

The Results of Inaction

Figure 13.8 lists the more common disciplinary problems identified by managers. Failure to take disciplinary action in any of these areas only serves to aggravate a problem that eventually must be resolved. Failure to act implies that the performance of the employee concerned has been satisfactory. If disciplinary action is eventually taken, the delay will make it more difficult to justify the action if appealed. In defending against such an appeal, the employer is likely to be asked why an employee who had not been performing or behaving satisfactorily was kept on the payroll. Or an even more damaging question might be "Why did that employee receive satisfactory performance ratings (or perhaps even merit raises)?"

Such contradictions in practice can only aid employees in successfully challenging management's corrective actions. Unfortunately, some supervisors try to build a case to justify their corrective actions only after they have decided that a particular employee should be discharged. The following are common reasons given by supervisors for their failure to impose a disciplinary penalty:[59]

1. The supervisor had failed to document earlier actions, so no record existed on which to base subsequent disciplinary action.

Figure 13.8 Common Disciplinary Problems

ATTENDANCE PROBLEMS
- Unexcused absence
- Chronic absenteeism
- Unexcused/excessive tardiness
- Leaving without permission

DISHONESTY AND RELATED PROBLEMS
- Theft
- Falsifying employment application
- Willfully damaging organizational property
- Punching another employee's time card
- Falsifying work records

WORK PERFORMANCE PROBLEMS
- Failure to complete work assignments
- Producing substandard products or services
- Failure to meet established production requirements

ON-THE-JOB BEHAVIOR PROBLEMS
- Intoxication at work
- Insubordination
- Horseplay
- Smoking in unauthorized places
- Fighting
- Gambling
- Failure to use safety devices
- Failure to report injuries
- Carelessness
- Sleeping on the job
- Using abusive or threatening language with supervisors
- Possession of narcotics or alcohol
- Possession of firearms or other weapons
- Sexual harassment

2. Supervisors believed they would receive little or no support from higher management for the disciplinary action.
3. The supervisor was uncertain of the facts underlying the situation requiring disciplinary action.
4. Failure by the supervisor to discipline employees in the past for a certain infraction caused the supervisor to forgo current disciplinary action in order to appear consistent.
5. The supervisor wanted to be seen as a likable person.

Setting Organizational Rules

The setting of organizational rules is the foundation for an effective disciplinary system. These rules govern the type of behavior expected of employees. Organizations as diverse as Gerber Products, Wal-Mart, Steelcase, and Pitney Bowes have written policies explaining the type of conduct required of employees. Because employee behavior standards are established through the setting of organizational rules and regulations, the following suggestions may help reduce problems in this area:

1. Rules should be widely disseminated and known to all employees. It should not be assumed that employees know all the rules.
2. Rules should be reviewed periodically—perhaps annually—especially those rules critical to work success.
3. The reasons for a rule should always be explained. Acceptance of an organizational rule is greater when employees understand the reasons behind it.
4. Rules should always be written. Ambiguity should be avoided, as this can result in different interpretations of the rules by different supervisors.
5. Rules must be reasonable and relate to the safe and efficient operation of the organization. Rules should not be made simply because of personal likes or dislikes.
6. If management has been lax in the enforcement of a rule, the rule must be restated, along with the consequences for its violation, before disciplinary action can begin.
7. Employees should sign a document stating that they have read and understand the organizational rules.

When seeking reasons for unsatisfactory behavior, supervisors must keep in mind that employees may not be aware of certain work rules. Before initiating any disciplinary action, therefore, it is essential that supervisors determine whether they have given their employees careful and thorough orientation in the rules and regulations relating to their jobs. In fact, the proper communication of organizational rules and regulations is so important that labor arbitrators cite *neglect in communicating rules* as a major reason for reversing the disciplinary action taken against an employee.[60]

hot-stove rule
A rule of discipline that can be compared with a hot stove in that it gives warning, is effective immediately, is enforced consistently, and applies to all employees in an impersonal and unbiased way

The Hot-Stove Approach to Rule Enforcement

Regardless of the reason for the disciplinary action, it should be taken as soon as possible after the infraction has occurred and a complete investigation has been conducted. HR professionals often use the **hot-stove rule** to explain the correct application of

discipline
(1) Treatment that punishes, (2) orderly behavior in an organizational setting, or (3) training that molds and strengthens desirable conduct—or corrects undesirable conduct—and develops self-control

discipline. A hot stove gives warning that it should not be touched. Those who ignore the warning and touch it are assured of being burned. The punishment is an immediate and direct consequence of breaking the rule never to touch a hot stove. Likewise, a work rule should apply to all employees and should be enforced consistently and in an impersonal and unbiased way. Employees should know the consequences of violating the rule, so that it has preventive value.

Defining Discipline

In management seminars conducted by the authors of this text, when managers are asked to define the word *discipline,* their most frequent response is that discipline means punishment. Although this answer is not incorrect, it is only one of three possible meanings. As normally defined, **discipline** has these meanings:

1. Treatment that punishes
2. Orderly behavior in an organizational setting
3. Training that molds and strengthens desirable conduct—or corrects undesirable conduct—and develops self-control

Discipline should never be viewed as punishment but rather as a way to correct undesirable employee behavior.

To some managers, discipline is synonymous with force. They equate the term with the punishment of employees who violate rules or regulations. Other managers think of discipline as a general state of affairs—a condition of orderliness in which employees conduct themselves according to standards of acceptable behavior. Discipline viewed in this manner can be considered positive when employees willingly practice self-control and respect organizational rules.

The third definition considers discipline a management tool used to correct undesirable employee behavior. Discipline is applied as a constructive means of getting employees to conform to acceptable standards of performance. Many organizations, such as Goodyear Aerospace and Arizona State University, define *discipline* in their policy manuals as training that "corrects, molds, or perfects knowledge, attitudes, behavior, or conduct." Discipline is thus viewed as a way to correct poor employee performance. As these organizations emphasize, discipline should be seen as a method of training employees to perform better or to improve their job attitudes or work behavior.

When taken against employees, disciplinary action should never be thought of as punishment. Discipline can embody a penalty as a means of obtaining a desired result; however, punishment should not be the intent of disciplinary action. Rather, discipline must have as its goal the improvement of the employee's future behavior. To apply discipline in any other way—as punishment or as a way of getting even with employees—can only invite problems for management, including possible wrongful discharge suits.

Investigating the Disciplinary Problem

It's a rare manager who has a good, intuitive sense of how to investigate employee misconduct. Too frequently investigations are conducted in a haphazard manner; worse, they overlook one or more investigative concerns.[61] In conducting an employee investigation, it is important to be objective and to avoid the assumptions, suppositions, and biases that often surround discipline cases. Figure 13.9 lists seven questions to consider in investigating an employee offense. Attending to each question will help ensure a full and fair investigation while providing reliable information free from personal prejudice.[62]

Figure 13.9 **Considerations in Disciplinary Investigations**

1. In very specific terms, what is the offense charged?
   - Is management sure it fully understands the charge against the employee?
   - Was the employee really terminated for insubordination, or did the employee merely refuse a request by management?
2. Did the employee know he or she was doing something wrong?
   - What rule or provision was violated?
   - How would the employee know of the existence of the rule?
   - Was the employee warned of the consequence?
3. Is the employee guilty?
   - What are the sources of facts?
   - Is there direct or only indirect evidence of guilt?
   - Has anyone talked to the employee to hear his or her side of the situation?
4. Are there extenuating circumstances?
   - Were conflicting orders given by different supervisors?
   - Does anybody have reason to want to "get" this employee?
   - Was the employee provoked by a manager or another employee?
5. Has the rule been uniformly enforced?
   - Have all managers applied this rule consistently?
   - What punishment have previous offenders received?
   - Were any other employees involved in this offense?
6. Is the offense related to the workplace?
   - Is there evidence that the offense hurt the organization?
   - Is management making a moral judgment or a business judgment?
7. What is the employee's past work record?
   - How many years of service has the employee given the organization?
   - How many years or months has the employee held the present job?
   - What is the employee's personnel record as a whole, especially his or her disciplinary record?

Documentation of Employee Misconduct

"It's too complicated." "I just didn't take time to do it." "I have more important things to do." These are some of the frequent excuses used by managers who have failed to document cases of employee misconduct. The most significant cause of inadequate documentation, however, is that managers have no idea of what constitutes good documentation. Unfortunately, the failure of managers to record employee misconduct accurately can result in the reversal of any subsequent disciplinary action. The maintenance of *accurate* and *complete* work records, therefore, is an essential part of an effective disciplinary system. For documentation to be complete, the following eight items should be included:

1. Date, time, and location of the incident(s)
2. Negative performance or behavior exhibited by the employee—the problem
3. Consequences of that action or behavior on the employee's overall work performance and/or the operation of the employee's work unit
4. Prior discussion(s) with the employee about the problem
5. Disciplinary action to be taken and specific improvement expected
6. Consequences if improvement is not made, and a follow-up date
7. The employee's reaction to the supervisor's attempt to change behavior
8. The names of witnesses to the incident (if appropriate)

When preparing documentation, it is important for a manager to record the incident immediately after the infraction takes place, when the memory of it is still fresh, and to ensure that the record is complete and accurate. Documentation need not be lengthy, but it must include the eight points in the preceding list. Remember, a manager's records of employee misconduct are considered business documents, and as such they are admissible as evidence in arbitration hearings, administrative proceedings, and courts of law. As noted by one manager at a seminar on discipline, "When taking corrective action against an employee, the importance of compiling a complete and objective disciplinary record simply cannot be overstated."

The Investigative Interview

Before any disciplinary action is initiated, an investigative interview should be conducted to make sure employees are fully aware of the offense.[63] This interview is necessary because the supervisor's perceptions of the employee's behavior may not be entirely accurate.[64] The interview should concentrate on how the offense violated the performance and behavior standards of the job. It should avoid getting into personalities or areas unrelated to job performance. Most important, the employee must be given a full opportunity to explain his or her side of the issue so that any deficiencies for which the organization may be responsible are revealed.

In the leading case *NLRB v Weingarten, Inc.*, the Supreme Court upheld a National Labor Relations Board ruling in favor of the employee's right to representation during an investigative interview in a unionized organization.[65] The Court reasoned that the presence of a union representative would serve the beneficial purpose of balancing the power between labor and management, because the union representative could aid an employee who was "too fearful or inarticulate to relate accurately the incident being investigated, or too ignorant to raise extenuating factors." In the *Weingarten* case, the Court decided that because the employee had reason to believe that the investigative interview might result in action jeopardizing her job security, she had the right to representation.

© DEBORAH SCHWARTZ/GETTY IMAGES

An investigative interview should always be held in private and should elicit the comments and concerns of the employee.

It is important to note also that an employee's right to representation in a unionized organization does not extend to all interviews with management. The *Weingarten* case places some carefully defined limits on an employee's representation rights. For example, representation rights apply only to *investigative interviews,* not to run-of-the-mill shop floor discussion, and the rights arise only in incidents when the employee requests representation and *reasonably believes that discipline may result* from the interview. Furthermore, the *Weingarten* decision does not automatically guarantee an employee an investigative interview. The law does permit employers to cancel the interview if a representative is requested, and management may then continue the investigation by other appropriate means.

Within the past twenty-five years the National Labor Relations Board has flip-flopped four times on whether nonunion employees enjoy *Weingarten* rights. Currently, nonunion employees do not have the right to have a co-worker present in an investigatory interview that may lead to disciplinary action.[66] It is recommended, however, that employers monitor NLRB decisions in this area.

Approaches to Disciplinary Action

If a thorough investigation shows that an employee has violated some organization rule, disciplinary action must be imposed. Two approaches to disciplinary action are progressive discipline and positive discipline.

Progressive Discipline

progressive discipline
Application of corrective measures by increasing degrees

Generally, discipline is imposed in a progressive manner. By definition, **progressive discipline** is the application of corrective measures by increasing degrees. Progressive discipline is designed to motivate an employee to correct his or her misconduct voluntarily. The technique is aimed at nipping the problem in the bud, using only enough corrective action to remedy the shortcoming. However, the sequence and severity of the disciplinary action vary with the type of offense and the circumstances surrounding it. Because each situation is unique, a number of factors must be considered in determining how severe a disciplinary action should be. Some of the factors to consider were listed in Figure 13.9.

The typical progressive discipline procedure includes four steps. From an oral warning (or counseling) that subsequent unsatisfactory behavior or performance will not be tolerated, the action may progress to a written warning, to a suspension without pay, and ultimately to discharge. The "capital punishment" of discharge is utilized only as a last resort. Organizations normally use lower forms of disciplinary action for less severe performance problems. It is important for managers to remember that three important things occur when progressive discipline is applied properly:

1. Employees always know where they stand regarding offenses.
2. Employees know what improvement is expected of them.
3. Employees understand what will happen next if improvement is not made.

Positive Discipline

Some HR professionals believe that progressive discipline has certain flaws, including its intimidating and adversarial nature that prevent it from achieving the intended purpose. For these reasons, organizations such as Saint Alphonsus Regional Medical Center, Ocean Spray, Banner Health, Pennzoil, and Bay Area Rapid Transit are using an approach called **positive,** or **nonpunitive, discipline.** Positive discipline is based on the concept that employees must assume responsibility for their personal conduct and job performance.[67]

positive, or nonpunitive, discipline
A system of discipline that focuses on early correction of employee misconduct, with the employee taking total responsibility for correcting the problem

Positive discipline requires a cooperative environment in which the employee and the supervisor engage in joint discussion and problem solving to resolve incidents of employee irresponsibility. The approach focuses on early correction of misconduct, with the employee taking total responsibility for resolving the problem. Nothing is imposed by management; all solutions and affirmations are jointly reached. HR managers often describe positive discipline as "nonpunitive discipline that replaces threats and punishment with encouragement."

While positive discipline appears similar to progressive discipline, its emphasis is on giving employees reminders rather than reprimands as a way to improve performance. The technique is implemented in three steps. The first is a conference between the employee and the supervisor. The purpose of this meeting is to find a solution to the problem through discussion, with oral agreement by the employee to improve his or her performance. The supervisor refrains from reprimanding the employee or threatening him or her with further disciplinary action. Supervisors may document this conference, but a written record of this meeting is not placed in the employee's file unless the misconduct occurs again.

If improvement is not made after this first step, the supervisor holds a second conference with the employee to determine why the solution agreed to in the first conference did not work. At this stage, however, a written reminder is given to the employee. This document states the new or repeated solution to the problem, with an affirmation that improvement is the responsibility of the employee and a condition of continued employment.

When both conferences fail to produce the desired results, the third step is to give the employee a one-day *decision-making leave* (a paid leave). The purpose of this paid leave is for the employee to decide whether he or she wishes to continue working for the organization. The organization pays for this leave to demonstrate its desire to retain the person. Also, paying for the leave eliminates the negative effects for the employee of losing a day's pay. Employees given a decision-making leave are instructed to return the following day with a decision either to make a total commitment to improve performance or to quit the organization. If a commitment is not made, the employee is dismissed with the assumption that he or she lacked responsibility toward the organization. The positive discipline process used by Banner Health is shown in Highlights in HRM 2.

Discharging Employees

When employees fail to conform to organizational rules and regulations, the final disciplinary action in many cases is discharge. Because discharge has such serious consequences for the employee—and possibly for the organization—it should be undertaken only after a deliberate and thoughtful review of the case. If an employee is fired, he or she may file a wrongful discharge suit claiming the termination was "without just or sufficient cause," implying a lack of fair treatment by management.

Highlights in HRM 2

The Banner Health System Performance Recognition Policy

Recognition

Recognition is the foundation of the Performance Recognition process. It is based on the belief that you have control over your own behavior and are accountable for your actions. Your desire to exhibit the behaviors that are expected of Banner Health employees can be directly affected by the feedback you receive. Sincerely expressed appreciation affirms that you are making a difference and adding value to the organization. Recognition can also indicate to you when performance enhancement or improvement needs to occur. When you experience this recognition, your efforts can increase, as well as your satisfaction with your workplace.

Coaching

Each of us has been involved in coaching at some time. When we coach each other, within or outside of our own department, we provide feedback, guidance, and training. Our goal is always to help someone be successful.

Coaching may be formal or informal, based upon the seriousness of the performance problem. Formal coaching is a structured process requiring you to develop a mutually agreed-upon plan of action for improvement.

Supervisors generally coach for one of two reasons:

- Performance Enhancement: these discussions help us by clarifying expectations, providing feedback, identifying opportunities for development in reaching our goals, and recognizing our accomplishments. The supervisor may document these discussions as a reminder to a follow-up, or as a means of tracking progress in meeting our goals.
- Performance Improvement: these discussions occur if there is a recognized need for improvement in performance. Coaching objectives include clarification of expectations, identification of the cause for current performance not meeting those expectations, development of effective solutions, and commitment to correct the problem.

Formal Discipline

If performance does not improve after coaching, or a single incident occurs which warrants a more serious response, the supervisor may apply the Formal Discipline levels of Performance Recognition. *This Formal Discipline process does not apply to employees in their Conditional Period or to those in a Supplemental position.* At each step in the Formal Discipline process, a sincere effort will be made to encourage you to take responsibility for your problem and commit to making a change. Recognition and coaching may occur between the levels of the Formal Discipline process to provide you feedback on your progress, and to identify concerns.

Levels of Formal Discipline

1. Initial Reminder

The Initial Reminder requires a formal discussion between the supervisor and the employee. This is the first level of Formal Discipline, and should be used when a performance problem has not been corrected through coaching. It may also be used if the seriousness of the problem warrants beginning at the Initial Reminder level without previous coaching.

(continued on next page)

(continued from previous page)

2. Advanced Reminder

The Advanced Reminder is the second level of the Formal Discipline process, and should be used if continued or additional performance problems have occurred following the Initial Reminder. The Advanced Reminder level of Formal Discipline may also be used if the seriousness of the problem warrants a more advanced level of Formal Discipline.

A memo summarizing the discussion and reinforcing the need for improvement will be written and discussed with you. Your supervisor will follow up to ensure the problem has been corrected and to recognize performance improvement.

3. Decision-Making Leave (DML)

The DML is the last formal level in the Performance Recognition process. This step is taken as a result of a sustained or serious performance problem. Following a discussion of the problem and your failure to live up to the agreement for correcting the problem, you will be given a day of leave with pay (*not* from your PTO hours) to seriously consider your intentions of making a total commitment to improve your performance.

Upon return from the DML, if your decision is to make an immediate and sustained improvement in your overall work performance, you will report this to your supervisor. You and your supervisor will develop an action plan. If you decide not to meet performance expectations, you may return to work under directed compliance or you may resign. You will be given a memo summarizing the DML discussion and your decision.

Deactivation

If you maintain an overall satisfactory work record after a formal level of discipline, your immediate supervisor will acknowledge improvement. If you have not received any additional Formal Discipline, the previous Formal Discipline will no longer be active after the following time periods: Initial Reminder, 6 months; Advanced Reminder, 12 months; Decision-Making Leave, 12 months.

Crisis Suspension

Certain types of incidents warrant removing you immediately from the workplace. These incidents would require the supervisor to address the problem immediately; for an example, a safety or security issue, or any offense when a DML or termination may be the appropriate level of response for the first occurrence. If termination is likely, you will be removed from the work schedule until the completion of the investigation. Crisis suspension requires consultation with Human Resources/Employee Relations.

Termination

Termination may occur when:

- Following the DML, you do not immediately improve and maintain an overall satisfactory work record, or
- You commit an offense so serious that progressing through the Formal Discipline levels of Performance Recognition is not warranted.

Termination is not a formal step in the Performance Recognition process, but is the result of your refusal or inability to meet the performance expectations.

Source: Adapted from Banner Health Performance Recognition Policy. Used with Permission of Banner Health, Phoenix, AZ.

Figure 13.10 "Just Cause" Discharge Guidelines

1. Did the organization forewarn the employee of the possible disciplinary consequences of his or her action?
2. Were management's requirements of the employee reasonable in relation to the orderly, efficient, and safe operation of the organization's business?
3. Did management, before discharging the employee, make a reasonable effort to establish that the employee's performance was unsatisfactory?
4. Was the organization's investigation conducted in a fair and objective manner?
5. Did the investigation produce sufficient evidence of proof of guilt as charged?
6. Has management treated this employee under its rules, orders, and penalties as it has other employees in similar circumstances?
7. Did the discharge fit the misconduct, considering the seriousness of the proven offense, the employee's service record, and any mitigating circumstances?

If an employee termination is to be upheld for good cause, what constitutes fair employee treatment? This question is not easily answered, but standards governing just cause discharge do exist, in the form of rules developed in the field of labor arbitration.[68] These rules consist of a set of guidelines that are applied by arbitrators to dismissal cases to determine if management had just cause for the termination. These guidelines are normally set forth in the form of questions, provided in Figure 13.10. For example, before discharging an employee, did the manager forewarn the person of possible disciplinary action? A no answer to any of the seven questions in the figure generally means that just cause was not established and that management's decision to terminate was arbitrary, capricious, or discriminatory. The significance of these guidelines is that they are being applied not only by arbitrators in discharge cases, but also by judges in wrongful discharge suits, and by the EEOC in discrimination violations such as sexual harassment.[69] It is critical that managers at all levels understand the just cause guidelines, including their proper application.

Informing the Employee

Regardless of the reasons for a discharge, it should be done with personal consideration for the employee affected. Every effort should be made to ease the trauma a discharge creates.[70] The employee must be informed honestly, yet tactfully, of the exact reasons for the action. Such candor can help the employee face the problem and adjust to it in a constructive manner.

Managers may wish to discuss, and even rehearse, with their peers the upcoming termination meeting. This practice can ensure that all important points are covered while giving confidence to the manager. While managers agree that there is no single right way to conduct the discharge meeting, the following guidelines will help make the discussion more effective:

1. Come to the point within the first two or three minutes, and list in a logical order all reasons for the termination.
2. Be straightforward and firm, yet tactful, and remain resolute in your decision.
3. Make the discussion private, businesslike, and fairly brief.
4. Don't mix the good with the bad. Trying to sugarcoat the problem sends a mixed message to the employee.
5. Avoid making accusations against the employee and injecting personal feelings into the discussion.
6. Avoid bringing up any personality differences between you and the employee.
7. Provide any information concerning severance pay and the status of benefits and coverage.
8. Explain how you will handle employment inquiries from future employers.[71]

Termination meetings should be held in a neutral location, such as a conference room, to prevent the employee from feeling unfairly treated. When discussing the termination, management must never provoke the employee or allow the employee to become belligerent toward management. Should the employee become agitated, or show signs of hostility, the meeting should be stopped immediately with notification given to security or the HR department.

Finally, when terminated employees are escorted off the premises, the removal must not serve to defame the employee. Managers should not give peers the impression that the terminated employee was dishonest or untrustworthy. Furthermore, managers are advised never to discuss the discharge or "bad-mouth" the terminated employee with other employees, customers, or other individuals. Managers should be very tight-lipped in this area.[72] Increasingly, terminated employees are pursuing lawsuits that go beyond the issue of whether their discharge was for business-related reasons.

Due Process

Management has traditionally possessed the right to direct employees and to take corrective action when needed. Nevertheless, when employees are alleged to have violated organizational rules, many individuals also believe that employees should not be disciplined without the protection of due process. HR managers normally define **due process** as the employee's right to be heard—the right of the employee to tell his or her side of the story regarding the alleged infraction of organizational rules. Due process serves to ensure that a full and fair investigation of employee misconduct occurs. Normally, due process is provided employees through the employer's appeals procedure. However, proactive employers will additionally incorporate the following principles—or rights—in their interpretation of due process:

due process
An employee's right to present his or her position during a disciplinary action

1. The right to know job expectations and the consequences of not fulfilling those expectations.
2. The right to consistent and predictable management action for the violation of rules.
3. The right to fair discipline based on facts, the right to question those facts, and the right to present a defense.
4. The right to progressive discipline.
5. The right to appeal disciplinary action.

Alternative Dispute Resolution Procedures

alternative dispute resolution (ADR) A term applied to different types of employee complaint or dispute resolution procedures

In unionized workplaces, grievance procedures are stated in virtually all labor agreements. In nonunion organizations, however, **alternative dispute resolution (ADR)** procedures are a developing method to address employee complaints.[73] The employer's interest stems from the desire to meet employees' expectations for fair treatment in the workplace while guaranteeing them due process—in the hope of minimizing discrimination claims or wrongful discharge suits.[74] ADR procedures received a boost from the U.S. Supreme Court when, in *Gilmer v Interstate/Johnson Lane Corp.*, the Court enforced a private agreement that required the arbitration of an age-discrimination claim.[75] The mandatory use of arbitration to resolve employment disputes received additional support when the U.S. Supreme Court held in *Circuit City Stores, Inc. v Adams*[76] that employers may require employees to bring their work-related disputes before an arbitrator rather than file a lawsuit. This major decision allows employers to establish arbitration programs as a means for employees to resolve employment complaints—replacing court action as an option.[77] Additionally, Section 118 of the Civil Rights act of 1991 encourages the use of ADR procedures, including arbitration.

USING THE INTERNET

Current federal and state laws and leading court decisions regarding alternative dispute resolution procedures can be found on the American Arbitration Association web site. Go to the Student Resources at:

http://bohlander.swlearning.com

While the right to adopt arbitration agreements is supported by court decisions, arbitration agreements—to be enforceable—must be fair and equitable to both employees and employers.[78] Employers cannot "stack the deck" against employees by imposing rules on employees that clearly favor the employer. As one legal expert has noted, "As much as possible, the agreement should provide employees with the same rights and remedies that they would have enjoyed had their day in court been available to them."[79]

Step-Review Systems

step-review system A system for reviewing employee complaints and disputes by successively higher levels of management

As Figure 13.11 illustrates, a **step-review system** is based on a pre-established set of steps—normally four—for the review of an employee complaint by successively higher levels of management. These procedures are patterned after the union grievance systems we will discuss in Chapter 14. For example, they normally require that the employee's complaint be formalized as a written statement. Managers at each step are required to provide a full response to the complaint within a specified time period, perhaps three to five working days.

An employee is sometimes allowed to bypass the meeting with his or her immediate supervisor if the employee fears reprisal from this person. Unlike appeal systems in unionized organizations, however, nonunion appeal procedures ordinarily do not provide for a neutral third party—such as an arbitrator—to serve as the judge

Figure 13.11 Conventional Step-Review Appeal Procedure

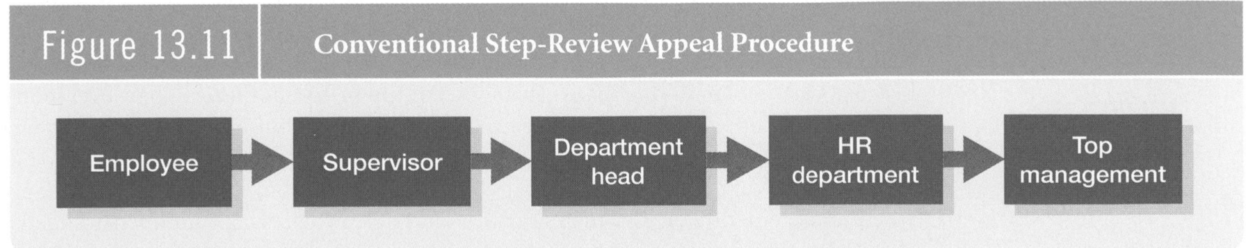

of last resort. In most step-review systems, the president, chief executive officer, vice president, or HR director acts as the final authority, and this person's decision is not appealable. Some organizations give employees assistance in preparing their complaint cases. For example, an employee who desires it may be able to get advice and counsel from a designated person in the HR department before discussing the issue with management.

Unfortunately, step-review systems may not yield their intended benefits. Employees may believe that management is slow in responding to complaints and that management's response often does not solve the problem. Furthermore, employees may believe that, regardless of policies forbidding reprisal, supervisors would still hold it against them if they exercised their rights as spelled out in the step-review system. These concerns should not lead to the conclusion that all step-review systems are ineffective, but rather that management must take special precautions to ensure that the systems work and provide the benefits intended.

Peer-Review Systems

peer-review system
A system for reviewing employee complaints that utilizes a group composed of equal numbers of employee representatives and management appointees, which functions as a jury because its members weigh evidence, consider arguments, and, after deliberation, vote independently to render a final decision

A **peer-review system,** also called a complaint committee, is composed of equal numbers of employee representatives and management appointees. Employee representatives are normally elected by secret ballot by their co-workers for a rotating term, whereas management representatives are assigned, also on a rotating basis. A peer-review system functions as a jury because its members weigh evidence, consider arguments, and, after deliberation, vote independently to render a final decision.

Organizations such as Turner Brothers Trucking, Northrop-Grumman, Polaroid, and Citicorp consider one of the benefits of the peer-review system to be the sense of justice that it creates among employees. The peer-review system can be used as the sole method for resolving employee complaints, or it can be used in conjunction with a step-review system. For example, if an employee is not satisfied with management's action at step 1 or 2 in the step-review system, the employee can submit the complaint to the peer-review committee for final resolution.

Open-Door Policy

open-door policy
A policy of settling grievances that identifies various levels of management above the immediate supervisor for employee contact

The open-door policy is an old standby for settling employee complaints. The traditional **open-door policy** identifies various levels of management above the immediate supervisor that an aggrieved employee may contact; the levels may extend as high as a vice president, president, or chief executive officer. Typically the person who acts as "the court of last resort" is the HR director or a senior staff official.

The problems with an open-door policy are well documented. Two of its major weaknesses are the unwillingness of managers to listen honestly to employee complaints and worker reluctance to approach managers with their complaints. As an employee once told the authors of this text, "My manager has an open-door policy but the door is only open one inch." Obviously this employee felt he had little opportunity to get through to his manager. Other problems are attributed to this system as well. The open-door policy generally fails to guarantee consistent decision making because what is fair to one manager may seem unfair to another. Higher-level managers tend to support supervisors for fear of undermining authority. And, as a system of justice, open-door policies may lack credibility with employees. Still, the open-door policy is often successful when it is supported by all levels of management and when management works to maintain a reputation for being fair and open-minded.

Ombudsman System

ombudsman
A designated individual from whom employees may seek counsel for resolution of their complaints

Rockwell, Johnson & Johnson, Herman Miller, Eastman Kodak, and Pace University are just a few organizations who employ ombudsmen. An **ombudsman** is a designated individual from whom employees may seek counsel for the resolution of their complaints. The ombudsman listens to an employee's complaint and attempts to resolve it by seeking an equitable solution between the employee and the supervisor. This individual works cooperatively with both sides to reach a settlement, often employing a problem-solving approach to the issue. Gordon Halfacre, ombudsman for faculty and graduate students at Clemson University, notes, "The ombuds is an advocate for a fair process, not an advocate on behalf of individuals or the institution."[80] Because the ombudsman has no authority to finalize a solution to the problem, compromises are highly possible and all concerned tend to feel satisfied with the outcome.

To function successfully, ombudsmen must be able to operate in an atmosphere of confidentiality that does not threaten the security of the managers or subordinates who are involved in a complaint. For example, complaints of sexual harassment, abuse of power, or issues that deal with circumstances that violate the law or unethical behavior (whistle-blowing) require high degrees of confidentiality to protect those involved. While ombudsmen do not have the power to decide employee complaints, it is recommended that they have access to high levels of management to ensure that employee complaints receive fair treatment.

Mediation

mediation
The use of an impartial neutral to reach a compromise decision in employment disputes

mediator
A third party in an employment dispute who meets with one party and then the other in order to suggest compromise solutions or to recommend concessions from each side that will lead to an agreement

Along with arbitration, mediation is fast becoming a popular way to resolve employee complaints. **Mediation** employs a third-party neutral (called a mediator) to help employees and managers reach voluntary agreement acceptable to both parties. The essence of mediation is compromise. The **mediator** holds a meeting with the employee and management, listens to the position of each side, gathers facts, then, through discussion, suggestions, and persuasion obtains an agreement that will satisfy the needs and requirements of both sides. A mediator serves primarily as a fact finder and to open up a channel of communication between the parties. Unlike arbitrators, mediators have no power or authority to force either side toward an agreement. They must use their communication skills and the power of persuasion to help the parties resolve their differences. A cornerstone of mediation is that the parties maintain control over the settlement outcome.

Mediation is a flexible process that can be shaped to meet the demands of the parties. Also, it can be used to resolve a wide range of employee complaints, including discrimination claims or traditional workplace disputes.[81] Employees like the process because of its informality. According to one authority, "Mediation might be described as a private discussion assisted by an impartial third party."[82] Settlements fashioned through mediation are readily acceptable by the parties, thus promoting a favorable working relationship.

Arbitration

Prompted by the *Gilmer* and *Circuit City* decisions, private employers may require that employees submit their employment disputes for a binding resolution through arbitration.[83] (Arbitration is fully explained in Chapter 14.) Arbitration is used primarily to resolve discrimination suits in areas of age, gender, sexual harassment, and race. Other workplace issues such as promotions, compensation, discipline, and application of company policies may be arbitrated if allowed in the employer's arbitration program. Employers cite savings in litigation costs and avoidance of time delays and unfavorable publicity as advantages for using arbitration.

While arbitration agreements normally mandate that employees arbitrate their discrimination claims and may prevent employees from suing their employer in court, they cannot prohibit employees from filing discrimination charges with the EEOC and pursuing other statutory rights with government agencies. In *EEOC v Waffle House Inc.,*[84] the U.S. Supreme Court ruled that employees can file discrimination suits with the EEOC even when the employer has a mandatory arbitration agreement and it is signed by the employee.[85] Writing for the Court, Justice John Paul Stevens noted, "The EEOC has the authority to pursue victim-specific relief regardless of the forum that the employer and the employee have chosen to resolve their dispute."[86]

Managerial Ethics in Employee Relations

ethics
A set of standards of conduct and moral judgments that help to determine right and wrong behavior

Throughout this textbook we have emphasized the legal requirements of HRM. Laws, agency rulings, and court decisions impact all aspects of the employment process—recruitment, selection, performance appraisal, safety and health, labor relations, and testing. Managers must comply with governmental regulations to promote an environment free from litigation.

However, beyond what is required by the law is the question of organizational ethics and the ethical—or unethical—behavior engaged in by managers. **Ethics** can be defined as a set of standards of acceptable conduct and moral judgment. Ethics provides cultural guidelines—organizational or societal—that help us decide between proper or improper conduct. Therefore, ethics, like the legal aspects of HR, permeates all aspects of the employment relationship. For example, managers may adhere to the organization's objective of hiring more protected-class members, but how those employees are supervised and treated once employed gets to the issue of managerial ethics.

Compliance with laws and the behavioral treatment of employees are two completely different aspects of the manager's job. While ethical dilemmas will always occur in the supervision of employees, it is how employees are treated that largely distinguishes the ethical organization from the unethical one. Interestingly, a recent research study, *Employee Trust and Organizational Loyalty*, sponsored by the Society for Human Resource Management, showed that employee perceptions of ethical behavior by their organizational leadership may be the most important driver of employee trust and loyalty. According to the study, of critical interest to employees is the consistent and credible communication of information about the organization's ethical standards and its values, the organization's mission, and its workplace policies.[87] We believe that managerial ethics in employee relations requires honesty in all dealings between employees and their managers, including mutual respect throughout the performance of workplace duties.

Many organizations have their own code of ethics that governs relations with employees and the public at large.[88] This written code focuses attention on ethical values and provides a basis for the organization, and individual managers, to evaluate their plans and actions. HR departments have been given a greater role in communicating the organization's values and standards, monitoring compliance with its code of ethics, and enforcing the standards throughout the organization. Organizations now have ethics committees and ethics ombudsmen to provide training in ethics to employees. The ultimate goal of ethics training is to avoid unethical behavior and adverse publicity; to gain a strategic advantage; and most of all, to treat employees in a fair and equitable manner, recognizing them as productive members of the organization.

SUMMARY

objective 1 Employees may claim that they have legal rights guaranteeing them fair and equitable treatment while on the job. Employee rights issues frequently involve employer searches, drug testing, and monitoring of an employee's personal conversations. Employers, however, have the responsibility to provide a safe and secure workplace free from harmful employee acts. When the perceived rights of employees differ from the reasonable responsibilities of management, conflict can result.

objective 2 Both employees and employers have rights and expectations in the employment relationship. The employment-at-will doctrine regards the rights of employees and employers to terminate the employment relationship; the implied-contract concept is an exception to the employment-at-will doctrine. Under this concept, an employer's oral or written statements may form a contractual obligation that can preclude automatic termination of employees. Constructive discharge occurs when an employee voluntarily terminates employment but subsequently alleges that he or she was forced to quit because of intolerable working conditions imposed by the employer. Employees may claim they are retaliated against when employers punish them for exercising their rights under law or for receiving favorable EEOC or court awards.

objective 3 Once employed, employees expect certain privacy rights regarding freedom from unwarranted intrusion into their personal affairs. These rights extend over such issues as substance abuse and drug testing; searches and monitoring; off-duty privacy rights; e-mail, Internet, and voice mail privacy; and genetic testing.

objective 4 The HR department, in combination with other managers, should establish disciplinary policies. This will help achieve both acceptance of the policy and its consistent application. To reduce the need for discipline, organizational rules and procedures should be widely known, reviewed on a regular basis, and written and explained to employees. The rules must relate to the safe and efficient operation of the organization. When managers overlook the enforcement of rules, they must re-emphasize the rule and its enforcement before disciplining an employee.

objective 5 The term *discipline* has three meanings—punishment, orderly behavior, and training of employee conduct. When used with employees, discipline should serve to correct undesirable employee behavior, creating within the employee a desire for self-control. This third definition of discipline can be achieved only when managers conduct a complete and unbiased investigation of employee misconduct.

Investigation of employee misconduct begins with proper documentation of wrongdoing. When managers are investigating employee problems they need to know specifically the infraction of the employee, whether the employee knew of the rule violated, and any extenuating circumstances that might justify the employee's conduct. When employees are to receive discipline, the rule must be uniformly enforced and the past work record of the employee must be considered.

objective 6 The two approaches to discipline are progressive discipline and positive discipline. Progressive discipline follows a series of steps based on increasing the degrees of corrective action. The corrective action applied should match the severity of the employee misconduct. Positive discipline, based on reminders, is a cooperative discipline approach in which employees accept responsibility for the desired employee improvement. The focus is on coping with the unsatisfactory performance and dissatisfactions of employees before the problems become major.

objective 7 Alternative dispute resolution procedures present ways by which employees exercise their due process rights. The most common forms of ADRs are step-review systems, peer-review systems, the open-door system, the ombudsman system, mediation, and arbitration.

objective 8 Ethics in HRM extends beyond the legal requirements of managing employees. Managers engage in ethical behavior when employees are treated in an objective and fair way and when an employee's personal and work-related rights are respected and valued.

KEY TERMS

alternative dispute resolution (ADR)
constructive discharge
discipline
due process
employee rights
employment-at-will principle
ethics
hot-stove rule
mediation
mediator
negligence
ombudsman
open-door policy
peer-review system
positive, or nonpunitive, discipline
progressive discipline
psychological contract
step-review system
whistle-blowing

DISCUSSION QUESTIONS

1. Explain three areas in which employee rights and employer responsibilities could result in conflict. How might this conflict arise?

2. Define the employment-at-will doctrine. What are the three major court exceptions to the doctrine?

3. What are the legislative and court restrictions on employer drug testing in both the private and the public sector?

4. If you were asked to develop a policy on discipline, what topics would you cover in the policy?

5. What should be the purpose of an investigative interview, and what approach should be taken in conducting it?

6. Discuss why documentation is so important to the disciplinary process. What constitutes correct documentation?

7. Describe progressive and positive discipline, noting the differences between these two approaches.

8. What do you think would constitute an effective alternative dispute resolution system? What benefits would you expect from such a system? If you were asked to rule on a discharge case, what facts would you analyze in deciding whether to uphold or reverse the employer's action?

9. Working by yourself, or in a team, identify ethical dilemmas that could arise in the HR areas of selection, performance appraisal, safety and health, privacy rights, and compensation.

BIZFLIX EXERCISES

In Good Company: Firing an Employee

This scene from the film *In Good Company* shows Mark Steckle's (Clark Greg) efforts to fire Dan Foreman (Dennis Quaid) and Carter Duryea (Topher Grace). Carefully assess Mark's behavior against the discussion of employee rights and discipline in this chapter.

A corporate takeover brings star advertising executive Dan Foreman a new boss who is half his age. Carter Duryea—Dan's new boss—wants to prove his worth as the new marketing chief at *Sports America,* Waterman Publishing's flagship magazine. Carter applies his unique approaches while dating Dan's daughter, Alex (Scarlett Johansson).

This scene comes from the "teddy k. is coming" sequence near the film's end. It starts with Mark Steckle saying to Dan Foreman, "Look, we've been carrying your fat, bloated salary for way too long." This scene follows Teddy K.'s (Malcolm McDowell) synergy speech to the assembled employees of his recent acquisition, Waterman Publishing. The film continues with Carter and Dan carrying out their plan to get some new magazine advertising.

What to Watch for and Ask Yourself

- This chapter opened with the observation that managers and supervisors find it hard to discipline employees. Does this observation apply to Mark Steckle? Why or why not?
- Does Mark follow the suggestions shown in Figure 13.2 in trying to end the employment of Dan and Carter?
- The earlier section "Disciplinary Policies and Procedures" offered guidelines and observations on correct approaches to employee discipline. Does Mark follow any of those procedures? If not, which aspects of his behavior deviate from the procedures described earlier?

HRM Experience

Learning about Employee Rights

In the constantly changing field of human resources it is imperative that both HR managers and supervisors be aware of changes that affect the organization and the process of managing employees. Nowhere is this more true than in the growing field of employee rights. As employees demand more job and employment rights regarding drug testing, monitoring, unjust dismissals, off-duty conduct, and genetic testing, employers must be knowledgeable about new laws, court rulings, and the policies of other organizations that influence each area. This knowledge will enable managers to respond to these employee concerns in a positive and proactive manner. Failure to provide employees their rights could lead to costly and embarrassing lawsuits, resulting in diminished employee loyalty or morale. The purpose of this exercise, therefore, is to enable you to familiarize yourself with issues of employee rights.

Assignment

Working individually or in teams, for each of the following employee rights topics, identify and discuss the privacy concerns for both employees and employers. You may wish to review articles in HR journals such as *Labor Law Journal, HRMagazine, Workforce,* and *Employee Relations Law Journal* as you complete this assignment. Answer the questions pertaining to each topic.

- Employment-at-will and wrongful discharge suits
- Substance abuse and drug testing
- Searches and monitoring
- Employee conduct away from the workplace
- Genetic testing
- E-mail, Internet

1. What is the issue concerned with?
2. Why is this issue of current interest to employees and managers?
3. What rights are employees demanding?
4. What, if any, laws or court cases affect this right?
5. Generally, how are employers responding to this employee right?

case study 1

Discharged for Off-Duty Behavior

The following case illustrates the off-duty privacy claim of an employee and management's right to uphold the reputation of the company.

Before his termination on Monday, May 6, 2004, John Hilliard worked as a senior sales representative for Advanced Educational Materials (AEM), a provider of high-quality educational books and supplies to junior and senior high schools. During his twelve years of employment, John was recognized as an outstanding employee with close working relationships with the schools he served. His sales record was excellent. John's discharge resulted from what AEM claimed was a serious breach of its code of conduct for employees.

On Saturday, May 4, 2004, due to a chance meeting between John and his manager, Jean Ellison, John was observed leaving an adult video store carrying what his manager described as pornographic magazines and an X-rated video. The following Monday, Jean discussed the incident with AEM's vice-president for sales and a representative from HR. All agreed that John's off-duty behavior constituted a serious violation of the company's code of conduct for employees, which read, in part, "Employee off-duty behavior in no way should reflect unfavorably upon the company, its employees, or sales of any educational materials." AEM has traditionally held its sales representatives to high moral standards because the company sells extensively to public school administrators and teachers.

At his discharge meeting John vigorously opposed his firing. While he acknowledged making the purchases, he argued strongly that what he did on his personal time was "no business of the company's" and his behavior in no way reflected unfavorably upon AEM or the sales of its products. Besides, he said, "The purchases were made as jokes for a stag party."

Source: This case is based on an actual termination for off-duty misconduct. All names are fictitious.

QUESTIONS

1. Given the facts of this case, should John have been discharged? Explain.
2. Should the sales representatives of AEM be held to a higher standard of personal conduct than sales representatives for other types of organizations? Explain.
3. Should management have considered John's past work record before deciding on discharge? Explain.

case study 2

You Can't Fire Me! Check Your Policy

Supervisors report that discharging an employee is one of the toughest tasks they perform as managers. Furthermore, termination for absenteeism can be particularly difficult due to the causes of absenteeism, and, in some cases, the past work record of the employee. This case illustrates a typical absentee problem faced by management.

Mary Schwartz was employed by Beach Electrical Systems for nine years. For the first six years of her employment she was considered a model employee. Mary's annual performance reviews were always above average or exceptional and she was described by her managers as a loyal and dedicated employee. However, things changed rapidly in 2000 when Mary became, as her current manager stated, "an absentee problem."

According to HR department records, in 2001 and 2002 Mary was absent 12 percent and 19 percent of the time, respectively. Her worst year was 2003, when she was absent 27.2 percent of the time. However, unlike other absent employees, Mary was always absent because of genuine and verifiable illnesses or work-related accidents. Mary's supervisor had talked to her periodically about her attendance problem, but she was never given an official warning notice—oral or written—that she would be fired if her attendance record did not improve.

The incident that caused her termination occurred on Thursday, May 20, 2004. On that day her manager notified all department employees (eight in total) that they would need to work overtime on Saturday, May 22, 2004, to complete a critical order for a highly valued and important customer. All employees agreed to work Saturday, except Mary, who cited "personal reasons," which she refused to disclose, for her refusal to work.

On Monday, May 24, 2004, her supervisor, with concurrence from the department manager, terminated her employment for "unsatisfactory attendance." Mary did not dispute the attendance record; however, she filed a grievance through the company's alternative dispute resolution procedure alleging that management did not discharge her according to the organization's published disciplinary policy. She pointed to the section in the policy manual that states, "Employees will be warned for absenteeism before they are terminated." Mary maintained that she was never officially warned as required. Management replied that Mary was well aware of her absentee problem but that warning her would have served no purpose as she was unable to prevent her continued illnesses from occurring. Additionally, her refusal to work overtime on Saturday was a further indication of her lack of concern for her job or the welfare of her company.

Source: Based on an arbitration case heard by George W. Bohlander. Names have been changed.

QUESTIONS

1. What role, if any, should Mary's past work record play in this case? Explain.
2. Does management have a right to know why employees refuse to work overtime? Explain.
3. Evaluate the arguments of Mary Schwartz and management in this case.
4. If you were a member of the company's peer-review complaint committee, how would you vote in this case? What facts would cause you to vote this way?

NOTES AND REFERENCES

1. Robert J. Denny, interview by author, Phoenix, Arizona, December 8, 2004.
2. John D. Canoni, "Location Awareness Technology and Employee Privacy Rights," *Employee Relations Law Journal* 30, no. 1 (Summer 2004): 26.
3. David J. Walsh, *Employment Law for Human Resource Practice* (Mason, OH: South-Western, 2004): Chapter 17. See also Barbara Kate Repa, *Your Rights in the Workplace*, 6th ed. (Berkeley, CA: Nolo Press, 2002).
4. Jeffery A. Mello, "Introduction: The Evolving Nature of the Employment Relationship: Reconsidering Employee Responsibilities and Rights," *Employee Responsibility and Rights Journal* 15, no. 3 (September 2003): 99.
5. Jonathan A. Segal, "Security vs. Privacy," *HRMagazine* 47, no. 2 (February 2002): 93–96.
6. "How to Do Background Checks Properly," *HRFocus* 81, no. 1 (August 2004): 11.
7. Mindie Le, Thanh Bao Nguyen, and Brian H. Kleiner, "Don't Be Sued for Negligent Hiring," *Nonprofit World* 21, no. 3 (May/June 2003): 14.
8. Luc Sels, Maddy Janssens, and Inge Van den Brande, "Assessing the Nature of Psychological Contracts: A Validation of Sex Dimensions," *Journal of Organizational Behavior* 25, no. 4 (June 2004): 461. See also Maddy Janssens, Luc Sels, and Inge Van den Brande, "Multiple Types of Psychological Contracts: A Six Cluster Solution," *Human Relations* 56, no. 11 (November 2003): 1349.
9. Jill Kickul and Mathew A. Liso-Troth, "The Meaning behind the Message: Climate Perceptions and the Psychological Contract," *Mid-American Journal of Business* 18, no. 2 (Fall 2003): 23.
10. Matthew Heller, "A Return to At-Will Employment," *Workforce* 80, no. 5 (May 2001): 42–46.
11. *Adair v United States*, 2078 U.S. 161 (1908).
12. Jeffery A. Mello, "Employment-at-Will vs. Wrongful Discharge," *Business Horizons* 45, no. 6 (November/December 2002): 3.
13. Lawrence Peikes, "Employer Pays for Reneging on a Promise," *HRMagazine* 49, no. 3 (March 2004): 109.
14. Janet E. Michael, "Investigate Thoroughly to Avoid Wrongful Termination Suits," *Nursing Management* 35, no. 5 (May 2004): 20.
15. Linda Goldman and Joan Lewis, "A Private Matter," *Occupational Health* 56, no. 10 (October 2004): 12.
16. Stefanie L. Lindquist, "Developments in Federal Whistleblower Protection Laws," *Review of Public Personnel Administration* 23, no. 1 (March 2003): 78.
17. 18 U.S.C.S. § 1514A (a) (2002).
18. 5 U.S.C.S. § 2302 (2002).
19. P.L. No. 107-174 (2002).
20. 31 U.D.C.S. §§ 3729–3730 (2002).
21. Charles Haddad and Amy Barrett, "A Whistle-Blower Rocks an Industry," *Business Week* (June 24, 2002): 126–30.
22. Matthew Arnold, "MWC Reaches Settlement for Mail Fraud," *Medical Marketing and Media* 38, no. 8 (August 2003): 16.
23. Benisa Berry, "Organizational Culture: A Framework and Strategies for Facilitating Employee Whistleblowing," *Employee Responsibilities and Rights Journal* 16, no. 1 (March 2004): 1.
24. *Toussaint v Blue Cross and Blue Shield of Michigan*, 408 Mich. 579, 292 N.W.2d 880 (1980).
25. Bill Schaefer, Dyane Holt, and Rebecca R. Hastings, "Employee Handbooks, W-4s, Unpaid Suspensions," *HRMagazine* 49, no. 11 (November 2004): 43.
26. Margaret M. Clark, "Constructive Discharge Is Tangible Employment Action," *HRMagazine* 48, no. 7 (July 2003): 105.
27. John H. Gray, "Is a Constructive Discharge Resulting from a Supervisor's Environmental Harassment a Tangible Employment Action?" *Labor Law Journal* 55, no. 3 (Fall 2004): 179.
28. Jathan W. Janove, "Don't Add Insult to Injury," *HRMagazine* 47, no. 5 (May 2002): 113–20.
29. "Companies Need to Take Extra Care with Employees Who Sue," *HRFocus* 78, no. 4 (April 2001): 2.
30. Wayne Outten, "Insider Tips from a Plaintiff's Lawyer," *HRFocus* 78, no. 6 (June 2001): 3–4.
31. 29 U.S.C.A. §§ 2101–2109 (2001).
32. Margaret M. Clark, "Employers Fail to Give Required Notice in Majority of Mass Layoffs and Closures," *HRMagazine* 48, no. 12 (December 2003): 34.
33. Maria Greco Danaher, "Loss of Client 'Unforeseeable' Despite Shaky Relationship," *HRMagazine* 48, no. 2 (February 2003): 105.
34. The common definition of privacy as a "general right of the individual to be let alone" is captured in the words of Samuel Warren and Louis Brandeis in their seminal article "The Right to Privacy," *Harvard Law Review* 193, 205 (1890).
35. Justin Juozapavius, "Ban on Firefighter Drug Test Upheld," *The Arizona Republic*, October 5, 2004, Section B.
36. Janis Procter-Murphy, employment attorney, interview by author, December 9, 2004.
37. Carolyn Mei-Sha Chieh and Brian H. Kleiner, "How Organizations Manage the Issue of Employee Privacy Today," *Managerial Research News* 2, no. 4 (2003): 82.
38. Diana Cadrain, "Are Your Employee Drug Tests Accurate?" *HRMagazine* 48, no. 1 (January 2003): 41.
39. Sandy Smith, "What Every Employer Should Know about Drug Testing in the Workplace," *Occupational Hazards* 66, no. 8 (August 2004): 45. See also William F. Current, "Improving Your Drug Testing ROI," *Occupational Safety and Health* 73, no. 4 (April 2004): 40.
40. Cadrain, "Are Your Employee Drug Tests Accurate?," 42.
41. Walsh, *Employment Law for Human Resource Practice*, 132.

42. Ibid.
43. 41 U.S.C.S. § 701 (a) (1) (2001).
44. 42 U.C.S. § 12210 (b).
45. The following states have laws making drug-test fraud a crime: New Jersey, North Carolina, Virginia, Oregon, South Carolina, Pennsylvania, Louisiana, Texas, and Nebraska.
46. "Employee Crime Prevention," *Risk Management* 50, no. 10 (October 2003): 8.
47. James Weber, Lance B. Kurke, and David W. Pentico, "Why Employees Steal," *Business and Society* 42, no. 3 (September 2003): 359.
48. Jonathan A. Segal, "Searching for Answers," *HRMagazine* 47, no. 3 (March 2002): 85–91.
49. Matthew J. Camardella, "Electronic Monitoring in the Workplace," *Employment Relations Today* 30, 3 (Fall 2003): 91.
50. Electronic Communications Privacy Act, 18 U.S.C. §§ 2510–2720.
51. Walsh, *Employment Law for Human Resource Practice*, 461.
52. Robin L. Wakefield, "Computer Monitoring and Surveillance," *CPA Journal* 74, no. 7 (July 2004): 52.
53. Gillian Flynn, "Internet Issues at Work," *Workforce-Vendor Directory* 80, no. 10 (2002): 33–34.
54. Jack Harari, "HIPAA Takes Effect," *Risk Management* 49, no. 6 (June 2002): 54.
55. John Swenney, "Camera Use," *HRMagazine* 49, no. 7 (July 2004): 42.
56. Sheila Anne Feeney, "Love Hurts," *Workforce Management* 83, no. 2 (February 2004): 36.
57. Larry Hicks, "Counting Your Genomes before They're Mapped: Patients' Privacy Yet in Danger," *Workspan* 44, no. 6 (June 2001): 19. See also Steve Bates, "Science Fiction: Sparks Fly When Advances in Genetics Collide with Employee Concerns," *HRMagazine* 46, no. 7 (July 2001): 35–44.
58. Mark A. Hoffman, "Genetic Bias Legislation Not Needed—Some Say," *Business Insurance* 37, no. 42 (October 20, 2003): 4.
59. One of the original studies on this topic can be found at Edward L. Harrison, "Why Supervisors Fail to Discipline," *Supervisory Management* 30, no. 4 (April 1985): 17.
60. George W. Bohlander and Donna Blancero, "A Study of Reversal Determinants in Discipline and Discharge Arbitration Awards: The Impact of Just Cause Standards," *Labor Studies Journal* 21, no. 3 (Fall 1996): 3–18.
61. "Steps to Take before Recommending Disciplinary Action," *PM Public Management* 86, no. 6 (July 2004): 43.
62. "22 Tips for Avoiding Employee Lawsuits," *HRFocus* 80, no. 12 (December 2003): 4.
63. Jathan W. Janove, "Private Eye 101," *HRMagazine* 49, no. 7 (July 2004): 127.
64. Kelly Mollica, "Perceptions of Fairness," *HRMagazine* 49, no. 6 (June 2004): 169.
65. *NLRB v Weingarten, Inc.*, 95 S.Ct. 959 (1975), 402 U.S. 251, 43 L.Ed.2d. 171.
66. D. Diane Hatch, James Hall, and Mark T. Kobata, "NLRB Eliminates Nonunion-Employee Weingarten Rights," *Workforce Management* 83, no. 12 (November 2004): 18.
67. Readers interested in the pioneering work on positive discipline should see James R. Redeker, "Discipline, Part I: Progressive Systems Work Only by Accident," *Personnel* 62, no. 10 (October 1985): 8–12; James R. Redeker, "Discipline, Part 2: The Nonpunitive Approach Works by Design," *Personnel* 62, no. 11 (November 1985): 7–14.
68. For an excellent explanation of just cause discharge guildeines, see Frank Elkouri and Edna Asper Elkouri, *How Arbitration Works*, 5th ed. (Washington, DC: Bureau of National Affairs, 1997).
69. Mollie H. Bowers, W. Sue Reddich, and E. Patrick McDermott, "Just Cause in the Arbitration of Sexual Harassment Cases," *Dispute Resolution Journal* 55, no. 4 (January 2001): 40–55.
70. Richard Bayer, "Firing: Letting People Go with Dignity Is Good for Business," *HRFocus* 77, no. 1 (January 2000): 10. See also Paul Falcone, "Give Employees the (Gentle) Boot," *HRMagazine* 46, no. 4 (April 2001): 121–28.
71. "The New Rules of Termination," *HRFocus* 78, no. 5 (May 2001): 1, 11–15.
72. Carol Hymowitz, "Just How Much Should a Boss Reveal to Others about a Staffer's Firing?" *The Wall Street Journal*, March 19, 2002, B-1.
73. Elizabeth Hill, "AAA Employment Arbitration: A Fair Forum at Low Cost," *Dispute Resolution Journal* 58, no. 2 (May–June 2003): 8.
74. Theodore Eisenberg and Elizabeth Hill, "Arbitration and Litigation of Employment Claims," *Dispute Resolution Journal* 58, no. 4 (November 2003–January 2004): 44.
75. *Gilmer v Interstate/Johnson Lane Corp.*, 111 S.Ct. 1647 (1991).
76. *Circuit City Stores, Inc. v Adams*, 121 S.Ct. 1302 (2001).
77. Gillian Flynn, "High Court Weighs in on Arbitration," *Workforce* 80, no. 6 (June 2001): 100–101. See also Arthur F. Silbergeld and Gayle Wasserman, "U.S. Supreme Court Gives Arbitration of Employment Disputes Another Boost," *Employment Relations Today* 28, no. 2 (Summer 2001): 123–37.
78. Louise Lamothe, "Avoiding Potholes in Mandatory Arbitration: A Look at Recent California Decisions," *Dispute Resolution Journal* 58, no. 2 (May–June 2003): 18. See also George W. Bohlander and Robert J. Denny, "Designing a Legally Defensible Alternative Dispute Resolution Agreement," *Journal of Individual Employment Rights* 7, no. 3 (January 1999): 189.
79. Walsh, *Employment Law for Human Resource Practice*, 22.
80. Carolyn Hirchman, "Someone to Listen," *HRMagazine* 48, no. 1 (January 2003): 47.
81. Margaret M. Clark, "EEOC's Effort to Expand Mediation Gains Momentum," *HRMagazine* 48, no. 5 (May 2003): 32.

82. "How Best to Avoid Mediation Mistakes," *HRFocus* 77, no. 9 (September 2000): 2. See also Nancy Kauffman and Barbara Davis, "What Type of Mediation Do You Want?" *Dispute Resolution Journal* 53, no. 2 (May 1998): 10.
83. Cristina Fahrbach, "From *Gardner* to *Circuit City*: Mandatory Arbitration of Statutory Employment Disputes Continues," *Dispute Resolution Journal* 56, no. 4 (January 2002): 64–76. See also Carolyn Hirschman, "Order in the Hearing," *HRMagazine* 46, no. 7 (July 2001): 58–64.
84. *EEOC v Waffle House, Inc.*, 534 U.S. 279 (2002).
85. Chad Egan Burton, "EEOC v. Waffle House: Employers Win, Again," *Defense Counsel Journal* 71, no. 1 (January 2004): 52.
86. "EEOC May Sue Even If Arbitration Agreement Exists," *HRFocus* 79, no. 3 (March 2002): 2.
87. Jennifer Schramm, "Perception on Ethics," *HRMagazine* 49, no. 11 (November 2004): 176.
88. "Ethical Corporate Behavior Begins with a Code of Conduct," *HRFocus* 79, no. 7 (July 2002): 8–9.

UNION
UAW
YES
UNION
UAW
YES

chapter 14

The Dynamics of Labor Relations

After studying this chapter, you should be able to

Identify and explain the principal federal laws that provide the framework for labor relations.

Explain the reasons employees join unions.

Describe the process by which unions organize employees and gain recognition as their bargaining agent.

Discuss the bargaining process and the bargaining goals and strategies of a union and an employer.

Differentiate the forms of bargaining power that a union and an employer may utilize to enforce their bargaining demands.

Describe a typical union grievance procedure and explain the basis for arbitration awards.

Discuss some of the contemporary challenges to labor organizations.

Mention the word *union* and most people will have some opinion, positive or negative, regarding U.S. labor organizations. To some, the word evokes images of labor-management unrest—grievances, strikes, picketing, boycotts. To others, the word represents industrial democracy, fairness, opportunity, equal representation. Many think of unions as simply creating an adversarial relationship between employees and managers.

Regardless of attitudes toward them, since the mid-1800s unions have been an important force shaping organizational practices, legislation, and political thought in the United States.[1] Today unions remain of interest because of their influence on organizational productivity, U.S. competitiveness, the development of labor law, and HR policies and practices. Like business organizations themselves, unions are undergoing changes in both operation—such as mergers and coalitions—and philosophy. Furthermore, after years of declining membership, unions are again actively organizing unrepresented employees. For example, recently autoworkers have won representation rights for tens of thousands of workers at major U.S. auto parts makers including Johnson Controls, Collins and Aidman, Dana, Lear, and Metaldyne.[2] The Service Employees International Union, one of the nation's fastest-growing unions, organized 9,000 employees at twenty hospitals owned by Catholic Health Care West. In 2004, large national unions such as the United Food and Commercial Workers and the Teamsters have joined hands to organize workers at Wal-Mart, the nation's largest employer.[3] The AFL-CIO and national unions have targeted organizing as a top priority for the revival of the labor movement in the twenty-first century.

In spite of the long history of unions, the intricacies of labor relations are unfamiliar to many individuals. Therefore, this chapter describes government regulation of labor relations, the labor relations process, the reasons why workers join labor organizations, and the structure and leadership of labor unions. Importantly, according to labor law, once the union is certified to negotiate for bargaining-unit members, it must represent everyone in the unit equally, regardless of whether employees subsequently join the union or elect to remain nonmembers. Therefore, in the latter sections of the chapter, we discuss the important topics of contract administration, particularly the handling of employee grievances and arbitration. The chapter concludes with a discussion of contemporary challenges to labor organizations.

Unions and other labor organizations can affect significantly the ability of managers to direct and control the various functions of HRM. For example, union seniority provisions in the labor contract may influence who is selected for job promotions or training programs. Pay rates may be determined through union negotiations, or unions may impose restrictions on management's employee appraisal methods. Therefore, it is essential that managers in both the union and nonunion environment understand how unions operate and be thoroughly familiar with the important body of law governing labor relations. Remember, ignorance of labor legislation is no defense when managers and supervisors violate labor law. Before reading further, test your knowledge of labor relations law by answering the questions in Highlights in HRM 1.

Highlights in HRM 1

Test Your Labor Relations Know-How

1. An auto mechanic applied for a job with an automotive dealership. He was denied employment because of his union membership. Was the employer's action lawful?
   ___Yes ___No
2. During a labor organizing drive, supervisors questioned individual employees about their union beliefs. Was this questioning permissible?
   ___Yes ___No
3. When members of a union began wearing union buttons at work, management ordered the buttons to be removed. Was management within its rights?
   ___Yes ___No
4. While an organizing drive was under way, an employer agreed—as a social gesture—to furnish refreshments at a holiday party. Was the employer acting within the law?
   ___Yes ___No
5. A company distributed to other antiunion employers in the area a list of job applicants known to be union supporters. Was the distribution unlawful?
   ___Yes ___No
6. During a union organizing drive, the owner of Servo Pipe promised her employees a wage increase if they would vote against the union. Can the owner legally make this promise to her employees?
   ___Yes ___No
7. Employees have the right to file unfair labor practice charges against their employer even when the organization is nonunion.
   ___Yes ___No
8. The union wishes to arbitrate a member's grievance, which management has demonstrated is completely groundless. Must management arbitrate the grievance?
   ___Yes ___No
9. John Green, a maintenance engineer, has a poor work record. Management wishes to terminate his employment; however, Green is a union steward and he is highly critical of the company. Can management legally discharge this employee?
   ___Yes ___No
10. During an organizing drive, an office manager expressed strong antiunion beliefs and called union officials "racketeers," "big stinkers," and a "bunch of radicals." He told employees who joined the union that they "ought to have their heads examined." Were the manager's comments legal?
   ___Yes ___No

Answers are found at the end of this chapter.

Government Regulation of Labor Relations

The development of U.S. labor legislation has its foundation in the social, economic, and political climate of America. Generally, we can say that the growth of the labor movement has paralleled the passage of prolabor legislation and the ability of workers to impose their economic demands on management.[4] Clearly labor laws passed in the 1920s and 1930s favored the growth and stability of labor organizations. As unions became stronger under federal laws, legislation was passed to curb union abuses of power and to protect the rights of union members from unethical union activities. Today the laws governing labor relations seek to create an environment in which both unions and employers can discharge their respective rights and responsibilities. Knowledge of labor relations laws will assist the understanding of how union-management relations operate in the United States. The first federal law pertaining to labor relations was the Railway Labor Act of 1926. Other major laws that affect labor relations in the private sector are the Norris-LaGuardia Act, the Wagner Act, the Taft-Hartley Act, and the Landrum-Griffin Act.

The Railway Labor Act

The primary purpose of the Railway Labor Act (RLA), enacted in 1926, is to avoid service interruptions resulting from disputes between railroads and their operating unions. To achieve this end, the RLA contains two extensive procedures to handle these labor-management disputes. First, the National Mediation Board resolves negotiating impasses by using mediation and/or arbitration. The board is additionally charged with holding secret-ballot elections to determine whether employees desire unionization. Second, the National Railway Adjustment Board handles grievance and arbitration disputes arising during the life of an agreement. In 1936, the RLA was amended to extend coverage to the airline industry.

The Norris-LaGuardia Act

USING THE INTERNET

The U.S. National Labor Relations Board has its own web site. There you can find details of its organization, current cases, and decisions. Go to the Student Resources at:

http://bohlander.swlearning.com

The Norris-LaGuardia Act, or Anti-Injunction Act, of 1932 severely restricts the ability of employers to obtain an injunction forbidding a union from engaging in peaceful picketing, boycotts, or various striking activities. Previously, federal court injunctions had been an effective anti-union weapon because they forced unions to either cease such activities or suffer the penalty of being held in contempt of court. Injunctions may still be granted in labor disputes. Before an injunction may be issued, however, employers must show that lack of an injunction will cause greater harm to the employer than to the union. Like the RLA, this act promotes collective bargaining and encourages the existence, formation, and effective operation of labor organizations.

The Wagner Act

The Wagner Act of 1935 (or National Labor Relations Act) has had by far the most significant impact on union-management relations. It placed the protective power of the federal government firmly behind employee efforts to organize and bargain collectively through representatives of their choice.

The Wagner Act created the National Labor Relations Board (NLRB) to govern labor relations in the United States. Although this act was amended by the Taft-Hartley Act, most of its major provisions that protected employee bargaining rights were retained. Section 7 of the law guarantees these rights as follows:

> Employees shall have the right to self-organization, to form, join, or assist labor organizations, to bargain collectively through representatives of their own choosing, and to engage in concerted activities, for the purpose of collective bargaining or other mutual aid or protection, and shall also have the right to refrain from any or all of such activities except to the extent that such right may be affected by an agreement requiring membership in a labor organization as a condition of employment.[5]

To guarantee employees their Section 7 rights, Congress outlawed specific employer practices that deny employees the benefits of the law. Section 8 of the act lists five **unfair labor practices (ULPs)** of employers:

unfair labor practices (ULPs)
Specific employer and union illegal practices that deny employees their rights and benefits under federal labor law

1. Interfering with, restraining, or coercing employees in the exercise of their rights guaranteed in Section 7
2. Dominating or interfering with the formation or administration of any labor organization, or contributing financial or other support to it
3. Discriminating in regard to hiring or tenure of employment or any term or condition of employment so as to encourage or discourage membership in any labor organization
4. Discharging or otherwise discriminating against employees because they file charges or give testimony under this act
5. Refusing to bargain collectively with the duly chosen representatives of employees

Many ULPs are either knowingly or unknowingly committed each year by employers. In fiscal year 2004, for example, 26,890 unfair labor practices were filed with the NLRB. Alleged violations of the act by employers were filed in 19,446 cases.[6] Most charges against employers concerned illegal discharge or other discrimination against employees. It is therefore imperative that managers at all levels receive training in employee rights and unfair labor practices. When employers violate employee rights, the NLRB can "take such affirmative action including reinstatement of employment with or without back pay, as well as effectuate the policies of the Act, and make discriminated employees whole."[7] In 2004, the NLRB won for employees $205.7 million in back pay because of employer violations of the act.[8]

The National Labor Relations Board

The agency responsible for administering and enforcing the Wagner Act is the National Labor Relations Board (NLRB). It serves the public interest by reducing interruptions in production or service caused by labor-management strife. To accomplish this goal the NLRB is given two primary charges: (1) to hold secret-ballot elections to determine whether employees wish to be represented by a union and (2) to prevent and remedy unfair labor practices. The NLRB does not act on its own initiative in either function. It processes only those charges of unfair labor practices and petitions for employee elections that may be filed at one of its thirty-two regional offices or other smaller field offices.

The NLRB operates in a dynamic field in which information about the operation of the agency and answers to legal questions can be critical to both employees and managers. In 2003, the NLRB launched a toll-free telephone number designed to provide cost-free and easy access about the agency to the public.[9] Additionally, each regional office has an "information officer" available to answer specific legal questions about the law and the NLRB.

The Taft-Hartley Act

Passage of the Wagner Act spurred the huge growth of unionization during the 1930s and 1940s. Union membership in the United States reached 9 million in 1940, and with membership gains, labor's increased use of the strike became problematic to employers. With the bargaining power of unions now significantly increased, coupled with reports of union abuses of employee rights, certain restraints on unions were considered necessary. The Taft-Hartley Act of 1947 (also known as the Labor-Management Relations Act) met these objectives by defining unfair labor practices of unions and curbing various strike activities of labor organizations. The unfair labor practices of unions are as follows:

1. Restraint or coercion of employees in the exercise of their rights
2. Restraint or coercion of employers in the selection of the parties to bargain in their behalf
3. Persuasion of employers to discriminate against any of their employees
4. Refusal to bargain collectively with an employer
5. Participation in secondary boycotts and jurisdictional disputes
6. Attempt to force recognition from an employer when another union is already the certified representative
7. Charge of excessive initiation fees and dues
8. "Featherbedding" practices that require payment of wages for services not performed

In short, by passing the Taft-Hartley Act, Congress balanced the rights and duties of labor and management in the collective bargaining arena. No longer could the law be criticized as favoring unions.[10]

The Federal Mediation and Conciliation Service

Because of the high incidence of strikes after World War II, the Taft-Hartley Act created the Federal Mediation and Conciliation Service (FMCS) to help resolve negotiating disputes. The function of this independent agency is to help labor and management reach collective bargaining agreements through the processes of mediation and conciliation. These functions use a neutral party who maintains communications between bargainers in an attempt to gain agreement. Unlike the NLRB, the FMCS has no enforcement powers, nor can it prosecute anyone. Rather, the parties in a negotiating impasse must voluntarily elect to use the service. Once the FMCS is asked to mediate a dispute, however, its involvement in the process can greatly improve labor-management relations while providing a vehicle for the exchange of collective bargaining proposals.[11] According to Ron Collotta, commissioner of FMCS in Phoenix, Arizona, the agency mediates between 6,000 and 7,000 bargaining disputes annually.[12] In recent years, the FMCS has been highly visible in resolving deadlocks involving the communications, sports, education, and transportation industries.

The Landrum-Griffin Act

In 1959 Congress passed the Landrum-Griffin Act (also known as the Labor-Management Reporting and Disclosure Act) to safeguard union member rights and prevent racketeering and other unscrupulous practices by employers and union officers. One of the most important provisions of the Landrum-Griffin Act is the Bill of Rights of Union Members, which requires that every union member must be given the right to (1) nominate candidates for union office, (2) vote in union elections or referendums, (3) attend union meetings, and (4) participate in union meetings and vote on union business. Union members are also granted the right to examine union accounts and records in order to verify information contained in union reports and to bring suit against union officers as necessary to protect union funds. Moreover, under the act, unions are required to submit a financial report annually to the secretary of labor, and employers must report any expenditures that are made in attempting to exercise their bargaining rights.

The Labor Relations Process

labor relations process
A logical sequence of five events: (1) workers desire collective representation, (2) the union begins its organizing campaign, (3) the NLRB representation process begins, (4) collective negotiations lead to a contract, and (5) the contract is administered

Individually, employees may be able to exercise relatively little power in their relationship with employers. Of course, if they believe they are not being treated fairly, then Section 7 of the National Labor Relations Act grants them the legal right to organize and bargain with the employer collectively. When employees pursue this direction, the labor relations process begins. As Figure 14.1 illustrates, the **labor relations process** consists of a logical sequence of five events: (1) workers desire collective representation, (2) the union begins its organizing campaign, (3) the NLRB representation procedure begins, (4) collective negotiations lead to a contract, and (5) the contract is administered. Laws and administrative rulings influence each of the separate events by granting special privileges to, or imposing defined constraints on, workers, managers, and union officials.[13]

Why Employees Unionize

The majority of research on why employees unionize comes from the study of blue-collar employees in the private sector. These studies generally conclude that employees unionize as a result of economic need, because of a general dissatisfaction with managerial practices, and/or as a way to fulfill social and status needs. In short, employees see unionism as a way to achieve results they cannot achieve acting individually.

union shop
A provision of the labor agreement that requires employees to join the union as a requirement for their employment

It should be pointed out that some employees join unions because of the union-shop provisions of the labor agreement. In states where it is permitted, a **union shop** is a provision of the labor agreement that requires employees to join as a condition of employment. Even when compelled to join, however, many employees accept the concept of unionism once they become involved in the union as a member.

Economic Needs

Whether employees select unionization will greatly depend on whether the employees perceive the union as likely to be effective in improving various economic conditions

Figure 14.1 The Labor Relations Process

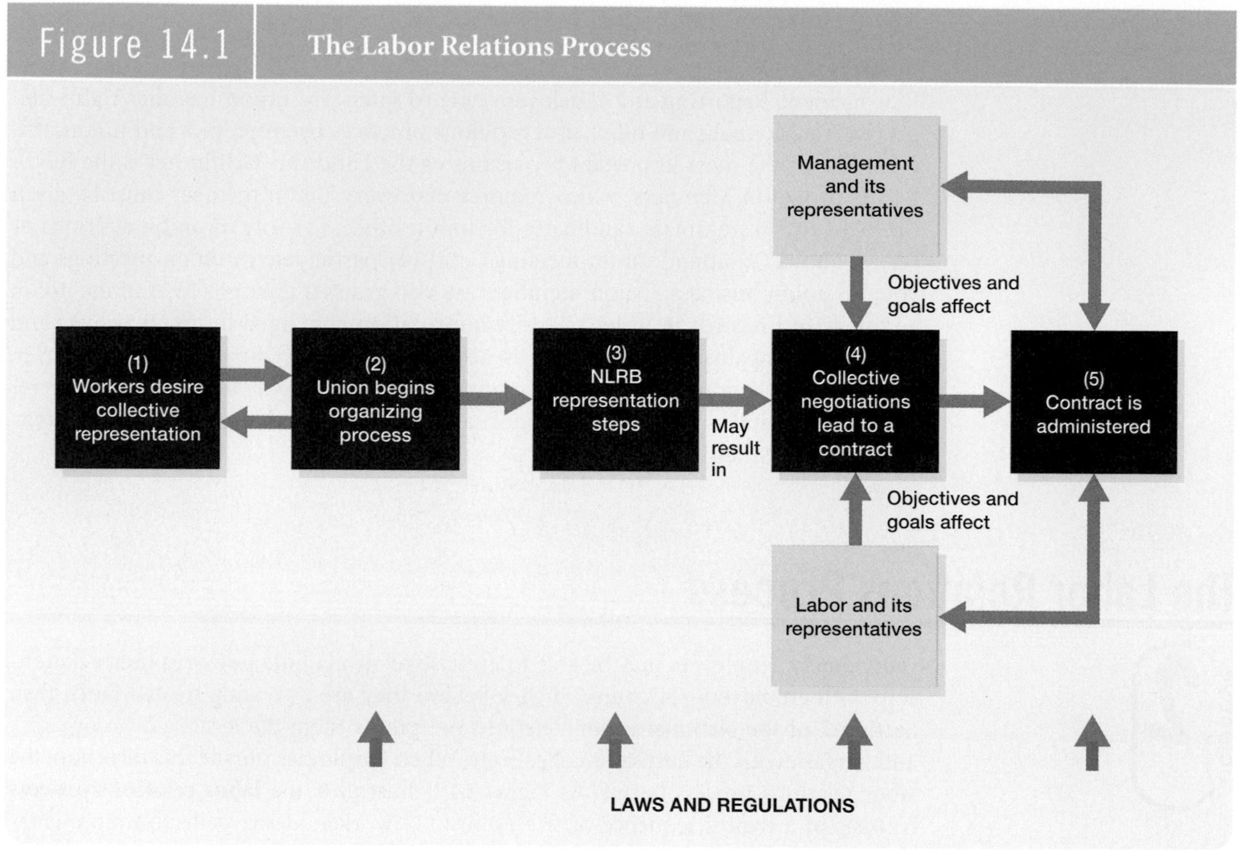

of employment—often referred to as the union's instrumentality. Dissatisfaction with wages, benefits, and working conditions appears to provide the strongest reason to join a union. This point is continually supported by research studies that find that both union members and nonmembers have their highest expectations of union performance regarding the "bread and butter" issues of collective bargaining.[14] It is these traditional issues of wages, benefits, and working conditions on which unions are built.

Dissatisfaction with Management

Employees may seek unionization when they perceive that managerial practices regarding promotion, transfer, shift assignment, or other job-related policies are administered in an unfair or biased manner. Employees cite favoritism shown by managers as a major reason for joining unions. This is particularly true when the favoritism concerns the HR areas of discipline, promotion, job assignments, and training opportunities.

We have noted throughout this book that today's employees are better educated than those of the past, and they often express a desire to be more involved in decisions affecting their jobs. Chapter 4 discussed the concept of employee empowerment and highlighted various employee involvement techniques. The failure of employers to give employees an opportunity to participate in decisions affecting their welfare may encourage union membership. It is widely believed that one reason managers

© SPENCER GRANT/PHOTOEDIT

These teachers are exercising their legal rights to protest perceived unfair management actions.

begin employee involvement programs and seek to empower their employees is to avoid collective action by employees. For example, employers in the auto, semiconductor, and financial industries involve employees in collaborative programs as a means to stifle unionization. In one organizing effort by the United Auto Workers at a Nissan plant, the union lost the election because workers were satisfied with the voice in decision making that Nissan's participatory style of management gave them.

Social and Leadership Concerns

Employees whose needs for recognition and social affiliation are being frustrated may join unions as a means of satisfying these needs. Through their union, they have an opportunity to fraternize with other employees who have similar desires, interests, problems, and gripes. Simply, employees may join unions for the same reason they would join a civic organization, club, or sports team, namely to enjoy the companionship of others and to benefit in the prestige and value that organization may provide. Additionally, the union also enables them to put leadership talents to use as officers of the union and representatives of fellow employees. One study found that employees became union stewards so that they could be seen as "a fellow your buddies look to" and as a person who "stands up to the boss."[15]

Organizing Campaigns

Once employees desire to unionize, a formal organizing campaign may be started either by a union organizer or by employees acting on their own behalf.[16] Contrary to popular belief, most organizing campaigns are begun by employees rather than by union organizers. Large national unions like the United Auto Workers, the United Brotherhood of Carpenters, the United Steelworkers, and the Teamsters, however, have formal organizing departments whose purpose is to identify organizing opportunities and launch organizing campaigns.

Organizing Steps

Terry Moser, former president of Teamster Local 104, once told the authors that the typical organizing campaign follows a series of progressive steps that can lead to employee representation. The organizing process as described by Moser normally includes the following steps:

1. Employee/union contact
2. Initial organizational meeting
3. Formation of in-house organizing committee
4. Election petition and voting preparation
5. Contract negotiations

Step 1. The first step begins when employees and union officials make contact to explore the possibility of unionization. During these discussions, employees investigate the advantages of labor representation, and union officials begin to gather information on employee needs, problems, and grievances. Labor organizers also seek specific information about the employer's financial health, supervisory styles, and organizational policies and practices. To win employee support, labor organizers must build a case *against* the employer and *for* the union.

Step 2. As an organizing campaign gathers momentum, the organizer schedules an initial union meeting to attract more supporters. The organizer uses the information gathered in Step 1 to address employee needs and explain how the union can secure these goals. Two additional purposes of organizational meetings are (1) to identify employees who can help the organizer direct the campaign and (2) to establish communication chains that reach all employees.

Step 3. The third important step in the organizing drive is to form an in-house organizing committee composed of employees willing to provide leadership to the campaign. The committee's role is to interest other employees in joining the union and in supporting its campaign. An important task of the committee is to have employees sign an **authorization card** (see Highlights in HRM 2) indicating their willingness to be represented by a labor union in collective bargaining with their employer. The number of signed authorization cards demonstrates the potential strength of the labor union.[17] At least 30 percent of the employees must sign authorization cards before the National Labor Relations Board will hold a representation election.

authorization card
A statement signed by an employee authorizing a union to act as a representative of the employee for purposes of collective bargaining

Step 4. If a sufficient number of employees support the union drive, the organizer seeks a government-sponsored election. A representation petition is filed with the NLRB, asking that a secret-ballot election be held to determine whether employees actually desire unionization. Before the election, a large publicity campaign is directed toward employees, seeking their support and election votes. This is a period of intense emotions for the employees, the labor organization, and the employer.

Step 5. Union organizing is concluded when the union wins the election. The NLRB "certifies" the union as the legal bargaining representative of the employees. Contract negotiations now begin; these negotiations represent another struggle between the union and employer. During negotiations each side seeks employment conditions favorable to its position. Members of the in-plant organizing committee and the union organizer attempt to negotiate the employees' first contract. In about one out of four union campaigns, unions are unable to secure a first contract after winning a representation election.[18] Should the union fail to obtain an agreement

Highlights in HRM 2

United Food and Commercial Workers International Union Authorization Card

United Food & Commercial Workers International Union
Affiliated with AFL-CIO-CLC
AUTHORIZATION FOR REPRESENTATION

I hereby authorize the United Food & Commercial Workers International Union, AFL-CIO-CLC, or its chartered Local Union(s) to represent me for the purpose of collective bargaining.

(Print Name) (Date)

(Signature) (Home Phone)

(Home Address) (City) (State) (Zip)

(Employer's Name) (Address)

(Hire Date) (Type Work Performed) (Department)

(Hourly Rate) (Day Off) Day Shift ____ Night Shift ____ Full Time ____ Part-Time ____

Would you participate in an organizing committee? Yes ____ No ____

within one year from winning the election, the Taft-Hartley Act allows the employees to vote the union out through an NLRB "decertification" election.

Aggressive Organizing Tactics

Without question, a strategic objective of the labor movement is to become more aggressive and creative in its organizing tactics. Unions have been shocked into developing these "revolutionary" organizing strategies to compensate for a decline in membership and to counteract employer antiunion campaigns.[19] (Both topics will be discussed later.) To accomplish their agenda of "vitalizing" the labor movement, unions employ the following organizing weapons—in varying degrees—to achieve their goals:

1. *Political involvement.* Unions have become more selective in their support of public officials, giving union funds to candidates who specifically pledge support for prolabor legislation. One union, the Service Employees International Union, shelled out an astonishing $65 million to support John Kerry in the 2004 presidential election.[20] According to one union official, organized labor needs to generate "Street Heat" during political struggles.[21]
2. *Union "salting."* Paid union organizers apply for employment at a company targeted for organizing, normally a nonunion construction firm. Once hired, these

trained organizers actively work to unionize other employees. In *NLRB v Town and Country Electric, Inc.*, the U.S. Supreme Court (1995) held that employers cannot discriminate in regard to hire or other terms of employment against union salts.[22] A real thorn to managers, salting campaigns have been successful in the growth regions of our nation.[23]

3. *Organizer training.* Traditionally, organizing has been part-time work. Today, the AFL-CIO's Organizing Institute is actively training a new generation of professional, highly skilled, full-time organizers. The current goal is to train 1,000 new organizers. Additionally, the AFL-CIO has challenged local unions to mobilize the local's entire membership around organizing—including spending 30 percent of local monies on recruitment efforts.
4. *Corporate campaigns.* Unions may enlist political or community groups to boycott the product(s) of a targeted company. Other tactics include writing newspaper editorials chastising specific company decisions; filing charges with administrative agencies such as OSHA, the Department of Labor, and the NLRB; and pressuring an organization's financial institution to withhold loans or demand payments. In a recent strategy, the AFL-CIO has asked the Internal Revenue Service and the Department of Labor to investigate financial practices at nineteen chapters of Associated Builders and Contractors (ABC), an industry group that supports GOP causes.[24] In 2003, the American Federation of State, County and Municipal Employees union pressured several pension funds holding its members' money to not invest in companies that privatize public jobs. The purpose is to stop the transfer of public unionized jobs to nonunion independent businesses.[25]
5. *Information technology.* E-mail and the Web are fast becoming effective union organizing tools. Web sites exist that link employees to union literature, union membership applications, and individual union web pages. "Cyberunions" seek to apply computer technology to all aspects of organizing activity.[26]

Employer Tactics Opposing Unionization

Employers use a two-pronged campaign to fight unionization. First, when possible, employers stress the favorable employer-employee relationship they have experienced in the past without a union. Employers may emphasize any advantages in wages, benefits, or working conditions the employees may enjoy in comparison with those provided by organizations that are already unionized. "While you have a right to join a union," the employers may remind their employees, "you also have a right not to join one and to deal directly with the organization free from outside interference."

Second, employers emphasize any unfavorable aspects of unionism including strikes, the payment of union dues and special assessments, and published abuses of members' legal rights, along with any false promises made by the union in the course of its campaign. Union rules on member conduct, such as being fined for crossing a picket line, are emphasized to employees. Employers may also use government statistics to show that unions commit large numbers of unfair labor practices. For example, 6,917 unfair labor practices were charged against unions in 2004; the majority (5,976) alleged illegal restraint and coercion of employees.[27] Employers may initiate legal action should union members and/or their leaders engage in any unfair labor practices during the organizing effort.

Within the limits permitted by the Taft-Hartley Act, employers can express their views about the disadvantages of being represented by a union. However, when

Highlights in HRM 3

Employer "Don'ts" during Union Organizing Campaigns

Union organizing drives are emotionally charged events. Furthermore, labor law, NLRB rulings, and court decisions greatly affect the behavior and actions of management and union representatives. During the drive, managers and supervisors should avoid the following:

- Attending union meetings, spying on employee-union gatherings, or questioning employees about the content of union meetings
- Questioning present or current employees about their union sentiments, particularly about how they might vote in a union election
- Threatening or terminating employees for their union support or beliefs
- Changing the working conditions of employees because they actively work for the union or simply support its ideals
- Supplying the names, addresses, and phone numbers of employees to union representatives or other employees sympathetic to the union
- Promising employees improvements in working conditions (wage increases, benefit improvements, and so on) if they vote against the union
- Accepting or reviewing union authorization cards or prounion petitions, because employees' names are listed on these documents

counteracting a union campaign, managers must not threaten employees with loss of jobs or loss or reduction of other employment benefits if they vote to unionize. Nor may employers offer new or improved employee benefits or higher wages as a means of getting employees to vote "no union." Highlights in HRM 3 lists some of the activities in which managers or supervisors should not engage.[28]

How Employees Become Unionized

bargaining unit
A group of two or more employees who share common employment interests and conditions and may reasonably be grouped together for purposes of collective bargaining

The employees to be organized constitute the bargaining unit to be covered by the labor agreement. The NLRB defines a **bargaining unit** as a group of two or more employees who have common employment interests and conditions and may reasonably be grouped together for purposes of collective bargaining. If an employer and a union cannot agree on who should be in the bargaining unit, an appropriate bargaining unit will be determined by the NLRB on the basis of a similarity of interests (such as wages, job duties, or training) among employees within the unit. For example, in hospitals, the NLRB has designated separate units for nurses, technicians, doctors, maintenance employees, office clerical personnel, all other nonprofessionals, and guards.

NLRB Representation Election

If it succeeds in signing up 30 percent of employees within the bargaining unit, the union petitions for an NLRB-conducted election. The petition to hold representation elections usually is initiated by the union, although employers, under certain circumstances, have the right to petition for one (see Highlights in HRM 4). Prior to the election, the NLRB holds a *pre-election hearing* with the employer and union, or unions, seeking to represent the employees. At this meeting several important issues are determined, including verification of the authorization cards, the NLRB's jurisdiction to hold the election, determination of the bargaining unit (if contested by the parties), the date of the election, and the voting choice(s) to appear on the ballot. The ballot lists the names of the unions that are seeking recognition and also provides a choice of "no union."

After the election is held, the winning party is determined on the basis of the number of actual votes, not on the number of members of the bargaining unit. For example, suppose the bargaining unit at XYZ Corporation comprised 100 employees, but only 27 employees voted in the election. A union receiving 14 yes votes among the 27 voting (a majority) would be declared the winner, and the union would bargain for all 100 employees. By law the union would be granted **exclusive representation** over all bargaining-unit employees. The union is *certified* by the NLRB as the bargaining agent for at least a year, or for the duration of the labor agreement. Once the union is certified, the employer is obligated to begin negotiations leading toward a labor agreement.

exclusive representation
The legal right and responsibility of the union to represent all bargaining-unit members equally, regardless of whether employees join the union or not

An important statistic in labor relations is the win/loss record of unions in certification elections. In 1950, the union win rate in elections held by the NLRB was 74.5 percent. This percentage dropped dramatically to 60.2 percent in 1965 and to 48.2 percent in 1995. The percentage win rate for unions has stabilized at around 50 percent since 1995. For example, in 2004, the NLRB held 2,719 conclusive representation elections, of which 1,579 resulted in union wins—a 53.2 percent win rate.[29] Recent statistics show that unions have lost much of their ability to win bargaining representation for employees.

Employees can unionize without an NLRB election. This NLRB procedure is referred to as "certification on a card check." If the union succeeds in signing up at least 50 percent of employees within the bargaining unit, the union may request recognition by the employer. Typically, evidence is produced in the form of authorization cards signed by employees. However, if the employer believes that a majority of its employees do not want to belong to the union or if the employer questions the authenticity of the cards, the employer can insist that a representation election be held. In recent years a growing number of unions, including the Communications Workers of America (CWA) and the United Auto Workers, have turned to card checks as an expedient way to organize employees. The AFL-CIO estimates that unions enlist about 150,000 to 200,000 new members a year through card checks.[30]

Impact of Unionization on Managers

Why do employers aggressively oppose the unionization of their employees? First, studies from the field of labor economics routinely show that wages and benefits are higher in union organizations compared to similar nonunion organizations. Second, unions can have a significant effect on the prerogatives exercised by management in making decisions about employees. Third, unionization restricts the freedom of management to formulate HR policy unilaterally and can challenge the authority of supervisors.

Challenges to Management Prerogatives

Unions typically attempt to achieve greater participation in management decisions that affect their members. Specifically, these decisions may involve such issues as the

Highlights in HRM 4

NLRB Election Poster

NOTICE TO EMPLOYEES

FROM THE

National Labor Relations Board

A PETITION has been filed with this Federal agency seeking an election to determine whether certain employees want to be represented by a union.

The case is being investigated and NO DETERMINATION HAS BEEN MADE AT THIS TIME by the National Labor Relations Board. IF an election is held Notices of Election will be posted giving complete details for voting.

It was suggested that your employer post this notice so the National Labor Relations Board could inform you of your basic rights under the National Labor Relations Act.

YOU HAVE THE RIGHT under Federal Law

- **To self-organization**
- **To form, join, or assist labor organizations**
- **To bargain collectively through representatives of your own choosing**
- **To act together for the purposes of collective bargaining or other mutual aid or protection**
- **To refuse to do any or all of these things unless the union and employer, in a state where such agreements are permitted, enter into a lawful union-security agreement requiring employees to pay periodic dues and initiation fees. Nonmembers who inform the union that they object to the use of their payments for nonrepresentational purposes may be required to pay only their share of the union's costs of representational activities *(such as collective bargaining, contract administration, and grievance adjustments).***

It is possible that some of you will be voting in an employee representation election as a result of the request for an election having been filed. While NO DETERMINATION HAS BEEN MADE AT THIS TIME, in the event an election is held, the NATIONAL LABOR RELATIONS BOARD wants all eligible voters to be familiar with their rights under the law IF it holds an election.

The Board applies rules that are intended to keep its elections fair and honest and that result in a free choice. If agents of either unions or employers act in such a way as to interfere with your right to a free election, the election can be set aside by the Board. Where appropriate the Board provides other remedies, such as reinstatement for employees fired for exercising their rights, including backpay from the party responsible for their discharge.

NOTE:

The following are examples of conduct that interfere with the rights of employees and may result in the setting aside of the election.

- **Threatening loss of jobs or benefits by an employer or a union**
- **Promising or granting promotions, pay raises, or other benefits to influence an employee's vote by a party capable of carrying out such promises**
- **An employer firing employees to discourage or encourage union activity or a union causing them to be fired to encourage union activity**
- **Making campaign speeches to assembled groups of employees on company time within the 24-hour period before the election**
- **Incitement by either an employer or a union of racial or religious prejudice by inflammatory appeals**
- **Threatening physical force or violence to employees by a union or an employer to influence their votes**

Please be assured that IF AN ELECTION IS HELD every effort will be made to protect your right to a free choice under the law. Improper conduct will not be permitted. All parties are expected to cooperate fully with this Agency in maintaining basic principles of a fair election as required by law. The National Labor Relations Board, as an agency of the United States Government, does not endorse any choice in the election.

NATIONAL LABOR RELATIONS BOARD
an agency of the
UNITED STATES GOVERNMENT

THIS IS AN OFFICIAL GOVERNMENT NOTICE AND MUST NOT BE DEFACED BY ANYONE

FORM NLRB-666 (5-90)

* U.S. Government Printing Office: 1990-270-693/10127

subcontracting of work, productivity standards, and job content. Employers quite naturally seek to claim many of these decisions as their exclusive *management prerogatives*—decisions over which management claims exclusive rights. However, these prerogatives are subject to challenge and erosion by the union. They may be challenged at the bargaining table, through the grievance procedure, and through strikes.

Loss of Supervisory Authority

At a recent labor-management conference a union official commented, "Contract terms covering wages, benefits, job security, and working hours are of major importance to our membership." However, for managers and supervisors, the focal point of the union's impact is at the operating level (the shop floor or office facility), where the terms of the labor agreement are implemented on a daily basis. For example, these terms can determine what corrective action is to be taken in directing and in disciplining employees. When disciplining employees, supervisors must be certain they can demonstrate *just cause* (see Chapter 13) for their actions, because these actions can be challenged by the union and the supervisor called as defendant during a grievance hearing. If the challenge is upheld, the supervisor's effectiveness in coping with subsequent disciplinary problems may be impaired. Specific contract language can also reduce the supervisor's ability to manage in such areas as scheduling, training, transfers, performance evaluation, and promotions. Under provisions of the labor agreement, supervisors may have to promote employees by seniority rather than by individual merit.

Structures, Functions, and Leadership of Labor Unions

craft unions
Unions that represent skilled craft workers

industrial unions
Unions that represent all workers—skilled, semiskilled, unskilled—employed along industry lines

Unions that represent skilled craft workers, such as carpenters or masons, are called **craft unions.** Craft unions include the International Association of Iron Workers, the United Brotherhood of Carpenters, and the United Association of Plumbers and Pipefitters. Unions that represent unskilled and semiskilled workers employed along industry lines are known as **industrial unions.** The American Union of Postal Workers is an industrial union, as are the United Auto Workers; the United Steelworkers; the American Federation of State, County, and Municipal Employees; and the Office and Professional Employees International Union. While this distinction still exists, technological changes, union mergers, and competition among unions for members have helped reduce it. Today skilled and unskilled workers, white-collar and blue-collar workers, and professional groups are being represented by both types of union.

employee associations
Labor organizations that represent various groups of professional and white-collar employees in labor-management relations

Besides unions, **employee associations** represent various groups of professional and white-collar employees. Examples of employee associations include the National Education Association, the Michigan State Employees Association, the American Nurses' Association, and the Air Line Pilots Association. In competing with unions, these associations, for all purposes, may function as unions and become just as aggressive as unions in representing members.

Regardless of their type, labor organizations are diverse organizations, each with its own method of governance and objectives. Furthermore, they have their own structures that serve to bind them together. For example, when describing labor

USING THE INTERNET

Many national unions have web sites for their members. For information on sites for auto and transport workers, office and professional employees, and the AFL-CIO, go to the Student Resources at:

http://bohlander.swlearning.com

organizations most researchers divide them into three levels: (1) the American Federation of Labor–Congress of Industrial Organizations (AFL-CIO), (2) national unions, and (3) local unions belonging to a parent national union. Each level has its own purpose for existence as well as its own operating policies and procedures.

Structure and Functions of the AFL-CIO

In 1955 the American Federation of Labor—composed largely of craft unions—and the Congress of Industrial Organizations—made up mainly of industrial unions—merged to form the AFL-CIO. The AFL-CIO is a federation of fifty-three autonomous national and international unions.[31]

In effect, the AFL-CIO is the "House of Labor" that serves to present a united front on behalf of organized labor. It disseminates labor policy developed by leaders of its affiliated unions, assists in coordinating organizing activities among its affiliated unions, and provides research and other assistance through its various departments. Most major unions belong to this federation.[32] The affiliated unions pay per capita dues (currently 50 cents per member per month) to support federation activities. Specifically, the AFL-CIO serves its members by:

1. Lobbying before legislative bodies on subjects of interest to labor
2. Coordinating organizing efforts among its affiliated unions
3. Publicizing the concerns and benefits of unionization to the public
4. Resolving disputes between different unions as they occur

A goal of the AFL-CIO is to build solidarity among its member unions. However, the interests and organizing activities of AFL-CIO unions do not always coincide. A chief advantage of belonging to the federation is a provision that affords protection to member unions against "raiding" by other unions within the federation.[33] A violation of this no-raiding provision can lead to sanctions or expulsion from the AFL-CIO.[34] Besides offering these services, the AFL-CIO maintains an interest in international trade and domestic economic issues, foreign policy matters, social issues, and national and regional politics.

Structure and Functions of National Unions

The center of power in the labor movement resides with national and international unions. These organizations set the broad guidelines for governing union members and for formulating collective bargaining goals in dealing with management. National unions hold conventions to pass resolutions, amend their constitutions, and elect officers. The president of the national union is responsible for the overall administration of the unions and he or she exerts a large influence—if not control—over the union's policies and direction.

A national union, through its constitution, establishes the rules and conditions under which the local unions may be chartered. Most national unions have regulations governing dues, initiation fees, and the internal administration of the locals. National unions also may require that certain standard provisions be included in labor agreements with employers. Standard contract terms covering safety or grievance procedures and seniority rights are examples. In return for these controls, they provide professional and financial assistance during organizing drives and strikes and help in the negotiation and administration of labor agreements. Other services provided by national unions include (1) training of union leaders, (2) legal assistance, (3) leadership in political activity, (4) educational and public relations programs, and (5) discipline of union members.

Structure and Functions of Local Unions

To the "rank-and-file" union member the importance of unionism resides in the activities of the local union and its leaders. The officers of a local union are usually responsible for negotiating the local labor agreement and for investigating and processing member grievances. Most important, they assist in preventing the members of the local union from being treated by their employers in ways that run counter to management-established HR policies.

The officers of a local union typically include a president, vice president, secretary-treasurer, and various committee chairpeople. Depending on the size of the union, one or more of these officers may be paid by the union to serve on a full-time basis. The remaining officers are members who have regular jobs and who serve the union without pay except perhaps for token gratuities and expense allowances. Paid officers from the national union—called CWA Representatives by the Communication Workers of America—will assist the local union with functions such as organizing, negotiating the labor agreement, the arbitration of member grievances, and legal matters.

union steward
An employee who as a nonpaid union official represents the interests of members in their relations with management

An extremely important position in the local union is the union steward. The **union steward** represents the interests of union members in their relations with their immediate supervisors and other members of management. Stewards are normally elected by union members within their department and serve without union pay. Because stewards are full-time employees of the organization, they often spend considerable time after working hours investigating and handling member problems. When stewards represent members during grievance meetings on organizational time, their lost earnings are paid by the local union.

A union steward can be viewed as a "person in the middle," caught between conflicting interests and groups. It cannot be assumed that stewards will always champion union members and routinely oppose managerial objectives. Union stewards are often insightful individuals working for the betterment of employees and the organization. Therefore it is *highly* encouraged that supervisors and managers at all levels develop a professional working relationship with stewards and all union officials. This relationship can have an important bearing on union-management cooperation and on the efficiency and morale of the workforce.[35]

Union Leadership Commitment and Philosophies

To evaluate the role of union leaders accurately, one must understand the nature of their backgrounds and ambitions and recognize the political nature of the offices they occupy. Union leaders—at all levels—often possess enthusiasm and a commitment to the ideals of unionism and employee welfare that is difficult for managers to understand and accept. To some managers, union officials have a "religious" zeal toward the labor movement and the advancement of member bargaining rights. Additionally, it is important for managers to understand that union officials are elected to office and, like any political officials, must be responsive to the views of their constituency. The union leader who ignores the demands of union members may risk being voted out of office or having members vote the union out as their bargaining agent.

business unionism
A term applied to the goals of U.S. labor organizations, which collectively bargain for improvements in wages, hours, job security, and working conditions

To be effective leaders, labor officials must also pay constant attention to the general goals and philosophies of the labor movement. **Business unionism** is the general label given to the goals of American labor organizations: increased pay and benefits, job security, and improved working conditions. Furthermore, union leaders also know that unions must address the broader social, economic, and legislative issues of concern to members. For example, the United Auto Workers continually lobbies Congress for protective legislation affecting the auto industry. The American Federation of State, County, and Municipal Employees; the Union of Needletrades, Industrial and Textile Employees; and the Association of Flight Attendants, representing flight attendants at America West Airlines, have been active supporters of women's issues at both the state and national levels.

Labor Relations in the Public Sector

Collective bargaining among federal, state, and local government employees has been an area of important activity for the union movement since the early 1960s. Today 7 million public workers belong to unions or employee associations. They constitute about 40 percent of government employees. The latest union membership figures show that some of the nation's largest labor organizations represent employees in the public sector—the National Education Association (2.7 million members), American Federation of Teachers (1.3 million members), and State, County, and Municipal Employees (1.1 million members), for instance.[36] As unions and employee associations of teachers, police, firefighters, and state employees have grown in size and political power, they have demanded the same rights to bargain and strike that private-sector employees have.

While public- and private-sector collective bargaining have many features in common, a number of factors differentiate the two sectors. First, there are no national laws, like the National Labor Relations Act in the private sector, governing public-sector labor relations. Public-sector collective bargaining falls within the separate jurisdiction of each state, and great diversity exists among the various state laws.[37] For example, some states, such as Arizona, Utah, and Mississippi, have no collective bargaining laws; other states, such as Florida, Hawaii, and New York, have comprehensive laws granting collective bargaining rights to all public employees. Between these extremes are state laws granting collective bargaining rights only to specific employee groups such as teachers and the uniformed services (police and fire). For federal employees, collective bargaining is governed by executive orders (regulations issued by the U.S. president) and the Civil Service Reform Act of 1978.[38]

USING THE INTERNET

Many unions representing public-sector employees also have active web sites. A few examples are the National Education Association, American Federation of Teachers, and American Postal Workers. Go to the Student Resources at:

http://bohlander.swlearning.com

Second, public jurisdictions often establish the wages, employee benefits, and organizational rules under which their employees work. Public *civil service systems* exist to address employee complaints or grievances. With wages and working conditions set by law, unions are largely denied the opportunity to negotiate for the traditional bread-and-butter issues of collective bargaining.[39] Unions see this arrangement as a loss of opportunity to "champion" their cause to employees.

Lastly, striking in the public sector is largely prohibited. Because the services that government employees provide are often considered essential to the well-being of the public, public policy is opposed to such strikes. Thus most state legislatures have not granted public employees the right to strike. In those states where striking is permitted, the right is limited to specific groups of employees—normally nonuniformed employees—and the strike cannot endanger the public's health, safety, or welfare. Public-employee unions contend, however, that denying them the same right to strike as employees in the private sector means that their power during collective bargaining is greatly reduced. Union officials often describe negotiating with public officials as a process of "meet and beg."

In order to provide some equity in bargaining power, various arbitration methods are used for resolving collective bargaining deadlocks in the public sector.[40] One is *compulsory binding arbitration* for employees such as police officers, firefighters, and others in jobs for which strikes cannot be tolerated. Another method is *final-offer arbitration*, under which the arbitrator must select one or the other of the final offers submitted by the disputing parties. With this method, the arbitrator's award is more likely to go to the party whose final bargaining offer has moved the closest toward a reasonable settlement.

The Bargaining Process

collective bargaining process
The process of negotiating a labor agreement, including the use of economic pressures by both parties

Those unfamiliar with contract negotiations often view the process as an emotional conflict between labor and management, complete with marathon sessions, fist pounding, and smoke-filled rooms. In reality, negotiating a labor agreement entails long hours of extensive preparation combined with diplomatic maneuvering and the development of bargaining strategies. Furthermore, negotiation is only one part of the **collective bargaining process.** (See Figure 14.2.) Collective bargaining also may include the use of economic pressures in the form of strikes and boycotts by a union. Lockouts, plant closures, and the replacement of strikers are similar pressures used by an employer. In addition, either or both parties may seek support from the general public or from the courts as a means of pressuring the opposing side.

Preparing for Negotiations

Preparing for negotiations includes assembling data to support bargaining proposals and forming the bargaining team. This permits collective bargaining to be conducted on an orderly, factual, and positive basis with a greater likelihood of achieving desired goals. Negotiators often develop a bargaining book that serves as a cross-reference file to determine which contract clauses would be affected by a demand. The bargaining book also contains a general history of contract terms and their rela-

Figure 14.2 The Collective Bargaining Process

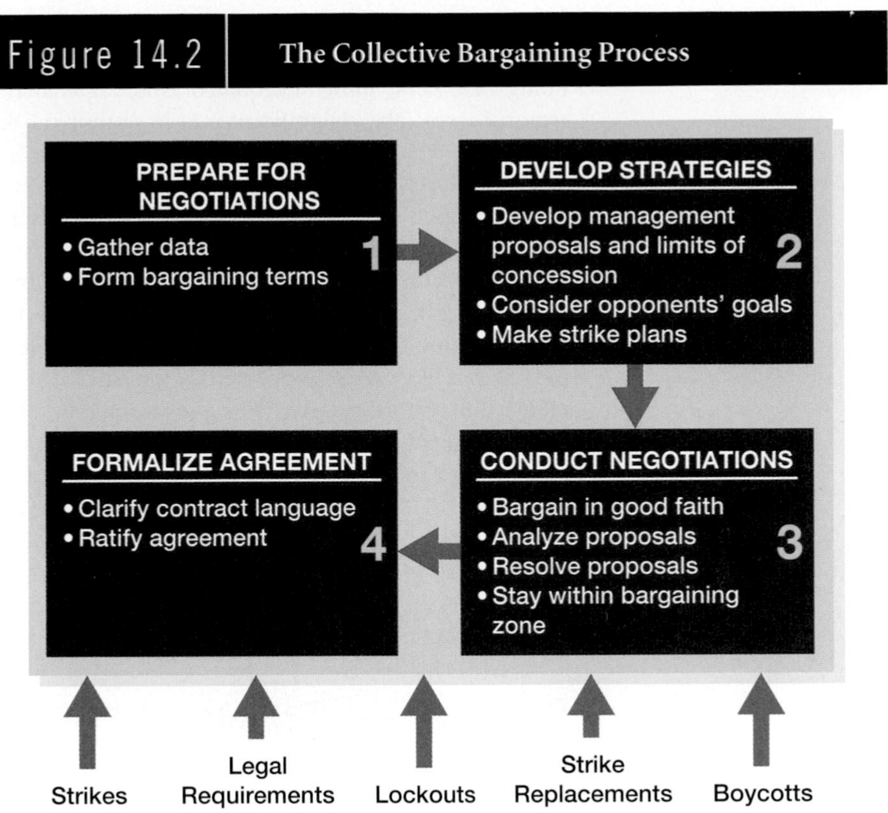

tive importance to management.[41] Assuming that the labor agreement is not the first to be negotiated by the parties, preparation for negotiations ideally start soon after the current agreement has been signed. This practice allows negotiators to review and diagnose weaknesses and mistakes made during the previous negotiations while the experience is still current in their minds.

Gathering Bargaining Data

Employers gather economic data primarily in the areas of wages and benefits. However, internal data relating to grievances, disciplinary actions, transfers, promotions, overtime, and former arbitration awards are useful in formulating and supporting the employer's bargaining position. The supervisors and managers who must live with and administer the labor agreement can be very important sources of ideas and suggestions concerning changes that are needed in the *next* agreement. Their contact with union members and representatives provides them with a firsthand knowledge of the changes that union negotiators are likely to propose.

When negotiating contracts, union bargainers talk about "taking wages out of competition." This term refers to having similar contract provisions—particularly concerning wages and benefits—between different companies in order to prevent one employer from having a favorable labor cost advantage over another. For example, the United Auto Workers representing workers at both General Motors and Ford will seek similar contract provisions. Furthermore, this allows unions to show their members that they are receiving wages and benefits comparable to those of other employees doing like work. Other negotiated labor agreements, particularly at the local and regional levels, play a significant part in settling the terms of the labor agreement.

Bargaining Teams

Normally, each side has four to six representatives at the negotiating table. The chief negotiator for management is the vice president or manager for labor relations; the chief negotiator for the union is the local union president or national union representative. Others making up management's team may include representatives from accounting or finance, operations, employment, legal, or training. The local union president is likely to be supported by the chief steward, various local union vice presidents, and a representative from the national union.

The initial meeting of the bargaining teams is a particularly important one because it establishes the climate that will prevail during the negotiations that follow. According to one experienced negotiator, "The conduct of negotiations largely depends on the relationship and attitude of negotiators toward one another. If you want conflict in your bargaining sessions just start off attacking the other side." This *attitudinal structuring* is done to change the attitudes of the parties toward each other, often with the objective of persuading one side to accept the other side's demands.[42]

Developing Bargaining Strategies and Tactics

Both management and union negotiators approach bargaining with a defined strategy. In tough economic periods, the employer's strategy might be cost containment or specific reductions in wages or benefits. Conversely, in times of economic growth—when a union strike would harm sales—the employer will be more willing to meet union demands. The employer's strategy should also consider proposals the union is likely to submit, goals the union is striving to achieve, and the extent to which it may be willing to make concessions or to resort to strike action in order to achieve these goals.

At a minimum, the employer's bargaining strategy must address these points:

- Likely union proposals and management responses to them
- A listing of management demands, limits of concessions, and anticipated union responses
- Development of a database to support management bargaining proposals and to counteract union demands
- A contingency operating plan should employees strike

Certain elements of strategy are common to both the employer and the union. Generally, the initial demands presented by each side are greater than those it actually may hope to achieve.[43] This is done in order to provide room for concessions. Moreover, each party usually avoids giving up the maximum it is capable of conceding in order to allow for further concessions that may be needed to break a bargaining deadlock.

The negotiation of a labor agreement can have some of the characteristics of a poker game, with each side attempting to determine its opponent's position while not revealing its own.[44] Each party normally tries to avoid disclosing the relative importance that it attaches to a proposal so that it will not be forced to pay a higher price than is necessary to have the proposal accepted. As in buying a new car, the buyer and seller employ a lot of strategy in order to obtain the best outcome possible.

Negotiating the Labor Agreement

bargaining zone
An area in which the union and the employer are willing to concede when bargaining

While there is no "exact" way to negotiate a labor agreement, typically each side focuses on one issue or several related issues until agreement is reached. For each bargaining issue to be resolved satisfactorily, the point at which agreement is reached must be within limits that the union and the employer are willing to accept. In a frequently cited bargaining model, Ross Stagner and Hjalmar Rosen call the area within these two limits the **bargaining zone.** In some bargaining situations, such as the one illustrated in Figure 14.3, the solution desired by one party may exceed the limits of the other party. Thus that solution is outside the bargaining zone. If that party refuses to modify its demands sufficiently to bring them within the bargaining zone or if the opposing party refuses to extend its limit to accommodate the demands of the other party, a bargaining deadlock results.[45] For example, when bargaining a wage increase for employees, if the union's lowest limit is a 4 percent increase and management's top limit is 6 percent, an acceptable range—the bargaining zone—is available to both parties. If management's top limit is only 3 percent, however, a bargaining zone is not available to either side and a deadlock is likely to occur. Figure 14.3, which is based on the original model by Stagner and Rosen, shows that as bargaining takes place, several important variables influence the negotiators and their ability to reach agreement within the bargaining zone.

The Taft-Hartley Act requires an employer to negotiate in good faith with the union's representatives over conditions of employment (the same obligation applies to the union representatives). Good faith requires meetings to be held at reasonable times and places to discuss employment conditions. It requires also that the proposals submitted by each party be realistic. In discussing the other party's proposals, each side must offer reasonable counterproposals for those it is unwilling to accept. Finally, both parties must sign the written document containing the agreement reached through negotiations.

The National Labor Relations Board (NLRB) defines the duty to bargain as bargaining on all matters concerning rates of pay, wages, hours of employment, or other conditions of employment.[46] These topics are called *mandatory subjects* of bargaining, and both the employer and the union must bargain in good faith over these issues. The law, however, does not requires either party to agree to a proposal or to make concessions while negotiating these subjects. On other topics, called *permissive issues*—matters that are lawful but not related to wages, hours, or other conditions of employment—the parties are free to bargain, but neither side can force the other side to bargain over these topics. Permissive subjects might include a union demand to ratify supervisory promotions or consultation on setting the price of the organization's product or service. *Illegal subjects* of bargaining would include such issues as the closed shop or compulsory dues checkoff. If a demand is made concerning an illegal item, the NLRB finds a violation of good-faith bargaining under section 8(a)(5) of the Taft-Hartley Act. When labor and management negotiators cannot agree on whether a bargaining proposal is a mandatory or a permissive issue, the NLRB decides the dispute.

Figure 14.3 The Bargaining Zone and Negotiation Influences

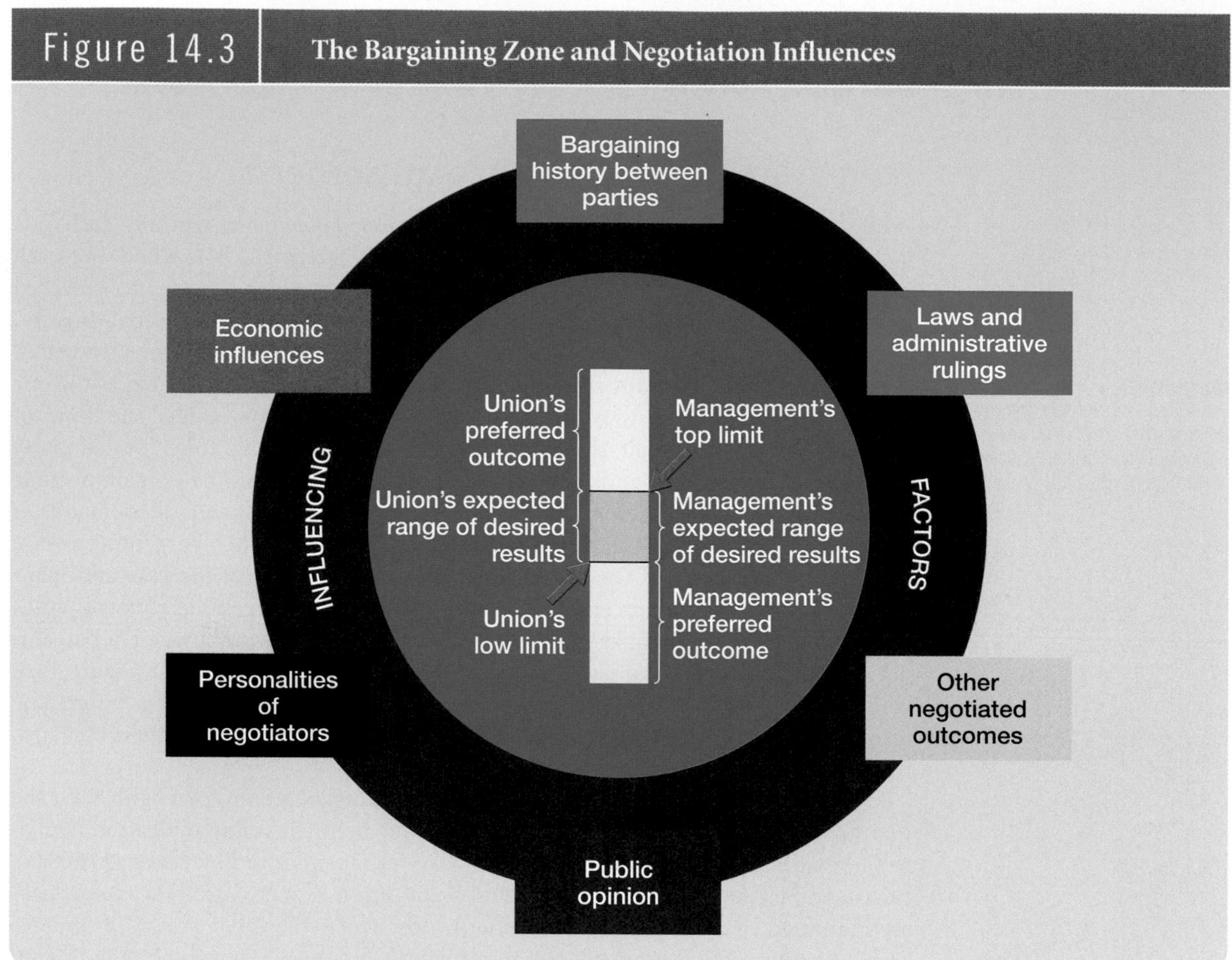

Source: Adapted from Ross Stagner and Hjalmar Rosen, *Psychology of Union-Management Relations* (Belmont, CA: Wadsworth Publishing Company, 1965), 96. Adapted with permission from Brooks/Cole Publishing Co.

Interest-Based Bargaining

U.S. labor-management negotiations are characterized as adversarial. With adversarial bargaining, negotiators start with defined positions and through deferral, persuasion, trade, or power, the parties work toward the resolution of individual bargaining demands. With traditional bargaining—and its give-and-take philosophy—the results may or may not be to the complete satisfaction of one or both parties.[47] In fact, when one side feels it received "the short end of the stick," bitter feelings may persist throughout the life of the agreement. As noted by one labor negotiator, "adversarial bargaining does little to establish a long-term positive relationship based on open communications and trust. By its nature, it leads to suspicion and compromise."[48] To overcome these negative feelings, labor and management practitioners may use a nonadversarial approach to negotiating.

interest-based bargaining Problem-solving bargaining based on a win-win philosophy and the development of a positive long-term relationship

Interest-based bargaining is based on the identification and resolution of mutual interests rather than the resolve of specific bargaining demands.[49] As defined by the Federal Mediation and Conciliation Service, interest-based bargaining is "a problem-solving process conducted in a principled way that creates effective solutions while improving the bargaining relationship."[50] The focus of bargaining strategy is to discover mutual bargaining interests with the intent of formulating options and solutions for mutual gain.

Interest-based bargaining is novel in both its philosophy and its bargaining process. Also distinct are the bargaining tools used to expedite a successful nonadversarial negotiating experience. Rather than using proposals and counterproposals as a means of reaching agreement (as with adversarial negotiations), participants use brainstorming, consensus decision making, active listening, process checking, and matrix building to facilitate the settlement of issues. An underlying goal of interest-based bargaining is to create a relationship for the future based on trust, understanding, and mutual respect.

Management and Union Power in Collective Bargaining

bargaining power
The power of labor and management to achieve their goals through economic, social, or political influence

Fortunately, the great majority of labor-management negotiations are settled peacefully. However, should negotiations become deadlocked, bargaining can become highly adversarial as each side will now employ its bargaining power to achieve its desired ends. The party's **bargaining power** consists of its economic, political, and social influence to achieve its demands at the expense of the other side.

Union Bargaining Power

The bargaining power of the union may be exercised by striking, picketing, or boycotting the employer's products or services. A strike is the refusal of a group of employees to perform their jobs. Unions usually seek strike authorization from their members to use as a bargaining ploy to gain concessions that will make a strike unnecessary.[51] A strike vote by the members does not mean they actually want or expect to go out on strike. Rather, it is intended as a vote of confidence to strengthen the position of their leaders at the bargaining table.

Of critical importance to the union is the extent, if any, to which the employer will be able to continue operating through the use of supervisory and nonstriking personnel and employees hired to replace the strikers. In organizations with high levels of technology and automation, and consequently fewer employees, continuing service with supervisors and managers is more likely. Among the highly automated telephone companies, most services can be maintained by supervisors during a strike. According to one authority, "Because of technological change, striking in many industries no longer has the effect of curtailing the employer's operations significantly."[52] Consequently, the greater the ability of the employer to continue operating, the less the union's chances of gaining its demands through a strike.

When a union goes on strike, it pickets the employer by placing people at business entrances to advertise the dispute and to discourage others from entering the premises. Because unions often refuse to cross another union's picket line, the pickets may serve to prevent the delivery and pickup of goods or performance of other services. For example, a Teamster truck driver may refuse to deliver produce to a food store whose employees are out on strike with the United Food and Commercial Workers Union.

These picketers are encouraging a boycott of the employer's products.

Another economic weapon of the union is the *boycott*, which is a refusal to patronize the employer. For example, production employees on strike against a hand tool manufacturer might picket a retail store that sells the tools made by the struck employer. Unions will also use handbills, radio announcements, e-mail campaigns, and newspaper ads to discourage the purchase of the employer's product or service.

Management Bargaining Power

When negotiations become deadlocked, the employer's bargaining power largely rests on being able to continue operations in the face of a strike *or* to shut down operations entirely.

Should employees strike the organization (referred to as an economic strike), employers have the legal right to hire replacement workers. With this right, employers acquire a bargaining weapon equal in force to the union's right to strike. As one observer noted, "The availability of a worker replacement strategy improves management's ability to battle a union head-on in the way that unions have battled employers for decades."

Should *permanent* replacement workers be hired, under NLRB rulings, economic strikers have re-employment rights for one year, beginning when they indicate a desire to return to work. This right, however, exists only if permanent job openings become available. Should the employer hire *temporary* replacement workers, economic strikers will go back to work after an agreement is reached and the temporary replacements will be dismissed. [53]

Another prevalent bargaining strategy is for the employer to continue operations by using managers and supervisors to staff employee jobs. In one case, nearly 30,000 managers left their offices to serve as operators, technicians, and customer service representatives during a strike between Verizon and the Communications Workers of America. As noted previously, technological advances enhance the employer's ability to operate during a strike.

In extreme situations, the employer may elect to lock out its employees. The lockout is a bargaining strategy by which the employer denies employees the opportunity to work by closing its operations. In a highly publicized case, during the 2004–2005 National Hockey League season, management locked out players represented by the National Hockey League Players Association. Besides being used in bargaining impasses, lockouts may be used by employers to combat union slowdowns, damage to their property, or violence within the organization that may occur in connection with a labor dispute.[54] Employers may still be reluctant to resort to a lockout, however, because of their concern that denying work to regular employees might hurt the organization's image.

Resolving Bargaining Deadlocks

arbitrator
A third-party neutral who resolves a labor dispute by issuing a final decision in the disagreement

Unions and employers in all types of industries—sports, transportation, entertainment, manufacturing, communication, and healthcare—have used mediation and arbitration to help resolve their bargaining deadlocks. As discussed in Chapter 13, mediation is a voluntary process that relies on the communication and persuasive skills of a mediator to help the parties resolve their differences. The federal government is likely to become involved in labor disputes through the services of the FMCS.

USING THE INTERNET

Information about the responsibilities of the Federal Mediation and Conciliation Service, as well as a description of its history and current service, may be found via the Student Resources at:

http://bohlander.swlearning.com

Unlike a mediator, an **arbitrator** assumes the role of a decision maker and determines what the settlement between the two parties should be. In other words, arbitrators write a final contract that the parties *must* accept. Compared with mediation, arbitration is not often used to settle private-sector bargaining disputes. In the public sector, where strikes are largely prohibited, the use of *interest arbitration* is a common method to resolve bargaining deadlocks. Generally, one or both parties are reluctant to give a third party the power to make the settlement for them. Consequently, a mediator typically is used to break a deadlock and assist the parties in reaching an agreement. An arbitrator generally is called on to resolve disputes arising in connection with the administration of the agreement, called *rights arbitration* or *grievance arbitration*, which will be discussed shortly.

The Labor Agreement

When negotiations are concluded, the labor agreement becomes a formal *binding* document listing the terms, conditions, and rules under which employees and managers agree to operate. Highlights in HRM 5 shows some of the major articles in a labor agreement and also provides examples of some new and progressive contract clauses. Two important items in any labor agreement pertain to the issue of management rights and the forms of security afforded the union.

The Issue of Management Rights

Management rights have to do with the conditions of employment over which management is able to exercise exclusive control. Almost without exception, the labor agreement contain a *management rights* clause. This clause states that "management's authority is supreme in all matters except those it has expressly conceded in the collective agreement, or in those areas where its authority is restricted by law." Management

Highlights in HRM 5

Items in a Labor Agreement

Typical clauses will cover

- Wages
- Vacations
- Holidays
- Work schedules
- Management rights
- Union security
- Transfers
- Discipline
- Training
- Grievance procedures
- No strike/no lockout clause
- Overtime
- Safety procedures
- Severance pay
- Seniority
- Pensions and benefits
- Outsourcing
- Work rules

Progressive clauses will cover

- Employee access to records
- Limitations on use of performance evaluation
- Elder care leave
- Flexible medical spending accounts
- Protection against hazards of technology equipment (VDTs)
- Limitations against electronic monitoring
- Procedures governing drug testing
- Bilingual stipends
- Domestic partnership benefits
- Employee involvement programs

rights might include the right of management to determine the products to produce, to determine the location of production or service facilities, or to select production equipment and procedures. The following is an example of a clause defining management rights in one labor agreement:

> It is agreed that the company possesses all of the rights, powers, privileges, and authority it had prior to the execution of this agreement; and nothing in this agreement shall be construed to limit the company in any way in the exercise of the regular and customary functions of management and the operation of its business, except as it may be specifically relinquished or modified herein by an express provision of this agreement.[55]

Union Security Agreements

As we noted at the beginning of this chapter, unions must represent all bargaining-unit members equally regardless of whether employees join the union or not. In exchange for this obligation, union officials will seek to negotiate some form of compulsory membership as a condition of employment. Union officials argue that compulsory membership precludes the possibility that some employees will receive the benefits of unionization without paying their fair share of the costs. A standard union security provision is dues checkoff, which gives the employer the responsibility of withholding union dues from the paychecks of union members who agree to such a deduction.

Other common forms of union security found in labor contracts are different types of "shop" agreements. These agreements—in varying degrees—attempt to require employees to join the union. For example, the *union shop* provides that any employee who is not a union member upon employment must join the union within thirty days or be terminated. Another, the *agency shop*, provides for voluntary membership. However, all bargaining-unit members must pay union dues and fees.

Few issues in collective bargaining are more controversial than the negotiation of these agreements.[56] The most popular union security clause, the union shop, is illegal in twenty-two states having right-to-work laws.[57] Right-to-work laws ban any form of compulsory union membership. Section 14(b) of the Taft-Hartley Act permits individual states to enact legislation prohibiting compulsory union membership as a condition of employment.

Administration of the Labor Agreement

Negotiation of the labor agreement, as mentioned earlier, is usually the most publicized and critical aspect of labor relations. Strike deadlines, press conferences, and employee picketing help create this image. Nevertheless, as managers in unionized organizations know, the bulk of labor relations activity comes from the day-to-day administration of the agreement, because no agreement could possibly anticipate all the forms that disputes may take. In addition, once the agreement is signed, each side will naturally interpret ambiguous clauses to its own advantage.[58] These differences are traditionally resolved through the grievance procedure.

Negotiated Grievance Procedures

grievance procedure
A formal procedure that provides for the union to represent members and nonmembers in processing a grievance

The **grievance procedure** typically provides for the union to represent the interests of its members (and nonmembers as well) in processing a grievance. It is considered by some authorities to be the heart of the bargaining agreement, or the safety valve that gives flexibility to the whole system of collective bargaining.[59]

The grievance procedure is normally initiated by the union—or an individual employee—when it feels management has violated some article of the labor agreement. In one case, the union filed a grievance against a supervisor when it believed the supervisor promoted an employee out of seniority order—called a bypass grievance. A significant benefit of the grievance procedure is that it provides a formal and orderly procedure for the union to challenge the actions of management without resort to force. One authority has noted, "The grievance procedure fosters cooperation, not conflict, between the employer and the union."[60]

The operation of a grievance procedure is unique to each individual collective bargaining relationship, although there are common elements among systems. For example, grievance procedures normally specify how the grievance is to be initiated, the number and timing of steps that are to compose the procedure, and the identity of representatives from each side who are to be involved in the hearings at each step. (See Figure 14.4.) When a grievance cannot be resolved at one of the specified steps,

Figure 14.4 Five-Step Grievance Procedure

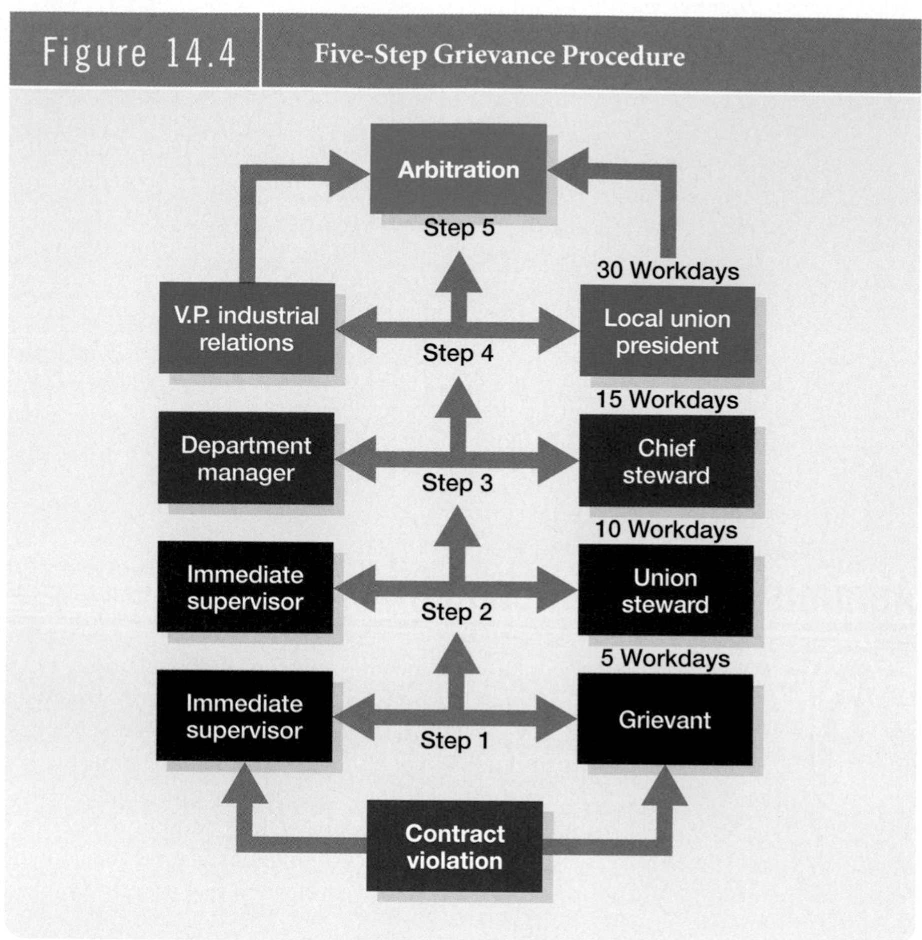

most agreements provide for the grievance to be submitted to a third party—usually an arbitrator—whose decision is final. Some labor agreements provide for mediation as a way to resolve employee grievances. When used, *grievance mediation* will be listed as a formal step in the grievance procedure preceding arbitration.[61]

The Grievance Procedure in Action

In order for an employee's grievance to be considered formally, it must be expressed orally and/or in writing, ideally to the employee's immediate supervisor (see Highlights in HRM 6). Because grievances are often the result of an oversight or a misunderstanding, many of them can be resolved at this point. Whether it is possible to resolve a grievance at the initial step will depend on the supervisor's ability and willingness to discuss the problem with the employee and the steward. Additionally, HR professionals acknowledge that grievance handling is more successful when supervisors are trained formally in resolving grievances, including familiarization with the terms of the labor agreement and the discussion of the problem in a rational and objective manner. A grievance should not be viewed as something to be won or lost. Rather, both sides must view the situation as an attempt to solve a human relations problem.

Highlights in HRM 6

Grievance Form: Phoenix Transit System and Teamsters, Local 104

COMPLAINT RECORD

Transport, Local Delivery and Sales Drivers, Warehousemen and Helpers, Mining and Motion Picture Production, State of Arizona, Local Union No. 104

an Affiliate of the International Brotherhood of Teamsters, Chauffeurs, Warehousemen and Helpers of America

Member's name____________________ Date__________

Member's address____________________ Home phone__________

City____________________ State__________ Zip Code__________

Name of company against whom you are filing complaint____________________

Explain complaint in detail____________________

If complaint is for discharge (give exact reason given by Co.)____________________

This will constitute full authority for Transport and Local Delivery Drivers Local 104 or any employee or agent designated by them as my attorney-in-fact, to fully represent me in the processing of this complaint in any manner they deem is in the best interest of myself as the complainant and the Union, and to receive on my behalf any monies due me.

Should this complaint be processed through the grievance procedure,

(a) I request notification of the time, date and place of hearing ☐

(b) I do not request notification of the time, date and place of hearing ☐

I understand and agree that if I attend any hearing on my behalf, I will do so at my own personal expense, and the Union will in no way be obligated for same.

____
MEMBER'S SIGNATURE

Record of action by Union:____________________

Case settled:____________________
AGENT

Source: Courtesy of Phoenix Transit System and Teamsters, Local 104, Phoenix, Arizona.

In some instances a satisfactory solution may not be possible at the first step because there are legitimate differences of opinion between the employee and the supervisor or because the supervisor does not have the authority to take the action required to satisfy the grievant. Personality conflicts, prejudices, emotionalism, stubbornness, or other factors may also be barriers to a satisfactory solution at this step.

Grievance Arbitration

rights arbitration
Arbitration over interpretation of the meaning of contract terms or employee work grievances

The function of **rights arbitration** is to provide the solution to a grievance that a union and an employer have been unable to resolve by themselves. As mentioned earlier, arbitration is performed by a neutral third party (an arbitrator or impartial umpire). This third party's decision dictates how the grievance is to be settled.[62] Both parties are obligated to comply with the decision.

The Decision to Arbitrate

fair representation doctrine
A doctrine under which unions have a legal obligation to assist both members and nonmembers in labor relations matters

In deciding whether to use arbitration, each party must weigh the costs involved against the importance of the case and the prospects of gaining a favorable award. It would seem logical that neither party would allow a weak case to go to arbitration if there were little possibility of gaining a favorable award. Logic, however, does not always prevail. For example, it is not unusual for a union to take a weak case to arbitration in order to demonstrate to the members that the union is willing to exhaust every remedy in looking out for their interests. Union officers also are not likely to refuse to take to arbitration the grievances of members who are popular or politically powerful in the union, even though their cases are weak. Moreover, under the **fair representation doctrine,** unions have a legal obligation to provide assistance to members who are pursuing grievances. Because members can bring suit against their unions for failing to process their grievances adequately, many union officers are reluctant to refuse taking even weak grievances to arbitration.

USING THE INTERNET

Check out the American Arbitration Association's web site for more information about the organization and its work. Go to the Student Resources at:

http://bohlander.swlearning.com

Management, on the other hand, may allow a weak case to go to arbitration to demonstrate to the union officers that management "cannot be pushed around." Also, managers at lower levels may be reluctant to risk the displeasure of top management by stating that a certain HR policy is unworkable or unsound. Stubbornness and mutual antagonism also may force many grievances into arbitration because neither party is willing to make concessions to reach an agreement, even when it may recognize that it is in the wrong.

The Arbitration Hearing

In our experience, employees unfamiliar with arbitration find the process confusing and often stressful. This is true for employees in the nonunion, as well as the union, setting. Arbitration hearings have the appearance of a court hearing but without many of the formalities of a court proceeding. The process begins with the swearing-in of witnesses and the introduction of the *submission agreement.* The submission agreement is a statement of the problem to be resolved. Such a statement might read: "Was the three-day suspension of Alex Hayden for just cause? If not, what is the appropriate remedy?" The parties will then make opening statements, followed by the presentation of facts and evidence, and the oral presentation of witnesses. The hearing will conclude with each side making summary statements that are arguments in support of its position.

Source: PEANUTS ©UFS. Reprinted by Permission.

In arbitrating a dispute, it is the responsibility of the arbitrator to ensure that each side receives a fair hearing during which it may present all of the facts it considers pertinent to the case. The primary purpose of the hearing is to assist the arbitrator in obtaining the facts necessary to resolve a human relations problem rather than a legal one. The arbitrator, therefore, has a right to question witnesses or to request additional facts from either party. After conducting the hearing and receiving post-hearing briefs (should the parties choose to submit them), the arbitrator customarily has thirty days in which to consider the evidence and render an award. In most labor contracts, the costs of arbitration are shared equally by the parties.

The Arbitration Award

The arbitration award is a formal written document given to both sides. As in grievance procedures, there is no specific format to an arbitration award but typically the award contains five parts: (1) the submission agreement, (2) the facts of the case, (3) the positions of the parties, (4) the opinion of the arbitrator, and (5) the decision rendered. As might be expected, the decision of the arbitrator is of major importance to the parties. However, the reasoning behind the decision—the opinion—is equally important as it can provide guidance concerning the interpretation of the labor agreement and the resolution of future disputes arising from its administration. In pointing out the merits of each party's position, the reasoning that underlies the award can help lessen the disappointment and protect the self-esteem of those representing the unsuccessful party. The opinion will also evaluate the evidence presented by each side in support of its position and, in discipline cases, whether management had just cause for the action taken against an employee. (See Chapter 13 for a discussion of just cause in arbitration.) Importantly, in deciding a case, the arbitrator has the power to modify the outcome requested by both sides. It is not uncommon, for example, for an arbitrator to reduce a discharge to a suspension without pay for a specific time period.

Because of the importance and magnitude of arbitration in both the union and nonunion setting, the process by which arbitrators make decisions and the factors that influence those decisions are of continuing interest to managers. Typically, arbitrators use four factors when deciding cases:

1. The wording of the labor agreement (or employment policy in nonunion organizations)
2. The submission agreement as presented to the arbitrator

3. Testimony and evidence offered during the hearing
4. Arbitration criteria or standards (similar to standards of common law) against which cases are judged

When deciding the case of an employee discharged for absenteeism, for example, the arbitrator would consider these factors separately and/or jointly. Arbitrators are essentially constrained to decide cases on the basis of the wording of the labor agreement, or employment policy, and the facts, testimony, and evidence presented at the hearing.

In practice, arbitration decision making is not an exact science. In fact, the decisions of arbitrators can be rather subjective. Arbitrators can, and do, interpret contract language differently (for example, What does "just cause discharge" actually mean?), they assign varying degrees of importance to testimony and evidence, they judge the truthfulness of witnesses differently, and they give arbitration standards greater or lesser weight as they apply to facts of the case. Each of these influences introduces subjectivity into the decision-making process.

Contemporary Challenges to Labor Organizations

We conclude our discussion of labor relations by highlighting three important issues facing unions today: foreign competition and technological advances, the decrease of union membership, and employers' focus on maintaining nonunion status.

Foreign Competition and Technological Change

The importation of steel, consumer electronics, automobiles, clothing, textiles, and shoes from foreign countries creates a loss of jobs in the United States for workers who produce these products. Furthermore, foreign subsidiaries of American corporations such as Nike, Westinghouse, and Xerox have been accused by labor unions of exporting the jobs of American workers. As a result, unions are demanding more government protection against imports, seeking to protect American jobs from low-cost overseas producers. Furthermore, in recent years the service sector of the U.S. economy has witnessed the outsourcing of white-collar jobs to foreign employers in locations such as India and Indonesia.

Coupled with the threat of foreign competition is the challenge to labor brought about by rapid technological advances. Improvements in computer technology and highly automated operating systems have lowered the demand for certain types of employees. Decline in membership in the auto, steel, rubber, and transportation unions illustrates this fact. As previously discussed, technological advances have also diminished the effectiveness of strikes because highly automated organizations are capable of maintaining satisfactory levels of operation with minimum staffing levels during work stoppages.

Decrease in Union Membership

A major challenge confronting organized labor is to halt the decline in union membership. The magnitude of the problem is illustrated by statistics that show how union membership has declined in total numbers and as a percentage of the total civilian labor force. In 1970, union membership totaled approximately 21 million, or 25 percent of the civilian labor force. In 1990, those figures dropped to 16.7 million union members, or slightly more than 16 percent of the civilian workforce. In 2004, union membership was approximately 15.5 million, or 12 percent of the civilian workforce—both 2004 figures are modern-era lows.[63] In the private sector, union membership accounted for approximately 10 percent of all those employed, or about 9 million workers. The loss of union jobs reflects, in part, the decline in U.S. manufacturing jobs, coupled with the failure of unions to draw membership from among the white-collar ranks, where the labor force is growing more rapidly.[64] Other reasons for the decline in union membership include the following:

- A shift from traditional unionized industries (manufacturing, mining) to high-technology industries (computers, pharmaceuticals).
- Growth in the employment of part-time and temporary workers.
- Growth in small businesses, in which unionization is more costly and difficult to perform.

What are labor organizations doing to stem the decline in union membership?[65] The answer, according to one union official, is "energized organizing." First, unions are targeting workers they have long ignored: low-wage service workers on the bottom tier of the U.S. economy—for example, janitors, maids, and service workers; food service employees; and retail clerks. Furthermore, unions see recent immigrants, the fastest-growing segment of working people, as potent prospects for union growth. Haitian cab drivers, Latino airport workers, Vietnamese warehouse distribution workers, Russian truck drivers, and Asian American service workers are targeted for union representation.[66]

Second, the AFL-CIO has embraced an aggressive unionization strategy. John Swenney, president of the AFL-CIO, adopted "America Needs a Raise" as the AFL-CIO's motto for a $20-million-a-year organizing drive. In 2003, the AFL-CIO held an Organizing Summit for 250 organizers to adopt innovative organizing strategies. The AFL-CIO has placed greater emphasis on its Organizing Institute, which recruits, trains, and places talented individuals in organizing opportunities where workers appear "ripe" for unionization.

Finally, national unions are restructuring in order to increase their ability to effectively organize. Two examples are noteworthy. In 2004, two unions—the Union of Needletrades, Industrial and Textile Employees (UNITE) and the Hotel Employees and Restaurant Employees (HERE)—merged to become UNITE HERE. According to Chris Chafe, spokesperson for the union, "We all benefit from working more closely together on solidarity issues, organizing campaigns, and contract battles."[67] Also, in 2004, five unions formed a coalition—the New Unity Partnership—aimed at improving organizing efforts. David Denholm, a union researcher, states, "The New Unity Partnership wants to organize for 'density' meaning not only increasing total national membership within a union but also increasing the percentage of members within key industries and geographical areas."[68]

Employers' Focus on Maintaining Nonunion Status

A significant fact in U.S. labor relations during the 1990s and into the twenty-first century is the prevalence of union avoidance programs. Managers in all types of

Highlights in HRM 7

Strategies to Remain Union-Free

- Offer competitive wages and benefits based on labor market comparisons and salary and benefit surveys.
- Train supervisors in progressive human relations skills, including employee motivation, job design, and employment law.
- Institute formal procedures to resolve employee complaints and grievances; these may include peer-review committees, step-review complaint systems, or open-door policies.
- Involve employees in work decisions affecting job performance or the quality or quantity of the product or service provided.
- Give attention to employee growth and development needs; recognize that the workforce is growing older, more female, more vocal, better educated, less patient, and more demanding.
- Draft HR policies that reflect legal safeguards and that are fair and equitable in employment conditions such as discipline, promotions, training, and layoffs.

organizations are vocal in their desire to maintain a union-free environment. To support this goal, employers are providing wages, benefits, and services designed to make unionism unattractive to employees.[69] In addition, a participative management style, profit-sharing plans, and alternative dispute resolution procedures (see Chapter 13) are offered to counteract the long-established union goals of improved wages and working conditions. Highlights in HRM 7 lists the key strategies identified by HR specialists as means of avoiding unionization. It is important to recognize that these strategies react to the conditions cited at the beginning of the chapter as the main reasons why workers unionize. Because these conditions are under the direct control of management, they can be changed to help discourage or prevent unionism.

SUMMARY

objective 1

The Railway Labor Act (1926) affords collective bargaining rights to workers employed in the railway and airline industries. The Norris-LaGuardia Act (1932) imposes limitations on the granting of injunctions in labor-management disputes. Most private employees are granted representation rights through the Wagner Act (1935), which has helped protect and encourage union organizing and bargaining activities. The passage of the Taft-Hartley Act (1947) and the Landrum-Griffin Act (1959) has served to establish certain controls over the internal affairs of unions and their relations with employers.

objective 2 Studies show that workers unionize for different economic, psychological, and social reasons. While some employees may join unions because they are required to do so, most belong to unions because they are convinced that unions help them improve their wages, benefits, and various working conditions. Employee unionization is largely caused by dissatisfaction with managerial practices and procedures.

objective 3 A formal union organizing campaign is used to solicit employee support for the union. Once employees demonstrate their desire to unionize through signing authorization cards, the union petitions the NLRB for a secret-ballot election. If 51 percent of those voting in the election vote for the union, the NLRB certifies the union as the bargaining representative for all employees in the bargaining unit.

objective 4 Negotiating a labor agreement is a detailed process. Each side prepares a list of proposals it wishes to achieve while additionally trying to anticipate proposals desired by the other side. Bargaining teams must be selected and all proposals must be analyzed to determine their impact on and cost to the organization. Both employer and union negotiators are sensitive to current bargaining patterns within the industry, general cost-of-living trends, and geographical wage differentials. Managers establish goals that seek to retain control over operations and to minimize costs. Union negotiators focus their demands around improved wages, hours, and working conditions. An agreement is reached when both sides compromise their original positions and final terms fall within the limits of the parties' bargaining zone.

Traditionally, collective bargaining between labor and management has been adversarial. Presently, there is an increased interest in nonadversarial negotiations—negotiations based on mutual gains and a heightened respect between the parties. What the FMCS calls interest-based bargaining is one form of nonadversarial negotiations.

objective 5 The collective bargaining process includes not only the actual negotiations but also the power tactics used to support negotiating demands. When negotiations become deadlocked, bargaining becomes a power struggle to force from either side the concessions needed to break the deadlock. The union's power in collective bargaining comes from its ability to picket, strike, or boycott the employer. The employer's power during negotiations comes from its ability to lock out employees or to operate during a strike by using managerial or replacement employees.

objective 6 When differences arise between labor and management they are normally resolved through the grievance procedure. Grievance procedures are negotiated and thus reflect the needs and desires of the parties. The typical grievance procedure consists of three, four, or five steps—each step having specific filing and reply times. Higher-level managers and union officials become involved in disputes at the higher steps of the grievance procedure. The final step of the grievance procedure may be arbitration. Arbitrators render a final decision to problems not resolved at lower grievance steps.

The submission agreement is a statement of the issue to be solved through arbitration. It is simply the problem the parties wish to have settled. The arbitrator must answer the issue by basing the arbitration award on four factors: the contents of the labor agreement (or employment policy), the submission agreement as written, testimony and evidence obtained at the hearing, and various arbitration standards developed over time to assist in the resolution of different types of labor-management disputes. Arbitration is not an exact science, because arbitrators give varying degrees of importance to the evidence and criteria by which disputes are resolved.

objective 7 Challenges facing union leaders today include declining membership caused by technological advancements and increased domestic and global competition. Labor organizations experience less success in organizations when employers establish progressive HR policies in the areas of wages, employee benefits, and organizational policies that enhance job security and the dignity of employees. To counteract a declining membership base, unions have become aggressive in organizing employees in lower-skilled occupations, recent immigrants, and employees in white-collar jobs. Through union mergers and coalitions, labor organizations seek to become more effective in their organizing efforts.

KEY TERMS

arbitrator
authorization card
bargaining power
bargaining unit
bargaining zone
business unionism
collective bargaining process
craft unions
employee associations
exclusive representation
fair representation doctrine
grievance procedure
industrial unions
interest-based bargaining
labor relations process
rights arbitration
unfair labor practices (ULPs)
union shop
union steward

DISCUSSION QUESTIONS

1. Under the provisions of the Taft-Hartley Act, which unfair labor practices apply to both unions and employers?

2. Contrast the arguments concerning union membership that are likely to be presented by a union with those likely to be presented by an employer.

3. Describe the steps in the traditional organizing drive. What "nontraditional" organizing tactics are unions using to increase their membership ranks?

4. Of what significance is the bargaining zone in the conduct of negotiations? What are some influences affecting negotiated outcomes?

5. The negotiations between Data Services International and its union have become deadlocked. What form of bargaining power does each side possess to enforce its bargaining demands? What are the advantages and disadvantages of each form of bargaining power for both the employer and union?

6. Nancy Buffett has decided to file a grievance with her union steward. The grievance alleges that she was "bypassed" by a junior employee for a promotion to senior technician.
   a. Explain the steps her grievance will follow in a formal union-management grievance procedure.
   b. Should her grievance go to arbitration, explain the process of an arbitration hearing and identify the criteria used by the arbitrator to resolve her claim.

7. a. What are some of the actions being taken by unions to cope with the contemporary challenges they face?
   b. Why have attitudes toward organized labor, on the part of certain segments of our society, become less favorable than they were in the past?

Learn about Unions

Unions, like business organizations, are dynamic and varied organizations. Some unions are very large, such as the United Auto Workers (UAW) and the American Federation of State, County and Municipal Employees (AFSCME) and represent workers nationally or even internationally. Others are smaller in size—for example, the Writers Guild of America (WGA) or the Air Traffic Controllers Association (ATCA)—and represent only specific groups of employees or organize only in a designated geographic area. This exercise will help you learn more about unions.

Assignment

Working individually or in teams, select four or five different unions or employee associations and report on the following. Vary your selections (large/small, public/private, and so on) to widen your understanding of labor organizations.

- History of the union
- Membership size and type of employees represented
- Mission of the union
- Structure of the union, including its major departments
- National officers
- Names of employers with whom they have an agreement
- Special benefits they offer members
- Other interesting or pertinent information

The AFL-CIO web site (http://www.afl-cio.org) provides a list of all unions—and their web sites—affiliated with the federation. National unions and their locals along with library research can also provide information. Be prepared to present your findings during a class discussion.

BIZFLIX EXERCISES

Bread & Roses: Join the Union; Get Bread and Roses

Make sure you have read this chapter before watching this scene from *Bread & Roses.* Before viewing the scene, note your perceptions of unions. Do the same after watching the scene. It strongly relates to discussions of why employees unionize and of union-organizing campaigns.

"Justice for Janitors" is the union-organizing slogan that drives Sam Shapiro's (Adrien Brody) efforts to organize the janitors who work for Angel Services in Los Angeles. Unionized janitors earn over $8.00 an hour plus benefits; nonunionized janitors earn $5.75 an hour with no benefits. These nonunionized janitors are mainly immigrants from different countries. Maya (Pilar Padilla) becomes an early supporter of the cause, although she risks losing her job and getting deported. Director Ken Loach launches a political polemic that grippingly tells the story of workers calling for fair wages and fair treatment by their employers.

This scene comes from the "Standing Strong" segment near the end of the film. Sam has worked untiringly to organize the Angel Services workers who work in a building with a prominent law firm as a major tenant. A large group of janitors, both union and nonunion, have marched to the building's lobby. Sam rallies them to continue their fight for fair wages, benefits, and reinstatement of the workers fired by Perez (George Lopez) at Angel Services. The film continues after this scene to show that the workers won. Angel Services agrees to reinstate all fired workers plus higher wages and benefits.

What to Watch for and Ask Yourself

- What was your perception of unions and union organizers before you watched this scene? What was your perception after you watched this scene? If your perception changed, why do you think it changed?
- An earlier chapter section, "Why Employees Unionize," describes several factors that motivate people to become union members. Based on this scene, which factors do you think drive these janitors to want to join a union? You also can refer to Figure 14.1, "The Labor Relations Process," for guidance with this question.
- An earlier section, "Organizing Campaigns," describes many parts of a union-organizing campaign. Sam Shapiro is the union organizer. Compare the chapter section to this scene, and infer which steps occurred. Also, assess Sam Shapiro's effectiveness as a union organizer.

case study 1

The Union Drive at Apollo Corporation: ULPs and Organizing Tactics

Bob Thomas was discharged after nineteen years as a plant maintenance engineer with Apollo Corporation. During that time he had received average, and sometimes below-average, annual performance appraisals. Thomas was known as something of a complainer and troublemaker, and he was highly critical of management. Prior to his termination, his attendance record for the previous five years had been very poor. However, Apollo Corporation had never enforced its attendance policy, and Thomas had never been disciplined for his attendance problems. In fact, until recently, Apollo management had been rather laid-back in its dealings with employees.

Apollo Corporation produces general component parts for the communications industry—an industry known for intense competitive pressures. To meet this competitive challenge, Jean Lipski, HR director, held a series of meetings with managers in which she instructed them to tighten up their supervisory relationship with employees. They were told to enforce HR policies strictly and to begin disciplinary action against employees not conforming to company policy. These changes did not sit well with employees, particularly Bob Thomas. On hearing of the new management approach, Thomas became irate and announced, "They can't get away with this. I wrote the book around here." But secretly Thomas believed his past conduct was catching up with him, and he became concerned about protecting his job.

One night after work, Thomas called a union organizer of the Brotherhood of Machine Engineers and asked that a union drive begin at Apollo. Within a week employees began handing out flyers announcing a union meeting. When Lipski heard of the organizing campaign and Thomas's leadership in it, she decided to terminate his employment. Thomas's termination paper read: "Discharged for poor work performance and unsatisfactory attendance." Thomas was called into Lipski's office and told of the discharge. After leaving her office, Thomas called the union organizer, and they both went to the regional office of the NLRB to file an unfair labor practice charge on Thomas's behalf. The ULP alleged that he was fired for his support of the union and the organizing drive.

Jean Lipski had little experience with unions in general and no specific experience with union-organizing campaigns. Unfortunately for Lipski, the Brotherhood of Machine Engineers, Local 1463, began an organizing drive against Apollo on June 1. Although the union's initial efforts were confined to passing out flyers about an organizational meeting, by June 10 it was obvious that employee support for the union had grown and union campaigning had greatly intensified. The question faced by Lipski was no longer "Should Apollo do something?" but rather "What should Apollo do?" It was obvious to Lipski that the union was committed to a full-fledged effort to unionize the company's employees. Supervisors reported to her that union supporters were passing out authorization cards in order to petition the NLRB for a certification election.

QUESTIONS

1. What, if any, violation of the law did Apollo Corporation commit?
2. What arguments will Jean Lipski and Bob Thomas use to support their cases?
3. List things that managers should *not* do lest they commit unfair labor practices.

case study 2

The Arbitration Case of Jesse Stansky

At the arbitration hearing, both parties were adamant in their positions. Nancy Huang, HR manager of Phoenix Semiconductor, argued that the grievant, Jesse Stansky, was justly terminated for arguing and hitting a co-worker—a direct violation of company policy and the employee handbook. Stansky argued that he had been a good employee during his ten years of employment.

The submission agreement governing the case read, "It is the employer's position that just cause existed for the discharge of Mr. Jesse Stansky and the penalty was appropriate for the offense committed." Additionally, the employer introduced into evidence the labor agreement, which defined just cause termination as follows:

> Just cause shall serve as the basis for disciplinary action and includes, but is not limited to: dishonesty, inefficiency, unprofessional conduct, failure to report absences, falsification of records, violation of company policy, destruction of property, or possession or being under the influence of alcohol or narcotics.

Stansky was hired as a systems technician on November 20, 1994, a position he held until his termination on October 25, 2004. According to the testimony of Huang, Phoenix Semiconductor strived to maintain a positive and cordial work environment among its employees. Fighting on the job was strictly prohibited. Stansky's performance evaluation showed him to be an average employee, although he had received several disciplinary warnings for poor attendance and one three-day suspension for a "systems control error." Stansky was generally liked by his co-workers, and several testified in his behalf at the arbitration hearing.

The termination of Stansky concerned an altercation between himself and Gary Lindekin, another systems technician. According to witnesses to the incident, both Stansky and Lindekin became visibly upset over the correct way to calibrate a sensitive piece of production equipment. The argument—one witness called it no more than a heated disagreement—lasted approximately three minutes and concluded when Stansky was seen forcefully placing his hand on Lindekin's shoulder. Lindekin took extreme exception to Stansky's behavior and immediately reported the incident to management. After interviews with both Stansky and Lindekin, and those who observed the incident, Huang; Samantha Lowry, the employee's immediate supervisor; and Grant Ginn, department manager, decided that Stansky should be terminated for unprofessional conduct and violation of company policy.

Source: Adapted from an arbitration heard by George W. Bohlander. All names are fictitious.

QUESTIONS

1. Which arguments should be given more weight: those based on company policy, the employee handbook, and the labor agreement, or mitigating factors given by the grievant and his witnesses? Explain.
2. How might unprofessional conduct be defined? Explain.
3. If you were the arbitrator, how would you rule in this case? Explain fully the reasons for your decision.

NOTES AND REFERENCES

1. Bruce E. Kaufman, "Reflections on Six Decades in Industrial Relations: An Interview with John Dunlop," *Industrial and Labor Relations Review* 55, no. 2 (January 2002): 324–48.
2. Aaron Bernstein, "A Breakthrough for Labor," *Business Week* (August 2, 2004): 86.
3. Aaron Bernstein, "Up against the Wal-Mart," *Business Week* (August 2, 2004): 9.
4. Cindy Fazzi, "All You Need to Know about the History of Labor Union Law," *Dispute Resolution Journal* 59, no. 2 (May–June 2004): 87.
5. *Labor-Management Relations Act*, Public Law 101, 80th Cong., 1947.
6. *Annual Report of the National Labor Relations Board—2004 (Washington, DC: U.S. Government Printing Office, 2004), 7.*
7. *Labor-Management Relations Act*, sec. 10(c), as amended.
8. *Annual Report of the National Labor Relations Board*—2004, 11.
9. The NLRB toll-free telephone number is (866) 667-NLRB.
10. Stan Greer and Charles W. Baird, "The Phony Case against Taft-Hartley and the Real One," *Labor Law Journal* 55, no. 1 (Spring 2004): 25.
11. Douglas E. Noll, "A Theory of Mediation," *Dispute Resolution Journal* 56, no. 2 (May–June 2001): 78–84.
12. Ron Collotta, FMCS commissioner, interview by author, Phoenix, Arizona, January 5, 2005.
13. For an expanded model of the labor relations process, see John Dunlop, *Industrial Relations Systems* (New York: Henry Holt, 1958), Chapter 1. This book is a classic in the labor relations field. Also, those interested in labor relations may wish to explore in greater detail the historical developments of the U.S. labor movement. Much can be learned about the current operations of labor organizations and the philosophies of labor officials from labor's historical context. A brief but comprehensive history of labor unions can be found in undergraduate labor-management textbooks such as those listed among these references.
14. Maureen Hannay, "The Unionization of Professionals," *Journal of Labor Research* 23, no. 3 (Summer 2002): 487–98. See also John A. McClendon, Hoyt N. Wheeler, and Roger D. Weikle, "The Individual Decision to Unionize," *Labor Studies Journal* 23, no. 3 (Fall 1998): 34–54.
15. For a pioneering study on why workers unionize, see E. Wight Bakke, "Why Workers Join Unions," *Personnel* 22, no. 7 (July 1947): 3.
16. Kate Bronfenbrenner and Robert Hickey, "Successful Union Organizing in the United States—Clear Lessons, Too Few Examples," *Multinational Monitor* 24, no. 6 (June 2003): 9.
17. William H. Holley, Kenneth M. Jennings, and Roger S. Wolters, *The Labor Relations Process*, 8th ed. (Mason, OH: South-Western, 2005).

18. While most employers will readily negotiate with the union once it is certified as the bargaining representative of employees, other employers will continue to vigorously oppose unionization. This may be accomplished by taking a very aggressive bargaining posture against union demands. NLRB statistics show that unions file a large number of unfair labor practice charges [8(a)(5) violations] when they believe employers illegally hinder the bargaining process.
19. "Declining Unionization: Rising Inequality," *Multinational Monitor* 24, no. 5 (May 2003): 21.
20. Aaron Bernstein, "Can This Man Save Labor?" *Business Week* (September 13, 2004): 83.
21. Richard S. Dunham and Aaron Bernstein, "Dancing with Hardhats: Bush's Strategy Starts to Work," *Business Week* (April 15, 2002): 51.
22. *NLRB v Town and Country Electric, Inc.*, 116 S.Ct. 450 (1995).
23. Cory R. Fine, "Union Salting: Reactions and Rulings since *Town and Country*," *Journal of Labor Research* 23, no. 3 (Summer 2002): 475–85.
24. Jessi Hempel, "Labor Calls in the Feds," *Business Week* (September 27, 2004): 13.
25. Aaron Bernstein, Amy Borrus, and Christopher Palmeri, "Labor Sharpens Its Pension Sword," *Business Week* (November 24, 2003): 62.
26. Arthur B. Shostak, ed., *The CyberUnion Handbook* (Armonk, NY: M. E. Sharpe, 2002).
27. *Annual Report of the National Labor Relations Board—2004* (Washington, DC: U.S. Government Printing Office), 7.
28. Jonathan A. Segal, "Labor Pains for Union-Free Employers," *HRMagazine* 49, no. 3 (March 2004): 113.
29. *Annual Report of the National Labor Relations Board—2004*, 16.
30. Bernstein, "Can This Man Save Labor?," 86.
31. The number of unions associated with the AFL-CIO has steadily declined during the past twenty years. The decline has largely been caused by the mergers of unions through absorptions, amalgamations, or affiliations. Several prominent mergers have seen the merger of the International Ladies Garment Workers Union and the Amalgamated Clothing and Textile Workers Union into the Union of Needletrades, Industrial and Textile Employees; the merger of the Packinghouse and Industrial Workers with the United Food and Commercial Workers; and the merger of the Woodworkers with the Machinists.
32. Statistical information on the AFL-CIO can be obtained at http://www-aflcio.org.
33. George W. Bohlander and G. Ryan Bohlander, "The AFL-CIO Internal Dispute Plan: Public Sector Arbitration Experience," *Journal of Collective Negotiations in the Public Sector* 28, no. 3 (2000): 195–205.
34. George W. Bohlander, "Keeping the Peace: AFL-CIO's Internal Dispute Plan," *Dispute Resolution Journal* 57, no. 1 (February–April 2002): 21–27.
35. Researchers have discussed the erosion of union steward power in contract administration. The loss of power has been attributed to bureaucratization and centralization of labor relations activity within both union and management hierarchies. While no one doubts the influence—positive or negative—that stewards can have on labor-management relations, the shifting power of the steward is important in deciding labor-management controversies.
36. Data obtained from union web pages, January 11, 2005.
37. John A. Fossum, *Labor Relations Development, Structure, Process*, 8th ed. (Homewood, IL: Irwin, 2002). See also Steven Kreisberg, "The Future of Public Sector Unionism in the United States," *Journal of Labor Research* 25, no. 2 (Spring 2004): 223.
38. The two executive orders pertaining to public-sector collective bargaining are EO 10988, signed by President Kennedy in 1962, and EO 11491, issued in 1971 by President Nixon.
39. Jeffery K. Guiler and Jay M. Shafritz, "Dual Personnel Systems—Organized Labor and Civil Service: Side-by-Side in the Public Sector," *Journal of Labor Research* 25, no. 2 (Spring 2004): 199.
40. Kathleen L. Pereles and Edward A. Pereles, "Arbitral Finality: The Current Interpretation of the Public Policy Exception," *Journal of Collective Negotiations in the Public Sector* 30, no. 3 (2003): 223.
41. Fossum, *Labor Relations Development, Structure, Process*, 312.
42. For the original description of attitudinal structuring, see Richard E. Walton and Robert B. McKersie, *A Behavioral Theory of Labor Negotiations* (New York: McGraw-Hill, 1965). This book is considered a classic in the labor relations field.
43. Leigh Thompson, *The Mind and Heart of the Negotiator*, 3rd ed. (Upper Saddle River, NJ: Prentice Hall, 2004).
44. Thomas R. Colosi, "The Principles of Negotiation," *Dispute Resolution Journal* 57, no. 1 (February–April 2002): 28–31.
45. Ross Stagner and Hjalmar Rosen, *Psychology of Union-Management Relations* (Belmont, CA: Wadsworth, 1965): 95–97. This is another classic in the field of labor-management relations.
46. The National Labor Relations Board offers an excellent book on the National Labor Relations Act. This book discusses good-faith bargaining as well as other important legal issues—for example, employers covered by the law, unfair labor practices, and election procedures. See *Basic Guide to the National Labor Relations Act* (Washington, DC: U.S. Government Printing Office, 1997).
47. Nils O. Fonstad, Robert B. McKersie, and Susan C. Eaton, "Interest-Based Negotiations in a Transformed Labor-Management Setting," *Negotiation Journal* 20, no. 1 (January 2004): 5. See also Robert B. McKersie, Susan E. Eaton, and Thomas A. Kochan, "Kaiser Permanente: Using Interest-Based Negotiations to Craft a New Collective Bargaining Agreement," *Negotiation Journal* 20, no. 1 (January 2004): 13.
48. Joe Stanley, interview by author, Phoenix, Arizona, January 5, 2005.
49. The FMCS has a complete and comprehensive program to train labor and management negotiators in the art and techniques of interest-based bargaining (IBB). Information on the

IBB program can be obtained from the FMCS national headquarters at 2100 K Street, N.W., Washington, DC 20427, or from FMCS district offices.

50. *Interest-Based Negotiations: Participants' Guidebook* (Washington, DC: Federal Mediation and Conciliation Service, 1998): 11.
51. "US Airways Group Inc.: Flight Attendants Union Mails Strike-Authorization Ballots," *The Wall Street Journal* (Eastern Edition), November 20, 2004, 1.
52. Bill McDonough, president of United Food and Commercial Workers Union Local 99, interview by author, January 12, 2005, Phoenix, Arizona.
53. Holley, Jennings, and Wolters, *The Labor Relations Process*, 406–408.
54. Bill Coffin, "Labor Lockout Hurts More Than Shipping," *Risk Management* 49, no. 12 (December 2002): 8.
55. Labor agreement, Wabash Fibre Box Company and Paperworkers.
56. Raymond Hogler, Steven Shulman, and Stephan Weiler, "Right-to-Work Laws and Business Environments: An Analysis of State Labor Policy," *Journal of Management Issues* 16, no. 3 (Fall 2004): 289.
57. Right-to-work states are Idaho, Nevada, Wyoming, Utah, Arizona, North Dakota, South Dakota, Nebraska, Kansas, Oklahoma, Texas, Iowa, Arkansas, Louisiana, Mississippi, Tennessee, Alabama, Georgia, Virginia, North Carolina, South Carolina, and Florida.
58. John B. Larocco, "Ambiguities in Labor Union Contracts: Where Do They Come From?" *Dispute Resolution Journal* 59, no. 1 (February–April 2004): 38.
59. *Grievance Guide*, 11th ed. (Washington, DC: BNA Books, 2003).
60. Vera Riggs, Labor-Management Relations Conference, August 11, 2004, Phoenix, Arizona.
61. Peter J. Conodeca, "Ready . . . Set . . . Mediate," *Dispute Resolution Journal* 56, no. 4 (November 2001–January 2002): 32–38.
62. Arbitration awards are not final in all cases. Arbitration awards may be overturned through the judicial process if it can be shown that the arbitrator was prejudiced or failed to render an award based on the essence of the agreement.
63. Statistics are from the U.S. Department of Labor, Bureau of Labor Statistics web site at http://www.bls.gov.
64. Richard D. Kearney, "Patterns of Union Decline and Growth: An Organizational Ecology Perspective," *Journal of Labor Research* 24, no. 4 (Fall 2003): 581. See also Henry S. Farber and Bruce Western, "Accounting for the Decline of Unions in the Private Sector," *Journal of Labor Research* 22, no. 2 (Spring 2001): 459–83.
65. Robert Bussei, "State of the Union: A Century of American Labor," *Industrial and Labor Relations Review* 58, no. 1 (October 2004): 160.
66. Bruce Nissen, "The Role of Labor Education in Transforming a Union toward Organizing Immigrants: A Case Study," *Labor Studies Journal* 27, no. 1 (Spring 2002): 109–27.
67. Ibid., 38.
68. Cora Daniels, "Up against the Wal-Mart," *Fortune* 149, no. 10 (May 17, 2004): 112.
69. Nancy J. King, "Labor Law for Managers of Non-union Employees in Traditional and Cyber Workplaces," *American Business Law Journal* 40, no. 4 (Summer 2003): 827.

ANSWERS TO HIGHLIGHTS IN HRM 1

1. No. Applicants are considered as employees and, as such, are protected under the law.
2. No. Individual questioning of employees about their union membership or activities is unlawful.
3. No. Except in specific situations (for example, to promote safety), employees have the right to wear union insignia.
4. Yes.
5. Yes. Blacklisting of job applicants or employees is against labor law.
6. No. During an organizing drive, an employer cannot promise improvements in wages or benefits as a means of defeating the union.
7. Yes. Both nonunion and union employers are subject to unfair labor practice charges.
8. Yes. When a grievance arbitration clause exists in a labor agreement, management must arbitrate cases that seem baseless.
9. Yes. Employees can be disciplined or discharged for work-related misconduct but not solely because of their union affiliations or union sentiments.
10. Yes. Antiunion remarks are not unlawful, provided they are not coercive.

chapter 15

International Human Resources Management

After studying this chapter, you should be able to

Identify the types of organizational forms used for competing internationally.

Explain the economic, political-legal, and cultural factors in different countries that HR managers need to consider.

Explain how domestic and international HRM differ.

Discuss the staffing process for individuals working internationally.

Identify the unique training needs for international assignees and their employees.

Identify the characteristics of a good international compensation plan.

Reconcile the difficulties of home- and host-country performance appraisals.

Explain how labor relations differ around the world.

When you pick up a newspaper or turn on the TV, you'll notice that stories are constantly being told about companies competing globally. These stories might include mergers of U.S. and international companies, such as Daimler-Benz and Chrysler a few years ago. Or they might highlight companies expanding into other markets, such as Starbucks in Asia or Wal-Mart in Mexico. Or the stories might focus on international companies gaining dominance here in the United States, such as Sony or Toyota. "No matter what kind business you run, no matter what size you are, you're suddenly competing against companies you've never heard of all around the world that make a very similar widget or provide a very similar service," as one global manager put it. In fact, nearly three-quarters of HR professionals from companies large and small in a wide range of industries and countries say they expect their company's international business to grow in the coming years.[1] Some of these companies are handling the challenge well. Others are failing miserably as they try to manage across borders. More often than not, the difference boils down to how people are managed, the adaptability of cultures, and the flexibility of organizations.

Up until this point in the book, we have emphasized HRM practices and systems as they exist in the United States. This is not so much an oversight on our part as it is a deliberate decision to explain the HR practice in the most fundamental manner possible. Nonetheless, the topic of international HRM is so important that we wanted to dedicate an entire chapter to its discussion. In this chapter we will observe that much of what has been discussed throughout this text can be applied to international operations, provided one is sensitive to the requirements of a particular international setting.

USING THE INTERNET

The Society for Human Resource Management Global Forum provides current news updates on issues concerning HRM from around the world. Go to the Student Resources at:

http://bohlander.swlearning.com

The first part of this chapter presents a brief introduction to international business firms. In many important respects, the way a company organizes its international operations influences the type of managerial and human resources issues it faces. In addition, we briefly describe some of the environmental factors that also affect the work of managers in a global setting. Just as with domestic operations, the dimensions of the environment form a context in which HRM decisions are made. A major portion of this chapter deals with the various HR activities involved in the recruitment, selection, development, and compensation of employees who work in an international setting.

Managing across Borders

international corporation A domestic firm that uses its existing capabilities to move into overseas markets

International business operations can take several different forms. A large percentage carry on their international business with only limited facilities and minimal representation in foreign countries. Others, particularly Fortune 500 corporations, have extensive facilities and personnel in various countries of the world. Dell, for example, actually employs more people outside the United States than within it. Managing these resources effectively and integrating their activities to achieve global advantage is a challenge to the leadership of these companies.

Figure 15.1 shows four basic types of organizations and how they differ in the degree to which international activities are separated to respond to the local regions and integrated to achieve global efficiencies. The **international corporation** is essen-

Figure 15.1 Types of Organizations

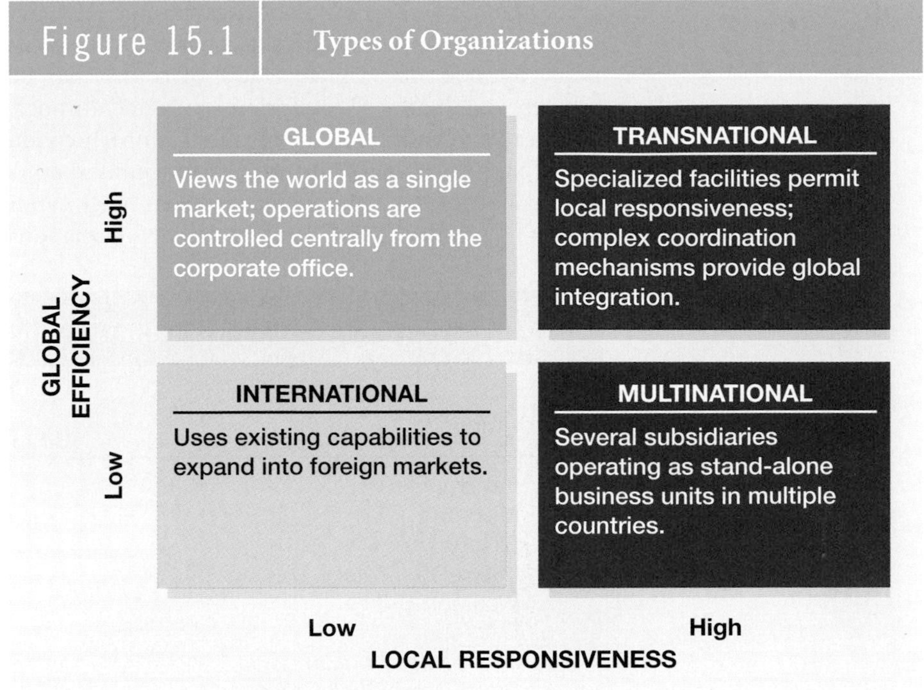

tially a domestic firm that builds on its existing capabilities to penetrate overseas markets. Companies such as Honda, General Electric, and Procter & Gamble used this approach to gain access to Europe—they essentially adapted existing products for overseas markets without changing much else about their normal operations. (One such adaptation, for example, was P&G's extremely successful introduction of a detergent brick used on washboards in India.)

multinational corporation (MNC) A firm with independent business units operating in multiple countries

A **multinational corporation (MNC)** is a more complex form that usually has fully autonomous units operating in multiple countries. Shell, Philips, and ITT are three typical MNCs. These companies have traditionally given their foreign subsidiaries a great deal of latitude to address local issues such as consumer preferences, political pressures, and economic trends in different regions of the world. Frequently these subsidiaries are run as independent companies, without much integration. The **global corporation,** on the other hand, can be viewed as a multinational firm that maintains control of operations back in the home office. Japanese companies, such as Matsushita and NEC, tend to treat the world market as a unified whole and try to combine activities in each country to maximize efficiency on a global scale. These companies operate much like a domestic firm, except that they view the whole world as their marketplace.

global corporation A firm that has integrated worldwide operations through a centralized home office

transnational corporation A firm that attempts to balance local responsiveness and global scale via a network of specialized operating units

Finally, a **transnational corporation** attempts to achieve the local responsiveness of an MNC while also achieving the efficiencies of a global firm. To balance this "global/local" dilemma, a transnational uses a network structure that coordinates specialized facilities positioned around the world. By using this flexible structure, a transnational provides autonomy to independent country operations but brings these separate activities together into an integrated whole. For most companies, the transnational form represents an ideal, rather than a reality. However, companies such as Ford, Unilever, and Shell have made good progress in restructuring operations to function more transnationally.[2]

Although various forms of organization exist, in this chapter we will generally refer to any company that conducts business outside its home country as an international business. The United States, of course, has no monopoly on international business. International enterprises are found throughout the world. A number of European and Pacific Rim companies have been conducting business on an international basis much longer than their U.S. counterparts. The close proximity of European countries, for example, makes them likely candidates for international trade. Figure 15.2 shows a list of some of the top international companies.[3]

Figure 15.2 Top International Companies

	MARKET VALUE (BILLIONS OF U.S. DOLLARS)
1. General Electric	$286.10
2. Microsoft	263.99
3. ExxonMobil	244.93
4. Pfizer	244.89
5. Wal-Mart Stores	232.22
6. Citigroup	210.86
7. Johnson & Johnson	161.36
8. Royal Dutch/Shell Group	158.48
9. BP	153.24
10. AIG	150.97

	SALES (BILLIONS OF U.S. DOLLARS)
1. Wal-Mart Stores	$244.52
2. ExxonMobil	204.51
3. General Motors	184.21
4. Royal Dutch/Shell	179.43
5. BP	178.72
6. Ford Motor	162.59
7. DaimlerChrysler	156.84
8. Toyota Motor	134.23
9. General Electric	131.70
10. Allianz	126.80

	PROFITS (BILLIONS OF U.S. DOLLARS)
1. Citigroup	$15.32
2. General Electric	15.13
3. Altria Group	11.10
4. ExxonMobil	11.01
5. Royal Dutch/Shell	9.42
6. Bank of America	9.25
7. Pfizer	9.18
8. Wal-Mart Stores	8.04
9. Toyota Motor	7.90
10. Microsoft	7.83

Source: Chester Dawson, "The Global 1000," *Business Week*, July 14, 2003, 34.

These companies are in a strong position to affect the world economy in the following ways:

1. Their production and distribution extend beyond national boundaries, making it easier to transfer technology.
2. They have direct investments in many countries.
3. They have a political impact that leads to cooperation among countries and to the breaking down of barriers of nationalism.

How Does the Global Environment Influence Management?

In Chapter 1, we highlighted some of the global trends affecting human resources management. One of the major economic issues we discussed was the creation of free-trade zones within Europe, North America, and the Pacific Rim. Twenty-five member countries now comprise the European Union (EU), whose goal is to facilitate the flow of goods, services, capital, and human resources across national borders in Europe in a manner similar to the way they cross state lines in the United States.[4] A similar transition occurred within North America with the passage of the North American Free Trade Agreement (NAFTA) in 1994. NAFTA created the world's largest free market. Since its passage, commerce between the United States, Canada, and Mexico has nearly tripled, growing twice as fast as U.S. trade with the rest of the world. There has been a great deal of debate about whether NAFTA has cost Americans jobs. Economists don't deny that an estimated 500,000 to 1 million U.S. jobs have been lost, primarily in the manufacturing sector. But this is only part of the picture: The agreement has also resulted in lower product prices for Americans overall, giving them more money to spend, thereby stimulating other parts of the U.S. economy. The net result is that the United States has added an average of 2 million jobs a year since NAFTA's passage—far more than the number it has lost.[5]

USING THE INTERNET

The Outpost Expatriate Network is an online information center for Shell expatriates and their families. Go to the Student Resources at:

http://bohlander.swlearning.com

Like NAFTA, numerous trade agreements, including the Association of Southeast Asian Nations (ASEAN), East Asia Economic Group, Asia-Pacific Economic Cooperation (APEC), and South Asian Association for Regional Cooperation (SAARC), have significantly facilitated trade among Asian countries, making Asia the fastest-growing region in the world. China—its fastest-growing country—has emerged as a dominant trade leader since instituting trade reforms in the late 1970s. In the last decade and a half, China's economy has grown fourfold, drastically altering political and trading relations among nations. Some industry analysts estimate that the country now produces 50 percent of the world's cameras, 30 percent of air conditioners and televisions, 25 percent of washing machines, and 20 percent of refrigerators worldwide. In addition, China's 1.3 billion people represent a massive, largely untapped consumer market for global companies. Today more cars are sold in China than in Europe, for example. Driving this trend are big multinational corporations such as General Electric, Toyota, and Intel, which are building or expanding their manufacturing units in the country. But many smaller firms are heading to China as well. "It's not so much that [companies] want to go East: They feel that they have no choice," said one international HR staffing consultant. "They must be in China. It's not a question of if, but a question of how." In addition to China, India's economy is also growing very quickly.[6]

The fact that international corporations can choose the countries in which they do business or relocate operations generally results in the selection of countries that have the most to offer. In addition to economic factors, political-legal factors are a huge consideration. In many countries, particularly those in Africa, property rights are poorly protected by governments. Whoever has the political power or authority can seize others' property with few or no repercussions. Civil unrest can also lead to the poor enforcement of property rights. This gives companies less incentive to locate factories or invest there. Another issue relates to intellectual property rights—rights related to patents, trademarks, and so forth. Despite the fact that private property rights are now generally enforced in China, intellectual property rights have seen little protection. For example, when General Motors formed a joint venture with a Chinese company to produce and sell a new automobile in the country, a knockoff version of the car could be seen on China's streets even before GM and its partner were able to manufacture their first car. Environmental restrictions also make some countries more attractive to do business in than others.

cultural environment
The communications, religion, values and ideologies, education, and social structure of a country

Beyond the economic and political-legal issues just mentioned, a country's **cultural environment** (communications, religion, values and ideologies, education, and social structure) also has important implications when it comes to a company's decision about when and how to do business there. Because of language and culture similarities, many U.S. companies are finding Canada, Ireland, and the United Kingdom attractive places to locate their facilities, particularly call centers. Eastern Europe has also begun to attract interest because citizens there are well educated and largely possess English-speaking skills. Similarly, the U.S. military's departure from Panama in recent years left that country with a bilingual workforce that is very attuned to the American work culture.[7]

host country
A country in which an international corporation operates

Figure 15.3 summarizes the complexity of the cultural environment in which HR must be managed. Culture is an integrated phenomenon. By recognizing and accommodating taboos, rituals, attitudes toward time, social stratification, kinship systems, and the many other components listed in Figure 15.3, managers stand a better chance of understanding the culture of a **host country**—a country in which an international business operates. Different cultural environments require different approaches to human resources management. Strategies, structures, and management styles that are appropriate in one cultural setting may lead to failure in another. Even in countries that have close language or cultural links, HR practices can be dramatically different. In some countries night shifts are taboo. In other countries employers are expected to provide employees with meals and transportation between home and work. In India, workers generally receive cash bonuses on their wedding anniversaries which with to buy their spouses gifts, and dating allowances are provided to unmarried employees. These are practices that would never occur to American managers and HR practitioners.[8] Throughout this chapter we will discuss several HR issues related to adapting to different cultural environments.

Domestic versus International HRM

International HRM differs from domestic HRM in several ways. In the first place, it necessarily places a greater emphasis on functions and activities such as relocation, orientation, and translation services to help employees adapt to new and different environments outside their own countries and to help newly hired employees in foreign countries adapt to working for companies headquartered outside their borders. In years, past, the internationalization has grown at a faster pace than the interna-

Figure 15.3 Cultural Environment of International Business

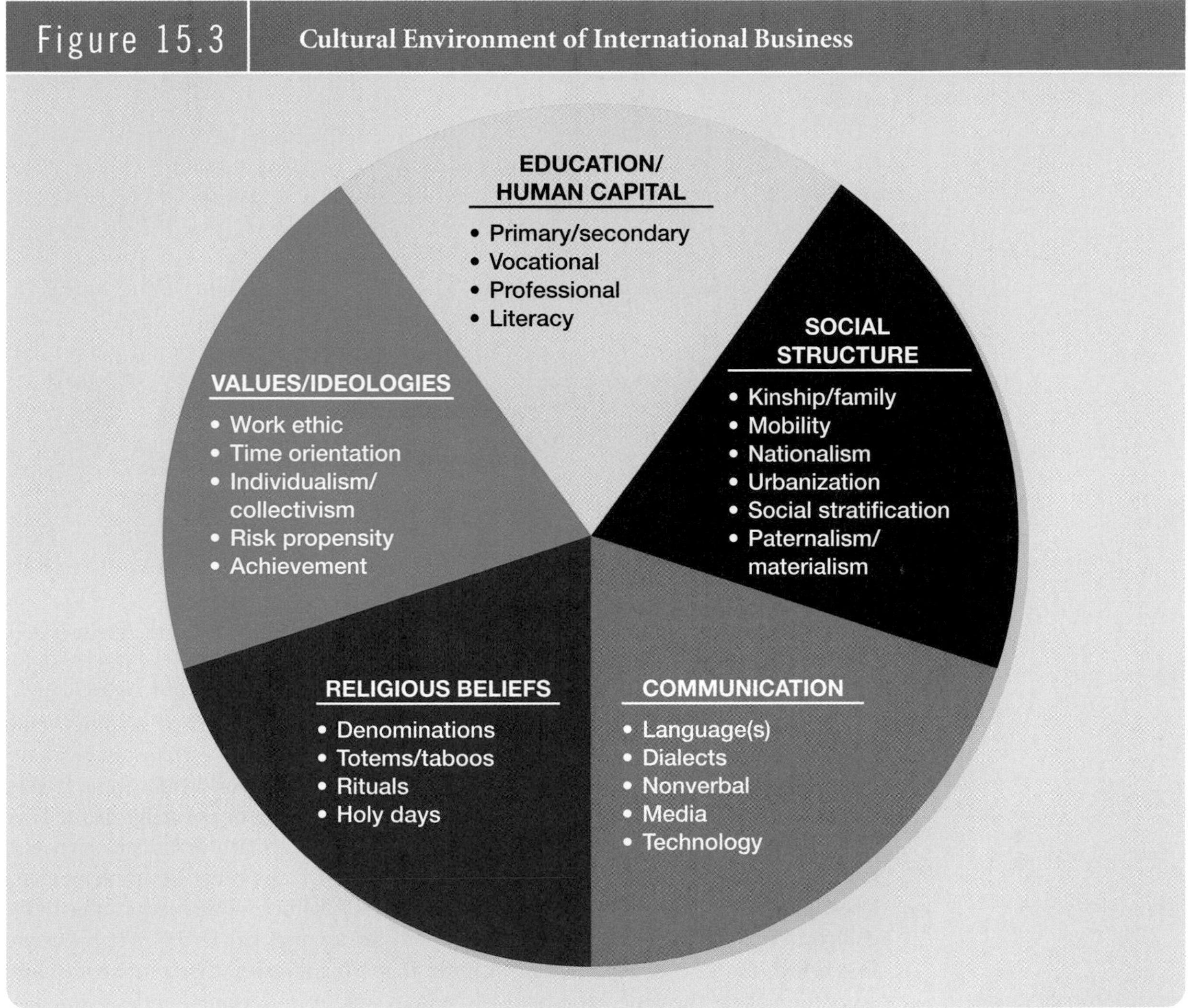

tionalization of the HRM profession, causing executives in the very best of companies to lament that their HR policies have not kept pace with the demands of global competition. But this is changing. Today, global HR management has become a front-and-center issue for a wide variety of firms. Many larger corporations, and even smaller ones doing business in key international markets, now have full-time HR managers devoted solely to assisting with the globalization process. British Airways, for example, has a team of HR directors who travel around the world to help country managers stay updated on international concerns, policies, and programs. Coca-Cola provides support to its army of HR professionals working around the world. A core HR group in the company's Atlanta headquarters holds a two-week HR orientation twice a year for the international HR staff. This program helps international HR practitioners share information about HR philosophies, programs, and policies established either in Coca-Cola's headquarters or in another part of the world that can be successfully adopted by others.[9] Because doing business internationally can be extremely complex, many companies also hire international staffing

Global companies have the challenge of managing operations—and people—in many different countries.

© JEREMY HORNER/CORBIS

firms such as Boston Global Consulting and Cendant Mobility, a Connecticut-based company. These firms have expertise when it comes to relocating employees, establishing operations abroad, and helping with import/export and foreign tax issues.

HR information systems have also come a long way in terms of helping firms improve their international coordination. A good HR information system can facilitate communication, record keeping, and a host of other activities worldwide. Some HRISs are designed to track the whereabouts of employees traveling or on assignment. This can be important in the event of a transportation accident, a natural disaster such as a tsunami, a terrorist attack, or civil strife if evacuation plans must be implemented. Occasionally, however, even the seemingly simplest of cultural differences can be difficult to overcome when a company attempts to set up a global HRIS: When Lucent first rolled out a PeopleSoft system to more than 90 countries, the company's managers found that the order of employees' names was so important—and so varied—that it took two months to settle on a name format allowing employees to be entered into the system. As you can see, even seemingly small cultural differences can create major headaches for the international HR manager.[10]

expatriates, or home-country nationals
Employees from the home country who are on international assignment

International Staffing

When a company expands globally, HR managers are generally responsible for ensuring that operations are staffed. There are three main ways a company can staff a new international operation. First, the company can send people from its home country. These employees are often referred to as **expatriates,** or **home-country nationals.** Second, it can hire **host-country nationals,** natives of the host country, to do the managing. Third, it can hire **third-country nationals,** natives of a country other than the home country or the host country.

host-country nationals
Employees who are natives of the host country

third-country nationals
Employees who are natives of a country other than the home country or the host country

Each of these three sources of overseas workers provides certain advantages and certain disadvantages. Most corporations use all three sources for staffing their multinational operations, although some companies exhibit a distinct bias for one or another of the three sources.[11]

As shown in Figure 15.4, at early stages of international expansion, organizations often send home-country expatriates to establish activities (particularly in less-developed countries) and to work with local governments. This is generally very costly. Expatriate assignments cost companies, on average, $1 million over a three-year period. This can be three to five times what a domestic assignment costs. As result, many companies are taking greater pains to more clearly outline the overall goal of the foreign assignment and its timetable for completion. Ingersoll-Rand, an international equipment maker, now carefully documents in detail what should be accomplished during an assignment abroad—whether the assignment is designed to enhance an assignee's leadership skills, improve productivity and sales targets abroad, transfer specific technology to a foreign operation, or staff it with local, expatriate, or third-country nationals.

In recent years, there has also been a trend to send expatriates on shorter, project-based assignments (two to twelve months versus one to three years) and to shift more quickly toward hiring host-country nationals. This has three main advantages:

1. Hiring local citizens is generally less costly than relocating expatriates.
2. Since local governments usually want good jobs for their citizens, foreign employers may be required to hire locally.
3. Most customers want to do business with companies (and people) they perceive to be local versus foreign.

Because U.S. companies want to be viewed as true international citizens, there has also been a trend away from hiring expatriates to head up operations in foreign countries, especially European countries. ABB, Eli Lilly, and PepsiCo, which have strong regional organizations, tend to replace their U.S. expatriate managers with local managers as quickly as possible. In addition to hiring local managers to head their foreign divisions and plants, more companies are using third-country nationals. Third-country nationals are often multilingual and already acclimated to the host

Figure 15.4 Changes in International Staffing over Time

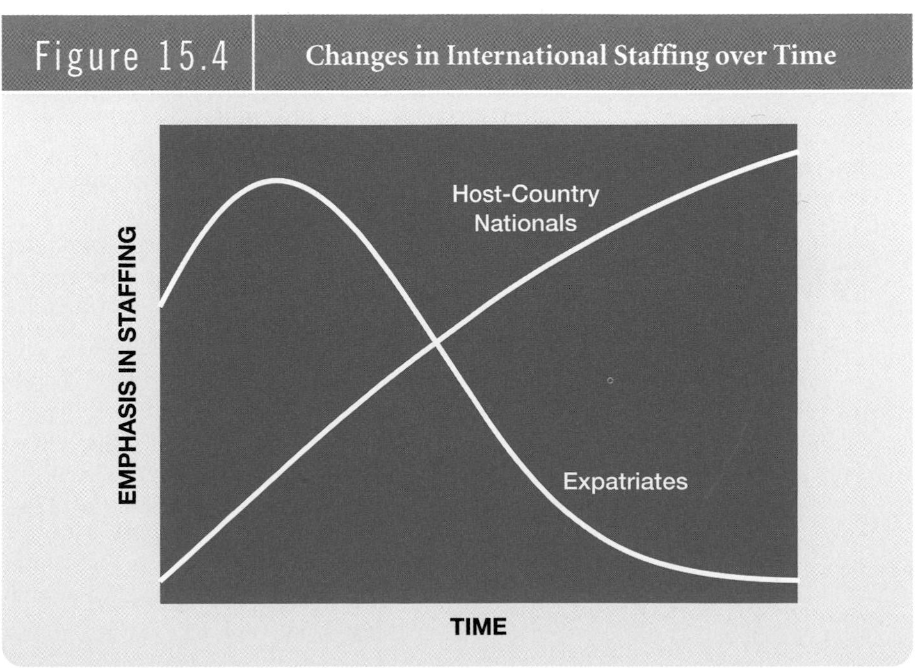

country's culture—perhaps because they live in a nearby region. Thus, they are also less costly to relocate and sometimes better able to cope culturally with the foreign environment.

Companies tend to continue to use expatriates only when a specific set of skills is needed or when individuals in the host country require development. For example, after embarking on a joint venture in China with a formerly state-owned enterprise, Ingersoll-Rand discovered that it had to educate its Chinese employees not only on the company's practices and culture, but also on free-market, Western business practices. This required the company's expatriates to stay in China longer than planned.[12] It's important to note, however, that while top managers may prefer one source of employees over another, the host country may place pressures on them that restrict their choices. Such pressure takes the form of sophisticated government persuasion through administrative or legislative decrees designed to employ host-country individuals. Tax incentives, tariffs, and quotas are frequently implemented by the host country to encourage local hiring.

Recruiting Internationally

Improved telecommunications and travel have made it easier to match up employers and employees of all kinds worldwide. As we mentioned earlier in the chapter, most of Dell's employees work outside the United States. Rolls-Royce, headquartered in the United Kingdom, hires 25 percent of its 25,000 employees abroad. Because its customers come from around the globe, Rolls-Royce figures its workforce should as well. Airbus, the European commercial jet maker, recruits engineers from universities and colleges all over Europe. American-based Boeing's need for engineers is so great that it also recruits internationally and has even opened a design center in Moscow. The trend is likely to continue as the populations in developed countries age and HR managers search for talent elsewhere. Even China, despite its massive population, faces labor shortages because laws there prohibit couples from having more than one child.

HR departments must be particularly responsive to the cultural, political, and legal environments both domestically and abroad when recruiting internationally. Companies such as Starbucks, Levi Strauss, Digital, and Honeywell have made a special effort to create codes of conduct for employees throughout the world to ensure that standards of ethical and legal behavior are known and understood. PepsiCo has taken a similar approach to ensuring that company values are reinforced (even while recognizing the need for adapting to local cultures). The company has four core criteria that are viewed as essential in worldwide recruiting efforts: (1) personal integrity, (2) a drive for results, (3) respect for others, and (4) capability. Zurich, a Swiss financial and insurance company with operations in the United States and Europe, makes sure its inbound U.S. assignees take diversity and sexual harassment courses. This training is rarely provided in other parts of the world.[13]

In general, however, employee recruitment in other countries is subject to more government regulation than it is in the United States. Regulations range from those that cover procedures for recruiting employees to those that govern the employment of foreign labor or require the employment of the physically disabled, war veterans, or displaced people. Many Central American countries, for example, have stringent regulations about the number of foreigners that can be employed as a percentage of the total workforce. Virtually all countries have work permit or visa restrictions that

work permit, or visa A government document granting a foreign individual the right to seek employment

apply to foreigners. A **work permit** or **visa** is a document issued by a government granting authority to a foreign individual to seek employment in that government's country. Since 9/11 there has been a backup in the number of visas granted to foreign workers and students entering the United States. U.S. managers complain that this is making it harder for them to hire top talent. Whatever the employee's destination, HR managers need to ensure that work permits and visas are applied for early in the relocation process.[14]

MNCs tend to use the same kinds of internal and external recruitment sources as in their home countries. At the executive level, companies use search firms such as Korn/Ferry and Heidrick & Struggles in the United States or Spencer Stuart in the U.K. At lower levels more informal approaches tend to be useful. While unskilled labor may be readily available in a developing country, recruitment of skilled workers may be more difficult. Many employers have learned that the best way to find workers in these countries is through referrals and radio announcements because many people lack sufficient reading or writing skills. Other firms use international recruiting firms to find skilled labor abroad. Some countries, in fact, require the employment of locals if adequate numbers of skilled people are available. Specific exceptions are sometimes granted (officially or unofficially) for contrary cases, as for Mexican farm workers in the United States and for Italian, Spanish, Greek, and Turkish workers in Germany and the Benelux countries (Belgium, the Netherlands, and Luxembourg). Foreign workers invited to perform needed labor are usually referred to as **guest workers.** In the United States, a law currently under consideration by Congress would allow foreign farm workers to enter the country and stay for three years, provided they have jobs lined up. Although hiring nonnationals may result in lower direct labor costs for a company, the indirect costs—those related to housing, language training, health services, recruitment, transportation, and so on—can be substantial. Some companies competing in industries with acute talent shortages are nonetheless finding the expenditures worthwhile. Nursing is one such industry. (See the case at the end of the chapter.)[15]

guest workers Foreign workers invited to perform needed labor

Apprenticeships

A major source of trained labor in European nations is apprenticeship training programs (described in Chapter 7). On the whole, apprenticeship training in Europe is superior to that in the United States. In Europe, a dual-track system of education directs a large number of youths into vocational training. The German system of apprenticeship training, one of the best in Europe, provides training for office and shop jobs under a three-way responsibility contract between the apprentice, his or her parents, and the organization. At the conclusion of their training, apprentices can work for any employer but generally receive seniority credit with the training firm if they remain in it. France has been able to draw on its "Grandes Ecoles" for centuries. Created during the Renaissance to fulfill a need that universities weren't meeting at the time, the Grandes Ecoles educate prospective engineers up to the equivalent level of Master of Engineering. Snecma, an international equipment supplier headquartered in Paris, hires about 80 percent of its employees from the Grandes Ecoles.[16]

Staffing Transnational Teams

In addition to focusing on individuals, it is also important to note that companies are increasingly using transnational teams to conduct international business.

transnational teams
Teams composed of members of multiple nationalities working on projects that span multiple countries

Transnational teams are composed of members of multiple nationalities working on projects that span multiple countries. General Electric's LightSpeed VCT, a state-of-the art medical scanner, was designed with input from cardiologists around the world. The machine's innards were designed by GE engineers in four different countries, and the software to run it written by multiple teams working together from India, Israel, France, and Wisconsin.[17] Teams such as these are especially useful for performing tasks that the firm as a whole is not yet structured to accomplish. For example, they may be used to transcend the existing organizational structure to customize a strategy for different geographic regions, transfer technology from one part of the world to another, and communicate between headquarters and subsidiaries in different countries. In GE's case, the company realized its competitors were developing their own medical scanning technology more quickly. GE decided it could no longer afford to duplicate its efforts in different divisions around the world—that these groups would have to work together as a team.

Sometimes companies send employees on temporary assignments abroad as part of transnational teams lasting, say, a few months. This might be done to break down cultural barriers between international divisions or disseminate new ideas and technologies to other regions. In other instances employees are transferred for extended periods of time. Years ago, Fuji sent fifteen of its most experienced engineers from Tokyo to a Xerox facility in Webster, New York. Over a five-year period, the engineers worked with a team of American engineers to develop the "world" copier. The effort led to a joint venture that has lasted for decades. Fuji-Xerox now employs approximately 34,000 people globally at sixty member companies around the world.[18]

The fundamental task in forming a transnational team is assembling the right group of people who can work together effectively to accomplish the goals of the team. For GE's LightSpeed team, this frequently meant holding eight-hour global conference calls encompassing numerous time zones. (The call times were rotated so that no single team had to stay up all night for every call.) Many companies try to build variety into their teams in order to maximize responsiveness to the special needs of different countries. For example, when Heineken formed a transnational team to consolidate its production facilities, it ensured that team members were drawn from each major region within Europe. Team members tended to have specialized skills, and members were added only if they offered some unique skill that added value to the team.

Selecting Employees Internationally

As you might imagine, selection practices vary around the world. In the United States managers tend to emphasize merit, with the best-qualified person getting the job. In other countries, however, firms tend to hire on the basis of family ties, social status, language, and common origin. The candidate who satisfies these criteria may get the job even if otherwise unqualified. Much of this is changing—there has been a growing realization among organizations in other nations that greater attention must be given to hiring those most qualified. In addition to a person's qualifications, various other hiring laws, particularly those related to discrimination, are enforced around the world. Highlights in HRM 1 outlines some of the U.S. and international laws and pacts companies must adhere to when hiring in the United States and elsewhere. Labor union restrictions, which we will discuss later in the chapter, can also have an impact on hiring.

USING THE INTERNET

For an example of HR services concerning expatriate employees that might be purchased by an organization, see Expatriate Essentials. Go to the Student Resources at:

http://bohlander.swlearning.com

Global Laws and Pacts Prohibiting Discrimination

U.S. laws affecting firms conducting business outside the United States:

- Title VII of the Civil Rights Act of 1964
- Age Discrimination in Employment Act (ADEA)
- Americans with Disabilities Act (ADA)

International laws that require nondiscrimination in employment:

- European Union (EU)—Equal Pay Directive
- International Labour Organization (ILO)—Equal Remuneration Convention No. 100
- Organization for Economic Cooperation and Development (OECD)—Guidelines for Multinational Enterprises
- United Nations—Global Compact

Selecting Global Managers

Selecting a global manager depends on a variety of different employment factors, including the extent of contact the manager will have with local citizens and the government and the degree to which the foreign environment differs from the home environment. For example, if the job involves extensive contacts with the community, as with a chief executive officer, this factor should be given appropriate weight. The magnitude of differences between the political, legal, socioeconomic, and cultural systems of the host country and those of the home country should also be assessed.[19]

global manager
A manager equipped to run an international business

Levi Strauss has identified the following six skill categories for the **global manager,** or manager equipped to run an international business:

- Ability to seize strategic opportunities
- Ability to manage highly decentralized organizations
- Awareness of global issues
- Sensitivity to issues of diversity
- Competence in interpersonal relations
- Skill in building community[20]

If a candidate for expatriation is willing to live and work in a foreign environment, an indication of his or her tolerance of cultural differences should be obtained. On the other hand, if local nationals have the technical competence to carry out the job successfully, they should be carefully considered for the job before the firm launches a search (at home) for a candidate to fill the job. As stated previously, most corporations realize the advantages to be gained by staffing international operations with host-country nationals wherever possible.

Selecting home-country and third-country nationals requires that more factors be considered than in selecting host-country nationals. While the latter must of course possess managerial abilities and the necessary technical skills, they have the

Figure 15.5 Comparison of Advantages in Sources of Overseas Managers

HOST-COUNTRY NATIONALS	HOME-COUNTRY NATIONALS (EXPATRIATES)	THIRD-COUNTRY NATIONALS
Less costly	Talent available within company	Broad experience
Preferred by host-country governments	Greater control	International outlook
Intimate knowledge of environment and culture	Company experience	Multilingualism
Language facility	Mobility	
	Experience provided to corporate executives	

advantage of familiarity with the physical and cultural environment and the language of the host country. Figure 15.5 compares the advantages and disadvantages of hiring global managers from these three different groups. The discussion that follows, however, will focus on the selection of expatriate managers from the home country, along with their compensation and performance appraisals.

core skills
Skills considered critical to an employee's success abroad

augmented skills
Skills helpful in facilitating the efforts of expatriate managers

Colgate-Palmolive, Whirlpool, and Dow Chemical have further identified a set of **core skills** that they view as critical for success abroad and a set of **augmented skills** that help facilitate the efforts of expatriate managers. These two types of skills are shown in Highlights in HRM 2. Many of these skills are not significantly different from those required for managerial success at home. Although in years past the average U.S. expatriate manager was an American-born Caucasian, more companies today are seeing the advantages of assigning expatriates depending on their ethnicity. But such a decision needs to be considered carefully. For example, an Indian candidate applying for a position in India may never have actually visited the country or may not relate well to the culture. Ultimately, the candidate best qualified for the job should be sent. Unfortunately, talented women are frequently overlooked for global managerial positions—perhaps because companies believe they will fare poorly in foreign, male-dominated societies or because they believe women have less desire to go abroad. Highlights in HRM 3 show some of the obstacles women face in being selected for an overseas assignment. However, many women who have been given international assignments have performed quite well. Because locals know how unusual it is for a woman to be given a foreign assignment, they frequently assume that the company would not have sent a woman unless she was the very best. In addition, because women expatriates are novel (particularly in managerial positions), they are very visible and distinctive and may even receive special treatment not given to their male colleagues.[21]

Several steps are involved in selecting individuals for an international assignment, and the sequencing of these activities can make a big difference:

Step 1: Begin with self-selection. Employees should begin the process years in advance by thinking about their career goals and interest in international work. By beginning with self-selection, companies can more easily avoid the problems of forcing otherwise promising employees into international assignments where they would be unhappy and unsuccessful. For individuals with families, decisions about reloca-

Highlights in HRM 2

Skills of Expatriate Managers

CORE SKILLS
Experience
Decision making
Resourcefulness
Adaptability
Cultural sensitivity
Team building
Maturity

AUGMENTED SKILLS
Technical skills
Negotiation skills
Strategic thinking
Delegation skills
Change management

tion are more complicated. Employees should seek information to help them predict their chances of success living abroad. Companies such as EDS and Deloitte & Touche give their employees self-selection instruments to help them consider the pros and cons of international assignments. Other companies give these tools to candidates' spouses as well. At Solar Turbines, a San Diego–based manufacturer of industrial gas turbines, a candidate's spouse and sometimes his or her children undergo a day of assessment to see how well they are likely to respond to an international assignment.[22]

Step 2: Create a candidate pool. After employees have self-selected, organizations can build a database of candidates for international assignments. Information in the database might include availability, languages, country preferences, and skills.

Step 3: Assess core skills. From the short list of potential candidates, managers can assess each candidate on technical and managerial readiness relative to the needs of the assignment. Although many factors determine success abroad, the initial focus should be on the requirements of the job.

Highlights in HRM 3

Top Three Barriers for Women Attempting to Gain Global Managerial Experience

- Getting selected—the biggest hurdle to entering the global business arena
- Being perceived as less internationally mobile than men due to work and personal responsibilities
- Lack of mentors and networks on international assignments

Source: Adapted from *Passport to Opportunity: U.S. Women in Global Business* (New York: Catalyst, 2000).

© THE IMAGE BANK/GETTY IMAGES

Expatriate employees receive intensive training on their host countries, the cultural differences, negotiation tactics, business practices, everyday living, and other aspects of working and living successfully in a foreign country.

Step 4: Assess augmented skills and attributes. As shown in Figure 15.6, expatriate selection decisions are typically driven by technical competence as well as professional and international experience. In addition, however, an increasing number of organizations have also begun considering an individual's ability to adapt to different environments. Satisfactory adjustment depends on flexibility, emotional maturity and stability, empathy for the culture, language and communication skills, resourcefulness and initiative, and diplomatic skills.[23]

failure rate
The percentage of expatriates who do not perform satisfactorily

Even companies that believe they have selected the best candidates frequently experience high expatriate **failure rates.** Figure 15.7 shows the major causes of assignment failure. By far, the biggest factor tends to be a spouse's inability to adjust to his or her new surroundings.[24] There are number of ways to improve the success of expatriate assignments. One important step is to involve spouses early on in the process. In addition, training and development for both expatriates and their spouses can have a big impact. We discuss this next.

Training and Development

Although companies try to recruit and select the very best people to send abroad, once they are selected it is often necessary to provide them with some type of training. Not only is this type of training important for expatriate managers, it is also important for the foreign employees they will ultimately supervise. To know and understand how the Japanese or Chinese negotiate contracts or how businesspeople from Latin America view the enforcement of meeting times, for example, can help expatriate managers and their employees deal with each other more successfully. The biggest mistake managers can make is to assume that people are the same every-

Figure 15.6 Expatriate Selection Criteria

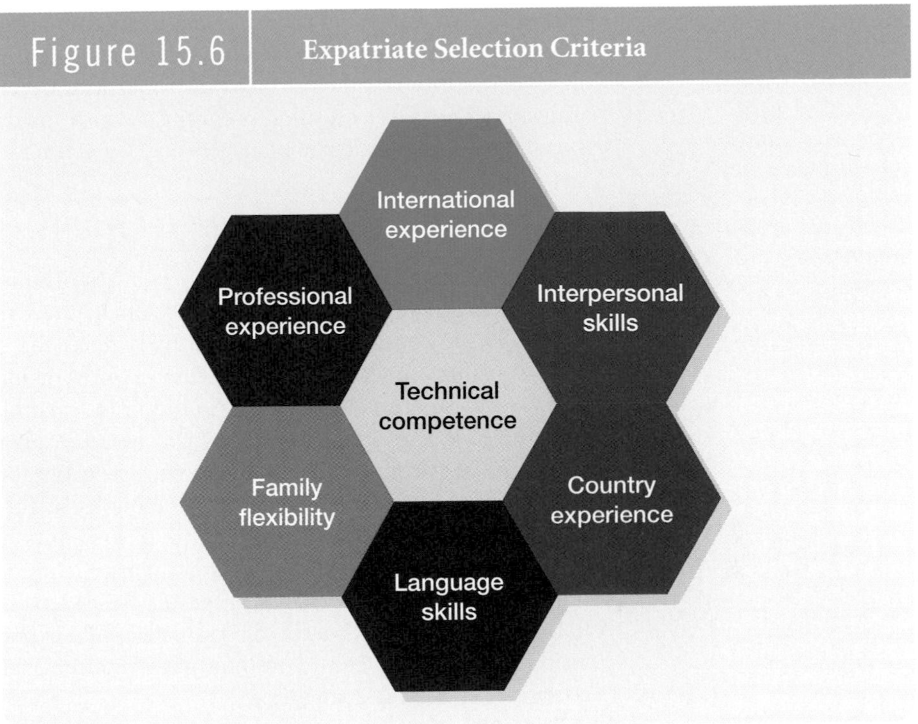

where. Corporations that are serious about succeeding in global business are tackling these problems head-on by providing intensive training. At Motorola this type of training is conducted at divisions worldwide by Motorola University, the company's educational arm. All employees, including division heads, receive forty hours of training each year to learn, in part, how to work together as "Motorola People." [25]

Apart from developing talent for overseas assignments, most companies have found that good training programs also help them attract needed employees from the host countries. In less-developed countries especially, individuals are quite eager to receive the training they need to improve their work skills. One of the greatest contributions that the United States has made to work organizations is in improving the competence of managers. Americans have a facility for analytical reasoning that is part of their lives. They tend to make decisions on a rational basis, giving them a better background for decision making. Foreign nationals have generally welcomed

Figure 15.7 Causes of Expatriate Assignment Failure

- Family adjustment
- Lifestyle issues
- Work adjustment
- Bad selection
- Poor performance
- Other opportunities arise
- Business reasons
- Repatriation issues

the type of training they have received through management development programs offered by American organizations. Increasingly, organizations such as the World Bank, ExxonMobil, and Petroleos de Venezuela are entering into partnerships with university executive education programs to customize the training experiences to the specific needs of expatriate managers and foreign nationals.

Content of Training Programs

Lack of training is one of the principal causes of failure among employees working internationally. Those working internationally need to know as much as possible about (1) the country where they are going, (2) that country's culture, and (3) the history, values, and dynamics of their own organizations. Figure 15.8 gives an overview of what one needs to study for an international assignment. In many cases, the employee and his or her family can obtain a great deal of general information about the host country, including its culture, geography, social and political history, climate, food, and so on, via the Internet, books, lectures, videotapes, and DVDs. The knowledge gained will at least help the participants have a better understanding of their assignments. Sensitivity training can also help expatriates overcome ethnic prejudices they might harbor. The Peace Corps uses sensitivity training supplemented by field experiences. Expatriates can simulate a field experience in sensitivity training by visiting a nearby subculture in their native countries or by actually visiting a foreign country prior to relocating there.

However, at least five essential elements of training and development programs prepare employees for working internationally: (1) language training, (2) cultural training, (3) assessing and tracking career development, (4) managing personal and family life, and (5) repatriation—a final, but critical, step.[26]

Figure 15.8 Preparing for an International Assignment

To prepare for an international assignment, one should become acquainted with the following aspects of the host country:

1. Social and business etiquette
2. History and folklore
3. Current affairs, including relations between the host country and the United States
4. Cultural values and priorities
5. Geography, especially its major cities
6. Sources of pride and great achievements of the culture
7. Religion and the role of religion in daily life
8. Political structure and current players
9. Practical matters such as currency, transportation, time zones, hours of business
10. The language

Language Training

Communication with individuals who have a different language and a different cultural orientation is extremely difficult. Most executives agree that it is among the biggest problems for the foreign business traveler. Unfortunately, only a small percentage of Americans are skilled in a language other than English. But this is changing. Students who plan careers in international business should start instruction in one or more foreign languages as early as possible. Penn State University changed its requirements for all students in business management so that they now include four college semesters of a foreign language. Other programs designed to train participants for international business, such as those offered at the American Graduate School of International Management in Glendale, Arizona, and the Global Management Program at the University of South Carolina, provide intensive training in foreign languages. The top-ranked China Europe International Business School (CEIBS), jointly founded by the Chinese government and the European Union in 1994, also offers language training. Some companies do their own language training. When ARCO Products, a U.S. firm, began exploring potential business opportunities in China, its HR department set up a language training class (with the help of Berlitz International) in conversational Mandarin Chinese. Multinational companies as well as businesses that outsource work abroad stand to benefit from this type of training.

USING THE INTERNET

Thunderbird at the American Graduate School of International Management is devoted solely to the education of college graduates for international careers. Native speakers of English receive thorough training in nine languages. Go to the Student Resources at:

http://bohlander.swlearning.com

Fortunately for most Americans, English is almost universally accepted as the primary language for international business. Particularly when many people from different countries are working together, English is usually the designated language for meetings and formal discourse. Many companies provide instruction in English for those who are required to use English in their jobs. Dow Chemical requires that all employees across the globe be fluent in English so they can communicate more easily with one another. At Volkswagen's Shanghai operation, only after workers pass German-language examinations do they become eligible for further training in Germany. Learning the language is only part of communicating in another culture, though. Even with an interpreter, much is missed. The following list illustrates the complexities of the communication process in international business.

1. In England, to "table" a subject means to put it on the table for present discussion. In the United States, it means to postpone discussion of a subject, perhaps indefinitely.
2. In the United States, information flows to a manager. In cultures in which authority is centralized (such as Europe and South America), the manager must take the initiative to seek out the information.
3. Getting straight to the point is uniquely American. Many Europeans, Arabs, and others resent American directness in communication.
4. In Japan, there are sixteen ways to avoid saying "no."
5. When something is "inconvenient" to the Chinese, it is most likely downright impossible.
6. In most foreign countries, expressions of anger are unacceptable; in some places, public display of anger is taboo.

7. The typical American must learn to treat silences as "communication spaces" and not interrupt them.
8. In general, Americans must learn to avoid gesturing with the hand. A couple of cases in point: When Richard Nixon traveled to Brazil in the 1950s, he waved and gave the "A-OK" sign to the country's citizens. But in Brazil, the gesture is considered obscene and insulting. Similarly, a college sports–related hand signal made by George W. Bush and his family members during his second inauguration shocked Norwegians around the world; in Norway, the gesture is a satanic symbol. Nonverbal communication training can help businesspeople avoid some of these communication pitfalls. Highlights in HRM 4 illustrates that some of our everyday gestures have very different meanings in other cultures.[27]

Cultural Training

Cross-cultural differences represent one of the most elusive aspects of international business. Brazilians tend to perceive Americans as always in a hurry, serious, reserved, and methodical, whereas the Japanese view Americans as relaxed, friendly, and impulsive. Why do these different perceptions exist and how do they affect the way we do business across borders?

Managerial attitudes and behaviors are influenced, in large part, by the society in which managers have received their education and training. Similarly, reactions of employees are the result of cultural conditioning. Each culture has its expectations for the roles of managers and employees. On her first day on the job abroad, one expatriate manager recalls her boss ordering a bottle of wine to split between the two of them at lunch. Although this is a common practice in Britain, the expatriate manager was initially taken aback. Likewise, in what one culture encourages as participative management another might see as managerial incompetence: An American manager in Asia once complained that meetings held in his foreign place of employment accomplished nothing. He was used to arriving at a final decision during meetings. But to his Asian co-workers, meetings were solely a place in which to share ideas. Decisions were to be made only later.[28] Being successful depends on one's ability to understand the way things are normally done and to recognize that changes cannot be made abruptly without considerable resistance, and possibly antagonism, on the part of local nationals.

A wealth of data from cross-cultural studies reveals that nations tend to cluster according to similarities in certain cultural dimensions such as work goals, values, needs, and job attitudes. Using data from eight comprehensive studies of cultural differences, Simcha Ronen and Oded Shenkar have grouped countries into the clusters shown in Figure 15.9.

Ronen and Shenkar point out that while evidence for the grouping of countries into Anglo, Germanic, Nordic, Latin European, and Latin American clusters appears to be quite strong, clusters encompassing the Far Eastern and Arab countries are ill defined and require further research, as do clusters of countries classified as independent. Many areas, such as Africa, have not been studied much at all. It should also be noted that the clusters presented in Figure 15.9 do not include Russia and the former satellites of the Soviet Union. Those countries, if added to the figure, would likely fall between the Near Eastern and Nordic categories. Studying cultural differences can help managers identify and understand work attitudes and motivation in other cultures. When compared with the Japanese, for example, Americans may feel little loyalty to their organizations. In Japan, employees are more likely to feel a

Highlights in HRM 4

Nonverbal Communications in Different Cultures

CALLING A WAITER

In the United States, a common way to call a waiter is to point upward with the forefinger. In Asia, a raised forefinger is used to call a dog or other animal. To get the attention of a Japanese waiter, extend the arm upward, palm down, and flutter the fingers. In Africa, knock on the table. In the Middle East, clap your hands.

INSULTS

In Arab countries, showing the soles of your shoes is an insult. Also, an Arab may insult a person by holding a hand in front of the person's face.

A-OKAY GESTURE

In the United States, using the index finger and the thumb to form an "o" while extending the rest of the fingers is a gesture meaning okay or fine. In Japan, however, the same gesture means money. Nodding your head in agreement if a Japanese uses this sign during your discussion could mean you are expected to give him some cash. And in Brazil the same gesture is considered a seductive sign to a woman and an insult to a man.

EYE CONTACT

In Western and Arab cultures, prolonged eye contact with a person is acceptable. In Japan, on the other hand, holding the gaze of another is considered rude. The Japanese generally focus on a person's neck or tie knot.

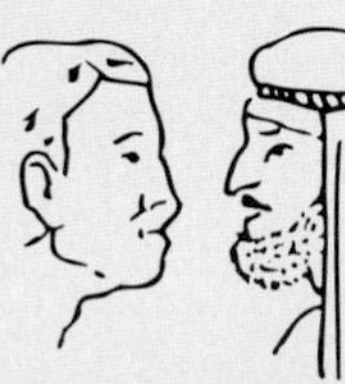

HANDSHAKE AND TOUCHING

In most countries, the handshake is an acceptable form of greeting. In the Middle East and other Islamic countries, however, the left hand is considered the toilet hand and is thought to be unclean. Only the right hand should be used for touching.

SCRATCHING THE HEAD

In most Western countries, scratching the head is interpreted as lack of understanding or noncomprehension. To the Japanese, it indicates anger.

INDICATING "NO"

In most parts of the world, shaking the head left and right is the most common way to say no. But among the Arabs, in parts of Greece, Yugoslavia, Bulgaria, and Turkey, a person says no by tossing the head to the side, sometimes clicking the tongue at the same time. In Japan, no can also be said by moving the right hand back and forth.

AGREEMENT

In addition to saying yes, Africans will hold an open palm perpendicular to the ground and pound it with the other fist to emphasize "agreed." Arabs will clasp their hands together, forefingers pointed outward, to indicate agreement.

Source: S. Hawkins, *International Management* 38, no. 9 (September 1983): 49.

Figure 15.9 A Synthesis of Country Clusters

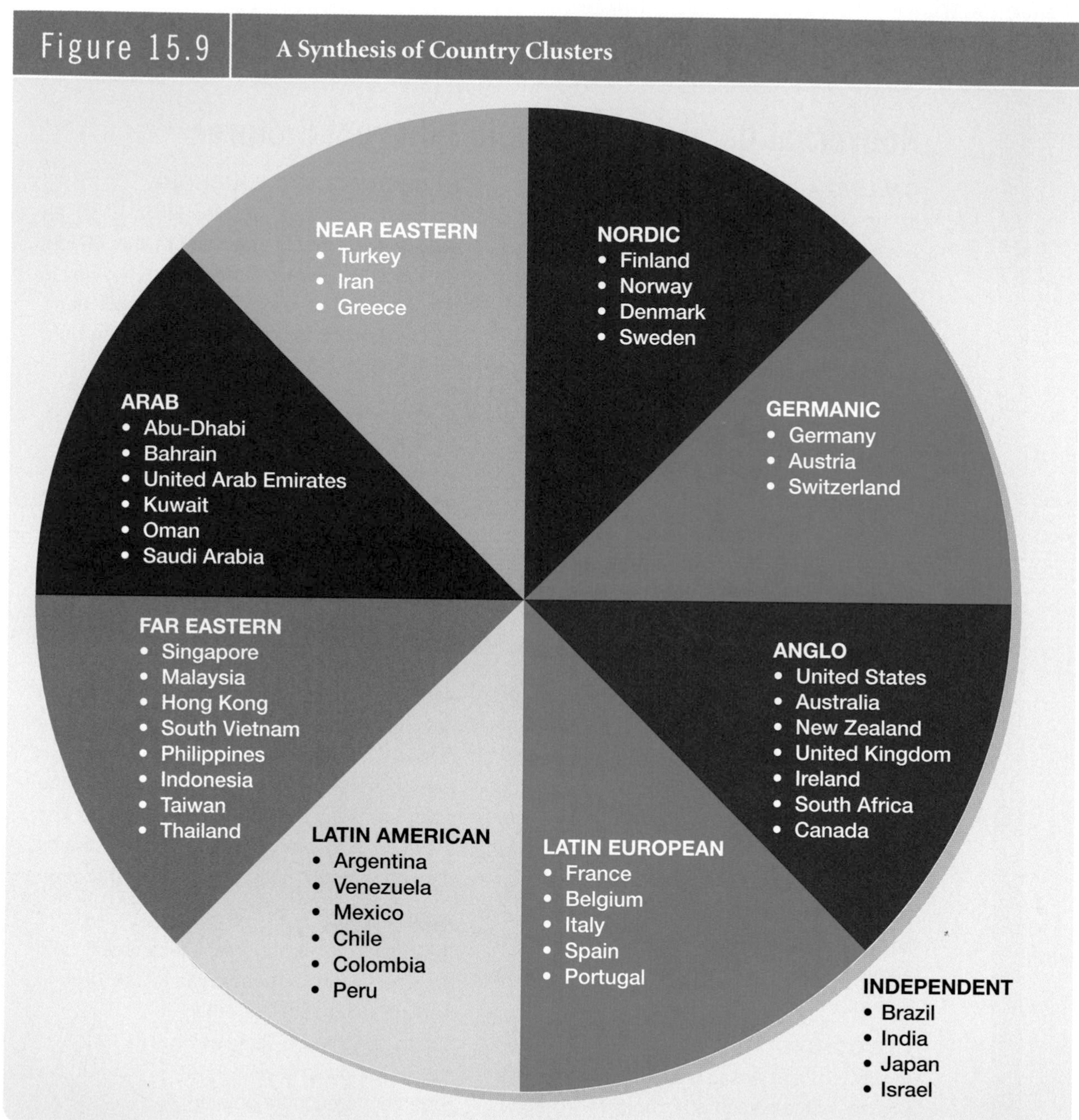

Source: Simcha Ronen and Oded Shenkar, "Clustering Countries on Attitudinal Dimensions: A Review and Synthesis," *Academy of Management Review* 10, no. 3 (July 1985): 435–54. Copyright © 1985 by *Academy of Management Review.* Reprinted with permission of the *Academy of Management Review* via Copyright Clearance Center.

strong loyalty to their company, although this may be changing. Japanese companies no longer universally guarantee an employee a job for life, and layoff decisions are increasingly being made based on merit, not seniority—a practice unthinkable in the country in the past. Latin Americans tend to view themselves as working not only for a particular company but also for an individual manager. Thus managers in Latin

American countries can encourage performance only by using personal influence and working through individual members of a group. In the United States, competition has been the name of the game; in Japan, Taiwan, and other Asian countries, cooperation is more the underlying philosophy.[29]

One of the important dimensions of leadership, whether in international or domestic situations, is the degree to which managers invite employee participation in decision making. While it is difficult to find hard data on employee participation across different countries, careful observers report that American managers are about in the middle on a continuum of autocratic to democratic decision-making styles. Scandinavian and Australian managers also appear to be in the middle. South American and European managers, especially those from France, Germany, and Italy, are toward the autocratic end of the continuum; Japanese managers are at the most participatory end. Because Far Eastern cultures and religions tend to emphasize harmony, group decision making predominates there.[30]

Assessing and Tracking Career Development

International assignments provide some definite developmental and career advantages. For example, working abroad tends to increase a person's responsibilities and influence within the corporation. In addition, it provides a person with a set of experiences that are uniquely beneficial to both the individual and the firm. In this way, international assignments enhance a person's understanding of the global marketplace and offer the opportunity to work on a project important to the organization.[31]

In recent years, U.S. companies have become a virtual melting pot of CEOs: In 2002, foreign-born CEOs filled 57 of the Fortune 500 top slots—a fourfold increase over the previous six years. Coke's Irish-born E. Neville Isdell is one of a growing number of foreign-born chief executive officers at the helm of American companies. Schering-Plough CEO Fred Hassan is from Pakistan. Alcoa boasts a Moroccan CEO, as does Eli Lilly. Figure 15.10 presents a number of other foreign-born CEOs.

Figure 15.10 Selected Foreign-Born Executives

NAME, COMPANY, AND COUNTRY OF ORIGIN
Charles Bell, McDonald's (Australia)
Fernando Aguirre, Chiquita Brands International (Mexico)
Matthew Barrett, Barclays (Canada)
Jean-Pierre Garnier, GlaxoSmithKline (France)
Douglas Daft, Coca-Cola (Australia)
Neville Isdel, Coca-Cola (Ireland)
Sidney Taurel, Eli Lilly (Morocco)
Mahendra Vora, Intelliseek (India)
Carlos Gutierrez, Kellogg (Cuba)
Raj Gupta, Rohm and Haas (India)
Fred Hassan, Schering-Plough (Pakistan)

"Having a foreign perspective gives you an advantage not only for doing business outside the United States but also domestically, where we have the most diverse society in the world," remarked Carlos Gutierrez, who was born in Cuba and is now the CEO of Kellogg in the United States.[32]

To maximize the career benefits of a managerial assignment, a candidate should ask two key questions before accepting a foreign post:

1. Do the organization's senior executives view the firm's international business as a critical part of their operation? Research shows that expatriates with clear goals that truly need to be accomplished are likely to find their assignments more rewarding. Realizing this, fewer companies are sending expatriates abroad for career development purposes only.
2. Within top management, how many executives have a foreign-service assignment in their background, and do they feel it important for one to have overseas experience? Colgate-Palmolive sees a foreign assignment as part of an extended career track rather than as a one-off assignment. A successful foreign assignment tends to lead to another and another. "Our top priority is to identify, develop and retain the next two to three generations of leaders," said one Colgate-Palmolive manager. Part of that strategy includes directly using the knowledge of the company's current and former expatriates.

Managing Personal and Family Life

culture shock Perpetual stress experienced by people who settle overseas

As noted previously, one of the most frequent causes of an employee's failure to complete an international assignment is personal and family stress. **Culture shock**—a disorientation that causes perpetual stress—is experienced by people who settle overseas for extended periods. The stress is caused by hundreds of jarring and disorienting incidents such as being unable to communicate, having trouble getting the telephone to work, being unable to read the street signs, and a myriad of other everyday matters that are no problem at home. Soon minor frustrations become catastrophic events, and one feels helpless and drained, emotionally and physically. Highlights in HRM 5 shows some of the primary sources of stress at different stages of an international assignment, as well as some of the responses that individuals and organizations use to cope with these types of stress.

© PHOTODISC/GETTY IMAGES

For many reasons, women often make very successful expatriates.

In Chapter 5, we observed that more and more employers are assisting two-career couples in finding suitable employment in the same location. To accommodate dual-career partnerships, some employers are providing informal help finding jobs for the spouses of international transferees. However, other companies are establishing more formal programs to assist expatriate couples. These include career- and life-planning counseling, continuing education, intercompany networks to identify job openings in other companies, and job-hunting/fact-finding trips. In some cases, a company may even create a job for the spouse—though this is not widely practiced. The available evidence suggests that while a spouse's career may create some problems initially, in the long run it actually may help ease an expatriate's adjustment process.[33]

Highlights in HRM 5

Stressors and Coping Responses in the Developmental Stages of Expatriate Executives

	PRIMARY RESPONSE	EXECUTIVE COPING RESPONSE	EMPLOYER COPING STAGE STRESSORS
Expatriate selection	Cross-cultural unreadiness.	Engage in self-evaluation.	Encourage expatriate's self- and family evaluation. Perform an assessment of potential and interests.
Assignment acceptance	Unrealistic evaluation of stressors to come. Hurried time frame.	Think of assignment as a growth opportunity rather than an instrument to vertical promotion.	Do not make hard-to-keep promises. Clarify expectations.
Pre- and post-arrival training	Ignorance of cultural differences.	Do not make unwarranted assumptions of cultural competence and cultural rules.	Provide pre-, during, and post-assignment training support-seeking behavior.
Arrival	Cultural shock. Stressor reevaluation. Feelings of lack of fit and differential treatment.	Do not construe identification with the host and parent cultures as mutually exclusive. Seek social support.	Provide post-arrival training. Facilitate integration in expatriate network.
Novice	Cultural blunders or inadequacy of coping responses. Ambiguity owing to inability to decipher meaning of situations.	Observe and study functional value of coping responses among locals. Do not simply replicate responses that worked at home.	Provide follow-up training. Seek advice from locals and expatriate network.
Transitional	Rejection of host or parent culture.	Form and maintain attachments with both cultures.	Promote culturally sensitive policies at host country. Provide Internet access to family and friends at home. Maintain constant communication and periodic visits to parent organization.
Mastery	Frustration with inabiliity to perform boundary spanning role. Bothered by living with a cultural paradox.	Internalize and enjoy identification with both cultures and walking between two cultures.	Reinforce rather than punish dual identification by defining common goals.
Repatriation	Disappointment with unfulfilled expectations. Sense of isolation. Loss of autonomy.	Realistically reevaluate assignment as a personal and professional growth opportunity.	Arrange pre-repatriation briefings and interviews. Schedule post-repatriation support meetings.

Source: J. Sanchez, P. Spector, and C. Cooper, "Adapting to a Boundaryless World: A Developmental Expatriate Model," *Academy of Management Executive* 14, no. 2 (May 2000): 96–106.

Repatriation

repatriation
The process of employee transition home from an international assignment

An increasing number of companies such as Monsanto, 3M, EDS, and Verizon are developing programs specifically designed to facilitate **repatriation**—that is, helping employees make the transition back home. Repatriation programs are designed to prepare employees for adjusting to life at home (which at times can be more difficult than adjusting to a foreign assignment). ExxonMobil employees are given a general idea of what they can expect following a foreign assignment even before they leave home. Unfortunately, not all companies have career development programs designed for repatriating employees. Several studies have found that the majority of companies do not do an effective job of repatriation. Here are some general findings:

1. Only about one-third of companies had a repatriation plan.
2. Another third typically don't begin formal repatriation discussions until two to six months before the end of an expatriate's assignment.
3. The remaining third of companies never engage in a repatriation discussion with their employees.[34]

Employees often lament that their organizations are vague about repatriation, their new roles within the company, and their career progression. In many cases, employees abroad have learned how to run an entire international operation—or at least significant parts of it. When they return home, however, their responsibilities are often significantly diminished. In fact, the evidence suggests that only a fraction of them are actually promoted. It is also not at all uncommon for employees to return home after a few years to find that there is *no* position for them in the firm and that they no longer know anyone who can help them—their longtime colleagues have moved to different departments or even different companies. This frequently leaves the repatriated employee feeling alienated.

USING THE INTERNET

Published by West Virginia University, the *U.S. Expatriate Handbook,* available online, provides extensive information on working and living outside the United States. Go to the Student Resources at:

http://bohlander.swlearning.com

Even when employees are successfully repatriated, their companies often do not fully utilize the knowledge, understanding, and skills developed on their assignments. This hurts the employee, of course, but it also hurts the firm's chances of utilizing the employee's expertise to gain a competitive advantage. Not surprisingly, expatriates frequently leave their companies within a year or two of coming home. Some experts say the number of expatriates who do so is as high as 50 percent.

At companies with good repatriation processes, employees are given guidance about how much the expatriate experience may have changed them and their families. Some firms introduce former expatriates and their spouses to other former expatriates at special social events. And more companies are making an effort to keep in touch with expatriates while they are abroad, which has been made easier by e-mail, instant messaging, and videoconferencing. Colgate's division executives and other corporate staff members frequently visit international transferees. Dow appoints a high-level manager who serves as a stateside contact for information about organizational changes, job opportunities, and anything related to salary and compensation. Monsanto's repatriation program is designed not only to smooth the employee's return to the home organization but also to ensure that the expatriate's knowledge and experience are fully utilized. To do so, returning expatriates get the chance to showcase their new knowledge in debriefing sessions. Some companies also create databases of expatriates to help other employees who go abroad later.[35] A repatriation checklist is shown in Highlights in HRM 6.

Highlights in HRM 6

Repatriation Checklist

Before they go:

- Make sure there is a clear need for the international assignment. Don't send someone abroad unnecessarily. Develop a clear set of objectives and expectations and timeframes in which they should be met.
- Make sure that your selection procedures are valid. Select the employee and also look at and involve the employee's family.
- Provide (or fund) language and cultural training for the employee and the employee's family.
- Offer counseling and career assistance for the spouse.
- Establish career-planning systems that reward international assignments and lead to promotion and knowledge sharing.

While they are away:

- Jointly establish a developmental plan that focuses on the goal to be achieved.
- Tie performance objectives to the achievement of the goal.
- Identify mentors who can be a liaison and support person from home.
- Keep communications open so that the expatriate is aware of job openings and opportunities.
- Arrange for frequent visits back home (for the employee and the family). Make certain they do not lose touch with friends and relatives.

When they come back home:

- Throw a "welcome home" party and arrange for a meeting with other former expatriates.
- Offer counseling to ease the transition.
- Arrange conferences and presentations to make certain that knowledge and skills acquired away from home are identified and disseminated.
- Set up an expatriate database to help other employees who go abroad later.
- Get feedback from the employee and the family about how well the organization handled the repatriation process.

Sources: Adapted from Bennet & Associates, Price Waterhouse, and Charlene Marmer Solomon, "Repatriation Planning Checklist," *Personnel Journal* 14, no. 1 (January 1995): 32; Charlene Marmer Solomon, "Global HR: Repatriation Planning," *Workforce* 2001, special supplement: 22–23.

Compensation

One of the most complex areas of international HRM is compensation. Different countries have different norms for employee compensation. For Americans, while nonfinancial incentives such as prestige, independence, and influence may be motivators, money is likely to be the driving force. Other cultures are more likely to emphasize respect, family, job security, a satisfying personal life, social acceptance, advancement, or power. Since there are many alternatives to money, the rule is to match the reward with the values of the culture. In individualistic cultures, such as the United States, pay plans often focus on individual performance and achievement. However, in collectively oriented cultures such as Japan and Taiwan, pay plans focus more on internal equity and personal needs.[36]

Figure 15.11 shows some of the primary forces shaping global pay strategies. In general, a guiding philosophy for designing pay systems might be "think globally and act locally." That is, executives should normally try to create a pay plan that supports the overall strategic intent of the organization but provides enough flexibility to customize particular policies and programs to meet the needs of employees in specific locations. After a brief discussion of compensation practices for host-country employees and managers, we will focus on the problems of compensating expatriates.

Compensation of Host-Country Employees

As shown in Figure 15.12, hourly wages vary dramatically from country to country, from more than $30 on average in Norway and Germany to just $5–$10 in Taiwan and Portugal and less than a dollar in developing countries. Host-country employees are generally paid on the basis of productivity, time spent on the job, or a combination of these factors. In industrialized countries, pay is generally by the hour; in developing countries, by the day. The piece-rate method is quite common. In some countries, including Japan, seniority is an important element in determining employees' pay rates. When companies commence operations in a foreign country, they usually set their wage rates at or slightly higher than the prevailing wage for local companies. Eventually, though, they are urged to conform to local practices to avoid "upsetting" local compensation practices. In Italy, Japan, and some other countries, it is customary to add semiannual or annual lump-sum payments equal to one or two months' pay. These payments are not considered profit sharing but an integral part of the basic pay package. Profit sharing is legally required for certain categories of industry in Mexico, Peru, Pakistan, India, and Egypt among the developing countries and in France among the industrialized countries. Compensation patterns in Eastern Europe are in flux as these countries make the adjustment to more-capitalistic systems.

Figure 15.11 Forces Driving Global Pay

CULTURAL PREFERENCES
Importance of status
Role of individual vs. organization vs. government
Equality vs. disparity
Achievement vs. relationships

ECONOMIC CONDITIONS
Size of economy
Types of industries, natural resources
Inflation, unemployment
Protectionism vs. open market

PERSONAL PREFERENCES
Attitudes toward risk
Quality of life vs. work
Short- vs. long-term
Competitiveness vs. solidarity

SOCIAL CONSTRAINTS
Income tax rates, social costs
Laws and regulations
Collective bargaining, worker participation
Skills, education of workforce

Source: Steven Gross and Per Wingerup, "Global Pay? Maybe Not Yet!" *Compensation and Benefits Review* 31, no. 4 (July/August 1999): 25–34.

Figure 15.12 **Hourly Wages in Different Countries***

COUNTRY	$/HOUR
Norway	31.55
Germany (former West)	31.25
Switzerland	27.87
Belgium	27.73
Sweden	25.18
United States	21.97
France	21.13
Britain	20.37
Japan	20.09
Australia	20.05
Canada	19.28
Italy	18.35
Spain	14.96
Israel	11.73
Korea	10.28
Portugal	6.23
Taiwan	5.84
Brazil	2.67
Mexico	2.48
China	0.63
Sri Lanka	0.49

*Hourly compensation costs in U.S. dollars for production workers in manufacturing.

Source: U.S. Department of Labor, Bureau of Labor Statistics, November 2004.

Employee benefits can range dramatically from country to country as well. In France, for example, benefits are about 70 percent, compared with around 40 percent in the United States. In contrast to ten vacation days in the United States, workers in the United Kingdom, France, and the Netherlands receive about twenty-five days of paid vacation. Workers in Sweden and Austria receive thirty. Whereas in the United States most benefits are awarded to employees by employers, in other industrialized countries most of them are legislated or ordered by governments. Some of these plans are changing. Defined contribution plans are on the rise, sex equality is becoming important, and stock ownership is being tried.[37]

Because the largest cost for most companies is labor, it plays a prime role in international HR decision making. However, some people believe that companies are overcapitalizing on worldwide compensation differences. Many firms (Nike included) have generated bad press for charging hundreds of dollars for their individual products while the people who make them—sometimes children in developing countries working under terrible conditions—earn only a few cents on the dollar. This has led to international political protests, as we mentioned in Chapter 1, and pressure on firms to exercise greater global social responsibility. As Nike discovered, it's pressure they can't afford not to take seriously. Starbucks clearly takes good corporate citizenship seriously. Among Starbucks' many initiatives is its association with Fair Trade and Conservation International to help farmers in third-world countries get a premium for

USING THE INTERNET

What salary would a manager need to receive to maintain his or her real current income while working in a foreign city? See the international salary calculator. Go to the Student Resources at:

http://bohlander.swlearning.com

the coffee they grow. We will discuss more on the fair treatment of workers in third-world countries toward the end of the chapter.

Compensation of Host-Country Managers

In the past, remuneration of host-country managers has been ruled by local salary levels. However, increased competition among different companies with subsidiaries in the same country has led to a gradual upgrading of host-country managers' salaries. Overall, international firms are moving toward a narrowing of the salary gap between the host-country manager and the expatriate. Unilever, for example, used to leave the compensation arrangements largely to the boss of a region or a big country. Now brand managers in different countries increasingly compare notes, so they see potential discrepancies based on market differences and expatriate assignments. So the company moved from a narrow grading structure to five global work levels. Managers' pay is still based on the country they work in, but there will be regional convergence so that in time there will be a pan-European rate.[38]

Compensation of Expatriate Managers

If the assignment is going to be successful, the expatriate's compensation plan must be competitive, cost-effective, motivating, fair, easy to understand, consistent with international financial management, relatively easy to administer, and simple to communicate. To be effective, an international compensation program must:

1. Provide an incentive to leave the United States
2. Allow for maintaining an American standard of living
3. Provide for security in countries that are politically unstable or present personal dangers
4. Include provisions for good healthcare
5. Take into account the foreign taxes the employee is likely to have to pay (in addition to domestic taxes) and help him or her with tax forms and filing
6. Provide for the education of the employee's children abroad, if necessary
7. Allow for maintaining relationships with family, friends, and business associates via trips home and other communication technologies
8. Facilitate reentry home
9. Be in writing[39]

For short-term assignments, usually those that are project-based, expatriates are frequently given per-diem (per-day) compensation. These managers might reside in hotels and service apartments instead of leasing houses. They are also less likely to bring their family members with them. The assignment becomes more like a commuting assignment in which the expatriate spends the week in the host country and returns home on the weekend.

home-based pay
Pay based on an expatriate's home country's compensation practices

balance-sheet approach
A compensation system designed to match the purchasing power in a person's home country

For longer-term assignments, there are two basic types of compensation systems. The first is **home-based pay,** based on the **balance-sheet approach,** a system designed to equalize the purchasing power of employees at comparable positions living overseas and in the home country and to provide incentives to offset qualitative differences between assignment locations.[40] The balance-sheet approach generally comprises the following steps:

Step 1: Calculate base pay. Begin with the home-based gross income, including bonuses. Deduct taxes, Social Security, and pension contributions.

Step 2: Figure cost-of-living adjustment (COLA). Add a cost-of-living adjustment to the base pay. Typically, companies don't subtract when the international assignment has a lower cost of living. Instead, they allow the expatriate to benefit from the negative differential. Often a housing allowance is added in here as well.

Step 3: Add incentive premiums. General mobility premiums and hardship premiums compensate expatriates for separation from family, friends, and domestic support systems, usually 15 percent of base salary, although in recent years, some companies have reduced this amount. Sometimes incentive premiums are paid for hazardous duty or harsh conditions the expatriate might experience while abroad.

Step 4: Add assistance programs. These additions are often used to cover added costs such as moving and storage, automobile, and education expenses.

The differentials element is intended to correct for the higher costs of overseas goods and services so that in relation to their domestic peers expatriates neither gain purchasing power nor lose it. It involves a myriad of calculations to arrive at a total differential figure, but in general, as we have said, the cost typically runs between three and five times the home-country salary. Fortunately, employers do not have to do extensive research to find comparative data. They typically rely on data published quarterly by the U.S. State Department for use in establishing allowances to compensate American civilian employees for costs and hardships related to assignments abroad. Alternately, they consult international relocation experts to make sure all of the relocation bases are covered. For example, in some countries expatriates are mandated by local law to participate in host-country programs—whether or not their pay packages are home- or host-based. Other countries have negotiated bilateral agreements that allow expatriates to opt out of state-sponsored benefit programs such as Social Security, as long as the expatriates are covered by similar programs in their home countries. The United States currently has bilateral agreements of this type with twenty countries.[41]

host-based pay
Expatriate pay comparable to that earned by employees in a host country

localization
Adapting pay and other compensation benefits to match that of a particular country

The second type of compensation system is **host-based pay.** Companies are under pressure to move expatriates to host-based pay because it is generally less costly. Host-based pay is compensation that is equivalent to that earned by employees in the country where the expatriate is assigned. This process is called **localization.** When an employee is localized, his or her compensation is set on par with local standards and practices. Incentive premiums are generally phased out, and the employee pays only local taxes and falls under the social benefit programs established by the government of the host country. Some companies localize only certain aspects of the pay package or do so gradually over a course of three to five years.

Usually the decision to localize an employee depends on whether he or she will ultimately remain abroad or return home. In many companies the decision depends on whether the employee or the employer is the driving force behind the localization. An expatriate employee with a strong desire to remain in the host country beyond the planned length of assignment (perhaps because he or she married a local or has simply fallen in love with the country), is likely to be more amenable to localization. Localization shouldn't be viewed as a cost-saving panacea, however. There are many countries in which expatriates would refuse to "go local." Forcing an employee to do so can ultimately result in a failed assignment costing the company much more money than it would have saved by localizing him or her.

Another serious issue related to expatriate compensation is medical care. Employees are unlikely to consent to going aboard if they cannot get healthcare comparable to what's available in their home countries. Often U.S.-based plans can't cover expatriate employees or efficiently deal with claims that need to be reimbursed in foreign currency. Drugs prescribed abroad that are not FDA approved can also cause reimbursement problems for U.S. expatriates. One solution is to provide the expatriate with a global health benefits plan such as Cigna International Expatriate Benefit. The Cigna plan covers 200,000 expatriates and their dependents for 700 different international client companies. Another alternative is to transfer the employee to a global employment company that can provide these types of benefits. A global employment company is similar to a PEO (professional employer organization), discussed in Chapter 5. Basically, the employee is transferred to the global employment company, which administers all of his or her benefits as well as those of numerous employees working for other companies. Still another issue is the need to provide expatriates and employee who travel abroad with security. Citigroup hires private drivers for employees doing business in countries such as Mexico—even for employees on extended stays. Archer Daniels Midland uses a travel management company that provides travel security climate information to employees as soon as they book their trips. Companies can also purchase travel-related insurance covering a range of services such as evacuation and disability or travel-related injuries.[42] HR managers are generally responsible for evaluating and implementing these different types of programs.

Performance Appraisal

As we noted earlier, individuals frequently accept international assignments because they know that they can acquire skills and experiences that will make them more valuable to their companies. Frequently, however, it can be difficult for the home office to evaluate the performance of employees working abroad. Even the notion of performance evaluation is indicative of a U.S. management style that focuses on the individual, which can cause problems in Asian countries such as China, Japan, and Korea and Eastern European countries such as Hungary and the Czech Republic. Performance appraisal problems can contribute to failure rates among expatriates and actually derail an individual's career rather than enhance it.[43]

Who Should Appraise Performance?

In many cases, an individual working internationally has at least two allegiances: one to his or her home country (the office that made the assignment) and the other to the host country in which the employee is currently working. Superiors in each location frequently have different information about the employee's performance and may also have very different expectations about what constitutes good performance. For these reasons, the multirater (360-degree) appraisal discussed in Chapter 8 is gaining favor among global firms. There are exceptions, however. Thai workers do not see it as their business to evaluate their bosses, and Thai managers do not think subordinates are in any way qualified to assess them. Before implementing a different appraisal process, HR managers need to understand how the process is likely to be received in the host country.[44]

Home- versus Host-Country Evaluations

Domestic managers are frequently unable to understand expatriate experiences, value them, or accurately measure their contribution to the organization. Geographical distances create communication problems for expatriates and home-country managers, although e-mail, instant messaging, and other HR information systems technologies have begun to help close the gap.[45] Still, local managers with daily contact with the expatriate are more likely to have an accurate picture of his or her performance. Host-country evaluations can sometimes be problematic, though. First, local cultures may influence one's perception of how well an individual is performing. As noted earlier in the chapter, participative decision making may be viewed either positively or negatively, depending on the culture. Such cultural biases may not have any bearing on an individual's true level of effectiveness. In addition, local managers sometimes do not have enough of a perspective on the entire organization to know how well an individual is truly contributing to the firm as a whole.

Given the pros and cons of home-country and host-country evaluations, most observers agree that performance evaluations should try to balance the two sources of appraisal information. Although host-country employees are in a good position to view day-to-day activities, in many cases the individual is still formally tied to the home office. Promotions, pay, and other administrative decisions are connected there, and as a consequence, the written evaluation is usually handled by the home-country manager. Nevertheless, the appraisal should be completed only after vital input has been gained from the host-country manager. As discussed in Chapter 8, multiple sources of appraisal information can be extremely valuable for providing independent points of view—especially if someone is working as part of a team. If there is much concern about cultural bias, it may be possible to have people of the same nationality as the expatriate conduct the appraisal.

Performance Criteria

Because expatriate assignments are so costly, many HR managers are increasingly under pressure to calculate the return on investment of these assignments. What did the firm get for the million dollars it spent to send an expatriate abroad? Has the expatriate achieved the goals set forth in the assignment in the appropriate time frame? Obviously the goals and responsibilities inherent in the job assignment are among the most important criteria used to evaluate an individual's performance, and different goals necessitate measuring different criteria. The Expatriate Technology Forum (ETF), comprising multinational companies such as Philips, Shell, and Heineken, has developed benchmarks and other standards HR professionals can use to calculate ROI. The criteria are tied to the various reasons employees were sent abroad in the first place—whether the goal was to transfer technical skills or best practices, improve a division's financial performance, or develop managerial talent.[46] Figure 15.13 outlines various other initiatives companies can undertake to improve ROI.

The danger with ROI calculations, however, is that there is a temptation to resort to using "easy" criteria such as productivity, profits, and market share to measure an expatriate's performance. These criteria may be valid—but they are still deficient if they do not capture the full range of an expatriate's responsibility. Other, more subtle factors should be considered as well. Leadership development, for example, involves a much longer-term value proposition. In many cases, an expatriate is

Figure 15.13 Boosting ROI of Expatriates

Major initiatives planned to improve assignment return on investment (ROI):

Initiative	%
Better candidate selection	32%
Career-planning skills	26
Communicating objectives	24
Assignment preparation	20
Monitoring program	17
Cross-cultural training	10
Developing or expanding intranet	7
Communication/recognition	6
Web-based cultural training	5
Mandating destination support	4
Other	17

Source: Andrea Poe, "Selection Savvy," *HRMagazine* 47, no. 4 (April 2002): 77–83.

an ambassador for the company, and a significant part of the job is cultivating relationships with citizens of the host country. As we discussed at the beginning of this chapter, an individual's success or failure is affected by a host of technical and personal factors. For example, as one might guess, it is much easier to adjust to similar cultures than to dissimilar ones. An American can usually travel to the United Kingdom or Australia and work with locals almost immediately. Send that same individual to Hungary or Malaysia, and the learning curve is more steep. And the expatriate's adjustment period may be even longer if the company has not yet established a good base of operations in the region. The first individuals transferred to a country have no one to show them the ropes or to explain local customs. Even relatively simple activities such as navigating the rapid-transit system can prove to be problematic. The U.S. State Department and defense forces have developed rating systems that attempt to distinguish the different degrees of difficulty associated with different regional assignments. These difficulty factors need to be considered and built into the appraisal system.[47]

Providing Feedback

Performance feedback in an international setting is clearly a two-way street. Although the home-country and host-country superiors may tell an expatriate how well he or she is doing, it is also important for expatriates to provide feedback regarding the support they are receiving, the obstacles they face, and the suggestions they have about the assignment. More than in almost any other job situation, expatriates are in the very best position to evaluate their own performance.

In addition to ongoing feedback, an expatriate should have a debriefing interview immediately on returning home from an international assignment. These repatriation interviews serve several purposes:

1. They help expatriates reestablish old ties with the home organization and may prove to be important for setting new career paths.
2. The interview can address technical issues related to the job assignment itself.
3. The interview may address general issues regarding the company's overseas commitments, such as how relationships between the home and host countries should be handled.
4. The interview can be very useful for documenting insights an individual has about the region. These insights can then be incorporated into training programs for future expatriates. However, if the learning is not shared, then each new expatriate to a region may have to go through the same cycle of adjustment.[48]

The Labor Environment Worldwide

A country's labor environment plays a large role in international business and HR decisions. As we have said, wages and benefits vary dramatically across the world as do safety, child, and other legal regulations. In many countries, the state's regulation of labor contracts is profound and extensive. Labor unions around the world differ significantly as well. Differences exist not only in the collective bargaining process but also in the political-legal conditions. For example, the EU prohibits discrimination against workers in unions, but in many other countries, including countries in Central America and Asia, labor unions are illegal. China has only one union, the All-China Federation of Trade Unions, an eighty-year-old Communist Party institution that for decades has aligned itself more closely with management than workers. In some countries, only workers at larger firms are allowed to organize.[49]

Union strength depends on many factors, such as the level of employee participation, per capita labor income, mobility between management and labor, homogeneity of labor (racial, religious, social class), and unemployment levels. These and other factors determine how well a union will be able to represent labor effectively. Nearly all of Sweden's workers are organized, giving the unions in this country considerable strength and autonomy. By contrast, in countries with relatively high unemployment, low pay levels, and no union funds with which to support social welfare systems, unions are driven into alliance with other organizations: political party, church, or government. This is in marked contrast to the United States, where the union selected by the majority of employees bargains only with the employer, not with other institutions. By contrast, the unions in many European countries (such as Sweden) have a great deal of political power and are often allied with a particular political party. When employers in these countries deal with unions, they are, in effect, dealing indirectly with governments.

Job Outlook
The supply of teachers is expected to increase during the next ten years in response to reports of improved job prospects, better pay, more teacher involvement in school policy, and greater public interest in education. An option for teachers is to teach English abroad.

Sources: *Occupational Outlook Handbook,* 2004–05 Edition, http://www.bls.gov/oco and http://teflintl.com.

In a number of countries, however, including Japan, Germany, New Zealand, and the United Kingdom, unions have been losing some of their power. Ironically, the power of the unions to gain high wages and enforce rigid labor rules has been blamed for hurting competitiveness, particularly in European countries. Laws make it difficult to fire European employees, so workers are hired only sparingly. Unemployment benefits are very generous, so people tend to remain unemployed for longer rather than seek work. But because companies are increasingly tempted to off-shore jobs to lower-labor-cost countries, unionized workers are beginning to make more concessions. For example, at Bosch in France, union bosses opposed management's plan to lengthen the workweek. But fearful workers overruled the union bosses, voting instead for the longer workweek.[50] As the power of unions declines a bit, the trend has been to demand compensation in other ways—through benefits or through greater participation in company decision making. Various approaches to participation will be discussed later.

Collective Bargaining in Other Countries

We saw in Chapter 14 how the collective bargaining process is typically carried out in companies operating in the United States. When we look at other countries, we find that the process can vary widely, especially with regard to the role of government. Collective bargaining can take place at the firm, local, or national level. In Australia and New Zealand for most of the twentieth century, labor courts had the authority to impose wages and other employment conditions on a broad range of firms (many of which were not even privy to the suits brought before the courts). In the United Kingdom and France, the government intervenes in all aspects of collective bargaining. Government involvement is only natural where parts of industry are nationalized. Also, in countries with heavy nationalization government involvement is more likely to be accepted, even in the nonnationalized companies. At Renault, the French government–owned automobile manufacturer, unions use political pressures in their bargaining with managers, who are essentially government employees. The resulting agreements then set the standards for other firms. This is true in spite of the fact that union membership rates in France have declined dramatically since the 1970s. In developing countries the governments commonly have representatives present during bargaining sessions to ensure that unions with relatively uneducated leaders are not disadvantaged in bargaining with skilled management representatives. Still, in these countries a union may do little more than attempt to increase wages and leave the rest of the employment contract unchanged. In more-developed countries, goals related to other aspects of the employment relationship, such as workweek lengths, safety requirements, and grievance procedures, are more likely to be pursued.

International Labor Organizations

The most active of the international union organizations has been the International Confederation of Free Trade Unions (ICFTU), which has its headquarters in Brussels. The ICFTU is a confederation of 215 national trade union centers, representing 125 million trade union members in 145 countries and territories. Cooperating with the ICFTU are numerous International Trade Secretariats (ITSs), which are really international federations of national trade unions operating in the same or related industries. In addition to the ITSs, the ICFTU also cooperates with the European Trade Union Confederation (ETUC). The ETUC represents 60 million trade unionists from 76 organizations and 11 industry federations in 34 Western, Central and Eastern Europe countries. Another active and influential organization is the International Labour Organization (ILO), a specialized agency of the United Nations created in 1919. The ILO perhaps has had the greatest impact on the rights of workers throughout the world. It promotes the rights of workers to organize, eradication of forced and child labor, and elimination of discrimination. Over the decades, 178 countries have voluntarily committed to nearly 200 international conventions proposed by the ILO. The organization has been effective because it involves nation-states as well as workers and their employers. In recent years, the ILO has redefined its mission based on the "Decent Work Agenda." The Decent Work Agenda promotes the idea that there is an ethical dimension of work. This ethical dimension includes decent homes, food, education, the right to organize, and social programs to protect workers when they are elderly, disabled, or unemployed. Moreover, the agenda pertains to workers worldwide, including the self-employed—a situation common in agricultural-based, developing countries. Given the fact that half of the world's population lives on $2 a day or less, that 250 million children around the world are forced to work, and only 20 percent of people globally are covered by any sort of social insurance programs, these are worthy goals. Some companies, however, oppose the decent pay initiative, believing it promotes unionization.[51]

Labor Participation in Management

In many European countries, provisions for employee representation are established by law. An employer may be legally required to provide for employee representation on safety and hygiene committees, worker councils, or even boards of directors. While their responsibilities vary from country to country, worker councils basically provide a communication channel between employers and workers. The legal codes that set forth the functions of worker councils in France are very detailed. Councils are generally concerned with grievances, problems of individual employees, internal regulations, and matters affecting employee welfare.

codetermination
Representation of labor on the board of directors of a company

A higher form of worker participation in management is found in Germany, where representation of labor on the board of directors of a company is required by law. This arrangement is known as **codetermination** and often by its German word, *Mitbestimmung*. While sometimes puzzling to outsiders, the system is fairly simple: Company shareholders and employees are required to be represented in equal numbers on the supervisory boards of large corporations. Power is generally left with the shareholders, and shareholders are generally assured the chairmanship. Other European countries and Japan either have or are considering minority board participation.[52]

Each of these differences makes managing human resources in an international context more challenging. But the crux of the issue in designing HR systems is not choosing one approach that will meet all the demands of international business. Instead, organizations facing global competition must balance multiple approaches and make their policies flexible enough to accommodate differences across national borders. Throughout this book we have noted that different situations call for different approaches to managing people, and nowhere is this point more clearly evident than in international HRM.

SUMMARY

There are four basic ways to organize for global competition: (1) The international corporation is essentially a domestic firm that has leveraged its existing capabilities to penetrate overseas markets; (2) the multinational corporation has fully autonomous units operating in multiple countries in order to address local issues; (3) the global corporation has a worldview but controls all international operations from its home office; and (4) the transnational corporation uses a network structure to balance global and local concerns.

In addition to economic considerations, political-legal and cultural factors in different parts of the world make some countries more desirable to do business in than others.

International HRM places greater emphasis on a number of responsibilities and functions such as relocation, orientation, and translation services to help employees adapt to a new and different environment outside their own country.

Many factors must be considered in the selection and development of employees. Though hiring host-country nationals or third-country nationals automatically avoids many potential problems, expatriates are preferable, but more costly, in some circumstances. When expatriates are hired, most companies try to minimize their stay. Operations are handed off to host-country nationals as soon as possible.

Once an expatriate is selected, an intensive training and development program is essential to qualify that person and his or her spouse for the assignment. Wherever possible, development should extend beyond information and orientation training to include sensitivity training and field experiences that will enable the manager to understand cultural differences better. Those in charge of the international program should provide the help needed to protect managers from career development risks, reentry problems, and culture shock.

Compensation systems should support the overall strategic intent of the organization but be customized for local conditions. Compensation plans must give expatriates an incentive to leave the United States; meet their standard-of-living, healthcare, and safety needs; provide for the education of their children, if necessary; and facilitate repatriation.

Although home-country managers frequently have formal responsibility for appraising individuals on foreign assignments, they may not be able to fully understand expatriate experiences because geographical distances pose communication problems. Host-country managers may be in the best position to observe day-to-day performance but may be biased by cultural factors and may not have a view of the organization as a whole. To balance the pros and cons of home-country and host-country evaluations, performance evaluations that combine the two sources of appraisal information is one option.

In many European countries—Germany, for one—employee representation is established by law. Organizations typically negotiate the agreement with the union at a national level, frequently with government intervention. In other countries union activity is prohibited or limited to only large companies. European unions have much more political power than many other unions around the world, although their power has declined somewhat, due to globalization forces. The International Confederation of Free Trade Unions (ICFTU), the European Trade Union Confederation (ETUC), and the International Labour Organization (ILO) are among the major worldwide organizations endeavoring to improve the conditions of workers.

KEY TERMS

augmented skills
balance-sheet approach
codetermination
core skills
cultural environment
culture shock
expatriates, or home-country nationals
failure rate
global corporation
global manager
guest workers
home-based pay
host-based pay
host country
host-country nationals
international corporation
localization
multinational corporation (MNC)
repatriation
third-country nationals
transnational corporation
transnational teams
work permit, or visa

DISCUSSION QUESTIONS

1. What major HR issues must be addressed as an organization moves from an international form to a multinational, to a global, and to a transnational form?

2. In recent years we have observed an increase in foreign investment in the United States. What effect are joint ventures, such as those between General Motors and Toyota and Daimler-Benz and Chrysler, having on HRM in the United States?

3. If you were starting now to plan for a career in international HRM, what steps would you take to prepare yourself?

4. Describe the effects that different components of the cultural environment can have on HRM in an international firm.

5. Starbucks is opening new stores abroad every day, it seems. If you were in charge, would you use expatriate managers or host-country nationals to staff the new facilities? Explain your thinking.

6. In what ways are American managers likely to experience difficulties in their relationships with employees in foreign operations? How can these difficulties be minimized?

7. This chapter places considerable emphasis on the role of the spouse in the success of an overseas manager. What other steps should companies take to increase the likelihood of a successful experience for all parties involved?

8. Talk with a foreign student on your campus; ask about his or her experience with culture shock on first arriving in the United States. What did you learn from your discussion?

9. If the cost of living is lower in a foreign country than in the United States, should expatriates be paid less than they would be at home? Explain your position. Who should ultimately decide whether an employee should be localized or not?

10. If grooming a talented individual for a leadership role is an important outcome of a foreign assignment, how can this be worked into a performance appraisal system? How would a manager assess leadership accomplishments?

11. What are the major differences between labor-management relations in Europe and those in the United States?

12. Do you believe that codetermination will ever become popular in the United States? Explain your position.

An American (Expatriate) in Paris

There is often a great deal of work involved in setting up expatriate assignments. The administrative requirements can be far ranging and extend beyond the employee to also include family issues. Suppose you were faced with the following scenario. What would be the most pressing considerations that you would need to address?

The Scenario

You are the head of HR for Sarip International, a consulting firm specializing in hotel and restaurant management. Your firm is opening an office in Paris, France, and Jim Verioti, director of sales and marketing, has been asked to assume responsibilities for the expansion. Jim understands that the expatriate assignment will last two to three years, and although he has traveled to Europe for work on several occasions, this is his first long-term assignment overseas. He has a lot of questions about what he can expect and also some personal constraints.

Jim and his wife Betty have just moved into their new home (their mortgage is around $1,500 per month). In addition, Betty is an elementary school teacher and doesn't really know how the move will affect her job security. Their three children, Veronica (14), Reggie (12), and Archie (10), are of an age at which school considerations are very important. A friend told them about the American School in Paris, and this is a consideration. None of the Veriotis speak French.

Assignment

Working in teams of four to six individuals, put together the package that would allow Jim to move his family to Paris while still maintaining his present lifestyle (his current annual salary is $140,000 plus incentives). Address at least the following issues:

1. Visas and permits
2. Relocation allowance and housing
3. Language and culture training
4. Spousal employment concerns
5. Health/medical/insurance issues
6. Compensation and incentives
7. Education for the children

The following web sites may be helpful to you, but other resources may prove valuable as well.

- U.S. Embassy in Paris (http://www.amb-usa.fr/)
- French Consulates in the United States (http://www.ambafrance-us.org/intheus/consulates.asp)
- Expatica.com (http://www.expatica.com/france.asp)
- Americans in Paris (http://www.americansinfrance.net/)
- The Paris France Guide (http://www.parisfranceguide.com/)
- Easy Expat (http://www.easyexpat.com/en/pa/index_city.htm)
- Center for Disease Control (http://www.cdc.gov/travel/)
- American School in Paris (http://www.asparis.org/about/)
- Medibroker (insurance) (http://www.medibroker.com/homecom.html?id=1js10)
- Access USA (mail) (http://www.myus.com/)
- Travlang (currency calculator) (http://www.travlang.com/money/)

BIZFLIX EXERCISES

Mr. Baseball: Tolerance of Cultural Differences

This chapter emphasized the importance of tolerance of cultural differences for success as an expatriate. Watch this *Mr. Baseball* scene carefully while considering the questions below.

The New York Yankees trade aging baseball player Jack Elliot (Tom Selleck) to the Chunichi Dragons, a Japanese team. This lighthearted comedy traces Elliot's bungling entry into Japanese culture. It exposes his cultural misconceptions, which almost cost him everything—including his new girlfriend, Hiroko Uchiyama (Aya Takanashi). After Elliot slowly begins to understand Japanese culture and Japanese baseball, his teammates finally accept him. This film shows many examples of Japanese culture, especially its love for baseball.

This scene is an edited version of the "Welcome to Japan" sequence that appears early in the film. Jack Elliot arrives at Nogoya International Airport, Tokyo, Japan. Yoji Nishimura (Toshi Shioya) meets him and acts as Jack's interpreter and guide. The film continues after this scene with the unfolding adventure of Jack Elliot playing for the Chunichi Dragons.

What to Watch for and Ask Yourself

- Is Jack Elliot culturally sensitive or culturally insensitive?
- Does he make any cross-cultural errors on his arrival in Japan? If yes, what are they?
- Review the earlier chapter section "Training and Development." What type of training would you recommend for Jack Elliot?

case study 1

How about a 900 Percent Raise?

Registered nurse Carmen Lopez wants a raise—so she's leaving Mexico and moving to California to take a job at Desert Valley Medical, a hospital near Los Angeles, where her income will increase tenfold. "I was making US$500 a month in Mexico, and in the U.S. I will be making between $25 to $28 an hour," Lopez says. Lopez, upon finishing her U.S. nursing exam, will be joining nine other Mexican nurses at Desert Valley Medical.

As U.S. baby boomers—now in their early sixties—age, the number of registered nurses in the United States is not keeping up. The U.S. government forecasts that by 2020 the demand for registered nurses will have increased by 40 percent while number of nurses will have risen by just 6 percent. There are currently 2.2 million working nurses.

Lopez and her colleagues were recruited by MDS Global Medical Staffing in Los Angeles. Roger Viera, co-founder of MDS Global Staffing, says he and his business partner have invested $1 million, and the Mexican government added another $1 million, to open a nurse residency program in Mexico that trains and certifies nurses to work in the United States. "We only recruit qualified nurses. They must have a four year Bachelor of Science degree and four years of work experience," Viera says. MDS expects to recruit from Mexico's twelve nursing schools and from Costa Rica in the near future.

MDS has also recruited Maria de la Cruz Gonzalez, who says she's excited about this opportunity to emigrate with her husband and work as a nurse in the United States. "The hospitals offer us a two-year contract where our nuclear family can come along to live with us in the U.S.," she says. MDS gives the nurses three months of paid rent and transportation, provides placement with client hospitals, and provides training in technology and language. They will be able to work in U.S. hospitals for two years under a North American Free Trade Agreement visa.

Donna Smith, chief nursing officer at Desert Valley Medical, says she is happy to have the Mexican nurses join her staff and believes that they are as qualified as U.S. nurses. But, she says, they will need more technical experience before they can go to work, since technology is different in the hospitals of Mexico. "We will provide them with extra training once they get here," she says.

Source: Condensed from Aisha Belone, "How about a 900 Percent Raise? Mexican Nurses Head North to Cure the Ballooning U.S. Health Care Labor Shortage," *Latin Trade* 12 no. 7 (July 2004): 30.

QUESTIONS

1. Is recruiting nurses abroad a good idea for U.S. hospitals facing worker shortages?
2. Can you think of any cultural problems U.S. hospitals might encounter as a result?
3. What long-term recruiting measures should U.S. hospitals strive for?

case study 2

A "Turnaround" Repatriate Plan: U.S. Company Moves Indian Workers Back Home

In an unusual move, a seriously ailing Dallas software company, i2 Technologies, resettled 209 Indian engineers, programmers, and managers in their South Asian homeland on a voluntary basis to help stem losses as it laid off thousands of other employees. A series of corporate crises led to the mass repatriation back to India beginning in 2001.

Many returnees had worked in Texas, Massachusetts, and California for five to seven years on H-1B visas designed for temporary, highly skilled workers, although about 10 percent had acquired permanent-residency green cards or U.S. citizenship. They found the company's Move to India Program too good to turn down—even if it meant a pay cut of 50 percent or more. None was pressured by management to return, said Gunaranjan "Guna" Pemmaraju, a 30-year-old engineer, who returned home. The returnees, many graduates of India's top technical universities, were confident of finding other U.S. jobs if i2 laid them off and were prepared to "change industries if need be," he asserted.

"When I left America, I actually kissed the ground," Pemmaraju said. "It helped me grow as an individual, and it enriched my thought process." Significantly, though, Pemmaraju says the quality of life in his middle-class Bangalore neighborhood is comparable—with a few minor downsides that he and his wife are willing to accept. Although their pay shrank in dollar terms, the repatriates are relatively better off in India.

"If we were in the top 25 percent in the United States, we're in the top 5 percent here," said one repatriate.

"We may not have 54-inch TV sets, but we have more of a sense of community and belonging here," another added.

Pemmaraju relies on DSL Internet access, fields morning calls from Dallas colleagues on a cell phone, and watches satellite TV while pedaling his new exercise bike. Instead of a Honda Accord, he drives a much smaller Suzuki Zen sedan.

For i2, the wage and benefit savings are helping it edge toward profitability. The company says the savings have been substantial. At its peak, i2 employed 6,349 people, with about 800 in India. It has since scaled down to 2,500 workers, 1,100 of whom are based in Bangalore.

Pemmaraju's family expresses no regrets about returning, yet they retain fond memories of the United States, a country of "milk and honey"—not to mention seven-layer Taco Bell burritos and Krispy Kreme doughnuts. Pemmaraju was tickled by a recent call to a fast-food restaurant in Bangalore: "A guy answered the phone saying, 'Thank you for calling Pizza Hut. Would that be for delivery or carry out?' he said. It's just what they said in Arlington [Texas]!"

Source: Condensed from Barry Shlachter, "Software Firm Resettles Indian Workers in Turnaround Plan," *Fort Worth* (Texas) *Star-Telegram* (via Knight-Ridder/Tribune Business News), June 24, 2004.

QUESTIONS

1. Does repatriation represent a good financial strategy for firms with international employees?
2. Besides cost savings, does i2 have anything to gain by repatriating its Indian employees?
3. What type of repatriation preparation training do you think i2's repatriates should receive before going home?

case study 3

How Deloitte Builds Global Expertise

Although he is based in the medium-sized city of Leon, northwest of Mexico City, Fabian Gomez spends much of his time working with clients who don't speak Spanish. He is an audit partner for the Mexican branch of Deloitte Touche Tohmatsu, a global accounting and business-services organization with 700 offices and 95,000 employees in 140 countries. "A lot of our business is serving Mexican subsidiaries of international companies, and the executives usually come from other places," he says. "Tomorrow, for example, I have a meeting where six of the executives from one company are Americans, and ten from another company are Japanese."

To best serve his clients, Gomez has to reconcile Mexican-style accounting documents and data with U.S. or Japanese standards. He also has to deal with business nuances that are often quite different from his own Mexican cultural roots. "For example, in Mexico, when you meet with clients, you're expected to spend some time talking with them about their families, how their grandfathers and children are doing. That's an important part of the relationship with them. The American style, in contrast, is very direct and to the point. You have to be very conscious of respecting a client's time."

Gomez is well equipped to handle the challenges. He spent eighteen months training and working in New York as a participant in Deloitte's Global Development Program (GDP), an HR curriculum in which promising midcareer employees from throughout the world are assigned to work in other countries. Participants further develop their foreign-language skills, study the business practices and cultures of other countries, and network with people from other countries to broaden their business perspective. "We take great pride in preparing our people to help clients excel in a marketplace without borders," says CEO James E. Copeland, Jr. But the Global Development Program provides more than just a boost to corporate self-esteem. Management views it as a key part of the organization's strategic objective of expanding and integrating its business operations around the world. "The GDP isn't just about learning the accounting practices of another country," says Lynda Spielman, deputy director of deployment. "It's about taking all these promising leaders from different countries and reinforcing the concept that they're in a global organization."

The value of such a program to an international company might seem fairly obvious. Yet when Deloitte management made the decision to focus more strongly on developing its international talent in the late 1990s, the company found itself in an odd dilemma. Graduates of the program could not only help their home-country operations acquire new clients and keep existing ones happy, but also burnish their own credentials and career prospects. Despite such clear advantages, the corporation had difficulty getting people to participate. In 1997, for example, the program managed to attract only 128 participants, barely 1 percent of the organization's vast global workforce. Only 25 out of 140 of the company's international subsidiaries sent participants to other locations or hosted them, and a disproportionate number of employees in the program came from just a few countries, such as the United Kingdom.

Deloitte's corporate HR team saw that it needed to get the Global Development Program off the ground in many more countries, and that it had to sell both employees and executives on the value of participation. HR was tapped to help redesign the program to make it more appealing.

The next phase was to launch an ambitious multimedia internal marketing campaign. The core element was a self-assessment tool artfully designed to help employees from a wide range of cultural backgrounds to decide whether they were good candidates for the program.

Reshaping a Program to Fit Global Needs

When Deloitte's corporate HR team started pondering how to jump-start the organization's international development efforts in 1998, they realized that effective marketing often starts with understanding the audience, and tweaking the product to better serve them.

At the time, Spielman says, the Global Development Program was called the Strategic Career Development Program. The internal promotion efforts emphasized how international experience could help participants rise higher on the career ladder. After corporate HR sought feedback from company operations throughout the world, however, the team saw that the approach wasn't working. Too often, what attracted potential candidates to the program was the opportunity to live in a particular country. They didn't grasp the program's strategic mission and how it related to the Deloitte operation in their home country.

Worse, the executives who headed the organization's far-flung outposts often didn't encourage staff members to participate. They didn't see how allowing valued employees to spend a couple of years working in another country would benefit their own operations. And they weren't always eager to bring in someone from another country and allow him or her to work for important clients just to gain experience—especially if they had to cover the salary cost.

As a result, the company decided to make some small but significant changes. The program was given a new name, carefully chosen to focus on its real mission—helping Deloitte increase its global business capabilities. Instead of simply depending on employees to choose countries that appealed to them, HR coordinators began working with applicants to identify other places in the world that offered experience relevant to work in their own countries. For example, an accountant whose office worked with the Mexican subsidiary of General Motors might be sent to Michigan to provide services to GM headquarters.

"Today, about 25 percent of the participants are placed so that they can work with the same global client in another location," Spielman says. If that isn't feasible, the HR coordinator will look for a country where the employee can work with a client in the same industry as a major client at home. Establishing that sort of tangible linkage between the assignment and home-country needs has helped make the program easier to sell. Additionally, Deloitte sought to encourage its operations in emerging countries to accept placements by agreeing to underwrite the employees' salaries. The company also made the length of the assignment flexible.

To ensure that those improvements registered with the decision makers at Deloitte operations throughout the world, HR put considerable effort into marketing the program to executives as well as potential candidates. "In order to undertake something like this, you need to have your business leaders on board," Spielman says. "There are so many things that can deter them—if they had a bad experience [with an expatriate] four years ago, for example, they're still going to have a memory that you'll need to overcome." To address this problem, HR designed its video and print materials to emphasize the value that the program would provide to the executives. "For example, we found Deloitte clients to talk about the importance of international knowledge and skills," Spielman says. "Those interviews were something that our leaders found very appealing."

Marketing the Program to Employees from Diverse Cultures

Another problem, corporate HR learned, was that good candidates for the program were sometimes deterred by anxiety about leaving their families behind and coping with life in an unfamiliar place.

"In many other parts of the world, life tends to be more collectivist," Spielman says. "People tend to do things together, or else divide the responsibilities. A professional from another country may have great skills on the job, but he may never have turned on a stove or shopped for groceries. I had a forty-year-old Brazilian professional who still lived at home. Despite her accounting skills, she'd never actually managed her own money, because she just turned her paycheck over to her parents." Going from that situation to living alone in an apartment in New York or Detroit can be a difficult experience. An American who takes an international assignment may have to make very different adjustments. "If you're used to watching Monday night football, you have to deal with the fact that they don't have anything like that in Malaysia," Spielman says. According to a 1997 study by the company's Employee Relocation Council, 58 percent of employees on international assignments fail because of an inability to adapt to life in another country.

That's why marketing materials were carefully designed to help employees feel more comfortable with the idea of an international development assignment. The "Experience the World" booklet, for example, included profiles of program participants from Chile, South Africa, Belgium, China, and the United States. "We also tried to balance men and women, married and single people," Spielman says. "We wanted to create a message that everyone could identify with, no matter what country or background that person came from."

To reduce potential candidates' uncertainty, Spielman—who also teaches a class in cross-cultural management at New York University—felt it was crucial to develop a self-assessment tool that would help potential participants evaluate whether they were ready for a developmental placement elsewhere in the world. That wasn't an easy task. "We needed something that would work for everybody, but also would dig deeper. We needed to force people to think introspectively and to be more culturally self-aware, so they could identify the issues that might affect them on an international assignment." Spielman hired an outside consultant to redesign an existing tool, and then made additional modifications to ensure that the tool was culturally neutral. The finished product includes a case study that features a fictional Deloitte employee, Mark Peterson, and his wife, Linda.

Candidates evaluate the Petersons' strengths and weaknesses, a drill that gives them comparative insights into their own real-life situations. Questionnaires and checklists help candidates zero in on their biggest concerns. "They take the questions home and share them with their spouses. Each person takes the test separately, and they compare their answers." The results can be scored numerically, so that the employee can get a more precise indication of whether he or she is a good candidate for the program.

Impressive Results

The results of the program revamping and marketing campaign have been impressive. Since 1997, Deloitte has increased the number of participating countries in the Global Development Program from twenty-five to fifty, and the number of employees has more than doubled, to 288. While it's difficult to separate out the precise economic impact of that improvement, Deloitte executives see it as a factor in the company's 11 percent growth in global revenue in fiscal 2001, to $12.4 billion. But the biggest benefit of successfully promoting the Global Development Program may lie a few years down the road. "Having more people with international training and experience may mean increasing the revenue we get from a client from $20 million to, say, $23 million, because we can handle the client's subsidiary in Mexico," Spielman says. In other cases, the added revenue isn't as important as protecting a larger client relationship. "If you do a bad job on a $50,000 contract in Brazil, you may risk millions of dollars in revenue from the company's parent in the United States."

In Leon, Mexico, the success of the program is seen in management's eagerness to have more participants. "We now have three people with international experience in our office, and we're hoping to add one more each year," Gomez says. "People are very excited about it, because they know that if they have international experience, both they and the company are going to get ahead."

Source: Patrick Kiger, "How Deloitte Builds Global Expertise," *Workforce* 81, no. 6 (June 2002): 62–66. Used with permission of ACC Communications/*Workforce*, Costa Mesa, CA via Copyright Clearance Center.

QUESTIONS

1. What were the goals of Deloitte's Global Development Program?
2. What were the most noteworthy features of the program for career development?
3. What concerns do you have as the company looks toward the future?

NOTES AND REFERENCES

1. Peter Dowling, Denice E. Welch, and Randall S. Schuler, *International Human Resource Management: Managing People in a Multinational Context*, 3rd ed. (Cincinnati, OH: South-Western, 1999); Nancy J. Adler, *International Dimensions of Organizational Behavior* (Cincinnati, OH: South-Western, 1997); J. Michael Geringer, Colette Frayne, and John Milliman, "In Search of 'Best Practices' in International Human Resource Management: Research Design and Methodology," *Human Resource Management* 41, no. 1 (Spring 2002): 5–30; "Cendant Mobility Survey Shows Continued Challenges around Repatriation Management; Focus on Cost Control Also Driving New Approaches to Global Assignments, Say Global Mobility Practitioners," *PR Newswire* (April 28, 2004).
2. Abagail McWilliams, David Van Fleet, and Patrick Wright, "Strategic Management of Human Resources for Global Competitive Advantage," *Journal of Business Strategies* 18, no. 1 (Spring 2001): 1–24.
3. Charles Dawson, "The Global 1000," *Business Week*, no. 3841 (July 14, 2003): 34; Cristina Lindblad, "The Global 1000: The World's Most Valuable Companies," *Business Week*, no. 3791 (July 15, 2002): 58–80.
4. M. F. Wolff, "Innovation and Competitiveness among EU Goals for Knowledge Economy," *Research Technology Management* 44, no. 6 (November/December 2001): 2–6; Tony Emerson, "The Great Walls: The United States and Europe Are Leading the Race to Carve Up the Trading World," *Newsweek*, April 23, 2001, 40. For more information about the European Union online, see the Europa web site at http://europa.eu.int.
5. Kris Axtman, "NAFTA's Shop-Floor Impact; Ten Years Later, The Trade Deal Costs Some U.S. Jobs But Buoys Trade and Efficiency," *Christian Science Monitor*, November 4, 2003, 1; Sarah Schweitzer, "As Jobs Fall, Maine Blames Free Trade; Anti-NAFTA Rhetoric Echoes U.S. Anxiety," *The Boston Globe* (via Knight-Ridder/Tribune Business News), March 28, 2004.
6. Sadanand Dhume, "Just Quit It," *Far Eastern Economic Review* 165, no. 36 (September 12, 2002): 46–50; George Koo, "Fast Lane to China: Companies That Never Thought of Doing Business Overseas Are Now Looking to the Thriving Chinese Economy," *Computer Technology Review* 24, no. 4 (April 2004): 42.
7. Julia Christensen Hughes, "HRM and Universalism: Is There One Best Way?" *International Journal of Contemporary Hospitality Management* 14, no. 5 (2002): 221–28; "What's Keeping HR from Going Global?" *HRFocus* 77, no. 8 (August 2000): 8; "Culture: A Key Ingredient for International HR Success," *HRFocus* 78, no. 7 (July 2001): 1–3.
8. Interested readers can access this journal online at http://www.tandf.co.uk/journals/online/0958-5192.html; Beth McConnell, "Global Forum Speakers to Share Insights on International HR," *HRMagazine* 48, no. 3 (March 2003): 115–17.
9. DeeDee Doke, "Perfect Strangers: Cultural and Linguistic Differences between U.S. and U.K. Workers Necessitate Training for Expatriates," *HRMagazine* 49, no. 12 (December 2004): 62.
10. Readers interested in codes of conduct and other ethical issues pertaining to international business might read the following: Bill Roberts, "Going Global," *HRMagazine* 45, no. 8 (August 2000): 123–28.
11. Carla Joinson, "No Returns," *HRMagazine* 47, no. 11 (November 2002): 70–77; Frank Jossi, "Successful Handoff," *HRMagazine* 47, no. 10 (October 2002): 48–52; Steve Bates, "Study Discovers Patterns in Global Executive Mobility," *HRMagazine* 47, no. 10 (October 2002): 14; Morgan McCall and George Hollenbeck, "Global Fatalities: When International Executives Derail," *Ivey Business Journal* 66, no. 5 (May/June 2002): 74–78; Leslie Gross Klass, "Fed Up with High Costs, Companies Thin the Ranks of Career Expats," *Workforce Management* 83, no. 10 (October 1, 2004): 84.
12. David Lipschultz, "Bosses from Abroad," *Chief Executive* 174 (January 2002): 18–21.
13. Readers interested in codes of conduct and other ethical issues pertaining to international business might read Nadar Asgary and Mark Mitschow, "Toward a Model for International Business Ethics," *Journal of Business Ethics* 36, no. 3 (March 2002): 238–46; Diana Winstanley and Jean Woodall, "The Adolescence of Ethics in Human Resource Management," *Human Resource Management Journal* 10, no. 4 (2000): 45; J. Brooke Hamilton and Stephen Knouse, "Multinational Enterprise Decision Principles for Dealing with Cross-Cultural Ethical Conflicts," *Journal of Business Ethics* 31, no. 1 (May 2001): 77–94; Michael Maynard, "Policing Transnational Commerce: Global Awareness in the Margins of Morality," *Journal of Business Ethics* 30, no. 1 (March 2001): 17–27.
14. "Keeping Out the Wrong People: Tightened Visa Rules Are Slowing the Vital Flow of Professionals into the U.S.," *Business Week*, no. 3902 (October 4, 2004): 90; "Security Delays Hurt U.S. Business," *Legal Times*, August 23, 2004.
15. Anne E. Kornblut, "Bush Cites Political Hurdles in Plan for 'Guest Workers,'" *The New York Times*, March 24, 2005, A6.

16. "Society: Affirmative Action? Oui! At Long Last, France Takes a Page from America in Order to Manage Diversity—and Bring Minorities into Elite Schools," *Newsweek International*, April 12, 2004, 30.
17. Snell et al., "Designing and Supporting Transnational Teams," 147–58; Debra Shapiro, Stacie Furst, Gretchen Spreitzer, and Mary Ann Von Glinow, "Transnational Teams in the Electronic Age: Are Team Identity and High Performance at Risk?" *Journal of Organizational Behavior* 23 (June 2002): 455–67; Claude Philipps, Harold Sirkin, Duane Filtz, and Scott Kirsner, "Time [Zone] Travelers: They Bounce from Beijing to Bangalore at a Moment's Notice," *Fast Company*, no. 85 (August 2004): 60-67.
18. Snell et al., "Designing and Supporting Transnational Teams," 147–58; Leslie Gross Klass, "Fed Up with High Costs, Companies Thin the Ranks of Career Expats," *Workforce Management* 83, no. 10 (October 1, 2004): 84.
19. Andrea Poe, "Selection Savvy," *HRMagazine* 47, no. 4 (April 2002): 77–83; "Exploiting Opportunity: Executives Trade Stories on Challenges of Doing Business in Global Economy," *Business Mexico* 15, no. 2 (February 2005): 54–58.
20. Yehuda Baruch, "No Such Thing as a Global Manager," *Business Horizons* 45, no. 1 (January/February 2002): 36–42.
21. Sheree R. Curry, "Offshoring Swells Ranks of 'Returnees' Working Back in Their Native Countries," *Workforce Management* 84, no. 2 (February 1, 2005): 59; Margaret Linehan and Hugh Scullion, "Selection, Training, and Development for Female International Executives," *Career Development International* 6, no. 6 (2001): 318–23; Nancy Lockwood, "The Glass Ceiling: Domestic and International Perspectives," *HRMagazine* 49, no. 6 (June 2004): S1–11.
22. Nancy Wong, "Mark Your Calendar! Important Tasks for International HR," *Workforce* 79, no. 4 (April 2000): 72–74; Robert O'Connor, "Plug the Expat Knowledge Drain," *HRMagazine* 47, no. 10 (October 2002): 101–107; Andrea Graf and Lynn K. Harland, "Expatriate Selection: Evaluating the Discriminant, Convergent, and Predictive Validity of Five Measures of Interpersonal and Intercultural Competence," *Journal of Leadership & Organizational Studies* 11, no. 2 (Winter 2005): 46–63.
23. McCall and Hollenbeck, "Global Fatalities: When International Executives Derail," 74–78; Poe, "Selection Savvy," 77–83; Juan Sanchez, Paul Spector, and Cary Cooper, "Adapting to a Boundaryless World: A Developmental Expatriate Model," *Academy of Management Executive* 14, no. 2 (May 2000): 96–106; Eric Krell, "Evaluating Returns on Expatriates: Though Difficult to Ascertain, Measuring the Return on the Cost of Expatriate Assignments Is Necessary to Justify the Expensive Investment," *HRMagazine* (March 2005): 12.
24. Riki Takeuchi, Seokhwa Yun, and Paul Tesluk, "An Examination of Crossover and Spillover Effects of Spousal and Expatriate Cross-Cultural Adjustment on Expatriate Outcomes," *Journal of Applied Psychology* 87, no. 4 (August 2002): 655–66; Poe, "Selection Savvy," 77–83; Talya Bauer and Sully Taylor, "When Managing Expatriate Adjustment, Don't Forget the Spouse," *Academy of Management Executive* 15, no. 4 (November 2001): 135–37; Iris I. Varner and Teresa M. Palmer, "Role of Cultural Self-Knowledge in Successful Expatriation," *Singapore Management Review* 27, no. 1 (January–June 2005): 1–25.
25. "Motorola to Increase Operations in China," *The New York Times*, November 8, 2001, C4; Peter J. Buckley, Jeremy Clegg, and Hui Tan, "Knowledge Transfer to China: Policy Lessons from Foreign Affiliates," *Transnational Corporations* 13, no. 1 (April 2004): 31–73.
26. Lionel Laroche, John Bing, and Catherine Mercer Bing, "Beyond Translation," *Training & Development* 54, no. 12 (December 2000): 72–73; Sabrina Hicks, "Successful Global Training," *Training & Development* 54, no. 5 (May 2000): 95.
27. Managers who are interested in setting up a language-training program or who wish to evaluate commercially available language-training programs should consult the "Standard Guide for Use-Oriented Foreign Language Instruction." The seven-page guide is put out by the American Society for Testing and Materials (ASTM), (610) 832-9585, http://www. astm.org. See also "Why Top Executives Are Participating in CEIBS and IESE's Joint Global Management Programme," *PR Newswire*, July 19, 2004.
28. Jared Wade, "The Pitfalls of Cross-Cultural Business," *Risk Management* 51, no. 3 (March 2004): 38–43.
29. Vipin Gupta, Paul Hanges, and Peter Dorman, "Cultural Clusters: Methodology and Findings," *Journal of World Business* 37, no. 1 (Spring 2002): 11–15; Jane Terpstra-Yong and David Ralston, "Moving toward a Global Understanding of Upward Influence Strategies: An Asian Perspective with Directions for Cross-Cultural Research," *Asia Pacific Journal of Management* 19, no. 2 (August 2002): 373–404.
30. Ping Ping Fu et al., "The Impact of Societal Cultural Values and Individual Social Beliefs on the Perceived Effectiveness of Managerial Influence Strategies: A Meso Approach," *Journal of International Business Studies* 35, no. 4 (July 2004): 33; Geert Hofstede, *Culture's Consequences: Comparing Values, Behaviors, Institutions, and Organizations across Nations* (Thousand Oaks, CA: Sage, 2001).
31. Lisa Bohannon, "Going Global," *Career World* 29, no. 6 (April/May 2001): 28–30; Aimin Yan, Guorgong Zhu, and Douglas T. Hall, "International Assignments for Career Building: A Model of Agency Relationships and Psychological Contracts," *Academy of Management Review* 27, no. 3 (July 2002): 373–91; Justin Martin, "The Global CEO: Overseas Experience Is Becoming a Must on Top Executives' Resumes, According to This Year's Route to the Top," *Chief Executive* no. 195 (January–February 2004): 24–31.
32. David Lipschultz, "Bosses from Abroad," *Chief Executive* 174 (January 2002): 18–21; Denis Lyons and Spencer Stuart, "International CEOs on the Rise," *Chief Executive* 152 (February 2000): 51–53; U.S. Companies with Foreign-Born Executives," *Workforce Management* 83, no. 7 (July 1, 2004): 23.
33. "Prudential Relocation Survey Finds Spouses' Experiences a Key Factor in the Success of International Work Assignments," *Canadian Corporate News*, December 7, 2004.
34. "Plug the Expat Knowledge Drain," 101–107; Charlene Marmer Solomon, "Global HR: Repatriation Planning," *Workforce* 2001,

special supplement: 22–23; Leslie Gross Klaff, "The Right Way to Bring Expats Home," *Workforce* 81, no. 7 (July 2002): 40–44; Avan Jassawalla, Traci Connolly, and Lindsay Slojkowski, "Issues of Effective Repatriation: A Model and Managerial Implications," *SAM Advanced Management Journal* 69, no. 2 (Spring 2004): 38–47.

35. Mila Lazarova and Paula Caligiuri, "Retaining Repatriates: The Role of Organizational Support Practices," *Journal of World Business* 36, no. 4 (Winter 2001): 389–401; "Expatriate Administration: New Realities and HR Challenges," *Employee Benefit News* (March 1, 2005) pITEM05090007; "For Those Working Abroad, Moving Home Can Be Jarring," *The Kansas City (Missouri) Star* (via Knight-Ridder/Tribune Business News), February 22, 2005.
36. Calvin Reynolds, *Guide to Global Compensation and Benefits* (New York: Harcourt, 2001); Gary Parker, "Establishing Remuneration Practices across Culturally Diverse Environments," *Compensation & Benefits Management* 17, no. 2 (Spring 2001): 23–27; Timothy Dwyer, "Localization's Hidden Costs," *HRMagazine* 49, no. 6 (June 2004): 135–141.
37. Caroline Fisher, "Reward Strategy Linked to Financial Success: Europe," *Benefits & Compensation International* 32, no. 2 (September 2002): 34–35; "Comparative Analysis of Remuneration: Europe," *Benefits & Compensation International* 31, no. 10 (June 2002): 27–28; Fay Hansen, "Currents in Compensation and Benefits: International Trends," *Compensation and Benefits Review* 34, no. 2 (March/April 2002): 20–21.
38. Chao Chen, Jaepil Choi, and Shu-Cheng Chi, "Making Justice Sense of Local-Expatriate Compensation Disparity: Mitigation by Local Referents, Ideological Explanations, and Interpersonal Sensitivity in China-Foreign Joint Ventures," *Academy of Management Journal* 45, no. 4 (August 2002): 807–17.
39. Patricia Zingheim and Jay Schuster, "How You Pay Is What You Get," *Across the Board* 38, no. 5 (September/October 2001): 41–44; "Benefits for Expatriate Employees: International," *Benefits & Compensation International* 31, no. 10 (June 2002): 26–27; Steven P. Nurney, "The Long and Short of It: When Transitioning from a Short-Term to a Long-Term Expatriate Assignment, Consider the Financial Implications," *HRMagazine* 50, no. 3 (March 2005): 91–95.
40. Stephan Kolbe, "Putting Together an Expat Package: As More and More Companies Adopt an International Outlook, They Are Increasingly Sending Staff on Overseas Assignments—Usually Involving a Complex Relocation Package," *International Money Marketing* (September 2004): 33.
41. The U.S. State Department Index of Living Costs Abroad can be found on the Web at http://www.state.gov/travel/.
42. Barbara Hanrehan and Donald R. Bentivoglio. "Safe Haven: Accommodating the Needs of Employees and Families in Hostile Environments Can Increase Expenses and Alter Tax Liability," *HRMagazine* 47, no. 2 (February 2002): 52–54.
43. Paul Hempel, "Differences between Chinese and Western Managerial Views of Performance," *Personnel Review* 30, no. 2 (2001): 203–15.
44. "Cross-Cultural Lessons in Leadership: Data from a Decade-Long Research Project Puts Advice to Managers in Context, Country by Country," *MIT Sloan Management Review* 45, no. 1 (Fall 2003): 5–7.
45. Paula Caligiuri, "The Big Five Personality Characteristics as Predictors of Expatriate's Desire to Terminate the Assignment and Supervisor-Rated Performance," *Personnel Psychology* 53, no. 1 (Spring 2000): 67–88; Calvin Reynolds, "Global Compensation and Benefits in Transition," *Compensation and Benefits Review* 32, no. 1 (January/February 2000): 28–38; Charlene Marmer Solomon, "The World Stops Shrinking," *Workforce* 79, no. 1 (January 2000): 48–51; Stephenie Overman, "Mentors without Borders: Global Mentors Can Give Employees a Different Perspective on Business Matters," *HRMagazine* 49, no. 3 (March 2004): 83–87.
46. Frank Jossi, "Successful Handoff," *HRMagazine* 47, no. 10 (October 2002): 48–52; Paula Caligiuri and David Day, "Effects of Self-Monitoring on Technical, Contextual, and Assignment-Specific Performance," *Group & Organization Management* 25, no. 2 (June 2000): 154–74.
47. Mendenhall and Oddou, eds., *Readings and Cases.*
48. Ariane Berthoin, "Expatriates' Contributions to Organizational Learning," *Journal of General Management* 26, no. 4 (Summer 2001): 62–84; Peter J. Buckley, Jeremy Clegg, and Hui Tan, "Knowledge Transfer to China: Policy Lessons from Foreign Affiliates," *Transnational Corporations* 13, no. 1 (April 2004): 31–73.
49. Bernhard Ebbinghaus and Jelle Visser, *The Societies of Europe: Trade Unions in Western Europe since 1945* (London, England: Palgrave Macmillan, 2000); John Pencavel, "Unionism Viewed Internationally," *Journal of Labor Research* 26, no. 1 (Winter 2005): 65–98.
50. Christopher Rhoads, "Germany Faces Storm over Tech Staffing—Labor Groups Are Enraged by Proposal to Import Badly Needed Workers," *The Wall Street Journal,* March 7, 2000, A23; "European Workplaces Tighten Policies as Countries Struggle to Compete Worldwide," *Pittsburgh (Pennsylvania) Post-Gazette* (via Knight-Ridder/Tribune Business News), November 28, 2004.
51. Dharam Gahi, "Decent Work: Universality and Diversity" (discussion paper, International Institute for Labour Studies 2005), 1–22; Jean-Michael Servais, "Globalization and Decent Work Policy: Reflections upon a New Legal Approach," *International Labour Review* 143, no. 1–2 (Spring–Summer 2004): 104–108; "Philosophical and Spiritual Perspectives on Decent Work," *International Labour Review* 143, no. 3 (Autumn 2004): 290–292. Interested readers can find more information about international trade unions by checking out the web sites of the ICFTU (http://www.icftu.org) and the ILO (http://www.ilo.org).
52. Dirk Kolvenbach and Ute Spiegel, "The Reform of the Works Council Constitution Act in Germany and Its Effects on the Co-Determination Rights of the Works Council," *International Financial Law Review* (2001): 59–65; Pencavel, "Unionism Viewed Internationally," 65–98.

chapter

Creating High-Performance Work Systems

After studying this chapter, you should be able to

Discuss the underlying principles of high-performance work systems.

Identify the components that make up a high-performance work system.

Describe how the components fit together and support strategy.

Recommend processes for implementing high-performance work systems.

Discuss the outcomes for both employees and the organization.

Explain how the principles of high-performance work systems apply to small, medium-sized, and large organizations.

So, you've finished reading fifteen (or so) chapters on HRM. Congratulations—textbooks do not always make for the most gripping reading. And if you read this one cover to cover, you were probably cramming for an exam. But before you close this book, think about the following question: What is more difficult—designing effective HR practices or managing them all together as one system?

In the past, HR textbooks simply ended after each individual aspect of HRM was introduced and explained. But in today's competitive environment, many organizations are discovering that it's how the pieces are combined that makes all the difference. After all, managers typically don't focus on staffing, training, and compensation practices in isolation from one another. These HR practices are combined into an overall system to enhance employee involvement and performance. So now that we have talked about the individual pieces, we thought it might be useful to spend some time talking about how they fit together into *high-performance work systems.*

high-performance work system (HPWS)
A specific combination of HR practices, work structures, and processes that maximizes employee knowledge, skill, commitment, and flexibility

A **high-performance work system (HPWS)** can be defined as a specific combination of HR practices, work structures, and processes that maximizes employee knowledge, skill, commitment, and flexibility. Although some noteworthy HR practices and policies tend to be incorporated within most HPWSs, it would be a mistake for us to focus too much, or too soon, on the pieces themselves. The key concept is the *system.* High-performance work systems are composed of many interrelated parts that complement one another to reach the goals of an organization, large or small.

We will start by discussing the underlying principles that guide the development of high-performance work systems and the potential benefits that can occur as a result. Then we will outline the various components of the system, the work-flow design, HR practices, management processes, and supporting technologies. (See Figure 16.1.) We will also describe the ways in which organizations try to tie all the pieces of the system together and link them with strategy. We end the chapter with a discussion of the processes organizations use to implement high-performance work systems as well as the outcomes that benefit both the employee and the organization as a whole.

Fundamental Principles

In Chapter 1, we noted that organizations face a number of important competitive challenges such as adapting to global business, embracing technology, managing change, responding to customers, developing intellectual capital, and containing costs. We also noted some very important employee concerns that must be addressed, such as managing a diverse workforce, recognizing employee rights, adjusting to new work attitudes, and balancing work and family demands. We now know that the best organizations go beyond simply balancing these sometimes competing demands; they create work environments that blend these concerns to simultaneously get the most from employees, contribute to their needs, and meet the short-term and long-term goals of the organization.

The notion of high-performance work systems was originally developed by David Nadler to capture an organization's "architecture" that integrates technical and social

Figure 16.1 Developing High-Performance Work Systems

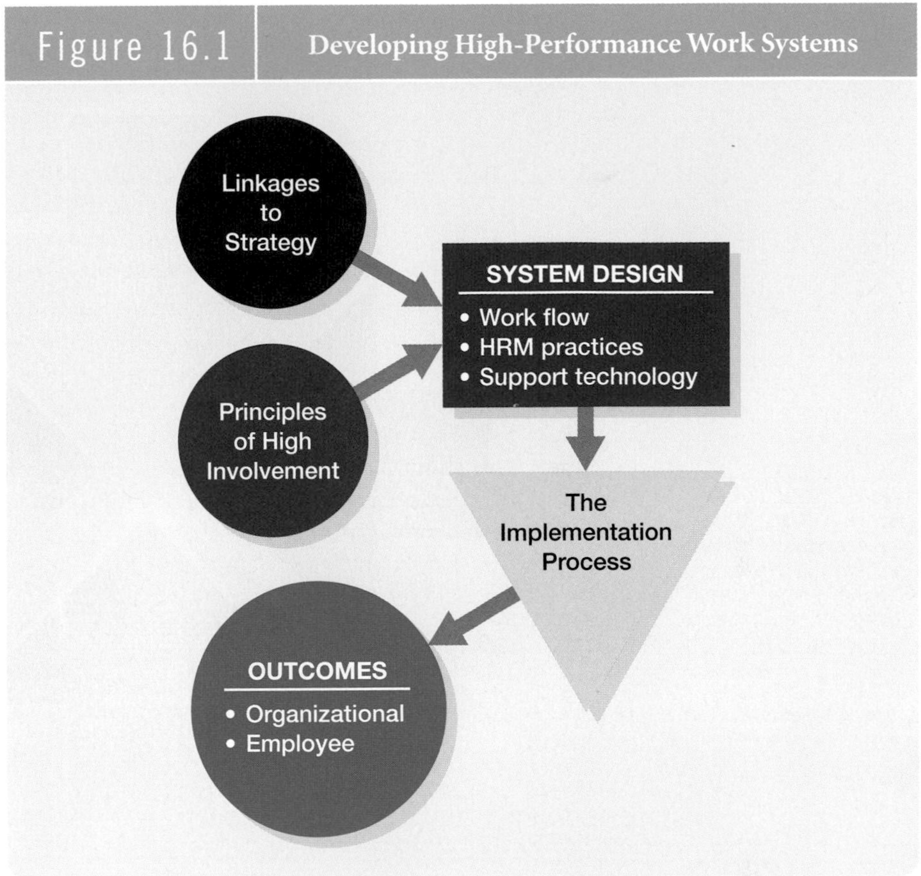

aspects of work. Edward Lawler and his associates at the Center for Effective Organization at the University of Southern California have worked with Fortune 1000 corporations to identify the primary principles that support high-performance work systems. There are four simple but powerful principles, as shown in Figure 16.2:

- Shared information
- Knowledge development
- Performance-reward linkage
- Egalitarianism[1]

In many ways, these principles have become the building blocks for managers who want to create high-performance work systems. More important, they are also quickly becoming the foundation for current theories of human resources management. We will use them as a framework for the rest of the chapter.

The Principle of Shared Information

The principle of shared information is critical for the success of empowerment and involvement initiatives in organizations. In the past, employees traditionally were not given—and did not ask for—information about the organization. People were hired

Figure 16.2 Underlying Principles of High-Performance Work Systems

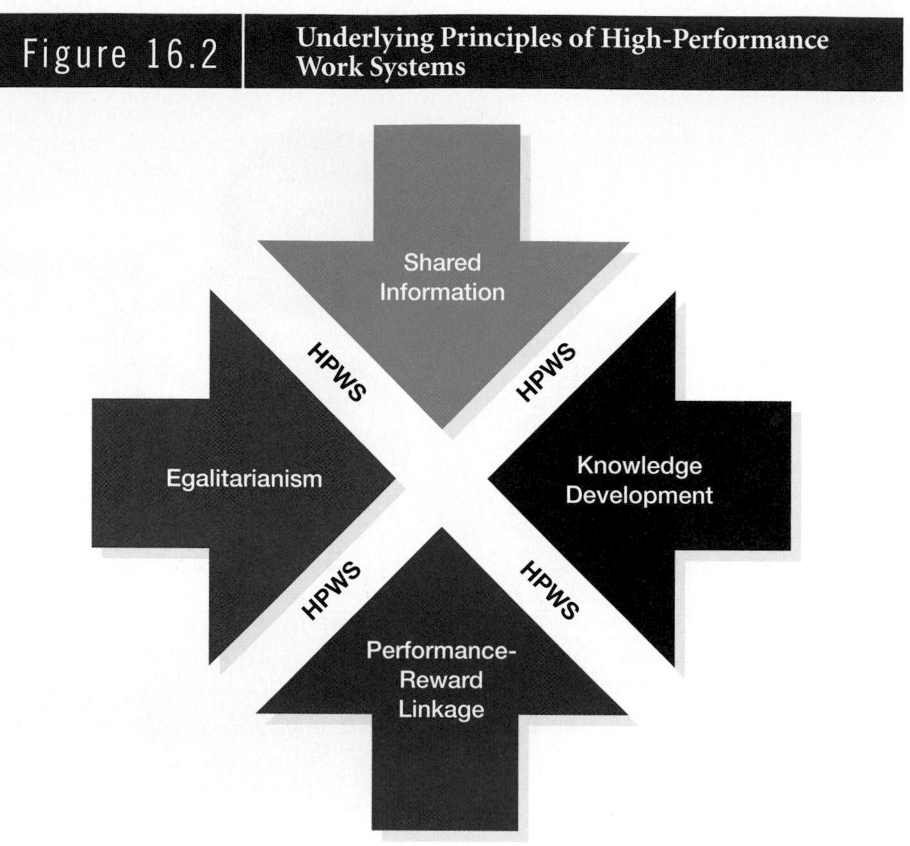

to perform narrowly defined jobs with clearly specified duties, and not much else was asked of them. One of the underlying ideas of high-performance work systems is that workers are intimately acquainted with the nature of their own work and are therefore in the best position to recognize problems and devise solutions to them. Today organizations are relying on the expertise and initiative of employees to react quickly to incipient problems and opportunities. Without timely and accurate information about the business, employees can do little more than simply carry out orders and perform their roles in a relatively perfunctory way. They are unlikely to understand the overall direction of the business or contribute to organizational success.

On the other hand, when employees are given timely information about business performance, plans, and strategies, they are more likely to make good suggestions for improving the business and to cooperate in major organizational changes. They are also likely to feel more committed to new courses of action if they have input in decision making. The principle of shared information typifies a shift in organizations away from the mentality of command and control toward one more focused on employee commitment. It represents a fundamental shift in the relationship between employer and employee. If executives do a good job of communicating with employees and create a culture of information sharing, employees are perhaps more likely to be willing (and able) to work toward the goals for the organization. They will "know more, do more, and contribute more."[2]

The Principle of Knowledge Development

Knowledge development is the twin sister of information sharing. As Richard Teerlink, former CEO of Harley-Davidson, noted, "The only thing you get when you empower dummies is bad decisions faster." Throughout this text, we have noted that the number of jobs requiring little knowledge and skill is declining while the number of jobs requiring greater knowledge and skill is growing rapidly. As organizations attempt to compete through people, they must invest in employee development. This includes both selecting the best and the brightest candidates available in the labor market and providing all employees opportunities to continually hone their talents.

High-performance work systems depend on the shift from touch labor to knowledge work. Employees today need a broad range of technical, problem-solving, and interpersonal skills to work either individually or in teams on cutting-edge projects. Because of the speed of change, knowledge and skill requirements must also change rapidly. In the contemporary work environment, employees must learn continuously. Stopgap training programs may not be enough. Companies such as DaimlerChrysler and Roche have found that employees in high-performance work systems need to learn in "real time," on the job, using innovative new approaches to solve novel problems. Likewise, at Ocean Spray's Henderson, Nevada, plant, making employees aware of the plant's progress has been a major focus. A real-time scoreboard on the Henderson plant floor provides workers with streaming updates of the plant's vital stats, including average cost per case, case volumes filled, filling speeds, and injuries to date. When people are better informed, they do better work. "We operate in real time and we need real-time information to be able to know what we have achieved and what we are working towards," says an Ocean Spray manager. (See the case at the end of the chapter for more on Ocean Spray's HPWS initiative.)[3]

The Principle of Performance-Reward Linkage

A time-tested adage of management is that the interests of employees and organizations naturally diverge. People may intentionally or unintentionally pursue outcomes that are beneficial to them but not necessarily to the organization as a whole. A corollary of this idea, however, is that things tend to go more smoothly when there is some way to align employee and organizational goals. When rewards are connected to performance, employees naturally pursue outcomes that are mutually beneficial to themselves and the organization. When this happens, some amazing things can result. For example, supervisors don't have to constantly watch to make sure that employees do the right thing. But in fact, employees may go out of their way—above and beyond the call of duty, so to speak—to make certain that co-workers are getting the help they need, systems and processes are functioning efficiently, and customers are happy.

Connecting rewards to organizational performance also ensures fairness and tends to focus employees on the organization. Equally important, performance-based rewards ensure that employees share in the gains that result from any performance improvement. For instance, Lincoln Electric has long been recognized for its efforts in linking employee pay and performance.

The Principle of Egalitarianism

People want a sense that they are members, not just workers, in an organization. Status and power differences tend to separate people and magnify whatever disparities

USING THE INTERNET

Nucor makes no secret of the importance of its employees. Read about its management philosophy and incentive-based compensation plans at About Nucor. Go to the Student Resources at:

http://bohlander.swlearning.com

exist between them. The "us versus them" battles that have traditionally raged between managers, employees, and labor unions are increasingly being replaced by more-cooperative approaches to managing work. More-egalitarian work environments eliminate status and power differences and, in the process, increase collaboration and teamwork. When this happens, productivity can improve if people who once worked in isolation from (or in opposition to) one another begin to work together.

Nucor Steel has an enviable reputation not only for establishing an egalitarian work environment but also for the employee loyalty and productivity that stem from that environment. Upper levels of management do not enjoy better insurance programs, vacation schedules, or holidays. In fact, certain benefits such as Nucor's profit-sharing plan, scholarship program, employee stock purchase plan, extraordinary bonus plan, and service awards program are not available to Nucor's officers at all. Senior executives do not enjoy traditional perquisites such as company cars, corporate jets, executive dining rooms, or executive parking places. On the other hand, every Nucor employee is eligible for incentive pay and is listed alphabetically on the company's annual report.

Moving power downward in organizations—that is, empowering employees—frequently requires structural changes. Managers often use employee surveys, suggestion systems, quality circles, employee involvement groups, and/or union-management committees that work in parallel with existing organizational structures. In addition, work flow can be redesigned to give employees more control and influence over decision making. At Old Home Foods in St. Paul, Minnesota, one of the few independent, exclusively cultured dairy product manufacturers in the country, all employees are involved in the decision-making process of the business. "It's part of the Old Home Foods culture," says owner Peter Arthur "P. A." Hanson. "To be a successful independent, you need to empower your employees and let them know they are critical to success."[4] Job enlargement, enrichment, and self-managing work teams are typical methods for increasing the power of employees to influence decisions, suggest changes, or act on their own. With decreasing power distances, employees can become more involved in their work; their quality of work life is simultaneously increased, and organizational performance is improved.

These four principles—shared information, knowledge development, performance-reward linkage, and egalitarianism—are the basis for designing high-performance work systems. They also cut across many of the topics and HR practices we have talked about elsewhere in this textbook. These principles help us integrate practices and policies to create an overall high-performance work system.

Anatomy of High-Performance Work Systems

We said at the beginning of this chapter that high-performance work systems combine various work structures, HR practices, and management processes to maximize employee performance and well-being. And although we outlined the principles underlying such systems, their specific characteristics have not as yet been described in detail.

Although it may be premature to claim that there is a foolproof list of "best practices" that can be implemented by every organization for every work situation, some clear trends in work design, HR practices, leadership roles, and information technologies tell us what high-performance work systems look like.[5] Some of these are summarized in Figure 16.3.

Work-Flow Design and Teamwork

High-performance work systems frequently begin with the way work is designed. Total quality management (TQM) and reengineering have driven many organizations to redesign their work flows. Instead of separating jobs into discrete units, most experts now advise managers to focus on the key business processes that drive customer value—and then create teams that are responsible for those processes. Federal Express, for example, redesigned its delivery process to give truck drivers responsibility for scheduling their own routes and for making necessary changes quickly. Because the drivers have detailed knowledge of customers and routes, Federal Express managers empowered them to inform existing customers of new products and services. In so doing, drivers now fill a type of sales representative role for the company. In addition, FedEx drivers also work together as a team to identify bottlenecks and solve problems that slow delivery. To facilitate this, advanced communications equipment was installed in the delivery trucks to help teams of drivers balance routes among those with larger or lighter loads.[6]

Figure 16.3 Anantomy of High-Performance Work Systems

	Shared Information	Knowledge Development	Performance-Reward Linkage	Egalitarianism
Work flow				
• Self-managed teams	■	□	□	■
• Empowerment	■	■	□	■
Staffing				
• Selective recruiting	□	■	□	□
• Team decision making	■	□	□	■
Training				
• Broad skills	□	■	□	□
• Cross-training	■	■	□	■
• Problem solving	■	■	□	■
• Team training	■	■	□	□
Compensation				
• Incentives	□	□	■	■
• Gainsharing	■	■	■	■
• Profit sharing	■	■	■	■
• Skill-based pay	□	■	■	■
Leadership				
• Few layers	■	■	□	■
• Coaches/facilitators	■	■	□	■
Technologies				
• HRIS	■	□	□	□
• Communications	■	■	□	■

Similarly, when Colgate-Palmolive opened a plant in Cambridge, Ohio, managers specifically designed teams around key work processes to produce products such as Ajax, Fab, Dynamo, and Palmolive detergent. Instead of separating each stage of production into discrete steps, teams work together in a seamless process to produce liquid detergent, make polyurethane bottles, fill those bottles, label and package the products, and deliver them to the loading dock.

By redesigning the work flow around key business processes, companies such as Federal Express and Colgate-Palmolive have been able to establish a work environment that facilitates teamwork, takes advantage of employee skills and knowledge, empowers employees to make decisions, and provides them with more meaningful work.[7]

Complementary Human Resources Policies and Practices

Work redesign, in and of itself, does not constitute a high-performance work system. Neither does total quality management or reengineering. Other supporting elements of HRM are necessary to achieve high performance. Several recent studies suggest that both performance and satisfaction are much higher when organizations combine their changes in work-flow design with HR practices that encourage skill development and employee involvement.[8]

Staffing Practices

Many high-performance work systems begin with highly directive recruitment and selection practices. Recruitment tends to be both broad and intensive in order to get the best pool of candidates from which to choose. Then, by selecting skilled individuals with the ability to learn continuously and work cooperatively, organizations are likely to make up for the time and expense they invested in selection. The good news is that human resources information systems have made it easier for firms to compile an inventory of their talent and search for employees with the specific skills they need. Talented employees "come up to speed" more quickly and take less time to develop. Too often organizations try to save money by doing a superficial job of hiring. As a consequence, they run the risk of hiring the wrong people and spending more on training and/or outplacement, severance, and recruitment of replacements. Especially in organizations that try to stay lean, perhaps after a painful cycle of downsizing, HPWS can be instrumental for effective performance.[9]

In organizations such as Nissan's Smyrna, Georgia, plant, potential job applicants are drawn from a pool of individuals who have been trained at the state's expense and who seem best suited to working in high-performance teams. In other organizations, such as Macy's, General Motors's Saturn division, and Weyerhaeuser, team members select their teammates. This practice gives employees more control over decisions about who their co-workers will be and forges relationships more quickly than if new members were simply assigned to a team.[10]

Training and Development

Like recruitment and selection, training focuses on ensuring that employees have the skills needed to assume greater responsibility in a high-performance work environment. For example, Schindler Elevator Corporation, the world's second-largest man-

© JOHN MADERE/CORBIS

High-performance work systems have helped companies such as Nissan and Saturn improve production and quality.

ufacturer of elevators, provides a sixty-hour prehire training program of instruction and testing in such subjects as orientation/company history, safety, plant policies and procedures, just-in-time (JIT) techniques, and basic shop math. The company also has an apprenticeship program that focuses on key areas based on its specific business needs. Apprentices are hired as machinists, tool and die makers, welders, electricians, mechanics, and so forth. In addition, Schindler gives each of its employees at least five days of classroom training every year. Similarly, team members at Saturn receive up to several hundred hours of training in their first few months. Typically, training focuses on technical, problem-solving, and interpersonal skills. Emphasis on teamwork, involvement, and continuous improvement requires that employees develop a broader understanding of work processes performed by others around them rather than rely on just knowing their own jobs. To accomplish this, organizations increasingly use cross-training, discussed earlier in the book. Recall that this involves training employees in jobs in areas closely related to their own. For example, nurses in the perinatal unit of Cincinnati-based TriHealth System implemented cross-training to facilitate teamwork and cooperation across units; even more, it helps nurses identify trouble spots that cut across several jobs and allows them to suggest areas for improvement.

Beyond individual training, Eastman Chemical has established a training certification process that helps ensure that intact teams progress through a series of maturity phases. The teams certify their abilities to function effectively by demonstrating knowledge and skills in such areas as customer expectations, business conditions, and safety. Because these skills must be continually updated, Eastman Chemical requires that even certified teams periodically review their competencies.[11]

Compensation

Another important piece of a high-performance work system is the compensation package. Because high-performance work systems ask many different things from

Source: © Randy Glasbergen. Reprinted by permission.

employees, it is difficult to isolate one single approach to pay that works for everyone. As a consequence, many companies are experimenting with alternative compensation plans. In order to link pay and performance, high-performance work systems often include some type of employee incentives. For example, an average of 10 percent of Saturn employees' pay is linked to goals for quality and training. Other organizational incentives such as gainsharing, profit-sharing, and employee stock ownership plans focus employee efforts on outcomes that benefit both themselves and the organization as a whole. The Scanlon Plan, the Rucker Plan, and Improshare, three systems discussed in Chapter 10, have been used by companies such as TRW, Weyerhaeuser, and Xaloy to elicit employee suggestions and reward them for contributions to productivity.

High-performance work systems may also incorporate skill-based pay plans. By paying employees based on the number of different job skills they have, organizations such as Shell Canada, Nortel Networks, and Honeywell hope to create both a broader skill base among employees and a more flexible pool of people to rotate among interrelated jobs. Both of these qualities are beneficial in a high-performance work environment and may justify the added expense in compensation. Honeywell has even experimented with what it calls "intracapital"—a pool of money employees can spend on capital improvements if the company meets profitability goals.[12]

Recall that in addition to linking pay and performance, high-performance work systems are also based on the principle of egalitarianism. To reinforce this principle in plants utilizing high-performance work systems, Monsanto, AES, and Honeywell recently implemented an all-salaried workforce. The open pay plan, in which everyone knows what everyone else makes, is yet another feature of compensation systems used to create a more egalitarian environment that encourages employee involvement and commitment.[13]

Management Processes and Leadership

Leadership issues arise at several levels with high-performance work systems. At the executive level there needs to be clear support for a high-performance work environment, for the changes in culture that may accompany this environment, and for the modification of business processes necessary to support the change. These concerns will be addressed in more detail shortly in our discussion of implementation issues.

Organizations such as Doubletree Hotels, American Express, and Reebok International found that the success of any high-performance work system depends on first changing the roles of managers and team leaders. With fewer layers of management and a focus on team-based organization, the role of managers and supervisors is substantially different in an environment of high-performance work systems. Managers and supervisors are seen more as coaches, facilitators, and integrators of team efforts.[14] Rather than autocratically imposing their demands on employees and closely watching to make certain that the workers comply, managers in high-performance work systems share responsibility for decision making with employees. Typically, the term *manager* is replaced by the term *team leader.* And in a growing number of cases, leadership is shared among team members. Kodak, for example, rotates team leaders at various stages in team development. Alternatively, different individuals can assume functional leadership roles when their particular expertise is needed most.

Supportive Information Technologies

Communication and information technologies are yet one more piece that has to be added to the framework of high-performance work systems. Technologies of various kinds create an infrastructure for communicating and sharing information vital to business performance. Federal Express, for example, is known for its use of information technology to route packages. Its tracking system helps employees monitor each package, communicate with customers, and identify and solve problems quickly. Sally Industries in Jacksonville, Florida, uses information technology to assign employees to various project teams. The company specializes in animatronics, the combination of wires and latex that is used to make humanoid creatures such as are found in Disney's Hall of Presidents. Artisans employed by Sally Corporation work on several project teams at once. A computerized system developed by the company helps budget and track the employee time spent on different projects.

But information technologies need not always be so high-tech. The richest communication occurs face to face. The important point is that high-performance work systems cannot succeed without timely and accurate communications. (Recall the principle of shared information.) Typically the information needs to be about business plans and goals, unit and corporate operating results, incipient problems and opportunities, and competitive threats.[15]

Fitting It All Together

Each of these practices highlights the individual pieces of a high-performance work system. And while we have emphasized throughout this text that certain HR practices are better than others, recall that in high-performance work systems the pieces are particularly valuable in terms of how they help the entire system function as a whole. As discussed in Chapter 2, careful planning helps ensure that the pieces fit together and are linked with the overall strategic goals of the organization. This philosophy is reflected in the mission statement of Saturn Motors, a model organization for HPWS. Saturn's mission is to "Market vehicles developed and manufactured in the United States that are world leaders . . . through the integration of people, technology, and business systems." Figure 16.4 summarizes the internal and external linkages needed to fit high-performance work systems together.

Ensuring Internal Fit

internal fit
The situation in which all the internal elements of the work system complement and reinforce one another

Recall from Chapter 2 that **internal fit** occurs when all the internal elements of the work system complement and reinforce one another. For example, a first-rate selection system may be of no use if it is not working in conjunction with training and development activities. If a new compensation program elicits and reinforces behav-

Figure 16.4 Achieving Strategic Fit

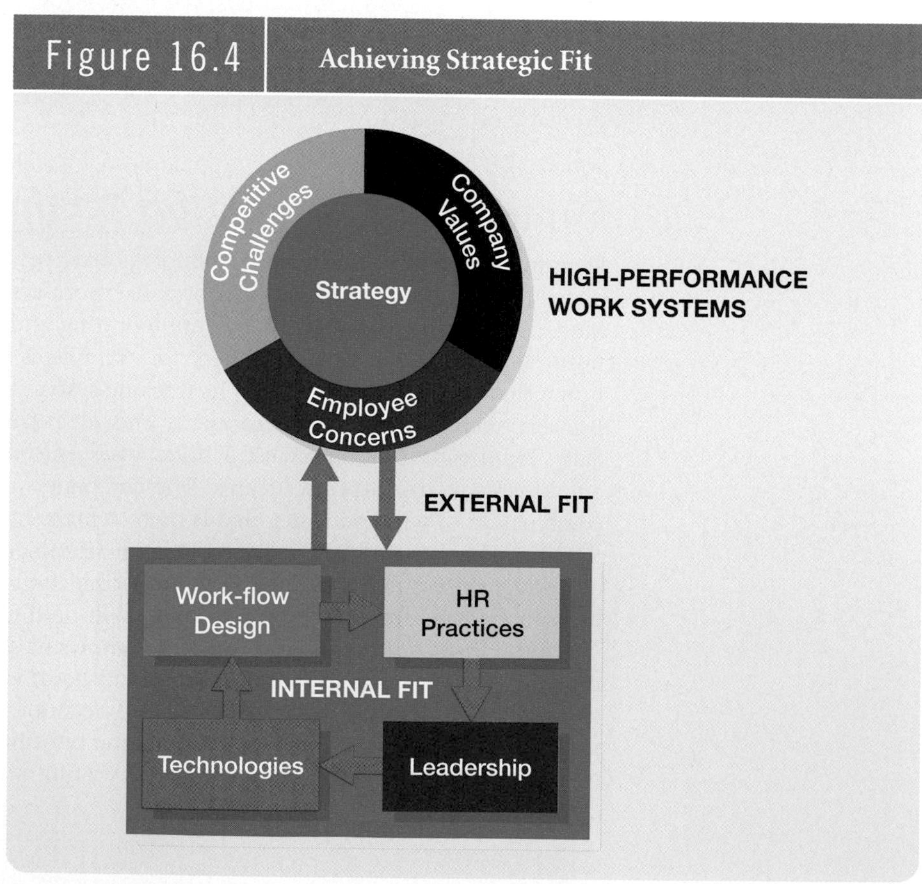

iors that are directly opposed to the goals laid out in performance planning, the two components would be working at cross purposes.

This is the true nature of systems. Changes in one component affect all the other components. Because the pieces are interdependent, a new compensation system may have no effect on performance if it is implemented on its own. Horizontal fit means testing to make certain that all of the HR practices, work designs, management processes, and technologies complement one another. The synergy achieved through overlapping work and human resources practices is at the heart of what makes a high-performance system effective.

Establishing External Fit

external fit
The situation in which the work system supports the organization's goals and strategies

To achieve **external fit,** high-performance work systems must support the organization's goals and strategies. This begins with an analysis and discussion of competitive challenges, organizational values, and the concerns of employees and results in a statement of the strategies being pursued by the organization.[16]

Xerox, for example, uses a planning process known as "Managing for Results," which begins with a statement of corporate values and priorities. These values and priorities are the foundation for establishing three-to-five-year goals for the organization. Each business unit establishes annual objectives based on these goals, and the process cascades down through every level of management. Ultimately, each employee within Xerox has a clear "line of sight" to the values and goals of the organization so he or she can see how individual effort makes a difference.[17]

Efforts such as this to achieve vertical fit help focus the design of high-performance work systems on strategic priorities. Objectives such as cost containment, quality enhancement, customer service, and speed to market directly influence what is expected of employees and the skills they need to be successful. Terms such as *involvement, flexibility, efficiency, problem solving,* and *teamwork* are not just buzzwords. They are translated directly from the strategic requirements of today's organizations. High-performance work systems are designed to link employee initiatives to those strategies.

Assessing Strategic Alignment: The HR Scorecard

In Chapter 2 we introduced the balanced scorecard as a tool that helps managers evaluate the link between strategic goals and operational activities. Professors Brian Becker, Mark Huselid, and Dave Ulrich have adapted that model to create an *HR Scorecard* that helps managers assess the strategic alignment of their work systems.[18]

The HR Scorecard can be used to diagnose internal fit and external fit in a relatively straightforward way: First, managers diagnose internal fit by assessing whether particular HR practices reinforce one another or work at cross purposes (see Highlights in HRM 1A). Second, managers assess whether the HR practices significantly enable key workforce deliverables such as employment stability and teamwork (see Highlights in HRM 1B). Third, the degree of external fit is evaluated by assessing the degree to which the workforce deliverables are connected with key strategic performance drivers (see Highlights in HRM 1C). These three assessments are extremely useful not just for deriving measures of internal and external fit of high-performance work systems, but for engaging a broader set of managers and employees in the discussion of how to best implement the system.

Highlights in HRM 1A

Diagnosing Internal Fit

In the following chart, please estimate the degree to which the various HR management subsystems work together harmoniously or "fit" together. Think of the degree of fit and internal consistency as a continuum from −100 to +100, and assign a value in that range to each relationship. Examples of the extremes and midpoints on that continuum are as follows:

−100: The two subsystems work at cross purposes.
0: The two subsystems have little or no effect on one another.
+100: Each subsystem is mutually reinforcing and internally consistent.
DNK: Don't know or have no opinion.

	HR Planning	Recruiting and Selection	Training and Development	Performance Management and Appraisal	Compensation and Benefits	Work Organization (e.g., Teams)	Communication Systems	HR Performance Measurement	
								Cost	Value Creation
HR planning	—	−30	0	−20	0	0	0	0	0
Recruiting and selection		—	0	−10	−20	−30	0	+30	−40
Training and development			—	0	0	0	0	+30	−10
Performance management and appraisal				—	0	−30	+20	0	−20
Compensation and benefits					—	−50	0	+40	0
Work organization (e.g., teams)						—	0	0	0
Communication systems							—	0	0
HR performance measurement								—	

Source: Brian Becker, Mark Huselid, and Dave Ulrich, *The HR Scorecard* (Cambridge, MA: Harvard University Press, 2001).

Implementing the System

So far we have talked about the principles, practices, and goals of high-performance work systems. Unfortunately, these design issues compose probably less than half of the challenges that must be met in ensuring system success. Much of what looks good on paper gets messy during implementation. The American Society for Training and Development (ASTD) asked managers and consultants to identify the critical

Highlights in HRM 1B

Testing Alignment of the HR System with HR Deliverables

Please indicate the degree to which the following elements of the HR system facilitate the HR deliverables shown, on a scale of −100 to +100. Examples of the extremes and midpoints on that continuum are as follows:

−100: This dimension is counterproductive for enabling this deliverable.
0: This dimension has little or no effect on this deliverable.
+100: This dimension significantly enables this deliverable.
DNK: Don't know or have no opinion.

	HR Planning	Recruiting and Selection	Training and Development	Management and Appraisal	Compensation and Benefits	Work Organization (e.g., Teams)	Communication Systems
Employment stability	0	0	0	0	−50	−20	0
Team-based behaviors	0	0	−30	−20	−40	0	0
Strategy-focused behaviors	0	0	0	0	+40	0	0
High-talent staffing level	0	−50	0	−50	0	0	0

factors that can make or break a high-performance work system. The respondents identified the following actions as necessary for success (see Figure 16.5):

- Make a compelling case for change linked to the company's business strategy.
- Ensure that change is owned by senior and line managers.
- Allocate sufficient resources and support for the change effort.
- Ensure early and broad communication.
- Ensure that teams are implemented in a systemic context.
- Establish methods for measuring the results of change.
- Ensure continuity of leadership and champions of the initiative.[19]

Many of these recommendations are applicable to almost any change initiative, but they are especially important for broad-based change efforts that characterize high-performance work systems. Some of the most critical issues are discussed next.

Building a Business Case for Change

Change can be threatening because it asks people to abandon the old ways of doing things and accept new approaches that, to them at least, are untested. To get initial commitment to high-performance work systems, managers have to build a case that the changes are needed for the success of the organization. In a recent study on the implementation of high-performance work systems, it was found that a member of top management typically played the role of sponsor/champion and spent a substantial

Highlights in HRM 1C

Testing Alignment of HR Deliverables

Please indicate the degree to which each HR deliverable in the chart below would *currently* enable each strategic driver, on a scale of −100 to +100. Empty cells indicate this is not a key deliverable for a particular driver. Examples of the extremes and midpoints on that continuum are as follows:

−100: This deliverable is counterproductive for enabling this driver.
0: This deliverable has little or no effect on this driver.
+100: This deliverable significantly enables this driver.
DNK: Don't know or have no opinion.

	HR Deliverable			
Strategic Performance Drivers	Employment Stability among Senior R&D Staff	Team-Based Behaviors	Strategy-Focused Performance	High-Talent Staffing Level
1. Shorten product development times	−80	−30	+30	
2. Enhance customer focus and responsiveness	−20		−20	
3. Enhance productivity		−10	−50	−40
4. Develop and successfully manage joint ventures	−10	−50		

portion of his or her time in that role communicating with employees about the reasons and approaches to change. Major transformation should not be left to middle managers. Rather, the CEO and the senior management team need to establish the context for change and communicate the vision more broadly to the entire organization. For example, executives at Harley-Davidson tried to institute employee involvement groups without first demonstrating their own personal commitment to the program. Not surprisingly, employees were apathetic and in some cases referred to the proposed changes as just "another fine program" put in place by the personnel

Figure 16.5 Implementing High-Performance Work Systems

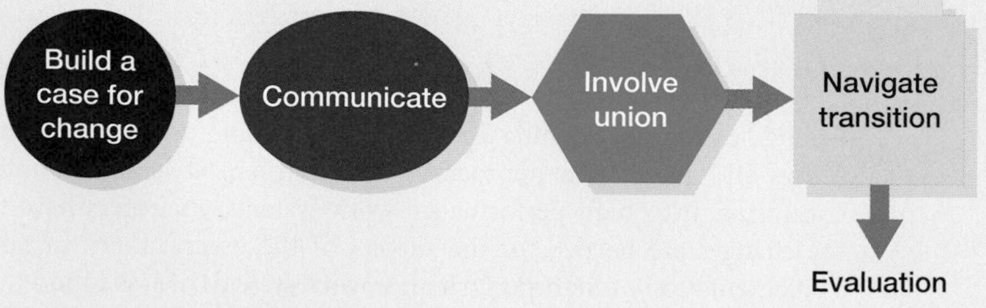

department. Harley-Davidson executives learned the hard way that commitment from the top is essential in order to establish mutual trust between employees and managers. Similarly, the CEO of a business-consulting company was adamant that his twenty-four vice presidents understand a new initiative and give a short speech at an introductory session. On the day of the program's launch, however, the CEO himself did not show up. The message to the vice presidents was clear: The CEO didn't think the change was important enough to become an active participant. Not surprisingly, the change was never implemented.[20]

One of the best ways to communicate business needs is to show employees where the business is today—its current performance and capabilities. Then show them where the organization needs to be in the future. The gap between today and the future represents a starting point for discussion. When executives at TRW wanted to make a case for change to high-performance work systems, they used employee attitude surveys and data on turnover costs. The data provided enough ammunition to get conversation going about needed changes and sparked some suggestions about how they could be implemented.

Highlights in HRM 2 shows what happened when BMW bought British Land Rover and began making changes without first talking through the business concerns. Ironically, in this case, BMW unwittingly dismantled an effective high-performance work system. Now that Ford owns the company, will things work differently?

Establishing a Communications Plan

The ASTD council on high-performance work systems noted that providing an inadequate communication system is the most frequent mistake companies make during implementation. While we have emphasized the importance of executive commitment, top-down communication is not enough. Two-way communication not only can result in better decisions, it may help to diminish the fears and concerns of employees.

For example, Solectron Corporation, winner of the Baldrige National Quality Award, tried to implement high-performance work systems to capitalize on the knowledge and experience of its employees. A pilot program showed immediate gains in productivity of almost 20 percent after the switch to self-managed teams and team-based compensation. Although Solectron's rapid growth of more than 50 percent per year made it unlikely that middle managers would be laid off, many of them resisted the change to a high-performance work system. They resented the loss of status and control that accompanied the use of empowered teams.

If Solectron managers had participated in discussions about operational and financial aspects of the business, they might not have felt so threatened by the change. Open exchange and communication at an early stage pay off later as the system unfolds. Ongoing dialogue at all levels helps reaffirm commitment, answer questions that come up, and identify areas for improvement throughout implementation. Recall that one of the principles of high-performance work systems is sharing information. This principle is instrumental to success both during implementation and once the system is in place.

Involving the Union

We mentioned in Chapter 14 that autocratic styles of management and confrontational approaches to labor negotiations are being challenged by more-enlightened

Highlights in HRM 2

Land Rover, BMW, and Ford Crash Head-On

Some years ago, the British Land Rover Company, a leading manufacturer of four-wheel-drive vehicles, found itself saddled with a notorious reputation for poor quality and productivity. Then it underwent a fundamental transformation. The company instituted extensive training (including giving every employee a personal training fund to be used on any subject), implemented more team-based production methods, reduced the number of separate job classifications, developed more cooperative relations with organized labor, and began a total quality program.

As a result of these changes, productivity soared by 25 percent, quality action teams netted savings worth millions of dollars, and the quality of products climbed. Operating in a very competitive environment, Land Rover produced and sold one-third more vehicles. On the basis of these changes, the company was certified as an "Investors in People—U.K." designee. This national standard recognizes organizations that place the involvement and development of people at the heart of their business strategy.

So far, so good. Then BMW bought the company. In spite of massive evidence documenting the effectiveness of the new management methods and changed culture, BMW began to dictate changes within a manner of months. Unfortunately, the changes undid the cultural transformation.

Land Rover never fully recovered under the new management. After losing more than $6 billion, BMW sold off the company. Land Rover was later purchased by Ford Motor Company. Ford bought Land Rover and put it under one roof with Volvo, Jaguar, and Aston Martin to create the Premier Auto Group. Ford has continued to manufacture the Land Rover in England while improving its quality, but this hasn't been enough to turn Land Rover around. In 2003, Land Rover finished near the bottom of the J.D. Power Initial Quality Study, thirty-sixth out of thirty-seven brands, and the division has been showing losses.

Land Rover's 8,000-strong workforce in Solihull, England, has been put on notice by group chairman Mark Fields that it needs to alter its culture and working practices to match those embraced by Ford. In the Ford production system, teams of workers are supposed to take charge of and improve quality in their areas. Fields wants the Solihull plant to operate like a nearby Jaguar plant in Halewood, England, which formerly built Ford Escorts. The Halewood plant had been notorious for militancy, work stoppages, absenteeism, and quality problems. Halewood later became Ford's top factory after a decision was made to transform into a Jaguar factory, and a sweeping series of cultural, productivity and working practice changes were put into place.

"We've taken a very positive set of first steps but there's a lot of pavement in front of us," said Fields about Land Rover.

Sources: Jeffrey Pfeffer, "When It Comes to 'Best Practices'—Why Do Smart Organizations Occasionally Do Dumb Things?" Reprinted from *Organizational Dynamics,* Summer 1996 with permission from Elsevier; Cordelia Brabbs, "Rover's White Knight," *Marketing,* May 18, 2000, 28; Georg Auer, "Burela to Instill Quality Culture at Land Rover," *Automotive News* 75, no. 5902 (November 6, 2000): 32x–32z; Ronald W. Pant, "Land Rover History Lesson," *Truck Trend* 8, no. 3 (May–June 2005): 12; Bradford Wernle, "Solihull Must Do 'a Halewood' to Survive; Jaguar Plant Is the Example Land Rover Factory Must Follow," *Automotive News Europe* 9, no. 19 (September 20, 2004): 39.

USING THE INTERNET

Read the full story of how Selectron won the Baldrige Award at a special web site devoted to the subject. Go to the Student Resources at:

http://bohlander.swlearning.com

approaches that promote cooperation and collaboration. Given the sometimes radical changes involved in implementing high-performance work systems, it makes good sense to involve union members early and to keep them as close partners in the design and implementation process. Figure 16.6 shows how to "build a bridge" toward a cooperative relationship with unions in implementing high-performance work systems.[21]

Cultivating Mutual Gains

In order to establish an alliance, managers and labor representatives should try to create "win-win" situations, in which all parties gain from the implementation of high-performance work systems. In such cases, organizations such as Shell and Weyerhaeuser have found that "interest-based" (integrative) negotiation rather than positional bargaining leads to better relationships and outcomes with union representatives. Trust is a fragile component of an alliance and is reflected in the degree to which parties are comfortable sharing information and decision making. Manitoba Telecom Services has involved union members in decisions about work practices, and because of this, company managers have been able to build mutual trust and respect with the union. This relationship has matured to a point at which union and company managers now design, select, and implement new technologies together. By working hard to develop trust up front, in either a union or a nonunion setting, it is more likely that each party will understand how high-performance work systems will benefit everyone; the organization will be more competitive, employees will have a higher quality of work life, and unions will have a stronger role in representing employees.[22]

Figure 16.6 Building Cooperation with Unions

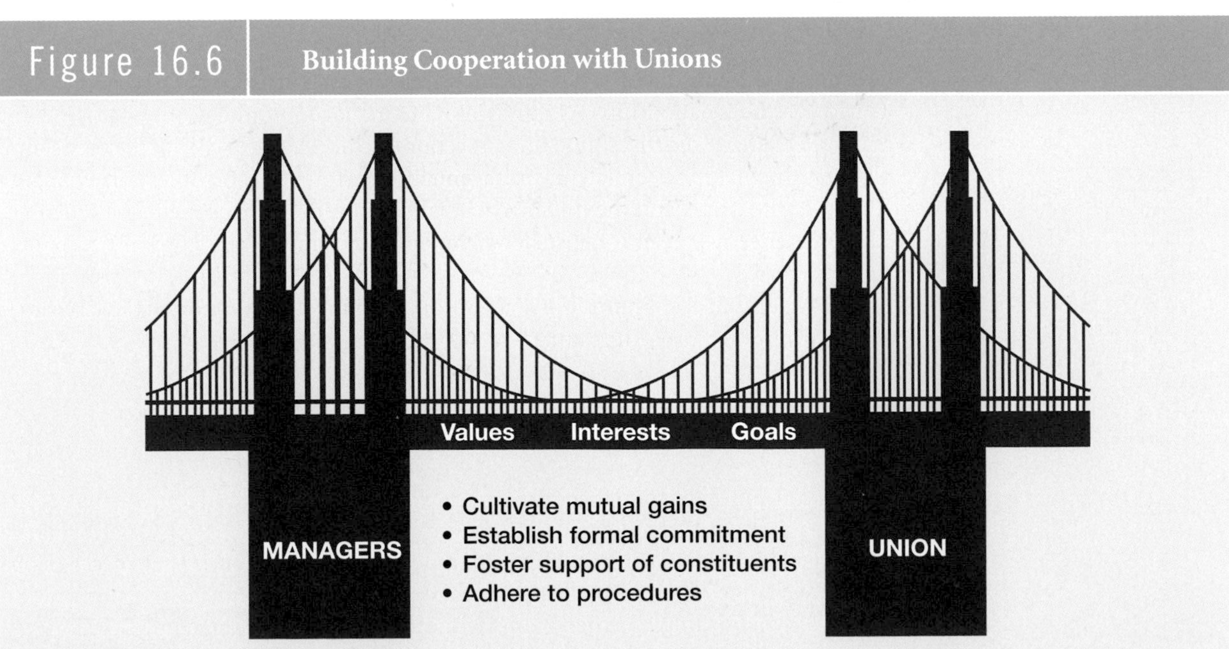

Source: The Conference Board of Canada.

Establishing Formal Commitment

Most labor-management alliances are made legitimate through some tangible symbol of commitment. This might include a policy document that spells out union involvement, letters of understanding, clauses in a collective bargaining agreement, or the establishment of joint forums with explicit mandates. MacMillan Bloedel, a Canadian wood products company now owned by Weyerhaeuser, formed a joint operations committee of senior management and labor representatives to routinely discuss a wide range of operational issues related to high-performance work systems. These types of formal commitments, with investments of tangible resources, serve two purposes: (1) They are an outward sign of management commitment, and (2) they institutionalize the relationship so that it keeps going even if key project champions leave.[23]

Fostering Support of Other Key Constituents

In addition to union leadership, it is critical to have the support of other key constituents. Leaders must ensure that understanding and support are solid at all levels, not just among those in the executive suite. To achieve this commitment, some organizations have decentralized the labor relations function, giving responsibility to local line managers and human resources generalists, to make certain that they are accountable and are committed to nurturing a high-performance work environment. Nortel Networks, for example, formally transferred accountability for labor relations to its plant managers through its collective bargaining agreement with the union. Line managers became members of the Employee Relations Council, which is responsible for local bargaining as well as for grievance hearings that would formerly have been mediated by HR. Apart from the commitment that these changes create, perhaps the most important reason for giving line managers responsibility for employee relations is that it helps them establish a direct working relationship with the union.

Adhering to Procedures

Once processes, agreements, and ground rules are established, they are vital to the integrity of the relationship. As Ruth Wright, manager of the Council for Senior Human Resource Executives, puts it, "Procedure is the 'rug' on which alliances stand. Pull it out by making a unilateral management determination or otherwise changing the rules of the game, and the initiative will falter. Procedure keeps the parties focused, and it is an effective means of ensuring that democracy and fairness prevail."[24]

In most cases, a "home-grown" process works better than one that is adopted from elsewhere. Each organization has unique circumstances, and parties are more likely to commit to procedures they create and own.

Navigating the Transition to High-Performance Work Systems

Building commitment to high-performance work systems is an ongoing activity. Perhaps, in fact, it is never fully completed. And as in any change activity, performance frequently falters as implementation gets under way. One reason is that pieces of the system are changed incrementally rather than as a total program. Xerox Corporation found that when it implemented teams without also changing the compensation system to support teamwork, it got caught in a bad transition. The teams actually showed poorer performance than did employees working in settings that supported individual contributions. Company executives concluded that they needed to change the entire system at once, because piecemeal changes were actually detrimental.

The other mistake organizations often make is to focus on either top-down change driven by executives or bottom-up change cultivated by the employees. In reality, firms such as Champion International, now a part of International Paper, and ASDA, a low-cost British retailer, are among the many companies that have found that the best results occur when managers and employees work together. The top-down approach communicates manager support and clarity, while the bottom-up approach ensures employee acceptance and commitment.[25]

Building a Transition Structure

Implementation of high-performance work systems proceeds in different ways for different organizations. In organizational start-ups, managers have the advantage of being able to put everything in place at once. However, when organizations have to be retrofitted, the process may occur a bit more clumsily. When Honeywell switched to high-performance work systems in its plant in Chandler, Arizona, employees attended training programs and participated in the redesign of their jobs while the plant was shut down to be reequipped with new technology. When the new plant was reopened, self-managing teams were put in place and a new pay system was implemented for the high-performance workforce.[26]

Not every organization has the luxury of suspending operations while changes are put in place. Nevertheless, establishing an implementation structure keeps everyone on track and prevents the system from bogging down. The structure provides a timetable and process for mapping key business processes, redesigning work, and training employees.

Incorporating the HR Function as a Valuable Partner

One of the mistakes that organizations can make in implementing high-performance work systems is allocating too few resources to the effort. This means money, of course, but it also means time and expertise. Although line managers typically own the responsibility for implementation, HR managers can be invaluable partners in leading the charge for and managing change. Because change is difficult, HR managers need to understand what employees in transition are going through and help them handle it. When the "old ways" of doing things are abandoned, many experienced employees begin to feel like "beginners" again on the job. This can be stressful and sometimes polarize employees. As a coping mechanism, many are likely to fall back on older routines. Texas Instruments created its High Performance Organization Development unit to facilitate the transition to a high-performance work system. Other organizations such as Merck, Ford, and Deutsche Bank have also developed special HR units to manage organizational change. Unilever created a transition team of senior line and HR managers to oversee the implementation of high-performance teams and develop an implementation road map.[27]

Evaluating the Success of the System

Once high-performance work systems are in place, they need to be monitored and evaluated over time. Several aspects of the review process should be addressed. First, there

process audit
Determining whether the high-performance work system has been implemented as designed

should be a **process audit** to determine whether the system has been implemented as it was designed and whether the principles of high-performance work systems are being reinforced. Questions such as the following might be included in the audit:

- Are employees actually working together, or is the term "team" just a label?
- Are employees getting the information they need to make empowered decisions?
- Are training programs developing the knowledge and skills employees need?
- Are employees being rewarded for good performance and useful suggestions?
- Are employees treated fairly so that power differences are minimal?

Second, the evaluation process should focus on the goals of high-performance work systems. To determine whether the program is succeeding, managers should look at such issues as the following:

- Are desired behaviors being exhibited on the job?
- Are quality, productivity, flexibility, and customer service objectives being met?
- Are quality-of-life goals being achieved for employees?
- Is the organization more competitive than in the past?

Finally, high-performance work systems should be periodically evaluated in terms of new organizational priorities and initiatives. Because high-performance work systems are built on key business processes that deliver value to customers, as these processes and customer relationships change so too should the work system. The advantage of high-performance work systems is that they are flexible and, therefore, more easily adapted. When change occurs, it should be guided by a clear understanding of the business needs and exhibit a close vertical fit to strategy.

Outcomes of High-Performance Work Systems

Organizations achieve a wide variety of outcomes from high-performance work systems and effective human resources management. We have categorized these outcomes in terms of either *employee concerns* such as quality-of-work-life issues and job security or *competitive challenges* such as performance, productivity, and profitability. Throughout the text we have emphasized that the best organizations find ways to achieve a balance between these two sets of outcomes and pursue activities that improve both.

Employee Outcomes and Quality of Work Life

There are a myriad of potential benefits to employees from high-performance work systems. In high-performing workplaces, employees have the latitude to decide how to achieve their goals. In a learning environment, people can take risks, generate new ideas, and make mistakes, which in turn lead to new products, services, and markets. Because employees are more involved in their work, they are likely to be more satisfied and find that their needs for growth are more fully met. Because they are more informed and empowered, they are likely to feel that they have a fuller role to play in

High-performance work systems benefit employees by keeping them involved and informed.

the organization and that their opinions and expertise are valued more. This of course underlies greater commitment. With higher skills and greater potential for contribution, they are likely to have more job security as well as be more marketable to other organizations.

Additionally, as we discussed in Chapter 1, individuals with two- and four-year college degrees are a growing segment of the workforce. If employees with advanced education are to achieve their potential, they must be allowed to utilize their skills and abilities in ways that contribute to organizational success while fulfilling personal job growth and work satisfaction needs. High-performance work systems serve to mesh organizational objectives with employee contributions. Conversely, when employees are underutilized, organizations operate at less than full performance, while employees develop poor work attitudes and habits.[28]

Organizational Outcomes and Competitive Advantage

Several organizational outcomes also result from using high-performance work systems. These include higher productivity, lower costs, better responsiveness to customers, greater flexibility, and higher profitability. Highlights in HRM 3 provides a sample of the success stories that companies have shared about their use of high-performance work systems.[29]

Recall that in Chapter 2 we said that organizations can create a sustainable competitive advantage through people if they focus on four criteria. They must develop competencies in their employees that have the following qualities:

- *Valuable:* High-performance work systems increase value by establishing ways to increase efficiency, decrease costs, improve processes, and provide something unique to customers.
- *Rare:* High-performance work systems help organizations develop and harness skills, knowledge, and abilities that are not equally available to all organizations.
- *Difficult to imitate:* High-performance work systems are designed around team processes and capabilities that cannot be transported, duplicated, or copied by rival firms.
- *Organized:* High-performance work systems combine the talents of employees and rapidly deploy them in new assignments with maximum flexibility.[30]

These criteria clearly show how high-performance work systems in particular, and human resources management in general, are instrumental in achieving competitive advantage through people.

However, for all their potential, implementing high-performance work systems is not an easy task. The systems are complex and require a good deal of close partnering among executives, line managers, HR professionals, union representatives, and employees. Ironically, this very complexity leads to competitive advantage. Because high-performance work systems are difficult to implement, successful

Highlights in HRM 3

The Impact of High-Performance Work Systems

- Ames Rubber Corporation, a New Jersey–based manufacturer of rubber products and office machine components, experienced a 48 percent increase in productivity and five straight years of revenue growth.
- Sales at Connor Manufacturing Services, a San Francisco firm, grew by 21 percent, while new orders rose 34 percent and the company's profit on operations increased 21 percent to a record level.
- Over a seven-year period, Granite Rock, a construction material and mining company in Watsonville, California, experienced an 88 percent increase in market share, its standard for on-time delivery grew from 68 to 95 percent, and revenue per employee was 30 percent above the national average.
- At One Valley Bank of Clarksburg, West Virginia, employee turnover dropped by 48 percent, productivity increased by 24 percent, return on equity grew 72 percent, and profits jumped by 109 percent in three years.
- The Tennessee Eastman Division of the Eastman Chemical Company experienced an increase in productivity of nearly 70 percent, and 75 percent of its customers ranked it as the top chemical company in customer satisfaction.
- A study by John Paul MacDuffie of sixty-two automobile plants showed that those implementing high-performance work systems had 47 percent better quality and 43 percent better productivity.
- A study by Jeff Arthur of thirty steel minimills showed a 34 percent increase in productivity, 63 percent less scrap, and 57 percent less turnover.
- A study by Mark Huselid of 962 firms in multiple industries showed that high-performance work systems resulted in an annual increase in profits of more than $3,800 per employee.

Source: Martha A. Gephart and Mark E. Van Buren, "The Power of High Performance Work Systems," *Training & Development* 50, no. 10 (October 1996): 21–36.

organizations are difficult to copy. The ability to integrate business and employee concerns is indeed rare, and doing it in a way that adds value to customers is especially noteworthy. Organizations such as Wal-Mart, Microsoft, and Southwest Airlines have been able to do it, and as a result they enjoy a competitive advantage.

High-Performance Work Systems and the Small and Medium-Sized Employer

We conclude our discussion of high-performance work systems by noting their applicability to small and medium-sized organizations. While many of the examples

used to illustrate the popularity of HPWSs come from large, well-known companies, the philosophies, principles, and techniques that underlie HPWSs are equally appropriate to the management of enterprises of all sizes. It would be wrong to think that the four principles of HPWSs identified by Lawler (sharing information with employees, linking pay to performance, training and developing employees, and fostering an egalitarian work culture) are somehow unique to Fortune 1000 organizations. Nor would it be correct to surmise that the anatomy of HPWSs is applicable only to large corporations. Progressive organizations of all sizes have successfully implemented team-based work systems, implemented staffing practices that select high-quality employees, developed training programs that continually update employee skills, and utilized compensation practices that support specific organizational goals. The key is that they have done these things in a coordinated, integrative manner. These smaller organizations have simply achieved a system approach to organizational design that combines HR practices, work structures, and processes that effectively utilize employee competencies.

Readers of this text will find the principles of HPWSs of great assistance as they manage human resources, regardless of organizational size.

SUMMARY

objective 1 High-performance work systems are specific combinations of HR practices, work structures, and processes that maximize employee knowledge, skill, commitment, and flexibility. They are based on contemporary principles of high-involvement organizations. These principles include shared information, knowledge development, performance-reward linkages, and egalitarianism.

objective 2 High-performance work systems are composed of several interrelated components. Typically, the system begins with designing empowered work teams to carry out key business processes. Team members are selected and trained in technical, problem-solving, and interpersonal skills. To align the interests of employees with those of the organization, reward systems are connected to performance and often have group and organizational incentives. Skill-based pay is regularly used to increase flexibility and salaried pay plans are used to enhance an egalitarian environment. Leadership tends to be shared among team members, and information technology is used to ensure that employees have the information they need to make timely and productive decisions.

The pieces of the system are important only in terms of how they help the entire system function. When all the pieces support and complement one another, high-performance work systems achieve internal fit. When the system is aligned with the competitive priorities of the organization as a whole, it achieves external fit as well.

Implementing high-performance work systems represents a multidimensional change initiative. High-performance work systems are much more likely to go smoothly if a business case is first made. Top-management support is critical, and so too is the support of union representatives and other important constituents. HR representatives are often helpful in establishing a transition structure to help the implementation progress through its various stages. Once the system is in place, it should be evaluated in terms of its processes, outcomes, and ongoing fit with strategic objectives of the organization.

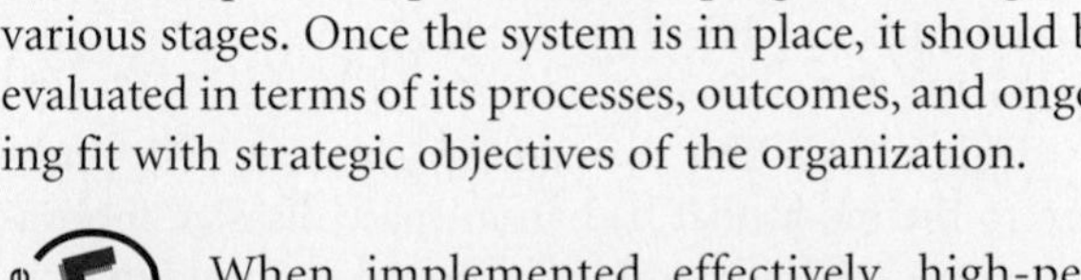

When implemented effectively, high-performance work systems benefit both the employees and the organization. Employees have more involvement in the organization, experience growth and satisfaction, and become more valuable as contributors. The organization also benefits from high productivity, quality, flexibility, and customer satisfaction. These features together can provide an organization with a sustainable competitive advantage.

The principles of HPWS apply in small and medium-sized organizational work settings as well as in large organizations. Progressive organizations of all sizes have successfully implemented high-performance work systems.

KEY TERMS

external fit
high-performance work system (HPWS)
internal fit
process audit

DISCUSSION QUESTIONS

1. Do you think the four principles of high involvement provide an adequate context for designing high-performance work systems? What other concerns or guidelines for developing high-performance work systems would you suggest?

2. In many cases, organizations use teams as a part of their high-performance work systems. Could such systems be useful in organizations that do not use teams? What special concerns might you have to address?

3. Although both internal and external fit are important concerns with high-performance work systems, which do you consider more critical and why?

4. This chapter places considerable emphasis on the processes involved in implementing high-performance work systems. What are the most critical steps to successful implementation?

5. How do you think employee-related outcomes and organizational outcomes are related to one another? Is it possible to achieve one set of outcomes without the other? Why or why not?

6. What concerns must a smaller employer address in trying to implement high-performance work systems? What advantages would a smaller organization have in using such systems?

BIZFLIX EXERCISES

Apollo 13: Houston, We Have a Problem

This chapter discussed some principles that underlie high-performance work systems. Watch for these principles in action while viewing this scene from the film *Apollo 13.*

This superb film dramatically shows a NASA mission to the moon that had an in-space disaster. Innovative problem solving and decision making amid massive ambiguity saved the crew. *Apollo 13* shows many examples of problem solving and decision making throughout the film. The zero-gravity simulator, a KC-135 four-engine jet aircraft (NASA's "Vomit Comet"), helped create the film's realistic weightless scenes. These scenes required 600 parabolic loops over 10 days of filming.

The chosen scene is an edited version of the "Houston, We Have a Problem . . ." sequence that appears a third of the way into the film. It starts as Jim Lovell (Tom Hanks) says, "Houston, we have a problem." This scene ends after Lovell tells Mission Control that they are venting something into space. The film continues with frenzied activity in Mission Control. Flight Director Gene Krantz (Ed Harris) asks people to work the problem and stop guessing about it.

What to Watch for and Ask Yourself

- Which principles of high-performance work systems appear in this scene? Note some examples from the scene of the principles you identify. You also can refer to Figure 16.2 while viewing the scene.
- The chapter earlier noted that training and development is a human resource practice that is important for high-performance work systems. What type of training do you believe the astronauts receive? Does it appear effective for them to carry out their mission? Why or why not?
- Jim Lovell is the commander of the Apollo 13 mission. During this scene, does he show the management and leadership characteristics discussed earlier in the chapter?

HRM Experience

Assessing the Strategic Fit of High-Performance Work Systems

High-performance work systems (HPWSs) are potentially powerful tools for managing employee commitment, involvement, and excellence. However, ensuring that all of the HR practices support one another—and the principles underlying the HPWS—is not always easy. At times, certain HR practices may support the HPWS while others actually may work against the principles. But if all the HR practices are not aligned, the system may be doomed. It takes only one misaligned practice to crash the whole system. Recall that the HPWS principles include the following:

- Shared information
- Egalitarianism
- Knowledge development
- Performance-reward linkage

Assignment

The figure on the following page lists the main HR practices used at Egan Clothiers, Ltd. Working in teams of four to six, assess the extent to which you believe each HR practice supports (or works against) each of the HPWS principles.

1. For each cell in the matrix, insert a number indicating the extent to which you believe the HR practice supports the principle or is counterproductive. The scale runs from −5 (strongly counterproductive) to 5 (very supportive). Zero indicates neither support nor detriment.
2. When you are done filling in each cell, add the numbers across each row to determine how supportive each HR practice is of all of the principles. Which HR practice is most supportive of the HPWS principles? Which HR practice is of most concern?
3. Add each column to see how the overall set of HR practices supports each principle. Which principle is most strongly supported? Which principle is the biggest concern?
4. Add the rows and/or columns to see how well the HPWS is supported overall. What changes would you recommend to improve the system?

Note: This figure corresponds to the integrative case on Egan Clothiers, Ltd., in the back of the text. The exercise can be used in conjunction with the case, or you may simply refer to the case as background reading.

EGAN CLOTHIERS, LTD.

HPWS PRINCIPLES

HR PRACTICES	Shared Information	Egalitarianism	Knowledge Development	Performance-Reward Linkage		
STRUCTURE						
• Cross-functional team						Row 1
• Department rotation						Row 2
STAFFING						
• Select for experience						Row 3
• Promote from within						Row 4
TRAINING						
• Retail selling skills						Row 5
• Customer service						Row 6
REWARDS						
• Results appraisal						Row 7
• Forced distribution						Row 8
• Individual incentives						Row 9
TECHNOLOGY						
• HR Info System						Row 10
• Post performance						Row 11
	Column 1	Column 2	Column 3	Column 4	TOTAL	

SCORING KEY

5 = strongly supports the principle
0 = neutral
–5 = strongly counterproductive

case study 1

HPWS Transforms Nevada Plant into One in a Million

In the world of beverage plants, this milestone at Ocean's Spray's Henderson, Nevada, plant is virtually unheard of—1 million operating hours without a lost-time accident. "This is an accomplishment that very few in our industry ever achieve," says Mike Stamatakos, vice president of operations for Ocean Spray. "A plant's safety record is a reflection of how well it is run. This milestone is an indication that Henderson does most—if not everything—well."

The fact that Ocean Spray Henderson is one of the safest beverage plants around is no accident. The plant's impressive operations milestone is the result of a two-and-a-half-year effort to improve safety awareness, uptime, and overall operations. When the plant was built in 1994 to serve Ocean Spray customers west of the Rockies, Ocean Spray had a vision to create a high-performance work system. The goal was to have an educated and involved workforce that would raise the bar in terms of plant performance and operations.

As part of that effort, in 2001 Henderson managers began a dedicated environmental health and safety (EHS) program. An early step in the process was bringing in an occupational therapist to perform a job safety analysis on the plant. The EHS program ranges from formal computer-based training—required of every employee—to fun promotions designed to get employees engaged with the safety message. The

Ocean Spray Henderson plant staff is divided into four teams and each is measured on just how well it performs. A bulletin board posts each team's days without a recordable accident. A real-time scoreboard on the plant floor provides workers a streaming update of the plant's vital performance statistics. The idea is that an informed worker is a stronger team member. The plant operates on a just-in-time delivery and shipment schedule that helps keep things running on time and within budget.

Reaching the 1-million-hour milestone was a twenty-five-year journey. "It's not just a case of the people in the front office talking the talk. It is the people on the floor and everyone in the facility walking the walk," says Jim Colmey, a safety specialist at the plant.

Source: Condensed from Andrea Foote, "One in a Million: Ocean Spray Henderson Has Parlayed Hard Work and Dedication into a Remarkable Operations Milestone," *Beverage World* 122, no. 8 (August 15, 2003): 22–29.

QUESTIONS

1. What are the key aspects of Ocean Spray's high-performance work system?
2. Do you think the system achieves both internal and external fit?
3. What other HR practices might the company consider implementing?

case study 2

HPWS at Xerox Corporation

One of the largest companies in the United States to implement high-performance work systems is the Xerox Corporation. The company employs 58,100 people worldwide. Its revenues in 2004 were $15.7 billion. As a result of a total quality management mandate that "improving quality is every employee's job," Xerox introduced its version of empowered teams, what it called "family groups." These family groups became the cornerstone for high-performance work systems throughout the company's service organization around the globe. Xerox service managers realized that they could improve productivity if responsibility for decision making moved closer to the point of customer contact. As empowered work groups evolved, the company began to realize that the groups could not function effectively unless other aspects of the company changed as well. Employees complained that they were evaluated and rewarded as individuals despite being organized as teams. Team members were not receiving the kind of information they needed to make decisions. This led Xerox to consider the entire system in which teams operated. And thus high-performance systems were born.

Perhaps the best example of a transition to HPWS is the Ohio Customer Business Unit (CBU), based in Columbus, Ohio. High-performance work systems were not introduced overnight, but through an incremental process that has taken nearly ten years. The first few steps were timid ones, consisting primarily of training in team dynamics and facilitation skills. Next, Xerox realized the importance of analyzing and reengineering work processes. All of the primary processes such as reliability, parts planning, and team facilitation were analyzed and documented. In each work group, process owners were identified and each team member took on a different role.

As process owners, team members had decision-making responsibility and accountability for such day-to-day decisions as work scheduling and for larger decisions such as hiring and performance reviews. The new responsibilities created some problems. Work-group members were expected to make decisions, but they often lacked relevant information.

In response, Xerox created a management information system to track and summarize key business indicators. Most of the business information is updated monthly. Some information, such as expense reports, is updated weekly. The system also provides teams with indicators of customer satisfaction levels several times a month. At each team meeting, members share information about the company's business plan and its financial performance.

The communication system wasn't the only thing that had to be modified to support high-performance work systems. Teams had to be tied together by common objectives and incentives. They had to be compensated in a way that fostered collaboration between team members and motivated them to work toward team goals. As a result, Xerox moved to a pay-for-performance compensation system called "Work-group Excellence," which rewards the performance of a team as a whole. Then, within each team, rewards are distributed on the basis of such factors as experience.

Some managers struggled with the new work systems. To increase their understanding, some were sent to Xerox's service operation in Phoenix, Arizona, which had also been experimenting with empowered teams. There they learned that the key to managerial support for work groups was to have managers structured into the work groups themselves. Only after experiencing team dynamics and acquiring the skills to work in teams were the managers able to address the needs of the teams they oversaw.

The Ohio CBU became the top service organization within Xerox, with customer satisfaction levels around 94 percent on service calls. It also has the lowest maintenance expenses per vehicle of any service unit within Xerox. Evidence of success for other high-performance work systems at Xerox is easy to find. Service organizations reported increases in all their target areas. Customer satisfaction increased by as much as ten points, with each point representing millions of dollars of business. Employee satisfaction improved 15 percent. Increases of 10 to 15 percent in response time and reliability occurred as well.

Source: Martha A. Gephart and Mark E. Van Buren, "The Power of High Performance Work Systems," *Training & Development* 50, no. 10 (October 1996): 21–36; Julie Demers, "Service Drives a New Xerox Program," *CMA Management* 76 no. 3 (May 2002): 36–39.

QUESTIONS

1. If you were a manager at Xerox, what concerns would you have with the way the company initially implemented high-performance work systems?
2. What role did information technology play in supporting high-performance work systems?
3. Why do you suppose some Xerox managers resisted the new systems?

case study 3

Iams's Pet Project

Iams Pet Food Company holds quarterly communication meetings with its employees at all of its eleven major facilities worldwide and has been doing so since 1985—even after being acquired by Procter & Gamble in 2000. Several members of the leadership team, including the owner and the president, have attended every one of these meetings. This method of communication helped pump the company's growth. In 1985, Iams had about $50 million in sales, with a couple of hundred employees in three major locations. At the end of 2004, its sales were over $1.6 billion, and the company had thousands of employees worldwide.

In 1985, Iams's HR Department performed its first employee attitude survey. The overall scores on the twenty-one-question survey were very good. But one statement on the survey had a very low score, which caught the attention of the ownership and the leadership team. The statement was: "We do not get enough information about how well our work group and company are doing." Employees were telling management that they felt left out of the picture as the company was growing. Something was not right when it came to communication.

This was a wake-up call to the ownership and leadership team because the company philosophy was built around Culture, Customers, Products, and People (CCPP). Because top management truly believed in this philosophy, they felt it was critical to improve the overall communication process in the company. Management decided they needed to report information to the employees as if they were stockholders, even though Iams was a privately held company.

The leadership team also knew that if they did not take action to improve communication, a third party might be needed to represent Iams employees in communications with Iams management. This could put even more distance between management and employees and further complicate the open communication process management envisioned. The process they finally settled on was to hold information-sharing "Quarterly Meetings" as if their employees were indeed stockholders.

How It Works

How does this "Quarterly Meetings" communication process work? Iams employee quarterly meetings are held four times a year at the home office, R&D, the plants, and key international locations. Senior managers travel to each location and share business results, as well as other pertinent information (future plans, products, strategies, and so on). The leadership at each of the company's locations also shares local results. This is done in a group setting with all employees attending the meeting.

The importance of real two-way communication became clear when this process became a platform for all types of improvements. First, this forum allows all employees to become active "shareholders" as they receive up-to-date key company results. This is important, because each employee is on a bonus incentive plan tied into sales, profit, and ROI.

The forum also allows for open dialogue between the employee audience and senior management after the presentations are completed. The meetings allow a great amount of information to be passed along in a timely manner and add to team speed. Even though quarterly all-employee meetings would seem to take away from team speed and production, they really have enhanced both.

Building Trust

Another important aspect of the quarterly meetings is the trust that develops between employees and management. The meetings are characterized by total openness, acceptance of criticism, demand for feedback, a nonthreatening atmosphere, and honest responses to open-ended questions, without prefabricated answers. This type of atmosphere creates a learning process for all participants in the meetings.

The "Trust Factor" is a personal growth issue for everyone. For instance, a unique feature at every meeting is the president or a senior vice president speaking directly to new employees in front of all employees about the company's vision, values, and strategies as a welcome to the company. This sets the tone for the whole meeting and encourages employee trust and participation. The secret of success is in an honest, plainly worded presentation of facts, placing all the cards on the table. Sharing important company information and organizational performance results with the entire company community shows a genuine concern from leadership.

Finally, holding these meetings on a regular basis is critical to building trust. As a result, all team members now hold themselves publicly accountable for what they say they are going to do. When this happens, trust comes alive. More and more positive performances start to happen within the organization.

Through this process, expectations of high performance for every member of the organization (including the leaders) are communicated. It is a two-way street: The leadership looks for feedback and ideas from every level of the company and employees are kept well-informed, focused on company goals, and motivated to follow through. Confidence and trust are continually established between the leadership and the members because they truly understand one another and have the opportunity to talk to each other.

Through this process the leadership of the company keeps everyone focused on the vision, mission, strategies, and goals of the organization. Because this is done every quarter, major changes, missed directions, and communication issues can quickly be corrected and action taken to get back on course.

Administration

Holding company-wide meetings is always a challenge. Deciding where to hold them and the best time of the week to hold them is tricky. The Iams Company uses local high school auditoriums and community centers as well as its own meeting rooms at remote locations. The best days of the week for Iams are Thursday, Friday, or Monday; the meetings are spread out over a three-week period to reach the various locations. Human Resources orchestrates the agenda, the mechanics, and the delivery.

At the end of the program, all local and home office leadership stands in front of the audience to answer questions. If a member of the leadership team does not know an answer, he or she is charged with finding the answer, getting back to the individual questioner, and posting it for everyone to see. This shows that the leadership can be trusted to follow through and respond to employees—that they care about and respect their employees.

The Results

So what does this communication process do for the company? First, it provides direction to the entire company team. It provides the answers to what is being done, where the company is going, and how it will get there.

Second, it provides definition. It helps everyone understand why certain actions are being taken, certain products made, certain methods used. It helps establish the importance of everyone's job in the overall scheme of things. It sets the definitions for quality and productivity. It responds to individual and group concerns about company social and administrative programs. Most important, it explains why we are doing the things we do.

Third, it is about drive. It provides for the spirit of togetherness. It makes the vision, values, and strategies of the company come alive to everyone. It keeps the team focused and moving forward toward the common goal.

Finally, this forum is an opportunity for senior management to develop their leadership skills. Having location, division, or department heads stand before those they lead and provide current performance updates and answer questions develops their leadership abilities. Answering why and how, clarifying issues that might be starting to fester, handling questions without threatening the individual—these are some of the critical elements company leadership must master. Iams's management gets plenty of opportunities to demonstrate courage, passion, integrity, and empathy.

The Cost

This type of program requires a great deal of effort and cost: shutting down part or all of an office or plant operation for three to four hours once a quarter, the time and travel of presenters, IT and audiovisual support. Is this type of human resource strategic effort worth the cost and effort involved? Each company or organization will have to make that determination, depending on its size and number of locations. For Iams, the benefits are real and this forum supports the concepts of performance management and management performance.

HR Catalyst

HR leadership can be the strategic catalyst to move this type of organizational communication forward. Creativity needs to come forward no matter what the size of the organization to make this two-way communication process become a reality. Communication technology (such as videoconferencing) is readily available to support the effort. But never forget the power of face-to-face contact and the importance of top management's willingness to be there to answer the organization's questions. Current business events continue to point toward the need for establishing trust.

Source: John Meyer, "Strategic Communication Enhances Organizational Performance." Reprinted with permission from *Human Resource Planning* 25, no. 2 (2002): 7–9. Copyright 2002 by The Human Resource Planning Society, 317 Madison Avenue, Suite 1509, New York, NY 10017, Phone: (212) 490–6387, Fax: (212) 682–6851. See also "The Fast 50: Peak Performers," *Fast Company* (March 2005): 52.

QUESTIONS

1. What aspects (principles, practices, and so on) of high-performance work systems are represented at Iams?
2. If you were a consultant to this company, what recommendations would you make to enhance the system?
3. Does anything concern you about what Iams is doing? Why or why not?

NOTES AND REFERENCES

1. D. A. Nadler and M. S. Gerstein, "Designing High-Performance Work Systems: Organizing People, Work, Technology, and Information," *Organizational Architecture* (San Francisco: Jossey-Bass, 1992): 195–208; E. Lawler III, Susan Albers Mohrman, and Gerald E. Ledford, *Creating High Performance Organizations: Practices and Results of Employee Involvement and Total Quality Management in Fortune 1000 Companies* (San Francisco: Jossey-Bass, 1995); Edward Lawler III, Susan Albers Mohrman, and George Benson, *Organizing for High Performance: Employee Involvement, TQM, Reengineering, and Knowledge Management in the Fortune 1000: The CEO Report* (San Francisco: Jossey-Bass, 2001). See also David Nadler, Michael Tushman, and Mark Nadler, *Competing by Design: The Power of Organizational Architecture* (New York: Oxford University Press, 1997); Cameron Allan and Ken Lovell, "The Effects of High Performance Work Systems on Employees in Aged Care," *Labour & Industry* 13, no. 3 (April 2003): 1–17.
2. Carlton P. McNamara, "Making Human Capital Productive," *Business and Economic Review* 46, no. 1 (October–December 1999): 10–13; Meagan Stovel and Nick Bontis, "Voluntary Turnover: Knowledge Management—Friend or Foe?" *Journal of Intellectual Capital* 3, no. 3 (2002): 303–22.
3. Martin Eppler and Oliver Sukowski, "Managing Team Knowledge: Core Processes, Tools and Enabling Factors," *European Management Journal* 18, no. 3 (June 2000): 334–41; Andrea Foote, "One in a Million: Ocean Spray Henderson Has Parlayed Hard Work and Dedication into a Remarkable Operations Milestone," *Beverage World* 122, no. 8 (August 15, 2003): 22–29.
4. Anil Gupta and Vijay Govindarajan, "Knowledge Management's Social Dimension: Lessons from Nucor Steel," *Sloan Management Review* 42, no. 1 (Fall 2000): 71–80; Patricia Panchack, "Putting Employees First Pays Off," *Industry Week* 251, no. 5 (June 2002): 14; Donna Berry, "Commitment to Culture: Old Home Foods Invests in Technology and Intellectual Capital," *Dairy Foods* 104, no. 4 (April 2003): 32.
5. This section is based on several studies related to best practices in human resources management and the development of high-performance work systems. See Arup Varma, Richard W. Beatty, Craig Eric Schneier, and David O. Ulrich, "High Performance Work Systems: Exciting Discovery or Passing Fad?" *Human Resource Planning* 22, no. 1 (1999): 26–37; J. B. Arthur, "Effects of Human Resource Systems on Manufacturing Performance and Turnover," *Academy of Management Journal* 37 (1994): 670–87; M. Huselid, "The Impact of Human Resource Management Practices on Turnover, Productivity, and Corporate Financial Performance," *Academy of Management Journal* 38 (1995): 635–72; P. Osterman, "How Common Is Workplace Transformation and Who Adopts It?" *Industrial and Labor Relations Review* 47, no. 2 (1994): 173–88; Craig Olson and Casey Ichniowski, "What Works at Work: Overview and Assessment," *Industrial Relations* 35, no. 3 (1996): 299–333; Mark A. Youndt, Scott A. Snell, James W. Dean, Jr., and David P. Lepak, "Human Resource Management, Manufacturing Strategy, and Firm Performance," *Academy of Management Journal* 39, no. 4 (August 1996): 836–66; John F. Tomer, "Understanding High-Performance Work Systems: The Joint Contribution of Economics and Human Resource Management," *The Journal of Socio-Economics* 30, no. 1 (January 2001): 63.
6. Jeffrey Kling, "High Performance Work Systems and Firm Performance," *Monthly Labor Review,* May 1995, 29–36. See also Chad Kaydo, "Top of the Charts: FedEx," *Sales and Marketing Management* 150, no. 7 (July 1998): 46, 48; Michael Trachtman, "Roving Internet Appliances," *Web Techniques* 6, no. 10 (October 2001): 55–57; Richard Shulman, "Just Say the Word," *Supermarket Business* 56, no. 6 (June 15, 2001): 19–20; "Customer Service Excellence: Continuously Delighting Your Customers," *PR Newswire* (February 24, 2005).
7. For more information about designing teams around critical work processes, see Mark Chen, "Applying the High Performance Work Team to EPC," *AACE International Transactions* (2002): PM61–PM67; Valerie Sessa, "Supporting Work Team Effectiveness: Best Management Practices for Fostering High Performance," *Personnel Psychology* 53, no. 2 (Summer 2000): 457–60.
8. See Lawler, Mohrman, and Ledford, *Creating High Performance Organizations;* Eileen Appelbaum, Thomas Bailey, Peter Berg, and Narne Kalleberg, *Manufacturing Advantage: Why High-Performance Work Systems Pay Off* (Ithaca, NY: Cornell University Press, 2000); Gil Preuss and Brenda Lautsch, "The Effect of Formal versus Informal Job Security on Employee Involvement Programs," *Relations Industrielles* 57, no. 3 (Summer 2002): 517–39; Wendy S. Becker, "Manufacturing Advantage: Why High-Performance Work Systems Pay Off," *Personnel Psychology* 56, no. 2 (Summer 2003): 549–53; "Nike Factories to Get Help from MIT's Sloan School," *InformationWeek* (April 13, 2005).
9. Laurie J. Bassi and Mark E. Van Buren, "Sustaining High Performance in Bad Times," *Training & Development* 51, no. 6 (June 1997): 32–42; Katie Thomas, "Short-Term Downsizing, Long-Term Performance," *Incentive* 171, no. 4 (April 1997): 14; Nik Theodore and Rachel Weber, "Changing Work Organization in Small Manufacturers: Challenges for Economic Development," *Economic Development Quarterly* 15, no. 4 (November 2001): 367–79.
10. Michael J. Stevens and Michael A. Campion, "Staffing Work Teams: Development and Validation of a Selection Test for

Teamwork Settings," *Journal of Management* 25, no. 2 (1999): 207–28; Leaetta Hough and Frederick Oswald, "Personnel Selection: Looking toward the Future—Remembering the Past," *Annual Review of Psychology* 51 (2000): 631–64.

11. Cristina Gibson and Mary Zellmer-Bruhn, "Metaphors and Meaning: An Intercultural Analysis of the Concept of Teamwork," *Administrative Science Quarterly* 46, no. 2 (June 2001): 274–303; Diane Bailey, "Modeling Work Group Effectiveness in High-Technology Manufacturing Environments," *IIE Transactions* 32, no. 4 (April 2000): 361–68; Mark E. Van Buren and Jon M. Werner, "High Performance Work Systems," *B&E Review* (October–December 1996): 15–23; "Schindler Elevator Announces Center for Service Excellence; Holland, OH Facility to Serve as National Support Center," *PR Newswire* (July 21, 2004); "Large Organizations That Focus on Excellence in Human Capital Management May Be More Likely to Outperform the Market, According to Taleo Customer Study," *PR Newswire* (March 30, 2005).
12. Rosemary Batt and Lisa Moynihan, "The Viability of Alternative Call Centre Production Models," *Human Resource Management Journal* 12, no. 4 (2002): 14. For more information on the potential application of "intracapital," see Gifford Pinchot, "Free Intraprise," *Executive Excellence* 18, no. 1 (January 2001): 10.
13. David Paper, James Rodger, and Parag Pendharker, "A BPR Case Study at Honeywell," *Business Process Management Journal* 7, no. 2 (2001): 85–93. See also Robert McNabb and Keith Whitfield, "Job Evaluation and High Performance Work Practices: Compatible or Conflictual?" *Journal of Management Studies* 38, no. 2 (March 2001): 293–312; Leslie A. Weatherly, "Performance Management: Getting It Right from the Start," *HRMagazine* 49, no. 3 (March 2004): S1–S11.
14. Warren Bennis, "The Future Has No Shelf Life," *Executive Excellence* 17, no. 8 (August 2000): 5–6; Peggy Holman, "Culture Change," *Executive Excellence* 17, no. 7 (July 2000): 16; Clinton Longenecker, "Building High Performance Management Teams," *Industrial Management* 43, no. 6 (November/December 2001): 21–26; Wendy S. Becker, "Manufacturing Advantage: Why High-Performance Work Systems Pay Off," *Personnel Psychology* 56, no. 2 (Summer 2003): 549.
15. Keith Newton, "The High Performance Workplace: HR-Based Management Innovations in Canada," *International Journal of Technology Management* 16, no. 1–3 (1998): 177–92; Georg Von Krogh, Kazuo Ichijo, and Ikujiro Nonaka, *Enabling Knowledge Creation: How to Unlock the Mystery of Tacit Knowledge and Release the Power of Innovation* (New York: Oxford University Press, 2000); Lawler, Mohrman, and Benson, *Organizing for High Performance.*
16. Patrick M. Wright and Scott A. Snell, "Toward a Unifying Framework for Exploring Fit and Flexibility in Strategic Human Resource Management," *Academy of Management Review* 23, no. 4 (October 1998): 756–72; Clair Brown and Michael Reich, "Micro-Macro Linkages in High-Performance Employment Systems," *Organization Studies* 18, no. 5 (1997): 765–81; S. A. Snell, M. Shadur, and P. M. Wright, "Human Resources Strategy: The Era of Our Ways," in M. A. Hitt, R. E. Freeman, and J. S. Harrison (eds.), *Handbook of Strategic Management* (London: Blackwell, 2002), 627–49.
17. Van Buren and Werner, "High Performance Work Systems," 15–23; Gilbert Probst, Steffen Raub, and Kai Romhardt, *Managing Knowledge—Building Blocks for Success* (New York: Wiley, 2000). For a similar example of vertical fit within European firms, see Sue Hutchinson, John Purcell, and Nick Kinnie, "Evolving High Commitment Management and the Experience of the RAC Call Center," *Human Resource Management Journal* 10, no. 1 (2000): 63–78.
18. Brian Becker, Mark Huselid, and Dave Ulrich, *The HR Scorecard: Linking People, Strategy, and Performance* (Cambridge, MA: Harvard Business School Press, 2001).
19. Varma, Beatty, Schneier, and Ulrich, "High Performance Work Systems," 26–37; Gephart and Van Buren, "Power of High Performance Work Systems," *Training & Development* 50, no. 10 (October 1996): 21–36; Foote, "One in a Million: Ocean Spray Henderson," 22–29.
20. Varma, Beatty, Schneier, and Ulrich, "High Performance Work Systems," 26–37; Gephart and Van Buren, "Power of High Performance Work Systems"; "Making Change Work—for Real," *HRFocus* 80, no. 1 (January 2003): S1.
21. Louise Clarke and Larry Haiven, "Workplace Change and Continuous Bargaining," *Relations Industrielles* 54, no. 1 (Winter 1999): 168–91; Ruth Wright, "Forging Sustainable Alliances in a New Economy," *Canadian Business Review* (Summer 1995): 20–24.
22. Clarke and Haiven, "Workplace Change," 168–91; Wright, "Forging Sustainable Alliances," 20–24; Joel Cuthcer-Gershenfeld, Thomas Kochan, and John Calhoun Wells, "In Whose Interest? A First Look at National Survey Data on Interest-Based Bargaining in Labor Relations," *Industrial Relations* 40, no. 1 (January 2001): 1–21.
23. Wright, "Forging Sustainable Alliances," 20–24; Hannele Rubin, "How CEOs Get Results," *Chief Executive* (February 2001): 8.
24. Wright, "Forging Sustainable Alliances," 20–24.
25. Gephart and Van Buren, "Power of High Performance Work Systems"; Michael Beer, "How to Develop an Organization Capable of Sustained High Performance: Embrace the Drive for Results-Capability Development Paradox," *Organizational Dynamics* 29, no. 4 (Spring 2001): 233–47.
26. Neal and Tromley, "From Incremental Change to Retrofit," *The Academy of Management Executive* 9, no. 1 (February 1995): 42–54.
27. Nicolay A. M. Worren, Keith Ruddle, and Karl Moore, "From Organizational Development to Change Management: The Emergence of a New Profession," *Journal of Applied Behavioral Science* 35, no. 3 (September 1999): 273–86; Randa A. Wilbur, "Making Changes the Right Way," *Workforce,* Supplement

(March 1999): 12–13; Gephart and Van Buren, "Power of High Performance Work Systems"; Irena St. John-Brooks, "CEOs See HR as Helping to Lead Organizational Efforts: USA," *Benefits & Compensation International* 32, no. 1 (July/August 2002): 73–74; "Human Resources Role Transformed at Deutsche Bank," *Human Resource Management International Digest* 10, no. 5 (2002): 12–14; Michael Svoboda and Silke Schroder, "Transforming Human Resources in the New Economy: Developing the Next Generation of Global HR Managers at Deutsche Bank AG," *Human Resource Management* 40, no. 3 (Fall 2001): 261–73; "HR Advice: Manage Transition—Not Just Change," *HR Briefing* (November 15, 2002): 1–2; "HR Must Seize Major Role over Change Management," *Personnel Today* (May 20, 2003): 8.

28. Berg, "The Effects of High Performance Work Practices"; Peter Cappelli and Nikolai Rogovsky, "Employee Involvement and Organizational Citizenship: Implications for Labor Law Reform and Lean Production," *Industrial & Labor Relations Review* 51, no. 4 (July 1998): 633–53; D. J. Storey, "Education, Training and Development Policies and Practices in Medium-Sized Companies in the UK: Do They Really Influence Firm Performance?" *Omega* 30, no. 4 (August 2002): 249–64; Paul Osterman, "Work Reorganization in an Era of Restructuring: Trends in Diffusion and Effects on Employee Welfare," *Industrial & Labor Relations Review* 53, no. 2 (January 2000): 179–96; "How to Take the 'Non' out of Your 'Non-Performers'" *Human Resource Department Management Report* (February 2005): 1–5.

29. Robert J. Vandenberg, Hettie A. Richardson, and Lorrina J. Eastman, "The Impact of High Involvement Work Processes on Organizational Effectiveness: A Second-Order Latent Variable Approach," *Group & Organization Management* 24, no. 3 (September 1999): 300–39; Jeffrey Pfeffer and John F. Veiga, "Putting People First for Organizational Success," *Academy of Management Executive* 13, no. 2 (May 1999): 37–48; Laurie J. Bassi and Mark E. Van Buren, "The 1999 ASTD State of the Industry Report," *Training & Development*, Supplement (1999): 1–26.

30. John Purcell, "Best Practice and Best Fit: Chimera or Cul-de-Sac?" *Human Resource Management Journal* 9, no. 3 (1999): 26–41; Snell, Shadur, and Wright, "Human Resources Strategy: The Era of Our Ways," 627–649; Patrick M. Wright, Benjamin Dunford, and Scott A. Snell, "Human Resources and the Resource-Based View of the Firm," *Journal of Management* 27, no. 6 (2001): 701–21.

HR Proves Its Value at SYSCO Foods

Case 1

For evidence that SYSCO Corporation's innovative Virtual Human Resource Center is making an impact, consider this. It motivated Jim Hope, president of a Kansas City subsidiary of SYSCO, to station himself in the warehouse one morning before dawn so that he could give a presentation on stock options to the company's truck drivers. "We did a workplace climate survey," Hope says, "and one of the things it showed was that employees wanted to see top management in person more."

Undoubtedly, there are companies where regional management might gripe at having to implement initiatives flung down from corporate headquarters. But SYSCO—the largest food-service company in North America, with $29 billion in annual revenues—isn't one of them. One reason is simple: Regional executives such as Hope are free to accept or reject the programs pitched by the Virtual Resource Center. The program uses a "market-driven" approach to HR, in which SYSCO's corporate HR professionals have to persuade regional subsidiaries to "buy" its initiatives—and to pay for them.

"We get to choose what we think will help us," Hope says. All the same, he and other regional managers—as well as SYSCO's top management—are enthusiastic about the results that the Virtual Resource Center's unorthodox approach has produced. Since the center's inception in 1998, for example, SYSCO has experienced a big drop in workers' compensation claims—a $10 million annual savings, the company estimates. It also reports a significant improvement in the retention rate for tough-to-keep night warehouse employees, at an estimated yearly cost savings of about $15 million. Corporate management is also impressed by HR's contribution to bottom-line performance at SYSCO. "I really feel like HR has helped our profits," says SYSCO president and chief operating officer Richard Schnieders.

SYSCO isn't the kind of business that would lend itself to a conventional top-down approach to HR. The company's 47,000-some employees work to supply food and other products to more than 400,000 establishments, ranging from fancy restaurants and posh hotels to corner delis and hospital cafeterias. In addition to selling food and beverages, the firm supplies items such as napkins and kitchen equipment and provides consulting advice about menus and food safety issues. SYSCO is able to serve the diverse needs of its vast clientele by allowing the regional managements of its more than 120 far-flung business units to operate with a high degree of autonomy.

Over the years, the HR department at SYSCO's Houston headquarters has developed an approach that mimics the corporate culture. Corporate HR functions as an entrepreneurial entity, with the regional SYSCO subsidiaries acting as its customers. HR has to sell every initiative it develops to the regional companies, which generally are free to accept a particular program—and fund it out of their own regional budgets—or reject it. The system puts pressure on corporate HR to figure out which programs and services the subsidiaries really need, and to demonstrate how those initiatives will affect the subsidiaries' bottom line. That may sound like a tough sale, but SYSCO's HR team has become adept at closing the deal, by providing information that shows how its programs can enhance a regional subsidiary's bottom line. They make innovative use of workplace climate surveys, correlating the findings to data on customer satisfaction and business performance. And they've developed a company-wide intranet database that enables the subsidiaries' executives to see which HR programs are achieving results at other company facilities.

"SYSCO has taken a very traditional approach to HR and turned it absolutely upside down," says Patrick Wright, director at the Center for Advanced HR Studies at Cornell University, which has assisted SYSCO as a consultant. With the creation of the Virtual Resource Center, the business has achieved demonstrable results.

Creating and Selling an HR "Brand"

SYSCO's corporate and regional HR group has evolved into a collaborative, innovative team. For most of the company's 35-year history, it wasn't so innovative. But as the company grew, its thinking about corporate HR did too. SYSCO wanted to provide services to its employees and help them improve their performance. But the company didn't want to force them on the local subsidiaries, whose managements traditionally had been free to run things as they saw fit. That independence, after all, had been a crucial element of SYSCO's success at serving markets large and small across the continent. The company brought in Ken Carrig, a former HR executive for Continental Airlines and PepsiCo, to oversee the delicate task of creating a new corporate HR program. "Early on, I sat down with [SYSCO founder] John Baugh, to learn his thoughts and values," Carrig recalls. "I followed up with a meeting with our current executive team. From those conversations, it was obvious to me that the SYSCO culture was intensely entrepreneurial, and that HR had to find a way to complement that."

As a result of those discussions, Carrig and SYSCO created the Virtual Resource Center concept. Instead of replacing the regional units' existing HR practices, corporate HR teamed up with regional HR to provide them with additional tools and resources. Management at the subsidiaries would be free to choose which services and programs they wanted. And since the funding for those initiatives came out of their own budgets, they also got to decide whether they wanted to purchase services from corporate headquarters or hire an outside vendor.

Since the Virtual Resource Center had to depend on financing from the SYSCO subsidiaries to fund its programs, Carrig and his staff were forced to pay very close attention to regional needs. "I have to say to our president, 'This program will cost us $50,000, and I can get 10 companies to kick in $5,000,'" he says.

Had SYSCO corporate tried to dictate its HR programs, Wright says, it wouldn't have worked. "You'd have a lot of defensive reactions from the regional companies, because they're not getting dictates in other areas," he says. "Instead, Ken Carrig and his team have done a good job of developing relationships and credibility. Corporate works with them as a consultant, not as a director."

When executives of several SYSCO subsidiaries came to Carrig early on for help with a pressing problem—staff retention—he was eager to find a way to help. "We discovered that we didn't have any systematic tools to address the problem, to get a handle on what was good and what was not so good about our operations." That got Carrig thinking. And that's when he and Susan Billiot, assistant vice president of HR, went to Wright for help in designing a new survey program.

Innovative Use of Surveys

Companies have conducted workplace climate surveys for decades, but Carrig and SYSCO wanted to go beyond what others had done. Sears, for example, already had shown that positive employee attitudes had a good effect on customer satisfaction, and that a combination of the two improved a company's profits. Carrig wanted to gather that kind of data, too, but he wanted to keep compiling it over time, and to study the impact of specific management practices at SYSCO companies.

"This is a step up from the classic Sears Employee-Customer-Profit-Chain model," Wright says. "That approach tells you the consequences of employee attitudes. The SYSCO model, hopefully, can tell you how to fix them."

When Carrig presented the new survey concept to a conference of regional executives, he was so confident of the initiative's promise that he offered the subsidiaries a money-back guarantee if they weren't satisfied. Fifty percent of the regional companies agreed to participate in the first year. In the past five years, the vast majority have signed on.

The wealth of data has helped SYSCO make useful discoveries. Corporate HR learned, for example, that one of the key discontents of delivery associates was the way their compensation was determined. "Generally, the only way they could make more money was to work overtime, or to stall so that they would be away from the warehouse longer," Carrig says. But HR also noticed that a few companies got higher quality-of-life scores from their drivers than the others did. They investigated further and found that those companies were paying activity-based compensation, which augmented a base pay rate with incentives for drivers who made more deliveries and fewer mistakes, and maintained good safety records.

"Once we figured out what they were doing, we developed a compensation program around that concept and made it available to all of our companies." As a result, the retention rate for drivers jumped 8 percent. "We've found that it wasn't a fluke," Carrig explains. "Every company that went on ABC [activity-based compensation] the first year has had significantly higher satisfaction." Delivery expenses also dropped, and customer satisfaction levels improved.

Sharing Information Online

To help SYSCO companies use the data, corporate HR developed powerful analytical tools and made them available on the corporate intranet. A benchmarking system gives regional executives scorecards showing their companies' performance compared to that of others in SYSCO's realm.

Even more innovative is the online database that enables executives to find subsidiaries of similar size that are strong performers in particular areas so that they can learn about the practices that make them successful.

"For example, if you're not in the 50th percentile in a particular performance area, we give you a message that says, 'You may want to actually call this company and/or do a site visit,'" Carrig says. "Or we may alert you that your company has enough other things happening that fixing this particular factor may not be enough to improve performance."

The portal also helps a regional executive find a higher-performing SYSCO subsidiary that would make an appropriate model. Instead of emulating a company that's been operating consistently well for fifteen years, Carrig says, subsidiaries are likely to get more benefit from studying a company that's gone from the bottom to the top 25 percent in a short time.

One of the benefits of SYSCO's entrepreneurial, data-driven approach to HR is that the company's regional HR professionals can see more definitively which initiatives work and which ones don't, and why. That enables them to tinker with the system and subtly improve it over time. The need to continually sell its initiatives keeps corporate HR on its toes.

"We've got plenty of room to grow," Carrig says. And that's good. By its very nature, SYSCO acquires businesses and spins off new regional companies from existing ones all the time. As the corporation continues to evolve and change, the services offered by the Virtual Human Resource Center are bound to be in even greater demand.

Source: Patrick J. Kiger, "HR Proves Its Value," *Workforce* 81, no. 3 (March 2002): 28–33. Reprinted by permission of the publisher via Copyright Clearance Center. See also Wayne F. Cascio, "From Business Partner to Driving Business Success: The Next Step in the Evolution of HR Management," *Human Resource Management* 44, no. 2 (Summer 2005): 159-164.

QUESTIONS

1. What are the fundamental aspects of SYSCO's Virtual HR system that add value to the organization?
2. What concerns would you have in implementing such a system in other organizations?
3. What other elements would you recommend to enhance SYSCO's HR system?

Golden Values: Molson Coors Brewing Co.

Case 2

In the aftermath of events at Enron, WorldCom and Tyco, the emphasis on ethical business operations has reached a fever pitch. But it didn't take a scandal or the wrath of the press for Molson Coors Brewing Co. to put a comprehensive program in place. Over the last decade, the brewer has provided an array of tools to help employees understand ethical issues and effectively cope with them.

The Golden, Colorado, company has developed one of the nation's most comprehensive ethics programs. The company emerged as a model by offering its 8,500 employees a spate of resources, including interactive online courses, ethics leadership training, a decision map, a highly detailed set of policies and a help line.

"The goal of the program is to step beyond rules and guidelines and teach employees how to think, clarify and analyze situations," says Warren Malmquist, who developed the program and serves as director of Molson Coors Audit Services. When he started the program in 1990, the company's ethics policy was little more than a basic code of conduct and set of guidelines. Since then, the firm has continually added features that are deliberately focused on a strategy of "prevention" rather than "investigation."

In 1996, the beer maker introduced a company-wide affirmation process. Initially there was some resistance from union and employee groups that didn't like certain provisions in the ethics policy. With education and training, however, it was better understood and accepted.

"We realized that it was essential to develop a code of ethics that is meaningful rather than a legal-based document that's difficult to understand," says Caroline McMichen, group manager of ethics and audit services.

A cross-functional team rewrote the code of conduct to make it more user-friendly and accessible to workers. Then in 2002, the company invested $250,000 in an interactive Web-based module to help guide employees through real-world scenarios and ensure that they understand key principles of ethics. The program uses an "ethics expedition" theme that requires employees to ascend from a base camp to the top of a mountain by completing activities in each of four camps. As the employee ascends, the topics evolve from rules to values, from black-and-white issues to shades of gray.

All new hires must complete the online course within 90 days as a condition of employment. Existing employees must take a refresher course every year or two. All employees, from senior executives to those loading trucks in the warehouse, must partake in a Web-based ethics training module. All employees have access to the help line, which they can call with questions about an event or relay concerns about an ethical breach. Today, the help line receives about 25 calls per quarter, and Molson Coors investigates each one, McMichen says.

Employee evaluations at Molson Coors factor in how well workers model the behavior outlined in the company's ethical code of conduct. McMichen notes that while it's difficult to measure results in terms of numbers or dollars, there's no question that the program has paid handsome dividends. "People understand ethical issues and concerns more clearly and they are able to face situations more proactively," she says.

Source: Samuel Greengard, "Golden Values," *Workforce Management* 84, no. 3 (March 1, 2005): 52.

QUESTIONS

1. Why is it important to teach employees how to reason through ethical business dilemmas?
2. If you were an employee, do you think specific ethical "tools," such as a decision map, ethical hotline, and so forth, would help you make the right decision?
3. Why is it important to appraise employees on the basis of their ethics?

Job Analysis and Hiring Decisions at Ovania Chemical

Case 3

Company Background

Ovania Chemical Corporation is a specialty chemical producer of polyethylene terephthalate (PET) thermoplastic resins primarily used to make containers for soft drinks and bottled water, as well as packaging for food and pharmaceutical products.

Though smaller than other chemical producers that produce globally, Ovania has competed successfully in its niche of the U.S. specialty chemical business. Its main plant is located in Steubenville, Ohio, positioned along the Ohio River midway between Pittsburgh, Pennsylvania, and Wheeling, West Virginia. In recent years, advances in technology have altered the nature of chemical production, and like other firms in the industry, Ovania Chemical is taking steps to modernize its facilities. Not surprisingly, these technological changes have been accompanied by redesign in employee jobs. In fact, over the last three years, there have been drastic changes in both the number and the kinds of jobs being performed by employees. The latest change at the Steubenville plant involves the job transformations of the system analyzer position.

The System Analyzer

Because chemical production involves highly integrated process technologies, someone must monitor all of the individual components simultaneously. The system analyzer is primarily responsible for this monitoring function. It is one of the most prestigious nonmanagerial jobs in the entire plant, and its importance is likely to grow.

Formerly the position was classified as that of a semiskilled maintenance technician, but as the plant has become more automated, the requirements for the system analyzer job have become much more extensive. Knowledge of pneumatics, hydraulics, information technology, programming, and electrical wiring are all increasingly critical aspects of this job. As these up-skilling trends continue, the three men who currently hold the position admit that they will be incapable of performing adequately in the future. It is estimated that within two years, the tasks, duties, and responsibilities of the system analyzer will have changed by more than 70 percent. For these reasons, management decided to recruit and select three new people for the rapidly transforming position.

Job Analysis and New Position Analysis

Ovania's Steubenville plant manager, Jack Sarabe; the HR manager, Emily Claire; and two senior engineers, Dave Packley and Mark Young, formed a selection committee. With the help of two consultants, they first conducted a job analysis for the new position of system analyzer. Although they had to project into the future regarding the specific nature of the job, they collectively felt they had created an accurate depiction of the requirements for someone who would occupy the position. Figure 3-1 shows a list of the major performance dimensions of the job and a subsample of specific tasks characteristic of each dimension.

From this list of tasks, the selection committee then delineated a set of personal qualities required for anyone who would hold the system analyzer position. These qualities included the twelve abilities shown in Figure 3-2. The numbers beside each ability indicate the tasks (see Figure 3-1) to which it is related. The abilities marked with an asterisk (*) were considered by the committee to be "critical." Any applicant not scoring well on each of the critical dimensions would be considered unqualified for the job.

Anticipated Selection Process

The committee hoped to gain "new blood" for the redesigned system analyzer job and therefore wanted to recruit externally for the best available talent they could find. However, as a matter of policy, management was also deeply committed to the

Figure 3-1 Performance Dimensions (Duties and Tasks)

MAINTAINING SPARES AND SUPPLIES

1. Anticipates future need for parts and supplies and orders them.
2. Stocks parts and supplies in an orderly fashion.
3. Maintains and calibrates test equipment.

TROUBLESHOOTING

4. Applies calibration standards to verify operation by subjecting the system to known standards.
5. Decides whether the problem is in the sensor, in the processor, in the process stream, and/or in the sample system.
6. Uses troubleshooting guides in system manuals to determine the problem area.
7. Uses test equipment to diagnose the problem.
8. Makes a general visual inspection of the analyzer system as a first troubleshooting step.
9. Replaces components such as printed circuit boards and sensors to see if the problem can be alleviated.

HANDLING REVISIONS AND NEW INSTALLATIONS

10. Makes minor piping changes such as size, routing, and additional filers.
11. Makes minor electrical changes such as installing switches and wires and making terminal changes.
12. Uses common pipefitting tools.
13. Uses common electrical tools.
14. Reads installation drawings.

RECORD KEEPING

15. Maintains system files showing the historical record of work on each system.
16. Maintains loop files that show the application of the system.
17. Updates piping and instrument drawings if any changes are made.
18. Maintains Environmental Protection Agency records and logbooks.
19. Disassembles analyzers to perform repairs onsite or back in the shop.
20. Replaces damaged parts such as filters, electronic components, light source, lenses, sensors, and valves.
21. Uses diagnostic equipment such as oscilloscopes, ohmmeters, and decade boxes.
22. Tests and calibrates repaired equipment to ensure that it works properly.
23. Reads and follows written procedures from manuals.

ROUTINE MAINTENANCE

24. Observes indicators on systems to ensure proper operation.
25. Adds reagents to systems.
26. Decides whether the lab results or the system is correct regarding results (resolves discrepancies between lab and analyzer results).
27. Performs calibrations.

Figure 3-2 **Abilities and Tasks**

Numbers represent tasks cited in Figure 3-1. Asterisks indicate abilities considered critical by the committee.

SKILLS	TASK NUMBERS
*Finger dexterity	3, 4, 7, 9, 10, 11, 12, 13, 19, 20, 21, 22, 25, 27
*Mechanical comprehension	3, 5, 6, 8, 9, 10, 12, 13, 7, 14, 19, 20, 22, 23, 24, 27, 11, 17
*Numerical ability	11, 3, 4, 24, 10, 21, 12, 13, 14, 27
*Spatial ability	2, 4, 5, 9, 10, 11, 14, 19, 20
*Visual pursuit	3, 4, 5, 6, 7, 8, 9, 10, 11, 14, 16, 17, 19, 20, 21, 22, 27
*Detection	2, 3, 5, 6, 8, 9, 10, 14, 19, 20, 23, 7
Oral comprehension	1, 2, 5, 6, 26, 7, 8, 9, 19, 21, 25
Written comprehension	1, 15, 16, 17, 18
Deductive reasoning	1, 5, 3, 6, 7, 8, 9, 10, 11, 19, 21, 20, 22, 2, 26, 27
Inductive reasoning	1, 3, 5, 6, 7, 8, 9, 10, 11, 19, 21, 20, 22, 2, 26, 27
Reading comprehension	3, 6, 14, 7, 22, 23, 21, 9, 27
Reading scales and tables	3, 4, 7, 8, 9, 21, 23, 24, 27, 2, 6, 14

idea of promoting from within. After deliberation, the committee decided to recruit both internally and externally for the new position. It also decided to especially encourage current system analyzers to "reapply" for the job.

Because of the two-year lead time before the newly transformed position would be put in place, the committee was very careful not to include in the selection battery any skills or knowledge that could reasonably be trained within that two-year period. Only aptitude or ability factors were incorporated into the selection process, rather than achievement tests.

In a private session, a few of the selection committee members admitted candidly that they had serious doubts whether any woman or minority member currently in the relevant labor market would have requisite credentials to be competitive for the position. The three present system analyzers were white males. However, because Ovania Chemical had a rather unenviable history of employment discrimination charges, the committee decided to do no unnecessary prescreening of applicant qualifications, previous experience, and so on. This strategy was thought to encourage minorities and women to apply for the new position irrespective of their prior employment history.

However, there was some concern about prejudice if a woman or minority member were to get the job. According to the grapevine, many did not consider a woman or minority suitable for such a prestigious position. Moreover, several people commented that a woman would not get down into the treatment tanks to check gauge readings. All of these factors, taken together, made for a very sensitive selection process. Ovania's management, however, was dedicated to making the procedures and decisions fair and objective.

Fifty-six employees applied for the new position of system analyzer. Twenty-one were female; fifteen were black. Only two of the three current system analyzers reapplied for the new position. For now, the company decided that an overall total score of 800 on the twelve tests would be the cutoff score in order for an applicant to be

Figure 3-3 Primary Pool of Candidates

NAME	RACE	SEX	EXTERNAL/ INTERNAL	Finger dexterity	Mechanical comprehension	Numerical ability	Spatial ability	Visual pursuit	Detection	Oral comprehension	Written comprehension	Deductive reasoning	Inductive reasoning	Reading comprehension	Reading scales and tables		TEST SCORES
Baldwin, T.	W	M	I	83	76	78	76	69	71	90	70	74	72	88	92	=	941
Bittner, D.	W	M	E	92	62	88	89	96	85	90	94	93	89	97	87	=	1062
Bohlander, G.	W	M	E	67	78	74	70	76	62	80	69	71	76	78	82	=	883
Buffett, J.	B	M	E	87	97	89	61	94	93	75	90	85	96	85	80	=	1032
Denny, A.	B	F	I	92	88	72	72	78	79	69	76	81	83	81	78	=	949
Egan, M.	W	F	E	93	80	76	98	76	88	93	92	93	78	81	92	=	884
Granger, D.	W	F	I	82	82	79	75	77	73	72	80	81	77	70	80	=	856
Haney, H.	W	M	E	82	76	76	71	69	80	62	76	75	74	78	67	=	810
Kight, G.	W	F	E	65	75	72	67	80	74	62	47	66	67	60	80	=	815
Kovach, S.	W	M	E	82	87	85	85	83	88	81	80	80	83	84	80	=	998
Laukitis, T.	B	F	E	87	97	63	89	93	90	91	85	86	96	88	89	=	1054
Lesko, B. J.	B	F	I	83	84	89	91	80	82	86	88	85	84	90	89	=	1031
Rom, D.	B	M	I	80	60	67	66	67	62	74	80	67	72	75	66	=	835
Sara, E.	W	F	I	89	91	77	93	90	91	88	78	98	80	80	76	=	1021
Sauder, C.	W	F	E	76	72	78	81	80	72	73	77	75	79	82	82	=	927
Sherman, A.	W	F	I	91	82	78	93	92	94	89	77	95	77	81	92	=	1041
Snell, J.	W	M	E	80	85	84	81	81	80	89	88	84	86	81	82	=	1001
Timothy, S.	W	F	E	82	78	76	71	69	80	62	76	76	70	71	67	=	878
Whitney, J.	W	M	I	67	71	70	76	76	62	81	69	71	76	78	82	=	815
Wright, P.	W	M	I	80	60	57	56	57	62	74	80	69	72	75	65	=	887

seriously considered for the system analyzer position. This criterion resulted in the primary pool of twenty candidates shown in Figure 3-3. It should be noted that although each of the aptitude tests has been published, standardized (100 points possible for each test), and validated on other jobs, there are no normative data or validity information for the specific job of the system analyzer. Therefore, the defensibility of the test battery is founded solely on content validity judgments. Issues regarding the final cutoff scores and method for combining the multiple predictors are problematic for the selection committee.

QUESTIONS

1. How would you conduct a job analysis for a job that does not yet exist?
2. Do you think the abilities chosen for selection are content-valid? What other kinds of predictors might be generally useful for employee selection?
3. What reasons did the selection committee have for selecting only the factors that could not be acquired in a two-year training program?
4. Should the concern about women getting down into the dirty treatment tanks have been a selection issue? How might you include this factor in a selection battery?

5. For the abilities termed "critical," what score should someone receive in order to be considered scoring "well" on that test (that is, what should be the cutoff scores)? How should the test scores be combined (for example, compensatory, multiple hurdle, or combination)?
6. Which three candidates appear most qualified? What are your reservations, if any, about this recommendation?
7. Would this test battery and selection procedure be defensible in court?

UPS: Empowering Employees to Be Safe

Case 4

Confronted with unacceptably high injury rates, United Parcel Service Inc. took a chance and flipped its traditional top-down management approach to a ground-up safety program fashioned by drivers and parcel handlers. It worked.

Today, injury rates among the company's 327,600 U.S. employees are tumbling, turnover is down, and UPS reports that company-wide attitudes toward safety have improved significantly. The company began implementing the new safety program in 1996. Committees of drivers and parcel handlers were given broad new powers to design and implement safety strategies under a company-wide initiative called the Comprehensive Health and Safety Process.

Keith Jones, director of health and safety for UPS, says the goal of the CHSP program was to make safety a personal value of every UPS employee. "We challenged our employees," Jones says. "They rose to the occasion."

When the program began, UPS workers were reporting injuries—mostly sprains and strains—at a rate of 27.2 injuries per 200,000 hours worked. By the end of 2004, UPS got the injury rate down to 10.2 for every 200,000 hours worked. By 2007, the company wants the injury rate down to 3.2.

The company's 2,400 CHSP committees are driving the improved numbers. Each group has at least five members, composed of both management and nonmanagement employees. The committees investigate accidents, conduct facility and equipment audits, counsel employees on how they can perform their jobs more safely and make a full report on every accident.

Activities like loading and unloading packages and getting into and out of trucks seem like fairly straightforward jobs. But UPS' safety program breaks down the mechanics of such things as bending the knees properly when picking up a parcel or backing up a delivery truck. Then it empowers safety committee members to make sure the jobs are done the right way.

Nonmanagement employees on the safety committees are schooled in health and safety issues such as eating properly, stretching and getting enough rest. One manual alone has a checklist of 60 safety items. If committee members see someone engaged in an unsafe activity, such as bending from the waist rather than the knees, they are required to approach the employee immediately or face a reprimand themselves.

Initially, management was reluctant to give up the reins. "We are talking about 90 years of culture," Jones says. "It was really a challenge for us culturally to give up some of our authority to nonmanagement folks."

At the same time, workers on the loading docks wondered whether the nonmanagement safety committee members, with their distinctive T-shirts, were representatives of management. Committee members say they are now widely accepted, even among workers who have to be retrained in the proper way to do a job.

"Most people react to it in a positive way," says Alberto Ruiz, who works in the UPS facility in Richmond, California. "Five years ago, maybe it wasn't like that, but now it is part of our culture. They know we are working in their best interest."

Source: Douglas P. Shuit, "A Left Turn for Safety," *Workforce Management* 84, no. 3 (March 1, 2005): 49.

QUESTIONS

1. Why was it a good idea for UPS to put its employees in charge of their own safety?
2. Should all companies make employees responsible for their own safety? What drawbacks do you see to such a plan?
3. Do you think UPS could empower its employees to improve their performance in other areas of the business? What might those areas be?

The Training and Development Dilemma at Whitney and Company

Case 5

Company Background

Whitney and Company is a global management consulting firm that has been growing rapidly, particularly in the United States and Western Europe. The firm provides comprehensive business planning and analysis as well as consulting in operational and technical areas such as finance, operations, and information technology. Its client list includes medium-sized firms but its growth tends to focus on Fortune 1000 companies. Whitney contracts include manufacturing and service organizations as well as government, healthcare, and religious organizations. The firm has offices in twenty-four U.S. cities and offices in sixteen other countries. With its world headquarters in Chicago, Whitney employs nearly 27,000 people, the vast majority of whom are young, aggressive professionals.

In light of the tremendous growth of the consulting industry, Whitney has ambitious plans for expanding the firm. It is estimated that in the next five years alone they will need 1,200 new managers and about 200 new partners. Because Whitney maintains a policy of promotion from within, these people will come mainly from the ranks of entry-level employees. There is plenty of incentive for these young professionals to do well; starting salaries for partners average $250,000 (although normally individuals do not reach partner status until they have been with the firm for ten years).

Training and Development

Given the critical importance of professional talent, Whitney has devoted millions of dollars over the years to create in-house educational and training facilities that are the envy of the industry. The most observable indicator of this dedication is the very plush Corporate Education and Development Center (CEDC) in St. Charles, Illinois, thirty minutes west of Chicago. The 100-acre center provides living and meeting accommodations for approximately 500 people and includes an impressive facility of classrooms, conference rooms, libraries, and even a television studio. The center also employs a staff of nearly 50 instructors, mostly field managers who rotate on a two-year basis into the CEDC.

Every new Whitney employee spends two weeks at CEDC before receiving three additional months of training at one of nine other regional facilities in Atlanta, Boston, Cleveland, Chicago, Dallas, Denver, Los Angeles, Seattle, and New York. All told, Whitney spends almost $4,500 per employee for training and education each year.

The majority of this investment is on technical and systems training for entry-level consultants. Additionally, employees receive extensive training in the specific industries where they will predominantly work (such as oil and gas, telecommunications, banking, or healthcare). The senior staff is particularly aware that Whitney's public image is largely a function of the actions and work quality of its first-level associates. Executives clearly recognize the importance of an expert workforce and spare no expense in this regard.

Employee Performance

While Whitney affords many opportunities to its employees and spends a great deal of money on professional development, it expects a great deal from its employees in return. Especially in the first two years, it is not at all uncommon for a beginning associate to work seventy-hour weeks. The schedules and traveling are often grueling, and the rewards in the first few years are typically not commensurate. For example, salaries are generally in the mid-$50,000s, and the benefit package is only average for a firm of Whitney's size and reputation. The greater payoffs, as indicated before, come when one achieves partner status, but not much earlier.

Nevertheless, Whitney has little trouble attracting very aggressive, energetic students generally right out of college who are eager "to pay their dues" for success in a major firm. Occasionally, however, this aggressiveness has come across as being boorish and callous with clients, especially in the healthcare industry. There are even situations in which clients have discontinued business with Whitney, not because of concerns about expertise, but because of the "fast-in, fast-out style of big-time consulting." While in most cases, Whitney employees gradually learn to interpret the subtleties of client needs, occasionally (and increasingly), employees have been let go because of their lack of personal acumen.

In view of the importance of interpersonal competence at Whitney, some of the training staff have suggested that more attention should be placed on that part of the development of entering employees. But others on staff point out that only two years ago a series of lectures was put into the training program dealing with clients and customer relations. The consensus has been that the program addition has not been well received. They simply do not feel that the added expense would be justified. In fact, a growing group of senior partners believe that too much is already being spent on education and training, as so many of those trained employees subsequently leave to take jobs with other companies.

The facts in this regard are clear. Only about 50 percent of new hires stay with Whitney beyond their first five years. Approximately 90 percent leave the firm within ten years of employment. Most of these people either start their own firms or go to work for one of Whitney's clients. Comparatively few are fired. Many people think this turnover rate is terribly detrimental to the success of Whitney, especially given the immense expense for training and development. Many others, however, feel that the departures are inevitable, given the promotion-from-within policies. Some feel that the turnover actually helps business because those who go to work for other companies often persuade them to become clients of Whitney—the logic being that former employees are familiar with Whitney's procedures and generally will respect the quality of the firm's work.

The Training and Development Dilemma

Not surprisingly, there is increasing debate regarding the role and importance of education and training at Whitney. It is very difficult to know which parts of the current programs are good and which are not. Likewise, there is the problem of determining if additional training is needed. As Anthony Blaine, one of the training directors, summarized it: "For years we've been throwing tons of training at these people, but we aren't sure if it's the right kind, if it's too much, or even if they're catching what we're throwing. We've got to start coming up with some good questions, and then figure out some pretty intelligent answers."

QUESTIONS

1. What could Whitney do to enhance the value of training?
2. Is the company using the most effective techniques, especially with regard to training for client and customer service? What technique changes would you recommend?
3. How should Whitney decide specifically who needs training? Is it advisable, even cost-efficient, to send everyone through the program?
4. How would Whitney determine whether its education and training programs are of sufficient utility? How would you specifically evaluate the programs?

Realigning HR Practices at Egan's Clothiers

Case 6

At the end of fiscal year 2004, revenues at Egan's Clothiers had increased 21 percent over 2003 and had increased at a compounded rate of 24 percent over the past five years. That's the good news. The bad news is that costs have risen at an even more rapid rate, thereby shrinking the company's gross margins. As a consequence, Egan's profitability (measured as return on sales and return on net assets) has actually fallen by 14 percent over the past three years.

The drop in profitability at Egan's is particularly worrisome. In fact, according to Egan's chief financial officer, Richard Coyle, if something isn't done immediately to control material and labor costs as well as administrative expenses, the company may need to restructure its operations. In the short run, Coyle, company president Karen Egan, and vice president of HR Jim Rooney have put an indefinite freeze on all hiring. Further, they are contemplating layoffs of nearly one-quarter of Egan's sales staff and are weighing the benefits of cutting back on HR-related expenses such as training. Compared to others in the industry, their labor costs are very high.

Company Background

Gene Egan and Pat Pollock opened their first store in Baldwin, New York, in 1958. The company grew rapidly during the 1980s and now operates a chain of thirty-four medium-sized stores located throughout Connecticut, New York, Pennsylvania, and New Jersey. Since the beginning, Egan's customers have been primarily middle- and upper-middle-class families purchasing sportswear, dresswear, and fashion accessories. The company has established a long-standing tradition of quality and customer service. In addition to its thirty-four stores, the company also maintains two distribution centers and its administrative offices in Stamford, Connecticut. Total employment currently stands at approximately 2,400 people: 15 executives, 40 staff specialists, 40 store managers, 215 sales managers, 250 administrative personnel, 1,600 salespeople, and 240 distribution workers. Except for the employees at the distribution centers, the company is not presently unionized. However, it is no secret that Egan's management has been trying very hard recently to keep current labor-organizing activities to a minimum. Especially in these times of growth and change, management views unionism as a threat to the company's success. In this regard, the HR office has been asked to conduct a program audit of various HR practices at Egan's. The purpose of this audit is to assess the impact of HR policies and practices on employee outcomes (such as performance, satisfaction, absenteeism, and turnover). The corollary objective of this audit is to identify specific problem areas in which policy adjustments may be necessary. The final report to the executive staff will include the HR department's evaluation of current problems and recommendations for implementing changes in HR practices.

Human Resources Management History

Over the past five years, Egan's has made several changes in order to implement the best HR practices possible. Partially, this has been to circumvent unionization efforts, but primarily it reflects Egan's long-standing belief that success in retailing depends on the competencies and efforts of its employees.

The commitment to HR is demonstrated by the fact that in 2004 the company spent $1.3 million on an intranet-based human resources information system (HRIS). The HRIS has successfully automated most employment records (for example, job titles, salary information, sales levels, attendance, and demographics) and connects each of the retail stores, distribution centers, and executive offices. Also, Egan's has maintained an ongoing training program for the past five years to help salespeople improve their retail selling skills (RSS) and customer service. The annual cost of this program has been roughly $750,000. To further ensure high ability levels in their workforce, the company sets selection standards substantially higher than those of its competitors. Whereas other retail companies typically hire inexperienced high school students, Egan's generally requires some retailing or sales experience before considering an applicant for employment. While this policy increases overall labor costs, Egan's management has been confident that the added expense is well justified over the long run. However, recently even the strongest proponents of HR have been wondering whether it might be a good idea to cut back on training, given the company's current financial picture.

By far the most problematic and volatile HR issues at Egan's have involved promotions and salary increases. Because the company promotes from within and distributes raises on a company-wide basis, comparisons generally have to be made across employees in different jobs and departments. To combat arguments of subjectivity and bias pertaining to these decisions, Egan's links these rewards to objective measures of performance. Specifically, rather than utilizing subjective managerial evaluations of employee performance, ongoing accounts of sales results are maintained for each employee via the HRIS. On the basis of this information, each department manager assigns each employee to one of five categories:

Superior—top 10 percent
Very good—next 20 percent
Good—middle 40 percent
Fair—lower 20 percent
Poor—lowest 10 percent

Administrative decisions are then made across departments utilizing these standardized distributions. Additionally, in order to provide constant feedback to each employee concerning his or her relative performance, data are updated and posted daily. It is hoped that this feedback is motivating to employees, and in this way there are no surprises when the time comes for semiannual performance appraisal interviews. It is interesting to note that since these changes have been made in the performance appraisal system, not one formal complaint has been registered regarding salary or promotion decisions. However, sales managers themselves have mentioned occasionally that they do not feel as comfortable now that they are required to assign employees to the "fair" and "poor" categories.

HR Outcomes

Despite the concerted efforts of Egan's management to create a first-rate system of human resources management, several troubling issues face the company. The HR practices are not having their desired effects. For example, there have been recent complaints that employees have not been as patient or courteous with customers as they should be. This was best summarized by Paul Kelly, a store manager in White Plains, New York, who noted, "My people are beating up the clientele in order to make a sale—the very opposite of what the RSS program trains them to do." This lapse in customer service is frustrating to management because the RSS training has proven effective in the past. Additionally, there seems to be a great deal of competition *within* departments that is hurting team effort. Although intergroup rivalries *between* departments has always been viewed as normal and healthy, the lack of intragroup cohesiveness is seen as a problem.

Additionally, Egan's has been plagued with increases in lost and damaged merchandise. Management attributes this to the fact that storage rooms are disorganized and unkempt. This is in sharp contrast to the selling floors, which have remained fairly well orderly and uncluttered. Nevertheless, inventory costs have been increasing at an alarming rate.

Everyone notices that something is wrong. But the behavior patterns are perplexing. Absenteeism has decreased by 23 percent, but employee turnover has actually increased from 13 to more than 29 percent, thereby increasing labor costs overall. Unfortunately, many of those leaving the company (43 percent) are rated as very good to superior employees.

As executives in the company look at these trends, they are understandably concerned. The success of the company and its reputation for quality and service depend on solid investments in HR to ensure the best possible workforce. However, the expenses are eroding the company's profits, and worse, it looks now like these investments are not paying off.

QUESTIONS

1. What overall changes could you recommend to the executive team at Egan's about its HR practices?
2. What are the pros and cons of Egan's performance appraisal system? Do you think it identifies the best employees? Do you think it helps develop employees to perform the best they can?
3. Can increased sales be linked directly and/or indirectly to the appraisal system? How about some of the other performance effects? How would you change the system?
4. How do you account for the fact that absenteeism has decreased at Egan's while turnover has increased?

A Performance Appraisal Snafu

Case 7

Research has shown that the performance appraisal process, and particularly the interaction between employees and managers, is a key determinant affecting employee motivation and productivity. Understandably, managers can view the appraisal of employee performance as a "Catch-22" in which the slightest mistake can cause employee resentment, as this case illustrates.

Marcus Singh, a naturalized U.S. citizen from India, is a research economist in the Office of Research and Evaluation in the City of Newport, Oregon. He is forty years old and has worked for the City of Newport for the past ten years. During that time, Singh has been perceived by his supervisors as an above-average performer. However, due to the small size of the department and the close working relationship between employees and management, a formal evaluation of employees was considered unnecessary. About ten months ago Singh was transferred from the department's Industrial Development unit to the newly formed Office of Research and Evaluation. Other employees were also transferred as part of an overall reorganization.

Out of concern for equal employment opportunity, plus the realization that employee performance should be evaluated formally and objectively, Victor Popelmill, department director, issued a directive to all unit heads to formally evaluate the performance of their subordinates. Attached to his memorandum was a copy of a new performance appraisal form to be used in conducting the evaluations. Garth Fryer, head of the Office of Research and Evaluation, decided to allow his subordinates to have some input in the appraisal process. (In addition to Garth Fryer, the Office of Research and Evaluation comprised Marcus Singh, five other research economists—

Jason Taft, Susan Mussman, Richard Gels, Marsha Fetzer, and Juan Ortiz—and one secretary, Connie Millar.) Fryer told each of the researchers to complete both a self-appraisal and a peer appraisal. After reviewing these appraisals, Fryer completed the final and official appraisal of each researcher. Before sending the forms to Popelmill's office, Fryer met with each researcher individually to review and explain his ratings. Each researcher signed his appraisal and indicated agreement with the ratings.

About one week after submitting the appraisals to the director, Fryer received a memorandum from Popelmill stating that his evaluations were unacceptable. Fryer was not the only unit head to receive this memorandum; in fact, they all received the same note. On examination of the completed appraisal forms from the various departments, the director had noticed that not one employee was appraised in either the "fair" or "satisfactory" category. In fact, most employees were rated as "outstanding" in every category. Popelmill felt that his unit heads were too lenient and asked them to redo the evaluations in a more objective and critical manner. Furthermore, because the department's compensation budget for salary increases was largely based on a distribution of employee ratings, evaluating all employees as outstanding exceeded budget limits.

Garth Fryer explained the director's request to his subordinates and asked them to redo their appraisals with the idea of being more objective this time. To Fryer's astonishment, the new appraisals were not much different from the first ones. Believing he had no choice in the matter, Fryer unilaterally formulated his own ratings and discussed them with each employee.

Marcus Singh was not pleased when he found out that his supervisor had rated him one level lower on each category. (Compare Figures 7-1 and 7-2.) Although he signed the second appraisal form, he indicated on the form that he did not agree with the evaluation. Jason Taft, another researcher in the Office of Research and Evaluation, continued to receive all "outstanding" ratings on his second evaluation.

Like Singh, Taft has a master's degree in economics, but he has been working for the City of Newport for less than two years and is only twenty-four years old. Taft had also worked closely with Garth Fryer before being transferred to his new assignment ten months ago. Recently, the mayor of the city had received a letter from the regional director of a major government agency praising Jason Taft's and Garth Fryer's outstanding research. Marcus Singh's working relationship with Garth Fryer and Jason Taft and with others in the department has been good. On some occasions, though, he has found himself in awkward disagreements with his co-workers in areas where he holds strong opinions.

After Singh and Taft had signed the appraisals, Garth Fryer forwarded them to Popelmill's office, where they were eventually added to the employees' permanent files. When pay raises were awarded in the department three weeks later, Marcus Singh did not receive a merit raise. He was told that it was due to his less-than-outstanding appraisal. He did, however, receive the general increase of $1,200 given to all employees regardless of their performance appraisal. This increase matched the increase in the CPI for the Newport, Oregon, area.

Singh has refused to speak one word to Garth Fryer since they discussed the appraisal, communicating only through Connie Millar or in writing. Singh has lost all motivation and complains bitterly to his colleagues about his unfair ratings. While he reports to work at 8 A.M. sharp and does not leave until 5 P.M. each day, he has been observed to spend a lot of time reading newspapers and books while at work.

Source: This case was adapted from a case prepared by James G. Pesek and Joseph P. Gronenwald of Clarion University of Pennsylvania.

QUESTIONS

1. What do you see as the problems in this case? Explain.
2. Could these problems have been avoided? How?
3. Comment on the advantages and disadvantages of using peer evaluations in the appraisal process.
4. What can be done to correct the problem with Marcus Singh?

Figure 7-1 Employee Appraisal Form

Employee Name: Marcus Singh Date: October 4, 2004

Job Title: Economist/Researcher

Please indicate your evaluation of the employee in each category by placing a check mark (✓) in the appropriate block.

	Outstanding	Good	Satisfactory	Fair	Unsatisfactory
KNOWLEDGE OF JOB Assess overall knowledge of duties and responsibilities of current job.	☑	☐	☐	☐	☐
QUANTITY OF WORK Assess the volume of work under normal conditions.	☐	☑	☐	☐	☐
QUALITY OF WORK Assess the neatness, accuracy, & effectiveness of work.	☐	☑	☐	☐	☐
COOPERATION Assess ability & willingness to work with peers, superiors, & subordinates.	☐	☑	☐	☐	☐
INITIATIVE Assess willingness to seek greater responsibilities & knowledge. Self starting.	☐	☑	☐	☐	☐
ATTENDANCE Assess reliability with respect to attendance habits.	☑	☐	☐	☐	☐
ATTITUDE Assess disposition & level of enthusiasm. Desire to excel.	☑	☐	☐	☐	☐
JUDGMENT Assess ability to make logical decisions.	☐	☑	☐	☐	☐

Comments on ratings: Valuable employee!

Supervisor's signature: Garth Fryer Date: Oct. 4, 2004

Department: Office of Research and Evaluation

Employee's signature: Marcus Singh

Does the employee agree with this evaluation? _X_ Yes ___ No

Figure 7-2 **Employee Appraisal Form**

Employee Name: Marcus Singh   Date: October 18, 2004

Job Title: Economist/Researcher

Please indicate your evaluation of the employee in each category by placing a check mark (✓) in the appropriate block.

	Outstanding	Good	Satisfactory	Fair	Unsatisfactory
KNOWLEDGE OF JOB Assess overall knowledge of duties and responsibilities of current job.	☐	☑	☐	☐	☐
QUANTITY OF WORK Assess the volume of work under normal conditions.	☐	☐	☑	☐	☐
QUALITY OF WORK Assess the neatness, accuracy, & effectiveness of work.	☐	☐	☑	☐	☐
COOPERATION Assess ability & willingness to work with peers, superiors, & subordinates.	☐	☐	☑	☐	☐
INITIATIVE Assess willingness to seek greater responsibilities & knowledge. Self starting.	☐	☐	☑	☐	☐
ATTENDANCE Assess reliability with respect to attendance habits.	☐	☑	☐	☐	☐
ATTITUDE Assess disposition & level of enthusiasm. Desire to excel.	☐	☑	☐	☐	☐
JUDGMENT Assess ability to make logical decisions.	☐	☐	☑	☐	☐

Comments on ratings: Marcus needs to increase the quantity of his work to receive higher ratings. Also, he should take a greater initiative in his job.

Supervisor's signature: Garth Fryer   Date: Oct. 18, 2004

Department: Office of Research and Evaluation

Employee's signature: Marcus Singh

Does the employee agree with this evaluation? ____ Yes _X_ No

Someone Has to Go: A Tough Layoff Decision

Case 8

The figures are staggering—8.7 million workers were involuntarily displaced in the United States between 2000 and 2003. In 2004 alone, there were 4,879 mass layoffs that affected 956,327 individuals.* The reasons for mass layoffs include expanding global competition, a dynamic domestic business environment, organizational mergers, and companies unable or unwilling to adapt to rapid change.

Beyond layoffs of large numbers of employees at major corporations, the economic environment of recent years has forced layoffs of small groups of employees—or a single employee—when economic conditions warrant a reduction in company size. These incidents affect the lives of both employees and their managers, as this case illustrates.

Located in the Los Angeles area, Aero Performance, with twenty-seven employees, is a sales and maintenance company that provides equipment upgrades and general aircraft maintenance to regional airlines, corporate aircraft, and small international carriers. When Aero Performance was created twelve years ago, the company faced little competition and a robust airline market seemed to present an unlimited potential for growth. Unfortunately, industry economics, coupled with cost-cutting measures by airlines and new competition from similar airline service companies, means that Aero's business has stabilized with actual losses in certain specialized areas.

One area of concern is the company's "technology advanced" airplane equipment. However, with cost control a major objective of airline companies as well as owners of corporate jets, these organizations have delayed the purchase and installation of advanced electronic equipment.

Mike Martinez, manager of the technology upgrade unit, faces a tough decision. With a significant downturn in his unit's work, he must lay off one employee. The decision is made particularly difficult because all employees of the unit are qualified employees with average or better work records. Additionally, each employee has a unique personal background directly affecting his or her work life. A summary of the background and work record of each of the four employees follows. No question, Martinez faces a difficult decision.

Gary Meadors is married and has two children in high school. He lives modestly in order to send his kids to college. His wife works evenings at a convenience store to assist with family expenses. Meadors has worked nine years with Aero Performance, six years in airline maintenance and three years in the technology upgrade unit. He has learned airline technology largely through technical articles, trade journals, and on-the-job experience. His performance evaluations are average and he is considered a consistent and reliable employee. His attendance and company loyalty are exceptional.

Brenda Baldwin is the only woman in the technology upgrade unit. She is a single mother with a child in elementary school. Brenda has three years of service with Aero Performance, all in Martinez's unit. She joined the company after obtaining an airline technology degree from a well-respected four-year university. Brenda continues to take evening classes in her field and seems to have, according to Martinez, "the most potential for growth in the company." However, her performance has slipped the past year and she has been counseled for an attendance problem. She has felt somewhat resented as a female in a traditionally male-dominated industry.

Udit Chopra is a dedicated employee. In fact, everyone says he is "married to his job." He will work long hours to complete technical installations and is regarded as a perfectionist. Udit has a college degree in marketing but has found his home in airline technology. He possesses an excellent ability to persuade Aero Performance customers to upgrade their technology systems. Udit drives a new BMW and is reported to come from a wealthy family.

Craig Cottrell joined Aero Performance three years ago, having been hired away from a competitor. He has a total of twelve years of experience in the airline service industry. Craig has a complete understanding of airline technology. Cottrell's work performance the first two years with Aero Performance was barely average; however, his work record the past year was evaluated as very high. Currently he is the top performer in the unit. There has been work friction between him, Baldwin, and Chopra over the selection and installation of cockpit instruments.

	SENIORITY (YEARS)	SALARY	PERFORMANCE 1999	2000	2001	2002
Gary Meadors	9	$42,250	Avg	Good	Avg	Avg
Brenda Baldwin	3	$48,190		High	Good	Avg
Udit Chopra	5	$45,500	Avg	Good	Good	Good
Craig Cottrell	3	$43,960		Avg	Avg	High

Mike Martinez must make his decision by this Friday. Aero Performance will grant the laid-off employee a severance package to assist transition to other employment. Martinez is committed to aiding his employee in finding another job in the airline service industry.

*Figures are from Mass Layoff Statistics, 2002. Bureau of Labor Statistics, http://www.bls.gov. (See mass layoff statistics.)

QUESTIONS

1. What criteria should be used to determine potential laid-off candidates? What emphasis, if any, should be given to non-job-related factors such as personal problems or a spouse's need to work? Explain.
2. What should be included in a severance package for laid-off employees? How long should the severance package last? Explain.
3. Are there any potential legal implications in Martinez's decision? Explain your answer.
4. How would you handle the termination interview? Explain.

Ethics: Doing It Right at Lockheed

Case 9

In 2001, a man named Ron Covais, a vice president for business development at aerospace giant Lockheed Martin, received an "inappropriate request for payment" during the bidding process for a contract with a foreign customer. Covais not only turned down the bribe request flat but also immediately removed his company from the bidding process. He reported the incident to his bosses and met with top-level U.S. and foreign officials to discuss the matter. His action cost his employer a multi-million-dollar business opportunity.

But in March 2002, Covais was presented with the first annual Chairman's Award, a crystal bowl symbolizing "the highest standards for integrity and business conduct." Lockheed Martin's chairman and CEO, Vance Coffman, presented the award in a special ceremony. "Ron's action in resolving this complex ethical issue followed our ethical guidelines to the letter," Coffman declared. In March 2003, the second annual Chairman's Award was presented to Vic LaRosa, a software engineer who inadvertently received two e-mails containing proprietary information belonging to a competitor. LaRosa immediately deleted the messages and reported the incidents to his manager.

These aren't the kinds of stories that get much ink these days. There's much more interest in plumbing the murkier depths of the military-industrial relationship. But perhaps the primary reason why Lockheed Martin, unlike Boeing and Halliburton, has been out of the headlines lately is that the formulation, dissemination and enforcement of ethical standards is one of the company's strategic priorities. It is this company-wide commitment that singled out Lockheed Martin as the 2004 *Optimas Award* winner for Ethics.

"Our belief is that good ethics is good business," says Maryanne Lavan, Lockheed Martin's vice president for ethics and business conduct. "The competition in this business is fierce, but if our company wins through underhanded means, we don't consider it a win. Because eventually there'll be someone uncomfortable enough to report it." Lavan emphasizes that her company's ethics policy, in effect since the 1995 merger of Lockheed and Martin Marietta, works from the top down. To illustrate, she points out that each year, every senior leader in the company is asked to find an example of exemplary ethical behavior in his business unit and recommend the responsible employee for the Chairman's Award. If he fails to do this, he receives a negative evaluation.

No one, from the CEO down, is exempt from inquiries and complaints phoned in to an anonymous ethics hotline. Every one of Lockheed Martin's 130,000 employees—again from the CEO down—receives a mandatory hour of ethics training each year. To carry out such ambitious tasks, Lockheed Martin employs 65 ethics officers, divided among its Bethesda, Maryland, headquarters and its five business units. The ethics department produces training materials that stress guided role-playing exercises simulating "gray area" ethical quandaries. For instance, what do you do if you accidentally receive information from a U.S. government employee about a rival company's bid? If a manager asks you to fudge financial information on an internal report? If a vendor's representative offers to pay for TGIF drinks for your entire work team? Many of the scenarios are based on actual experiences of workers at Lockheed Martin and other corporations.

To keep its messages fresh, the Lockheed Martin ethics department turns out a newspaper and calendar and an "Ethics Zone" site on the company intranet. There is even an annual Lockheed Martin Ethics Film Festival. Prizes are awarded to the best tongue-in-cheek amateur ethics "infomercials" submitted by auteurs from throughout the company. Some of the entries are surprisingly well produced and powerful. Some are not, but the ethical messages still get through. In 1997 the company contracted with *Dilbert* creator Scott Adams to spice up the training materials with pertinent examples of his satirical comic strip. Then-CEO Norman Augustine, a particularly vocal advocate of ethical conduct and education, appeared with Dilbert in an introductory video.

The roots of Lockheed Martin's ethics program go back to the 1970s, when Lockheed was caught in a messy scandal involving kickbacks to foreign customers, which resulted in a major congressional investigation and the passage of the Foreign Corrupt Practices Act. In the intervening years, there has been much heated discussion about the cozy relationship between the defense industry and the U.S. government as well as some of its more byzantine contracting and pricing methods. It's a measure of the company's progress that when the Sarbanes-Oxley Act was passed in 2002, Lockheed Martin was already in compliance with most of its provisions and proscriptions.

Calculating the ethics program's return on investment is difficult, especially since its budget, about which Lavan will say only that it's "millions of dollars," is secret. But another way to look at it is that in an era when Enron, WorldCom, Parmalat and Tyco have become household names, public scrutiny is closer and illegal corporate conduct costlier. Last year's ethical lapse by Boeing—to be precise, an ex-employee's pilfering of proprietary information connected to an Air Force missile contract—cost the Chicago-based company an estimated $1 billion. Says Brian Sears, Lockheed Martin's director of ethics services, "You lose a billion dollars in business, it gets people's attention in a hurry."

Source: Andy Meisler, "Lockheed Is Doing It Right and Doing It Well," *Workforce Management* 83, no. 3 (March 1, 2004): 50.

QUESTIONS

1. How does Lockheed's approach to ethics add value to the firm?
2. Suppose you were a Lockheed shareholder. If the company lost a large contract because it failed to make a kickback and its share price dropped dramatically as a result, how would you feel?
3. What more can Lockheed do to ensure that ethical principles are followed at the company?

Newell's Decision to Downsize: An Ethical Dilemma

Case 10

Introduction

A particular issue in business ethics is, "What exactly does the term *ethics* mean?" Various writers have described ethics as rules that govern behavior; desired societal values such as respect for justice, or accepted principles of right or wrong. Furthermore, the subject of ethics embraces the study of morals and virtues. One author noted, "While laws concern what we *must* do, ethics concerns what we *should* do."*

In the practice of HR, managers and supervisors are continually faced with ethical dilemmas regarding the fair and equitable treatment of employees. Ethical choices abound in areas such as recruitment and selection, employee privacy, whistle-blowing, sexual harassment, and diversity or affirmative action. An important ethical dilemma faced by managers today is the fair and correct way to downsize organizations. At conflict are organizational goals and strategies, HR policy and practices, and, of course, the lives of those affected. The facts of the following case are straightforward. The decisions involved in downsizing a workforce are complex, and as one manager stated, "gut-wrenching."

The Need to Downsize

Newell Corporation is a medium-sized manufacturer of navigational systems for commuter-size and larger airplanes. The company operates two plants—one in Atlanta, Georgia, the other in Norwood, California. In 2000, the Norwood plant employed 273 employees, most of them engaged in the manufacture and technical support of company products.

Important to this case is that Newell is regarded as an excellent place to work by its employees and within the surrounding communities. Employee morale and loyalty have always been high and job satisfaction studies conducted by the company consistently rate the organization as a fair and equitable place to work. HR policies can be described as proactive and progressive. With its positive reputation, Newell has been able to select new employees from a large pool of job applicants.

One cornerstone of HR policy has been the use of seniority in training, job assignment, transfers, and promotion. Additionally, with Newell's emphasis on employee retention, employees have experienced—some say, "have come to expect"—long tenure and steady employment. Prior to 2004, Newell has never downsized its workforce. Employment growth at the Norwood facility can be described as moderate and steady.

The racial composition of the company has been predominately Caucasian, for two reasons. First, the racial composition of the company's local labor market has historically been Caucasian. Second, the skill level needed for the company's technical jobs has come primarily from a trained Caucasian labor force. A review of the company's federally required EEO-1 report for 2001 showed that Newell had few employees in each of the minority categories listed. This is true for both hourly and managerial positions. However, since approximately 1995, the demographic characteristics of the local labor market have changed dramatically to include more Hispanics, African Americans, and Asian Americans. Minority job applicants have generally not possessed the skills needed for entry-level manufacturing and technical support jobs.

In 2001, Newell experienced a large increase in the demand for its products. To meet customer orders the Norwood plant hired twenty-seven new manufacturing assemblers and fourteen new technical support technicians. With the increased diversity of the external labor force, plus the desire to increase the minority composition of its internal workforce, thirty-four of the forty-one new hires were minorities. It is noteworthy that Newell welcomed the opportunity to rapidly increase the diversity of its workforce for both business and ethical reasons. The following is an excerpt from Newell's statement of vision and values published in July 2000:

> *Newell Corporation believes that a work environment that reflects a diverse workforce, values diversity, and honors the worth of its employees benefits the company, its customers, and its employees. Employment decisions will be made on these principles while also considering the efficient and effective operation of the organization.*

Because new minority employees generally did not possess the skills needed for its manufacturing and technical jobs, the company spent approximately $1.7 million on entry-level skills training. The integration of minorities into the Norwood facility was seamless and without racial tension.

In 2002, sales for Newell's products once again followed historical patterns. Unfortunately, sales then unexpectedly took a sharp downturn: a 12 percent decline in 2003 and a 23 percent decline in 2004. Causes for the decline in sales were attributed to two new low-wage foreign competitors who entered the market in 2003, a slight decline in market demand for company products, and higher-than-average production costs due to Newell's older, less-efficient manufacturing equipment. Future demand for company products was projected to be moderate for 2005, 2006, and 2007.

In February 2005, Tom Malcom, Norwood's director of HR; Steven L. Davis, corporate vice president for manufacturing; and Mary Umali, Norwood's plant manager, decided to downsize the workforce at the Norwood facility. Specifically, they decided to lay off thirty-seven manufacturing employees and eleven technical support personnel. The difficult question faced by senior management was how to lay off employees in a manner that would be fair and equitable to individuals and legally defensible, while maintaining the integrity of Newell's HR policies and the productivity of the Norwood plant.

Source: This case was adapted from an actual case known to the authors. All names are fictitious.

*Terry Halbert and Elaine Ingulli, *Law and Ethics in the Business Environment,* 4th ed. (Mason, OH: Thompson, South-Western, 2003).

QUESTIONS

1. What is the ethical dilemma faced by management in this case. Explain fully.
2. What specific problems might Newell face in its downsizing decision?
3. What options might Newell employ in its downsizing decision? Explain fully.
4. How would you downsize the Norwood facility? Explain fully.

OK—Who's Telling the Truth?

Case 11

Introduction

When employees are questioned during an investigative hearing with management, it is reasonable to assume that they will provide the story that best supports their case. In some instances their statements will be based on their subjective perceptions and feelings. In other cases, they may lie in order to lessen or avoid possible disciplinary action. If the punishment received is later appealed through either a grievance/arbitration procedure or an alternative dispute resolution system, some third party must determine whether the discipline imposed was supported by the evidence presented during the hearing. Typically, much of the evidence is in the form of testimony presented by witnesses on behalf of the employer and the employee. Unfortunately there are often significant differences in the testimony presented by the witnesses for each side. In such situations it is up to the neutral third party to try to evaluate the credibility of the testimony in order to determine which witnesses to believe. This is the problem confronting the arbitrator in this case, although the situation is likely to surface in any employee appeals hearing.

The Issues to Be Arbitrated

Oscar Grimes was employed by the Lenz and Klass Optical Company from August 1999 until his discharge on May 10, 2004, by Harvey Lenz. Lenz is the company president and principal stockholder. Reporting to Lenz is Irma Holman, the general manager. Reporting to her are Thomas Lee, supervisor of the surface room where the lenses are ground according to prescription, and Washington Jones, supervisor of the bench room where the lenses are cut, tinted, and fitted into frames. The stated cause for discharging Grimes was that he did poor-quality work, had excessive breakage, and displayed a poor attitude in his job. Furthermore, on several occasions he had challenged his supervisor to fire him.

Grimes contested his discharge by filing a grievance through the company's ADR- complaint resolution procedure. The final step in the ADR is arbitration. The substance of the testimonies presented during the arbitration hearing by the witnesses on behalf of each party is summarized as follows.

Testimony of Witnesses for the Company

Harvey Lenz's Testimony

Lenz testified that Grimes had been a problem to Thomas Lee, his supervisor, during the time Grimes had worked in the surface room. Grimes had been tried out on a number of different jobs and, according to Lenz, did not do well in any of them. Lenz stated, "Lee kept coming to me saying, 'This fellow, I can't keep him here. Every time I move him, he tells me to fire him.' So we transferred him to the bench room. I have had discussions with Grimes five or ten times over the last couple of years. I would tell him, 'I don't hire people to fire them. It takes a lot of time to train people and we don't want to fire you, but you've got to shape up.' Every time I had him in for talks, I had Holman and Lee or Jones present."

Lenz testified further that when Grimes was transferred to the bench room, Lenz called him in for a talk, with Holman present. "I told him, 'Look, we moved you to the bench room because Mr. Lee doesn't want you in the surface room any more. Every time he asked you to do something, you would argue and tell him to fire you.' However, it was not until I called the grievant in on May 10, with Holman and Jones present, that I heard the 'fire me' bit personally. When I called him in, I had no intention of firing him but only wanted to give him one final warning. I explained to him what he was doing wrong and then told him to get back to work and straighten out. He said he wouldn't leave until Joseph Rudinski, a fellow employee, was brought in. I called Rudinski in and explained the whole thing to him. The grievant then stated, 'Yes, that's about the size of it and you better fire me.' I replied, 'But I didn't bring you in here to fire you. I've already told you to leave the room and go back to work.' Grimes then insisted, 'I want to be fired.' I then told him, 'Fine, you're fired.'"

Lenz also testified that the easiest job in the company was that of dyeing lenses—the job Grimes held at the time of his discharge. The grievant, according to Lenz, was put on this job because, in Lenz's words, "I really didn't want to fire him. I didn't want to train someone else." Lenz stated further that he did not put warnings in writing because he did not want to "start writing people up." He admitted, however, that in the past he had issued perhaps a couple of written warnings and had fired at least one person.

Thomas Lee's Testimony

Lee testified that the grievant had worked in the surface room for nearly four years. He maintained that the grievant had excess breakage and that Lee could not find a place to put Grimes where he didn't have problems. He would ask the grievant to go some other place and Grimes would not go. On numerous occasions, Lee claimed, the grievant would say, "Fire me." Lee added that he would tell Grimes, "I don't want to fire you. If you want to quit, quit." Grimes replied, at least once, "Well, then, I can't draw unemployment."

Lee maintained that he was present six or seven times at meetings when Lenz told Grimes he would have to do better or be let go. "After Grimes had given me that 'fire me' routine several times," Lee testified, "I told Lenz that I couldn't keep this guy and that Lenz should do something about it. So they moved him to the bench room." Lee could not recall the date he requested that Grimes be moved, and Lee didn't keep records on breakage. He insisted that the grievant had had more breakage than anyone else.

Mike Murphy's Testimony

Murphy testified that he had trained the grievant when Grimes worked in the surface room. In his words, "Grimes's work performance was slow and he became upset when I brought poor work back to him. He had more breakage than others and would stand there running the machine, just like he was daydreaming." Murphy also stated that the grievant would rush through jobs too quickly and rebelled when Murphy tried to correct him. Murphy admitted that he and the grievant "butted heads on occasion."

Testimony of Witnesses for the Grievant

Ian Dougal's Testimony

Dougal testified that he had worked for Lenz and Klass six years in the surface room. He wasn't aware of what Lee, the supervisor, thought about the grievant's work, but as far as he was concerned, Grimes's attitude and abilities were just fine. He knew the grievant had been called into Lenz's office about six months after starting work; perhaps there were also other occasions. The witness also knew of people who had received written notices.

Oscar Grimes's Testimony

Appearing as a witness in his own behalf, the grievant testified that when he came to work he had had no prior optical experience. By the time he was discharged, he was classified as a journeyman. He testified also that, except for the incident relating to his discharge, there had been only one other occasion when he had been called into Lenz's office. "My only other meeting with Lenz," Grimes states, "was about three years ago. He warned me my work wasn't good and to shape up or ship out. I told him I could do the job." Grimes admitted being moved around but maintained, "Lee told me it was so I could learn all operations. He never informed me about excessive breakage and he never asked me to quit. I never objected to being moved. I never received any written warnings."

Under direct examination Grimes denied ever having said that if he quit he wouldn't get unemployment insurance. He maintained that he never had any problems with respect to attendance or tardiness, and had never used up his sick leave. Recalling his meeting with Lenz on May 10, the grievant stated, "Mr. Lenz told me if I didn't improve he was going to fire me or I would have to quit. I told him I wasn't going to quit and if he wanted to fire me that was his option."

Grimes insisted that he never felt he had a problem with his boss, Thomas Lee, and he did not know why Lee would say so. Grimes thought his problems in the shop were the same as everyone's. In his opinion, the morale of most employees in the shop was low and none of them were particularly thrilled to be working for Lenz. In his testimony the grievant did admit that on one occasion in 2002 he told Lee that if Lee didn't like his work, Lee could fire him.

QUESTIONS

1. What do you believe to be the principal weakness of the company's position in this case? Explain.
2. Did Grimes have the right to request that his fellow employee be present during his meeting with Lenz? Explain.
3. Does the concept of progressive discipline require an employer to precede a discharge with a written warning and then a suspension without pay? Explain.
4. Which witnesses do you believe provide the more credible testimony, those for the employer or those for the grievant? Explain.
5. If you were the arbitrator, what would be your decision in this case and on what information or principle of HRM would you base your decision? Explain.

glossary

A

Achievement tests
Measures of what a person knows or can do right now.

Adverse impact
A concept that refers to the rejection of a significantly higher percentage of a protected class for employment, placement, or promotion when compared with the successful, nonprotected class.

Affirmative action
Policy that goes beyond equal employment opportunity by requiring organizations to comply with the law and correct past discriminatory practices by increasing the numbers of minorities and women in specific positions.

Alarm reaction
Response to stress that basically involves an elevated heart rate, increased respiration, elevated levels of adrenaline in the blood, and increased blood pressure.

Alternative dispute resolution (ADR)
Term applied to different types of employee complaint or dispute resolution procedures.

Apprenticeship training
System of training in which a worker entering the skilled trades is given thorough instruction and experience, both on and off the job, in the practical and theoretical aspects of the work.

Aptitude tests
Measures of a person's capacity to learn or acquire skills.

Arbitrator
Third-party neutral who resolves a labor dispute by issuing a final decision in the disagreement.

Assessment center
Process by which individuals are evaluated as they participate in a series of situations that resemble what they might be called upon to handle on the job.

Augmented skills
Skills helpful in facilitating the efforts of expatriate managers.

Authorization card
A statement signed by an employee authorizing a union to act as a representative of the employee for purposes of collective bargaining.

B

Balance-sheet approach
Compensation system designed to match the purchasing power in a person's home country.

Balanced Scorecard (BSC)
A measurement framework that helps managers translate strategic goals into operational objectives.

Bargaining power
The power of labor and management to achieve their goals through economic, social, or political influence.

Bargaining unit
Group of two or more employees who share common employment interests and conditions and may reasonably be grouped together for purposes of collective bargaining.

Bargaining zone
Area within which the union and the employer are willing to concede when bargaining.

Behavior modeling
Approach that demonstrates desired behavior and gives trainees the chance to practice and role-play those behaviors and receive feedback.

Behavior modification
Technique that operates on the principle that behavior that is rewarded, or positively reinforced, will be exhibited more frequently in the future, whereas behavior that is penalized or unrewarded will decrease in frequency.

Behavior observation scale (BOS)
A behavioral approach to performance appraisal that measures the frequency of observed behavior.

Behavioral description interview (BDI)
An interview in which an applicant is asked questions about what he or she actually did in a given situation.

Behaviorally anchored rating scale (BARS)
A behavioral approach to performance appraisal that consists of a series of vertical scales, one for each important dimension of job performance.

Benchmarking
Process of measuring one's own services and practices against the recognized leaders in order to identify areas for improvement.

Bona fide occupational qualification (BFOQ)
Suitable defense against a discrimination charge only where age, religion, sex, or national origin is an actual qualification for performing the job.

Bonus
Incentive payment that is supplemental to the base wage.

Burnout
Most severe stage of distress, manifesting itself in depression, frustration, and loss of productivity.

Business necessity
Work-related practice that is necessary to the safe and efficient operation of an organization.

Business unionism
Term applied to the goals of U.S. labor organizations, which collectively bargain for improvements in wages, hours, job security, and working conditions.

C

Career counseling
Process of discussing with employees their current job activities and performance, their personal and career interests and goals, their personal skills, and suitable career development objectives.

Career networking
The process of establishing mutually beneficial relationships with other business people, including potential clients and customers.

Career paths
Lines of advancement in an occupational field within an organization.

Career plateau
Situation in which for either organizational or personal reasons the probability of moving up the career ladder is low.

Charge form
Discrimination complaint filed with the EEOC by employees or job applicants.

Codetermination
Representation of labor on the board of directors of a company.

Collective bargaining process
Process of negotiating a labor agreement, including the use of economic pressures by both parties.

Combined salary and commission plan
Compensation plan that includes a straight salary and a commission.

Comparable worth
The concept that male and female jobs that are dissimilar, but equal in terms of value or worth to the employer, should be paid the same.

Compensatory model
Selection decision model in which a high score in one area can make up for a low score in another area.

Competence-based pay
Pay based on an employee's skill level, the variety of skills possessed, or increased job knowledge of the employee.

Competency assessment
Analysis of the sets of skills and knowledge needed for decision-oriented and knowledge-intensive jobs.

Concurrent validity
The extent to which test scores (or other predictor information) match criterion data obtained at about the same time from current employees.

Construct validity
Extent to which a selection tool measures a theoretical construct or trait.

Constructive discharge
An employee voluntarily terminates his or her employment because of harsh, unreasonable employment conditions placed upon the individual by the employer.

Consumer price index (CPI)
Measure of the average change in prices over time in a fixed "market basket" of goods and services.

Consumer-driven health plan (CDHP)
A medical insurance plan financed by employer contributions to an employee's individual healthcare spending account.

Content validity
Extent to which a selection instrument, such as a test, adequately samples the knowledge and skills needed to perform a particular job.

Contrast error
Performance-rating error in which an employee's evaluation is biased either upward or downward because of comparison with another employee just previously evaluated.

Contributory plan
A pension plan where contributions are made jointly by employees and employers.

Cooperative training
Training program that combines practical on-the-job experience with formal educational classes.

Core competencies
Integrated knowledge sets within an organization that distinguish it from its competitors and deliver value to customers.

Core skills
Skills considered critical to an employee's success abroad.

Core values
The strong and enduring beliefs and principles that the company uses as a foundation for its decisions.

Corporate social responsibility
The responsibility of the firm to act in the best interests of the people and communities affected by its activities.

Craft unions
Unions that represent skilled craft workers.

Criterion-related validity
Extent to which a selection tool predicts, or significantly correlates with, important elements of work behavior.

Critical incident
Unusual event that denotes superior or inferior employee performance in some part of the job.

Critical incident method
Job analysis method by which important job tasks are identified for job success.

Cross-training
Training of employees in jobs in areas closely related to their own.

Cross-validation
Verifying the results obtained from a validation study by administering a test or test battery to a different sample (drawn from the same population).

Cultural audits
Audits of the culture and quality of work life in an organization.

Cultural environment
Communications, religion, values and ideologies, education, and social structure of a country.

Culture shock
Perpetual stress experienced by people who settle overseas.

Cumulative trauma disorders
Injuries involving tendons of the fingers, hands, and arms that become inflamed from repeated stresses and strains.

Customer appraisal
Performance appraisal, which, like team appraisal, is based on TQM concepts and seeks evaluation from both external and internal customers.

D

Defined-benefit plan
A pension plan in which the amount an employee is to receive upon retirement is specifically set forth.

Defined-contribution plan
A pension plan that establishes the basis on which an employer will contribute to the pension fund.

Depression
Negative emotional state marked by feelings of low spirits, gloominess, sadness, and loss of pleasure in ordinary activities.

Differential piece rate
Compensation rate under which employees whose production exceeds the standard amount of output receive a higher rate for all of their work than the rate paid to those who do not exceed the standard amount.

Disabled individual
Any person who (1) has a physical or mental impairment that substantially limits one or more of the person's major life activities, (2) has a record of such impairment, or (3) is regarded as having such an impairment.

Discipline
(1) Treatment that punishes; (2) orderly behavior in an organizational setting; or (3) training that molds and strengthens desirable conduct—or corrects undesirable conduct—and develops self-control.

Disparate treatment
Situation in which protected-class members receive unequal treatment or are evaluated by different standards.

Distress
Harmful stress characterized by a loss of feelings of security and adequacy.

Downsizing
The planned elimination of jobs.

Dual-career partnerships
Couples in which both members follow their own careers and actively support each other's career development.

Due process
Employee's right to present his or her position during a disciplinary action.

E

E-learning
Learning that takes place via electronic media.

EEO-1 report
An employer information report that must be filed annually by employers of 100 or more employees (except state and local government employers) and government contractors and subcontractors to determine an employer's workforce composition.

Elder care
Care provided to an elderly relative by an employee who remains actively at work.

Employee assistance programs (EAPs)
Services provided by employers to help workers cope with a wide variety of problems that interfere with the way they perform their jobs.

Employee associations
Labor organizations that represent various groups of professional and white-collar employees in labor-management relations.

Employee empowerment
Granting employees power to initiate change, thereby encouraging them to take charge of what they do.

Employee involvement groups (EIs)
Groups of employees who meet to resolve problems or offer suggestions for organizational improvement.

Employee leasing
Process of dismissing employees who are then hired by a leasing company (which handles all HR-related activities) and contracting with that company to lease back the employees.

Employee rights
Guarantees of fair treatment from employers, particularly regarding an employee's right to privacy.

Employee stock ownership plans (ESOPs)
Stock plans in which an organization contributes shares of its stock to an established trust for the purpose of stock purchases by its employees.

Employee teams
An employee contributions technique whereby work functions are structured for groups rather than for individuals and team members are given discretion in matters traditionally considered management prerogatives, such as process improvements, product or service development, and individual work assignments.

Employment-at-will principle
The right of an employer to fire an employee without giving a reason and the right of an employee to quit when he or she chooses.

Entrepreneur
One who starts, organizes, manages, and assumes responsibility for a business or other enterprise.

Environmental scanning
Systematic monitoring of the major external forces influencing the organization.

Equal employment opportunity
The treatment of individuals in all aspects of employment—hiring, promotion, training, etc.—in a fair and nonbiased manner.

Ergonomics
An interdisciplinary approach to designing equipment and systems that can be easily and efficiently used by human beings.

Error of central tendency
Performance-rating error in which all employees are rated about average.

Escalator clauses
Clauses in labor agreements that provide for quarterly cost-of-living adjustments in wages, basing the adjustments on changes in the consumer price index.

Essay method
A trait approach to performance appraisal that requires the rater to compose a statement describing employee behavior.

Ethics
Set of standards of conduct and moral judgments that help to determine right and wrong behavior.

Eustress
Positive stress that accompanies achievement and exhilaration.

Exclusive representation
The legal right and responsibility of the union to represent all bargaining unit members equally, regardless of whether employees join the union or not.

Exempt employees
Employees not covered in the overtime provisions of the Fair Labor Standards Act.

Expatriates, or home-country nationals
Employees from the home country who are on international assignment.

External fit
Situation in which the work system supports the organization's goals and strategies.

F

Failure rate
Percentage of expatriates who do not perform satisfactorily.

Fair employment practices (FEPs)
State and local laws governing equal employment opportunity that are often more comprehensive than federal laws.

Fair representation doctrine
Doctrine under which unions have a legal obligation to provide assistance to both members and nonmembers in labor relations matters.

Fast-track program
Program that encourages young managers with high potential to remain with an organization by enabling them to advance more rapidly than those with less potential.

Flexible benefits plans (cafeteria plans)
Benefit plans that enable individual employees to choose the benefits that are best suited to their particular needs.

Flextime
Flexible working hours that permit employees the option of choosing daily starting and quitting times, provided that they work a set number of hours per day or week.

Forced-choice method
A trait approach to performance appraisal that requires the rater to choose from statements designed to distinguish between successful and unsuccessful performance.

Four-fifths rule
Rule of thumb followed by the EEOC in determining adverse impact for use in enforcement proceedings.

Functional job analysis (FJA)
Quantitative approach to job analysis that utilizes a compiled inventory of the various functions or work activities that can make up any job and that assumes that each job involves three broad worker functions: (1) data, (2) people, and (3) things.

G

Gainsharing plans
Programs under which both employees and the organization share financial gains according to a predetermined formula that reflects improved productivity and profitability.

Global corporation
Firm that has integrated worldwide operations through a centralized home office.

Global manager
Manager equipped to run an international business.

Globalization
Trend toward opening up foreign markets to international trade and investment.

Graphic rating-scale method
A trait approach to performance appraisal whereby each employee is rated according to a scale of characteristics.

Grievance procedure
Formal procedure that provides for the union to represent members and nonmembers in processing a grievance.

Guest workers
Foreign workers invited to perform needed labor.

H

Hay profile method
Job evaluation technique using three factors—knowledge, mental activity, and accountability—to evaluate executive and managerial positions.

Health maintenance organizations (HMOs)
Organizations of physicians and health-care professionals that provide a wide range of services to subscribers and dependents on a prepaid basis.

High-performance work system (HPWS)
A specific combination of HR practices, work structures, and processes that maximizes employee knowledge, skill, commitment, and flexibility.

Home-based pay
Pay based on an expatriate's home country's compensation practices.

Host country
Country in which an international corporation operates.

Host-based pay
Expatriate pay comparable to that earned by employees in a host country.

Host-country nationals
Employees who are natives of the host country.

Hot-stove rule
Rule of discipline that can be compared with a hot stove in that it gives warning, is effective immediately, is enforced consistently, and applies to all employees in an impersonal and unbiased way.

Hourly work
Work paid on an hourly basis.

Human capital
The knowledge, skills, and capabilities of individuals that have economic value to an organization.

Human resources information system (HRIS)
Computerized system that provides current and accurate data for purposes of control and decision making.

Human resources management (HRM)
The process of managing human talent to achieve an organization's objectives.

Human resources planning (HRP)
Process of anticipating and making provision for the movement of people into, within, and out of an organization.

I

Improshare
Gainsharing program under which bonuses are based upon the overall productivity of the work team.

Industrial engineering
A field of study concerned with analyzing work methods and establishing time standards.

Industrial unions
Unions that represent all workers—skilled, semiskilled, unskilled—employed along industry lines.

Instructional objectives
Desired outcomes of a training program.

Interest-based bargaining
Problem-solving bargaining based on a win-win philosophy and the development of a positive long-term relationship.

Internal fit
Situation in which all the internal elements of the work system complement and reinforce one another.

International corporation
Domestic firm that uses its existing capabilities to move into overseas markets.

Internship programs
Programs jointly sponsored by colleges, universities, and other organizations that offer students the opportunity to gain real-life experience while allowing them to find out how they will perform in work organizations.

J

Job
A group of related activities and duties.

Job analysis
Process of obtaining information about jobs by determining what the duties, tasks, or activities of jobs are.

Job characteristics model
Job design that purports that three psychological states (experiencing meaningfulness of the work performed, responsibility for work outcomes, and knowledge of the results of the work performed) of a jobholder result in improved work performance, internal motivation, and lower absenteeism and turnover.

Job classification system
System of job evaluation in which jobs are classified and grouped according to a series of predetermined wage grades.

Job description
Statement of the tasks, duties, and responsibilities of a job to be performed.

Job design
Outgrowth of job analysis that improves jobs through technological and human considerations in order to enhance organization efficiency and employee job satisfaction.

Job enrichment
Enhancing a job by adding more meaningful tasks and duties to make the work more rewarding or satisfying.

Job evaluation
Systematic process of determining the relative worth of jobs in order to establish which jobs should be paid more than others within an organization.

Job family
A group of individual jobs with similar characteristics.

Job posting and bidding
Posting vacancy notices and maintaining lists of employees looking for upgraded positions.

Job progressions
Hierarchy of jobs a new employee might experience, ranging from a starting job to jobs that successively require more knowledge and/or skill.

Job ranking system
Simplest and oldest system of job evaluation by which jobs are arrayed on the basis of their relative worth.

Job specification
Statement of the needed knowledge, skills, and abilities of the person who is to perform the job.

K

Knowledge workers
Workers whose responsibilities extend beyond the physical execution of work to include planning, decision making, and problem solving.

L

Labor relations process
Logical sequence of five events: (1) workers desire collective representation, (2) union begins its organizing campaign, (3) NLRB representation process, (4) collective negotiations lead to a contract, and (5) the contract is administered.

Leniency or strictness error
Performance-rating error in which the appraiser tends to give employees either unusually high or unusually low ratings.

Localization
Adapting pay and other compensation benefits to match that of a particular country.

Lump-sum merit program
Program under which employees receive a year-end merit payment, which is not added to their base pay.

M

Management by objectives (MBO)
Philosophy of management that rates performance on the basis of employee achievement of goals set by mutual agreement of employee and manager.

Management forecasts
The opinions (judgments) of supervisors, department managers, experts, or others knowledgeable about the organization's future employment needs.

Manager and/or supervisor appraisal
Performance appraisal done by an employee's manager and often reviewed by a manager one level higher.

Managing diversity
Being aware of characteristics common to employees, while also managing employees as individuals.

Markov analysis
Method for tracking the pattern of employee movements through various jobs.

Material Safety Data Sheets (MSDSs)
Documents that contain vital information about hazardous substances.

Mediation
The use of an impartial neutral to reach a compromise decision in employment disputes.

Mediator
Third party in an employment dispute who meets with one party and then the other in order to suggest compromise solutions or to recommend concessions from each side that will lead to an agreement.

Mentors
Executives who coach, advise, and encourage individuals of lesser rank.

Merit guidelines
Guidelines for awarding merit that are tied to performance objectives.

Mission
The basic purpose of the organization as well as its scope of operations.

Mixed-standard scale method
A trait approach to performance appraisal similar to other scale methods but based on comparison with (better than, equal to, or worse than) a standard.

Multinational corporation (MNC)
Firm with independent business units operating in multiple countries.

Multiple cutoff model
Selection decision model that requires an applicant to achieve some minimum level of proficiency on all selection dimensions.

N

Negligence
Failure to provide reasonable care where such failure results in injury to consumers or other employees.

Nepotism
A preference for hiring relatives of current employees.

Noncontributory plan
A pension plan where contributions are made solely by the employer.

Nondirective interview
An interview in which the applicant is allowed the maximum amount of freedom in determining the course of the discussion, while the interviewer carefully refrains from influencing the applicant's remarks.

Nonexempt employees
Employees covered by the overtime provisions of the Fair Labor Standards Act.

O

Offshoring
The business practice of sending jobs to other countries.

Ombudsman
Designated individual from whom employees may seek counsel for the resolution of their complaints.

On-the-job training (OJT)
Method by which employees are given hands-on experience with instructions from their supervisor or other trainer.

Open-door policy
Policy of settling grievances that identifies various levels of management above the immediate supervisor for employee contact.

Organization analysis
Examination of the environment, strategies, and resources of the organization to determine where training emphasis should be placed.

Organizational capability
Capacity of the organization to act and change in pursuit of sustainable competitive advantage.

Orientation
Formal process of familiarizing new employees with the organization, their jobs, and their work units.

Outplacement services
Services provided by organizations to help terminated employees find a new job.

Outsourcing
Contracting outside the organization to have work done that formerly was done by internal employees.

P

Panel interview
An interview in which a board of interviewers questions and observes a single candidate.

Pay equity
An employee's perception that compensation received is equal to the value of the work performed.

Pay grades
Groups of jobs within a particular class that are paid the same rate.

Pay-for-performance standard
Standard by which managers tie compensation to employee effort and performance.

Peer appraisal
Performance appraisal done by one's fellow employees, generally on forms that are compiled into a single profile for use in the performance interview conducted by the employee's manager.

Peer-review system
System for reviewing employee complaints that utilizes a group composed of equal numbers of employee representatives and management appointees, which functions as a jury because its members weigh evidence, consider arguments, and, after deliberation, vote independently to render a final decision.

Performance appraisal
A process, typically performed annually by a supervisor for a subordinate, designed to help employees understand their roles, objectives, expectations, and performance success.

Performance management
The process of creating a work environment in which people can perform to the best of their abilities.

Perquisites
Special benefits given to executives; often referred to as perks.

Person analysis
Determination of the specific individuals who need training.

Piecework
Work paid according to the number of units produced.

Point system
Quantitative job evaluation procedure that determines the relative value of a job by the total points assigned to it.

Position
The different duties and responsibilities performed by only one employee.

Position analysis questionnaire (PAQ)
Questionnaire covering 194 different tasks which, by means of a five-point scale, seeks to determine the degree to which different tasks are involved in performing a particular job.

Positive, or nonpunitive, discipline
System of discipline that focuses on the early correction of employee misconduct, with the employee taking total responsibility for correcting the problem.

Predictive validity
Extent to which applicants' test scores match criterion data obtained from those applicants/employees after they have been on the job for some indefinite period.

Preferred provider organization (PPO)
A group of physicians who establish an organization that guarantees lower healthcare costs to the employer.

Proactive change
Change initiated to take advantage of targeted opportunities.

Process audit
Determining whether the high-performance work system has been implemented as designed.

Profit sharing
Any procedure by which an employer pays, or makes available to all regular employees, in addition to base pay, special current or deferred sums based on the profits of the enterprise.

Progressive discipline
Application of corrective measures by increasing degrees.

Promotion
Change of assignment to a job at a higher level in the organization.

Protected classes
Individuals of a minority race, women, older people, and those with disabilities who are covered by federal laws on equal employment opportunity.

Psychological contract
Expectations of a fair exchange of employment obligations between an employee and employer.

R

Reactive change
Change that occurs after external forces have already affected performance.

Real wages
Wage increases larger than rises in the consumer price index; that is, the real earning power of wages.

Realistic job preview (RJP)
Informing applicants about all aspects of the job, including both its desirable and undesirable facets.

Reasonable accommodation
Attempt by employers to adjust, without undue hardship, the working conditions or schedules of employees with disabilities or religious preferences.

Recency error
Performance-rating error in which the appraisal is based largely on the employee's most recent behavior rather than on behavior throughout the appraisal period.

Recordable case
Any occupational death, illness, or injury to be recorded in the log (OSHA Form 300).

Red circle rates
Payment rates above the maximum of the pay range.

Reengineering
Fundamental rethinking and radical redesign of business processes to achieve dramatic improvements in cost, quality, service, and speed.

Reliability
Degree to which interviews, tests, and other selection procedures yield comparable data over time and alternative measures.

Relocation services
Services provided to an employee who is transferred to a new location, which might include help in moving, in selling a home, in orienting to a new culture, and/or in learning a new language.

Repatriation
Process of employee transition home from an international assignment.

Replacement charts
Listings of current jobholders and persons who are potential replacements if an opening occurs.

Reverse discrimination
Act of giving preference to members of protected classes to the extent that unprotected individuals believe they are suffering discrimination.

Right-to-know laws
Laws that require employers to advise employees about the hazardous chemicals they handle.

Rights arbitration
Arbitration over interpretation of the meaning of contract terms or employee work grievances.

Rucker Plan
Bonus incentive plan based on the historic relationship between the total earnings of hourly employees and the production value created by the employees.

S

Scanlon Plan
Bonus incentive plan using employee and management committees to gain cost-reduction improvements.

Selection
Process of choosing individuals who have relevant qualifications to fill existing or projected job openings.

Selection ratio
The number of applicants compared with the number of people to be hired.

Self-appraisal
Performance appraisal done by the employee being evaluated, generally on an appraisal form completed by the employee prior to the performance interview.

Sexual harassment
Unwelcome advances, requests for sexual favors, and other verbal or physical conduct of a sexual nature in the working environment.

Silver handshake
An early-retirement incentive in the form of increased pension benefits for several years or a cash bonus.

Similar-to-me error
Performance-rating error in which an appraiser inflates the evaluation of an employee because of a mutual personal connection.

Situational interview
An interview in which an applicant is given a hypothetical incident and asked how he or she would respond to it.

Six Sigma
A process used to translate customer needs into a set of optimal tasks that are performed in concert with one another.

Skill inventories
Files of personnel education, experience, interests, skills, etc., that allow managers to quickly match job openings with employee backgrounds.

Spot bonus
Unplanned bonus given for employee effort unrelated to an established performance measure.

Staffing tables
Graphic representations of all organizational jobs, along with the numbers of employees currently occupying those jobs and future (monthly or yearly) employment requirements.

Standard hour plan
Incentive plan that sets rates based on the completion of a job in a predetermined standard time.

Step-review system
System for reviewing employee complaints and disputes by successively higher levels of management.

Straight commission plan
Compensation plan based on a percentage of sales.

Straight piecework
Incentive plan under which employees receive a certain rate for each unit produced.

Straight salary plan
Compensation plan that permits salespeople to be paid for performing various duties that are not reflected immediately in their sales volume.

Strategic human resources management (SHRM)
The pattern of human resources deployments and activities that enable an organization to achieve its strategic goals.

Strategic planning
Procedures for making decisions about the organization's long-term goals and strategies.

Strategic vision
A statement about where the company is going and what it can become in the future; clarifies the long-term direction of the company and its strategic intent.

Stress
Any adjustive demand caused by physical, mental, or emotional factors that requires coping behavior.

Structured interview
An interview in which a set of standardized questions having an established set of answers is used.

Subordinate appraisal
Performance appraisal of a superior by an employee, which is more appropriate for developmental than for administrative purposes.

Succession planning
Process of identifying, developing, and tracking key individuals for executive positions.

Supplemental unemployment benefits (SUBs)
A plan that enables an employee who is laid off to draw, in addition to state unemployment compensation, weekly benefits from the employer that are paid from a fund created for this purpose.

SWOT analysis
A comparison of strengths, weaknesses, opportunities, and threats for strategy formulation purposes.

T

Task analysis
Process of determining what the content of a training program should be on the basis of a study of the tasks and duties involved in the job.

Task inventory analysis
An organization-specific list of tasks and their descriptions used as a basis to identify components of jobs.

Team appraisal
Performance appraisal that recognizes team accomplishment rather than individual performance.

Team incentive plan
Compensation plan where all team members receive an incentive bonus payment when production or service standards are met or exceeded.

Telecommuting
Use of personal computers, networks, and other communications technology such as fax machines to do work in the home that is traditionally done in the workplace.

Third-country nationals
Employees who are natives of a country other than the home country or the host country.

Total quality management (TQM)
A set of principles and practices whose core ideas include understanding customer needs, doing things right the first time, and striving for continuous improvement.

Transfer
Placement of an individual in another job for which the duties, responsibilities, status, and remuneration are approximately equal to those of the previous job.

Transfer of training
Effective application of principles learned to what is required on the job.

Transnational corporation
Firm that attempts to balance local responsiveness and global scale via a network of specialized operating units.

Transnational teams
Teams composed of members of multiple nationalities working on projects that span multiple countries.

Trend analysis
A quantitative approach to forecasting labor demand based on an organizational index such as sales.

U

Unfair labor practices (ULPs)
Specific employer and union illegal practices that operate to deny employees their rights and benefits under federal labor law.

Uniform Guidelines on Employee Selection Procedures
Procedural document published in the *Federal Register* to assist employers in complying with federal regulations against discriminatory actions.

Union shop
Provision of the labor agreement that requires employees to join the union as a requirement for their employment.

Union steward
Employee who as a nonpaid union official represents the interests of members in their relations with management.

V

Validity
Degree to which a test or selection procedure measures a person's attributes.

Validity generalization
Extent to which validity coefficients can be generalized across situations.

Value creation
What the firm adds to a product or service by virtue of making it; the amount of benefits provided by the product or service once the costs of making it are subtracted.

Value-added compensation
Evaluating the individual components of the compensation program to see if they advance the needs of employees and the goals of the organization.

Variable pay
Tying pay to some measure of individual, group, or organizational performance.

Vesting
A guarantee of accrued benefits to participants at retirement age, regardless of their employment status at that time.

Virtual team
A team with widely dispersed members linked together through computer and telecommunications technology.

W

Wage and salary survey
Survey of the wages paid to employees of other employers in the surveying organization's relevant labor market.

Wage curve
Curve in a scattergram representing the relationship between relative worth of jobs and wage rates.

Wage-rate compression
Compression of differentials between job classes, particularly the differential between hourly workers and their managers.

Whistle-blowing
Complaints to governmental agencies by employees about their employers' illegal or immoral acts or illegal practices.

Work permit, or work certificate
Government document granting a foreign individual the right to seek employment.

Work valuation
A job evaluation system that seeks to measure a job's worth through its value to the organization.

Workers' compensation insurance
Federal- or state-mandated insurance provided to workers to defray the loss of income and cost of treatment due to work-related injuries or illness.

Workforce utilization analysis
Process of classifying protected-class members by number and by the type of job they hold within the organization.

Y

Yield ratio
Percentage of applicants from a recruitment source that make it to the next stage of the selection process.

name index

A

B

E

F

G

H

I

J

K

N

O

P

Q

R

organization index

A

B

C

D

E

subject index

D

P

Q

R

T

U

V

W

Y

Z